Dutton's
Navigation
& Piloting

Dutton's Navigation & Piloting

FOURTEENTH EDITION

By Elbert S. Maloney

Naval Institute Press
Annapolis, Maryland

Library of Congress Cataloging in Publication Data
Dutton, Benjamin, 1883–1937.
    Dutton's Navigation & piloting.
    Includes index.
    1. Navigation. 2. Nautical astronomy. I. Maloney,
Elbert S. II. Title. III. Title: Navigation and
piloting. IV. Title: Dutton's Navigation and piloting.
VK555.D96   1985   623.89   85-3004
ISBN 0-87021-157-9
Printed in the United States of America on acid-free paper ∞

10 9 8 7 6 5

Contents

Preface

Time marches on—and so does the art and science of navigation! Since the first edition of *Navigation and Nautical Astronomy* (as it was then titled) was written by Commander Benjamin Dutton, U.S. Navy, and published in 1926, this book has been often updated and revised. The title was changed after his death to both honor the originator and to more accurately reflect its focus; thus, the 11th edition was the first with the present title of *Dutton's Navigation and Piloting*. (And please, do *not* write to me to say that this title is redundant, that "piloting" is a subdivision of "navigation"; I know that—see the very first page of the text—but tradition being what it is, the decision was made not to change the title for this edition.)

Many, but not all, of the revisions in successive editions have resulted from the rapid technological advances of recent decades. This new 14th edition of *Dutton's* continues that trend, accelerating it with the wonders of solid-state integrated circuits that are now available—radars and depth sounders with square or rectangular TV-like screens, some even in color; radionavigation receivers that combine two or more systems, such as Loran-C, Omega, and SatNav, and which can be interfaced into vessel steering systems; and many others. And of course, computers, computers, and more computers! The availability of microprocessors on a single chip has made it possible to integrate them into a wide variety of navigation equipment, often without their presence even being recognized. Even the time-honored Mercator chart can now be stored in binary digital form, and many can be carried on board a vessel in the form of a single magnetic disk or tape.

But technological advances are not the only

changes in the 14th edition. A new set of inspection tables for celestial sight reduction is introduced and described. There has been some regrouping of major topics and rearranging of chapters for a smoother flow of subject matter. Many new illustrations have been included, and numerous ones from the previous edition were revised. Greater attention is given in this edition to the needs of navigators of merchant ships and small craft of all types. Even the basic format and layout of the book has been changed to enhance its usefulness to the reader. A thorough revision of the index was made, using—what else—a computer, my own Apple IIe.

As in the case of earlier versions, this edition is intended for use by practicing navigators at sea, as well as by students of the subject, either enrolled in a class or engaged in independent study. While not intended to be encyclopedic in scope, it should well meet the needs of both experienced and neophyte navigators.

Although the 14th edition of *Dutton's Navigation and Piloting* represents more than a year's work by the author, it is far from a "one-man job." My principal source of assistance has been my son, Lieutenant Commander Elbert S. Maloney, Jr., U.S. Navy. Barney, as he is better known, reviewed the entire 13th edition and offered many useful comments, even pointing out a few errors; he also did much research on specific assigned topics. Individuals who reviewed chapters within their areas of special expertise include Lieutenant Commander J. Dennis Gay, U.S. Maritime Service; James E. Gearhart; Robert C. Middaugh; and Commander G. R. Siddall, U.S. Coast Guard. (In my acknowledgments, I have listed names alphabetically, as any attempt to rank each contribution in order of importance would be hopeless.) Technical information and suggestions were received from many offices of the Coast Guard, Navy, National Ocean Service, Defense Mapping Agency Hydrographic/Topographic Center, and the Maritime Institute of Technology and Graduate Studies—and from many manufacturers of navigation equipment. Individuals whose assistance is gratefully acknowledged include Chester Amicone, Melvin E. Cruser, Edward Danforth, LeRoy E. Doggett, Randolph Doubt, William Foushee, John Hanna, John Hird, Paul Janiczek, Donald R. Lesnick, William T. McMullen, John Quill, George Sokol, Samuel Smith, John Underhill, and Alden (Buzz) West.

A general acknowledgment is also due to the lengthy list of those who contributed to the 13th edition, much of which has been carried over in whole or part into this edition. And a general "thank you" to the readers of the 13th edition who wrote in with criticisms and suggestions.

Special thanks are extended to Richard R. Hobbs of the Naval Institute staff for a critical review of the entire book, who offered many valuable suggestions for changes. My thanks also go to two other Institute staff members, Moira Megargee, who is responsible for the handsome new layout, and Carol Swartz, who has been my editor for the last two editions.

No author can end his acknowledgments without stating his appreciation to the typists who put in so many hours puzzling out my longhand penciled drafts with many revisions, inserts, and deletions. Miss Anne Baubie did the initial draft, and Mrs. Jeanne Renick typed the final manuscript.

And as in the previous edition, I end with my thanks, and apologies, to my wife, Mary, for her understanding and patience during the many months of the preparation of this edition when I was all too often unavailable for family duties and activities.

Dutton's
Navigation
& Piloting

Chapter 1

Introduction to Navigation

Origins and Definitions

101 Man has traveled on the waters of the world since the dawn of recorded history—and perhaps even earlier than that. At first, he probably drifted at the whim of waves and currents, but soon he faced up to the problem of getting from where he was to where he wanted to be. Thus was born navigation, the process of directing the movement of a vehicle from one point to another; the "vehicle" can be a surface craft or ship, a submarine, an aircraft, or a space craft. To make the definition complete, the qualifier of "safely" or "efficiently" should be added.

Undoubtedly, navigation was first an art, but soon elements of science were added. Today it has aspects of both. It is a science in that it involves the development and use of instruments, methods, tables, and almanacs. It is an art in that it involves the proficient use of these tools and the application and interpretation of information gained from such use. Much work must be done with precise instruments and exact mathematical tables, yet when the observations have been taken, and the calculations made, the seasoned navigator applies a measure of judgment when he says, "We are here on the chart."

Primary Categories of Navigation

102 Navigation can be divided into four primary classifications: piloting, dead reckoning, celestial navigation, and radionavigation. These are convenient and logical categories; this is also the sequence in which they probably developed as man's knowledge and abilities grew over the centuries.

Piloting

Piloting may be defined as the determination of the position and the direction of the movements of a vessel involving frequent or continuous reference to landmarks, aids to navigation, and depth soundings. Man first directed his movements on land by referring to familiar objects and views. When he took to the water to transport himself and his goods, he carried over the same techniques. Later, when water travel became more widely practiced, man-made aids to navigation, at first quite primitive but soon more advanced, were needed and were developed. Piloting is now done by referring to natural land features and structures and other objects ashore that, although not constructed for

Figure 102. Plotting on charts is a part of all forms of navigation.

that purpose, can guide the mariner; by making use of specific aids to navigation such as lights, buoys, daybeacons, and fog signals; and by measuring the depth of the water. Under normal circumstances, piloting will establish a vessel's position with precision and accuracy.

Man once depended entirely on his senses of sight and sound for piloting. Now he is aided by modern developments such as radio, radar, and electronic depth sounders that vastly expand a navigator's range of perception. Because these devices are electronic extensions of the senses of sight and sound and are frequently used in modern-day piloting, they are treated in the section on piloting rather than in the section on complex radionavigation systems.

Dead Reckoning

Dead reckoning (DR) is the projection of a present position, or anticipated future position, from a previous known position using the best available information on directions and distances. As man became bolder in his ventures on the seas, he traveled beyond the range of visual references to natural or man-made landmarks and into waters too deep to measure. He then developed procedures to help him estimate his position. The term is derived from the "deduced reckoning" of sailing ships, which was abbreviated "ded. reckoning." In basic applications of dead reckoning, projections are made from planned courses and speeds without allowance for wind or current. Courses are determined from the compass, magnetic or gyro, and distance is taken from a log, a count of engine revolutions, or a multiplication of speed and time. The plot of DR positions can be done either manually or by a dead reckoning tracer that automatically analyzes directions and distances and plots a continuous track. The very modern systems of inertial and Doppler navigation are, in reality, extensions of dead reckoning using the capabilities of present-day technology.

Celestial Navigation

Celestial navigation is the determination of position by observing the celestial bodies—the sun, moon, planets, and stars. Navigators, recognizing the deficiencies of dead reckoning when carried on for days without knowing the effects of wind and current, soon developed techniques for observing heavenly bodies. Instruments were crude at first, but soon became more precise; even today, improvements are still being made in observational instruments and the techniques for using them.

The angle of elevation above the horizon is measured for an identified heavenly body. This is compared with a mathematical calculation of that angle for the position of the body at that time, and the difference between the observed angle and the calculated angle is used to fix the location of the observer. The necessary mathematics may make use of precomputed tables, an electronic calculator, or a computer.

Although presently somewhat overshadowed by electronic systems, celestial navigation remains a basic and widely used procedure for determining positions at sea.

Radionavigation

Radionavigation is the determination of position—and to a lesser extent, course direction—using information gained from radio waves received and processed on board a vessel or aircraft. Radar navigation and satellite navigation are a part of this primary classification, but will be considered separately from radionavigation systems. Radar is essentially "electronic piloting," and the use of satellites is a unique application of radio waves. (The term "electronic navigation," which is sometimes used, more properly includes *all* of the electronic devices from depth sounders and gyrocompasses to inertial systems and Doppler equipment.)

Radionavigation systems in general provide coverage of a few hundred to many thousands of miles with accuracies from ±5 miles or so down to a hundred yards or less. Radionavigation systems and celestial techniques complement each other well at sea—celestial navigation is simple and self-contained, but requires fair weather in order to observe the heavens and horizon; radio systems are generally usable regardless of the weather, but are subject to power and equipment failures. Radionavigation systems are continually being improved by research and development; already some earlier systems have been phased out and replaced with improved versions or entirely new systems. Recent developments include "interface" equipment that will allow positional information from the Loran-C radionavigation system to be fed to a vessel's automatic steering mechanism (the so-called "autopilot") to provide continuous steering corrections to maintain a preset track. Another new device is a radionavigation receiver that combines data from two systems—typically, satellite navigation signals and Loran-C—for greater accuracy, or even information from three systems, the above two plus Omega.

The Problems of Navigation

103 Regardless of the specific method of navigation, or combination of methods, used by a navigator, the procedures he applies must furnish him with a solution to the three basic problems of navigation. These problems are:

1. How to determine his *position;*
2. How to determine the *direction* in which to proceed to gct from one position to another; and
3. How to determine *distance,* and the related factors of *time* and *speed* as he proceeds.

Position

Of these three problems facing every navigator, the most basic is that of determining his position. Unless he knows where he is, he cannot direct the movements of his vessel with accuracy, safety, and efficiency. The term *position* refers to an identifiable location on the earth or a point within a man-made system of artificial coordinates. The word *position* is frequently qualified by such adjectives as "known," "estimated," or "dead reckoning"; these will be further discussed in later chapters.

Direction

Direction is the orientation of an imaginary line joining one point to another without regard to the distance between them. Direction is measured in angular units—*degrees* of arc from a reference—using a polar coordinate system. The usual reference is *true north,* although others will be defined and used later in this book. A degree may be subdivided either into *minutes* and *seconds* (1° = 60'; 1' = 60"), or into *decimal fractions.* Geographic directions are stated as a three-digit number, with leading zeros as required; for example, a direction

Figure 103b. Accurate and precise time is essential to all forms of navigation.

of 7° east of north would be written as 007°, and one of 36° east of north would be stated as 036°.

It is the knowledge of the spatial relationship between two positions—the direction from one to another—that makes it possible for a navigator to lay a course from where he is to where he wants to go, and then to proceed to that destination.

Distance

Distance is the spatial separation between two points without regard to direction. In navigation, it is measured by the length of a line on the surface of the earth from one point to the other; customary units are yards, miles, or kilometers. The "mile" commonly used by navigators is the *international nautical mile* of 6,076.1 feet (approximately). This is longer than the *statute mile* used on land, 5,280 feet; a close approximation of the ratio is 38/33, but 8/7 or 1.15/1 is often used because of its simplicity.

Time may be either the time of day of an event as indicated by a watch or clock or the interval between two successive events. Units used are hours, minutes, and seconds; decimal fractions of a second are rarely needed. Time is written as four digits in a 24-hour system. Four minutes after midnight is 0004; 9:32 A.M. would be written as 0932; and 8:15 P.M. would appear as 2015. (The word "hours" is *not* written or spoken after the four digits.)

Speed is defined as the rate of movement and in navigation is usually measured in nautical miles per hour, or *knots.* Note that the time element is included in the definition of "knot"; the use of "knots per hour" is incorrect.

Figure 103a. Chart plots indicate a vessel's position, course, speed, and other essential information.

Metric System of Measurement

104 The "metric system of measurements"—more correctly known as the *International System of Units*, abbreviated as *SI* (from the name in French), has been adopted in nearly all countries of the world. It is a logical, systematic series of inter-related units with larger and smaller units based on multiples of ten.

The Metric Conversion Act of 1975 declared that the policy of the United States was to increase the use of metric units on a voluntary basis with the goal of a "nation predominately, although not exclusively, metric." Progress towards this goal has slowed in recent years, but the global use of metric units makes this system of vital interest to navigators. Accordingly, this book will note metric units where appropriate as approximate equivalents to the customary (English) units.

The nautical mile is expected to remain the basic unit of distance at sea. Depths and heights, however, are increasingly being shown in meters and decimeters (tenths of meters). (1 nautical mile = 1.852 km; 1 fathom = 1.829 m; 1 foot = 0.3048 m.)

Additional information on the metric system of measurement is given in appendix D.

Navigational Mathematics

105 A navigator will constantly be working with mathematics regardless of the type of navigation being practiced or the particular problem being solved. Standards of accuracy and precision, and general mathematical rules, are given in appendix C.

Summary

106 The study of navigation is the learning of how to measure and use position, direction, distance, time, and speed. The practice of navigation, in any of its forms, is the application of this knowledge to ensure the safe and expeditious passage of a vessel.

Chapter 2

The Earth and Geographic Coordinates

Shape and Size of the Earth

201 The earth is often considered a true sphere, and for nearly all practical applications it is so used. Actually, however, it is a less-than-perfect sphere, technically an *oblate spheroid* or an *ellipsoid of revolution*. The equatorial diameter of the earth is not quite 6,888 nautical miles (12,756 km); the polar diameter is nearly 6,865 nautical miles (12,714 km), or about 23 miles (43 km) less.

If the earth is represented by a globe with an equatorial diameter of 12 inches (30.48 cm), the polar diameter, to be exact, should be 11.96 inches (30.38 cm), or 0.04 inches (0.10 cm) less.

The earth has a much smoother surface than might be imagined. Mt. Everest reaches a little less than 30,000 feet (9,144 m) above mean sea level; the greatest ocean depths yet known extend a little more than 35,000 feet (10,668 m) below the water's surface. On the same globe as above, these heights and depths would only be about 0.01 inch (0.025 cm) above or below the mean surface, unless the vertical scale was deliberately much exaggerated for emphasis and clarity. Without vertical expansion it would take a fine craftsman to make a globe with a surface so smooth!

Since these variations from a truly spherical shape are so slight, for most navigational purposes the earth can be considered a sphere, and solutions of navigational problems based on this assumption are of practical accuracy. In charts, however, consideration is given to the oblateness of the earth.

Reference Lines on the Earth

202 Points on the surface of a sphere at rest are similar because all are equidistant from its center.

Lines passing through the center of the sphere, between two points on its surface, are also similar. None of the lines have any distinguishing characteristics that would render them suitable as a reference for navigational measurements.

But if the sphere is rotated, one line becomes distinguishable from all others; this line is the *axis* on which the sphere rotates. The earth's axis meets its surface at the *North Pole* and *South Pole*.

Halfway between the two poles, a plane perpendicular to the axis intersects the surface of the earth in a line known as the *equator*. All points on the equator are equidistant between the two poles, and the plane of the equator divides the earth in half, into the *Northern* and *Southern Hemispheres*.

Great and Small Circles

203 A *great circle* is a circle formed on the surface of the earth by the intersection of a plane passing through the center of the earth, thereby dividing the earth into two equal parts. Great circles are illustrated in figure 203a.

A *small circle* is a circle formed on the surface of the earth by the intersection of a plane that does *not* pass through the center of the earth and thus does not divide the earth into two equal parts. Although "small circles" may actually be quite large, they are always smaller than any great circle of the earth. Figure 203b illustrates several examples of small circles.

Parallels and Meridians

204 Certain great and small circles have special applications in navigation. A *parallel* is a small circle on the earth's surface whose plane of intersection is parallel to the plane of the equator. The

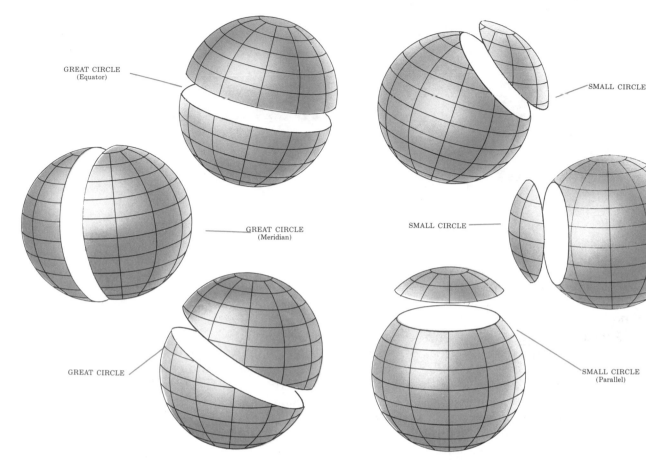

Figure 203a. Great circles.

Figure 203b. Small circles.

equator itself is a special parallel in that it is a great circle. See figures 204a and b.

A *meridian* is a great circle formed by a plane that contains the earth's axis and its poles; see figure 204c. That half of a meridian extending from the north to the south pole on the *same* side of the earth as an observer is considered by him as the *upper branch* of the meridian. The other half of the meridian, which is on the *other* side of the earth and seems to the observer to be beneath him is referred to as the *lower branch*. (The simple term "meridian" is commonly applied to the upper branch only.)

Note that parallels and meridians always intersect at 90° angles. Parallels are always equidistant from each other in contrast to meridians, which converge and then meet at the poles. This difference should be clearly understood, as it is of critical importance in practical navigation when measuring distances on nautical charts.

Geographic Coordinates

205   The location of any point on earth may be defined by using a system of *geographic* (or *terres-*

trial) *coordinates*. The earth's surface is laid out in a grid of *parallels of latitude* (usually referred to merely as "parallels") and *meridians of longitude*.

Latitude

Latitude (abbreviated as Lat., symbol L, or occasionally ϕ, the Greek letter phi) is measured north or south from the equator, where it is 0°, to the poles, where it is 90°. The latitude of a point may be considered either as the angular distance measured from the center of the earth or as an arc on the surface. Latitude is normally measured in degrees, minutes, and seconds, or in degrees, minutes, and decimal fractions of a minute; the suffix "north" or "south" is an essential part of the description and must always be included. Figure 205a shows measurements of the angles for 15° and 45° *north* latitude and for 30° *south* latitude.

Longitude

Longitude (abbreviated as Long., symbol Lo or λ, the Greek letter lambda) is measured using meridians, but a particular meridian must be selected as the starting point. In the early days of map making,

Figure 204a. Parallels of latitude are formed by planes perpendicular to the earth's axis.

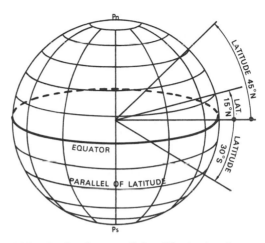

Figure 205a. Latitude; parallels of latitude; the equator.

Figure 204b. The equator is formed by a plane perpendicular to the axis of the earth and equidistant from the poles.

Figure 205b. Longitude; meridians; prime meridian; east and west longitude.

Figure 204c. Meridians of longitude are formed by planes that contain the earth's axis.

a number of meridians were used for starting points. Each map maker or seafaring nation used its own reference meridian, and charts often had four or more longitude scales. Now, however, the *prime meridian*, longitude 0°, is universally taken as the upper branch of the meridian that passes through the original site of the Royal Observatory, Greenwich, England. All modern charts use the prime meridian as the starting point for the measurement of longitude.

Figure 205b illustrates the measurement of longitude. The longitude of any point on earth may be defined as the angular distance between the meridian of Greenwich and the meridian passing through the point. It is measured in degrees of arc, from 0° to 180° east (*east longitude*) or west (*west longitude*) from the prime meridian (Greenwich). It may be thought of:

1. As measured along a parallel of latitude, as in the figure;
2. As measured along the equator; or
3. As the angle between the two meridians as they converge and meet at the pole.

Having established a set of reference lines for the sphere (parallels and meridians), any position on earth may be precisely pinpointed as "so many degrees north (or south) latitude, and so many degrees east (or west) longitude." (Latitude is always stated first.)

Degree Length

The length of a degree of latitude (measured along a meridian) is essentially the same everywhere on the earth from the equator to the poles. There are very slight variations due to the oblateness of the earth. For practical navigation purposes, 1 degree is equal to 60 nautical miles (111.12 km), and 1 minute of latitude is equal to 1 nautical mile (1.852 km).

The situation with longitude, however, is quite different. The length of one degree (measured along a parallel) decreases from 60 nautical miles (111.12 km) at the equator to 52.10 nautical miles (96.48 km) at latitude 30° north or south, and to 30.13 nautical miles (55.80 km) at latitude 60°; it is zero at latitude 90° at the north and south poles. See figure 205c.

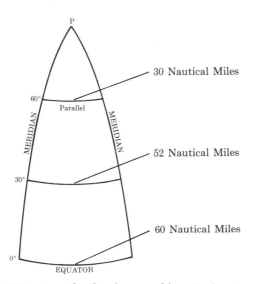

Figure 205c. Length of a degree of longitude at various latitudes.

Departure

The linear distance between two meridians at any given parallel of latitude is termed *departure* (abbreviated Dep., symbol p); it is normally expressed in nautical miles.

Difference of Latitude or Longitude

206   In some problems of navigation it is necessary to know the *difference of latitude (l)*, or the *difference of longitude* (DLo) between two points.

In determining the difference of latitude, the two points may both be on the same side of the equator, in which case they are said to be of the "same name" (that is, both are *north* latitude, or both are *south* latitude); or they may be on opposite sides of the equator, and of "contrary name" (one *north* latitude, one *south*). The difference of latitude *(l)* is always measured as though the two points were both on the same meridian, with one point due north or south of the other, regardless of the direction between them. Thus, in figure 206a, A is 45° north, B is 30° south *(contrary name)*; obviously, the total difference of latitude between them is obtained by *adding* the two distances from the equator: 45° + 30° = 75° = *l*. The formal rule for this is:

for latitudes of contrary name, add.

Again, in figure 206a, A is 45° north, C at 15° north *(same name)* and the difference of latitude, 30°, is obtained by subtracting the smaller from the larger. The rule in this case becomes:

for latitudes of same name, subtract.

In the same way, the *difference of longitude* (DLo) is always measured as though both points were on the same parallel, or on the equator.

Both points may be on the same side of the prime meridian (Greenwich), and therefore of the "same name"—both *east* longitude, or both *west* longitude. They may also be on opposite sides of the prime meridian, and therefore of "contrary name" —one in *east* longitude, the other in *west* longitude.

In figure 206a, B is at longitude 30° west, C at 30° east *(contrary name)*; the total DLo is obtained by adding the two distances from the prime meridian: 30° + 30° = 60° = DLo, and the rule is still:

for contrary name, add.

A slight complication may appear if the sum of the two longitudes is greater than 180°, but in this case the DLo is 360° *minus the sum*. This may be seen from figure 206b, in which the circumference GWE is the equator, and P is the North Pole. PG is

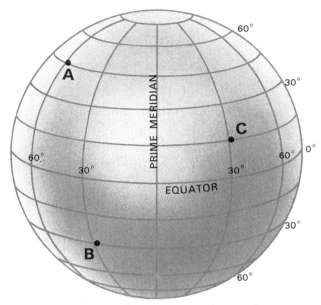

Figure 206a. Difference of latitude *(l)* and difference of longitude (DLo).

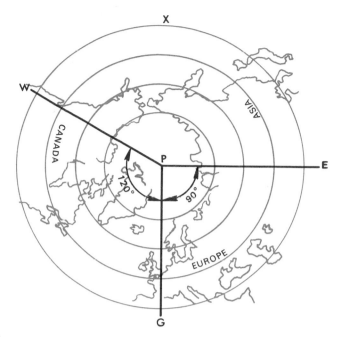

Figure 206b. Difference of longitude (DLo) for "contrary names"; and when greater than 180°.

the meridian of Greenwich. PW is the meridian through the point W, at 120° west longitude, PE the meridian through E, at 90° east longitude *(contrary name):* sum, 120° + 90° = 210°. Obviously, the DLo sought is the *shorter* arc between them (WXE), or 360° − 210° = 150°, not the longer arc of 210°.

Again, in figure 206a, A is at 60° west longitude, B at 30° west longitude *(same name)*. The DLo of 30° is obtained by subtracting the smaller from the larger, and the rule again is:

for same name, subtract.

Some navigation problems are solved by means of *latitude* and *departure (latitude,* here, is the difference of latitude already discussed). *Departure* is the difference in longitude, but here expressed in nautical miles rather than degrees and minutes of arc; mathematically, it is DLo multiplied by the cosine of the latitude. As described in chapter 20, DLo or departure can be found graphically; it can be computed; or it can be found using table 3 of Volume II, DMAHTC Publication No. 9, *American Practical Navigator* (generally referred to as *Bowditch*).

Mid-latitudes

For some navigational calculations, the *mid-latitude* (Lm) is needed. To be quite precise, this is the latitude at which the arc length of the parallel between the meridians of the two points concerned is

exactly equal to the departure when proceeding from one point to the other. As this is difficult to calculate, the *mean* latitude is normally used; this gives fully satisfactory results for practical navigational purposes. When both points are on the same side of the equator, this is the arithmetical mean of the two latitudes. For example, in figure 206a, Lm for points A and C is (45° + 15°) ÷ 2 = 60° ÷ 2 = 30°.

If Lm is ever required for points on opposite sides of the equator, the procedure is more complex, but can be readily deduced from figure 206a. For A and B *(contrary names)*, the computation is as follows: (45° + 30°) ÷ 2 = 75° ÷ 2 = 37°30'. In this case, however, 37°30' is *not* the Lm sought. Lm is found by subtracting this initial result from *either* of the two latitudes; that is, Lm can be found as either 45° − 37°30' = 7°30' (that is, 7°30' on the other side of the equator from B, which is, as before, at 7°30' north latitude).

Although charts and globes are printed with meridians and parallels at regular intervals of 1, 2, 5, or more degrees, a navigator must remember that *any* point on earth lies on *a meridian* and on *a parallel;* and that the absence of a printed line does not alter the fact that the longitude and latitude of a point is the measurement of the meridian and parallel passing through that point, as described earlier.

Distance in Navigation

207   On a *plane* surface, a straight line is defined as "the shortest distance between two points." With the help of a straightedge, such a line may be drawn on an engineering plan and the *distance* measured at the scale of the drawing. Similarly, the *direction* from one point to another may be measured by using an ordinary protractor to determine the angle that the line makes with the rectangular reference lines of the drawing.

Great Circles

The shortest *distance* (abbreviated as Dist., symbol D) between any two points on the surface of the earth is always along the great circle between them. The more closely the plane of a small circle approaches the center of the earth, the more closely will distance measured along it approach the shortest distance. The converse is also true, of course.

Since a great circle is the shortest distance between two points on the surface of a sphere, it might be supposed that it would always be the route selected unless there were intervening dangers, such as reefs or shoals. The practical objection to following a great-circle route is that the direction of that great circle is constantly changing; it makes a different angle with each meridian it crosses from the starting point to the destination. This means that the ship's course on a great-circle route would be subject to continuous alterations.

Rhumb Lines

Since constant course changes are scarcely practical, it is customary to follow a *rhumb line,* or a series of rhumb lines, rather than to follow a great circle. For practical purposes, a *rhumb line* (also known as a loxodrome or loxodromic spiral) can be defined as a line that crosses every meridian of the terrestrial sphere at the same angle. In other words, a ship may maintain a true heading without change from starting point to destination (if, for the moment, one disregards factors such as currents, wind, and changing magnetic variation). Figure 207a shows a rhumb line extending in a continuous spiral from the equator to the north pole, crossing each meridian at a constant angle of about 70°.

Figure 207b shows a great circle and a rhumb line, both from a point on the equator to a point about 135° of longitude eastward and at a latitude near 52° north. In this view of the earth it is not possible to show angular relationships correctly, but reference to a globe will show that the great

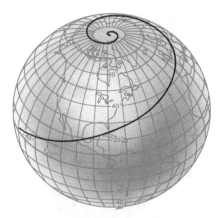

Figure 207a. A rhumb line or loxodrome.

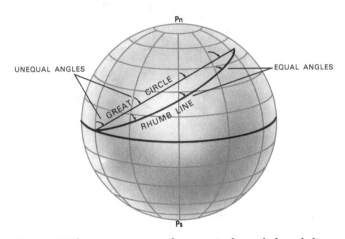

Figure 207b. Comparison of great circle and rhumb line.

circle leaves the equator at an angle of a little less than 30° with the meridian there; near the middle of the route, the angle with the meridian has increased to about 50° and, near the end of the route, to more than 100°. The rhumb line crosses each successive meridian at a constant angle of about 65°.

Comparison of Distances

208   A navigator is concerned with both great-circle distances and rhumb-line distances. Except for a few special cases where they are the same, great-circle distances are always shorter than rhumb-line distances, the amount of difference depending upon various combinations of latitude and longitude. The difference increases (1) as the latitude increases, (2) as the difference in latitude at the two points decreases, and (3) as the difference of longitude increases.

In article 204 it was seen that the equator is a great circle. But the equator is also a rhumb line, with a constant direction of 090° or 270°. Along the equator, then, great-circle and rhumb-line distances are identical; there is no difference at all.

As a vessel moves farther from the equator toward either pole, the saving in distance by way of a great circle becomes greater, and is always greatest for east-west courses (090° or 270°).

All meridians, too, are great circles by definition; they are also rhumb lines of constant direction, 000° or 180°. It thus can be quickly seen that along a meridian (as along the equator) great-circle distances and rhumb-line distances are identical; there is no difference. The difference begins to increase as the great-circle direction moves away from a north-south direction, reaching a maximum when east-west.

Near the equator, then, the saving in distance by use of a great-circle track is negligible, and it increases only slowly with increasing latitude. For an east-west distance of 1,000 miles, the saving is only 2.5 miles at latitude 40° (North or South), increasing to 10.6 miles at latitude 60°. For the route from New York City to London (mid-latitude about 40°), the great-circle distance is 3,016 nautical miles, and the rhumb-line distance is 3,139 miles—a difference of 123 miles.

Great-circle distances are often calculated, rather than measured on a chart. When so computed, they are measured in degrees and minutes of arc. As is true for any great circle, one degree of arc is equal, for all practical navigational purposes, to 60 nautical miles, and one minute essentially equals 1 mile. The total number of minutes can thus be taken as the distance in nautical miles.

Directions in Navigation

209 From the preceding discussion, it is apparent that there are two different kinds of direction, both of which are of interest to the navigator:

Rhumb-line directions, most commonly used in determining the course to be followed, or the track to be made good.

Great-circle directions, used chiefly in connection with radio direction finding or star sights, and generally referred to as *bearings* or *azimuths*.

In navigation, *true direction* is the direction from one point on the earth's surface to another, without regard to the distance between them; it is expressed as an angle in degrees from 000° to 360°, referenced to true north. True north may be considered as either 000° or 360°, according to the problem at hand.

In figure 209, the true direction from A to B is 060°. The true direction from B to A is 240°; this is

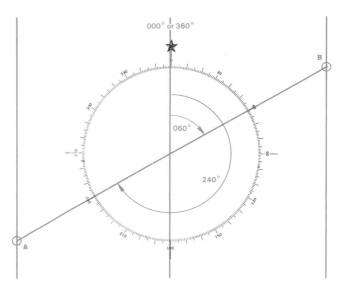

Figure 209. Measurement of direction (course, track) in navigation.

called the *reciprocal* direction and is 180° greater, or less, than the other direction. It is axiomatic that every line has two directions, hence the direction intended should be clearly indicated on a chart by arrow heads or some system of labeling. Direction can be shown as clearly by the *order of letters* used: thus AB is the direction from A to B; the reciprocal direction from B to A is BA.

All directions, whether great circle, rhumb line, or other, are *true directions* when measured from the true geographic meridian printed on the chart; *magnetic directions* when measured from magnetic north; and *compass directions* when measured with respect to compass north as indicated by the vessel's compass. *Relative directions* are those measured from the ship's head (the direction in which the ship is pointed).

Definitions, Abbreviations, and Symbols

210 Certain terms are widely used in navigation. A few that have already been touched upon, together with several related ones, will be defined here, together with their commonly used abbreviations and symbols. Others will be defined later as they are introduced and used.

Azimuth (Zn). The great-circle direction of any place or object from a given point; chiefly used to designate the direction of a heavenly body in celestial navigation. When referred to true north, azimuth is written as Zn. *Azimuth angle* (Az or Z) is measured either east or west to 90° using either north or south as the reference direction.

Bearing (B). Same as azimuth, but commonly used in radio direction finding, or in visual sights. As mentioned in article 208, azimuths and bearings (or any other directional term) may be true, magnetic, compass, or relative, according to the reference line or point used.

Course (C). As applied to marine navigation, the direction in which a vessel is to be steered, or is being steered; the direction of travel through the water. Course may be designated as *true, magnetic, compass,* or *grid* as determined by the reference system in use. The course is measured from 000° clockwise from the reference direction to 360°.

Heading (Hdg. or SH). The direction in which a ship points or heads at any instant, expressed in angular units, 000° clockwise through 360°, from a reference point. The heading of a ship is also called ship's head. Heading is a constantly changing value as a ship oscillates or yaws across the course due to effects of the sea and of steering error.

Track (TR). The intended (anticipated, desired) direction of movement with respect to the earth.

Course Over Ground (COG). The actual path of a vessel with respect to the earth; this will not be a straight line if the vessel's heading varies as she yaws back and forth across the course.

Course Made Good (CMG). The single resultant direction from a given point of departure to a subsequent position; the direction of the net movement from one point to the other. This may differ from the track by inaccuracies in steering, varying current effects, etc.; see figure 210.

Mile. The unit of distance used in navigation at sea is the *international nautical mile* (n.mi.) of 6,076.1 feet (1.852 km). In practical terms it is equivalent to one minute of latitude, or one minute of arc of any great circle. The *statute mile* (st.mi.) of 5,280 feet (1.609 km) is used on land and some inland U.S. waters such as the Great Lakes and the Intracoastal Waterways. One nautical mile equals approximately 1.15 statute miles. Unless otherwise qualified, the term "mile (mi.)" in this book will mean the international nautical mile. (For short distances, a nautical mile and 2,000 yards are often used interchangeably; the error is only 1¼ percent.)

Knot (kn, or occasionally kt). The unit of speed; one knot equals one nautical mile per hour. It is redundant and incorrect to refer to speeds in "knots *per hour.*"

Latitude (Lat., L or occasionally ϕ, the Greek letter phi). The arc distance of a point measured from the equator toward either pole. In problems involving latitude at two or more points, latitude of the

Figure 210. Course, track, course over ground (exaggerated), and course made good.

first point is usually written as L_1; second point L_2, etc. *Difference* of latitude between two places is indicated by l; *mid-latitude* (the mean latitude) is indicated by Lm.

Longitude (Long., Lo or λ, the Greek letter lambda). The angular distance along the equator or a parallel between the prime meridian at Greenwich and the meridian of a particular point. In problems involving the longitude of two or more points, the longitude of the first point is written as Lo_1 or λ_1), the second point as Lo_2 (or λ_2), etc. The east-west separation of two points is termed *difference of longitude* (DLo) when expressed in angular units, or as *departure* (p) when expressed in linear units such as nautical miles.

Time. In navigation, time is stated on the basis of a 24-hour clock rather than the typical 12-hour timepiece. This method removes the dangers of confusing "A.M." and "P.M." time; it is used by the U.S. Armed Forces and by the civilian population of many foreign countries.

In many applications, such as piloting and dead reckoning, seconds are not needed, and time is normally stated as a four-digit number without spaces; the first two digits represent the hours, from 00 to 24, and the latter two the minutes, from 00 to 59.

Hours and minutes before 10:00 A.M. are preceded by a zero, to maintain the four-digit system. Thus, 9:30 A.M. is written 0930, and 4:37 P.M. becomes 1637. When spoken, the former would be "oh-nine-thirty," and the latter "sixteen thirty-seven." Exact hours are said as "oh-five-hundred" or "seventeen hundred," for example. The times 1000 and 2000 are spoken "ten hundred" and "twenty hundred" respectively; not as "one thousand" or "two thousand." It is *incorrect* in nautical usage to add "hours" to the expression of time, as in "sixteen hundred hours."

In other applications, such as celestial navigation, time measurement to seconds is critical. In this case time is normally expressed by writing hours, minutes, and seconds separated by dashes. Thus a clock time of 10 hours, 57 minutes, and 17 seconds P.M. is written 22-57-17. If the number of hours, minutes, or seconds is less than 10, a "0" is placed in front of each so that the hour, minutes, and seconds are each expressed by two digits; a time of 4 hours, 9 minutes, and 7 seconds A.M. is written as 04-09-07. Since the connotation of hours, minutes, and seconds is understood, no further labeling is required.

Time zone descriptions may be applied if necessary; see articles 2213–2215.

Chapter 3

Compasses

THE MAGNETIC COMPASS

Introduction

301 The origins of the *magnetic compass* are not precisely recorded by history; it is one of the oldest—if not the oldest—of a navigator's instruments. It was almost certainly developed independently in several different seagoing cultures. The Vikings were apparently familiar with it in the eleventh century, and the Chinese at the same time, or even earlier, as seamen in those areas were familiar with the natural magnetic properties of lodestone, a type of iron ore. Although historical records are lacking, the first compasses most likely consisted of a piece of lodestone placed on a chip of wood floating in a bowl of water. Soon this developed into an iron needle thrust through a straw and floated on the surface of a container of water; a lodestone had to be applied to the needle each time that this "compass" was to be used.

Initially, a compass was used only to indicate north, but subsequently the concept of marking other directions around the rim of the bowl was introduced. The directions were given the names of the various winds, now known as North, East, South, and West; these are the *cardinal* directions. Next are the *intercardinal* directions: NE, SE, SW, and NW. Still finer subdivisions are the *combination* directions: NNE, ENE, ESE, etc., and the *by-points:* NxE, NNExN, NNExE, etc. This system results in a complete circle divided into 32 points (1 point = $11\frac{1}{4}°$), and there are half-points and quarter points. The point system was widely used until relatively modern times, but is now obsolete except for some minor use on sailing craft and generalized use in indicating the direction of wind.

Because of the difficulty at sea in using a needle floating freely in an open bowl of water, the next development was that of using a pivot at the center of a dry bowl. Not for some centuries was the liquid put back in, this time in an enclosed chamber, as now is the case with the modern magnetic compass.

The magnetic compass still retains its importance despite the invention of the gyrocompass. While the latter is an extremely accurate instrument, it is highly complex, dependent on an electrical power supply, and subject to mechanical damage. The magnetic compass, on the other hand, is entirely self-contained, fairly simple, and not easily damaged.

Standard and Steering Compasses

Many vessels carry two magnetic compasses; these are the *standard compass* and the *steering compass.* The standard compass, whenever possible, is located on the ship's centerline, and on a weather deck near the bridge, at a point where it will be least affected by unfavorable magnetic influences. Headings read from this compass are termed *per standard compass (psc).* The steering compass in most ships is also located near the centerline, just forward of the steering wheel, where it can be seen easily by the helmsman. Its headings are termed *per steering compass (p stg c).*

Many small craft will have only a single magnetic compass to serve both functions described above for larger vessels. In some instances it will not be possible to mount it on the centerline, but it still must be properly aligned parallel to the vessel's keel. Another useful form of magnetic compass usually found on boats is a *hand-bearing* compass.

	Points	Angular measure ° ′ ″		Points	Angular measure ° ′ ″
NORTH TO EAST			**SOUTH TO WEST**		
North	0	0 00 00	South	16	180 00 00
N¼E	¼	2 48 45	S¼W	16¼	182 48 45
N½E	½	5 37 30	S½W	16½	185 37 30
N¾E	¾	8 26 15	S¾W	16¾	188 26 15
N by E	1	11 15 00	S by W	17	191 15 00
N by E¼E	1¼	14 03 45	S by W¼W	17¼	194 03 45
N by E½E	1½	16 52 30	S by W½W	17½	196 52 30
N by E¾E	1¾	19 41 15	S by W¾W	17¾	199 41 15
NNE	2	22 30 00	SSW	18	202 30 00
NNE¼E	2¼	25 18 45	SSW¼W	18¼	205 18 45
NNE½E	2½	28 07 30	SSW½W	18½	208 07 30
NNE¾E	2¾	30 56 15	SSW¾W	18¾	210 56 15
NE by N	3	33 45 00	SW by S	19	213 45 00
NE¾N	3¼	36 33 45	SW¾S	19¼	216 33 45
NE½N	3½	39 22 30	SW½S	19½	219 22 30
NE¼N	3¾	42 11 15	SW¼S	19¾	222 11 15
NE	4	45 00 00	SW	20	225 00 00
NE¼E	4¼	47 48 45	SW¼W	20¼	227 48 45
NE½E	4½	50 37 30	SW½W	20½	230 37 30
NE¾E	4¾	53 26 15	SW¾W	20¾	233 26 15
NE by E	5	56 15 00	SW by W	21	236 15 00
NE by E¼E	5¼	59 03 45	SW by W¼W	21¼	239 03 45
NE by E½E	5½	61 52 30	SW by W½W	21½	241 52 30
NE by E¾E	5¾	64 41 15	SW by W¾W	21¾	244 41 15
ENE	6	67 30 00	WSW	22	247 30 00
ENE¼E	6¼	70 18 45	WSW¼W	22¼	250 18 45
ENE½E	6½	73 07 30	WSW½W	22½	253 07 30
ENE¾E	6¾	75 56 15	WSW¾W	22¾	255 56 15
E by N	7	78 45 00	W by S	23	258 45 00
E¾N	7¼	81 33 45	W¾S	23¼	261 33 45
E½N	7½	84 22 30	W½S	23½	264 22 30
E¼N	7¾	87 11 15	W¼S	23¾	267 11 15

	Points	Angular measure ° ′ ″		Points	Angular measure ° ′ ″
EAST TO SOUTH			**WEST TO NORTH**		
East	8	90 00 00	West	24	270 00 00
E¼S	8¼	92 48 45	W¼N	24¼	272 48 45
E½S	8½	95 37 30	W½N	24½	275 37 30
E¾S	8¾	98 26 15	W¾N	24¾	278 26 15
E by S	9	101 15 00	W by N	25	281 15 00
ESE¾E	9¼	104 03 45	WNW¾W	25¼	284 03 45
ESE½E	9½	106 52 30	WNW½W	25½	286 52 30
ESE¼E	9¾	109 41 15	WNW¼W	25¾	289 41 15
ESE	10	112 30 00	WNW	26	292 30 00
SE by E¾E	10¼	115 18 45	NW by W¾W	26¼	295 18 45
SE by E½E	10½	118 07 30	NW by W½W	26½	298 07 30
SE by E¼E	10¾	120 56 15	NW by W¼W	26¾	300 56 15
SE by E	11	123 45 00	NW by W	27	303 45 00
SE¾E	11¼	126 33 45	NW¾W	27¼	306 33 45
SE½E	11½	129 22 30	NW½W	27½	309 22 30
SE¼E	11¾	132 11 15	NW¼W	27¾	312 11 15
SE	12	135 00 00	NW	28	315 00 00
SE¼S	12¼	137 48 45	NW¼N	28¼	317 48 45
SE½S	12½	140 37 30	NW½N	28½	320 37 30
SE¾S	12¾	143 26 15	NW¾N	28¾	323 26 15
SE by S	13	146 15 00	NW by N	29	326 15 00
SSE¾E	13¼	149 03 45	NNW¾W	29¼	329 03 45
SSE½E	13½	151 52 30	NNW½W	29½	331 52 30
SSE¼E	13¾	154 41 15	NNW¼W	29¾	334 41 15
SSE	14	157 30 00	NNW	30	337 30 00
S by E¾E	14¼	160 18 45	N by W¾W	30¼	340 18 45
S by E½E	14½	163 07 30	N by W½W	30½	343 07 30
S by E¼E	14¾	165 56 15	N by W¼W	30¾	345 56 15
S by E	15	168 45 00	N by W	31	348 45 00
S¾E	15¼	171 33 45	N¾W	31¼	351 33 45
S½E	15½	174 22 30	N½W	31½	354 22 30
S¼E	15¾	177 11 15	N¼W	31¾	357 11 15
South	16	180 00 00	North	32	360 00 00

Figure 301. Conversion table, points to degrees (from DMAHTC Pub. No. 9).

This is a small, lightweight unit that is used for taking bearings all around the horizon from many locations on the craft; see figure 309d.

The articles that follow take note of the continuing importance of the magnetic compass, despite the great advances made in the field of the gyrocompass. They will deal only briefly with the theory of magnetism, and are not intended as a treatise for the professional compass adjustor. The theory of compass adjustment is covered in detail in the *Handbook of Magnetic Compass Adjustment and Compensation*, DMAHTC Pub. No. 226.

Magnetic Principles

302 Magnetism is a fundamental physical phenomenon that occurs both naturally, as in a lodestone mentioned above, and artificially by induction. It is the property of certain metals to attract or repel items of like material or certain other metals; it is also an effect of electrical currents. An object that exhibits the property of magnetism is called a *magnet*. It can be elongated, as in a *bar* magnet, shaped like a horseshoe, or take other forms. The space around each magnet in which its

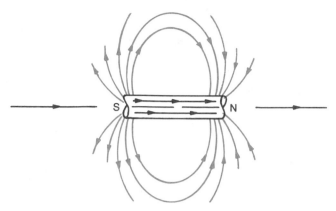

Figure 302. Lines of force representing the field around a bar magnet.

influence can be detected is called its *field;* this can be pictured as being composed of many lines of force that represent its field. The lines concentrate at both ends, or *poles,* of a magnet. Each magnet always has two areas of opposite polarity; one is termed *north* and the other *south.*

The Basic Law of Magnetism

The basic law of magnetism is that poles of the *same polarity repel* each other and those of *opposite polarity attract.* Thus an *N* pole (sometimes colored red in illustrations) attracts an *S* (blue) pole, but repels another *N* pole.

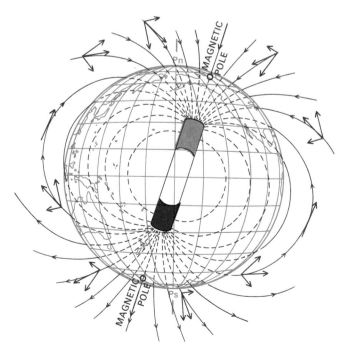

Figure 303. The earth's magnetic field.

The Earth as a Magnet

303   The earth may be visualized as having a bar magnet within it, radiating lines of force that may be detected on the surface; figure 303 illustrates this concept. This "internal magnet" is not exactly aligned with the earth's axis. The consequence of this divergence is that the magnetic poles are *not* at the same locations as the geographic poles; furthermore, the locations of the magnetic poles vary with time. These two factors complicate the use of a magnetic compass. The *north magnetic pole* is currently in the vicinity of latitude 78.9° N, longitude 103.8° W, and the *south magnetic pole* is near 65.4° S, 139.5° E; these positions are somewhat indefinite and change irregularly over the years. Some studies have shown that the poles appear to move in daily cycles over an elliptical path having a major axis of about 50 miles; such movement is, of course, too slight to affect practical navigation in nonpolar latitudes.

Magnetic Meridians

At the surface of the earth, the lines of force become *magnetic meridians.* The irregularity of these lines is primarily caused by the non-uniform distribution of magnetic material within the earth.

The magnetic lines of force can be divided into two components, horizontal and vertical. For a navigator, both the horizontal and vertical components are important, and are discussed as *variation* and *dip* in subsequent articles.

Variation

304   Magnetic meridians indicate the direction of the earth's magnetic field, but only in a very few places do the magnetic and geographic meridians coincide. The difference at any location between the directions of the magnetic and true meridians is the *variation,* sometimes called *magnetic declination.* It can also be described as the difference between true north and the direction that a compass would point if free of all local influences. Variation is labeled easterly *(E)* if the compass needle, aligned with the magnetic meridian, points eastward or to the right of true north; and westerly *(W),* if it points to the left. Variation results from the horizontal component of the earth's magnetic field.

Variation is important to the navigator because a magnetic compass, responding to the earth's magnetic field, is in error in measuring true geographic direction by the amount of the variation (Var. or *V*). The magnetic variation and its annual rate of change are shown on charts, so that directions indicated by the magnetic compass can be corrected to true directions. Since variation is caused by the earth's magnetic field, its value changes with the geographic location of a vessel, but is the same for all headings of that vessel at any specific position and for all vessels at or near that position.

Secular Change

The earth's magnetic field is not constant in either intensity or direction. The changes are *diurnal* (daily), *yearly*, and *secular* (occurring over a longer period of time). The changes in intensity are too small to have any effect in navigation. The same is true of diurnal changes in direction, except in polar regions, where diurnal changes of as much as 7° have been observed.

The secular change in direction, however, can be a practical factor in navigation. Although it has been under observation for more than 300 years, the length of its period has not been fully established. The change generally consists of a reasonably steady increase or decrease in *variation*. This change may continue for many years, sometimes reaching large values, remain nearly unvarying for a few years, and then reverse its trend.

Another change, although not one of immediate importance to a navigator, is the long-term fading of the earth's magnetic field as a whole. Although the causes are not well understood, it is known that there have been 12 reversals of magnetic polarity over the past nine million years, and that we are overdue for another. The earth's field intensity has decreased 50 percent in the last 4,000 years, and one study predicts that in 1,200 years or so magnetic compasses will become useless—there will be no field to direct them and they will point in any direction. Although all decreases do not result in reversal, when the field returns a few centuries later, its polarity is more likely than not to have reversed!

Updating Charted Variation

The secular change is extremely complex. However, if the change of inclination of the magnetic meridian to the geographic meridian is measured over a period of years at a given location, its future values for the next few years can be predicted with reasonable accuracy. Charts generally indicate the value of the variation for a stated year, and the annual amount and direction of the secular change, so that the variation for any subsequent year, within a reasonable period, can be calculated. This annual change is printed within each compass rose on a chart as shown in figure 304. Predictions of the

change of variation are intended for short-term use—a period of a few years. Since values derived from the predictions on an older chart may be in error, the latest chart editions available should always be used.

Dip

305 The earth and its surrounding magnetic field are illustrated in figure 303. Note that the lines of force are horizontal, or parallel to the earth's surface, only at the *magnetic equator*, which is defined as the line connecting points of zero dip. At all other points they are inclined to the horizontal, the degree of inclination increasing as the magnetic poles are approached, where the inclination reaches 90°. The amount of this inclination is called the *dip* or *magnetic inclination*, and the instrument that measures it is called a *dip circle*.

As the compass magnets are constrained to remain essentially horizontal, they are acted on only by the horizontal component of the earth's total magnetic force. This is greatest at the magnetic equator, where the dip is 0°, and it disappears altogether at the magnetic poles, where the dip is 90°. Thus it can be seen that the aligning force on a magnetic compass will be considerably diminished at the higher magnetic latitudes.

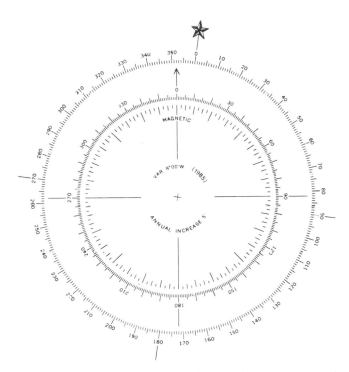

Figure 304. Compass rose, showing variation and annual rate of change.

Magnetic Charts

306 Lines on a chart that connect points of equal magnetic variation are called *isogonic lines;* the line of zero variation is the *agonic line.* The Defense Mapping Agency Hydrographic Topographic Center publishes a series of magnetic charts of the earth as a whole (Mercator projection) and for the north and south polar areas (azimuthal equidistant projection). Separate charts are prepared for variation and vertical inclination (dip) and for intensity of field—horizontal, vertical, and total; they are revised when required by changes in the earth's magnetic field. Of greatest interest to a navigator is DMAHTC Chart 42, Magnetic Variation Chart of the World (printed for various years); a simplified adaptation of the one for 1985 is shown in figure 306.

While these charts are useful for planning purposes, the large-scale chart of the area involved should always be consulted in setting a course by magnetic compass or converting a magnetic compass bearing to a true bearing for plotting, since there are many small irregularities in variation that cannot be shown on small-scale world charts. In addition, there are very small areas of local magnetic disturbance that may or may not be indicated on charts. At one place off the coast of Australia, near Cossack, the variation changes from 56° E to 26° W in a distance of about 180 yards, less than the length of a ship; areas of local disturbance of lesser magnitude extend over nearly three miles of navigable water. There are many others of less extreme nature, but still of a magnitude and extent that must be taken into account by a navigator.

Modern Compass Construction

307 The basic mechanism of modern magnetic compasses is exactly the same as that of the very earliest ones used—a small bar magnet freely suspended in the magnetic field of the earth. Refinements have been added for greater accuracy, steadiness of indication, and ease of reading, but the fundamental mechanism remains unchanged.

Compass Components

The modern marine magnetic compass is contained in a glass-topped bowl made of nonmagnetic material. Figure 307a presents a sectional view, and figure 307b a photograph, of a Navy standard No. 1 seven-and-one-half-inch compass. The letter C indicates the bowl with its cover secured by the bezel ring, G. The letters in the following description refer to the corresponding components in this illustration. At the forward side of the bowl is the *lubber's line,* which indicates the direction of the vessel's head (355° in the photograph). At the center of the bottom of the bowl is a vertical pin, the pivot,

Figure 306. Simplified chart of magnetic variation worldwide, showing agonic and isogonic lines (from Chart 42).

Figure 307a. Cutaway view of a magnetic compass.

Figure 307b. U.S. Navy standard No. 1, 7½-inch varsol-filled compass.

The bowl is supported in *gimbals*, or double rings, hinged on both the fore and aft and athwartships axes. These gimbals permit the compass bowl to remain horizontal, or nearly so, regardless of the vessel's rolling or pitching. A gimbal is illustrated in figure 307b.

The gimbaled compass is mounted in a *binnacle*, or stand, made of nonmagnetic material. A typical binnacle is shown in figure 307c. (The balls on either side are called "quadrantal spheres"; their function is explained in article 315.)

A recent development of advanced technology is the *remote-reading magnetic compass*, particularly useful on small craft where a suitable location for the magnetic compass at the helm is difficult or impossible to obtain. With this equipment, the direction-sensing unit can be located at any place on the vessel where the magnetic environment is favorable. Directional information is transmitted electronically to a digital readout at the helm that need not be critically positioned. The electronic signals can also be fed into other navigational equipment requiring direction as an input, such as dead reckoning plotters or satellite navigation receivers.

Requirements for a Marine Compass

308 Much research has gone into the development of the magnetic compass to bring it to its present high state of accuracy and reliability. Metallic alloys have been intensively studied in order

upon which the compass card (B) rests. To the bottom of this card are attached two or more magnets (A) aligned with the north-south axis of the compass card. The card is marked around its outer edge with graduations at suitable intervals—1°, 2°, or 5°—from 000° at the point where the card indicates compass north clockwise through 360°; cardinal and intercardinal directions may also be shown on the card in some designs.

In order to reduce friction on the pivot and to dampen vibration, the compass bowl is filled with a clear fluid (D) that is not subject to freezing at normal temperatures. The card has a *float* or air chamber (E), designed so that it will support all but a minute percentage of the weight of the card with its attached magnets. Lastly, the bowl is fitted with an *expansion bellows* (F), which permits the bowl to remain filled as the liquid expands and contracts with temperature changes.

Figure 307c. Binnacle for standard U.S. Navy compass.

that magnets of increased strength and retentivity might be produced. Alloys of nickel, cobalt, and other metals have proven far superior to the iron formerly used in both these respects. In addition, great advances have been made in protecting the needle from mechanical disturbances, in reducing its oscillations, or *hunting*, and in the presentation of the directional readout.

On some modern compasses a circular or ring magnet is used, replacing the bar magnets attached to the compass card. The ring magnet, due to its circular shape, causes less friction with the fluid in the compass bowl as the ship turns, producing an exceptionally steady card.

Typical Marine Compasses

309   The No. 1 *seven-and-one-half-inch compass* described in article 307 is the magnetic compass used most widely in the U.S. Navy. It has proven itself to be an excellent instrument. Two other typical compasses are the five-inch model shown in figure 309a and the three-inch model illustrated in figure 309b. Merchant ships use compasses of generally similar design. A specialized type of magnetic compass—the hand-bearing compass—is described in article 707.

A *spherical compass* is illustrated in Figure 309c. This type of compass is becoming increasingly popular among yachtsmen, as well as with commercial operators, as it offers several advantages compared to the conventional flat-topped compass. These compasses are internally gimbaled, and the compass card is pivoted at the center of the sphere, assuring maximum stability of the card in all conditions of pitch, roll, and heave. In addition, the transparent spherical dome of the compass acts as a powerful magnifying glass, and greatly increases the apparent size of the compass card in the area of the lubber's line. A "dished" card, slightly concave,

Figure 309b. U.S. Navy standard No. 5, 3-inch varsol-filled top-reading compass.

together with spherical dome, permits such a compass to be read accurately from a distance of 10 feet (3 m) or more. When fitted with shock-absorbing mounts, a spherical compass functions very well in high-speed boats, despite continuous vibration and shock in heavy seas.

Operation of a Magnetic Compass

310   When a compass is mounted on a vessel, its magnets align themselves with the magnetic field in which they exist. Assuming for the moment that there are no local influences (objects of magnetic material or electrical currents), this alignment will be parallel to the horizontal component of the earth's magnetic field. *The compass card will maintain this alignment regardless of the vessel's heading.*

As the compass card is attached to the magnets, the 000° mark on the card always points in the direction of *compass north*, and the ship's *compass heading* is indicated by the lubber's line. If there are no local disturbing influences, no *deviation* (see article 311 below), then this is also the *magnetic heading*. When a compass is installed, great care must be taken to align the lubber's line exactly parallel to the centerline of the ship. The compass bowl and lubber's line turn with the vessel, thus the direction of the lubber's line from the center of the compass always represents the direction of the ship's head. Since the 000° mark on the card is always toward the magnetic north, the direction indicated on the compass card opposite the lubber's line is the ship's heading. As the ship turns, the lubber's line turns with it, while the compass card remains aligned with compass north, so that the

Figure 309a. U.S. Navy standard No. 3, 5-inch alcohol-filled compass in binnacle.

Figure 309c. A spherical compass.

Figure 309d. A hand-bearing compass.

heading at any moment is indicated at the lubber's line. *Remember—it is the lubber's line, and not the compass card, that turns.*

Deviation

311 As stated above, a compass needle free to turn horizontally tends to align itself with the earth's magnetic lines of force. Unfortunately, it is not free to do so in a steel ship; such ships have marked magnetic properties of their own, and these tend to deflect the compass from the magnetic meridian. The divergence thus caused between the north-south axis of the compass card and the magnetic meridian is called *deviation* (Dev. or D). Even in a vessel made of wood or fiberglass there is enough magnetic material on board— engines, fuel and water tanks, rigging, etc.—to cause deviation.

The possibility of deviation from electrical circuits must not be overlooked. Direct currents flowing in straight wires create magnetic fields. Care must be taken that all wiring in the vicinity of a compass is properly installed to eliminate or reduce any effect on the compass; checks must be made for deviation with the circuits turned on and off.

Although deviation differs from variation in that the latter is caused by the *earth's* magnetism, the two are designated in the same manner. Thus, if no deviation is present, the compass card lies with its axis in the magnetic meridian, and its north point indicates the direction of *magnetic* north. If deviation is present and the north point of the compass points eastward of magnetic north, the deviation is named *easterly* and marked *E*. If it points westward

of magnetic north, the deviation is named *westerly* and marked *W*.

The navigator can easily find the correct variation by referring to the chart of his area. Deviation, however, is not so simple to ascertain. It varies not only on different ships, but on any particular ship it varies with changes in the ship's heading. Also, it changes somewhat with large changes in the vessel's latitude, as a result of change in the relative strengths of local disturbing influences and the horizontal component of the earth's magnetic field.

Compass Error

312 The algebraic sum of variation (article 304) and deviation (article 311) is termed *compass error.* The navigator must understand thoroughly how to apply variation, deviation, and compass error, as he is frequently required to use them in converting one kind of direction to another.

From the foregoing it should be apparent that there are three ways in which a direction can be expressed:

As *true*, when referred to the *true* (geographic) meridian as the origin of measurement.

As *magnetic*, when referred to the *magnetic* meridian as the origin of measurement.

As *compass*, when referred to the axis of the *compass* card as the origin of measurement.

Any given direction may be expressed in all three of these ways, if it is understood that:

True differs from *magnetic* by *variation.*
Magnetic differs from *compass* by *deviation.*
Compass differs from *true* by *compass error.*

Figure 312a. Compass error.

Figure 312a outlines a vessel in which is shown the card of the standard compass. OC is the direction of the compass needle. OM is the magnetic meridian, and OT the true meridian. The two outer circles, concentric with the standard compass card, represent magnetic and true compass roses, thus indicating magnetic and true directions. The observer is at O. The magnetic meridian is 12° eastward (right) of the true meridian; therefore, the variation at that position is 12° E. It is added to the magnetic direction of M (0° on magnetic rose) to obtain the true direction of M (12° on true rose). The compass needle is 8° eastward (right) of the magnetic meridian; therefore, the deviation is 8° E on the ship's heading shown. It is added to the compass direction of C (0° on compass card) to obtain the magnetic direction of C (8° on magnetic rose). The compass error is the algebraic sum of the variation and deviation or CE = 20° E. It is added to the compass direction of C (0° on compass card) to obtain the true direction of C (20° on true rose). The bearing of object A from the ship is shown as 20° psc, 28° magnetic, and 40° true. In practice, bearings are expressed in three-numeral groups—e.g., 020°, 028°, and 040°. The ship's heading is 300° psc (note lubber's line LL), 308° magnetic, and 320° true.

As already noted, easterly deviation is added (+) to magnetic in converting to true. Conversely, they are subtracted (−) when converting in the reverse order.

Figures 312b and c show westerly variation and deviation and demonstrate that the above rules of application should be reversed for westerly errors.

Rules for Applying Compass Errors

It is convenient to have a rule of thumb to serve as an aid to the memory in applying the above principles. The following will serve: *When correcting, easterly errors are added*, or simply, *correcting add east*. When applying this rule, it is necessary to consider a *compass* direction as the "least correct" expression of direction, as it contains two "errors," variation and deviation. *Magnetic* direction is thus "more correct" than compass as it contains only *one error*, variation. This is so even when the axis of the compass card is closer to the true meridian than is the magnetic meridian. Magnetic direction is, however, "less correct" than *true* direction, which contains *no errors*. Hence the process of converting a compass direction to a magnetic or true direction or of converting a magnetic direction to a true direction is one of "correcting," or removing errors. If easterly errors are added, it is obvious that westerly errors are subtracted, and no separate rule is needed.

Correcting and Uncorrecting

The opposite of *correcting* is called *uncorrecting*. The process of uncorrecting is one of converting a true direction to a magnetic or compass direction or a magnetic direction to a compass direction by applying errors. If easterly errors are added and westerly errors subtracted when correcting, then the reverse is true when uncorrecting. Hence, the one rule, *correcting add east*, is sufficient to cover all four possible situations:

Correcting—add east, subtract west.
Uncorrecting—add west, subtract east.

C-D-M-V-T

Another method for remembering the rules of correcting and uncorrecting involves using the first letters of the following words: Compass, Deviation, Magnetic, Variation, and True and letting these be the initial letters of words that form an easy-to-remember sentence. A convenient one to use is Can Dead Men Vote Twice? Using this sentence to remember the order, write down just the initial letters and arrange them vertically:

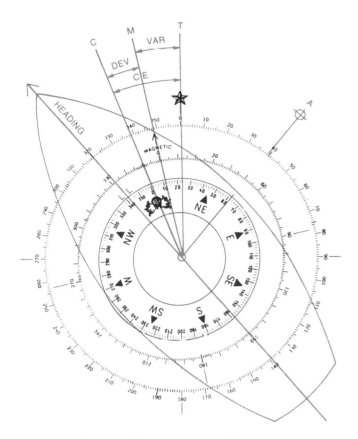

Figure 312b. Westerly variation and deviation.

Figure 312c. Westerly variation, but easterly deviation.

W   C _____
↑   D _____
+   M _____
↓   V _____
E   T _____

To the left of the column, draw a double-ended arrow, placing a W at the top, an E at the bottom, and a *plus* sign in the center as illustrated. The addition of "At Elections" to the sentence above will assist in remembering that in the direction C-D-M-V-T the procedure is to *Add East*. The arrowheads have nothing to do with actual direction, but apply only to the direction of proceeding through the initial letters of the memory phrase, whether correcting from compass to true or uncorrecting from true to compass.

Now, by placing the given information in the corresponding blanks, the unknown values can easily be computed following the rule of the form.

Examples of Correcting and Uncorrecting

Example 1: A ship is heading 127° per standard compass. For this heading the deviation is 16° E, and the variation is 4° W in the area.

Required: (1) The magnetic heading. (2) The true heading.

Solution: The problem is one of correcting. Since the deviation is easterly, it must be added. Hence, the magnetic heading is 127° + 16° = 143°. To find the true direction we are again correcting, and since the variation is westerly, it is subtracted. Hence, the true heading is 143° − 4° = 139°. In this case the compass error is 16° E − 4° W = 12° E. Applying this directly to the compass heading, we find the true heading is 127° + 12° = 139°, as previously determined.

Answers: (1) MH 143°, (2) TH 139°.

Example 2: A ship's course is 347° psc. The deviation is 4° W and the variation is 12° E.

Required: (1) The magnetic course. (2) The true course.

Solution: Again the problem is one of correcting. The deviation is subtracted and the magnetic course is 347° − 4° = 343°. The variation is added and the true course is 343° + 12° = 355°.

Answers: (1) MC 343°, (2) TC 355°.

Example 3: A ship's course is 009° psc. The deviation is 2° W and the variation is 19° W.

Required: (1) The magnetic course. (2) The true course.

Solution: The problem is one of correcting, and since both errors are westerly, they are subtracted. The magnetic course is 009° − 2° = 007°. The true course is 007° − 19° = 348°. Since 000° is also 360°, this is the same as 367° − 19° = 348°.

Answers: (1) MC 007°, (2) TC 348°.

Example 4: From a chart the true course between two places is found to be 221°. The variation is 9° E and the deviation is 2° W.

Required: (1) The magnetic course. (2) The compass course.

Solution: It is necessary to uncorrect; the easterly variation is subtracted and the westerly deviation is added. The magnetic course is 221° − 9° = 212°. The compass course is 212° + 2° = 214°.

Answers: (1) MC 212°, (2) CC 214°.

Naming Variation, Deviation, or Compass Error

Another problem that can arise is that of assigning a "name"—east or west—to variation, deviation, or compass error when the numerical value has been found by subtraction between two directions. Here, the simple phrase rhymes as follows:

Compass least, error east.
Compass best, error west.

"Least" means lesser numerically, and "best" means greater numerically. For variation from true directions, "magnetic" can be substituted for "compass" in the rhyme.

Example 5: A navigator sets up a compass at a spot on shore near the ship's anchorage. This compass, not being affected by the iron and steel of the ship, is free from deviation and indicates magnetic direction. From the chart the navigator determines the true bearing of a distant mountain peak to be 320°. By compass it bears 337°. The ship bears 076° by compass from the observation spot ashore.

Required: (1) The variation. (2) The true bearing of the ship.

Solution: The numerical difference between the true and magnetic bearings is 17°; since the magnetic bearing is greater—"best" by the rhyme—the variation is westerly, 17° W. To find the true bearing of the ship is "correcting," and we use the previous rule—correcting, subtract west: thus, the true bearing of the ship is 076° − 17° = 059°.

Answers: (1) V 17° W, (2) TB 059°.

Example 6: Two aids to navigation are so placed that when seen in line from seaward they mark the direction of a channel, 161° T. Seen in line from a ship heading up the channel, they bear 157.5° by compass. The chart shows the variation for the locality to be 2.5° E.

Required: (1) The compass error. (2) The deviation.

Solution: The numerical difference is 161° − 157.5° = 3.5°. Since "compass is least," the "error is east." The compass error is the algebraic sum of the variation and deviation. Hence, the deviation is the algebraic *difference* or 3.5° − 2.5° = 1.0° E.

Answers: (1) CE 3.5° E, (2) D 1.0° E.

The table below summarizes the six examples; answers that were determined in each problem are underscored. A line for compass error (CE) has been added.

Deviation Table

313 As stated in article 311, the deviation changes with a change in the vessel's heading. The deviation is determined by comparing a direction shown on the compass with the known magnetic direction. Several methods of accomplishing this will be explained later. The deviation on various headings is tabulated on a form called *a deviation table* (or *magnetic compass table*) and posted near the compass. A copy of the table should also be kept posted in the charthouse.

Figures 313a and 313b illustrate the standard U.S. Navy form, used for tabulating deviation, compass history, and performance data.

It provides blanks for filling in certain information regarding the compass and the correctors used to reduce the deviation. Two different columns of deviation are shown, one marked "DGOFF" and the other "DGON." "DG" refers to the ship's de-

		1	2	3	4	5	6
W							
↑	C	127°	347°	009°	214°	337°	157°.5
+	D	16° E	4° W	2° W	2° W	0°	1° E
↓	M	143°	343°	007°	212°	337°	158°.5
E	V	4° W	12° E	19° W	9° E	17° W	2°.5 E
	T	139°	355°	348°	221°	320°	161°
	CE	12° E	8° E	21° W	7° E	17° W	3°.5 E

Figure 313a. Left, deviation table (front), NAVSHIPS 3120/4; 313b, right, deviation table (reverse), NAVSHIPS 3120/4.

gaussing coils. Since the deviation may be somewhat different when the degaussing coils are energized, it is necessary to determine the deviation under both conditions. Merchant ships and small craft would use a roughly comparable form. A deviation table for a vessel without degaussing coils would be simpler by half.

The deviations shown in this illustration are somewhat larger than would be acceptable under normal conditions of a properly adjusted compass. Such larger values are given here to provide practice in calculation and interpolation, the procedure for determining an intermediate value between two tabular listings.

A deviation table can be made for ship's heading by compass as in figure 313c or, more commonly, by vessel's heading magnetic as shown in figure

313a. *When the deviations are small (5° or less), compass and magnetic courses being close together, little significant error is introduced in entering the deviation table with either compass or magnetic heading.* When the deviations are large and change rapidly, great care must be exercised in using the table of deviation to ensure that the proper deviation is obtained for the heading desired.

To find the compass course when a magnetic heading deviation table is available, proceed in the manner discussed in the following examples.

Example 1: A ship is to steer course 201° true. The variation is 10.5° W. DG is off.

Required: The compass course using deviation table of figure 313a.

Solution: Applying the variation, the magnetic course is 201° + 10.5° = 211.5°.

SHIPS HEAD COMPASS	DEVIATIONS		SHIPS HEAD COMPASS	DEVIATIONS	
	DG OFF	DG ON		DG OFF	DG ON
0	4.0 W	4.5 W	180	4.5 E	4.0 E
15	4.0 W	4.0 W	195	6.0 E	5.5 E
30	3.5 W	4.0 W	210	7.0 E	6.0 E
45	3.0 W	3.5 W	225	6.5 E	6.0 E
60	2.5 W	3.0 W	240	5.5 E	5.5 E
75	2.5 W	2.5 W	255	4.0 E	3.5 E
90	2.0 W	2.5 W	270	2.5 E	2.5 E
105	2.0 W	2.0 W	285	0.5 E	0.5 E
120	2.0 W	2.0 W	300	1.0 W	1.0 W
135	1.5 W	1.5 W	315	2.5 W	3.0 W
150	0.5 W	0.5 W	330	3.5 W	3.5 W
165	2.0 E	1.5 E	345	4.0 W	4.0 W

Figure 313c. Deviation tabulated by compass headings.

Enter the table with 211.5°. The deviation is 6.5° E. The compass course is 211.5° − 6.5° = 205.0°.

Example 2: The ship's head is 210° magnetic. A lighthouse bears 136° by compass. The variation is 3° E. DG is off.

Required: The true bearing using deviation table of figure 313a.

Solution: The deviation depends on the ship's head, *not* the bearing. Hence, we enter the table with 210°. The deviation is 6.5° + 3.0° E = 9.5° E. The true bearing is then 136° + 9.5° = 145.5°.

Answer: TB 145.5°.

Example 3: Using the deviation table of figure 313a, determine the compass courses corresponding to the following true courses in an area where the variation is 12° W and the DG off: 093°, 168°, 238°.

Answers: CC 107°, CC 176°, CC 245°.

When it is desired to find a compass course if deviations for compass headings only (figure 313c) are available, proceed as shown in example 4.

Example 4: A vessel is to steer course 187° true. The variation is 6° E. DG off.

Required: The compass course (CC) using the deviation table of figure 313c.

Solution: Find the magnetic course first: 187° − 6° = 181°. Enter the deviation table with the compass courses, which when converted to magnetic courses, will bracket the desired magnetic course of 181° as follows:

Ships Hd. Compass	Deviation	Ships Hd. Magnetic
165°	2.0° E	167.0°
		181.0°
180°	4.5° E	184.5°

Interpolate between 167.0° and 184.5° to find the deviation corresponding to MH 181° as follows: for a change in magnetic heading of 17.5° (184.5° − 167.0°), the corresponding change of deviation is +2.5 E. For a change of magnetic heading of 14° (181.0° − 167.0°), the change of deviation is found by the ratio $2.5/17.5 = \Delta d/14$, and $\Delta d = 2.0°$ E. The deviation for MH 181° is then the deviation for MH 167° plus Δd determined above, or 2.0° E + (+2.0° E) = 4.0° E. Combining this deviation with the magnetic course of 181° corresponds to the true course given of 187°, the compass course is found to be 177°.

Answer: CC 177°.

The degree of precision to which calculations are carried should be determined by the application of the final figures. In this book, interpolation and other calculations of direction will be carried out to the nearest half-degree. In the practice of navigation at sea, it is not likely that any greater degree of precision in the steering of a vessel could be obtained, and in smaller craft it is probable that the nearest whole degree would be used.

It should be noted that the deviation tables illustrated above list deviations for either compass or magnetic headings. Usually only one or the other of these deviations is prepared by the navigator and is available.

A simplified form of deviation table is discussed in article 326. It is easier to use, eliminating interpolation, and the table is frequently employed on small craft, although it is applicable to any size vessel.

Napier Diagram

314 If the deviations are large, 10° or more, interpolating for headings between those tabulated can be difficult. A convenient way of graphically determining intermediate values is to use a *Napier Diagram*, also called a *Curve of Deviations*. This permits quick, easy, and accurate interpolation between recorded values of deviation. The user can find the deviation for any heading, compass or magnetic, and obtain the magnetic course corre-

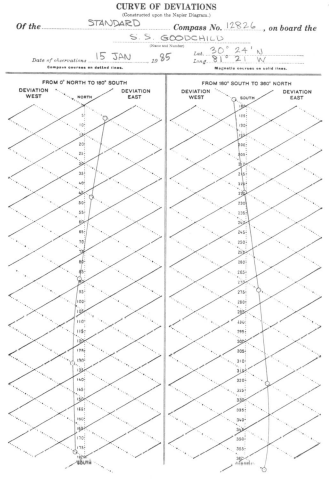

CURVE OF DEVIATIONS
(Constructed upon the Napier Diagram.)

Of the _____ STANDARD _____ Compass No. 12826 _____, on board the
S. S. GOODCHILD
(Name and Number)

Date of observations 15 JAN, 19 85 Lat. 30° 24' N
Long. 81° 21' W

Compass courses on dotted lines. Magnetic courses on solid lines.

Figure 314. Napier diagram, with curves drawn.

sponding to a compass course, or vice versa, simply by drawing two short lines.

Figure 314 shows a Napier diagram. The solid blue curves are drawn through the points established by plotting the deviations given in the following table:

Compass		Magnetic	Deviation
N	000°	012°	12° E
NE	045°	049°	4° E
E	090°	087°	3° W
SE	135°	128°	7° W
S	180°	174°	6° W
SW	225°	224°	1° W
W	270°	278°	8° E
NW	315°	328°	13° E

For simplicity, only whole degrees have been used in this table and there are fewer data points than would be normal. The values here are exces-

sive; they indicate that the compass is in need of adjustment (see article 315), but they serve to illustrate the construction and use of a Napier diagram.

The central dotted line of the diagram with the numerals of every fifth degree represents the rim of a compass card cut at the north point and straightened into a vertical column. For convenience, it is usually arranged in two columns, as shown in the illustration. The method of constructing and using the curve can best be explained by describing the preparation of the *curve of deviations* shown in the figure, and by examples.

Just above the left half of the curve is the precept, "compass courses on dotted lines." This means that to plot the deviation of 12° E on north (000°) by compass, the dotted line is followed toward "deviation east" from the "0" to the twelfth dot. This dot is enclosed in a small circle. (Because the table is in two halves, the full circle back to zero ends with the "360" at bottom of the right half of the diagram; here again the twelfth dot toward "deviation east" is circled for the deviation of 12° E.) In similar fashion, the deviation of 4° E on compass heading of 045 is represented by a circle around the fourth dot from the "45" toward "deviation east," and the 3° W on 090 by compass is shown by the circle around the third dot from the "90" toward "deviation west," etc. A faired curve is drawn through as close as possible to the circled points. When a deviation to a fraction of a degree is to be plotted, the correct position between the dots for the whole degrees on each side is estimated by eye and marked by a circled dot.

Wherever the curve crosses a diagonal dotted line, the deviation for that 15° rhumb of the compass headings may be read directly, as 15° E for 330° and 345° and 5° W for 105°. For a compass heading that does not have a diagonal dotted line through it, a broken line drawn parallel to those dotted lines, from the dot of the desired heading to the curve, will give the deviation. For example, for compass heading 009° the broken line, from the ninth dot on the central line to the curve, will be found to be about 11 dots long toward "deviation east," showing the deviation to be 11° E.

The second precept, "magnetic courses on solid lines," is applied this way: A *solid* line drawn parallel to the *solid* lines, say, from the 323d dot to the curve will be found to be 13 dots long toward "deviation east." This shows that the deviation for 323° *magnetic* is 13° E.

When using the "curve of deviations" to determine directly the magnetic courses corresponding to compass courses, or vice versa, the following old jingle may help in applying the two precepts:

> From compass course, magnetic course to gain,
> Depart by dotted and return by plain.
> From magnetic course to steer the course allotted,
> Depart by plain and then return by dotted.

The first half of this jingle is applied as follows: From the point on the central dotted line, draw a light penciled line from the known compass heading, parallel to the *dotted* diagonal lines, out until it intersects the curve. From this point draw a light line, parallel to the *solid* diagonal lines back until it intersects the central dotted line. At this point, read the value for the desired magnetic heading.

Example 1: The compass heading is 310°. What is the correct magnetic heading? *Answer:* 323°.

The second half of the jingle is applied in a similar fashion. Draw a light construction line from the known magnetic course, parallel to the solid diagonal lines, out to its intersection and then parallel to the dotted diagonal lines, back to the central vertical line where the intersection is the value of the desired compass course.

Example 2: A magnetic course of 020° is desired. What is the compass course to be steered? *Answer:* 009°.

PRACTICAL COMPASS ADJUSTMENT

Introduction

315 Article 311 stated that deviation of a magnetic compass is caused by the magnetic properties of metallic objects on a vessel and/or the vessel itself. A complete analysis of the many separate magnetic components that combine to cause deviation is beyond the scope of this book; however, an understanding of the basic concepts and terminology is desirable. The various magnetic components or parameters of the total magnetic field of a vessel are referred to as *coefficients*, and different correcting magnets are used to compensate for their effects on the compass. Figure 303 illustrates the concept of the earth as a magnet, with the north magnetic pole colored blue, in accordance with the usual practice. Article 302 states that materials of opposite polarity attract each other; the polarity of the magnetic hemisphere and the north-seeking end of a compass magnet are therefore opposite. To identify their polarity, the ends of compensating bar magnets used in binnacles are color-coded, the *north* end being painted *red*, and the *south*, *blue*.

Coefficients of Deviation

The components of the total magnetic forces causing deviation, the coefficients, are arbitrarily defined and designated by letters. As used below, "soft iron" is material in which magnetism is induced by the earth's magnetic field. This magnetism changes as its orientation with respect to the earth's magnetic field changes. In contrast, a ship's "hard iron" has the relatively permanent magnetism acquired during construction and fitting-out. Soft and hard iron are also classified as "horizontal" or "vertical" as determined by the orientation of their magnetic axes when induced by components of the earth's field.

Coefficient A is constant on all headings and may be a combination of other parameters or may be mechanical, as from an incorrectly placed lubber's line.

Coefficient B is maximum on compass headings east or west and zero on compass headings north or south.

Coefficient C is maximum on compass headings north or south and zero on east or west.

Coefficients B and C are caused by permanent magnetism and to some extent by induced magnetism in vertical soft iron. On small craft constructed mainly of wood and/or fiberglass, adjustment is normally made only for these coefficients. Most boat compasses or their mountings will have built-in small correcting magnets for this purpose.

Coefficient D is quadrantal deviation. It is maximum on intercardinal headings: 045°, 135°, 225°, 315°, and zero on cardinal compass headings: north, south, east, west.

Coefficient E is quadrantal deviation, which is maximum on the cardinal compass headings and zero on the intercardinal headings.

Coefficients D and E are caused by induced magnetism in horizontal soft iron and are compensated for by the use of the soft iron *quadrantal spheres* normally mounted on brackets athwartships on the binnacle. These spheres should be used on all vessels constructed of steel.

Heeling Error

Coefficient J is defined as the change of deviation for a heel of 1° while the vessel is on compass heading 000°. It is, in effect, the error caused because the compass, with its gimballing arrangement, remains in a horizontal plane while the vessel, with its magnetic field, rolls and pitches. A slight change in the relative positions of the compass and ship is therefore introduced. This change in deviation caused by the motion of the vessel can cause the compass card to oscillate. Coefficient J is compensated for by a heeling magnet placed in a vertical tube directly below the center of the compass.

Flinders Bar

On the magnetic equator (article 305) there is no vertical component of the earth's magnetic field and consequently no induced magnetism in vertical soft iron. At other locations, notably in higher latitudes, the vertical component can cause the compass to become unreliable over a much larger area than if the force is neutralized. This statement represents an oversimplification of the problem, as the various coefficients are, of course, interrelated. To compensate for or neutralize any induced magnetism in vertical soft iron, a *Flinders bar* is used. This consists of sections of soft iron having no permanent magnetism; as many sections as are required are installed vertically in a tube on the side of the compass opposite to the effective pole of the ship's field.

The theory of compass adjustment hinges on a more complete analysis. The following articles will dispense with theory, and follow empirically the procedure that experience indicates is satisfactory for adjusting the great majority of compasses. It is assumed that the compass is in correct alignment with the ship's centerline, has no internal malfunctions, and that only comparatively minor adjustment is required.

If the procedure outlined hereinafter does not give acceptable results, the services of a professional compass adjustor should be sought. For a detailed discussion of compass adjustment, see *Handbook of Magnetic Compass Adjustment.* DMAHTC Pub. No. 226.

Correctors in Compass Binnacle

316 The *compass binnacle* is the case and stand in which a magnetic compass is mounted. The type used by the Navy for mounting its standard 7½-inch compass is illustrated in figure 307c. It consists of a casting of nonmagnetic material about 3½ feet (1.1 m) high, with an opening in the top to receive the compass and with a place for the correctors used for adjusting the compass. Inside the binnacle, which has access doors, are trays or holders for fore-and-aft magnets and for athwartship magnets. The trays are supported on screws so they can be raised or lowered, with about 12 inches (30 cm) of travel available, and provision is made for as many

as eight 4-inch (10-cm) magnets in each set of trays. These are the B and C correcting magnets. Most modern binnacles now have provision for underlighting the compass. In the center of the interior of the binnacle there is a tube to hold the heeling magnets, which can be moved up and down in the tube and secured as desired. The soft-iron spheres are mounted on either side of the binnacle in grooved brackets that permit the spheres to be moved in a horizontal plane, toward or away from the binnacle. The binnacle in figure 307c is also equipped with degaussing compensating coils shown near the base of the stand. Binnacles for non-naval vessels are generally of similar design, but without degaussing coils.

Preparations for Adjustment

317 The preparatory steps for adjusting the compass can be made before getting underway. The vessel should be on an even keel. All movable magnetic gear in the vicinity of the compass should be secured in the position it will occupy at sea. Several types of personal articles occasionally taken onto the bridge of a vessel—small transistor radios, photoelectric light meters, and hand calculators—are highly magnetic and should never be permitted in the vicinity of the compass, nor should any hand- or electric-powered tools.

Degaussing coils should be secured and compass coils given a "dockside" compensation.

The binnacle should be exactly on the midship line and should be so solidly secured as to avoid any chance of movement.

The compass bowl should be in the center of the binnacle. To center a compass bowl in its binnacle, with the ship heading north or south, or nearly so, and on an even keel, put the compass bowl in place and adjust its position by the screws at the ends of the outer gimbal ring knife-edges, until no change of heading by compass is observed as the heeling magnet is raised and lowered. Secure the compass bowl in this position by tightening the screws. If the gimbal rings are loose from wear, they should be repaired or new ones obtained. The compass bowl should not move either fore-and-aft or athwartships in the gimbal rings.

The lubber's line of the compass should be exactly in the fore-and-aft plane of the ship. This should be carefully verified. It is best done by sighting with the azimuth circle on straightedges erected on the midship line at some distance forward and abaft the compass; this may be done very accurately when in drydock.

The lubber's line of each pelorus should also be checked. This can be done by taking simultaneous bearings of a distant object from the magnetic compass and the pelorus.

Preparations should be made to record details of the adjustment.

Position of the Magnets

318 If the *Flinders bar* is in place, leave it there. If not, do not use it until expert advice has been obtained.

The *quadrantal spheres* should be left in the same position they were in when the compass was last adjusted. If there is uncertainty as to where they should go, place them in the middle of each athwartship arm.

If the *heeling magnet* is in place, with the correct end up—*red* end *up, north* of the magnetic equator, and *blue* end *up, south* of the magnetic equator—leave it in place. If not, place it in the bottom of the tube with the appropriate end up. The proper height for the heeling magnet can be determined after the other steps of the adjustment are completed, by heading north or south when the ship has a steady roll. Observe the oscillations of the compass, and raise the magnet until the compass steadies. This can readily be accomplished on smaller vessels; it is more difficult on larger ones. The position of the heeling magnet may have to be readjusted to keep the compass steady if the ship moves to a substantially different magnetic latitude.

Remove all other correctors, except the degaussing coils.

Underway Procedures

319 Having arrived in a clear area, with plenty of room to maneuver, the vessel must be steadied *accurately* on selected *magnetic* headings in a definite sequence. Then when the proper corrector described below is so placed as to cause the compass to read the known *magnetic* heading, the deviation becomes zero. For example, if the vessel is on magnetic north, but the compass shows the heading is 358° when it should read 000°, the deviation is 2° E, and the corrector should be so placed as to cause the compass to read 000°. Various methods of putting the vessel on the desired magnetic headings are given later in this chapter.

The sequence of magnetic headings is as follows:
1. A cardinal point—E or W (preferably), or N or S.
2. The cardinal point 180° from the first point.
3. A cardinal point 90° from the first.
4. The cardinal point 180° from the third.

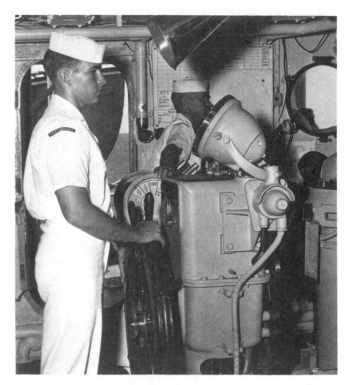

Figure 318. Using compass on bridge of ship.

5. An intercardinal point—NE, SE, SW, or NW.
6. An intercardinal point 90° from the point used in step 5.
7. Separate runs, steadying for at least one minute on headings 15° apart—000°, 015°, 030°, etc., through 360°—to find the residual deviations.

Assume that the first heading is *east*. After the vessel has been steadied on 090° *magnetic*, the compass is read and the deviation noted. The required correcting magnets will go in the *fore-and-aft* holders below the compass, which should be cranked down to near, but not quite at, the bottom of their travel. The correct direction in which to place the red ends of the magnets may be determined by holding one magnet above the compass parallel to the position it will have in the holder. If the card swings in the proper direction, magnets should be inserted in the holders with that orientation; if the swing is in the wrong direction, the magnet should be turned end for end before it is inserted. The number of magnets to be used is determined by trial and error. *Several magnets near the bottom of travel are preferable to one or two close to the compass;* if more than one magnet is used, all red ends must point in the same direction. When enough magnets have been put in the holder to remove approximately all the deviation on that heading, a fine adjustment is made by cranking the holders up or down until the compass indicates the correct magnetic heading, zero deviation.

The vessel is now brought to the second heading, 180° from the first—in this case, *west*. After she steadies down, the deviation, which should be small, is again noted. *Half* of the deviation is removed, by cranking the holders containing the *fore-and-aft* magnets up or down, as necessary.

Proceed next to the third heading, which in this case will be north or south. All deviation on this heading is removed by using magnets in the athwartship holders. Determine the correct direction of the red ends as on the first heading. The holders should again be cranked down almost to the lower end of their travel; insert the magnets as required. Crank the holders up or down to remove all deviation.

The vessel now comes to the fourth heading, 180° from that of the third. *Half* the deviation is removed by cranking the fore-and-aft magnets up or down as required.

She is next brought to the fifth heading, an intercardinal point, and all deviation found on this heading is removed by moving the two iron spheres. *Move both the spheres equally in or equally out*, as required, until the magnetic heading and heading by compass are identical. If the inboard limit of travel is reached without fully removing the deviation, larger spheres are needed; if overcorrection exists at the outward limit of movement of the spheres, smaller ones must be used. It is preferable to use large spheres farther away from the compass rather than smaller ones nearer the compass.

Come next to the sixth heading, an intercardinal point 90° from the one used for the fifth heading, and remove *half* the deviation found by moving the iron spheres. Again, both spheres must be moved in, or out, and by the same amount.

At this point the number and positions of all correctors should be carefully logged.

Finally, the vessel is swung through 360°, steadying on each 15° heading *for not less than a minute;* if the compass appears sluggish, steady up for at least two minutes on each heading. The *residual deviation*, the deviation remaining after adjustment, is recorded for each 15° change of heading. If time is short, or the residuals only 2° or less, deviations may be taken on only eight headings, or every 45°.

If the vessel is fitted with degaussing gear, all circuits for normal operation are now energized, the procedures are repeated, and the residuals for degaussing on (DG ON) are noted on each 15° heading.

The degaussing equipment is intended to give a ship some measure of protection against magnetic mines and torpedoes by reducing the ship's magnetic field. The degaussing currents do, however, have a strong effect on the magnetic compass, and the deviation caused by these currents is usually larger than that caused by the vessel's magnetism. Some of the deviation caused by the degaussing circuits is offset by degaussing compensation coils mounted in the binnacle as described in article 316. These are not completely effective, however, and hence deviation must be determined with the degaussing gear activated as well as off.

A deviation table as described in article 313 or 326 is now prepared; also a Napier diagram, if desired. Copies of the deviation table should be posted at the compass, in the compass record book, and in the vessel's log.

Procedures for Small Craft

Procedures for small craft follow the same basic principles as those for large vessels, but are somewhat simplified. Compensating magnets are normally contained within the mounting for the compass and are adjusted with a *nonmagnetic* screwdriver; these serve the same purpose as the bar magnets placed in binnacle trays and raised or lowered. Occasionally a compass will not have built-in compensating magnets, and in this case a small external bar magnet is placed at either side of the instrument with another just forward or aft of the compass. These must be accurately aligned with the fore-and-aft and athwartship axes of the compass; they are reversed end for end and moved nearer or farther away until the correct amount of compensation is achieved on E-W and N-S headings. Except in the unlikely event of a craft with a steel hull, no quadrantal spheres are used; deviation on intercardinal headings—NE, SE, SW, and NW—is recorded, but no effort is made to adjust the compass for it.

Sailing craft normally carry an angle of heel when underway, and will often require the installation and adjustment of a *heeling magnet*. The heeling magnet is placed vertically beneath the compass and the correct end to be up is determined by trial and error. The proper up-down placement of this compensator is normally determined at the dockside, and will require the services of a skilled compass adjustor.

Establishing a Magnetic Heading

320 There are at least five methods for coming to a specified magnetic heading in order to determine deviation. The first two listed below are more accurate and are the most commonly used:

By taking azimuths of a celestial body;
By comparison with a gyrocompass;
By comparison with a magnetic compass having known deviations;
By using ranges.

Azimuths of a Celestial Body

321   The body most frequently used for this purpose is the sun. A time of day should be selected when the sun's altitude is below about 30°, because it is more difficult to measure its azimuth accurately at high altitudes. The azimuths must be computed in advance, usually for every eight minutes of the period that it is anticipated will be required for the adjustment. Azimuths can be computed from DMAHTC Pub. No. 229, or from special tables of azimuths of the sun, such as Pub. No. 260 (no longer published, but possibly available). Having determined the azimuth at eight-minute intervals, the variation for the locality is applied to obtain magnetic azimuths. These are plotted on graph paper, and a smooth curve is drawn through the various points; the coordinates are time and magnetic azimuths. The method of computing the azimuths and plotting the curve is discussed in chapter 28.

To put the ship on a desired magnetic heading, pick the magnetic azimuth off the curve for the appropriate time, then find the angle between the desired magnetic heading and the magnetic azimuth. Rotate the azimuth circle on the compass so that the line of sight through the vanes forms this same angle with the lubber's line. Adjust course right or left until the sun appears in the vanes. Recheck the time and the corresponding magnetic azimuth, and adjust the setting of the azimuth circle, if necessary.

Example: How would you place a ship on magnetic heading 225° when the magnetic azimuth of the sun is 101°?

Solution: When the ship is on the required heading, the sun will be 225° − 101° = 124° to the *left* of the ship's head. See figure 321.

Answer: Place the far vane 124° to the left of the ship's head and maneuver the ship until the sun is in line with the vanes.

If a pelorus is used, it can be set with the required magnetic heading, 225°, at the lubber's line and the far vane at the magnetic azimuth, 101°.

The deviation is determined by comparing the observed azimuth with its computed value at that moment. The difference is the deviation, which is easterly if the computed azimuth is the greater,

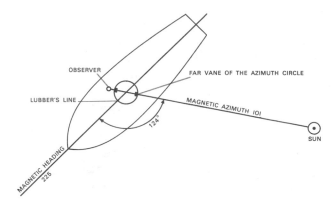

Figure 321. Placing a vessel on a magnetic heading of 225° by azimuth of the sun.

and westerly if the observed azimuth is the greater. Again the jingle "Compass least, error east; compass best, error west" can serve as a memory aid.

Example: At a given time the azimuth of the sun is observed by the standard compass, and is found to be 105.5°. The magnetic azimuth taken from the curve for the same moment is 103.5°.

Required: The deviation of the standard compass on the present heading.

Answer: Dev. 2.0° W.

Comparison with a Gyrocompass

322   When a gyrocompass is available, the comparison of the course as shown by gyro and the course as shown by magnetic compass will give the compass error, provided the gyro is running true. If the gyro has an error, it must be allowed for (see article 347). The deviation can then be found by combining the compass error thus determined and the charted variation. This is the method most frequently used by ships with a reliable gyrocompass.

To bring the ship to a desired magnetic heading, apply the variation to the desired magnetic heading to obtain the corresponding true heading, and bring the ship to this heading by gyro.

Example 1: A ship is heading 214° by gyrocompass and 201° by magnetic compass. The gyro error is 1° W and the variation is 5° E.

Required: The deviation of the standard compass on the present heading.

Solution: If the ship is heading 214° by gyrocompass and the gyro error is 1° W, the heading is 213° true. Applying the variation, the magnetic heading is found to be 213° − 5° = 208°. The deviation is 208° − 201° = 7° E.

Answer: Dev. 7° E.

Example 2: Find the gyro heading to place a ship on magnetic heading 000°, if the variation is 23° E and the gyro error is 1° W.

Solution: The true heading is 000° + 23° = 023°. The gyro heading is 023° + 1° = 024°.

Answer: GH 024°.

Comparison with a Compensated Compass

323 Comparison with a magnetic compass of known deviation (compensated) is a similar method to that of comparison with a gyrocompass, except that it is not necessary to know the variation, as it will be the same for both compasses. The method is often used when two or more magnetic compasses are adjusted at the same time. For example, the deviation of the standard compass may be found by a curve of magnetic azimuths or some other method and the steering compass then compared with it. This is a method frequently used when there is no gyrocompass installed in the boat or ship.

To bring the vessel to a desired magnetic heading, apply the deviation to the desired magnetic heading to obtain the compass heading.

Example 1: A ship is heading 173° by standard compass and 175° by steering compass. The deviation of the standard compass on this heading is 4° E.

Required: The deviation of the steering compass.

Solution: The magnetic heading is 173° + 4° = 177°. The deviation of the steering compass is 177° − 175° = 2° E.

Answer: Dev. 2° E.

Example 2: Find the compass heading to place a ship on magnetic heading 180°, using the deviation table of figure 323 (DG OFF).

Solution: The deviation table is made out for compass headings. Entries of compass headings 165° and 180° are converted to magnetic headings of 167° (Dev. 2.0° E) and 184.5° E. Interpolation is done for a magnetic heading of 180° (rounded to the nearest half degree), and deviation is found to be 4° E. Applying this to the magnetic heading, the required compass heading is found to be 180° − 4° = 176°.

Answer: CH 176°.

Bearings on a Distant Object

324 Despite any swinging of any but the largest of vessels about her anchor, the bearings of a fixed object at least six miles distant will not change materially during the swing. By observing the bearing of the object by a magnetic compass as the vessel heads in various directions, the deviation can be obtained for each heading for which an observation is taken by comparison with the magnetic bearing.

If the distant object is shown on the chart, its magnetic bearing is obtained simply by applying the charted variation to the true bearing by compass rose. If not charted, its magnetic bearing may be taken as the average of a round of compass bearings of the object, observed on equidistant headings of the vessel. The explanation of the last statement is that, theoretically, if a vessel is swung through a circle and deviations are determined on equidistant compass headings, the sum of the easterly deviations found will equal numerically the sum of the westerly deviations, the resulting net deviation for all headings being zero. The error introduced by this assumption is generally very small unless there is a constant error, such as a misaligned lubber's line.

A ship or boat may be under way when obtaining a table of deviations by this method. In this case an object at a great distance must be chosen, and the vessel should remain in as small an area as possible while making the observations. A buoy in place can be used (if there is safe water all around it) or one can be anchored for this specific purpose; the vessel is maneuvered to keep as close as possible to the buoy while taking the observations.

Example 1: A small craft establishes a buoy, and remaining close to this buoy, takes bearings of an unidentified prominent peak on a distant mountain.

Required: The deviations of the standard and steering compasses, the observations being as shown in the columns below:

Solution:

Columns A, B, and F (see table on following page) are observed during the swing. Column C is the average of column B. Column D is the difference between columns B and C. Column E is found by applying column D to column A. Column G is the difference between columns E and F.

If bearings can be read to one- or two-tenths of a degree, it is good practice to so measure, but then to round off to the nearest half-degree when preparing the deviation table. (With boats, yachts, and other small craft, it is probable that readings and tabulated values will not be more precise than whole degrees.) When deviation values have been determined for headings at irregular intervals, as with the steering compass in the above example, it is desirable to calculate values for the more normal intervals of the table. Plot the deviation on graph paper and fair a curve through the points. The deviation at regular intervals such as 000°, 045°, 090°, etc., can then be read from the curve to the nearest half degree.

With deviations as large as those shown, the ship should be swung on headings differing by 15°,

A	B	C	D	E	F	G
Ship's head psc	Bearing of peak psc	Magnetic bearing of peak	Deviation standard compass	Ship's head magnetic	Ship's head per steering compass	Deviation of steering compass
°	°	°	°	°	°	°
000	340.7	330.5	10.2 W	349.8	342.4	7.4 E
045	338.0	330.5	7.5 W	037.5	038.0	0.5 W
090	332.5	330.5	2.0 W	088.0	097.0	9.0 W
135	328.0	330.5	2.5 E	137.5	154.0	16.5 W
180	325.0	330.5	5.5 E	185.5	193.7	8.2 W
225	321.5	330.5	9.0 E	234.0	232.6	1.4 E
270	326.0	330.5	4.5 E	274.5	263.5	11.0 E
315	332.3	330.5	1.8 W	313.2	294.0	19.2 E
Sum	2644.0					
Mean	330.5					

rather than 45° as shown, if it is not possible to adjust the compasses and reduce the deviations. The example uses headings differing by 45° for brevity.

Note that this example includes the method of comparing a compass with one of known deviation.

To bring the vessel to a desired magnetic heading, determine the magnetic bearing of the object, and find the difference between this and the desired magnetic heading. Set the far vane of the bearing circle to the right or to the left as with an azimuth of a celestial body, and maneuver the vessel until the distant object is in line with the vanes.

Example 2: How would you place a yacht on magnetic heading 180° if the true bearing of a distant radio tower is 227° and the variation is 12° W?

Solution: The desired magnetic bearing is 227° + 12° = 239°. Since 239° is greater than 180° it will be necessary to set the far sight vane to the *right* of the yacht's centerline; the amount is 239° − 180° = 59°. See figure 324.

Answer: Set the far vane 59° to the right of the yacht's head and maneuver until the radio tower is in line with the vanes.

Ranges

325 Two fixed, identifiable objects appearing in line constitute a *range*. Aids to navigation consisting of two range marks are often used to mark mid-channels, turning points, measured mile courses, etc. Ranges of natural or man-made objects can frequently be found. If it is intended to use these to *swing ship*—take multiple bearings for compass compensation—it should be done where it will not interfere with normal vessel traffic. The true direction of the range is determined by measurement on

Figure 324. Placing a ship on a magnetic heading of 180° by bearings on a distant object.

the chart. (The direction of ranges that are aids to navigation can be found in the *Light List;* see article 604.) The magnetic direction is then determined by applying the variation of the locality. The deviation is found by crossing the range on the desired heading and observing the compass bearing at the instant the objects are in line.

To bring the vessel to a desired magnetic heading, proceed as outlined in article 324.

Refer to figure 325. Beacons A and B form a range, the direction of which is 030.5° true. The local variation is 20° W. Hence, the magnetic direction of the range is 050.5°. If the observed bearing of the range is 045°, the deviation is 050.5° − 045.0° = 5.5° E.

Example: For determining the deviations of the standard compass, a boat uses one of the two ranges marking the measured mile off Kent Island, Chesapeake Bay. The true direction of the ranges is

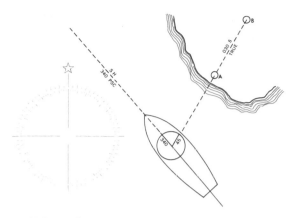

Figure 325. Finding compass deviation by a range.

091.5°, and the variation for the locality is 7.8° W. As the craft crosses a range on the headings shown in the first column of the following table, the navigator observes the corresponding directions of the range as noted in the third column.

Required: The deviations of the standard compass.

Ship's head psc	Magnetic direction of range	Direction of range psc	Deviation
°	°	°	°
000	099.3	103.2	3.9 W
015		103.1	3.8 W
030		102.6	3.3 W
045		102.1	2.8 W
060		101.8	2.5 W
075		101.7	2.4 W
090		101.5	2.2 W
105		101.4	2.1 W
120		101.3	2.0 W
135		100.8	1.5 W
150		099.9	0.6 W
165		097.2	2.1 E
180		094.8	4.5 E
195		093.3	6.0 E
210		092.5	6.8 E
225		092.9	6.4 E
240		093.8	5.5 E
255		095.3	4.0 E
270		096.8	2.5 E
285		098.8	0.5 E
300		100.3	1.0 W
315		101.8	2.5 W
330		102.7	3.4 W
345		103.3	4.0 W

Ships Heading Compass	Deviation DG Off
000–034	4W
035–077	3W
078–133	2 W
134–150	1 W
151–159	0 W
. . . .	. . . .
286–293	0 W
294–303	1 W
304–314	2 W
315–330	3 W
331–360	4 W

Figure 326. Deviation shown by a table of critical values (extract).

Critical Values Table

326 A different style of deviation table is often used on smaller vessels where deviation and headings are only used in whole degrees. It is considerably quicker and easier to use, requiring no interpolation for any heading. This is a *critical values* table. The spread of headings is shown for each one-degree increment of deviation. For example, the DG-OFF portion of figure 323, disregarding fractions of a degree, might appear as seen in figure 326.

GYROCOMPASSES

Introduction

327 The first portion of this chapter was devoted to the magnetic compass, which was for many centuries the only instrument available at sea for the determination of direction. In the search for an instrument that would indicate true north rather than magnetic north, the gyrocompass was developed early in this century. Parallel advances have been made in America and Europe; the American Sperry gyrocompass was developed on the basis of using a single rotor or spinning wheel as compared with the multiple rotors of the early Anschutz gyrocompasses built in Germany.

Schuler Pendulum

As will be explained in article 333, the gyrocompass inherently is capable of oscillating about its vertical, or azimuth-indicating axis. Damping is employed to suppress this tendency. Professor Max Schuler showed that the effects of accelerations, due to speed and course changes, are minimized when the period of this oscillation is made equal to approximately 84 minutes. This is the period a simple pendulum would have if its length were equal to the radius of the earth. This has come to be known as the Schuler pendulum, and the principle has basic application in all inertial navigation systems.

One or more gyrocompasses are basic components of an inertial navigation system (chapter 35). The gyro is being used increasingly in navigation aboard ships, not only as a heading or steering reference, but also to provide rolling and pitching data as input to the vessel's integrated navigation system (chapter 38).

Gyroscopic Laws

Of the four natural laws or principles upon which gyrocompass operation depends, the first two are inherent properties of the gyroscope, namely, *gyroscopic inertia* (rigidity in space) and *precession*. The third and fourth relate to the earth and are the earth's rotation and gravitation. The interrelationship of these natural phenomena is explained briefly in this chapter to enable a navigator to understand the basic concept of a gyrocompass and, more importantly, to enable him to realize the limits of its accuracy, and to know the sources of inherent error of the gyroscope when used as a compass in the shipboard environment.

A Basic Gyroscope

328   A rapidly spinning body having three axes of angular freedom constitutes a gyroscope. This is illustrated by a heavy wheel rotating at high speed in supporting rings or gimbals, as shown in figure 328. One degree of freedom for the mass of the wheel or rotor is provided by the spin axis (1) itself. The remaining two degrees of freedom, which allow the spin axis to be pointed in any direction, are provided by the axes of the supporting gimbals. Corresponding to the arrangement used in the simple gyrocompass, these are designated in figure 328 as the horizontal axis (2) and the vertical axis (3).

Gyroscopic Inertia

329   Newton's First Law of Motion states that a body in motion will continue to move at constant speed in the same direction unless it is acted upon by an outside force. If the gyroscope could be constructed entirely free of mechanical error, with no bearing friction on the axis of the rotating wheel or its gimbals, and operated in a vacuum with no air friction on the rotating wheel, the result would be a

Figure 328. A gyroscope has three axes of freedom.

perpetual-motion machine. The direction of the spin axis would be fixed *in inertial space* parallel to its original position when placed in motion, and the gyroscope would rotate forever. Obviously this perfection has not been accomplished, although electrostatically supported gyros have been constructed that could spin, or coast, for many months. Gyroscopic inertia thus tends to keep the rotating wheel in the same plane and resists any force that tries to change its plane of rotation. The strength of this force depends on the moment of inertia and velocity of the spinning rotor.

A basic model of the gyroscope as shown in figure 328 can be used to illustrate the principle if the rotor is kept spinning with sufficient velocity. If the base of the gyroscope is slowly tipped, the rotor or wheel will maintain its original plane of rotation as the base is moved about in any direction and the relative position of the gimbals is changed. A simple model of this type is useful in demonstrating gyroscopic inertia and precession.

Precession

330   If force is applied to the axis of the spinning gyroscope, the axis rotates not in the direction in which the force is applied, but 90° from this. This reaction is known as *precession*, which is defined as that property of a gyroscope that causes the spin axis to change direction when a torque or force is applied to the gyro. The phenomenon was observed by Foucault, the French physicist who first observed the laws of the gyroscope and gave the device its present name. Figure 330a illustrates precession when a force is applied to the horizontal axis. (Note that here the horizontal axis is the outer axis, rather than the inner axis of figure 328; this does not affect the gyroscope.) The applied force or torque, T, meets with resistance and the reaction of

Figure 330a. Left: precession about the vertical axis; 330b, right: precession about the horizontal axis.

the gyro, rather than turning about its horizontal axis as it would do if the rotor were stationary, is to rotate about the other, vertical, axis in the direction indicated by the arrow P in the figure. Similarly, in figure 330b, if the force (torque), T, is applied around the vertical axis, the gyro turns (precesses) about its horizontal axis in the direction shown by the arrow P. A convenient way to remember the direction in which precession takes place is to regard the pressure or torque as though it acted at a single point on the rim of the wheel, as indicated by the black dot in figure 330a and 330b. This point will not move in response to the pressure, but a point 90° beyond (in the direction of the wheel's rotation) will move away instead. The speed of precession is directly proportional to the force applied and to the speed of rotation of the wheel.

Effect of Rotation of the Earth

331 As stated in article 329, the direction of the spin axis tends to be fixed in inertial space due to gyroscopic inertia. Inertial space may be considered as a region in which the sum of all acceleration and gravity forces is zero. For purposes of illustration, if the spin axis were directed toward a star, the axis would continue to point toward the star during its apparent motion across the sky.

To an observer on earth the spin axis would appear to change direction as the earth rotated eastward. This is illustrated in figure 331a, in which it can be seen that with one rotation of the earth the direction of the spin axis relative to the earth would have moved through a complete 360°; it

therefore becomes apparent that the gyroscope in this form is not suitable as a compass as it is not *north-seeking*. To make the gyroscope useful as a direction-indicating instrument with respect to the earth rather than space, a torque must be applied that causes it to precess an amount exactly opposite to the apparent movement caused by the rotation of the earth.

Earth Rate

In figure 331b, the gyroscope is considered to be mounted at the equator with its spin axis pointing east and west. From a point in space beyond the South Pole, the relative position of the gyro and of the earth is illustrated for a 24-hour period. If observed while standing on the earth the gyro appears to rotate about its horizontal axis with a velocity equal to, but in the opposite direction of, the rotation of the earth. This effect is commonly referred to as *horizontal earth rate*. Similarly, if the gyro is assumed to be mounted at the North or South Pole with its axis horizontal as shown in figure 331c, the gyro will appear to rotate about its vertical axis. This effect is commonly referred to as *vertical earth rate*. At points between the poles and the equator, the gyro appears to turn partly about the horizontal axis and partly about the vertical axis. This can be visualized in figure 331a. The relative magnitudes of the vertical and horizontal rates are a function of latitude. The effect of horizontal earth rate is maximum at the equator and zero at the poles, and varies as the cosine of the latitude. The effect of the vertical earth rate will vary as the

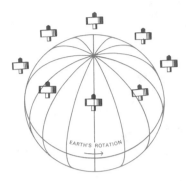

Figure 331a. A gyroscope with its spin axis horizontal at any point away from the equator; observed from a point in space above the gyroscope.

Figure 331b. A gyroscope with its spin axis set in an east-west position at the equator; observed from a point in space beyond the earth's South Pole.

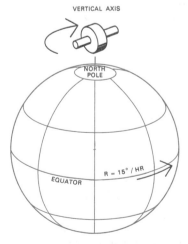

Figure 331c. A gyroscope set with its spin axis horizontal at the North Pole; observed from a point in space beyond the equator.

sine of the latitude, being maximum at the poles and zero at the equator.

In general, the horizontal earth rate causes the gyro to tilt, and the vertical earth rate causes it to move in azimuth with respect to the earth.

Gravity Effect

332 As previously stated, the horizontal earth rate causes the gyro spin axis to tilt in relation to the surface of the earth. The precession effect on a gyroscope when a force or torque is applied has been discussed briefly. The effect of this application of force is precisely the same whether it be a force applied mechanically or whether it be the force of gravity, or of acceleration. The use of gravity to cause the spin axis to precess into a north-south plane, in a pendulous type gyro, can be visualized in an overly simplified manner as follows: picture the spinning gyroscope mounted in a hollow sphere with the spin axis horizontal and aligned in an east-west direction and with a weight mounted in the bottom of the sphere. The unit is located on the equator (figure 332 at A). As the earth rotates, the spin axis, which is fixed in space, tends to become inclined to the horizontal, with the east end rising. The weight applied to the bottom of the sphere is therefore raised against the pull of gravity and consequently causes a torque about the horizontal axis of the gyro, as at position B.

This torque causes a precession about the vertical axis causing the *spin axis* of the gyroscope to align itself with the axis of rotation of the earth, the north-south direction, position C. When this alignment has taken place, there will no longer be a tendency for the heavy bottom of the sphere to rise and produce further precession. The gyroscope now performs as a crude north-seeking instrument, a gyrocompass. Gravity reference systems vary with different designs and will be discussed in the following articles. Older designs of gyrocompasses were described as *pendulous* or *nonpendulous* according to the type of mechanical device used. Newer models use an electronic gravity reference system. There are, however, other essential elements of a practical gyrocompass, such as *damping*, plus *latitude* and *speed correction*.

Basic Gyrocompasses

333 A gyrocompass fundamentally consists of one or more north-seeking gyroscopes with suitable housing, power supply, etc. To each gyroscope there must be added control elements to apply

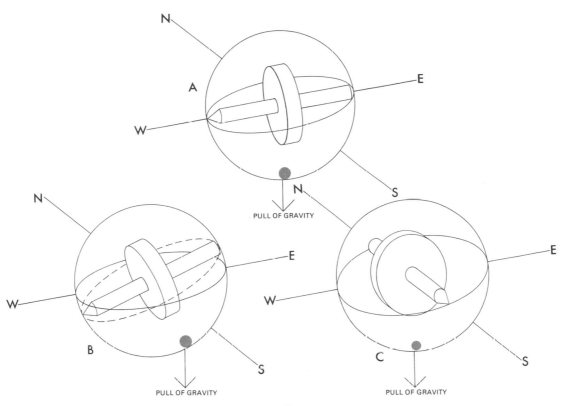

Figure 332. Gravity effect on a gyroscope.

torques of the correct phase and magnitude in order that it will precess in such a manner that the spin axis is brought parallel to the geographic meridian within a reasonable time (a few hours) after the wheel is set spinning, and is quickly returned to the meridian if it becomes displaced. The gyroscope will precess about the vertical axis at the proper rate and in the proper direction so as to cancel the effect of the earth's rotation; the spin axis will remain nearly level when parallel to the meridian and prevent the instrument from oscillating across the meridian.

So that it may act as a "compass," there must also be a scale for reading direction, and electronic components to sense direction and transmit this information as signals to other equipment.

Various mechanical and electrical arrangements have been devised to take advantage of the natural laws described in the preceding articles. The mercury ballistic method described below is employed in the nonpendulous systems of older Sperry gyrocompasses. A pendulous system is used in Arma compasses and by some European manufacturers to achieve the same results.

One way in which precession is used to cause a gyroscope to seek north is illustrated in figure 333a.

Two reservoirs connected by a tube are attached to the bottom of the case enclosing the gyro rotor, with one reservoir north of the rotor and one south of it. These are filled with mercury to such a level that the weight below the spin axis is equal to the weight above it, so that the gyroscope is nonpendulous. The system of reservoirs and connecting tubes is called a *mercury ballistic*. In practice, there are usually four symmetrically placed reservoirs.

Suppose that the spin axis is horizontal, but is directed to the eastward of north. As the earth rotates eastward on its axis, the spin axis of the gyroscope tends to maintain its direction in space; that is, it appears to follow a point, such as a star rising in the northeastern sky. With respect to the earth, the north reservoir rises, and some of the mercury flows under the force of gravity into the south reservoir. The south side becomes heavier than the north side, and a torque is thus applied to the rotor case; this is equivalent to a force being applied to the rotor at point A. If the rotor is spinning in the direction shown, the north end of the spin axis precesses slowly to the westward, following an elliptical path. When it reaches the meridian, upward tilt reaches a maximum. Precession continues, so that the axis is carried past the meridian

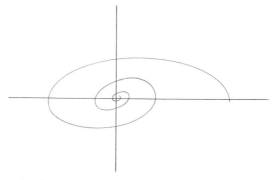

Figure 333a. A mercury ballistic (left) and the elliptical path (right) of the axis of spin without damping.

Figure 333b. Spiral path of axis of spin with damping.

and commences to sink as the earth continues to rotate. When the sinking has continued to the point where the axis is horizontal again, the excess mercury has returned to the north reservoir and precession stops. As sinking continues, due to continued rotation of the earth, an excess of mercury accumulates in the north reservoir, thus reversing the direction of precession and causing the spin axis to return slowly to its original position with respect to the earth, following the path shown at the right of the illustration. One circuit of the ellipse requires about 84 minutes. This is the Schuler period mentioned previously.

The elliptical path is symmetrical with respect to the meridian, and neglecting friction, would be retraced indefinitely, unless some method of damping the oscillation were found. One method is by offsetting the point of application of the force from the mercury ballistic. Thus, if the force is applied not in the vertical plane, but at a point to the eastward of it, as at B in figure 333a, the resulting precession causes the spin axis to trace a spiral path as shown in figure 333b and eventually to settle near the meridian. The gyroscope is now north-seeking and can be used as a compass. Some compasses are provided with automatic means for moving the point of application to the centerline during a large change of course or speed, to avoid introduction of a temporary error.

Another method of damping the oscillations caused by the rotation of the earth is to reduce the precessing force of a pendulous gyro as the spin axis approaches the meridian. One way of accomplishing this is to cause oil to flow from one damping tank to another in such a manner as to counteract some of the tendency of an offset pendulous weight to cause precession. Oscillations are completely damped out in approximately one and one-half swings.

Details of construction differ considerably in the various models. Each instrument is provided with a manual giving such information and operating instructions. A navigator should carefully read the instruction manual accompanying the gyrocompass installed in his vessel. In the latest designs, methods have been developed to measure the tilt of the gyro axis due to earth rate, and to use control devices about the vertical and horizontal axes to produce torques proportional to such tilt. This eliminates the necessity for using weights or a mercury ballistic to produce the needed torques and damping.

Detailed descriptions of various systems using sensing devices in the form of electrolytic levels, special pendulums, and electro-mechanical pick-off units for sensing orientation are included in the operating and technical manuals provided with each gyrocompass. A comparative analysis of mechanical and electrical features of various compass designs is beyond the scope of this book.

Gyrocompass Components

334 A modern gyrocompass system consists of a *master unit*, a *control cabinet*, a *power supply unit*, a *speed unit*, and *auxiliary electrical transmission* and *alarm units*.

The master unit is the heart of the compass system and contains the gyroscopic north-seeking element (and in the more complex newer compasses, the vertical-seeking sensitive element), necessary gimballing, and related electrical components and wiring.

The control cabinet is the "nerve center" of the system. It contains all the computing and amplifying circuitry and components, and in addition provides on its front panel all the controls, meters, and dials necessary for proper control of the operation of the compass.

On major U.S. naval ships, present standards provide for two master compasses with the necessary control units and auxiliary apparatus. At steering stations, two repeaters are installed in order that indications of both master compasses can be constantly available for purposes of comparison and checking. On smaller naval vessels, and on merchant ships, only one gyrocompass is installed; repeater compasses are provided as necessary for navigation and fire control.

Most naval vessels are also equipped with dead-reckoning equipment to plot automatically, to the scale of various charts, the track of the vessel while maneuvering. Latitude and longitude readouts and course recorders are also a part of the tracking equipment.

On both naval and merchant vessels, most gyrocompasses provide an electrical output that can be connected to the steering system, causing the rudder to respond instantly to any deviation from the preset heading.

Gyro repeater compasses mounted as peloruses on the wings of the bridge give true bearings. Self-synchronous alidades also include gyro repeaters. In the event of gyrocompass failure, gyro or self-synchronous alidade repeaters, set to the true course, may be used as ordinary peloruses.

Gyrocompass Transmission Systems

335 One of the features of the gyrocompass system is the ability of the master compass to transmit to remotely located indicators electrical data representing the ship's heading, and on the more complex newer compasses, electrical data representing ship's roll and pitch. These data are used in various kinds of navigational equipment, and on warships, provide as well a necessary input to radar, sonar, fire-control, and other ship's systems.

Gyrocompass Repeaters

336 Gyrocompass repeaters (ship's heading indicators) are accurate electronic servomechanisms that reproduce the indications of the master gyrocompass at remote locations anywhere on the vessel.

Older types of repeater compasses consist essentially of a compass card fixed to the end of the shaft of a step or synchromotor, the rotor of which turns in synchronism with the transmitter indications of the master gyrocompass. In appearance it looks much the same as any compass, but it may be mounted rigidly in any position; it may be attached to a bulkhead as well as placed horizontally in a

Figure 336. Gyro repeater.

pelorus stand or binnacle. There are several models, each best adapted for a specific use.

Most repeaters are entirely self-synchronous, so that if they become out of step with the master gyro, as through temporary power failure, they will automatically line up with the transmitter when power is restored. Repeaters are generally provided with a damping device to prevent undesirable oscillation when the heading is changed rapidly.

A gyro repeater is used as a compass. As far as the user is concerned, the repeater *is* a compass. Lighting is provided by marking the dial of translucent material with dark or colored markings or of opaque material with translucent markings, and placing a light behind the dial.

There is no practical limit to the number of repeaters that can operate from a single master gyrocompass.

Preparation for Use

337 The gyrocompass is normally kept in continuous operation at sea. Most compasses are equipped with a stand-by power supply and a compass failure alarm to indicate any malfunction of the compass or failure of the power supply. The stand-by power supply will automatically operate the compass for a short period of time until ship's power can be restored. When in port for a considerable period of time, the gyro can be switched off. A navigator must be aware of the fact that when the gyro is restarted, several hours will be required for the rotor to attain operating speed and for the compass to settle on the meridian. Instruction manuals contain methods to externally precess the compass to speed up this settling period. If a vessel is apt to be ordered to get underway on short notice, her gyrocompass should be kept running. Modern merchant vessels, particularly container ships, are often in port for cargo handling for relatively short periods only, and gyrocompasses are normally not secured.

Latitude, Speed, and Course Corrections

338 When a vessel is underway, the movement over the earth resulting from course and speed, as well as the latitude in which the vessel is operating, is detected by the gyroscope as a change in the horizontal and vertical earth rate (article 331). The gyro cannot distinguish between a force caused by movement of the vessel and that caused by the rotation of the earth. On an east or west course there is no effect on the gyrocompass, as the vessel's movement merely adds to or subtracts from the rate of rotation of the earth. This motion is in the plane of the rotor when the spin axis is settled on a meridian and therefore causes no precession. A vessel steaming north or south produces a maximum effect upon the compass indication.

Applying Corrections

On older models of gyrocompasses, speed and latitude were compensated for by applying a torque that could be set by hand, generally by moving pointers along speed and latitude scales. Course was compensated for by the use of a built-in cosine cam automatically driven by the compass itself. On the Mark 19 and other new models, no insertion of latitude and speed correction by the navigator is necessary. The control cabinet contains an electronic computer that generates an electrical signal to torque the gyro. The computer has an input for speed directly from the vessel's speed-measuring instrument and an input for heading generated from within the compass itself. The computer is set for latitude when started and thereafter produces both a constant display of latitude and the appropriate electrical compensating signal to the gyrocompass.

U.S. Navy Mark 19, Mod 3 Gyrocompass

339 The Mark 19, Mod 3 gyrocompass, manufactured by Sperry, is in general use on larger ves-

sels of the U.S. Navy. It constitutes a system that includes two gyroscopes within a sensitive element, the meridian and slave gyros, to which certain control devices have been added. The Mark 19 consists of four principal components: the master compass, the control cabinet, the compass failure annunciator, and the standby power supply.

The spin axis of the meridian gyro is aligned with the earth meridian as in any gyrocompass. The slave gyro mounted on the same platform or support has its spin axis oriented in an east-west direction. In addition to indicating the meridian, this arrangement defines the true vertical, useful for fire control and other purposes.

The force of gravity, instead of acting directly to control the compass, merely acts on a special type of electrolytic bubble level, called the gravity reference, which generates a signal proportional to the tilt of the gyro axle. This signal is used to apply torque electromagnetically about the vertical or horizontal axes to give the compass the desired period and damping. Each gyro unit is enclosed in a *gyrosphere*.

The gyrosphere is the heart of the meridian gyro assembly, as it is the north-seeking component of the compass. It derives its name from the fact that the gyro wheel is mounted within a spherical enclosure. This gyrosphere, and the one for the slave gyro, is immersed in oil, and is of the same specific gravity as the oil. It is therefore neutral in buoyancy and exerts no load on the vertical bearings, which then serve only as guides. This flotation not only reduces pivot friction and wear, but also serves to protect the gyroscope from damaging shock.

Figure 339 shows the sensitive element in the master compass—the gyrosphere for the meridian gyro in the upper part of the sensitive element, and that for the slave gyro in the lower portion.

Mark 23, Mod 4 Gyrocompass

340 The Sperry Mark 23, Mod 4 gyrocompass was designed as a small compass capable of withstanding the severe operating conditions encountered by amphibious vessels, such as LSTs, without sacrificing the primary function of furnishing accurate heading data. It is also used as an auxiliary compass aboard larger ships. It combines electronic compass control and oil flotation, and uses an electronic control to make it north-seeking.

The electrolytic bubble level is used to sense the force of gravity in the same manner as on the Mark 19 compass.

Figure 339. Master gyrocompass with sensitive element components labeled.

AN/WSN-2 Gyrocompass

341 The latest gyrocompass design for the U.S. Navy is the AN/WSN-2, manufactured by the Guidance & Control Systems division of Litton Industries; it will be used aboard vessels from patrol boats to cruisers. Its components, within a single console, can provide for full inertial navigation: weapons system, radar, and ship's stabilization; automatic piloting; and collision avoidance. The AN/WSN-2 will combine improved performance with significantly reduced weight and volume.

Figure 340. Mark 23 Mod 4 (Sperry) gyrocompass.

Advantages of Gyrocompasses

342 The gyrocompass has the following advantages over the magnetic compass:

It seeks the true meridian instead of the magnetic meridian.

It can be used near the earth's magnetic poles, where the magnetic compass is useless.

It is not affected by surrounding magnetic material that might seriously reduce the directive force of the magnetic compass.

If an error exists, it is the same on all headings, and correction is a simple process.

Its information can be fed electronically into automatic steering equipment, course (DR) recorders, and inertial navigation systems. On warships, data can be injected into weapons control systems.

Limitations

343 In spite of the many advantages and undoubted capabilities of a modern gyrocompass, there are certain disadvantages inherent in its design:

It requires a constant source of electrical power.

It requires intelligent care and attention if it is to give the kind of service of which it is inherently capable.

The accuracy decreases when latitudes above 75 degrees are reached.

If operation is interrupted for any length of time long enough for it to become disoriented, a considerable period of time, as much as four hours, may be required for it to settle back into reliable operation.

Despite these limitations, the modern gyrocompass, if given proper attention, will render reliable and satisfactory service. This should not cause the navigating officer to neglect his magnetic compass. When the gyrocompass does fail, as any intricate instrument may, the prudent navigator who has a properly adjusted magnetic compass, with an accurate deviation table, will be well repaid for his efforts.

Accuracy

344 Even after all the corrections have been made, a gyrocompass is not perfect. However, the error of a modern, properly adjusted gyrocompass seldom exceeds 1°, and is usually such a small fraction of this that for practical purposes it can be considered zero. This does not mean that it must not be checked frequently. A small error carried for a long time will take a vessel far to one side of the desired objective. Large errors introduced by temporary mechanical failure, when undetected, have meant disaster.

Gyrocompass Errors

345 When a gyrocompass is mounted on land, it is affected only by gravity and the earth's motion. When it is mounted in a ship at sea, consideration must be given to additional factors due to motions of the ship—such as roll, pitch, turning, speed over the ground, and course being steered—and the latitude. The effect of these factors differs in compasses of different basic design. Reference should be made to the appropriate instruction books for a detailed exposition of the theory of a particular compass design, including a description of the automatic and manual corrective features incorporated in the design.

Determining Gyrocompass Errors

346 At both the gyrocompass itself and its repeaters, a compass card is attached to or activated by the sensitive element and is graduated in degrees from 0° to 360°. Just as with a magnetic compass, the direction of the ship's head is indicated by a *lubber's line*, a vertical line on the compass housing exactly aligned in the fore-and-aft axis of the ship. As the ship turns, the lubber's line turns with it so that the changing heading is properly indicated on the card. *It is the lubber's line and not the compass card* that actually turns. The 0° point on the card always points toward true north if there is no compass error. If there is compass error, the 0°

point on the compass will not indicate true north but a direction either to the left or to the right of the meridian. If the 0° point is to the left or west of the meridian, gyro error (GE) is the numerical difference between the two directions and is labeled west (W). If the 0° point is to the right or east of the meridian, gyro error is again the numerical difference between the two directions and is labeled east (E).

When a ship is at sea, the navigator should determine the gyrocompass error at least once each day; this is required for naval vessels and is desirable on any ship. Over and above this bare minimum, the prudent navigator will take advantage of every opportunity to check the accuracy of his gyro. The importance of so doing is emphasized by a grounding case on record where the failure of a ship's gyro went undetected for a period of over twelve hours, with the result that, at the time of grounding, the vessel was more than 110° off course and more than 200 miles from the DR position.

There are several methods of checking the accuracy of a gyrocompass, the most important of which are summarized and briefly discussed as follows.

1. By comparing the observed gyro bearing of an artificial or natural range with the charted true bearing of the range. When entering or leaving a port, the method of checking the gyrocompass by ranges should be used regularly, as the varying speed of the ship, even though compensated for by the proper setting of the speed corrector, causes the compass to oscillate to a certain extent across the meridian. The navigator must be constantly on the alert to note in which direction and by what amount his compass is swinging off and correct his bearings accordingly.

2. By comparing the gyro bearing of an object ashore with the charted true bearing of the same object from a fixed position. The fixed position is obtained by means of the three-point problem using a sextant and a three-arm protractor. (See article 1110.) The right and left angles for any three well-defined objects are taken with the sextant at the gyro repeater that is to be used in the checking. At the same time, the bearings of the three objects are taken with the repeater. By means of the sextant angles set on the three-arm protractor, the position of the ship at the time of observation can be accurately plotted on the chart. From this position, the bearings of the three objects can be found by plotting. A comparison of the bearings so found, with the bearing taken by the repeater, shows the error of the

gyrocompass. The repeater should be checked against the master gyro each time a set of these observations is made.

3. By comparing the gyro bearing of a celestial body, usually the sun, with the computed true bearing (azimuth) of the same body. At sea, the azimuth method is the only one available, and any time a sight of a celestial body is taken for a line of position, the bearing of the body observed may be taken at the same instant (see chapter 28). Azimuths of the sun at sunrise and sunset, and when its altitude is low in the early morning and late afternoon, are particularly useful for this purpose. The azimuth obtained by computation, when compared with the gyro azimuth, gives a check on the accuracy of the compass. Polaris is very useful for checking the azimuth at night in low northern latitudes.

4. By "trial and error" adjustment of the observed bearings of three or more lines of position obtained on charted objects equally spaced around the ship until a point fix is obtained. A set of bearings are taken with the repeater on three objects that will yield suitable angles of intersection; these are plotted on the chart. If they meet in a point, the repeater is "on" and there is no gyro error. If the three lines form a triangle, the lines can be adjusted to meet in a point by trial and error; that is, 1° is added to or subtracted from each bearing, and they are again plotted. If the size of the triangle is reduced, the proper estimate of the direction of the error has been made, and after a proper correction is applied, the lines should meet in a point. When they do meet, the total amount of correction applied to any one bearing is the error of the compass.

5. By comparison with a compass of known error, as for example, a standby gyro compared with a master gyro. If a compass of unknown error is compared with one whose errors are known, the difference in their readings on various headings will provide information from which the errors of the former can be determined. This comparison is generally only possible in ships having two gyrocompasses installed aboard.

As previously mentioned, error as determined by using one of these methods is known as *westerly* or *easterly* gyro error, depending upon its direction. If the 0° point on the compass card is to the *west* of true north, the card has been rotated counterclockwise and all readings of course and bearing made with this error will be too high. If the 0° point on the compass card is to the *east* of true north, the card has been rotated clockwise and all readings will be too low. The principles of applying compass error to obtain true course and bearing hold true both for the application of magnetic compass error discussed in article 312 and for the application of gyro error discussed in the next article.

Gyrocompass Error Calculations

347 By any one of several methods it is a relatively easy process for a navigator to determine the numerical value of the gyro error using simple arithmetic. The difficulty arises in determining the *label*, east or west, of the error. A simple memory-aid phrase can be used as before.

Compass least, error east;
Compass best, error west.

As with magnetic compasses, "compass best" means that the compass reading is numerically greater than the true value.

Example 1: Two fixed aids to navigation in line are sighted with a gyrocompass repeater, and found to be bearing 136.5° per gyrocompass. According to the chart, the bearing of these aids when in line is 138° true.

Required: The gyro error (GE).

Solution: Numerically, the gyro error is the difference between gyro and true bearings of the objects in range, or 138° − 136.5° = 1.5°. Since this 1.5° would have to be added to the gyro bearing to obtain true bearing, the direction of the error is easterly.

Answer: GE 1.5° E.

Example 2: A light ashore is sighted, and by gyrocompass repeater is observed to bear 310.0° per gyrocompass. From the ship's fixed position, the charted true bearing of the light is measured as 308.5° true.

Required: The gyro error (GE).

Solution: As before, the gyro error is the difference between the gyro and the true bearing, or 310° − 308.5° = 1.5°. Since this 1.5° would have to be subtracted from the gyro bearing to obtain true bearing, and since westerly errors are subtracted, the direction of the error is westerly.

Answer: GE 1.5° W.

Example 3: A round of gyro bearings was taken on three terrestrial objects with the following results:

Tower: 058.0°
Light: 183.0°
Beacon: 310.0°

The three lines of position, when plotted, formed a small triangle. By trial and error, it was found that when 2.0° was *added* to each bearing, a point fix resulted.

Required: The gyro error (GE).

Solution: Since 2.0° had to be added to each bearing to obtain a perfect fix, and since easterly errors are added, the gyro error is 2.0° E.

Answer: GE 2.0° E.

Gyro error must be added to or subtracted from true or gyro headings and bearings to go from one form of direction to the other. The two basic rules to be applied in such calculations can be stated as follows:

When converting from gyro to true, add easterly error and subtract westerly error.

When converting from true to gyro, add westerly error and subtract easterly error. Here, too, the memory aid for magnetic compasses, Correcting Add East (C-A-E) is applicable.

Example 4: A ship is heading 130° per gyrocompass (GH). The gyro error (GE) is 1° E.

Required: The true heading (TH).

Solution: Since error is easterly, it must be added. Hence the true heading is 130° + 1° = 131°.

Answer: TH 131°.

Example 5: A ship is heading 020° per gyrocompass. The gyro error is 1° W.

Required: The true heading.

Solution: Since the error is west it must be sub-

tracted. Hence, the true heading is 020° − 1° = 019°.

Answer: TH 019°.

Example 6: From a chart the true course between two places is found to be 151°; the GE is 1° E.

Required: The heading per gyrocompass to steer 151° true.

Solution: Since easterly errors are added to gyro to obtain true, they must be subtracted when converting from true to gyro, or 151° − 1° = 150°.

Answer: GH 150°.

Another simple, easily remembered expression combines the first letters of the words Gyro, Error, and True to form the short word GET. This is then written as G + E + T indicating that from Gyro to True it is Plus (add) East. The westerly error procedure and the reverse direction, True to Gyro, can be worked out from the basic equation.

Comparing Gyro and Magnetic Compasses

348 Whenever a new course is set, and at regular intervals thereafter, the magnetic compass, master gyrocompass, and all gyro repeaters should be compared. A record of these comparisons should be kept in a compass comparison book. Any erratic behavior of either gyrocompass or of any repeater will be apparent at once by such comparisons.

Chapter 4   Aids to Navigation

Introduction

401 A navigator usually needs more than just the charts and instruments on his vessel to fix her position and direct her course. Prominent features ashore, both natural—such as mountain peaks and points of land—and man-made—such as water tanks and radio towers—are frequently used, but more often a navigator will make use of an *aid to navigation* (ATON). In this chapter, these include lights, lightships, buoys, daybeacons, and fog signals. Landmarks are excluded from the definition of an "aid to navigation," which includes only objects established solely or primarily for that purpose. Electronic aids to navigation, such as radiobeacons, Loran, Omega, and other systems are discussed in later chapters.

The *U.S. Coast Guard* has responsibility for the operation and maintenance of all lights and other aids to navigation along 40,000 miles of coastline in the United States and its possessions, plus additional thousands of miles along the shores of the Great Lakes and on most inland rivers. There are more than 12,000 primary, secondary, and minor lights; over 24,000 lighted and unlighted buoys; and 10,000+ daybeacons. There are some "private aids," those maintained by individuals, local governments, or federal agencies other than the Coast Guard, but these are relatively few in number, except in the Gulf of Mexico where thousands of oil rigs are marked with private aids.

Importance

Aids to navigation are of vital assistance to a navigator in making a landfall when approaching from seaward, when navigating along a coast, and when piloting on inland waters. Their importance was first recognized by the ancient Mediterranean mariners; a lighthouse was built at Sigeum, near Troy, before 600 B.C., and the famous Pharos of Alexandria was built in the third century B.C. Wood fires furnished their illumination, and wood and sometimes coal remained in general use for this purpose until the eighteenth century. The first lighthouse in the United States was built at Boston in 1716, and logs and kegs were used as buoys in the Delaware River in 1767. Compressed gas was used in lighted buoys as late as the 1950s, but now all have been converted to electricity.

Major Categories

402 Aids to navigation take a wide variety of forms. Some are very simple unmanned objects; others are complex and costly devices, sometimes with operating crews in attendance. All serve the same goal—the safety of vessels and those on board; differences in type, size, etc., are determined by the circumstances of location and use.

Buoys

Buoys are perhaps the most numerous aids to navigation, and they come in many shapes and sizes. These are floating objects, heavily anchored to the bottom, that are intended to convey information to a navigator by their shape or color, by the characteristics of a visible or audible signal, or a combination of two or more such features. (Lightships fit such a definition, but form a separate category by themselves.) Buoys have bands of retroreflective material to enhance their detection at night; these reflect brightly in the beam of a vessel's searchlight (or even a hand-held flashlight on

Figure 402. Buoys are found in almost all waters.

smaller craft.) Most buoys now have *radar reflectors* (see article 1617).

Daybeacons

In shallower inland waters, *daybeacons* are often used instead of buoys because they are less expensive to maintain. These are single piles or multiple-pile structures (dolphins) driven into the bottom, on which are placed one or more signboards called *"daymarks"* that convey information through their color, shape, and lettering or numbers. Daymarks normally have retroreflective material as part of their design.

Lights and Lightships

The term "light" covers a wide variety of aids to navigation—from the simple short-range *minor light* on a single pile in inland waters to the multi-million-candlepower *primary seacoast light* in a structure a hundred feet or more tall established to aid ships in making a safe landfall. These lights, and the *secondary lights* between these extremes, are assigned characteristics of color and rhythm (off-on periods) for ease of identification. In some instances, the shape and color of the supporting structure will be of assistance in identification.

(The classification of "major light" includes both primary seacoast and secondary lights.)

When a light is required offshore, a *lightship* may be established. This is a specially designed vessel, anchored in a precisely determined position, equipped with a high-intensity light of specified characteristics and usually with other types of aids to navigation as well. The current trend is to replace lightships with fixed structures or with *large navigational buoys*—termed "LNBs" in U.S. waters, "Lanbys" in Europe. Either of these is much more economical to operate and maintain.

Ranges

Ranges are pairs of aids to navigation, lighted or unlighted, so positioned with respect to each other that a line between them, extended over water, marks a channel. (In Europe, a range is known as a *leading line*.) When the *front* and *rear* daymarks or lights are aligned, a navigator is guided safely through the channel. Ranges can also be used to mark turning points on channels or to establish specific directions for compass adjustment; they are especially useful in places where tidal currents set across or at an angle to a dredged channel that has shoal water on either side.

Fog Signals

Fog signals are audible signals used to indicate the location of an aid to navigation when it cannot be seen due to conditions of reduced visibility. They serve to warn the mariner of a danger or to indicate a general direction to steer. They are usually co-located with another form of aid such as a light; they may be on shore, on a fixed structure in the water, or most often on a buoy.

Radio and Radar Beacons

Radiobeacons supplement visual aids to navigation and permit bearings to be obtained at greater distances, at night, and under conditions of reduced visibility; they are often co-located with primary or secondary lights. See articles 3203–3209.

Radar beacons, known as *racons* and *ramarks*, are used to give a stronger radar return from specific locations; they are often co-located with other aids to navigation; as with fog signals, they may be on shore or in water areas on lights and buoys. See article 1618.

Light Lists

403 Light Lists for the United States and its possessions, including the Intracoastal Waterway, the Mississippi and its navigable tributaries, and the

Great Lakes—both the U.S. and Canadian shores—are published annually by the U.S. Coast Guard. A portion of a typical page is reproduced in figure 403.

Similar publications, called *Lists of Lights*, covering foreign coasts, are prepared by the Defense Mapping Agency Hydrographic/Topographic Center as Publications No. 110 through 116. See article 604.

These lists give detailed information regarding navigational lights, light structures, radiobeacons, and fog signals. In addition, the *Light Lists* for the United States give data on lighted and unlighted buoys and daybeacons.

Corrections to both sets of lists are published weekly in *Notices to Mariners* (and *Local Notices to Mariners* for USCG *Light Lists* only); see article 610. It is of the utmost importance that all corrections be entered in the appropriate list (or similar publication from other countries), as well as on any applicable chart, before either of these is used for navigation.

BUOYAGE SYSTEMS

Introduction

404 A *buoyage system* consists of those aids to navigation, floating and fixed, lighted and unlighted, that have been established to mark a nation's waterways. Aids can be used in either a *lateral* system or a *cardinal* system, or a combination of both. In the lateral system, aids are placed to indicate the sides of a navigable channel; they also mark junctions and bifurcations in channels, indicate the safe side on which to pass a hazard, and mark the general safe centerline of wide bodies of water. In the cardinal system, the aid generally is used to mark the geographic relationship to the aid of a hazard in terms of 90° quadrants centered on the cardinal directions of north, east, south, and west.

Over the years, more than 30 different buoyage systems have been used at one time or another by the world's maritime nations. Some features had exactly opposite meanings in different countries. Efforts toward standardization were made, but achieved little until in the mid-1970s the International Association of Lighthouse Authorities (IALA) developed and secured acceptance of two systems—two, because certain basic long-established international differences precluded adoption of a single system worldwide. Both systems, designated System A and System B, use a combination of cardinal marks and lateral marks plus unique marks

for isolated dangers, safe-water areas, and special purposes. The cardinal and unique marks are the same in both systems; the lateral marks have exactly *opposite* meanings in the two systems. To convey the desired information to the navigator, the IALA systems use buoy shape, color, and if lighted, the *rhythm* of the flashes; they also provide for a pattern of "topmarks," small distinctive shapes above the basic aid to facilitate its identification in the daytime from a distance, or under light conditions when the color might not be easily ascertained.

IALA system A is used in Europe, Africa, and most of Asia, including Australia and New Zealand. It makes much use of cardinal marks and places red buoys to port and green buoys to starboard when entering from seaward.

The IALA-B system is used in North, Central, and South America, plus Japan, South Korea, and the Philippines. Although cardinal marks are permitted, less frequent use of them is made. Buoys to port (entering from seaward) are green, and those on the starboard side are red.

IALA-B System

405 On 15 April 1982, the United States agreed to make the necessary changes in its buoyage to bring it into conformity with the IALA-B system. The U.S. Lateral System was not materially changed—only details of its features. An estimated 70 percent of all U.S. aids to navigation already conformed—red buoys and daymarks to starboard, green daymarks to port. The nonconforming aids—chiefly *black* buoys to port—will be converted on a gradual basis as they are routinely replaced or serviced.

The description of the U.S. lateral system of buoyage that follows is that of the new IALA-B system. Aids in the older U.S. system, some of which may remain in service until about 1989, are described in article 428. Until the conversion program is completed, mariners must be familiar with both systems and alert to the fact that conversions may not be immediately reflected on published charts. Individual conversions will be announced in *Notices to Mariners* and *Local Notices to Mariners* as applicable; see article 610.

The characteristics of buoys and other aids to navigation along the coasts, in the Intracoastal Waterways, and on the Great Lakes are determined as if a vessel were "returning from seaward" when she is proceeding in a westerly and southerly direction along the Maine coast, and in a southerly direction along the remainder of the Atlantic coast, in a

(1) No. Characteristic	(2) Name	(3) Location Lat. N. Long. W.	(4) Nominal Range	(5) Ht. above water	(6) Structure Ht. above ground Daymark	(7) Remarks Year
	(Chart 13260) (For Gulf of Maine, see No. 199)					
1 227 J048	**MOUNT DESERT LIGHT** . . . . . . , Fl. W., 15s	On Mount Desert Rock, 20 miles south of Mount Desert Island. 43 58.1 68 07.7	24	75	Conical gray granite tower . . . 58	HORN: 2 blasts ev 30s (2s bl-2s si-2s bl-24s si). Emergency light of reduced intensity when main light is extinguished. 1830
2 239 J116	**MATINICUS ROCK LIGHT** . . . . . Gp. Fl. W., (1 + 2), 15s 0.2s fl., 5.8s ec. 0.2s fl., 2.8s ec. 0.2s fl., 5.8s ec. (3 flashes.)	On south part of rock. 43 47.0 68 51.3	23	90	Cylindrical gray granite tower and dwelling. 48	RBN: 314 kHz MR(■ ■ ● ■ ●). Antenna on light tower. HORN: 1 blast ev 15s (2s bl). 1827—1857
3 282 J128	**MONHEGAN ISLAND LIGHT** . . . Fl. W., 30s (2.8s fl)	Near center of island. 43 45.9 69 19.0	21	178	Gray conical tower covered way to dwelling. 47	Within 3 miles of island the light is obscured between west and southwest. 1824—1850
283 J130	Manana Island Fog Signal Station.	On west side of island, close to Monhegan Island. 43 45.8 69 19.7	. . . .	. . . .	Brown brick house	RBN: 286 kHz MI(■ ■ ● ●)VI. Antenna 2,880 feet 259° from Monhegan Island light tower. HORN: 2 blasts ev 60s (3s bl-3s si-3s bl-51s si). 1855—1870
5 297 J146	**SEGUIN LIGHT** . . . . F. W.	On island, 2 miles south of mouth of Kennebec River. 43 42.5 69 45.5	18	180	White cylindrical granite tower connected to dwelling. 53	HORN: 2 blasts ev 20s (2s bl-2s si-2s bl-14s si). 1795—1857
6 320 J176	**HALFWAY ROCK LIGHT** . . . . . . Fl. R., 5s	On rock, midway between Cape Small Point and Cape Elizabeth. 43 39.4 70 02.2	19	77	White granite tower attached to dwelling. 76	Emergency light of reduced intensity when main light is extinguished. RBN: 291 kHz HR(● ● ● ● ■ ■ ●). Antenna on light tower. HORN: 2 blasts ev 30s (2s bl-2s si-2s bl-24s si). 1871
	(Chart 13286)					
7.10 334.10 J211	**Portland Lighted Horn Buoy** P (LNB). Fl. W., 2s F. W.	In 160 feet 43 31.6 70 05.5	14 8	42	Red	Equipped with passing light. RBN: 301 kHz PH(● ■ ■ ● ● ● ● ●). HORN: 1 blast ev 30s (3s bl). RACON: M(■ ■).
7.60 334.60	*Disposal Area Dumping Ground. Lighted Buoy DG.* Fl. W., 2.5s	In 181 feet 43 34.3 70 01.9	5	. . . .	Orange and white horizontal bands.	Ra ref. Private aid.
7.70 334.70	*Portland Disposal Area Lighted Buoy.* Fl. Y., 4s	In 220 feet 43 34.1 70 01.9	. . . .	. . . .	Orange and white horizontal bands.	Ra ref. Private aid.
	(For Portland Harbor, see No. 334.10)					
8 338 J208	**CAPE ELIZABETH LIGHT** . . . . . . Gp. Fl. W., 30s 0.2s fl., 2.3s ec. 0.2s fl., 2.3s ec. 0.2s fl., 2.3s ec. 0.2s fl., 2.3s ec. 0.2s fl., 2.3s ec. 0.2s fl., 17.3s ec. (6 flashes)	South of entrance to Portland Harbor. 43 34.0 70 12.0	27	129	White conical tower 67	HORN: 2 blasts ev 60s (3s bl-3s si-3s bl-51s si). Located 266 yards 146° from light tower. 1829—1874
	Taylor Reef Buoy 1TR	In 75 feet, off southeast side of reef.	. . . .	. . . .	Black can	Ra ref. Green reflector.
	Alden Rock Buoy 2AR	In 28 feet, 0.3 mile southwest of rock.	. . . .	. . . .	Red nun	Ra ref. Red reflector.

Figure 403. *Light List* (extract).

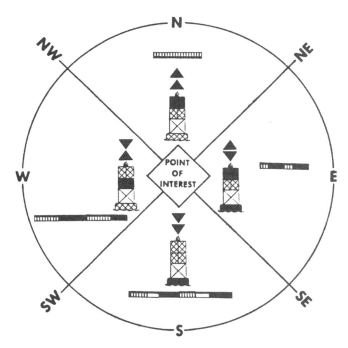

Figure 404a. The cardinal system of buoyage.

Red buoys (and aids with red triangular daymarks) mark the starboard (right) sides of channels, or the location of wrecks or obstructions that must be passed by keeping the buoy on the starboard (right) hand when returning from seaward.

Buoys with horizontal red and green bands (and aids with red and green horizontally divided daymarks) mark junctions or bifurcations in the channel, or wrecks or obstructions that may be passed on either side. If the topmost band is green, the preferred channel will be followed by keeping the buoy on the port (left) hand, as if the whole buoy were green. If the topmost band is red, the preferred channel will be followed by keeping the buoy to starboard.

However, in some instances it may not be feasible for larger vessels to pass on either side of such a buoy, and the chart should always be consulted.

Buoys with red and white vertical stripes (and aids with red and white vertically divided daymarks) are "safe-water marks" used to indicate the fairway or mid-channel, or a landfall. Such buoys are also used at the beginning of some vessel Traffic Separation Schemes at the entrances to busy ports, or in narrow passages congested with heavy traffic.

All special-purpose buoys—typically marking anchorages, fishnet areas, and dredging sites—are colored solid yellow. These buoys have no lateral system significance, but as most are shown on charts they can often serve to assist in determining one's position. They can be of any shape.

northerly and westerly direction along the Gulf coast, in a northerly direction on the Pacific coast, and in a northerly and westerly direction on the Great Lakes (except southerly in Lake Michigan). See figure 405a.

Buoy Colors

Green buoys (and aids such as daybeacons and minor lights with green square daymarks) mark the port (left) side of channels, or the location of wrecks or obstructions that must be passed by keeping the buoy on the port (left) hand *when returning from seaward.*

Types of Buoys

406 A complete system of buoyage includes several different types of buoys, each type designed to

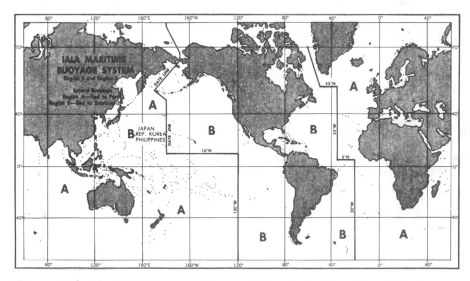

Figure 404b. The IALA Buoyage System differs in Regions A and B; see text.

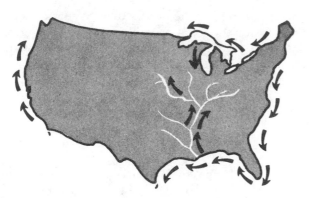

Figure 405a. Direction of increasing numbers for coastal buoys—as if "returning from sea."

Figure 405b. Buoys in the IALA-B lateral system. More complete illustrations will be found in the back pages of this book.

meet the requirements of certain specific conditions. All buoys serve as guides during daylight; those having lights are also available for navigation at night; those having sound signals are more readily located in times of fog or other conditions of reduced visibility.

Can buoy. A buoy built of steel plates with the portion above water having the shape of a tin can, flat on top when seen from a distance. In inland waters, small can buoys may be made of plastic material. (This is termed a *cylindrical buoy* in some systems.) These are green or have red and green horizontal bands where the topmost band is green.

Nun buoy. A buoy built of steel plates with the portion above water terminating in a cone, usually with a rounded tip. In inland waters, small nun buoys may be made of plastic materials. (This is termed a *conical buoy* in some systems.) These are red or have red and green horizontal bands where the topmost band is red.

Spherical buoy. A buoy of metal or plastic that has the shape of a sphere or globe. These buoys have red and white vertical stripes.

Spar buoy. A buoy with an elongated cylindrical shape, usually of wood resembling a pile. Closely related are *pillar buoys*, a low circular base with a tall cylindrical shape of smaller diameter mounted on top.

Lighted buoy. A steel float on which is mounted a short skeleton tower at the top of which a light is placed. (The majority of U.S. lighted buoys can be termed *pillar buoys*.) A set of electric batteries (or other source of power) that operates the light is placed in the body of the buoy.

Bell buoy. A steel float topped with a short skeleton tower in which there is a bell with several clappers—usually four—hung externally so that they will strike the bell as it rocks with the motion of the sea.

Gong buoy. Generally similar in construction to a bell buoy except that rather than a bell it has several, usually four, gongs mounted in a vertical stack, each of which sounds a *different* note; each gong has its own clapper of a length so as to strike only that gong.

Whistle buoy. A buoy generally similar in construction to a bell or gong buoy, but which has a low-pitched whistle signal that is activated by the rise and fall of the buoy in a seaway. A *horn buoy* is

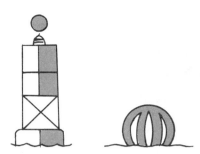

Figure 405c. Topmarks may be added to lighted buoys to aid in daytime identification. Here a spherical topmark has been added, corresponding to an unlighted spherical buoy.

much the same except that its sound signal is electrically powered by batteries within the lower part of the buoy.

Combination buoy. A buoy having a light signal and a sound signal; for example, a lighted bell buoy, a lighted gong buoy, etc.

Significance of Buoys

407 The primary function of buoys is to warn the mariner of some danger, some obstruction, or change in the contours of the sea bottom, and to delineate the channels leading to various points; occasionally, a buoy may be placed offshore merely to assist a navigator in establishing his position before approaching a harbor (a "sea buoy"). Valuable information is obtained from buoys when they are considered as marking definitely identified spots, for if a mariner knows his location at the moment and is properly equipped with charts, he can plot a safe course on which to proceed. Such features as size, shape, coloring, numbering, and signaling equipment of buoys are but means to warn, orient, and guide the navigator.

Buoy Shapes

The overall shape and general physical characteristics of these buoys may be seen in figure 407b. Small lifting rings or "ears" on buoys such as can, nun, or spherical are not considered to affect the basic shape. The shape of the superstructure on lighted, sound, and combination buoys has no navigational significance.

In order to provide easier identification under certain light conditions where the color may not be readily discerned, certain *unlighted* buoys—nuns, cans, and spherical buoys—can be differentiated by their shape. Special-purpose buoys, solid yellow, may be of any shape.

Full reliance should not be placed on the shape alone of an unlighted buoy. Charts and light lists should be consulted to ascertain the significance of unlighted buoys as determined by their colors.

The only *topmark* presently used in the U.S. lateral system is a single small red sphere (approximately ⅕ of the diameter of the buoy) on *lighted* red-and-white vertically striped safe water aids; it is placed above the light.

As noted before, lighted, sound, and combination buoys are not differentiated by shape to indicate the side on which they should be passed. Since no special significance is attached to the shapes of these buoys, *their purpose is indicated by the coloring, numbering, light characteristics (color and rhythm), and topmarks.*

Buoy Numbers

Most buoys are given numbers, letters, or combinations of numbers and letters that are painted conspicuously on them, or are applied in white retroreflective material. These markings facilitate identification and location of the buoys on the charts.

All solid-colored red or green buoys are given numbers or combinations of numbers and letters. Other colored buoys may be given letters. Numbers increase sequentially from seaward; numbers are sometimes omitted when there are more buoys of one type than another. Odd numbers are used *only* on solid green buoys. Even numbers are used *only* on solid red buoys. Numbers followed by letters are used on solid-colored red or green buoys when a letter is required so as not to disturb the sequence of numbers, such as when an additional buoy is placed after the numbering system has been established. Letters may also be used on certain important buoys, particularly those marking isolated offshore dangers. An example of the latter case would be a buoy marked "6 WQS." In this instance the number has the usual significance, while the letters "WQS" indicate the place as Winter Quarter Shoal. Letters without numbers are applied in some cases to red-and-white vertically striped buoys, red-and-green horizontally banded buoys, and solid yellow buoys.

The numbers and letters (as well as portions of the buoy) are of reflective material for better visibility at night.

Buoy Sound Signals

The IALA systems make no mention of sound signals—bells, gongs, whistles, horns—on buoys. In U.S. waters such fog signals will continue to be used as they have been in the past.

In some areas, if both bell and gong buoys are used to mark a channel, the gongs are placed to port and the bells to starboard when entering from seaward. In other areas, different local arrangements are used to aid a navigator traversing a channel in fog or other reduced visibility situation.

Station Buoys

Buoys do not always maintain exact positions; therefore, they should always be regarded as warnings and not as fixed navigational marks, especially during the winter months, or when moored in exposed waters or in heavy currents. A smaller nun or can buoy called a *station buoy* is sometimes placed in close proximity to a large lighted buoy or lightship to mark the station in case the regular aid is accidentally shifted from its designated location. Station buoys are colored and numbered in the same manner as the larger buoy or lightship.

Reflectors

Buoys and daybeacons are marked with retroreflective tape. This greatly facilitates locating them at night with a searchlight. Reflective areas may be red, green, white, or yellow, and have the same significance as lights of these colors.

Caution in Using Buoys

Despite their usefulness, buoys must be used with caution. The buoy symbol on a chart is used to indicate the *approximate* position of the buoy. This position is termed "approximate" because of the practical limitations in positioning and maintaining buoys in precise geographic locations. These limitations include, but are not limited to, imprecise position-fixing methods, prevailing wind and sea conditions, the slope and the make-up of the seabed, and the fact that buoy positions are not under continuous surveillance, but are normally checked only during periodic maintenance visits that may occur a year or more apart. It must also be remembered that buoys are moored to an anchor with varying lengths of chain (a scope of three times the depth of the water is typical, but it may be more), and a buoy can be expected to swing in a circle under the varying influences of current, wind, and waves. Buoys are subject to being carried away, shifted, capsized, or sunk; lighted buoys may become extinguished, and sound signals may malfunction.

Buoys marking wrecks will normally *not* be directly over the hazard, due to possible danger to the vessel that places the buoy in position. Such buoys are usually put on the seaward or chan-nelward side of the wreck; if two buoys are used, the wreck may lie between them. Wrecks may shift position due either to normal currents or storm conditions; care must always be exercised in the vicinity of buoys marking wrecks.

As useful as buoys are, a prudent navigator will not rely completely on the position or operation of floating aids to navigation, especially those in exposed waters. He will, whenever possible, give preference to bearings on fixed aids to navigation or natural landmarks, and will always navigate with reference to the appropriate nautical chart.

Daybeacons

408   Where daybeacons are substituted for unlighted buoys in the U.S. lateral system, the color of the daymark will be the same and the shape will be roughly similar—red daymarks will be triangular, approximating the shape of the top of a nun buoy; square daymarks, corresponding to can buoys, will be green.

Daymarks equivalent to spherical buoys are octagonal in shape. The daymarks on a daybeacon replacing a yellow special-purpose buoy are diamond shape (a square rotated through 45°).

Daybeacons will be numbered (and/or lettered) with retroreflective material in the same manner as a buoy and have a border of that material. Many have panels of red or green reflective material. Some channels may be marked with a combination of buoys, daybeacons, and lights.

Minor Lights

409   In a similar fashion to daybeacons replacing unlighted buoys, *minor lights* may be used in lieu of lighted buoys. In physical appearance, these are much like daybeacons to which a light has been added; daymarks are used in the same way.

Articulated Lights

A recent addition to the types of aids to navigation operated by the U.S. Coast Guard is the *articulated light*. This is something of a cross between a minor light and a lighted buoy. A sealed hollow metal cylinder a foot or so in diameter and up to 50 or more feet in length is attached at one end by a swivel to a normal buoy "sinker." Because the cylinder is buoyant, it floats in an essentially vertical position (in some locations, an additional buoyancy chamber may be attached to the cylinder just below the water surface). Because no scope of chain is used, the aid is always precisely over the sinker with a negligible swinging circle. The length of the

Figure 409. An articulated light.

cylinder is selected to be the normal depth of water, plus tide, plus 10–15 feet above the surface. At the top is mounted a typical light mechanism and daymarks. Articulated lights will be used when a position must be marked more precisely than is possible with a buoy, yet the depth of water, up to 40 feet, is too great for normal pile or dolphin minor light structure. See figure 409.

An unlighted aid of this construction is termed an *articulated daybeacon*.

Light Characteristics

410   Lights shown from buoys and other aids to navigation have distinct characteristics (rhythms) to assist in their identification. These are illustrated, and their abbreviations are given, in figure 410. Lights are described as *flashing* when the time on is less than the time off. Lights are termed *occulting* when they are on more than they are off ("eclipsed"). If the times on and off are equal, the light is designated as *equal interval* or *isophase*. A *group-flashing* light is one that shows more than one flash in quick sequence with a longer dark interval between groups. A *composite group-flashing* light shows more than one group separated by an interval that is longer than those within a group,

but less than the interval that separates complete cycles. The *period* of a light is the time for it to complete one full cycle of on-and-off changes. By varying the lengths of the periods and the elements of a cycle, a considerable variety of light rhythms can be obtained. Advantage is taken of this to provide the necessary distinction between aids in the same area.

Lighted ATONs in the U.S. Lateral System

411   Lighted aids in the U.S. lateral system may be identified at night by the color of the light and its rhythm. Lights are not on in daylight, and identification of the ATON then is by its basic shape and color, or by its daymark.

Figure 410. Light phase characteristics (rhythms).

The four standard light colors for lighted ATONs are red, green, white, and yellow. *Red* lights only are used on red buoys, or red-and-green horizontally banded buoys with the topmost band red; *green lights* only are used on green buoys, or red-and-green horizontally banded buoys with the topmost band green. White lights only are used on safe-water marks, red-and-white vertically striped buoys. Yellow is the only color of light used on special-purpose buoys.

Light Rhythms

Flashing lights (flashing at regular intervals and at a rate of not more than 30 flashes per minute) are used only on solid-color red, green, or yellow buoys, and on minor lights equivalent to such buoys.

Quick-flashing lights (not less than 50 but not more than 80 flashes per minute) are placed only on green buoys and red buoys, and on equivalent minor lights, at points where it is desired to indicate that special caution is necessary—for example, at sharp turns, where a channel narrows, or to mark wrecks or other obstructions that must be passed *on one side only*.

Composite group-flashing (2 + 1) lights are used on red-and-green horizontally banded buoys; the color of the light matches the upper band on the structure.

Morse (A) lights (groups consisting of a short flash and a long flash repeated at intervals of eight seconds) are placed on buoys with red-and-white vertical stripes, and on minor lights whose daymarks are octagonal, colored red and white vertically, and placed at points where it is desired to indicate fairways or mid-channels; they should be passed close aboard on either side. These lights are always white.

Lights on special-purpose aids may *not* be any one of a long list of specialized characteristics. In actual practice these lights will most probably be normal flashing; consult your chart or *Light List* to positively identify a yellow light on an ATON.

Other rhythms—fixed, occulting, equal interval, very quick flashing—are also permitted in the IALA-B System, but these are not normally used on buoys in the U.S. lateral system.

Aids to Navigation on the ICW

412 The Intracoastal Waterway (ICW) is a largely sheltered waterway, suitable for year-round use, extending some 2,400 miles along the Atlantic and Gulf coasts of the United States. In general it follows natural waterways.

Aids to navigation along the ICW carry special identification marks. The usual daymark and buoy painting schemes are used, but an additional *yellow* stripe is added *under* the number on daymarks and a yellow band is painted on buoys; see the color illustrations in the back pages of this book (*Chart No. 1*) or any volume of the *Light Lists*.

Colors

The colors used for ICW aids are governed by the following rules:

The *left side* of the channel, entering from the north and east, and traversing towards the south and west, is marked with *green aids*, bearing *odd numbers*.

The *right side* of the channel, entering from the north and east, is marked with *red aids*, bearing *even numbers*.

All *green* daymarks on daybeacons are *square*, while the *red* daymarks are *triangular* in shape.

In certain areas, the ICW coincides with other waterways that are buoyed in accordance with the standard practice—that is, green buoys on the left hand when proceeding from seaward, and red buoys on the right, as described in article 405. In such joint waterways the standard system of coloring for entering from seaward prevails for the ATONS, and the ICW numbers and yellow markings are omitted; but yellow triangles or squares are added to the regular markings to designate the ICW. The system of marking where the ICW and another waterway coincide is shown in the color illustrations referenced above. An inspection of the sketch on that page shows that the color of aids may be reversed under such conditions. A vessel proceeding south down the ICW has red aids on her right hand until the nun "6" is reached, where the channel becomes a joint waterway; at this point the red aids will be on her left hand. However, along this reach of the channel the yellow shapes painted on the buoys can be of assistance, as squares will be on the red buoys as a reminder that in this joint waterway a red buoy may be on the left hand for vessels proceeding south.

Buoyage on the Western Rivers

413 Aids to navigation on the "Western Rivers" of the U.S.—the Mississippi River and its tributaries—are generally similar to those on other U.S. waters, but there are a few differences that should be noted. Buoys are not numbered; their color system conforms to the U.S. lateral system or red-right-returning from sea. (The descriptions "right side" and "left side" are sometimes used, but in terms of a vessel proceeding downstream *toward* the sea.) Lights and daybeacons are numbered, but *not* in the even-odd style of the lateral system; numbers relate to the distance upstream in *statute* miles from some arbitrary point of origin. Lights and lighted buoys on the starboard side proceeding downriver show a single green or white flash; those on the port side show a *double* red or white flash. Special diamond-shape "crossing" daymarks are used at bends where the deeper channel crosses from one side of the river to the other. See color illustrations in the back pages of this book or any volume of the *Light Lists*.

Uniform State Waterway Marking System

414 To provide for consistent marking of U.S. internal waters not subject to federal jurisdiction, the Uniform State Waterway Marking System (USWMS) has been established. This consists of regulatory buoys and signs, plus buoys in either the lateral system or a cardinal system. See color illustrations referenced above. (Black lateral buoys may be changed to green at a later date.)

Range Lights

415 Two lights, located some distance apart and one higher than the other, visible usually in one direction only, are known as *range lights*. Technically these are not a part of a lateral system of buoyage, but they are usually found in waters that are marked in a lateral system. Range lights are so positioned that a mariner can place his vessel on the axis of a channel by steering to make the lights appear one above the other (the farther "rear" light above the nearer "front" light). If he continues to steer his vessel so that the lights stay aligned vertically, his vessel will remain within the limits of the channel.

Entrance channels are frequently marked by range lights. The Delaware River and the St. Johns River on the Atlantic coast, and the Columbia River on the Pacific coast are examples of successive straight reaches marked in this manner.

The lights of ranges may be any of the four standard colors, and may also be fixed, flashing, or occulting, the principal requirement being that they stand out distinctly from their surroundings. Range light structures are usually fitted with conspicuously colored daymarks for daytime use. Most range lights lose brilliance rapidly as a ship di-

Figure 415. A range is formed by two aids to navigation in line, with the rear aid higher than the front aid.

verges from the range line. On some ranges, the sector of visibility of the lights is very narrow; for example, the Cape May Harbor range lights are described in the *Light List* as "visible on range line only"; other range lights are variously listed as "visible 2° (or 4°) each side of range line."

Ranges should be used only after a careful examination of the charts, and *it is particularly important to determine how far the range line can be followed safely.* This is not obtainable from the *Light Lists*, and a chart must be consulted.

The proper turning point for leaving, or joining, any range must be known and the turn itself anticipated.

Directional Lights

In a limited number of situations, it is not practical for one reason or another to install a pair of range lights. A less effective, but generally acceptable, substitute is a *directional light*. This is a single light that projects a high-intensity beam of very narrow width; often three colors are used, with a sharp white beam flanked on one side by a broader, but still rather narrow, red sector and with a similar green sector on the other side. The red sector will be on the red buoy side of the channel, with the green sector appearing over the green buoys.

The same cautions regarding use apply as were discussed above for range lights. The entry in the *Light List* must be consulted for information on the beam-width(s) involved, as normally there is space on the chart for only the color(s) and rhythms.

Miscellaneous Light Information

416 The lights on U.S. buoys are operated by means of electricity supplied from batteries wired to a flashing mechanism in the base of the lantern. At minor lights, the batteries are in a weatherproof box on a platform near the top of the structure.

In order that lighted buoys and minor lights may function for a reasonably long period of time without requiring replacement of the batteries, the length of the light flashes is quite short in comparison with the intervening periods of darkness. To further conserve electricity, lights are now equipped with a "daylight control" (photoelectric cell) to turn the lights off during the day. Battery power supplies at isolated locations can often last for a year or more. An automatic bulb-changing mechanism is included to increase the dependability of the light; if a bulb burns out, an internal device puts into use one of several spare bulbs.

Electrical Power Changes

A program is underway to add solar panels to about 65 percent of the more than 16,000 lighted aids, both lighted buoys and minor lights. This will permit the use of a smaller storage battery in lieu of large, heavy primary cells that cannot be recharged and present a disposal problem.

Another technical development is the use on offshore lighted buoys of a wave-actuated generator to maintain the charge of a storage battery.

Navigation Lights on Bridges

417 In U.S. waters, the Coast Guard prescribes certain combinations of fixed lights for bridges and other structures extending over waterways. In general, red lights are used to mark piers and supports, and green lights mark the centerline of the navigable channel through a fixed bridge; if there is more than one channel through the bridge, the preferred route is marked by three white lights placed vertically. Green lights are also used on some drawbridges to indicate that the draw is open and the vessel may proceed. Some bridges may also be equipped with sound signals (see article 427).

ATONS NOT IN BUOYAGE SYSTEMS

Lighthouses

418 Lighthouses, called "lights" in the *Light Lists*, are found along most of the world's navigable coastlines and many of the interior waterways. Lighthouses are placed where they will be of most use, on prominent headlands, at entrances, on isolated dangers, or at other points where it is necessary that mariners be guided or warned. Their principal purpose is to support a light at a considerable height above the water. The same structure may also house a fog signal and radiobeacon equipment and contain quarters for the keepers. However, in the majority of instances, the fog signal, the radiobeacon equipment, and the operating personnel are housed in separate buildings grouped around the tower. Such a group of buildings constitutes a *light station*.

The location of a lighthouse, whether in the water or on shore, the importance of the light, the kind of soil upon which it is to be built, and the prevalence of violent storms have a direct bearing upon the type of structure erected and on the materials with which it is built. Engineering problems will not be discussed here, but it is important to note that the materials used and types of construction assist in differentiating one lighthouse from another and hence aid in identification.

Lighthouses vary markedly in their outward appearance because of the points already mentioned and also because of the great difference in the distances from which their lights need to be seen. Where the need for a powerful light is great and the importance and density of traffic warrant, a tall tower with a light of great candlepower is erected. Conversely, at points intermediate to the major lights, where the traffic is light, or where long range is not so necessary, a less expensive structure of more modest dimensions and capabilities suffices.

Classes of Lights

The terms *primary seacoast light*, *secondary light*, and *river* or *harbor light* (there are also *minor lights*) indicate in a general way the wide variety of lighted aids to navigation that are "fixed" as distinguished from "floating," as a buoy. The specific definition of each class is not of importance to a navigator. Such lights may be displayed from massive towers or may be shown from almost any type of inexpensive structure. The essentials of a light structure are: best possible location dependent upon physical conditions of the site, sufficient height for the location, a rugged support for the lantern (and solar panel if used), and a housing for the tanks of compressed gas or electric batteries by which the light is operated. There are many types of structures meeting these essentials—small tank houses surmounted by a short skeleton tower, a cluster of piles, or even a single pile supporting a battery box and the light, as well as countless other forms.

Lighthouses and major light structures are painted to make them readily distinguishable from the background against which they are seen, to distinguish one structure from others in the same vicinity, and for positive identification by a navigator making an uncertain landfall. Solid colors, and various patterns are used for these purposes; see figure 418. Minor lights, such as river or harbor lights that are part of a lateral system, will normally have a numbered daymark of the appropriate shape and color.

Many primary and secondary lights that formerly were manned by resident keepers are now *automated;* often the proper operation of such lights is remotely monitored so that any failure is immediately known at a central control point. The automation program has progressed to the point where in U.S. waters there are now less than 50 manned lights as compared with more than 12,000 unmanned major and minor lights.

Lightships

419 Lightships serve the same purpose as lighthouses, being equipped with lights, fog signals, and

Figure 418. A primary seacoast light (Cape Hatteras Light).

radiobeacons. Ships are used only when it is impracticable or impossible to construct a lighthouse at the desired location. Lightships mark the entrances to important harbors or estuaries, dangerous shoals lying in much-frequented waters, and they serve as points of departure for both transoceanic and coastwise traffic.

Relief vessels may be placed at any lightship station, and when practicable, will exhibit lights and sound signals having the characteristics of the station. They may differ in outward appearance from the regular station ship in certain minor details. Relief lightships are painted the same color as the regular station ships, with the word "RELIEF" in white letters on the sides.

The masthead lights, fog signals, and radiobeacon signals of lightships all have distinguishing characteristics, so that each lightship may be differentiated from others and also from nearby lighthouses. As with lighthouses, details regarding these signals are shown briefly on charts and more completely in the *Light Lists* and *Lists of Lights*.

A lightship under way or off station will fly the International Code signal flags "LO," signifying that the lightship is not at anchor on her station. It will not show or sound any of the signals of a lightship, but will display the lights prescribed by the International or Inland Rules for a vessel of her class. While on station a lightship shows only the ATON light and a less brilliant light on the forestay. As lightships ride to a single anchor, the light on the forestay indicates the direction from which the combined wind and current effect is coming and the direction in which the ship is heading. By day, whenever it appears that an approaching vessel does not recognize the lightship or requests identification, the lightship will display the call letters of the station in flags of the International Code.

Lightships are anchored to a very long scope of chain, and thus the radius of the swing circle is considerable. The charted position is the approximate location of the anchor. A navigator must set his course to pass lightships with sufficient clearance to avoid any possibility of collision. Experience has shown that lightships cannot be safely used as "leading marks" to be passed close aboard; they must always be left broad off the course whenever sea room permits. Many lightships have a station buoy that must also be avoided.

All U.S. lightships have been replaced with aids more economical in terms of manpower and operating funds.

Light Towers

420 A number of the aids replacing lightships are *offshore light towers*, one of which, the Ambrose Offshore Light Station, is shown in figure 420. This is a red tower on a white square superstructure supported by four steel piles. Quarters for the crew are located just below the helicopter landing platform. Ambrose Light is located at the approach to New York Harbor approximately seven miles east of Sandy Hook, New Jersey, in 75 feet of water. The main light, 136 feet (41.4 m) above the water, operates at a high intensity of 6,000,000 candlepower and at a low intensity of 600,000 candlepower, with a nominal range of 26 miles. A fog horn signal with an audible range of 4 miles and a radiobeacon with a range of 125 miles are mounted on the tower. Facilities for an oceanographic laboratory are also located on the tower.

Some offshore light stations have resident crews; others are automated and unmanned.

Large Navigational Buoys

421 The light towers were developed as a more economical means than a lightship for maintaining a light in an offshore location. Now, however, the trend is toward the use of *large navigational buoys*, also called "LNBs" or "Lanbys," figure 421. These provide a platform for a light, a fog signal, and a radiobeacon, plus sensors for sea and weather conditions that can be telemetered ashore over a radio

Figure 420. An offshore primary light tower (Ambrose Light).

link. Such buoys can be put on station at only a small fraction of the cost of a light tower and require no on-board operating crews. They may have a smaller station buoy.

Light Sectors

422 *Sectors* of colored glass are placed in the lanterns of certain lights to mark shoals or to warn mariners away from nearby land. Lights so equipped show one color from most directions and a different color or colors over definite arcs of the horizon indicated in the *Light Lists* and upon the charts. A sector changes the color of a light, when viewed from certain directions, but *not* the rhythm. For example, a flashing white light having a red sector, when viewed from within the sector, will appear as flashing red. (But remember, the red flashes may not be visible from such distances as the white flashes can be seen.)

Sectors may be but a few degrees in width, marking an isolated rock or shoal, or of such width as to extend from deep water to the shore. Bearings referring to sectors are expressed in degrees as observed *from a vessel toward the light*. Charts normally show sector limits by a line of short dashes and include an arc labeled with the color of the light in that sector.

For example, the *List of Lights* describes a certain light as having a red sector from 045° to 120°. Both are true bearings as observed toward the light.

Figure 421. A large navigational buoy (LNB) (Delaware Lighted Horn Buoy "D").

Figure 422 is a sketch of this light, indicating the limits through which it would appear red to an observer on a vessel.

In the majority of cases, water areas covered by red sectors should be avoided, the exact extent of the danger being determined from an examination of the chart. In some cases, instead of using red sectors to indicate danger, a narrow sector of white may mark the best water across a shoal.

In some atmospheric conditions, a white light may have a reddish hue; the mariner should therefore not trust solely to color where there are sectors, but should verify his position by taking a bearing of the light. On either side of the line of separation between white and a colored sector there is always a small sector (about 2°) of uncertain color, as the edges of a sector cannot be cut off sharply.

When a light is cut off by adjoining land or structures, the *obscured sector* is shown on the chart and described in the *Light List*. The bearings on which the light is cut off are stated as for colored sectors, from a vessel toward the light. The exact bearings of cut-off may vary with the distance of the observer and his height of eye.

Identification of Lights

423 In order to obtain full benefit from lights, the navigator must not only understand their use and be able to interpret all data concerning them given in the *Light Lists* and on charts, but he must also be able to identify each light correctly.

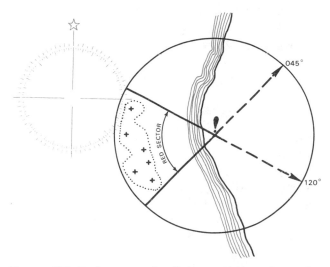

Figure 422. Red sector of a light marking a hazardous area (reef).

One of the most frequent causes of groundings is the failure to identify lights correctly. When making a landfall, the navigator should consult the charts and *Light Lists* to learn the exact characteristics of the light or lights that he expects to see first. When a light is observed, its color is noted, and by means of a watch or clock with a second hand, a note is made of the time required for the light to go through its full cycle of changes. If color, period, and number of flashes per period agree with the information in the *Light List*, correct identification has been made. The *Light List* should also be examined to ascertain if any other light in the general locality might be seen and mistaken for the desired light. If there is any doubt, a careful timing of the length of all flashes and dark intervals, and comparison with the *Light List* is usually conclusive.

To help locate specific aids in the *Light List*, different styles of lettering are used for lighted buoys (italics) and the various categories of other lights (normal roman type, bold, all uppercase, and combinations thereof).

In approaching a light with a complex characteristic of different colors and intensities, allowance must be made for the lesser range of the portion with inferior brightness. For example, a *fixed-and-flashing* light will have flashes much brighter than the fixed light. When initially seen from a distance, it is most likely that only the flashes will be bright enough to be seen, and the full characteristic will not develop until the observer has come within range of the fixed light. Another example might be a light with a characteristic of alternating flashing, white and red. The red flashes will be less bright, and such a light when first seen from a distance will probably be considered to have a simple flashing white characteristic; the intervening red flashes will be seen only after the observer comes closer. At short distances and in clear weather, some flashing lights may show a continuous faint light; this is because the light does indeed burn continuously, with the "flashes" being created by a revolving lens.

It is important to note that in *Light Lists* all bearings are stated in degrees true, reading clockwise from 000° at north; bearings relating to visibility of lights are given as observed *from a vessel*; distances are in nautical miles unless otherwise stated; heights are referred to mean high water; depths are referred to the plane of reference on charts. The great majority of lights have no resident crew tending them; such lights are called "unwatched" or "unmanned." Unwatched lights have a high degree of reliability but they may become irregular or extinguished. Latitudes and longitudes in the *Light Lists* are approximate, and are intended only to facilitate reference to a chart.

Visibility of Lights

424 In order for a lighted navigational aid such as a lighthouse to be seen at a distance, it must have sufficient elevation above sea level, and sufficient intensity or power. A navigator frequently wants to know at what specific distance he can expect to sight a given light. The first step is always to refer to the appropriate *Light List* or *List of Lights* for the necessary data.

The following terms and their definitions as used in current editions of the *Light Lists* are employed in connection with the range of visibility of a light.

Horizon distance (or distance of visibility) is the distance, expressed in nautical miles, from a position above the surface of the earth along the line of sight to the horizon. It is the approximate range of visibility of an object of known height to an observer whose eye is at sea level. Horizon distances for various heights are given in Table 8 of *Bowditch*, an extract from which appears as figure 424. A similar table can be found in the introductory pages of each volume of the *Light Lists*. These tables are calculated for standard conditions of weather and refraction.

The distance to the horizon, D, in nautical miles, may be calculated by the formula $D = 1.17\sqrt{h}$, where h is the height of eye in feet. For height of eye in meters, the constant is 2.12, and D is still in nautical miles (factors are 1.35 and 2.44 for distance in statute miles).

Nominal range is the maximum distance at which a light may be seen in clear weather (meteorological visibility of 10 nautical miles—see International Visibility Code, figure 425a) expressed in nautical miles. Nominal range is listed for all Coast Guard lighted aids except for range and directional lights.

Luminous range is the maximum distance at which a light may be seen under the existing visibility conditions. By use of the diagram in figure 425b, luminous range may be determined from the known nominal range and the existing visibility conditions. Nominal and luminous ranges take no account of elevation, observer's height of eye, or the curvature of the earth.

Geographic range is the maximum distance at which a light may be seen under conditions of perfect visibility, limited only by the curvature of the

Height Feet	Nautical Miles	Height Feet	Nautical Miles	Height Feet	Nautical Miles
1	1.2	33	6.7	125	13.1
2	1.7	34	6.8	130	13.3
3	2.0	35	6.9	135	13.6
4	2.3	36	7.0	140	13.8
5	2.6	37	7.1	145	14.1
6	2.9	38	7.2	150	14.3
7	3.1	39	7.3	160	14.8
8	3.3	40	7.4	170	15.3
9	3.5	41	7.5	180	15.7
10	3.7	42	7.6	190	16.1
11	3.9	43	7.7	200	16.5
12	4.1	44	7.8	210	17.0
13	4.2	45	7.8	220	17.4
14	4.4	46	7.9	230	17.7
15	4.5	47	8.0	240	18.1
16	4.7	48	8.1	250	18.5
17	4.8	49	8.2	260	18.9
18	5.0	50	8.3	270	19.2
19	5.1	55	8.7	280	19.6
20	5.2	60	9.1	290	19.9
21	5.4	65	9.4	300	20.3
22	5.5	70	9.8	310	20.6
23	5.6	75	10.1	320	20.9
24	5.7	80	10.5	330	21.3
25	5.9	85	10.8	340	21.6
26	6.0	90	11.1	350	21.9
27	6.1	95	11.4	360	22.2
28	6.2	100	11.7	370	22.5
29	6.3	105	12.0	380	22.8
30	6.4	110	12.3	390	23.1
31	6.5	115	12.5	400	23.4
32	6.6	120	12.8	450	24.8

Figure 424. Table of distance to the horizon for various heights of eye.

earth. It is expressed in nautical miles for a height of observer's eye at sea level.

Computed range is the geographic range plus the observer's distance to the horizon based on his height of eye.

Computed visibility is the visibility determined for a particular light, taking into consideration its height and nominal range and the height of eye of the observer. In computing the visibility of a light, it is assumed that the computed visibility will never exceed the light's nominal range; however, under certain atmospheric conditions a light may occasionally be visible far beyond its nominal range.

Determining Visibility

425 The following examples illustrate the recommended form for determining the visibility of a light. *The computed visibility is the lesser of the computed range or the luminous range.*

Example 1: Determine the visibility of Mount Desert Light (L.L. No. 1) for an observer with a height of eye of 70 feet.

Solution: From the *Light List* (figure 403) determine the nominal range (column 4), 24 miles; and the height above water (column 5), 75 feet, of the light. Determine horizon distance from figure 424 and place in the form shown below.

Geographic Range for 75 feet	10.1 miles
Horizon Distance for 70 feet	9.8 miles
Computed range	19.9 miles
Nominal range	24 miles

Answer: 19.9 miles

Example 2: Determine the visibility of Seguin Light (L.L. No. 5) for an observer with a height of eye of 11 meters.

Solution: From the *Light List* determine the nominal range (column 4), 18 miles, and the height of the light above water, 180 feet. Determine geographic range for the light from figure 419, 15.7 miles. Determine horizon distance for height of eye using the equation, 7.0 miles.

Geographic range for 180 feet	15.7 miles
Horizon distance for 11 meters	7.0 miles
Computed visibility	22.7 miles
Nominal range	18 miles

Answer: 18 miles (assuming standard "clear visibility")

Variations Due to Refraction

As stated earlier, the distance at which a light may be sighted may, as a result of abnormal atmospheric refraction, be far greater than its nominal range. Conversely, the nominal range may be greatly lessened by fog, haze, rain, snow, or smoke. In clear weather, the loom of a powerful light may appear before the light itself comes into sight.

Variations Due to Weather Conditions

The nominal ranges, tabulated in column 4 of the *Light Lists* for major lights, are predicted on the existence of "clear" weather, with a meteorological visibility of 10 nautical miles; this falls in code No. 7 of the International Visibility Code, reproduced in figure 425a. It may be noted that under "very clear" and "exceptionally clear" conditions, visibility is greatly increased, and the luminous range of a given light may be increased by several miles. Conversely, in the lower ranges, visibility tends to fall off very rapidly. By means of the diagram in each *Light List*, figure 425b, the luminous range of a light may be approximated for existing conditions of visibility. The diagram is entered vertically from either top or bottom using the nominal range in column 4, figure 403. The selected vertical line is followed until the appropriate curve for the existing visibility is reached (intermediate values are interpolated by eye, taking note that the scale is logarithmic). Horizontally opposite this point on the scale at the left, the approximate luminous range for the existing meteorological conditions may be read off. For example, using the diagram, the luminous range of Monhegan Island Light (L.L. No. 3) may be determined for different conditions of visibility. The nominal range, from figure 403, is 21 nautical miles. When the meteorological visibility is 20 miles, the light could be sighted at a distance of about 35 miles, but this would require a height of eye of roughly 300 feet. When the meteorological visibility is only 2 miles, it would be sighted at 6½ miles.

The diagram can also be used to obtain an approximate value for meteorological visibility. For example, Monhegan Island Light with a nominal range of 21 miles is sighted at 10 miles; the meteor-

METEOROLOGICAL OPTICAL RANGE					
Code	Weather	Yards	Code	Weather	Nautical Miles
0	Dense fog	Less than 50	5	Haze	1 to 2
1	Thick fog	50 to 200	6	Light haze	2 to 5½
2	Moderate fog	200 to 500	7	Clear	5½ to 11
			8	Very clear	11.0 to 27.0
3	Light fog	500 to 1000	9	Exceptionally clear	Over 27.0
4	Thin fog	½ to 1			

Figure 425a. International Visibility Code.

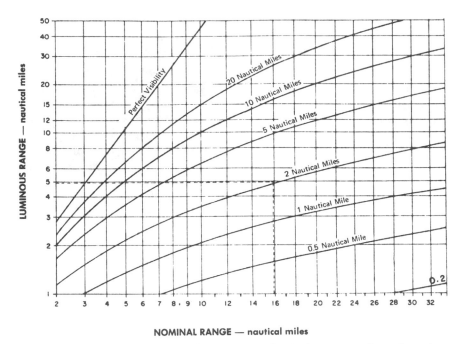

Figure 425b. Luminous Range Diagram; its method of use is explained in the text.

ological visibility is about 4 miles, or International Code 6, light haze.

Predicting Time and Bearing for Sighting a Light

426 When the visibility of a light for the appropriate height of eye has been determined, an arc representing this visibility can be drawn on the chart; this arc is centered at the charted position of the light, and its radius is the computed visibility. It is labeled with the name of the light above the arc, and the visibility below it. The point at which this circle intersects the dead reckoning plot indicates the position at which the light should become visible. The time of arrival at this point is determined by dead reckoning; the bearing on which the light should be sighted is its direction from this point. Such a plot is illustrated in figure 426. The true bearing obtained from the chart is frequently converted to a relative bearing to assist lookouts in locating the light. If the dead reckoning plot crosses the computed visibility arc at an acute angle, the predicted time and bearing may be considerably in error, as a small set to the right or left will make a considerable difference in the location of the point of intersection.

Bobbing a Light

When a light is first seen on the horizon, it will disappear if the observer tries to sight it from a point several feet, or one deck, lower, and reappear when he returns to his original position. This is called *bobbing a light*, and can be helpful in estimating its distance. When a light can be bobbed, it is at the limit of its visibility for the observer's height of eye. By determining geographic range for the height of the light, and for the observer's height of eye, and combining these two values, an approximation of the distance may be obtained. This distance, combined with a bearing will give an *estimated position;* distances obtained in this way are not sufficiently accurate to yield a fix.

Fog Signals

427 Any sound-producing instrument operated in time of reduced visibility (caused by fog, snow, haze, smoke, etc.) from a definite point shown on the charts, such as a lighthouse, lightship, or buoy, serves as a useful fog signal. To be effective as an aid to navigation, a mariner must be able to identify it and know from what location it originates. The simpler fog signals are bells, gongs, or whistles

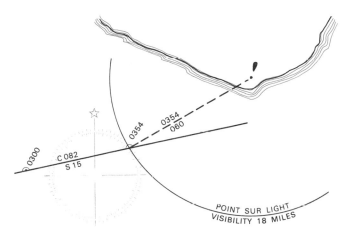

Figure 426. Predicting the time and bearing for sighting a light.

on buoys. As such signals on buoys are operated by the motion of the sea, they will not produce sounds in a calm sea without swells. The only buoy that will signal its location under such conditions is a horn buoy, whose sounds are electronically produced by power from the buoy's batteries.

At primary and secondary lights, and on lightships, fog signals are operated mechanically. There are several types of such fog signals.

Diaphones produce sound by means of a slotted reciprocating piston actuated by compressed air. Blasts may consist of two tones of different pitch, in which case the first part of the blast is high and the last part is low. These alternate-pitch signals are called "two-tone."

Diaphragm horns produce sound by means of a disc diaphragm vibrated by compressed air, steam, or electricity. Duplex or triplex horn units of differing pitch produce a chime signal.

Reed horns produce sound by means of a steel reed vibrated by compressed air.

Sirens produce sound by means of either a disc or a cup-shaped rotor actuated by compressed air, steam, or electricity.

Whistles produce sound by compressed air or steam directed through a circumferential slot into a cylindrical bell chamber.

Bells are sounded by means of a hammer actuated by hand, by a descending weight, compressed gas, or electricity; on buoys, wave action is used.

Identification

As signals on buoys that are operated by the motion of the sea do not produce sounds on a regular time schedule, identification may be difficult or impossible. While it is easy to differentiate a bell

buoy from a whistle buoy, it is often not as simple to distinguish a bell buoy from a gong buoy by their sounds.

Mechanically operated fog signals, however, are placed on a regular cycle of operation, and different types of signals and characteristics can be assigned various locations in the same general area for identification purposes. Fog signals at primary seacoast and secondary lights are usually *horns* with characteristics varying from one to three blasts in cycles of 10 to 60 seconds length; each blast is normally two or three seconds in duration with pauses of similar duration between blasts if there are more than one. Lightships are usually fitted with a *two-tone diaphone*; these, too, are assigned an identifying characteristic in terms of number of blasts and length of a cycle. Occasionally, a diaphone is installed on shore, or a siren or bell is used for some local purpose.

Operation

Fog signals of the U.S. Coast Guard at locations where a continuous watch is maintained are placed in operation when the visibility decreases to 5 miles, or when the fog signal of a passing ship is heard. Fog signals at stations where no continuous watch is maintained may not always be sounded promptly when fog conditions develop or may operate erratically due to mechanical difficulties. At some stations, fog signals are operated continuously for a portion of each year; the operation period is stated in the *Light Lists*.

Caution

The navigator must always bear in mind that sound signals in fog can be very deceptive. At times, they may be completely inaudible even when near at hand. Again, they may be somewhat refracted; that is, they may appear to be coming from a direction other than the actual bearing of the signal source. Constant soundings should be obtained when operating in fog in coastal areas.

The "Old" U.S. Lateral System of Buoyage

428 As noted in article 405, buoyage in U.S. waters prior to the adoption of the IALA-B system was different in a number of features, and these differences will continue to be seen until the completion of the conversion program, scheduled for 1989. Only the differences will be considered here; where a type or use of an ATON is *not* mentioned, the "old" and "new" systems are the same.

Can buoys marking the port side of a channel when entering from seaward are painted *black*.

Similarly, junction buoys, can or nun, have *black-and-red horizontal* bands.

Buoys marking a fairway or mid-channel have *black and white vertical stripes,* and are can or nun shape if unlighted.

Buoys marking anchorage areas are all *white* in color; those marking fishnet areas are *black-and-white horizontally banded.* Buoys used in connection with dredging operations are *white with green tops.* Special-purpose buoys, for applications not otherwise covered, are *white-and-orange horizontally banded.*

Red and black buoys and minor lights along a channel may have a *white* light in lieu of a red or green light where they must be seen from a greater distance.

Preferred-channel buoys and minor lights show an *interrupted quick flashing* light—red, green, or white. This is a group of six quick flashes repeated at intervals of ten seconds.

Lights on special-purpose aids may be of any color other than red or green.

Figure 429. Chart symbols for aids to navigation (typical).

Aids to Navigation Chart Symbols

429   Aids to navigation are shown on charts by a combination of symbols and abbreviations; color is used with many of the symbols. See article 532.

Buoyage Systems of Other Nations

430   The buoyage system used in the waters of other countries *may* or *may not* be similar to that of the United States. Conversion to IALA-A or IALA-B may not have been completed.

A navigator must be familiar with the system of buoyage that he will encounter before he enters the pilot waters of a foreign country. Advance study of the appropriate *List of Lights* or the appropriate volume of *Sailing Directions* is absolutely essential.

Chapter 5   Nautical Charts

Introduction

501 For many centuries mariners have used some form of nautical chart, a graphic representation of shorelines and ports, hazards and safe waters, landmarks, and other features essential for the safe guidance of ships. Yet as old as these are, they were undoubtedly preceded by, and derived from, *sailing directions*, written accounts of harbors, courses, seasonal weather conditions, etc., that were compiled by voyagers on the early trading routes. There are records verifying the use of sailing directions by the Greeks several hundred years before the birth of Christ. They may also have had charts, as it is easier to draw a diagram to show how to get to a place than it is to explain the process in writing; there is, however, no proof that such charts actually existed. Sailing directions—and charts, if any—were not normally published, but were often kept secret for the personal advantage of the captain/navigator who had prepared them.

In the third century B.C., the Greek scientific writer Eratosthenes of Alexandria reasoned that the earth must be a sphere, as at high noon on the day of the summer solstice objects of the same height at two locations on the same meridian did not cause shadows of the same length. He proceeded to make observations at Alexandria and at Syene (now Aswan), which he estimated to be the equivalent of 500 statute miles to the south. At both places he measured the angle from directly overhead to a selected star, and found them to differ by about 7.5°. Since 7.5° is 1/48 of the circumference of a circle, he reasoned that the earth's circumference must be 48 × 500 = 24,000 statute miles. This was

a surprisingly accurate determination, as the actual length of a meridian is 24,818 statute miles. This seems to be the first recorded measurement of latitude using the degree as a unit of measurement.

In the second century A.D., the great astronomer and mathematician Ptolemy constructed many maps, among them a famous chart of the then-known world that listed several thousand places by latitude and longitude. Unfortunately, he did not use Eratosthenes' calculations but rather those of a Greek philosopher, who had estimated the earth's circumference as the equivalent of 18,000 statute miles. Ptolemy's work remained a standard through the Middle Ages and led Columbus to believe that he had reached the East Indies in 1492 when he had not gone nearly far enough.

The earliest charts of the Middle Ages still in existence are the Portolan charts prepared in Spain in the fourteenth century. They are remarkably accurate in their portrayal of the Mediterranean. In 1515, Leonardo da Vinci drew his famous map of the world, which shows America extending farther east and west than north and south.

Gerardus Mercator, the Flemish cartographer who produced a world chart constructed on the basis of the projection that bears his name, is the father of modern cartography. The accuracy of charts continued to improve, but as they had to be printed by hand, they were extremely expensive. The mariner considered them much too valuable to be used for plotting; this led to wide use of the *sailings* (various forms of calculated dead reckoning). These mathematical methods of determining DR position remained in wide use aboard ship through much of the nineteenth century. (See chapter 30.)

Charts

A *nautical chart* is a representation on a two-dimensional surface of a portion of the earth's surface, but one that has been specially designed for convenient use in navigation and therefore has to do primarily with areas of navigable water. A modern chart is intended to be worked upon, not merely to be looked at, and should readily permit the graphic solution of navigational problems, such as distance and direction, or the determination of position in terms of latitude and longitude. It features such information as coastlines and harbors, depths of water, channels and obstructions, and landmarks and aids to navigation. Charts provide a means of describing a position in terms of latitude and longitude.

For use at sea there are also a number of "special-purpose" charts, such as pilot charts that provide weather and other information, tidal current charts, star charts, etc. In the remainder of this chapter, primary consideration will be given to nautical charts, to the projections upon which they are constructed, and to a navigator's use of them.

A *map* is a representation, at reduced scale, on a flat surface, of a portion of the earth's surface. It shows physical features; cities, towns, and roads; political boundaries; and other geographic information. A map is not so often written upon as is a chart.

U.S. Chart Agencies

The governmental agency for charting the coastal waters of the United States and its possessions is the *National Ocean Service (NOS)*, a unit of the National Oceanic and Atmospheric Administration (NOAA) within the Department of Commerce. NOS conducts hydrographic, topographic, and geodetic surveys from which charts are produced for coastal waters, most rivers, and the Great Lakes. The Army Corps of Engineers prepares navigational charts and maps for the Mississippi River and its tributaries and some larger inland lakes.

Nautical charts (and related publications) for much of the rest of the world are the responsibility of the *Hydrographic/Topographic Center* of the *Defense Mapping Agency*. This activity produces charts from its own field work, using U.S. Navy survey ships or by reproducing charts of other nations. Both NOS and DMAHTC conduct continuing surveys, and their highly accurate charts are generally available to the mariners of all nations (some DMAHTC charts are restricted to official govern-

mental use only.) Specialized charts for aviation interests and for other purposes are published by various other government agencies.

CHART PROJECTIONS

The Round Earth on Flat Paper

502 Simple experimentation will show you that no significant portion of a hollow rubber ball can be spread out flat without some stretching or tearing. Conversely, a sheet of tissue paper cannot be wrapped smoothly around a sphere; there will be numerous wrinkles and overlaps.

The earth also being round (a "spheroid"), it cannot be represented on a flat piece of paper without some distortion. The smaller the portion of the globe to be mapped, the less the distortion that will be present—conversely, the greater the area, the greater the distortion.

Because the surface of a sphere cannot be represented accurately upon a plane surface, it is called "undevelopable." There are other surfaces, however, that *are* developable, and can be spread out flat without change in any design or pattern drawn upon them. Two such surfaces are those of a cone and a cylinder. A paper cone or cylinder can be cut from top to bottom and rolled out flat without distortion of any kind, as indicated in figure 502. It is also true that a *limited portion* of the earth's surface

Figure 502. Development of a cylinder and a cone.

can be shown ("projected") directly upon a plane surface while keeping distortion within acceptable limits.

Reference Lines

It is customary to think of the reference lines of the nondevelopable sphere as first projected upon some developable surface (a plane, cone, or cylinder) and then developed or spread out flat. A chart projection may be loosely defined as any orderly arrangement on paper of the meridians and parallels of the sphere. There are several hundred projections, each with some particular property that may make it desirable for some specific purpose. Of these, not more than about half a dozen have ever been much used for navigation.

Properties and Projections

503 For navigation, certain properties are desirable in a projection. Among them are:
1. *True shape* of physical features such as bodies of land or water;
2. *True scale and size* of various areas of land or water;
3. *Correct angular relationships;*
4. *Great circles as straight lines;*
5. *Rhumb lines as straight lines.*

A chart of a very small area may closely achieve most or all of these characteristics with any method of projection. As the area grows larger, however, only one or two of the characteristics can be achieved; for example, in a large-area chart either great circles or rhumb lines can be straight lines, but not both. The projection method used for any particular application must weigh and balance the various characteristics against each other. *All* of them can be obtained *only* on a *spherical* surface.

All of the projections commonly used for navigational charts (with one exception) are *conformal*. This is generally interpreted to mean depiction of both *true shape* and *correct angular* relationships, but this is true only in a quite limited sense.

Conformality does provide true shape for small areas. For example, the Mercator projection (see article 505) is conformal. Along the rugged coast of Alaska it preserves the shape of a single inlet accurately enough, but for Alaska as a whole this projection stretches out the northerly portion much more than the southerly portion, and the overall shape is not true at all.

Conformality is also said to yield correct angular relationships. It might therefore be expected that on a Lambert conformal map (see article 510) of the United States, one might draw a straight line from Miami to Seattle, and that the line so drawn would make the correct angle with each of the meridians between, but this is not the case (see figure 510a). With only minor exceptions, no straight line "from A to B" can be said to represent *exactly* correct angular relationships, even on a conformal map or chart.

Projection Classifications

504 It is perhaps most practical to classify chart projections in accordance with the developable surface from which they are considered to be derived—plane, cylindrical, or conical projections.

The *plane* projections best known to navigators are the various forms of *gnomonic;* the *stereographic* projection is infrequently used.

The most-used cylindrical projection is the *Mercator;* it has several variations.

Conic projections include those with a tangent cone, those with a cone cutting the earth's surface at two parallels of latitude, and those with multiple cones tangent at several parallels. The two best known are the *polyconic* and *Lambert conformal* projection.

Plane Projections

Classification by developable surfaces can be further broken down in some cases according to the *point* from which the reference lines are projected onto the developable surface.

For plane projections, figure 504a shows the method of projection for the *gnomonic, stereographic,* and *orthographic.*

For the *gnomonic* projection the points D and D' on the sphere in figure 504a are projected from A, the center of the sphere, upon a plane tangent at the equator. Because of the point of projection, this is classed as a *central perspective* (or geometrical) projection. Since the plane is tangent at the equator, it is also known as the *equatorial* gnomonic. For a chart of the north polar regions, the plane could have been made tangent at the pole, and the resulting projection from A would have been a *polar* gnomonic. The plane could also have been made tangent at any point between the equator and either pole, in which case the projection obtained from the same central point A would have been an *oblique* gnomonic.

Figure 504a also shows the method of projection for the *stereographic.* Instead of being projected from the center of the sphere, points are projected upon the tangent plane from the opposite end of the diameter from the point of tangency (from B in the

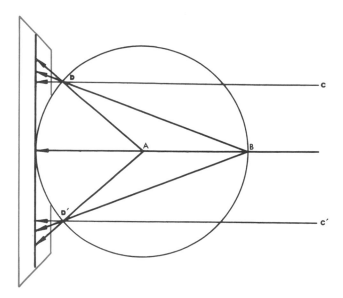

Figure 504a. Gnomonic projection from center of sphere A; stereographic projection from B; orthographic projection from C and C′ (parallel rays).

figure). As described in the preceding paragraph, the case shown in the figure yields an equatorial stereographic. A *polar* stereographic or an *oblique* stereographic is as readily obtained. In each case, the point of projection is always the opposite end of the diameter from the point of tangency.

The third type of projection onto a tangent plane illustrated by figure 504a is the *orthographic*. Here the projection "rays" are from infinity, shown as C and C′, and thus are all parallel. The plane of the projection is usually tangent at the equator to depict half of the earth, such as the Western Hemisphere, although without conformality or equal area representation.

Cylindrical Projections

A central perspective projection can readily be obtained by projecting the reference lines of the sphere upon a cylinder tangent to the sphere along the equator. The resulting projection is shown in figure 504b (at left), with the meridians represented by a series of equally spaced vertical lines, the parallels by a series of lines at right angles to the meridians; spacing between the parallels expands rapidly with increasing distance from the equator. This expansion is, in fact, so great that the *central perspective cylindrical* projection is never used.

A *Mercator projection* is often visualized as the placement of a cylinder around the earth touching it at a great circle; see figure 504b. For this reason, it is generally classified as a cylindrical projection. Strictly speaking, however, the modern Mercator chart is derived from complex mathematical equations in order that a straight line between any two points will represent a rhumb line; this is a property that the central perspective projection does not have. The Mercator is conformal, and its distortion in high latitudes is less than that which would occur with a central perspective chart.

Accepting the general classification of the Mercator as a cylindrical projection, the "cylinder" may be thought of as tangent along the equator (its most common form), and become the *equatorial* case. The cylinder may also be turned through 90° and become tangent along a selected meridian, and thus tangent also at both poles. According to previous terminology, this should be known as the polar case, but is actually called the *transverse Mercator*— or, sometimes, the *inverse Mercator*.

The cylinder may also be made tangent to some selected great circle, in any direction, anywhere on the surface of the sphere, as along a great-circle route. This is generally known as the *oblique Mercator*, since the cylinder in this case is neither vertical nor horizontal with reference to the earth's axis; only a small area on either side of the line of tangency is used.

Conic Projections

A conic projection using a single tangent cone is termed a *simple conic* projection. The height of the cone increases with decreasing latitude of the parallel of tangency *(standard parallel)*; at the equator, the cone has become infinitely high, in effect a cylinder. Such a projection is not conformal.

The *polyconic* projection uses a series of tangent cones; see figure 504c. At the edges of the chart the overlap between the standard parallels is expanded to eliminate gaps. In this way improved conformity is achieved. Parallels appear as nonconcentric circles, and meridians as curved lines converging toward the pole and slightly concave to the central meridian. The scale—the ratio of the distance between any two points to the actual distance between those points on the earth—is correct along any parallel and along the central meridian.

A single cone with two standard parallels—the Lambert conformal projection—is discussed in article 510.

For conic projections, the axis of the cone usually coincides with the axis of the earth, but it also may be turned to any other position, resulting in a transverse or oblique conic.

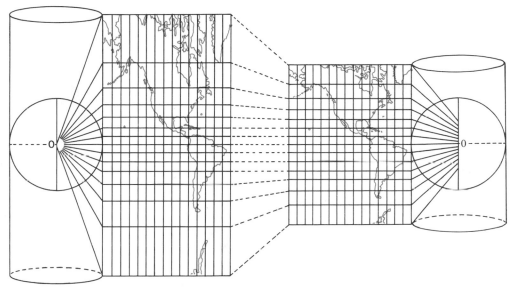

Figure 504b. Central projection upon a cylinder (left) compared with Mercator conformal projection (right).

Azimuthal Projections

Other classifications are common. For example, most polar projections are *azimuthal* (or zenithal). By this it is meant that all directions (azimuths) from the center of the projection are true. The polar stereographic projection is azimuthal as well as conformal. All gnomonic projections are azimuthal, affording true directions from the point of tangency, regardless of the position of the point on the sphere.

In any family of projections, it is possible to obtain different properties simply by varying the spacing of the parallels. The *polar stereographic* projection is conformal, and scale along the meridians varies. The *polar equidistant* yields true scale along each meridian. A *polar equal area* projection is also obtainable by another variation in the spacing of the parallels. All three are azimuthal.

In the same way, a cylindrical projection may be conformal (the ordinary Mercator) or equal area, by varying the spacing of the parallels. Conic projections, too, may be either conformal (as the Lambert conformal) or equal area (as the Albers).

The Mercator Projection

505 Most of the charts used for marine navigation, and many of those used for air navigation, are based on the Mercator projection. For this reason, it is essential that a navigator have a thorough understanding of such charts.

For conventional methods of navigation—largely based on dead reckoning, or the determination of position by course and distance from some charted point—the Mercator projection has its advantages. On its rectangular graticule, latitude and longitude are conveniently plotted; the *rhumb line* (see article 207) between any two points is the straight line between them; and the direction of a rhumb line may be measured at any convenient meridian.

Figure 504c. Polyconic projection.

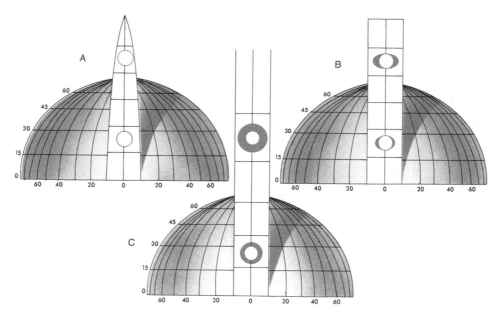

Figure 505. Relationship between areas on a globe and their representation on a Mercator projection.

Distances along a course line can be determined without great difficulty. Great-circle distances and directions are not readily determinable without first plotting the great circle on a gnomonic chart (article 509) and transferring points along the line to the Mercator.

When compared with a globe, a Mercator projection shows great exaggeration of shape and area in high latitudes. The example most often cited is that of Greenland, which when shown complete on the Mercator, appears to be larger than South America, although it actually is only one-ninth as large as that continent.

Figure 505 will aid in understanding this weakness of the projection. In the figure, at A, one "gore" or section of an ordinary globe has been peeled off and stands vertically. Two true circles of the same size have been drawn on the gore, to serve as "test patterns."

At B the sides of the gore have been stretched horizontally so that the two outer meridians are parallel to the central meridian of the gore. In the stretching the two circles have become ellipses (represented by the shaded areas), the northerly one having been stretched much more than the southern one.

Since the Mercator projection is to be conformal, true shapes of small areas must be preserved, so the horizontally stretched gore must now be stretched vertically until the ellipses again become (approximately) circles, the diameter in each case approxi-

mately the major axis of the ellipse. The result is shown in figure 505.

Distortion

Note that, since the upper part of the gore has been stretched more than the lower part, the upper circle has become appreciably greater in diameter than the lower one. Also, the upper edge of the gore at C is shown ragged and broken. It can no longer be extended all the way to the pole, for the pole has been stretched northward all the way to infinity. Consequently, most Mercator projections extend no farther from the equator than about 70°, rarely beyond 80°.

Part of the definition of *conformality* is that the scale at any point must be the same in all directions. This means that when a given parallel of latitude has been expanded from its length as shown at A to the length indicated in B, the scale of the meridian at that latitude must be expanded proportionately. It can be shown mathematically that the expansion at any place on the Mercator approximates the secant of the latitude of that place. Figure 504b (right) shows the graticule of a Mercator projection for the Western Hemisphere.

Many navigation charts cover a much smaller area, on which the distance scale is almost constant and there is little variation between the rhumb line and great circle. It is on the small-scale charts of large areas (see article 523) that distinctive features become evident.

Position on a Mercator Chart

506 A position of known latitude and longitude can be quickly plotted on a Mercator projection, using a plotter or straightedge and a pair of dividers. For example, a navigator's position at 1635 (Lat. 41°09'N, Long. 70°44'W) may be plotted as follows: first find the given latitude, 41°09'N, on the latitude scale. Place a straightedge through this point parallel to any convenient parallel of latitude, aligning it in an east-west direction. Then set one point of the dividers at 71°00'W on the longitude scale and the other at 70°44'W, a spread of 16.0 minutes of longitude. Without changing the setting of the dividers, lay off this distance along the straightedge from the 71st meridian eastward, in the direction of the position. Circle this point and label with the appropriate time (1635).

The reverse problem—determining the latitude and longitude of a position that has been plotted on the chart—is also easily accomplished; see figure 506. Place one point of a pair of dividers on the 1635 position and swing the other point in an arc, while adjusting its radius, until it becomes tangent to a parallel of latitude. The spread of the dividers then equals the difference of latitude from this reference parallel. Transfer the dividers to the latitude scale, and placing one point at the reference parallel, read the latitude of the position at the other point. A similar procedure, measuring from the position to a meridian of longitude, will provide the longitude of the point. Be careful in each case to lay off the difference of latitude and longitude in the proper direction from the reference parallel or meridian. With practice, this can easily be done with one hand while aligning the straightedge or recording with the other.

Direction on a Mercator Chart

507 As pointed out in article 209, two kinds of direction are important to a navigator; *great-circle* directions and *rhumb-line* directions.

On a sphere, a great circle is the most direct (shortest) route, and may be thought of as a straight line, while the rhumb line is a longer curved line, always between the great circle and the equator; see figure 507a. The purpose of the Mercator projection is to introduce exactly the right amount of distortion to show every rhumb line as a straight line; see figure 507b. When this has been done, in order to keep all parts of the chart in their correct *relative* positions, the great circle has been distorted into a curved line, always far-

Figure 506. Locating a position on a Mercator chart.

Figure 507a. On a Mercator chart, a great-circle course plots as a curve with its vertex on the side of the equivalent rhumb line *away* from the equator.

Figure 507b. Measuring direction on a Mercator chart.

ther from the equator than the rhumb line, and always concave toward the equator; see figure 507a. If a mental picture of this relationship is kept in mind, it will help in the solution of navigational problems.

Measurement of the rhumb-line direction (figure 507b) can be made at any convenient meridian, with any available protractor; or the direction of the rhumb line can be transferred to a nearby compass rose by means of parallel rulers or a drafting machine (see articles 720–723), and read from the compass rose (see article 529). In any case, care must be taken to read the direction at the circumference of the compass rose *toward* the destination, not in the opposite direction, a difference of 180°.

Distance on a Mercator Chart

508   For practical purposes, 1° of latitude everywhere on the earth's surface may be considered to be 60 nautical miles in length; the length of 1° of longitude varies with the latitude, from 60 miles at the equator to zero at the poles (figure 205c). Since 1 *minute* of latitude, then, is everywhere equal to 1 *mile*, it is the *latitude scale* that must be used for measuring distance—*never the longitude scale.*

Measure at Mid-latitude of the Path

Because the latitude scale of a Mercator chart expands increasingly with distance from the equator, the scale of miles is increasing accordingly. That is, in the northerly part of a Mercator chart in the Northern Hemisphere, the length of each mile on the chart has been stretched, and there are fewer miles in an inch than in the southerly part. That part of the latitude scale should be used which is at the mean latitude of the distance to be measured (figure 508a). Except for small-scale charts, this may usually be done with sufficient accuracy by placing one point of a pair of dividers (see article 718) at A, the other point at B, then placing the dividers on the latitude scale with the middle of the dividers at about the mid-latitude. The difference of latitude in minutes on the latitude scale, is the distance in nautical miles.

Measuring Longer Distances

When the distance is great enough that the dividers cannot reach all the way from A to B in one step, one point of the dividers might be placed at A, the other point at a position about halfway between A and B. The length of this portion of the route could then be measured from the latitude scale with the dividers centered at about the mid-latitude of that part. Similarly, the length of the

Figure 508a. Measuring distance on a Mercator chart.

remainder could be read with the dividers centered at about the mid-latitude of the other part. The two distances then would be added to obtain the total distance.

When the distance is too great for one or two settings of the dividers, some convenient unit (10 miles, in figure 508a) can be taken from the latitude scale at the mid-latitude and stepped off along the route, as shown. In the figure, it was stepped off five times: 5 × 10 = 50 miles, with a little left over. The small amount left over is then set on the dividers and laid off along the latitude scale, where it is found to measure 2 miles: 50 + 2 = 52 miles, the total distance from A to B.

Using Graphic Scales

Large-scale charts, which cover a limited area, with little change of scale, often carry a simple graphic "bar scale" for measuring distance. This may be simply a line, or a double line, divided into miles, or some other appropriate unit such as yards or kilometers; fractions of one major unit are marked to the *left* of the zero point. Frequently, such a chart will carry two or three such graphic scales, each with different units; see figure 508b.

To use a bar scale, set the dividers to cover the space between the two locations on the chart. Then move the dividers to the bar scale, placing the right-hand point on a mark for a whole unit so that the left-hand point is to the left of the 0 mark on the subdivided unit. For example: assume that the distance to be measured is between 2 and 3 miles; one point of the dividers is set on the bar scale graduation for 2 miles, and the other falls on the mark for 0.4 miles to the *left* of the 0 mark. The total distance is thus determined to be 2.4 miles.

For smaller scale charts covering a wide band of latitude, a "scale diagram" (figure 508c) is sometimes used. This is, in effect, simply a series of bar scales, in parallel lines, with zero of each scale in

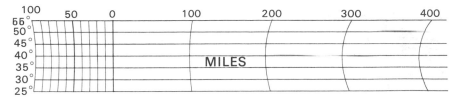

Figure 508b. Various chart graphic (bar) scales.

Figure 508c. Scale diagram for a Lambert conformal chart of the United States; scale 1:5,000,000.

Figure 508d. Great circle and rhumb line on a Mercator chart.

the same vertical line. Smooth curves are then drawn through the corresponding graduations of each scale.

Each scale in the diagram is correct for the latitude indicated, and distances should be measured with the scale for the average latitude of the distance required. Obviously, the correct scale for any latitude intermediate between two adjacent lines is also available. For example, if the average latitude between A and B is determined to be about 27°30′ the dividers can be set on the diagram about halfway between the scales for 25° and 30°.

Rhumb Line–Great Circle Comparison

Figure 508d is a portion of a Mercator chart showing both the great-circle route and the rhumb line between Norfolk, Virginia (Chesapeake Bay Entrance), and Brest, France. As always on a Mer-

cator chart, the great-circle route *appears* to be appreciably longer; but, when measured as shown in figure 508a, the apparently longer line is found to cover fewer miles.

Special Mercator Projections

Transverse and *oblique* Mercator projections are described in article 511.

Gnomonic Projection

509   The gnomonic projection (figure 504a) is a perspective (geometrical) projection in which the reference lines of the sphere are projected from the center of the earth upon a tangent plane. The point of tangency may be on the equator *(equatorial)*; at either pole *(polar)*; or at any other latitude *(oblique gnomonic)*. For the oblique gnomonic, shown in figure 509a, convergency of the meridians increases

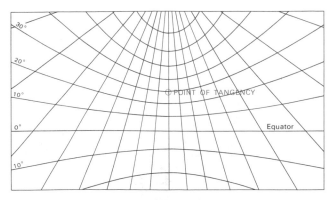

Figure 509a. Gnomonic great-circle chart.

Figure 509b. Rhumb line and great circle on a gnomonic chart.

with the latitude of the point of tangency, from 0° in the equatorial case to 1° for each degree of longitude in the polar case.

Great Circle as a Straight Line

The Mercator projection was developed for the purpose of showing every rhumb line as a straight line. The gnomonic projection has been adapted to a number of special uses, but in navigation it is chiefly used because it shows every *great circle* as a straight line. Figure 509b shows the great circle and rhumb line of figure 508d. For the latter figure, the great circle was first drawn as a straight line on the gnomonic, then transferred to the Mercator by plotting a number of geographic positions along it. For the navigator, this is the principal use of the gnomonic or great-circle charts. If a rhumb line is desired on the gnomonic, this process must be reversed: a straight line is first drawn on the Mercator, then transferred to its geographic position on the gnomonic.

Combining Great-circle and Rhumb-line Courses

Great-circle courses yield the shortest distances; rhumb-line courses are easier to steer because of the unvarying heading. For routes where the saving in distance is sufficient to justify it, the advantages of great-circle *and* rhumb-line navigation can be combined. As it is obviously impractical to follow a path of constantly changing direction (great circle), the course is changed in steps at convenient intervals; the result is a series of rhumb lines closely approximating the great-circle course. This is done by first plotting the great-circle route on a *gnomonic* chart, on which every straight line is a great circle (figure 509a). The great-circle route is then subdivided into segments of convenient length—usually where it crosses meridians at reg-

ular intervals of longitude. These points are next transferred to the Mercator chart, as described above, and connected by straight lines. In this manner, the great-circle track is approximated by a series of rhumb line "chords." (See, also, article 3008.)

Great-circle courses and intermediate points can also be calculated mathematically; see articles 3012–3015.

Gnomonic Distortion

In all three cases of gnomonic charts, distortion of shape and scale increases as distance from the center of the projection (the point of tangency) increases. Within about 1,000 miles of the point of tangency, this distortion is not objectionable; beyond that, it increases rapidly. Distance and direction cannot be measured directly, but instructions are usually printed on the chart for determining great-circle distances and the initial direction of a great circle. It is not usable as a working chart for normal plotting of navigational data.

It is impossible to include as much as a hemisphere in a single gnomonic chart. At 90 degrees from the center of the projection (the point of tangency) the projecting line is parallel to the plane of the projection, and would meet it only at infinity.

Lambert Conformal Projection

510 Like the Mercator, the Lambert is derived from mathematical equations. To aid in visualizing the general form of the projection, it is convenient to think of it as in figure 510a, which illustrates a Lambert chart of the United States.

The cone is represented, not as tangent to the earth, but as *intersecting* the earth along two *standard parallels* of true scale. Between the standard parallels the scale is somewhat compressed, the maximum error being about 1/2 of 1 percent (minus); outside them, the scale is slightly expanded, reaching a maximum of nearly 2½ percent at the tip of Florida. Stated another way, the *total* change in scale within the United States is about 3 percent. That is, from a point in the central United States to the tip of Florida, each 100-mile section

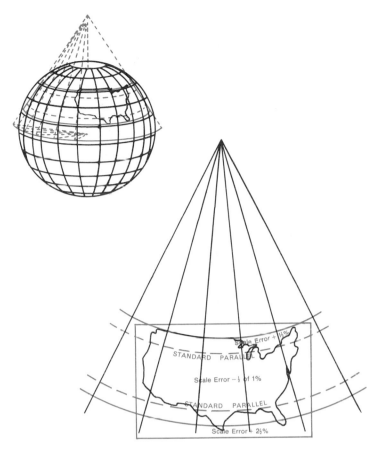

Figure 510a. Development and scale properties of Lambert conformal projection.

would measure about 103 miles (figure 510a). By way of comparison, the total change of scale for a Mercator chart of the United States would be approximately 40 percent.

As illustrated in figure 510a, all parallels are concentric circles, all meridians are straight-line radii of the parallels, meeting when extended at a common point, the apex of the developed cone.

This projection first came into use during World War I, for military maps. Since then it has been widely used for aeronautical charts; its use for marine navigation has been largely limited to higher latitudes.

On a Lambert chart, a great circle is very nearly a straight line, close enough so for purposes of practical navigation; see figure 510c. Points along such a line can be transferred to a Mercator chart for a series of rhumb lines in the same manner as for a gnomonic chart.

Transverse and Oblique Mercator Projections

511 When one speaks of a "Mercator chart" it is commonly understood that the reference is to the

Mercator *conformal* projection. There are, however, other forms of this cylindrical projection.

For the *transverse* Mercator projection the cylinder has been turned through 90° and is tangent along a selected meridian; see figure 511a.

Figure 511b shows a transverse Mercator chart. For the polar regions it has the same desirable properties that the original Mercator possesses near the equator. As with the original Mercator projection, there has to be expansion of the parallel as one moves away from the line of tangency in order to maintain the relative shape of areas. Now, however, the areas of size distortion are those *distant from the pole*.

The transverse mercator has been used for some charts of the polar regions. Its chief disadvantage is the curvature of the meridians, making them less suitable for direction measurements using a protractor. Within the limits of a single chart, however, this distortion is usually negligible. The transverse Mercator is also known, confusingly enough, as the *inverse* Mercator. If its use is confined to regions not too far removed from the central (vertical) meridian—the shaded area of figure 511b—it portrays meridians and parallels with little distortion.

The cylinder of the Mercator projection could have been turned through some angle other than 90°—any angle, and at any latitude between the equator and either pole. This is known as an *oblique Mercator* projection.

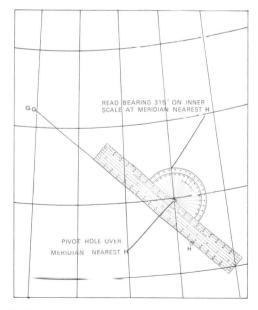

Figure 510b. Measuring a bearing on a Lambert chart using an AN plotter. Note that measurement is made at the meridian nearest the vessel's position.

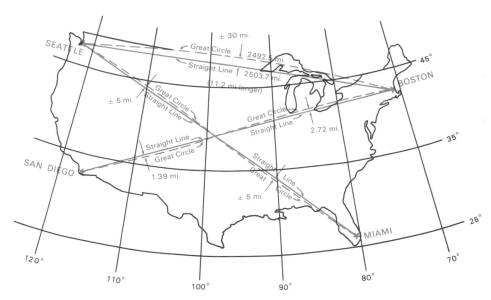

Figure 510c. Straight lines on a Lambert chart are close approximations of great circles.

Figure 511c shows a portion of a cylinder tangent to the great circle joining Miami and Lisbon. On the resulting *oblique Mercator* projection, whether it is visible or not, this great circle becomes, in effect, the "equator" of the projection. Meridians will be curves, the direction of curvature reversing as the meridian crosses the fictitious "equator," but the curvature is scarcely noticeable for areas within 700 to 800 miles on either side of this central line. Parallels are also curved lines.

Stereographic Projection

512 The *polar stereographic* projection is used for aeronautical (and some nautical) charts of the polar regions, from about 75° latitude poleward. Figure 512 shows a polar stereographic map of the Northern Hemisphere, another application of this projection. Note that in this case the parallels are concentric·circles and all meridians are straight-line radials.

Azimuthal Equidistant Projection

513 A specialized type of chart is the *azimuthal equidistant*, which is actually mathematically derived rather than being "projected." It is always centered on some place of particular significance, such as a nation's capital city or a major communications center. On this projection, it is possible to show the *entire* surface of the earth in one flat chart, though with *great* distortion. For example, the *point* at the opposite end of the earth's diameter from the central point of the projection is stretched into a *line* throughout the entire 360° of the limiting circle, as in figure 513.

From the chosen central point of the projection all distances are true (equidistant), and the distance to any place on earth may be measured as accurately as the scale of the chart permits.

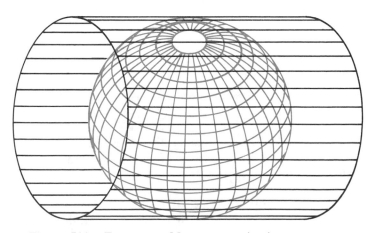

Figure 511a. Transverse Mercator projection.

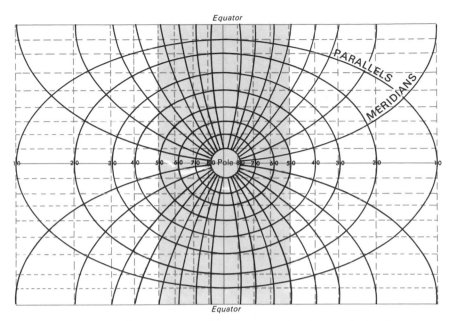

Figure 511b. Transverse Mercator projection as derived from a Mercator conformal projection.

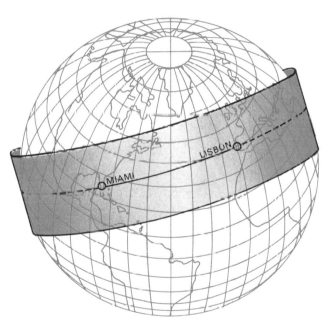

Figure 511c. Oblique Mercator projection in which a selected great circle (Miami to Lisbon) serves as the "equator" of the projection.

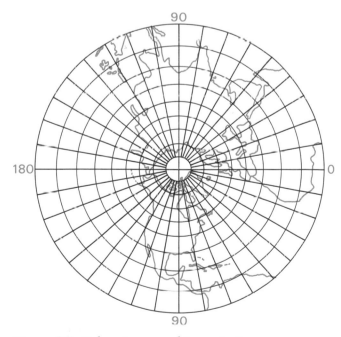

Figure 512. Polar stereographic projection.

Figure 513. An azimuthal equidistant chart centered on Washington, D.C.

From the same central point all directions are true, and the direction (azimuth) of any place on earth may also be measured directly. A 360° scale is usually printed around the edge of the chart for this purpose.

Charts using the azimuthal equidistant projection are particularly useful in communications as the great-circle paths followed by radio waves appear as radial lines, and the proper orientation for a directional antenna is easily obtained. For aviation interests, direct great-circle routes are easily plotted, and the various areas to be overflown are readily apparent. A number of these charts, centered on points of typical interest, are published by the Defense Mapping Agency Hydrographic/Topographic Center.

Other Projections

514 There is a considerable number of other types of projections that can be used for making charts. Most, but not all, of these are variations of the types just discussed. They will not, however, be of general interest to the marine or air navigator.

Computer-based Charts

515 The National Ocean Service has established an automated information system with a database that can store all chart information in digital form. Every point, line, symbol, letters, and numbers—*everything*—is being stored in digital form on tapes or discs.

Negatives are prepared for each color using a laser-beam raster plotter guided by digital information fed through a computer. To the user, the resulting chart will be indistinguishable from previous charts, except for a somewhat sharper image appearance and a brief note in the margin advising him that a computer-assisted cartographic compilation system was used. Not only are the man-hours reduced for initially preparing these automated charts, but there are also great savings of effort in keeping charts up to date. Information on any point is entered only once in the data base and is equally available to all charts concerned, such as for overlapping areas or charts of the same area at different scales. A single correction to the data base will serve to correct all applicable items. Instead of working at a drafting table, a cartographer works with a computer terminal and a video screen, making changes via the keyboard and a cursor. When a chart is revised, the old data will be preserved in a separate file for historical or legal purposes, but the master data base is continuously kept up to date.

Plotting Sheets

516 At sea, where no large-scale charts are available, navigators use *plotting sheets*. These are basically Mercator charts showing only the grid of meridians and parallels with a compass rose, without any other chart data. Plotting sheets are particularly useful in plotting celestial fixes on a large scale. The position of the fix is then transferred to the working chart. There are two types available: those printed for a given band of latitude, and Universal Plotting Sheets (UPS), which can be used at any latitude.

The DMA Hydrographic/Topographic Center publishes several series of plotting sheets at different scales; the value of the latitude is printed on the parallels of latitude. The meridians are left blank, and the user inserts the longitude of his area of operations. When labeling the meridian, it must be remembered that in west longitude the longitude becomes numerically greater towards the west, to the left on the sheet. In east longitude it increases numerically to the east, to the right on the sheet. The same plotting sheets can be used for either north or south latitudes by inverting the sheet. As on nearly all charts, north is always at the top. When plotting sheets are used in north latitude, the value of the latitude becomes numerically larger towards the north or top of the sheet. In south latitude the reverse is true. DMAHTC charts No. 900 through 910 are position plotting sheets 20 × 38 inches in size with a longitude scale of 1° = 4 inches. Charts 920 to 933 are larger in overall size

(35 × 46 inches) at the same longitude scale; latitude coverage ranges from 8° at the equator to 3° at 65° latitude. Charts 934 to 936 are the same size, but at higher latitudes with a scale of 1° of longitude = 2 inches. Charts 960 to 975 are smaller than either of the above sets (17 × 22 inches), covering 3° or 4° of latitude at a scale of 1° of longitude = 4 inches. The smallest of all (10 × 18 inches) are charts 960 to 975 intended for use in lifeboats; the highest latitude available is 49°.

Universal plotting sheets (UPS) have a compass rose, unnumbered parallels of latitude, and a single meridian in the center of the sheet. They are unusual in that they can be used for any latitude and longitude, exclusive of the polar areas where a Mercator chart is not practical. On the UPS the navigator draws in meridians properly spaced for the mid-latitude of the area to be covered. To draw meridians on the UPS, the mid-latitude of the area desired is determined and the parallels labeled accordingly. Points on the compass rose, representing angles from the horizontal numerically equal to the mid-latitude, are determined and a meridian drawn through these points, as in figure 516. The Universal Plotting Sheets are published by DMA Aerospace Center with the designation of VP-OS. They are 13″ by 14″ and have a scale of 20 miles per inch. The AN plotter shown in figure 510b has distance scales to fit the UPS; this greatly facilitates plotting distance and direction.

If a small-area plotting sheet is needed, and no printed forms are available, a navigator can construct his own by drawing a circle of convenient size and marking it as a compass rose for the latitudes with which he is concerned. Lines are then drawn for parallels and meridians in the same manner as for a universal plotting sheet.

Comparison of Chart Projections

517 In the preceding articles of this chapter, the basic principles of chart projection have been presented, with comments on the selection of the different projections and how to use them.

By way of summary, the items of practical importance for selected projections have been combined into the table on page 82, for further study and convenient reference.

THE USE OF NAUTICAL CHARTS

Introduction

518 Nautical charts can provide a navigator with a vast amount of information including the depth of the water and objects under and on the surface; features of the land, primarily those of spe-

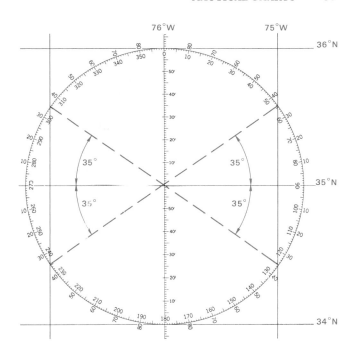

Figure 516. Universal plotting sheet.

cific interest to those traveling the waters; man-made features, again with emphasis on those that assist in navigation; information on tides and currents, facilities ashore, and restrictive laws and regulations; and more. All this is conveyed through the use of symbols, various colors, and written statements and abbreviations—even by the style of lettering used.

Charts come in a wide range of sizes, and even in different shapes. Most are *conventional* charts, large sheets of high-quality paper, usually printed on one side only, and intended for flat or rolled storage. Recognizing that small craft will have difficulty both in using and storing a large flat chart, the National Ocean Service has printed some in a special format; see article 525. Regardless of the format, nautical charts should be treated with respect and provided adequate storage.

Although there are publications that list and explain the symbols, colors, abbreviations, etc.—including Chart No. 1 and this book—a navigator must have a wide and detailed knowledge of the system used to convey chart information if he is to travel on the water safely and efficiently. There may be times when a source of information is not available or there is not time to consult it.

Editions and Revisions

519 Charts are published with an *edition* number and the *date* to which the information it contains has been corrected. When a high number of revisions have been made to the information on a

	Mercator	Lambert*	Oblique gnomonic
Parallels	Horizontal straight lines	Arcs of concentric circles	Curved (conic sections), except equator
Meridians	Vertical straight lines perpendicular to parallels	Straight-line radii of parallels, converging at the pole	Straight lines
Appearance	See figure 504b	See figure 510	See figure 509a
Conformal	Yes	Yes	No
Great circle	Curved lines (except meridians and equator)	Approximates straight line	Straight line
Rhumb line	Straight line; course angle measured with *any* meridian	Curved line; course angle measured at intersection of straight line and mid-meridian	Curved line
Distance scale	Varies; scale at mid-latitude of a particular course to be used	Nearly constant	No constant scale; can be measured by rules printed on most charts
Increase of scale	Increases with distance from equator	Increases with distance from central parallel of projection	Increases with distance from center of projection (point of tangency)
Derivation	Mathematical; tables available (only one table required)	Mathematical; tables available for various standard parallels	Graphic or mathematical
Navigational uses	Dead reckoning; may be adapted to almost any type	Dead reckoning and electronic; may be used for almost any type	Great-circle determination

*Includes Lambert conformal, transverse, and oblique Mercator, and polar stereographic; statements in this column are true for the Lambert conformal, approximately correct for others. The statements are also essentially true for polyconic projection charts.

chart, a new edition is published; the interval between editions can vary from a year or less to more than 12 years. A chart is sometimes issued with a "Revised" date when the stock level requires another printing, and only a few changes have been incorporated; in this case, a new edition number is not warranted.

All charts in regular use on board ships and boats should be kept corrected according to the latest information from all official sources such as *Notices to Mariners* and *Local Notices to Mariners:* urgent information on chart discrepancies or changes is disseminated by radio in the appropriate series of warning notices (see article 611). Also, procedures should be established whereby charts that are not used regularly can be quickly brought up to date when needed; the use of a file of *Chart/Publication Record* cards (DMAHTC No. 8860/9) will help to organize and expedite this task.

For safety in navigation, every chart when used must be the latest printing and fully corrected for changes that have occurred since the edition date. An old edition of a chart, or an uncorrected chart, is *not* safe to use.

Chart Numbering System

520 To provide an orderly system for the numbering of U.S. charts, a worldwide scheme is used that generally identifies a chart by means of a scale range and geographic location. U.S. charts have numbers consisting of one to five digits as follows:

One digit	No scale involved
Two digits	1:9,000,001 and smaller
Three digits	1:2,000,001 to 1:9,000,000
Four digits	Various non-navigational items
Five digits	1:2,000,000 and larger

The one-digit category comprises the symbol and abbreviation charts for the United States and some other nations. Also included is the chart of International Code Flags and Pennants published by DMAIITC.

The two- and three-digit categories contain charts of very large areas such as entire oceans or major portions thereof. For these numbers, the world's waters have been divided into nine *ocean basins* numbered as shown in figure 520a. The first digit of a two- or three-digit chart number (with limited exceptions) indicates the ocean basin concerned. (There are no two-digit chart numbers used for Ocean Basins 3 and 4, as the limited areas of the Mediterranean and Caribbean seas make such very small scale charts inappropriate; thus two-digit chart numbers beginning with 3 or 4 do not fit into the overall numbering scheme.)

The four-digit category consists of a series of *non-navigational*, special-purpose charts. These are numbered by arbitrarily assigning blocks of new numbers to existing series and to new series when originated.

The five-digit category includes those charts most often used by navigators. Except for bathymetric charts, the first of the five digits indicates one of the nine *coastal regions* of the world in which the chart is located; see figure 520b. (Note that this "coastal region" number is *not* the same as the "ocean basin" number used in the two- and three-digit number series.) The second of the five digits identifies a subregion; again see figure 520b. The final three digits associate the chart with a specific location; they are assigned in rough counterclockwise fashion around the subregion.

Many gaps are left in the assignment of numbers so that any future charts may be smoothly fitted into the system. Although the numbering system covers the world, it has as yet been applied only to U.S.-produced charts and foreign charts reissued by DMAHTC.

By virtue of their scale, DMAHTC bottom contour bathymetric charts would normally be assigned a five-digit number. However, these charts, available only to the U.S. Navy, are not of coastal areas as are others in the five-digit series, and to distinguish them they are assigned a one-letter, four-digit number. The letter "B" indicates an interim version; the letter "C" indicates the inclusion

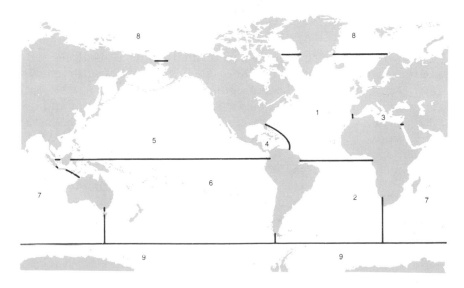

Figure 520a. The "ocean basins" of the DMA chart numbering system; the first digit of a two- or three-digit chart number.

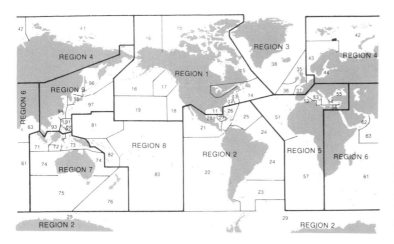

Figure 520b. The "coastal regions" of the DMA chart numbering system; the first digit of a five-digit chart number. The two-digit numbers are designations of sub-regions.

of Loran-C lines; and the letter "E" indicates the Omega version. (Eventually, there will be only the Omega versions.) The first two digits indicate a band of longitude, and the second pair of digits designate a latitude band. See figure 520c.

Chart Catalogs

521 The National Ocean Service and DMAHTC publish *chart catalogs* consisting of various pages or panels showing the area covered by each chart. Generally similar catalogs are issued by the hydrographic survey authorities of other countries.

NOS has five marine chart catalogs: *Nautical Chart Catalog 1, the Atlantic and Gulf Coasts, including Puerto Rico and the Virgin Islands; Nautical Chart Catalog 2, the Pacific Coast, including Hawaii, Guam, and Samoa Islands; Nautical Chart Catalog 3, Alaska, including the Aleutian Islands;* and *Nautical Chart Catalog 4, the U.S. Great Lakes and Adjacent Waterways;* also *Map and Chart Catalog 5, Bathymetric Charts and Special-Purpose Charts.* These useful, free publications also contain information on other NOS publications and where they may be obtained.

Charts and other publications prepared by DMAHTC are listed in the *DMA Catalog of Maps, Charts, and Related Products, Part 2—Hydrographic Products.* This is divided into nine regional volumes, I through IX, plus Volume X—*Miscellaneous and Special-Purpose Navigational Charts, Sheets and Tables.* (Volume X was formerly designated as Pub. 1-N-A, and this shorter name is still used informally.) There is also Volume XI (ex-Pub. 1-N-S) for security classified charts and publications. These volumes are issued to naval units, and Volumes I through X can be purchased by civilian navigators

from local sales agents for DMAHTC products (these are listed in each volume).

Portfolios

522 The chart-numbering system based on regions and subregions provides an organized method of keeping track of charts issued by many various agencies, such as DMAHTC, NOS, Canadian Hydrographic Service, British Admiralty, and others. For U.S. naval vessels, the required charts for each of the 52 subregions are grouped into a *portfolio* designated with the number of that subregion. This is further subdivided into "A" and "B" sections; for example, the charts of Subregion 26 are placed in Portfolios 26A and 26B (these include most, but not all, of the charts of that subregion).

Portfolios are indicated by the charts' DMA stock numbers. The first letter following the initial two digits of the stock number (the number of the subregion) will be either an A or a B for the respective portfolio section (or an X if the chart is not a part of a portfolio). For each subregion, the A portfolio contains all the general charts and the principal approach and harbor charts; the B portfolio supplements the A coverage of the nautical charts within the subregion.

There are also three portfolios of general and international charts, Atlantic, Pacific, and the World; stock numbers of such charts will begin with WOA, WOP, or WOB respectively (or WOX for charts of this type not in a portfolio). There are four other portfolios, each containing Bottom Contour charts of a major area; the distribution of these charts is limited to naval activities.

The chart portfolio system provides a simple method for ordering all the charts of a subregion,

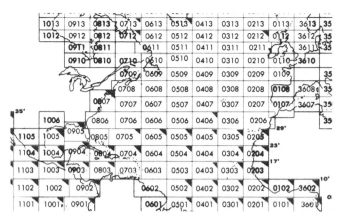

Figure 520c. Numbering system for bottom contour charts.

rather than ordering them individually. Although intended primarily for use by navigators of Navy, Coast Guard, and other federal vessels, it may also be used by nongovernmental individuals and activities.

Chart Scales

523 The *scale* of a chart is the ratio of a distance unit on the chart to the actual distance on the surface of the earth; as this is a ratio, it does not matter what size the unit is, or in what system it is measured. For example, a scale of 1:80,000 means that one unit (inch, foot, meter, etc.) on the chart represents 80,000 such units on the earth. Such a ratio is commonly called the *natural* or *fractional scale*.

At times, the scale will be stated in descriptive terms, such as "4 miles to the inch" or "2 inches to a mile"; these are called *numerical* or *equivalent scales*, and are often used as a generalization rather than an exact statement of scale. On a Mercator chart it may be stated that "1° of longitude equals 1.25 inches." Scale is stated in this form because the spacing between meridians is the one constant on a Mercator projection.

All charts have their scale shown in fractional form; charts on a scale of 1:80,000 or larger will generally also carry *graphic (bar) scales* of distance, usually in more than one set of units; see figure 508b.

"Large-scale" and "Small-scale" Charts

The terms "large scale" and "small scale" are often confusing to persons who are not accustomed to using charts.

For example, if a chart is printed at scale 1:5,000,000, the very "bigness" of the second number makes it seem of larger scale than one at 1:150,000. But remember that these scales can also be written as fractions—1/5,000,000 or 1/150,000— and the larger the denominator of a fraction, the smaller is the quantity.

At a scale of 1:5,000,000, one mile is only 0.015 inch in length; at 1:150,000, it is 0.486 inch— roughly 33 times as long.

The 1:5,000,000 means that 1 inch on the chart represents 5,000,000 inches on the earth's surface; or 1 centimeter represents 5,000,000 cm.; or 1 of any other unit represents 5,000,000 of the same units.

There is no firm definition for the terms "large-scale charts" and "small-scale charts"; the two terms are only relative. Thus, as compared with a chart at 1:40,000, the chart at 1:500,000 is a *small-scale* chart; it becomes a *large-scale* chart when it is compared with one at 1:5,000,000. The chart that shows any particular feature, such as an island or bay, at a larger size and in more detail is considered—comparatively, at least—as a *large-scale* chart.

In summary, remember that opposites go together: "Small scale, large area; large scale, small area."

Chart Series

524 The scales of nautical charts range from about 1:2,500 to about 1:5,000,000. Charts published by the National Ocean Service are classified into the following "series" according to their scale.

Sailing charts. Scales 1:600,000 and smaller. These are used in fixing the mariner's position as he approaches the coast from the open ocean, or for sailing between distant coastwise ports. On such charts, the shoreline and topography are generalized and only offshore soundings, the principal lights, outer buoys, and landmarks visible at considerable distances are shown. Charts of this series are also useful for plotting the track of major tropical storms.

General charts. Scale 1:150,000 to 1:600,000. These are used for coastwise navigation outside of outlying reefs and shoals when the vessel is generally within sight of land or aids to navigation and her course can be directed by piloting techniques.

Coast charts. Scale 1:50,000 to 1:150,000. These are used for inshore navigation, for entering bays and harbors of considerable width, and for navigating large inland waterways.

FLUSHING BAY
NEW YORK

Mercator Projection
Scale 1:10,000 at Lat. 40°47′

SOUNDINGS IN FEET
AT MEAN LOW WATER

TIDAL INFORMATION

Place	Height referred to datum of soundings (MLW)			
	Mean High Water	Mean Tide Level	Mean Low Water	Extreme Low Water
	feet	feet	feet	feet
College Point	6.5	3.2	0.0	−4.0
Flushing	6.8	3.4	0.0	−4.0

HEIGHTS
Heights in feet above Mean High Water.

Figure 524a. Chart legend showing title, projection, scale, datum used for heights and depths, and other information.

Harbor charts. Scales larger than 1:50,000. These are used in harbors, anchorage areas, and the smaller waterways.

Small-craft charts. Scale of 1:80,000 and larger. These are special charts of inland waters, including the Intracoastal Waterways, or special editions of conventional charts. They are printed on lighter weight paper and folded. These "SC" charts contain additional information of interest to small-craft operators, such as data on facilities, tide predictions, weather broadcast information, and so forth.

Charts published by the Defense Mapping Agency Hydrographic/Topographic Center are classed as *general* or *approach* charts, with the latter category being used for those with scales of roughly 1:150,000 or larger.

Mariners are urged to obtain and study thoroughly the largest scale charts available for a particular route, even if a smaller scale is used for keeping track of position in passage.

General Information

525 Each chart has a *title block,* placed where it does not interfere with the presentation of essential navigational information. This block includes the title of the chart and a statement of the projection; if the chart is based on foreign sources, as many DMAHTC charts are, the original authority and date of surveys will appear here. The number of the chart does not appear here; it is printed in several places around the margins, with the chart number and date in the lower-left corner.

Planes of Reference

Also in the title block are statements regarding the *planes of reference* used for heights and depths. The *datum* for soundings (depth measurements) is generally some form of average low water so that at most states of the tide the mariner has at least the charted depth. Among the various levels used are *mean low water, mean lower low water,* and *mean low water springs;* for more details see article 905. It must always be remembered that tidal stages *below* a mean level will occur at times, and the depths will then be less than charted. The sounding datum used on the U.S. Pacific Coast and Gulf Coast is mean lower low water (MLLW). Although MLLW has been authorized for the U.S. Atlantic Coast, this has not yet been implemented, and it is expected that mean low water (MLW) will remain in use for some time. There is little difference between MLW and MLLW along the east coast. On bodies of water not significantly affected by tidal action, such as the Great Lakes and the Baltic Sea, an arbitrary reference plane is designated. The unit of measurement—feet, meter, or fathom (1 fathom = 6 feet)—is also stated as part of the title block.

The plane of reference for the measurements of heights is usually chosen so that the mariner will have, at least at most times, the charted vertical clearance under bridges and other overhead obstructions such as power transmission lines. Mean high water is commonly used and is assumed to be the reference plane on U.S. charts unless information to the contrary is shown. As with mean lows, some observed or predicted high-tide levels will be *above* mean high water, and caution must be exercised if vertical clearances are critical.

Chart Notes

Much valuable information is printed on charts in the form of *notes* and as *boxes* of data. Notes will relate to such topics as regulatory restrictions, cautions and warnings, unusual magnetic conditions,

NOTE B
SPECIAL ANCHORAGES – anchor lights not required on vessels less than sixty-five feet long.

NOTE A
Navigation regulations are published in Chapter 2, Coast Pilot 2, or subsequent yearly supplements and weekly Notices to Mariners. Copies of the regulations may be obtained at the office of the District Engineer, Corps of Engineers in New York.
Refer to section numbers shown with area designation.

NOTE C
All vessels traversing the area shall pass directly through without unnecessary delay. No vessels having a height of more than 35 feet with reference to the plane of mean high water shall enter or pass through the area whenever visibility is less then one mile.

Figure 524b. Chart "notes" are used to provide information that cannot be shown by symbols or abbreviations.

etc. The boxes may show depths in major dredged channels, mean and extremes of tidal stages at selected points on the chart (charts with scales of 1:75,000 and larger), etc. Notes and boxes may be printed in the margins or on the face of the chart at locations where they will not obscure navigational information.

Distance

526 The unit of *distance* on most marine charts is the *nautical mile* (see article 210); this is measured using a graphic scale, if available on larger-scale charts (see article 523), or on the *latitude* scale as described in article 508. On some charts, distances can be measured in *kilometers;* here a graphic scale is a necessity. Charts of U.S. inland and some coastal waters will have graphic scales for measurement of distances in *statute miles*. Charts with graphic scales may also have one marked off in yards for the measurement of shorter distances.

Latitude and Longitude

527 As noted under the section on chart projections, each chart will have lines marking parallels and meridians—these are used to measure the geographic location of any point in terms of latitude and longitude. The intervals between these lines may be 2′, 5′, 10′ or more as determined by the scale of the chart. Latitude scales will appear at the sides of conventional charts, with longitude scales at the top and bottom. (Small-craft charts may be oriented so as to make the best use of rectangular sheets of paper; north may *not* be "up," towards the top of the sheet.)

Latitude and longitude scales will be marked with *degrees* and *minutes*. NOS charts with a scale larger than 1:49,000 will have minutes divided into *seconds* or multiples of seconds. Charts of a smaller scale will have subdivisions of tenths of minutes, while still smaller-scale charts will use fifths or halves of minutes, or no subdivision.

Direction

528 Navigational directions on a chart may be referenced to either true north or magnetic north. *True directions* can be referenced to the meridians and parallels using techniques discussed in chapter 7; techniques will vary for different projections. *Magnetic directions* can be calculated from true directions by applying variation as discussed in chapter 3.

Charts also carry *compass roses* in several locations; see figure 304. These have an outer circle ref-erenced to true north; true directions may be measured here rather than using parallels and meridians. Graduations around this circle may be at intervals of 1°, 2°, or more as determined by the scale and use of the chart; note carefully the interval between adjacent marks. An inner circle is offset from true north by the amount of variation and can be used for the direct measurement of magnetic directions without arithmetical calculations; the subdivisions on this inner scale may be different from those on the outer circle, typically 2° rather than 1°; carefully check each compass rose used. There may also be a second inner circle subdivided according to the "point" system described in article 301. On smaller scale charts covering wider areas the variation may be different at different locations—always use the compass rose *nearest* the line whose direction is being measured.

Use of Color

529 Nearly all charts employ color to distinguish various categories of information such as deep water, shoal water, and land areas; "screening" is used to produce variations of the basic colors of black, blue, green, grays, magenta, gold, and white.

Deep-water areas are white (uncolored). Shoal areas are colored blue; there may be two shades, and the dividing depth between white and blue will vary with the scale and use of the chart. Areas that cover and uncover with tidal changes are colored green. If a chart includes an area that has had a wire-drag survey to ensure the absence of all obstructions—wrecks, rocks, coral heads, etc.—this may be indicated in a screened-green tint with the depth of the drag indicated by words or symbols. (All white may also be used on areas such as harbors that are not shown in detail on that chart, but are so shown on larger scale charts.)

Figure 529. Vertical lettering is used for features that are dry at high water; slant letters for submerged and floating features.

On NOS charts, land areas are shown in a screened gold tint. On charts published by DMAHTC, land areas are represented in a screened black tint that appears as gray. On larger scale charts, built-up areas of cities may be indicated by a darker land tint. "Nautical purple" ink has been widely used in the past for much information on charts, as it is more easily read under the red night-time illumination normally used on the bridge of a ship to avoid interference with watchstanders' vision. This is used for printed information, compass roses, and some symbols for aids to navigation. This purple, however, is now being changed to a dark magenta color.

Lettering Styles

530   Even the style of lettering on a chart provides information. For example, features that are dry at high water are identified in roman type; submerged and floating hydrographic features (except the sounding figures, showing depths) are identified in *italics*. Often on small-scale charts it may be difficult to distinguish a small reef from a small islet, but the type of lettering will indicate the difference. To avoid confusion, periods are not used with abbreviations. Dots are used, however, above each lower-case "i" and "j"; and periods are used normally in chart notes and general statements.

Symbols and Abbreviations

531   Many symbols and abbreviations are used on charts. These constitute a shorthand that tells the navigator the physical characteristics of the charted area and details of the available aids to navigation. The symbols used are standardized, but are subject to some variation depending on the scale of the particular chart or chart series. It is not possible on a small-scale chart to show all the details that can be shown on a large-scale chart.

Many pages of text would be needed to describe all the symbols and abbreviations used to present the detailed information available on a modern chart. Only the more important will be described here. The full set is included in *Chart No. 1* issued jointly by the National Ocean Service and the Defense Mapping Agency Hydrographic/Topographic Center; see the back pages of this book, following the index. New editions of *Chart No. 1* are published at irregular intervals as required by changes.

Features of Water Areas

532   In water areas, *soundings* (depths) are the items of greatest concern to navigators. These are shown as many small numbers in roman type. The

Steep coast (Bluff)   Rocky coast

Figure 530. Charts can show the nature of the coastline, such as bluffs or cliffs.

Figure 532. File card for recording chart and publication corrections.

unit of measurement and the datum from which measured are stated in the title block. (Actual depths will, of course, vary in tidal waters.) Most charts will have lines connecting points of equal depth; these *contour lines* are generally termed *depth curves* or *fathom curves*. The number of such lines and the depth for which they are drawn will depend upon the type and scale of the chart. One of them will serve as the boundary between deeper areas in white and shallower water tinted blue; typically this is the 6-foot curve on harbor charts and the 12-, 18-, or 30-foot line on coastal charts, as determined by the rate of slope of inshore waters.

Artificial Channels

Dredged channels, deeper than the surrounding waters, are shown by a pair of parallel dashed lines. Information is normally printed within the lines or just outside for the depth and width of the channel and the date on which the last depth survey was taken; for major channels, this data may be presented in tabular form in a box elsewhere on the chart.

Information on channel depth and width is frequently updated between chart editions by items in *Notices to Mariners*.

Character of the Bottom

Information on the composition of the bottom—mud, sand, rocks, coral, etc.—is of interest to mariners primarily when anchoring. This is shown on charts by abbreviations; many of these are self-evident; they may or may not be explained on the chart itself, but all are in *Chart No. 1*.

Features of the Shoreline

A chart will include information regarding the nature of the shoreline, the mean high-water mark on most charts. Marshy areas or vegetation extending out into the water will be noted by symbols and abbreviations. A surveyed low-water line is marked by a series of dots. A natural shoreline is indicated by a slightly heavier line than a man-made shoreline such as a seawall. Unsurveyed stretches of any type are shown by a broken line.

Aids to Navigation

Information on aids to navigation, being of prime importance to a navigator, is as complete as possible. Both symbols and abbreviations are used to this end; a mariner must be fully knowledgeable of these and able to read his charts without reference to other sources.

Buoys, except large navigational buoys and mooring buoys, are shown by a diamond shape above a very small circle. (A dot may still be found instead of the small circle on some older charts.) The circle indicates the position of the buoy and the diamond shape may be at any angle as required to avoid interference with other charted detail. For most single-color buoys, the diamond may be filled in with that color—green, or magenta (for red buoys). Other colors, such as yellow, are shown with an "open"—uncolored—diamond. To facilitate color identification, a letter abbreviation—G, R, Y—is printed near the buoy symbol; two letters are used where necessary, such as "RG" for red and green.

A horizontally banded buoy will have a line across the *shorter* axis of the diamond shape, and the two halves will be colored magenta and green with the half away from the position circle matching the top-most band on the buoy; abbreviation "RG" or "GR" will be used as appropriate. A vertically striped buoy will have an open diamond symbol with a line along the *longer* axis and the letter abbreviation RW to identify the colors. The symbol

for a special-purpose buoy is an open diamond with the letter "Y" for yellow.

Lighted buoys have a small magenta disc or flare printed over the position circle (or dot) of the symbol. The color and rhythm of the light are identified by readily understood abbreviations placed close to the symbol. (No letter abbreviation is used for a white light.)

A mooring buoy is represented by a downward tapering solid black trapezoid with a position circle on the lower side (⬇). A "superbuoy" has an open trapezoid with the shorter side upward; a large navigational buoy or an offshore data buoy has a "mast" pointing upward in addition to the position circle (⚓), and purple "flare" if lighted.

Daybeacons have a small triangular symbol if the daymarks are triangular; this is colored magenta if the daymark is solid red or is open, with "RG" if it is red over green. All other daymarks, regardless of shape, are represented by small square symbols. A square green daymark shows as a square green symbol, all other colors and shapes are shown as open squares with letter abbreviations for the colors.

Lights of all sizes, from minor lights to primary seacoast lights, are shown by a small black dot and magenta "flare"—the combination is much like an exclamation mark. The size of the symbol normally has no significance, except that on some DMAHTC charts a larger symbol is used for lights with greater distances of visibility. The color (other than white) and rhythm of the light are shown by abbreviations as for lighted buoys. Additional abbreviations may be included for the height of the light (*not* the top of the structure) and its nominal range.

The newer articulated lights (see article 409) are shown by a unique symbol. This combines a very small position circle, smaller than that used for buoys, with the magenta flare used for lights. The italic letters *"Art"* are placed nearby to further indicate this type of aid; light color, rhythm, and other identification data are shown in normal fashion. An explanatory note is placed on all charts with articulated lights.

Sound (fog) signals on buoys and at lights or elsewhere are labeled with the type of signal—BELL, GONG, HORN, or WHIS.

The number and/or letter identification of a buoy, daybeacon, or minor light is printed near the symbol and is enclosed in quotation marks to prevent confusion with depth figures. Lights that have names may have this printed near the symbol in full or shortened form; quotation marks are not used.

Ranges are shown by a pair of symbols for the front and rear markers. A solid line is printed for the length on the chart that the range is intended for navigational use. This is extended as a broken line to the front marker and continued on to the rear marker.

The symbol for a radiobeacon is a magenta circle around the basic symbol for that aid at which it is located or around a position dot if separately located. The frequency, identifying signal (in dots and dashes and in letters), and operating periods (if not continuous) are shown near the abbreviation "RBn"; aeronautical radiobeacons are further identified by "AERO."

Other Buoyage Systems

The foregoing paragraphs on symbols for aids to navigation are based on the IALA-B system of buoyage, the implementation of which began in U.S. waters in 1982.

Minor differences in the aids themselves and their symbols will exist until the former colors used in the U.S. lateral system have been completely phased out.

Differences will also be encountered in the symbols on charts of foreign waters, but these will in general conform to one of the variations permitted in *Chart No. 1*. NOS metric charts of the Great Lakes, coproduced with the Canadian Hydrographic Service, will have specialized pictorial symbols for buoys, both lighted and unlighted.

Hazards to Navigation

Many types of symbols are used to show the location of dangers to navigation. These can indicate whether the particular hazard is above water at all times, is submerged at all times (with the clearance over it), or covers and uncovers with tidal changes. Some symbols reveal the nature of the hazard; others are more generalized, some with a word or words, or abbreviations nearby. These are shown in detail and explained in *Chart No. 1*.

Land Features

Information shown on nautical charts that relates to land features is generally limited to items that will assist a navigator in establishing his position and directing his vessel's movements safely. These will relate to the shoreline that can be observed from the sea.

Land Forms

533   The general form of the land may be shown by the use of *contours*, lines connecting points of equal elevation. The height above datum, measured in feet or meters, is given by figures placed at intervals along the lines; the interval between contours will be uniform, but may vary from chart to chart based on the nature of the terrain and the scale of the chart. The height of conspicuous hills may be given within the closed lines of the highest contour. Contours are often omitted, however, if the land is relatively flat and featureless. Where contours would be useful, but exact surveys have not been made, generalized *form lines*, or *sketch contours* may be used. These are broken lines, and no height figures are placed on them.

Cliffs and steep slopes are shown by *hatchures*, short lines or bands of such lines at right-angles to the rise of land. The length of such lines may indicate the height or steepness of the slope.

The nature of the shore may be shown by symbols—fine dots for sand, small circles of varying diameters for rocks or boulders—or by words such as "sand," "gravel," or "rocks." The presence of breakers in the surf is likewise indicated to warn mariners of this hazard.

Vegetation

Various forms of vegetation may be shown on a chart by symbols and/or abbreviations. This is not uniformly done, generally being omitted unless the information will assist the navigator. Specific types of trees (and especially single or small groups of isolated trees), and types of cultivation such as rice paddies or trees in rows (orchards) are shown where they can help establish a position offshore.

Man-made Features

534   Man-made features will be shown for both water and land areas. In water areas these include both aids and hazards to navigation. Bridges, piers, platforms, and overhead power cables are typical items above the water's surface; cable areas and pipelines are the most often below-surface man-made features.

On land, man-made features include landmarks—towers, stacks, tanks, etc.; buildings such as customs houses, post offices, and health offices; and structures of interest to mariners—breakwaters and jetties, wharves, and drydocks. Depending upon the scale of the chart, streets and roads may be shown in some detail; railroads are almost always indicated by a symbol and are often identified by lettering.

Metric System

535   A program is under way in the United States to make use of the metric system of measurement on nautical charts issued by DMAHTC, and, to a much lesser degree, on those published by NOS. The object of this program is to conform to bilateral chart-reproduction agreements with other nations. Heights and water depths will be shown in meters. Land contours will be shown in meters. As the program progresses, the change to the metric system will have widespread effects and will, for example, necessitate changes in echo-sounder equipment to provide dual scales for use with either the customary (English) or the metric system.

Nautical charts that use the metric system will carry in *bold magenta* type the legend "Soundings in Meters" on the upper and lower margins or the word "Meters" superimposed over the metric depths on the face of the chart where space allows.

Appendix E to this book provides a table for the easy and accurate conversion of measurements in feet, fathoms, or meters to both of the other two units.

Using a Chart

536 Charts must be used intelligently, not blindly. The degree of reliance to be placed on a given chart or portion of a chart is no less of an art than is navigation itself. With experience, however, comes the skill that makes the chart a much more useful and dependable aid.

Read carefully all notes appearing on the chart. Do not merely look at it as though it were a picture. Check the scale, note the date of the survey on which it is based, if given, and see whether or not the chart is corrected and up-to-date. Check whether soundings are in feet, fathoms, or meters. Check that the sounding coverage is complete, and if not, note the areas where lack of information may indicate danger. Note the system of projection used, so that you can be sure how to measure direction and distance. Check the tidal reference plane. Remember that a chart is a basic tool in the art of navigation. Learn to use it skillfully.

Cautions

A chart is no more accurate than the survey on which it is based. In order to judge the accuracy and completeness of a survey, note its source and date (which may be given in the title). Beside the changes that may have taken place since the date of the survey, earlier surveys often were made under circumstances that precluded great accuracy and completeness of detail. Until a chart based on such a survey is tested, it should be regarded with caution. Except in well-frequented waters, few surveys have been so thorough as to make certain that *all*

WEST INDIES
BAHAMAS
LITTLE BAHAMA BANK
GREAT ABACO ISLAND
SOUTHERN EXTREMITY
From British surveys in 1836 and 1885
SOUNDINGS IN FATHOMS
For Symbols and Abbreviations, see Chart No. 1

SCALE 1: 73,170

Figure 535. Always check a chart for the date of the original and subsequent surveys.

dangers have been found. Noting the abundance or scantiness of the soundings is usually a dependable method of estimating the completeness of the survey, but it must be remembered that the chart seldom shows all soundings that were obtained. If the soundings are sparse or unevenly distributed, it should be assumed, as a precautionary measure, that the survey was not in great detail.

Large or irregular blank spaces among soundings mean that no soundings were obtained in those areas. Where the nearby soundings are deep, it may be logically, but incorrectly, assumed that in the blanks the water is also deep; but when the surrounding water is shallow, or if it can be seen from the rest of the chart that reefs or banks are present in the vicinity, such blanks should be regarded with suspicion as though they also were hazardous. This is particularly true in coral regions and off rocky coasts. These areas should be given a wide berth.

Compromise is sometimes necessary in chart production, as scale, congestion, and various other factors may preclude the presentation of all data that have been collected for a given area.

The National Ocean Service publishes nearly 1,000 charts covering shorelines in excess of 86,000 miles. DMAHTC is responsible for an even greater number of charts. It is obvious that changes can and do occur in considerable quantities and may be detected by official survey parties only years later, if ever. Thus it is clear that charts must be used with all due caution—they are a navigational "aid," not a guarantee of safety. It should be equally clear that it is the *duty* of every mariner to observe and report—promptly and in as full detail as possible—all inaccuracies noted in his charts to the appropriate agency.

Chapter 6

Navigational Publications

Introduction

601 A vessel's navigator uses many types and forms of written documents to make possible the full and efficient execution of his duties. The majority of these are prepared by various governmental agencies, although some originate from commercial sources. The term "document" here is used in a broad sense to include charts, tables, books, and pamphlets, and devices that relate to navigation. (Charts were considered in chapter 5; the other types are the subject of this chapter.) Government agencies conduct field surveys and research studies of their own and collaborate with each other and with similar activities in many foreign nations in order that their charts and other publications will contain the most recent and accurate information. A very valuable input to all types of navigational documents results from reports made by vessels' crews as to new and changed situations.

U.S. Agencies

602 The documents of the following U.S. agencies will be discussed in this chapter.

Defense Mapping Agency Hydrographic/Topographic Center (DMAHTC), Department of Defense.

National Ocean Service (NOS), a part of the National Oceanic and Atmospheric Administration (NOAA) in the Department of Commerce.

Naval Observatory, Department of the Navy.

U.S. Coast Guard (USCG), Department of Transportation.

Corps of Engineers, Department of the Army.

National Weather Service, NOAA, Department of Commerce.

Naval Oceanographic Office, Department of the Navy.

Hydrographic services of varying degrees of comprehensiveness are maintained by practically all maritime countries. The smaller countries restrict such service to their own coastal waters, but the larger countries, whose maritime interests embrace large parts of the globe, issue charts and other publications that cover the entire world. Most of these institutions are members of the International Hydrographic Organization, which holds periodic conferences to promote international uniformity in nautical publications and to coordinate the collecting and disseminating of hydrographic information. As a result of this effort, there has been a marked improvement in the quality and coverage of hydrographic surveys in many parts of the world and an increasing uniformity in charts and nautical books, both of which make navigating easier for mariners of all nations. There is a free exchange of hydrographic publications among the various maritime countries. As a result of this arrangement, the U.S. agencies, in preparing nautical documents for any particular area, make full use of the hydrographic and other marine information that has been compiled and published by the country having jurisdiction.

The various agencies responsible for navigational publications do not depend solely upon official sources of information. They serve as clearing houses for appropriate nautical data from any and all sources and in this way give navigators in general the benefit of observations noted by ships' officers in the routine performance of their duties. Many observers from time to time contribute valuable data concerning currents, aids and dangers to navigation, port facilities, and related subjects, which help materially in keeping charts, *Sailing Directions, Coast Pilots,* and *Light Lists* in agreement with prevailing conditions. These publications solicit such cooperation, and they greatly appreciate the receipt of any data that may increase their accuracy and completeness. Direct contact with ships' officers is facilitated by branch offices maintained at a number of ports in the United States and its possessions where the most recent marine information is made available to ships' masters and navigators.

Nautical Charts

603 The principal U.S. agencies involved with nautical charts are the National Ocean Service (NOS) and the Defense Mapping Agency Hydrographic/Topographic Center (DMAHTC). Both of these agencies have branch or regional offices, plus a network of local sales agents from whom charts and other publications can be obtained. Charts of some inland rivers, chiefly the Mississippi, Ohio, Tennessee, and their tributaries are prepared by the Army Corps of Engineers; these are sometimes called "navigational maps." Such charts or maps are normally purchased from District Engineer Offices.

Nautical charts are discussed in detail in chapter 5.

Light Lists

604 Charts show as much information as possible regarding the many aids to navigation, but practical limitations of space necessitate a less-than-complete description. To supplement what is shown on the chart, and to provide the full amount of data to assist a navigator in locating, identifying, and using aids to navigation, there are two other series of publications; these are the *Light Lists* (see figure 403) prepared by the U.S. Coast Guard (printed and sold by the Government Printing Office) and the *Lists of Lights* published by DMAHTC.

The Coast Guard *Light Lists* are published in seven volumes covering the U.S. coasts (including island possessions), the Great Lakes, and the Mississippi River system. These are complete listings of all lights, buoys, daybeacons, ranges, fog signals, radiobeacons, and radar beacons (RACONs); detailed information is given on each aid including position (where necessary), shape, color, and characteristics. Typical of details *not* shown on a chart, but shown in a *Light List,* is information that the

aids to navigation along a certain channel are 150 feet back from the channel limits rather than at the edge, or that certain lighted buoys are removed or replaced by unlighted buoys during specified months because they may be endangered by ice.

In addition, each *Light List* volume contains introductory pages with general information on aids to navigation and their use, and the Loran radionavigation system; color illustrations are included of various aids in the U.S. lateral system and the Uniform State Waterway Marking System. Aids are tabulated in the same sequence as lights are numbered—basically, clockwise around the U.S. coasts from Maine to Florida to Texas, California to Washington, east to west on the Great Lakes, and upriver in the Mississippi River System; seacoast aids are listed first in the applicable volumes, followed by harbor and river aids, and then Intracoastal Waterways aids, if applicable. Each volume of the *Light Lists* is republished annually, but during the year should be kept continuously corrected from *Notices to Mariners* and *Local Notices to Mariners* (see article 611).

The DMAHTC *Lists of Lights,* seven volumes, cover foreign coasts of the world (and limited portions of U.S. coasts); these are Pubs. No. 110 through 116 (see figure 604). They include descriptive information similar to *Light Lists,* but because of their greater coverage areas, they list only lighted aids to navigation and fog signals (lighted buoys within harbors are omitted). Each *List of Lights* is published in a new edition at intervals of approximately twelve months; changes and corrections are included frequently, as they are required, in *Notices to Mariners.*

Coast Pilots and Sailing Directions

605 Just as for aids to navigation, charts are limited in what can be shown by symbols and abbreviations regarding channels, hazards, winds and currents, restricted areas, port facilities, pilotage service, and many other types of information needed by a navigator for safe and efficient navigation. These deficiencies are remedied by the *Coast Pilots* published by NOS and the *Sailing Directions* published by DMAHTC.

U.S. Coast Pilots are published in nine numbered volumes to cover the waters of the United States and its possessions. They are of great value to a navigator when used with charts of an area both during the planning stage of a voyage and in the actual transit of the area. The contents of *Coast Pilots* have been stored in a computerized data bank,

(1) No.	(2) Name and location	(3) Position lat. long.	(4) Characteristic and power	(5) Height	(6) Range (miles)	(7) Structure, height (feet)	(8) Sectors. Remarks. Fog signals
	FRANCE—WEST COAST						
		N. W.					
	GIRONDE ENTRANCE:						
	— Passe Sud:						
2390 D 1310	— — Entrance range, front, Saint Nicolas.	45 34 1 05	F. G . . . . Cp. 100,000	72 **22**	14	White quadrangular tower; 29.	Intensified 2° each side of axis.
2390.1 D 1310.1	— — — Rear, **Pointe de Grave**, 63° from front.	45 34 1 04	Occ. W. R. G. . . . . period 4ˢ lt. 3ˢ, ec. 1ˢ Cp. W. 20,000 R. 4,000 G. 2,500	85 **26**	14	Square white tower, angles and top black; 82.	W. 330°–233°30', R.–303°, W.–312°, G.–330°. **Radiobeacon.**
2395 D 1312	— — **Le Chay** Range, front.	45 37 1 03	F. R . . . . Cp. 20,000	105 **32**	16	White tower, red top; 44 . . .	Intensified 1°30' each side of axis.
2395.1 D 1312.1	— — — Rear, **Saint Pierre**, about 1,990 yards 41° from front.	. . . .	F. R . . . . Cp. 10,000	197 **60**	14	Light gray water tower, red support; 128.	Intensified 2ˢ each side of axis.
	GIRONDE:						
2400 D 1314	— Port Bloc, head of N. mole.	45 34 1 04	Fl. G . . . . period 4ˢ fl. 1ˢ, ec. 3ˢ Cp. 60	18 **5**	7	Black pylon; 13	
2410 D 1316	— — Head of S. mole	. . . .	Iso. W . . . . period 4ˢ Cp. 120	26 **8**	8	White tower, red top; 20 . . .	
2420 D 1328	— Le Verdon sur Mer, head of pier.	45 33 1 02	Gp. Fl. W. G. (3) . . . . . period 12ˢ Cp. W. 500 G. 60	56 **17**	W. 12 G. 7	White pylon, green top; 42 .	G. 215°–172°, W.–215°.
2425	— — Range, front	45 32 1 02	Qk. Fl. W . . . . Fl. G . . . . period 2ˢ	16 **5**	9	White rectangular daymark with black stripe on dolphin. On same dolphin	
2425.1	— — — Rear, 435 yards 172° from front.	. . . .	Qk. Fl. W . . . . Fl. G . . . . period 2ˢ	30 **9**	11	White rectangular daymark with black stripe on dolphin. On same dolphin.	
2430 D 1330	— Pointe de la Chambrette .	45 33 1 03	F. G	25 **8**	3	Iron column	2 F. G. lights are shown 185 yards 73°, marking extremities of a jetty.
	— Royan:						
2460 D 1304	— — South Jetty	45 37 1 02	Gp. Occ. W. R. (1+3) . period 12ˢ lt. 1ˢ, ec. 1ˢ lt. 1ˢ, ec. 1ˢ lt. 3ˢ, ec. 1ˢ lt. 3ˢ, ec. 1ˢ Cp. W. 1,200 R. 240	36 **11**	10	White tower, red base; 30 . .	R. 199°–220°, W.–116°. **Horn:** 2 bl. ev. 30ˢ.
2470 D 1306	— — North Jetty	45 37 1 02	Gp. Occ. W. R. (1+3) . period 12ˢ lt. 3ˢ, ec. 1ˢ lt. 3ˢ, ec. 1ˢ lt. 1ˢ, ec. 1ˢ lt. 1ˢ, ec. 1ˢ Cp. W. 1,200 R. 240	52 **16**	W. 11 R. 10	White pylon, red base; 43 . .	W. 95°–285°, R.–35°. Synchronized with No. 2460.

Figure 604. *List of Lights* (extract from DMAHTC Pub. No. 113).

and volumes are reprinted annually with all intervening changes included (except CP8 and CP9, which are revised every two years). Interim changes are published in *Notices to Mariners* and *Local Notices to Mariners*.

The DMAHTC *Sailing Directions* provide information comparable to the *Coast Pilots*, but for foreign coasts and coastal waters, and again contain much data that cannot conveniently be shown on charts. The appropriate volume of *Sailing Directions*, used with charts of a suitable scale, should enable a navigator to approach strange waters with adequate information for his vessel's safety. The conversion from the former series of 70 looseleaf volumes to a new set of 43 publications—8 *Planning Guides* for ocean basin transits and 35 *Enroute* directions for coastal waters and ports—is essentially completed.

The new-style *Sailing Directions* are based on a division of the world's waters into eight "ocean basins" (but these are *not* the same as those used for two- and three-digit chart numbers). The revised *Sailing Directions* are given three-digit DMAHTC Pub. Nos. starting with a "1"; the second digit is a number according to the ocean basin concerned; the third digit is "0" for the *Planning Guide*, and "1" through "9" for the various *Enroute* directions. (Exceptions are ocean basin 5, the North Pacific; here the *Planning Guide* is Pub. No. 152, as the number "150" was already assigned to the *World Port Index*, and "151" to the *Table of Distances Between Ports;* and ocean basin 2, the South Atlantic Ocean, where the *Planning Guide* is Pub. No. 121.)

The two components of the new *Sailing Directions* contain information as follows.

Planning Guide. Each covers an ocean basin containing chapters of useful information about countries adjacent to that particular ocean basin; information relative to the physical environment and local coastal phenomena; references to publications and periodicals listing danger areas; recommended ship routes; detailed electronic navigation systems and buoyage systems pertaining to that ocean basin.

Enroute. Each includes detailed coastal and port approach information, supplementing the largest scale chart available from DMAHTC. It is intended for use in conjunction with the *Planning Guide* for the ocean basin concerned. Each *Enroute* volume is divided into a number of *sectors*, and for each sector information is provided on available charts (with limits shown on an overall diagram as in U.S. chart catalogs); winds, tides, and currents (shown on an outline chart); off-lying dangers; coastal features; anchorages; and major ports (an annotated chartlet with line drawings of aids to navigation and prominent landmarks). Figure 605 shows the limits for the various enroute guides of the North Atlantic Ocean basin.

Changes for each *Planning Guide* and *Enroute* volume are prepared and published on an as-required basis determined by the number of accumulated revisions.

The port facilities data, formerly scattered throughout the old *Sailing Directions*, has been computerized and tabulated in an expanded edition of Pub. No. 150, *World Port Index*, designed as a companion volume to be used in conjunction with the new *Sailing Directions*.

Fleet Guides

606 The Defense Mapping Agency Hydrographic/Topographic Center publishes, for U.S. Navy use only, *Fleet Guides*. These are Pub. No. 940, Atlantic Area, and Pub. No. 941, Pacific Area. These guides contain a number of chapters, each of which covers a port of major interest to naval vessels. They are prepared to provide important command, navigational, repair, and logistic information. This information is much like that contained in *Coast Pilots* and *Sailing Directions*, but is oriented toward naval interests and requirements; they are not needed by, nor are they available to, non-naval vessels.

Data in *Fleet Guides* are corrected and updated through the publication of changes and/or new editions when required; interim corrections are published in *Notices to Mariners* if the urgency so warrants.

Navigational Tables

607 Navigational tables are published to meet many different needs. Some of those most often used by navigators include:

Tide Tables: prediction tables published by National Ocean Service, in four volumes—*East Coast of North and South America, including Greenland; West Coast of North and South America, including the Hawaiian Islands; Europe and the West Coast of Africa, including the Mediterranean Sea;* and *Central and Western Pacific Ocean and the Indian Ocean* (annual editions). Each volume includes data on the height and time of high and low water at thousands of locations; also included are data on times of sunrise and sunset, moonrise and moonset, and other astronomical phenomena (see chapter 9).

Tidal Current Tables: prediction tables published by NOS, in two volumes—*Atlantic Coast of North*

Figure 605. Limits for *Enroute* volumes of *Sailing Directions, North Atlantic Ocean.*

America, and *Pacific Coast of North America and Asia* (annual editions); each volume includes data on the times and strengths of flood and ebb currents and the time of slack water for thousands of locations; also included are diagrams for certain heavily traveled bodies of water that facilitate determination of optimum transit times and speeds, and astronomical data similar to that in *Tide Tables* (see chapter 10).

Tables of Distances Between United States Ports: published by NOS; tabulates approximately 10,000 distances along the shortest routes marked by aids to navigation.

Table of Distances Between Ports, Pub. No. 151; published by DMAHTC; supplements the NOS publication with more than 40,000 distances between U.S. and foreign ports, and between foreign ports.

Sight Reduction Tables for Marine Navigation, Pub. No. 229, published by DMAHTC, in six vol-

umes, each volume covering 16° of latitude, North or South (1° overlap between volumes) (see chapter 24).

Sight Reduction Tables for Air Navigation, Pub. No. 249, published by DMAHTC in three volumes; offers somewhat greater ease and speed in sight reduction, but has a limited range of declination and gives a lower order of precision as to position (see chapter 24).

Almanacs

608 Volumes tabulating the position of various celestial bodies used by navigators, and the times of sunrise and sunset, moonrise and moonset, and other astronomical data of interest to navigators, are prepared jointly by the U.S. Naval Observatory and the Royal Greenwich Observatory in England. However, the almanacs are printed separately (in the United States by the Government Printing Office). The *Nautical Almanac,* published annually,

Figure 608. The *Nautical Almanac,* published in annual editions.

and the *Air Almanac,* published twice each year, give ephemeristic data for marine and air navigation respectively (the *Air Almanac* can be, and sometimes is, used by marine surface navigators). These volumes are used in many other countries with minor modifications, chiefly changes in the language used for page headings and in the explanatory material. The *Almanac for Computers* is also published by the U.S. Naval Observatory with mathematical data and instructions for the computation of ephemeristic data using electronic computers or advanced models of calculators. These almanacs are discussed in chapter 23.

The *Astronomical Almanac* (formerly the *American Ephemeris and Nautical Almanac*), published annually by the Naval Observatory, contains the information in the *Nautical Almanac* plus a considerable amount of data of interest primarily to astronomers.

Books and Manuals

609 Perhaps the best-known and most encyclopedic of all navigation books is the *American Practical Navigator,* DMAHTC Pub. No. 9, generally referred to simply as *Bowditch.* It first appeared in 1802 and has since been revised many times. The book was originally published because of the need for a simply written, complete text on navigation, with the necessary tables and explanations to permit the relatively uneducated mariner of a century and a half ago to navigate. The book immediately became popular because it was so much better and more reliable than any other book of its time. It has

now become primarily a reference book, and will be found in any collection of books on navigation. The latest revision is printed in two volumes: Volume I, 1984, and Volume II, 1981.

Other useful and often used navigation books are:

Handbook of Magnetic Compass Adjustment & Compensation: DMAHTC Pub. No. 226.

Maneuvering Board Manual: DMAHTC Pub. No. 217.

Radar Navigation Manual: DMAHTC Pub. No. 1310.

Other Publications

610 There are other publications that are of interest to navigators, but which do not fit easily into one of the above categories; among these are:

Pilot Charts. Published by DMAHTC for the North Atlantic Ocean, *Chart No. 16,* and for the North Pacific Ocean, *Chart No. 55.* These charts present available data in graphic form that will assist the mariner in selecting the safest and fastest routes. Besides timely information of a varied nature, pilot charts graphically depict magnetic variation, currents, prevailing winds and calms, percentage of gales, tracks of tropical and extratropical cyclones, wave heights, surface air and water temperatures, percentage of fog, surface barometric pressure, ice and iceberg limits, the location of ocean weather-station ships, and recommended routes for steam and sailing vessels. Additionally, such topics as winds (including gales and cyclones), pressures, temperatures, visibilities, and wave heights are discussed in brief paragraphs at the sides of each chart. Pilot charts are published quarterly with each sheet containing three monthly charts and an article of general information. They are furnished without charge to contributing observers, and automatically to naval vessels after an initial request; they may be purchased in the usual manner by others interested in their contents.

Pilot charts are published in atlas form (for certain specific prior years) for the South Atlantic Ocean, Pub. No. 105; for Central American Waters and the South Atlantic, Pub. No. 106; for the South Pacific Ocean, Pub. No. 107; for the Northern North Atlantic, Pub. No. 108; and Indian Ocean, Pub. No. 109.

Radio Navigational Aids. Pub. No. 117, published by DMAHTC, contains information on marine direction-finder stations, radiobeacons, Consol stations, Loran, Decca, Racon, Radar, time signals, times and transmission frequencies of navigational warnings, the delineation of *Hydro-*

lant and *Hydropac* areas, medical advice and quarantine stations, long-range navigational aids, and radio regulations for territorial waters.

Worldwide Marine Weather Broadcasts. Published by the National Oceanic and Atmospheric Administration.

Catalog of Maps, Charts, and Related Products. Published by the Defense Mapping Agency (DMA); Part 2 relates to hydrographic products and contains 11 volumes. These volumes are described in article 521.

Guide to Marine Observing and Reporting. Pub. No. 606 is a collaborative effort of several U.S. governmental agencies to provide detailed guidance for submitting hydrographic and oceanographic reports. Check lists of key questions are included, where appropriate, as a means of ensuring that no essential facts will be inadvertently omitted from a report.

Loran-C User Handbook. Published by the U.S. Coast Guard as COMDTINST M16562.3; contains descriptive information, in an easy-to-read style, regarding the Loran-C system and its use. This is supplemented by the quarterly *Radionavigation Bulletin* from the same office, which also covers radiobeacons, Omega, and other systems as well as Loran.

Corrective Information

611 As charts and other publications accumulate a sufficient number of changes and corrections, they are reprinted as a revision with the same edition number or as a new edition. Certain publications, such as *Light Lists* and *Coast Pilots*, are reprinted on an annual schedule. Other publications may have numbered "changes" issued, usually in the form of reprinted pages for direct insertion into the volume after the superseded pages are removed.

Notice to Mariners

In many instances the importance of the corrected or updated information is such that it cannot be delayed until the next scheduled transmittal of changes, or the revised or new edition. In such cases, the information is included in the weekly *Notice to Mariners* published by DMAHTC with the cooperation of NOS and the Coast Guard. This printed pamphlet includes corrections for charts, listed in numerical order, with a separate entry for each chart affected; in order that corrections will not be overlooked, each entry also indicates the number of the *Notice* carrying the last previous correction. New charts and publications and new or revised editions are announced in *Notice to Mari-*

ners. This publication also carries corrections for other publications such as *Coast Pilots, Sailing Directions, Light Lists* and *Lists of Lights, Radio Navigational Aids,* and *Fleet Guides.* Small chartlets for pasting onto charts to correct limited areas are printed in the weekly *Notice,* as well as information of general interest to navigators. Broadcast NAVAREA WARNINGS for Areas IV and XII and *Hydrolant* and *Hydropac* messages for the preceding week are printed in each *Notice.* Quarterly, an issue of *Notice to Mariners* will contain a summary, listing by number the charts affected by changes during that period, with the numbers of applicable *Notices. Notice to Mariners No. 1* of each year includes additional information of continuing interest.

Modern technology has made possible the *Automated Notice to Mariners System* (ANMS). The weekly *Notices* are compiled from a digitalized data base tied in with that which is now producing computerized nautical charts (see article 515). Publication is expedited, and users can query the data base using modern communications links from anywhere in the world at any time. This means, for example, that a ship entering a port or area of hazardous waters can obtain up-to-the-minute information on chart changes or navigational warnings. A navigator in a distant port can obtain all the latest information on the route and ports ahead of him before he departs. Use is made of dial-up telephone lines with a small portable terminal or Telex links. Satellite transmissions are used from vessels on the high seas. Users pay the cost of communication links that can also be used in the reverse direction to feed information into the data base. A *Users Manual* is available from DMAHTC for the Automated Notice to Mariners System.

A separate edition of *Notice to Mariners* for the Great Lakes is published by the 9th Coast Guard District for those waters and tributaries east to Montreal, Canada.

Summary of Corrections

Semiannually, DMAHTC publishes a *Summary of Corrections* in six volumes—Volume 1 for the East Coast of North and South America; Volume 2 for the Eastern Atlantic and Arctic Oceans and Mediterranean Sea; Volume 3 for the West Coast of North and South America, including Antarctica; Volume 4 for the Western Pacific and Indian Oceans; and Volume 5 for World and Ocean Basin Charts, *Coast Pilots, Sailing Directions, Fleet Guides,* and miscellaneous publications. Volume 6 is for classified charts and publications, with distribution limited to government activities on a need-to-

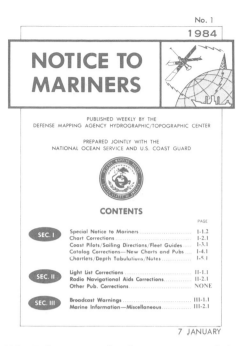

Figure 611a. Information for the correction of charts and certain publications is published weekly in *Notices to Mariners*.

know basis. Volumes of the *Summary of Corrections* are published on a staggered basis; the schedule of publications for each volume is listed in *Volume X of the DMA Chart Catalog, Part 2*. Each issue contains the full text of all applicable corrections; when any volume gets too large for convenient use, DMAHTC will begin a new series. If a new edition of a chart is issued in the six-month period between issues, corrections for the old edition are omitted. Changes listed in a previous *Summary* are not repeated.

Paste-on corrections as chartlets, depth tabulations, and chart notes are included in the back portion of the appropriate region. In cases where the paste-on corrections supersede previously issued similar items, only the latest item is included.

The *Summary of Corrections*, with the full text of all changes, is easier to use than the quarterly listings in *Notices to Mariners*, which give only the numbers of the charts affected without providing the information necessary to make the change. The *Summary* is particularly valuable in bringing charts fully up-to-date when they have been obtained some time after their publication date, such as the initial set of charts for a newly commissioned vessel, or when charts have not been used and kept corrected for some time. The *Summary* is *not* a complete substitute for the *Notices to Mariners*; these must still be used for changes affecting

Light Lists, Lists of Lights, and other navigational publications.

It should be noted that copies of the *Summary of Corrections* are not furnished without charge to nongovernmental navigators, as in the case of *Notices to Mariners*. Copies must be purchased individually or as part of an annual subscription (two issues).

Local Notices to Mariners

Since the publications just described are worldwide in scope, changes that are of local interest only, of no concern to ocean-going ships, are omitted. Such information is published in *Local Notices to Mariners*, which are issued separately by each U.S. Coast Guard District at weekly intervals, or as required. The type of information is generally the same as for the worldwide *Notices;* items from those *Notices* are repeated in *Local Notices* if they are of interest to small vessels and craft of the waters covered.

Radio Broadcast Warnings

Often it is necessary for the safety of navigation to promulgate information without delay; radio broadcasts serve to accomplish this action. A worldwide navigational broadcast warning system having 16 long-range warning areas is operated by member nations of the International Hydrographic Organization; these NAVAREAs are shown in figure 611b. An Area Coordinator is designated for each and is responsible for assembling and evaluating information from various sources and then issuing an appropriate NAVAREA *Warnings* broadcast by a powerful radio station to cover the whole of that Area and parts of adjacent Areas. The various NAVAREAs are subdivided into *Sub-areas* (in which a number of countries have established a coordinated system of the transmission of coastal warnings) and *Regions* (portions of an Area or Sub-area in which one country has accepted responsibility for the transmission of coastal warnings). Radio broadcast details are contained in **DMAHTC Pub. No. 117, as kept current by changes published in** *Notices to Mariners*.

The United States is Area Coordinator for Areas IV and XII, and is also providing worldwide coverage by continuing the *Hydrolant* and *Hydropac* Navigational Warning System outside Areas IV and XII. (*Hydrolant*s cover the Atlantic Ocean, Gulf of Mexico, Caribbean Sea, and contiguous areas; *Hydropac*s cover the Pacific Ocean, Indian Ocean, and contiguous areas.) The location that is affected in these messages is indicated by the chart numbering system—region or subregion numerical de-

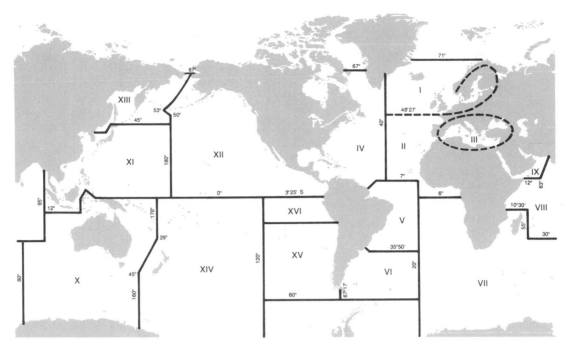

Figure 611b. A system of area responsibilities for radio broadcasts has been established to disseminate navigational safety information.

signators are a part of the *Hydrolant/Hydropac* number.

For U.S. coastal and inland waters, Coast Guard radio stations transmit *Broadcast Notices to Mariners;* in some instances, these may also be transmitted by Navy and/or commercial (public correspondence) radio stations. Information remaining in effect is included in the next issue of *Local Notices to Mariners.* Other countries will generally have somewhat similar local broadcasts of warnings relating to defective aids to navigation and other hazards; details on stations, frequencies, time, etc., will be found in *Radio Navigational Aids,* Pub. No. 117.

Other Warnings

The DMAHTC *Daily Memorandum* is issued in two editions, Atlantic and Pacific; both are prepared at DMAHTC headquarters, Washington, D.C. This publication is of value to ships in port, both naval and merchant. Together with other items of navigational interest, each *Daily Memorandum* contains the text of applicable NAVAREA WARNINGS for Areas IV and XII and *Hydrolant* and *Hydropac* messages broadcast in the previous 24 hours, or since the last previous working day, with the exception of messages containing satellite ephemeral data.

Special Warnings supplement regular DMAHTC messages such as *Hydrolant* and *Hydropac;* they are used primarily for the dissemination of official governmental proclamations affecting commercial shipping restrictions. These warnings are consecutively numbered and are given further publicity in the *Daily Memorandum* and *Notices to Mariners.*

The Importance of Accurate, Up-to-date Information

612 A navigator has many sources of information available to him to ensure the safe and efficient passage of his ship; a well-organized system exists to provide the latest data for keeping charts and other publications up to date. He should know what is available to him and how to obtain it. The navigator of a vessel of any size should *study* the applicable publications and charts covering his operating areas; such studying should be done well in advance of the need for the knowledge—a time of danger or emergency is *not* the time to be hastily thumbing through an unfamiliar publication.

Failure to have on board and use the *latest* charts and other publications, *and to keep them corrected,* may adversely affect a mariner's legal position should he have a grounding, collision, or other mishap in which chart or publication information is involved.

Chapter 7

Instruments for Piloting

Introduction

701 As noted in chapter 1, navigation is both an art and a science, and this is reflected in the "tools of the trade." This chapter will describe some of the instruments and devices available to a navigator for determining the position of his vessel and guiding it safely and efficiently on its way.

Navigational instruments can be classified in various ways, any of which will result in some overlap. They will be considered here in groups according to their primary purpose—for measuring *direction*, *speed* and *distance*, *depth*, and *weather conditions;* for use in *plotting;* and for *miscellaneous* use. Earlier chapters have considered the compass and other "instruments" such as charts and publications. Sextants and chronometers will be covered later in the chapters relating to celestial navigation.

DIRECTION

Compasses

702 The two general types of compasses are: *magnetic compass*, which depends on the earth's magnetic field for its directive force; and *gyrocompass*, which depends upon the inherent stability in space of a rapidly spinning wheel plus mechanical or electrical torquing to keep its axis aligned with that of the earth. Marine compasses were discussed in chapter 3.

Gyrocompass Repeaters

703 A gyrocompass can transmit constant indications of true headings electrically to *gyrocompass repeaters* located at various positions throughout the ship. These repeaters resemble a magnetic compass in appearance, but unlike a magnetic compass they may be mounted in any position.

Azimuth Circle

704 The term *azimuth* is most often used for stating the direction of a celestial body, with *bearing* used for the direction of terrestrial objects. This division, however, is not rigid, and at times the terms are used interchangeably. Bearings and azimuths are expressed in degrees, using three digits, from 000° at north clockwise through 360°. True azimuth or bearing refers to direction with respect to true north, magnetic azimuth with respect to magnetic north, and compass azimuth with respect to north as indicated by the compass being used. A *relative* bearing or azimuth is reckoned from the ship's head, measuring clockwise with 000° being dead ahead.

An *azimuth circle* (see also *bearing circle* below) can be used for determining both *azimuths* of celestial bodies and bearings of terrestrial objects. It consists of a nonmagnetic ring formed to fit snugly over the top of a compass bowl (or onto the top of a gyrocompass repeater), about which it can be turned to any desired direction. Its inner lip is graduated from 0° to 360°, *counterclockwise*, for measuring relative bearings. An azimuth circle is shown in figure 704. On one diameter of this ring is mounted a pair of sighting vanes, consisting of a peep vane (A) at one end of the diameter and a vertical wire mounted in a suitable frame at the other end (B). To observe the bearing of a terrestrial object, the observer looks through the peep vane in the direction of the object, and by means of the finger lugs (C, C') provided on the circle, he turns the

Figure 704. Azimuth circle to fit U.S. Navy standard 7½-inch compass.

latter until the observed object appears on the vertical wire of the opposite vane. At the base of the opposite vane is a mirror (D) marked with a centerline agreeing with the vertical wire of the vane. This mirror reflects the compass card into the observer's field of view so that he can see the observed object and the compass card at the same time. The compass bearing of the observed object is then read by the position of the vertical wire on the reflected compass card.

There is a reflector of dark glass (E) attached to the far vane (called *far* vane because it is *farther* from the eye, in observing, than the peep vane). The reflector is movable about a horizontal axis, enabling the observer to adjust it so that the reflected image of a celestial body can be brought to his eye, and a compass azimuth obtained as has been described for a terrestrial object.

At right angles to the line of sight of the pair of vanes just described, there is a second set of observing devices, designed especially for obtaining a compass azimuth of the sun. At one extremity of the diameter on which these appliances are mounted is a 45° reflecting prism encased in a metal housing (F). This housing is provided with a narrow slit in which light may be received from a concave mirror diametrically opposite (G), the slit being at the focus of the concave mirror. Light so received is reflected downwards by the prism and appears on the graduations of the compass card as a bright narrow band. To observe the compass bearing of the sun with this arrangement, the observer turns the azimuth circle until the sun's rays are reflected by the mirror across the card to the prism, when the bearing can be read on the compass card by means of the narrow band of light.

Two leveling bubbles (H, H′) are provided, one under each far sight vane. The appropriate bubble

is used to level the instrument in the vertical plane through the line of sight, and so eliminate a possible source of inaccuracy.

Relative bearings or azimuths can be obtained by reading the graduations of the azimuth circle against a mark on the bezel ring, colinear with the lubber's line of the compass. (See article 307.)

An azimuth circle without the prism-mirror appliance for sun observation is called a *bearing circle*. It serves the same purpose as an azimuth circle, except that azimuths of the sun are not as conveniently measured.

Telescopic Alidade

705 A *telescopic alidade* is similar to a bearing circle except that the alidade circle mounts a telescope instead of the sighting vanes. The telescope contains a reticle for greater precision in taking bearings. The image is magnified, making distant objects appear larger to the observer. A prism arrangement that reflects the bearing of the object from the compass card enables the observer to sight the object and its bearing simultaneously.

Pelorus

706 Since a clear view in all directions may be unobtainable from the compass, a *pelorus* (figure 706) or dumb compass may be mounted at convenient points, such as the wing of a bridge. It is less desirable than a gyrocompass repeater fitted with an azimuth or bearing circle, but it will meet the needs of small craft or vessels lacking more sophisticated equipment.

A pelorus consists essentially of a flat, nonmagnetic, metallic ring mounted in gimbals on a vertical stand. The inner edge of the ring is graduated in degrees from 0° at the ship's head clockwise through 360°. This ring snugly encloses a compass card called a *pelorus card*. The card, flush with the ring and the top of the bowl, is rotatable, so that any chosen degree of its graduation may be set to the lubber's line. A small set screw is provided for temporarily securing the card to the ring. Upon the card is mounted a pair of sighting vanes similar to those of a bearing circle. They may be revolved about the center of the card, *independently of the card itself*, and held in any desired position by a central clamp screw. On some models an electric light inside the stand illuminates the card from underneath for night work.

Taking True Bearings

True bearings are obtained as follows: set the pelorus to the ship's *true* course, by turning the card

Figure 706. A pelorus, used for taking relative bearings.

until its true-course graduation coincides with the lubber's line. Secure the card. Line up the sighting vanes approximately on the object to be observed. Direct the steersman to say "Mark! Mark! Mark!" when he is steady on his steering compass course, and when he does so, take the bearing exactly, and read the degree on the card as indicated by the sighting vanes.

As an alternative method of obtaining a true bearing, the navigator gives the steersman a warning "Stand by!" followed by a "Mark!" at the instant of the observation. If the steersman was on his course, the bearing was *true*. If not, it may be corrected by applying the number of degrees the steersman was off, being careful to apply the correction in the proper direction.

Magnetic Bearings

Magnetic or compass bearings are taken in exactly the same manner as true bearings, the pelorus card being set beforehand to the magnetic or compass course, respectively. By applying to such bearings the variation or the compass error, as appropriate, they can be converted to true bearings (article 312) for plotting on a chart.

Relative Bearings

The pelorus is used for taking relative bearings by setting the 0° graduation of the card to the lubber's line and observing the object. Relative bearings are converted to true bearings for plotting by

adding the true heading of the ship to the bearings observed. In most modern installations on large ships, a gyro repeater is mounted in the pelorus stand in place of the pelorus card, so that gyro bearings can be obtained directly.

Hand-bearing Compass

707 On small craft, bearings are often taken with a *hand-bearing* compass. This is a small, portable compass that has sighting vanes or marks, may have a handle, and usually has some form of internal illumination for use at night. See figure 707. Its advantages stem from its ability to be carried to any place on deck from which a bearing can be taken on an object that might not be visible from the steering station due to the vessel's superstructure, sails, etc. Deviation may or may not exist at locations from which a hand-bearing compass is used; caution is advised. In the event of a failure (unlikely, but possible) of a boat's steering compass, a hand-bearing compass can be used quite adequately if consideration is given to the probability of different values of deviation.

SPEED AND DISTANCE

Types of Logs

708 A *log* is any device used to determine a vessel's *speed* or *distance traveled through the water*. Allowances or calculations must be made to determine speed and distance with respect to the bottom.

To determine a vessel's speed, the *chip log*, or *ship log*, was invented in the sixteenth century; it consisted of a piece of wood in the shape of a quadrant, weighted with lead at the center of the circular side. This log chip, as it was called, was secured to a bridle at each corner; the bridle, in turn, was secured to the log line. At one corner of the log chip, the bridle was held by a wooden peg so arranged that a sharp tug on the log line would pull out the peg, allowing the chip to be hauled back on board readily.

The log line was wound on a free-turning reel. To determine speed, the log chip was put overboard where it floated vertically due to its ballasting. A considerable length of log line was let out to get the log chip into undisturbed water astern where its resistance to forward motion kept it essentially stationary in the water; as the ship moved forward, the line was pulled off the reel. When the first knotted marker on the line passed off the reel, timing was started; at the end of a definite period, the line was seized and the number of knots in the line that

Figure 707. A hand-bearing compass.

had paid out were counted to determine the vessel's speed. From this arose the present use of the term *knot* to designate one nautical mile per hour.

The timing was originally done by reciting certain religious sentences, which, in theory, required an exact amount of time. Later, a sand glass was employed. This was usually a 30-second timer, and gave far more accurate results.

Modern Logs

Three types of modern logs are in general use on ships; some of these integrate values of speed to determine distance traveled as well as speed. These are: the pitot-static log, the impeller type, and the electromagnetic (EM) log. These logs all require the use of a *rodmeter* projecting through the bottom of the ship into the water. The rodmeter contains the sensing device used to determine speed. As the rodmeter can be damaged by striking submerged objects, it may be necessary to retract the unit in shallow water. A sea valve forms a support for the rodmeter and provides a means for closing the hull opening when the rodmeter is withdrawn or housed. The various logs have a remotely located *indicator-transmitter* housing the electrical or electromechanical parts. The signal received from the sensing device is converted into a readout of speed and distance traveled that can be transmitted by

synchronous motors or electronically to display units throughout the ship.

The dead-reckoning analyzer (article 724), the modern gyrocompass, and various navigational computers require an automatic input of speed that is also transmitted from the indicator-transmitter unit of the log.

Speed can also be measured using the *Doppler principle* (see chapter 37); this gives speed (and distance) with respect to the bottom rather than through the water.

Pitot-static Log

709 The rodmeter assembly of a *pitot-static* log detects both dynamic and static pressure. As a ship moves through the water, the forward side of the rodmeter is exposed to *dynamic* pressure that is proportional to the speed of the ship. Dynamic pressure is defined as the pressure on a surface resulting from a fluid in motion against that surface; it includes static pressure as well as that from the flow of the fluid. The pressure of still water is called *static* pressure. A *pitot tube* is a device by which the difference in dynamic and static pressures may be detected. Obviously, the difference of the two pressures will vary with the speed of the ship. The device consists of two tubes, one inside the other. One tube opens forward and is subjected to dynamic pressure when the ship is in motion; the other

Figure 708. A chip log, or ship log, for measuring a vessel's speed (now obsolete).

Figure 711a. Underwater log equipment; electromagnetic type, 0–40 knots.

opens athwartship and is exposed only to static pressure.

The control unit for converting the pressure indications into speed units consists of a sensitive bellows arrangement connected to the dynamic and static orifices of the rodmeter. Suitable mechanical and electrical linkage converts the movement of the bellows into rotary motion for transmission to the speed and distance indicators by self-synchronous motors.

Two types differing slightly in construction but using the pitot-static principle are in general use. They are commonly known as the Pitometer Log and the Bendix Underwater Log.

Impeller-type Log

710 An *impeller-type* log uses a propeller to produce an electrical signal by which the speed and distance traveled are indicated at one or more remote locations. Typically, a rodmeter head is projected about two feet out from the vessel's hull through a sea valve. The head assembly contains an 8-pole, two-phase, propeller-driven frequency generator. The impeller is driven by the water as the impeller moves through it. The frequency generated is directly proportional to ship's speed.

The output of the generator is amplified and passed to a master transmitter indicator where the number of alternations, reduced by gears, shows the mileage on a dial. The frequency of the alternating current, being proportional to the speed of the ship, is transmitted to the display mechanism that indicates the speed of the ship.

Electromagnetic Log

711 The *electromagnetic* (EM) log is generally calibrated for speeds from 0 to 40 knots. Components are shown in figure 711a. The rodmeter (A), which can be fixed to the hull, is generally retractable through a sea valve (B), as described in article 708. It is an induction device which produces a signal voltage that varies with the speed of the ship through the water. Any conductor will produce an electromagnetic field or voltage when it is moved across a magnetic field, or when a magnetic field is moved with respect to the conductor. It is this relative movement of the conductor and the magnetic field producing a measurable induced signal voltage that is used in the EM log. Figure 711b shows a cutaway view of the sensing unit in the rodmeter. The magnetic field, produced by a coil in the sensing unit, is set up in the water in which the ship is floating. Two Monel buttons, one on each side of the rodmeter, pick up the induced voltage as the ship moves through the water. A complete discussion of the principle involved and instructions for adjustment and repair are included in the manual supplied with each instrument.

The *indicator-transmitter*—labeled (C) in figure 711a—contains all the electrical and electromechanical parts of the log except the components in the rodmeter and remote-control unit. It indicates

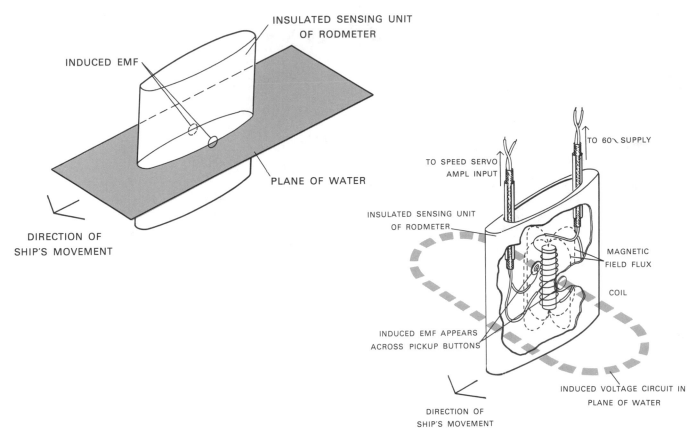

Figure 711b. Functional schematic of a rodmeter sensing unit.

the ship's speed on a dial, and operates synchro-transmitters to generate corresponding synchro-signals for transmission to receivers located elsewhere in the ship. It also registers the number of miles the ship has steamed. Provision is made in the indicator-transmitter for calibrating the log.

The *remote-control unit*—labeled (D) in figure 711a—is used to set speed into the indicator-transmitter when the equipment is being operated as a dummy log. (See article 712.)

In addition to the ship's forward motion, pitching and rolling will produce output signals from the rodmeter, which could lead to an indicated speed that is too high. Provision is made in the indicator-transmitter so that these undesirable signals can be rejected.

Continuing progress in solid-state electronics is being reflected in advances in the design of ships' logs, and a Doppler log is under development for naval vessels.

RPM Counters

712 An *engine revolution counter* provides a convenient means of determining speed and distance; these are widely used, especially on merchant ships. One of these instruments is in the engine room for each shaft; repeating indicators may be installed on the bridge. They automatically count the revolutions of the propellers and show the total count continuously on their dials. By means of a master counter connected to the individual counters, the average revolutions made by all propellers can be obtained. The output from these devices may be either a total number of revolutions or the rate in revolutions per minute (RPM), or both. The records of the acceptance trials of a ship furnish data as to the revolutions required for a mile, as well as RPM for various speeds. Such data can be derived, or verified, from later runs by the vessel over a measured mile, a number of which are available for this purpose. (A measured mile is not necessary; trials can be run over any known distance, with only slightly more complicated calculations required.) This information is used to construct a curve with RPM as ordinates and corresponding speed in knots as abscissas. From the curve, a *revolution table* is prepared for use on the bridge while underway. It gives the RPM required for each knot

Figure 713. Speedometer/log for small craft, impeller type.

of speed. In making use of engine revolutions as speed indicators, the draft of the ship, the condition of its bottom as to cleanliness, and the state of the sea must be considered.

When a vessel's regular log is not operating, speed information, based on shaft RPM, can be set by hand into a *dummy log*. This is necessary to supply speed data to the gyrocompass, a dead reckoning tracer (DRT) (article 724), and various computers that may be in use.

Small-craft Logs and Speedometers

713 On small craft, the term *speedometer* is commonly used to designate devices that measure only speed. The term *log* is applied to instruments that measure speed or distance, or both. Simplified versions of all three types discussed for larger vessels are used on commercial and recreational boats.

On smaller, faster boats, the common type of speedometer is a simple form of *pitot-static log*, with the indicating meter coupled directly to the sensing head by a length of tubing. The principal fault of this type is its lack of sensitivity at low speeds. On larger and slower boats, the *impeller type* is used in a "miniaturized" version. A small propeller-shaped or millwheel-design rotor projects from the hull a few inches; it may be fixed, or retractable for cleaning (problems of fouling with grass and weeds are not unknown). Indications of speed may be transmitted from the sensor to the indicator either mechanically or electrically.

A few models of the *electromagnetic* type have appeared for boats; the sensing elements are flush

with the hull or even entirely internal. Although more expensive than the impeller type, this design avoids the problem of fouling with weeds or marine growth that will adversely affect an impeller that cannot be withdrawn into the hull when not in use.

The indicator unit of impeller-type and electromagnetic logs may include additional circuitry for sensing small speed changes—useful in trimming sails—and/or for *integrating* speed measurements with respect to time in order to provide an output of distance traveled.

Many boats depend upon a *tachometer* giving engine RPM for a determination of speed. An RPM vs. speed table is prepared on a measured mile or other course of known length, and a graph is plotted as described for ships in article 712.

A few small craft, chiefly ocean-cruising sailboats, still use the traditional *taffrail log*. This consists of a rotor streamed at the end of a braided log line sufficiently far astern to be clear of the wake effect. The log line is connected to an indicating device, usually reading nautical miles and tenths on two separate dials. In sailing ships, this indicator was frequently attached to the taffrail, the hand rail at the after end of the ship, hence the name.

Good taffrail logs are quite reliable if kept clean of weeds and other floating debris, although all logs tend to over-read slightly when moving through a head sea, and to under-read with a following sea.

Stadimeters

714 A *stadimeter* is an instrument for measuring the distance of objects of known heights, between 50 and 200 feet, covering ranges from 200 to 10,000 yards. Other ranges can be measured by using a scale factor for the graduations. The two general types in use, the Fisk and the Brandon sextant type, are illustrated in figure 714.

The Fisk type stadimeter consists of a rectangular metal frame upon which is pivoted an index arm graduated in feet. The arm bears an index mirror directly above the pivot. By moving the arm this mirror is rotated through a small arc, providing the necessary adjustment between the direct and reflected images as viewed through the sighting telescope. The stadimeter measures the angle subtended by the object of known height and converts it into range, which is read directly from a micrometer drum attached to a pointer that moves the index arm. The instrument is initially set for the known height of the object by moving the carriage holding the drum and pointer along the index arm. The drum is then turned until the top of the

Figure 714. Stadimeters; Brandon sextant type (upper), and Fisk type (lower).

reflected image is brought into coincidence with the bottom of the direct image, and the range read.

The Brandon sextant-type stadimeter uses the same principle as the Fisk type, but the construction is different. The frame, similar in appearance to a sextant frame, has mounted upon it two pivoted arms, the index arm and radius arm. The radius arm is first positioned using the scale for the known height of the distant object sighted upon. Rotation of the micrometer drum moves the index arm, accomplishing the rotation of the index mirror necessary for the desired coincidence of images.

The adjustment of a stadimeter is similar to that of a sextant as described in chapter 24.

Distances of objects can also be ascertained by determining the angle subtended by an object of known height, as measured by a sextant. The angle so measured can be converted to distance by means of trigonometry or Table 9 in *Bowditch.*

DEPTH

Hand Lead and Deep-sea Lead

715 The *lead* (pronounced led), or *lead line,* for determining the depth of water consists essentially of a lead weight attached to one end of a suitably marked line. It is undoubtedly one of the oldest of piloting instruments.

Since the days of man's first ventures onto the waters, a mariner's major concern has been the depth of the water, the prevention of grounding. The first man who ran his dugout onto a shoal soon learned that he needed some way to find the depth of the water. Probably his first tool was a marked pole—a *sounding pole*—but the sounding line soon followed. From these developed the *deep-sea lead,* which could be used for greater depths. The base of the lead was concave, so that the hollow could be *armed* with tallow or salt-water soap, thus yielding both a sounding and a sample of bottom sediment to assist in determining position. From the *Historia* of the Greek historian, Herodotus, one learns that this technique was in use in and around the mouth of the Nile in the fourth century B.C.: "When one gets 11 fathoms and ooze on the lead, he is one day's journey from Alexandria." Even so long ago the nature of the bottom was of navigational significance.

Such soundings could be obtained only in the vicinity of the continental shelf, and only at comparatively long intervals, due to the time consumed in recovering by hand a lead of fifty or more pounds and a hundred or more fathoms of line. Later, greater depths could be measured with a *sounding machine* that used fine steel wire and mechanical methods for retrieving the weight and devices at its end. Due to currents and the forward motion of the ship, the sounding wire was normally not vertical, and so its length did not give a true indication of depth. *Sounding bottles* attached to the wire measured pressure at the bottom that could be translated to a measurement of depth. The sounding machine allowed accurate measurements of considerable depths, but only a very few measurements could be taken in an hour of continuous effort.

Modern technology has now eliminated the difficulties described above, but a lead line can still be a very valuable backup "tool" for a navigator, particularly when proceeding slowly in "thick" (foggy) weather and shallow waters. Of the various types of lead lines used for taking soundings, the two most common are the *hand lead,* weighing from 7 to 14 pounds, with a line marked to about 25 fathoms; and the *deep-sea lead*, weighing from 30 to 100 pounds, the line being 100 fathoms or more in length.

Lines are generally marked as follows:	*Metric Equivalent*
2 fathoms from the lead, with 2 strips of leather	3.66 meters
3 fathoms from the lead, with 3 strips of leather	5.49
5 fathoms from the lead, with a white rag	9.14
7 fathoms from the lead, with a red rag	12.80
10 fathoms from the lead, with leather having a hole in it	18.29
13 fathoms from the lead, same as at 3 fathoms	23.77
15 fathoms from the lead, same as at 5 fathoms	27.43
17 fathoms from the lead, same as at 7 fathoms	31.09
20 fathoms from the lead, a line with 2 knots	36.58
25 fathoms from the lead, a line with 1 knot	45.72
30 fathoms from the lead, a line with 3 knots	54.86
35 fathoms from the lead, a line with 1 knot	64.01
40 fathoms from the lead, a line with 4 knots	73.15

Fathoms that correspond with the marked depths are termed *marks* and intermediate fathoms are called *deeps*. The only fractions of a fathom used are a half and a quarter. A practice sometimes followed is to mark a hand lead line at the critical depths of the vessel using it.

Lead lines should be measured frequently while wet and the correctness of the markings verified. The distance from the leadman's hand to the water's surface should be known in order that proper allowance may be made in taking soundings at night.

Small vessels often use a lead line with a weight of 2 to 5 pounds on a line of 20 to 30 feet. The line is normally marked with plastic tags giving the depth directly in feet or meters. Boatmen may find a sounding pole useful in some circumstances, particularly if it is marked with the craft's draft and at whole feet above that depth.

Electronic Depth Sounders

716 A sound pulse generated in the water will echo from the bottom and can be received by a microphone. Since the speed of sound in water is known fairly closely, the depth can be determined by measuring the time interval between the generation of the sound and the return of the echo, according to the equation: depth = speed $\times \frac{1}{2}$ time interval between sound pulse and echo.

The speed of sound waves in water varies with the salinity of the water, its temperature, and the pressure (depth). The variation is not great, and most echo-sounding equipment of American manufacture is calibrated for a speed of 4,800 feet per second (1,463 m/s). At sea, the actual speed of travel of sound waves is nearly always slightly greater than this calibration speed, and any error introduced lies on the side of safety, except where the water is fresh or extremely cold. (If the equipment used in surveying the depths used the same calibration speed, there would be no error.) This assumed speed being equivalent to 800 fathoms per minute, an elapsed time of one second would indicate a depth of 400 fathoms.

Devices for measuring depth in this manner are variously known as *echo sounders* or *electronic depth sounders*. (The term "Fathometer" is often used, but this is properly applied only to the equipment of one manufacturer whose trademark it is.) The essential components of an electronic depth sounder are a *transmitter*, a *transducer*, a *receiver*, and a *display* (indicator or recorder). The transmitter and receiver are normally combined into a single unit; there may be both an indicator and a recorder.

Transmitter-receiver

The transmitter generates a pulse of electrical energy at either a *sonic* (audible) frequency in the range of 20 to 20,000 hertz or at an *ultrasonic* frequency, usually 150–200 kHz; the trend is now toward the higher frequencies, as these permit smaller transducers and sharper beams. The receiver amplifies the very weak returned echo and converts it to a form suitable for visual display.

Transducer

An electrical cable carries the electrical pulse from the transmitter to the transducer mounted on the vessel's hull where it is converted to sound (pressure) waves and sent directly downward in the shape of a cone. The returning echo is picked up by

Figure 716. Electronic depth sounder, commercial type.

the same transducer, converted to electrical energy, and sent back to the receiver by the same cable. (In a few instances, a separate receiving transducer and cable are used.)

On most large ships, the echo-sounding equipment generates a cone of 30° to 60° apex angle. The area of the bottom covered by such a cone is a function of depth; in deep water this can be quite large. The trend in the development of newer echo-sounding equipment is toward narrower beams, obtained by using higher frequencies (generally around 200 kHz), or larger transducers, or both. Higher frequencies, however, have the disadvantage of greater attenuation and lesser depth range; practical installation considerations place a restraint on transducer size. For survey work, complex arrays of multiple transducers may be used; transducers may be stabilized to counter ship's rolling and pitching motions that could result in erroneous data.

Depth sounders for smaller vessels commonly use either 50 or 200 kHz. Deeper depth penetration is achieved by the lower frequency pulses that employ transducers with sound cones of 40° to 60°. The higher frequency pulses are sent and received with transducers having sound cones of 8° to 12° that provide much sharper definition. Some more expensive models operate on either frequency as selected by a front-panel switch; these use a specially designed dual-frequency transducer that has a sound cone to match the frequency being used.

Display

Electronic depth sounder displays vary greatly in detail, but all operate on the same principle of indicating the elapsed time for a pulse to go to the bottom and return. Display types include rotary flashing light, digital readout, electrical meter, and bottom profile, which may be recorded on a moving paper chart or shown on a TV-like screen. Some models have the capability of operating on more than one range or displaying depth measurements in a choice of units—feet, fathoms, or meters; *it is essential that the navigator be certain what range and unit of measurement is being used.*

The flashing-light type has an arm that is mounted on the end of a shaft of a constant-speed motor. A flash occurs when the pulse is sent out—zero depth—and again when the echo returns. A scale is mounted over or just outside the end of the arm and calibrated in units of depth. One revolution of the arm corresponds to the range of the sounder, and the fraction of a revolution when the light flashes for the echo is proportional to the

depth. A recent development is a liquid-crystal display (LCD) that has the appearance of a rotating flashing light, but no moving parts.

Digital-readout models use electronic circuitry to provide a direct display of depth. Meter type units use a similar technique, but have now been largely displaced by the more easily read digital displays. Two or more ranges are available in some models.

Depth recorders provide a permanent indication, usually by means of a hot stylus and sensitized paper that moves across the face of the device. Some recorders also show instantaneous depth in a flashing-light or digital display. Many models include the "white (or gray) line" feature that electronically emphasizes the bottom contour and makes possible the detection of fish just above the bottom.

A more recent development is the echo sounder that displays a profile of the bottom on a rectangular TV-like picture tube. The profile moves across the screen as the vessel travels forward; no permanent record is made. Multiple colors may be used on some models to indicate different intensities of echos, and thus give an indication of the object—bottom or fish—that is returning the echo.

Electronic depth sounders used on small craft may use any of the displays discussed above. Because of the greater interest in shallower waters, maximum ranges will be less, and transmitters will operate at higher frequencies with less power; digital displays commonly show depths in tenths of a foot up to 10 feet, and in whole feet beyond that. Alarm buzzers are included in many units that will sound when depths decrease below a preset figure; on some models, an anchor alarm will sound when the depth either decreases or increases.

A U.S. Navy precision echo sounder of recent design, the AN/UQN-4, is described in article 3603.

PLOTTING EQUIPMENT

717 Most lines on a chart are made by means of a straightedge. Because of the width of the pencil lead and the conical shape of the sharpened end, the line ruled on the chart is a slight distance from the straightedge. Allowance for this distance must be made when placing the straightedge in position. The actual amount is easily determined by trial and error. The important point to remember is that the pencil must make the same angle with respect to the straightedge throughout the length of the line.

Use No. 2 pencils for plotting, and keep a number of them handy and well sharpened. Hexagonal pencils are less likely to roll off a chart table than are round pencils.

Draw only light lines on the chart, so that they can be easily erased. Avoid drawing lines longer than necessary, and erase extra lengths. Label all lines and points as soon as drawn. An unlabeled line on a chart is a possible source of error. Avoid drawing lines through symbols for navigational aids, so that the symbols will not be made less distinct when the line is later erased.

A soft eraser, such as the "Pink Pearl" type, should be used for making small erasures. An "art gum" eraser is best for a more general cleaning of a chart.

Dividers

718 Dividers are frequently used by the navigator. He keeps them handy for immediate use, primarily for measuring distance on the chart, but they have many other uses, also.

Learn to use the dividers with one hand, keeping the other hand free for other purposes. With a little practice this can be done easily and it will speed up plotting considerably. The dividers should be tight enough to remain as set, but not so tight that setting is difficult. If there is any choice, pick a pair of dividers with long legs, so that considerable distances can be measured with one setting. Some navigators prefer to use traditional "one-hand" dividers that are shaped so that a squeeze in one position closes the distance between the points, while a squeeze in another position opens the gap. See figure 718a.

It is frequently desirable to have a second pair of dividers of the "bow" style in which the distance between the points is set, and maintained, by a cross arm with a setting screw; see figure 718b. These can be set to a specific distance and left with assurance that they will not be changed accidentally.

Compasses

719 Drafting compasses (not to be confused with magnetic compasses) are convenient for drawing circles and arcs. They are used most frequently for drawing in computed visibility circles of lights, but they are also useful in drawing circles of position when the range of an object is known, for drawing circles of position for high-altitude celestial observations, and other purposes.

The statement regarding the use, adjustment, and selection of dividers applies also to compasses. The pencil point must be kept well sharpened for neat and accurate work.

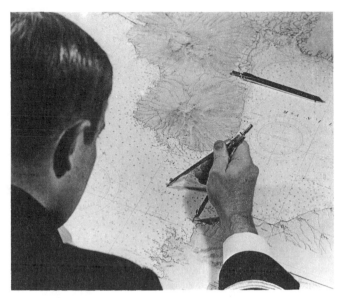

Figure 718a. Dividers are a basic piloting tool for measuring distances and plotting positions.

Figure 718b. "Bow" dividers are particularly useful as their setting cannot be accidentally changed.

Parallel Rulers

720 Although various types of plotters have appeared, and some are widely used, parallel rulers are still used by some navigators for measuring direction on a chart. Several types of parallel rulers are available. The best known consists of two bars—the "rulers"—of the same length connected by a mechanical linkage in such a manner that when one ruler is held in place on the chart and the other moved, the orientation of the ruler that is moved will remain parallel to the stationary ruler, and thus a line drawn using it is parallel to the original direction.

Parallel rulers are used for drawing straight lines, moving lines parallel to themselves (as in advancing lines of position), and for measuring direction. When the direction of a line is to be measured, one of the rulers is placed on the line and held firmly in place; the other ruler is opened away from the fixed ruler in the direction of the nearest *compass rose*. This ruler is then aligned with the center of the compass rose and the direction is read from its graduations. It may be necessary to "walk" the ruler through several steps to reach the compass rose, alternating the two rulers as stationary and moving. The key to successful operation is to press the stationary ruler *firmly* against the chart while the other ruler is being moved—slippage at this time will destroy the accuracy of the measurement. To plot a desired direction from a point on the chart, the direction is transferred by the parallel rulers from the compass rose to the given point.

Plotters

721 Parallel rulers are somewhat slow, and it is sometimes difficult to keep them from slipping when a direction is to be moved a considerable distance across the chart. Moreover, they are of little value for measuring direction when no compass rose is shown on the chart, as on those of polyconic or Lambert conformal projection.

For these reasons and as a matter of personal preference, many navigators use one of the various plotters that are available. Most of these consist of some form of protractor and a straightedge.

A typical plotter-protractor is shown in figure 721a. The rectangular piece of plastic has a 180° scale for measuring directions relative to any meridian; an auxiliary scale, rotated 90°, permits measuring relative to any parallel of latitude (as shown, it is measuring 186° from A to B). Some such plotters have distance markings on the longer edges at typical chart scales.

The Parallel Plotter, figure 721b, is a device that can be used as either a plotter or a roller-type parallel ruler. It is convenient for use on small craft and has been adopted by many ship navigators.

A pair of ordinary draftsman's triangles is also useful in plotting; they need not be of the same type or size. The two hypotenuse (longest) sides are placed together, and the pair is aligned so that the chart line or desired direction is along one of the other four sides; see figure 721c. By holding one triangle firmly in place and sliding the other with respect to it, alternating between them if the distance is great, the original direction, or one at right angles to it, can be transferred across the chart. The

Figure 721a. Aircraft-type "AN" plotter, often used in marine navigation.

use of two triangles provides an easy and accurate means of drawing both a line and another line at right angles to the first one as is needed when plotting celestial sight reductions.

Protractors

722 While not essential, a common protractor is sometimes useful for measuring angles. Any type will do, but a fairly large one made of transparent plastic is most desirable. One model has several small cutouts in its face so that it can be used for drawing standard plotting symbols.

A special type of protractor with three arms is useful for plotting the position of a vessel. The middle arm is fixed and the others movable so that they can be set at essentially any angle to the fixed arm. A complete description of this instrument and the method of using it is given in article 1110; the instrument is illustrated in figure 1110a.

Drafting Machines

723 Chart plotting on most large ships is done with a *drafting machine*, also called a parallel motion protractor. Figure 723 shows such a device; smaller and simplified models are sometimes used

Figure 721b. Parallel plotter.

Figure 721c. Two drafting triangles can be used to transfer a direction across a chart.

Figure 723. A universal drafting machine is excellent for plotting.

on recreational and commercial boats. A typical unit consists of a protractor carried on a parallel-motion linkage system fastened to the upper left-hand corner of the chart table. The linkage permits the movement of the protractor to any part of the chart without change of orientation. Several graduated rulers of different length are provided. On some models any two of these can be mounted, one as shown and the other at right angles to the first, to facilitate plotting of lines of position from celestial observations. However, most navigators prefer to use a right triangle to obtain the perpendicular. The graduated protractor rim, or compass rose, can be rotated and clamped in any position desired. Hence, it can be oriented to directions on the chart.

Dead Reckoning Equipment

724 Many large vessels are equipped with a dead reckoning electro-mechanical computer. The basic part of this device is its *analyzer* (DRA); heading information is fed into the DRA from the ship's gyrocompass, and speed information is supplied by the log. The speed input is integrated with time to read distance. The DRA has three readouts: miles steamed north or south, miles steamed east or west, and total number of miles steamed.

Some DRAs also give latitude and longitude readouts, in which case they are usually called Dead Reckoning Analyzer-Indicators (DRAI). A Mark 9 Mod 4 DRAI is shown in figure 724a. There is also a DRAI Mark 10.

The *Dead Reckoning Tracer* (DRT) receives its heading and speed inputs from the DRA, and provides a graphic trace of the ship's travel through the water. Some new models also trace the paths of two or more targets, permitting a constant readout of target range and bearing; target data are supplied from radar or sonar inputs. The DRT permits the choice of one of a number of scales, depending on the tactical situation, and the trace may be on a Mercator chart or a polar coordinate chart. The "own ship" trace may be made by a pencil moved across the chart; alternately, the ship's position as well as that of the targets may be indicated by spots of light focused on the chart from underneath. Such a DRT is shown in figure 724b; it is the PT-512 plotting table, designed primarily for use aboard ASW vessels. This plotting table permits a

Figure 724a. Dead Reckoning Analyzer-Indicator, Mark 9, Mod 4.

Figure 724b. Plotting Table, PT-512.

choice of eight scales, ranging from 200 yards per inch to 5 miles per inch, and gives a plotting area of 30 by 30 inches (76 by 76 cm). There is also a DRT Mark 6 Mod 4.

Nautical Slide Rule

725 Circular plastic slide rules (figure 725 is typical) are widely used for the rapid solution of problems involving time, distance, and speed. Given any two of these factors, the third may be

obtained. The time scale gives hours in red figures and minutes and seconds in black figures. Seconds are shown separately to 120; this scale may be used only for times of 120 seconds or less. Hours and minutes are both stated in units and decimals. If the hour scale is set to 2.5, the minute scale will read 150. Similarly, if the minute scale is set to 1.5, 90 seconds may also be read.

In the model shown, the distance scale is in miles in red figures and in yards in black figures. The yards scale is based on the assumption that 1 nautical mile equals 2,000 yards; this is an assumption frequently used in marine surface navigation—the slight error, $1\frac{1}{4}$ percent, is ignored for the convenience gained. Therefore, if the distance scale is set at 3 miles, it will also read 6,000 yards. The figures on the distance scale may also be used in solving problems involving statute miles; however, in this case, the yard scale must *not* be used.

In using the slide rule, when the distance is one of the known factors, the distance setting should be made *first*. When speed is a known factor, it should always be set last, as the speed scale is read through both dials.

Electronic Calculators and Computers

726 The rapid development of small hand-held electronic calculators has brought them onto the bridge of both large and small vessels for the solution of many navigational problems. These have essentially replaced conventional slide rules; they permit quick, easy, and accurate solutions of problems of speed-time-distance, dead reckoning, current sailing, metric conversions, and many others related to navigation or general "ship's business." The more sophisticated personal calculators can be programmed and approach the capabilities of microcomputers. See appendix F for more on these mathematical instruments.

Many modern naval vessels are equipped with a number of computers, usually specialized ones "dedicated" to some specific function such as weapons control. Minicomputers and microcomputers of a more general type are being increasingly found on merchant ships and yachts. Consideration of the use of computers in navigation will be found in chapter 38 and appendix F.

TIME MEASUREMENTS

727 Knowledge of the time of day and of elapsed time is essential in many phases of piloting. An accurate, easily read clock, indicating seconds, should be mounted near the navigator's station. This may be a conventional analog clock with

Figure 725. Nautical slide rule.

sweep-second hand, but digital models showing time directly in the 24-hour system are becoming more widely used.

A stopwatch or a navigational timer, which can be started and stopped at will, is of particular value in timing the period of a navigational light to determine its characteristic for purposes of identification. When equipped with a luminous dial and sweep-second hand, the watch may be read without the use of artificial light, thereby maintaining night-adapted vision.

Split-second timers, sometimes referred to as split-action stopwatches, are now available. With this feature the watch continues to run and measure elapsed time while simultaneously timing events of short duration; there are, in effect, two second hands that run together. When the side push button on the stopwatch is depressed, one of these second hands is stopped so that the exact interval can be read from the face of the watch. A second depression of the side push button causes the second hands to run together. This feature is also available on chronographs that can be kept running on GMT, with the split-second feature being used to determine the exact time of an event, such as passing a buoy, without disturbing the time-keeping function of the watch.

Electronic watches and stopwatches are now available with direct digital readouts. These gener-

ally have several modes of split-second operation suitable for the timing of different types of events. Some models have alarms that can be set to a specific time, or to count down and sound at the end of a preset interval. Also available are electronic wristwatches that can show time in a second zone, such as GMT, by the press of a button.

WEATHER INSTRUMENTS

Barometer

728   A *barometer* is an instrument for determining the atmospheric pressure, a meteorological ele-

Figure 726. A personal electronic calculator. Courtesy Texas Instruments, Inc.

Figure 727. A stopwatch (left) and a chronograph with split-second capability.

ment of considerable interest to a mariner, as its fluctuations provide an index useful in predicting weather, an important factor in navigation and ship handling. Because bad weather is usually associated with regions of low atmospheric pressure and good weather with areas of high pressure, a rapidly falling barometer usually indicates the approach of a storm.

Two general types of barometers are used. The *mercurial* barometer consists essentially of a column of mercury in a tube, the upper end of which is closed and the lower end open to the atmosphere. The height of the column of mercury supported by the atmosphere is read by a suitable scale. Readings are in inches of mercury. The *standard* atmospheric pressure is 29.92 inches or 1013.2 millibars.

An *aneroid* barometer consists essentially of a short metal cylinder from which the air has been partly exhausted. The ends of the cylinder, being of thin metal, expand or contract as the external atmospheric pressure changes. This motion is transferred by a suitable mechanical linkage to a registering device that may be graduated in either inches of mercury or millibars, or both. A reading of one scale can be converted to one of the other by table or arithmetically if both scales are not shown.

A *barograph* is a recording instrument that provides a permanent record of atmospheric pressure over a period of time. It is a relatively sensitive instrument and must be protected from shock and vibration; it is not normally affected by motions of the vessel, including rough weather.

Thermometer

729   For measuring temperature on board vessels *thermometers* are usually graduated to the Fahrenheit scale (water freezes at 32° and boils at 212° at standard atmospheric pressure), but use of the metric scale of Celsius (formerly centigrade) degrees (0° is freezing, 100° is boiling) is increasing, particularly in international applications. The reading of one scale can be easily converted to that of the other by means of Table 15, *Bowditch*, or mathematically, since

$$°F = \tfrac{9}{5}C° + 32°$$
$$°C = \tfrac{5}{9}(F° - 32°)$$

in which °F = degrees Fahrenheit, and °C = degrees Celsius.

Two thermometers are often mounted together in an *instrument shelter*, a wooden box with louvered sides to protect the instruments from direct rays of the sun and other conditions that would render their readings inaccurate. The instrument shelter is installed at some exposed position aboard ship. One of the thermometers has its bulb covered with a wet fabric, and the other is exposed to the air. The rate of evaporation of the water is dependent upon the *relative humidity* of the air, or the relative amount of water vapor in the air. The evaporating water cools the bulb of the thermometer, resulting in a lower temperature. Knowing the air temperature (reading of the *dry bulb thermometer*) and the difference between this and the reading of the *wet bulb thermometer*, the relative humidity and *dew point* (the temperature to which the air must be cooled for condensation to take place) can be easily determined; Tables 16 and 17 of *Bowditch* are applicable. Calculations of relative humidity and dew point are of special interest to the mariner in connection with the formation of fog. A combination of wet and dry thermometers is known as a *psychrometer*.

Anemometer

730   An *anemometer* is an instrument for measuring wind force or speed, usually in knots. It must always be remembered that wind speed measured on a moving vessel is *apparent* wind, or wind relative to the moving ship or both. Apparent wind can be converted to true wind, or vice versa, by means of a simple graphic solution (see article 1417) or by the use of tables such as Table 10 in *Bowditch*.

MISCELLANEOUS EQUIPMENT

Binoculars

731   The term "pair of binoculars" is commonly used for a single unit, but this is not strictly correct; the proper term is "binocular"—as in "bicycle." However, since the plural form is usually used, that form will be used here. Good binoculars are useful for visually detecting aids to navigation, especially small ones such as buoys, and in reading their identifying markings. The navigator should have binoculars for his own exclusive use; they should be kept in a handy location, but sufficiently protected to prevent damage from dropping, being knocked off a table by the motion of the ship, or by weather. When they are being used, the strap should be placed around the user's neck. Like the other instruments used by the navigator, binoculars must receive proper care if they are to give reliable service.

The size of binoculars deemed most useful for marine work is 7 × 50; this describes glasses with a magnification of 7 powers and an objective lens

Figure 731. A good pair of binoculars is essential to the navigation of a vessel of any size.

50 mm in diameter. This ratio of magnification is a satisfying compromise between need for magnification and the reduction of field of view that results as the magnification is increased. Objective lenses of 50-mm diameter have excellent light-gathering characteristics, making them particularly suitable for night use.

Other models, such as 6 × 30, may be used, but these are generally somewhat less satisfactory. The style in which each eye is *individually focused* has been adopted by the U.S. Navy, but many civilian mariners and boatmen use the *center-focusing* style that focuses for both eyes simultaneously after an initial correction is made for any difference between the user's two eyes. Either style will serve the purpose; the choice can be made on personal preference.

Much higher powered binoculars may be found on pedestals on the wings of many ships' bridges; the mounting is necessary because of the much greater weight of these larger glasses.

Flashlight

732 At least one good flashlight should be kept handy for an accurate reading of watches and sextants during twilight observations if the latter are not equipped with their own light, and for timing light characteristics, etc., during the hours of darkness. To protect dark-adapted vision, this flashlight should be equipped with a red bulb, or a red lens. Lacking these, a red plastic or cellophane filter should be fitted.

If accurate twilight or night observations are to be made, the navigator must protect his eyes from any direct white light. If no red flashlight is available, the person who is acting as recorder should stand with his back to the observer, with his light shielded and close to the watch. After the altitude is obtained, if the sextant has no readout light the navigator should hand it to the recorder for reading.

Chapter 8

Dead Reckoning

Introduction

801 Once primitive man took to the larger bodies of water and developed enough skills in piloting to venture long distances from home port, it became necessary for him to keep track of his vessel's movements and position. Thus was developed *dead reckoning* (DR), now one of the four principal divisions of navigation. The term is derived from *deduced*, or *ded*, reckoning, the process by which a vessel's position was *deduced* or computed trigonometrically in relation to a known point of departure. While modern charts permit solutions by graphic methods, rather than by laborious mathematics, the term *dead reckoning* continues in use. Although treated as a separate division of navigation in this text, DR is actually basic to all phases of navigation.

DR Defined

802 Dead reckoning is the process of determining a ship's approximate position by applying from its last known position a vector or a series of consecutive vectors representing the run that has since been made, using only the courses steered, and the distance run as determined by log, engine revolutions, or calculations from speed measurements, *without considering current*. By projecting these course and speed vectors ahead of the present position, the ship's predicted DR position for any desired time can be determined. Dead reckoning is normally a process carried out as a vessel proceeds along its passage. It can, however, be done in advance to plot an intended track.

The key elements of dead reckoning may be summarized as follows:

Only the courses steered are used to determine a DR position.

The distance used in determining a DR position is obtained by multiplying the ordered engine speed by the time involved in the run.

A DR plot is always started from an established position, that is, a fix or running fix. (See article 804.)

The effects of current are *not* considered in determining a DR position. If the effects of known or anticipated currents are included, the result is a plot of *estimated positions* (EPs). (See article 1205.)

The Importance of DR

803 The importance of maintaining an accurate dead reckoning plot cannot be overemphasized. Other means of fixing the ship's position are not always available, due to weather, equipment failure, etc. Under such conditions, a navigator must rely on his dead reckoning. It is obvious that a DR position must be used with extreme caution in the vicinity of shoal water or other dangers to navigation; if adequate information is available, an EP plot should be maintained in addition to, but *not* in lieu of, the DR plot.

If a ship made good the exact course and speed ordered, and there was no wind or current, dead reckoning would at all times provide an accurate indication of position. Such conditions rarely exist, however, and a DR position is only an approximation of the true position. A navigator must know his position, or approximate position, to determine when to make changes in course and/or speed, to predict the time of sighting lights or other aids to navigation, and to identify landmarks.

Although dead reckoning can be quickly and accurately done on a computer or calculator, it is almost always done graphically on a chart or plotting sheet appropriate to the area in which the vessel is operating. Graphic solutions are advantageous in that they enable the navigator to visualize his vessel's position relative to landmarks, aids to navigation, and hazards.

DR Terms Defined

804 A number of terms used in dead reckoning must be defined. Not all books on navigation use exactly the same terms and definitions; the terms used in this book are defined below.

Heading (Hdg. or SH). The direction in which a ship points or heads *at any instant*, expressed in angular units, clockwise from 000° through 360°, from a reference direction—true, magnetic, or compass—(figure 804). The heading of a ship is also called *ship's head*. Heading is a constantly changing value as a ship oscillates or yaws across the course due to the effects of the sea and of steering error.

Course (C). As applied to marine navigation, the direction in which a vessel is to be steered, or is being steered; the direction of travel through the water. The course is measured from 000° clockwise from the reference direction to 360°. Course may be designated as *true, magnetic, compass, or grid* as determined by the reference direction.

Course line. The graphic representation of a vessel's course, normally used in the construction of a dead reckoning plot.

Speed (S). The ordered rate of travel of a vessel through the water; normally expressed in knots. (In some areas, where distances are stated in statute miles, such as on the Great Lakes and other inland waters, speed units will be "miles per hour.") It is used in conjunction with time to establish a distance run on each of the consecutive segments of a DR plot.

DR position. A position determined by plotting a vector or series of consecutive vectors using only the course, and distance determined by speed through the water, without considering current.

DR plot. The graphical representation on the nautical chart of the line or series of lines that are the vectors of the ordered true courses, and distance run on these courses at the ordered speeds, while proceeding from a fixed point. The DR plot originates at a fix or running fix; it is suitably labeled as to courses, speeds, and times of various dead reckoning positions, usually at hourly intervals or at times of change of course or speed. A DR plot prop-

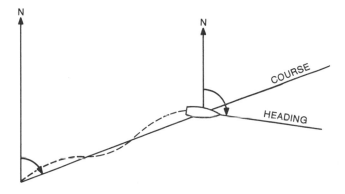

Figure 804. Heading and course.

erly represents courses and speeds that have been used; a similar plot may be made in advance for courses and speeds that are expected to be used.

Estimated position (EP). The more probable position of a vessel determined from incomplete data or data of questionable accuracy. In practical usage it is often the DR position modified by the best additional information available.

Fix. A position established at a specific time to a high degree of accuracy; it may be determined by any of a number of methods discussed in chapter 11. A *running fix* is a position of lesser accuracy based in part on present information and in part on information transferred from a prior time.

Estimated time of departure (ETD). The estimate of the time of departure from a specified location in accordance with planned courses and speeds and anticipated currents.

Course, speed, time, distance, and position will be stated to an order of precision suitable to the vessel concerned and prevailing conditions; see appendix C.

A planned or intended path *with respect to the earth* rather than the water is labeled *Track* and *Speed of Advance;* see chapter 12.

Labeling a DR or EP Plot

805 It is of the utmost importance that all points and lines plotted on a chart be properly labeled. The use of standardized methods will ensure that the plot will mean the same thing to others as it did to the navigator who made it; this is essential to the safety of the vessel.

The principal rules for labeling DR plots are:

Immediately after drawing any line or plotting any point, it should be labeled.

Labels indicating direction and speed along a course line should be written *along* that line.

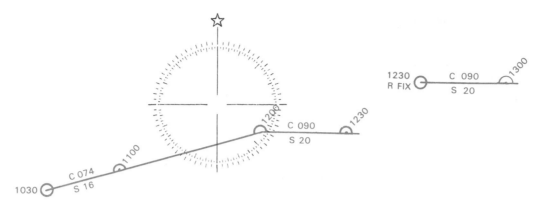

Figure 805. Labeling a DR plot.

The label for direction should be the letter *C* followed by three digits indicating the *true* course in degrees (the degree symbol is not used); this is placed *above* the course line. (Should course be stated with reference to another base direction, an appropriate letter is added following the digits, such as *M* for magnetic.)

The label indicating the rate of movement along the course line is the letter *S* followed by digits indicating the speed; the name of the units being used is normally omitted. This is placed *below* the course line, usually directly beneath the direction label.

The label for any point on a line should *not* be placed close alongside that line. Labels for fixes, running fixes, and estimated positions should be written horizontally as the chart is normally viewed; labels for time of DR positions should be placed at an angle to the horizontal.

The symbol for a DR position is a small semi-circle around a small dot on a straight segment of a course line; it will be more or less than a semicircle when plotted at a change in direction. The letters "DR" are *not* used. Time, to the nearest minute—stated in the 24-hour system as a four-digit number without a colon or a dash (see article 210)—is written nearby *at an angle to the horizontal and to the course line.*

The symbol for an estimated position is a small square. Time is written *horizontally* close nearby.

The symbol for a fix is a small circle (with a dot if needed); the word "FIX" is *not* used. Time is written nearby *horizontally.* The symbol for a running fix is the same as for a fix, but the letters "R FIX" are added following the time.

If a DR plot is drawn in advance of actual vessel movement, distances are known; speeds may or may not be known prior to departure. If it is desired to label a DR plot with distance, this is done with the letter *D* followed by the distance in nautical miles (statute miles in some areas), usually to the nearest tenth of a mile; this is placed below the course line. (Some navigators will label a destination, usually in pilot waters, with its ETA and then intermediate points, marked by a heavy dot, with the ETA there plus the distance measured back from the final destination along the intended track.)

All labels should be printed clearly and neatly.

The dot in a fix, estimated position, or DR position symbol is used to emphasize the point of the position; it should be small and neat, and is not needed if the position is at the intersection of two lines. Course lines, properly labeled, are shown in figure 805.

When DR Positions Are to Be Plotted

806 In addition to the rules for symbols and labels, there are also standard rules that will guide a navigator as to *when* DR positions and course lines are required to be plotted:

A DR position shall be plotted every hour on the hour.

A DR position shall be plotted at the time of every course change.

A DR position shall be plotted at the time of every speed change.

A DR position shall be plotted at the time of obtaining a fix or a running fix.

A DR position shall be plotted at the time of obtaining a single line of position.

A new course line shall be plotted from each fix or running fix as soon as the fix or running fix has been determined and plotted on the chart.

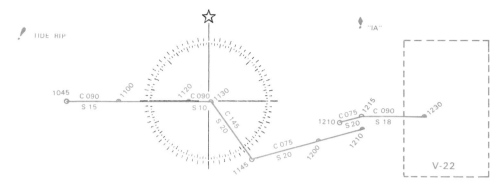

Figure 807. A typical navigator's DR plot.

These rules of dead reckoning are considered adequate to meet the needs and requirements of navigation in the open waters of the sea. There are occasions, however, when a *more frequent* plot of the vessel's dead reckoning position is essential to safe navigation, as when in the confined waters of channels, bays, straits, and harbors. Knowledge of when to plot frequent fixes and even more frequent dead reckoning positions when in such waters will come with experience and judgment. This subject will be discussed more fully in chapter 15.

Example of a DR Plot

807   The following example illustrates a typical dead reckoning plot; see figure 807.

A partial extract from a ship's deck log reads as follows:

1045.   With Tide Rip Light bearing 315°, distant 6 miles, took departure for operating area V-22 on course 090°, speed 15 knots.

1120.   Changed speed to 10 knots.

1130.   Changed course to 145° and increased speed to 20 knots.

1145.   Changed course to 075°.

1210.   Made radar contact on Buoy 1A bearing 010°, distant 8 miles.

1215.   Changed course to 090° and changed speed to 18 knots to arrive at the rendezvous point at 1230.

Note the applicability of the rules for dead reckoning as they pertain to this example. Commencing at the initial known position, the 1045 fix, the navigator plotted the course line in a direction of 090°, the ordered course. The rate of travel, speed 15 knots, for an elapsed time of 15 minutes and then 20 minutes enabled the navigator to make a scaled plot of the 1100 DR and 1120 DR positions on his chart. Labeling the fix, the 1100 DR, the 1120 DR, and the course line itself completes the graphic

description of the ship's travel until 1120. At 1120, only the speed was changed. At 1130, both the course and speed were changed, while at 1145, only the course was changed. Each of these occurrences requires a separate DR position on the plot, while segments of the course lines are labeled to indicate what the course and speed were at that time. The 1200 DR was plotted on the whole hour as prescribed. At 1210, since the navigator fixed his position by radar, he must then plot both the 1210 DR on the former course line and the 1210 radar fix from which he commences a new course line. The navigator plots the ship from the fix on a course of 075° at a speed of 20 knots to 1215, at which time the course is changed to 090° and the speed is reduced to 18 knots in order to arrive at the operating area at 1230 as scheduled. (Note that while a new course line is drawn from the fix, the ship continues on briefly on the old course and speed while a revised course and speed are being determined—in this example, for five minutes. See article 809.) The DR plot reflects the new course and speed and includes the 1230 DR as shown.

Planned Track

808   In actual practice, a preplanned track line is often plotted on a tentative basis before a ship ever gets underway. Called "navigational planning," it is a fundamental principle of safe navigation. Every passage, every departure from and entry into port, must be planned in advance, based on all information available to the navigator. The material studied in the course of this planning includes the charts of the areas to be traversed, the navigational aids expected to be sighted, the availability of radionavigation systems, estimates of currents and weather to be encountered, the contour of the bottom, and other factors that will be discussed in this book. The preplanning phase also includes the plotting of danger bearings, ranges,

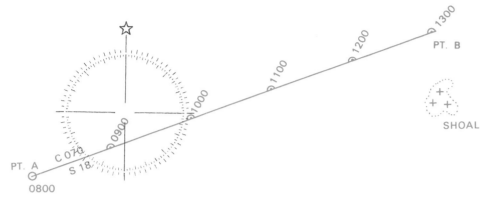

Figure 808a. Intended DR, plotted and labeled in advance.

etc. The following description of a short voyage will serve to illustrate many of the principles and concepts enumerated so far in this chapter.

Referring to figure 808a, assume that a ship is located at point A, and receives orders to depart at 0800 for point B, 90 miles distant, arriving at 1300. Immediately upon receipt of this information, the navigator locates points A and B on the appropriate small-scale chart of the area. By measuring the direction of B from A, the course of 070° is determined and noted on the DR plot as "C 070." Dividing the rhumb-line distance between A and B by five hours, the required speed is computed to be 18 knots and labeled accordingly. Next, starting at the known position, or fix, at 0800, the navigator steps off and marks the successive hourly positions that the ship is expected to occupy. The plot is now complete and barring any unforeseen circumstances, represents the track that the ship will follow from the point of departure to her destination. Note that in this case the vessel was able to order the planned course and speed and arrive at the destination as planned; this very seldom happens in actual practice. The technique of handling deviations from the plan is the subject of the next article.

An alternative procedure of labeling is shown in figure 808b. Here *distances to go* are given at each change of course, and the line is labeled for track (TR) and speed of advance (SOA). Actual courses and speeds ordered will differ as allowance is made for the river's current.

Departures from Plan

809 The ship gets underway as scheduled in figure 808a and sets course 070° true and speed 18 knots to arrive at B at 1300. If the calculations are correct and there is no current or change of course to avoid shipping, the ship should arrive at B as planned. The navigator's work now consists of trying to establish his actual position from time to time, in order to be sure that the ship is following the intended track, or if it is not following it, to recommend changes in course or speed, or both, that will bring the ship safely back to the intended track at any selected point on it.

The navigator had poor weather and was unable to establish his position until about noon, at which time he obtained a 1200 fix. When the fix was plotted, he found that the ship was actually about 10 miles south and a bit east of his 1200 DR position; see figure 809. He further noted that if his ship maintained the same course from the 1200 fix as it had from point A, she would be in danger of grounding on the indicated shoal.

Since the ship will not reach the desired destination on a course of 070° and a speed of 18 knots, the navigator must determine a new course and speed to arrive at point B by 1300, based upon the relationship between point B and the latest fix at 1200.

Since time was required to record the fix, evaluate it, and decide upon a new course and speed, this change cannot be effected from the 1200 fix, but rather from a DR position some time later. Making a rough estimate of how long it will take him to determine a new course and speed, and get approval, the navigator plots a 1215 DR position based on the old, and still maintained, course and speed. From here he calculates a new course and a new speed (or new ETA if the ship is not capable of the greater speed needed to reach point B by 1300). It is very important to remember that *the course line will continue in the direction and at the speed originally ordered during the time required to obtain and plot the fix and decide upon a new course of action.* Upon the advice of the navigator in this instance, the captain ordered a course of 028° and a

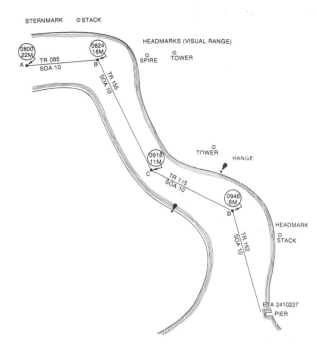

Figure 808b. Alternative labeling of a proposed track.

Figure 809. The practice of dead reckoning.

speed of 24 knots at 1215 so that the ship would arrive at point B at 1300. Although it is apparent that a current existed, it is not considered in this simplified example. The technique and procedures of computing and allowing for current are explained later in chapter 12; they would have been used by the navigator in the computation of the new course and speed through the water.

The navigator believed that the ship was following the intended track until he obtained and plotted his 1200 fix. This illustrates the fundamental weakness of relying solely on dead reckoning, for dead reckoning is dependent upon the assumption that the ship makes good over the ground the same direction that it is traveling through the water, and that the ship makes good over the ground the same speed that it is traveling through the water. Therefore, the dead reckoning position should not be relied upon if it is possible to obtain information to determine the position by other means. The many

volumes of records on maritime disasters are filled with reports of vessels having been put aground and lost because of a navigator's adherence to a course that was laid in safe waters, while the actual movement was an unknown path leading to danger.

Plotting Techniques

810 As stated above, neatness and accuracy in plotting are essential for safe navigation. Skill will come with experience and practice, but a few hints and suggestions may be of assistance toward both accuracy and speed in plotting.

A drafting machine should be used whenever available to determine the direction of a line, as it is both more rapid and accurate than other methods. When a drafting machine is not available, a course plotter (or protractor or parallel rulers) is used. Various types are shown in chapter 7.

Tape the chart to the table or desk used. This will maintain proper orientation of the chart. Tape is preferable to thumbtacks for this purpose, and masking tape should be used, as it will not harm the surface of the chart when removed provided it has not been left in place for an extended time and allowed to harden.

If the chart is too large to fit on the table used, determine the extent of the chart that must be used, then fold under the portions of the chart that will not be required. Be sure to leave one latitude scale and one longitude scale available for measurement.

Use a *sharp* No. 2 pencil. A harder pencil will not erase well, and a softer pencil will smear.

Draw lines heavy enough to be seen readily, but light enough so that they do not indent the chart paper.

Avoid drawing unnecessary lines, and erase any lines used only for the purpose of measurement. Do not extend course lines excessively beyond the point at which their direction is to be changed or bearing lines much beyond the anticipated fix.

Hold the pencil against the straightedge in a vertical position throughout the entire length of a line when drawing it.

Measure all directions and distances carefully. Accuracy is the mark of good navigation. On Mercator charts, measure distance on the graphic bar scale or on the *latitude* scale using the portion of the scale that is opposite the line that is being measured. Be neat and exact in plotting work. Use standard symbols and labels and print neatly.

Lay down a new DR (or EP) track from each new fix or running fix. Plot a DR position at every change of course, at every change of speed, at the

Figure 811. Logarithmic scales for determining speed or distance.

time of obtaining a fix, a running fix, or a single line of position, and on the whole hour.

Time-speed-distance Calculations

811 The navigator may find it convenient to use a *nautical slide rule* (figure 725) for the solution of time, speed, and distance problems. Small hand-held electronic calculators (appendix F) are also useful for the easy, quick, and very accurate solution of these problems. Alternatively, he may use precomputed tables, such as those in *Bowditch*, Volume II, for such solutions. He must, however, always be able to solve these problems quickly and accurately without the use of any equipment beyond pencil and paper.

Regardless of the tools used, however, *it must always be remembered in adding or subtracting values of time, there are 60 minutes in an hour, and 60 seconds in each minute;* don't forget and work in decimal terms of 100 units.

Time, distance, and speed calculations—finding the third quantity if the other two are known—can also be worked graphically using the logarithmic scale printed on larger-scale NOS and DMAHTC charts, on some plotting sheets, and as the top line of the nomogram printed near the bottom of Maneuvering Board sheets, DMAHTC Pub. No. 5090 and 5091; see figure 811. The scale, together with a pair of dividers, is used as a slide rule. Let the right leg of a pair of dividers represent time in minutes and the left leg, distance. Consider speed as distance in 60 minutes. Then, to obtain time, place the left leg of the dividers on the speed and the right leg on 60. Without changing the spread of the dividers, place the left leg on the required distance and read off the time at the right leg. If distance in a given time is desired, place the right leg on the given time and read off the distance at the left leg. If speed is required, set the left leg of the dividers at distance and the right leg at time, and then, without chang-

ing the spread, place the right leg on 60 and read the speed at the left leg.

If the problem runs off the scale, the solution can be found by using a fraction of the speed, or distance (only one), and multiplying the answer by the inverse of that fraction.

If in doubt as to the accuracy of a solution, check it mentally or by simple arithmetic using the formula $D = S \times T$, where D is distance in miles, S is speed in knots, and T is time in hours (or 60D if T is in minutes).

The Maneuvering Board sheets also have a three-scale nomogram that can be used as described in article 1404.

A useful rule to use in plotting in confined waters where frequent fixes and DR positions are required is the so-called *three-minute rule,* applied as follows: the travel of a ship *in yards* in three minutes is equal to the speed of the ship in knots multiplied by 100. (This uses the assumption that one nautical mile is equal to 2,000 yards—not exact, but close enough for practical use.) Where a *six-minute* DR would be more appropriate than a three-minute plot, the travel of a ship *in miles* in six minutes is equal to the speed of the vessel divided by 10, a shift of the decimal point one place to the left.

Example 1: A navigator desires to plot a three-minute DR from his last fix in Brewerton Channel. The ship is making a speed of 12 knots. To compute the travel of the ship in yards in three minutes, he multiplies the speed in knots, 12, by the factor 100 and determines the DR advance to be 1,200 yards.

Answer: Distance 1,200 yards.

Example 2: A navigator desires to plot a six-minute DR from his last fix in Chesapeake Bay. The ship is making a speed of 15 knots. To compute the travel of the ship in miles, he divides the speed in knots, 15, by the factor 10 and determines the DR advance to be 1.5 miles.

Answer: Distance 1.5 miles.

Chapter 9

Tides and Tide Predictions

Introduction

901 When approaching a harbor, or pilot waters generally, one of the most important preparatory actions to be taken by a vessel's navigator is consideration of the available depths of water at the expected time of arrival. The natural phenomenon known as *tide* will cause such depths to vary from time to time in most areas of the world. Anyone who would call himself a navigator must have a thorough knowledge of tidal action and how the height of tide—which in turn determines the depth of water—can be predicted and calculated.

In addition to concern over adequate depths of water in channels, across bars, alongside piers and wharves, etc., in some locations there may be concern as to sufficient vertical clearance beneath a fixed bridge. Here, too, tides play a major role, for as depths increase for improved clearance under the hull, available vertical clearances for masts and superstructures decrease by the same amount.

Definitions

902 The *vertical* rise and fall of the ocean level due to gravitational and centrifugal forces between the earth and the moon, and, to a lesser extent, the sun, is called *tide*. Local conditions cause considerable variations in tidal phenomena from place to place, but most places on the earth's oceans and connecting waters experience two high tides and two low tides each lunar day. *High tide*, or *high water*, is the highest level reached by an ascending tide. From high tide the level of the water decreases until it reaches a minimum level called *low tide*, or *low water*. At high water and at low water there is a brief period when no change in the water level can be detected. This period is called *stand*. The total rise or fall from low water to high water, or vice versa, is called the *range* of the tide. *Mean sea level* is the average height of the surface of the sea for all stages of tide, differing slightly from *half-tide level*, which is the plane midway between mean high water and mean low water.

Causes of Tide

903 In any consideration of tidal theory, it is convenient to start with a spherical earth uniformly covered with water. It is also convenient to consider separately the effects of the moon and sun, following this with a consideration of the combined effects of both bodies; the effects of the moon will be studied first as that body exerts the larger influence. Before 100 A.D. The Roman naturalist Pliny observed and wrote of the influence of the moon on tides, but a full understanding had to wait for Newton's scientific description of gravity in 1687.

Effect of the Moon

The oceans are affected by the gravitational attraction between the earth and the moon, and by the centrifugal forces resulting from the rotation of these bodies around a common center, a point located *within* the earth about 810 miles (1,500 km) beneath the surface. The gravitational and centrifugal forces are in balance, and so the earth and moon neither collide nor fly away from each other. The centrifugal force is the same everywhere on the earth's surface, since all points describe the same motion around the center of mass; these forces are all parallel to each other and to a line joining the centers of the earth and moon. On the other hand, the gravitational force is *not* everywhere the same;

particles at points nearer the moon feel a greater attractional force than those on the far side of the earth; these forces are *not* parallel, each being in the direction from that point to the center of the moon. The combination of these forces, much exaggerated for emphasis, is shown in figure 903a. Note that there are a series of resultant forces that will cause the surface water to flow toward the points on the earth's surface that are then nearest and farthest from the moon. This flow causes higher than normal levels of water at these points, and lower than normal levels at the areas from which the flow comes. Although at the nearest and farthest points there is an indicated outward force, this is very slight and not nearly enough to cause an appreciable tide; the true tide results from the near-horizontal forces causing the flow described above.

As the earth rotates each day on its axis, the line of direction toward the moon changes, and so each point has two highs and two lows. As a result of the tilt of the earth's axis, the highs and lows are not normally of equal levels.

Effect of the Sun

This overly simplified explanation must now be complicated by the presence of the sun, a body of immensely greater mass than the moon, but relatively so much more distant that its effect is less (only about 46 percent as great). The tides that occur on earth are the result of both lunar and solar influences. When these two bodies are in line with the earth—as at both new and full moon—the two influences act together, and the result is higher than average high tides and lower than normal low tides; these are called *spring tides* (the word "spring" here has nothing to do with the season of the year of the same name). This is true regardless of whether the moon is between the earth and the sun or on the opposite side. Figure 903b illustrates these situations.

When the directions of the sun and moon are 90° apart—as at both first- and third-quarter moons—the effect of the sun is to partially counteract the moon's influence. At these time, the high tides are lower and the low tides are higher than normal; these are *neap* tides; figure 903c shows this alignment of the moon and sun.

As the moon revolves about the earth once each lunar month of roughly 29½ days, its transit of any meridian on earth occurs approximately every 24 hours and 50 minutes. This is the period for two high waters and two low waters and is called a *tidal day;* the period of one high and one low is referred to as a *tidal cycle.* In actuality, the daily rotation of

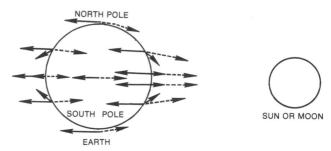

Figure 903a. Gravitational forces (dashed lines) and centrifugal forces (solid lines). (Not to scale)

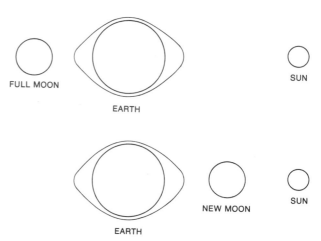

Figure 903b. Moon and sun acting together to produce spring tides.

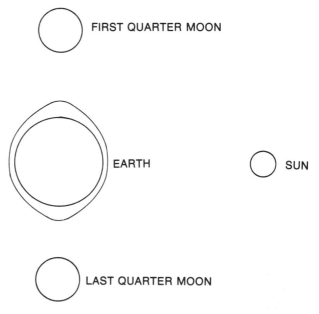

Figure 903c. Moon and sun in quadrature acting to produce neap tides.

the earth on its axis has a frictional effect on the tides, so that high tides normally lag the time of the moon's transit across the meridian of any location. Additional irregularities are introduced into heights and times of tide by the moon's varying declination and distance from the earth (see article 1805). The many effects result in a pattern of tides that repeats only at intervals of roughly 19 years.

The assumption of a spherical earth uniformly covered with water is, of course, purely hypothetical. Tides in the open oceans are probably only one to two feet high (0.3–0.6 m). Actual coastal tides are often much greater, in some places as much as 40 or 50 feet (12 to 15 m) or more. This is the result of large land masses restricting the flow of water, of ocean bottom and shoreline variations, the internal friction (viscosity) of the flowing water, and other factors. These interrelate to establish natural periods of oscillation for seas, gulfs, large bays, and estuaries, which combine with the basic tidal influences as described in the following article.

Types of Tides

904 A body of water has a natural period of oscillation that is dependent upon its dimensions. No ocean appears to be a single oscillating body, but rather each one is made up of a number of oscillating basins. As such basins are acted upon by the tide-producing forces, some respond more readily to daily or diurnal forces, others to semidiurnal forces, and still others respond almost equally to both. Hence, tides at a given place are classified as *semidiurnal*, *diurnal*, or *mixed*—according to the characteristics of the tidal pattern occurring at that place.

Semidiurnal. In this type of tide, there are two high and two low waters each tidal day with relatively small inequality in the consecutive high and low water heights. Tides on the Atlantic coast of the United States are representative of the semidiurnal type, which is illustrated in figure 904a.

Diurnal. In this type of tide, only a single high and a single low water occur each tidal day. Tides of the diurnal type occur along the northern shore of the Gulf of Mexico, in the Java Sea, in the Gulf of Tonkin (off the Vietnamese-Chinese coast), and in a few other localities. The tide curve for Pakhoi, China, illustrated in figure 904b is an example of the diurnal type.

Mixed. In this type of tide the diurnal and semidiurnal oscillations are both important factors, and the tide is characterized by a large inequality in the high-water heights, low-water heights, or in both.

Figure 904a. Semidiurnal type of tides.

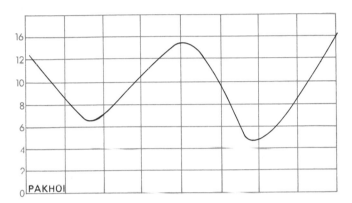

Figure 904b. Diurnal type of tides.

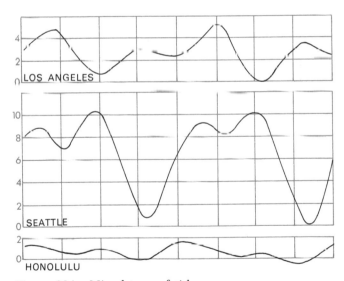

Figure 904c. Mixed type of tides.

There are usually two high and two low waters each day, but occasionally the tide may become diurnal. Mixed tides are prevalent along the Pacific Coast of the United States and in many other parts of the world. Examples of mixed types of tides are shown in figure 904c. At Los Angeles, it is typical that the inequalities in the high and low waters are about the same. At Seattle the greater inequalities are typically in the low waters, while at Honolulu the high waters have the greater inequalities.

Reference Planes for Tidal Data

905 The expression *height of tide* is not to be confused with *depth of water*. The latter refers to the vertical distance from the surface of the water to the bottom; the former refers to the vertical distance from the surface of the water to an arbitrarily chosen *reference plane* or *datum*, such plane being based as a selected *low-water* average. The *charted depth* is the vertical distance from this reference plane to the ocean bottom. A second reference plane based on a selected *high-water* average is used as a basis for the measurement of *charted heights* of objects above the water and *vertical clearances* under structures such as bridges and power lines. The difference between the selected high-water and low-water averages is called the *mean range of the tide*. The relationship of these terms is illustrated in figure 905.

The arbitrarily chosen reference plane differs with the locality and the country making the survey on which the chart is based. The principal planes of reference used are derived from the approximation of the following:

Mean low water (MLW), the average of *all* low tides. This plane was used for many years on NOS charts of the Atlantic coast and on nearly all DMAHTC charts, but is now in the process of being discontinued.

Mean lower low water (MLLW), the average of only the lower of the two daily low tides. This plane has long been used on charts of the Pacific Coast of the United States, the Hawaiian Islands, the Philippines, and Alaska. It has now been adopted for the Atlantic and Gulf of Mexico coasts; charts will be gradually changed over, but the change has no practical significance for navigators. The Gulf Coast Low Water Datum (GCLWD), now also discontinued, was essentially the same plane.

Mean low-water springs, the average of the low waters at spring tides, or *mean lower low-water springs*, the average of the lower of the two daily low tides at springs. Most British Admiralty charts are based on one of these two reference planes.

Each chart normally carries a statement of the datum used for soundings. For U.S.-produced charts, it is not necessary to consider the reference planes for various localities, as the *Tide Tables* (see article 906) are always based on the same datum as used for the largest scale chart of the area.

However, the plane of reference may be in doubt on charts compiled from old or questionable data.

Figure 905. Relationship of terms used in measurement of depths and heights. Low water datum may be mean low water, mean lower low water, or as otherwise specified on a chart.

If there is any doubt, assume that it is mean low water, for this assumption allows for the greatest margin of safety in that it is the *highest* of the low water datum planes in use on nautical charts. The depth of the water will seldom be lower than the charted depth, *regardless of the state of the tide*, if mean lower low-water springs was used as a tidal reference plane.

Caution

It is important to remember that the water level will at times be *below the reference plane*. In other words, *the actual depth of water can be less than the charted depth*. This is indicated by a minus sign (−) placed before the height of tide shown in the *Tide Tables*. (Note that for the month of August in figure 906a, of the 59 low tides, 14 are minus heights.)

The predicted depth of water is equal to the algebraic sum of the charted depth and the height of tide, so that when there is a negative tide, the numerical value of the height of tide is subtracted from the charted depth to find the depth of water.

In many coastal areas, the actual height of tide at any time may be considerably influenced by winds from a particular direction, especially if the winds are strong and persist for several days. At such times, the predicted tide variations may be completely masked by the temporary conditions. Periods of abnormally low barometric pressure may result in higher water levels for both high and low tides.

In computing vertical clearance when the chart datum is mean lower low water, it is necessary to use mean tide level in Table 2 (figure 906b). Mean tide level is midway between mean high water and mean low water, and its tabulated value is above the chart datum (mean lower low water). Thus, one-half of the mean range added to mean tide level will give the elevation of mean high water (the vertical clearance datum) above mean lower low water (chart datum).

Tide Tables

906 Predictions of tidal heights have been published annually by the National Ocean Service (and its predecessor agencies, the Coast & Geodetic Survey and National Ocean Survey) since 1853. The *Tide Tables* now appear in four volumes as follows: *Europe and West Coast of Africa (including the Mediterranean Sea); East Coast, North and South America (including Greenland); West Coast, North and South America (including the Hawaiian Islands); Central and Western Pacific Ocean and Indian Ocean.* Together they contain daily predictions for about 200 reference ports and difference data for approximately 6,000 other stations.

Reference Stations

The format of the *Tide Tables* is shown in the following series of extracts. Table 1 lists the time and height of the tide at each high water and low water in chronological order for each day of the year at a number of places that are designated as *reference stations;* the year for which the data are valid is shown at the top of each page of Table 1 following the name of the reference station. Figure 906a is an extract from Table 1 of the *Tide Tables for the West Coast of North and South America, including the Hawaiian Islands* for the months of July, August, and September (of a certain year) at the reference station, Humboldt Bay, California. Depths are given in feet and meters.

All times stated in the *Tide Tables* are *standard times;* each page of Table 1 indicates the central meridian of the time zone used. Adjustment must be made for the use of daylight time or any other deviation from standard time at the locality concerned; see article 2213.

Because the lunar or tidal day is a little more than 24 hours in length (an average of about 24^h50^m), the time between successive high or low tides is a little more than 12 hours. When a high (or low) tide occurs just before midnight, the next high (or low) tide occurs about noon of the following day, and the next one occurs just after midnight. Under these conditions, three consecutive high (or low) tides may occur on three different dates, although the total interval may be no more than the

average period of a lunar day, 24^h50^m. This means that on the middle of the three days, there is but one high (or low) water. An example of this is seen in figure 906a; only one high tide occurs at Humboldt Bay, California, on 9 August.

During portions of each month, the tide becomes diurnal at some stations; that is, there is only one high tide and one low tide each lunar or tidal day. This is indicated by blanks in the tabulated data.

Subordinate Stations

Secondary or *subordinate stations* are listed in geographical order in Table 2; see figure 906b. Each subordinate station is given a number, its location is described, and its position in latitude and longitude is given to the nearest minute. Data are then given that are to be applied to the predictions at a specified reference station (shown in bold type) to obtain the tidal information for the subordinate station; if there is more than one reference station shown on a page of Table 2, a navigator must be careful to use the one printed *nearest above* the subordinate station line. For example, in figure 906b, Nestucca Bay entrance in Oregon is Subordinate Station No. 763 at 45° 10′ N, 123° 58′ W; the time and height differences are to be applied to the daily predictions for the reference station of Humboldt Bay, California.

Table 2 also includes a listing for each reference station; this is used only for the geographic coordinates of the station (not given in Table 1), tidal ranges, and mean tide level data.

Determining Time of High or Low Tide

A separate time difference is tabulated for high and low water as shown in figure 906b. Each time difference is added to or subtracted from the time of the respective high or low water at the reference station in accordance with its sign. A navigator must be alert to *changes of date*, either forward or backwards, when the time difference is applied. For example, if a high water occurs at a reference station at 2200 on 23 March and the tide at the subordinate station occurs 3 hours later, then high water will occur at 0100 on *24* March at the subordinate station. Conversely, if a high water at a reference station occurs at 0200 on 29 March, and the tide at the subordinate station occurs 5 hours earlier, the high water at the subordinate station will occur at 2100 on *28* March.

Determining Height of High or Low Tide

The height of the tide is found in several ways, depending on local conditions. If a difference for

HUMBOLDT BAY, CALIFORNIA

Times and Heights of High and Low Waters

JULY

Day	Time (h m)	Height (ft)	Height (m)	Day	Time (h m)	Height (ft)	Height (m)
1 F	0251	5.2	1.6	16 Sa	0414	5.1	1.6
	1003	0.2	0.1		1043	0.4	0.1
	1703	5.1	1.6		1725	6.2	1.9
	2245	2.8	0.9		2354	1.4	0.4
2 Sa	0347	4.7	1.4	17 Su	0536	4.5	1.4
	1043	0.6	0.2		1133	1.1	0.3
	1741	5.3	1.6		1814	6.4	2.0
	2351	2.4	0.7				
3 Su	0456	4.2	1.3	18 M	0107	0.9	0.3
	1129	1.1	0.3		0707	4.1	1.2
	1817	5.6	1.7		1224	1.8	0.5
					1903	6.5	2.0
4 M	0059	1.9	0.6	19 Tu	0211	0.4	0.1
	0616	3.9	1.2		0837	4.0	1.2
	1214	1.5	0.5		1323	2.3	0.7
	1854	5.9	1.8		1953	6.6	2.0
5 Tu	0155	1.2	0.4	20 W	0311	0.0	0.0
	0744	3.8	1.2		0951	4.2	1.3
	1303	2.0	0.6		1419	2.7	0.8
	1935	6.3	1.9		2039	6.6	2.0
6 W	0251	0.4	0.1	21 Th	0400	-0.4	-0.1
	0904	4.0	1.2		1052	4.4	1.3
	1359	2.3	0.7		1516	2.9	0.9
	2017	6.6	2.0		2122	6.6	2.0
7 Th	0340	-0.3	-0.1	22 F	0445	-0.6	-0.2
	1012	4.2	1.3		1142	4.6	1.4
	1451	2.6	0.8		1604	3.0	0.9
	2103	7.0	2.1		2204	6.6	2.0
8 F	0429	-1.0	-0.3	23 Sa	0526	-0.8	-0.2
	1111	4.5	1.4		1223	4.7	1.4
	1546	2.7	0.8		1649	3.0	0.9
	2149	7.3	2.2		2241	6.6	2.0
9 Sa	0515	-1.6	-0.5	24 Su	0603	-0.8	-0.2
	1202	4.8	1.5		1256	4.8	1.5
	1636	2.8	0.9		1732	3.0	0.9
	2237	7.6	2.3		2319	6.6	2.0
10 Su	0602	-1.9	-0.6	25 M	0637	-0.8	-0.2
	1249	5.0	1.5		1328	4.9	1.5
	1731	2.7	0.8		1811	3.0	0.9
	2326	7.6	2.3		2355	6.4	2.0
11 M	0647	-2.0	-0.6	26 Tu	0711	-0.7	-0.2
	1334	5.2	1.6		1400	4.9	1.5
	1826	2.6	0.8		1850	2.9	0.9
12 Tu	0018	7.5	2.3	27 W	0030	6.3	1.9
	0734	-1.9	-0.6		0743	-0.5	-0.2
	1420	5.4	1.6		1425	5.0	1.5
	1923	2.5	0.8		1935	2.8	0.9
13 W	0110	7.1	2.2	28 Th	0105	6.0	1.8
	0820	-1.6	-0.5		0815	-0.2	-0.1
	1505	5.6	1.7		1457	5.1	1.6
	2023	2.3	0.7		2018	2.7	0.8
14 Th	0206	6.6	2.0	29 F	0147	5.6	1.7
	0906	-1.0	-0.3		0847	0.2	0.1
	1551	5.8	1.8		1525	5.3	1.6
	2129	2.1	0.6		2107	2.5	0.8
15 F	0305	5.9	1.8	30 Sa	0233	5.2	1.6
	0954	-0.3	-0.1		0919	0.6	0.2
	1639	6.0	1.8		1556	5.4	1.6
	2240	1.8	0.5		2206	2.3	0.7
				31 Su	0321	4.7	1.4
					0954	1.1	0.3
					1632	5.6	1.7
					2305	2.0	0.6

AUGUST

Day	Time (h m)	Height (ft)	Height (m)	Day	Time (h m)	Height (ft)	Height (m)
1 M	0431	4.3	1.3	16 Tu	0033	0.7	0.2
	1033	1.6	0.5		0659	4.1	1.2
	1711	5.8	1.8		1152	2.5	0.8
					1818	6.2	1.9
2 Tu	0011	1.5	0.5	17 W	0140	0.4	0.1
	0552	3.9	1.2		0831	4.1	1.2
	1121	2.1	0.6		1255	2.9	0.9
	1756	6.1	1.9		1915	6.2	1.9
3 W	0116	0.9	0.3	18 Th	0242	0.1	0.0
	0727	3.8	1.2		0939	4.3	1.3
	1220	2.5	0.8		1403	3.1	0.9
	1846	6.4	2.0		2012	6.2	1.9
4 Th	0219	0.2	0.1	19 F	0335	-0.1	0.0
	0854	4.0	1.2		1031	4.6	1.4
	1323	2.8	0.9		1502	3.1	0.9
	1942	6.7	2.0		2101	6.3	1.9
5 F	0316	-0.4	-0.1	20 Sa	0420	-0.3	-0.1
	1002	4.3	1.3		1113	4.8	1.5
	1429	2.9	0.9		1553	3.0	0.9
	2037	7.1	2.2		2147	6.4	2.0
6 Sa	0407	-1.0	-0.3	21 Su	0500	-0.4	-0.1
	1054	4.7	1.4		1148	4.9	1.5
	1531	2.8	0.9		1638	2.8	0.9
	2133	7.4	2.3		2230	6.4	2.0
7 Su	0457	-1.4	-0.4	22 M	0535	-0.4	-0.1
	1141	5.0	1.5		1217	5.0	1.5
	1627	2.6	0.8		1718	2.6	0.8
	2225	7.6	2.3		2307	6.4	2.0
8 M	0543	-1.7	-0.5	23 Tu	0607	-0.3	-0.1
	1223	5.3	1.6		1245	5.1	1.6
	1723	2.3	0.7		1757	2.4	0.7
	2318	7.6	2.3		2343	6.3	1.9
9 Tu	0627	-1.6	-0.5	24 W	0639	-0.2	-0.1
	1302	5.6	1.7		1307	5.3	1.6
	1816	2.0	0.6		1833	2.2	0.7
10 W	0013	7.4	2.3	25 Th	0021	6.1	1.9
	0709	-1.4	-0.4		0708	0.1	0.0
	1341	5.8	1.8		1335	5.4	1.6
	1913	1.7	0.5		1914	2.1	0.6
11 Th	0105	7.0	2.1	26 F	0057	5.8	1.8
	0755	-0.9	-0.3		0736	0.4	0.1
	1423	6.0	1.8		1357	5.5	1.7
	2009	1.5	0.5		1956	1.9	0.6
12 F	0201	6.3	1.9	27 Sa	0135	5.5	1.7
	0837	-0.2	-0.1		0808	0.8	0.2
	1505	6.2	1.9		1425	5.6	1.7
	2110	1.3	0.4		2038	1.7	0.5
13 Sa	0301	5.6	1.7	28 Su	0221	5.1	1.6
	0919	0.5	0.2		0836	1.3	0.4
	1547	6.3	1.9		1454	5.8	1.8
	2215	1.1	0.3		2129	1.5	0.5
14 Su	0408	4.9	1.5	29 M	0315	4.7	1.4
	1005	1.3	0.4		0911	1.8	0.5
	1633	6.3	1.9		1529	5.9	1.8
	2322	0.9	0.3		2226	1.2	0.4
15 M	0528	4.4	1.3	30 Tu	0421	4.3	1.3
	1056	2.0	0.6		0951	2.3	0.7
	1723	6.3	1.9		1612	6.0	1.8
					2331	0.9	0.3
				31 W	0545	4.0	1.2
					1042	2.7	0.8
					1705	6.1	1.9

SEPTEMBER

Day	Time (h m)	Height (ft)	Height (m)	Day	Time (h m)	Height (ft)	Height (m)
1 Th	0041	0.5	0.2	16 F	0205	0.4	0.1
	0720	4.0	1.2		0913	4.6	1.4
	1149	3.0	0.9		1352	3.2	1.0
	1808	6.3	1.9		1943	5.7	1.7
2 F	0149	0.1	0.0	17 Sa	0300	0.3	0.1
	0842	4.3	1.3		1001	4.8	1.5
	1307	3.1	0.9		1450	3.0	0.9
	1915	6.5	2.0		2042	5.8	1.8
3 Sa	0248	-0.4	-0.1	18 Su	0345	0.2	0.1
	0940	4.6	1.4		1033	5.0	1.5
	1421	3.0	0.9		1542	2.7	0.8
	2022	6.8	2.1		2132	5.9	1.8
4 Su	0344	-0.8	-0.2	19 M	0424	0.1	0.0
	1027	5.0	1.5		1105	5.2	1.6
	1524	2.6	0.8		1624	2.3	0.7
	2124	7.1	2.2		2217	6.0	1.8
5 M	0433	-1.0	-0.3	20 Tu	0500	0.2	0.1
	1109	5.4	1.6		1129	5.4	1.6
	1624	2.1	0.6		1702	2.0	0.6
	2221	7.2	2.2		2255	6.0	1.8
6 Tu	0519	-1.1	-0.3	21 W	0531	0.3	0.1
	1148	5.8	1.8		1152	5.6	1.7
	1716	1.6	0.5		1740	1.6	0.5
	2315	7.2	2.2		2334	5.9	1.8
7 W	0602	-0.9	-0.3	22 Th	0600	0.5	0.2
	1223	6.1	1.9		1218	5.7	1.7
	1808	1.1	0.3		1816	1.3	0.4
8 Th	0011	6.9	2.1	23 F	0013	5.8	1.8
	0641	-0.4	-0.1		0629	0.8	0.2
	1258	6.3	1.9		1239	5.9	1.8
	1859	0.7	0.2		1855	1.1	0.3
9 F	0103	6.5	2.0	24 Sa	0052	5.6	1.7
	0722	0.1	0.0		0658	1.2	0.4
	1337	6.5	2.0		1304	6.0	1.8
	1952	0.5	0.2		1930	0.8	0.2
10 Sa	0159	6.0	1.8	25 Su	0133	5.3	1.6
	0802	0.8	0.2		0729	1.6	0.5
	1413	6.5	2.0		1330	6.1	1.9
	2048	0.4	0.1		2012	0.6	0.2
11 Su	0254	5.4	1.6	26 M	0220	5.0	1.5
	0843	1.5	0.5		0801	2.1	0.6
	1454	6.4	2.0		1402	6.2	1.9
	2144	0.4	0.1		2101	0.5	0.2
12 M	0403	4.8	1.5	27 Tu	0315	4.7	1.4
	0929	2.2	0.7		0836	2.5	0.8
	1538	6.3	1.9		1441	6.2	1.9
	2246	0.4	0.1		2157	0.4	0.1
13 Tu	0519	4.4	1.3	28 W	0425	4.4	1.3
	1021	2.7	0.8		0921	2.9	0.9
	1627	6.0	1.8		1527	6.2	1.9
	2352	0.5	0.2		2259	0.3	0.1
14 W	0651	4.3	1.3	29 Th	0548	4.3	1.3
	1123	3.1	0.9		1024	3.2	1.0
	1727	5.8	1.8		1627	6.1	1.9
15 Th	0101	0.5	0.2	30 F	0011	0.1	0.0
	0813	4.4	1.3		0717	4.4	1.3
	1239	3.3	1.0		1146	3.4	1.0
	1834	5.7	1.7		1738	6.1	1.9

Time meridian 120° W. 0000 is midnight. 1200 is noon.
Heights are referred to mean lower low water which is the chart datum of soundings.

Figure 906a. *Tide Tables,* Table 1 (extract).

TABLE 2. - TIDAL DIFFERENCES AND OTHER CONSTANTS

NO.	PLACE	POSITION Lat.	POSITION Long.	DIFFERENCES Time High water	DIFFERENCES Time Low water	DIFFERENCES Height High water	DIFFERENCES Height Low water	RANGES Mean	RANGES Diurnal	Mean Tide Level
		° ' N	° ' W	h. m.	h. m.	ft	ft	ft	ft	ft
	CALIFORNIA Outer Coast-Continued Time meridian, 120°W			on SAN FRANCISCO, p.72						
683	Bodega Harbor entrance....................	38 18	123 03	-0 42	-0 22	-0.1	+0.1	3.8	5.7	3.1
685	Fort Ross................................	38 31	123 15	-0 55	-0 36	-0.1	0.0	3.9	5.7	3.0
687	Point Arena..............................	38 57	123 44	-0 46	-0 27	0.0	0.0	4.0	5.8	3.1
689	Albion...................................	39 14	123 46	-0 35	-0 25	0.0	0.0	4.0	5.8	3.1
691	Little River Harbor......................	39 16	123 47	-0 35	-0 25	0.0	0.0	4.0	5.8	3.1
693	Mendocino, Mendocino Bay.................	39 18	123 48	-0 42	-0 27	0.0	0.0	4.0	5.8	3.1
695	Fort Bragg Landing.......................	39 27	123 49	-0 34	-0 26	+0.1	0.0	4.1	5.8	3.1
696	Noyo River...............................	39 25	123 48	-0 35	-0 18	+0.2	+0.1	4.1	6.0	3.2
697	Westport.................................	39 38	123 47	-0 35	-0 28	0.0	0.0	4.0	5.8	3.1
699	Shelter Cove.............................	40 02	124 04	-0 43	-0 23	+0.3	+0.1	4.2	6.0	3.3
701	Cape Mendocino...........................	40 26	124 25	-0 32	-0 05	0.0	0.0	4.0	5.7	3.1
				on HUMBOLDT BAY, p.76						
703	Eel River entrance.......................	40 38	124 19	-0 36	-0 32	-0.1	0.0	4.4	6.3	3.4
	Humboldt Bay									
705	Entrance.............................	40 46	124 15	-0 14	-0 09	-0.2	0.0	4.3	6.2	3.3
707	HUMBOLDT BAY (South Jetty)...........	40 45	124 14	Daily predictions				4.5	6.4	3.4
709	Fields Landing.......................	40 43	124 13	+0 03	+0 03	+0.3	-0.1	4.9	6.7	3.6
711	Hookton Slough.......................	40 41	124 13	+0 10	+0 09	+0.3	0.0	4.8	6.6	3.6
713	Bucksport............................	40 46	124 12	+0 07	+0 07	+0.1	0.0	4.6	6.5	3.5
715	Eureka...............................	40 48	124 10	+0 28	+0 32	+0.3	0.0	4.8	6.7	3.6
716	Samoa................................	40 49	124 11	+0 32	+0 21	+0.6	0.0	5.1	7.0	3.8
717	Arcata Wharf.........................	40 51	124 07	+0 43	+0 38	+0.6	+0.1	5.0	7.0	3.8
719	Trinidad Harbor..........................	41 03	124 09	-0 37	-0 40	+0.1	0.0	4.6	6.4	3.5
721	Crescent City............................	41 45	124 12	-0 32	-0 29	+0.6	0.0	5.1	6.9	3.7
	OREGON									
723	Brookings, Chetco Cove...................	42 03	124 17	-0 30	-0 26	+0.6	0.0	5.1	6.9	3.7
725	Wedderburn, Rogue River..................	42 26	124 25	-0 22	-0 14	+0.3	-0.1	4.9	6.7	3.6
727	Port Orford..............................	42 44	124 30	-0 24	-0 21	+0.9	+0.1	5.3	7.3	3.9
729	Bandon, Coquille River...................	43 07	124 25	-0 08	-0 02	+0.6	-0.1	5.2	7.0	3.7
	Coos Bay									
731	Charleston...........................	43 21	124 19	-0 01	0 00	+1.2	0.0	5.7	7.5	4.1
733	Empire...............................	43 24	124 17	+0 41	+0 50	+0.3	-0.1	4.9	6.7	3.5
735	Coos Bay.............................	43 23	124 13	+1 30	+1 28	+1.0	-0.1	5.6	7.3	3.9
	Umpqua River									
737	Entrance.............................	43 41	124 12	+0 09	+0 03	+0.6	0.0	5.1	6.9	3.7
739	Gardiner.............................	43 44	124 07	+1 00	+1 09	+0.4	-0.2	5.1	6.7	3.5
741	Reedsport............................	43 42	124 06	+1 15	+1 24	+0.4	-0.2	5.1	6.7	3.6
	Siuslaw River									
743	Entrance.............................	44 01	124 08	-0 02	+0 03	+1.0	0.0	5.5	7.3	4.0
745	Florence.............................	43 58	124 06	+0 48	+0 58	+0.3	-0.2	5.0	6.6	3.5
747	Waldport, Alsea Bay......................	44 26	124 04	+0 25	+0 31	+1.3	0.0	5.8	7.7	4.1
	Yaquina Bay and River									
749	Bar at entrance......................	44 37	124 05	+0 03	+0 09	+1.5	+0.1	5.9	7.9	4.2
751	Newport..............................	44 38	124 03	+0 13	+0 12	+1.6	+0.1	6.0	8.0	4.3
752	Southbeach...........................	44 39	124 03	+0 02	+0 01	+1.9	+0.1	6.3	8.3	4.5
753	Yaquina..............................	44 36	124 01	+0 24	+0 25	+1.8	+0.1	6.2	8.0	4.4
755	Winant...............................	44 35	124 00	+0 32	+0 46	+1.8	0.0	6.3	8.2	4.3
757	Toledo...............................	44 37	123 56	+0 68	+1 09	+1.7	-0.1	6.3	8.1	4.2
759	Taft, Siletz Bay........................	44 56	124 01	+0 17	+0 43	+0.2	-0.3	5.0	6.6	3.4
761	Kernville, Siletz River.................	44 54	124 06	+0 53	+1 23	*0.95	*0.67	4.6	6.1	3.1
763	Nestucca Bay entrance...................	45 10	123 50	+0 24	+0 42	+1.2	-0.1	5.8	7.6	4.0
	Tillamook Bay									
765	Barview..............................	45 34	123 57	+0 11	+0 26	+1.1	-0.1	5.7	7.5	3.9
766	Garibaldi............................	45 34	123 55	+0 43	+0 46	+1.4	0.0	5.9	7.8	4.2
767	Miami Cove...........................	45 33	123 54	+0 44	+0 56	+1.0	-0.1	5.6	7.4	3.9
769	Bay City.............................	45 31	123 54	+1 02	+1 30	+0.7	-0.1	5.4	7.1	3.7
771	Tillamook, Hoquarten Slough..........	45 28	123 51	+1 21	+2 45	*1.03	*0.58	5.2	6.6	3.3
	Nehalem River									
773	Brighton.............................	45 40	123 56	+0 20	+0 24	+1.4	0.0	5.9	7.8	4.1
775	Nehalem..............................	45 43	123 53	+0 46	+1 26	+0.8	-0.3	5.6	7.2	3.7
	OREGON and WASHINGTON Columbia River <5>			on ASTORIA, p.80						
777	Columbia River entrance (N. Jetty)......	46 16	124 04	-0 46	-1 10	-0.7	+0.1	5.6	7.5	4.0
779	Ilwaco, Baker Bay, Wash.................	46 18	124 02	-0 15	-0 09	-0.5	-0.1	6.0	7.6	4.0
781	Chinook, Baker Bay, Wash................	46 16	123 57	-0 15	-0 44	-0.2	0.0	6.2	7.9	4.2
783	Hungry Harbor, Wash.....................	46 16	123 51	+0 02	-0 19	+0.1	+0.1	6.4	8.2	4.4
785	Point Adams, Oreg.......................	46 12	123 57	-0 27	-0 48	+0.1	+0.1	6.4	8.3	4.4
787	Warrenton, Skipanon River, Oreg.........	46 10	123 55	-0 15	-0 29	+0.2	+0.1	6.5	8.3	4.4
789	Astoria (Youngs Bay), Oreg..............	46 10	123 50	-0 15	-0 24	+0.4	+0.1	6.7	8.6	4.5
791	Astoria (Port Docks), Oreg..............	46 11	123 52	-0 10	-0 13	-0.2	0.0	6.2	8.0	4.2
793	ASTORIA (Tongue Point), Oreg............	46 13	123 46	Daily predictions				6.5	8.2	4.3
795	Settlers Point, Oreg....................	46 10	123 41	+0 20	+0 43	-0.2	-0.1	6.3	8.0	4.1
797	Harrington Point, Wash..................	46 16	123 39	+0 19	+0 42	-0.5	-0.2	6.1	7.7	3.9

Endnotes can be found at the end of table 2.

Figure 906b. *Tide Tables*, Table 2 (extract).

TABLE 3.—HEIGHT OF TIDE AT ANY TIME

Duration of rise or fall, see footnote	Time from the nearest high water or low water														
h. m.	h. m.	h. m.	h. m.	h. m.	h. m.	h. m.	h. m.	h. m.	h. m.	h. m.	h. m.	h. m.	h. m.	h. m.	h. m.
4 00	0 08	0 16	0 24	0 32	0 40	0 48	0 56	1 04	1 12	1 20	1 28	1 36	1 44	1 52	2 00
4 20	0 09	0 17	0 26	0 35	0 43	0 52	1 01	1 09	1 18	1 27	1 35	1 44	1 53	2 01	2 10
4 40	0 09	0 19	0 28	0 37	0 47	0 56	1 05	1 15	1 24	1 33	1 43	1 52	2 01	2 11	2 20
5 00	0 10	0 20	0 30	0 40	0 50	1 00	1 10	1 20	1 30	1 40	1 50	2 00	2 10	2 20	2 30
5 20	0 11	0 21	0 32	0 43	0 53	1 04	1 15	1 25	1 36	1 47	1 57	2 08	2 19	2 29	2 40
5 40	0 11	0 23	0 34	0 45	0 57	1 08	1 19	1 31	1 42	1 53	2 05	2 16	2 27	2 39	2 50
6 00	0 12	0 24	0 36	0 48	1 00	1 12	1 24	1 36	1 48	2 00	2 12	2 24	2 36	2 48	3 00
6 20	0 13	0 25	0 38	0 51	1 03	1 16	1 29	1 41	1 54	2 07	2 19	2 32	2 45	2 57	3 10
6 40	0 13	0 27	0 40	0 53	1 07	1 20	1 33	1 47	2 00	2 13	2 27	2 40	2 53	3 07	3 20
7 00	0 14	0 28	0 42	0 56	1 10	1 24	1 38	1 52	2 06	2 20	2 34	2 48	3 02	3 16	3 30
7 20	0 15	0 29	0 44	0 59	1 13	1 28	1 43	1 57	2 12	2 27	2 41	2 56	3 11	3 25	3 40
7 40	0 15	0 31	0 46	1 01	1 17	1 32	1 47	2 03	2 18	2 33	2 49	3 04	3 19	3 35	3 50
8 00	0 16	0 32	0 48	1 04	1 20	1 36	1 52	2 08	2 24	2 40	2 56	3 12	3 28	3 44	4 00
8 20	0 17	0 33	0 50	1 07	1 23	1 40	1 57	2 13	2 30	2 47	3 03	3 20	3 37	3 53	4 10
8 40	0 17	0 35	0 52	1 09	1 27	1 44	2 01	2 19	2 36	2 53	3 11	3 28	3 45	4 03	4 20
9 00	0 18	0 36	0 54	1 12	1 30	1 48	2 06	2 24	2 42	3 00	3 18	3 36	3 54	4 12	4 30
9 20	0 19	0 37	0 56	1 15	1 33	1 52	2 11	2 29	2 48	3 07	3 25	3 44	4 03	4 21	4 40
9 40	0 19	0 39	0 58	1 17	1 37	1 56	2 15	2 35	2 54	3 13	3 33	3 52	4 11	4 31	4 50
10 00	0 20	0 40	1 00	1 20	1 40	2 00	2 20	2 40	3 00	3 20	3 40	4 00	4 20	4 40	5 00
10 20	0 21	0 41	1 02	1 23	1 43	2 04	2 25	2 45	3 06	3 27	3 47	4 08	4 29	4 49	5 10
10 40	0 21	0 43	1 04	1 25	1 47	2 08	2 29	2 51	3 12	3 33	3 55	4 16	4 37	4 59	5 20

Range of tide, see footnote	Correction to height														
Ft.	Ft.	Ft.	Ft.	Ft.	Ft.	Ft.	Ft.	Ft.	Ft.	Ft.	Ft.	Ft.	Ft.	Ft.	Ft.
0.5	0.0	0.0	0.0	0.0	0.0	0.0	0.1	0.1	0.1	0.1	0.1	0.2	0.2	0.2	0.2
1.0	0.0	0.0	0.0	0.0	0.1	0.1	0.1	0.2	0.2	0.2	0.3	0.3	0.4	0.4	0.5
1.5	0.0	0.0	0.0	0.1	0.1	0.1	0.2	0.2	0.3	0.4	0.4	0.5	0.6	0.7	0.8
2.0	0.0	0.0	0.0	0.1	0.1	0.2	0.3	0.3	0.4	0.5	0.6	0.7	0.8	0.9	1.0
2.5	0.0	0.0	0.1	0.1	0.2	0.2	0.3	0.4	0.5	0.6	0.7	0.9	1.0	1.1	1.2
3.0	0.0	0.0	0.1	0.1	0.2	0.3	0.4	0.5	0.6	0.8	0.9	1.0	1.2	1.3	1.5
3.5	0.0	0.0	0.1	0.2	0.2	0.3	0.4	0.6	0.7	0.9	1.0	1.2	1.4	1.6	1.8
4.0	0.0	0.0	0.1	0.2	0.3	0.4	0.5	0.7	0.8	1.0	1.2	1.4	1.6	1.8	2.0
4.5	0.0	0.0	0.1	0.2	0.3	0.4	0.6	0.7	0.9	1.1	1.3	1.6	1.8	2.0	2.2
5.0	0.0	0.1	0.1	0.2	0.3	0.5	0.6	0.8	1.0	1.2	1.5	1.7	2.0	2.2	2.5
5.5	0.0	0.1	0.1	0.2	0.4	0.5	0.7	0.9	1.1	1.4	1.6	1.9	2.2	2.5	2.8
6.0	0.0	0.1	0.1	0.3	0.4	0.6	0.8	1.0	1.2	1.5	1.8	2.1	2.4	2.7	3.0
6.5	0.0	0.1	0.2	0.3	0.4	0.6	0.8	1.1	1.3	1.6	1.9	2.2	2.6	2.9	3.2
7.0	0.0	0.1	0.2	0.3	0.5	0.7	0.9	1.2	1.4	1.8	2.1	2.4	2.8	3.1	3.5
7.5	0.0	0.1	0.2	0.3	0.5	0.7	1.0	1.2	1.5	1.9	2.2	2.6	3.0	3.4	3.8
8.0	0.0	0.1	0.2	0.3	0.5	0.8	1.0	1.3	1.6	2.0	2.4	2.8	3.2	3.6	4.0
8.5	0.0	0.1	0.2	0.4	0.6	0.8	1.1	1.4	1.8	2.1	2.5	2.9	3.4	3.8	4.2
9.0	0.0	0.1	0.2	0.4	0.6	0.9	1.2	1.5	1.9	2.2	2.7	3.1	3.6	4.0	4.5
9.5	0.0	0.1	0.2	0.4	0.6	0.9	1.2	1.6	2.0	2.4	2.8	3.3	3.8	4.3	4.8
10.0	0.0	0.1	0.2	0.4	0.7	1.0	1.3	1.7	2.1	2.5	3.0	3.5	4.0	4.5	5.0
10.5	0.0	0.1	0.3	0.5	0.7	1.0	1.3	1.7	2.2	2.6	3.1	3.6	4.2	4.7	5.2
11.0	0.0	0.1	0.3	0.5	0.7	1.1	1.4	1.8	2.3	2.8	3.3	3.8	4.4	4.9	5.5
11.5	0.0	0.1	0.3	0.5	0.8	1.1	1.5	1.9	2.4	2.9	3.4	4.0	4.6	5.1	5.8
12.0	0.0	0.1	0.3	0.5	0.8	1.1	1.5	2.0	2.5	3.0	3.6	4.1	4.8	5.4	6.0
12.5	0.0	0.1	0.3	0.5	0.8	1.2	1.6	2.1	2.6	3.1	3.7	4.3	5.0	5.6	6.2
13.0	0.0	0.1	0.3	0.6	0.9	1.2	1.7	2.2	2.7	3.2	3.9	4.5	5.1	5.8	6.5
13.5	0.0	0.1	0.3	0.6	0.9	1.3	1.7	2.2	2.8	3.4	4.0	4.7	5.3	6.0	6.8
14.0	0.0	0.2	0.3	0.6	0.9	1.3	1.8	2.3	2.9	3.5	4.2	4.8	5.5	6.3	7.0
14.5	0.0	0.2	0.4	0.6	1.0	1.4	1.9	2.4	3.0	3.6	4.3	5.0	5.7	6.5	7.2
15.0	0.0	0.2	0.4	0.6	1.0	1.4	1.9	2.5	3.1	3.8	4.4	5.2	5.9	6.7	7.5
15.5	0.0	0.2	0.4	0.7	1.0	1.5	2.0	2.6	3.2	3.9	4.6	5.4	6.1	6.9	7.8
16.0	0.0	0.2	0.4	0.7	1.1	1.5	2.1	2.6	3.3	4.0	4.7	5.5	6.3	7.2	8.0
16.5	0.0	0.2	0.4	0.7	1.1	1.6	2.1	2.7	3.4	4.1	4.9	5.7	6.5	7.4	8.2
17.0	0.0	0.2	0.4	0.7	1.1	1.6	2.2	2.8	3.5	4.2	5.0	5.9	6.7	7.6	8.5
17.5	0.0	0.2	0.4	0.8	1.2	1.7	2.2	2.9	3.6	4.4	5.2	6.0	6.9	7.8	8.8
18.0	0.0	0.2	0.4	0.8	1.2	1.7	2.3	3.0	3.7	4.5	5.3	6.2	7.1	8.1	9.0
18.5	0.1	0.2	0.5	0.8	1.2	1.8	2.4	3.1	3.8	4.6	5.5	6.4	7.3	8.3	9.2
19.0	0.1	0.2	0.5	0.8	1.3	1.8	2.4	3.1	3.9	4.8	5.6	6.6	7.5	8.5	9.5
19.5	0.1	0.2	0.5	0.8	1.3	1.9	2.5	3.2	4.0	4.9	5.8	6.7	7.7	8.7	9.8
20.0	0.1	0.2	0.5	0.9	1.3	1.9	2.6	3.3	4.1	5.0	5.9	6.9	7.9	9.0	10.0

Figure 906c. *Tide Tables*, Table 3.

height of high water is given, with 0.0 feet tabulated as the low-water difference, apply the high-water difference in accordance with its sign to the height of high water at the reference station. The height of low water will be, of course, the same as that at the reference station. If a difference for height of low as well as high water is given, each must be applied in accordance with its sign to the height of the corresponding tide at the reference station, adding the difference if its sign is plus (+) and subtracting if its sign is minus (−). Note that height differences are only in terms of feet; if a final height is desired in meters, conversion is made after the addition or subtraction is done. If a *ratio* of rise is given, the heights of the tides at the subordinate station can be obtained by *multiplying* the heights of both high and low tides at the reference station by the respective ratios.

Any unusual conditions pertaining to a subordinate station, or any complex calculations required, are explained in keyed endnotes that will be found following Table 2.

Tidal Ranges

The mean tide level and the ranges of tide (mean, plus spring, diurnal, or tropic) are listed in Table 2, but are seldom used by a navigator except as items of general interest. An explanation of them is given in the *Tide Tables*.

Height of Tide at Intermediate Time

The height of the tide at a specific time other than those tabulated in Table 1 or computed using Table 2 can be found by means of Table 3, illustrated in figure 906c. This table is easy to use, and the instructions given below the table are explicit.

Note that interpolation is not done when using Table 3. The predictions of times and heights of tide are influenced by local conditions to the extent that they are not exact enough to make meaningful any interpolation for more precise values.

Other Information in Tide Tables

The various volumes of the *Tide Tables* also contain other information that may be of interest to a navigator.

The local mean time of sunrise and sunset is given in Table 4 for each two degrees of latitude. While this information is usually obtained from an *almanac*, it should be noted that values in Table 4 extend to latitude 76° N; this is 4° beyond the latitude range of American almanacs.

Table 5 provides a quick and convenient method for converting local mean time to standard time when the difference in longitude is known.

Table 6 lists the time of moonrise and moonset for a few selected locations.

Table 7 provides a convenient means of converting feet to meters, and vice versa.

A glossary of terms precedes the index of reference and subordinate stations. The inside back cover of each volume gives data for the phases of the moon, apogee, perigee, and greatest north and south declinations, and crossing of the equator; it also gives solar data on equinoxes and solstices.

Examples of Tidal Calculations

907 The following examples illustrate the use of *Tide Tables;* all data are taken from the extracts shown in figures 906a, b, and c.

Example 1: Determination of predicted time and height of a tide at a reference station.

Required: The time and height of morning high water at Humboldt Bay, California, on 6 August. (Local time is then Pacific Daylight Time, PDT.)

Solution: The desired information can be extracted directly from Table 1 (figure 906a) without calculation.

Answer: High water is predicted for 1054 Pacific Standard Time (PST) which would be 1154 PDT. The height of tide is predicted to be 4.7 feet (1.4 meters). Note that if the date had been 7 August, the PST of 1141 would move across noon when changed to PDT and this would be an *afternoon* high tide; on 7 August there is no morning high water.

Example 2: Determination of predicted time and height of a tide at a subordinate station.

Required: The time and height of morning low water at Port Orford, Oregon, on 10 August.

Solution: Determine the time and height differences for the location from Table 2; apply these to the appropriate tide at the reference station.

Differences at subordinate station for low water: time − 0ʰ21ᵐ; height +0.1 feet.

Reference station: Humboldt Bay; low water at 0709; height −1.4 feet (−0.4 meters).

07 09	−1.4 feet
− 0 21	+0.1
06 48	−1.3 feet

Answer: The morning low water is predicted to be at 0648 PST, or 0748 PDT; predicted height is 1.3 feet (0.4 m) *below* the datum of lower low water. Note that at this time *actual depths of water are less than charted soundings.*

Example 3: Determination of predicted height of tide at a specified time at a reference station.

Required: Height of tide at Humboldt Bay at 1100 on 23 August.

TABLE 4.-SUNRISE AND SUNSET

Date	30° N. Rise	30° N. Set	32° N. Rise	32° N. Set	34° N. Rise	34° N. Set	36° N. Rise	36° N. Set	38° N. Rise	38° N. Set	40° N. Rise	40° N. Set
	h. m.	h. m.	h. m.	h. m.	h. m.	h. m.	h. m.	h. m.	h. m.	h. m.	h. m.	h. m.
Jan. 1	6 56	17 11	7 01	17 07	7 06	17 02	7 11	16 57	7 16	16 51	7 22	16 45
6	6 57	17 15	7 02	17 11	7 06	17 06	7 11	17 01	7 17	16 56	7 22	16 50
11	6 57	17 19	7 02	17 15	7 06	17 10	7 11	17 05	7 16	17 00	7 22	16 55
16	6 57	17 23	7 01	17 19	7 05	17 15	7 10	17 10	7 15	17 05	7 20	17 00
21	6 55	17 28	6 59	17 24	7 04	17 20	7 08	17 15	7 12	17 11	7 17	17 06
26	6 54	17 32	6 57	17 28	7 01	17 25	7 05	17 21	7 09	17 16	7 14	17 12
31	6 51	17 36	6 55	17 33	6 58	17 29	7 02	17 26	7 06	17 22	7 10	17 18
Feb. 5	6 48	17 41	6 51	17 37	6 54	17 34	6 58	17 31	7 01	17 27	7 05	17 24
10	6 44	17 45	6 47	17 42	6 50	17 39	6 53	17 36	6 56	17 33	6 59	17 30
15	6 40	17 49	6 43	17 46	6 45	17 44	6 48	17 41	6 50	17 39	6 53	17 36
20	6 36	17 53	6 38	17 50	6 40	17 48	6 42	17 46	6 44	17 44	6 47	17 41
25	6 31	17 56	6 32	17 55	6 34	17 53	6 36	17 51	6 38	17 49	6 40	17 47
Mar. 2	6 25	18 00	6 27	17 58	6 28	17 57	6 29	17 56	6 31	17 54	6 32	17 53
7	6 20	18 03	6 21	18 02	6 22	18 01	6 23	18 00	6 24	17 59	6 25	17 58
12	6 14	18 06	6 14	18 06	6 15	18 05	6 16	18 05	6 16	18 04	6 17	18 04
17	6 08	18 10	6 08	18 09	6 08	18 09	6 09	18 09	6 09	18 09	6 09	18 09
22	6 02	18 13	6 02	18 13	6 01	18 13	6 01	18 13	6 01	18 14	6 01	18 14
27	5 56	18 16	5 55	18 16	5 55	18 17	5 54	18 18	5 53	18 18	5 53	18 19
Apr. 1	5 50	18 19	5 49	18 20	5 48	18 21	5 47	18 22	5 46	18 23	5 45	18 24
6	5 44	18 22	5 43	18 23	5 41	18 24	5 40	18 26	5 38	18 27	5 37	18 29
11	5 38	18 25	5 36	18 26	5 35	18 28	5 33	18 30	5 31	18 32	5 29	18 34
16	5 33	18 28	5 30	18 30	5 28	18 32	5 26	18 34	5 24	18 37	5 21	18 39
21	5 27	18 31	5 25	18 33	5 22	18 36	5 20	18 39	5 17	18 41	5 14	18 44
26	5 22	18 34	5 19	18 37	5 17	18 40	5 13	18 43	5 10	18 46	5 07	18 49
May 1	5 17	18 37	5 14	18 40	5 11	18 43	5 08	18 47	5 04	18 51	5 00	18 54
6	5 13	18 40	5 10	18 44	5 06	18 47	5 03	18 51	4 59	18 55	4 54	18 59
11	5 09	18 44	5 06	18 47	5 02	18 51	4 58	18 55	4 54	19 00	4 49	19 04
16	5 06	18 47	5 02	18 51	4 58	18 55	4 54	18 59	4 49	19 04	4 44	19 09
21	5 03	18 50	4 59	18 54	4 55	18 59	4 50	19 03	4 45	19 08	4 40	19 14
26	5 01	18 53	4 57	18 57	4 52	19 02	4 47	19 07	4 42	19 12	4 36	19 18
31	5 00	18 56	4 55	19 00	4 50	19 05	4 45	19 11	4 40	19 16	4 34	19 22
June 5	4 59	18 58	4 54	19 03	4 49	19 08	4 43	19 14	4 38	19 19	4 32	19 25
10	4 58	19 01	4 53	19 05	4 48	19 11	4 43	19 16	4 37	19 22	4 31	19 28
15	4 58	19 02	4 53	19 07	4 48	19 13	4 43	19 18	4 37	19 24	4 30	19 30
20	4 59	19 04	4 54	19 09	4 49	19 14	4 43	19 20	4 37	19 26	4 31	19 32
25	5 00	19 05	4 55	19 10	4 50	19 15	4 44	19 21	4 38	19 26	4 32	19 33
30	5 02	19 05	4 57	19 10	4 52	19 15	4 46	19 21	4 40	19 27	4 34	19 33

Figure 906d. *Tide Tables,* Table 4 (extract).

Solution: Convert daylight time to standard time. Use Table 1 to determine times and heights of high and low tides on either side of the specified time. Use Table 3 to determine height at the specified time.

1100 PDT is 1000 PST, the zone time used in Table 1 for this area.

The applicable times and heights of tide from Table 1 are:

0607	−0.3 feet
1245	5.1 feet

To use Table 3, calculate the range of the tide: 5.1 − (−0.3) = 5.4 feet. Calculate duration of rise or fall: 1245 − 0607 = 6^h38^m rising. Calculate time interval from the specified time to the *nearest* high or low water: 1245 − 1000 = 2^h45^m (from high water).

Entering Table 3 on the line for the nearest tabulated duration, 6^h40^m, go across to the nearest tab-

ulated value for the time interval 2^h40^m. Go down this column to the line in the lower part of Table 3 for the nearest value of range, 5.5 feet; here read the correction to height, 1.9 feet.

Since the time interval is taken from high water, the correction is subtracted from the height at high water: 5.1 − 1.9 = 3.2.

Answer: The predicted height of tide at 1100 PDT is 3.2 feet (1.0 m) above datum.

Example 4: Determination of predicted height of tide at a subordinate station at a specified time.

Required: Height of tide at Kernville, Oregon, on the Siletz River, at 0930 PDT on 21 August.

Solution: (See figure 907.) Convert daylight time to standard time. Use Table 2, then Table 1, to determine the times and heights of high and low waters on either side of the specified time. Use Table 3 to determine height at specified time.

0930 PDT is 0830 PST, the time zone of Table 1 for this area.

Difference of longitude between local and standard meridian	Correction to local mean time to obtain standard time	Difference of longitude between local and standard meridian	Correction to local mean time to obtain standard time	Difference of longitude between local and standard meridian	Correction to local mean time to obtain standard time
° ′ ° ′	*Minutes*	° ′ ° ′	*Minutes*	°	*Hours*
0 00 to 0 07	0	7 23 to 7 37	30	15	1
0 08 to 0 22	1	7 38 to 7 52	31	30	2
0 23 to 0 37	2	7 53 to 8 07	32	45	3
0 38 to 0 52	3	8 08 to 8 22	33	60	4
0 53 to 1 07	4	8 23 to 8 37	34	75	5
1 08 to 1 22	5	8 38 to 8 52	35	90	6
1 23 to 1 37	6	8 53 to 9 07	36	105	7
1 38 to 1 52	7	9 08 to 9 22	37	120	8
1 53 to 2 07	8	9 23 to 9 37	38	135	9
2 08 to 2 22	9	9 38 to 9 52	39	150	10
2 23 to 2 37	10	9 53 to 10 07	40	165	11
2 38 to 2 52	11	10 08 to 10 22	41	180	12
2 53 to 3 07	12	10 23 to 10 37	42		
3 08 to 3 22	13	10 38 to 10 52	43		
3 23 to 3 37	14	10 53 to 11 07	44		
3 38 to 3 52	15	11 08 to 11 22	45		
3 53 to 4 07	16	11 23 to 11 37	46		
4 08 to 4 22	17	11 38 to 11 52	47		
4 23 to 4 37	18	11 53 to 12 07	48		
4 38 to 4 52	19	12 08 to 12 22	49		
4 53 to 5 07	20	12 23 to 12 37	50		
5 08 to 5 22	21	12 38 to 12 52	51		
5 23 to 5 37	22	12 53 to 13 07	52		
5 38 to 5 52	23	13 08 to 13 22	53		
5 53 to 6 07	24	13 23 to 13 37	54		
6 08 to 6 22	25	13 38 to 13 52	55		
6 23 to 6 37	26	13 53 to 14 07	56		
6 38 to 6 52	27	14 08 to 14 22	57		
6 53 to 7 07	28	14 23 to 14 37	58		
7 08 to 7 22	29	14 38 to 14 52	59		

Figure 906c. *Tide Tables*, Table 5.

The applicable factors from Table 2 are: high water $+0^h53^m$, 0.95 ratio; low water $+1^h23^m$, 0.67 ratio.

Use these factors to determine the applicable high and low waters at Kernville on either side of 0930 PDT (0830 PST).

Low water   05 00   −0.4   feet
              + 1:23   ×0.67
              ──────   ───────
                06 23   −0.268
                             −0.3   (rounded)

High water   11 48   4.9   feet
              + 0:53   ×0.95
              ──────   ───────
                12 41   4.655
                             4.7   (rounded)

With these data, calculate the range of the tide: 4.7 − (−0.3) = 5.0 feet. Calculate the duration of the rise or fall: 1241 − 0623 = 6^h18^m. Calculate the time interval from the specified time to the time of the nearest high or low water: 0830 − 0623 = 2^h07^m (from low water).

Entering Table 3 on the *line* for the nearest value of duration, 6^h20^m, go across to the nearest tabulated value of time interval, 2^h07^m (in this particular instance the "nearest" value is exact). Go down this *column* to the *line* for the nearest value of range (again, this happens to be an exact value), 5.0 feet; here read the correction for height, 1.2 feet.

Since the interval was from low water, the tide is rising; add the correction to the height at low water: −0.3 + 1.2 = 0.9 feet.

Answer: The predicted height of the tide at 0930 PDT is 0.9 feet (0.3 m) above datum.

Example 5: Determination of the predicted time that a specific height of tide will be reached during a specified portion of a day at a reference station.

Required: How early in the afternoon of 9 August at Humboldt Bay is it predicted that the rising tide reach the datum plane, a height of 0.0 feet?

TABLE 6—MOONRISE AND MOONSET
SAN FRANCISCO, CALIF.

Day	January Rise	January Set	February Rise	February Set	March Rise	March Set	April Rise	April Set	May Rise	May Set	June Rise	June Set	Day
	h. m.	h. m.	h. m.	h. m.	h. m.	h. m.	h. m.	h. m.	h. m.	h. m.	h. m.	h. m.	
1	14 26	03 58	15 36	05 09	14 20	03 44	16 12	04 13	17 13	03 58	19 28	04 52	1
2	15 10	04 51	16 35	05 52	15 20	04 26	17 19	04 50	18 24	04 39	20 31	05 51	2
3	15 58	05 42	17 36	06 33	16 22	05 05	18 28	05 27	19 36	05 24	21 27	06 56	3
4	16 51	06 30	18 39	07 11	17 27	05 43	19 38	06 07	20 44	06 15	22 16	08 02	4
5	17 47	07 15	19 43	07 47	18 33	06 20	20 49	06 50	21 49	07 11	22 58	09 09	5
6	18 46	07 57	20 48	08 23	19 40	06 56	21 58	07 37	22 47	08 11	23 35	10 14	6
7	19 47	08 36	21 54	08 59	20 49	07 34	23 02	08 28	23 37	09 15	.. ..	11 16	7
8	20 49	09 12	23 01	09 35	21 57	08 14	.. ..	09 25	.. ..	10 20	00 16	12 17	8
9	21 52	09 47	.. ..	10 15	23 05	08 57	00 02	10 25	00 21	11 24	00 43	13 16	9
10	22 57	10 21	00 08	10 58	.. ..	09 44	00 54	11 27	01 00	12 26	01 14	14 13	10
11	.. ..	10 56	01 13	11 45	00 10	10 35	01 41	12 29	01 35	13 26	01 46	15 09	11
12	00 02	11 33	02 17	12 38	01 11	11 31	02 22	13 32	02 08	14 25	02 19	16 04	12
13	01 09	12 13	03 17	13 36	02 07	12 31	02 59	14 32	02 39	15 22	02 54	16 58	13
14	02 15	12 58	04 11	14 37	02 57	13 33	03 33	15 32	03 11	16 18	03 33	17 50	14
15	03 22	13 49	05 00	15 41	03 41	14 35	04 05	16 30	03 43	17 14	04 15	18 41	15
16	04 26	14 45	05 43	16 45	04 21	15 37	04 36	17 27	04 17	18 09	05 00	19 29	16
17	05 26	15 47	06 23	17 48	04 57	16 39	05 08	18 24	04 54	19 03	05 49	20 14	17
18	06 20	16 51	06 58	18 50	05 31	17 39	05 41	19 19	05 33	19 55	06 41	20 56	18
19	07 07	17 57	07 32	19 50	06 04	18 37	06 16	20 14	06 16	20 44	07 36	21 34	19
20	07 49	19 02	08 04	20 49	06 35	19 35	06 54	21 07	07 03	21 31	08 33	22 10	20
21	08 27	20 05	08 36	21 46	07 08	20 32	07 35	21 59	07 53	22 14	09 32	22 44	21
22	09 02	21 06	09 08	22 42	07 41	21 27	08 19	22 47	08 46	22 54	10 32	23 18	22
23	09 34	22 05	09 43	23 38	08 17	22 22	09 07	23 33	09 42	23 32	11 33	23 52	23
24	10 05	23 03	10 20	.. ..	08 56	23 14	09 59	.. ..	10 40	.. ..	12 37	.. ..	24
25	10 36	23 59	11 00	00 31	09 38	.. ..	10 53	00 15	11 39	00 08	13 42	00 28	25
26	11 09	.. ..	11 43	01 23	10 24	00 04	11 50	00 55	12 41	00 42	14 50	01 06	26
27	11 45	00 54	12 31	02 13	11 14	00 52	12 50	01 32	13 45	01 16	15 58	01 49	27
28	12 23	01 48	13 24	03 00	12 07	01 37	13 52	02 08	14 51	01 52	17 06	02 37	28
29	13 05	02 41	.. ..	.. ..	13 04	02 19	14 57	02 44	16 00	02 30	18 11	03 32	29
30	13 51	03 33			14 04	02 59	16 04	03 20	17 10	03 12	19 11	04 34	30
31	14 41	04 22			15 07	03 37			18 21	03 59			31

Figure 906f. *Tide Tables*, Table 6 (extract).

Solution: Study Table 1 and note the trend of the tide; low water at 0627, −1.6 feet rising to high water at 1302, 5.6 feet.

Determine the duration of rise: $1302 − 0627 = 6^h35^m$. Determine the range: $5.6 − (−1.6) = 7.2$ feet. Determine the correction for height needed: $0.0 − (−1.4) = 1.4$ feet.

Use the lower part of Table 3 with the nearest tabulated values of range, 7.0, and correction for height, 1.4, to determine the column to be used. Go up this column to the line for the nearest tabulated value of duration, 6^h40^m; here read the time interval, 2^h00^m.

Since the interval is that of rising from low water, add this time to the time of low water: $0627 + 2:00 = 0827$ PST or 0927 PDT.

Answer: By 0927 PDT the tide is predicted to have risen to a level of 0.0 feet, the local datum for charted depths. Note that this problem at a subordinate station would be solved in a similar manner after first calculating the times and heights of high and low waters at that location.

Example 6: Determination of the available clearance under a fixed bridge at a given time and location.

Required: The available clearance under a bridge charted with a vertical clearance of 19 feet; the chart datum for heights is mean high water, and for depths it is mean lower low water.

Solution: Determine the height of tide at the specified time in accordance with prior examples; assume for this example that it is 6.9 feet. Determine mean tide level from Table 2; assume for this example that it is 5.6 feet. Determine the mean range from Table 2; assume for this example that it is 5.6 feet. Take one-half of the mean range and add it to the mean tide level—$5.6 ÷ 2 = 2.8$ feet; $2.8 + 3.9 = 6.7$ feet. Calculate the water level at the specified time with respect to mean high water—$6.9 − 6.7 = 0.2$ feet. The water level is thus 0.2 feet above the datum for heights; there is that much less clearance; $19 − 0.2 = 18.8$ feet.

Answer: The available vertical clearance at the specified time is 18.8 feet (5.7 m).

ASTRONOMICAL DATA

Greenwich mean time of the moon's phases, apogee, perigee, greatest north and south declination, moon on the Equator, and the solar equinoxes and solstices.

January

	d.	h.	m.
N	3	17	..
O	5	12	10
E	10	17	..
◑	12	19	55
P	16	10	..
S	17	01	..
●	19	14	11
E	23	15	..
◐	27	05	11
A	28	06	..
N	31	02	..

February

	d.	h.	m.
O	4	03	56
E	7	00	..
P	11	04	..
◑	11	04	07
S	13	09	..
●	18	03	37
E	20	01	..
A	25	03	..
◑	26	02	50
N	27	11	..

March

	d.	h.	m.
O	5	17	13
E	6	08	..
P	8	23	..
◑	12	11	35
S	12	15	..
E	19	09	..
●	19	18	33
O₁	20	17	43
A	24	22	..
N	26	19	..
◐	27	22	27

April

	d.	h.	m.
E	2	18	..
O	4	04	09
P	5	21	..
S	8	21	..
◑	10	19	15
E	15	15	..
●	18	10	35
A	21	12	..
N	23	02	..
◐	26	14	42
E	30	05	..

May

	d.	h.	m.
O	3	13	03
P	4	05	..
S	6	06	..
◑	10	04	08
E	12	21	..
●	18	02	51
A	18	18	..
N	20	09	..
◐	26	03	20
E	27	14	..

June

	d.	h.	m.
P	1	15	..
O	1	20	31
S	2	17	..
◑	8	15	07
E	9	04	..
A	14	21	..
N	16	16	..
●	16	18	23
O₂	21	12	14
E	23	22	..
◐	24	12	44
P	30	00	..
S	30	04	..

July

	d.	h.	m.
O	1	03	24
E	6	13	..
◑	8	04	39
A	12	08	..
N	14	00	..
●	16	08	37
F	21	05	..
◐	23	19	38
S	27	15	..
P	28	02	..
O	30	10	52

August

	d.	h.	m.
E	2	23	..
◑	6	20	40
A	9	00	..
N	10	08	..
●	14	21	31
E	17	11	..
◐	22	01	04
S	23	22	..
P	24	09	..
O	28	20	10
E	30	09	..

September

	J.	h.	m.
◑	5	14	33
A	5	18	..
N	6	17	..
●	13	09	23
E	13	19	..
P	18	09	..
S	20	04	..
◐	20	06	18
O₃	23	03	30
E	26	17	..
O	27	08	17

October

	d.	h.	m.
A	3	14	..
N	4	01	..
◑	5	09	21
E	11	04	..
●	12	20	31
P	15	09	..
S	17	10	..
◐	19	12	46
E	24	00	..
O	28	23	35
A	31	08	..
N	31	08	..

November

	d.	h.	m.
◑	4	03	58
F	7	15	..
●	11	07	09
P	12	12	..
S	13	19	..
◐	17	21	52
E	20	06	..
O	25	17	31
N	27	16	..
A	27	21	..

December

	d.	h.	m.
◑	3	21	16
E	5	01	..
●	10	17	33
P	10	23	..
S	11	06	..
◐	17	10	37
E	17	13	..
O₄	21	23	24
A	24	21	..
N	24	23	..
O	25	12	49

●, new moon; ◐, first quarter; O, full moon; ◑, last quarter; E, moon on the Equator; N, S, moon farthest north or south of the Equator; A, P, moon in apogee or perigee; O₁, sun at vernal equinox; O₂, sun at summer solstice; O₃, sun at autumnal equinox; O₄, sun at winter solstice.

0^h is midnight. 12^h is noon. The times may be adapted to any other time meridian than Greenwich by adding the longitude in time when it is east and subtracting it when west. (15° of longitude equals 1 hour of time).

This table was compiled from the American Ephemeris and Nautical Almanac.

Figure 906g. *Tide Tables,* inside back cover.

HT OF TIDE	
Date	21 August 1985
Location	Kernville, #761
Time	.0930 PDT (0830 PST)
Ref Sta	Humboldt Bay
HW Time Diff	+0 53
LW Time Diff	+1 23
HW Ht Diff	0.95 ratio
LW Ht Diff	0.67 ratio
Ref Sta HW/LW Time	1148 / 0500
HW/LW Time Diff	+0 53 +1 23
Sub Sta HW/LW Time	1241 0623
Ref Sta HW/LW Ht	4.9 / -0.4
HW/LW Ht Diff	.95 .67
Sub Sta HW/LW Ht	4.7 -0.3
Duration Rise/Fall	6:18 rising
Time Fm Near Tide	2:07 fm LW
Range of Tide	5.0
Ht of Near Tide	-0.3
Corr Table 3	1.2
Ht of Tide	0.9
Charted Depth	
Depth of Water	
Draft	
Clearance	

Figure 907. Calculation of the predicted height of tide at a given time at a subordinate station.

Tidal Data by Calculator or Computer

908 The NOS *Tide Tables* state that Table 3, Height of Tide At Any Time, is based on the assumption that the rise and fall conform to a simple cosine curve. (This is actually only an approximation, but it is sufficiently precise for practical purposes since the actual heights and times will vary somewhat from predicted values due to short-term local effects of winds and barometric pressure.) With this cosine relationship, a personal electronic calculator (or computer) makes the determination of height of tide at any time an easy task (see appendix F).

For this procedure, the correction is always calculated *up* from low water, rather than up or down from the nearest low or high water as when using Table 3. The predicted height of tide at any desired time (Ht_D) is the low-water predicted height (Ht_{LW}) plus a correction (C).

$$Ht_D = Ht_{LW} + C$$

The correction is equal to the product of the range of tide and a factor (F) based on time.

$$C = F(Ht_{HW} - Ht_{LW})$$

The factor, F, is found using a haversine relationship.

$$F = \frac{1 - \cos\left(\frac{T_D \sim T_{LW}}{T_{HW} \sim T_{LW}} \times 180°\right)}{2}$$

Where T_{HW} is the time of high water
T_{LW} is the time of low water
T_D is the desired time, and $\sim$ indicates absolute difference, the smaller quantity subtracted from the larger.
(Times may be subtracted in either the format of hours and minutes or hours and decimal fractions, but must be stated decimally for division.)

Combining the above equations, the height of tide at any given time may be found from the following expression:

$$Ht = Ht_{LW} + (Ht_{HW} - Ht_{LW})$$
$$\left[\frac{1 - \cos\left(\frac{T_D \sim T_{LW}}{T_{HW} \sim T_{LW}} \times 180°\right)}{2}\right]$$

This equation may be used directly for predictions at reference stations, and for predictions at subordinate stations after applying time and height differences. Solutions for the time of a desired height of tide may be found by rearranging the knowns and unknowns in the equation.

Example: Determination of the predicted height of tide at a reference station at a specified time by use of a calculator.

Required: Predicted height of tide at Humboldt Bay at 1100 on 23 August.

Solution: Daylight time is changed to standard time by subtracting one hour. Values of time and height on either side of the given time are taken from Table 1 and entered into the equation.

T_D = 1300 PST
LW = -1.4 feet at 0849
HW = 5.5 feet at 1537

Therefore:

$$Ht_D = (-1.4) + [5.5 - (-1.4)]$$

$$\left[\frac{1 - \cos\left(\frac{1300 - 0849}{1537 - 0849} \times 180°\right)}{2} \right]$$

$$= 3.27 \text{ feet.}$$

Expressed to the nearest tenth of a foot, as specified for height of tide, this is 3.1 feet. In some instances, a difference of one or two tenths may exist between the results obtained by the two procedures, as Table 3 is used to the nearest tabulated values without interpolation. The calculator solution might be said to be "more precise," but as noted above, normal variations in local conditions will render the predictions less accurate in practice than the calculations would indicate.

Graphic Solution

909 Each volume of the *Tide Tables* now includes in the explanatory material for Table 3 a description of a graphic method of determining the height of tide at any time, or the time of a desired height. This method, while interesting, offers no improvements over other methods and is of little interest to a navigator at sea.

Notes on Tide Problem Solutions

910 The use of a standard printed form (such as figure 907) will expedite calculations and help ensure accuracy. On U.S. naval ships, a standard workbook must be used unless an exception has been specifically authorized. A qualified navigator, however, *must* be able to solve any tide problem *without* dependence on such forms, as these may not always be available.

In cases of doubt, particularly in working with Table 3 in the Tide Tables, reference to the explanatory notes accompanying the tables will clarify the method of solution.

The most common errors in the completion of a tide table for a subordinate station are: applying the high-water difference to the height of low water at the reference station as well as to the height of high water; not being alert to a change in date at the subordinate station after applying the high-water or low-water time difference to the reference station; and failure to apply the difference factor from Table 3 (with the proper sign) to a rising or a falling tide at the station in question.

When the nearest tide is high water, subtract the correction factor of Table 3 from nearest high tide; when the nearest tide is low water, add the correction to nearest low tide.

Chapter 10

Currents and Current Prediction

Introduction

1001 In addition to the vertical changes in water levels—tides—discussed in the preceding chapter, a navigator must be concerned with *currents*, horizontal movements of the body of water in which his vessel floats and moves. Currents can be the result of several causes: the daily changes in tidal levels, the normal flow of rivers from higher elevations to the sea, the steady blowing of wind from approximately the same direction for several days or more, or long-term climatic and weather conditions. Often two or more of these causes combine in temporary local conditions, such as when tidal action is superimposed on a river's natural flow, or when a number of days of steady winds alter a normal ocean current. The effect of current on a vessel, whatever its cause, is to set it off course, change its speed with respect to the earth, or, more likely, both of these actions combined.

The first part of this chapter will deal with the various *ocean current systems*, their location, and where data concerning them may be found. In considering these current systems, it must be borne in mind that strong winds, blowing contrary to the prevailing wind pattern for prolonged periods, can have a marked effect on the *drift* (speed) of an ocean current, and, to a lesser degree, on its *set* (direction) in the affected area. (Drift for ocean currents is often described in terms of miles per day, rather than knots.) When the weather returns to normal, the current system will also return to its usual flow, which can often be predicted with considerable precision and accuracy.

Ocean Current Systems

1002 A number of well-defined, permanent current systems exist in the open oceans, as charted in figure 1002. The chief cause of these currents is wind. Winds, such as the various *trade winds*, blow almost continuously with considerable force, and in the same general direction, over large areas of the globe. The direction, steadiness, and force of a prevailing wind determine to a large extent the set, drift, depth, and permanence of the current it generates. However, currents with a generally northerly or southerly drift are considerably affected by the *Coriolis force*. This is an apparent force, acting on a body in motion, caused by the rotation of the earth. In the Northern Hemisphere deflection is to the right, in a clockwise direction; in the Southern Hemisphere the deflection is counterclockwise. The Coriolis force is largely responsible for the circular pattern of the slow flow of currents in the North and South Atlantic, the North and South Pacific, and in the Indian Ocean. Because of seasonal variations in the wind systems, and due to other seasonal changes, the characteristics of most ocean currents change considerably, but quite predictably, at certain times of the year.

Currents are often described as warm or cold. These terms are relative, and are based on the latitudes in which they originate, and on the effect they have on climate. For example, the northeast drift current off the northern coast of Norway is a "warm" current, although it may be lower in temperature than the southern extremity of the "cold" Labrador Current off the New England coast.

Warm and Cold Currents

Currents as well as winds were of great importance in the days of sail. Clipper ships in the nineteenth century wool trade, bound from England for Australia, would go out via the Cape of Good Hope,

Figure 1002. The principal ocean currents.

but return via Cape Horn, thus taking advantage of both the strong prevailing westerlies in the "Roaring Forties" and the resultant westerly ocean currents; see figure 1002. Similarly, the sixteenth century Spanish "treasure galleons" sailed from Acapulco, Mexico, for Manila via the North Equatorial Current, but returned via the Japan Stream and the California Current. Much useful information on these currents may be obtained from the *Pilot Charts* and *Pilot Chart Atlases* published by the Defense Mapping Agency Hydrographic/Topographic Center; see article 610. These publications, covering the principal ocean areas of the world, are, in most instances, designed to show for each month the mean direction and force of the surface currents in specific quadrangles of latitude and longitude, as well as the frequency of direction and average drifts. Brief summaries of the chief currents of the Atlantic and Pacific Oceans follow.

Atlantic Ocean Currents

1003 The effect of the trade winds is to form two *equatorial currents* flowing westward across the Atlantic at the rate of about two thirds of a knot. Between the *North* and *South* Equatorial Currents the somewhat weaker *Equatorial Counter Current* flows to the eastward under the influence of the southwest monsoon.

At the western edge of the Atlantic, the South Equatorial Current divides at the eastern tip of South America, part of it flowing southward and part continuing on into the Caribbean or northwestward along the West Indies. This current is joined by the North Equatorial Current of the Atlantic, which has flowed westward from an area to the north of the Cape Verde Islands. Water flows up the Caribbean, through the Yucatan Strait, across the Gulf of Mexico, and back into the Atlantic through the Straits of Florida. Here it meets with the flow that came up to the eastward of the West Indies to form the famous Gulf Stream, which flows northerly along the east coast of the United States, picking up even more flow from currents eastward of the Bahamas.

The indigo-blue water of this sharply defined current of warm water roughly follows the coastline as far as Cape Hatteras, where it curves eastward, widens, and gradually loses some of its velocity.

Off the Grand Banks, the Gulf Stream loses its identity as such, but continues on eastward as a general circulatory flow or drift. It meets the cold water of the *Labrador Current* in this area, part of which accompanies it towards the east. However, the water mass remains comparatively warm, and has a very marked effect on the climate of north-western Europe. On the eastern side of the Atlantic it divides to form the *northeast, easterly,* and *southeast drift currents.*

The circulation of the South Atlantic is generally similar. That part of the South Equatorial Current curving southward forms the *Brazil Current,* which roughly follows the coast of South America. Off the coast of Uruguay the current divides further, part of it continuing on to the south and part curving eastward back across the South Atlantic. This part, known as the *Southern Current,* is joined in the eastern Atlantic by water flowing northward from the Antarctic, and flows along the western coast of Africa to connect with the South Equatorial Current and complete the circulation, much as does the southeast drift current in the North Atlantic. The following are the principal Atlantic currents.

North Equatorial (warm)
South Equatorial (warm)
Equatorial Counter (warm)
Gulf Stream (warm)
Labrador (cold)
Brazil (warm)
Southern (cold)

Pacific Ocean Currents

1004   The circulation in the Pacific is similar to that in the Atlantic. Here, as in the Atlantic, the *North* and *South Equatorial Currents* set westward, with the *Equatorial Counter Current* between them setting to the east.

In the western Pacific the North Equatorial Current curves northward forming the *Japan Stream,* which is similar to the Gulf Stream, roughly following the coastline of the Japanese islands. The Japanese name for this current is *Kuroshio,* or "black stream," named for the dark color of the water. Part of this stream flows west of Japan into the Sea of Japan, but the main stream passes east of Japan and flows northward and eastward, widening as it does so, with a loss of velocity.

Part of the stream continues northerly as well as easterly to the region of the Aleutian Islands, and part continues on east where it joins the weak north and northeast drift currents in this area.

Similar to the Labrador Current, the cold *Oyashio* flows out of the Bering Sea to the south and west close to the shores of the Kuril Islands and Japan. Like the Labrador Current, the Oyashio often brings ice from the Arctic Ocean.

Along the Pacific coast of the United States the cold *California Current* flows southward, generally following the coastline. This current, being 200 to 300 miles wide, is not as strong as narrower currents, but flows with an average velocity of about 0.8 knot.

In the western Pacific the South Equatorial Current divides, part of it continuing on to the west and part of it, the *Australia Current,* curving southward past the east coast of Australia, where it bends toward the east and spreads out and is lost as a well-defined stream.

A current of cold water sets out of the Antarctic southwest of South America. The current divides at the southern tip of Patagonia, part of it, the *Cape Horn Current,* crossing into the southern Atlantic and part of it continuing up the west coast of South America, as the *Peruvian Current.* Near Cape Blanco it curves to the west past the Galapagos Islands and finally joins the South Equatorial Current. The following are the principal Pacific Ocean currents.

North Equatorial (warm)
South Equatorial (warm)
Equatorial Counter (warm)
Japan Stream (warm)
Oyashio (cold)
California (cold)
Australia (warm)
Peruvian or Humboldt (cold)

Temporary Wind-driven Currents

1005   Temporary, local *wind-driven currents* at times develop outside the well-defined ocean current systems. The drift of such a current depends largely on the force of the wind and its duration. If a wind has been blowing fairly steadily for some time at sea, a reasonable assumption would be that the drift of the current roughly equals 2 percent of the wind speed.

In the open ocean the set of a temporary wind current is *not* in the direction the wind is blowing. It is deflected by the *Coriolis force* (article 1002); in the Northern Hemisphere, this deflection is to the right; in the Southern Hemisphere it is to the left. In the open sea, the deflection is about 40°; near a coastline it is considerably less, probably nearer 20°. Deflection of a wind-driven current is affected by the land structure and varies with depth, being more deflected at greater depths. The *Tidal Current Tables* (see article 1010) give information on offshore conditions that may be expected in certain areas.

TIDAL CURRENTS

Basic Causes

1006   Chapter 9 discussed briefly the causes of tides and noted that the waters in the oceans and connecting waterways rise and fall periodically. It is obvious that if the amount of water changes, thus varying its level, there must be a flow back and forth between different areas; these flows are *tidal currents.* Such water movements are little noticed on the high seas, but they become of significance, and sometimes of critical importance, along coasts and in bays, estuaries, and the lower reaches of rivers; this is particularly so in fog or thick weather. The horizontal movement of the water toward the land is called *flood current,* and the horizontal movement away from the land is called *ebb current.* Between these two, when the current changes direction, there is a brief period when no horizontal motion can be detected; this is *slack water.*

Rotary Tidal Currents

1007 Offshore, where the direction of flow under tidal influence is not restricted by any barriers, the tidal current is *rotary;* that is, it flows continuously, with the direction changing through all points of the compass during the tidal period. Because of the effect of the earth's rotation, the change is clockwise in the Northern Hemisphere, and counterclockwise in the Southern Hemisphere, except where modified by local conditions. The speed usually varies throughout the tidal cycle, passing through two maximums in approximately opposite directions, and two minimums about halfway between the maximums in time and direction. Rotary currents can be depicted as in figure 1007 by a series of arrows representing the direction and speed of the current at each hour. This is sometimes called a *current rose.*

A distinguishing feature of a rotary current is that it has no time of slack water. Although the current varies in strength, the variation is from a maximum to a minimum and back to the next maximum without any occurrence of slack; see figure 1010e.

Reversing Tidal Currents

1008 In rivers, bays, and straits, where the direction of flow is more or less restricted to certain channels, the tidal current is called a *reversing current;* that is, it flows alternately in approximately opposite directions, with a short period of slack water at each reversal of the current. During the flow in each direction, the speed varies from zero at the time of slack water to the *maximum flood* or *ebb* about midway between the slacks. The symmetry of reversing currents is affected in certain areas by the configuration of the land and/or the presence of the natural flow of a river. Occasionally a river current will merely lessen in forward speed rather

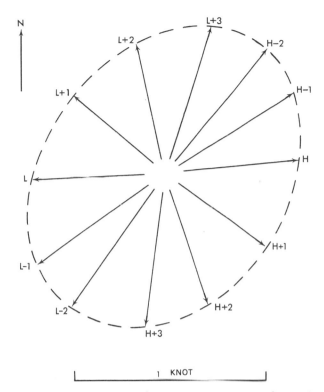

Figure 1007. Rotary tidal currents. Times are hours before and after high and low tides at a specified reference station (former location of Nantucket Lightship). The bearing and length of each arrow represent the direction and strength of the current at the labeled time.

than fully reverse. Reversing currents can be represented graphically by arrows or curves that indicate the strength of the current at each hour, as in figure 1008.

In navigation, the effect of tidal current is at times of more importance than the height of tide; in any body of water subject to tidal action, both must be considered. Mariners will sometimes speak of "the tide" as ebbing or flooding; this is incorrect terminology and should be avoided.

Along a relatively straight coast with shallow indentations, there is usually little difference between the time of slack water and high or low tide, but where a large bay connects with the ocean through a narrow channel, the tide and current may be out of phase by as much as several hours.

The effect of the tide in causing currents may be illustrated by two cases:

Where there is a small tidal basin connected with the sea by a large opening.
Where there is a large tidal basin connected with the sea by a small opening.

In the first case, the velocity of the current in the opening has its maximum value when the height of

Figure 1008. Reversing tidal currents; note asymmetrical nature of flood and ebb currents. (Some such graphs may show only the curve without the arrows.)

the tide within is changing most rapidly, i.e., at a time about midway between high and low water. The water in the basin stays at approximately the same level as the water outside. The flood current corresponds with the rising of the tide and the ebb current with the falling of the tide.

In the second case, the velocity of the current in the opening has its maximum value when it is high water or low water outside the basin, for then there is the greatest difference in levels and the maximum hydraulic pressure for producing motion. The flood current in such cases generally begins about three hours after low water and the ebb current about three hours after high water, slack water thus occurring about midway between the tides.

Along most shores not much affected by bays, tidal rivers, etc., the current usually turns soon after high water and low water.

The swiftest current in straight portions of tidal rivers is usually in the middle of the river, but in curved portions the most rapid current is toward the outer edge of the curve, and here the deepest water will generally be found.

Counter currents and eddies may occur near the shores of straits, especially in bights and near points of land. A knowledge of them is useful, so as to either take advantage of them or avoid them.

A swift current often occurs in a narrow passage connecting two large bodies of water, owing to their considerable difference of level at the same instant. The several passages between Vineyard Sound and Buzzards Bay are cases in point. A similar situation also occurs in connecting waterways such as the Cape Cod and Chesapeake & Delaware Canals, at Hell Gate in New York City, in passages between the Florida Keys, and on the Pacific Coast at such locations as Deception Pass and in Seymour and Sergious Narrows. With these *hydraulic currents*, strength is reached much more quickly after

a very brief period of slack water, and the current remains strong for a greater part of the cycle than with normal reversing tidal currents.

Tide rips generally occur when a rapid current sets over an irregular bottom, as at the edges of banks where the change of depth is considerable, but they also sometimes occur on the high seas.

Tidal Current Predictions

1009 Annual tables of predicted tidal currents have been published by the National Ocean Service (and its predecessor agencies) since 1890. Originally these also contained tide predictions, but were made separate publications in 1923. There are now two volumes: *Tidal Current Tables for the Atlantic Coast of North America*, and *Tidal Current Tables for the Pacific Coast of North America and Asia*. Related publications by NOS include *Tidal Current Charts* and *Tidal Current Diagrams*.

Tidal Current Tables

1010 The *Tidal Current Tables* have an organization and format generally similar to the *Tide Tables* discussed in chapter 9 and are used in much the same manner.

For a number of principal locations, called *reference stations*, Table 1 of these tables (figure 1010a) lists the predicted times of slack water in chronological order in the left-hand column, and the predicted times and velocities of maximum flood (F) and ebb (E) currents, also in chronological order, in the center and right-hand columns respectively for each day of the year; the year for which the tables are valid is shown at the top of each page following the name of the reference station. Flood and ebb current directions are also shown at the top of each page of Table 1.

All times in the *Tidal Current Tables* are *standard times;* each page of Table 1 indicates the central

ST. JOHNS RIVER ENTRANCE, FLORIDA

F-Flood, Dir. 275° True   E-Ebb, Dir. 100° True

JULY

Day	Slack Water Time h.m.	Maximum Current Time h.m.	Vel. knots	Day	Slack Water Time h.m.	Maximum Current Time h.m.	Vel. knots
1 F	0220	0506	2.1E	16 Sa		0014	2.1F
	1001	1209	1.4F		0302	0603	2.5E
	1441	1724	1.9E		1024	1246	2.2F
	2204				1543	1839	2.1E
					2259		
2 Sa		0031	1.5F	17 Su		0111	1.8F
	0304	0553	2.1E		0355	0658	2.3E
	1044	1301	1.5F		1120	1344	2.1F
	1536	1815	1.9E		1644	1953	2.0E
	2303						
3 Su		0120	1.4F	18 M	0003	0208	1.6F
	0349	0642	2.1E		0448	0757	2.1E
	1128	1350	1.6F		1216	1443	2.1F
	1632	1910	1.9E		1744	2110	1.9E
4 M	0004	0213	1.3F	19 Tu	0106	0306	1.4F
	0438	0730	2.1E		0542	0857	2.0E
	1212	1443	1.8F		1311	1540	2.1F
	1730	2009	1.9E		1842	2232	1.9E
5 Tu	0103	0306	1.3F	20 W	0204	0403	1.3F
	0528	0823	2.2E		0635	0953	2.0E
	1256	1534	2.0F		1403	1632	2.1F
	1828	2108	2.0E		1936	2333	1.9E
6 W	0158	0400	1.4F	21 Th	0316	0457	1.3F
	0621	0918	2.3E		0727	1047	1.9E
	1341	1625	2.2F		1453	1723	2.1F
	1924	2206	2.2E		2026		
7 Th	0250	0451	1.5F	22 F		0018	1.9E
	0714	1013	2.4E		0348	0548	1.3F
	1428	1717	2.5F		0816	1133	1.9E
	2018	2307	2.4E		1540	1810	2.1F
					2112		
8 F	0340	0544	1.6F	23 Sa		0053	2.0E
	0808	1106	2.6E		0435	0630	1.3F
	1516	1809	2.7F		0903	1211	2.0F
	2111				1624	1853	2.1F
					2154		
9 Sa		0002	2.5E	24 Su		0117	2.0E
	0429	0635	1.7F		0518	0715	1.4F
	0903	1200	2.7E		0948	1247	2.0E
	1606	1900	2.9F		1707	1934	2.1F
	2202				2234		
10 Su		0053	2.7E	25 M		0143	2.0E
	0517	0726	1.9F		0559	0756	1.5F
	0957	1253	2.8E		1030	1323	2.1E
	1658	1950	2.9F		1748	2015	2.1F
	2252				2313		
11 M		0147	2.8E	26 Tu		0209	2.1E
	0605	0817	2.0F		0639	0838	1.5F
	1053	1348	2.9E		1112	1400	2.1E
	1752	2041	2.9F		1828	2058	2.1F
	2342				2351		
12 Tu		0236	2.9E	27 W		0238	2.2E
	0653	0909	2.2F		0717	0920	1.5F
	1148	1445	2.8E		1154	1441	2.1E
	1848	2133	2.8F		1908	2139	2.0F
13 W	0031	0327	2.9E	28 Th	0028	0313	2.2E
	0743	1001	2.2F		0754	1004	1.6F
	1245	1539	2.7E		1237	1523	2.2E
	1947	2226	2.6F		1949	2224	1.8F
14 Th	0121	0417	2.8E	29 F	0105	0350	2.2E
	0835	1055	2.2F		0831	1049	1.6F
	1343	1634	2.6E		1321	1608	2.1E
	2049	2319	2.4F		2034	2309	1.7F
15 F	0211	0509	2.6E	30 Sa	0143	0431	2.3E
	0929	1150	2.2F		0908	1137	1.6F
	1442	1737	2.3E		1409	1653	2.1E
	2153				2125	2356	1.5F
				31 Su	0223	0514	2.2E
					0946	1222	1.7F
					1501	1744	2.1E
					2224		

AUGUST

Day	Slack Water Time h.m.	Maximum Current Time h.m.	Vel. knots	Day	Slack Water Time h.m.	Maximum Current Time h.m.	Vel. knots
1 M		0047	1.4F	16 Tu		0139	1.4F
	0305	0602	2.2E		0414	0717	2.0E
	1028	1315	1.7F		1147	1412	1.9F
	1557	1835	2.0E		1713	2039	1.7E
	2327						
2 Tu		0136	1.3F	17 W	0042	0237	1.2F
	0353	0653	2.2E		0510	0818	1.8E
	1118	1408	1.9F		1245	1510	1.9F
	1656	1937	2.0E		1812	2203	1.7E
3 W	0031	0234	1.2F	18 Th	0141	0337	1.2F
	0447	0750	2.3E		0606	0923	1.7E
	1212	1502	2.0F		1340	1605	1.9F
	1757	2036	2.0E		1907	2330	1.7E
4 Th	0130	0328	1.3F	19 F	0235	0432	1.2F
	0545	0845	2.3E		0701	1026	1.8E
	1308	1557	2.2F		1432	1658	1.9F
	1857	2141	2.1E		1958		
5 F	0225	0424	1.4F	20 Sa		0010	1.8E
	0646	0945	2.4E		0323	0523	1.3F
	1405	1654	2.5F		0753	1114	1.8E
	1954	2242	2.3E		1520	1746	2.0F
					2044		
6 Sa	0316	0520	1.6F	21 Su		0028	1.9E
	0747	1046	2.6E		0408	0609	1.4F
	1500	1746	2.7F		0842	1155	1.9E
	2049	2342	2.5E		1604	1829	2.0F
					2127		
7 Su	0405	0614	1.9F	22 M		0051	2.0E
	0847	1145	2.7E		0449	0650	1.5F
	1554	1839	2.8F		0927	1230	2.0E
	2141				1647	1910	2.1F
					2207		
8 M		0039	2.7E	23 Tu		0114	2.0E
	0452	0705	2.1F		0527	0729	1.6F
	0944	1242	2.9E		1009	1305	2.1E
	1648	1931	2.9F		1727	1950	2.1F
	2232				2244		
9 Tu		0130	2.9E	24 W		0138	2.1E
	0539	0757	2.3F		0604	0812	1.7F
	1040	1338	2.9E		1050	1340	2.2E
	1742	2023	2.9F		1806	2031	2.0F
	2320				2321		
10 W		0219	2.9E	25 Th		0207	2.2E
	0626	0848	2.4F		0638	0853	1.8F
	1135	1431	2.9E		1130	1417	2.3E
	1837	2113	2.8F		1845	2114	2.0F
					2356		
11 Th	0008	0306	2.9E	26 F		0243	2.3E
	0714	0939	2.5F		0710	0926	1.8F
	1229	1526	2.8E		1211	1458	2.3E
	1933	2203	2.6F		1924	2155	1.0F
12 F	0056	0354	2.8F	27 Sa	0031	0316	2.4E
	0804	1030	2.5F		0740	1017	1.0F
	1324	1621	2.6E		1254	1539	2.3E
	2031	2255	2.3F		2006	2239	1.7F
13 Sa	0143	0439	2.6E	28 Su	0106	0359	2.4E
	0856	1124	2.4F		0811	1104	1.9F
	1419	1714	2.4F		1340	1624	2.3E
	2132	2347	2.0F		2055	2325	1.5F
14 Su	0232	0528	2.4E	29 M	0145	0440	2.4E
	0952	1219	2.2F		0847	1153	1.9F
	1516	1813	2.1E		1430	1714	2.2E
	2236				2153		
15 M		0042	1.7F	30 Tu		0016	1.3F
	0322	0619	2.2E		0227	0529	2.3E
	1049	1313	2.1F		0933	1244	1.9F
	1614	1919	1.9E		1526	1809	2.1E
	2340				2259		
				31 W	0318	0109	1.2F
						0622	2.3E
					1032	1338	1.9F
					1627	1906	2.0E

Time meridian 75° W.   0000 is midnight.   1200 is noon.

Figure 1010a. *Tidal Current Tables,* Table 1 (extract).

TABLE 2. - CURRENT DIFFERENCES AND OTHER CONSTANTS

NO.	PLACE	POSITION Lat. (N)	POSITION Long. (W)	METER DEPTH (ft)	TIME DIFFERENCES Min. before Flood (h. m.)	TIME DIFFERENCES Flood (h. m.)	TIME DIFFERENCES Min. before Ebb (h. m.)	TIME DIFFERENCES Ebb (h. m.)	SPEED RATIOS Flood	SPEED RATIOS Ebb	Minimum before Flood (knots)	Minimum before Flood (deg.)	Maximum Flood (knots)	Maximum Flood (deg.)	Minimum before Ebb (knots)	Minimum before Ebb (deg.)	Maximum Ebb (knots)	Maximum Ebb (deg.)
	ST. JOHNS RIVER Time meridian, 75°W																	
	on ST. JOHNS RIVER ENTRANCE, p.94																	
7641	St. Johns Bluff..................	30 23.4	81 29.5		+0 13	+0 43	+0 02	+1 02	0.8	1.0	0.0	---	1.6	244	0.0	---	2.2	059
7651	Drummond Point, channel south of..	30 24.55	81 36.17		+1 31	+2 03	+2 25	+2 57	0.7	0.7	0.0	---	1.3	232	0.0	---	1.6	060
7661	Phoenix Park....................	30 22.92	81 37.72		+2 17	+2 55	+3 01	+3 30	0.6	0.4	0.0	---	1.1	192	0.0	---	1.0	352
7671	Chaseville, channel near........	30 22.6	81 37.4		+2 35	+3 20	+3 20	+3 20	0.6	0.7	0.0	---	1.1	151	0.0	---	1.6	337
7681	Quarantine Station.............	30 21.42	81 37.08		+2 17	+2 41	+2 35	+3 32	0.6	0.5	0.0	---	1.1	183	0.0	---	1.2	001
7691	Commodore Point, terminal channel	30 19.05	81 37.58		+2 14	+2 50	+2 49	+3 27	0.6	0.4	0.0	---	1.0	209	0.0	---	1.2	062
7701	Jacksonville, off Washington St..	30 19.3	81 39.2		+1 59	+2 31	+2 39	+3 14	0.9	0.8	0.0	---	1.8	281	0.0	---	1.9	118
7711	Jacksonville, F.E.C. RR. bridge..	30 19.3	81 39.9		+1 59	+2 45	+2 44	+3 20	0.8	0.7	0.0	---	1.6	240	0.0	---	1.7	060
7721	Winter Point...................	30 18.5	81 40.5		+1 59	+2 43	+3 49	+3 40	0.8	0.5	0.0	---	1.1	200	0.0	---	1.1	015
7731	Mandarin Point................	30 09.3	81 41.1		+3 00	+3 07	+3 02	+3 36	0.3	0.3	0.0	---	0.6	179	0.0	---	0.7	013
7741	Red Bay Point, draw bridge.....	29 59.1	81 37.8		+2 34	+3 27	+4 59	+4 01	0.5	0.3	0.0	---	0.9	115	0.0	---	0.6	300
7751	Tocoi to Lake George..........	---	---		Current weak and variable													
	FLORIDA COAST																	
	on MIAMI HARBOR ENTRANCE, p.100																	
7761	Ft. Pierce Inlet..............	27 28.3	80 17.5		+1 03	+0 20	+0 34	+0 30	1.4	1.5	0.0	---	2.6	250	0.0	---	3.1	072
7771	Lake Worth Inlet (between jetties)	26 46.33	80 02.13		-0 03	-0 26	-0 15	-0 05	1.3	1.7	0.0	---	2.4	273	0.0	---	3.6	094
7781	Fort Lauderdale, New River.....	26 06.73	80 07.18		-0 59	-0 58	-0 20	-0 21	0.4	0.2	0.0	---	0.8	005	0.0	---	0.5	130
	PORT EVERGLADES																	
7791	Pier 2, 1.3 miles east of <41>..	26 05.63	80 05.78		---	---	---	---	0.3	0.3	0.0	---	0.2	275	0.0	---	0.4	095
7801	Entrance (between jetties).....	26 05.58	80 06.32		-0 24	-1 08	-0 57	-0 39	0.7	0.8	0.0	---	0.6	167	0.0	---	0.7	358
7811	Entrance from southward (canal).	26 05.2	80 06.9		+0 24	-0 12	+0 17	-0 14	0.1	0.2	0.0	---	1.3	320	0.0	---	1.7	155
7821	Turning Basin.................	26 05.70	80 07.1		-1 17	-1 26	-1 16	-1 19	0.1	0.9	0.0	---	0.2	349	0.0	---	0.5	160
7831	Turning Basin, 300 yards north of	26 05.8	80 07.1		-0 36	-1 28	-0 41	-0 19	0.5	0.9	0.0	---	0.9	349	0.0	---	1.8	160
7841	17th Street Bridge...........	26 06.02	80 07.13		-0 54	-1 10	-0 42	-1 00	1.0	0.9	0.0	---	1.9	350	0.0	---	1.9	170
	MIAMI HARBOR																	
7851	Bakers Haulover Cut..........	25 54.0	80 07.4		-0 17	-0 12	0 00	-0 22	1.5	1.2	0.0	---	2.9	270	0.0	---	2.5	090
7861	North Jetty (east end).......	25 45.65	80 07.47		-0 30	-0 21	-0 53	-0 48	0.4	0.6	0.0	---	0.8	250	0.0	---	1.3	105
7871	Miami Outer Bay Cut entrance..	25 45.7	80 05.8		See table 5.													
7881	MIAMI HARBOR ENTRANCE (between jetties)	25 45.7	80 07.8		Daily predictions — See table 5.													
7891	Fowey Rocks Light, 1.5 miles SW of	25 35	80 07								0.0		1.9	290	0.0		2.1	126
	on KEY WEST, p.106																	
	FLORIDA REEFS to MIDNIGHT PASS																	
7901	Caesar Creek, Biscayne Bay....	25 23.2	80 13.6		+0 07	-0 08	-0 14	-0 05	1.2	1.0	0.0	---	1.2	316	0.0	---	1.8	123
7911	Long Key, drawbridge east of..	24 50.4	80 46.2		+0 58	+1 27	+2 21	+1 33	1.1	0.7	0.0	---	1.1	000	0.0	---	1.2	202
7921	Long Key Viaduct.............	24 48.1	80 51.9		+1 34	+1 28	+2 02	+1 57	0.9	0.7	0.0	---	0.9	349	0.0	---	1.2	170
7931	Moser Channel, swingbridge....	24 42.0	81 10.2		+1 07	+1 30	+1 50	+1 47	1.4	1.0	0.0	---	1.4	339	0.0	---	1.8	166
7941	Bahia Honda Harbor, bridge....	24 39.4	81 17.3		+1 01	+0 39	+1 53	+1 05	1.4	1.2	0.0	---	1.4	004	0.0	---	2.1	182
7951	No Name Key, northeast of.....	24 42.3	81 18.8		+0 55	+1 24	+1 20	+0 53	0.7	0.5	0.0	---	0.7	312	0.0	---	0.9	142

Figure 1010b. *Tidal Current Tables,* Table 2 (extract).

meridian of the time zone used. Adjustments must be made for the use of daylight time or any other deviation from standard time; see article 2213.

Due to the length of the lunar day, approximately 24^h50^m, all days in Table 1 will not have a full set of four maximum currents and four slack waters.

Table 2 (figure 1010b) contains a list of secondary or *subordinate stations*, arranged in geographic order. Given for each station is its position in latitude and longitude to the nearest minute, its reference station, the difference in times of minimum and maximum currents in hours and minutes with respect to the reference station, the maximum flood and maximum ebb velocity *ratios* with respect to similar current at the reference station, and the direction and average velocity of the maximum flood and ebb currents. (Separate time differences may be given for minimum current before flood begins and before ebb begins; note also that the term used is "minimum current" rather than "slack.")

The factors for any subordinate station are applied to the predictions of the reference station whose name is printed *next above* the subordinate station's listing in Table 2.

The respective time differences are added to or subtracted from, according to their signs, the time of slack water and strength of current (maximum flood or ebb) at the reference station to obtain the times of occurrence of the respective events in the current cycle at the subordinate station. The velocity of the maximum currents at the subordinate station is found by multiplying the velocity of either the flood or ebb current at the reference station by the respective velocity ratio listed for the subordinate station. Where unusual conditions exist, keyed endnotes, applicable to specific subordinate stations, appear at the end of the table. The average flood velocity is the mean of all the maximum flood currents, and the average ebb velocity is the mean of all the maximum ebb currents.

Primary reference stations are also included in Table 2 in proper sequence; this listing is used only for the geographic coordinates of the station (not given in Table 1) and average values of flood and ebb currents.

Table 3, figure 1010c, is used to determine the velocity of a current at any intermediate time between slack and maximum current. Instructions on its use appear beneath the tabulated factors. This table is in two parts, A and B. Table A is for use at nearly all locations. Table B is used for a limited number of places where there are "hydraulic" currents (see article 1008); these locations for each volume of the *Tidal Current Tables* are listed beneath Table 3.

Table 4 (figure 1010d) is used to find the duration of slack. Although slack water, or the time of zero velocity, lasts but an instant, there is a period on each side of slack during which the current is so weak that for practical purposes it can be considered as being negligible. From Table 4, the period (half on each side of slack) during which the current does not exceed a given velocity (0.1 to 0.5 knot) is tabulated for various maximum currents. (This table also has a "Table B" whose use is similar, but which is limited to a few specified locations.)

Table 5 (Atlantic tables only—figure 1010e) gives information regarding *rotary tidal currents*, or currents that change their direction continually and never come to a slack, so that in a tidal cycle of about $12\frac{1}{2}$ hours they set in all directions successively. Such currents occur offshore and in some wide indentations of the coast. The values given are average velocities due to tidal action only. When a steady wind is blowing, the effect of the current due to wind should be added vectorially to the current due to tidal action. This table is seldom used. Instructions for the use of this table as well as for Tables 1 through 4 are given in the publications themselves.

A limited amount of information is given on *wind-driven currents* and how such currents can be combined with predicted tidal currents to obtain a prediction of greater velocity. The astronomical data on the inside back cover is the same as that given in the *Tide Tables*—dates and times for the phases of the moon, apogee, perigee, greatest north and south declinations, and crossing of the equator; also included are solar data on equinoxes and solstices.

Use of Tidal Current Tables

1011 The use of the *Tidal Current Tables* will be illustrated by a series of examples. All problems will be worked from the tabular extracts of figures 1010a, b, c, and d. These examples are sample calculations and do not cover all possible uses and computations.

Example 1: Determination of predicted time of slack water, and time, strength, and direction of a maximum current at a reference station.

Required: The time of the mid-morning slack water at St. John's River Entrance, Florida, on 12 August, and the time, strength, and direction of the next subsequent maximum current.

Solution: The desired information is obtained

TABLE 3.—VELOCITY OF CURRENT AT ANY TIME

TABLE A

Interval between slack and desired time	Interval between slack and maximum current													
h. m.	h. m. 1 20	h. m. 1 40	h. m. 2 00	h. m. 2 20	h. m. 2 40	h. m. 3 00	h. m. 3 20	h. m. 3 40	h. m. 4 00	h. m. 4 20	h. m. 4 40	h. m. 5 00	h. m. 5 20	h. m. 5 40
	f.	f.	f.	f.	f.	f.	f.	f.	f.	f.	f.	f.	f.	f.
0 20	0.4	0.3	0.3	0.2	0.2	0.2	0.2	0.1	0.1	0.1	0.1	0.1	0.1	0.1
0 40	0.7	0.6	0.5	0.4	0.4	0.3	0.3	0.3	0.3	0.2	0.2	0.2	0.2	0.2
1 00	0.9	0.8	0.7	0.6	0.6	0.5	0.5	0.4	0.4	0.4	0.3	0.3	0.3	0.3
1 20	1.0	1.0	0.9	0.8	0.7	0.6	0.6	0.5	0.5	0.5	0.4	0.4	0.4	0.4
1 40	------	1.0	1.0	0.9	0.8	0.8	0.7	0.7	0.6	0.6	0.5	0.5	0.5	0.4
2 00	------	------	1.0	1.0	0.9	0.9	0.8	0.8	0.7	0.7	0.6	0.6	0.6	0.5
2 20	------	------	------	1.0	1.0	0.9	0.9	0.8	0.8	0.7	0.7	0.7	0.6	0.6
2 40	------	------	------	------	1.0	1.0	1.0	0.9	0.9	0.8	0.8	0.7	0.7	0.7
3 00	------	------	------	------	------	1.0	1.0	1.0	0.9	0.9	0.8	0.8	0.8	0.7
3 20	------	------	------	------	------	------	1.0	1.0	1.0	0.9	0.9	0.9	0.8	0.8
3 40	------	------	------	------	------	------	------	1.0	1.0	1.0	0.9	0.9	0.9	0.9
4 00	------	------	------	------	------	------	------	------	1.0	1.0	1.0	1.0	0.9	0.9
4 20	------	------	------	------	------	------	------	------	------	1.0	1.0	1.0	1.0	0.9
4 40	------	------	------	------	------	------	------	------	------	------	1.0	1.0	1.0	1.0
5 00	------	------	------	------	------	------	------	------	------	------	------	1.0	1.0	1.0
5 20	------	------	------	------	------	------	------	------	------	------	------	------	1.0	1.0
5 40	------	------	------	------	------	------	------	------	------	------	------	------	------	1.0

TABLE B

Interval between slack and desired time	Interval between slack and maximum current													
h. m.	h. m. 1 20	h. m. 1 40	h. m. 2 00	h. m. 2 20	h. m. 2 40	h. m. 3 00	h. m. 3 20	h. m. 3 40	h. m. 4 00	h. m. 4 20	h. m. 4 40	h. m. 5 00	h. m. 5 20	h. m. 5 40
	f.	f.	f.	f.	f.	f.	f.	f.	f.	f.	f.	f.	f.	f.
0 20	0.5	0.4	0.4	0.3	0.3	0.3	0.3	0.3	0.2	0.2	0.2	0.2	0.2	0.2
0 40	0.8	0.7	0.6	0.5	0.5	0.5	0.4	0.4	0.4	0.4	0.3	0.3	0.3	0.3
1 00	0.9	0.8	0.8	0.7	0.7	0.6	0.6	0.5	0.5	0.5	0.4	0.4	0.4	0.4
1 20	1.0	1.0	0.9	0.8	0.8	0.7	0.7	0.6	0.6	0.6	0.5	0.5	0.5	0.5
1 40	------	1.0	1.0	0.9	0.9	0.8	0.8	0.7	0.7	0.7	0.6	0.6	0.6	0.6
2 00	------	------	1.0	1.0	0.9	0.9	0.9	0.8	0.8	0.7	0.7	0.7	0.7	0.6
2 20	------	------	------	1.0	1.0	1.0	0.9	0.9	0.8	0.8	0.8	0.7	0.7	0.7
2 40	------	------	------	------	1.0	1.0	1.0	0.9	0.9	0.9	0.8	0.8	0.8	0.7
3 00	------	------	------	------	------	1.0	1.0	1.0	0.9	0.9	0.9	0.9	0.9	0.8
3 20	------	------	------	------	------	------	1.0	1.0	1.0	1.0	0.9	0.9	0.9	0.8
3 40	------	------	------	------	------	------	------	1.0	1.0	1.0	1.0	0.9	0.9	0.9
4 00	------	------	------	------	------	------	------	------	1.0	1.0	1.0	1.0	0.9	0.9
4 20	------	------	------	------	------	------	------	------	------	1.0	1.0	1.0	1.0	0.9
4 40	------	------	------	------	------	------	------	------	------	------	1.0	1.0	1.0	1.0
5 00	------	------	------	------	------	------	------	------	------	------	------	1.0	1.0	1.0
5 20	------	------	------	------	------	------	------	------	------	------	------	------	1.0	1.0
5 40	------	------	------	------	------	------	------	------	------	------	------	------	------	1.0

Use table A for all places except those listed below for table B.
Use table B for Cape Cod Canal, Hell Gate, Chesapeake and Delaware Canal and all stations in table 2 which are referred to them.

Figure 1010c. *Tidal Current Tables,* Table 3.

TABLE A

Maximum current	Period with a velocity not more than—				
	0.1 knot	0.2 knot	0.3 knot	0.4 knot	0.5 knot
Knots	*Minutes*	*Minutes*	*Minutes*	*Minutes*	*Minutes*
1.0	23	46	70	94	120
1.5	15	31	46	62	78
2.0	11	23	35	46	58
3.0	8	15	23	31	38
4.0	6	11	17	23	29
5.0	5	9	14	18	23
6.0	4	8	11	15	19
7.0	3	7	10	13	16
8.0	3	6	9	11	14
9.0	3	5	8	10	13
10.0	2	5	7	9	11

Figure 1010d. *Tidal Current Tables,* Table 4A (there is a Table 4B for locations with hydraulic currents).

TABLE 5.—ROTARY TIDAL CURRENTS

Great Round Shoal Channel, 4 miles NE. of Great Pt., Nantucket Sound. Lat. 41°26′ N., long. 69°59′ W.

Time (Hours after maximum flood at Pollock Rip Channel, see page 28)	Direction (true)	Velocity
	Degrees	*Knots*
0	80	0.8
1	88	1.1
2	96	1.3
3	104	1.0
4	129	0.5
5	213	0.5
6	267	1.1
7	275	1.4
8	280	1.2
9	284	0.7
10	328	0.2
11	42	0.4

Cuttyhunk I., 3¼ miles SW. of Lat. 41°23′ N., long. 71°00′ W.

Time (Hours after maximum flood at Pollock Rip Channel, see page 28)	Direction (true)	Velocity
	Degrees	*Knots*
0	356	0.4
1	15	0.3
2	80	0.2
3	123	0.3
4	146	0.5
5	158	0.5
6	173	0.4
7	208	0.3
8	267	0.2
9	306	0.3
10	322	0.3
11	335	0.4

Gooseberry Neck, 2 miles SSE. of Buzzards Bay entrance. Lat. 41°27′ N., long. 71°01′ W.

Time (Hours after maximum flood at Pollock Rip Channel, see page 28)	Direction (true)	Velocity
	Degrees	*Knots*
0	52	0.6
1	65	0.4
2	108	0.2
3	168	0.3
4	210	0.4
5	223	0.5
6	232	0.5
7	249	0.3
8	274	0.2
9	321	0.2
10	14	0.3
11	38	0.5

Browns Ledge, Massachusetts. Lat. 41°20′ N., long. 71°06′ W.

Time (Hours after maximum flood at Pollock Rip Channel, see page 28)	Direction (true)	Velocity
	Degrees	*Knots*
0	330	0.3
1	12	0.3
2	26	0.3
3	104	0.4
4	118	0.4
5	123	0.4
6	168	0.3
7	205	0.2
8	201	0.3
9	270	0.3
10	282	0.4
11	318	0.5

Point Judith, Harbor of Refuge, Block Island Sound (west entrance). Lat. 41°22′ N., long. 71°31′ W.

Time (Hours after maximum flood at The Race, see page 34)	Direction (true)	Velocity
	Degrees	*Knots*
0	197	0.2
1	160	0.2
2	151	0.4
3	159	0.5
4	146	0.5
5	124	0.5
6	109	0.4
7	104	0.2
8	90	0.1
9	30	0.1
10	336	0.1
11	209	0.1

Point Judith, 4.5 miles SW. of, Block Island Sound. Lat. 41°18′ N., long. 71°33′ W.

Time (Hours after maximum flood at The Race, see page 34)	Direction (true)	Velocity
	Degrees	*Knots*
0	264	0.6
1	270	0.6
2	270	0.5
3	280	0.2
4	62	0.2
5	70	0.6
6	78	0.7
7	95	0.5
8	105	0.3
9	120	0.1
10	286	0.1
11	277	0.3

Figure 1010e. *Tidal Current Tables,* Table 5 (extract).

directly from Table 1 without calculation except to add one hour for Eastern Daylight Time (EDT).

Answer: The predicted time of mid-morning slack water is 0904 EDT; the next maximum current is at 1130, 2.5 knots, flooding 275°. (These times are one hour later than the tabulated values to allow for daylight time (+4) that would be used locally at this time of the year.)

Example 2: Determination of the predicted time of slack and following maximum current at subordinate station.

Required: The time of afternoon slack water in the channel of the St. John's River just south of Drummond Point on 12 August, and the time and the strength of the next subsequent maximum current.

Solution: From Table 2, obtain the time difference and strength ratios as follows:

Time difference, minimum before ebb	$+2^h25^m$
Time difference, maximum ebb	$+2^h57^m$ (060°)
Strength ratio, maximum ebb	0.7

From Table 1 for the reference station, St. John's River Entrance, the following times are extracted:

Slack	1324
Maximum ebb	1621

The differences are applied as follows:

```
  13 24 (slack at reference station)
+  2 25 (Table 2 difference)
  15 49 (+5)
+  1 00 (for daylight time)
  16 49 (+4) slack, local time
```

```
  16 21 (max. ebb at reference station)
+  2 57 (Table 2 difference)
  19 18 (+5)
+  1 00 (for daylight time)
  20 18 (+4) maximum ebb, local time
```

The strength is calculated by multiplying the maximum current at the reference station by the table 2 factor.

$2.6 \times 0.7 = 1.82$ kn (which is rounded to nearest tenth of a knot).

Answer: The afternoon slack is predicted to occur at 1649 EDT, with the next maximum current at 2018 EDT, which will be 1.8 knots, ebbing (060°).

Example 3: Determination of predicted current conditions at an intermediate time at a reference station.

Required: The strength and direction of the current at St. John's River Entrance at 1600 local time on 12 August.

Solution: The applicable entries, those bracketing the desired time, in Table 1 are:

Slack	1324	
Maximum ebb	1621	2.6 kn

To use Table 3, the calculations below are made: Interval between slack and maximum current:

```
  16 21
− 13 24
   2:57
```

Interval between slack and desired time after changing 1600 EDT to 1500 EST as used in the tables:

```
  15 00
− 13 24
   1:36
```

Note: Caution must be used when subtracting times to remember that there are 60 minutes, and not 100, in an hour; this seemingly obvious fact is often overlooked, resulting in simple mathematical error. It is convenient when subtracting a larger number of minutes from a smaller number to restate the time as one hour less but 60 minutes more; for example.

```
1621 =   15 81        1500 =   14 60
       − 13 24               − 13 24
          2:57                  1:36
```

Now applying these intervals to Table 3A, we use the line for 1^h40^m and the column for 3^h00^m. The factor thus found is 0.8. (Note that the nearest values were used; predictions of current strength are not precise enough to justify the use of interpolation.) The factor from Table 3A is applied to the Table 1 value of maximum current.

$2.6 \times 0.8 = 2.08$ kn

Answer: The predicted current for 1600 EDT is 2.1 knots, ebbing (100°).

Example 4: Determination of predicted current conditions at an intermediate time at a subordinate station.

Required: The strength and direction of the current in the channel of the St. John's River at Jacksonville off of Washington Street at 1600 EDT on 12 August.

Solution: (See figure 1011.) The time differences of Table 2 are first applied to the predictions for the reference station (Table 1) to obtain the times

VEL OF CURRENT	
Date	12 August
Location	Jacksonville, Wash. St. 7701
Time	1600 EDT (1500 EST)
Ref Sta	St. Johns River Entrance
Time Diff Minimum before Ebb	+ 2:39
Time Diff Max Flood	+ 2.31
Vel Ratio Max Flood	0.9
Vel Ratio Max Ebb	0.8
Flood Dir	281°
Ebb Dir	118°
Ref Sta Slack Water Time	1324
Time Diff	2:39
Local Sta Slack Water Time	1603
Ref Sta Max Current Time	1030 flooding
Time Diff	+ 2:31
Local Sta Max Current Time	1301
Ref Sta Max Current Vel	2.6
Vel Ratio	0.9
Local Sta Max Current Vel	2.2
Int Between Slack and Desired Time	1:03
Int Between Slack and Max Current	3:02
Max Current	
Factor Table 3	0.5
Velocity	1.1
Direction	Flooding, 281°

Figure 1011. Calculation of the predicted velocity of current at a given time at a subordinate station.

(EST) at the subordinate station that bracket the desired times; the applicable velocity ratio is noted at the same time.

10 30	2.5 kn, flooding	13 24
+ 2:31	ratio 0.9	+ 2:39
12 61 = 1301		15 63 = 1603 slack

Note that the bracketing times are those at the subordinate station, which may be different from those of the reference station.

The maximum velocity at the subordinate station is obtained by applying the appropriate ratio.

$2.5 \times 0.9 = 2.25 = 2.2$ kn (rounding is to nearest even tenth; see appendix C).

Next, the desired time of 1600 EDT is converted to the standard time of the tables, 1500, and the intervals are calculated as in the preceding example.

Interval between slack and maximum current:

$$\begin{array}{r} 16\ 03 \\ -13\ 01 \\ \hline 3{:}02 \end{array}$$

Interval between slack and desired time:

$$\begin{array}{r} 16\ 03 \\ -15\ 00 \\ \hline 1{:}03 \end{array}$$

Entering Table 3A on the line for 1^h00^m and the column for 3^h00^m, the factor of 0.5 is obtained; this is applied to the maximum current *at the subordinate station* as previously calculated.

$2.2 \times 0.5 = 1.1$ kn

Answer: The predicted current at 1600 EDT is 1.1 knots, flooding (281°).

Example 5: Determination of the predicted duration of a weak current (specified maximum strength) at a given point. (This information is frequently of considerable value when docking or undocking in a tidal current that has appreciable maximum velocities.)

Required: The times between which the current will be less than 0.3 knots in the terminal channel at Commodore Point on the St. John's River approximately midday on 15 July.

Solution: The time of applicable slack water is calculated from Tables 1 and 2; the velocity of the maximum current on either side of this slack is also calculated.

$$\begin{array}{l} 09\ 29\ \text{slack} \\ +\ 2{:}14\ \text{Table 2 difference} \\ \hline 11\ 43 \end{array}$$

05 09	2.6 ebbing
+ 3:27	×0.4
08 36	1.0 maximum ebbing

11 50	2.2 flooding
+ 2:50	×0.5
14 40	1.1 maximum flooding

Table 4 is entered for a 1.0 maximum current, as the difference between the two maximums is slight in this case. (If, however, the difference were great, separate periods on either side of slack water toward their respective maximums could be calculated.) One half of the duration of 70 minutes is taken on either side of the predicted time of slack water.

11 43	11 43
− :35	+ :35
11 08	12 18

These times are standard and must be converted to local daylight time by adding one hour.

Answer: It is predicted that the current will be less than 0.3 knots between 1208 and 1318 EDT.

Example 6: Determination of the predicted time of a current of specified velocity.

Required: The time at which the velocity of the ebbing current at St. John's River Entrance will have decreased to 1.6 knots following its first maximum for 13 August.

Solution: From Table 1,

0439	2.6 kn max, ebbing
0856	slack

Calculating the interval and factor to use in Table 3:

$$\begin{array}{r} 08\ 56 \\ -04\ 39 \\ \hline 4{:}17\ \text{interval max–slack} \end{array}$$
$1.6 \div 2.6 = 0.615 = 0.6$ factor

Table 3A is entered on the column for 4^h20^m; the line for a factor of 0.6 is located and identified as an interval between slack and desired time of 1^h40^m. This is applied to the time of slack water, and the result is converted to local (daylight) time.

$$\begin{array}{l} 08\ 56 \\ -\ 1{:}40 \\ \hline 07\ 16\ \text{(EST)} \\ +\ 1{:}00 \\ \hline 08\ 16\ \text{(EDT)} \end{array}$$

Answer: It is predicted that by approximately 0816 local time, the ebbing current will have decreased to 1.6 knots.

Current Determination by Calculator

1012 In a manner generally similar to that used for the determination of tidal heights in article 908, predictions of current strength at any given time can be made with a personal calculator or computer. The equation used is based on a cosine-curve variation in strength from one maximum to slack water; this is not exact, but sufficiently accurate for practical predictions.

$$S_D = S_M \times \text{Cos}\left[90° - \left(\frac{T_D \sim T_S}{T_M \sim T_S} \times 90°\right)\right]$$

Where S_D is strength at desired time
S_M is maximum current strength
T_D is desired time
T_S is time of slack water
T_M is time of maximum current, and $\sim$ indicates absolute difference, the smaller quantity subtracted from the larger.

The direction of the current will be the same as that for the maximum current used in the equation; this should be the maximum current the time of which, with the time of slack water, brackets the desired time.

Example: Determination of the current strength and direction for a given time at a reference station using a calculator.

Required: The strength and direction of the current at St. John's River Entrance at 1600 local time on 12 August.

Solution: The desired time is converted to standard time by subtracting one hour to get 1500 EST. The slack water and maximum current that bracket the desired time are taken from table 1:

Slack   1324
Maximum current   1621, 2.6 kn, ebbing
Therefore

$$S_D = 2.6 \times \text{Cos}\left[90° - \left(\frac{1500 - 1324}{1621 - 1324} \times 90°\right)\right]$$

$$= 1.96 \text{ knots}$$

Expressed to the nearest tenth of a knot, as specified for currents, this is 2.0 knots and the direction is ebbing. This is not quite the same answer as was obtained in Example 3 of article 1012 by use of Table 3. In some instances, the solution by calculator will yield an answer that is one or two tenths of a knot different from that obtained through use of Table 3. This results from the use of tabulated values in Table 3 without interpolation; the difference is of no practical significance.

This equation can also be expressed in a form so as to permit the calculation of the time at which a current of specific strength is predicted; the direction of this current is the same as that of the maximum current used in the equation.

$$T_D = T_S + \left[\left(\frac{90° - \text{Cos}^{-1}\dfrac{S_D}{S_M}}{90°}\right)(T_M \sim T_S)\right]$$

Where T_D is the time of desired strength
S_D is the desired strength

As before, the time determined by computer or calculator may vary a few minutes from that obtained by the use of Table 3, but the difference is of no practical significance, and neither is more truly "accurate" than the other.

Diagrams in Tidal Current Tables

1013 The *Tidal Current Tables* for the Atlantic Coast contain diagrams of current direction and strength for certain bodies of water; this information is shown as a function of conditions at a specified reference station. These diagrams are very useful in determining a time of departure and speed so as to make maximum use of favorable ("fair") currents or minimize adverse ("foul") currents. Figure 1013 illustrates such a diagram for Chesapeake Bay. Note the "speed lines" for travel in each direction. A speed for a northbound ship can be selected which, with a properly selected starting time, will permit it to "ride the tide," have a favorable current, all the way from the Bay entrance to Baltimore near its northern end. Conversely, departure time and speed for a southbound passage can be selected to minimize the effects of unavoidable adverse flood currents up the Bay.

In using these diagrams, as in using any of the predictions of the *Tidal Current Tables*, it must be remembered that they are for "normal" or "average" conditions. Periods of sustained winds of moderate or greater strength from certain directions will considerably alter both the times and strengths predicted.

Tidal Current Charts

1014 The National Ocean Service also publishes a series of *Tidal Current Charts*. These cover eleven areas of heavy maritime activity.

Boston Harbor
Narragansett Bay to Nantucket Sound
Narragansett Bay
Long Island and Block Island Sounds
New York Harbor

Figure 1013. Current Diagram from *Tidal Current Tables* (typical).

Figure 1014. *Tidal Current Chart* (extract).

Figure 1015. *Tidal Current Diagrams* are available for a few bodies of water; they are used with the corresponding *Tidal Current Chart* (extract).

Delaware Bay and River
Upper Chesapeake Bay
Charleston (S.C.) Harbor
Tampa Bay
San Francisco Bay
Puget Sound, Southern Part
Puget Sound, Northern Part

Tidal Current Charts each consist of a set of twelve reproductions of a small-scale chart of the area concerned. There is one chart for each hour of a tidal current cycle in terms of time before or after a stated event such as "slack, flood begins"; on each chart, there are numerous arrows and numbers that represent the current flow at that time; see figure 1014.

The conditions for any hour of interest can be easily visualized. Some caution is necessary, however, as these are only for "normal" conditions, and currents can vary significantly under unusual circumstances; currents can also vary considerably over small distances, and the *Tidal Current Charts* should be used as no more than a general guide. By following through a sequence of charts, the changes in currents at any point can be readily discerned.

The *Tidal Current Chart* for Narragansett Bay is used with the effective annual edition of *Tide Tables;* all others must be used with the effective edition of *Tidal Current Tables.* The former are prepared with respect to predicted tides, the latter with respect to predicted currents. *Tidal Current Charts* may be used for any year. New editions are published whenever conditions change, or when additional information becomes available; only the latest edition should be used.

Tidal Current Diagrams

1015 For certain limited areas, there are now available *Tidal Current Diagrams* that are published separately and should not be confused with the "current diagrams" contained in the East Coast volume of *Tidal Current Tables;* see article 101.

Tidal Current Diagrams are available for the following areas:

Boston Harbor
Long Island and Block Island Sounds
New York Harbor
Upper Chesapeake Bay

These are annual publications, sets of twelve monthly graphs to be used with the appropriate *Tidal Current Chart.* The *Diagrams* are more convenient than the *Tables* for determining conditions at any point, as the graphs indicate directly from the date and time which chart is to be used and what the strength correction factor is.

Importance of Currents

1016 Currents can help or hinder the passage of a vessel on the high seas or in pilot waters; they can set her off course and into hazardous waters. Every navigator must know where to get information on the various currents that may be encountered, and he must be able to make all the necessary calculations.

Broad, general information on ocean currents can be found in books such as this or *Bowditch.* More specific information and predictions of ocean currents under *normal* conditions can be obtained from *Pilot Charts, Pilot Chart Atlases, Sailing Directions,* and *Coast Pilots.* These can be used for planning purposes, but navigation should be based on the actual currents encountered as measured by the differences between DR positions and fixes (see article 1207).

Reversing tidal currents in bays, rivers, and harbors may affect the efficiency of a vessel's progress, or her safety in docking and undocking. Predictions of these are generally available in publications; they must, however, be used with a degree of caution, as short-term, unusual local conditions may have made them inaccurate.

The solutions to problems relating to tidal current predictions may be expedited, and the possibility of error lessened, by the use of standard printed forms, but a navigator must *never* become dependent on the use of such forms since they are not always available.

Chapter 11   Visual Piloting

Introduction

1101 Determining the position and directing the movements of a vessel by reference to land and sea marks, by measurements of depth, or by radar is termed *piloting*. Waters in which piloting is the normal method of navigation—rather than electronic methods, although these may be concurrently employed—are termed *pilot waters*. This chapter deals with *visual piloting*, including a limited use of soundings; radar piloting is considered in chapter 17.

Piloting requires the greatest experience and nicest judgment of any form of navigation. Constant vigilance, unfailing mental alertness, and a thorough knowledge of the principles involved are essential. Mistakes in navigation on the open sea can generally be discovered and corrected before the next landfall. In pilot waters there is little or no opportunity to correct errors. Even a slight blunder may result in disaster, perhaps involving the loss of life. The problems of piloting are fundamentally very simple, both in principle and in application. It is the proximity of danger that makes piloting so important. Avoiding a collision in the heavy traffic that exists in the harbors and along coastlines is essentially a problem of *seamanship*, not piloting. The navigator is concerned with the problem of keeping his ship in navigable waters. Throughout this chapter a deep-draft vessel is hypothesized. The principles and procedures that will keep sufficient water under the keel of a large vessel will unquestionably bring safety to a smaller one.

In all phases of piloting, the navigator must constantly realize that he is dealing with the past, the present, and the future. He must continually analyze the situation that existed in the recent past, and that exists at present, in order to plan for the future. He should constantly use every logical means at his disposal to:

> *obtain warnings* of approaching danger;
> *fix the position* of the ship accurately and frequently; and
> *determine the proper course* of immediate action.

The keeping of a dead reckoning plot was described in chapter 8. There it was noted that the plot was maintained without considering any offsetting effects of currents. Since it was seen in chapter 10 that currents, both ocean and tidal, do exist, sometimes with considerable velocities, it becomes obvious that the ship may well *not* be where its DR plot indicates. Thus it is necessary to have techniques to determine not just where a vessel could be, but where she actually is; this is *positioning* and is the major topic of this chapter; the integration of known or predicted currents into the determination of courses and speeds is *current sailing,* covered in chapter 12.

Lines of Position (LOP)

1102 Probably the most important concept in piloting, as in nearly all phases of navigation, is that of the *line of position (LOP)*. A single observation does not establish a position; it does, however, provide the observer with a line on some point of which he is located. This line is a segment of a great circle, but in visual piloting the segment is so short that it may be plotted as a straight, or rhumb, line on a Mercator chart. In this chapter, only visual lines of position established by various methods will be discussed.

It should also be noted that a line of position can provide useful *negative* information. If the LOP is valid, then the observer, and his vessel, are *not* somewhere else, such as in shoal water. A single LOP of good quality, therefore, while not establishing a position, can at least rule out some worries if it has no hazards along its length or nearby.

It must be borne in mind that there is no connection between the DR course line and lines of position. The DR course line is a statement of *intention*, a graphic representation of ordered courses and speeds; a DR position is a *calculated* position. Accurately obtained lines of position are statements of *fact*, as the vessel is somewhere on the LOP, regardless of courses steered and speeds used.

Labeling Lines of Position

1103 A single line of position, whether a bearing (article 1105), a range (article 1104), or a distance (article 1106), is labeled on the upper side of the line with the time of observation expressed in four digits. A single line of position advanced to form a running fix (article 1111) is labeled with the original time of observation and the time to which it has been advanced. (The actual numeric value of direction is of little value after the line is drawn and normally is omitted, provided that it has been recorded elsewhere; if labeled on the chart, it is shown as a three-digit number directly beneath the time label; true direction is assumed unless "M" is suffixed indicating magnetic direction.) Simultaneous lines of position forming a fix need not be labeled, the time of the fix being sufficient. Similarly, the second line of position in a running fix need not be labeled, taking its time as that of the running fix. Use sufficient labels, but the fewer the better, as the chart will thus be less cluttered and more easily read.

Every line must be labeled as soon as it is plotted; an unlabeled line can be a source of error, especially after a change of watch. There is enough uncertainty in piloting without adding to it by leaving doubt as to the meaning of a line. Care must be taken not to confuse a course line with a line of position.

Using a Range

1104 The simplest way to establish a line of position is to observe a *range* (called a *leading line* by some navigators). If two fixed objects of known

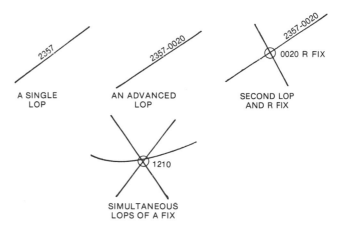

Figure 1103. Labels for lines of position and fixes.

position appear to the observer to be in line, he must at that instant be somewhere on the line passing through the objects and extending beyond it. He can also take comfort from the negative implications of his line of position; if he is on the range line, he is certainly *not* somewhere off of it such as in shoal water or headed into some other hazard. To be plotted, both objects must, of course, be identified from their symbols on the chart.

Example: (Figure 1104). At 1205 a tower and stack appear in line. The ship must then be somewhere along the straight line drawn through the symbols on the chart for these two objects.

Draw light lines on the chart and make them no longer than necessary. Particularly avoid drawing them through chart symbols for aids to navigation and other objects that might be made indistinct by erasures. In illustrations for this chapter, broken lines will be extended from the symbols on the chart to illustrate principles; *the solid segment of the line of position is all that is normally plotted on the chart.* Time is labeled on the plot, but the numeric direction of the range line is seldom measured or recorded; this would be useful only if the LOP were to be advanced to a later time.

Most ranges used for navigation consist of two fixed aids to navigation, usually, but not always, lighted, and specifically established to constitute a range; these are called *range markers* or *leading marks.* A navigator, however, must not overlook the possibility of using natural or man-made objects fortuitously located to meet his needs, as in the example above.

In addition to using two objects in line to obtain a line of position, a *steering range* may often be used to direct the course of a vessel. These consist of pairs of aids to navigation specifically located to

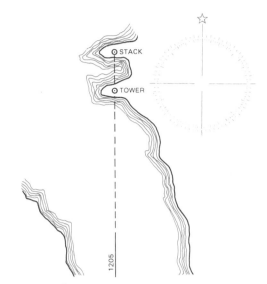

Figure 1104. Plotting a range.

assist a vessel in staying within a channel; see articles 402 and 415. The danger in using any range, formal or informal, is that it can be used *beyond its safe limits*. A navigator must be careful to use any range over only that portion that is safe. He must be especially careful not to follow a range too far, either towards the front marker or away from it; he must be continually alert as to his position along the range line.

Using Bearings

1105   Usually a navigator will not be able to find two fixed objects in line, identifiable on his chart, at the time he wishes to make an observation. Consequently, a line of position is normally obtained by plotting a *bearing* on the chart. The observer sights across his pelorus, hand-bearing compass, bearing circle, or gyro repeater toward a fixed, known object and thus determines the direction of the line of sight to that object; this is the *bearing* of the object. (On small craft, a frequent practice if the distant object is not far off-course is to turn and head directly for the object taking a bearing over the steering compass; this can eliminate one step of calculation.) He then plots the reciprocal of this bearing from the known object on his chart.

Example: (Figure 1105). At 1200 a spire bears 050°. The navigator plots this line as shown; at 1200 his ship must be somewhere on this line. Direction is not labeled in figure 1105; if it had been desirable to show it, the direction *toward the spire* would have been shown as a three-digit number beneath the time label.

Using Distance Measurements

1106   If the distance to an object is known, the ship must lie somewhere on a circle centered on the object, with the known distance as the radius. This circle is termed a *distance circle of position*. Figure 1106 illustrates a distance circle; at 1600, the navigator found the distance of the lighthouse, *D*, to be 6 miles. Obviously the ship must be somewhere on a circle of 6-mile radius, centered on the light. In most cases only a segment of the circle will be drawn on the chart. Distance may be obtained by radar, by range finder, or if the height of the object is known, by stadimeter or sextant; the latter two instruments are used for measuring angles by which distance may be determined. Table 9 in *Bowditch* permits a rapid solution for sextant angles. The distance can also be calculated with an accuracy sufficient for practical navigation using the equation D = H ÷ tan A, where *D* is the distance to the object, *H* is its height, and *A* is the vertical angle measured. *D* will be in the same units as *H* and should be converted to yards or nautical yards; a pocket calculator is useful for this equation. If the object observed is a lighthouse, the known height may be stated either as "height above water," "height of structure," or "height of light"; the angle must be measured accordingly.

A distance circle is frequently combined with a bearing, as described in article 1107 (example 6).

Obtaining a Fix

1107   As noted in article 1102, a single line of position does not give a navigator full and complete information as to his location—he is somewhere along that LOP, but just exactly where is undetermined. If, however, he has *two* simultaneous LOPs, he is on both of them and his only possible position (assuming that the LOPs are accurate) is at their intersection—he has fixed his position; he has established a "fix." Obviously, if his vessel is moving, he is at his fix only at the time that the LOPs were obtained. Thus a time label must be added (horizontally) to the circle symbol of a fix. The two lines of position should cross at angles as near 90° as possible to define the position most precisely. Even more desirable would be three LOPs; in this case the bearings should differ by as close to 120° (or 60°) as possible. See article 1109.

Lines of position can be combined to obtain fixes as follows:

Example 1: Two cross bearings (figure 1107a). At 1545 a ship steaming on course 000°, speed 10

Figure 1105. A line of position from a bearing.

Figure 1106. A circular line of position (or "circle of position") from a distance measurement.

Figure 1107a. A fix from two crossed bearings.

knots, observes a tower bearing 288°, and Danger Shoal Buoy bearing 194°.

The 1545 fix must lie at the intersection of the two lines of position; it is obtained by plotting the *reciprocals* of the observed bearings *from* the symbols of the tower and lightship on the chart of the area.

The intersection of the two lines of position at the 1545 fix is labeled as shown in figure 1107a. A new DR course is then started from this position.

Example 2: Three cross bearings (figure 1107b). At 1351, with the vessel on course 285°, speed 15 knots, the navigator observes the following bearings by gyrocompass (gyro error is zero); left tangent of Smith Point, 005°; left tangent of Jones Bluff, 130°; Hall Reef Light, 265°.

Required: Plot and label the 1351 fix.

Solution: See figure 1107b.

Note that in Examples (1) and (2) the bearings were taken simultaneously to obtain the fix, which is often the case in observing terrestrial objects. However, as will be explained more fully in article 1111, if the bearings are taken at times differing by more than a fraction of a minute or so, they must be adjusted to a common time to determine what is known as a *running fix*. (On small craft and slow-moving vessels, a time difference of a minute or two is usually ignored.)

Example 3: Two ranges. A ship entering a harbor at 10 knots steams so as to keep range lights W and X (figure 1107c) in line. At 2153, with W and X exactly in line, light Y and church spire Z are observed to be in line, and the ship changes course to 057°.

Required: Plot and label the 2153 fix.

Solution: See figure 1107c. The 2153 fix is at the intersection of the two range lines of position.

Example 4: One range and a bearing (figure 1107d). A vessel is on course 090°, speed 10 knots. At 1227 Radio Tower A and a cupola are in range. At the same time the right tangent of Burke Point bears 057°.

Required: Plot and label the 1227 fix.

Solution: The 1227 fix is at the intersection of the two lines of position.

Example 5: Bearing and distance on different objects (figure 1107e). At 1425 radio tower A bears 350 degrees. At the same time, the radar range to Sandy Point Light is four miles. The ship is on course 050°, speed 18 knots.

Required: Plot and label the 1425 fix.

Solution: The 1425 fix is at the intersection of the line of position and the distance circle of position.

Figure 1107b. A fix from three intersecting bearings.

Figure 1107c. A fix from two ranges.

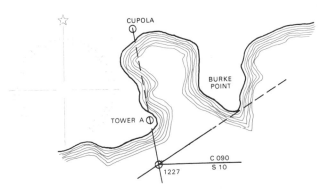

Figure 1107d. A fix from one range plus one bearing.

Example 6: Bearing and distance of the same object (figure 1107f). At 1314, Double Point Light bears 347°. From a 1314 sextant observation its distance is computed to be 3 miles. Ship is on course 225°, speed 10 knots.

Required: Plot and label the 1314 fix.

Solution: Plot the observed bearing, 347°. With the lighthouse as the center, plot the distance circle of position. The point where the line of position is intersected by the circle of position is the 1314 fix.

Example 7: Passing close aboard an aid to navigation. A vessel's position can also be determined approximately by passing close aboard a navigational aid, such as a buoy or offshore light tower, the position of which is indicated on the chart. The accuracy of a position obtained in this manner depends upon two factors: the accuracy of the measurement of the relationship between the ship and the observed aid, and the amount of displacement between the actual and plotted positions of the aid. If the aid is a fixed structure, this displacement is likely to be too small to be significant; the fix will be as accurate as the determination of distance off. If a floating aid is involved, or there is any doubt as to its distance away, this procedure should be used only when more accurate means are not available to establish a position.

Using Relative Bearings

1108 The *relative bearing* of an object is its direction from the ship, relative to the ship's head. It is the angle between the fore-and-aft line of the vessel and the bearing line of the object, measured clockwise from 000° at the ship's head through 360°. In figure 1108 the relative bearings of objects *A*, *B*, *C*, and *D* are 135°, 180°, 270°, and 340°, respectively. A pelorus can be used for taking relative bearings by setting the 000° graduation of the pelorus card to the lubber's line, then observing the object and reading the card. An azimuth circle or the bearing circle are more frequently used, however.

Relative bearings are converted to true bearings before they are plotted. This is done simply by adding their value to the vessel's true heading when the relative bearings were taken (subtracting 360° if the sum equals or exceeds that amount). Thus, assuming the vessel is steady on 045° true during observations, the corresponding true bearings of *A*, *B*, *C*, and *D* are 180°, 225°, 315°, and 025°. Conversely, true bearings can be converted to relative bearings by subtracting from them the vessel's true heading (first adding 360° if necessary).

TB = RB + SH(−360°)
RB = TB(+360°) − SH

Figure 1107e. A fix by a bearing on one object and distance from another.

Figure 1107f. A fix by a bearing on and distance from the same object.

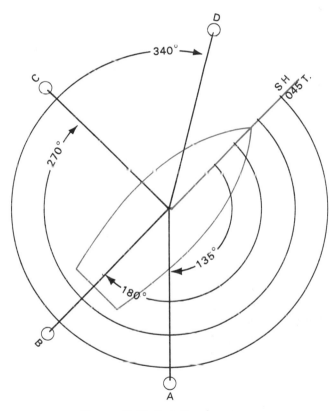

Figure 1108. Relative bearings.

Selecting Objects for Obtaining a Fix

1109 When selecting objects from which to obtain a fix, the primary consideration is the angle between the bearings. If only two visual bearings are available, the best fix results from two bearings crossing at 90°, in which case an error in either bearing results in minimal error in the plotted fix.

As the angle between the objects decreases, a small error in either bearing throws the fix out by an increasing amount. Bearings of objects intersecting at less than 30° should be used only when no other objects are available, and the resulting fix should be regarded with caution. Figure 1109 illustrates the deterioration in accuracy of a fix caused by a given error in one bearing. (See also article 3008.)

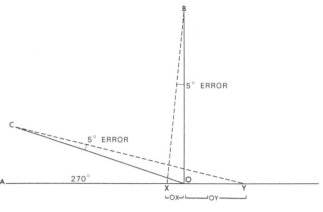

5° ERROR IN ANGLE AOB = DISTANCE ERROR OX
5° ERROR IN ANGLE AOC = DISTANCE ERROR OY

Figure 1109. Effect on error by change in angle of intersection of two lines of position.

To check two bearings and to minimize fix error, three or more bearings should always be taken if possible. If three are taken, the optimum angle is 120° (or 60°) between bearings.

Figure 1109 compares the errors to a fix arising from a 5° error in one bearing, when the observed objects differ 90° in bearing and when they differ 20°. *A*, *B*, and *C* each represent known objects. *O* is the observer's true position. *AOC* = 20°, and AOB = 90°. If *A* and *B* are the objects sighted upon, and a 5° error is made in taking or plotting the bearing of *B*, *OX* shows the resulting error. If, however, *A* and *C* are the objects and a similar 5° error is made in the bearing of *C*, the much larger error, *OY*, results.

Using Horizontal Angles

1110   A fix can also be determined by the measurement of the two horizontal angles between the lines of sight to three identifiable objects. The actual *directions* of these lines of sight are *not* measured; but the two angles must be measured simultaneously, usually when the vessel has no way on. The angles are normally measured by a sextant held horizontally.

The Three-arm Protractor

The two angles so measured are usually plotted with a *three-arm protractor*. This instrument, made of brass or plastic, consists of a circular scale that can be read to fractions of a degree or minutes of arc, and to which the three arms are attached (figure 1110a). The center or index arm is fixed, and the zero graduation of the protractor coincides with the straightedge of this arm. The other arms

are rotatable, and can be set and locked at any angle relative to the fixed arm.

To obtain a fix, three fixed objects that can be identified on the chart must be visible. The angles between the right and central objects, and the left and central objects, are measured with the sextant. The two movable arms are set to these angles and locked, and the protractor is placed on the chart, with the index arm passing through the center object. The instrument is now moved slowly across the chart until all three arms are aligned with the three objects. The vessel's position may now be marked on the chart with the point of a pencil through the hole at the center of the protractor.

Care must be used in selecting the three objects to be observed; if they and the vessel all lie on the circumference of a circle, no fix can be obtained. To avoid this possibility, the objects should be so selected, if a choice is available, that the center one is closer to the estimated position than the right and left objects.

The three-arm protractor gives chart positions of great accuracy; these positions are not affected by any error of the compass. If a three-arm protractor is not available, the method can be used by drawing straight lines on clear plastic or transparent paper, which is then placed on the chart and moved about until the lines pass over all three objects; the position is beneath the intersection point of the lines.

If a navigator does not have a sextant available, a *position finder* can be substituted, because the accuracy required, for purposes other than surveying, is considerably less than the inherent accuracy of the sextant. The position finder is, in effect, a three-arm protractor with mirrors attached that permit using the same instrument for observing and plotting. It is unnecessary to read the value of the angles measured, as the plotting arms are properly positioned for plotting when making the observa-

Figure 1110a. A three-arm protractor.

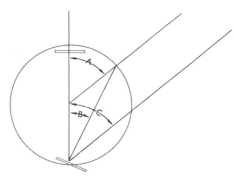

Figure 1110b. Optical principle of a position finder; B = A, C = A.

Figure 1110c. Using a position finder on a chart.

tions. Figure 1110b illustrates the optics of the position finder, and figure 1110c shows it positioned on the chart for plotting.

The Running Fix

1111 It is not always possible to obtain two simultaneous observations. At such times a navigator must resort to a *running fix,* using two lines of position that are obtained by observations at *different times.* In order to plot a running fix, he must make allowance for the time elapsed between the first observation and the second. This is done by *advancing* the carlier line of position to the time of the second observation. (It is also possible to obtain a running fix by *retiring* the second LOP to the time of the first observation, but this is seldom desirable in actual navigation, as the first method gives a more recent position.)

The navigator assumes that, for the limited period of time between the two observations, the vessel makes good over the ground a definite distance in a definite direction. He moves the earlier line of position, parallel to itself, to this advanced position. The new advanced line now represents possible positions of the vessel at the time of the second observation.

When an accurate position has been determined by a fix or a good running fix, the old DR plot is discontinued and a new one started.

There is no rule as to how far a line of position can be advanced and still give a well-determined position. This is a matter of judgment and depends upon individual circumstances. But until judgment is developed, a good general rule in piloting is to avoid advancing a terrestrial line of position more than 30 minutes. The length of time should be kept as short as possible, consistent with other considerations.

In the examples below, current effects are not considered.

Example 1: Advancing a line of position (figure 1111a). A ship on course 012°, speed 12 knots, observes Light *E,* at 1500, bearing 245°. A subsequent observation on another object is made at 1520, at which time Light *E* is no longer visible.

Required: Advance the 1500 line of position until it becomes a 1520 line of position.

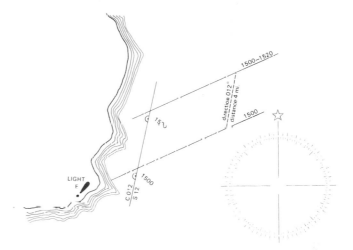

Figure 1111a. Advancing a line of position without consideration of current.

Solution: In this case the navigator assumes that for the limited period of time (20 minutes) involved, the ship makes good both course 012° and speed 12 knots, or 4 miles in the direction of 012°. Plot and label the 1500 DR and the 1500 line of position. This line represents all possible positions of the ship at 1500. Note that the 1500 DR is not on the 1500 line of position, indicating that the DR position does not coincide with the true position of the ship, the location of which is not as yet known. From *any* point on the 1500 line of position (including but not limited to the point where the course line intersects this line of position), measure off 4 miles in the direction of 012°, and draw a line through this point parallel to the original 1500 line. Label the new line with both the original time of observation, 1500, and the time to which the line has been advanced, 1520, as shown. Note that *any point* on the 1500 line advanced 4 miles in direction 012° arrives at the advanced line.

The label "1500–1520" really means "a 1500 line that has become a 1520 line by advancing all points of the 1500 line in a given direction at a given speed for the time interval indicated (1500–1520)." The given direction and given speed are the ordered course and the ordered speed, respectively.

Consider now the full problem of determining a ship's position by running fix.

Example 2: A running fix with bearings on different objects (figure 1111b). The 1440 DR position of a ship is as shown. The ship is on course 012°, speed 12 knots. The weather is foggy. At 1500 Light *E* is sighted through a rift in the fog bearing 245°. No other landmark is visible at this time. At 1520 stack *F* is sighted bearing 340°. Light *E* is no longer visible.

Required: Plot and label the running fix (1520 R Fix).

Solution: Plot and label both the 1500 and 1520 DR positions. (A DR position should be determined and plotted every time an LOP or fix is obtained.) Plot the bearing of Light *E* as a line of position and label with time. Advance this line parallel to itself in the direction (012°) of the ship's course being steered and a distance (4 miles) determined by the speed of the ship divided by elapsed time. (Depending upon the plotting technique used, it may be desirable to label the 1500 LOP with its direction, so that this direction can be used to draw an advanced line through an advanced point.) This distance will be the same as that between the 1500 and 1520 DR positions. Label this advanced line of position as shown in figure 1111b. Plot the second line of position through stack *F* bearing 340°. It is only necessary to draw a segment of this line, long enough to intersect the advanced LOP. The intersection of the two LOPs is the 1520 running fix; this is labeled with the time (horizontally), and with the abbreviation "R FIX" so that the small circle symbol will not be thought of as a true "fix," a position determined to a higher degree of accuracy. Since the position of the vessel has been relatively well established along an LOP to a better degree of accuracy than the simultaneous DR position, a new DR course and speed line is plotted from the running fix.

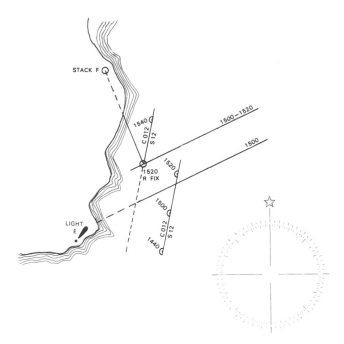

Figure 1111b. A running fix.

Care must be exercised when plotting a running fix to ensure that the earlier line is advanced in the proper direction. This may be determined by close inspection of the labels on the DR course line and the lines of position.

Example 3: A running fix from successive bearings on the same object (figure 1111c). A running fix can also be obtained by plotting two bearings on the same object as illustrated in this example.

A ship is on course 018°, speed 12 knots. At 1430, Light *G* bears 042° and at 1452, it is observed to bear 083°.

Required: Plot and label the 1452 running fix.

Solution: Plot the 1430 DR position on the course line that corresponds with the time of the first observation and plot the 1430 line of position on a bearing of 042° to the light, labeling the plot as indicated. In a like manner, plot the 1452 DR and its corresponding line of position on a bearing of 083°. Then advance any point on the earlier line of position in the direction of the course, 018°, for a distance of 4.4 miles ($22/60 \times 12$ kts = 4.4 miles). Through this advanced point, construct a line parallel to the original 1430 line of position. (Again, it may be desirable to label direction on the initial LOP so that this information can be used for drawing the advanced LOP.) The intersection of the 1430

Figure 1111c. A running fix from two bearings on the same object at different times.

Figure 1111d. Advancing a circle of position.

LOP advanced to 1452 with the 1452 LOP determines the 1452 running fix. A new course line is started from the 1452 running fix as indicated.

Example 4: A running fix advancing a distance circle of position (figure 1111d). A distance circle of position is advanced by moving the center of the circle as illustrated in this example.

A ship is on course 076°, speed 15 knots. The 1440 DR position has been plotted as shown. At 1440, the distance to Buoy *J*, obscured by fog, is found by radar to be 4.7 miles. At 1508, Light *H* is sighted bearing 040°, and the radar has become inoperable.

Required: Plot and label the 1508 running fix.

Solution: Note that the center of the circle (the buoy) is advanced in the direction 076° for a distance of seven miles (28/60 × 15 knots = 7 miles). From this point, the distance circle of position is constructed again with a radius of 4.7 miles and labeled as indicated. The 1508 line of position to Light *H* is plotted on a bearing of 040°. The intersection of this line of position with the advanced distance circle of position determines the 1508 running fix, from which a new course line is started.

Note also that there are two possible intersections of a bearing line of position with a distance circle of position, only one of which is shown. In ordinary circumstances, the intersection nearer the DR position is termed the running fix. In cases of doubt and in the absence of additional information that will confirm either one as the true running fix, commence a DR plot from both positions, assume the ship to be on the course that is potentially more dangerous, and govern future actions accordingly.

A Running Fix with Change in Course or Speed

1112 A line can be advanced to determine a running fix even though the vessel's course or speed is changed in the period between the two observations, as illustrated in the following examples.

Example 1: A running fix with a single course change (figure 1112a). A ship is on course 063°, speed 18 knots. The 2100 DR position is plotted as shown. At 2105 Light *P* bears 340° and disappears shortly thereafter. The 2105 DR position is plotted. At 2120 the course is changed to 138° and the 2120 DR position plotted. At 2132 Light *Q* is sighted bearing 047°.

Required: Plot and label the 2132 running fix.

Solution: Plot the 2105 DR and 2132 DR positions. The 2105 line of position is advanced by using the course and distance *made good* through the water between the DR position corresponding

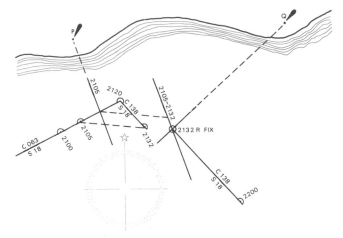

Figure 1112a. A running fix with a change of course between times of bearings.

Figure 1112b. A running fix with multiple changes of course and speed.

to the time of each visual observation. This is shown by a dashed line, usually not drawn in practice, but used here for clarity, connecting the 2105 DR and the 2132 DR. By advancing the 2105 line of position parallel to itself in the direction of the *course made good*, a distance equal to the *distance made good* between the 2105 and the 2132 DR, the 2105 line of position advanced becomes the 2105–2132 line of position. In this example, the point of origin for the measurement of this advance was at the intersection of the 2105 LOP with the DR course line as shown. Similar advance of any other point on the 2105 LOP would have produced the identical result.

Plot the 2132 line of position to Light Q on a bearing of 047°. The intersection of this line of position with the 2105–2132 LOP determines the 2132 running fix, from which a new DR is started. The plot is labeled as indicated.

Example 2: A running fix with multiple course and speed changes (figure 1112b). At 0300, a ship is on course 125°, speed 20 knots. At 0302, Light A is observed on a bearing of 040° and is soon lost sight of in the haze. At 0310 course is changed to 195°, and speed is reduced to 18 knots. At 0315, course is changed to 220°. At 0319, course is changed to 090°, and speed is increased to 24 knots. At 0332, Light B is sighted on a bearing of 006°.

Required: Plot and label the 0332 running fix.

Solution: Use the "course and distance made good" technique described in the foregoing example to construct the 0332 running fix. The accuracy of measurement of "course made good–distance made good" displacement will depend, of course, upon the accuracy with which the DR plot was

maintained between 0302 and 0332. *This principle is true for any running fix obtained by construction.*

The 0302 line of position is advanced parallel to itself in the direction of the course made good a distance equal to the distance made good between the 0302 and 0332 DR position. This advanced line now defines the 0302–0332 LOP. The intersection of this line of position with the 0332 line of position on a bearing of 006° to Light B establishes the 0332 running fix, from which a new DR plot is started. The plot is labeled as indicated.

Example 3: A running fix using the DRT (figure 1112c). A ship is maneuvering with frequent changes of course and speed. The 0900 DR position is as shown. At 0900, Light D bears 220° by visual observation, and at 0925 it bears 150°, at which time the ship is on course 270°, speed 10 knots. The DRT (article 724) indicates that between 0900 and 0925 the ship makes good 2.5 miles north and 4.0 miles west.

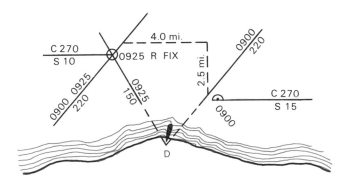

Figure 1112c. A running fix using a DRT.

Required: Plot and label the 0925 running fix.

Solution: Any point on the 0900 bearing line is advanced 2.5 miles north and 4.0 miles west, as indicated by the dashed line, and the advanced line of position is drawn through the point thus determined. A new DR track is started from the 0925 running fix.

Running Fix Using Trigonometry

1113 It is possible to solve the running fix by trigonometry; two angles are determined by measurement, and the length of the side between them is determined by the ship's run between the bearings. The distance off at the time of the second bearing can readily be found, as can the predicted distance off when the object is abeam. These calculations can easily be done on any small hand calculator that has trigonometric functions; see appendix F.

Solution by Table 7, Bowditch

It is not necessary to resort to trigonometry to obtain the solution. Table 7 of *Bowditch* Volume II (figure 1113) tabulates both distance off at the second bearing and predicted distance off when abeam, for a run of one mile between relative bearings from 20° on the bow to 30° on the quarter. Since the distance rarely equals exactly one mile, the tabulations are in reality *multipliers* or *factors*, which when multiplied by the actual run, give the distance from the object at the time of the second

bearing and the *predicted* distance at which the object should be passed abeam.

Arguments for entering Table 7 are arranged across the top and down the left side of each page. The multipliers or factors are arranged in *double columns.* The left-hand column lists the factors for finding the distance at the time of the second bearing. The right-hand column contains the factors for finding the predicted distance when abeam.

Whenever the second bearing is 90° (relative), the two factors are the same. In this case the second bearing *is* the beam bearing and the element of prediction no longer exists.

In case the second bearing is greater than 90° (relative), the right-hand factor obviously no longer gives a predicted distance abeam, but the estimated distance at which the object *was passed* abeam.

Caution

It must be remembered that the ship's heading (SH) may *not* be the same as the course being made good over the bottom (CMG); for example, the vessel may be "crabbing" slightly, heading a bit into a cross current in order to make good a desired track. In the general cases of this article, and in the more special cases of the following article, *the angles must be measured with respect to the course being made good over the bottom.* If there are any currents influencing the track of the ship with respect to the earth, appropriate corrections must be applied.

TABLE 7
Distance of an Object by Two Bearings.

Difference between the course and second bearing.	Difference between the course and first bearing.												
	20°		22°		24°		26°		28°		30°		32°
30°	1.97	0.98												
32	1.64	0.87	2.16	1.14										
34	1.41	0.79	1.80	1.01	2.34	1.31								
36	1.24	0.73	1.55	0.91	1.96	1.15	2.52	1.48						
38	1.11	0.68	1.36	0.84	1.68	1.04	2.11	1.30	2.70	1.66				
40	1.00	0.64	1.21	0.78	1.48	0.95	1.81	1.16	2.26	1.45	2.88	1.85		
42	0.91	0.61	1.10	0.73	1.32	0.88	1.59	1.06	1.94	1.30	2.40	1.61	3.05	2.04
44	0.84	0.58	1.00	0.69	1.19	0.83	1.42	0.98	1.70	1.18	2.07	1.44	2.55	1.77
46	0.78	0.56	0.92	0.66	1.09	0.78	1.28	0.92	1.52	1.09	1.81	1.30	2.19	1.58
48	0.73	0.54	0.85	0.64	1.00	0.74	1.17	0.87	1.37	1.02	1.62	1.20	1.92	1.43
50	0.68	0.52	0.80	0.61	0.93	0.71	1.08	0.83	1.25	0.96	1.46	1.12	1.71	1.31
52	0.65	0.51	0.75	0.59	0.87	0.68	1.00	0.79	1.15	0.91	1.33	1.05	1.55	1.22
54	0.61	0.49	0.71	0.57	0.81	0.66	0.93	0.76	1.07	0.87	1.23	0.99	1.41	1.14
56	0.58	0.48	0.67	0.56	0.77	0.64	0.88	0.73	1.00	0.83	1.14	0.95	1.30	1.08
58	0.56	0.47	0.64	0.54	0.73	0.62	0.83	0.70	0.94	0.80	1.07	0.90	1.21	1.03
60	0.53	0.46	0.61	0.53	0.69	0.60	0.78	0.68	0.89	0.77	1.00	0.87	1.13	0.98
62	0.51	0.45	0.58	0.51	0.66	0.58	0.75	0.66	0.84	0.74	0.94	0.83	1.06	0.94

Figure 1113. Extract from Table 7 of *Bowditch*, Volume II.

There is usually no need to interpolate when using Table 7, even though only the even-numbered relative bearings are given. As a rule it is easy to obtain even-numbered relative bearings if the bearing-taker or navigator exercises a little patience.

Example 1: A ship is on course 187°, speed 12 knots. At 1319 Light *A* bears 161°, and at 1334 it bears 129° true.

Required: (1) Distance from Light *A* at 1334. (2) Predicted distance at which Light *A* should be passed abeam.

Solution: (figure 1113) Difference between course and *first* bearing (first relative bearing or first angle on the bow) = 26°. Difference between course and *second* bearing (second relative bearing or second angle on the bow) = 58°.

Factors (multipliers) = 0.83 and 0.70.

Run (1319 to 1334) = 15 minutes = 3 miles $(12 \times \frac{15}{60})$. (1) 3 × 0.83 = 2.49 = 2.5 miles (distance at 1334). (2) 3 × 0.70 = 2.10 = 2.1 miles (predicted distance abeam).

Example 2: A ship is on course 235° psc, speed 14 knots. At 2054 Light *X* bears 267° psc, at which time the patent log reads 26.7. At 2129 Light *X* bears 289° psc, at which time the patent log reads 34.9.

Required: (1) Distance from Light *X* at 2129. (2) Predicted distance at which Light *X* should be passed abeam.

Solution: (figure 1113) Difference between course and *first* bearing (first relative bearing or first angle on the bow) = 32°. Difference between course and *second* bearing (second relative bearing or second angle on the bow) = 54°.

Factors = 1.41 and 1.14.

Distance run = 8.2 miles. (1) Distance at 2129 (time of second bearing) = 11.6 miles. (2) Predicted distance when abeam = 9.3 miles.

Special Cases

1114 Certain cases of this problem (two bearings of an object and the intervening run) do not require the use of tables. Some of these *special cases* are as follows:

The *bow and beam* bearing (figure 1114a and 1114b) in which the known run between the bow (45°) and beam (90°) bearings equals the object's distance abeam.

Doubling the angle on the bow (figure 1114c). This is developed as follows:

$$b = 180° - 2a$$
$$a + b + c = 180°$$
$$a + 180° - 2a + c = 180°$$
$$a - 2a + c = 0°$$
$$\text{and } a = c$$

Therefore, *ABC* is an isosceles triangle, and *AB = BC*.

Hence, when the angular distance of the object on the bow is doubled, the run between bearings equals the object's distance at the second bearing.

The $22\frac{1}{2}°$–45° *case*, or $\frac{7}{10}$ *rule*. This is a case of doubling the angle on the bow, explained in the preceding case, the distance run being equal to the

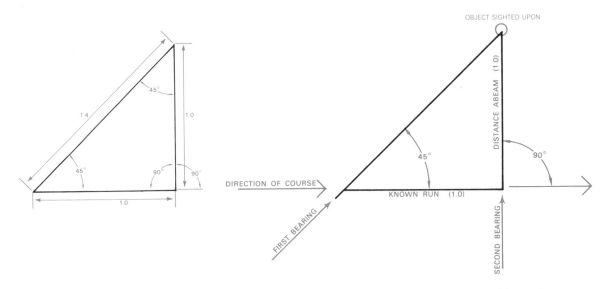

Figure 1114a, left. Portions of a right isosceles triangle. Figure 1114b, right. Bow and beam bearings.

DIRECTION OF COURSE
FIRST BEARING

Figure 1114c. Do

object's distanc
particular case
distance the ob

The 30°–60°
bearings are 3
another case of
distance run b
distance at the
tance run equ
passed abeam.

The 26½°–45°
the bow and th
when abeam e
is true in other
ral cotangents
binations are li
The asterisked
since they invo
the distance r
tance of passin
is reached.

Keeping in Safe Water without a Fix

It is at times possible to ensure the safety
essel without obtaining a fix, even in the ab-
of a range. Under some conditions, such a
d might be even more certain and even easier
than those discussed previously.

g a straight coast where the various depth
s roughly parallel the shore, the echo sounder
d can be kept going and any tendency of the
o be set in toward the beach will soon be ap-
t. Such a method, of course, must be used in-
ntly. If a given fathom curve is blindly fol-
, it may lead into trouble. It is necessary to
head and anticipate the results. If the given
n curve makes a sharp turn, for instance, a
ollowing a steady course might find itself in
y shoaling water before it could make the
The given fathom line, while affording plenty
er under the keel, might pass close to isolated
rs, such as wrecks, shoals, or rocks. Use this
dure *only with due caution.*

ollowing a narrow channel, particularly one
s not well marked, a constant bearing on a
t object ahead or a range can be of inestima-
lue. A very slight deviation from the desired
is immediately apparent when piloting by
s of a range dead ahead (or dead astern). Aids
vigation are often established in such a posi-
s to form ranges to guide ships along chan-
but when such an aid is not available, natural
s can sometimes be found. A navigator should
ert to recognize such a situation, for the value
nges, either artificial or natural, as guides in
navigation cannot be overemphasized. In using a
range, it is important to know how far the range

1st Bearing	2d Bearing	1st Bearing	2d Bearing	1st Bearing	2d Bearing
°	°	°	°	°	°
20	29¾	28	48½	37	71¼
21	31¼	*29	51	38	74¼
*22	34	30	53¾	39	76¾
23	36¼	31	56¼	*40	79
24	38¾	*32	59	41	81¼
*25	41	33	61½	42	83½
26	43½	34	64¼	43	85¾
26½	45	35	66¾	*44	88
*27	46	36	69¼	*45	90

Figure 1114d. Pairs of relative bearings.

Figure 1115. Passing around a point of land.

can be followed, that is, when to turn. Turns in a channel are usually marked by turn buoys. Excellent fixes to check the progress of a ship can be obtained by following a range and noting the instant other pairs of objects near the beam are in range. A study of the chart in advance will often reveal several good natural ranges to use as check points along a channel. One near a turn is especially valuable.

A vessel can usually be taken safely on a change of course around a point of land that has a prominent, identifiable landmark by using the following procedure (see figure 1115): The vessel proceeds down the coast maintaining a specified distance off. As the landmark draws abeam, course is gradually altered (to starboard in this example) in such a manner that the landmark continues to be abeam and *never forward of the beam*; frequent small changes of course are made to maintain this condition. Caution: this technique is subject to errors, and could be hazardous if there is appreciable current or leeway.

Danger Bearings

1116 A *danger bearing* is used by the navigator to keep his ship clear of an outlying area of danger close to which the *ship* must pass. The area has been previously surveyed and is plotted on his chart, but in the vast majority of cases, it will give no warning of its presence to the eye. Examples of such dangers are submerged rocks, reefs, wrecks, and shoals. A danger bearing must be established between two fixed objects, one of which is the danger area. The other object must be selected to satisfy these conditions: visible to the eye; indicated

on the chart; true bearing from the danger area should be in the same general direction as the course of the ship as it proceeds past the area.

As shown in figure 1116, a ship is standing up a coast on course 000°, speed 15 knots. The 0430 DR is at Point *A*. A charted area of shoal water and sunken rocks off the coast must be avoided. On the chart draw line *GO* from Light *O* (the visible object), tangent to the danger area (the invisible object). The measured direction of this line from *G* to *O*, 015°, is the danger bearing. It is habitually drawn in red pencil, hachured on the dangerous side, and is labeled, also in red pencil, with "NLT 015" (meaning *Not Less Than* 015°) on the side opposite the hachures; any bearing less than 015° could indicate a hazardous situation. (If the chart is to be used under a red light at night, some other dark color may be desirable.)

As the ship proceeds up the coast, frequent visual bearings of Light *O* are taken. If each such bearing is numerically *greater* than the charted bearings *GO*, such as *EO* or *FO*, the ship must be in safe water. If, however, a bearing is observed to be *less* than *GO*, such as *HO*, the ship *may* be standing into danger as illustrated. In this case, if the position of the ship cannot be determined by a fix, the ship should change course radically to the left until the danger bearing is reached, after which it is safe to resume the original course.

Similarly, if the hazard were to the left of the course, a danger bearing could be plotted with hachures on the other side and a label reading "NMT" meaning *Not More Than*. In some waters, it is useful to use a pair of danger bearings, one NLT and one NMT, to keep the vessel on a safe course between hazards to either side.

The value of this method decreases as the angle between the course and the danger bearing increases. Unless the visible object is nearly *dead ahead*, the danger bearing is of little value in keeping the vessel in safe water as the danger is approached. If there is a large angle between the course and the danger bearing, the object might better be used to obtain running fixes as the vessel proceeds. However, if there is but one object in sight and that nearly ahead, it would be very difficult to get an exact position, but a danger bearing will show whether or not the vessel is on a good course, and will, in consequence, be of the greatest value. Even if there were other objects visible by which to plot accurate fixes, it is a simple matter to note, by an occasional glance over the sight vane of the pelorus or compass, between fixes, that the vessel is making good a safe course. It occasionally

Figure 1116. A danger bearing.

will occur that two natural objects will so lie that when in range, they mark a danger bearing. Advantage should be taken of all such ranges.

When stated or recorded for use, a "danger bearing" should include not only the numerical value of the bearing, but also an amplifying statement of whether the bearing tendency should be greater or less for safety. In the previous example, the personnel concerned should be informed that *"bearings to Light O greater than 015° are safe"* or *"bearings to Light O less than 015° are dangerous,"* (but to avoid confusion, not both statements) in order that the danger bearing be meaningful.

Danger Angles

1117 To avoid sunken rocks or shoals, or other dangerous obstructions that are marked on the chart, a navigator may use what is known as a *danger angle*. There are two kinds, the *horizontal* and the *vertical* danger angle. The former requires two well-marked objects indicated on the chart, lying in the direction of the coast, and sufficiently distant from each other to give a fair-sized horizontal angle; the latter requires a well-charted object of known height.

Horizontal Danger Angle

In figure 1117a, let *AMB* be a portion of the coast along which a ship is making her way on course *CD*. *A* and *B* are two prominent objects shown on the chart; *S'* is an outlying shoal or reef, or other danger. In order to pass offshore of the danger, *S'*, take the middle point of the danger as a center and the distance from that center at which it is desired to pass as a radius, and draw a circle. Pass a circle through points *A* and *B* tangent to the offshore side of the first circle *(E)*. To do this, it is only necessary to draw a line joining *A* and *B* and draw a line per-

pendicular to the middle of *AB*, and then find by trial and error the location for the center of circle *AEB*. Measure the angle *AEB*; this is the *horizontal danger angle*, 60° in the example of figure 1117a. (From any point on arc *AEB*, the same angle will be measured.) A sextant is set to the danger angle and frequent measurements are taken of the angle between *A* and *B*. In this situation, if the angle gets *less*, 50° in figure 1117a, the trend is farther *away* from the danger, and the course is *safe*. If, on the other hand, the angle becomes *greater*, the ship is closer in to the danger and the course is *hazardous*.

Alternatively, if the danger area is farther offshore and it is desired to pass between it and the coastline, as at *S* in figure 1117b, the danger angle is established by again drawing the smaller circle around the hazard and the larger circle tangent to it as before. Here any *decrease* in the observed hori-

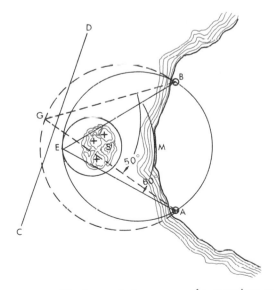

Figure 1117a. Horizontal danger angle, passing safely offshore of the hazard.

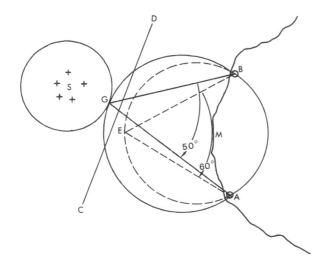

Figure 1117b. Horizontal danger angle, passing safely inshore of the hazard.

zontal angle between *A* and *B* would indicate that the vessel was getting farther out from the coastline and hence *closer to the danger area*. If the danger angle *increased*, it would indicate greater clearance from the danger area and greater safety, provided that the shore was not approached too closely.

The two situations described above can be combined into one if it is necessary to pass between two hazards, and suitable objects exist to serve as points *A* and *B*. In this case, the *safe* sextant angle will be between two limiting values with a decrease or increase beyond these limits being dangerous.

To simplify reference to the danger angle and to make the plot more meaningful, a notation can be made on the chart in red (or other color for night work) of the numerical value or values of the horizontal danger angles. In addition, trace over in red pencil the arc of the inscribed circle about shoal *S* and the arc of the circle *AEB* adjacent to which the ship will pass in the safe-passage corridor between the danger areas. Unless the danger covers a large area, it is generally not necessary to draw the cir-

cles as described above. In many cases points *E* and *G* can be selected by eye at a safe distance from the dangers.

Vertical Danger Angle

A vertical danger angle involves the same general principle, as can be seen by reference to figure 1117c, in which *AB* represents a vertical object of known height. In this case the tangent circles are drawn with the charted position of the object as a center. The limiting angles are determined by computation or by means of Table 9, *Bowditch* Volume II. The addition of the measured values of the respective vertical danger angles and the marking of the limits of the safe-passage corridor between the shoals in red pencil will measurably improve the graphic value of the plot.

An Estimated Position

1118   At times, the information available to a navigator is insufficient to fix the position of the vessel accurately. However, under these conditions it is often possible to improve on the DR by using the data at hand. A position determined under these conditions is called an *estimated position* (EP). An EP is indicated on the chart by a small square with the corresponding time, written horizontally.

Estimated positions are determined in a variety of ways. In a heavy sea, it is sometimes impossible to obtain accurate bearings. Bearing lines determined electronically may vary considerably in accuracy; they are seldom as reliable as good visual bearings. Bearings obtained by magnetic compass are no more accurate than the deviation table. Estimates of current and leeway due to wind are rarely accurate enough to use in obtaining a fix. However, any of these factors may supply information, which, while not exactly correct, will tend to indicate the more probable position of the vessel than that indicated by the DR.

An estimated position is the best position obtainable short of a fix or good running fix. A doubtful fix or running fix should appropriately be consid-

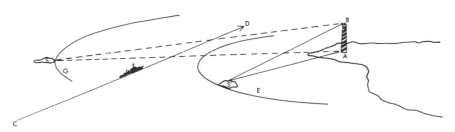

Figure 1117c. A vertical danger angle.

Figure 1118. Estimated position (EP).

ered an EP. An estimated position is determined by gathering all the data available and giving due consideration to each factor. Each additional item of information results in a reconsideration of the estimated position and the possible revision of the estimate.

One method of obtaining an estimated position from limited information involves the ship's DR position. The DR position at the time of observation represents the best position available before a line of position is plotted. Once plotted, a line of position represents the locus of all the possible points the ship could have occupied at the time of the observation. The most probable estimated position (EP) of the ship is defined as that point on the line of position that is *closest* to the DR position.

Example 1: (figure 1118) The 0600 DR of a ship is as indicated. Course is 025°, speed 10 knots. At 0627, Light A was observed through a rift in the fog, bearing 260°.

Required: Plot and label the 0627 EP.

Solution: Plot the 0627 LOP and the corresponding 0627 DR. From the 0627 DR, draw a perpendicular to the LOP. The intersection of the LOP and the perpendicular locates the 0627 EP, labeled as shown. This is the most probable position of the ship on the 0627 LOP, as it is not only on the observed line of position, but it also represents the nearest point thereon to the 0627 DR.

EP from Depth Information

1119 The use of depth information to obtain an estimated position must not be overlooked. With modern electronic equipment, charts now show a number of precise depth soundings; on many charts depth contours (lines of equal depths) are shown as light blue lines. If the bottom has a general slope, or there are areas of pronounced features, such as a sharp "valley" or ridge, a sounding can be combined with other positioning information to establish at least an estimated position. (This will not be possible on a flat, featureless bottom.)

One of the best ways to establish an estimated position from depth information is to use a *line of soundings.* The manner of employing this method is largely determined by the chart covering the area.

Either of the two procedures requires a piece of transparent paper or plastic, on which is drawn a straight line representing the ship's course. If bottom contour lines are printed on the chart, the depth values of the contour lines should be noted; assume that these are given for every 20 fathoms. The echo sounder is now turned on, and when a sounding of a multiple of 20 fathoms true depth is obtained, a mark is made at one end of the course line on the tracing paper, the depth is noted opposite the mark at one side of the line, and the time at the other. When the depth changes by 20 fathoms, the time is again noted, and using the latitude scale of the chart, the vessel's run for the time interval is calculated, and another mark is made at the appropriate distance from the first, and depth and time are again noted. After this process has been repeated several times, the paper is placed on the chart in the vicinity of the vessel's DR position, with the vessel's line oriented in the proper direction. It is now moved across the chart, with the course line always oriented in the proper direction, until the depth marks on the paper agree with the contour lines on the chart. The vessel's position may now usually be determined with reasonable accuracy.

Note that if the echo sounder reads depth under the keel, the soundings must be adjusted to represent depth below the surface. In this case, if the vessel draws 24 feet (4 fathoms), use echo-sounder readings of 16, 36, 56, etc. fathoms. If the vessel is in tidal waters, all charted depths must be adjusted for the height of the tide at the time that this method is used. Do not forget the possibility of a current setting the vessel to one side of its intended track or affecting the speed made good.

When contour lines are not shown on the chart, mark off the course line in equal distances, each representing the vessel's advance for a convenient length of time such as 6 or 10 minutes, or perhaps one mile. On small-scale charts, these intervals will be greater than when using a large-scale chart. When a number of soundings have been recorded, the paper strip is oriented to the course line and moved about the chart in the same manner as described above to determine an estimated position.

A generally similar, but more complex, procedure is described in article 3607.

It is suggested that navigators use depth contours for position determination and for planning courses in advance, particularly where characteristic bottom features are available. These may be combined with other information such as radio bearings, visual bearings, or lines of position from celestial bodies.

In thick weather, or at times of poor radio reception, depth-sounding navigation can provide, where bottom characteristics permit, a highly practical means of obtaining an acceptable estimated position.

Using an EP

1120 Often the two methods just described in articles 1118 and 1119 can be combined for a better EP than could be obtained from either alone. The negative value of depth information should never be overlooked—if the depths being measured at a location vary markedly from those shown on the chart, you are *not* at the position indicated by whatever other method is being used. Depth soundings may not be able to conclusively confirm an EP, but they can emphatically point to its inaccuracy.

Since an EP is not a well-determined position, it is not customary to run a new DR plot from such a position. However, a light line representing the estimated course and speed being made good should be run from an EP to indicate any possibility of the ship standing into danger, allowing the navigator to take appropriate avoiding action before a dangerous situation develops.

Responsibilities of a Navigator

1121 One of the most important responsibilities of a navigator is to *fix* the position of his vessel often and accurately. He can direct its further movement safely and efficiently *only* if he knows from where he is starting; he can be assured of his vessel's safety *only* if he knows where he is at a given time.

Lines of position are among the most valuable and useful "tools" of the navigator. An LOP of good quality tells a navigator that he is somewhere along that line, and *not* somewhere else. A single LOP provides useful information, but a second (and preferably more) are required to establish a *fix*. If he is on both lines, he can only be at their intersection. A *running fix* is a position obtained when two simultaneous observations cannot be made, and one of the LOPs is advanced or retired in time to match the other; it is of lesser validity than a fix, but of sufficient value to be used as a starting point for a new DR track. An *estimated position* is of still lesser validity, but contains more input information than a *dead reckoning* position, which is the least likely to be the actual position of the vessel.

At all times, a navigator must know to the best of his capabilities the position of his vessel and plan ahead for its safe future movement.

Chapter 12   Current Sailing

Introduction

1201 Preceding chapters have considered the movement of a vessel through the water without regard to current—chapter 8, Dead Reckoning—and then the movement of the water itself—chapter 10, Currents and Current Prediction. Chapter 11 presented methods by which the actual, rather than DR, position of the vessel could be fixed, and thus the DR plot verified—or the need for correction could be seen. This chapter carries the process further showing how the net effect of current can be determined from the difference between DR positions and actual fixes, and also how allowances can be made in advance for the anticipated effect of currents. This is *current sailing*.

Actually, the term used in this chapter should be stated as "current"—in quotation marks—for more is to be considered than the horizontal movement of the waters. In navigation, especially in *current sailing*, the total of *all* the factors that may cause a ship to depart from its intended course and DR are lumped together and termed *current*. Among the factors included in the term are:

    Ocean current
    Tidal current
    Wind current
    Windage on the ship
    Heavy seas
    Inaccurate steering
    Undetermined compass error
    Inaccurate determination of speed
    Error in engine calibration
    Error in log calibration
    Excessively fouled bottom
    Unusual conditions of trim

From the foregoing, it can be seen that *current*, unfortunately, has two meanings as commonly used in marine navigation. First, it refers to the horizontal movement of water due to ocean currents, tidal currents, or wind currents. Second, in common usage it refers to the combined effect of all the factors listed above. Thus, the term current, as used in navigation, may or may not solely involve the motion of the water through which the ship is passing; in most cases, however, this factor, if it exists, will have the greatest effect on the ship's course.

Current Sailing Defined

1202 Current sailing is the art of selecting course and speed through the water, making due allowance for the effect of a predicted or estimated current, so that upon completion of travel, the intended track and the actual track will coincide, and you will have arrived at your desired destination.

Primarily, current sailing is the application to the intended track of the best available current information to determine what course and speed to use. Additionally, however, the term is expanded to include the determination of actual current—by comparison of DR position and fixes—and the prediction of anticipated track if course and speed are specified.

Types of Current

1203 As considered in greater detail in chapter 10, three types of current are of interest to a navigator:

    Ocean current is a well-defined current, extending over a considerable oceanic area.
    Tidal current is one resulting from tidal action. It will normally be of a *reversing* nature in har-

bors and estuaries, etc.; velocities are often enough to be significant in navigation. Along coasts, tidal currents are usually *rotary* in nature, with weak strength, but these must still be taken into consideration in some navigational situations.

Wind currents are currents affecting a limited area that are created by the action of a strong wind blowing in a relatively constant direction for 12 hours or more; they usually do not flow in the direction of the wind, as they tend to be deflected by the Coriolis force.

Current Terms Defined

1204 *Estimated current* is found by evaluating all the known forces that will make up the sum total of current effects in a given area.

Actual current is determined by measurement of the distance and direction between a fix and the DR position of a vessel for the same time; it is determined only when an accurate fix can be obtained.

An *estimated position (EP)* is the most probable position of a vessel, determined from all available data, when a fix or a running fix cannot be obtained; it includes the effect of estimated current or the probable effect of an earlier-determined actual current.

A *current triangle* is a graphic *vector diagram*, in which one side represents the set and drift of the current, one side represents the ship's course and speed, and the third side represents the actual track. If any two sides are known, the third can be determined by measurement or calculation.

The terms *heading, course,* and *speed* were employed in the discussion of dead reckoning in chapter 8. Some additional terms to be introduced here include:

Track (TR). The intended (anticipated, desired) horizontal direction of travel with respect to the earth, taking into consideration known or predicted offsetting effects such as current, wind, and seas.

Speed of Advance (SOA). The intended (anticipated, desired) speed along the track with respect to the earth, taking into consideration the effect of known or predicted current; speed along the track. SOA is also used to designate the average speed that must be made good to arrive at a destination at a specified time.

Set. The direction *toward* which the current is flowing; if the broader definition of "current" is used, the resultant direction of all offsetting influ-

ences. Note carefully that the description of the set of a current is directly *opposite* from the naming of a wind—a westerly *current* sets *toward* the west, a westerly *wind* blows *from* the west.

Drift. The speed of a current (or the speed of the resultant of all offsetting influences), usually stated in knots. Some publications, however, notably pilot charts and atlases, express drift in terms of nautical miles per day.

Course Made Good (CMG). The resultant direction from a given point of departure to a subsequent position; the direction of the net movement from one point to another, disregarding any intermediate course changes en route. This will differ from the track if the correct allowance for current was not made.

Speed Made Good (SMG). The net speed based on distance and time of passage directly from one point to another, disregarding any intermediate speed change; speed along the course made good.

Course Over the Ground (COG). The actual path of the vessel with respect to the earth; this may differ from CMG if there are intermediate course changes, steering inaccuracies, varying offsetting influences, etc. (Not used in current sailing triangles; CMG is used.)

Speed Over the Ground (SOG). The actual ship's speed with respect to the earth along the COG. (Not used in current sailing; SMG is used.)

The Two Current Triangles

1205 Note carefully that there are *two* current triangles: before and after movement—anticipated and actual conditions. Track and speed of advance are used with the "before" triangle. Course made good and speed made good are the corresponding components of the "after" triangle. Set and drift are used with both triangles, although, of course, in one case it is estimated current and in the other, actual current. Course and speed can be components of either the "anticipated" or the "actual" triangle.

Practical Current Sailing

1206 In figure 1206, point *D* lies 20 miles, 090° from point *A*. A current with an estimated set of 180°, and drift of 4 knots flows between the two points. If a ship were ordered to steam from *A* to *D* in a total elapsed time of two hours, her navigator would be faced with a typical problem in current sailing. It is obvious that the direction of the *TR* is 090°, and the *SOA* is 10.0 knots. It is equally obvious that if course 090°, and speed 10.0 knots, were

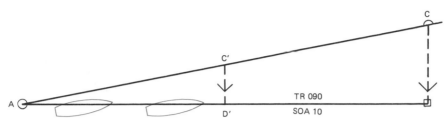

Figure 1206. Allowing for current.

ordered, the ship two hours later would be some eight miles south of D. To allow for the estimated current on this two-hour trip, the ship should be steered on a course somewhat into the current in the direction of Point C some eight miles to the north of D, and at a speed slightly greater than 10 knots. *Provided the estimate of the current was correct*, the ship would arrive at D in two hours, the current effects having exactly countered the course and speed offset from the intended track.

Figure 1206 illustrates what has occurred. The ship headed for Point C on course 070°, but actually made good 090°, constantly "crabbing" into the current, as shown. At the end of the first hour she reached D', rather than C', and at the end of the second hour she reached Point D rather than C. The track, AD, is the resultant of the vector sum of the velocity of the ship with respect to the water *(AC)* and the velocity of the current with respect to the earth *(CD)*, both of which were in action for the same length of time.

Point C represents the ship's DR position at the end of two hours, and Point D represents the *estimated position*, EP, which is the most probable position, short of a fix or running fix.

This situation in current sailing is considered in greater mathematical detail in the second examples of article 1208 and figure 1208b.

An EP Plot

1207 It has been pointed out that in the absence of a fix or running fix, the navigator, on the basis of available information, may often estimate his ship's position to a greater accuracy than that indicated by the DR. For instance, if a navigator has good reason to believe that a current of well-determined set and drift exists, he can find the EP for a given time by plotting the predicted movement of the ship away from the DR position for a given time, due to the effect of the current. To do this, he plots the *set* and measures off along this line the *drift* multiplied by the number of hours it has been or will be acting. An alternate method, used chiefly when a vessel proceeds on a single course at a constant speed, is to solve graphically a current triangle.

Example: (Figure 1207) The 0500 fix of a ship is as shown. The ship is on course 300°, speed 6 knots. A current has been estimated with a set of 250°, drift 1.0 knot.

Required: Plot and label the hourly DR positions and hourly EPs from 0500 to 0800.

Solution: Plot the course and the hourly DR positions up to 0800. From each DR position plot a line in the direction 250° and measure off 1 mile from the 0600 DR, 2 miles from the 0700 DR, and 3 miles

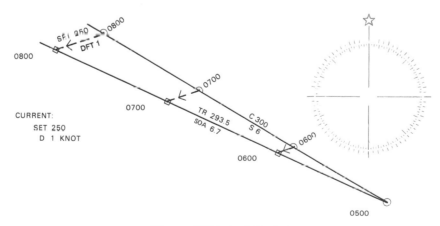

Figure 1207. An EP plot.

Part	Using Estimated Current	Using Actual Current
Point A	Present position (fix) of ship	Previous position (fix) of ship
Point D	DR position of ship at future time	DR position of ship at present time
Point B	Estimated position at future time	Present position (fix) at present time
Side AD	Course and speed vector	Course and speed vector
Side AB	Track and SOA	CMG and SMG
Side DB	Anticipated or expected current	Actual current encountered

Note: Points B and D are always for the *same* time.

Figure 1208. The current triangle and its parts.

from the 0800 DR. Enclose the points so obtained in small squares and label as shown in figure 1207.

The accuracy of an estimated position depends on the accuracy with which the current is estimated. It is not safe to assume that a current determined by the last fix will continue, unless there is evidence to indicate that this is so. Unless there is information available to permit a reasonably accurate estimate of the current, it is best to assume zero current. It is especially unwise to expect a current to be regular and uniform near a coast, for local conditions are likely to cause irregularity, and tidal currents have greater effects here than on the open sea. When approaching pilot waters, it is often desirable to maintain two plots, allowing for anticipated current in one (the EP plot) and not in the other (the DR plot), and to consider *both* plots when laying a course to avoid danger.

Labeling Current Sailing Triangles

1208 Many times it is a good idea to construct a current sailing vector triangle to assist in the graphic solution of the problem. In all cases the solution of the unknown part of the triangle must be in terms of the given information of the known parts.

A complete current triangle equally applicable to the solutions of the current problem prior to departure, as well as to its solution after arrival, is illustrated in figure 1208. A tabulation of the respective parts of each triangle is given in the accompanying table.

Various Current Sailing Problems

1209 Three problems frequently arise in connection with currents of estimated set and drift:

Finding the anticipated track and speed of advance of a vessel proceeding on a specified course at a specified speed through an estimated current.

Finding what course a vessel proceeding at a given speed through an estimated current should take to make good an intended track.

Finding what course and speed must be ordered to proceed through an estimated current to arrive at the destination on time.

If a current is setting in the same direction as the course, or its reciprocal, the track is the same as the course through the water. The effect on speed can be found by simple addition or subtraction—if in the same direction, the speeds are added; if in opposite directions, the smaller is subtracted from the larger. This situation happens frequently when a vessel encounters tidal currents upon entering or leaving a port. If a vessel is crossing a current, either at right angles or at a lesser or greater angle, the solution can be found graphically by a vector diagram, since the velocity over the ground is the vector sum of the vessel's velocity through the water and the current effects over the ground.

Such vector solution can be made to any convenient scale and at any convenient place, such as at the center of a compass rose, on a separate sheet, or directly on the plot. The following examples will illustrate the method of graphic solution:

Example 1: (Figure 1209a) Given the course and speed of the vessel, and the estimated set and drift of the current, find the anticipated track (TR) and the anticipated speed (SOA) along this track. This example illustrates how the navigator not only finds the TR and SOA, but also, and perhaps more

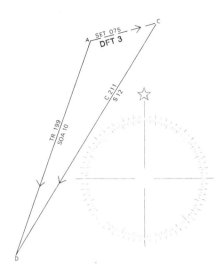

Figure 1209a. Determining track and speed of advance to determine an estimated position.

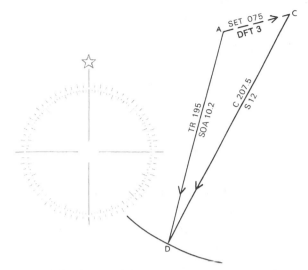

Figure 1209b. Determining course to steer to make good a desired track.

importantly, how he establishes an estimated position (D). It illustrates the first of the three cases of current sailing stated at the beginning of this article.

Required: A vessel is to proceed at 12 knots on a course of 211° true, through a current estimated to be setting 075° at drift of 3 knots. Find the anticipated track and speed of advance along that track.

Solution: In figure 1209a, let point A be the location of the vessel. From A, lay off the vector AC in the direction of the set of the current, 075°, for a length equal to the drift, 3 knots, at the scale selected (this represents motion of the ship due to current alone). From C, lay off a vector in the direction of the course, 211°, with length to scale of the speed, 12 knots (this represents the travel of the vessel through the water with no consideration of current). Complete the current sailing vector diagram by drawing AD. The direction of AD is the direction of the anticipated track while its length represents, to the established scale, the speed that is anticipated along this track, if the current was predicted or estimated correctly. D is an *estimated* position only and must be used with caution until a fix can be obtained. The navigator is now able to apply this solution to the DR track from his last fix to obtain an estimated position.

Example 2: (Figure 1209b) Given the estimated set and drift of the current and the ordered speed of the vessel, find what course must be steered to make good a given intended track (find also what the expected SOA will be along this TR).

Required: Let the estimated set of the current be 075°, drift 3 knots. The vessel will proceed at 12 knots. The direction of the desired (intended) track

is 195°, the speed of advance along that track is not specified and can be of any value.

Solution: In figure 1209b, from point A, the position of the vessel, lay off the line AD of indefinite length in the direction 195°. Plot the current vector, AC, in the direction of the set, 075°, for a distance equal to the velocity of the drift, 3 knots. With C as a center, swing an arc of radius equal to the vessel's speed through the water, 12 knots, intersecting AD at D. The direction, CD, 207.5°, is the course to order and the length AD, 10.2 knots, is the estimated SOA. Notice that vectors AD and AC, representing intended track and current respectively, have been plotted with respect to the earth (point A), while vector CD has been plotted with respect to the water.

Example 3: (Figure 1209c) Given the set and drift of the estimated current, and the direction of the desired track and the required speed of advance, find the course and speed to be used.

Required: A vessel at 1300 is 100 miles due west of her desired destination. If the ship is to arrive at her destination at 1800, find the course and speed to order if a 2-knot current southeast (135°) is predicted.

Solution: In figure 1209c, the vessel is located at point A with point D as its destination, 100 miles due east. With five hours to reach this destination, she obviously must maintain a speed of advance of 20 knots. Lay off AD in the direction 090° to represent the intended track and of a length equal to the intended SOA, 20 knots. Lay off the current vector, AC, in the direction of its set, 135°, from Point A and of a length equal to the drift, 2 knots. Complete the current sailing vector diagram by drawing CD. The

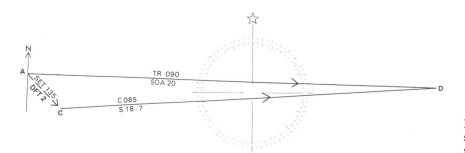

Figure 1209c. Determining course and speed to make good a desired track and speed of advance.

direction of *CD*, 085°, is the course to steer, while its length, 18.7 knots, is the speed to order to make the passage. Again notice that vectors *AD* and *AC*, representing *intended track* and current respectively, have been plotted with respect to the earth, while vector *CD* has been plotted with respect to the water.

Determining Actual Current

1210 The preceding three examples have all included the use of "estimated currents." Another use of a current sailing triangle is the graphic determination of "actual current" from a comparison of a DR position with a fix for the same time. If a course line is laid down from a fix (not a running fix), and at a later time a new fix is obtained that does not agree with the corresponding DR position, the difference between these two positions can be assumed to represent the actual "current" encountered during passage. It is immediately apparent that current so determined will include all of the factors mentioned in article 1201 and, in addition, any errors in the fixes. (If the course line of the DR plot was last started from a *running* fix, actual current can still be determined, but special procedures are needed; see example 2 below.)

It should also be apparent that if the estimated position on the intended track coincides with the fix on the actual track, the estimated current computed prior to departure was exactly equal to the actual current encountered during passage. If the two positions are *not* identical, then the estimated current was in error by an amount directly proportional to the rate and direction of separation of the two positions.

Three problems most frequently arise in determining the set and drift of an actual current:

Finding the set and drift of an actual current, given the DR position based on a plot run from an earlier fix, and a new fix for the same time as the DR position.

Finding the set and drift of an actual current, given a DR position on a plot last started at a *running* fix, and a new fix at the same time as the DR position.

Finding the set and drift of an actual current, given a DR position and an estimated position, both based on an earlier fix, and a new fix for the same time as the DR position and EP.

Example 1: (Figure 1210a) Given the DR position based on an earlier fix and a new fix for the time of the DR position, find the set and drift of the actual current.

The DR plot has been run forward from a fix obtained at 0545 the same day. At 1815 a fix is obtained and when plotted, is located 7.5 miles from the 1815 DR position.

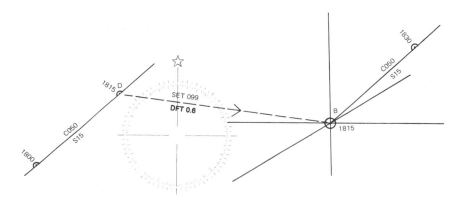

Figure 1210a. Determining the set and drift of a current.

Required: The set and drift of the actual current.

Solution: The set is the direction *from the DR position to the fix* for the same time. Drift is determined by measuring the distance between the DR position and the fix for the same time, and dividing it by the number of hours *since the last fix.* This is true regardless of the number of changes of course and speed since the last fix. Since the 1815 DR position represents the position the vessel would have occupied had there been no current, and the 1815 fix represents the actual position of the ship, the line *DB* joining them is the direction and distance the vessel has been moved by current. The direction of this line from the DR to the fix, 099°, is the *set* of the current. The *drift* is its distance, 7.5 miles, divided by the time between the fixes, 12.5 hours, or 7.5 ÷ 12.5 = 0.6 knots.

Answer: Set 099°, drift 0.6 knots.

Example 2: (Figure 1210b) Given the DR position based on an earlier running fix, and a fix for the same time, find the set and drift of the actual current.

Two methods may be used to determine the actual current when the DR position has been run forward from a running fix. Each method is explained below. At 0700 the navigator obtained a fix as shown. At 1152 a running fix is obtained from two LOPs, one at 0919, and the other at 1152, and a new DR plot is begun. At 1710 another fix is obtained as shown.

Required: The set and drift of the current.

Solution: (Method 1) The plotted DR position at 1710 (point *D′*) has been run forward from a running fix, and therefore cannot be used to obtain the set and drift of the current. Ignore the 1152 running

fix, and continue the original DR course from point *C* until the DR position for time 1710 (point *D*) is determined. The set of the current is the direction from point *D*, to the 1710 fix (point *B*), 357°, and the drift is this distance, 12.7 miles, divided by the time since the last fix, 10.2 hours, or 1.2 knots. (In this example the extension of the original course from *C* to *D* is shown as a broken line for clarity.)

Solution: (Method 2) Measure the direction and distance *CC′* from the original 1152 DR to the 1152 running fix. By applying the reciprocal of this direction and the same distance to the 1710 DR position, point *D* is established. It is noted that this is the same position as determined in method 1. The set of 357° and drift of 1.2 knots are obtained as before.

Answer: Set 357°, drift 1.2 knots.

Example 3: (Figure 1210c) Given a DR position and an estimated position based on an earlier fix, and a fix for the same time, find the set and drift of the actual current.

At 0900, a navigator fixed his position at *A* as shown. While proceeding to Point *D* bearing 090°, 20 miles from *A*, he estimated that the current would be 135°, 6 knots, and therefore he set course 075°, speed 16.3 knots, to make good the intended track to Point *D*. At 1000, the navigator fixed his position at Point *B*.

Required: The set and drift of the actual current.

Solution: Since the 1000 DR represents the position the vessel would have occupied had there been no current, and the 1000 fix represents her actual position, the line *CB* joining them is the direction and distance she has been moved by the actual current. The direction of this line from the DR to the

Figure 1210b. Determining the current when the DR plot has been carried forward from a running fix.

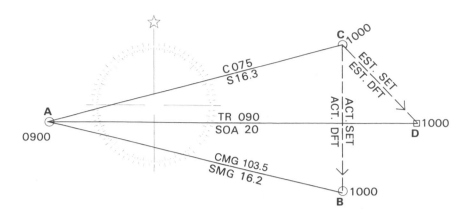

Figure 1210c. Determining actual current after having allowed for an estimated current.

fix, 180°, is the set of the current. The drift is its distance, 8.0 miles, divided by the time between fixes, 1 hour, or drift = 8.0 knots.

As is evident from an inspection of the figure, the navigator's estimate of current was in error by the vector difference of CD and CB.

Other Methods of Solution

1211 Although the normal method of solving current sailing triangles is the graphic procedure described above, solutions are also possible by mathematics. In any of these triangles, there are six components, three sides and three angles (derived from the three directions); four of these factors will be known, two unknown. Solutions by plane trigonometry are unduly laborious if attempted by use of tables, but they can be quickly and easily found using a computer or a small electronic calculator, especially a programmable model. Calculators with a "polar-rectangular conversion" capability are particularly suitable for current sailing problems; vectors are resolved into their N-S and E-W components, these are added, and the sums reconverted back to polar directions and speeds.

Advancing an LOP with Current

1212 Article 1210 considered the fact that a running fix could not be used in the determination of current, as the earlier LOP used to obtain the running fix had in fact been acted upon by current during the time intervening between it and the second LOP. It follows, therefore, that if the navigator believes he knows the set and drift of the current within reasonable limits, he can increase the accuracy of the running fix by allowing for them when he advances the earlier LOP.

The following example illustrates the technique of plotting a running fix with a known current.

Example 1: (Figure 1212) The navigator of a ves-

sel on course 012°, speed 12 knots, observes Light *E* bearing 311° at 1500. He has reason to believe that a current exists with set 030°, drift 3.0 knots. Light *E* is subsequently observed bearing 245° at 1520.

Required: Plot the 1520 running fix, allowing for current.

Solution: In the twenty minutes between LOPs, the vessel advanced 4.0 miles in the direction 012°, so the navigator advances the 1500 LOP as shown by line *AA'*. During this time the current has also moved the ship 1.0 mile in the direction 030°. The navigator must further advance the 1500 LOP to represent the additional travel of the vessel caused by the current, or to the 1500–1520 LOP shown in the figure. The intersection of the 1500 LOP so advanced and the 1520 LOP marks the 1520 running fix. Had current not been taken into consideration, the running fix (see article 1111) would have been located at the dotted circle, over one mile from the established running fix.

Errors Inherent in Running Fixes

1213 In working with current, an inexperienced navigator may well make one of two errors, both about equally dangerous for his vessel. He may either allow for too little or no current, or he may assume that a current is continuing without change when he is not justified in so doing. Judgment born of experience is the best guide, but there are some considerations that even a beginner can learn to apply. The estimates of current given in official tables, pilot charts, etc., are usually quite accurate under normal conditions; these should not be ignored, but neither should they be accepted as a proven "fact." When there is a strong, steady wind, its effect both in causing a temporary wind-driven current, or increasing or decreasing the predicted current, and in slowing the vessel or blowing her off course downwind should be considered. The effect of wind on a vessel differs with the type of vessel, her draft, and the relative direction of the wind. The current acting on a vessel is generally changing because of the tidal cycle, changes in wind, changes in geographical position, etc. Any steering error normally changes with a change of helmsman. Hence, it is generally unwise to blindly assume that the "current" that has acted since the last fix will continue. All the factors mentioned above should go into an estimate of the present current. In estimating current, the most unfavorable conditions possible should be assumed in order to best assure the safety of the vessel.

It must be remembered that a running fix obtained from two bearings not taken simultaneously will be in error unless the movement of the vessel between the observations is correctly estimated—the actual course and distance made good over the ground are required. Difficulty will occur in estimating the exact course when there is bad steering, a cross current, or when the vessel is making leeway; errors in the estimated run will arise when the vessel is being set ahead or held back by a current or when the distance shown by the log is inaccurate. Since the actual current is seldom known, the run between two bearings will often be in error, and therefore a running fix will give an incorrect position, the amount and direction of the error depending upon the difference between estimated and actual values of current during the run.

Often a plot is made by taking a number of successive bearings on the same object, and plotting a series of running fixes, each using the three most recent lines of position. If the current is parallel to the course, but actually greater or less than esti-

mated, the run between successive bearings will be in error, and a line between the successive running fixes will *not* indicate the track made good. If an opposing ("foul") current is not allowed for, or is underestimated, the plot will give an indication of position that is too far from the object; the actual track will be closer inshore and hence potentially less safe. The same situation would result from an overestimation of an aiding ("fair") current, as both cases result in actual runs between bearings being less than the values used for the plot. See figure 1213a. The opposite situation would result from an overestimation of an opposing current or an underestimation of an aiding current. The existence of error in current estimates will *not* be apparent from a plot of this type; for the greatest measure of safety, a navigator should use the *minimum* estimate of speed over the ground, except where hazards are on the side of the track opposite to that of the object on which the first bearing was taken.

If the current is oblique to the vessel's course, a more complex situation develops. A current at 90° to the course results in a plot as shown in figure 1213b. The successive running fixes from sets of LOPs will be triangles, the size of which depends upon the relative magnitude of the crosscurrent, and the line through the mean points of the successive actual positions will show a track oblique to the course steered. At other angles, the effect will be governed by whether the along-course component of the current opposes or aids the vessel's movement.

Obviously, the presence of a current acting against a vessel's forward progress presents a possible hazard, since in this case her position as plotted by running fixes indicates a greater margin of safety relative to shoals and rocks extending out from shore than actually exists. Hence, where the possibility of an opposing current exists, all inshore dangers to navigation should be given a wider berth than indicated by the running fixes. A better plan, where possible, would be to obtain frequent fixes by simultaneous bearings on two or more stationary objects.

Summary

1214 The preceding consideration of current sailing has involved aspects of dead reckoning and piloting that are inseparable. Examples as "simple" or "pure" as those used in this chapter will not normally be encountered in actual navigation, but the ones shown serve to illustrate the vector analy-

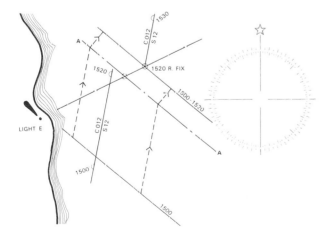

Figure 1212. Plotting a running fix with known current.

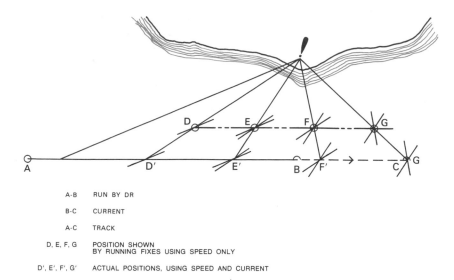

A-B RUN BY DR

B-C CURRENT

A-C TRACK

D, E, F, G POSITION SHOWN BY RUNNING FIXES USING SPEED ONLY

D', E', F', G' ACTUAL POSITIONS, USING SPEED AND CURRENT

Figure 1213a. Error of a running fix with current parallel to course (following current).

A-B RUN BY DR

B-C CURRENT

A-C TRACK

D, E, F, G POSITION SHOWN BY RUNNING FIXES USING SPEED ONLY

D', E', F', G' ACTUAL POSITIONS USING SPEED AND CURRENT

Figure 1213b. Error of a running fix with cross current.

sis involved. Solutions are also possible using the considerable mathematical capabilities of computers, or even small hand-held electronic calculators.

A DR plot must always be maintained. If data on current are not available, or cannot be trusted, the course and anticipated track are considered one and the same. If data of acceptable reliability are available, they should be used and an EP plot maintained. If the vessel is in waters containing hazards, both plots should be maintained, at least to the extent of determining any possible danger. All possible data should be evaluated to give an estimated position, as it is a rare occasion when a fix is obtained that coincides precisely with the DR position, indicating no current effect whatsoever.

Chapter 13

Ship Characteristics in Piloting

Introduction

1301 The term "handling characteristics" refers to the way a vessel responds to engine and rudder orders. For naval vessels, this is termed the "tactical characteristics of the ship." Tables of tactical characteristics are maintained on the bridge of all U.S. naval vessels. Coast Guard regulations require that U.S. merchant ships post data on handling characteristics where they can easily be seen by bridge watchstanders. On smaller craft the data will not normally be formalized, but they do exist even if only in the mind of the skipper.

Up to this point it has been conveniently assumed that at the instant of an ordered course change the vessel came immediately to the new course, and that when a new speed was ordered, the ship attained that speed instantly. Such, of course, is not the case in "real life." To increase or decrease speed by 10 knots may require from one to twenty minutes or more, depending on the initial speed, the power available, and the flexibility of the engineering plant. A course change of 90° may require as much as a half mile, or more, of sea room to complete, depending on the type of ship, the rudder angle used, the wind and sea, and other factors. Each ship reacts in a different way to a given rudder or speed order and reacts differently under different conditions of wind and sea. A navigator must know his ship's handling characteristics—how she will respond to a given order under existing conditions, and what order must be given to achieve a desired result.

Speed and Course Changes

1302 When a ship is traveling singly at sea, her navigator may ignore the time and travel required to effect course and speed changes, for the scale of his plot is too small to be affected by the resulting errors. In restricted waters the situation is entirely different. Here, the navigator frequently needs to know his position within 10 yards, and the effect of the ship's travel in the time required to complete a change of course or speed is so comparatively large that it must be taken into account. The navigator must know his ship's handling characteristics, that is, how she will respond to a given order under existing conditions. Much the same is true for vessels of a naval formation or in a convoy.

This chapter is concerned with the quantitative effects of course and speed changes on the travel of the ship, and the techniques and methods that a navigator uses to allow for these effects when piloting a ship in restricted waters. The term "precise piloting" is sometimes applied to the navigation of a vessel taking into consideration these small, but very important, factors. Bringing a ship to anchor in an assigned berth, which requires the use of these same techniques, will also be discussed in some detail.

Turning Characteristics

1303 When approaching an anchorage, turning onto a range, piloting in a restricted channel, maintaining an intended track, or at any time when precise piloting is necessary, the navigator must allow for the *turning characteristics* of the ship. The standard method of finding a ship's turning characteristics is to turn her in a number of complete circles under varying conditions and to record the results for each. The variables used are: right and left rudder of specified angles, steady speeds of different value, and differences in draft and trim. When taking turning data, effects of wind and sea are allowed for. Most course changes are not as much as 360°, but by studying the complete turning circle, the ship's behavior for turns of any extent can be determined.

In considering the track actually followed by a ship during a turn, an understanding of the following definitions is essential. These terms may be understood more easily by reference to figure 1304a, in which a right turn is shown; a left turn would be generally similar, but the actual distances would probably be slightly different in a single-screw vessel.

Definitions

1304 Turning circle is the path followed by the pivoting point of a ship in making a turn of 360° or more at a constant rudder angle and speed; the *pivoting point* is typically about one-third the way aft from the bow, but will vary from one vessel to another and may vary for a given vessel under different conditions of a longitudinal trim. The stem will turn on the inside of the turning circle and the stern outside this circle. The diameter of a turning circle for a given ship will vary with both her rudder angle and her speed through the water. See figure 1304a.

Advance is the distance gained in the original direction until the vessel steadies on her new course; it is measured from the point at which the rudder is put over. The advance will be maximum when the ship has turned through 90°.

Transfer is the distance gained at right angles to the original course, measured from the line representing the original direction of travel to the point of completion of the turn.

Tactical diameter is the distance gained to the right or left of the original course when a turn of 180° has been completed.

Final diameter is the distance perpendicular to the original course between tangents drawn at the points where 180° and 360° of the turn have been completed. Should the ship continue turning indefinitely with the same speed and rudder angle, she will keep on turning in a circle of this diameter. It will nearly always be less than the tactical diameter.

Standard tactical diameter is a specific distance that varies according to naval ship type. It is laid down in tactical publications and is used when ships are maneuvering in company.

Standard rudder is the amount of rudder angle necessary to cause the ship to turn in the standard tactical diameter at standard speed.

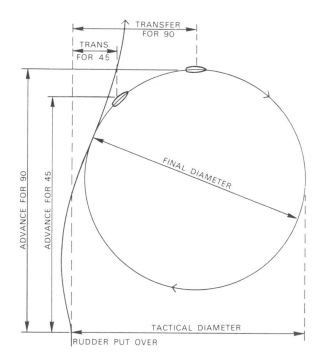

Figure 1304a. Advance, transfer, and tactical and final diameters.

Angle of turn (figure 1305) is the arc, measured in degrees, through which the ship turns from the original course to the final course.

The speed at which a ship makes a turn may affect the turning diameter markedly if the "speed-length ratio" (ratio of speed to the square root of the length) is high enough. Thus a 300-foot ship at 30 knots has a considerably larger turning circle than at 15 knots. Tactical diameters are *not* inversely proportional to the rudder angle. While turning diameters decrease with increase in rudder angle (up to a certain point), the relationship is not an inverse proportion. Furthermore, the rudder angle for minimum turning diameter varies from one design to another. The rudder angle for minimum diameter depends upon many factors of ship and appendage form, as well as speed. The majority of ships have a limiting rudder angle of 35°; some have larger ones. A short vessel will have a smaller turning circle than a longer one with the same general tonnage.

Sample Turning Data

Figure 1304b is a partial set of typical data on the turning characteristics of a naval ship; other values would be applicable for different speeds and rudder angles. These figures are representative of one particular ship and are for use *only* with problems

Standard Tactical Diameter, 1500 Yards—Standard Rudder 15°

Angle of Turn	Advance	Transfer	Angle of Turn	Advance	Transfer
15°	500	38	105°	993	853
30°	680	100	120°	933	1013°
45°	827	207	135°	827	1140
60°	940	347	150°	687	1247
75°	1007	513	165°	533	1413
90°	1020	687	180°	367	1500

Figure 1304b. Typical amounts of advance and transfer for various angles of turn for a specific vessel.

in this book. It must be understood that the proper tactical data for the specific vessel in which a navigator is embarked must be used when actually working under service conditions.

Handling characteristics are usually determined during the builder's trials of a new vessel (for the first of a class of naval ships). Values of advance and transfer can vary slightly as a ship ages or is modified; they should be verified or updated when circumstances permit.

It will be noted that the table in figure 1304b is prepared for every 15° of turn. Data required for increments between these 15-degree points may be obtained by interpolation. Instructions for obtaining tactical data for U S Navy ships are contained in NWP 50-A, *Shipboard Procedures,* and in the *Technical Manual,* NAVSEA 59086-C4-STM-000.

Using a Turning Bearing

1305 From the preceding discussion it can be seen that during conditions when precise piloting is required a navigator must know at what point the rudder must be put over, so that when allowance has been made for the advance and transfer of the ship, she will steady on the desired heading at the time the desired track or point is reached. Having determined this point on his plot, his next task is to establish a means by which he will know when he has arrived at that point. This is done by selecting a prominent mark, such as an aid to navigation or a landmark ashore, and predetermining the bearing to that mark from the point at which the turn is to begin; this is the *turning bearing.* For some time ahead, continuous observations are made on the selected mark, and when the predetermined bearing is observed, the appropriate rudder angle is ordered. Ideally, the object upon which the turning bearing is taken would be abeam at the time of starting the turn; this would give the greatest rate of change of bearing and hence the most

precisely determined point. In actual practice, relative bearings from roughly 30° to 150°, or 210° to 330° can be used if care is taken at the extremes of these ranges. If practicable, preference is given to taking the turning bearing on the side toward which the turn is to be made, as the conning officer will be giving that side of the vessel the greater part of his attention.

In precise piloting, bearings will often be taken on objects that are at relatively close distances. Allowances must be made for the conditions of *parallax* that will then exist. Bearings on close objects will *not* be the same from peloruses on opposite wings of the bridge; directions, such as head bearings (article 1307), will not be the same from bridge wings as those seen by the helmsman on the ship's centerline.

In allowing for the advance and transfer, the navigator should use standard tactical diameter and commence the turn using standard rudder. By so doing a margin for the compensation of any error remains, and the rudder angle can be increased if the turn is commenced too late.

Example: (Figure 1305) A ship is standing up a channel on course 000°T and after rounding the point of land with Light *M*, must take up a new course of 075°T to continue up the river.

Required: The turning bearing on light *M* so as to be on course 075° upon completing the turn to proceed up the next reach of the river.

Solution: Draw the desired course line up the next reach of the river. Draw a line parallel to the vessel's present track at a distance out to the side equal to the transfer for a 75° turn (513 yards). The intersection of this line with the final course, 075°T, will be the point *B* at which the turn must be completed. From this point, measure back along the line a distance equal to the advance, 1,007 yards, locating point *X*. From point *X*, drop a perpendicular to the original course line. This will locate the

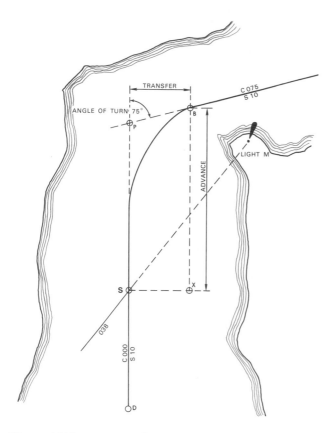

Figure 1305. A turning bearing.

point at which the rudder must be put over to complete the turn at the required point. The bearing, determined from the chart to be 038°, from that point to Light *M* is the *turning bearing*.

The problem is now complete and the data obtained are: The ship continuing on course 000°T arrives at a point *S*, from where Light *M* bears 038°T; here the order *"Right standard rudder"* is given. The turn is complete, and the ship is heading on the final course at point *B*. The solid line *DB* represents the actual track of the ship (ignoring the slightly different turning paths of the bow and stern as shown in figure 1303).

Acceleration and Deceleration

1306 Speed changes are usually of less concern to a navigator than are course changes. There are many times, however, when one may desire to or must allow for the acceleration or deceleration as in the cases described here.

Values for acceleration and deceleration rates vary widely for different vessels. The values given in figure 1306 are illustrative for one particular ship and are to be used *only* for examples in this

book. A similar table must be prepared for or by a navigator on his own specific vessel.

The term *head reach* is used for the distance that a ship will travel from the point where action is taken to stop it to the point where it is dead in the water; this distance can be as much as several miles for large vessels of considerable tonnage but modest horsepower.

Determining Time to Change Speed

Example 1: A ship is standing up a channel at speed 15 knots, and the captain desires to slow to 10 knots at the latest possible time so as to pass a construction barge at that speed.

Required: How far before reaching the barge should speed 10 knots be rung up so as to slow the ship to an actual speed of 10 knots at the time the barge is abeam?

Solution: The table in figure 1306 shows that to decelerate from 15 to 10 knots requires 1 minute. Since the rate of deceleration between these speeds is assumed to be constant, the average of the initial speed and the final speed will be the average speed for that minute, or 12½ knots. In a minute at 12½ knots a ship will travel 422 yards. Measure back 422 yards along the DR track from a point abeam of the construction barge to locate the point at which speed 10 knots should be rung up on the engines. (Note: A slightly different value, 417 yards, will be obtained if 2,000 yards is used for a nautical mile rather than the more precise value of 2,025.4 yards; the slight difference is of no practical significance.)

Example 2: A ship is standing down the channel at speed 10 knots. The captain has stated that he desired to order speed 24 knots as soon as the ship is clear of the channel, in order to make a rendezvous on time.

Required: How far along the DR track line should the navigator consider the ship to have traveled between the time speed 24 is rung up on the engines, and the time the ship actually gets up to speed 24 knots through the water, and how much time is required?

Solution: (Figure 1306) Note that three different rates of acceleration will be used for this speed change. For this reason it will be necessary to calculate the distance traveled during the period of acceleration in three separate parts, one part for each rate of acceleration. From speed 10 to speed 15 knots requires 1 minute, at an average speed of 12½ knots. During this time the ship will travel 422 yards. From speed 15 to speed 20 requires 2 min-

Knots		Minutes		Rate
Change of Speed From	To	Time Required for Change	Total Elapsed Time	Knots Change per Minute
Acceleration				
0	10	3	3	$3\frac{1}{3}$
10	15	1	4	5
15	20	2	6	$2\frac{1}{2}$
20	24	4	10	1
24	28	6	16	$\frac{2}{3}$
28	31	9	25	$\frac{1}{3}$
Deceleration				
31	28	3	3	1
28	24	4	7	1
24	20	2	9	2
20	15	1	10	5
15	10	1	11	5
10	0	2	13	5

Figure 1306. Acceleration and deceleration table.

utes at an average speed of $17\frac{1}{2}$ knots. During this time the ship will travel 1,181 yards. From speed 20 to speed 24 requires 4 minutes at an average speed of 22 knots. During this time the ship will travel 2,971 yards. Add the three distances computed to find the total distance traveled from the time the new speed is rung up until the ship is actually making it; the answer is 4,574 yards, or about $2\frac{1}{4}$ miles. Elapsed time, the total of that noted in the table and used above, is 7 minutes.

As can be seen from these examples, the determination of distance traveled between the time a speed is ordered and the time a ship actually is making it good through the water is easily accomplished and can be quite accurate. The time involved can be determined by reading directly from the table. Many navigators use the average of the initial and final speeds as the effective average speed during the time of acceleration or deceleration. Although this is not as accurate as the method used in the examples above (it would yield 4,017 yards, a difference of 557 yards, or 12 percent), it is usually sufficiently accurate for most navigational work.

Anchoring in a Specific Spot

1307 Charts showing specific anchorage berths are published for many ports by either the National Ocean Service, the Defense Mapping Agency Hydrographic/Topographic Center, or the local maritime authorities for a foreign port. They are simply harbor charts with anchorage berths over-printed in colored circles of various diameters corresponding to the swinging area required by vessels of various types and sizes. On these charts, berths of like size are laid out in straight lines, referred to as *lines of anchorages*. Often, adjacent circles are tangent to each other. The center of the circle marks the center of the berth, and each berth is designated by a number or letter printed inside the circle.

This orderly arrangement greatly simplifies the assignment of anchorages, especially when a large group of ships in company is to occupy a harbor. In harbors for which no standard anchorage chart is available, berths are assigned by giving the bearing and distance of the berth from a landmark or aid to navigation, together with its diameter. It is the duty of the navigator to cause the ship to be maneuvered in such a manner that the anchor may be let go in the center of the ship's assigned berth. This should be accomplished with a maximum permissible error of 10–50 yards (9–46 m), depending upon the type of ship.

Definitions of Anchoring Terms

For this discussion, the following terms are defined:

Approach track is the track that a vessel must make good in order to arrive at the center of her assigned berth.

Letting-go circle is a circle drawn around the

center of the berth with a radius equal to the horizontal distance from the hawsepipe to the instrument used for taking bearings.

The *letting-go bearing* is the bearing from the point of intersection of the letting-go circle and the final approach track to any convenient landmark, generally selected near the beam.

Range circles are distance circles of varying radii from the center of the berth, with distances measured from the letting-go circle.

Preparations

When the ship has been ordered to anchor in a specific berth (figure 1307), the navigator consults the chart and prepares for the approach to the anchorage by laying off from the center of the berth the following.

The *letting-go circle* as described above.

The *intended track*, selecting appropriate approach courses and navigational aids for fixing the ship's position en route, and locating turning bearing marks at predetermined points where turns are necessary. The final approach should, if possible, be made with the vessel heading into the current, or if the wind has the greater effect, then into the wind. The approach track must be long enough for the final turn to have been completed and any last-minute adjustments of track accomplished before reaching the center of the berth; this distance will vary with the ship concerned, but should not be less than 500 to 1,000 yards, increasing as the size of the vessel increases. It is also desirable that the approach track be directly toward an identifiable aid to navigation or landmark; as the approach is made, the constant bearing (termed a *head bearing*) of the aid or landmark can then be maintained. If no such aid is available, or if the aid previously selected becomes obscured, the positions of consecutive fixes with respect to the approach track (to the right of it or to the left of it) will permit the navigator to recommend a change of course to conn the ship back on the approach course.

Range circles of varying radii, including the radius of the letting-go circle. In most cases it is necessary to draw in only the arcs of the range circle adjacent to the approach track. In practice it is usual to draw arcs every 100 yards out to 1,000 yards; then at 1,200 yards, 1,500 yards, and 2,000 yards. The *letting-go circle* is labeled 0 yards; the other range circles are labeled with their distance from the *letting-go point*, which is the intersection of the approach track and the letting-go circle.

When planning to bring a ship to anchor, the navigator should determine the depth of the water and the characteristics of the bottom as they may be shown on the chart, as well as the nature of and distance to any nearby areas of shoal water or other hazards. This information should then be passed to the captain and other officers directly concerned with the anchoring.

Execution

Example: A ship is assigned Berth 21 for anchoring, figure 1307. The initial approach into the harbor is on a course of 350°T. An approach track directly toward Light *M* is possible and is selected. Distance from the hawsepipe to the gyro repeater used for taking bearings is 75 yards.

Required:
1. Approach track to the berth.
2. Letting-go bearing on Light *H*.
3. Turning point.
4. Turning bearing on Light *H*.

Solution: The selected approach track is plotted back from Light *M* through the center of the berth; its direction is measured (295°). The *letting-go circle* with a radius of 75 yards is plotted around the center of the berth. The intersection of this circle and the approach track is the *letting-go point* and is labeled 0 yards.

The initial approach track into the harbor is plotted. By use of the table of the ship's characteristics, the navigator can determine the advance and transfer of the final turn at the speed to be used. With this data, he determines the point at which the turn is to be completed and the point at which the rudder is to be put over. He plots this and determines the *turning bearing* on Light *H* (291°).

Range circles are plotted from the center of the berth, *but distances are measured from the letting-go point.* Thus, the radius used to plot the "100-yard" range circle is actually 100 + 75 = 175 yards; similarly, all other range circles are plotted with a radius 75 yards greater than the labeled distance.

As the ship enters the harbor and proceeds along the track, frequent bearings are taken and fixes plotted to ensure that the desired track is maintained. As the range circles are crossed, the navigator advises the captain of the distance to the letting-go point so that the speed may be adjusted to bring the ship nearly dead in the water when the letting-go point is reached.

When Light *H* bears 291° the rudder is put over and the turn commenced. The rate of turn is adjusted so that upon completion Light *M* bears 295° dead ahead. The heading of the ship is adjusted so that a constant bearing of 295° is maintained on Light *M*. Bearings on Lights *H* and *M* are plotted

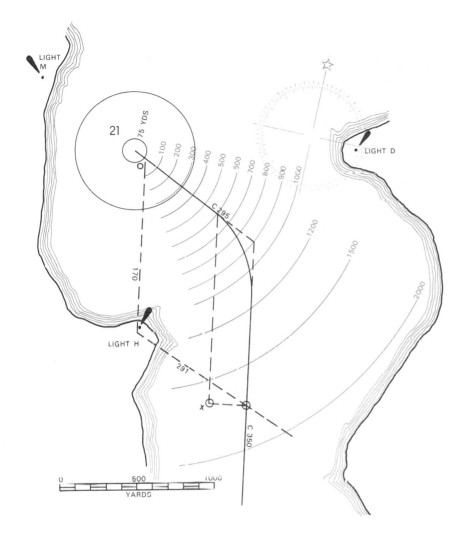

Figure 1307. Anchoring in an assigned berth.

continuously, and the captain advised of the distance to go. When Light *H* bears 170° and Light *M* 295°, the anchor is let go, and at that instant bearings are taken on all navigational aids visible, in order that the exact location of the anchor can be accurately determined. The ship's exact heading at the time of the final fix is also observed. A distance of 75 yards is then plotted from the fix, in the direction of the observed heading. The exact position of the anchor is then known. The anchor should be within 10 yards of the center of the berth.

Answers:

(1) Approach track 295°;
(2) Letting-go bearing 170°;
(3) See figure 1306;
(4) Turning bearing 291°.

Procedures after Anchoring

Immediately after the anchor is down and holding, and the intended length of anchor chain or line has been let out, the navigator should plot the ac-

tual position of the anchor from the bearings taken at the moment it was dropped. Using this as a center, and radius equal to the ship's length plus the horizontal component of the length of anchor cable in use, a *swing circle* is plotted, and the chart is closely examined to be sure that no hazards exist within this circle, nor does it infringe on any other anchoring berth.

The navigator can also plot a *drag circle*, using the actual anchor position as a center and the horizontal component of the anchor cable length plus the hawsepipe-to-bearing-instrument distance as the radius. Therefore, any check bearing, taken to determine if the anchor is holding, must fall within this circle, which is of smaller diameter than the swing circle.

Effects of Wind and Current

1308 In discussing the computation of the turning bearing, the effects of acceleration and deceleration, and anchoring in an assigned berth, the assumption was made that these maneuvers were being carried out under conditions with no wind or current. In actual practice there almost always is some wind or current, and frequently both. Before entering or leaving harbor, and particularly if the channel is restricted in any way, the navigator must determine what currents may be encountered, and what effect they may have on the ship as she negotiates the channel. The effect of wind must also be taken into consideration; at times a strong wind may have a greater effect than the existing current. A navigator must always be prepared to modify his original plans to meet existing conditions.

When possible, constricted channels should be negotiated at slack water, or if this is impractical, when the ship can head into the current.

Importance

1309 Precise piloting becomes a necessity when in confined waters, anchoring in a precisely defined berth, or traveling in close company with other vessels. Every vessel has its own handling characteristics; the details for each will be different in varying degrees. The data must be available on the bridge at all times when underway, and in the most convenient form for use by the captain, the officer of the deck, and the navigator.

Chapter 14

Relative Motion

Introduction

1401 The principal concern of this book is the safe and efficient direction of a vessel to her destination by avoiding fixed hazards such as shoals. These are stationary hazards; to avoid them a navigator must know the actual or geographic movement of his vessel. But moving hazards, such as other ships underway, are also encountered in the course of a voyage, and introduce a second kind of movement with which a navigator must become familiar. This is *relative movement,* which deals with the apparent motion of moving objects. Sometimes, as when meeting another ship underway in constricted waters, both types of motion must be considered simultaneously.

The purpose of this chapter is to define the movement of a vessel underway with respect to another moving vessel, and to the earth, and to show how the relationship between these two motions can be solved accurately and quickly, primarily to avoid the hazard of collision. For this purpose, it is assumed that all bearings and ranges on other vessels are obtained by radar, although the principles and procedures would be equally valid for visual bearings and distance measurements. The technical and operational characteristics of radar equipment are covered in chapter 17.

The Maneuvering Board here described can be used for many additional types of problems involving relative motion. In naval formations the conning officer is required to maintain a position relative to the guide, and to determine course and speed to move to a new station. These ship-handling problems and many other uses of this device are discussed in Pub. No. 217, *Maneuvering Board*

Manual, published by the Defense Mapping Agency Hydrographic / Topographic Center (DMAHTC). Useful information will also be found in Pub. No. 1310, *Radar Navigation Manual.*

Types of Motion

1402 Motion is the movement of an object from one point to another; it can be stated in terms of the direction and distance from the first point to the second. Alternatively, it can be measured in terms of the direction and speed of the object, as it moves from the first point to the second. All motion is relative to some reference, and it is necessary when discussing motion to define the reference. For purposes of this discussion, all fixed objects on the earth will be considered as being without motion.

To the navigator, the motion of his ship over the earth's surface is of primary importance. Assuming that there is no current, the course and speed of the ship through the water represents its movement *over the ground.* This is called *actual movement;* it is defined as *motion measured with respect to the earth.*

Relative movement is motion measured *with respect to a specified object,* which may or may not have actual movement itself.

To illustrate the difference between relative and actual motion, suppose two vessels are proceeding on the same course and at the same speed. Both of these vessels have actual movement, the same actual movement, relative to the earth, but relative to each other there is no motion.

Problems in relative movement are solved subconsciously in everyday life. A pedestrian walking across a street sees a car coming. Without conscious thought, he determines the car's approximate speed and converts it to speed relative to himself when walking; based on this determination he either crosses ahead of the car or waits for it to pass. The same type of reasoning, but at a conscious level, applies to the solution of problems of relative motion at sea.

In general, the problem aboard ship is to determine the course and speed required to bring about the desired change in relative position. A navigator must learn to plot the position of any ship relative to any other ship. How this is done is discussed in the following articles.

General Considerations for the Use of Radar and Relative Motion Plotting

1403   A navigator must be concerned with the accuracy of any radar bearings and ranges that he will be using, and that of the relative motion plot. The three factors involved are the technical characteristics of his radar set, his ability to read ranges and bearings accurately, and his care in plotting.

Assuming that the radar, when set on the 8-mile scale, gives bearings accurate to 0.5°, and ranges accurate to ±0.2 miles, and that the navigator uses reasonable care in plotting, he should be able to determine the *closest point of approach (CPA)* within 0.5 miles, the other vessel's course within 2°, and her speed within 0.2 knots. Times are stated to the nearest whole minute.

It is most important that bearings and ranges be obtained on a continuing basis; the more of each there are, the more accurate and reliable the plot will be. Situations are known in which the other ship (in radar terms, the "target") has changed course or speed, or both, just after a navigator had decided that no more bearings were required as the separation at the closest point of approach would be sufficient to be safe.

It is vital that the Rules of the Road be observed in making any decisions on course or speed changes based on radar or any other information. Article 1412 describes a situation in which two vessels are on a collision course, and one correctly changes course to the right, while the other changes to the left, contrary to the rules and common sense. But such things do happen. Some years ago the *Andrea Doria* and the *Stockholm*, both large passenger liners and both equipped with radar, collided under rather similar conditions resulting in the loss of the *Andrea Doria*. The admonition to motorists to "drive defensively" applies equally well to navigating officers on the high seas.

Tips on Plotting

The following suggestions are offered to simplify the task of relative plotting: A stopwatch is a great convenience in timing. It, as well as a pad of Maneuvering Board sheets or Radar Transfer Plotting Sheets (see article 1404), pencils, dividers, and

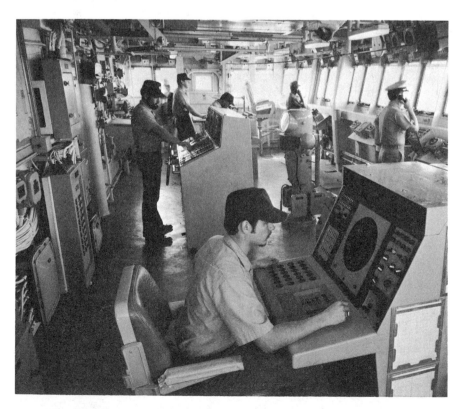

Figure 1403. Radar serves the dual function of navigation and collision avoidance.

plotting instruments should be ready to use at a moment's notice.

A series of readings should be made at convenient, but constant, time intervals. Readings should be made as long as there is *any* possibility that a change of course and speed on the part of the target ship might result in collision.

If a risk of collision exists, and action on your part is called for, make *big* changes in your course and/or speed, rather than small ones, so that your actions will be readily apparent on the radar screen of the other vessel.

If the radar has concentric range rings, but no other range indicator, take bearings of the echo as it crosses these rings, and record the times.

Plot all bearings as true. If the radar does not have a gyro repeater, set the movable azimuth circle so that the bearings are true.

Plot all targets.

Aids for Graphic Solutions

1404   The plotting necessary to obtain a solution to problems in relative motion could be done on plain paper. The solution is greatly facilitated, however, if the work is done on a polar coordinate form or "board."

Two such forms or boards designed especially for solving relative movement problems are available. These are the *Maneuvering Board* and the *Radar Transfer Plotting Sheet*. The former is intended to assist in the solution of all types of relative movement and related problems; the latter is intended primarily for plotting radar contacts.

The Maneuvering Board comes in pads of 50 sheets; each sheet can be used on both sides. It is published by DMAHTC as Chart No. 5090 or 5091; the difference is in size—No. 5090 has a 10-inch diameter for the plot, while No. 5091 is larger with a 20-inch diameter. Sheets from the No. 5090, used to illustrate problems in this chapter, have ten concentric, equally spaced rings numbered 2 to 10 (the first ring is not numbered). All rings are dotted lines except the innermost and outermost; dotted arcs of rings beyond the tenth appear in each corner of the square working area. Dotted radial lines at 10° intervals extend out from the inner ring to the edge of the plotting area. These radials are labeled with 0° at the top of the sheet for the larger figures around the outside of the outer ring and with 0° at the bottom of the sheet for the smaller figures around the inside of that ring. All dots indicate one-tenth subdivisions between concentric circles and the radial lines; every fifth dot is replaced with a small + for more accurate plotting. Arranged vertically on either side of the paper are scales designed for rapid conversion for measuring distance or the length of vectors when a ratio other than 1:1 in circle spacing is desired.

Aboard most vessels, moving targets are detected at 20 miles or less, and since most speeds are less than 20 knots, a scale of 2:1 is generally convenient for plotting both ranges and speeds. (In U.S. Navy usage, ranges are measured in yards, and the 4:1 scale is used for distances, but 2:1 for speeds.)

A nomogram is provided at the bottom of the Maneuvering Board form, consisting of three logarithmic scales: one each for time, distance, and speed. If any two are known, the third can be determined by connecting the two known points with a straight line (extended if necessary) and noting where it intersects the third scale; the point so determined is the unknown quantity. If distance (D) is one of the known quantities, the nomogram can be used with a pair of dividers rather than by drawing a line. Place one point of the dividers on the D value on the center scale; place the other point on the known value of S or T; swing the dividers, keeping the first point on the center scale; the second point will fall on the third scale at the unknown value of T or S. (The distance scale is marked off in both nautical miles and yards on the basis of one mile equalling 2,000 yards.)

Time, speed, and distance problems may also be solved by using only the top logarithmic scale in the same manner as with the similar scale printed on many larger-scale charts; see article 811. This method can be more accurate than using all three scales as a nomogram.

The Radar Transfer Plotting Sheet (figure 1413) is DMAHTC Chart No. 5089. It has a 10-inch circle with six concentric rings. Distance scales, of different values, appear in the left margin, and there is a single speed scale at the right. A logarithmic S-D-T scale is printed at the bottom. Boxes are included in each corner of the sheet for recording data from each radar observation.

This sheet is extremely useful in the solution of radar plotting problems; solution is accomplished in the same manner as by the Maneuvering Board. (For relative movement problems other than those involving radar plots, the Maneuvering Board is generally more convenient.) The *Radar Navigation Manual*, DMAHTC Pub. No. 1310 covers the use of this sheet in detail.

The Geographic Plot

1405   A plot showing the successive positions of one or more vessels moving over the earth's surface is called a *geographic* or *navigational plot;* this represents motion with reference to the earth. Such a

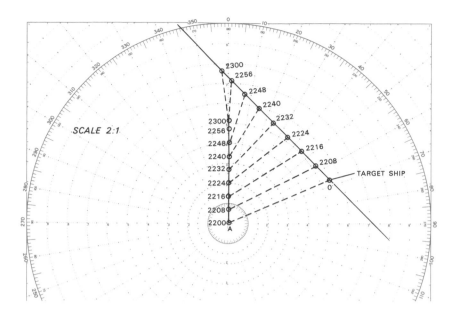

Figure 1405. Geographic plot shown on Maneuvering Board form.

plot is presented in figure 1405; it can best be illustrated by an example. Your ship is on course 000°, speed 10.0 knots. At 2200, your ship is at point *A*, and a radar contact on another ship is obtained, bearing 067°, distance 10.8 miles.

Required: The other vessel's course and speed, and the closest point of approach (CPA).

Solution: Draw your ship's course line from *A*, marking off the distance run for convenient periods of time; for this example, use 8 minutes. Then plot the target vessel's 2200 position, bearing 167° distant 10.8 miles from *A*. Radar ranges and bearings on the target are obtained every 8 minutes, as shown in the table, and plotted from the position of your ship at that time.

Time	Bearing	Range (Miles)
2200	067°	10.8
2208	063°	9.4
2216	058°	8.2
2224	052°	7.2
2232	043°	6.2
2240	032°	5.4
2248	017°	4.9
2256	001°	4.8
2300	352°	4.9

Inspection will show that the bearing changed to the left, and that the range closed steadily until the target crossed ahead at about 2256, the CPA being about 4.8 miles (the actual CPA was about 4.76 miles, on bearing 003°). The plot will show that the target was on course 315°, speed 15.0 knots. Actu-

ally, all this information could have been predicted after the first few points were plotted.

This geographical plot provides the required information; the difficulty is that its construction is extremely time consuming, some 30-odd steps being required. Fortunately, there is a simpler method of obtaining the desired information by means of the relative plot.

The Relative Plot

1406 In the geographical plot, the positions of both ships were plotted, using the earth as a reference; that is, course lines had to be drawn for both ships. But the requirement in that problem was the movement of the target ship, *relative* to your own. Now, consider that your ship remains fixed at the center of the Maneuvering Board, which, of course, is the way it appears on most radar screens, and plot only the position of the target relative to your ship, using the same bearings and ranges as in article 1405.

Relative Movement

This plot of the same situation is shown in figure 1406. The line joining M_1, M_2, M_3 through M_9 represents the movement of the target (other vessel) in one hour, *relative to your vessel*; it is the *relative movement line*, and the direction of relative movement (DRM) is 274°. Measurement shows it is 10.6 miles long; as the target moved this distance in 60 minutes, target speed along this line must be 10.6 knots. This is the target speed with respect to your ship, or *speed of relative movement (SRM)*.

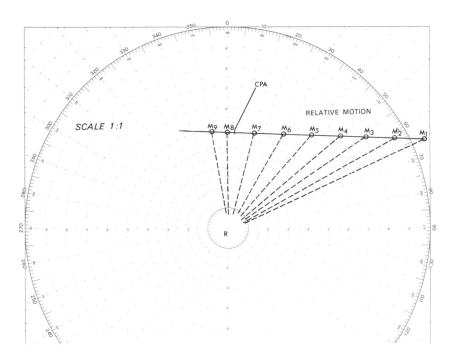

Figure 1406. Relative motion plot.

This plot has provided data necessary to determine with a minimum amount of work, by inspection, the CPA (about 4.8 miles on bearing 003° at 2255), as well as the SRM and the DRM. It is frequently desirable to determine the distance at which another ship will pass ahead or astern of your ship. This is done by drawing a line from your ship's position (R, at center of the Maneuvering Board) in the direction of the course; where this line crosses the direction of relative movement line is the point where the other vessel will be directly ahead or astern.

Problems in relative motion require the use of two diagrams; the relative plot just discussed, and the speed triangle, which will be discussed in the following article. These diagrams are entirely separate, although the solution to the problem consists of developing one diagram with the information gained from the other until the desired result is reached. Inasmuch as this development of the two diagrams consists largely in transferring similar directions from one to the other, it simplifies matters to use a common origin of direction (north) for the two, so that these similar directions become parallel lines, readily transferred with parallel rulers, plastic triangles, or a drafting machine. It may also prove more convenient and will also save space if both diagrams are constructed from a common point of origin, but the diagrams as such remain separate and distinct, and must not be confused. To help prevent confusion, it is wise to use different types of lettering in the two diagrams. The

common practice is to use *lowercase* letters in the *speed diagram* and *capital letters* in the *relative plot*, but the same letter of the alphabet should be used to represent the same unit in both diagrams. In this text, *e* is used for earth, *r* (R) for own ship, and *m* (M) for the target vessel.

The relative plot is a diagram comprising a fixed point of origin and one or more straight lines called relative movement lines. In the problems concerning collision avoidance illustrated in this chapter, own ship is used as the point of origin, as the basis of the problem is the movement and position of other ships *relative to own ship*. In tactical naval maneuvers a guide ship is generally used as the origin, as the position and movement of your ship and others in the formation *relative to the guide* are the primary concerns. The fixed point of origin is always plotted at the center of the Maneuvering Board.

The Speed Triangle

1407 So far, use of the relative plot has determined the relative speed and the direction of relative movement of the target, as well as the CPA. Still to be obtained are the target's true course and actual speed; these may be determined by means of the *speed triangle*, sometimes called the vector triangle.

The speed triangle (figure 1407) consists of a system of properly related straight lines called "vectors." Each vector has a pointed end called the "head," and a plain end called the "foot," both

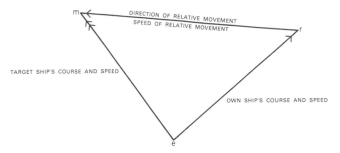

Figure 1407. The speed (or vector) triangle.

appropriately lettered to indicate the units represented. These vectors indicate direction and rate of travel in accordance with the following vector definition applying to relative movement: "A *vector* is a straight line indicating by its orientation the direction, and by its length the ratio, of travel of a moving element, represented by the head of the vector, with respect to another element that is represented by the foot of the vector." It is essential that the distinction between the head and the foot of a vector be kept clearly in mind—the element or unit represented by the head moves relative to the element or unit represented by the foot of the vector. In order to form a vector diagram, the component vectors must represent movement taking place concurrently, they must be referred to a common origin of direction, and they must all be to the same scale. Since the vector diagram is composed entirely of vectors, and since vectors indicate only direction and speed, it follows that the diagram deals exclusively with direction and speed and will therefore yield only what is called course and speed.

The center of the plot is labeled with the lower-case letter *e* for the "earth," since that is the reference for actual movement. The course and actual speed of own ship is represented by the vector *er*, while the course and actual speed of the target ship is represented by the vector *em*. the vector *rm* can be remembered as standing for relative movement; it represents both the direction of relative movement (DRM), and the speed of relative movement (SRM). *All actual course and speed vectors are drawn from e*. The directions of the vectors are also shown by arrows; the vector *rm* is always drawn in the direction from *r* towards *m*.

It is important not to confuse the speed triangle with the relative plot. The *relative plot* represents direction and *distance;* the *speed triangle* represents direction and *speed*.

Having plotted any two sides or vectors of the speed triangle, it is obvious that the third side is

determined and can be measured, thus obtaining the direction and speed that is required.

Use of the Relative Plot and Speed Triangle

1408   The procedure for obtaining the required data from the relative plot and speed triangle is illustrated in the following example.

Example: (Figure 1408) Own ship is on course 020°, speed 10.0 knots; at 2312, radar picks up a contact bearing 337°, distant 16.0 miles.

Required: The time and distance of the CPA, and course and speed of the vessel.

Solution: As the initial range to the target is 16.0 miles, 2:1 appears to be a convenient scale for distance. Accordingly, plot *M*, bearing 337° on the 8 circle; this is the first step in preparing the relative plot. As own ship speed is 10.0 knots, 2:1 also is a convenient scale for the speed triangle; draw *er*, course and speed vector.

Bearings and ranges are obtained on the target as tabulated below; the successive positions of the target are plotted as soon as noted.

Time	Bearing	Range (Miles)
2312	337°	16.0
2324	342°	15.0
2336	348°	14.0
2348	354°	13.3
0000	002.5°	12.6
0012	011°	12.3
0024	019°	12.2

After the third bearing has been obtained, it is evident that the bearing is changing quite rapidly and that *no danger* of collision exists, *as long as both ships maintain their present course and speed*. When the 019° bearing and range are plotted at 0024, sufficient data are on hand to furnish answers of acceptable accuracy. A line is drawn through all the bearings and range points that have been plotted and labeled M_1–M_2. Measure it, remembering to use a 2:1 scale to find the relative distance of 10.8 miles. The target vessel, therefore, has traveled a *relative* distance of 10.8 miles in 72 minutes; by simple arithmetic, determine the *relative speed,* which is 9.0 knots $\left(\dfrac{10.8}{72} \times 60\right)$, and check this answer by putting a straightedge across the nomogram at the bottom of the board as indicated.

Now draw the second vector or side in the speed triangle. From *r*, the head of own ship's course and speed vector, draw a line parallel to M_1–M_2, and to the *right*, as this is the direction of relative movement. This line is $4\frac{1}{2}$ units in length, to correspond

Figure 1408. Speed triangle and relative motion plot.

to the relative speed of 9.0 knots. The head of this line is drawn joining *em* to complete the triangle. This line, or vector, represents the target vessel's course and speed; inspection shows target course 060.5°, speed 13.8 knots.

Data on the CPA is obtained by dropping a perpendicular from *e* to the line of relative movement, M_1–M_2. Measurement of this perpendicular shows that at the CPA, the target will be distant 12.2 miles, and the bearing will be 017.5°. To determine the time of the CPA, first determine its relative distance from M_1 which is 5.2 units or 10.4 miles. As the relative speed is 9.0 knots, it will take 68 minutes to move 10.4 miles. The time of CPA is 0020 (2312 + 68 min.). The nomograph or log scale may also be used to advantage in determining the time of CPA. Often the time of CPA can be estimated closely enough for practical purposes by judging its location with respect to time-labeled points on the relative motion line.

Change of Course Involved

1409 The preceding article used an example in which the target was crossing the bow of your own ship, but the CPA was 12.2 miles. This is a comfortable distance at which to pass another ship, and obviously no change of course or speed was indicated in the interests of safety.

Now consider the relative movement problem, when it appears that at the CPA the target vessel will be uncomfortably close to your ship, and you desire to take corrective action.

Example: (Figure 1409) Your ship is on course 200°, speed 14.0 knots. A pip appears on the radar screen, bearing 212°, range 20.0 miles. Plot the contact on the Maneuvering Board, using a scale of 2:1 and label it M_1, as shown. Observation of the pip shows that it is drawing left slowly, and that the range is closing. Ten minutes after the first contact, the bearing is 211.5°, the range 18.2 miles. Ten minutes later the bearing is 211°, range 16.3 miles.

Enough data are now available to determine the CPA if both ships maintain present course and speed. Draw the relative movement line through the three points marking the target's bearings and ranges, and extend it past *e*, at the center of the Maneuvering Board. Note that this relative move-

Figure 1409. Own ship changes course.

ment line shows that the range at the CPA will be slightly less than 2 miles.

The decision is made to pass the target at a range of 4.0 miles, by altering course immediately to starboard. To obtain the new course, first determine the target's course and speed. To do this, plot er own ship's present course and speed vector. Measure the relative distance traveled by the target between the first and third bearings (20 min); it is 3.6 miles. This gives a relative speed of 10.8 knots. Draw in the relative vector from r and parallel to the direction of relative movement (M_1–M_2). Now draw the target's course and speed vector from e to the end of the relative speed vector m. By inspection, the target is on course 160°, speed 5 knots.

To determine the new course, draw a line from M_2 tangent to the circle centered on e, and representing a distance of 4 miles. This line, M_2–M_3, will be the new direction of relative movement. From m the end of the target's course and speed vector, draw the new relative speed vector parallel to the new line of relative movement, M_2–M_3. The point

where this relative speed vector crosses the speed circle for 14.0 knots, r_1, defines the new course, 206°. Note that the target's range can be determined for the moment it crosses your ship's bow. The range is 12.3 miles.

Collision Course; Own Ship Stops

1410   The following situation is that of a "giveway" vessel that must stop or proceed at a reduced speed to avoid endangering the "stand-on" vessel.

Example: (Figure 1410) Your ship is on course 145°, speed 10.0 knots. A radar contact is picked up, bearing 220°, range 18.0 miles, and a relative plot of the target is commenced, with its present position labeled M_1. The range is closing, and there is no apparent change in the bearing. After 17 minutes, the range has closed to 14.0 miles, but the bearing remains unchanged. At 34 minutes after first contact the range is 10.0 miles; this position is M_3. Immediate corrective action is required—it is not possible for your ship to change course to starboard as this would turn you into the other vessel's

Figure 1410. Collision situation.

path—so you must stop engines, then back them until your ship has lost all headway.

First, determine the target's course and speed. The direction of the relative movement is indicated by the successive plots of the target's position, along the line M_1–M_3, 040° as shown, and the relative distance traveled by the target is indicated by the length of the line M_1–M_2, which is 8.0 miles. The relative speed is 14.0 knots. With this data and own ship's course and speed vector, er, construct the speed triangle, erm. From the target's vector, em, determine the target to be on course 080°, speed 15.0 knots.

Next determine what the bearing and range of the target will be at 39 minutes, 5 minutes after your ship stopped. (For purposes of this problem, assume that your ship stopped short, with no advance while losing way.) Remember that your ship is now dead in the water and the situation has become a geographic plot rather than a relative movement plot. Draw a line in the direction 080°, the target's course, from M_3, its position at 34 minutes. Target speed is 15.0 knots, therefore in 5 minutes it will have moved 1.25 miles along this course

line, and its position will be at M_4, bearing 215°, distant 9.2 miles.

At 39 minutes, you decide to go ahead on the original course, but at a speed of 6.0 knots. You wish to determine how far ahead of you the target will pass. You return to the speed triangle; the target's vector, em, remains the same, as it has not changed course or speed. Your own ship's vector, er, remains unchanged in direction, but is shortened to represent the new speed of 6.0 knots; call this vector er_2. By drawing in r_2m, obtain the new direction of relative motion, as well as the relative speed. Draw a line through M_4 the 39-minute position, parallel to r_2m; this crosses your own ship's course line at a distance of 3.2 miles, which will be the range when the target crosses ahead of you.

In actual practice the time and distance for coming to a stop, and for accelerating to 6.0 knots, must be determined and worked into the solution.

Collision Situation; Target Alters Course

1411   In the following situation, your vessel is the "stand-on" vessel, and the other, being the "give-way" vessel, is the one to alter course or

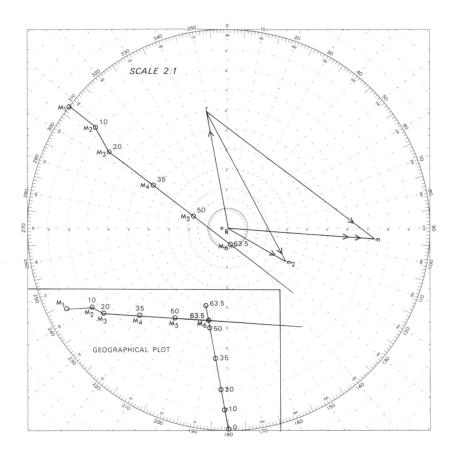

Figure 1411. Target ship changes course.

speed. This problem, using a Maneuvering Board, requires only a relative plot. By now, the basic problems involved in solving relative movement problems should be coming clearer. A geographic plot is also shown in the lower left corner of figure 1411 to assist in comprehension; it is not necessary to the solution of the problem at hand, nor is it normally drawn.

Example: (Figure 1411) Your ship is on course 350°, speed 12.0 knots. At 00 minutes a pip is seen on the radar screen, bearing 308°, range 20.0 miles. At 10 minutes, the range has closed to 16.5 miles; the bearing remains the same, and a plot is commenced. Subsequent plots show the bearing falling off to the left, and at 20 minutes, the target bears 303°, range 14.0 miles, indicating a new relative movement line. A partial list of bearings and ranges appears below. (In actual practice, many additional bearings would have been obtained. Only the more important ones are included here.)

Required:
1. Target's course and speed from time 00 to 10.
2. What maneuver the target made at time 10.
3. What the target did at time 20.
4. The CPA.
5. The time of the CPA.

Time	Bearing	Range (Miles)
00 (M_1)	308°	20.0
10 (M_2)	308°	16.5
20 (M_3)	303°	14.0
35 (M_4)	300°	8.8
50 (M_5)	290°	3.7
63.5 (M_6)	170°	1.7

Solution: (Figure 1411)
1. Plot the ranges and bearings M_1 to M_6 establishing the relative motion line. Construct the speed triangle *erm*. From your ship's vector, *er*, lay off *rm* parallel to M_1–M_2, and for a relative speed of 21.0 knots (M_1–M_2 equals 3.5 miles; this distance was covered in 10 minutes). The vector *em* gives the target's course, 094°, and speed, 14.5 knots.

2. Draw a new relative speed vector from *r*. This vector, rm_2, is parallel to M_2–M_3, and for a relative speed of 16.8 knots. The vector em_2 shows that the target came right to course 120°, and slowed to 6.4 knots.

3. Use the relative movement line M_3–M_5, to obtain a new vector *rm*. This falls on the first vector *rm*, and is of the same length; the target

therefore returned to her original course, 094°, and speed, 14.5 knots, at time 20 minutes.

4. Drop a perpendicular from e to the line M_3–M_5 extended, and find that the range at the CPA will be 1.2 miles, on bearing 217.5°.

5. Measure the relative distance from M_3 to the CPA. It is 14.0 miles; 14.0 miles at the relative speed of 21.0 knots will require 40 minutes, so the CPA will be reached at 60 minutes (40 + 20).

It should be pointed out again that considerably more bearings and ranges must be obtained than those tabulated in this example. There would have been considerable doubt as to the direction of the short leg, M_2–M_3, if only these two bearings had been obtained.

Relative Movement; Both Ships Changing Course

1412 A more complicated situation exists if *both* vessels change course, but it remains susceptible to a graphic solution using the Maneuvering Board. This example highlights the need to keep a *constant* check on a radar contact when danger of

collision exists, and for plotting at frequent intervals.

Example: (Figure 1412) Your ship is steaming on course 000°, speed 10.0 knots. You obtain a radar contact bearing 029°, range 20.0 miles, start your stopwatch, and plot the target's relative position, M_1, as shown. At time 10 minutes the bearing has not changed, but the range has closed to 16.7 miles (M_2). You must obtain the target's course and speed. The relative speed is 19.8 knots (3.3 miles in 10 minutes) and the direction of relative movement is 209°. From the speed triangle, you determine that the target is on course 233°, speed 12.0 knots. The plot of the target's relative position is continued. At time 20 minutes, the bearing remains unchanged at 029°, but the range has closed at 13.4 miles (M_3). An immediate 20° course change to the right is ordered, and your ship steadies on course 020°.

This change of course should change the direction of the line of relative movement, as the latter is generated by the movement of one ship with relation to another, and any change in course or speed

Figure 1412. Own ship and target ship both change course.

by either ship will change the relative movement line. You plot er_1m vectors.

Obviously, your ship's change of course to the right should cause the bearing to change to the left. This can be checked from the plot r_1m, which will now be the direction of relative movement; this direction, laid down from M_3, passes to the left of e. The CPA, incidentally, should be slightly more than 2 miles.

With your ship on her new course, 020°, you continue to watch the radar contact. Surprisingly, the range steadily decreases, but the bearing remains unchanged. This can be due only to the fact that the target has also changed course or speed. You believe that it is probably maintaining a speed of 12.0 knots, and that a course change is causing the bearing to remain constant. The target's new course must be determined.

Construct a new speed triangle, starting with the vector of your ship's new course, and speed of 10.0 knots; this is er_1. The relative speed line (r_1m_1) is then drawn in parallel to the direction of the relative movement, which has not changed. The terminus of the line, m, is determined by where the line

cuts the 12-knot speed circle, at 217°. This shows the target's new course to be 217°, *and both ships are again on a collision course.*

The lower right corner of figure 1412 shows a geographic plot for greater clarity of the situation as it is developing for both vessels.

At this time you must take drastic evasive action, as the range is closing at about 21.7 knots. At time 30 minutes, the bearing is still 029°, but the range has decreased to 9.8 miles. If your ship maintains speed of 10.0 knots, but comes right to 080°, can you determine the range and bearing at the CPA, assuming that the target makes no further changes in course or speed? The plotting necessary to this solution is not included in figure 1412, which is already adequately complete. The answer is: Range 4.4 miles; bearing 327°.

Relative Movement; Own Ship Being Overtaken

1413 A quite different situation, but one which is frequently encountered at sea, is when your ship is being overtaken by another vessel.

Example: (Figure 1413) You are at sea, on course 320°, speed 10.0 knots. At 00 minutes a radar con-

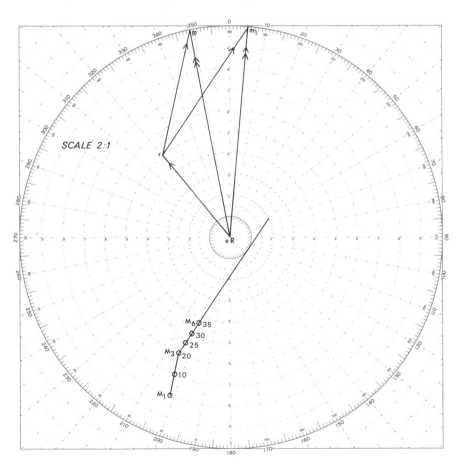

Figure 1413. Own ship is being overtaken.

tact is made, bearing 201°, range 16.0 miles. You continue to track and plot the target. A partial list of bearings and ranges is tabulated as follows:

Time (Min.)	Bearing	Range (Miles)
00	201°	16.0
10	202°	14.0
20 (M_3)	204°	12.0
25	203°	10.9
30	202°	9.7
35	200°	8.5

At time 20 minutes you decide to determine the target's course and speed based on the data so far obtained. The relative distance, M_1–M_3, is 4.1 miles, and this distance was traversed in 20 minutes: the relative speed is 12.3 knots, and the direction of relative movement is 012°. With these data draw the rm vector of the triangle: the target's vector, em, shows that it is on course 349°, speed 20.0 knots.

However, the bearings obtained after that are now changing in the opposite direction. As your ship has maintained course and speed, the target must have changed course and speed or both. With the data obtained after time 20 minutes, you must determine the target's new course and speed. The relative speed is 14.8 knots. By means of parallel rulers, the direction of relative movement is determined to be 033°. With these data, plot a new relative speed vector, rm_1, and determine that the target is now on course 005°, speed remaining at 20 knots. All that remains is to determine the range, the bearing, and the time of the CPA. Extend the M_3–M_6 line; it is tangent to the 2.0 miles circle, on bearing 123°. The target will reach the CPA at time 68 minutes (M_3 − CPA = 11.8 miles). The relative speed is 14.6 knots; 11.8 miles at 14.6 knots requires 48 minutes; 48 + 20 minutes (M_3) = 68 minutes.

Plotting Multiple Targets

1414 Particularly in pilot waters, several targets may be on the radar screen at one time. The following example illustrates the plot for two targets that are on the screen at the same time; the Maneuvering Board is well suited to the graphic solution of such a situation.

Example: (Figure 1414) Your ship is on course 000°, speed 8.0 knots. At time 00 there is a radar contact bearing 280.5°, range 10.0 miles. At time 43 there is another contact, bearing 070°, range 11 miles. Bearings and ranges are tabulated below:

Figure 1414. Multiple targets.

TARGET M		
Time (Min.)	Bearing	Range (Miles)
00	280.5°	10.0
30	286°	7.7
45	291°	6.5
61	300°	5.0
87	313°	4.0
105	336°	3.2

TARGET M'		
Time (Min.)	Bearing	Range (Miles)
43	070°	11.0
62	072°	8.1
76	074°	6.3
94	080°	3.8
103	090°	2.5

As the plot develops, it becomes obvious from the two lines of relative movement M_1–M_6, M'_1–M'_5, that both ships are going to pass clear of you. The speed triangles are interesting, as they are both based on your ship's vector. The course and speed of target M, from its triangle, are 030° and 10.0 knots. (The relative distance M_1–M_6 is 8.6 miles, time is 105 minutes; relative speed is 5 knots.)

Target M' is on course 298°, speed 9 knots. (The relative distance M'_1–M'_5 is 8.5 miles, the time is 60 minutes; the relative speed is 8.5 knots.)

You must determine the time each vessel will be at CPA, and the range at that time.

Interception of Another Vessel

1415 The following example is that of a ship ordered to intercept another vessel whose course and speed are known, as well as her relative position at the start of the problem.

This is a common problem for Navy and Coast Guard vessels; it arises at times for other ships, as when called on to lend assistance. It is not based on radar data. The solution, on a Maneuvering Board, illustrates the use of different scales for speed and distance.

Example: Your ship at sea receives a message from ship A that she requires assistance. She gives her position, and states that she will remain on course 090°, speed 6.0 knots. The plot shows her to bear 030° from your position, distant 200 miles. Your ship can maintain 20 knots.

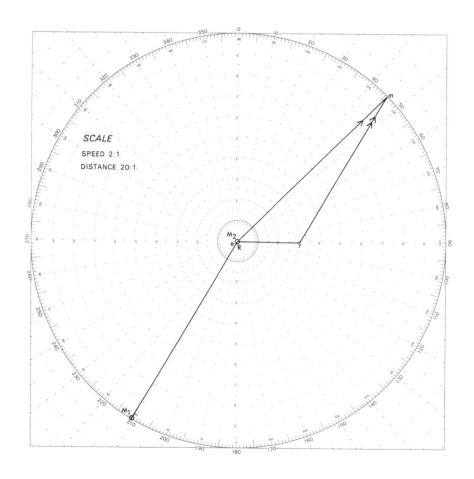

Figure 1415. Rendezvous problem.

Required: (Figure 1415) (1) The course to reach *A* in minimum time; (2) How long will it take to rendezvous?

This is merely a new application of the other problems in this chapter. The relative plot differs in that ship *A* is at the center; your vessel will be at M_1 initially and your final position, M_2, is also at the center. In the speed triangle, *A*'s course and speed vector will establish the base with which to determine your ship's course, at 20.0 knots.

Solution: Plot the initial position, M_1, bearing 210°, and distant 200 miles from *e* using a scale of 20:1. Plot *A*'s course and the speed vector, 090°, 6.0 knots, using a scale of 2:1. The direction of relative motion is from M_1 towards $M_2(e)$, this is 030°. Plot the relative speed vector parallel to M_1–M_2 from *r* to where it intersects the relative speed circle at 20.0 knots; this intersection establishes the point *m*.

Answer: (1) The vector *em* establishes the course, 045°, to steer at 20.0 knots.

Your course is now established; all that remains is to determine how long it will take to come alongside *A*. The relative distance is 200 miles, the relative speed, *rm*, is found to be 16.3 knots.

(2) The time required will therefore be 12.3 hours, to the nearest tenth.

Other information can be obtained for this plot. For example, how many miles must your ship steam to reach *A*? Answer: 246—12.3 hours at 20.0 knots. Again, when should you pick up *A* on radar, at a range of 20.0 miles? *A*'s echo should appear in slightly over 11 hours (180 miles at 16.3 knots).

Changing Position in a Formation

1416 A common problem on board naval vessels is that of changing station within a formation.

Example: (Figure 1416) Your ship is in formation on course 020°, speed 12 knots, 9 miles ahead of the guide. The formation commander orders your ship to take station on the port beam of the guide, at a distance of 7 miles. The following information will be necessary before you can decide the most expedient way to make the maneuver:

1. Direction or relative movement of the guide with respect to your ship;
2. Own ship course at 18 knots;
3. Own ship course at 12 knots;
4. Own ship speed if you steer 295°;
5. Own ship speed if you steer 350°.

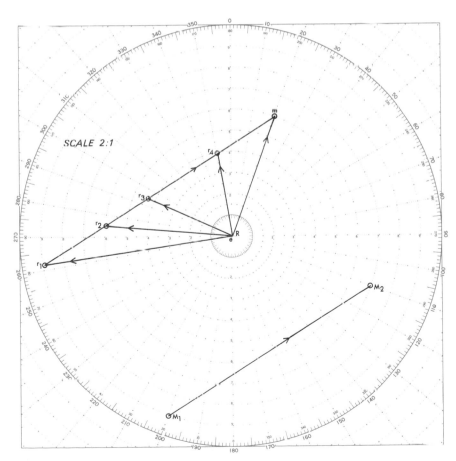

Figure 1416. Changing station maneuver.

Solution:

1. Draw vector *em* to represent the true course, 020°, and speed 12 knots, of the guide. Locate M_1 and M_2 as follows. Convert your relative bearing from the guide to true bearing as described above, which is 020°. Since own ship is the reference, M_1 bears the reciprocal of 020°, or 200° from the center. Hence, M_1 is located on the 9 circle in the direction 200° from the center. Similarly, M_2 is located on the 7 circle in the direction 110° from the center. The direction of relative movement (DRM) can now be determined.

2. Draw vector r_1m parallel to M_1M_2. Since the direction of relative movement is from *r* to *m*, and *r* is to be found, the reciprocal of *rm* is drawn from *m* until it intersects the 18-knot circle. Thus, *rm* is in the required direction M_1M_2.

3. Complete the speed triangle by drawing vector er_1 from the center of the diagram to r_1.

4. Draw vector er_2 from the center to the intersection of the r_1m vector with the 12-knot circle.

5. Draw vector er_3 in the direction 295°.

6. Draw vector er_4 in the direction 350°.

Answer: It can be seen that the DRM is 058°, the course at 18 knots is 262°, the course at 12 knots is 276°, the speed when steering 295° would be 8.8 knots, and the speed for course 350° would be 7.9 knots. From this information you would be able to pick the course and speed to put your ship on the new station in the most efficient manner.

Determining True Wind

1417 The Maneuvering Board lends itself well to determining the speed (force) and direction of the true wind by means of the speed triangle.

Apparent wind is the force and the relative direction from which the wind blows, as measured aboard a moving vessel. It can also be expressed as a true direction.

In this triangle, the vector *er* represents the course and speed of the ship, the vector *rw* the direction and speed of the relative or apparent wind, and the vector *ew* is the direction and speed of the true wind. The vector *er* is plotted first, the vector *rw* is then plotted from *r* in the direction the apparent wind is blowing, the length of *rw* representing the speed of the apparent wind. The third vector *ew* represents the direction and speed of the true wind. *True wind* is the force and the true direction from

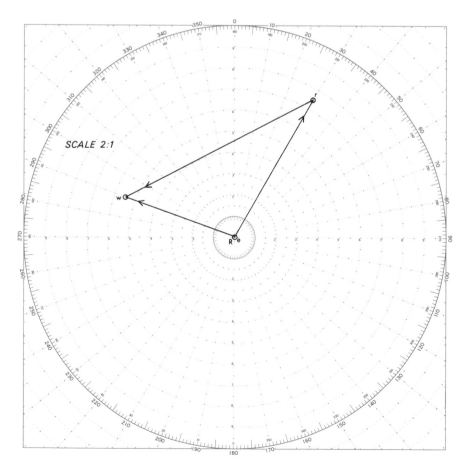

SCALE 2:1

Figure 1417. Wind triangle.

which the wind blows, as measured at a fixed point on the earth.

Example: (Figure 1417) Assume the ship is underway, on course 030°, speed 15 knots, and that true direction of the apparent wind is from 062° at 20 knots.

Required: Direction and speed of the true wind.

Solution: Draw the speed triangle as shown, using a scale of 2:1. The vector *er* represents your course and speed. From *r*, plot the relative speed vector *rw* in the direction of 242° (the apparent wind direction, 062° plus 180°), and to a length representing 20 knots; the terminus of this vector is labeled *w*; join *e* and *w*; this vector *ew* represents the true wind direction, from 109.5°, and its speed, 10.8 knots.

Allowing for Known Current

1418 It is easy to determine the course to steer at a given speed, and the speed over the bottom, when the set and drift of a current are known. Solution is by the speed triangle method.

In this example, *er* is the vector representing the set and drift of the current; it is the vector on which

the speed triangle is constructed. The vector *em* represents the intended track (TR) and speed of advance (SOA) to make good, and *rm* represents the course to steer and the speed through the water, to reach a given point at a desired time.

Example 1: (Figure 1418) You have an intended track of 285° at a speed of 10.0 knots. The current is setting 240°, drift 2.0 knots.

Required: Course and speed to make in order to stay on the track line.

Solution: First, draw the current vector *er* as shown in figure 1418 (solid lines). Next, draw in vector *em* for the intended track line in the direction 285°.

Answer: The vector *rm* represents the course to steer, 294.5°, and the speed to make, 8.6 knots, to travel along a track in the direction 285°, making 10.0 knots over the ground.

A similar problem arises when you want to travel through a known current along a given track line at a given speed, and you must determine the course to steer and the speed made good over the ground.

Example 2: (Figure 1418) A current sets 070°, drift 4.0 knots. You have an intended track of 180°, and have set a speed of 12.0 knots.

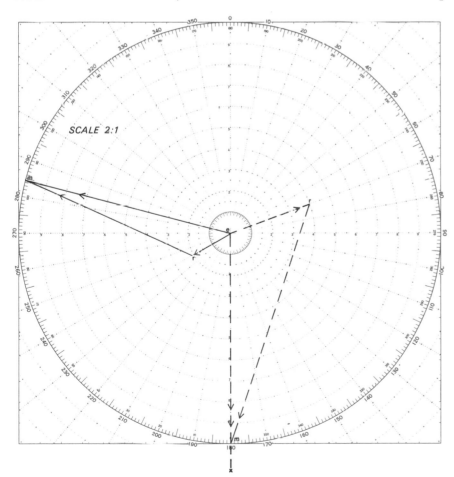

Figure 1418. Current vector problem.

Required: Course to steer to stay on the track line, and the speed made good over the bottom.

Solution: (Figure 1418, broken lines) Plot the current vector, *er,* in the direction 070°, and for a speed of 4.0 knots. Next, from *e,* plot a vector *ex* in the direction 180°, but of indefinite length. Now from *r* swing an arc of a radius equal to 12.0 knots. The point at which this arc cuts *ex* is labeled *m;* draw in *rm,* the vector representing the course you must steer. It is in the direction 198°; the length *em* indicates that you will need to make good 10.0 knots over the ground.

Importance of Relative Motion Plots

1419 Relative motion is of paramount importance to a navigator when his vessel is in the vicinity of others. A careful and continuous plot of bearings and distances, usually by radar, to the "target" ship or ships is necessary to determine the closest point of approach, and hence any danger of collision.

Relative-motion solutions are used for problems of movement within ship formations, for determining true wind, and for applying current vectors.

Chapter 15   The Piloting Team

Introduction

1501 The preceding chapters were concerned with piloting, using various data such as bearings, distances, and depths without regard to the methods used to obtain this data.

This chapter is concerned with the systematic and organized procedures and techniques used by a group of several persons to obtain the data and provide the navigator with the proper information at the proper time. This group, known as the *piloting team*, is stationed whenever the vessel gets underway or enters into pilot waters.

On the following pages, we will consider how this team is organized to furnish this information, and we will also consider some elements of doctrine and methods that have proven to be of assistance in solving this problem. Not all of the combinations of data available to the navigator are used in the example herein; only a representative sampling is shown for purposes of illustration. It should be emphasized at the outset that the methods outlined here are only *one* way to accomplish the result desired—namely, a smooth and timely flow of essential information to the navigator. Any method will do, provided it achieves this desired result.

Aboard most U.S. Navy vessels, the Combat Information Center (CIC) will also supply bearings and ranges, obtained by radar, to the bridge. The DRT in the CIC will also be in operation, and will be updated frequently. The navigator must always bear in mind, however, that he is charged with the safe navigation of the ship, and that the information passed on from CIC is for back-up purposes only.

Although this chapter is written largely in terms of the activities aboard a U.S. naval vessel, the same broad principles will apply both to merchant ships and small craft. It is recognized, however, that such vessels will be operating with far fewer personnel and with less formalized procedures, but the same basic information is required for safe pilotage, even if it can only be obtained in lesser detail.

Sources of Information for Naval Vessels

1502 The navigator is charged with using all available sources to fix the ship's position. The types of information needed, and the various places in a typical ship where it may be acquired, are listed in the following paragraphs.

Bearings of objects can be obtained by any of the following means in most ships of the navy:

> *Visually*, by means of a gyrocompass repeater, magnetic compass, pelorus, or self-synchronous alidade, or through use of one of several gun and missile fire-control systems.
>
> *By radar*, using the surface-search radar equipment (either in CIC or the bridge PPI), or using a fire-control radar.
>
> *By radio*, using radio direction finding equipment and various transmitters on shore or on other vessels.
>
> *By sonar*, using the echo-ranging equipment.

Ranges (distances) of objects can be obtained in most ships of the navy by the following means:

> *Optically*, using an optical rangefinder found in many gun directors.
>
> *Visually*, by use of a stadimeter or sextant.
>
> *By radar*, using the surface-search radar equipment (either in CIC or the bridge PPI), or using fire-control radar.
>
> *By sonar*, using the echo-ranging equipment.

Depths of water can usually be obtained for most ships of the navy by the following methods:

Echo-sounder readings
Lead-line soundings.

Sources of Information for Merchant Vessels

Sources for merchant ships are far fewer than for naval vessels. Sources of visual bearings include the gyrocompass or magnetic compass in combination with a bearing circle, alidade, or pelorus. Radar bearings can be taken from the wheelhouse display of either of the radars, also from the collision-avoidance system, if fitted. Radio bearings can be taken by RDF equipment, but this procedure is now infrequently used.

Distances to objects can be measured by vertical sextant angles, or through the use of the radars or the collision-avoidance system.

Depths can be determined by a depth sounder or depth recorder. A hand lead line is generally restricted to use around a vessel that is either berthed or aground.

Required Records

1503 Various U.S. Navy instructions require that a permanent record be maintained of all observations and computations made for the purpose of navigating the ship. This means that any team established by the navigator to obtain navigational data must be so organized that the necessary information is recorded without hampering its flow to the navigator.

Bearing Book

Since in piloting the navigator normally relies on visual bearings of landmarks and other aids to navigation to fix his position, the primary record that must be maintained is of the bearings used to navigate the ship. To be complete, the time of the bearings and the identification must also be included. To accomplish this, a *bearing book* is maintained in each ship of the navy; a standard form (OpNav Form 3530/2) is provided for this purpose. A sample page of a bearing book is shown in figure 1503. Note that there is a place for the date, the port the ship is entering or leaving, and the gyro error. If distances are measured, they are recorded under the bearing (or in lieu of it) in the column for the object to which they relate. In figure 1503, an entry of this nature is seen for 0621 under Thimble Shoals.

When bearings on one object are discontinued, the column previously used may be relabeled if it is desired to use it for an object that is not already listed. Using this manner of relabeling, any number and sequence of landmarks or aids employed for piloting can be recorded; for greater clarity, a horizontal line should be drawn between the last of the bearings on the previous object and the name of the new object. The right-hand column should also be carefully noted; it provides a record of the depths measured by echo-sounder (under the keel, unless otherwise noted) at the times indicated.

On non-naval vessels and small craft, a book of any convenient size may be used as a bearing book by simply ruling off the columns desired, and printing the appropriate information at the top of the page. The left-hand column is for the *time* of each observation; normally there are at least four columns for *bearings* (and distances), and the right-hand column is for depth information, depth under the keel unless stated otherwise.

On most naval ships, it is required that the man keeping the bearing book sign his name when the piloting is completed, to indicate that the record is a true one. Official instructions prohibit any erasures; if data must be corrected, a line is drawn through the mistake and the correct information entered in such a manner that both entries are legible.

Sounding Book

All depth readings may not be sent to the navigator, for reasons that will be discussed later. However, all readings must be recorded, and a special *sounding book* is established for this purpose. Note that the right-hand column of the bearing book normally indicates the depth under the keel. This reading may or may not be the depth indicated on the echo-sounder, depending upon the location of the transducer with respect to the keel; hence a correction factor may need to be applied. A record of this correction should be made on the inside front cover of the sounding book. A recommended procedure that can be considered the least subject to error is to have the echo-sounder operator record and report depth measurements as read; the bearing book recorder and navigator will then apply the correction factor, if any. (If desired, the draft of the ship can then be added to obtain the actual depth of the water for comparison with the charted depth, corrected for height of tide, corresponding to the estimate of the vessel's position.)

Records on Merchant Vessels

Merchant vessels are required by federal regulations to maintain a "smooth log" with certain

RECORD GYRO BEARINGS

Entering Norfolk, Va.
PLACE

GYRO ERROR   *1° W*

DATE TIME	Cape Henry Lt.	Cape Charles Lt.	Tunnel South Lt.	Thimble Shoal Lt.	East Tank Ocean View	DEPTH
9 August 0557	219.5	020.0	278.0			60
0600	199.0	024.0	278.5			56
0603	183.5	028.0	279.0			41
0606	152.0	030.5	280.0			26
0609	137.5	034.0	281.0			23
0612	131.0	037.5	274.0			21
0615	126.5	041.0	275.5			22
0618	124.0	044.0	267.0			21
0621	121.5	047.0	239.0	292.0 *14,300*		23
0624	120.0		158.5	292.5	257.0	22

Figure 1503. A U.S. Navy Bearing Book.

items of information; this is kept in the chartroom while the vessel is at sea. In normal circumstances, entries to this record will be made at the end of a watch, using data from a "rough log" entered as information is gained and events happen, and a "bell book" of engine orders. In addition to other required entries, the smooth log book is used in piloting waters to record officially such items as courses and speeds, with times of change of either; major aids to navigation encountered, with time, bearing, and range; the time of crossing of major fathom curves, such as the 100- or 50-fathom curve; the time that the ship's master assumes the conn; the names and times of arrival and departure of pilot and/or docking master; the position, time, and names of tugboats alongside and away; the time and details of the docking or undocking process; the time that the anchor is let go or weighed, the number of chain shots in the water, and the bearings on fixed objects; and compliance with federal regulations (33 CFR 164.25) regarding the testing of gear prior to arrival or departure. The format of the bell book varies—in some instances, only the times and engine orders are entered; in other instances, more space is available for the entry of such additional data as the aids to navigation encountered (if not entered in a rough log). Together with the course recorder and chart of the area, the bell book can be used, and often is, by an investigative board to re-create accurately the vessel's track and positions while being piloted.

Each mariner should maintain a notebook or workbook containing all navigation work done while on board ship. Although such a record is required by federal regulations (46 CFR 4.05-15), the individual will likely find that this diary of navigation provides a practical record-keeping format for personal use as well.

Selection of Information

1504   Article 1502 lists the considerable number of sources of information available to a naval navigator in piloting. It is essential that he organize his piloting team so that the aids to navigation are known in advance, and that he receives only the information that he requires at any particular time. Too much information flowing in can be nearly as undesirable as too little.

For normal piloting in good visibility, the navigator can accurately fix the position of the ship by using three bearings or other LOPs. As visual bearings are the most accurate, and normally the most easily obtained, they are the first choice. Should three objects not be visually available, the use of multiple *radar ranges* (article 1707) is the next most accurate method of positioning the ship.

When the ship is in pilot waters, continuous use of the echo sounder should be required. Depths obtained by the hand lead are useful in doubtful situations when the ship is proceeding slowly enough to permit accurate casts and readings. Both may then be used in comparison with charted depth data, corrected for height of tide, to ensure the greatest degree of safety. Merchant ships make little use of a hand lead line, except perhaps to take soundings around a vessel as she is loaded down to her safe loading lines, or when she is aground.

From this brief summary of the effectiveness and accuracy of different types of fixes, it has been determined that the piloting team should be so organized as to be able to obtain the following sources of piloting information:

Visual bearings.
Radar information (ranges and bearings) from CIC and the bridge PPI.
Depth information from the echo sounder and by a hand lead line.

Stationing of Personnel

1505 Since the chains (see figure 1509) will be manned in pilot waters for the taking of soundings by means of a hand lead line (if the speed of the ship is slow enough), and the echo sounder will also be manned, two members of the team are thus stationed. As the typical ship has at least two peloruses or alidades, a man is assigned to each to obtain visual bearings. The navigator will request the operations officer to station his radar navigation team in CIC, which will include two additional surface plotters and an additional officer to supervise radar navigation, augmenting the normal watch personnel.

Means must also be provided to transmit piloting information to the bridge on designated circuits. The echo-sounder operator can maintain the *sounding book* as well as operate the equipment, but an additional man is required to maintain the *bearing book.* Using these personnel, the basic team consists of the following:

The navigator, with possibly an assistant.
A primary navigation plotter.
One leadsman in the chains, plus a talker to report his readings.
One echo-sounder operator.
Two or more bearing takers, each assigned to a pelorus.
One bearing recorder to maintain the bearing book.
One or more men to maintain communication with and receive radar information from CIC.

Should information be required from gun directors, special provision for personnel to provide this must be made with the weapons officer. Sonar information is usually available from persons in CIC.

Communications

1506 Communications must be established between the various members of the team and the navigator. This is done in such a manner that the navigator has positive control of the communications used to reach any member of the team at any time. It is therefore customary for the piloting team to be connected by means of sound-powered telephones, with the bearing recorder acting as the navigator's talker on the circuit. In this way, the bearing recorder can obtain all information sent to the navigator and enter it in the bearing book as it is received. He can also act as a communication link with CIC, requesting and recording all radar data considered pertinent by the navigator. In practice, the talker for the leadsman is not normally on the same telephone circuit as the other members of the team, but sends his soundings over the anchoring and maneuvering circuit to the bridge. This information is usually desired by the captain and the officer of the deck as well as by the navigator. The lead-line soundings are repeated by the telephone talker on the bridge so that all can hear them, and the navigator notes the information as it is heard.

Thus, a piloting telephone circuit has been established with the following stations:

The *bearing recorder* (who is the navigator's talker and controls the circuit).
A *bearing taker* at each pelorus.
The *echo-sounder operator.*
A *talker* in CIC.

The specific circuit used for this purpose will vary from ship to ship, but most ships have provision for such communications. In addition to sound-powered communications, many ships have and use voice tubes connecting these stations. Many navigators have found it helpful to use a call bell or buzzer system to indicate to the bearing takers the times to take a round of bearings. This system limits talking on the circuit, thereby reducing the noise level on the bridge, which is always desirable.

In addition, a separate circuit from CIC to bridge is usually established to provide a clear channel for the transmission of evaluated radar information.

Duties and Procedures

1507 For each station it is desirable to establish specific duties and reporting procedures to assist the navigator in the selection of data that he will receive while piloting the ship.

Bearing Recorder

The bearing recorder is charged with four main duties:

Controlling the communication circuit and acting as the navigator's talker on that circuit.

Relaying all information received to the navigator.

Recording all bearings, ranges, and depths as he receives them.

At the direction of the navigator, giving *marks* to the bearing takers and CIC to indicate when to take bearings or ranges. In ships so equipped, the *"mark"* can be indicated by sounding a bell or buzzer, which is installed on the bridge for that purpose. If this latter system is used, the officer doing the plotting frequently gives his own marks.

Bearing Takers

The primary duty of each bearing taker is to take bearings on objects at times specified by the navigator, and to report them over the phone. In addition, a bearing taker should be familiar with the landmarks and aids to navigation expected to be used, and should report when they are in sight. He will also assist the navigator in identifying each landmark or aid as it is sighted. In addition, each bearing taker will assist the navigator by reporting other information, such as the set and estimated drift of current past buoys, other vessels that may lie along the intended track, when buoys and landmarks pass abeam, etc.

In most ships only two gyro repeaters are available, and since the navigator usually desires three LOPs to plot his fix, one bearing taker must take bearings on two objects. If it can be determined beforehand that a majority of the aids to navigation to be used will lie either to port or to starboard for the major part of the time traveling in pilot waters, the most experienced bearing taker should be assigned to the repeater on that side. In taking bearings of two objects from the same repeater, the two bearings should be taken as nearly simultaneously as possible. The bearing taker is trained to take the fastest-changing bearing first. By this is meant taking the bearing of an object closest to the beam first, as it will be changing bearing most rapidly, and then taking the bearing of the object more nearly ahead or astern. In this manner the effects of the advance of the ship in the time between the two bearings will be minimized. (In small craft and some merchant ships where fewer persons are available to take bearings, it is more likely that the person taking the bearings will note the time of taking the last bearing of a series, and this will be the time of the fix. In such cases, the fastest-changing bearing is taken last, rather than first as above.)

Echo-sounder Operator

The echo-sounding equipment is sometimes not on the bridge where the navigator can personally oversee the work of the operator. For this reason, the man assigned as echo-sounder operator should be thoroughly trained and should realize the importance of his duties. As depths are normally used by the navigator only as a safety factor, readings do not actually have to be sent continuously to the bridge. Most ships establish a procedure directing the operator to observe soundings continuously, to record the soundings every minute, and to send soundings to the bridge at regular specified intervals (usually timed to each round of bearings or ranges), and whenever called for or when a limiting depth is encountered. This depth is a safety factor determined by each navigator for his ship depending primarily upon the draft of the vessel. For instance, in a destroyer with a draft of 22 feet, the navigator may direct the echo-sounder operator to report to the bridge immediately any reading less than 40 feet, while the doctrine on a larger vessel may prescribe a report at 60 feet (below the transducer). In addition, most navigators have a standing order to report immediately any rapid shoaling of the water. These limiting factors must occasionally be changed, depending on the depth of water in which the ship expects to steam, because a minimum reading doctrine of 6 or 7 fathoms would have little practical significance if the destroyer were proceeding inside the 5-fathom curve.

CIC Talker

The navigator does not provide the talker in CIC in most ships, as he is assigned from the CIC personnel. This talker usually sends up to the bridge only the information requested, in accordance with procedures established by the navigator and approved by the commanding officer.

Assistant Navigator

Whenever possible, it is the practice in many ships to require the assistant navigator to assist in plotting under the supervision of the navigator. This procedure frees the navigator for overall piloting supervision, giving him the opportunity personally to check the identification of new landmarks and aids to navigation as they are sighted, and to instruct the team regarding which objects to plot and when. The task of a navigator in pilot waters is an exacting one, and is a full-time duty, even with the assistance of a well-trained piloting team.

Frequency of Fixes

1508 No fixed policy on the frequency of taking bearings and obtaining fixes by a navigator can be stated here. In practice, the frequency will vary with the situation, the navigator, and the wishes of the captain. If the ship is steaming comparatively slowly in coastal waters with no immediate dangers to navigation in the vicinity, a fix every 15 minutes could be sufficient. But if the ship is coming to anchor and exact accuracy is required, fixes should probably be taken every 30 seconds. However, a good rule for normal piloting in restricted waters, and at normal speeds, is to obtain a fix every three minutes. This will allow the plotter (or navigator) sufficient time to plot the fix, extend the DR track ahead for at least six minutes, compute the current effects, and keep the captain advised on how the ship is proceeding along the track and the distance to the next turn. In any event, the interval should be such that a minimum of two additional fixes will be taken between the last fix and any shoal water ahead.

An international conference on this subject resulted in a consensus that is reproduced as the table below for general information and guidance.

The Team in Operation

1509 A diagramatic sketch of the bridge and related navigational positions on a typical destroyer-type ship is shown in figure 1509 (not to scale). Personnel who wear sound-powered telephone headsets are shown, as are the telephone circuits. It should be noted in this diagram that the bearing recorder is located next to the navigator at the chart table. Frequently no provision has been made for the navigator to be on the open bridge, and consequently he must operate from inside the pilothouse. This is acceptable if there is sufficient visibility, but it is preferable to have his chart desk on the open bridge. The chart table should have a clock mounted over it, or readily visible from it, as a record of time is important in piloting.

Preparations

A destroyer is entering Chesapeake Bay en route to Norfolk, and is about to pass into *Inland Waters*. The piloting team has been stationed. The navigator has a man on both the port and starboard gyro repeaters, the echo sounder is manned, a talker is in CIC, and the bearing recorder is at his station. Communications as shown in figure 1509 have been established. It is a clear morning; Cape Charles Light, Cape Henry Light, and Thimble Shoal Tunnel South Light are in sight. The bearing book has been set up as shown in figure 1503, with columns headed by the names of the aids to navigation expected to be used. The navigator directs the bearing recorder to sound the buzzer (or to give a "mark" over the telephone circuit) every third minute, being careful to note exactly when the second hand of the clock reaches the whole minute. The navigator also directs the bearing recorder to tell the port bearing taker to report Cape Henry Light and the Tunnel South Light, and the starboard bearing taker to report Cape Charles Light.

Plotting Procedures

When he is ready to plot, the navigator directs the bearing recorder to obtain a round of bearings. At about 10 seconds before the minute, the bearing recorder informs the personnel on the circuit to "*stand by.*" When the second hand reaches 60, he sounds the buzzer (or says "*mark*" over the circuit). The man on the port repeater, who at this time has two bearings to take, will report first. The first bearing (in the extract shown in figure 1503), which he took on the buzzer or mark, will be on the object nearest the beam, Cape Henry Light. He reports, "Cape Henry bearing 219.5 degrees." The starboard bearing taker has taken a reading on Cape Charles Light when the buzzer/mark was heard, but he does not report until the port bearing taker has read off his first reading. The man on the star-

Area	Distance From Nearest Danger	General Order of Depth of Water	Order of Accuracy	Fix Frequency
Pilot waters	Less than 3 miles	Up to 20 fathoms	± 50 yds.	Every minute
Coastal waters	3–50 miles	20–100 fathoms	± $\frac{1}{4}$ mi.	Every 3–10 minutes
Ocean passage	Over 50 miles	Over 100 fathoms	± 2–3 mi.	As conditions warrant, and at least 3 times daily

Figure 1509. Navigational stations on a U.S. Navy destroyer.

board side now reports, "Cape Charles bearing 020.0 degrees." While this report is being made, the port bearing taker has taken an observation on the Tunnel South Light, which he now reports as "278.0 degrees." (As the Tunnel South Light is nearly dead ahead, its bearing will not have changed appreciably during the time interval between the buzzer/mark and the actual taking of the bearing.)

When the bearing recorder sounded the buzzer or gave the "mark," the time was noted and recorded in the time column of the bearing book. As each of the bearings were reported by the bearing takers, the recorder wrote it down in the appropriate column of the bearing book, *and repeated it back over the circuit for confirmation.* This procedure enabled the navigator and plotter to hear it. The plotter commenced work as soon as the first bearing was reported, and should have all three bearings plotted in less than 30 seconds. As soon as the plotter has the fix drawn and labeled, the navigator inspects it to see if it is on the intended track. If it is, he has DR positions plotted ahead from the fix for the next six minutes, which will enable him to be reasonably sure of his position at the next three-minute mark. If the fix is *not* along the intended track, the navigator determines the course that should be steered, and recommends the new course to the captain. The plotter marks the DR positions, using the old course, up to the time of the course change and then lays down a DR plot for the new

course for the remainder of the six minutes. In addition, the distance, time of arrival at an expected turning point, the identity of the turning point in terms of relative or true bearing, the range from an identifiable object, and the new course recommendation can be given to the captain. When the recorder, who has been watching the clock, sees that the next three-minute mark is about due, he gives "stand by" and "mark" (or sounds the buzzer) at the proper time and the procedure continues as before.

As an object being used for bearings starts to become unsuitable—the angle of intersection between LOPs getting too small or the distance becoming too great—a new object is added and bearings are taken on it for several 4-LOP fixes *before* discontinuing bearings on the older object.

Plotting the LOP

Previous chapters have covered the proper labeling of the DR plot, various lines of position, and fixes, including placing the time above an LOP and, in some instances, the direction below the line. The purpose of this was to ensure identification and to provide a record of the data used to plot each LOP. On board a naval ship, however, using a full piloting team, the time and observed (uncorrected) bearing of each LOP are recorded in the bearing book as described above, and by using the information recorded therein, all plotting can be reconstructed should it become necessary. To facilitate plotting, labels may be left off LOPs in actual practice and only the symbols, with times, used for fixes, EPs, and DR positions. If a series of fixes is being taken by two independent means, such as visually and by radar, a circle is used for fixes from primary (visual) data and a triangle symbol may be used for fixes from secondary (radar) information.

Depth Information

Suppose that at about this time the echo-sounder operator reports "depth 24 feet" (feet are used in preference to fathoms in shallower pilot waters). Since 24 feet is the depth of water from the transducer, the navigator must add to it the distance from the waterline to the transducer before he can compare it with the charted depth corrected for height of tide. If this distance is 12 feet, then the total depth according to the echo-sounder is 36 feet. The chart at the DR position for the time of the reading showed 34 feet; therefore, the two depths are basically in agreement, for the chart uses a mean-low-water datum and the height of the tide has been previously calculated to be approximately

2 feet. (For the approach to most harbors it is sufficient to calculate the height of the tide to the nearest foot for the mid-time of the entrance or departure. Where the range of the tide is considerable, and the entrance or departure will take several hours, the height of the tide should be calculated for several points of critical interest for the ETA at each such point.)

On some naval vessels, a system of "yellow" and "red" soundings is used. A *yellow sounding* is the depth beneath the keel established by the commanding officer of the vessel as indicating potential danger. Upon obtaining any sounding equal to or less than the established yellow value, the officer of the deck should call the navigator, initiate action to fix the vessel's position, and proceed with due caution. A *red sounding* is the minimum permissible depth under the keel authorized by the commanding officer. Upon obtaining any sounding equal to or less than the established red sounding, the OOD must take immediate correction action.

The Navigator in Piloting

1510   The foregoing example does not show all the preparation that the navigator and his assistants made to achieve smooth results.

Prior to reaching the entrance to Chesapeake Bay, the navigator reviewed his predeparture planning and updated any details as required. He marked on the chart(s) those landmarks and aids to navigation that he expected to use and noted the physical appearance of each of these so that he could readily recognize the objects as they were sighted. With his plans reviewed, and with the necessary notes on the charts, he assembled all persons concerned with navigating the ship—his piloting team, CIC radar personnel, and the OOD—for a briefing. During this briefing, he pointed out to each the location of every landmark expected to be used, its name, its appearance, and the order of expected sightings. In so doing he enabled each member of his team to become familiar, in some degree, with the objects they would be using. The bearing takers knew in advance where to look and what to look for, and the bearing recorder knew the names of the landmarks he would have to record and transmit over the phones. In cases of entry into unfamiliar pilot waters, there is particular benefit to be gained from preparing and issuing a written guide to each man on the team in order that he can later refer to the printed information rather than trust it to memory. The guide should contain a written description of each expected navigational aid as recorded in the *Light List* or *List of Lights* and

appropriate extracts from the *Coast Pilot* or *Sailing Directions*. Such a guide materially helps in the smooth operation of a piloting team, and is of particular importance when entering a strange port. If the port is a familiar one, such a written guide is usually not necessary.

When on the bridge, the navigator uses the knowledge he has gained in his preparation. As each landmark and aid to navigation is sighted, he personally checks its appearance to be sure it is correctly identified and compares it with the description in the *Light List* or *List of Lights*, not trusting to memory alone. The bearing takers, having been briefed in advance, can be of considerable help in preliminary identification, but the responsibility for positive identification rests on the navigator. As he plots his fixes, and as the ship proceeds up the channel, the prudent navigator visually checks all landmarks and aids to make sure that his ship is where it appears to be on the chart. The quick appraisal and good judgment of an experienced navigator have kept many ships out of danger, even though objects—particularly buoys—may previously have been incorrectly identified.

The navigator is responsible for the safe navigation of the ship, and if he is in doubt, *for any reason*, as to the ship's position, the only safe thing to do is so advise the captain and recommend slowing or stopping.

Procedures on Merchant Ships

1511   Since the merchant marine officer is often left to his own devices as both watchstander and navigator, it is best to prepare for the piloting sequence well in advance. This may often require that the individual come to the bridge early so as to acquaint himself with at least the following: the chart in use as well as those to be used during the next four-hour watch; the *Light List* or *List of Lights; Radio Navigation Aids*, Pub. No. 117A or 117B; tide and tidal current information; *Coast Pilot* or *Sailing Directions*; and the gyrocompass error. Having reviewed these charts, publications, and equipment, the officer should develop a written plan in his navigation workbook that in tabular form details the aids to navigation, their characteristics, expected time of sighting, expected time abeam, and the desired distance off. As each aid is passed, the plan can be updated for those not yet reached. At night, it is wise to inform the lookout as to the general direction of the next aid to navigation of importance.

Although the actual practice of piloting is the same for merchant and naval vessels, it must be

Figure 1511. A typical merchant ship pilothouse equipment installation reflects the much smaller manning level of this type of vessel, compared with the naval ship.

understood that the piloting team found aboard a naval vessel has no real counterpart on a merchant ship. Hence, the watchstanding officer must accomplish the piloting tasks by himself while still maintaining a proper lookout and coping with whatever vessel traffic is in the vicinity. Since speed and efficiency are of prime importance to the solitary watch officer, it is not uncommon for the mate on watch to rely primarily on radar bearings and ranges, occasional Loran or Decca fixes, and on visual bearings only for verification or where the need for accuracy dictates such a practice. The use of RDF in today's merchant marine has generally fallen into a decline, retaining importance only in areas of poor visibility or when the next aid to navigation cannot yet be detected visually or by radar. Whenever the mate on watch encounters difficulty in performing the full required piloting functions alone, or when the vessel traffic precludes the ability of one man to pilot and simultaneously negotiate traffic situations, assistance in the form of the master and/or another mate should be solicited. Upon arrival at a port, the common practice of merchant ships is to enlist the services of a licensed pilot. In such cases, it is typical for the mate to pilot

the vessel to within a few miles of the pilot station. At that point, the ship's master usually comes to the bridge and assumes the conn; he will then negotiate the various traffic situations and dictate the vessel's course and speed. The mate now is delegated the task of fixing the vessel's position, advising the master of that information, and handling the engine order telegraph and related bell book and rough log entries. Once the pilot is on board, the navigation of the vessel is usually conducted solely by that individual. The master of the ship remains on the bridge to interact with the pilot and in any case remains ultimately responsible for the safe navigation of the vessel. The mate on watch continues to handle the engine order telegraph, the bell book entries, and the fixing of the vessel's position as frequently as possible. Although it would seem ill-advised to inform the pilot of the vessel's position three minutes ago, the mate must be aware of the fallibility of pilots and is thus charged with fixing the vessel's position for record-keeping purposes as well as for the possibility of pilot error. In this regard, the mate should avoid making trips to the bridge wings, to the chart room, and back to the wheelhouse. Instead it is preferable to find some flat surface in the wheelhouse where plotting on a chart can be reasonably performed. Whatever procedure is finally chosen, the mate on watch must keep the vessel's position recorded in the rough log or bell book and the track clearly indicated on the appropriate chart. Smooth log book entries are often recorded after the act as time permits, using the bell book or rough log as the source of information, and transferring the required entries to the smooth log.

Chapter 16   Radar Piloting

Introduction

1601   *Radar* (*RA*dio *D*etection *A*nd *R*anging) is a method of determining the distance to and direction of objects by sending out a beam of microwave radio energy and detecting the returned reflections. Distance is determined by measuring the time between the transmission of the signal and the return of the "echo"—this is the same principle as with electronic depth sounders, except that times are very much shorter due to the vastly greater speed of radio waves as compared to sound waves. In a few instances, the returned signal is not a reflection, but a pulse from a small *transponder* that has been triggered by the radar signal; a transponder generates a return automatically when "interrogated" by a signal of the appropriate frequency. The bearing of an echo returned by a "target" or a transponder is determined from the orientation of a highly directional antenna, which has also served to concentrate the outgoing energy into a sharply defined "beam."

Radar equipment is used for many purposes, including detection of ships, aircraft, and weather activities, and gunfire control. Here we will be concerned only with its use in the piloting of surface vessels. Radars for this purpose send out pulses of energy with the reception of an echo before the next pulse is transmitted. (There are types of "continuous-wave" radars, but these are very little used in navigation.) Range measurements can be both highly precise and accurate and provide the data most useful in piloting. Radar bearings are less precise than visual bearings and less accurate than distance measurements.

Equipment

1602   Radar sets vary in size and design, but all contain five major components.

Transmitter. An oscillator that produces electromagnetic waves of energy. Super high frequencies (SHF) are used, generally 3,000 to 10,000 megahertz, but sometimes as high as 30,000 MHz; these are wavelengths of 10, 3, and 1 cm, respectively (see article 1604).

Modulator. Circuitry that turns the transmitter on and off so that the energy is sent out in *pulses* of about one microsecond (one millionth of a second) or less. From 500 to 3,000 very accurately timed pulses are transmitted each second by most radars of the type used for surface navigation, depending upon the range scale being used. The *timing base* circuitry in the modulator also controls and synchronizes several functions of the receiver and indicator units.

Antenna. A physical structure used to transmit the outgoing pulse and receive the returned signal. Antennas must be highly directional and capable of rotation; they can be relatively large and are often quite complex. A single antenna is normally used for both transmitting and receiving. Typical rotation rates are 15 to 25 rpm, clockwise, but some models may have faster or slower speeds. (Some radars can be set to "sector scan" within set limits.)

Receiver. Electronic circuitry to amplify the very weak incoming signal and demodulate it for display. A *duplexer*, or electronic switch, with a *transmit-receive tube* (T/R tube) or equivalent circuitry is provided between the receiver and antenna to electronically disconnect the receiver and thereby pre-

Figure 1602a. Diagramatic sketch of a cathode ray tube (CRT) using electrostatic deflection. Other radars use CRTs with magnetic deflection obtained from coils placed around the neck of the CRT.

Figure 1602b. Major components of a typical radar set.

vent damage during the interval of transmission of the energy pulse.

Indicator. Presents the information in a form for interpretation. It consists essentially of a cathode ray tube (CRT), the face or screen of which is commonly referred to as the *scope* (figure 1602a), and various timing circuits and controls. In the scope a stream of electrons is directed toward a fluorescent screen, appearing there as a dot of light. Various types of presentation are used on CRTs, but for radar navigation only one type is generally employed; this presentation is called a *Plan Position Indicator* (PPI).

A typical arrangement for the five parts of a radar system is shown in figure 1602b.

The Display

On a typical PPI scope, a faint radial line represents the outgoing beam of energy, a line that starts at the "own ship's" position at the center of the screen and extends to the outer edge, rotating in bearing synchronization with the rotation of the antenna. Around the outer edge of the PPI scope are bearing indications, clockwise from 000° at the top.

When the radiated energy from the antenna strikes a target, a weak echo is returned, is amplified, and causes a spot or area of the PPI scope to glow; the distance out from the center of the scope to this spot or area is a measure of the distance from the ship to the target. This spot or area on the screen (called a "blip" or "pip") will continue to glow, with slowly decaying brightness, after the radial line has continued to sweep around the face of the scope; on most sets, it will be "repainted" by the next sweep of the beam at about the time that it is fading from sight. Thus, a continuous chart-like picture of the surrounding area will be presented without undue smearing of the old traces into the new; see figure 1602c. The bright area surrounding the transmitting ship's ("own ship") posi-

tion at the center of the screen is *clutter* caused by *sea return*, which is described in article 1606.

On simpler radar sets, the display on the PPI screen is aligned so that 000° is dead ahead and thus all radar bearings are relative. On ships equipped with gyrocompasses, it is normal for gyro heading information to be fed into the radar system. The display can then present either relative bearings or true bearings (with north at the top of the screen) at the option of the operator.

The bearing of specific blips on the indicator scope can be estimated against the outer scale, usually as the spot is repainted by the sweeping beam. For more precise directions, a *bearing cursor* can be used; this is a faint radial line of light that can be manually rotated by the radar operator to alignment with the spot on the scope, the bearing then being read from a dial.

Some models of radar will permit a *true-motion* type of display. In such a mode of operation, one's own ship is no longer at the center of the display. Here, the center of the screen temporarily remains a fixed geographic point, and a true-motion picture

Figure 1602c. Radar PPI display.

is painted of all targets, including the vessel on which the radar is located. (The fixed point of the screen's center must be advanced as the own-ship position approaches the outer limits of the screen.)

Radar sets have a number of *range scales,* the distance to the outer edge of the sweep on the PPI display, such as $\frac{1}{4}$, $\frac{1}{2}$, 1, 2, 4, 8, 16, and 32 miles. The number of different range scales and the maximum range scale available on any particular radar set are determined by its design; these characteristics are selected to match the size and use of the vessel on which the radar is installed. The shorter ranges are used for close-in navigation, and the longer range scales to initially detect aids to navigation, landfalls, and other vessels. Most radars have several *range rings* that can be illuminated to give a rough measure of distance from own ship. For more precise measurements, a set may have a *range strobe* (a spot of light that can be moved in and out along the bearing cursor) or a *variable range ring;* these are manually controlled by the operator who places them over the desired spot and then reads the distance from a dial.

Some radar sets, particularly military models, may have a second type of display in addition to the PPI scope. Typically, this is a linear-base presentation with a portion of the range scale expanded. Such an *M-scope* display permits very accurate measurements of range with good discrimination between targets at nearly equal ranges; this capability is often of use in navigation.

Recent Developments

After color TV for many years, now it is "color radar"! Models are available that use various colors to aid in the identification of different types of echoes. Typically, the sea surface is shown in blue, with targets in red, green, or yellow depending upon the strength of the echoes being returned; white is used for range rings and the bearing cursor. Some additional familiarization may be required, but then the use of the radar is considerably enhanced. In many installations only a new display unit is needed, with the remainder of the equipment unchanged.

Another recent result of the advancing application of microelectronics to radar is the "raster-scan" type of display. Here the incoming signals are digitalized and applied to a square screen in much the same manner as a television picture is produced. Greater clarity and detail are produced; the "picture" is presented in a manner that stays sharp and clear even when the vessel is making fast, tight turns, as it is refreshed 30 times each

second. The display may be temporarily "frozen" at any time in order to make more precise measurements of range and bearing.

Accuracy

1603 Many factors affect the operational characteristics of radar sets. The accuracy of positions obtained by radar varies considerably with different types of radar and with the skill of the operator. In general, the accuracy of radar fixes compares favorably with those obtained by other methods (see article 1607). The limitations of each radar set should be thoroughly understood by those who are depending upon its information. Some of the factors affecting the accuracy are beam width, pulse length, mechanical adjustment, and interpretation of the return.

Resolution in Bearing

Radar signals are directional, transmitted as narrow, fan-shaped beams. While a beam may be less than 1° in width, it may be 15° or more in the vertical dimension; this greater vertical dimension permits illumination of targets from close to the ship out to the radar horizon and allows for the pitching and rolling motion of the vessel. (Antennas will also have minor "side lobes" of very much less power; these are normally of no importance.) See figures 1603a and 1603b. Echoes are received continuously as the beam sweeps across a *target,* or reflecting surface. The center of the arc thus indicated is the desired bearing. On a PPI scope the effect is to cause a target to appear wider than it actually is. On each side its width is increased by about half the beam width, or slightly less. If two or more targets are relatively close together at about the same range, their widened pips may merge, appearing as the single pip of a larger target. The minimum difference in bearing between two objects at the same range that can be separated by a radar is called its *resolution in bearing.* The ability to make this separation is directly dependent on beam width. A number of piles, rocks, or small boats near a shore may appear as a solid line, giving a false impression of the position of the actual shore line; or two small craft may appear as one larger vessel.

Resolution in Range

The outgoing pulse of radio energy has a finite length, and this affects the depth of the reflected signal in a manner generally similar to the widening by the beam width. Thus, a signal of one microsecond duration reflected from a flat, perpendicu-

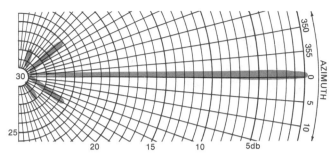

Figure 1603a. Horizontal radiation pattern of a radar antenna (typical).

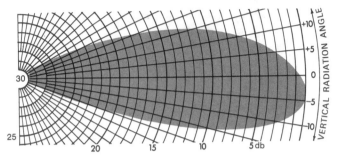

Figure 1603b. Vertical radiation pattern of a radar antenna (typical).

lar surface continues to be received for one microsecond. The depth of such a pip is equal to half the distance traveled by the signal in one microsecond, or 492 feet (150 m). The shorter the pulse, the less is the depth of the pip. This is the minimum difference in range between two objects on the same bearing that can be separated by a radar with this *pulse length*. *Resolution in range* is primarily dependent on pulse length, but to some extent also on the pulse shape and technical characteristics of the receiver. False interpretation may occur when two or more targets appear as a single long one, or when a ship, buoy, or rock is near shore and is not separated from it on the PPI.

Pulse length also determines the *minimum range* of the radar, a characteristic of considerable importance when navigating close to buoys and other aids to navigation (and other vessels) when proceeding along a channel.

Effects of Frequency Selection

It may be stated as a generality that radars operating in the radar frequency band of near 9,500 MHz (3 cm) may more easily be designed to have shorter pulse length and narrower beam width and therefore to give rather better resolution in both bearing and range than do those operating in a lower frequency band. On the other hand, for an equal output of power, sets operating at lower fre-

quencies can acquire targets at somewhat longer ranges.

Operating Adjustments

On modern radar sets special circuits are included with appropriate manual adjustments to permit improved resolution in both range and bearing. A *sensitivity time control (STC)* circuit (for clutter control) changes the gain characteristics of the receiver at close-in ranges. This circuit is valuable in reducing sea-return saturation at close ranges so that nearby targets can be seen; it does not affect targets beyond the limit of its time base. A *fast time constant (FTC)* circuit provides differentiation of the received signals and also helps to reduce *rain clutter*, the pale echoes on the PPI scope caused by rainfall. Often a change from the normal *horizontal polarization* of the antenna to *circular polarization* will reduce clutter from rain or sea return at a cost of slightly weakened pulses; this is not possible in all sets.

On many radars, different values for pulse length and repetition rate are used on different ranges. For example, a pulse repetition rate of 1,500 pulses per second and a pulse length of 0.1 microseconds is used on some sets for ranges under approximately 4 miles; this is changed to 750 pulses per second and 0.5 microseconds for longer ranges (there may be more than two combinations on some radars).

Frequency and Wavelength

1604 The great majority of marine surface-search radars, and the radar beacons designed for use with them, operate in frequency bands near 3,000 and 10,000 MHz (3 and 10 GHz). Radars are frequently described by the approximate wavelength they employ, or lettered "band" designation. Thus, a *10-centimeter* (S-band) radar is one operating in the frequency range of *3,000* to *3,246 MHz;* a *5-cm* (C-band) radar uses the *5,450* to *5,825 MHz* band; and a *3-cm* (X-band) radar is one in the *9,320* to *9,500* MHz band.

In the selection of a radar set for a vessel (or which set to use if more than one is on board), certain factors must be considered, such as:

Propagation conditions for the different wave lengths.

Size of antenna systems for the desired resolution and necessary gain (concentration of energy).

Comparative cost of components and complexity of design.

The first factor, propagation, is the one element affecting radar performance over which man has no control. Reliability of coverage regardless of meteorological conditions is an important consideration for navigational radars. Fog has a negligible effect on the strength of either 3-, 5-, or 10-centimeter signals. Rainfall is more serious, as the signal strength weakens more or less linearly with the density of the precipitation. The amount the signal is weakened is called the *attenuation constant* and varies approximately as the square of the frequency. This means that the effective range of the higher frequency 3-centimeter sets may be considerably less than the 10-centimeter sets during periods of rainfall. When the precipitation is heavy and the distance to the target is great, the effect becomes more serious. During cloudbursts a complete radar blackout may temporarily occur on a 3-centimeter set.

Higher frequencies permit smaller antennas (or sharper beams for the same size of antenna). The useful operational range of a given set depends not only on the frequency employed, but also on the height of its antenna above water, the power output, and its power of resolution. Lower-frequency radar, as a rule, permits better target acquisition in areas of heavy rain, and also tends to have a smaller area masked by *sea return* or *clutter*. Sea return is caused by a portion of the transmitted signal being reflected by wave tops. It occurs principally in the area immediately surrounding the ship, and can mask targets within its area. (See article 1606.) On the other hand, 3-cm radars operating at peak pulse powers far below the allowable maximum can detect targets at the horizon range of most radar antenna installations. A 3-cm radar at 25-kw peak pulse power can detect large ships at ranges above 60 miles (110 km) under certain atmospheric conditions.

Most small craft, such as yachts and the smaller commercial fishermen, use 3-cm radar so as to obtain maximum resolution in bearing and range; in most instances, they have neither the antenna height nor the power available to work at long ranges. Liners, large tankers, and freighters frequently are equipped with both 10-cm radar for target acquisition at maximum ranges, and 3-cm radar for use in piloting during periods of poor visibility. Various U.S. Navy surface-search radars operate on wavelengths of 10, 5, and 3 cm.

Interpretation

1605 Even after considerable training and ex-perience a radar operator may not always find it easy to interpret an echo correctly. Listed below are some factors that make the action difficult.

As noted earlier, *resolution* in bearing will be limited by the finite width of the radar beam; this will cause a target to appear wider than it actually is. False interpretation may occur as a result of this wider appearance or when two or more smaller targets appear as a single long one. Problems of *resolution in range*, caused by the finite length of the pulse, may cause faulty interpretation when a vessel, buoy, or rock is near shore and is not separated from it on the radarscope. Problems may also arise when two vessels are close together on the same bearing, or one vessel is similarly near a buoy.

False shore lines may appear on a PPI for any of several reasons. In figure 1605a false shore lines appear at B because of a pier, at C because of several small boats, and at D because of heavy surf over a shoal. Figure 1605b is a chart of the area shown in figure 1605a. The echoes of A and G make these appear as islands, where actually they are areas of high ground on the mainland. A shore line may be falsely indicated some distance inland if there are bluffs or cliffs back of a low and flat or gently sloping beach.

Shadows (figure 1605c) occur behind prominent objects. That is, no echo is returned from a surface that is completely shielded from radar pulses by higher targets nearer the antenna. Hence, mountains, towers, etc., inshore can be seen only if they extend above nearer objects by an essentially direct line of sight. Thus, a valley parallel to a high shore line will not return an echo, although the higher land on either side may be seen. Similarly, a rock or small boat too far beyond the horizon to be seen will not return an echo, although a high mountain beyond it can be picked up. Until the operator is thoroughly familiar with the interpretation of all echoes on the radar screen, he should take every opportunity to compare the picture shown on the PPI with the actual land area it portrays. Particular attention should be given to noting the difference in the appearance of echoes caused by buoys and by ships.

By comparing the screen with a chart of the area it will be noted that shore lines and prominent points will appear as bright areas against a dark background. The reflected echo will be very much like the actual view of the area. Small objects such as buoys will appear as small illuminated areas when picked up at a distance. The image will increase in size as range decreases in much the same

Figure 1605a. PPI pattern, ship off Pt. Loma, California.

Figure 1605b. Chart of area shown in figure 1605a.

Figure 1605c. Radar shadows.

way that it would appear visually larger at close range. At close range a buoy might give a stronger return than a small vessel situated at a greater distance; this is particularly true if the buoy is fitted with a *radar reflector* as nearly all now are (see article 402). (Small craft, particularly those of wood and fiberglass that have a very poor natural reflectivity, may hoist a radar reflector (see article 1618) in their rigging at night or in fog when in waters frequented by radar-equipped ships.) Such a reflector, despite its comparatively small size, returns a very strong echo. With practice, the size of different vessels can be estimated by the relative size of their images on the screen; allowance must be made for range. Low-flying aircraft can be identified by their speed of travel. High coastlines and mountain areas near the sea can be picked up at the extreme range of the equipment. Storm areas and rain squalls are easily recognized by their mass and hazy definition.

Interference from another radar-equipped vessel may occasionally appear on the screen as a patterned series of small dots. This effect is especially pronounced at the longer range scales. These dots appear to move to and from the center of the screen, often in long sweeping curves, sometimes in a straight line.

Ghost images of several types appear occasionally. They are easy to identify, as they maintain a fixed relationship with respect to the true image, they have more of an arc-like appearance than the true image, and they have a tendency to "smear." They are not generally troublesome, as they are easily recognized. They should be noted, with their probable cause, to assist in future recognition.

Limitations of Range

1606 Both minimum and maximum range is limited. The minimum range is dependent on several factors. Pulse length is a major factor in determining minimum range, as an echo from the leading edge of an outgoing pulse obviously cannot be received until the trailing edge of that pulse has cleared the antenna and the T/R has functioned to restore the signal path into the receiver. Minimum range is also affected by the frequency of the radar set; a 3-cm radar may have a minimum range as short as 12 yards (11 meters).

Excessive *sea return*, or echo from nearby water and other obstructions nearby, also affects the minimum effective range. Sea return can be reduced by judicious tuning, reducing the signal strength of close-in echoes, which, however, reduces maximum range. Sea return becomes less with increased range because of the change in the angle of incidence, more of the signal being reflected away from the ship and less returned in the form of an echo.

The STC (sensitivity time control) provides the operator with a means of controlling the receiver sensitivity near minimum operating range. The best results in reducing sea return and other clutter such as that caused by rain, snow, or sleet can generally be achieved by careful adjustment of both the STC and the fast time constant control (FTC).

When the ship is near land masses or large targets, echos picked up by the side lobes of the antenna may clutter the display and prevent the detection of close-in targets regardless of the direction in which the antenna is pointed.

Maximum Range

Maximum range is usually limited by the curvature of the earth to the line of sight or slightly more, because high-frequency radio waves travel in a straight line and do not follow the earth's curvature, except under abnormal atmospheric conditions. The approximate maximum range at which any given target will return an echo can be determined by use of the equation $D = 1.22\sqrt{H}$ where D is distance in nautical miles and H is the height of the antenna in feet. Table 8 of *Bowditch*, distance to the visible horizon, may also be used with distances increased by 4 to 5 percent to allow for the slight curvature of radar waves over the geometric horizon. A navigator should be alert to unusual ranges that may be obtained when a *temperature inversion* exists in the atmosphere.

Radar Fixes

1607 Radar can be used in several ways to obtain position. Well-determined positions are labeled as *fixes* and less reliable ones as *EPs*, depending on the judgment of the navigator after experience with his equipment. The accuracy of radar or radar-assisted position fixes follows in descending order:

Radar ranges and visual bearings of prominent isolated objects;
Radar ranges of several radar-conspicuous objects plotted as position circles;
Radar range and radar bearing of a single charted feature;
Radar bearings of two or more charted features.

Radar lines of position, no matter how they are determined, are plotted and labeled in the same manner as visual LOPs; see chapter 11. The only difference occurs in plotting radar bearings of tangents when the radar beam width must be taken into consideration. For this specific case a correction of one-half the beam width may be applied in the direction of the land. An example of this would be a radar with a beam width of 4° giving a bearing of 045° on the left tangent of a point of land. The actual bearing to be plotted on the chart would be 047°.

If a series of radar fixes are being plotted simultaneously with visual fixes, a different symbol, a small triangle, may be used for the radar fixes so that they may be readily distinguished from the visual fixes plotted with the usual small circle.

Advantages of Radar

1608 Radar has several advantages over other navigational aids for piloting:

It can be used at night and during periods of low visibility, when most other methods are limited, or are not available at all.
Navigation by radar is often more accurate than other methods of piloting during periods of reduced visibility.
Fixes may be available at greater distances from land than in most methods of piloting.
A fix can be obtained from a single object, since both range and bearing are provided. (This is less desirable than a fix by range to two or more objects.)
Fixes can be obtained rapidly. With the PPI, a continuous position is available.
It may be used to assist in the prevention of collision during periods of low visibility.
It can be used to locate and track heavy storms.

Disadvantages of Radar

1609 As a navigational aid, radar is subject to certain limitations and disadvantages:

It is subject to mechanical and electrical failure.
There are both minimum and maximum range limitations.
Interpretation of the information presented on the scope is not always easy, even after considerable training.
Charts do not always give information necessary for identification of radar echoes.
In some applications, it is less accurate than visual piloting; i.e., a radar bearing is less precise than a visual bearing. (Distance measurements, however, can be quite precise and accurate.)
Buoys, small boats, etc., may not be detected, especially if a high sea is running, or if they are near shore or other objects.

It requires transmission of signals from the vessel; this can be a limiting factor in naval operations and a problem on small craft with limited primary power sources.

Military and Commercial Radar Equipment

1610 Radar sets, while all consisting of the basic major components listed in article 1601, vary widely in design according to the primary use for which each model is designed. In the U.S. Navy, the variations run from extremely high frequency, high power, strictly line-of-sight radar for control of the ship's armament, to a much lower frequency, long-range radar for detecting aircraft. Somewhere in between lies navigational radar. Radar aboard naval vessels usually employs a *north up* presentation, that is, true north appears at the center of the top of the scope. Many commercial radar sets give relative indications only (own ship's head up) or have a switch to change from north up to a *ship's-head-up* presentation. Most military radars show own ship at the center of the scope with both fixed and moving targets having relative motion on the scope when own ship is in motion. Several commercial models now present *true motion* with both own ship and other moving target images moving across the scope, while land areas, fixed buoys, etc., remain motionless. Still another innovation permits an off-center relative motion display, with own ship position remaining motionless but offset from the center of the scope to permit a maximum view of the area lying in a desired relative direction, usually ahead.

Use of High-definition Radar

1611 The 3-cm band radar (9,500 MHz band) has come into general use both in the navies of the world, and with the merchant services as an adjunct to longer-wave radar. The high quality of the resolution it gives makes it particularly useful in pilotage. United States naval vessels of nearly all sizes and classes are now fitted with 3-cm radar to facilitate their entering or leaving port under conditions of zero visibility. Some merchant ships are now equipped with dual radar installations consisting of either a 10-cm and a 3-cm radar or two 3-cm sets. This practice is even gaining favor with many operators of seagoing tugs and larger fishing vessels in the United States.

Fishing fleets operating from U.S. ports are now widely equipped with the 3-cm band radar in order to allow greater mobility when fog, haze, or darkness might otherwise hinder operations. Smaller versions of the 3-cm band radar using solid-state electronics are available for use by yachtsmen in boats as small as 30 feet.

Navy Surface Radars

1612 The navy's search radar, like that used by the coast guard, army, and air force, differs from commercial radar, in that it is almost invariably equipped for Identification, Friend or Foe (IFF) operation, described below. Naval vessels commonly use their *surface-search* radars for navigation; these are currently models of the SPS-10 and SPS-53 series. The newer SPS-55 series, a 3-cm radar, is being installed in major combatant ships, particularly aboard new construction.

Some U.S. naval vessels are also equipped with commercial models of radars, primarily for use in navigation.

IFF

The IFF feature of a military radar set returns a predetermined coded identification signal automatically if this capability is switched on. Similarly, this radar can challenge "targets" who will return the properly coded signal if "friend" rather than "foe."

The AN/SPS-53 Radar

1613 The AN/SPS-53 is a surface-search radar in the 9345–9405 MHz band; it is used on medium-size vessels, and its maximum range is 32 miles. As it is typical of late-model radars now being used in the U.S. Navy and U.S. Coast Guard, it will be described in some detail. The pedestal-mounted antenna contains a horizontally polarized slotted waveguide radiating element. The "control-indicator" unit has a 10-inch (25.4 cm) PPI tube. A signal data converter provides either true or relative bearing inputs to the control indicator for display.

The RF energy output of the transmitter is conducted by a waveguide to the antenna where, after making a transition in the antenna pedestal, the energy is applied to the slotted array and then radiated in a fan-beam pattern. The antenna rotates at 15 RPM and provides search capability for both surface and low-flying targets.

The antenna picks up the portion of the transmitted energy that is reflected back by a target, and this weak signal is sent to the receiver via the waveguide. The detected echo pulse is amplified in the receiver and delivered to the control-indicator unit as a video signal whose amplitude is controlled at the desired level. The amplified video signal is applied to the grid of the cathode-ray tube, causing the echo signal to be converted into visual intelligence on the PPI screen, where the signal appears as a bright spot.

Antenna

The feedhorn, containing the slotted-array radiating element, produces a vertical beam width of 20° and a horizontal beam width of 1.6° at the half-power points. This is for a 5-foot (1.5 m) antenna; larger antennas that produce narrower horizontal beams are used on some models of the SPS-53A radars.

Receiver-transmitter

An RF pulse width of 0.1 microsecond with a pulse repetition rate of 1,500 pulses per second is used at short ranges; this may be switched to 0.5 microseconds and 750 pulses per second for improved longer-range performance.

Control-indicator Unit

The main display unit, shown in figure 1613, contains all the system controls. The set is turned on at this unit, the receiver is operated and adjusted, and true or relative bearing operation may be selected. The unit can be pedestal mounted; provision is also made for table-top, overhead, or bulkhead mounting.

The 10-inch (25.4 cm) electro-static-focus, magnetic-deflection cathode-ray tube provides a PPI

Figure 1613. AN/SPS-53 radar showing front panel controls.

presentation; a hood may be added for better daytime viewing. Range scales available are: 0.5, 1, 2, 4, 8, 16, and 32 miles, providing a wide choice of areas to be scanned; scales are multiples of two so that perspective is not lost when switching. Calibrated range markers are provided; the distance represented by each marker varies with the range being used. For example, the four markers will be at half-mile intervals when on the 2-mile range, but at 8-mile intervals when operating on the 32-mile maximum range.

Surrounding the radar screen is an azimuthal or bearing ring calibrated in degrees. A bearing cursor that intersects this azimuth ring can be rotated in either direction and aligned with an object on the screen to determine the direction to the target. A "ship's heading flasher" momentarily brightens the screen each time the PPI sweep goes through 000° relative, creating a definite line on the screen to indicate the vessel's heading. Figure 1613 shows the location of the controls on the SPS-53; the operator must be completely familiar with the use of these controls if he is to obtain optimum information from the scope picture.

The AN/SPS-55 Navy Radar

1614 The SPS-55 is the newest U.S. Navy surface-search radar; it has excellent capabilities for assisting in navigation. This radar operates in the 9.05–10.0 GHz band with 120 kw peak power. A 6-foot (1.8 m) antenna, which rotates at 16 rpm, provides a beam-width of 1.5° horizontally and 20° vertically; the antenna is actually a dual unit, back-to-back with one end-fed slotted waveguide radiating horizontally polarized pulses, and the other side circularly polarized pulses.

Two pulse repetition rates, 750 and 2,250 pps, are available, with corresponding pulse lengths of 1.0 and 0.12 microseconds. These are selected at the control panel; they are not automatically switched with the range selected as in some radar equipment. The minimum range is 50 yards (46 m) or 200 yards (183 m) for short or long pulses respectively; the corresponding range resolution figures are 75 feet (23 m) and 550 feet (168 m).

The various range scales are selected at the associated indicator unit, which is not a part of the SPS-55. The indicator has a 10-inch (25.4 cm) PPI scope and controls that are generally similar to other radar sets.

The LN66 Radar Set

1615 Many U.S. naval vessels have been equipped with the LN66 Radar Set. This equip-

Antenna
AS-2953/SPS-55

Pedestal
AB-1211/SPS-55

Antenna Pedestal
Unit
OE-172/SPS-55

Antenna
Safety
Switch
SA-1963/SPS-55

Plan Position
Indicator
(Not supplied)

Radar Set
Control Unit
C-9447/SPS-55

Receiver/Transmitter Unit
RT-1124/SPS-55

Surface Search and Navigation Radar System AN/SPS-55

Figure 1614. AN/SPS-55 radar.

ment is specifically designed as a shipboard navigation aid for the reliable detection of surface obstacles and other vessels. It permits surface surveillance through 360 degrees in azimuth within the range of 20 yards (18m) to 36 miles (67 km). The basic model operates in the relative bearing mode only, but a "true bearing unit" can be added to provide this additional feature.

Commercial Radar

1616 Typical of modern commercial radar equipment is the Furuno Model FR-1211. This X-band set operates at a frequency of 941 ± 30 MHz with a nominal peak power of 10 kw. There are ten selectable range scales from ¼ to 72 miles; the minimum range is 25 meters (27 yds). The display has fixed range rings appropriate to the range scale being used, plus a variable range marker with digital readout (a second digital readout is available as an option). Combinations of three different pulse lengths (0.08, 0.6, and 1.0 µs) and five pulse repetition rates (3,000 to 400 pps) are switched automatically with selection of a range scale; however, on each of the four ranges from 1.5 to 12 miles, the operator may choose between two combinations of pulse length and rate. Range accuracy is 1.5 percent or 70 meters (77 yds), whichever is the greater.

The display is a 12-inch (30.5 cm) PPI scope with a viewing hood for use in high-ambient-light conditions (the digital range readout is within the hood). The receiver can be manually tuned; an LED tuning indicator is also within the hood. Bearing accuracy is stated by the manufacturer as better than 1°; bearing discrimination varies from 1.0° to 1.2° depending upon the size of the antenna used. The presentation is normally relative to the ship's head, but with an optional gyrocompass interference unit it can be true north up. Front panel knobs are provided for receiver gain, variable sensitivity time control (STC), display and range ring brightness, and other features. The display unit is a free-standing console with front-opening access for easy maintenance. Slotted waveguide antennas are available with widths of 6.5 and 8 feet (2.0 and 2.4 m), having horizontal beamwidths of 1.23° and 0.9° respectively; polarization is horizontal. Vertical beamwidths are 25° and 20°; the antenna rotates at 24 RPM.

All electronics in the Furuno Model FR-1211 are solid-state except for the CRT display and the magnetron. Extensive use is made of integrated circuits on plug-in boards; standardized modules and sub-assemblies provide for ease of installation and maintenance. All RF transmitting and receiving stages are at the antenna, eliminating the need for any use of waveguide "plumbing."

Optional accessories include a Radar Alarm, Performance Monitor, Reflection Plotter, and an off-center capability for the display of up to ⅔ of the radius of the PPI.

A companion model is the FR-1221, which has a peak power of 25 kw and a range of 100 miles on the longest scale; other features are the same.

Other Uses of Radar

1617 Radar adapts itself quite readily to uses other than for navigation. As was previously pointed out, the military uses vary from fire control to detecting and tracking aircraft at long distances. Other uses include tracking weather disturbances, surveying, etc. However, in all probability, the most important use of radar is avoidance of collision.

Collision Avoidance

By means of radar-supplied data, proper plotting procedures, and common sense, information on the movements of other vessels can be properly evaluated. The conning officer can thus make decisions regarding course and speed changes in sufficient time to avoid the risk of collision.

Figure 1616. Commercial radar set, Furuno Model FR-1211.

The mariner must always bear in mind that even though other vessels may be detected by radar, there are no absolutely positive means of relating fog signals to objects detected by radar. Bridge-to-bridge radiotelephone (VHF Channel 13) can be of great value, but does not totally ensure identification. The International Rules of the Road (1972) and U.S. Inland Navigational Rules (1980) are specific and clear regarding the use of radar for collision avoidance in conditions of reduced visibility; if fitted on the vessel, radar *must* be used, including systematic observations and plotting (Rule 7), but radar is not a substitute for a "proper lookout" (Rule 5). The use of radar does *not* legally justify greater speeds under conditions of restricted visibility.

One of the most essential factors in the use of radar for collision avoidance is the use of proper procedures for plotting all available information, as described in chapter 14. As one knowledgeable mariner so aptly stated: "Many collisions have occurred because ships' officers were too busy to plot; but none, of which I have knowledge, has occurred because the officers were too busy plotting."

Radar Reflectors

1618 The use of a *radar reflector*—usually three flat metallic plates at right angles to each other,

called a "corner reflector"—greatly enhances the strength of a radar echo. This enables the detection of a small or nonmetallic object at greater range and/or enables it to be picked out of sea return. Radar reflectors are extensively used on buoys and other aids to navigation, and on small craft, especially those of wood or fiberglass construction.

Radar Beacons

1619 As useful as radar reflectors are, they are only *passive* devices, limited in the extent that they can enhance a radar echo. For stronger returns, and for positive identification, an *active* device, a *radar beacon*, is required. Such equipment transmits a signal that is much stronger at the receiving antenna than a mere reflected pulse; this signal can be *coded* for identification. Radar beacons can be of two different designs, racons and ramarks.

Racons

Racons transmit a pulse or pulses, but only when *triggered* by receipt of a pulse from a ship's radar; they not only give a stronger return than a reflector, they can be coded for positive identification and range measurement to the beacon.

In order to identify a racon, it is designed so that the reply to the received pulse consists of a number of pulses transmitted at selected intervals; these appear on the ship's PPI scope as segments of concentric arcs, figure 1619a. The number of segments, which can be short or long for reading as dots and dashes of the Morse code, provide an identification code. The usual procedure is that the racon can receive any frequency in the radar band, but transmits on a frequency in the adjacent beacon band. Thus the ship's radar must have the same capabilities as those mentioned below for ramark reception.

Figure 1619a. Racon signals as seen on a PPI scope.

Figure 1619b. Radar beacon presentation off Dungeness, England.

Since the racon reply pulses are initiated by the ship's radar pulses, the racon signal is in synchronism with the PPI display, and the range measurement is made to the inner edge of the pulse nearest the center of the scope. A correction, however, must be made, as it takes an appreciable time for the racon to react to the incoming pulse, causing the range to appear greater than it actually is. The true range is found by subtracting this difference, which can be the same for all racons. The bearing of the racon is taken to the middle of the arcs.

A racon is a saturable device and cannot reply to all received pulses over a certain number. Moreover, when interrogated by several radar sets simultaneously, interference from the replies to other ships' pulses can occur on the PPI display.

Ramarks

Ramarks are *continuously transmitting* beacons that display on the PPI scope a bright radial line or narrow sector on the bearing of the ramark; see figure 1619b. There are two general types of ramarks; one operates within the marine radar frequency band, the other transmits in the adjacent radar "beacon" band on a frequency of 9,310 MHz.

A ramark operating in the frequency band of radar equipment provides the advantage that no additional receiver is needed on the ship; the disadvantage is that the ramark design is more complex as it must *sweep* all frequencies in the band 9,320–9,500 MHz.

There are two methods of providing identification—by having the radial line on the PPI broken up into dots and dashes, or by transmitting the signal only during some of its antenna's revolutions and suppressing it during the next few revolutions (time coding). Specific identification by either method is achieved by assigning different codes to various ramarks. Time coding has a disadvantage for marine navigation in that a half-minute or so may be required to complete identification.

Ramarks operating in the beacon band are simpler, but require that the ship have either a separate receiver or a means of temporarily shifting the main radar set receiver from its normal working frequency to 9,310 MHz.

Chapter 17

The Practice of Piloting

Introduction

1701 The preceding chapters have considered in detail various aspects of piloting—charts, aids to navigation, instruments, personnel, procedures and techniques, etc.—required for the piloting of any vessel. Here in this chapter they will all be brought together in the practice of piloting in order that the interrelationship of each may be understood, and the importance of each to intelligent voyage planning and execution may be recognized. To accomplish this purpose, the initial articles discuss the steps that must be taken by a navigator in planning and executing any voyage in pilot waters, while the later articles illustrate how these general requirements are applied to a specific piloting situation.

The practice of piloting is illustrated here in terms of the plans and actions of a naval vessel and her crew, as this represents the highest degree of organization and complexity; see chapter 15. Many of the procedures described are applicable in general principles to merchant ships and yachts; others are of a purely naval nature. A non-naval navigator should carefully consider each step and adapt it to his needs if and as applicable.

Preliminary Preparations

1702 Well in advance of the time that a vessel will get underway for a specified destination, her navigator assembles various data, charts, and publications for study so that he can *plan* the voyage in detail before submitting his plan to the captain for approval. Once underway, the navigator and his assistants will find that their time is well occupied with the routine mechanics and techniques of piloting, and that little or no time is available for completing the planning phase. For this reason, it is essential that all planning be done well in advance of the sailing date. In the following paragraphs, essentials to the completion of adequate and safe planning are discussed. The order of accomplishing these steps may vary; an attempt has been made to place the various items in the sequence most frequently encountered in practice.

Determining ETD and ETA

1703 Authority for a naval ship to get underway and proceed to a specified destination will usually be in the form of a message, fleet or type employment schedule, or operation order. This authority should be carefully studied, with dates and times of departure and arrival noted, as well as the route, which may also be designated. It is customary for the authority directing the movement to specify only *dates* of departure and arrival, leaving the *times* of departure or arrival to the discretion of the commanding officer. This permits him to take advantage of the most favorable conditions of tide, current, and weather. Movement orders may specify other limiting factors such as SOA; or perhaps only the time and date of arrival will be prescribed. Where exact ETA and ETD are not given, the navigator must complete his study of the various charts and publications as outlined below before these times may be precisely determined.

Determining Chart Requirements

Once the destination and other information prescribed in the movement order, such as route, are known, the navigator must determine the charts available for use during the voyage. These are lo-

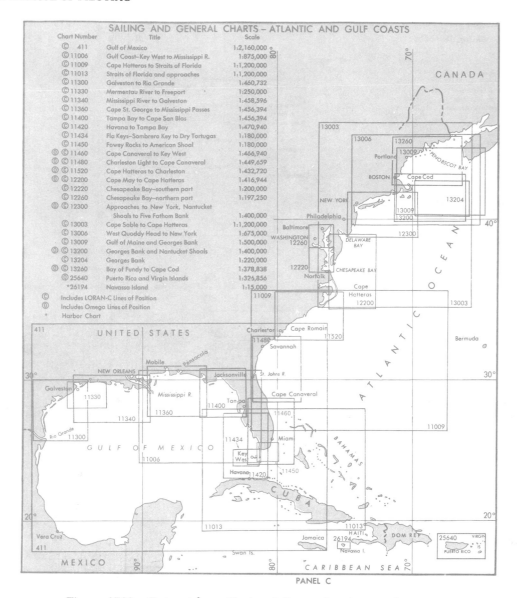

Figure 1703a. Extract from National Ocean Service Catalog No. 1.

cated by reference to the appropriate catalog of charts.

Most charts for United States waters are listed in the four catalogs of the National Ocean Service. Charts of foreign waters, bottom contour charts, and charts restricted to naval usage are listed in the various volumes of *DMA Catalog of Maps, Charts, and Related Products Part 2* (formerly Pub. No. 1-N). New editions of nautical chart catalogs are published when accumulated changes warrant such action; only the current edition of any catalog should be used. See also article 522.

Using the appropriate catalogs, the navigator examines the *index diagrams* covering the area of interest. Each such diagram shows by colored outlines the area covered by each chart, with its corre-

sponding number. With the chart numbers determined, he can consult a tabular listing for additional information such as chart name, scale, edition and date, and price.

From this information, the navigator compiles a list of the numbers of all available charts covering any part of the proposed route. These charts are then taken from the respective portfolios and are checked against the appropriate regional volume of the DMA catalog, which has been kept current by corrections from *Notices to Mariners*. As most naval vessels are on automatic distribution from DMAHTC, it is normal for the charts on board to be the latest edition.

If the latest edition is not on board, immediate steps should be taken to obtain it before departure.

Charts must be ordered by naval units using the quite complex procedures of the DMA Automated Distribution Management System (DADMS) as described in Volume X of the DMA catalog (formerly Pub. No. 1-N-A), which also lists the distribution points serving various geographical areas. Charts of the National Ocean Service may be obtained through DADMS except for a few charts that must be obtained directly from NOS sources. Civilian users will normally obtain DMAHTC charts from local sales agents, but can use the DADMS system with simplified procedures as set forth in Volume X; NOS charts should be purchased from local sales agents or directly from the NOS Distribution Division, Riverdale, MD 20737.

Determining Publication Requirements

The navigator should have available all pertinent *Light Lists, Lists of Lights, Coast Pilots, Sailing Directions*, and other navigational publications for the area to be traversed. On board naval ships, the current allowances established for the type of ship and the fleet to which it is assigned will normally be adequate.

Correction of Charts and Publications

After all necessary charts and publications have been assembled and checked to ensure that they are the latest edition, they must also be checked to verify that all pertinent corrections have been entered, or must be brought up to date if not already corrected.

Chart corrections. The Chart/Publication Correction Record card, DMAHTC Pub. No. 8660/9, for each chart to be used is consulted to determine those corrections that have been noted on the card, but which have not been entered on the chart. Each of these listed but unmade corrections must be completed before the chart can be used with safety. Charts may be corrected from either the on-board file of *Notices to Mariners* or a DMAHTC publication, *Summary of Corrections*, a consolidated reprint of all still-valid changes published in *Notices to Mariners*; see article 611. This semiannual *Summary* is more convenient to use for correcting charts than individual *Notices to Mariners*, but it does not contain chart corrections for the Great Lakes or inland bodies of water and routes that are not normally used by ocean-going vessels.

Corrections to publications. Each publication to be used must be checked to ensure that it has been fully corrected, or action must be taken to bring each volume up to date. The convenient *Summary of Corrections* can be used to correct *Coast Pilots*

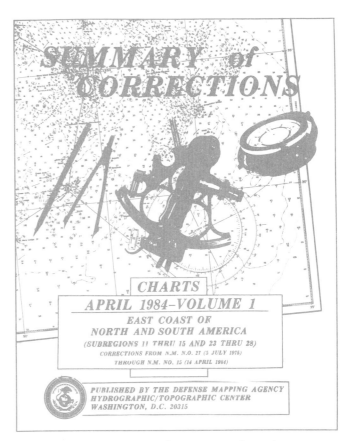

Figure 1703b. *Summary of Corrections* (cover).

and *Sailing Directions*, but the file of *Notices* must be used to update *Light Lists, Lists of Lights, Radio Aids to Navigation*, and other navigational publications. These publications are issued in annual editions (in a few cases, at somewhat longer intervals where the number of changes does not warrant annual editions). Between editions, changes are published in *Notices to Mariners*. In most instances, the change is published as an item that can be cut and pasted directly into the basic publication; few pen changes are required except for deletions. Each correction item published in *Notices to Mariners* carries information as to the last prior correction for that chart or publication published so that none will be inadvertently overlooked. Many publications contain a page where a record can be noted of the entry of each correction.

Prior to entering the destination port, the ship sends a LOGREQ (Logistics Request) message. Among the many items contained therein is the number of the last *Notice to Mariners* on board. The local command at the port will then advise the ship of any significant changes in aids to navigation, navigational hazards, etc. The ship may also listen for Broadcast Notices to Mariners from the local

U.S. Coast Guard Station or Base on 2670 kHz or VHF Channel 22A.

Consideration of Tides and Currents

It is usually desirable to get underway or enter port at high-water stand, and as near as possible to the time of slack water, although they seldom coincide. A large ship entering a harbor with comparatively shallow water will be primarily concerned with the time of high water, while a smaller vessel entering a harbor with deep water but variable current will be more interested in times when the current is slack.

Occasionally the draft of the ship will be greater than the charted depth (low water) of a portion of the channel or harbor. This requires the use of Table 3 in the *Tide Tables* to determine how long before and after high water the depth of the water will be sufficient to permit safe passage of the ship. Extreme care must be used in such cases, as the tide tables are only predictions, and there can be a significant difference between the predicted and the actual conditions.

Harbor Considerations

Many ports with large naval concentrations place sortie plans in effect on certain days of the week, specifying times and order for ships to get underway. This plan is normally arranged so that ships nearer the harbor entrance get underway first. The SOPA (Senior Officer Present Afloat) instructions should be consulted for such standing procedures.

Merchant vessels, particularly those with hazardous cargo, may be subject to restrictions and procedures established by the Coast Guard Captain of the Port (COTP).

Determining Distance and SOA

Since the navigator normally recommends the times of departure and arrival and the SOA to the commanding officer, it is essential that he first determine the total distance to be steamed. This distance may be obtained by measurement from the charts to be used, or, in many cases, by reference to available publications. DMAHTC Pub. No. 151, *Table of Distances Between Ports*, covering foreign ports throughout the world, or *Distance Between U.S. Ports*, published by the National Ocean Service, should be consulted. Distances between many other combinations of ports will also be found in the pertinent *Coast Pilots* and *Sailing Directions*. If it is intended to travel the regular route between ports, the distance given in these publications should be used, as it is more accurate than can normally be determined by chart measurement.

Once favorable hours of departure and arrival have been decided upon, the required speed of advance (SOA) can be determined. Care must be taken not to exceed the maximum steaming speeds prescribed by fleet or type commanders in current directives. After the SOA has been completed, the speed to be ordered can be determined, taking into account the ship's displacement, condition of bottom, and trim; currents expected to be encountered; and other applicable factors.

Planning the Passage

1704 After completing the preliminary preparations described above, the navigator is now ready to plan the voyage. Only by commencing the planning phase as far in advance as possible will a navigator have sufficient time to study the various publications, to give the proposed track careful consideration, and to obtain any needed charts and/or publications not presently on board.

Small-scale Charts

Many areas, such as the east coast of the United States, have charts available to four different scales. The overall plot referred to in the paragraph above will fit onto either one of the "sailing chart" series, such as Chart 13003, Cape Sable to Cape Hatteras at a scale of 1:1,200,000, or if not too great an area is required, one of the "general chart" series, such as Chart 12200, Cape May to Cape Hatteras at a scale of 1:416,944. Only occasionally will it be necessary to use a chart from both of these series.

Most captains and navigators prefer an overall plot of the entire voyage on one chart. This permits rapid determination of distance made good and distance to go at any desired time during the voyage, and presents clearly the relationship between the route selected and the coastline or adjacent land masses. For this reason, a small-scale (large-area) chart is initially used. Unless the voyage is very short, however, it is not possible to plot the entire track on one chart that is also suitable for piloting. In making this selection, two conflicting factors must be considered and balanced against each other. It is desirable to use a large-scale chart for the greater degree of detail provided. However, the use of the largest scale chart available may often require one or more changes of charts during a run through restricted waters; this is time consuming and could lead to errors at the time of shifting from one chart to the next. Use of a large-scale, small-area chart may also limit the navigator's concept of the "big picture," the area as a whole. It is the practice of some navigators to use the smallest scale chart that contains all essential aids to navigation.

It is quite helpful if any water area that is too shallow for safe navigation has been shaded on the chart in advance. This will permit the navigator to determine at a glance if his vessel is standing into danger.

It is important that all charts used be fully corrected according to the most recently received *Notices to Mariners* and radio broadcast navigational warning messages.

Large-scale Charts

For piloting during coastwise passages, the most commonly used chart is one from the "coast chart" series at a scale of 1:80,000. More detailed charts, at scales of 1:50,000 and larger, are desirable for harbor piloting, but are not useful for offshore waters or approaches.

In selecting a chart to be used for a voyage in pilot waters, consideration should be given to the scale used, ascertaining that it includes all of the landmarks and aids to navigation desired or required in any one area. If the scale is too small, the chart coverage may exclude features best suited for visual observation and fixes.

Once the charts to be used are selected, the navigator should ensure that he is familiar with the details shown on each. The following should be particularly noted:

Whether depths are indicated in feet or fathoms.

Whether heights are indicated in feet or meters.

The distance indicated by the smallest division of the latitude scale.

The distance indicated by the alternately shaded divisions of the latitude scale.

The distance between adjacent printed meridians and parallels.

The significance of the length of the ship and its handling characteristics in relation to the scale of the chart.

The geographical limits covered by each chart.

Variation of the magnetic compass, correction to variation since printing of the chart due to annual change, and the differences in variation at different points along the track.

The patterns of shoal and deep water, and depths, as indicated by the fathom lines; the depth at which water areas change from white to blue.

Abnormal patterns of bottom contour lines that may be useful for determining positions by echo sounder.

Land contours, marshes, bluffs, prominent mountain peaks, and landmarks that may be useful for radar piloting or identification, or which may affect radar PPI interpretation.

Intended Track

Having selected his charts, the navigator now plots the route to be followed on both the large- and the small-scale charts. The route is normally plotted first on the small-scale (large-area) chart or charts, and labeled as to track, speed, and distance between points. This permits the navigator to check visually the safety of the track as initially laid down, and to make any adjustments needed at this time.

DR positions for selected times are then plotted along the track, using the speed previously determined. The frequency with which these DR positions are plotted on the large-area chart will depend upon the judgment of the navigator, the proximity of land masses, and the desired course. When making an ocean passage, DR positions every twelve hours are normally sufficient; in coastal piloting, a DR position every hour is common practice.

At this time, any special information of interest in the broad planning of the voyage should be noted on the chart. These items may include limits of special danger, restricted areas, and for naval ships, limits of operational control areas and changes in communications responsibility. This information should be noted on the chart in the vicinity of the position at which the event is expected to occur.

The navigator should next translate the general information portrayed on the small-scale chart into detailed graphic representations on the large-scale charts covering the same areas. At this time, careful reference should be made to the instructions and information given in the *Coast Pilots* and *Sailing Directions* for the areas of each chart. If specific routes are recommended or overprinted on the charts, these should be used to the greatest extent possible, for they represent known safe tracks that have been tested over many years. In deciding on details of the final track, a careful navigator will not only avoid all obvious dangers, but will also allow himself as much sea room as possible in the areas of these dangers.

Critical points, points at which the course or speed must be changed, are of particular interest to navigators and should always be marked on the chart. In operational movements of ships in company, it is frequently desirable to assign a name or number designation to these points for ease of reference. The ETA at each critical point should be plainly marked on the charts.

Hazardous Areas, Danger Bearings, and Limits of Safe Water

Frequently the intended track may of necessity place the ship in close proximity to dangers to navigation during the voyage. In addition to such natural dangers as rocks, shoals, and bars, various governmental agencies have reserved certain designated areas for hazardous operations. Gunnery practice and testing ranges, ammunition disposal areas, special anchorages, and spoil grounds are a few examples. Where particularly confined waters or heavy shipping concentrations prevail, special rules may be in effect to limit maximum speed and otherwise restrict vessel movement. At the entrance to many ports, there have been established Vessel Traffic Services (VTS) or Traffic Separation Schemes (TSS) consisting of inbound and outbound lanes with a separation zone between them, special precautionary zones, and special communications arrangements. Each of these special areas, whether natural or man-made, constitutes an additional hazard for the mariner. Each chart should be carefully inspected to determine these dangers, and the *Coast Pilot, Sailing Directions*, and *Notices to Mariners* consulted for detailed information concerning them; appropriate annotations should then be made on each chart in question. In addition, it is a good practice to outline all danger areas and the limits of water considered safe for the draft of the ship, using a colored pencil. Do not use a red pencil if the chart will be used under a red light on the bridge at night, as the red marking will not be visible. For this reason, "nautical purple" (magenta) is frequently used instead.

Where appropriate, danger bearings should be located, plotted, and the information noted on the chart.

Aids to Navigation

Special attention should be given to the aids to navigation expected to be sighted during the voyage. A list recording a complete description of the structures and their light characteristics, the expected times of sighting, and the approximate bearings at sighting is of particular use to the navigator. A notation should be made on the chart for any ATON that is reported in *Notices to Mariners* as missing, defective, or temporarily replaced with an aid of another type.

Buoys

While the color and shape of buoys that are a part of the lateral system used in United States waters are evident from the printed chart information, it is not always possible to predict the characteristics of a special-purpose buoy by chart inspection alone. In like manner it is not possible to apply the rules pertaining to United States buoyage to the various buoyage systems in use in foreign countries; in such cases, careful reference to the *Lists of Lights* and *Sailing Directions* is necessary to avoid misinterpretation.

Lights and Lighted Buoys

Daytime identification. Under normal conditions of visibility, a primary seacoast light (a "lighthouse") can be seen in the daytime when within range and can be identified by its color and structural appearance. A complete description of the distinctive features of each is given in the appropriate *Light List* or *List of Lights*, and since this information seldom appears on the chart, notation should be made thereon. Photographs or drawings of many lights appear in the *Coast Pilots* and *Sailing Directions*, while many foreign charts include a sketch of the light near its symbol.

Nighttime identification. Harbor entrances, bays and rivers, coastal danger areas, and other hazards are normally well marked with lighted aids to navigation that the navigator should personally and positively identify on each initial sighting. Identification can be confirmed by using a stopwatch to time a light through a full cycle of its characteristics. Accurate identification of buoys is particularly important and should not be a matter of delegation, chance, or guesswork. The full characteristics of lighted buoys may not be printed on a chart, particularly small-scale charts, and even when using large-scale charts, information such as the length of each flash and eclipse of major aids does not normally appear. Only by use of the *Light List*, comparing the recorded information with those characteristics actually observed, can the navigator be absolutely certain of the identification of a lighted aid to navigation. Supplementary information appearing *only* in the *Light List* should be added to the chart in a box adjacent to the symbol.

Visibility of lights. While preparing for the voyage, the computed visibility of all lights expected to be sighted en route is plotted and labeled on the charts. In United States waters, the *nominal range* is the extreme distance in nautical miles at which a light may be seen in clear weather (as defined in the International Visibility Code) without regard to the elevation of the light, observer's height of eye, or the curvature of the earth; see article 424. In computing the geographic range at which the light might be sighted in clear weather, the navigator must allow for the elevation of the light and the height of his, and/or the lookout's eye; see article 425.

Tide and Tidal Current Data

Times and heights of the tides, and time and strengths of the currents, for the points of departure and arrival are computed for the respective dates. This information should be carefully studied before reaching a decision as to the time of departure and arrival. Some ports may have shoals or bars that can be crossed only near the time of high water, while others may have bridges of such vertical clearance that high-masted ships may be required to transit the channel at low water. Ships arriving at or leaving their berths will be assisted by a favorable current, while an unfavorable current may make the maneuver very difficult, especially for a single-screw ship.

When the decision as to the times of arrival and departure has been made, the navigator should consult the applicable National Ocean Service *Tidal Current Chart*, if available, for the ports or channels in question to determine the strength and direction of the current at selected reference points along the track noted on the chart. If none is published for the waters concerned, the *Tidal Current Tables* must be used and some calculations will probably be needed as described in chapter 10. The *Current Diagrams* contained in the *Tidal Current Tables*, if applicable, should be consulted to determine the average current expected en route. This information, combined with the chosen speed of advance, can be used to determine the speed to be ordered at selected stages of the voyage. Occasionally these diagrams are used to plan the time of departure in order that advantage may be taken of a favorable channel current.

For ocean passages, the estimates of predicted currents shown on the *Pilot Chart* for the month(s) concerned or in *Pilot Chart Atlases* should also be taken into consideration. These estimates have evolved after years of observation, and they warrant careful attention by navigators.

Port Information

Information concerning the anchorage or berthing space assigned to the ship may not be received until the ship has reported its ETA to the port authority. If the destination is a port frequently used by naval vessels, an anchorage chart is usually available showing the exact location of all berths, the radius of each, and the range and bearing of its center from a prominent landmark or aid to navigation. Additional information concerning the port such as pier space, tugs, pilots, communications, harbor facilities, and other pertinent items of interest is contained in the appropriate *Coast Pilot* (U.S. waters), or *Sailing Directions* (foreign waters), and *Fleet Guide* (for U.S. naval vessels only) which should be carefully read prior to arrival. In addition, the file of *NavArea Warnings*, *Hydrolant* or *Hydropac* messages, and *Local Notices to Mariners* (U.S. waters only) issued by the Coast Guard District concerned, should be checked to see if any recent changes in aids to navigation have been made, or if any special warnings about dangers to navigation have been issued for the area of interest.

Upon arrival, the latest copies of the *Daily Memorandum* and any other pertinent information available should be obtained from the DMAHTC Branch Office if there is one at that port.

Every week, the office of the Port Director distributes a list of the exercises to be conducted in the designated operating and training area. This list should be carefully checked to make sure that the ship, upon departure, does not interfere with any scheduled exercises.

Preparing to Get Underway

1705 The preceding articles have dealt with the preparations made in the planning stages by the navigator in advance of the day prescribed for getting underway. It is assumed that the navigator has conferred with the captain and that the latter has approved of the details of the plan proposed by the navigator, or that any changes directed by him have been incorporated into the final plan. There remain, however, certain other preparatory steps to be taken that have properly been postponed until the overall plan has been decided upon; the systematic accomplishment of these is no less important to the execution of a safe passage than was careful voyage planning.

Gyrocompass

A typical ship's organization book prescribes that the gyrocompass be started at least four hours before getting underway in order that the gyro may settle on the meridian. Many experienced navigators prefer to start the gyrocompass well in advance of this minimum. This provides them with sufficient time to detect and correct any minor mechanical or electrical malfunctioning before getting underway.

Degaussing Equipment

On a naval vessel, the proper settings for the degaussing equipment should be determined before getting underway by referring to the special charts prepared for that purpose, and the engineering department informed of the coil readings to be preset before departure. This equipment is always used in wartime and at any other time when it is known that influence mines may be encountered in a specified area. At the direction of the navigator, the degaussing equipment is energized before leaving protected waters, and periodic adjustments are made thereafter to the coil settings to maintain maximum protection.

Piloting Team

Prior to leaving or entering port, the navigator should assemble his piloting team for a briefing (see article 1510). While the bearing takers, bearing recorder, and radar operators will be most vitally concerned with the briefing, all other members of the piloting team and all members of the navigation department should also attend. During the briefing the navigator should point out all aids to navigation expected to be used, their name, appearance, and about where and when they will be sighted. All natural and man-made ranges are located in order that a check on the gyrocompass may be made whenever one is crossed. Any special information concerning soundings should be given to the echo-sounder operator at this time. This is also an excellent opportunity to brief the CIC officer on the plans for entering or leaving port.

It is advantageous that key members of the team be given the material covered in the briefing in written form in order that the detailed plan, the characteristics, and appearances of lights and other important features to be encountered will not be trusted entirely to memory.

Equipment Checks

The organization book of a ship, as well as the navigator's sea detail bill, prescribe certain readiness tests of various items of ship's equipment in accordance with a pre-underway time schedule. Again, forehanded testing will permit time to repair any casualties uncovered during this phase. The master gyro is first checked for error, after which the gyro repeaters on the bridge are checked against the master gyro. The steering engine and related electric and hydraulic transmission systems are tested as are the engine order telegraph,

the depth finder, the bridge radio, navigation and signal searchlights, and the navigational lighting circuits; appropriate check-off notations are made in the list maintained to record such test results. After the special sea detail has been set and all stations are manned, this equipment should be rechecked and all remaining items on the check-off list attended to, such as external and internal communication circuits, the bridge PPI, and the whistle and siren. In addition, the navigator should personally ascertain that all necessary charts, publications, and plotting instruments are available at his chart desk and ready for use.

Gyro Error

With the piloting team on station, a round of bearings is taken and plotted on the chart, or a gyro observation of a range is obtained and the amount and direction of gyro error, if any is present, is determined. When known, CIC should be notified of the results and an appropriate entry made in the bearing book. When the gyro error steadies down and remains constant, the navigator may offset the parallel motion dial of his drafting machine used for plotting by the amount of this error. This procedure permits plotting the reported bearings as they are received from the bearing takers without the necessity of applying gyro error before plotting each line of position.

Final Preparations

The navigator should personally check to see that his piloting team is on station and in all respects ready to function. A well-organized and efficient team requires a minimum of supervision, but the navigator should ensure that the more experienced bearing taker is on that side of the ship that will pass the larger number of aids to navigation, or who will have to take two bearings for each fix. Any final instructions pertaining to frequency of fixes, depth readings, draft, minor changes in plan, or bearing order should be announced at this time. A report of the vessel's draft should be made to the conning officer and the officer of the deck and entered in the log. To conclude all of the multitudinous preparations made by the navigator since the receipt of the original movement order, the navigator reports his department "ready for sea" to the executive officer, signifying that every phase of navigational planning and final checking under his cognizance has been accomplished to the best of his knowledge and ability.

So far, the navigator has been primarily concerned with the science of navigation, extracting information from a number of publications that will be of great value to him once the ship is underway. The manner in which the navigator employs the art of navigation—the practical use of the information made available to him from whatever source—will be the subject of the remainder of the chapter.

A TYPICAL PASSAGE

The Situation and Required Movement

1706 The USS *Nonesuch*, moored starboard side to Pier 4, U.S. Naval Shipyard, Philadelphia, Pennsylvania, has completed its overhaul and is preparing to make a coastal passage to Norfolk, Virginia, in accordance with the published Fleet Quarterly Employment Schedule. This schedule requires the ship to be at Pier 4, Norfolk, prior to 1200Q on 9 August, and the ship has been granted authority for an 0800Q arrival.

Preliminary Planning

1707 The navigator notes that a latest time of arrival has been specified and that the normal maximum speed of advance of 15 knots is applicable. Estimating that the trip will take about 16 hours, the ship should depart Philadelphia during the afternoon of 8 August in order to arrive on schedule. This is the navigator's initial estimate of the time of departure, which will be corrected after the exact length of the trip and current data have been determined.

Since both Philadelphia and Norfolk are deep-water ports, there are no restrictions placed on the times of departure or arrival by the state of the tide. As the time of arrival at Norfolk is specified, only the time of departure can be varied to allow for conditions en route. On consulting the captain, the navigator learned that he desired to take departure from Delaware Lighted Horn Buoy "D" (at the outer end of the Delaware to Cape Henlopen Traffic Lane) for Lighted Whistle Buoy "2JS" and hence to proceed directly to North Chesapeake Entrance Lighted Whistle Buoy "NCA" (at the start of an inbound traffic lane). The passage is planned accordingly.

Calculating the Departure Time

By reference to the table in *Coast Pilot 3* entitled "Atlantic Ocean Distances for Deep-Draft Vessels—Montreal, Canada, to Panama Canal Zone," the distance from Philadelphia to Norfolk was found to be 269 miles. As the speed of advance was specified as 15 knots, the navigator decided to allow about 19 hours for the trip. This is more than the time computed using distance and SOA, but makes allow-

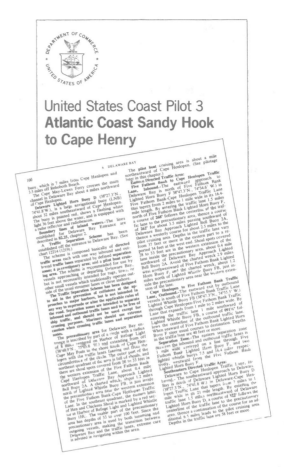

Figure 1707. U.S. *Coast Pilot 3* (cover and typical page).

ance for time expected to be lost in the transit of the Delaware River due to speed regulations and heavy traffic.

The time of departure from Philadelphia is now determined by subtracting 19 hours from the ETA, 0800, on 9 August.

Time of arrival		
Norfolk	9 August	0800 (Plus 4)
Length of trip		19 hours
Time of departure		
Phila.	8 August	1300 (Plus 4)

Both Philadelphia and Norfolk are keeping Daylight Saving Time (+4 or Q). If Norfolk were keeping Standard Time (+5), departure from Philadelphia could have been delayed by one hour. In such planning the navigator must always allow for any difference between the time kept at the port of departure and at the port of arrival.

Review of the Coast Pilot

The section of *Coast Pilot 3* covering Delaware Bay and River below the starting point was carefully studied to obtain all pertinent information relating to the waters to be used. The navigator made particular note of the following:

Channels: Federal project depth is 40 feet from the sea through the main channel in Delaware Bay and River to the Philadelphia Naval Shipyard.

Tides: The mean range of the tide varies from 4.1 feet at the entrance to Delaware Bay to 5.9 feet at Philadelphia.

Currents: At the Delaware Bay entrance the maximum currents are 1.8 knots flooding and 1.9 knots ebbing. Strengths upbay and upriver vary, reaching a maximum of 2.4 knots; predictions for many points are given in the *Tidal Current Tables*, together with a *Current Diagram* that will greatly aid in visualizing the changing effects of tidal current as the ship proceeds down Delaware River and Bay.

Speed: The Corps of Engineers has requested that vessels' speeds be limited when passing wharves and piers so as to avoid damage by suction or wave wash to property or persons; no specific maximum speed was prescribed.

Obstructions: At Mile 71, the Commodore John Barry Bridge has a clearance of 181 feet for a width of 1,600 feet over the main channel with 190 feet at the center. At Mile 60, the Delaware Memorial Bridge has twin spans with a clearance of 188 feet for the middle 800 feet.

Fogs: Most frequent along this part of the Atlantic coast during months of December, January, and February, but may be encountered at any time of the year.

Rules of the Road: Inland Navigational Rules shall be followed inside of a line from Cape May Light to Harbor of Refuge Light; thence to the northernmost extremity of Cape Henlopen.

Traffic Separation Scheme: A TSS has been established off the entrance to Delaware Bay. The ship will be using the Southeastern Directed Traffic Area, Delaware to Cape Henlopen Traffic Lane, outbound. This lane is described in detail, together with the Separation Zone between it and the corresponding inbound lane. There is a Precautionary Area inscribed in part by a circle with a radius of 8 miles centered on the Harbor of Refuge Light and extending from off Cape May Point to the shore south of Cape Henlopen; traffic lanes start at the circumference of this circle.

Local magnetic disturbance: Differences of as much as 2° to 5° from normal variation have been observed along the main channel from Artificial Island, Mile 44, to Marcus Hook, Mile 69.

A wealth of other information is available in this section of the *Coast Pilot*, but only that of direct concern in plotting the track down the bay has been noted above. In a similar manner, applicable portions of *Coast Pilot 3* were studied regarding the coastal passage and the entrance into Hampton Roads.

Chart Preparation

1708 To obtain the numbers of the charts to be used, the navigator consulted *DMA Catalog, Part 2, Volume I.* (As this voyage will be entirely in U.S. waters, he might alternatively have consulted *NOS Chart Catalog 1.*) These are shown as outlines on large-area diagrams. Figure 1708 shows the applicable portion from the NOS catalog for the passage from Philadelphia to Norfolk. Chart 12200 covers the offshore run at a scale of 1:416,944. Larger scale, more detailed charts that will be used for the passage are:

12313	12214	12222
12312	12211	12254
12311	12210	12256
12304	12221	12245

Since all charts required were in Portfolio 12, it was a simple matter to obtain them from chart stowage. Comparing each chart with the edition data shown in Volume I of the DMA catalog as kept corrected from *Notices to Mariners*, the navigator determined that all the charts he intended to use were in fact the latest edition.

Next, the Chart/Publication Correction Record card, DMAHTC Pub. No. 8660/9, for each chart to be used was removed from the file and checked to determine which *Notices to Mariners* contained changes that must be applied to the charts. The latest issue of *Summary of Corrections, Volume I*, together with any applicable individual *Notices to Mariners* since the date of the *Summary*, were consulted and the charts were brought up to date. Files of *Local Notices to Mariners* for the 3rd and 5th Coast Guard Districts were consulted, as the information in these publications may be fresher than in the weekly *Notices to Mariners*.

Plotting the Track

1709 With all charts up-to-date, the navigator was ready to plot his intended track, using as a guide information contained in *Coast Pilot 3*, the applicable *Fleet Guides*, and *Light List, Volume I*. These publications, before being used, were each checked to ensure that all changes had been entered.

Figure 1708. Portion of NOS Chart Catalog No. 1.

Figure 1709a. Intended track and notations shown on Chart 12313.

Using a time of departure of 1300, and a speed of 10 knots until abeam of New Castle, the ETA at every turn point was calculated and labeled on the intended track. The navigator made a mental note that adjustments might have to be made to these ETAs as the passage was made down the river; a precise estimate cannot be made of the effect on speed made good by the necessity to slow to perhaps 6 knots from time to time when passing piers and wharves. After passing New Castle, a speed of 15 knots was assumed to determine the ETA at the remainder of the turning points. The effect of the river's current will be compensated for by appropriate adjustments in the ordered shaft revolutions. (It will be seen later in article 1710 that the current was predicted to be as much as 1.8 knots, initially fair for the first 5 miles, but then turning foul.)

After plotting the track on all charts, the navigator computed the amount of advance and transfer for every turn, plotted the point at which the turn should commence, and located a landmark as near the beam as possible for use as a turning bearing. The turning point, turning bearing, and ETA were all noted on the chart. Two of these notations are illustrated in figure 1709a.

Continuing this procedure, all notations concerning tracks, ranges, turning points, turning bearings, areas requiring a speed reduction, and the ETA at the various points were made on the remaining charts to be used.

Ranges

As the navigator plotted the recommended track on the chart, he observed that the Delaware River Main Channel was exceptionally well marked with buoys and that every leg of the channel was marked by both day and night ranges. A notation was made on the chart of the bearing of each of the 12 ranges, observation of which would permit a continuous check of the gyrocompass while in the confined waters of the river.

After passing the Cohansey River, Chart 12304 must then be used to plot the track until abeam of Cape Henlopen. The navigator was alert to the fact that with this chart the scale would change from 1:40,000 to 1:80,000. (A previous scale change would occur from 12313 to 12312, from 1:15,000 to 1:40,000.) Subsequently, the track was plotted on NOS charts 12214, 12211, 12210, and 12221; the track for these charts was derived from the overall offshore track on chart 12200. Departure was to be taken from Delaware Lighted Horn Buoy "D" at the end of the Traffic Separation Scheme for Jack Spot Lighted Whistle Buoy "2JS," then to the start of North Chesapeake Bay Entrance Traffic Lanes.

NOS charts 12222, 12254, and 12245 were prepared for entry into Hampton Roads in the same

Figure 1709b. Arcs of visibility.

manner as the initial charts for departure from Philadelphia.

While proceeding down the Delaware River for the first 40 miles, every channel axis is marked by ranges providing a ready means of observing the ship's position in relation to the center of the channel. After leaving the Liston Range, no more ranges are available and the navigator must employ other means to keep the ship in safe water.

Danger Bearings

Besides taking frequent fixes, the navigator had previously decided that danger bearings would be very useful. An examination of the chart showed that the red sectors of the principal lights coincided with danger bearings. The limits of these sectors were outlined in magenta and the exact bearing obtained from the *Light List*. The information concerning the sectors, danger bearings, and the description of each light structure was placed in a box adjacent to the light symbol on the chart.

Lights

A list of all lights that would be seen from sunset until sunrise was then prepared, giving information as to the name and number of the light, light characteristics, length of flash and eclipse, and its sound signal, if any. The computed visibility of all lights that would be sighted after sunset was determined for this ship, using a height of eye of 36 feet (11 m), and the arcs of visibility plotted on the chart as in figure 1709b. From the intersection of the track with the arc of visibility, the predicted bearing and time of sighting was computed and added to the summary, an extract of which follows:

Time of Sighting	Bearing	Name of Aid	Characteristic	Fog Signal
1959	132°	BW Buoy "DA"	Fl.W., 4 sec. vis. 7 mi.	Whistle Radar reflector
2014	139°	Delaware Lighted Horn Buoy "D"	Fl.W., 5 sec. vis. 10 mi.	Horn, 1 bl ev 15 sec, (2 sec bl). Rbn 319 kHz, (D), Racon (D) Radar reflector
2231	281°	Red Buoy "2JS"	Fl.W., 4 sec. vis. 6 mi.	Whistle
0453	305°	BW Buoy "NCA"	Fl.W., 4 sec. vis. 7 mi.	Whistle Radar reflector

Arcs of visibility of the first two of these lights are shown in figure 1709b. Since sunset occurs at 2003, both of these lights will become visible almost immediately after sunset if the visibility is clear. In this figure, note the safety lanes established for vessels entering and departing Delaware Bay; the appropriate lanes must be used by all ships.

Tides and Currents

1710   The appropriate volumes of *Tide Tables* and *Tidal Current Tables*, as well as the *Tidal Current Charts*, were next inspected.

Tide summaries were prepared for Philadelphia and Norfolk as follows, all times (+4) (Q).

8 August
Philadelphia

Low water	0757	0.0 ft.
High water	1311	6.1
Low water	2007	0.2

9 August
Norfolk (Sewell's Point)

Low water	0329	−0.1 ft.
High water	0933	2.7
Low water	1538	−0.1

Tidal current summaries were prepared for Delaware Bay Entrance and Chesapeake Bay Entrance as follows, all times (+4).

8 August
Delaware Bay Entrance

Max. Flood	0617	1.6 kn.
Slack, Ebb begins	0919	
Max. Ebb	1221	1.7
Slack, Flood begins	1533	
Max. Flood	1830	1.8 kn.
Slack, Ebb begins	2146	

9 August
Chesapeake Bay Entrance

Max. Ebb	0323	1.5 kn.
Slack, Flood begins	0641	
Max. Flood	0910	0.9

From Table 2 of the *Tidal Current Tables*, the navigator found that the current at the Philadelphia Naval Shipyard would be negligible at the time of departure; a footnote to the table states that the "times of slack are indefinite," but it was noted that the time of departure was roughly midway between times of maximum currents, 1002 and 1606.

At Norfolk, the current was calculated to be at a maximum flood at 0735 at Sewell's Point; setting 195°, velocity 0.5 kn.

Using the publication *Tidal Current Charts— Delaware Bay and River*, the navigator determined the velocity and direction of the current at various points along the river for the estimated time of pas-

sage. Figure 1710a is a tidal current chart for a typical hour of the trip. These charts are related to the time of maximum or slack current at the entrance to the bay; the appropriate one must be used for each hour in the current cycle.

Using the Current Diagram

Reference was next made to the *Current Diagram for Delaware Bay and River*, which is included in the *Tidal Current Tables*. The starting point was estimated (the shipyard is at Mile 81), and the starting time, 1300, was found to be 2^h33^m "before flood begins at Delaware Bay Entrance." Consideration was then given to the speed to be run during the initial legs of the trip down the Delaware River, with attention being given to the fact that speed must be limited when passing wharves and piers. As an estimate, sufficiently accurate for use with the Current Diagram, speed would average 10 knots to New Castle and 15 knots thereafter. Appropriate speed lines were drawn on the Current Diagram (figure 1710b); these showed a fair current could be anticipated to about Mile 28, then a foul current for the remainder of the distance to the Delaware Bay Entrance. These conditions would be about as favorable as could be expected, inasmuch as it is not possible to "ride" a favorable current all the way when a vessel is outbound (as might be possible when inbound up the bay and river).

Completing the Planning

1711   The navigator then prepared his notebook, listing in chronological order every event of interest for the passage. Examples of typical entries are as follows:

Estimated Time	Event
1300	Underway.
1315	Set course 274°, speed 10.
1318	C/C to 233.5° on the Miflin Range.
1328	Reduce speed to 6 knots off Hog Island Billingsport.
1334	C/C to 250° on the Billingsport Range.
1341	C/C to 272° on the Tinicum Range.
	(Intervening entries omitted)
1723	R "32" Qk Fl Bell abeam. C/C to 156° (Cross Ledge Range)
1736	Cross Ledge Lt abeam. C/C to 145° (Miah Maull Range)
	(Intervening entries omitted)
1912	"5" Fl G Gong abeam. Special sea and anchor detail secured.
2003	Sunset.

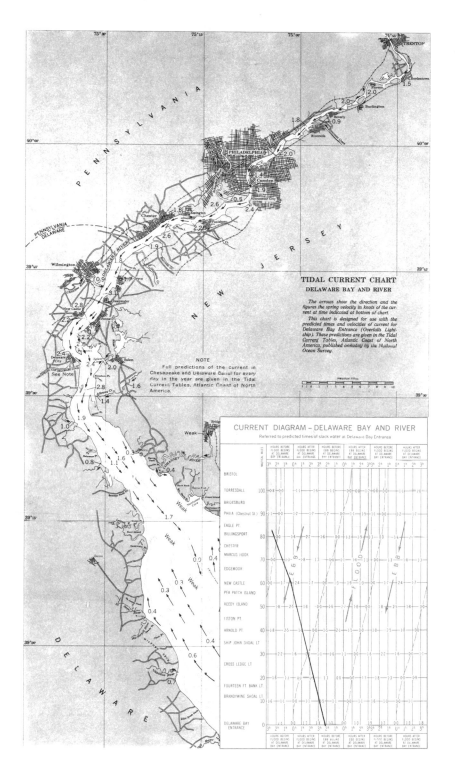

Figure 1710a. *Tidal Current Chart* for Delaware Bay and River for one particular hour of a tidal cycle (background). Figure 1710b. Current diagram for Delaware Bay and River (insert).

Based on the navigational planning as completed, a listing of all navigational events for the entire voyage is prepared, similar to that shown above. Such a listing is invaluable, especially when it is expected that the ship will be in pilot waters for an extended period of time, for it permits the assistant navigator or the officer of the deck to anticipate each item as the passage progresses, and permits the navigator greater freedom for supervision and observation.

Underway

1712 Prior to getting underway, all equipment checks mentioned in article 1704 were completed,

ETA	C/C to	Name	Distance	Bearing
2138	182°	Lighted Horn Buoy "D"	1.6 miles	044°
2314	218°	Buoy "2 JS"	0.5 mile	270°
		(intervening entries omitted)		
0243	—	Chesapeake Light	17 miles	195°
0520	251°	Lighted Whistle Buoy "NCA"	0.2 miles	140°

Figure 1712. Extracts from navigational data for preparation of night orders.

and all personnel concerned in the piloting team and the CIC piloting team were briefed and given last minute instructions. Gyro error was determined to be zero.

The ship got underway on time, and as the trip down the bay progressed, the assistant navigator plotted fixes on the chart every three minutes, while the navigator exercised supervision over the entire team, evaluated the information, and made recommendations to the commanding officer regarding changes of course and speed to carry out the voyage safely. Heavy river traffic slowed the ship so that by the time New Castle was reached, a speed of 8 rather than 10 knots had been made good. Since sufficient margin had been allowed in the planning phase, this caused no difficulties except for an adjustment to the schedule for arrival at subsequent significant points along the track. At 2138 departure was taken from Delaware Lighted Horn Buoy "D," and the SOA was adjusted to arrive at North Chesapeake Entrance Lighted Whistle Buoy at 0520 (+4) (Q).

Once the adjusted SOA for the next phase of the trip was known, the expected time of sighting each light was inserted in the summary prepared earlier, and one copy provided for the commanding officer, one for the officer of the deck, and one retained for the navigator's use. Using this same in-formation, the data for the Captain's Night Orders were prepared and sent to the commanding officer. See figure 1712. These data included the expected times of arrival at each turning point, with the new course and the bearing of aids to navigation used as markers for the course change, and any other pertinent data of interest to the safe navigation of the ship.

Entering Port at Norfolk

1713 At 0602 Cape Henry Light was passed abeam to port and the special sea detail had been set. Since Norfolk was the home port of the ship, no detailed briefing of the piloting team was necessary. Again, the assistant navigator did the actual plotting on the chart, while the navigator kept a continuous check on all the various phases of navigating the ship into port.

The piloting team was functioning smoothly, and the ship proceeded up the channel without incident. At 0703, speed was reduced after passing Fort Wool.

The tug and pilot met the ship as scheduled, and the first line was secured to the pier at 0744. The piloting team and all equipment except the gyro were secured after all lines were doubled-up. The navigator, knowing that the stay in Norfolk would be short, decided not to secure the gyro.

Chapter 18

Navigational Astronomy

Introduction

1801 Study of celestial navigation should properly start with a brief consideration of the basics of astronomy. A navigator need not be an astronomer, but a degree of knowledge of the stars and other celestial bodies—their size, distance, location, and movement—can aid in his understanding of the necessary calculations and diagrams.

Astronomy is one of the oldest—if not the oldest—of the sciences to which humans have devoted their attention; it is a fascinating subject, so broad that it can be studied for a lifetime. Undoubtedly, primitive men gazed at the sky in awe and wonderment; folklore and legends reflect their interest in the heavens and their crude explanations for the phenomena they saw. Progress in the science of astronomy is closely linked with the history of the human race. Each of the great civilizations of the ancient world recorded its findings in this field. The Egyptians, Babylonians, Chinese, Hindus, Mayas, and Aztecs all pursued the science of astronomy, which they associated with their religious beliefs. These studies were written down and have been well researched, and the science of astronomy has greatly advanced in recent years by scientists using the wonders of modern technology.

Here, however, consideration of this vast subject area must be limited to *navigational astronomy*—those aspects of astronomy of interest and value to a navigator in fixing his position and directing the course of his vessel.

The Universe

1802 The universe is generally considered to be infinite. Modern technology has made possible telescopes that have greatly increased man's ability to see farther into the vast reaches of space, and this capability continues to increase as telescopes are used on platforms in space. As a result, an immense number of galaxies have been discovered. Galaxies of stars are now observed at distances of approximately ten billion trillion (10^{22}) miles.

Units of Distance

Special units of measurement have been created for expressing such vast distances. In the measurement of distances within the solar system, the *astronomical unit* (AU) is used. To express distances to bodies outside the solar system, two terms are used, the *light-year*, and the *parsec*.

The value of the astronomical unit, the mean distance between the earth and the sun, is approximately 93 million statute miles, or 150 million kilometers. (In this chapter only, distances will be stated in statute miles, as used in texts on astronomy, rather than in nautical miles.)

A light-year is roughly 5.89 trillion miles (9.47 trillion or 9.47×10^{12} km); this is the distance that light travels in one year. The speed of light is approximately 186,282 miles (299,792.50 km) per second, and one year is equivalent to approximately 31.6 million seconds.

One parsec (from the words *parallax* and *second*) is the distance at which a body, viewed from the earth or sun, will differ in apparent position by one second of arc. This amounts to about 19.1 trillion miles (30.9×10^{13} km), or 3.24 light-years. Since this value is less than the distance from earth to Rigil Kentaurus, the navigational star nearest to our solar system at a distance of about 4.3 light-years, any star viewed from the sun and from the earth will differ in direction by less than one second of arc. This small angle is known as the

Figure 1802. Photograph of a spiral galaxy.

star's *heliocentric parallax* (not to be confused with *geocentric parallax*.)

Each galaxy is an assemblage of perhaps 100 billion stars, dust clouds, and masses of thin gas in rotation, held together by gravitational force in a lens-shaped formation. A typical galaxy may be some 100,000 light-years thick at the center, thinning to about 5,000 light-years near the rim. Most galaxies are spiral in shape (see figure 1802).

Magnitude

The brightness of a celestial body is expressed in terms of *magnitude*. The magnitude ratio is derived from Ptolemy's division of the visible stars into six groups according to brightness. The first group is considered to be 100 times brighter than the sixth group. Thus, the magnitude ratio is computed as the fifth root of 100 or 2.512, and a zero magnitude body is 2.512 times brighter than a first magnitude body, which is 2.512 times brighter than a second magnitude body, etc. Using this scale, the two brightest stars, Sirius and Canopus, have negative magnitudes of −1.6 and −0.9 respectively. Some are *variable stars* whose brightness varies slightly or considerably over regular or irregular intervals; for example, Betelgeuse varies in brightness by more than a factor of two over an irregular period.

The Milky Way

1803 Our own galaxy, the Milky Way, derives its name from the milky appearance of the night sky to the unaided eye as an observer looks along its major axis. This milky appearance is caused by the concentration of stars—uncounted and uncountable by the naked eye—in this area. The Milky Way is considered to be about average among galaxies in star population. The stars are not evenly distributed; they tend to be concentrated in two spiral arms extending outward from the center, with the whole galaxy in rotation. It is about 100,000 light-years in diameter, has a maximum thickness of some 10,000 light-years, and contains (perhaps!) 100 billion stars.

The stars of the Milky Way revolve around the center of the galaxy at speeds that decrease with increased distance from the center. At a distance of roughly 27,000 light-years from the center, the speed of revolution is approximately 140 miles per second (225 km/s). At this distance, near the inner edge of one of the spiral arms of the Milky Way and about halfway between the "top" and the "bottom" of the galaxy, there is a quite ordinary star, as stars go, but one of supreme importance to man—our *sun*.

The stars that make up the Milky Way galaxy vary greatly in size. The largest known star is Antares (Alpha Scorpii) with a diameter about 428 times that of our sun; the smallest, 48 light-years distant, was discovered only in recent years. Our sun, an average-sized star, is approximately 864,400 miles (1.39×10^6 km) in diameter.

Apart from the sun, the navigator is concerned only with stars within our galaxy—astronomically speaking, in our immediate neighborhood. The *Nautical Almanac* and the *Air Almanac* (chapter 23) tabulate data on a total of 173 stars suitable for use in celestial navigation. Only 58 of these are normally used; they are the 57 so-called "selected stars," plus Polaris, which is conveniently located for the determination of latitude in the Northern Hemisphere.

The stars are not the only celestial bodies employed in navigation. The *planets* of our solar system and the earth's *moon* (see article 1806) are also valuable to the navigator. Some of these bodies, with the sun, are suitable at times for daytime observations. However, the navigator's use of the bodies within the solar system differs from his use of the stars in two respects, both due to the vast difference in distance.

First, for navigation purposes, rays of light from any star may be considered to be parallel throughout the solar system. For example, Rigil Kentaurus, the nearest navigational star, is more than four light-years distant; the second nearest navigational star and the brightest in the sky, Sirius, is twice

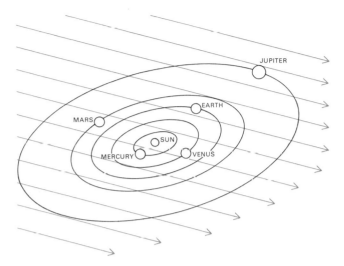

Figure 1803. Light rays from stars are essentially parallel all across the solar system.

that distance. Rigil Kentaurus, observed from opposite points on the earth's orbit around the sun (figure 1803), would differ in angle by approximately 1.5 seconds of arc. A navigator is not equipped to measure angles to this precision. Thus, in the observation of a star, *geocentric parallax*, that difference in apparent direction or position of a celestial body when observed from a point on the surface of the earth from the theoretical direction from the center of the earth (see figure 1806b), may be disregarded. For navigational purposes the stars can be considered as being at an infinite distance, while the sun, moon, and planets are at finite distances. The moon is only about $1\frac{1}{4}$ light seconds distant from the earth, and the sun is less than $8\frac{1}{2}$ light minutes away; these relatively close distances necessitate a correction for parallax.

Secondly, stars may be considered, for navigational purposes, as point sources of light with no measurable diameter when viewed through a sextant telescope. The sun, at an average distance from the earth of only 93,000,000 miles (1.5×10^8 km), and considered to be equivalent in mass to an average star, appears to us as a sphere.

Semidiameter

As a result of the nearness of the sun and the moon, a correction is necessary for *semidiameter*—which adjusts for the difference between an observation on the upper or lower edge, called *limb*, of the body and a true measurement to the center of the body. The semidiameter of planets, limited to not more than about 32 *seconds* of arc, is seldom considered in marine navigation.

The Sun

1804 The "star" at the center of our solar system, a rotating mass of very hot gases radiating energy at a fantastic rate, is called the *sun*. Every second it converts millions of tons of matter into energy, and it has been doing this for some five billion years. Its surface, at a temperature of about 10,000 degrees Fahrenheit, is in a constant state of agitation, emitting eruptions of burning gas to distances sometimes as much as hundreds of thousands of miles before they fall back to the surface.

A solar phenomenon of great interest is the *sun spot*, which appears dark on the surface of the sun. Sun spots are masses of comparatively cooler gas, sometimes 50,000 miles (80,000 km) in diameter.

Magnetic storms of the earth, which interfere with the propagation and reception of radio signals, such as those in radionavigation systems, are related to sun spots, which in recent times have occurred in eleven-year cycles.

The sun rotates about its axis, but because of its gaseous composition, the rotation is faster near the equator (25 days) than near the poles (34 days).

The Solar System

1805 The *solar system* consists of nine known major planets and thousands of planetoids or asteroids, traveling in elliptical orbits about the sun. Of these major planets, only Venus, Mars, Jupiter, and Saturn are normally used in navigation; they are often referred to as the *navigational planets* for this reason. Mean distances of the planets from the sun range from 67 million miles (1.08×10^8 km) for Venus, to 886 million miles (1.43×10^9 km) for Saturn; the periods required by each to complete a

Figure 1804. The surface of the sun. (Dot indicates the comparative size of the earth.)

revolution around the sun vary from about 225 days for Venus, to 29½ years for Saturn.

Pluto is about 5½ light-hours, or approximately 3,670 million miles (5.90×10^9 km) from the sun and requires more than 248 years to complete a revolution. Although it is generally referred to as "the most remote planet," its orbit is not circular and crosses Neptune's orbit; from 1979 to 1999 Neptune is farther from the sun than is Pluto.

Motions in the Solar System

All celestial bodies in our solar system *rotate* on their *axes* and *revolve* in their *orbits*. The solar system as a whole travels with the sun as it moves through space.

Planets, including the earth, rotate from west to east, except for Venus, which has an opposite rotation; the rotation axis of Uranus is very nearly in its orbit plane, being inclined at an angle of more than 82° (compared with the earth's inclination of roughly 23½°). All planets revolve in ellipses of quite slight eccentricities, one of the two focuses of which is the common center of mass of the sun and the body concerned. For any moon, the focus is the common center of mass of that satellite and its parent body.

In many instances, a smaller mass, called the *body*, orbits around a larger mass, called the *primary;* their relative motions are quite complex. The speed of a celestial body in its orbit varies in such a way that a line joining it with its primary sweeps over *equal areas* in equal times. Figure 1805a illustrates the orbit of a celestial body around its primary (somewhat exaggerated for emphasis). It could represent the orbit of a planet about the sun, or a satellite (moon) around a planet. Whatever the "system" of body and primary, the shaded sections of figure 1805a are equal in area, and in order for this to be so, the line joining the body and its pri-

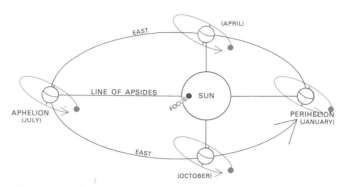

Figure 1805b. The body and its primary travel elliptical paths about a common focus.

mary must sweep faster as the body approaches the primary. Thus, the speed of a celestial body is greater when it is nearer the primary, and least when it is farthest from it.

Actually, the primary for any celestial body is itself affected by that body in such a way that the primary revolves in a small ellipse which is a miniature counterpart of the orbit of the body. This is illustrated, in a general way, by figure 1805b. In the earth-sun system, this focus is within the sun and very near its center. For the earth-moon pair, the focus is within the earth at about three-fourths radius from the center of the earth toward the moon. The orbit of the earth in relation to that of the moon is of particular significance in relation to the basic causes of tides (article 903).

The eccentricity of the earth's orbit about the sun is not great, but it is enough to result in a substantial change in the latter's apparent diameter. At *perihelion*, the point of nearest approach that follows the winter solstice (article 1815) by 10 to 12 days, the apparent diameter of the sun is approximately 32.6 minutes of arc. At *aphelion*, the point of greatest separation, which follows the summer solstice by about the same time interval, the apparent diameter is about 31.5 minutes. *Perihelion* and *aphelion* are illustrated in figure 1805b.

The Moon

1806 The earth's only natural satellite, the moon, is at an average distance of about 239,000 miles (385,000 km) from the earth. Its orbit is, of course, elliptical; a moderate degree of eccentricity results in a distance of approximately 221,000 miles (356,000 km) at *perigee*, and 253,000 miles (407,000 km) at *apogee*. As with the sun, this change in distance causes a variation in apparent diameter of the moon, as viewed from the earth, between 29.4 and 33.4 minutes of arc. The diameter of the

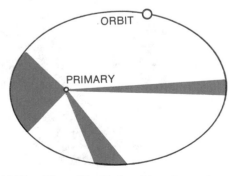

Figure 1805a. The elliptical orbit of a celestial body around its "primary" (exaggerated for emphasis).

moon is roughly 2,160 miles (3,480 km). Its period of revolution about the earth and its axial rotation are the same, $27\frac{1}{2}$ days, thus it always presents essentially the same face to the earth.

The moon illustrates why the navigator, in measuring altitudes, cannot use the nearest bodies in the solar system exactly as he does the stars. The altitude of the upper or lower limb of the body, as measured with the sextant, must be corrected to read as though made to the center of the body (a direct measurement not feasible by sextant). The moon's visible diameter changes in value as it moves in orbit from perigee to apogee. The *semidiameter*, illustrated in figure 1806a, must be applied as a correction to the sextant altitude.

The altitude observed by a navigator is measured up from the sea horizon, but it must be corrected to read as though it had been made at the center of the earth. This correction for *horizontal parallax* (figure 1806b) has a maximum value for bodies near the horizon, decreasing to zero for a body directly overhead. The greatest correction is on observations of the moon, as it is the nearest body used for navigational observations.

The Principal Planets

1807 The nearer planets, Venus and Mars, are at times observed at distances less than that of the sun. The distance of Venus varies from 0.28 astronomical units to 1.72 astronomical units; Mars, from 0.38 to 2.66 astronomical units. Venus, almost equal in diameter to the earth, provides an observable disc, rather than a true point of light, when nearest the earth. The sidereal period of revolution for Venus is only 224.7 days (for the earth it is 365.2 days). The maximum brilliance, as observed from the earth, occurs about 36 days prior to and after the inferior conjunction of the two planets, at which time it approaches a magnitude of −4.4. The minimum magnitude is about −3.3. For a considerable portion of the time, Venus is favorably situated for daytime celestial fixes in combination with

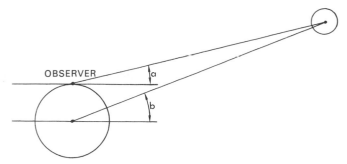

Figure 1806b. Parallax due to observer not being at the center of the earth.

lines of position acquired by sun or moon observations. Horizontal parallax is a small factor in planet observations.

Other planets may be observed during daylight hours, subject to the telescope used and atmospheric conditions. Jupiter varies in magnitude from −1.4 to −2.5, Mars from 1.6 to −2.8, Mercury from 1.1 to −1.2. These bodies compare very favorably in brilliance with the 57 selected stars that range from comparatively faint Zubenelgenubi with a magnitude of 2.9, to the brightest star, Sirius, with a magnitude of −1.6. The full moon has a magnitude varying slightly around −12.6; the magnitude of the sun is about −26.7.

Like the moon, the sun varies in apparent size, depending upon the earth's position in its elliptical orbit. Geocentric parallax, a value much smaller than that involved in moon observations due to the much greater distance of the sun, amounts to about 0.1° between altitudes 0° and 65°.

Data on the nine principal planets are given in figure 1807. It is interesting to note that nearly all of these planets have satellites, or "moons," revolving about them. These satellites, like the planets themselves, are relatively cold bodies, and shine

Figure 1806a. Semidiameter (scale greatly exaggerated).

Planet	Mean Distance from Sun		Mean Diameter (in miles)	Sidereal Period		Axial Rotation	Known Satellites
	Millions of Miles	Astronomical Units					
Mercury	36	0.4	3031	88	days	60^d	none
Venus	67	0.7	7521	224.7	days	243	none
Earth	93	1.0	7926	365.24	days	23^{h}56^m	1
Mars	142	1.5	4222	687	days	24^{h}37^m	2
Jupiter	484	5.2	88729	11.86	years	9^{h}50^m	16
Saturn	887	9.5	74565	29.46	years	10^{h}14^m	17
Uranus	1783	19.2	31566	84.02	years	17^{h}14^m	15
Neptune	2794	30.1	30199	164.8	years	15^{h}40^m	2
Pluto	3666	39.4	1423	248.4	years	6.4^d?	1

Figure 1807. Distance, diameter, and other data on planets.

only as a result of the light that is reflected from them.

Minor Planets and Asteroids

1808 The minor planets and asteroids differ from the principal planets chiefly in size and number; they are not of navigational interest. While Mercury, the smallest principal planet, is only about 3,100 miles (4,990 km) in diameter, the largest minor planet has a diameter of only 480 miles (770 km). Over 3,000 minor planets have been discovered, but many thousands more are believed to be circling the sun.

Most of the minor planets are in orbits lying between those of Mars and Jupiter. It is speculated that they may be the remains of a former principal planet, as there is mathematical support for the theory that such a planet once orbited there.

Meteors and Meteorites

1809 The so-called "shooting stars" are small, solid bodies of the solar system, often no larger than a grain of sand; they enter the earth's atmosphere and are heated to incandescence by friction. These are observed only when they enter the atmosphere, and most *meteors* are completely vaporized as they travel through the atmosphere. The small percentage that are not completely destroyed and strike the surface as solid particles are called *meteorites*. Most are composed largely of nickel and iron; the remainder are stone.

Some meteors are apparently small asteroids, which were drawn out of their elliptical orbits about the sun by the earth's gravity. Others, possibly remnants of comets, seem to travel in quasi-parabolic orbits; these latter are believed to cause the "showers of shooting stars" that occur periodically. The majority of meteors are believed to weigh only a small fraction of an ounce, but some can be of great size, and it seems probable that a large crater near Winslow, Arizona, was caused by a meteorite that weighed some 50,000 tons (4.5×10^7 kg).

Meteors enter the atmosphere at an estimated rate of 100 million each day. The dates of prominent annual meteor showers are listed in most astronomical texts. At such times, the observer may see ten or more, and on rare occasions sometimes hundreds, in an hour; the hours between midnight and dawn are the best for observation.

Comets

1810 Comets are composed chiefly of frozen methane, ammonia, and water, with clusters of

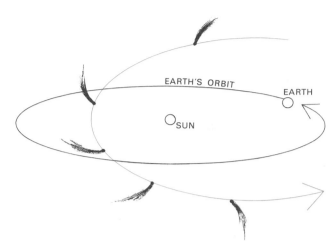

Figure 1810. Path of Cunningham's Comet. The tail of a comet always points away from the sun.

meteoric material in the nucleus. They travel in orbits that are elliptical (if periodic), parabolic, or hyperbolic. When a comet first becomes visible, it shines only by light reflected from the sun, but as it approaches the sun, solar radiation excites the gases within the comet and it becomes partly self-luminous.

As a comet approaches within 100 million to 200 million miles (1.6 to 3.2×10^8 km) of the sun, a tail generally begins to form as the result of the impact of the nucleus of the comet with the charged particles of the "solar wind." The tail may grow in length to 100 million miles (1.6×10^8 km) at perihelion and then gradually recede as the comet moves away from the sun.

This tail is always directed away from the sun (figure 1810) so that it precedes the comet as the latter recedes from the sun. Occasionally a comet is sufficiently brilliant to be seen in broad daylight, although this is a rare occurrence.

Comets are fairly plentiful in the solar system, and on most nights during the year at least one can be seen with a telescope. In general, they take many years to complete their orbits about the sun. Halley's comet, which is the best known, has a period of 76 years, and will next be visible in 1986.

Revolution and Rotation of the Earth

1811 The earth revolves about the sun in a slightly elliptical orbit; it is about 91,400,000 miles (1.47×10^8 km) from the sun in January, and 94,500,000 miles (1.52×10^8 km) in July. It rotates 360° about its axis once in 23 hours 56 minutes; this is termed the *sidereal day*, and differs from the solar

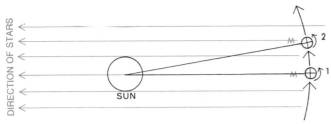

Figure 1811. Sidereal and solar days.

day, which averages 24 full hours, because of the earth's motion in its orbit. This difference between the sidereal and solar days is illustrated in figure 1811.

At position (1) the sun is over the meridian *M*; rotation is counterclockwise in this diagram. When the earth has arrived at position (2) in its orbit, it has rotated 360° on its axis, but the sun is still east of the meridian *M* and will not be on the meridian until the earth has rotated for an additional period averaging four minutes. This period varies slightly during the year, and depends on the earth's position in its orbit.

Inclination of the Earth's Axis

The earth's axis is not perpendicular to the plane of its orbit, but is inclined at an angle of about 23.5° from the vertical (figure 1815a), the north pole being inclined towards the sun from the latter part of March to the latter part of September. During the balance of the year, the south pole is inclined towards the sun. The resultant apparent annual path of the sun among the stars is called the *ecliptic*. This inclination of the equator is the cause of the change of seasons. The earth's axis remains rigidly inclined in space due to rotation of the mass, just as a spinning gyroscope's axis tends to be spacially fixed.

The Earth's Atmosphere

1812 The atmosphere of the earth has a major effect on celestial navigation; it is a great blanket of air, consisting principally of 78 percent nitrogen and 21 percent oxygen, with very small amounts and traces of other gases and contaminants. Half of the atmosphere is concentrated within about $3\frac{1}{2}$ miles ($5\frac{1}{2}$ km) of the surface; the remainder thins out to an altitude of roughly 1,000 miles (1,600 km).

Atmospheric Diffusion

Without the diffusing effect of the atmosphere, the stars and the sun would be visible at the same time. However, the molecules that make up the atmosphere, aided by suspended dust, scatter the sun's light in all directions and make it difficult to see the stars. Astronauts report that at altitudes of over 100 miles (160 km) they are still unable to see most stars in daytime, but that from true "outer space" they can. The short-wavelength blue light from the sun is particularly affected by this scattering, thus giving the sky its characteristic blue color.

When a celestial body is near the horizon, its light must pass through a greater volume of air than when it is overhead, as is shown in figure 1812. This causes additional scattering, and permits very little blue light to reach the observer, leaving only the long-wavelength red light. This causes the reddish-orange appearance of the sun and moon near the horizon.

Refraction of Light

The atmosphere also causes light rays to be *refracted*, or bent, as they enter it from space; this refraction of the sun's rays prolongs the twilight. In addition, except when a celestial body is directly overhead, refraction affects its apparent altitude, causing it to appear higher than it actually is. Refraction increases as altitude decreases; under "standard" atmospheric conditions it amounts to 34.5' at zero altitude. The entire disc of the sun can be visible after the upper limb has, in fact, passed below the celestial horizon (see article 1814) at sunset.

The atmosphere also reduces the apparent brightness of celestial bodies, again having its greatest effect when the body is on the horizon and its light rays are passing through the maximum distance and density of air. As its altitude decreases from 90° to 5°, a star's brightness may be reduced by a full magnitude. Atmospheric turbulence often

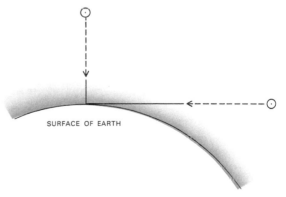

Figure 1812. At low altitudes, the sun's rays travel through greater distances in the earth's atmosphere, and the characteristic red color is a result.

causes the light from a star to fluctuate; hence the popular notion that stars "twinkle." The light from planets is normally much steadier, as they are comparatively near the earth and thus have appreciable size, rather than appearing as mere points of light.

Effects of Motions of the Earth

1813 The earth, in company with the entire solar system, revolves around the axis of our galaxy. This motion has very little effect on the apparent motion of the celestial bodies across the heavens. But there are three major and two minor types of earth motion or changes that do affect the apparent paths of these bodies. The three major motions of the earth are *rotation* about its axis, *revolution* about the sun, and *precession*. The two minor motions are the *wandering* of the terrestrial poles, and *variations* in the speed of rotation. These motions, and their effects, will be considered in the following articles.

Effects of the Earth's Rotation

1814 The daily rotation of the earth on its axis causes the principal apparent motion of the heavenly bodies across the sky from east to west. This motion is parallel to the plane of the earth's equator, occurs in circles whose centers are on the earth's axis or its extension, and is at an almost constant rate. These circles are called diurnal or daily circles. To be visible to an observer a body must, of course, be above his *celestial horizon*, which may be considered as a plane passing through the center of the earth, and perpendicular to a line connecting the observer's position and the earth's center (see figure 1814a). The plane of his horizon therefore changes as he changes latitude. If he is located at one of the poles, his horizon is parallel to the equator. If the body's brightness and atmospheric conditions are ignored, its visibility depends both upon the position of the body's diurnal circle, relative to the observer's latitude, and its location on that circle. The *declination* of a body on the celestial sphere (see article 1902) is identical to the latitude of the point on earth directly under the celestial body. This is referred to as the *geographical position* (GP) of the body. Declination and GP will be discussed in greater detail in chapter 19. The apparent motion of the celestial bodies caused by the rotation of the earth on its axis results in the GP of the body moving westward along a parallel of latitude equivalent in angular value to the declination of the body.

Figure 1814a. Diurnal circles.

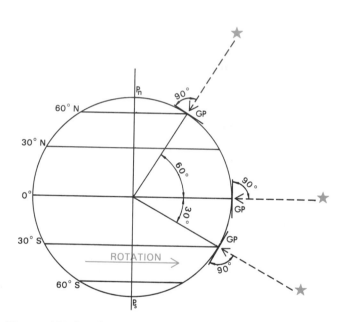

Figure 1814b. The declination of a star equals the latitude of its GP.

Figure 1814b illustrates three stars with declinations of 0°, 30° S, and 60° N. As the earth rotates, the GPs of the bodies will trace lines across the earth following the equator, the 30° south parallel of latitude, and the 60° north parallel of latitude respectively.

As illustrated in figure 1814a, an observer is in 30° north latitude; the plane of his horizon is shown as passing through the earth's center; circle 1 represents the apparent daily path or diurnal circle of a body having a declination of approximately 80° north. In moving along its diurnal circle, it is there-

Figure 1814c. Observatory photograph of circumpolar stars.

fore constantly above some point on the 80th parallel of north latitude. Note that for the observer in latitude 30° north this body never sets below the horizon. This, of course, will be equally true for all bodies having a declination of 60° or more north (90° minus observer's latitude of 30°). All such bodies will bear due north of the observer at the highest and lowest points on their diurnal circles, and since they do not set below the horizon they are referred to as *circumpolar* stars. Figure 1814c depicts the trace of circumpolar stars, showing their path around the earth's axis extended.

A star with a declination of 30° north (not shown in figure 1814a) will be above the horizon for about 14 hours and 40 minutes of the day. It rises over the horizon well north of east and will pass directly overhead and set north of west. Circle 2 in figure 1814a represents the diurnal circle of a star having a declination of 0°; it circles the equator. It rises due east of the observer, is due south of him when it reaches its maximum altitude of 60° and sets due west. It is above the horizon for 12 hours. Circle 3 represents the diurnal circle of a body with 60° south declination. Such a body or any with a declination greater than 60° south would never appear above the horizon for an observer in latitude 30° north.

The declination of each star changes so slowly that over a period of many years an observer in a given latitude will have essentially the same continuous view of the diurnal circle of that star. On the other hand, the declination of each body in the solar system changes with comparative rapidity,

and thus the apparent motion of these bodies changes at a similar rate. The declination of the sun, moon, and navigational planets varies between roughly 25° N and 25° S, and at any time their diurnal circles will lie between these limits.

Day and Night

One of the principal effects of the earth's rotation on its axis is the alternating phenomena known as *day* and *night*. Since the earth is approximately a sphere, half of it will be in sunlight and half in darkness at any given time. The length of the period of day or night varies with the observer's location on the surface of the earth as a result of the inclination of the earth's axis as discussed in articles 1811 and 1815.

Effects of the Earth's Revolution

1815   The annual revolution of the earth about the sun is illustrated in figure 1815a, which also shows the 23.5° inclination of the equator to the earth's orbit. About 21 June each year the north pole is at its maximum inclination towards the sun, and the declination of the latter is 23.5° *North*. As the earth moves on in its orbit about the sun, the northerly declination of the sun decreases slowly, and reaches 0° about 23 September; it continues to decrease at a constant rate until about 22 December, when it reaches 23.5° *South*, its maximum southerly declination. Moving on from this point, the declination increases at a constant rate, reaching 0° again about 21 March, and 23.5° North on 21 June.

First Point of Aries

The points of maximum declination are called the *solstices*; the points of 0° declination are called

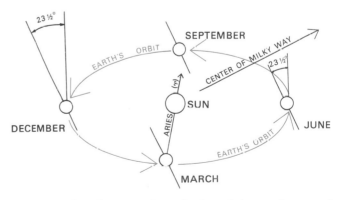

Figure 1815a. The annual revolution of the earth around the sun.

the *equinoxes*. These words are derived from the Latin, solstice meaning "sun standing still," and equinox meaning "equal night." The point in space at which the March equinox occurs is also called the *first point of Aries* ♈, or simply *Aries;* it is an important reference point in the system of celestial coordinates. It derives its name from the fact that when the celestial coordinate system was first established, the sun entered the constellation Aries as it passed from south to north declination. It has kept the name although this point has moved as a result of the earth's precession (article 1817).

The continuing change in the sun's declination throughout a yearly cycle explains the changing seasons experienced on earth; they are caused by the angle at which the sun's rays strike the earth, and the comparative length of daylight and darkness. In this connection the times of 0° declination are generally termed the vernal (spring) and the autumnal equinoxes; the time of maximum north declination is the summer solstice, and the time of maximum south declination is the winter solstice for the Northern Hemisphere; summer and winter are reversed for the Southern Hemisphere.

The revolution of the earth about the sun also affects the apparent positions of the stars, which surround the solar system on all sides. The ones that can be seen from the earth on a given night are those in a direction generally opposite to that of the sun. Because of this the stars appear to make one complete revolution around the earth each year independently of their nightly revolution, due to the earth's rotation on its axis; each succeeding night at the same time at a given place, each star will be almost one degree farther west; it requires an average of 365¼ days to complete the revolution of 360°. The early astronomers grouped the stars into arbitrary constellations; the twelve constellations along the plane of the ecliptic through which the sun passes during the year are called the *zodiac*. The zodiac, as such, has no navigational significance.

Superior Planets and Their Motions

The combination of the revolutions of the earth and the planets about the sun results in the comparatively rapid change of position of the planets. Mars, Jupiter, and Saturn, whose orbits lie outside that of the earth, are termed the *superior planets*. These appear to move steadily westward with respect to the sun, meaning that they rise earlier and cross the observer's meridian earlier on each succeeding day. They emerge from behind the sun as morning twilight bodies and continue to rise ear-

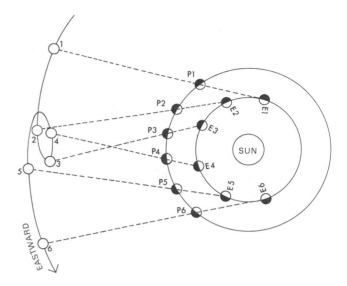

Figure 1815b. Retrograde movement of a superior planet.

lier each day until they again disappear behind the sun, last being seen as evening twilight bodies. With respect to the stars, the superior planets appear to move constantly eastward from night to night, except when they are nearest the earth. At this time their motion is *retrograde*, appearing to move westward among the stars. Figure 1815b illustrates the retrograde motion of a superior planet. When the earth is at E_1, E_2, E_3, etc., the superior planet is at P_1, P_2, P_3, etc., and appears at positions 1, 2, 3, etc., at the left.

Inferior Planets

Mercury and Venus are termed *inferior planets*, as their orbits lie inside that of the earth. They appear to oscillate with respect to the sun. Venus always appears comparatively near the sun; it alternates as a morning and evening planet, often popularly referred to as the "morning star" or "evening star," because it rises and sets within about three hours of sunrise and sunset.

Mercury is a bright celestial body, but because of its closeness to the sun it can be seen only rarely, and its coordinates are therefore not listed in the *Nautical Almanac*.

The planets shine by the reflected light of the sun; the inferior planets go through all the same phases as the moon (article 1816), being "full" when on the opposite side of the sun from the earth, and "new" when on the same side. The superior planets never pass between the earth and sun, and thus are never seen in the "new" phase; they vary only between "full" and "gibbous" (see article 1816) when viewed through a telescope.

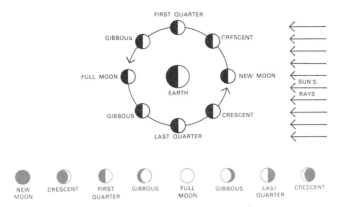

Figure 1816. Phases of the moon; symbols are shown below.

Effects of the Moon's Revolution

1816 The most obvious effect of the moon's revolution about the earth is the cycle of *phases* through which it passes. Like the planets, the moon shines by the sun's reflected light. Excluding occasional eclipses, the side facing the sun is lit, and the opposite side is dark; the moon's appearance from the earth depends on its orientation relative to the earth and sun.

Phases of the Moon

The moon passes through its cycle of phases during a 29.5 day *synodic period*. The synodic period of a celestial body is its average period of revolution with respect to the sun, as seen from the earth. It differs from the 360° sidereal period because of the motions of the earth and the moon in their orbits. Figure 1816 illustrates the positions of the moon relative to the sun and earth during its synodic period, and the resulting phases. When the moon is between the sun and the earth, its sunlit half faces away from the earth, and the body cannot be seen; this is the *new moon*. As it revolves in its orbit, (counterclockwise in figure 1816) an observer on earth first sees a part of the sunlit half as a thin *crescent*, which will then *wax* or grow slowly through first quarter, when it appears as a semicircle. After passing through the first quarter, it enters the *gibbous* phase until it becomes full, and the entire sunlit half can be seen. From full it is said to *wane*, becoming gibbous again to the last quarter, and then crescent until the cycle is completed.

Age of the Moon

The *age of the moon* at a given time is the number of days that have passed since the preceding new moon, and is an indication of the phase, and therefore of the amount of light it sheds. The full moon

rises in most latitudes about the same time the sun sets, and sets when the sun rises; the new moon rises and sets with the sun. On the average, the moon rises about 50 minutes later each day, although that interval varies considerably. The full moon that occurs near the time of the autumnal equinox actually has a small retardation, rising earlier each day. The illuminated side of the moon is always towards the sun with the *cusps* or points directed away from the sun.

Solar and Lunar Eclipses

Other effects of the moon's revolution about the earth are *solar* and *lunar eclipses* that occur when the sun, the earth, and the moon are in line. The earth and the moon both cast shadows into space, in a direction away from the sun. A solar eclipse occurs whenever the shadow of the moon falls on a part of the surface of the earth, blocking light from the sun. As determined by the alignment of the three bodies, an observer on the earth may witness a *total* eclipse, or only a *partial* eclipse if part of the disc of the sun is visible. A solar eclipse is defined as *annular* when the moon's distance from the earth is sufficiently great to permit a narrow ring of sunlight to appear around the moon. A lunar eclipse occurs when the moon passes through the shadow of the earth; it, too, may be partial or total.

Effects of Procession

1817 The earth is, in effect, a gigantic gyroscope, and is subject to the laws of gyroscopic motion. However, it is not a perfect sphere and has a bulge about its equator, which is inclined at 23.5° to the plane of its orbit. The moon and sun exert gravitational forces on the earth, and these forces would tend to make the polar axis perpendicular to the plane of its orbit. Due to its rotation the earth resists these strong forces, but reacts like a gyroscope when external force is applied. It precesses in a direction that is at right angles to the direction of the external force.

This precession causes a slow rotation of the earth's axis about an axis projected outward at right angles to the plane of its orbit, therefore slowly tracing a circle on the celestial sphere. The period of precession is about 25,800 years. Figure 1817 shows this path in space, and indicates various stars with the dates at which they will replace Polaris as the polestar.

Precession of the Equinoxes

As noted before, the apparent location of the sun among the stars when its declination is 0° is termed

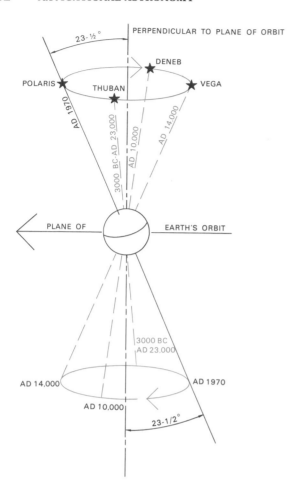

Figure 1817. Precession of the earth.

an *equinox;* this occurs each spring and fall. The gyroscopic action of the earth causes a *precession of the equinoxes;* this is at a rate of about 50 seconds of arc per year and is in a westerly direction—that is, clockwise from the north. This is the *opposite* direction to both the earth's rotation and its revolution. The period of the earth's precession is not uniform due to the varying positions of the moon relative to the earth's equator and some small effects of other bodies; this slight variation is termed *nutation.*

Minor Motions of the Earth

1818 In addition to the major motions described above, there are several motions of the earth of minor importance. Two of the more significant in navigation are the *wandering of the terrestrial poles* and the *variations in speed of rotation* of the earth.

The north and south terrestrial poles, or the points where the earth's axis of rotation theoretically pierces the earth's surface, are not stationary. Instead, they wander slightly in somewhat circular paths. The movement is believed to be caused by meteorological effects. Each pole wanders in an area smaller than a baseball diamond, and neither has been known to move more than 40 feet (12 m) from its average position. The phenomenon is also called "variation in latitude."

The rotational speed of the earth on its axis is steadily decreasing by a small amount, causing the length of the day to increase at the rate of about 0.001 seconds a century. There are also small irregular changes in the rotational period, the causes of which are uncertain. With the introduction of atomic time standards, which keep absolute time, variations in the speed of rotation of the earth—which affect its rotational position and hence astronomical observations—are of interest to the navigator; see chapter 22 for further discussion of the differences between "perfect" time and "correct" time for navigational use.

Astronomy and Celestial Navigation

1819 Navigational astronomy is that part of astronomy in general that is of interest and use to a navigator. It is concerned primarily with the *apparent motion* of celestial bodies. These apparent motions are *relative* motions as caused by the actual movements of the bodies as seen from the earth. Their apparent positions in space are tabulated in *Almanacs* (chapter 23), and are used by a navigator in solving the navigational triangle to determine his position (chapters 24–27).

Chapter 19

Introduction to Celestial Navigation

Introduction

1901 Even with the great technological advances in radionavigation over the past several decades, there is still very much a place for *celestial navigation* on the high seas. This may be defined as the art and science of navigation using observations of the sun, moon, certain planets, and the brighter stars. In order to use this method, however, until comparatively recent times a navigator had to be competent in spherical trigonometry. Now, modern inspection tables make celestial navigation possible with little mathematical skill beyond simple addition and subtraction. The user of tables should, however, be familiar with the basic geometry that underlies them. Use of an electronic calculator or computer further simplifies the determination of position from celestial observations, but increases the need for knowledge of the theory that leads to the equations being employed. Thus, the study of celestial navigation begins with a fundamental consideration of the geometry of the earth and the celestial sphere, the coordinate systems, and the angles used.

The Earth and the Celestial Sphere

1902 In celestial navigation, the earth is assumed to be a perfect sphere, located at the center of the universe. The universe is assumed to be a second sphere of infinite radius concentric with the earth. It is called the *celestial sphere*, and all heavenly bodies are considered to be located on it. The nearest of the "fixed stars" is at a distance of over six billion times the radius of the earth, resulting in that radius being infinite when using the "fixed stars" in celestial navigation.

Rotation of the Earth

The earth's rotation from west to east causes the celestial sphere to appear to rotate slowly in the opposite direction; bodies are seen to rise in the east, cross the observer's meridian, and then set in the west.

These assumptions ignore the vast variation in the distances of these bodies, and the fact that the earth is an oblate spheroid rather than a true sphere. Because of the latter, a number of the relationships stated herein are close approximations, rather than exact statements of fact. However, no significant error is introduced in celestial navigation, as it is usually practiced, by considering the earth as a sphere.

Celestial Poles, Equator, and Meridians

The earth's center is thus considered to be at the center of the celestial sphere, and the axis of its poles, extended outward, form the north and south *celestial poles*. Similarly, the plane of the earth's equator is extended outward to form the *celestial equator* on the sphere, and any of the earth's meridians can be projected out to form *celestial meridians*.

Celestial Coordinates

1903 In chapter 2, the earth's system of coordinates—latitude and longitude—was discussed; by means of these coordinates the location of any spot on earth can be precisely stated. A similar system of coordinates exists for the celestial sphere, by means of which a heavenly body can be located exactly on that sphere. The plane of reference is the *celestial equator* (the *equinoctial*), which is perpendicular to the axis formed by a line extending from the north celestial pole through the center of the earth and its poles to the south celestial pole.

Declination and Hour Angle

The celestial equivalent of latitude is *declination (Dec.)*. It may be defined as angular distance north or south of the celestial equator (figure 1903a). It is expressed in degrees and minutes of arc, generally to the nearest tenth of a minute, and is labeled N or S to indicate the direction of measurement. Declination is one of the coordinates for stating the location of any heavenly body.

The other celestial coordinate, equivalent to longitude on earth, is *hour angle*. Of particular importance is *Greenwich hour angle (GHA)*—the angular distance of a celestial body westward of the celestial meridian of Greenwich. GHA is measured in arc from 0° to 360° and is stated in degrees and minutes to the nearest tenth (in this it differs from longitude, which is measured east or west to 180°). This celestial meridian of Greenwich is formed by projecting the plane of the Greenwich meridian outward to the celestial sphere. Like all meridians, it is a great circle, in that it is formed on the sphere by a plane passing through the center of the sphere, as discussed in chapter 2.

Hour Circles

The observer's meridian is also projected out to the celestial sphere (figure 1903b), and like the

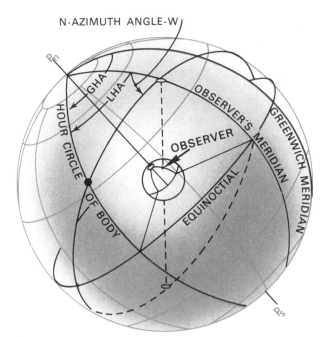

Figure 1903b. Celestial meridian, hour circles, and hour angle.

meridian of Greenwich, it forms an important reference in celestial navigation. Just as the special name of celestial meridian is given to the arc of a great circle on the celestial sphere that passes through the poles and remains fixed with respect to the earth, so the special name of *hour circle* is given to the arc of a great circle on the celestial sphere that passes through the celestial poles and a celestial body, and *moves with the body*.

Local Hour Angle (LHA) and Meridian Angle (t)

The *local hour angle (LHA)* of a celestial body is measured from 0° to 360° in arc *westward* from the observer's meridian to the hour circle of that body. In some celestial computations *meridian angle* (t) is used. It is equivalent to LHA, except that it is measured from 0° to 180° *east or west* from the observer's meridian to the hour circle of the body. Meridian angle, like longitude, is labeled with the suffix E or W, depending on whether the direction of measurement is east or west.

To determine LHA of a body apply longitude to the value of GHA by *adding* east longitude or *subtracting* west longitude.

The use of GHA relates the celestial sphere to the revolving earth by referring all values of hour angle to the earth's Greenwich meridian. The GHA of every celestial body is therefore constantly changing with time, as the earth containing the Greenwich meridian rotates around its axis. If the solar system, with the earth and navigational planets

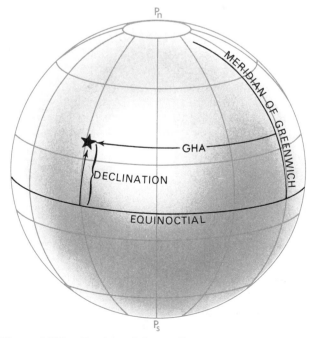

Figure 1903a. Equinoctial coordinates.

revolving around the sun, is ignored, there is a reference coordinate for locating the star positions in their east-west relationship to each other. Just as the meridian of Greenwich serves as the fixed reference on earth for terrestrial coordinates, so, on the celestial sphere, the hour circle through the *first point of Aries* (♈) is the fixed reference. In chapter 18 on navigational astronomy, Aries was described as the point in space represented by the vernal equinox, when the ecliptic crosses the equinoctial.

Sidereal Hour Angle (SHA)

Another angular measurement is the *sidereal hour angle (SHA)* of a celestial body; this is measured *westward* from the hour circle of Aries from 0° through 360°. All of the fixed stars can be positioned in space by their SHA and declination (see figure 1903c). (Astronomers use *right ascension* (RA), which is equivalent to SHA, but is measured eastward from the hour circle of Aries and expressed in units of time rather than arc; a navigator should understand what right ascension is, but need not be concerned with its use.) To tabulate the GHA of all the navigational stars in the *Almanac* would require publishing extremely large volumes. The GHA of the first point of Aries is therefore tabulated for various increments of time, and the slowly changing SHA and declination of the navigational stars are listed separately. The GHA of a star equals the GHA of Aries plus the SHA of the star. GHAs of the sun, moon, and navigational planets are tabu-

lated separately as they constantly move through the fixed pattern of the stars on the celestial sphere.

Horizon System of Coordinates

1904 A second system of coordinates is required in the practice of celestial navigation; this is termed the *horizon system of coordinates*. It differs from the celestial system in that it is based on the position of the observer, rather than on the celestial equator. The reference plane of the horizon system is the observer's *celestial horizon* (figure 1904a); this plane passes through the center of the earth, and is perpendicular to a line drawn from the position of the observer to the earth's center. This line, when extended outward from the earth's center through the observer's position, defines his *zenith* on the celestial sphere (figure 1904a). The zenith is exactly 90° above the celestial horizon; it could also be defined as the point on the celestial sphere directly above the observer. Extended in the opposite direction through the earth's center, this line marks the observer's *nadir* on the celestial sphere. The imaginary line from zenith to nadir forms the axis of the observer's celestial horizon system. The celestial horizon is parallel to the plane of the observer's visible horizon at sea. The *visible horizon*, also called the sea horizon, and sometimes the natural horizon, is the line at which, to an observer, sea and sky appear to meet.

This concept is important, as the celestial horizon is the reference plane to which the navigator's

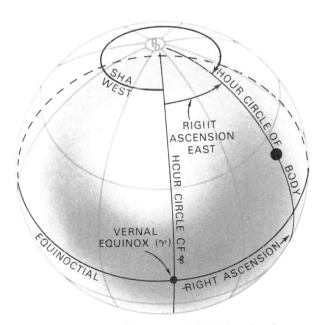

Figure 1903c. Sidereal hour angle (SHA) and right ascension.

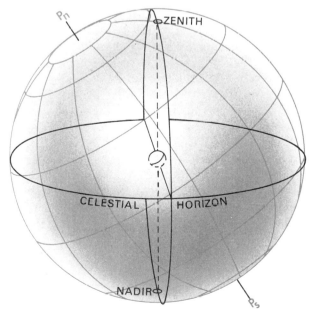

Figure 1904a. Zenith, nadir, and celestial horizon.

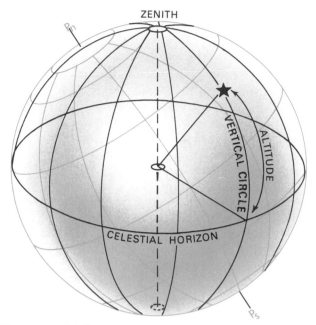

Figure 1904b. Altitude measured above the celestial horizon.

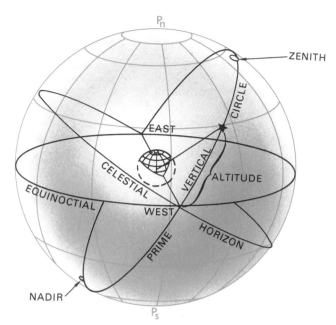

Figure 1904c. Horizon and equinoctial coordinates combined.

observations are referred. It is illustrated in figure 1904b.

Altitudes of *all* celestial bodies above the celestial horizon differ from those measured with the marine sextant aboard ship because of the height of the observer's eye above the plane of the visible horizon. The higher above the ocean surface the observer is situated, the more the visible horizon will be depressed below the true horizontal plane at his eye level. This causes the measured altitude of the body observed to read higher than its true altitude. A correction for the *dip of the horizon*, as it is termed, must be made to the measured altitude, as will be described in chapter 21.

A second correction is required for observations of the bodies within the solar system—the sun, moon, and planets. These bodies are much nearer the earth than are the fixed stars, which are considered to be at infinity; the light from such a body does not reach the earth in parallel rays, but diverges from the body's surface at a finite distance. The result is that a measurement of altitude taken at a point on the earth's surface will not be the same as an altitude measured from the center of the earth (center of the celestial sphere). The altitude of the body—sun, moon, or planet—above the celestial horizon will be greater than its altitude above the horizontal at the observer's eye, except when the body is on his zenith. This difference in altitude is called *parallax*. The required correction

to the altitude as measured above the visible horizon is described in chapter 21.

Altitudes of bodies, as measured with a sextant, and adjusted for dip (and parallax and other factors as appropriate), are angles above the plane of the celestial horizon, measured along a great circle, called the *vertical circle*, passing through the body as well as the observer's zenith and nadir; see figure 1904b. In the celestial equator system of coordinates there can be an infinite number of hour circles, so, in the horizon system of coordinates, there can be an infinite number of vertical circles each passing through a given body on the celestial sphere. In addition to the vertical circle passing through the celestial body being observed, there is one other important vertical circle. This is termed the *prime vertical* and is that vertical circle that passes through the east and west points of the observer's celestial horizon. Figure 1904c shows the two systems of coordinates superimposed, with the altitude of a star shown on the prime vertical.

The Astronomical Triangle

1905 The *astronomical* or *celestial triangle* is an area on the celestial sphere defined by the observer's celestial meridian, the hour circle passing through the observed celestial body, and the vertical circle passing through that body. The celestial triangle is illustrated in figure 1905. The vertices of the triangle are the elevated celestial pole, the ob-

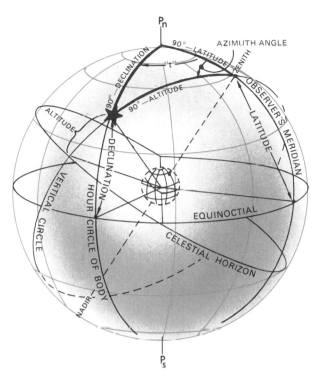

Figure 1905. Astronomical, or celestial, triangle.

Dec. and the one defined as 90° minus Lat. The third side, 90° minus altitude, has its angular distance determined by the altitude of the body above the celestial horizon, and therefore it uses the horizon system of coordinates. The relationship of the two systems, as projected on the celestial sphere, should now be clear. Only two of the angles within the celestial triangle are used in celestial navigation. Meridian angle (t), previously defined, is shown in figure 1905 as the angle at the pole between the observer's meridian and the hour circle of the body. *Azimuth angle* is the angle at the zenith between the celestial meridian of the observer and the vertical circle passing through the celestial body. Altitude and azimuth form the two horizon coordinates by means of which a celestial body is located with reference to the observer.

Geographical Position (GP)

1906   This chapter has considered the heavenly bodies only in relation to their positions on the celestial sphere, in order to show the fundamentals of the celestial triangle concept, and to define the terms used in celestial navigation. The understanding of celestial navigation is greatly simplified if the apparent position of each heavenly body is considered to lie on the surface of the earth rather than on another sphere. Imagine the earth to be a glass globe, with the observer located at its center. As the observer looks at a star or other celestial body its light rays pass through a single point on the earth's surface. This point is called the *geographical position* (GP) of the body (figure 1906); it is moving constantly westward, but its precise position on the earth's surface can be determined for any instant of time from information tabulated in an almanac

server's zenith, and the position of the celestial body.

In figure 1905 both the observer's zenith and the star being observed are shown in the Northern Hemisphere. The relationship of other possible positions will be discussed in detail later. It will be noted from this illustration that the angular distances representing two sides of the triangle are determined from the celestial equator system of coordinates, namely, the side defined as 90° minus

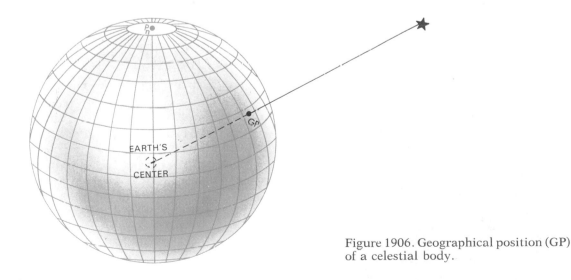

Figure 1906. Geographical position (GP) of a celestial body.

(chapter 23). Knowing the exact location of the GP of a body, a navigator can develop a line of position, by means of a sextant observation, very much as an LOP is obtained from observation of any landmark of known position on the earth's surface. To develop a celestial line of position, the navigator must obtain an accurate measurement of the altitude of a celestial body above the horizon. The following sections will explain the principles of developing such an LOP.

Circles of Equal Altitude

1907 To illustrate the basic concept involved in measuring an altitude, consider a pole of known height erected vertically on level ground, and stayed with a number of guy wires of equal length attached to the top of the pole and stretched taut to points on the ground equidistant from the base. The base of the pole establishes its GP. At the points where the guy wires meet the ground, angles are formed between the ground and the wires; these angles will be equal in value at each guy wire, and the points on the ground will describe a circle with the base of the pole at its center. It is evident then that anywhere on this circle the angle subtended by the height of the pole will be the same. This *circle of equal altitude* around the pole is illustrated in figure 1907a.

In the case of the pole of known height, the distance from the base of the pole can be determined by plane trigonometry if the angle it subtends is known. This is *partially* analogous to determining a ship's distance from the GP of a star by observing the star's altitude. The analogy, however, is not completely valid, as the ship is on the curved surface of the earth, rather than on a flat plane, and instead of dealing with a pole of known height, the navigator is concerned with a celestial body considered (in the case of stars) to be situated at an infinite distance above its GP. It is, in fact, because of the curvature of the earth's surface that the navigator can determine his distance from the GP of a celestial body by measuring its altitude above the visible horizon.

The problem here involved an angular measurement from a horizontal plane tangent to the earth's surface at the point of observation, followed by calculations in spherical trigonometry. As previously stated, most of the bodies used in navigation are at such great distances that their rays of light are parallel when they reach the earth. If the earth were flat, the angular altitude of each of these bodies would be the same at any point on the plane, regardless of distance from the GP, and the concept

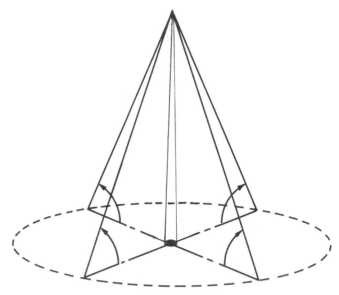

Figure 1907a. Circle of equal altitude around a pole.

of circles of equal altitude would not be valid. However, the angular altitude that the navigator actually uses is the angle between the lines of sight to the body and to the sea horizon. Because the earth's surface is curved, an observer's horizontal plane is tangent to the earth's surface at his position, and only at that one position on the surface of the earth. Hence, the angle between his horizon and the line of sight to a celestial body will vary if he moves his position toward or away from the GP of the body. This is illustrated in figure 1907b, which shows the light rays from a celestial body intersecting two different horizon planes on the surface of the earth at the same instant of time. At point A the altitude of the body above the horizon plane is considerably less than at point B, and the circle of equal altitude on which point A is located is farther away from the GP of the body than the circle of equal altitude passing through point B.

Celestial Lines of Position

As the altitude varies in proportion to an observer's distance from the GP, he can convert coaltitude (an angular distance on a great circle) into linear distance from the GP, and this distance will in turn be the radius of the circle of equal altitude since 1' of arc on a great circle equals 1 nautical mile. The entire circle is seldom drawn on the plotting chart as only a very short segment of its arc, in the vicinity of the DR position, is needed. Due to the usually large radius of the circle, this short segment can, for practical purposes, be represented as a straight line without causing significant distortion. This

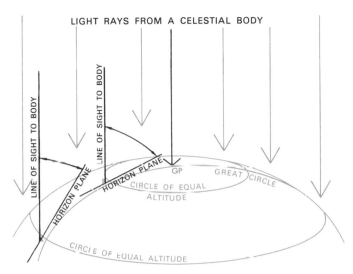

Figure 1907b. Parallel rays of light, angle of elevation.

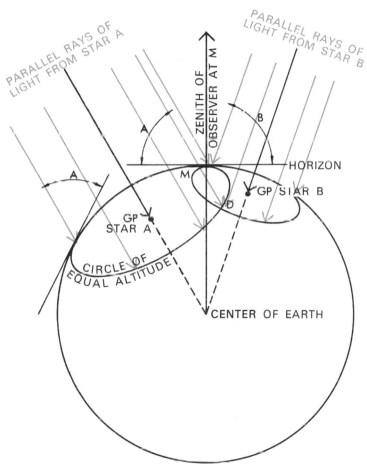

Figure 1907c. Circles of equal altitude for two stars. A—Altitude of star A from position of observer on circle of equal altitude. B—Altitude of star B from position of observer on circle of equal altitude. C and D—The two intersections of the circles of equal altitude.

small segment of a circle of equal altitude is a *celestial line of position* (chapter 25). Figure 1907c illustrates circles of equal altitude, or of position, derived from observations of two stars. One of the intersections of these two circles on the surface of the earth represents the navigator's position or "Fix." The other intersection of the two circles is located so far away from the DR position that in practical navigation there is no chance of error due to choosing the wrong intersection.

The Navigational Triangle

1908 The *navigational triangle* on the earth's surface is the counterpart of the astronomical or celestial triangle on the celestial sphere, as described in article 1905. It is the basis of celestial navigation, and as such it should be thoroughly understood by every person who would call himself a "navigator." The navigational triangle is defined by three points on the earth's surface, and it is formed by the arcs of the great circles connecting these points (figure 1909). These points are the position of the observer (*M*), the geographical position of the celestial body (GP), and the elevated pole. The elevated pole is the pole nearer the observer; it is the north pole for an observer in north latitude, and the south pole if he is in the Southern Hemisphere. It is called the elevated pole because it relates to the celestial pole above the observer's horizon. The GP may be in either the same or the opposite hemisphere to that of the observer.

Since the possible positions of *M* and GP are almost unlimited, this spherical triangle may take a great variety of shapes. For any particular moment of time, a navigational triangle can be constructed connecting an observer at any location on the earth, the elevated pole, and the GP of any celestial body within the observer's field of view. Having a complete understanding of the triangle, the navigator is able to solve any problem of celestial navigation. He can fix his position at sea, check the accuracy of his compasses, predict the time of rising or setting of any body in the heavens, determine the times of the beginning and ending of twilight, and locate and identify celestial bodies. The solution of the navigational triangle *is* celestial navigation.

The Sides of the Navigational Triangle

1909 The side of the triangle joining the observer and the elevated or nearer pole is called the *colatitude;* it is equal to 90° minus his latitude. The side joining the GP and the pole is called the *polar distance;* it can be equal to 90° minus the body's declination, or 90° minus the latitude of the body's GP when referred to the surface of the earth; but when the latitude of the observer and the declination of the body are of *contrary names,* polar distance is 90° *plus* declination, or 90° *plus* the latitude of the GP of the body. The side joining the GP and *M,* the position of the observer, is the *coaltitude,* sometimes called zenith distance; it is equal to 90° minus the altitude of the body. Each of these sides is an arc of a great circle through the two points it connects, and its angular distance in minutes of arc is the distance in nautical miles between those two points on the surface of the earth. The triangle shown in figure 1909a is for an observer in north latitude, with a celestial body setting to his west. Remember that two sides of the triangle, polar distance and colatitude, are defined by using the celestial equator system of coordinates, and the third side, coaltitude, is an arc of the vertical circle of the horizon system of coordinates. The three sides of the navigational triangle are illustrated and discussed in more detail in the following articles.

Colatitude

Latitude, described in chapter 2, is the angular distance north or south of the equator. It may also be defined as an angle at the center of the earth, measured along the observer's meridian from the equator to his position. Figure 1909b illustrates latitude and colatitude shown on the plane of the meridian of the observer. The line *QQ'* represents the equator and *O* the center of the earth. Since the maximum angle in the measurement of latitude is 90° (the latitude of the pole) it can be seen from the illustrations that colatitude will always be 90° minus the latitude.

Polar Distance

Since the geographical position, GP, of a body is a point on the earth's surface, it can be expressed in terms of latitude and longitude. Thus, the side of the navigational triangle joining the GP and the pole can be computed and used in the same manner as the side connecting the observer's position, *M,* and the pole. Although the observer is always on the same side of the equator as the elevated pole, at times he may observe a celestial body having a GP with a latitude of contrary name; that is, a navigator in north latitude may observe a celestial body whose GP is in south latitude or vice versa.

Polar distance, for a body having a GP in the same hemisphere as the observer's position, is

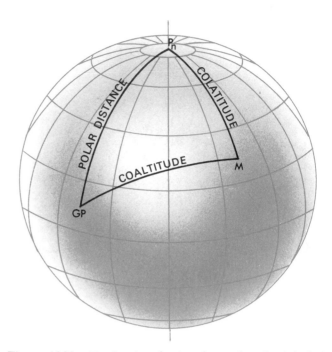

Figure 1909a. Navigational triangle, with sides labeled.

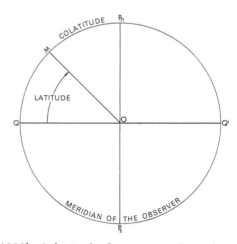

Figure 1909b. Colatitude shown as angle at the center of the earth.

shown in figure 1909c to be 90° *minus* the latitude of the GP. For any body observed with a GP in the latitude of opposite name, the polar distance will be 90° *plus* the latitude of the GP, as illustrated in figure 1911. In this illustration the line *QQ'* again represents the equator and point *O* the center of the earth.

Coaltitude

When a navigator observes a celestial body, he measures its angular altitude above the horizon. In figure 1909d the observer, *M,* is shown at the top of a great circle representing the earth's circumfer-

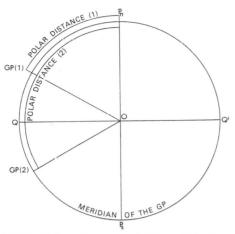

Figure 1909c. Polar distance of GP₁ = 90°—Lat. for GP₂ polar distance = 90° + latitude of GP₂.

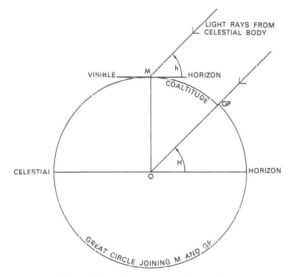

Figure 1909d. Coaltitude = 90° − altitude.

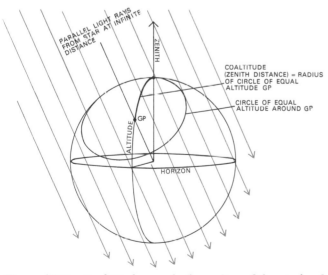

Figure 1909e. Coaltitude equals the radius of the circle of equal altitude.

ence. This great circle joins the position of the observer and the GP of the celestial body; it is not a meridian (except in the rare case in which the GP falls on the observer's meridian), but a vertical circle on which the body's altitude is measured from the celestial horizon toward the zenith.

In figure 1909d it can be seen that the light rays of a celestial body are assumed to be parallel, and that the angle (*h*) at the observer's visible horizon is the same as angle (*H*) at the center of the earth, measured from the celestial horizon. If altitude is illustrated as angle (*H*) in this figure, then it follows the coaltitude must be 90° minus the altitude. Although this presents no problem in the mathematical solution of the triangle, the visualization of this third side of the navigational triangle sometimes requires close attention. Figure 1909e presents a graphic illustration in which the arc segment labeled coaltitude is shown as both 90° minus altitude and as an arc of the circle of the equal altitude. This is true in all cases when using the basic relationship of one minute of arc on a great circle on the surface of the earth equaling one nautical mile.

The Angles of the Navigational Triangle

1910 Angles are, of course, as much a part of the navigational triangle as are its sides, and two of the three are routinely used in celestial navigation.

Meridian Angle

In the navigational triangle, the angle at the pole between the meridian of the observer and the meridian of the GP is called the *meridian angle*, and labeled "t"; refer back to figure 1903b, where this angle was labeled LHA. The local hour angle, LHA, is always measured in a westerly direction and from the meridian of the observer to the meridian of the GP, extending through an angle of 0° to 360°. In the computations involved in sight reduction, it is more convenient to be able to measure this angle either east or west from the meridian of the observer, hence the designation meridian angle. Meridian angle is the "difference of longitude" between the position of the observer and the GP of the body.

The use of a *time diagram* is explained in chapter 22. The meridian angle (t) is a vital part of the diagram. Figure 1910a illustrates the meridians of the observer and of the GP, with the resultant angle (t) as they will appear on a time diagram. The outer circle represents the earth's equator as viewed from a point in space on an extension of the earth's axis beyond the *south* pole. (This pole is selected so

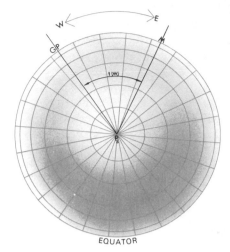

Figure 1910a. Meridian angle (t) is measured westerly from the observer's position.

as to place westerly directions to the left of north, and easterly to the right, a format familiar to a navigator from his use of charts.)

The center of this circle is labeled Ps to indicate the south pole. The lines in the illustration that connect both *M* and GP with the pole represent projections of meridians. *M* represents the intersection of the observer's meridian with the equator, and

GP represents the intersection of the meridian of the GP with the equator. In this diagram and in actual practice the meridian angle (t) is always measured from the observer's meridian toward the meridian of the GP and is labeled with the suffix "E" (east) or "W" (west) to indicate the direction of measurement. In a diagram of this type the use of the south pole does *not* imply that it is the elevated pole. The angle of intersection of the two meridians is identical at both poles.

Azimuth Angle

The other important angle within the navigational triangle is the *azimuth angle* (Z), measured at the observer's position, between the observer's meridian and the vertical circle running through the position of the GP and that of the observer (figures 1903b and 1905). Azimuth angle is always measured from the observer's meridian toward the vertical circle joining the observer and the GP. It is labeled with the prefix "N" (north) or "S" (south) to agree with the name of the observer's elevated pole, and with the suffix "E" (east) or "W" (west) to indicate the direction of measurement. Labeling the azimuth angle in this manner is necessary as it may be measured from either the north or south poles, and either in an easterly or westerly direction. In the final plotting of position this angle is

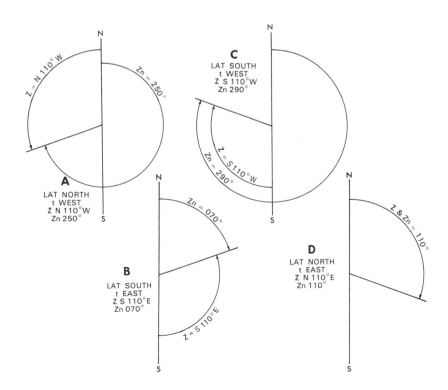

Figure 1910b. Azimuth angle (Z) and true azimuth (Zn).

converted to *true azimuth* (Zn), which is measured clockwise from the north through 360°, as illustrated in figure 1910b.

Parallactic Angle

The third angle in the navigational triangle is called the *parallactic angle*. It is not used directly in the ordinary practice of celestial navigation, and need not be considered here.

Use of the Navigational Triangle

1911   To obtain a position at sea, a navigator observes the altitude of a celestial body and simultaneously notes the exact time to the nearest second. Knowledge of the time of observation enables him to determine the exact position of the GP of that body from data in the *Nautical* or *Air Almanac* (chapter 23). Since the coaltitude has been previously described as equal to the arc of the circle of equal altitude, the observer is somewhere on the circumference of the circle of equal altitude. The exact position cannot be determined by a single observation (except for a meridian transit sight). If the azimuth of the GP at the instant of observation could be measured with the same accuracy as the attitude, the position of the observer could then be fixed mathematically. Unfortunately, at present it is not possible to measure azimuth with this degree of accuracy. A single observation only establishes that the observer is on the circle of equal altitude, a small segment of which can be assumed to be a straight line forming

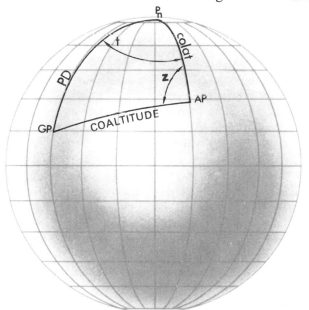

Figure 1911. Two sides and the included angle known; solve for Z and coaltitude.

a line of position in the close vicinity of his most probable position at the time of the sight.

Assumed Position

To use the navigational triangle to determine his position, a navigator first assumes that he is at some selected point, and then determines the error in this assumption. In some methods of celestial navigation this is the vessel's DR position or estimated position (EP). In other methods an artificial *assumed position* (AP) is used in order to simplify the use of precomputed tables.

Once an assumed position is selected and the GP of the celestial body at the exact time of observation is known, the colatitude, polar distance, and meridian angle can easily be computed. With these two sides and the angle formed by them known, the process of *sight reduction* can be undertaken to determine coaltitude and azimuth angle; see figure 1911. Modern "inspection" tables for sight reduction are conveniently arranged in a format that directly yields the desired value, altitude, rather than coaltitude.

Although a navigator using the precomputed tables will not use spherical trigonometry, the basic equations of use to those using an electronic calculator or a computer for sight reduction are listed below.

Altitude h
$$= \sin^{-1}[(\sin L \times \sin d) \pm (\cos L \times \cos d \times \cos t)]$$

Azimuth Angle $Z = \sin^{-1}\left(\dfrac{\cos d \times \sin t}{\cos h}\right)$

where d is declination and $\pm$ is interpreted as + when L and d are of the same name (N or S) and as - (algebraic difference) when L and d are of opposite name, with the smaller quantity being subtracted from the larger.

Compiled and Observed Altitudes

1912   As discussed in the preceding article, if an assumed position for the observer and the actual position of the GP for the body are used, the spherical triangle can be solved by tables or equations to produce a *computed altitude;* this value (h in the equations) is now labeled *Hc.* The *observed altitude* obtained from the sextant observation, with all corrections applied, is labeled *Ho.* Hc and Ho are each inversely proportional to the value of the radius of a circle of equal altitude, centered at the GP of the body, the first circle passing through the assumed position, the second through the observer's actual position.

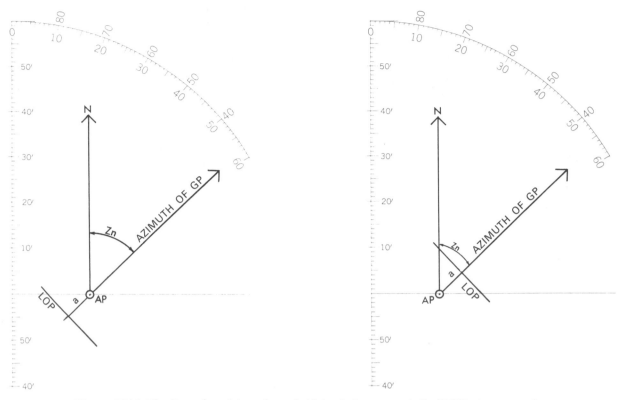

Figure 1912. The line of position plotted. Altitude intercept is "a." If Hc is *greater* than Ho, "a" is *away* from the GP (left). If Hc is *less* than Ho, "a" is *toward* the GP (right).

Altitude Intercept (a)

The difference between Hc and Ho is known as *altitude intercept (a);* this intercept represents the difference in length of the radii of the computed and observed circles of equal altitude. In article 1907 it was shown that a smaller altitude angle places the circle of equal altitude, and therefore the LOP, farther away from the GP of the body than does a larger altitude. Accordingly, if Hc—the computed altitude—for the assumed position is greater than Ho—the observed altitude—the actual position from which the observation was made would be farther from the GP of the body than the assumed position. Similarly, if Ho is the greater, the actual position would be nearer the GP. The intercept, a linear distance, must always be labeled either with the suffix T (toward) or A (away from) the GP as plotted from the AP (figure 1912).

Determining the Vessel's Position

1913   In addition to obtaining the value and direction of the intercept (a) in miles by solving the navigational triangle containing the AP, the navigator obtains the computed value of the azimuth angle (Z). By converting Z to azimuth measured from north (Zn), the navigator can conveniently plot on his chart the direction of the GP from the AP. This azimuth line drawn through the assumed position would indicate the direction of the GP even though that point is, in most cases, off the area of the chart being used. Since (a) is the difference in miles between the lines of position passing through the actual and assumed positions, the navigator can plot either toward or away for the value of (a) along this azimuth line. It is necessary to remember the direction of the intercept. From the description given in the preceding paragraph the phrase "Computed Greater Away" can be derived. A useful "memory aid" for CGA is "Coast Guard Academy"; another helpful acronym is "HoMoTo" for "Ho More Toward." The point on the azimuth line represented by marking off the intercept (a) is a point on the observer's circle of equal altitude. The celestial line of position is then drawn through this point and perpendicular to the azimuth line as shown in figure 1912.

Since a single celestial LOP does not produce an

absolute position or fix but merely a line some-where on which the observer is located, at least two LOPs are required to obtain a fix. Three LOPs from different bodies will give a fix with a greater degree of confidence, and four or five are not too many. The position of the vessel is determined by the intersection of the LOPs, a point for two lines and a single point for three or more lines if there is no error. In actual practice, however, three or more LOPs will rarely intersect at a point, but rather will form a small polygon, often popularly referred to as a "cocked hat." It is normally assumed that the actual position of the ship is at this figure's center, which can, for practical purposes, be estimated by eye; see also article 2909. In some instances, there can be an "exterior" fix in which the true position of the fix lies outside the polygon; see article 2910 for details of this situation.

Coordinates on the Plane of the Observer's Meridian

1914 Earlier in this chapter, two systems of celestial coordinates were described—one based on the celestial equator and the other on the observer's horizon. Both of these contain the celestial meridian of the observer, and celestial problems can be conveniently illustrated on the plane of this meridian. Should a neophyte observer become confused in the solution of a problem, he can often benefit by stopping to make sketches similar to these illustrations to clarify specific problems.

Horizon System of Coordinates

In figure 1914a the horizon system of coordinates is shown. The circle represents the plane of the observer's meridian, the line NS is the celestial horizon with north at the left and south at the right. It is obvious that the center of the circle can be either the east or west point on the horizon, and the NS line contains a locus of points representing all azimuths. Z represents the zenith of the observer, and Na the nadir. The line Z-Na passing through the zenith-nadir and the east-west point of the horizon is then, by definition, the prime vertical. Other vertical circles through celestial bodies will be shown on the diagram as curved lines passing through the observer's zenith, his nadir, and the celestial position of each body. The point where such a line intersects the celestial horizon determines the azimuth angle of the body. Lines parallel to the horizon will represent lines of equal altitude. The position of any body can be plotted on this diagram in terms of altitude and azimuth.

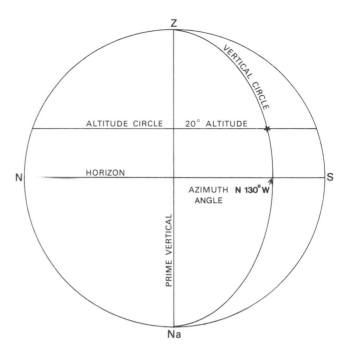

Figure 1914a. Horizon coordinates on the plane of the meridian.

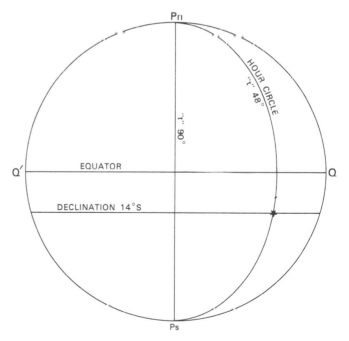

Figure 1914b. Celestial equator coordinates on the plane of the meridian.

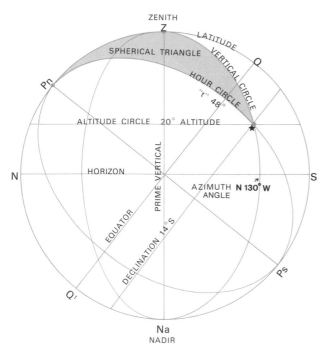

Figure 1914c. Combined coordinate systems.

Celestial Equator System of Coordinates

Figure 1914b illustrates the celestial equator system of coordinates on the plane of the celestial meridian. In this case the line *QQ'* is the celestial equator containing a locus of points representing a position on all hour circles. Pn and Ps are the north and south poles respectively. The hour circle 90° from the meridian of the observer appears as the straight line Pn-Ps (its LHA is 90° or 270° and t is 90° E or W); all other hour circles appear as curved lines. Lines parallel to the celestial equator are lines of equal declination. The position of any body can then be located on this diagram in terms of declination and hour angle.

Combining the Coordinate Systems

Combining the two systems of coordinates, if the observer were located at the north pole where his zenith and the north pole were identical, the diagrams could be superimposed on each other as drawn; this, obviously, is not a typical location for an observer on a vessel. For all other positions of an observer, the elevated pole must be placed on the plane of the observer's celestial meridian at a point above the horizon equal to the latitude of the observer. Figure 1914c illustrates the diagrams of figures 1914a and 1914b superimposed for a latitude of 40° N, with the area covered by the celestial triangle shaded; *B* indicates the position of the body observed.

Chapter 20

Identification of Celestial Bodies

Introduction

2001 Before a navigator can start a series of observations on celestial bodies, he must first decide which ones will be available, and which will give the better lines of position, primarily considering the angles between LOPs. With this information, he must next be able to identify these bodies in the sky. The sun and the moon obviously present no problem here; many, but far from all, navigational stars can be quickly identified from the constellations of which they are a part. Planets—the name is derived from "wanderer"—change their position in the sky and can present difficulties of identification except for special circumstances, such as the "morning star" and "evening star"—which are really planets, not stars, and not always the same planets. Lesser known stars, too, may require positive identification procedures; apparent differences in brightness, and occasionally in color, can be used to pick out the desired body.

The usual procedure in identifying stars and planets is to select, in advance of twilight, a number of these bodies, so located that lines of position obtained from them will result in a good fix. Only occasionally is an unknown body observed and identified afterward.

With experience, a navigator gains the ability to locate easily and quickly the most used navigational stars without the aid of mechanical or electronic devices. For the benefit of less-experienced navigators, this chapter will consider the use of such devices and the various "star charts" that are available in the *Nautical Almanac* and the *Air Almanac*. He must also learn how to predetermine the approximate altitude and azimuth of the navigational bodies, so that they may be located without

reference to other bodies. The modern sextant telescope enables the observer to sight a star in a comparatively bright sky when it is not visible to the unaided eye. Under such conditions he usually has the benefit of sharp horizon contrast, which permits accurate observations.

The "Star Finder and Identifier" 2102-D

2002 The Star Finder most used by navigators is generally referred to as "2102-D"; this was its "H.O." number when it was produced by the Navy Hydrographic Office. This navy star finder is no longer available to nongovernment personnel, but identical units can be obtained from civilian sources that continue to use the same number for identification. The device is a development from the original "Rude Starfinder" created by Captain G.T. Rude, USC&GS; it is still referred to by some people by its original name.

The 2102-D Star Finder and Identifier is designed to permit a user to determine the approximate altitude and azimuth of those of the 57 "selected navigational stars" listed on the daily pages of the *Nautical* and *Air Almanacs* (chapter 23) that are above his celestial horizon at any given place and time. With some minor additional effort, it can also be set up to indicate the positions of the navigational planets and other stars of interest (and even the sun and/or moon if desired, although this is rarely needed). The Star Finder can also be used in the reverse operation—identification of an unknown body whose altitude and azimuth have been measured. The accuracy of this device is roughly +3° to 5° in both altitude and azimuth.

The Star Finder consists of a *base* and ten circular *templates*, all contained in a case together with a sheet of instructions. The base, figure 2002a, is a

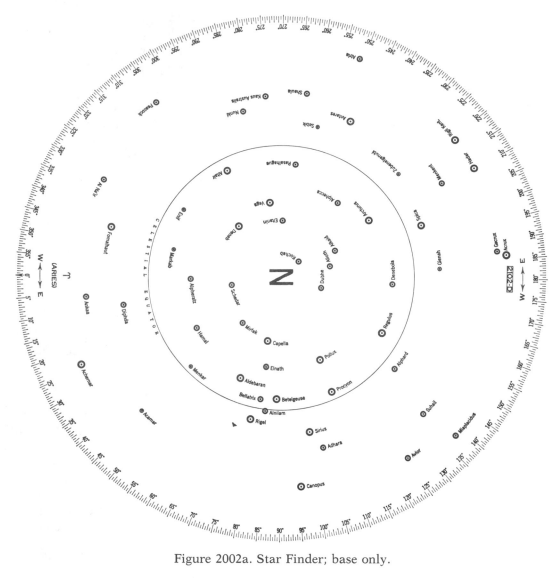

Figure 2002a. Star Finder; base only.

white opaque plastic disc, with a small pin at its center. On one side, the north celestial pole is shown at the center; on the opposite side the south celestial pole is at the center. On both sides the circumference is graduated in half degrees of LHA ♈, and labeled towards the east, at 5° intervals. All the stars are shown on each side of the base on a polar azimuthal equidistant projection extending towards the opposite pole. Each star is named, and the approximate magnitude is indicated by a symbol—a large heavy ring for first magnitude, a smaller heavy ring for second magnitude, and a yet smaller and thinner ring for third magnitude. The celestial equator is shown as a circle about half the diameter of the base. Because of the distortion caused by the projection, the relative positions of the stars shown on the base do *not* correspond to their apparent positions in the sky, and the device *cannot* be compared directly with the heavens.

There are ten templates of transparent plastic. Nine of these are printed with blue ink and are designed for apparent altitude and azimuth determinations, while the tenth, printed in red ink, is intended for the plotting of bodies other than the 57 selected stars on the base plate. There is one blue template for every 10° of latitude between 5° and 85°; one side of each template is for use in north latitudes, the other for south latitudes. Each of these "latitude" templates is printed with a set of oval blue *altitude* curves at 5° intervals, with the outermost curve representing the observer's celestial horizon, and a second set of radial *azimuth* curves, also at 5° intervals. The red template is printed with a set of concentric declination circles, one for each 10° of declination, and a set of radial meridian angle lines. In use, the appropriate template is placed on the star base much like a record on a phonograph turntable.

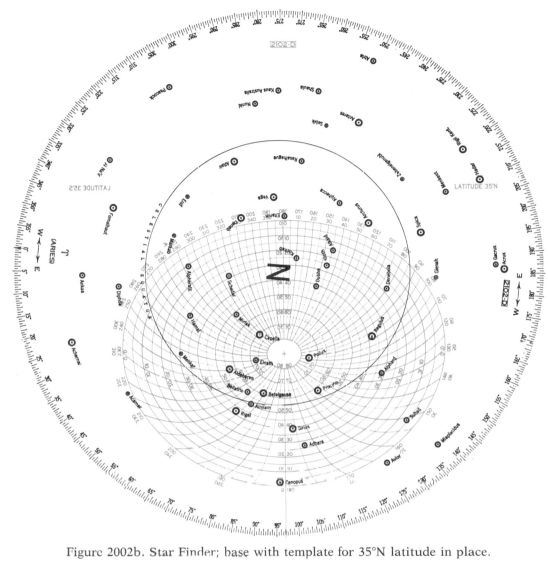

Figure 2002b. Star Finder; base with template for 35°N latitude in place.

Figure 2002b shows the north side of the Star Finder with the template for 35° north latitude set for a LHA ♈ of 97.2°.

Using the Star Finder to Determine Altitude and Azimuth

2003 The Star Finder is most convenient for determining which of the 57 selected stars will be favorably situated for observation at twilight and what their approximate altitudes and azimuths will be. First the LHA ♈ must be determined (article 1903) for the mid-time of the period during which observations are to be made. (LHA ♈ equals GHA ♈ from an almanac minus west longitude, or plus east longitude; LHA ♈ can also be determined graphically with a small circular plastic device marked with multiple scales.) For morning sights, the beginning of civil twilight (article 2320) or a time shortly thereafter is often used. For the eve-

ning, the time would be based on the ending of civil twilight. The most suitable time to select depends largely on the ability of the observer and the quality of his sextant, and can best be determined by experience; a few minutes' variation earlier or later is not significant.

The following examples illustrate the use of the Star Finder:

Example: A navigator, whose DR position at the time of the ending of civil twilight will be Lat. 37°14.8′N, Long. 144°25.6′E, determines the GHA of Aries to be 312°46.8′ at that time.

Required: The approximate altitudes and azimuths of all first magnitude stars above the horizon at that time, using the Star Finder.

Solution: (Figure 2002b) First, determine LHA in the usual manner; in this case, 312°46.8′ + 144°25.6′ = 457°12.4′ − 360° = 97°12.4′. Next, select the blue-ink template for the latitude closest to the DR latitude. Place this on the star base so that the labels for both correspond to the name of the DR latitude. In this case the template for Latitude 35° N is selected and placed over the side of the star base that has the letter "N" at the center, as shown. Orient the template so that the arrow extending from the 0°–180° azimuth line points to the value on the base plate of LHA ♈ for the time desired; in this case, the arrow is aligned, as closely as possible by eye, with 97.2°.

Finally, note the approximate altitudes and azimuths of the desired celestial bodies. The approximate altitudes and azimuths of the first magnitude stars are tabulated below, in order of increasing azimuth.

Body	ha	Zn
Regulus	36°	101°
Pollux	73°	110°
Procyon	56°	149°
Sirius	38°	171°
Canopus	1°	181°
Betelgeuse	61°	199°
Rigel	43°	206°
Aldebaran	58°	241°
Capella	73°	314°

GHA ♈ 312°46.8'
λ 144°25.6' E
LHA ♈ 97°12.4'

In this instance, there are a considerable number of first magnitude stars above the horizon, but they are not evenly distributed in azimuth. At sea, a navigator would include some tabulated stars of lesser magnitude to his north, such as Dubhe, Kochab, etc. He would probably not observe Canopus, except from necessity, due to its low altitude. Pollux and Capella might be difficult to observe, both being above 70° in altitude; Regulus and Mirfak would be easier to observe and give equivalent coverage in azimuth.

It is always wise to list more stars than the navigator actually expects to observe, as some may be obscured by clouds. The stars listed for observation should not be limited to those of the first magnitude; all the stars shown on the Star Finder are readily visible in clear weather. The stars should be selected so that good distribution in azimuth is obtained, and on the basis of altitude. The most convenient altitude band for observation lies roughly between 15° and 60°, but it is preferable to obtain observations considerably lower or higher than these approximate limits, rather than to have poor distribution in azimuth.

Using the Star Finder with Planets

2004   The Star Finder may be used in the same manner to predetermine the position in the heavens of the planets—or of additional fixed stars,

should this be required—if their positions are plotted on the star base (see below). (This may also be advisable to avoid confusing a star with a nearby planet.) While the planets move in position relative to the stars, their positions so plotted will be satisfactory for several days. Thus, for a vessel departing on a two-week passage, the positions of the planets could be plotted on the star base for a date approximately one week after departure.

To plot the position of a planet on the star base, the navigator first determines its declination for the desired time, as well as 360° minus its sidereal hour angle (SHA) as the relative positions of the stars are determined by their SHAs. This latter quantity is obtained by subtracting the GHA ♈ for the desired time from the GHA of the planet at that time, adding 360° to the GHA when necessary. This is equivalent to "right ascension" (article 1903) expressed in units of arc (degrees) rather than units of time (hours). For example, suppose a navigator in south latitude wishes to plot Venus on the star base. From the *Nautical* or *Air Almanac* for a time near the middle of the observation period, he obtains the data shown below, and then determines 360° − SHA.

GHA Venus	222°40.2'	Dec. S4°39.6'
GHA ♈	−213°29.3'	
SHA Venus	9°10.9'	
360° − SHA	350°49.1'	

This angle, and the declination, would be required to locate Venus on the star base: for plotting purposes, he would call them 350.8° and 4.5° south, respectively. (Alternatively, from the *Nautical Almanac* he could have directly read the SHA of Venus tabulated at the bottom of the left-hand page as an average for a three-day period and subtracted this value from 360°; this procedure is accurate enough for Star Finder use.)

Next, the red plotting template is placed, south latitude side up, on the south (S) side of the star base. On the red template, a radial line is printed to represent every 10° of meridian angle, and a concentric circle is printed for every 10° of declination, with the median circle being the celestial equator. When in place on the base plate, this median circle should be concurrent with the celestial equator circle on the base plate. The solid circles within the celestial equator circle then represent declination of the same name as the base plate, while the dashed circles outside the equator represent declinations of contrary name.

The index arrow is now aligned with 350.8°. The position of Venus is then plotted on the base by

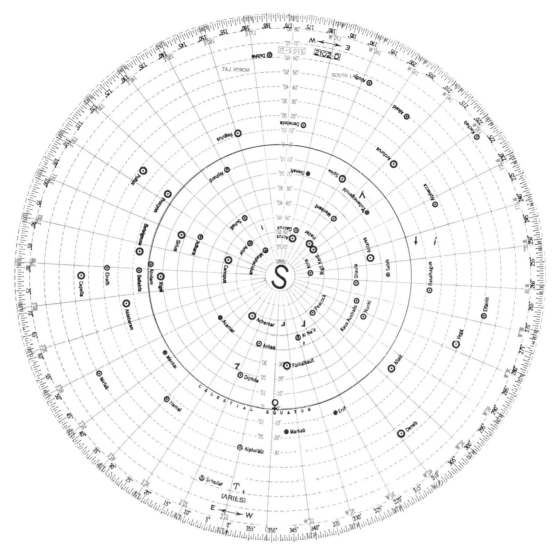

Figure 2004. Star Finder; base with red plotting template in place (shown here in blue).

marking with a pencil through the cut-out slot at the proper point on the declination scale. In this case, south declination is on the side of the circle for the celestial equator toward the S pole at the center of the base; if the declination of the body had been of the *contrary* name to the name of the center of the base plate, it would have been plotted on the side of the equatorial circle *away* from the center. The proper symbol for Venus, ♀, is drawn in on the base after the template is removed. Figure 2004 shows the star base with the plotting template set at 350.8° and a mark for Venus at 4.5° south declination. The date for this plot should be marked in some clear area of the base as a guide as to when the position will need to be recalculated and replotted.

Similar procedures can be followed to plot an unlisted star, the moon, or the sun. A star's plot will remain unchanged for an indefinite period, but any plot of the moon or sun must be corrected to a specific time of use.

Identifying Unknown Celestial Bodies

2005 At times, the navigator may obtain an observation of an unknown body. In such a case, if *both its altitude and azimuth* are noted as well as the time of the observation, it may be identified by means of the Star Finder.

If the star is one of those shown on the base plate of the star finder, the identification is quite simple. The index arrow of the blue template is aligned to the appropriate LHA ♈ for the time of the observation. The point of intersection of the altitude and azimuth curve of the body is then located on the blue template, and the body listed on the star base at or quite near this position can usually be assumed to be the one observed.

The visible planets should have been plotted on the star base as outlined above, as the observed body may have been a planet rather than a star.

If no star or planet appears at or near that point, the red template can be used to determine the approximate Dec. and SHA of the star. These two arguments can then be used with the list of stars in the *Almanac* for proper identification.

To determine the SHA and Dec., the blue template is left in place properly aligned with LHA of Aries; the red template is then placed over the blue template and rotated until the slotted meridian is over the intersection of the altitude and azimuth curve obtained from the observation of the star. The Dec. is read off the scale along the slotted meridian, or its imaginary extension for large values of Dec. the quantity 360° minus SHA is read from the base plate underneath the arrow on the red template. This figure subtracted from 360° equals the SHA of the star.

With the declination and SHA known approximately, the list of stars in the *Nautical* or *Air Almanac* can be consulted for identification and the exact values of these quantities.

U.S.A.F. Astrotracker Type CPU-300

2006 To avoid the inaccuracies introduced by the use of a template for a latitude that may be as much as 5° from the observer's actual latitude, there is a device based on the same principles as the 2102-D, but slightly more complex in operation. This is the U.S. Air Force *Astrotracker Type CPU-300*, also available commercially. Templates are provided for the same 10° intervals, and carry the same pattern of lines, but these do not fit over a central pin and are capable of adjustment over a 5° range so as to set the template for an exact value of latitude. Otherwise, use of this Astrotracker is exactly the same as for the 2102-D model.

Star Identification by Pub. No. 229

2007 Although no formal star identification tables are included in DMAHTC Pub. No. 229, *Sight Reduction Tables for Marine Navigation* (chapter 24), a simple approach to star identification is to scan the pages for the applicable latitude having a combination of arguments that give altitude and azimuth angle for the unidentified body. Thus the approximate declination and LHA of the body are

determined directly. The star's SHA is found from SHA star = LHA star − LHA ♈. With declination and SHA roughly known, the *Air* or *Nautical Almanac* is consulted for identification and exact values. Each volume of Pub. No. 229 describes this method, and an alternative, in greater detail.

Star Identifier by Calculator or Computer

2008 Several models of electronic calculators have available programs for star identification; if these are on magnetic cards or in insertable modules, they are easily used to get precise and accurate values of declination and SHA that can be used as described in the preceding articles.

If the vessel is equipped with a microcomputer or a minicomputer, it is possible for the navigator to write a program for star identification, or have one prepared for him.

Star Charts and Sky Diagrams

2009 In addition to the 2102-D Star Finder and Identifier, the identification of celestial bodies may be learned pictorially; remember that the Star Finder does *not* give a visualization of the heavens. *Sky charts* are photograph-like representations of the night sky at certain times of the year. *Sky diagrams* are drawings of the heavens as they would be seen from certain locations at various times. Although intended for the same purpose, there are differences in design and use.

Identification by Star Chart

Star charts are representations of the celestial sphere, or of part of it, on a flat surface. On most charts, north is at the top and south at the bottom, but east is at the *left*, and west at the *right;* this is the reverse of the terrestrial chart presentation. If the chart is held overhead, and the N-S axis is properly oriented, this presentation approximates the appearance of the heavens. Some star charts are polar projections; these show the star groups around the pole and are especially helpful in visualizing the movement and relationship of circumpolar stars. Star charts are more often used for learning the identification of stars than in the normal practice of navigation at sea.

Nautical Almanac Star Charts

The *Nautical Almanac* star charts consist of four charts; one polar projection for each hemisphere, covering declinations 10° through 90°, of the same name, and two rectangular projections covering Dec. 30° N to 30° S, around the celestial sphere. See figure 2009a.

Figure 2009a. Star Charts from the *Nautical Almanac*.

A planetary diagram giving LMT of meridian passage of the planets is also given in the *Nautical Almanac*. By means of this diagram, the approximate positions of the planets relative to the sun, and to each other, may be determined.

Air Almanac Star Charts

A fold-in, white-on-black star chart is located in the back of the *Air Almanac*. It presents the entire celestial sphere on a rectangular projection, the top and bottom edges representing the north and south celestial poles, respectively. This causes great distortion in the relative positions of stars near the poles, but provides a means of determining the order of appearance of the stars and constellations as they move across the heavens.

Air Almanac Sky Diagrams

The *Air Almanac* also contains a series of sky diagrams that show the appearance of the sky in various latitudes at different times of the day. They are helpful in selecting the most useful stars and planets for navigation, and for identifying prominent bodies when sighted. For each month, there is a series of diagrams for different latitudes (20° intervals from 70° N to 30° S) for two-hour intervals during the entire day. The diagrams for a given latitude are in a horizontal row and show the changes as the day progresses. The appearance of the sky for different latitudes and different times is shown on a pair of facing pages; thus, the appearance of the sky for an intermediate latitude and/or time is easily visualized. A separate set of diagrams is included for the north polar region.

The sky diagrams of the *Air Almanac* have an advantage over sky charts as they are prepared for each month; they are immediately usable without reference to tables or calculations. The diagram for a specific month also allows the inclusion of the planets and the moon, in addition to the 57 selected navigational stars and Polaris; the north and south celestial poles are also shown as NP and SP where appropriate. Stars are shown by a symbol indicating their magnitude and a number for identification; planets are identified by a single-letter abbreviation, and the sun by its symbol. The position of the moon is shown separately for each day by a small circle around figures representing the day of the month. See figure 2009b.

The positions of the stars and planets in each diagram are indicated for the 15th of the month and will usually serve for the entire month. If it is desired to allow for the motion of the stars during the month, it is necessary only to remember that a given configuration will occur at the beginning of each month one hour later than the time indicated, and at the end of the month one hour earlier. In those months during which Venus moves considerably with respect to the stars, the positions for the first and last of the month are shown; the position towards the west is for the first of the month.

As the sun moves with respect to the stars, its position is given for the first and last days of the month relative to the position of the stars and does not represent the true altitude and azimuth at those times; the position towards the west is for the first of the month. To obtain the altitude and azimuth of the sun at the beginning and end of the month, one must adjust the position of the sun by the amount the stars would have moved. The lengths of the arrows indicate the motion of the stars in 15 days. When the sun is above the horizon,

Figure 2009b. Star Diagrams from the *Air Almanac*.

only the moon and Venus can be seen with the naked eye, but the positions of the stars are given for use with astrotrackers.

The moon moves so rapidly with respect to the stars that its position at a given time of the night varies appreciably from night to night, and it is necessary to show on each diagram a succession of positions for various days of the month. Three or four such positions are indicated, and those for the intermediate dates may be estimated from those given. Since the moon moves completely around the sky in slightly less than a month, or a little over 13° in a day, it will appear on a given diagram for about half of each month. The position on the diagram for each successive night is always to the eastward; when it disappears off the eastern edge of the diagram, it will reappear on the western edge about two weeks later—except occasionally on the polar diagrams.

The sky diagrams, used in conjunction with the star chart previously mentioned and a planet location diagram also included in each *Air Almanac*, are very effective in star identification; the latter two are used for detailed verification of the identification made with the sky diagrams.

It must be remembered that the sky diagrams of the *Air Almanac* are to be used flat on the chart table and that they show bearings as they appear on the navigator's chart, east to the right. The star chart and the planet location diagram, on the other hand, are both designed to be held over the head for comparison with the sky, and on them east is to the left.

Additional Star Charts

2010   Six numbered star charts are included in this chapter as figures 2011 to 2016. They show all the brighter stars, necessarily with some repetition; the various constellations are described in addition to navigational stars. There are two charts of the polar skies usable all year long, plus four lower-latitude charts, one for each season of the year. The two charts of the polar regions are on the azimuthal equidistant polar projections; the others are on the transverse Mercator projection.

To use a polar chart, face the elevated pole and hold the correct chart with the name of the month on top. It will then be correctly oriented for that month for 2200 Local Mean Time (LMT) (see article 2210). For each hour that the LMT differs from 2200, rotate the chart one hour, as shown by the radial lines. These are labeled for LHA in *time units*, in which case it is called *local sidereal time* (LST), and for sidereal hour angle (SHA). The sidereal time indicates the direction of rotation, as earlier sidereal times occur at earlier solar times. The region about the *elevated* pole will be the only polar region visible.

To use a transverse Mercator star chart, hold it overhead with the top of the page toward north. The left edge will then be east, the right edge west, and the bottom south. The numbers along the central hour circle indicate declination and can be used to orient for latitude. The charts are made for LMT 2200 on the dates specified. For each half month later, subtract one hour to determine the time at which the heavens appear as depicted in the chart; for each half month earlier, add one hour to LMT 2200. The numbers below the celestial equator indicate local sidereal time; those above indicate sidereal hour angle. If the LMT of observation is not 2200, these can be used to determine which hour circle coincides with the celestial meridian. The lighter broken lines connect stars of some of the more easily distinguishable constellations. The heavier broken lines are shown to aid in the identification of stars of different constellations that have a spatial relationship to each other.

It should be kept in mind that the apparent positions of the stars are constantly changing because of the motions of the earth. If the observer changes his position on the earth, a further change in the apparent positions of the stars will result. Remember, too, that the limits of the transverse Mercator charts represent the approximate limits of observation only at the equator. Observers elsewhere will see below their elevated pole, and an equal amount of the opposite polar region will be hidden from view.

The approximate appearance of the heavens at any given time can be determined by obtaining LHA ♈ (from GHA ♈, tabulated in the almanacs, and the observer's longitude) and converting it to time units. The resulting local sidereal time (LST) is then found on the star charts. The celestial meridian on the transverse Mercator chart that is labeled with that time is the one that is approximately overhead. The same celestial meridian on the polar charts, labeled in the same way, is the one that is *up*. Thus if LHA ♈ is 225°, LST is 15ʰ. This appears on the transverse Mercator charts of both figures 2012 and 2013. The stars to the east of the celestial meridian at this time appear in figure 2013 (in the direction of increasing LST and decreasing SHA), and the stars to the west of the celestial meridian at this time appear in figure 2012 (in the direction of decreasing LST and increasing SHA). By orienting each polar chart so that the celestial meridian labeled 15ʰ is up, the stars toward and beyond each celestial pole can be seen. An observer can view only half of the celestial sphere at

a given time, of course, and the stars actually visible depend upon his latitude.

The North Polar Sky

2011   In the *north polar sky* (Star Chart 1, figure 2011) nearly everyone is familiar with the *Big Dipper*, the popular name for the constellation *Ursa Major* (the big bear). This is composed of seven stars in the shape of a dipper, with the open part toward the north celestial pole. For observers in the United States, most of the dipper is circumpolar and is therefore visible the year around. Dubhe, Alioth, and Alkaid are the stars of this constellation most used by navigators. Dubhe and Merak, forming part of the bowl of the dipper, are called the pointers, for if the line connecting them is extended northward, it passes very near Polaris, less than one degree from the north celestial pole. If the line is extended across the pole, it leads very near to Caph in *Cassiopeia*. These stars point straight *down* to Polaris in the evening sky of mid-April. By the middle of July they are to the left of Polaris. In mid-October they are directly below the pole, and three months later, in the middle of January, they are to the right. For other stars identified by means of the *Big Dipper*, see article 2012.

Ursa Minor (Little Dipper)

Polaris is part of the *Little Dipper*, as the constellation *Ursa Minor* (the little bear) is popularly known; this star is not conspicuous until the sky has become quite dark. Only Polaris at one end and Kochab at the other, both second-magnitude stars, are used by the navigator. The *Little Dipper* is roughly parallel to the *Big Dipper*, but upside down with respect to it. In the autumn the *Big Dipper* is under the *Little Dipper*, and there is a folktale that liquid spilling out of the little one will be caught by the big one. The handles of the two dippers curve in opposite directions, relative to their bowls.

Cassiopeia

Across the pole from the handle of the *Big Dipper*, and approximately the same distance from Polaris, will be found the constellation *Cassiopeia* (the queen), also known as *Cassiopeia's Chair*. The principal stars of this constellation form a well-defined *W* or *M*, depending on their position with respect to the pole. Schedar, the second star from the right when the figure appears as a *W*, is a second-magnitude star sometimes used by navigators. Second-magnitude Caph, the right-hand star when the figure appears as a *W*, is of interest because it is situated close to the hour circle of the vernal equinox.

Figure 2011. Star Chart 1, the north polar region. Hold the chart toward the north at 2200 LMT with the name of the current month at the top.

Draco

The constellation *Draco* (the dragon) is about halfway from *Cassiopeia* to the *Big Dipper* in a westerly direction, but its navigational star Eltanin probably is easier to identify by following the western arm of the *Northern Cross* as described in the *Scorpio* group (article 2013).

The Spring Sky

2012 In the *spring sky* (Star Chart 2, figure 2012) the *Big Dipper* is above the pole, high in the sky, and serves to point out several excellent navigational stars. Starting at the bowl, follow the curvature of the handle. If this curved arc is continued, it leads first to Arcturus, the only navigational star in *Boötes* (the herdsman) and then to Spica in *Virgo* (the virgin), both first-magnitude stars much used by the navigator.

Leo

A line northward through the pointers of the *Big Dipper* leads to Polaris. If this line is followed in the opposite direction, it leads in the general direction of Regulus, the end of the handle of the sickle in the constellation *Leo* (the lion). This much-used navigational star is of the first magnitude and the brightest star in its part of the sky. A line connecting Regulus and Arcturus passes close to second-magnitude Denebola (tail of the lion), sometimes used by navigators.

Corvus

The constellation *Corvus* (the crow) more nearly resembles a quadrilateral sail. It is not difficult to find, and contains the third-magnitude navigational star Gienah. Due south of *Corvus* is the *Southern Cross* (article 2016).

Hydra

The only navigational star in *Hydra* (the serpent), a long, inconspicuous constellation near *Corvus*, is the second-magnitude Alphard. This star is more easily identified by its being close to the extension of a line from the pointer of the *Big Dipper* through Regulus and extending southward.

The Summer Sky

2013 In the *summer sky* (Star Chart 3, figure 2013), *Scorpio* (the scorpion) is one constellation

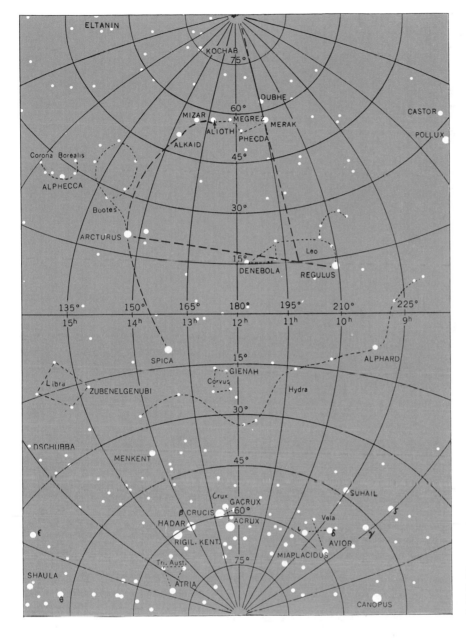

Figure 2012. Star Chart 2. The spring sky as seen at 2200 LMT on 22 April. Hold the chart overhead with the top of the page toward the north.

that resembles the animal for which it is named without too much imagination. The curve from Antares, the main navigational star, to Shaula is particularly suggestive of a scorpion's tail. Immediately to the east is a group forming the shape of a teapot with the star Nunki in the handle.

Cygnus

To the north of these are the first-magnitude stars Vega, Deneb, and Altair. They form a distinct right triangle (right angle at Vega), which many people use as an identification feature. However, each one is in a different constellation, which should enable one to identify it without reference to any other stars. Deneb is in the Northern Cross *(Cygnus);* the eastern arm of the cross points to Enif, the western arm to Eltanin, and the bisectors of the lower right angles point to Altair and Vega. Altair is readily identified by the small stars on either side of it, sometimes called the "guardians." It should be kept in mind, however, that the southern guardian is only a fourth-magnitude star and may not show too plainly on very hazy or bright moonlight nights. This configuration is unique and should identify Altair through a break in the overcast with no other stars showing. Vega may be identified under these conditions by an almost perfect parallelogram slightly to the south and east of

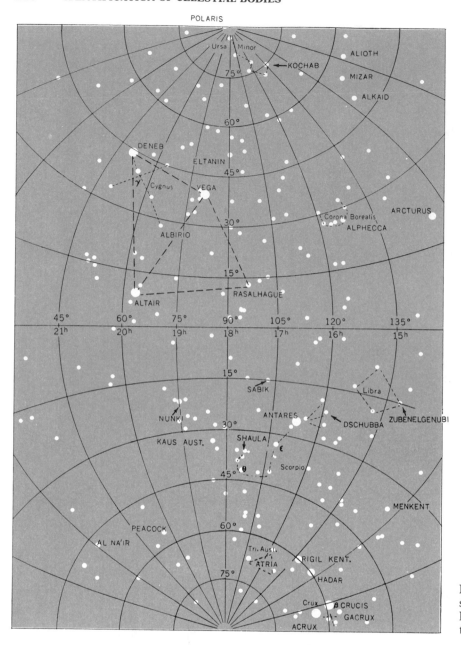

Figure 2013. Star Chart 3. The summer sky as seen at 2200 LMT on 22 July. Hold the chart overhead with the top of the page toward the north.

it. Again, however, these are fourth-magnitude stars and are not too distinct if the weather conditions are unfavorable.

Corona Borealis

The Northern Crown *(Corona Borealis)* is a group of stars shaped like a bowl about two thirds of the distance from Vega toward Arcturus. This constellation forms a distinctive pattern and connects the dipper group to the Northern Cross to the east. Second-magnitude Alphecca in this group is sometimes used by navigators.

Rasalhague forms nearly an equilateral triangle with Vega and Altair. This second-magnitude star

and third-magnitude Sabik, to the south, are occasionally used by navigators.

The Autumn Sky

2014 The *autumn sky* (Star Chart 4, figure 2014) is marked by a scarcity of first-magnitude stars. The *Northern Cross* has moved to a position low in the western sky, and *Cassiopeia* is nearly on the meridian to the north. A little south of the zenith for most observers in the United States, the great square of *Pegasus* (the winged horse) appears nearly on the meridian. The eastern side of this square, and Caph in *Cassiopeia*, nearly mark the hour circle of the vernal equinox. Alpheratz and

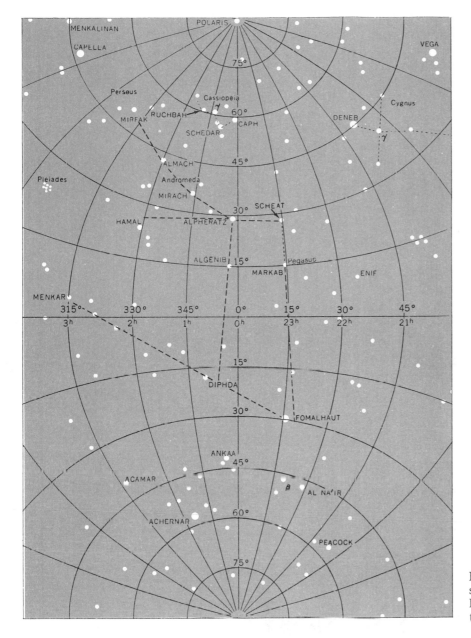

Figure 2014. Star Chart 4. The autumn sky as seen at 2200 LMT on 21 October. Hold the chart overhead with the top of the page toward the north.

Markab, second-magnitude stars at opposite corners of the square, are the principal navigational stars of this constellation. Second-magnitude Enif is occasionally used.

The square of *Pegasus* is useful in locating several navigational stars. The line joining the stars of the eastern side of the square, if continued southward, leads close to second-magnitude Diphda in *Cetus* (the sea monster). Similarly, a line joining the stars of the western side of the square, if continued southward, leads close to first-magnitude Formalhaut. A line extending eastward from the north side of the square leads close to second-magnitude Hamal, in *Aries* (the ram). This was the location of the vernal equinox some 2,000 years ago, when it was designated the "first point of Aries."

A curved line from Alpheratz through *Andromeda* leads to *Perseus*. The only navigational star frequently used in *Perseus* is the second-magnitude Mirfak. The curved line from Mirfak to Alpheratz forms a handle to a huge dipper of which the square of *Pegasus* is the bowl.

A line from Fomalhaut through Diphda extended about forty degrees leads to Menkar, an inconspicuous third-magnitude star in *Cetus;* and Ankaa, a second-magnitude star in *Phoenix,* is found about twenty degrees southeasterly from Fomalhaut. Both stars are listed among the navigational stars.

The navigational stars associated with *Pegasus* are Alpheratz, Markab, Diphda, Fomalhaut, and Hamal.

Capella, rising in the east as *Pegasus* is overhead, connects this group to the *Orion* group while Enif acts as a link to the west.

The Winter Sky

2015 At no other time do the heavens contain so many bright stars as in the *winter sky* (Star Chart 5, figure 2015). The principal constellation of this region is *Orion* (the hunter), probably the best-known constellation in the entire sky, with the exception of the *Big Dipper*. This figure is well known

to observers in both the Northern and Southern Hemispheres, as the belt of *Orion* lies almost exactly on the celestial equator. Brilliant Rigel and first-magnitude Betelgeuse are situated at approximately equal distances below and above the belt, respectively.

Stars Relative to Orion

Several good navigational stars may be found by the use of *Orion*. If the line of the belt is continued to the westward, it leads near first-magnitude, reddish Aldebaran (the "follower," so named because it follows the "seven sisters" of *Pleiades*), in the V-shaped head of *Taurus* (the bull). If the line of the

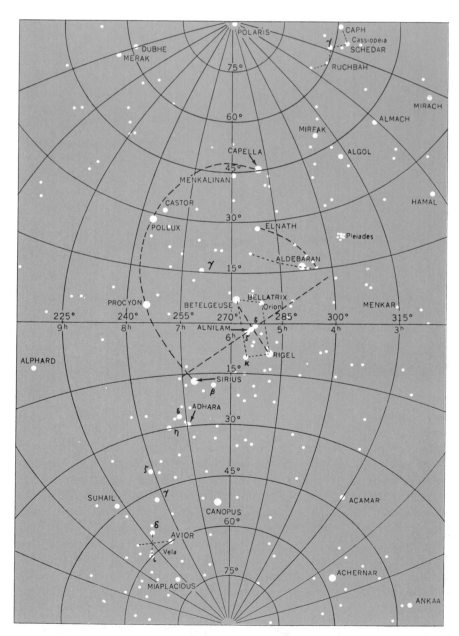

Figure 2015. Star Chart 5. The winter sky as seen at 2200 LMT on 21 January. Hold the chart overhead with the top of the page toward the north.

belt is followed in the opposite direction, it leads almost to Sirius, the brightest of all the stars; this is the principal star in the constellation of *Canis Major*, the hunter's large dog. Starting with Sirius, a rough circle can be drawn through Procyon in *Canis Minor* (the little dog), Pollux and Castor in *Gemini* (the twins), Capella in *Auriga* (the charioteer), Aldebaran, Rigel, and back to Sirius. All of these except Castor are first-magnitude stars.

Several second-magnitude stars in the general area of *Orion* are bright enough for navigational purposes, but are seldom used because there are so many first-magnitude stars nearby. Four of these second-magnitude stars are listed among the principal navigational stars of the almanac. These are Bellatrix, just west of Betelgeuse; Alnilam, the middle star (actually, a spiral nebulae) in the belt; Elnath, in *Taurus;* and Adhara, part of a triangle in *Canis Major*, and just south of Sirius.

Nearly on the meridian far to the south the brilliant Canopus, second brightest star, is visible only to observers in the United States south of latitude 37½°. This star is part of the constellation *Carina* (the keel).

The South Polar Sky

2016   While the *south polar sky* (Star Chart 6, figure 2016) contains a number of bright stars, a person who travels to the Southern Hemisphere for the first time is likely to be disappointed by the absence of any striking configuration of stars similar to those with which he is familiar. The famed *Southern Cross (Crux)* is far from an impressive constellation and such a poor cross it might easily be overlooked if two of its stars were not of the first magnitude. A somewhat similar "false cross" in the constellation *Vela* may be easily mistaken for the *Southern Cross*.

Canopus is almost due south of Sirius. The constellation *Carina*, of which Canopus is a part, was originally part of a larger constellation, *Argo* (the ship), which is now generally divided into *Carina* (the keel), *Puppis* (the stern), *Pyxis* (the mariner's compass), and *Vela* (the sails). Navigational stars included in *Argo* are, besides first-magnitude Canopus, Avior (part of the "false cross"), Suhail (figures 2010 and 2013) and Miaplacidus, all second-magnitude stars.

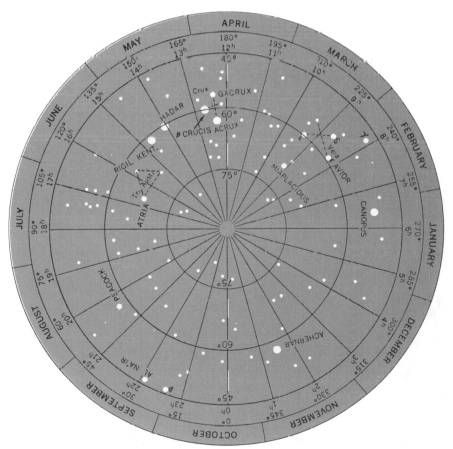

Figure 2016. Star Chart 6, the south polar region. Hold the chart toward the south at 2200 LMT with the name of the current month at the top.

Counterclockwise from *Argo* is *Crux*, the true *Southern Cross*. Acrux and Gacrux are listed among the principal navigational stars of the almanac. This constellation also contains the first-magnitude star β Crucis.

Centaurus

Two more good first-magnitude stars lie in nearby *Centaurus* (the centaur). These are Rigil Kentaurus and Hadar. The second-magnitude Menkent at the other end of the constellation (figures 2012 and 2013) is listed among the principal navigational stars and is used occasionally by navigators.

Near *Centaurus* and still in a counterclockwise direction around the pole is Atria, a commonly used navigational star in *Triangulum Australe*.

The half of the south polar region thus far described has a relatively large number of first- and second-magnitude stars. This area is actually a continuation of the bright area around *Orion*, as can be seen by referring to figure 2015.

In the remaining section of the south polar region, there are relatively few navigational stars. These are second-magnitude Peacock in *Pavo* (the peacock), second-magnitude Al Na'ir in *Grus* (the crane), and first-magnitude Achernar and third-magnitude Acamar (figure 2014 and 2015) in *Eridanus* (the river). All of these constellations are faint and poorly defined. Of these stars, Achernar and Peacock are good navigational stars; the others are seldom used.

Star Identification by Computer

2017 Programs are available for several models of microcomputers that will display a view of the sky upon entry of the geographic coordinates of a position and the time. Such a program should be readily adaptable to other models of microcomputers, and to minicomputers.

One program, *TellStar* ™, presents a high-resolution display of the sun, moon, planets, and stars (with an indication of their magnitude). Two displays are available—Overhead, a 360° view down to about 40° elevation, and Horizontal, covering various 90° sectors of azimuth from the horizon to the zenith. Distortion is present, as in any representation of a spherical surface on a two-dimensional plane, but it does not greatly handicap identification of the heavenly bodies. The name of a body can be entered on the keyboard, and if it is above the horizon, a set of cross-hairs will mark the body on the display. Conversely, the cross-hairs can be placed on the symbol for a body, and the computer will provide its name. A "statistical" display is also available that will provide information on a body's declination and elevation at a given time, and times of rising and setting with azimuths for these times. A paper copy of screen displays can also be made on some models of dot-matrix printers.

Programs are also available for advanced models of calculators that will give values of altitude and azimuth for given times, but these, of course, lack the capability for a visual display.

Chapter 21

The Marine Sextant: Its Use, Adjustment and Corrections

Introduction

2101 A *marine sextant* is one of the basic "tools" of celestial navigation (the others are a timepiece and tables or equations). It is used to make a highly precise and accurate measurement of the angle between lines from the observer to a celestial body and to the horizon; this is *sextant altitude, hs*, which must be corrected to *observed altitude, Ho*. In this chapter, the term "sextant" will be used for the standard marine sextant; other types will be specifically identified when discussed.

Development of the Sextant

The first successful instrument developed for measuring the altitude of celestial bodies while at sea was the *cross-staff*. It was unique in that it measured altitude from the sea horizon; its disadvantage was that it required the user to look at the horizon *and* at the body at the same time. This must have been quite a feat, particularly when the body was well above the horizon; an experienced navigator, however, could for the first time determine the altitude of a body at sea with an accuracy of about one degree.

In 1590, the *backstaff*, or *Davis's quadrant*, shown in figure 2101, was invented by John Davis; this was a great advancement over the cross-staff. To use this instrument the observer turned his back on the sun, and aligned a shadow cast by the sun with the horizon. Later designs of this instrument were fitted with a mirror so as to make possible observations of bodies other than the sun.

Today's *sextant* is an instrument designed to permit measurement of the angle between the lines of sight to two objects with great precision. It derives its name from the fact that its arc is approximately

Figure 2101. A Davis quadrant, 1775.

one-sixth of a circle; because of its optical principle, it can measure angles up to about 120°, or twice the value of the arc itself. Quintants and octants are similar instruments, named for the lengths of their arcs, but today it is the general practice to refer to all such instruments as sextants, regardless of the precise lengths of their arcs.

The optical principle of the sextant was first described by Sir Isaac Newton. However, its importance was not realized, and the information was long forgotten until it was applied to celestial navigation.

The double-reflecting principle of the sextant, described hereafter, was independently rediscovered in 1730 by Hadley in England and Godfrey in Philadelphia; it made possible a high standard of accuracy in celestial navigation.

Components of a Sextant

2102 A typical sextant is illustrated in figure 2102 with the principal parts labeled as follows:

H INDEX SHADE GLASSES
E INDEX MIRROR
G TELESCOPE
F HORIZON GLASS
I HORIZON SHADE GLASSES
A FRAME
B LIMB
B' ARC
C INDEX ARM
J HANDLE
D MICROMETER DRUM
D' RELEASE LEVER

Figure 2102. Component parts of a modern sextant.

A. The *frame*, on which the other parts are mounted. The frame is normally made of brass, but some "lightweight" models are of aluminum alloy. There are also less expensive models in which the frame is made of specially reinforced plastic material; see article 2105.

B. The *limb* is the lower part of the frame and carries the *arc* (B') graduated in degrees. The arc may be inscribed on the limb, or it may be inscribed on a separate plate permanently attached to the limb. The outer edge of the limb is cut into teeth, which are engaged by the teeth of the *tangent screw* (not visible).

C. The *index arm*, of the same material as the frame, is pivoted at the center of curvature of the arc and is free to move around it. Its lower end carries an *index mark* to indicate the reading in degrees on the arc.

D. The *micrometer drum* is used to make fine adjustments of the index arm. It is mounted on a shaft, having a pinion gear at the other end called the *tangent screw*. This tangent screw engages the worm teeth cut into the limb, and one full turn moves the index arm by one-half degree on the arc, thus changing the observed altitude by exactly one degree. The micrometer drum is generally graduated in minutes of arc. On some models there is only a single index mark for the micrometer drum, and fractions of a minute can only be estimated between gradu-

ations for whole minutes; see figure 2102. On other models there is a *vernier scale*, which permits readings to be taken to 0.1' (0.2'); see figure 2106a. A few sextants have vernier readings in tens of seconds of arc. The *release levers* (D') are spring-loaded clamps that hold the tangent screw against the teeth of the limb. When squeezed together, they release the tangent screw and allow the index arm to be moved easily along the arc to roughly the desired setting (which is then refined by use of the micrometer drum when pressure on these levers is loosened).

E. The *index mirror* is mounted at the upper end of the index arm directly over its pivot point; it is perpendicular to the plane of the instrument.

F. The *horizon glass* is mounted on the frame. It, too, is precisely perpendicular to the plane of the instrument. When the index arm is set to exactly 0°, the horizon glass is parallel to the index mirror. The "traditional" horizon glass is divided vertically into two halves. The part nearer the frame is silvered as a mirror; the other half is clear optical glass.

A recent development, using modern technology, is a horizon glass uniformly coated in a manner similar to a "one-way" mirror. The horizon can be seen all across the glass, as can the reflected image of the body.

G. The *telescope* is mounted with its axis parallel to

the plane of the frame. The magnification of the telescope permits the observer to judge contact between the celestial body and the sea horizon more exactly than is possible with the unaided eye, and it often makes it possible to pick up the image of a star when it cannot be seen by the naked eye. Telescopes are adjustable for the characteristics of the individual observer's eye, and on some models, the telescope can be moved towards or away from the frame as conditions warrant.

H. The *index shade glasses* are of optically ground glass mounted perpendicular to the arc, and are pivoted so that they can be swung into or out of the line of sight between the index and horizon mirrors. Two types of index shade glasses are employed on sextants. The first is a variable-density polarizing filter; the second consists of four or more shade glasses of neutral tint and increasing density. The shade glasses are employed when making observations of the sun, and sometimes when observing a bright planet or star above a dimly lighted horizon.

I. The *horizon shades* are similar to the index shades, but of lesser density, and serve to reduce the glare of reflected sunlight on the horizon.

J. The *handle*, usually of wood or plastic, is mounted on the frame at a location and angle for good balance and easy grip with the right hand. Some sextants provide for night lighting of the index marks of both the arc and the micrometer drum; the batteries for such lights are within the handle.

Optical Principles of a Sextant

2103 The optics of a sextant are based on a system of double reflection in that the image of the observed body is reflected from the upper, or index, mirror to the lower, or horizon, mirror, and thence into the field of view of the telescope, where it is brought into coincidence with the sea horizon, which is seen through the clear portion of the horizon mirror. The principle of optics involved is stated: *The angle between the first and last directions of a ray of light that has undergone two reflections in the same plane is twice the angle that the two reflecting surfaces make with each other.* This principle can be proven by geometry, and is illustrated in figure 2103. The sextant arc, however, is engraved to show the actual altitude of the body, rather than the number of degrees the index arm has been moved from the 0° setting. In figure 2103, angle *a*, the difference between first and last reflection, equals twice angle *b*, the angle between the reflect-

Figure 2103. The optical principle of a sextant.

ing surfaces. Angle *c* equals angle *d*, and angle *e* equals angle *f*, the angles of incidence and reflection, respectively, of the index and horizon mirrors.

Artificial Horizon Sextants

2104 The "bubble sextant" has long been used by aerial navigators for celestial observations. The vertical is established in these instruments by bringing the center of the observed body into coincidence with the center of a free-floating bubble. Most aviation artificial horizon sextants are fitted with an averaging device. This provides the determination of a mean of observations made over a considerable period of time, usually two minutes. On the latest models, the observation may be discontinued at any time after the first thirty seconds and the average altitude determined. It is usually desirable, however, to use the full one- or two-minute observation series, as it is assumed that this will at least cover the complete period of natural oscillation of the aircraft in pitch and roll.

The aircraft bubble sextant is difficult to use aboard most surface vessels, particularly in a seaway, due to the constant and often violent accelerations that occur and the relatively short period of roll of a ship or boat as compared to an aircraft. Useful results, however, have been obtained with them aboard large vessels and partially surfaced submarines. The Fleet ballistic missile submarines are now issued a marine sextant with special bubble attachment. For civilian use, artificial horizons (bubble devices) are available from some sextant manufacturers for attachment to their instruments.

In the past thirty years considerable experimentation has been conducted with sextants fitted with gyroscopic artificial horizon systems. Such a system holds great promise, but is very expensive and has not come into general usage.

The great advantage of an artificial horizon sextant is that it permits observations of celestial bodies when the sea horizon is obscured by darkness, fog, or haze. The accuracy obtainable with the bubble sextant lies in the range of minutes of arc, rather than the tenths of minutes obtained with a marine sextant using the natural horizon.

Other Sextants

2105 The sextants described above are high-precision instruments and are quite expensive. Models of lesser precision and accuracy are available for navigators whose requirements are less demanding. Sextants are also made of very stable plastic materials with optics of good, but lesser,

Figure 2105a. Sextant of modern design.

Figure 2105b. Sextant with a plastic frame and other parts.

Figure 2106a. Marine sextant, showing arc, micrometer drum, and vernier.

Figure 2106b. A U.S. Navy sextant showing the index mark opposite the 30° mark. The correct angle is 29°57′ and not 30°57′.

quality than those described in the preceding article. Such a sextant, sometimes carried as a back-up to a more refined instrument, can have a micrometer drum and read angles to a precision of 0.2′ with fully acceptable accuracy for ordinary navigation, yet cost one-tenth or less of the price of a first-line sextant.

There are also very simple plastic instruments often referred to as "practice" or "lifeboat" sextants. These operate on the same basic principles, but lack such features as a drum vernier, adjustable mirrors, and telescope; these can read angles no more precisely than 2′. Such sextants serve their intended purposes, however, and are relatively inexpensive.

Reading a Sextant

2106 In using a sextant to measure an angle, such as a celestial altitude, the spring release at the bottom of the index arm is disengaged, and the arm is moved until the body and the horizon are both seen in the field of view. The release is then freed so that the tangent screw re-engages the worm teeth on the arc and the micrometer drum is turned until the body is brought into coincidence with the horizon.

To read the altitude, the position of the arm's index mark against the scale of degrees on the arc is first read. In figure 2106a, the index mark is located between 29° and 30°, indicating that the altitude will be 29° plus the reading of minutes and tenths obtained from the micrometer drum and its vernier respectively.

The index mark for the micrometer drum is the zero mark on the vernier. In figure 2106a, it is between the drum markings for 42′ and 43′, indicating that the altitude will be 42′ plus the number of tenths obtained from the vernier. To read the ver-

nier, its graduation most nearly in line with a graduation on the drum is found. In figure 2106a, this is 5, indicating a reading of 0.5′. Adding each of these components, the altitude is found to be 29°42.5′.

Considerable care must be exercised in reading the micrometer drum if the index mark for the index arm is very close to a graduation on the arc. If, for example, that index mark was apparently right opposite the 30° mark on the arc, and the micrometer drum read 57′ and some tenths, then the true reading for the sextant would be 29°57′, *not* 30°57′. See figure 2106b. Similar care must be used in reading the micrometer drum when the vernier scale is at its upper end near 8 or 9 tenths.

SEXTANT ERRORS AND ADJUSTMENTS

Instrument Errors

2107 The sextant, being an optical-mechanical instrument, cannot be manufactured totally error-free. When a sextant is assembled by the manufacturer, it is tested for *fixed instrument errors*, and the combined values are recorded on a certificate attached to the inside of the sextant case. The error is usually listed for each 10° of the arc. Some manufacturers merely certify the instruments to be free of errors "for practical use." This implies that the error nowhere exceeds approximately 10 seconds of arc. In modern precision sextants, these nonadjustable errors are small and may usually be ignored. Specifications for the Navy Mark II sextant require that no errors be greater than 35 seconds of arc. Since this exceeds a half minute of arc, or half mile on the earth's surface, correction should be applied to the sextant reading for any errors approaching this magnitude.

The mirrors are mounted in a manner permitting adjustment to maintain their perpendicularity to

Figure 2108a. Sextant set at zero, with index error.

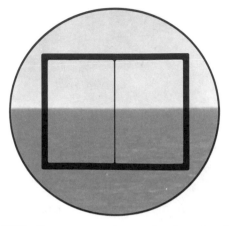

Figure 2108b. Sextant set at zero, horizon in alignment as seen through sextant telescope.

the sextant frame, and parallelism to each other. The line of sight of the telescope must be parallel to the plane of the sextant frame. Any necessary adjustment should, whenever possible, be accomplished in an optical repair shop.

Index Error

2108   Index error should be determined each time the sextant is used. In the daytime, this is usually done by an observation of the horizon. The index arm is first set at exactly 0°00.0' and with the sextant held in a vertical position, the horizon is observed. In nearly all instances, the horizon will not appear as a continuous line in the direct and reflected views; see figure 2108a. The micrometer drum is adjusted until the reflected and direct images of the horizon are brought into coincidence, forming a straight unbroken line, as is shown in figure 2108b. This operation should be repeated several times, the reflected image of the horizon being alternately brought down and up to the direct image. The value of the index error is read in minutes and tenths after each alignment, and the average of the readings is taken.

Index Correction

The *index correction (IC)* to be applied to an observed sextant angle is the index error *with the sign reversed*. If the error is positive—the micrometer drum reads more than 0.0'—the sign of the correction is negative. Conversely, if the drum reads less than 0.0', the error is negative and the sign of the correction is positive; for example, if the average reading of the micrometer drum is 58.5', the error is −1.5' and the IC is +1.5'. If the index error is small, less than about 4.0', it is best not to try to remove it. Where the error is negative, it is some-

times said to be "off the arc," conversely, when positive it is "on the arc."

At night the index error may be determined by observing a star. The direct and reflected images are brought into coincidence, or directly adjoining each other horizontally in the manner described above for the horizon.

Quite frequently two observers will not obtain the same value for the index error; their findings will represent a combination of the actual index error and of each observer's *personal error* (see article 2111).

Index error is caused by a lack of perfect parallelism between the index mirror and horizon glass when the sextant is set at 0°. This lack of parallelism causes a greater error in observations than would a slight error in the perpendicularity of the mirrors.

Adjusting the Mirrors

To eliminate or reduce excessive index error, the *horizon* glass must be adjusted. On a Mark II navy sextant the mirror is fixed within the mirror frame; adjustment is accomplished by moving the frame by means of two adjusting screws as shown in figure 2108c. This adjustment is a trial and error process; one screw is *first* loosened by a small fraction of a revolution, and *then* the other is tightened by an equal amount; the process is repeated until the error is removed, or brought within an acceptable limit.

With the Plath and several other fine commercial sextants, the horizon glass is adjusted within the mirror frame. When holding the sextant vertical, only the upper screw is used, as illustrated in figure 2108d. The procedure just described is followed except that only the one adjusting screw is turned

Figure 2108c. Adjusting screws, Navy Mark II sextant.

Figure 2108d. Adjusting screws, Plath sextant.

Figure 2109a. Checking perpendicularity of index mirror; here the mirror is not perpendicular.

slightly; this moves the mirror against the mounting springs. When the sextant is properly adjusted, the horizon will appear as in figure 2108b with the sextant reading zero.

Perpendicularity of Mirrors

2109 The sextant should occasionally be checked to see that the mirrors are perpendicular to the sextant frame, and adjusted if a misalignment is found to exist. Index mirror alignment is checked by holding the sextant in the left hand with the index mirror towards the observer; he then looks into the index mirror and shifts the position of the sextant until the reflected image of the limb in the index mirror appears as a continuation of the limb as seen directly, looking past the index mirror. This is illustrated in figure 2109a. If the reflected image is inclined to the limb as seen directly or is not in alignment with it, the index mirror is not perpendicular to the plane of the limb, and the alignment should be corrected by use of the adjusting screws on the back of the index mirror frame. Again, some sextants have two adjusting screws, one of which must first be loosened and then the other tightened. Other sextants use only one adjusting screw, which moves the mirror against retaining springs.

To check the perpendicularity of the horizon glass, the horizon should be sighted in the same manner as was discussed in article 2108 for determining the index error. The tangent screw is adjusted until the reflected and direct images of the horizon appear as a straight line with the sextant in a vertical position. The sextant is then turned or rocked around the line of sight; the reflected horizon and the direct horizon should remain in exact alignment as in figure 2109b. If they do not, as in figure 2109c, the horizon glass needs adjustment to make it perpendicular to the plane of the limb. On the navy Mark II sextant two adjusting screws (figure 2108c) are used to move the mirror frame assembly. Again, care must be used to loosen one before tightening the other. On sextants where the mirror is adjusted within the frame, the adjusting screw farthest away from the sextant frame is used (figure 2108d). When the mirror is properly ad-

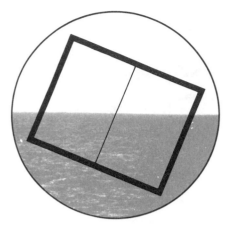

Figure 2109b. Horizon glass perpendicular to the sextant frame.

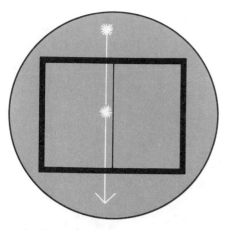

Figure 2109d. The reflected star image moves through the direct image.

Figure 2109c. Here the horizon glass is not perpendicular to the frame.

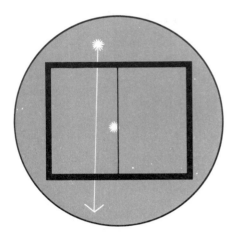

Figure 2109e. The images are not in line; the horizon glass is not perpendicular.

justed, the horizon will appear as a straight line while the sextant is rotated around the line of sight. To accomplish the adjustment at night the sextant is sighted directly at a star with the index set at 0°. When the tangent screw is turned, the reflected image of the star should move in a vertical line exactly through the direct image. If the line of movement is to one side or other of the direct image, the horizon mirror is not perpendicular to the frame and should be adjusted (figures 2109d and 2109e).

Proper Sequence of Adjustment

Since two different adjustments are made on the horizon glass, it is obvious that these adjustments are interrelated, and in making adjustment for the perpendicularity of the mirror, the index error will be affected. As a general rule, it is best to remove the index error first, adjust for perpendicularity, and then check again for the index error. Several series of adjustments may be necessary if the mirror is badly misaligned.

Telescope Alignment

2110 If extreme difficulty is encountered in bringing a star down to the horizon as discussed in article 2116, it is possible the line of sight of the telescope is not parallel to the plane of the sextant frame. This is usually difficult to adjust on board ship, but there is a quick practical check to determine if the telescope is out of alignment. The sextant is held in a horizontal position in the left hand with the horizon glass toward the observer, and the index arm set near 0°. The observer looks into the index mirror, holding the sextant in such a position that the reflected image of the center line of the horizon mirror is directly in line with the actual center line. In this position it should be possible to see straight through the telescope, the line of sight being the same as the path of light rays of a star when an observation is being made. If the telescope is out of alignment, the observer will be unable to look straight through it (figure 2110). Some sex-

Figure 2110. Checking telescope alignment.

tants have adjusting screws on the telescope for adjusting the line of sight; normally this should be accomplished in an optical shop.

Personal Error

2111 After all adjustable errors have been reduced or eliminated insofar as possible, the sextant will probably still retain some residual, variable, adjustable error as well as a small fixed nonadjustable instrument error. Additionally, a small variable error called *personal error* may often be produced as a result of the eye of the observer acting in conjunction with the optical system of the sextant. This might be different for the sun and moon than for planets and stars, and might vary with the degree of fatigue of the observer, and other factors. For this reason, a personal error should be applied with caution. However, if a relatively constant personal error persists, and experience indicates that observations are improved by applying a correction to remove its effect, better results might be obtained by this procedure than by attempting to eliminate it from one's observations. The *personal correction* (PC) is the personal error with the sign reversed.

SEXTANT OBSERVATIONS

Horizon System Coordinates

2112 As stated in article 1904, celestial observations are made with reference to the horizon system of coordinates. The axis of this system is dependent on the position of the observer, and its reference plane is the celestial horizon. The celestial horizon passes through the center of the earth and is perpendicular to the vertical circle passing from the observer's zenith on the celestial sphere, through his position and through the earth's center on to the observer's nadir.

Observing Altitudes

2113 Altitude observations of celestial bodies are made in the plane perpendicular to the celestial horizon, along the vertical circle passing through the body. They are measured upward from the visible, or sea horizon, and a correction is applied that adjusts the sextant altitude to read as though the observed angle had been measured from the earth's center, above the celestial horizon. The plane of the visible horizon may, for all practical purposes, be considered to be parallel to the celestial horizon. Figure 2113a illustrates the principle of a celestial altitude measurement.

The altitude of a body above the visible horizon as read from the sextant is termed the *sextant altitude*; its symbol is *hs*.

To make an observation, the observer stands facing the body, holding the sextant vertically in his right hand, and centers the horizon in his field of view. He then squeezes the release levers and moves the index arm until the body also appears in the field of view. The tangent screw is next allowed to engage the worm teeth on the arc, and the micrometer drum is turned until the horizon and the body are in coincidence.

Next, the sextant is tilted slightly from side to side slowly to determine that the sextant is being held vertically as is required for an accurate measurement. This rotation about the axis of the line of sight causes the body to swing like a pendulum across the horizon; this procedure is termed *swinging the arc*; see figure 2113b. The lowest point indicated on this arc marks the correct position for the sextant; the micrometer drum is again turned until the body makes contact with the horizon at the bottom of its swing. At this instant, the time is noted and the sextant altitude is read off.

With practice, it is easy to determine when the body is on the vertical. The eye tends to extend the line of the sea horizon into the mirrored portion of the sea horizon, and the arc of the reflected image appears not only in the mirrored half but also somewhat into the clear half as well.

Figure 2113a. An altitude measurement.

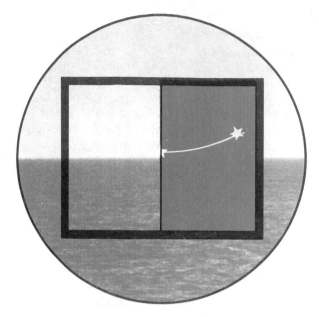

Figure 2113b. Swinging the arc.

Two recent developments of modern technology have made the task of correct vertical positioning much easier. The full-width horizon glass was described in article 2102F. Superimposing the image of the body and the horizon can be done essentially anywhere within the limits of the glass, thus minimizing the centering requirement. This ease is partially offset, however, by a loss of light transmitted through the glass. Such a horizon glass appears to be almost clear, just a hint of a tint; but there is a definite loss of transmitted light, perhaps 50 percent, and this can make the horizon less distinct under hazy conditions and will shorten the time available for sights at twilight. The full-width horizon glass is favored by some navigators, but rejected by others—it is a matter of personal preference.

A Prism-Level™ device may be attached to the outer edge of a horizon glass, either half-silvered or full-width clear. This splits the view of the horizon in much the same way as index error is checked (article 2108); when the horizon is seen as a continuous straight line, the sextant is exactly level.

Graphing Multiple Observations

Skill in obtaining accurate altitudes comes only with practice. Some individuals are markedly more accurate observers than others, but experiments conducted for the Office of Naval Research clearly indicate that the accuracy of even the best observers tends to increase with practice. Each of five observers made over 3,000 sextant observa-

tions, and for each observer the mean of his second thousand observations was better than his first thousand, and that of the third thousand showed still further improvement. The novice observer may find that his sights do not yield satisfactory lines of position. Working with an experienced navigator may improve his technique, or it may be helpful for him to make a string of 10 or more observations of the same body in a period of less than three minutes. These sights should then be plotted on a large sheet of plotting paper, using a horizontal scale of one inch to ten seconds of time, and a vertical scale of one inch to one minute of arc, if possible. A "line of best fit" is then drawn through the string. The divergence of the individual sights from this line will tend to indicate the magnitude of the observer's random errors; the random error of a single sight is the greatest hazard to the accuracy of celestial navigation. Where accuracy is required, a single observation should not be relied on to obtain a line of position. It is far better practice to take at least three sights of each body, and for maximum accuracy an even greater number of observations should be made and graphed as described above (because the body's altitude is constantly changing, simple averaging cannot be used). An altitude and time combination that lies on or near the mean line can then be selected as the sight to be reduced for the LOP.

Suggestions that may be helpful in obtaining good sights are included in the following articles.

Sun Observations

2114   As described in article 2102, the sextant is fitted with index shade glasses, either of the variable-density polarizing type, or neutrally tinted filters of varying degrees of density. To determine the degree of density best suited to the observer's eye under existing conditions, it is usually best to first look at the sun through the *darkest* index shade; if this dims the image too much, the next lightest shade should be tried. It should be noted that sometimes the best results are achieved by using two of the lighter filters, rather than a single dark one. When a polarizing filter is used, it should be set to *full dark* before looking at the sun; the rotatable portion can then be turned to lighten the image until the eye sees the image comfortably and clearly.

On a calm day, when the sun is low in altitude, the sea short of the horizon may reflect the sunlight so glaringly that it is desirable to employ a horizon shade. The most desirable shade must again be selected by trial and error.

Figure 2114. Observing the sun, lower limb.

The Sun's Limb

After the proper shade or shades are selected, the observer sets the index arm to 0°, faces the sun, and proceeds as described in article 2113 until the sun's *lower limb* is on the horizon; during this process the arc must be swung to establish the vertical. (The term "limb" is used to denote a portion of the circumference of the sun or moon.) At most altitudes, the best results are obtained by observing the sun's lower limb; however, at altitudes below about 5°, it is more desirable to observe the upper limb. In this case, the correction for *irradiation effect* should be applied to the sextant altitude, in addition to other corrections; see article 2127. The procedure for observing the sun's upper limb is the same as for the lower limb. Figure 2114 shows the sun's lower limb on the horizon, as seen through a sextant telescope.

Observing Local Apparent Noon (LAN)

When practicing with the sextant, a neophyte navigator should observe the sun at local apparent noon (LAN). In most latitudes, the sun changes altitude but little for a period of several minutes before and after LAN. (The determination of the time of LAN is covered in article 2702.) A string of 12 or more observations should be made, and the altitudes noted. After each sight, the micrometer drum should be moved so that the sun's image initially appears alternately above and below the horizon. It should then be brought to the horizon, and the arc

should be swung until the sun's image is brought into coincidence with the horizon on the vertical. When the novice is able to obtain a consistent string of altitudes at LAN, he should take a series of sights in the afternoon, or morning, when the sun is changing rapidly in altitude. The procedure for making sun sights is outlined earlier in this article. These should, if possible, be graphed as outlined above; by some means, it should be determined that the change in altitude is consistent with the time interval between each pair of sights.

Moon Observations

2115 Observations of the moon are made in the same manner as those of the sun, except that shades are not required during daylight hours.

Because of the various phases of the moon, upper limb observations are made about as frequently as those of the lower limb. Accurate observations of the moon can only be obtained if the upper or lower limb is brought to the horizon. This is not always possible, due to the moon's phase and its position in the sky.

Carefully made moon observations, obtained during daylight hours, under good observational conditions, yield excellent LOPs. If the moon is observed at night, it may be desirable to shade its image somewhat, in order that the horizon not be obscured by the moon's brilliance; nighttime observations of the moon using a moonlit horizon may be of less accuracy than a daytime sight or those taken at morning and evening twilight.

Star and Planet Observations

2116 Observations of stars and planets are made at twilight. More experience in the use of the sextant is required to obtain good twilight sights than is needed in daylight. This is chiefly the result of the fact that a star appears only as a point of light in the sextant telescope, rather than as a body of considerable size, as does the sun or moon. In addition, the stars fade out in the morning as the horizon brightens; in the evening this condition is reversed, and it is sometimes difficult to obtain a good star image and a well-defined horizon at the same time. The problem, however, is considerably simplified when a well-designed sextant, fitted with a good telescope, is employed.

Three methods of bringing the star and the horizon together are possible. The first is to bring the star's image down to the horizon, the second is to bring the horizon up to the star, and the third is to predetermine the approximate altitude and azimuth of the selected star. Of the three methods, the third is usually the most satisfactory, as it often permits locating the star before it can be seen by the unaided eye.

Bringing a Star Down

To employ the first method, the sextant is set within about 2' of 0°, and the line of sight is directed at the star, which will then appear as a double image. The index arm is then slowly pushed forward, while the sextant is moved downward, in order to keep the image of the body in the field of the telescope. When the index arm has reached the reading on the arc for the star's approximate altitude, the horizon will appear in the field. The micrometer drum is then allowed to engage the teeth on the arc, and the final contact between body and horizon is made by means of turning the drum, while rocking the arc to establish the vertical.

Some observers, when using a sextant with a small optical field of view, prefer to remove the telescope from the sextant while bringing the star down. The telescope should always be reinstalled before the altitude is read in order to obtain maximum accuracy.

Bringing the Horizon Up

The second method is sometimes employed when the horizon is bright, and the star is dim. To bring the horizon up to the star, the sextant is set at approximately 0°, and then held inverted in the left hand. The line of sight is then directed at the body, which will be seen through the clear portion of the horizon glass as shown in figure 2116. The index arm is next adjusted until the horizon appears in the field of view and then allowed to lock to the arc, the sextant is righted, and the altitude is determined in the usual way.

Using Precomputed Altitudes

The best procedure for star observations, in most cases, is to determine in advance the approximate altitude and azimuth of the stars to be observed, by means of a star finder, such as the "Star Finder and Identifier" 2102-D, which is described in article 2002. Another, and even easier, method is by inspection of the tables of DMAHTC Pub. No. 249, Volume I if that publication is on board for use in the reduction of sights (see article 2408). Predetermination of the approximate altitude permits full use to be made of the sextant telescope, which will usually make it possible to sight a star when it cannot be seen with the naked eye. Stars can thus be located at evening twilight, while the horizon is

Figure 2116. Using a sextant inverted.

still clearly defined, and can be observed in the morning after they have faded from view of the unaided eye.

When using this method, the altitude of the body to be observed is taken from the star finder, and set on the sextant. The observer then faces in the direction of the body's azimuth, usually determined by sighting over a gyro repeater or magnetic compass, and directs his line of sight at the horizon. After locating the star, its altitude is determined in the regular manner.

Notes Regarding Celestial Observations

2117   At times it is necessary to seize every opportunity to obtain one or more celestial observations, even under adverse conditions. Hints that may be helpful to the novice navigator in observing various bodies follow:

Sun

During extended periods of overcast, the sun may occasionally break through, appearing for only a minute or so. Under such conditions it is advisable to have a sextant set to the approximate altitude, with the telescope mounted, and located in a convenient spot where it can be picked up instantly if the sun appears. If necessary, the observer should be prepared to note his own time of observation rather than using another person for this. At times the sun shows through thin overcast, but its image is not sharply defined. It can nevertheless supply a helpful line of position.

When the sun is higher in altitude, as it transits the observer's meridian at LAN, its change in azimuth during the hour or so preceding and following LAN is very rapid. This permits obtaining excellent running fixes over a comparatively short period of time. The first observation should be made when the sun bears about 45° east of the meridian. This should be followed by the conventional noon sight and another set of observations made when the sun is about 45° west of the meridian.

Low-altitude sights of the sun (i.e., altitudes of 5° more or less) can be extremely helpful at times, and under most observational conditions will yield lines of position accurate to two miles or less when carefully corrected. When making low-altitude sun sights, the upper limb will usually yield better observations than the lower. The correction for sun, lower limb (page A3 of the *Nautical Almanac*) may be used, or a more precise calculation may be made using the correction for refraction listed for stars in the *Nautical Almanac*, as well as a correction for semidiameter, as found in the daily pages of the *Nautical Almanac*. The correction for index error, dip of the horizon, and an additional refraction correction for nonstandard conditions, all given in the *Nautical Almanac*, should be used.

Moon

Observations of the moon can often be used for valuable daytime fixes when made in conjunction with observations of the sun. When moon sights are to be taken at night, it is advisable to make them from a point as low in the ship as possible. This will minimize errors caused by cloud shadows, which can shade the true horizon and make the moon appear below its true position, causing the sextant altitude to read higher than it should.

Planets

Venus can frequently be observed with a sextant during daylight, particularly when its altitude is greater than that of the sun, and it is not too close to the latter in hour angle.

To locate Venus during daylight, its position (declination and angle relative to Aries) should be carefully plotted on the "Star Finder and Identifier" 2102-D, as discussed in article 2002. The latter is then set in the regular manner for the time of the desired observation and the corresponding DR position, and the approximate altitude and azimuth are read off.

Fixes based on sights of the sun, moon, and Venus made during daylight hours should be employed whenever possible.

The other planets, which are not as brilliant as Venus, are ordinarily observed only at twilight. Their positions may also be plotted on the Star Finder and Identifier, to aid in locating them in the sky. Twilight observation techniques, applicable to planets, are described in the following paragraph.

Stars

When the Star Finder and Identifier is used, altitudes and azimuths of twelve or more stars, preferably with altitudes of 20° or more, should be listed in advance for the time of twilight. It is desirable to list considerably more stars than will actually be observed, as not all the stars may be visible at twilight, due to clouds.

The visibility of a star at twilight depends primarily on its magnitude, or brilliance, and on its altitude; to a considerably lesser extent it depends on its azimuth relative to that of the sun. Remember that the lower the tabulated magnitude of a star, the greater the brilliance. All other factors being equal, a low-magnitude star will be visible against a brighter sky than one of higher magnitude, and hence of less brilliance. If two stars are of equal magnitude, and have the same azimuth, the star with the higher altitude will appear to be the brighter. Due to the polarization of the sun's light rays, stars situated at 90° to the sun's azimuth will appear to be slightly brighter than stars of the same magnitude and altitude having nearly the same azimuth as the sun or lying about 180° from it. This is equally true whether the sun be below or above the horizon.

The visibility of stars also depends on the sextant's mirrors, and on the quality and magnification of the telescope. The mirrors must be of a size that permits use of the full angular field of view of the telescope, as the larger the mirror, the larger is the bundle of light rays transmitted to the observer's eye; this is another way of saying the brighter will be the star's reflected image. In addition, the greater the magnification of the telescope, the more easily can the star be located against a bright sky; full daylight observations have been made of Sirius (Mag. −1.6) and Arcturus (Mag. 0.2) with a sextant fitted with a 20-power telescope; typically, however, sextant telescopes are only 2 to 7 power. A higher-power telescope is not necessarily advantageous due to any unsteadiness of the observer's hands (which may not be noticeable in everyday life). Although higher power results in light magnification, it reduces the field of view and makes it more difficult to keep the star in the field, particularly with vessel motion such as on small craft. Further, the higher the power of a telescope, the greater its weight. Although some navigators consider weight useful in steadying the instrument, it undoubtedly adds to muscular fatigue, with a resulting increase in shakiness. A 3- or 4-power telescope with a 21- or 28-mm objective (front) lens is a good overall choice for star observations.

Often the position of the telescope relative to the sextant frame may be adjusted to fit varying conditions of illumination at twilight. Article 2102G stated that some sextant telescopes are not permanently fixed in relation to the frame, and their axis may be moved in or out. This is generally true of sextants with small mirrors, which have less light-gathering power. When the telescope is moved as close as possible to the frame, the maximum amount of light is reflected from the elevated field of view. Conversely, when it is moved out from the frame, more light is transmitted from the horizon, and less from the sky. With a dim horizon, the telescope is moved out to the end of its travel. When the horizon is very dim, it may even be desirable to use a pale index filter when observing a brilliant star or planet; this will facilitate obtaining an accurate contact between the body and the horizon. A navigator should experiment in positioning the telescope in order to obtain the optimum balance of lighting between the body and the horizon. It should be noted that a telescope with good light-gathering powers will permit the observer to see a sharply defined horizon, when it appears "fuzzy" to the naked eye.

It is, of course, desirable to observe stars against a sharply defined horizon, which implies a fairly bright sky. At evening twilight, the eastern horizon will fade first; as a general rule, therefore, it is best to observe stars situated to the eastward first. At morning twilight, the eastern horizon will brighten first and so it would be best to observe first those stars generally toward the east. With experience, a navigator should be able to determine the most desirable sequence of star observation, balancing off the various factors involved, such as star magnitude and altitude and horizon lighting. An astigmatizing shade will also aid in determining star altitude with a faint horizon; see article 2907.

With a sextant telescope of good magnification and optical characteristics, it is possible to observe stars at any time on a clear night. However, the observer's vision must be completely dark adapted. Submarine navigators have regularly obtained very good star fixes in the middle of the night, using a sextant fitted with a 6-power prismatic telescope, having an objective lens 30 mm in diameter. Night-vision telescopes are now available that use an electronic unit to amplify the small amount of ambient light available at night. These light amplification scopes can be adapted to sextants for night observations.

SEXTANT ALTITUDE CORRECTIONS

Sextant Corrections

2118   The altitude of a celestial body as measured with a sextant is determined in accordance with article 2113. This value, hs, must be corrected for errors of the instrument and observer, and for the circumstances of the observation. The *observed altitude*, Ho, is the hs value corrected to read as though the altitude had been measured with reference to the celestial horizon, at the earth's center, on a perpendicular plane passing through the observer's zenith and the body. The Ho is the altitude used in all celestial navigation calculations. The significant corrections, and the order of their application to obtain Ho from hs, are described in the following articles. (If applicable, a personal correction, PC, must also be applied.) In order that these corrections may be applied in the correct order, an intermediate between hs and Ho is normally used. This intermediate is the *apparent altitude*, ha; its use is discussed in article 2123.

In addition to those listed in the following articles, other corrections are theoretically necessary in order to obtain Ho; however, these are so small (and in some cases so difficult to determine), that no appreciable error arises from omitting their use. These additional corrections are described in *Bowditch*, DMAHTC Pub. No. 9.

Correction for Nonadjustable Instrument Error

2119   Nonadjustable instrument error is the sum of the nonadjustable errors—prismatic, graduation, and centering—of a sextant (article 2107). The correction for these errors is called the *instrument correction* (I); it is determined by the manufacturer and recorded on a certificate framed in the sextant box. It varies with the angle, may be either *positive* or *negative*, and is applied to *all* angles measured by that particular sextant.

Correction for Index Error

2120   Index error is the residual error in a particular sextant, after the four adjustable errors have been corrected in so far as possible, as described in article 2108. It is compensated for by applying the *index correction* (IC).

The IC may be *positive* or *negative*, and is applied to *all* observations, whether they are celestial or terrestrial. When the IC is applied to the hs, the altitude is corrected to the value it would have if the instrument had no index error. The IC is not fixed, and its value should be determined each time the sextant is used.

Observational Corrections

2121 The remaining corrections are neither instrumental nor personal; they relate to the circumstances of the observation. Some will be required on all observations, others only as determined by the body observed.

Dip of the Horizon (D)

2122 Dip of the horizon is customarily referred to merely as "the dip." The D correction is required because of the height of the observer's eye above the level of the sea.

Celestial altitudes obtained with the marine sextant are measured relative to the visible, or sea, horizon. As the earth is spheroid, the higher the observer is situated above the surface, the more depressed the visible horizon will be below the celestial horizon or true horizontal at his eye. Figure 2122 shows two observers sharing a common zenith, but the observer at A'' is situated considerably higher than the observer at A'; both are observing the same star. The observer's height of eye is greatly exaggerated in the figure for illustrative purposes. It is obvious that the star's hs will be considerably larger for the observer at A'', than for the one at A', and that the latter will have a larger hs than he would at the point A, on the water surface directly beneath him. The value of the dip may be defined as the excess over 90° of the angular distance from observer's zenith to his visible horizon, since the reference plane for determining altitudes of celestial bodies is the observer's celestial horizon, which is perpendicular to his zenith. The D correction must be made for this excess. As the magnitude of the correction depends upon the observer's height above the water, it is sometimes called the "height of eye correction."

The value of the dip correction is somewhat decreased by atmospheric refraction between the observer and the horizon. Refraction causes the visible horizon to appear slightly higher than it would if the earth had no atmosphere. This refraction effect is not constant, but depends on atmospheric and sea conditions, chiefly on the difference between the temperature of the air at the observer's eye level, and that directly adjacent to the surface of the water. If the air is colder at the observer's level, the horizon tends to be depressed slightly; conversely, if it is warmer, it tends to be slightly elevated (article 2131).

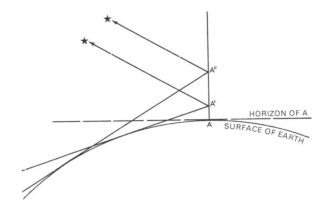

Figure 2122. Dip increases with greater height of eye above the water's surface.

The D correction is always *negative*, and is applied to all celestial altitude observations. Its application to the hs corrects the latter to the value it would have if the visible horizon were a plane passing through the eye of the observer and perpendicular to the line of his zenith.

Dip Short of Horizon

In some situations, the full distance to the natural horizon is not available—another ship, land, or other obstruction blocks vision. In this instance a *dip short* observation must be made and the dip correction taken from a special table such as table 22 in *Bowditch*, rather than from the *Nautical Almanac*. The distance to the foreshortened horizon must be accurately known, and the height of eye becomes a more critical factor than with sights taken on a natural horizon.

Apparent Altitude (ha)

2123 For purposes of routine navigation, corrections to the sextant altitude can be applied in any order using the hs as entering argument in the various correction tables. Where greater accuracy is desired, however, or at low altitudes where small changes in altitude can result in significant changes in the correction, the order of applying the corrections is important. To obtain maximum accuracy, the three corrections so far discussed, for nonadjustable instrument error (I), index error (IC), and dip (D), are first applied to the hs (plus PC if applicable). The hs so corrected is termed the *apparent altitude* (ha), and the value of ha is used in entering the tables to obtain corrections discussed in the following articles. (In some books this value is termed *rectified altitude*, hr.) For illustrative purposes in this chapter most of the corrections are shown as applied directly to hs. In chapter 26, calculations for the complete celestial solution will use the apparent altitude, ha, as an intermediate value.

Refraction (R)

2124   Refraction is caused by the bending of a light ray as it passes from a medium of one density into one of a different density. The increasingly dense layers of the earth's atmosphere cause the rays to be bent more and more downward in the vertical plane, as they approach the surface. Refraction, therefore, causes every heavenly body to appear higher than its actual position, as shown in figure 2124 (exaggerated for emphasis), except when the body is at the observer's zenith. In such a case, the light rays are traveling vertically, and there is no refraction.

The lower a body is located in altitude, the more atmosphere its light rays will penetrate in reaching the observer, and the greater, therefore, will be the refraction. This effect reaches its maximum at the horizon; in fact, when the sun's lower limb appears to just touch the visible horizon at sunset, its upper limb is actually below the horizon.

The refractive effect is not absolutely constant but varies slightly with the density of the atmosphere. This is discussed further in article 2125.

The R correction is always *negative*, and it is applied to all celestial altitude observations. Its application to hs corrects hs to the value it would have if the light rays from the body were not refracted by the earth's atmosphere.

Air Temperature (T) and Atmospheric Pressure (B) Corrections

2125   The R correction varies slightly with the density of the atmosphere; this, in turn, depends upon the air temperature and atmospheric pressure. The refraction correction table given in the *Nautical Almanac* is based on a standard or average atmospheric density, with a temperature of 50° Fahrenheit (10°C) and atmospheric pressure of 29.83 inches (1010 mb). An additional table of corrections is given in the *Almanac* to permit further correction for variations of temperature and pressure from the selected norms. The T and B corrections are ordinarily not required, except for low-altitude observations, unless temperature and pressure vary materially from the standard values. All observations at altitudes of 10° or less should be corrected for temperature and barometric pressure.

The *combined T and B* correction may be *positive* or *negative,* and is applied to all celestial altitudes

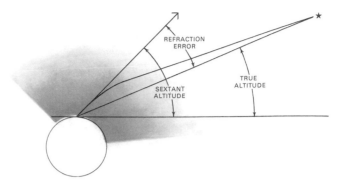

Figure 2124. Atmospheric refraction causes bending of light rays.

when conditions require it, in addition to the R correction. When applied to the hs, the sextant altitude is corrected to the value it would have under conditions of a standard atmospheric density.

Semidiameter Correction (SD)

2126   The values of Greenwich Hour Angle and declination tabulated in all almanacs are for the centers of the various celestial bodies. Because an observer using a marine sextant cannot readily determine the center of the sun or moon, he measures the altitude of one of the limbs of these two bodies. The *semidiameter* (SD) is the angular distance between the limb of the sun or moon and the center as illustrated in figure 2126. If a lower limb observation is made, the SD must be added to the hs to obtain the altitude of the center of the body; conversely, it is subtracted if the upper limb is observed.

The semidiameter varies with the distance of the body from the earth. The moon is comparatively near the earth, and the changes in its distance as it revolves about the earth have a comparatively large effect on its SD. At certain times, the moon's SD may change significantly from day to day. The sun is much more distant, and the eccentricity of the earth's orbit has a less pronounced effect on the sun's SD, which varies between about 15.8' and 16.3'.

The SD correction is *positive* for a *lower limb* observation and *negative* for the *upper limb*. It is applied only to observations of the sun and moon when their altitudes are measured above the visible horizon. It is not applicable to observations of stars or planets, as they have no significant apparent diameter when viewed through the telescopes normally used with sextants. When the SD is applied to the hs, the sextant altitude is corrected to the value it would have if the center of the body had been observed.

a—altitude of upper limb
b—altitude of center body
c—altitude of lower limb

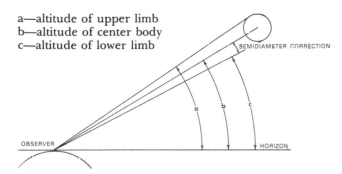

Figure 2126. Semidiameter correction for sun or moon (not to scale).

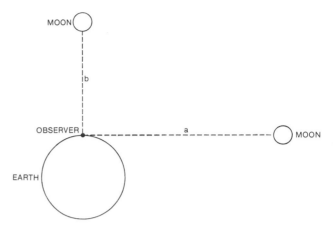

Figure 2127. Correction for augmentation; distance *a* is greater than *b* (not to scale).

Augmentation (A)

2127 The semidiameter of a body varies with its distance from the observer on earth. When a body is on the observer's horizon, its distance from him is greater than when it is at its zenith, the difference in distance being almost equal to the earth's radius; see figure 2127. As the earth's radius is extremely small in comparison to the distance to the sun, any correction for the difference in distance due to the observer's position on earth, which is termed *augmentation*, is not of practical significance in navigation. Augmentation for a planet would vary with the relative positions in their orbits of that body and the earth, but again this is too small to be considered.

As a result of the comparative nearness of the moon, its augmentation from the observer's horizon to his zenith is about 0.3' at mean lunar distance. No separate correction for augmentation need be applied, however, as allowance for this has been made in the moon correction tables of the *Nautical Almanac.*

Phase Correction (F)

2128 The planets go through phases that are quite similar to those of the moon. A planet's phase is not obvious to the unaided eye, but a telescope increases the phase effect and affects the positioning of a planet on the horizon by an observer using a sextant. The phase correction is generally similar to the semidiameter correction for the sun and moon. When applied to hs, the sextant altitude is corrected to the value it would have if the center of the planet had been observed.

Beginning with the *Nautical Almanac* for 1985, the phase correction for Venus is incorporated into the daily tabulated values of GHA and declination, and thus no separate correction value need be applied by a navigator. The phase effect does exist for Mars and the other navigational planets, but is too slight to require consideration in marine navigation.

Irradiation (J)

2129 *Irradiation* is the name applied to the optical illusion that causes the apparent size of a bright or light-colored object in juxtaposition with a darker one to appear larger than it actually is; conversely, a darker one appears smaller. Thus, when the sky is considerably brighter than the water, the horizon appears depressed. The apparent diameter of the sun is increased slightly by irradiation, and the brighter stars appear to have a measurable diameter. Altitudes of the sun's lower limb should not be affected, as the irradiation effect on the sun and on the horizon are in the same direction and effectively cancel out. The effect on the upper limb of the sun, however, is opposite to that on the horizon, and a subtractive correction would be applicable. Quantitatively, it decreases with increasing telescope magnification, and with increasing altitudes. Irradiation corrections are not included in the tabulated values of tables A2 and A3 of the *Nautical Almanac* and are seldom, if ever, calculated and applied in practical surface navigation.

Parallax Correction (P)

2130 *Parallax* is the difference in the direction of an object at a finite distance when viewed simultaneously from two different positions. It enters into the sextant altitude corrections because hs is measured from the earth's surface, but Ho is calculated from the earth's center. Since the moon is the celestial body nearest the earth, parallax has its greatest effect on lunar observations.

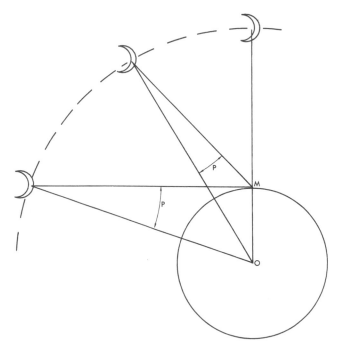

Figure 2130. The parallax correction varies with the altitude of the observed body (not to scale).

The effect of parallax is illustrated in figure 2130. If the moon is directly overhead, that is, with an altitude of 90°, there is no parallax, as its direction is the same at the center of the earth as for the observer. As the moon decreases in altitude its direction from the observer begins to differ with its direction from the earth's center, and the difference in direction increases continuously until the moon sets. The same effect, of course, occurs in reverse when a body is rising. Parallax ranges from zero for a body with an altitude of 90° to a maximum when the body is on the horizon, with 0° altitude. At altitude 0°, it is called *horizontal parallax* (HP).

In addition to increasing as altitude decreases, parallax increases as distance to a celestial body decreases. Venus and Mars, when close to the earth, are also appreciably affected by parallax. The sun is slightly affected, the parallax correction for the sun being +0.1' from zero altitude to 65°. All other celestial bodies are too far from the earth to require correction for parallax when observed with a sextant.

The correction for parallax is always positive, and is applied only to observations of the moon, sun, Venus, and Mars; its effect is to correct the sextant altitude to the value it would have if the observer were at the center of the earth. Parallax for the moon and sun is included with other correc-

tions such as those for refraction and semi-diameter. The star tables are used for the planets, but an additional correction for parallax (page A2) is required for Venus and Mars. (Alternatively, the "white pages" of the *Nautical Almanac* provide an equation by which this parallax may be computed.)

Sea-air Temperature Difference Corrections (S)

2131 In considering the dip of the horizon, it was pointed out that refraction affects the value of the dip. The various dip correction tables allow for such refraction, but the values given are based on a standard rate of decrease of temperature and atmospheric pressure with increased height above the surface. When, however, there is a difference between the sea water and the air temperatures *at the water surface*, the air in contact with the sea is warmed or cooled, and the normal rate no longer exists.

This may alter the value of the dip. If the water is warmer than the air, the horizon is depressed and the dip is increased, resulting in sextant altitudes that are too great. As a correction to hs, the sea-air temperature difference correction (S) is negative when the water is warmer than the air. Conversely, when the air is warmer, the reverse is true, and the correction is positive. This correction is small and is seldom used in routine navigation.

Summary of Effects and Corrections

2132 The various effects on observations and applicable corrections are summarized in figure 2132. In the following articles there are descriptions of the tables and procedures used to determine the specific corrections to be applied to an observation.

Applying Corrections from the Nautical Almanac

2133 All observations made with a marine sextant must first be corrected for fixed or instrument error (I), index error (IC), and dip (D); a personal correction (PC) is applied if one is known to be applicable. The sextant altitude thus corrected is termed the *apparent altitude*, ha. This apparent altitude is used as the argument for entering the appropriate correction tables described in the following articles. The I correction is obtained from the maker's certificate, furnished with the sextant. The IC should be determined each time that sextant is used, as described in article 2109. The correction for dip is found in a table on the inside front cover of the *Nautical Almanac*; it, and other often-used corrections, are also printed on a sheet of heavier

Correction	Symbol	Sign	Increases with	Bodies*	Sextants*	Source
Instrument	I	±	changing altitude	S, M, P, ☆	M, A	sextant box
Index	IC	±	constant	S, M, P, ☆	M, A	measurement
Personal	PC	±	constant	S, M, P, ☆	M, A	measurement
Dip	D	−	higher height of eye	S, M, P, ☆	M	almanacs
Sea-air temp. diff.	S	±	greater temp. diff.	S, M, P, ☆	M	computation
Refraction	R	−	lower altitude	S, M, P, ☆	M, A	almanacs
Air temp.	T	±	greater diff. from 50° F	S, M, P, ☆	M, A	almanacs, table 23 H. O. 9
Atmospheric pressure	B	±	greater diff. from 29.83 in. mercury	S, M, P, ☆	M, A	Nautical Almanac table 24 H. O. 9
Irradiation	J	−	constant	S	M, A	Nautical Almanac
Semidiameter	SD	±	lesser dist. from earth	S, M	M, A	almanacs
Phase	F	±	phase	P	M, A	Nautical Almanac
Augmentation	A	±	higher altitude	M	M, A	Nautical Almanac
Parallax	P	+	lower altitude	S, M, P	M, A	almanacs

* Bodies: S refers to sun, M to moon, P to planets, ☆ to stars.
* Sextants: M refers to Marine, A to artificial horizon.

Figure 2132. Summary of sextant corrections.

paper that is normally furnished with the almanac for use as a bookmark. This table, shown in figure 2133, is entered with the observer's height of eye above the water in feet or meters; it is a *critical-values* table in that the tabulated value of dip is correct for any height of eye between those printed half a line above and half a line below. If the entering height of eye is an exact tabulated value, the correction a half-line *above* it should be used.

More on the *Nautical Almanac* will be found in chapter 23.

Correcting Observations of the Sun

2134 The *Nautical Almanac* contains critical value tables for the correction of observations of the sun, as illustrated in figure 2133. The corrections are tabulated separately for the lower (☼) and upper limb sun (☼) sights, and are in two columns, titled Oct.–Mar., and Apr.–Sept., to approximate the change in the sun's semidiameter throughout the year. These tables combine the corrections for *refraction, semidiameter,* and *parallax.* If a navigator wants maximum accuracy, he may apply these corrections individually, using the more precise value for semidiameter for the specific date as obtained from the daily pages of the *Almanac.* The steps to follow are:

Apply I, IC, and D corrections to obtain ha.

With the apparent altitude thus found, extract the R correction from the "Stars and Planets" correction table (figure 2133).

Apply the SD correction obtained from the daily pages; this correction is positive for lower limb sights and negative for upper limb sights.

For altitudes below 65°, apply a positive correction of 0.1′ for parallax (P).

The procedure for individual corrections is rarely used in practical navigation; the combined value will usually be applied as in the following example:

Example: A navigator observes the upper limb of the sun with a marine sextant on 5 June with a height of eye of 48 feet. The sextant reading is

A2 ALTITUDE CORRECTION TABLES 10°–90°—SUN, STARS, PLANETS

SUN, OCT.–MAR.

App. Alt.	Lower Limb	Upper Limb
9 34	+10.8	−21.5
9 45	+10.9	−21.4
9 56	+11.0	−21.3
10 08	+11.1	−21.2
10 21	+11.2	−21.1
10 34	+11.3	−21.0
10 47	+11.4	−20.9
11 01	+11.5	−20.8
11 15	+11.6	−20.7
11 30	+11.7	−20.6
11 46	+11.8	−20.5
12 02	+11.9	−20.4
12 19	+12.0	−20.3
12 37	+12.1	−20.2
12 55	+12.2	−20.1
13 14	+12.3	−20.0
13 35	+12.4	−19.9
13 56	+12.5	−19.8
14 18	+12.6	−19.7
14 42	+12.7	−19.6
15 06	+12.8	−19.5
15 32	+12.9	−19.4
15 59	+13.0	−19.3
16 28	+13.1	−19.2
16 59	+13.2	−19.1
17 32	+13.3	−19.0
18 06	+13.4	−18.9
18 42	+13.5	−18.8
19 21	+13.6	−18.7
20 03	+13.7	−18.6
20 48	+13.8	−18.5
21 35	+13.9	−18.4
22 26	+14.0	−18.3
23 22	+14.1	−18.2
24 21	+14.2	−18.1
25 26	+14.3	−18.0
26 36	+14.4	−17.9
27 52	+14.5	−17.8
29 15	+14.6	−17.7
30 46	+14.7	−17.6
32 26	+14.8	−17.5
34 17	+14.9	−17.4
36 20	+15.0	−17.3
38 36	+15.1	−17.2
41 08	+15.2	−17.1
43 59	+15.3	−17.0
47 10	+15.4	−16.9
50 46	+15.5	−16.8
54 49	+15.6	−16.7
59 23	+15.7	−16.6
64 30	+15.8	−16.5
70 12	+15.9	−16.4
76 26	+16.0	−16.3
83 05	+16.1	−16.2
90 00		

SUN, APR.–SEPT.

App. Alt.	Lower Limb	Upper Limb
9 39	+10.6	−21.2
9 51	+10.7	−21.1
10 03	+10.8	−21.0
10 15	+10.9	−20.9
10 27	+11.0	−20.8
10 40	+11.1	−20.7
10 54	+11.2	−20.6
11 08	+11.3	−20.5
11 23	+11.4	−20.4
11 38	+11.5	−20.3
11 54	+11.6	−20.2
12 10	+11.7	−20.1
12 28	+11.8	−20.0
12 46	+11.9	−19.9
13 05	+12.0	−19.8
13 24	+12.1	−19.7
13 45	+12.2	−19.6
14 07	+12.3	−19.5
14 30	+12.4	−19.4
14 54	+12.5	−19.3
15 19	+12.6	−19.2
15 46	+12.7	−19.1
16 14	+12.8	−19.0
16 44	+12.9	−18.9
17 15	+13.0	−18.8
17 48	+13.1	−18.7
18 24	+13.2	−18.6
19 01	+13.3	−18.5
19 42	+13.4	−18.4
20 25	+13.5	−18.3
21 11	+13.6	−18.2
22 00	+13.7	−18.1
22 54	+13.8	−18.0
23 51	+13.9	−17.9
24 53	+14.0	−17.8
26 00	+14.1	−17.7
27 13	+14.2	−17.6
28 33	+14.3	−17.5
30 00	+14.4	−17.4
31 35	+14.5	−17.3
33 20	+14.6	−17.2
35 17	+14.7	−17.1
37 26	+14.8	−17.0
39 50	+14.9	−16.9
42 31	+15.0	−16.8
45 31	+15.1	−16.7
48 55	+15.2	−16.6
52 44	+15.3	−16.5
57 02	+15.4	−16.4
61 51	+15.5	−16.3
67 17	+15.6	−16.2
73 16	+15.7	−16.1
79 43	+15.8	−16.0
86 32	+15.9	−15.9
90 00		

STARS AND PLANETS

App. Alt.	Corrn
9 56	−5.3
10 08	−5.2
10 20	−5.1
10 33	−5.0
10 46	−4.9
11 00	−4.8
11 14	−4.7
11 29	−4.6
11 45	−4.5
12 01	−4.4
12 18	−4.3
12 35	−4.2
12 54	−4.1
13 13	−4.0
13 33	−3.9
13 54	−3.8
14 16	−3.7
14 40	−3.6
15 04	−3.5
15 30	−3.4
15 57	−3.3
16 26	−3.2
16 56	−3.1
17 28	−3.0
18 02	−2.9
18 38	−2.8
19 17	−2.7
19 58	−2.6
20 42	−2.5
21 28	−2.4
22 19	−2.3
23 13	−2.2
24 11	−2.1
25 14	−2.0
26 22	−1.9
27 36	−1.8
28 56	−1.7
30 24	−1.6
32 00	−1.5
33 45	−1.4
35 40	−1.3
37 48	−1.2
40 08	−1.1
42 44	−1.0
45 36	−0.9
48 47	−0.8
52 18	−0.7
56 11	−0.6
60 28	−0.5
65 08	−0.4
70 11	−0.3
75 34	−0.2
81 13	−0.1
87 03	−0.1
90 00	0.0

Additional Corrn

VENUS

Period	App. Alt.	Additional Corrn
Jan. 1–Jan. 29	0 / 47	+0.2
Jan. 30–Feb. 26	0 / 46	+0.3
Feb. 27–Mar. 14	0 / 11 / 41	+0.4 / +0.5
Mar. 15–Mar. 23	0 / 6 / 20 / 31	+0.5 / +0.6 / +0.7
Mar. 24–Apr. 19	0 / 4 / 12 / 22	+0.6 / +0.7 / +0.8
Apr. 20–Apr. 28	0 / 6 / 20 / 31	+0.5 / +0.6 / +0.7
Apr. 29–May 13	0 / 11 / 41	+0.4 / +0.5
May 14–June 8	0 / 46	+0.3
June 9–July 23	0 / 47	+0.2
July 24–Dec. 31	0 / 42	+0.1

MARS

Period	App. Alt.	Additional Corrn
Jan. 1–Nov. 12	0 / 60	+0.1
Nov. 13–Dec. 31	0 / 41 / 75	+0.2 / +0.1

DIP

Ht. of Eye (m)	Corrn	Ht. of Eye (ft.)
2.4	−2.8	8.0
2.6	−2.9	8.6
2.8	−3.0	9.2
3.0	−3.1	9.8
3.2	−3.2	10.5
3.4	−3.3	11.2
3.6	−3.4	11.9
3.8	−3.5	12.6
4.0	−3.6	13.3
4.3	−3.7	14.1
4.5	−3.8	14.9
4.7	−3.9	15.7
5.0	−4.0	16.5
5.2	−4.1	17.4
5.5	−4.2	18.3
5.8	−4.3	19.1
6.1	−4.4	20.1
6.3	−4.5	21.0
6.6	−4.6	22.0
6.9	−4.7	22.9
7.2	−4.8	23.9
7.5	−4.9	24.9
7.9	−5.0	26.0
8.2	−5.1	27.1
8.5	−5.2	28.1
8.8	−5.3	29.2
9.2	−5.4	30.4
9.5	−5.5	31.5
9.9	−5.6	32.7
10.3	−5.7	33.9
10.6	−5.8	35.1
11.0	−5.9	36.3
11.4	−6.0	37.6
11.8	−6.1	38.9
12.2	−6.2	40.1
12.6	−6.3	41.5
13.0	−6.4	42.8
13.4	−6.5	44.2
13.8	−6.6	45.5
14.2	−6.7	46.9
14.7	−6.8	48.4
15.1	−6.9	49.8
15.5	−7.0	51.3
16.0	−7.1	52.8
16.5	−7.2	54.3
16.9	−7.3	55.8
17.4	−7.4	57.4
17.9	−7.5	58.9
18.4	−7.6	60.5
18.8	−7.7	62.1
19.3	−7.8	63.8
19.8	−7.9	65.4
20.4	−8.0	67.1
20.9	−8.1	68.8
21.4		70.5

DIP (additional column)

Ht. of Eye	Corrn
m	
1.0	−1.8
1.5	−2.2
2.0	−2.5
2.5	−2.8
3.0	−3.0
See table ←	
m	
20	−7.9
22	−8.3
24	−8.6
26	−9.0
28	−9.3
30	−9.6
32	−10.0
34	−10.3
36	−10.6
38	−10.8
40	−11.1
42	−11.4
44	−11.7
46	−11.9
48	−12.2
ft.	
2	−1.4
4	−1.9
6	−2.4
8	−2.7
10	−3.1
See table ←	
ft.	
70	−8.1
75	−8.4
80	−8.7
85	−8.9
90	−9.2
95	−9.5
100	−9.7
105	−9.9
110	−10.2
115	−10.4
120	−10.6
125	−10.8
130	−11.1
135	−11.3
140	−11.5
145	−11.7
150	−11.9
155	−12.1

App. Alt. = Apparent altitude = Sextant altitude corrected for index error and dip.
For daylight observations of Venus, see page 260.

Figure 2133. *Nautical Almanac* correction tables for the sun, stars, and planets at altitudes between approximately 10° and 90°.

51°58.4'. The instrument correction is −0.2' and the sextant has an index error of 2.2' "off the arc."

Required: Ho at the time of observation using the *Nautical Almanac.*

Solution: (1) Record I and IC; in this case, they are −0.2' and +2.2'. (2) Enter the *Nautical Almanac* "Dip" table with height of eye; extract and record the D correction; in this case, it is −6.7'. (3) Determine the net correction and apply it to hs to obtain ha. (4) Using ha, in this case, 51°53.7', enter Table A2 in the inside front cover of the *Nautical Almanac*, SUN, Apr.–Sept., Upper Limb; extract the combined correction for refraction, parallax, and semidiameter; in this case, −16.6'. (5) Algebraically add this correction to ha to obtain Ho as 51°37.1′.

Answer: Ho 51°37.1′.

	+	☉	−
I			0.2′
IC	2.2′		
D			6.7′
Sum	2.2′		6.9′
Corr.		−4.7	
hs		51°58.4′	
ha		51°53.7′	
A2			16.6′
Corr.		−16.6′	
Ho		51°37.1′	

Correcting Observations of a Star

2135 In addition to the I, IC, and D corrections, star observations require only a correction for refraction, R. This is found in the appropriate column of Table A2 of the *Nautical Almanac,* headed "Stars and Planets."

Example: (Figure 2133) A navigator observes the star Zubenelgenubi with a marine sextant from a height of eye of 12 meters. The sextant altitude is 64°52.7′, and the instrument has an index error of 1.7′ "off the arc"; there is no applicable instrument correction.

Required: Ho at the time of observation.

Solution: (1) Record the IC. In this case it is +1.7′. (2) Enter the *Nautical Almanac* "Dip" table with height of eye, and extract and record the D correction. In this case it is −6.1′. (3) Determine the net correction and apply to hs to obtain ha. (4) Using ha, in this instance, 64°48.3′, enter the *Nautical Almanac,* Table A2, columns for "Stars and Planets"; extract the refraction correction, in this case −0.5′, and apply it algebraically to ha. Ho is found to be 64°47.8′.

Answer: Ho 64°47.8′.

	+	☆	−
IC	1.7′		
D			6.1′
Sum	1.7′		6.1′
Corr.		−4.4′	
hs		64°52.7′	
ha		64°48.3′	
A2-P			0.5′
Corr.		−0.5′	
Ho		64°47.8′	

Correcting Observations of Jupiter and Saturn

2136 The planets Jupiter and Saturn, due to their comparatively great distance from the earth, may be treated as stars in the ordinary practice of navigation.

Example: A navigator observes the planet Jupiter with a marine sextant from a height of eye of 29 feet. The sextant altitude is 18°20.2′, and the instrument has an IC of +2.2′.

Required: Ho at the time of observation.

Solution: (1) Record the IC. In this case, it is +2.2′. (2) Enter the "Dip" table with height of eye and extract and record the D correction. In this case, it is −5.2′. (3) Determine the next correction and apply it to hs to determine ha. (4) Using ha, in this case 18°17.2′, enter the *Nautical Almanac*— Table A2, Stars and Planets, left-hand column— and extract the correction for refraction, in this instance −2.9′. (5) Algebraically add this correction to ha to obtain Ho, which is 18°14.3′.

	+	JUPITER	−
IC	2.2′		
D			5.2′
Sum	2.2′		5.2′
Corr.		−3.0	
hs		18°20.2′	
ha		18°17.2′	
A2			2.9′
Corr.		−2.9′	
Ho		18°14.3′	

Correcting Observations of Venus and Mars

2137 Observations of Venus and Mars, in addition to being corrected for I, IC, D, and R, should be corrected for phase and parallax for observations made during the period of twilight. These latter two corrections are combined, under the names of the planets, in the "Stars and Planets" correction table shown in figure 2133.

Example: During morning twilight on 5 June a navigator with a marine sextant observes the planet Venus from a height of eye of 16.5 meters. The sextant altitude is 41°17.6′, and the instrument has an IC of −0.5′.

Required: Ho at the time of observation.

Solution: (1) Record the IC. In this case, it is −0.5′. (2) Enter the "Dip" table with a height of eye and extract and record the D correction. In this case, it is −7.1′. (3) Determine the net correction and apply it to hs to obtain ha, in this case 41°10.0′.

(4) Enter the *Nautical Almanac* Table A2—Stars and Planets—left-hand column and extract the refraction correction, which is −1.1'. (5) Enter the right-hand column of Stars and Planets and extract the additional correction, in this case +0.3'. (6) Determine the net correction to ha and apply it algebraically to determine Ho.

Answer: Ho 41°09.2'.

	+	VENUS	−
IC			0.5'
D			7.1'
Sum			7.6'
Corr.		−7.6'	
hs		41°17.6'	
ha		41°10.0'	
A2			1.1'
P add'l	0.3'		
Sum	0.3'		1.1'
Corr.		−0.8'	
Ho		41°09.2'	

Venus is occasionally observed in the daytime. Formerly a correction could be computed from an equation given in the explanation section of the *Nautical Almanac*, but beginning with the 1985 edition, this is no longer necessary as the phase correction is included in the basic tabulated values.

Correcting Observations of the Moon

2138 The tables for correcting observations of the moon are found on the inside back cover and the facing page of the *Nautical Almanac*, as shown in part in figure 2138. These tables combine the corrections for refraction, semidiameter, augmentation, and parallax.

To correct observations of the moon, the I, IC, and D corrections are applied to the sextant altitude. The upper portion of the moon correction tables are then entered with the apparent altitude thus obtained, and the first correction is found under the appropriate altitude heading. The moon's HP (Horizontal Parallax) is next obtained from the daily pages of the *Almanac* for the time of the observation. HP is the entering argument to obtain the second correction from the lower portion of the tables. These tables are entered in the same vertical column as was used to obtain the first correction. Two values are listed in each column under the headings L and U for each tabulated value of HP; the L value is for observations of the moon's lower limb ($\mathbb{D}$), and the U for those of the upper limb ($\mathbb{C}$). The second correction is extracted under the appropriate heading. It should be noted that as HP is tabulated in increments of 0.3', it is desirable to interpolate for nontabulated values of HP in obtaining the second correction.

Both the first and second corrections are *added* to the apparent altitude of all moon observations, but for *observations of the upper limb, 30.0' is to be subtracted from the sum of the corrections.*

Example: A navigator observes the lower limb of the moon with a marine sextant from a height of eye of 7.6 meters. The sextant reading is 56°39.7'; there is no instrument or index error. The HP from

ALTITUDE CORRECTION TABLES 35°–90°—MOON

App. Alt.	35°–39° Corrⁿ	40°–44° Corrⁿ	45°–49° Corrⁿ	50°–54° Corrⁿ	55°–59° Corrⁿ	60°–64° Corrⁿ	65°–69° Corrⁿ	70°–74° Corrⁿ	75°–79° Corrⁿ	80°–84° Corrⁿ	85°–89° Corrⁿ	App. Alt.
00	35 56·5	40 53·7	45 50·5	50 46·9	55 43·1	60 38·9	65 34·6	70 30·1	75 25·3	80 20·5	85 15·6	00
10	56·4	53·6	50·4	46·8	42·9	38·8	34·4	29·9	25·2	20·4	15·5	10
20	56·3	53·5	50·2	46·7	42·8	38·7	34·3	29·7	25·0	20·2	15·3	20
30	56·2	53·4	50·1	46·5	42·7	38·5	34·1	29·6	24·9	20·0	15·1	30
40	56·2	53·3	50·0	46·4	42·5	38·4	34·0	29·4	24·7	19·9	14·9	40
50	56·1	53·2	49·9	46·3	42·4	38·2	33·8	29·3	24·5	19·7	14·8	50
00	36 56·0	41 53·1	46 49·8	51 46·2	56 42·3	61 38·1	66 33·7	71 29·1	76 24·4	81 19·6	86 14·6	00
10	55·9	53·0	49·7	46·0	42·1	37·9	33·5	29·0	24·2	19·4	14·5	10
20	55·8	52·8	49·5	45·9	42·0	37·8	33·4	28·8	24·1	19·2	14·3	20
30	55·7	52·7	49·4	45·8	41·8	37·7	33·2	28·7	23·9	19·1	14·1	30
40	55·6	52·6	49·3	45·7	41·7	37·5	33·1	28·5	23·8	18·9	14·0	40
50	55·5	52·5	49·2	45·5	41·6	37·4	32·9	28·3	23·6	18·7	13·8	50

H.P.	L U	L U	L U	L U	L U	L U	L U	L U	L U	L U	L U	H.P.
57·0	4·3 3·2	4·3 3·3	4·3 3·3	4·4 3·4	4·4 3·4	4·5 3·5	4·5 3·5	4·6 3·6	4·7 3·6	4·7 3·7	4·8 3·8	57·0
57·3	4·6 3·4	4·6 3·4	4·6 3·4	4·6 3·5	4·7 3·5	4·7 3·5	4·7 3·6	4·8 3·6	4·8 3·6	4·8 3·7	4·9 3·7	57·3
57·6	4·9 3·6	4·9 3·6	4·9 3·6	4·9 3·6	4·9 3·6	4·9 3·6	4·9 3·6	5·0 3·6	5·0 3·6	5·0 3·6	5·0 3·6	57·6
57·9	5·2 3·7	5·2 3·7	5·2 3·7	5·2 3·7	5·2 3·7	5·1 3·6	5·1 3·6	5·1 3·6	5·1 3·6	5·1 3·6	5·1 3·6	57·9
58·2	5·5 3·9	5·5 3·8	5·5 3·8	5·4 3·8	5·4 3·7	5·4 3·7	5·3 3·7	5·3 3·6	5·3 3·6	5·2 3·6	5·2 3·5	58·2

Figure 2138. *Nautical Almanac* correction tables for moon observations.

the daily pages of the *Nautical Almanac* for the day concerned is found to be 57.6'.

Required: Ho for the time of observation.

Solution: (1) Record the IC. In this case there is no IC. (2) Enter the Nautical Almanac "Dip" table with height of eye, and extract and record the D correction. In this case it is −4.9'. (3) Apply the D correction to hs to obtain ha of 56°34.8'. (4) Enter the upper portion of the *Nautical Almanac* "moon" tables with ha and extract and record the first correction. In this case it is +41.8'. (5) Follow down the altitude column used in (4) above, and extract and record from the lower portion of the "moon" table the L correction for the HP found on the daily page. In this case HP is 57.6' and L is +4.9'. (6) Sum the corrections and apply algebraically to ha to obtain Ho.

Answer: Ho 57°21.5'.

	+	MOON	−
H.P. ☾		57.6'	
IC		0	
Dip (Ht 25')			4.9'
Sum		−4.9'	
hs		56°39.7'	
ha		56°34.8'	
First Corr.	41.8'		
L(HP = 57.6')			
Moon	4.9'		
Sum	+46.7' −		
Corr.		+46.7'	
Ho		57°21.5'	

Correcting for Nonstandard Refraction

2139 The refraction corrections included in the various altitude correction tables in the *Nautical Almanac* are based on an air temperature of 50°F (10°C), and an atmospheric pressure of 29.83 inches (1010 millibars) of mercury. When atmospheric conditions vary from these standard values, the light from celestial bodies is refracted to a greater or lesser value than is stated in the tables.

Additional corrections for nonstandard conditions of refraction are given in the *Nautical Almanac*, Table A4, which is reproduced in figure 2139. It is entered at the top with the temperature, and a line is projected down vertically until it intersects with a horizontal line drawn in from the appropriate point on the pressure scale. The intersection of these two lines will fall within one of the diagonal lettered zones; the name of this letter establishes the vertical correction column to be used. Using the

apparent altitude as the entering argument, the additional refraction correction is then found.

Except under extreme conditions, it is not necessary to use this table for altitudes above about 10°. However, due to the extremely rapid change in the value of the refraction at very low altitudes, this table should always be used for correcting such observations. Interpolation may be desirable at extremely low altitudes.

Example: A sextant observation of 7° is taken under conditions of air temperature +20°C and barometric pressure 1010 millibars.

Required: The additional correction for refraction.

Solution: Enter Table A4 of the *Nautical Almanac* for the stated conditions. These are found in area J of the upper portion. Following down column J to the line for an altitude of 7°, the value is found to be +0.4'.

Answer: Additional refraction correction is +0.4'.

Corrections Using the Air Almanac

2140 The *Air Almanac* can be used to obtain corrections for each of the categories of possible error discussed in the preceding sections, but the *Nautical Almanac* is generally preferred in marine navigation because of the greater precision of the tabulated corrections. In the *Air Almanac*, the refraction correction for all bodies is extracted from the same refraction table; see Figure 2140. When applicable, the effects of semidiameter, augmentation, phase, and parallax must be separately reckoned using data in the daily pages, and combined with the extracted refraction correction to form the total correction to ha for each body observed. An additional adjustment to the resulting line of position necessitated by the Coriolis effect on a fast-moving aircraft is also required in air navigation; tables for this correction are also contained in the *Air Almanac*.

More on the *Air Almanac* is found in chapter 23.

Care of a Sextant

2141 The modern marine sextant is a well-built, very precise optical instrument capable of rendering many years of service if it is properly maintained. Its usefulness can be greatly impaired, however, by careless handling or neglect. If a sextant is ever dropped, some error is almost certain to be introduced into all subsequent sightings.

When not in use, the sextant should always be kept in its case, and the case itself should be securely stowed in a location free from excessive

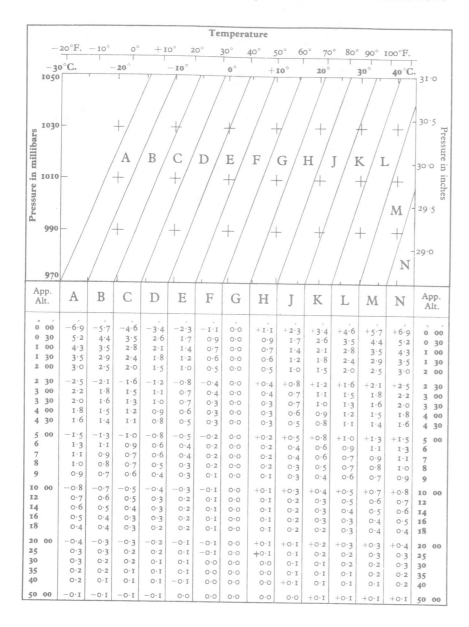

App. Alt.	A	B	C	D	E	F	G	H	J	K	L	M	N	App. Alt.
0 00	−6.9	−5.7	−4.6	−3.4	−2.3	−1.1	0.0	+1.1	+2.3	+3.4	+4.6	+5.7	+6.9	0 00
0 30	5.2	4.4	3.5	2.6	1.7	0.9	0.0	0.9	1.7	2.6	3.5	4.4	5.2	0 30
1 00	4.3	3.5	2.8	2.1	1.4	0.7	0.0	0.7	1.4	2.1	2.8	3.5	4.3	1 00
1 30	3.5	2.9	2.4	1.8	1.2	0.6	0.0	0.6	1.2	1.8	2.4	2.9	3.5	1 30
2 00	3.0	2.5	2.0	1.5	1.0	0.5	0.0	0.5	1.0	1.5	2.0	2.5	3.0	2 00
2 30	−2.5	−2.1	−1.6	−1.2	−0.8	−0.4	0.0	+0.4	+0.8	+1.2	+1.6	+2.1	+2.5	2 30
3 00	2.2	1.8	1.5	1.1	0.7	0.4	0.0	0.4	0.7	1.1	1.5	1.8	2.2	3 00
3 30	2.0	1.6	1.3	1.0	0.7	0.3	0.0	0.3	0.7	1.0	1.3	1.6	2.0	3 30
4 00	1.8	1.5	1.2	0.9	0.6	0.3	0.0	0.3	0.6	0.9	1.2	1.5	1.8	4 00
4 30	1.6	1.4	1.1	0.8	0.5	0.3	0.0	0.3	0.5	0.8	1.1	1.4	1.6	4 30
5 00	−1.5	−1.3	−1.0	−0.8	−0.5	−0.2	0.0	+0.2	+0.5	+0.8	+1.0	+1.3	+1.5	5 00
6	1.3	1.1	0.9	0.6	0.4	0.2	0.0	0.2	0.4	0.6	0.9	1.1	1.3	6
7	1.1	0.9	0.7	0.6	0.4	0.2	0.0	0.2	0.4	0.6	0.7	0.9	1.1	7
8	1.0	0.8	0.7	0.5	0.3	0.2	0.0	0.2	0.3	0.5	0.7	0.8	1.0	8
9	0.9	0.7	0.6	0.4	0.3	0.1	0.0	0.1	0.3	0.4	0.6	0.7	0.9	9
10 00	−0.8	−0.7	−0.5	−0.4	−0.3	−0.1	0.0	+0.1	+0.3	+0.4	+0.5	+0.7	+0.8	10 00
12	0.7	0.6	0.5	0.3	0.2	0.1	0.0	0.1	0.2	0.3	0.5	0.6	0.7	12
14	0.6	0.5	0.4	0.3	0.2	0.1	0.0	0.1	0.2	0.3	0.4	0.5	0.6	14
16	0.5	0.4	0.3	0.3	0.2	0.1	0.0	0.1	0.2	0.3	0.3	0.4	0.5	16
18	0.4	0.4	0.3	0.2	0.2	0.1	0.0	0.1	0.2	0.2	0.3	0.4	0.4	18
20 00	−0.4	−0.3	−0.3	−0.2	−0.1	−0.1	0.0	+0.1	+0.1	+0.2	+0.3	+0.3	+0.4	20 00
25	0.3	0.3	0.2	0.2	0.1	−0.1	0.0	+0.1	0.1	0.2	0.2	0.3	0.3	25
30	0.3	0.2	0.2	0.1	0.1	0.0	0.0	0.0	0.1	0.1	0.2	0.2	0.3	30
35	0.2	0.2	0.1	0.1	0.1	0.0	0.0	0.0	0.1	0.1	0.1	0.2	0.2	35
40	0.2	0.1	0.1	0.1	−0.1	0.0	0.0	0.0	+0.1	0.1	0.1	0.1	0.2	40
50 00	−0.1	−0.1	−0.1	−0.1	0.0	0.0	0.0	0.0	0.0	+0.1	+0.1	+0.1	+0.1	50 00

Figure 2139. *Nautical Almanac* additional refraction corrections for non-standard conditions. The graph is entered with values of temperature and pressure to find a "zone letter," A to L. Using the apparent altitude (sextant altitude corrected for dip) and column for appropriate zone letter, the proper correction is taken from the table. This correction is applied to the apparent altitude *in addition to* the corrections for standard conditions.

heat, dampness, and vibration. In particular, the sextant should never be left unattended and unsecured on the chartroom table or any other high place. When outside its case, a sextant should only be picked up by its handle—never by the telescope, limb, or index arm.

Next to careless handling, moisture is the greatest enemy of a sextant. The mirrors and lens should always be wiped off before a series of observations, because fogged optics make it very difficult to pick up dimmer stars; any moisture should also be wiped off before a sextant is placed back into its box after use. Lens paper should be used—cloth of any type tends to attract and retain dust particles that could scratch the mirror or lens surface; in particular, never use silk. Moisture in the sextant case can be controlled, at least partially, by keeping in the case a small bag of a desiccant, usually silica gel; the bag should occasionally be dehumidified by placing it in a moderately hot oven for a few hours.

Moisture has a particularly deleterious effect on the silvering of the mirrors and also on the graduations of the arc if they are on a bare, polished metal surface. Should resilvering of the mirrors become necessary, this task, like instrument alignment, is best left to an optical instrument repair facility. Materials can be obtained to perform resilvering on board ship, however, and *Bowditch* contains a description of the resilvering procedure.

CORRECTIONS TO BE APPLIED TO SEXTANT ALTITUDE

REFRACTION

To be subtracted from sextant altitude (referred to as observed altitude in A.P. 3270)

R_0	Height above sea level in units of 1 000 ft.												R_0	$R = R_0 \times f$			
	0	5	10	15	20	25	30	35	40	45	50	55		f			
														0·9	1·0	1·1	1·2
	Sextant Altitude													R			
	° ′	° ′	° ′	° ′	° ′	° ′	° ′	° ′	° ′	° ′	° ′	° ′		′	′	′	′
0	90	90	90	90	90	90	90	90	90	90	90	90	0	0	0	0	0
1	63	59	55	51	46	41	36	31	26	20	17	13	1	1	1	1	1
2	33	29	26	22	19	16	14	11	9	7	6	4	2	2	2	2	2
3	21	19	16	14	12	10	8	7	5	4	2 40	1 40	3	3	3	3	4
4	16	14	12	10	8	7	6	5	3 10	2 20	1 30	0 40	4	4	4	5	5
5	12	11	9	8	7	5	4 00	3 10	2 10	1 30	0 39	+0 05	5	5	5	5	6
6	10	9	7	5 50	4 50	3 50	3 10	2 20	1 30	0 49	+0 11	−0 19	6	5	6	7	7
7	8 10	6 50	5 50	4 50	4 00	3 00	2 20	1 50	1 10	0 24	−0 11	−0 38	7	6	7	8	8
8	6 50	5 50	5 00	4 00	3 10	2 30	1 50	1 20	0 38	+0 04	−0 28	−0 54	8	7	8	9	10
9	6 00	5 10	4 10	3 20	2 40	2 00	1 30	1 00	0 19	−0 13	−0 42	−1 08	9	8	9	10	11
10	5 20	4 30	3 40	2 50	2 10	1 40	1 10	0 35	+0 03	−0 27	−0 53	−1 18	10	9	10	11	12
12	4 30	3 40	2 50	2 20	1 40	1 10	0 37	+0 11	−0 16	−0 43	−1 08	−1 31	12	11	12	13	14
14	3 30	2 50	2 10	1 40	1 10	0 34	+0 09	−0 14	−0 37	−1 00	−1 23	−1 44	14	13	14	15	17
16	2 50	2 10	1 40	1 10	0 37	+0 10	−0 13	−0 34	−0 53	−1 14	−1 35	−1 56	16	14	16	18	19
18	2 20	1 40	1 20	0 43	+0 15	−0 08	−0 31	−0 52	−1 08	−1 27	−1 46	−2 05	18	16	18	20	22
20	1 50	1 20	0 49	+0 23	−0 02	−0 26	−0 46	−1 06	−1 22	−1 39	−1 57	−2 14	20	18	20	22	24
25	1 12	0 44	+0 19	−0 06	−0 28	−0 48	−1 09	−1 27	−1 42	1 58	−2 14	−2 30	25	22	25	28	30
30	0 34	+0 10	−0 13	−0 36	−0 55	−1 14	−1 32	−1 51	−2 06	−2 21	−2 34	2 49	30	27	30	33	36
35	+0 06	−0 16	−0 37	−0 59	−1 17	−1 33	1 51	−2 07	−2 23	−2 37	−2 51	−3 04	35	31	35	38	42
40	−0 18	−0 37	−0 58	−1 16	−1 34	1 49	−2 06	−2 22	2 35	−2 49	−3 03	−3 16	40	36	40	44	48
45		−0 53	−1 14	−1 31	−1 47	−2 03	−2 18	−2 33	−2 47	−2 59	−3 13	−3 25	45	40	45	50	54
50		−1 10	−1 28	−1 44	−1 59	−2 15	−2 28	−2 43	−2 56	−3 08	−3 22	−3 33	50	45	50	55	60
55			−1 40	−1 53	−2 09	−2 24	−2 38	−2 52	−3 04	−3 17	−3 29	−3 41	55	49	55	60	66
60				−2 03	−2 18	−2 33	−2 46	−3 01	−3 12	−3 25	3 37	−3 48	60	54	60	66	72
							−2 53	−3 07	−3 19	−3 31	−3 42	−3 53					

f	0	5	10	15	20	25	30	35	40	45	50	55	f	0·9 1·0 1·1 1·2
	Temperature in °C.													f
0·9	+47	+36	+27	+18	+10	3	− 5	−13					0·9	Where R_0 is
1·0	+26	+16	+ 6	4	−13	−22	−31	−40					1·0	less than 10′
1·1	+ 5	5	−15	−25	−36	−46	−57	−68					1·1	or the height greater than
1·2	−16	−25	−36	−46	−58	−71	−83	−95					1·2	35 000 ft. use
	−37	−45	−56	−67	−81	−95								$R = R_0$

For these heights no temperature correction is necessary, so use $R = R_0$

Figure 2140. *Air Almanac* corrections for refractions, all bodies.

Lubrication is important, but must not be over-done. The teeth of the tangent screw and those on the limb should always be kept lightly coated with a thin film of oil. The graduations on an arc that is bare, polished metal should be protected with a thin film of petroleum jelly.

If the sextant is normally stowed in an air-conditioned space and the ship is operating in a humid climate, it is a good practice to bring the sextant in its case out into the open an hour or so before use to prevent condensation forming on the mirror surfaces.

The sextant adjustments detailed in the articles 2108 and 2109 should be undertaken only by an experienced person and must be made with great care.

Chapter 22   Time

Introduction

2201 The single indispensable element of all forms of navigation from dead reckoning to celestial to the most advanced forms of radionavigation is *time*. In some instances—such as the determination of tides and currents, or celestial navigation—it is *actual time* ("clock" time) that is needed. Under other circumstances—dead reckoning, for example, or advancing a line of position in piloting—it is *elapsed time* that is required, and the accuracy of clock time is of little importance. But whichever kind it is, a navigator lives constantly with "time."

This chapter will first consider time in general terms, and then its specific application to celestial navigation. Other uses of time data occur in nearly every chapter of this book.

Basics of Time

2202 Most forms of time are based on the rotation of the earth in relation to various celestial bodies. Because of the different rates of motion (article 1811), these various forms of time may differ in the lengths of their standard unit, the *day*, which represents one rotation of the earth relative to the reference body, whatever that may be.

The Solar Day

The sun is the reference body most commonly used by man, and is the one principally used by the navigator; the period of the earth's rotation relative to the sun is called the *solar day*. The solar year is based on the period of the earth's revolution about the sun, which requires approximately $365\frac{1}{4}$ days. The *common year* is 365 days in length. In years exactly divisible by four, such as 1984 and

1988, known as *leap years*, an additional day—February 29—is usually inserted to adjust the calendar to the actual period of revolution. As the fraction in this period is not exactly $\frac{1}{4}$ of a day—it is some 11 minutes 14 seconds less—years ending in two zeros (1900, 2100) are not leap years, unless they are exactly divisible by 400 as are the years 2000 and 2400.

The other units of time, *month, week, hour, minute*, and *second* have origins deep in man's history. The ancient Egyptians used the rising of certain stars or star-groups to divide their calendar into ten-day periods. Such stars, or star-groups, rose successively at intervals of roughly 40 minutes, and so approximately 12 of them could be seen on any night. From this, the night was divided into 12 hours and the entire day became 24 hours. The division of hours into 60 minutes of 60 seconds each was a development of the ancient Babylonian culture.

In the metric (SI) system of measurements, the *second* is the basic unit of time. Contrary to the usage for larger values of other metric units, prefixes such as "kilo" and "mega" are not used for longer periods of time; hours, days, and years are acceptable units in the metric system. For shorter periods of time, however, metric prefixes such as "milli" and "micro" are used, as in microsecond.

The month is now an arbitrary, irregular unit of time, but it was originally the moon's period of revolution around the earth. The week, as a quarter of a month, was derived from the moon's four phases.

Apparent Solar Time

2203 As stated in article 2202, the sun has been the chief body by which man has controlled his life since prehistoric times. He used *apparent solar time*,

Figure 2203. Variation in the length of an apparent day due to the obliquity of the ecliptic.

which he read from a sun dial, as his criterion. Unfortunately, the speed of the apparent rotation of the sun around the earth, actually caused by the rotation of the earth on its axis, is *not* constant; as a result, the length of the *apparent day* varies throughout the year. This variation results, in part, from the fact that the revolution of the earth around the sun is in an elliptical orbit and thus is not at a constant speed; see article 1805. A second cause of the variation in the length of a day is the tilt of the axis of the earth's rotation with respect to its plane of revolution around the sun (figure 2203), causing the apparent path of the sun to be along the ecliptic.

Mean Solar Time

2204 The irregularities of apparent solar time resulted in numerous difficulties as civilization advanced and technology became more complex. To overcome these problems of a nonuniform rate, *mean solar time* was developed. This is based on a fictitious "sun," termed the *mean sun*, that has an hour circle moving westward along the celestial equator at a *constant* rate. Mean solar time is nearly equal to the average apparent solar time; see article 2209. This is the time used in everyday life, kept by the great majority of timepieces; it is the time kept by ships' chronometers and used in

almanacs for tabulating the position of celestial bodies; see figure 2204.

The method of stating time in navigation is described in article 210.

Equation of Time

The difference in length between any apparent and the mean day is never as great as a minute, but it is cumulative and amounts to approximately a quarter-hour at certain times of the year. The difference between mean and apparent time at any instant is called the *equation of time*. Values are tabulated in the *Nautical Almanac* for 00 and 12 hours each day; there is no comparable tabulation in the *Air Almanac*. Daily values of the equation of time are of little direct use in modern celestial navigation except for the determination of the time of local apparent noon (article 2702).

Upper and Lower Transit

2205 Transit signifies the instant a celestial body crosses or "transits" a given meridian. A meridian on the earth is a great circle, passing through the earth's geographical poles, at any given position.

The passage of a celestial body across the upper branch of the observer's meridian is called *upper transit*; in figure 2205, the sun at M is shown at upper transit. Depending on the observer's latitude and the body's declination, at this instant the body is either due north or due south of the observer (or directly overhead). The passage of a celestial body across the lower branch of an observer's meridian is called *lower transit;* in figure 2205, the sun is also shown at lower transit, at m. At this instant, the body will be either directly to his north, or south, or directly below him, again depending on his latitude and the body's declination. Bodies visible at the observer's position will be above the horizon at upper transit; the majority will be below the hori-

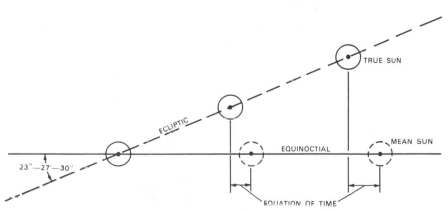

Figure 2204. Relationship of mean time to solar time.

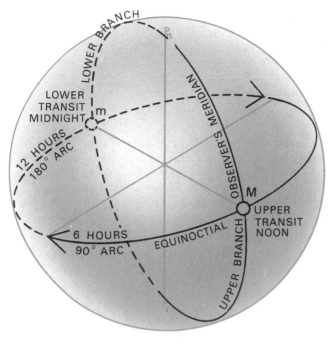

Figure 2205. Upper and lower transit.

zon at lower transit. *Circumpolar stars* are those that are above the horizon for both the upper and lower transits at the latitude of the observer; see article 1814.

At all times, one half of the earth is in sunlight, and the other is in darkness. The sun will be in upper transit on the central meridian of the half that is in sunlight, and it will be *midday* (noon, local time) at that meridian; on the lower branch of the same meridian the sun will be in lower transit; at that instant it will be *midnight*. Lower transit of the mean sun simultaneously marks the end of one day (24-00-00) and the beginning of the next (00-00-00). For the observer at *M* in figure 2205, this occurs when the mean sun is at *m*.

As the mean sun is considered to complete a revolution of 360° of arc about the earth in exactly 24 hours, it is evident that in one hour it will have traveled through 15°. In 6 hours it will have traveled through 90°, etc. Thus, there is a definite relationship between time and longitude; this will be discussed in article 2207.

Time Diagrams

2206 The transits of celestial bodies and the resultant time-arc relationships are, for navigational purposes, generally sketched on a *time* diagram rather than pictorially as in figure 2205. This is a most useful aid in visualizing any time and date problem; a navigator should be thoroughly

familiar with the preparation and use of such a diagram.

Essentially, it is a simple sketch showing the relative positions of the meridians and hour circles involved in a particular problem. It consists of a circle representing the equator, straight lines from the center to the circumference, representing the meridians and hour circles of the problem, and appropriate labels. In drawing a time diagram, the earth is always considered to be viewed from a point in space beyond the *south* pole. *East* is thus in a *clockwise*, and *west* in a *counterclockwise* direction; all celestial bodies are therefore considered to revolve in a counterclockwise direction about the circle. All time problems in this book are illustrated with the use of a time diagram prepared in this manner. The basic elements of the time diagram are shown in figure 2206a.

By convention, the observer's meridian is always drawn vertically, with the upper branch, *M*, shown as a solid line extending upward from the center. The lower branch, *m*, is shown as a broken line, extended downwards. In problems in which it is necessary to distinguish between local mean time and zone time (article 2217), the *M-m* line represents the observer's meridian, and a *Z-z* line represents the central meridian of his time zone, and these meridians will be quite close together. However, local mean time is involved in only a comparatively small percentage of problems. In the majority of cases, the central meridian of the zone is omitted. The approximate zone time (ZT) at *M* is shown by drawing in the hour circle of the sun (☉) for the time in question. As shown in figure 2206b, for an observer on the meridian *M-m*, the sun's

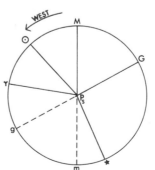

M Upper branch of observer's meridian.
m Lower branch of observer's meridian.
G Upper branch of Greenwich meridian.
g Lower branch of Greenwich meridian.
☉ Hour circle of sun
♈ Hour circle of Aries
☆ Hour circle of star
Ps South pole

Figure 2206a. Elements of a time diagram.

Figure 2206b. Time diagram illustrating the position of the sun at 2400-000, 0800, and 1200.

2400-0000 hour circle coincides with *m*, at 0800 it is 120° west or counterclockwise from *m*; at 1200 it coincides with *M* as it has moved through 180°. In figure 2206a, the sun is shown at approximately 1500.

A time diagram may be thought of as the face of a 24-hour clock, with *m* representing ZT 2400-0000, while *M* represents 1200, with the hour circles of the sun and other celestial bodies moving in a counterclockwise direction. Although most 24-hour clocks have a dial with 00 at the top, matching more conventional 12 hour clock faces, there is available at least one 24-hour clock with 12 at the top of its dial to match navigational time diagrams.

Time and Longitude

2207 The mean sun circles the earth's 360° of longitude in 24 hours, moving from east to west. In *one hour*, it passes over $\frac{1}{24}$ of the earth's meridians, or 15°. In *one minute* it covers $\frac{1}{60}$ of 15°, or 15 minutes of arc; in *four seconds* of time it covers one minute of arc, and in *one second*, it covers 0.25′ of arc.

The time-arc relationship may be summarized in tabular form.

Time	Arc
24 hours	360°
1 hour	15°
1 minute	15′
4 seconds	1′
1 second	0.25′

Due to the mean sun's motion from east to west,

it is always *later* by local mean time at places to the observer's *east*, and *earlier* at those to his *west*.

The relationship between time and longitude can be used to determine the difference in local mean time (see article 2210) between places in different longitudes. From the U.S. Naval Observatory in Washington, D.C., at longitude 77°04′ W, consider a ship in the Mediterranean at longitude 19°58′ E, and the lighthouse at Point Loma, California, at longitude 117°15′ W. These meridians are shown in figure 2207a, which again depicts the earth on a time diagram. West, the direction of the sun's motion, is in a counterclockwise direction. Ps-G represents the meridian of Greenwich, Ps-S that of the ship, Ps-N that of the Naval Observatory, and Ps-L that of the lighthouse. The difference in longitude between the ship and the observatory is 97°02′, since 19°58′ E + 77°04′ W = 97°02′, and the difference between the observatory and the lighthouse is 40°11′, since 117°15′ W − 77°04′ W = 40°11′. Converting these differences in longitude to time, we find that the difference in local time between the ship and the observatory is 6 hours, 28 minutes, and 08 seconds, and the difference between the observatory and the lighthouse is 2 hours, 40 minutes, and 44 seconds. Due to the sun's westerly motion, it is always later at the ship than at the other two positions. For example, when the local mean time at the observatory is 12-00-00, as shown by the sun over the meridian Ps-N in figure 2207a, the local mean time at S is 18-28-08, and that at L is 09-19-16. If subtracting a time difference results in a change of date, it is convenient to add 24 hours to the numerically smaller time in making the computation. For example, if the local mean time at the

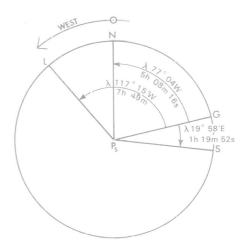

Figure 2207a. The difference in time between places is equal to the difference in their longitudes, converted into time units.

0°–59°		60°–119°		120°–179°		180°–239°		240°–299°		300°–359°			0'·00	0'·25	0'·50	0'·75
°	h m	°	h m	°	h m	°	h m	°	h m	°	h m	'	m s	m s	m s	m s
0	0 00	60	4 00	120	8 00	180	12 00	240	16 00	300	20 00	0	0 00	0 01	0 02	0 03
1	0 04	61	4 04	121	8 04	181	12 04	241	16 04	301	20 04	1	0 04	0 05	0 06	0 07
2	0 08	62	4 08	122	8 08	182	12 08	242	16 08	302	20 08	2	0 08	0 09	0 10	0 11
3	0 12	63	4 12	123	8 12	183	12 12	243	16 12	303	20 12	3	0 12	0 13	0 14	0 15
4	0 16	64	4 16	124	8 16	184	12 16	244	16 16	304	20 16	4	0 16	0 17	0 18	0 19
5	0 20	65	4 20	125	8 20	185	12 20	245	16 20	305	20 20	5	0 20	0 21	0 22	0 23
6	0 24	66	4 24	126	8 24	186	12 24	246	16 24	306	20 24	6	0 24	0 25	0 26	0 27
7	0 28	67	4 28	127	8 28	187	12 28	247	16 28	307	20 28	7	0 28	0 29	0 30	0 31
8	0 32	68	4 32	128	8 32	188	12 32	248	16 32	308	20 32	8	0 32	0 33	0 34	0 35
9	0 36	69	4 36	129	8 36	189	12 36	249	16 36	309	20 36	9	0 36	0 37	0 38	0 39
10	0 40	70	4 40	130	8 40	190	12 40	250	16 40	310	20 40	10	0 40	0 41	0 42	0 43
11	0 44	71	4 44	131	8 44	191	12 44	251	16 44	311	20 44	11	0 44	0 45	0 46	0 47
12	0 48	72	4 48	132	8 48	192	12 48	252	16 48	312	20 48	12	0 48	0 49	0 50	0 51
13	0 52	73	4 52	133	8 52	193	12 52	253	16 52	313	20 52	13	0 52	0 53	0 54	0 55
14	0 56	74	4 56	134	8 56	194	12 56	254	16 56	314	20 56	14	0 56	0 57	0 58	0 59

Figure 2207b. *Nautical Almanac* table "Conversion of Arc to Time" (extract).

Naval Observatory were 01-00-00 and it were desired to find the then local mean time at the Point Loma Lighthouse, 2-40-44 to the west, it is convenient to consider *0100 of today* as 0100 + 2400, or *2500 of the preceding day*. Then it is 25-00-00 minus 2-40-44 = 22-19-16, the *preceding day* at the lighthouse.

In doing any arithmetical calculations with time, but especially when subtracting, a navigator must be mentally alert to the fact that there are 60, not 100 minutes in an hour, and 60 seconds in a minute. One gets so used to decimal calculations that it is very easy to slip up on this "60" situation when "borrowing" or "carrying."

In the interconversion of time and arc, a navigator is aided by a conversion table published in the *Nautical Almanac*, an extract of which is shown in figure 2207b. A generally comparable table is included in each volume of the NOS *Tide Tables* and *Tidal Current Tables*.

Greenwich Mean Time (GMT)

2208 Greenwich Mean Time (GMT) is mean solar time measured with reference to the meridian of Greenwich, 0° longitude. The mean sun transits the lower branch of the meridian of Greenwich at GMT 00-00-00 and again at 24-00-00 (which is concurrently 00-00-00 of the following day); the mean sun transits the upper branch at 12-00-00. GMT is of great importance to the navigator, as it is the time used in almanacs as the argument for tabulating the coordinates of all celestial bodies. The choice of the meridian of Greenwich as the reference meridian for time is logical, as it is also the reference meridian that is used in reckoning longitude. Beginning with the 1989 edition, the *Nautical*

Almanac uses the description "UT" in preference to "GMT."

Universal Time (UT)

2209 Although it was stated in article 2204 that mean solar time was based on the *constant* motion of an imaginary sun, there are still slight variations. In contrast with this, man has developed a time standard that is essentially perfectly constant. The *second*, the basic unit of time in the metric system, is defined in terms of atomic vibrations using cesium beam oscillators; the "clocks" of various observatories and standards agencies are coordinated throughout the world by the International Time Bureau.

This steady, internationally adjusted time is termed *Coordinated Universal Time (UTC)*. This time scale meets the needs of most users; it is the time broadcast as radio time signals. Somewhat surprisingly, however, this near-perfect time is not the best for some purposes. In applications such as very precise navigation and satellite tracking, which must be referenced to the *actual* rotation of the earth, a time scale that speeds up and slows down with the earth's rotation rate must be used. This time scale is known as *UT1* and is inferred from astronomical observations.

To be responsive to the needs of such users, information is included in UTC broadcasts for adjustment to UT1. This increment, which may be either positive or negative, is termed DUT1 and is measured in tenths of a second. The relationships are as follows: UT1 = UTC + DUT1. The techniques used in transmitting and applying it are explained in article 2227.

For the navigator, and others who only need time to the nearest second, and to prevent DUT1 corrections from reaching too large a value, UTC is changed by occasional adjustments to UTC of exactly one second—a "leap second." These adjustments are inserted into UTC whenever needed to keep UTC time signals within ±0.9 seconds of UT1 at all times. Ordinarily, a positive leap second is required about once a year, usually at the end of December or June, depending upon how the earth's rotation rate is changing for that year.

For users who require the precision of time to the tenth of a second, UT1 can be calculated by adding the DUT1 correction. GMT is essentially UT1, but the fraction of a second difference from UTC is normally ignored by navigators (except that the insertion of a leap second must be taken into account in the determination of chronometer rate).

Local Mean Time (LMT)

2210 Just as Greenwich Mean Time is mean solar time measured with reference to the meridian of Greenwich, so *local mean time* (LMT) is mean solar time measured with reference to a given local meridian; this is the kind of time discussed in article 2207.

Zone Time (ZT)

2211 Local mean time was the standard generally used after the introduction of time based on a mean sun, and every city kept time based on the mean sun's transit of its meridian. As a result, a number of different time standards were used in comparatively small geographic areas. Before the days of modern electronic communications, and when physical travel was at the speed of a man, a horse, or the flow of a river, such disparities in time over relatively small areas were of no real importance. When electrical and mechanical develop-

ments made communications essentially instantaneous and transportation quite rapid, however, the differences in local times could no longer be tolerated. This led to the introduction of *zone time* to straighten out the confusion caused by the multiplicity of different local mean times in a given area. In zone time, all the places in a specified "zone" or band of longitude keep the same time, based on the local mean time of a single designated meridian, frequently the central meridian of the zone. Timepieces are reset only when moving into an adjoining time zone; they are advanced an hour if travel is to the east, and retarded an hour if to the west.

As a general rule, these zones are laid out so that they are not excessively wide; therefore, at no given place in the zone will the ZT vary greatly from the LMT, and the time will be in reasonably good agreement with the motions of the sun. At sea, the zones are usually equal bands of longitude 15° in width.

On land, the boundaries between adjacent zones are generally irregular, reflecting political boundaries and commercial influences; see article 2213.

Zone Description (ZD)

2212 In general, at sea the central meridians selected for time zones are longitudes that are exact multiples of 15°. There are 24 of these central or "standard" meridians, each one hour apart, and the longitude boundaries of each zone are 7½° on either side of the zone's standard meridian, as shown in figure 2212a. (For any one of several reasons, a ship at sea may elect to keep its clocks on a zone other than the one in which it is geographically located.)

The *zone description* (ZD) of a zone is the adjustment to be applied to the time of that zone to obtain GMT. For example, between longitudes 7½° east and 7½° west, the ZD is zero, and GMT will be used

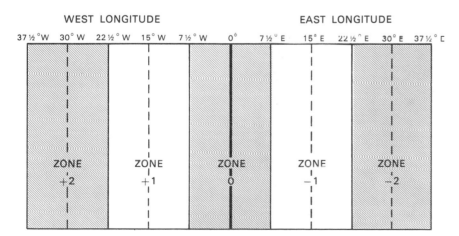

Figure 2212a. Time zone boundaries.

throughout the zone. In the zone bordered by longitudes 7°30′ E and 22°30′ E, the standard meridian is longitude (λ) 15° E. ZT in this zone will differ from GMT by one hour, and the zone being *east* of the meridian of Greenwich, it will be one hour *later*. One hour is *subtracted* from ZT to obtain GMT, and the ZD is (−1). Similarly, in the zone bordered by longitudes 7°30′ W and 22°30′ W, the ZT differs from GMT by one hour earlier, and the ZD is (+1), as one hour must be added to obtain GMT.

This procedure for determining the sign of time adjustments for various zones is valid for any longitude; the sign of the ZD of any zone in *east* longitude is *minus*, and that of the ZD of any zone in *west* longitude is *plus*. The numerical value of the adjustment for a zone can be determined by dividing the longitude of its standard meridian by 15°. Thus, the zone having λ 135° W as its standard meridian will have a ZD of (+9), the zone having λ 75° E as its standard meridian will have a ZD description of (−5).

The ZD at a given position can be similarly determined. The longitude of the place is divided by 15°, and the whole number of the quotient is determined. If the remainder is less than 7°30′, the whole number quotient establishes the numerical value of the ZD; if it is greater than 7°30′, the numerical value of the ZD is one more than the whole number of the quotient. Thus in λ 37°25.4′ W, the ZD will be (+2), while in λ 37°43.6′, the ZD will be (+3). These calculations refer to positions at sea where the zone boundaries are uniform; ashore, care must be taken with similar computations due to the frequently irregular boundaries of time zones.

The letter designations shown in each time zone in figure 2212b are those used by the U.S. Armed Forces in communications and operational planning for identification of the ZT in the various zones. These zone-descriptive letters have been widely adopted by other government and private activities. GMT (or Universal Time), which is zone time at Greenwich, is designated *Z* time. Zones to the east of Greenwich are designated alphabetically in order of increasing east longitude, commencing with *A*, and ending with *M*; the letter *J* is not used. Zones to the west of Greenwich are similarly designated, commencing with *N*, and ending with *Y* for the zone with ZD (+12).

The zone-description letters may be added to the four-digit statement of time. For example, a vessel off the east coast of the United States, keeping Eastern Standard Time (EST) could refer to the time of an event, for example, at "1715R"—*R* (Romeo) being the designator for zone (+5) which is EST. In communications involving ships or activities in different time zones, it is common to use *Z* (which is UTC). This is popularly known as "Zulu Time," as Zulu is the international phonetic alphabet equivalent for the letter *Z*.

Time Zone Plotter

Figure 2212b illustrates one form of Time Zone Plotter. On this device, which could be more accurately described as a "computer," the time zones and their variations are shown for both hemispheres. There is also DMAHTC Chart 76, which portrays this information on a Mercator chart of the world.

It should be noted that the 15°-wide zone centered on the 180th meridian is divided into two parts. The half in east longitude has a ZD of (−12), and that in west longitude has a ZD of (+12). This division of the zone having the 180th meridian as its standard is necessitated by the convention of the *International Date Line*, discussed in article 2215.

Figure 2212b. Time zone plotter.

With the use of the Time Zone Plotter one can easily determine the time at any other location in the world. The time zone diagram is pivoted to rotate over the base of the instrument, which contains a 24-hour time scale. Example: With the instrument set as in figure 2312b, it is 0700 in Washington, D.C., Zone (+5). In Kodiak, Alaska, it is 0200, Zone (+10). In Tokyo it is 2100 the following day (article 2215). If a message were received from a vessel near Kodiak containing a time designated 0200W, it would be easy to convert this to time at any other location, by reading time on the base plate opposite the time zone description on the movable dial.

It is also frequently desirable in communications to indicate the date as well as time. This is accomplished by *prefixing* the time group with two digits that indicate the date of the current month. Thus "121725Z" would indicate a *date/time* of GMT 1725 on the 12th of the current month. If a month other than the current one is to be described, the date/time group with the appropriate designator is used, and the name of the desired month is added as a suffix. If a year other than the current one is to be indicated, it is indicated after the month. If the date/time example previously used were for May 1985, the full group would read 121725Z May 85.

Many digital wristwatches or small timepieces have the capability of changing the hour, for a time zone switch, without interrupting the continuous count of minutes and seconds; some will internally keep two zone times, one of which can be local and the other GMT.

Variations in Zone Description; Standard and Daylight Time

2213 Zone time, based on uniform 15° bands of longitude, is a convenience at sea, but it can lead to complications on shore. For example, a city, or group of cities closely related by business ties, might lie astride the dividing line between zones. To avoid inconvenience to commerce and everyday life, such a territorial entity will often keep a single time that does not fully agree with the uniform zone system just described; boundaries between adjacent zones become quite irregular in many areas. This form of modified zone time is called *standard time*. In the 48 contiguous states of the U.S., it is designated as Eastern, Central, Mountain, and Pacific standard time. The "central" meridians of these zones are the 75°, 90°, 105°, and 125° of west longitude, respectively; the boundaries may be more or less than 7½° from a central meridian. Similarly, a nation which overlaps into two or three time zones may choose to keep one single ZT throughout its territory, thus eliminating any time difference problem within the country (figure 2212b).

Some places, for convenience, maintain a standard time that results in a ZD that is not a whole hour. The *Nautical Almanac* and *Air Almanac*, under the heading "Standard Times," tabulate the zone descriptions used in many areas of the world; the list is corrected as new countries come into existence or changes in standard time are made, but there may be a lag of several years in the publication of such corrections. The use, moreover, of "daylight time" will in some situations affect the given ZD values.

Daylight time (DT), also called *Daylight Saving Time* (DST) or *summer time*, is another variation of zone time. As a result of the early rising of the sun in summer, a certain amount of daylight would be "lost" to most people if the ZD were not adjusted. To avoid this loss, in many areas it is customary to adopt the time of the next adjacent zone to the *east*, during the period DT is in effect. This results in sunrise and sunset occurring one hour later. Along the east coast of the United States, where the ZD is usually (+5), based on the 75th meridian, during Daylight time the ZD becomes (+4). Similarly, a place using a ZD of (−9) might in summer advance its time so that the ZD becomes (−10).

Changing Time and Date at Sea

2214 When a vessel passes from one time zone into the next, it enters an area where it is desirable to keep a ZT differing by one hour from the previous one; if travel is toward the west, the ZT of the new zone will be one hour earlier than that of the old, and the ship's clocks would be set back one hour. If travel were eastward, the reverse would be true, and the clocks would be advanced one hour.

When a new time zone is about to be entered, a ship's navigator notifies the captain, who makes the decision as to the time that clocks will be reset. On smaller craft such as yachts the procedure is less formal, but essentially the same. Zone time is used as a matter of convenience, and the time that a change is made is selected with this in mind, to cause the minimal dislocation to the vessel's routine. The ZD does not change until the ZT is changed.

The International Date Line

2215 A vessel moving to the west sets its clocks back one hour in each new time zone; in a circumnavigation of the earth, it would therefore "lose" 24 hours. Conversely, if it were moving around the world in an easterly direction it would "gain" 24 hours in circling the globe. A method adjusting for the day lost or gained is necessary and this is accomplished by the *International Date Line,* which follows the 180° meridian, with some offsets so that it does not bisect an inhabited area. The adjustment to the date is made at some convenient time before or after the vessel crosses the date line. If a vessel has been proceeding *east,* its clocks have been steadily advanced, and this is compensated for by *retarding* the date one day. Conversely, a vessel traveling *west* has been setting back its clocks, so that the date is *advanced* one day. Note that the date change is in the *opposite* direction to the hour changes. This date change is made by every vessel crossing the date line, regardless of the length of the voyage.

The change of date accounts for the two zone descriptions associated with the 15° band of longitude centered on the 180th meridian. That part of the zone in west longitude has a ZD of (+12), and that part in east longitude has a ZD of (−12). The ZT is the same throughout the zone, but the date is *one day later* in the half that is in east longitude than it is in the half that is in west longitude. For example, aboard a ship in λ 175° W at 0900 ZT on 3 February, GMT is determined to be 2100, 3 February, by applying the ZD of (+12). At the same instant, on board a ship in λ 175° E, ZT is 0900 on 4 February; by applying the ZD (−12), GMT is also found to be 2100, 3 February.

The date line is used as a convenience, just as zone time is used as a convenience, and the change of date is made in the area of the date line at a time when the ship's routine will be disturbed as little as possible. Frequently, it is convenient to change the date at the midnight falling closest to the time the ship crosses the date line. However, it would generally be considered undesirable either to repeat a Sunday or a holiday, or to drop one. Under such conditions, ships have found it convenient to operate for a period using a ZD of either (+13), or (−13). Regardless of when the line is crossed, the *sign* of the ZD remains unchanged until the date is changed.

In summary, all changes in time and date are made solely for the purpose of convenience. The value of the zone time and the date used on board ship are of comparatively little importance in themselves; what is important is that the navigator be able to determine the time and date at Greenwich, so that he can obtain the coordinates of celestial bodies from the almanac. Also, navigators

should remember that the day that is added or subtracted when crossing the date line has *no effect* on the Greenwich date.

Using a Time Diagram

2216 In practical navigation, a navigator is concerned with using the preceding information on time to determine the GMT and date. The time diagram, introduced in article 2206 is generally sketched roughly by the navigator for each celestial problem to assist in visualizing the problem. Since GMT is used, the Greenwich meridian is shown on the diagram at an angular distance appropriate for the observer's longitude, east or clockwise from M if he is in west longitude, and west of M, if his longitude is east. The upper branch of the Greenwich meridian is drawn as a solid line and is labeled G, and the lower branch as a broken line and labeled g.

Figure 2216a shows on the left a time diagram for an observer in λ 60° W, with a ZT of about 1800. On the right, it shows a ZT of about 1800 for an observer in λ 15° E.

Since the sun is the basis of GMT as well as ZT, the approximate GMT can also be determined from a time diagram. In the time diagram in figure 2216a, with the observer at λ 60° W, the sun (☉) is approximately 90° west of the upper branch of the observer's meridian, M, and 150° or 10 hours west of the upper branch of the Greenwich meridian G; the GMT is therefore approximately 2200. Similarly, in the diagram at the right with the observer at λ 15° E, the sun is about 90° or six hours west of the local meridian M, but it is only about 75° or five hours west of the upper branch of the Greenwich meridian, G; the GMT is therefore about 1700. In this case, the sun will be a g in seven hours, which will signal the start of the next day for Greenwich.

A time diagram is particularly helpful when the date at the observer's meridian differs from that at another meridian, such as Greenwich. The time diagram in figure 2216b shows an observer in λ 115° E, at approximately 0500 ZT. Here the sun has already passed the lower branch of the observer's meridian m, and a new day has begun for him. At this moment the sun must travel approximately 40°, or some 2 hours and 40 minutes, before it transits the lower branch of the meridian of Greenwich to start the new day there; the date at Greenwich is therefore *the day preceding* the date for the observer at M. Thus, if it is ZT 0500, 10 January, for the observer at M, the GMT is 2100 on 9 January.

A difference in dates is readily apparent when a time diagram is used, as *the dates at two meridians*

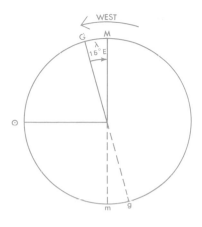

Figure 2216a. East and west longitude shown on a time diagram.

Figure 2216b. Time diagram illustrating a change in date

are always different if the sun's hour circle falls between the lower branches of the Greenwich meridian and the observer's meridian; the meridian whose *lower* branch is to the west of the sun's hour circle will have the earlier date.

Zone Time vs. Greenwich Mean Time

2217 Zone time differs from Greenwich Mean Time by the zone description.

To convert ZT to GMT, apply the ZD to ZT with the *sign as shown.*

To convert GMT to ZT, apply the ZD to GMT with the *opposite sign.*

These conversions are illustrated in the following examples:

Example 1: A navigator aboard a vessel at longitude 156°19.5' E observes the sun at 16-36-14 ZT on 26 April.

Required: GMT and date at the time of the observation.

Solution: First record the name of the body, the date based on ZT, and the ZT of the observation. Then sketch on a time diagram the relative positions of the observer, Greenwich, and the sun, to assist in visualizing the problem. Next, note the ZD of the time being kept aboard the vessel (longitude divided by 15° as described in article 2211). The ZD is (−)10 ("minus" because the observer is in east longitude; "10" because 156°10.5' ÷ 15° = 10, with remainder less than 7°30'). Then apply the ZD to ZT in accordance with its sign to determine GMT. Finally, record the date at Greenwich, which in this case is the same as the local date.

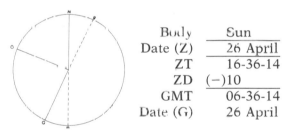

Body	Sun
Date (Z)	26 April
ZT	16-36-14
ZD	(−)10
GMT	06-36-14
Date (G)	26 April

Answer: GMT 06-36-14 on 26 April.

Example 2: A navigator aboard a vessel at longitude 83°17.9 W observes the star Arcturus at 19-15-29 ZT on 14 June.

Required: GMT and date at the time of the observation.

Solution: First record the name of the body, the date based upon ZT, and the ZT. Then sketch on a time diagram the relative positions of the observer, Greenwich, and the sun, to assist in visualizing the problem. Next, note the ZD (if necessary, dividing the longitude by 15°, to the nearest whole number). The ZD is (+)6 ("plus" because the observer is in west longitude; "6" because 83°17.9' ÷ 15° = 5, with remainder more than 7°30'). Then apply the ZD to ZT in accordance with its sign to determine GMT. Finally, record the date at Greenwich, which in this case is one day later than the local date—the sun having passed the Greenwich lower meridian (g) signaling the start of a new date there; it has not passed the lower branch of the local meridian that changes the local date.

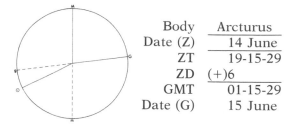

Body	Arcturus
Date (Z)	14 June
ZT	19-15-29
ZD	(+)6
GMT	01-15-29
Date (G)	15 June

Answer: GMT 01-15-29 on 15 June.

The relationship between Zone Time and Greenwich Mean Time can also be remembered by the following phrases:

Longitude west, Greenwich time best
Longitude east, Greenwich time least

in which "best" means greater and "least" means lesser.

Zone Time vs. Local Mean Time

2218 Local mean time (LMT) differs from zone time by the difference of longitude (DLo), expressed as time, between the meridian of the observer and the standard meridian of the zone. Local mean time is primarily of interest to the navigator in determining the zone time of phenomena such as sunrise and set, and moonrise and set.

If the observer is *east* of the central meridian of his zone, the phenomenon will occur for him *before* it will happen at the zone's central meridian. Conversely, if he is *west* of the standard meridian, the phenomenon will occur *later*, and LMT at his position will be earlier than ZT.

The following examples will serve to clarify the use of LMT, and its relationship to ZT.

Example 1: The navigator of a vessel at longitude 117°19.4' W determines from the almanac that sunrise is at LMT 0658 on 26 October. (The times of phenomena such as sunrise are given in the almanacs only to the nearest minute, which is fully adequate for practical navigation.)

Required: ZT of sunrise and local date.

Solution: First, record the name of the phenomenon, the date based on LMT, and the LMT of the event. Then sketch on a time diagram the relative positions of the observer, the sun, and the central meridian of the time zone (Z-z), to assist in visualizing the problem. Next determine the difference in longitude (DLo) between the meridian of the observer and the central meridian of the zone, and convert to units of time, to the nearest minute. In

this example the central meridian of the zone is 120° W (nearest whole multiple of 15°) and DLo equals 2°40.6'. Converting this value to time units by the rules of article 2207, DLo equals 11 minutes (to the nearest minute). (A convenient table for DLo time-units conversion is in each volume of the *Tide Tables* and *Tidal Current Tables*.) As the observer is east of the zone's central meridian, ZT is earlier than LMT, and the DLo, in time units, must be subtracted from LMT to obtain ZT.

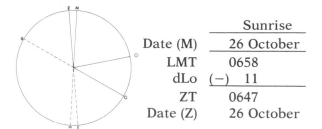

	Sunrise
Date (M)	26 October
LMT	0658
dLo	(−) 11
ZT	0647
Date (Z)	26 October

Answer: ZT 0647 on 26 October.

Example 2: The navigator of a vessel at longitude 38°58.5' E determines from the almanac that moonset is at LMT 2347 on 26 January.

Required: ZT of moonset, including local date.

Solution: First record the phenomenon, the date based upon LMT, and the LMT of the phenomenon. Then sketch on a time diagram the relative positions of the observer, the central meridian of the zone, and the sun, to assist in visualizing the problem. Next, determine the difference of longitude between the meridian of the observer and that of the central meridian of the zone and convert to time units, to the nearest minute. In this case, the central meridian of the zone is 45° E and DLo equals 6°01.5'. Converting this to time units, DLo equals 24 minutes (to the nearest minute). Since the observer is west of the central meridian, the ZT of moonset is later than LMT, and the DLo value must be added to LMT to obtain ZT.

Finally, record the date in the zone, which in this case is one day later than the date based upon LMT.

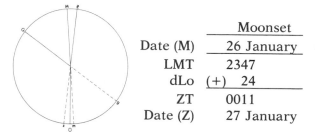

	Moonset
Date (M)	26 January
LMT	2347
dLo	(+) 24
ZT	0011
Date (Z)	27 January

Answer: ZT 0011 on 27 January.

In the practice of modern navigation, the navigator ordinarily has little occasion to convert ZT to LMT, except for sunrise and sunset, and moonrise and moonset computations.

Chronometers

2219 Time of day is used in many aspects of navigation, but nowhere is it more important than in the determination of longitude. The keeping of accurate time at sea was impossible until the invention of the chronometer by John Harrison in the early eighteenth century; voyages had to be sailed using techniques that accommodated the lack of knowledge of the vessel's longitude. Hour or sand glasses were satisfactory for rough dead reckoning, but were useless for sustained time keeping. Probably the best shipboard timekeeper before the eighteenth century was the compass. Many compasses were designed especially for this purpose, with a vertical pin at the center of the card. The compass card was in effect a sundial, and the pin was the gnomon.

The chronometer was important because it was sufficiently accurate to permit determining longitude afloat. The sextant offered both convenience and accuracy in measuring altitudes, not only of the sun, but also of the moon, planets, and stars. Until about 1880, it was the general practice to compute position by the time sight method. A latitude was obtained from an observation of Polaris or of the sun's transit. This latitude was carried forward by dead reckoning and used in determining longitude by a subsequent observation; latitude and longitude were both calculated, rather than being determined from plotting lines of position (LOPs) on a chart, as is done today.

A traditional chronometer is a very accurate spring-driven timepiece, usually about 4 or 5 inches in diameter, mounted in a heavy brass case, which is supported in gimbals in a wooden case. The gimbals take up much of the ship's motion, so that the chronometer remains in a nearly horizontal position. The wooden case is usually mounted in a very heavily padded second case, designed to give maximum protection against shock and sudden fluctuation of temperature. Chronometers are usually fitted with a detent escapement, and they beat, or tick, half-seconds, as compared to the five beats per second of most watches. This slow beat is of great convenience when comparing the instrument with radio time signals or other timepieces.

The great majority of chronometers have a 12-hour dial (see figure 2219); a few instruments have been produced that have a 24-hour face. A "winding indicator," showing how many hours have elapsed since the instrument was wound, is universally employed. Most chronometers will run for 56 hours before running down, although some 8-day models have been produced. However, *it is essential*

Figure 2219. A mechanical chronometer (Hamilton).

that the instrument be wound at the same time every day.

Marine chronometers are almost invariably set to GMT; they may, however, be adjusted to keep sidereal time. They are never reset aboard vessel; once the chronometer is started, the setting of the hands is not changed until it is removed for cleaning and overhaul. Due to the design of the escapement, a fully-wound mechanical chronometer will not start of its own accord. When a chronometer is to be started, the hands are set to the appropriate hour and minute of GMT. When the elapsed seconds of GMT agree with the second hand on the chronometer, the chronometer case is given a brisk horizontal turn through about 45°, and immediately turned back to its original position; this will start the movement.

The time indicated by a chronometer is chronometer time (C).

Although it is the actual time that is used in celestial navigation, equally important is *rate* of a timepiece, the amount it gains or loses in a specified time, usually 24 hours; see article 2222. It is usually expressed as seconds and tenths of seconds per day, and is labeled "gaining" or "losing." Temperature is the main factor affecting fine timepieces; in general, their rates will increase with rising temperatures.

Quartz Chronometers

A development of modern science is the *quartz chronometer,* in which a tiny quartz crystal is used to stabilize the frequency of an electronic oscillator. The stability of these newer chronometers far surpasses that of older mechanical designs; kept at a reasonably constant temperature, they are capable of maintaining an excellent rate, with the better models having a deviation of less than 0.01 second from their average daily rate that should not exceed 0.2 second per day. Many models have a sweep-second hand that can be advanced or retarded electronically in increments of one-tenth or one-hundredth of a second while the chronometer is running.

These quartz chronometers are powered by small "flashlight" batteries and thus do not require winding. They are highly resistant to shock and vibration and do not require gimbals; they may be mounted in a traditional box or on a bulkhead.

Quartz Wristwatches

A quartz-crystal-controlled movement is now used in a large percentage of wristwatches, replacing the tuning-fork technique, which was the first advancement from basic mechanical designs. Although the accuracy achieved will probably not be as great as that of a quartz chronometer, the daily rate will often be quite stable and adequate for practical navigation, especially if a few precautions are taken. A uniform "environment" should be established for the watch, such as always wearing it, or always not wearing it and keeping it in the same protected place, or wearing it a consistent number of hours each day. Before such a timepiece is used for navigation, its time should be regularly compared to time of known accuracy (radio time signals or a chronometer) for a sufficiently long period to establish both the amount and stability of its rate.

A useful feature found on many quartz wristwatches is an indication of the day of the month. If such a calendar watch is set to Greenwich time *and date,* one calculation (and possible error) can be eliminated. Care must be taken with ordinary watch dials as to whether GMT is between 00 and 12 or between 13 and 24 hours, but this is easily worked out mentally by adding the ZD to the hours of local time. (Many watches with digital dials can be set to show time in the 24-hour system.) Some watches may require a manual adjustment at the end of a month having less than 31 days in it, but many that show the date by month and day accomplish this automatically.

Atomic Time Standards Aboard Ship

With the ever-expanding use of highly sophisticated inertial and radionavigation systems and computers, there are more and more ships at sea equipped with their own atomic time standard. U.S. naval vessels, particularly nuclear-powered,

missile-launching submarines, are often equipped with one or more cesium- or rubidium-beam devices for time information that are orders of magnitude more precise than mechanical or quartz chronometers. With on-board time data of such extreme accuracy, equipment and systems can be synchronized independently with signals received from land-based or satellite transmitters.

Errors in Timepieces

2220 All timepieces are subject to certain errors, and at any given time nearly every timepiece probably will indicate a time that is somewhat fast or slow with respect to the correct time.

If the *error* (E) of a timepiece is *fast* (F), meaning that the time indicated is later than the correct time, the amount of error must be *subtracted* to obtain the correct time. If the error is *slow* (S), meaning that the time indicated is earlier than the correct time, the amount of error must be *added* to obtain the correct time.

Watch error (WE) is the difference between the indication of a watch and the correct time at any instant.

Chronometer Error

2221 The difference between chronometer time and GMT at any instant is called *chronometer error* (CE), labeled (F) or (S) as the chronometer is fast or slow on the correct (Greenwich) time. Since chronometers are not reset aboard ship, the accumulated error may become quite large. This is not important if the error is accurately known.

Chronometer error is usually determined by means of a radio time signal; see article 2226. The chronometer may be compared directly, or a *comparing watch* (see article 2224) may be used to avoid moving the chronometer.

Example 1: On 31 October, the navigator of a vessel at λ 118°36.6′ W desires to determine the chronometer error by direct comparison with a radio time signal. A time signal at 2000 UTC is used; at the moment of the "tick," the chronometer read 7-46-27.

Required: The chronometer error on GMT.
Solution:

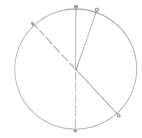

ZT	12-00-00 31 Oct.
ZD	(+) 8
GMT	20-00-00 31 Oct.
C	7-46-27
CE	(S) 13-33

Answer: The chronometer is 13^{m}33^s slow on GMT.

Note that the GMT is 20^h, while the chronometer reads 7-46-27. The CE shown is correct, since the chronometer face is graduated to only 12^h. Hence at GMT 20^h, the time in Greenwich is 8 P.M., as indicated approximately by the chronometer.

Example: On 10 July, the navigator of a vessel at 46°30.4′ W longitude desires to obtain the chronometer error from a radio signal. A comparing watch, set approximately to ZT (+3), is used in the radio room to note the watch time of the signal. A time signal for 1700 UTC is used. At the moment of the tick, the comparing watch reads 2-01-30 P.M. A little later the comparing watch reads 2-04-20 P.M. at the instant that the chronometer reads 4-38-00.

Required: The chronometer error on GMT.

Solution:

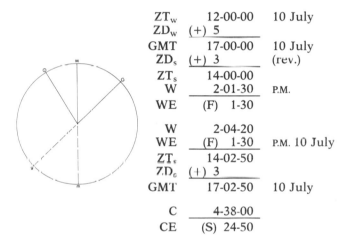

ZT$_w$	12-00-00	10 July
ZD$_w$	(+) 5	
GMT	17-00-00	10 July
ZD$_s$	(+) 3	(rev.)
ZT$_s$	14-00-00	
W	2-01-30	P.M.
WE	(F) 1-30	
W	2-04-20	
WE	(F) 1-30	P.M. 10 July
ZT$_s$	14-02-50	
ZD$_s$	(+) 3	
GMT	17-02-50	10 July
C	4-38-00	
CE	(S) 24-50	

Answer: The chronometer is 24^{m}50^s slow on GMT.

Rate Calculations

2222 The nearly constant rate (stated as either *gaining* or *losing*) of a fine chronometer is its most important feature, as it makes safe navigation possible on a long voyage without dependence on time signals. While the rate should be as small as possible, its consistency is more important.

A timepiece rate is determined by comparison with radio signals obtained several days apart.

Example 1: A navigator, desiring to determine the chronometer rate, compares his chronometer directly with a radio time signal at the same time on different days. On 6 April the chronometer reads 5-25-05 and on 16 April it reads 5-25-51.

Required: The chronometer error on each date and the chronometer rate.

Solution:

ZT	12-00-00	6 April
ZD	(+) 5	
GMT	17-00-00	6 April
C	5-25-05	
CE	(F) 25-05	6 April
GMT	17-00-00	16 April
C	5-25-51	
CE	(F) 25-51	16 April
CE	(F) 25-05	6 April
diff.	46	
rate	4.6	gaining

Answers: CE on 6 April is 25^{m}05^s fast on GMT. CE on 16 April is 25^{m}51^s fast on GMT. The chronometer rate over a ten-day period has been 4.6^s per day, gaining.

The chronometer rate provides a means of determining the chronometer error at any instant between time signals.

Example 2: At 1620 on 2 December the DR λ of a vessel is 147°40.6′ W when the navigator prepares to observe the sun. He compares his watch with a chronometer that was 17^{m}27^s fast on GMT at ZT 1200 (when the ship was keeping (+5) zone time on 20 November). The chronometer is 0.7^s gaining.

Required: The chronometer error.

Solution:

ZT	12-00-00	20 Nov.
ZD	(+) 5	
GMT	17-00-00	20 Nov.
ZT	16-20-00	2 Dec.
ZD	(+)10	
GMT	2-20-00	3 Dec.
GMT	17-00-00	20 Nov.
Elapsed time	9-20-00 + 12 days	
	= 12.4 days	
CE	(F) 17-27	20 Nov.
corr.	(+) 9	(12.4 × 0.7)
CE	(F) 17-36	2 Dec.

Answer: CE on 2 December is 17^{m}36^s fast on GMT.

Chronometer Records

2223 The *Navigation Timepiece Rate Book*, NAV-SEA 4270, is issued to every U.S. naval vessel; it permits the maintenance of complete records on three chronometers or other timepieces. These data include the daily error and the daily rate; each page has space for 31 daily entries. A portion of a sample page is reproduced in figure 2223.

DATE	A			B			C			OBSERVATION	
YEAR 19**84**	MAKE HAMILTON TYPE SC SERIAL NO. 4327			MAKE HAMILTON TYPE SC SERIAL NO. 1278			MAKE HAMILTON TYPE GCW SERIAL NO. 843				
MONTH July	ERROR RELATIVE TO G.C.T. +=FAST −=SLOW		SUCCESSIVE DAILY RATES	ERROR RELATIVE TO G.C.T. +=FAST −=SLOW		SUCCESSIVE DAILY RATES	ERROR RELATIVE TO G.C.T. +=FAST −=SLOW		SUCCESSIVE DAILY RATES	LOCAL TIME TO NEAREST MINUTE	
DAY	±	MIN. SECONDS	± SECONDS	±	MIN. SECONDS	± SECONDS	±	MIN. SECONDS	± SECONDS	TIME	INITIALS
1	+	1 4.5	.	−	2 4.6	.	+	12 42.4	.	1155	
2	+	1 6.0	+ 1.5	−	2 3.8	+ 0.8	+	12 40.0	− 2.4	1205	
3	+	1 7.5	+ 1.5	−	2 3.0	+ 0.8	+	12 37.5	− 2.5	1140	
4	+	1 9.0	+ 1.5	−	2 2.2	+ 0.8	+	12 35.1	− 2.4	1135	
5	+	1 10.6	+ 1.6	−	2 1.4	+ 0.8	+	12 32.7	− 2.4	1120	
6	+	1 12.1	+ 1.5	−	2 0.5	+ 0.9	+	12 30.2	− 2.5	1200	

Figure 2223. Page extract, filled in, from *Navigation Timepiece Rate Book* (Nav-SEC 9846/2).

Complete instructions for the care, winding, and transportation of chronometers are given in the *Navigation Timepiece Rate Book*. An officer assuming navigational duties should familiarize himself with these instructions as well as pertinent information in *NAVSEA Technical Manual* 0901-LP-252-0000.

The standard chronometer in the U.S. Navy is returned to a chronometer pool every three years for cleaning, lubrication, and any other work that may be necessary. It is the custom for a senior quartermaster to wind the chronometers and check the rates every day at about 1130. This is reported to the officer of the deck, who in turn advises the captain that "the chronometers have been wound and compared" as part of the routine 1200 report.

Procedures on non-naval vessels will be less formal, but they should be carried out systematically in order that correct time will always be available for navigation and other purposes.

Comparing Watch

2224 A *comparing watch* is a watch employed to time celestial observations, and to assist in checking a chronometer against a radio time signal. It is also sometimes called a *hack watch*. A good quality *split-second timer* makes the best comparing watch. It has two sweep second hands, one directly below the other, which can be started and stopped together, by means of a push button usually mounted in the center of the winding stem. A second push button stops the lower of the two sweephands, permitting an accurate readout. When this button is pushed again, the stopped hand catches up with the running hand. These watches are also fitted with a small dial to indicate the elapsed time after the continuously running sweep hand was started.

Lacking a split-second timer, any watch with a sweep second hand makes an acceptable comparing watch, as it facilitates reading time to the nearest second. A standard *stopwatch* may be used to advantage for this purpose, but should not be used for any extended period of time, as such units generally have low long-term accuracy.

Every watch used as a comparing watch should be checked regularly to determine that it will run free of appreciable error for the period of its normal maximum use; ordinarily this would be about 60 minutes.

A comparing watch can also be used in the determination of chronometer error and rate.

Second-setting Watch

A *second-setting watch* also makes a satisfactory comparing watch. In these watches, the hour, minute, and second hand are all mounted concentrically; the hour hand usually reads out to 24 hours. On this type of watch, the second hand is stopped when the winding stem is pulled out, and the hour and minute hands can then be set to any desired time by turning the stem. When the stem is pushed back in, the watch is restarted. This type of watch may be set very accurately by means of a radio time tick. Other models combine the features of keeping GMT with a stopwatch mechanism and are referred to as navigational time and stopwatches. Due to the ready availability of the radio time tick for checking purposes, many smaller vessels and seagoing recreational craft do not carry a marine chronometer, but depend on a high-quality watch or a mounted chronometer watch, plus radio time signals.

Timing Celestial Observations

2225 The coordinates of celestial bodies are tabulated with respect to GMT and date; it is therefore necessary that the navigator know the GMT and Greenwich date of each celestial observation.

This is accomplished most simply by using a time-piece set precisely to GMT, and noting the time at the instant of each observation. This is far superior to using a watch set either to zone or chronometer time, as it both speeds the operation, and reduces the hazard of error.

A split-second timer, or lacking such, a stop-watch, should be used for celestial observations. The watch should, if possible, be started against a radio time signal (see article 2226), using the tick that marks any exact minute; the GMT and Greenwich date at which the watch was started should be noted. If a radio time signal is unavailable, the watch should be started against the best chronometer. To do this, the local time zone description is applied to the ship's time to determine the Greenwich date, and whether the time there is A.M. or P.M. The updated chronometer error is then determined. The chronometer error must be applied to the chronometer time, *with the opposite sign*, in order to obtain GMT. With the error known, the watch is started at the proper time. This procedure is illustrated in the following example.

Morning star observations are to be obtained, and the recorder's watch is to be started on a 5-minute increment of GMT. The ship's clocks are set to Zone (−10) time. (Calculations are shown in figure 2225.)

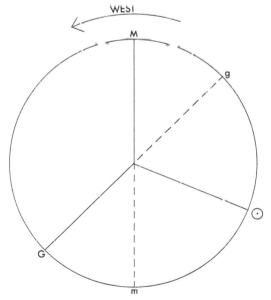

Figure 2225. Time diagram for a celestial observation using a stopwatch.
Ship's time and date: 0543 (−10), 7 April
GMT time and date: 1943, 6 April
Chronometer error: + (fast) 2 min, 41.5 sec
At GMT 19-45-00, a chronometer with a 12-hour dial will read 7 hours, 47 minutes, 41.5 seconds, and the comparing watch is started at this reading.

TIME SIGNALS

Radio Time Signals

2226 Radio time signals, often called "time ticks," are broadcast from many stations throughout the world. Complete information on the time signals of all countries is given in *Radio Navigational Aids* (DMAHTC Publications No. 117A and 117B), and in various publications of the U.S. Naval Observatory and the National Bureau of Standards, an activity of the Department of Commerce.

The signals most commonly used by United States vessels are broadcast from the Bureau of Standards radio stations WWV at Fort Collins, Colorado, and from WWVH on the island of Kauai, Hawaii. These signals have an accuracy far greater than is required for ordinary navigation.

Stations WWV and WWVH

2227 Stations WWV and WWVH broadcast time signals continuously during each day. Frequencies and radiated power in kilowatts are as follows:

Frequency MHz	Radiated power, kw.	
	WWV	WWVH
2.5	2.5	5
5.0	10	10
10.0	10	10
15.0	10	10
20.0	2.5	—

The selection of frequency for best reception will depend on the time of day, and on atmospheric conditions. As a general rule, the 15 MHz band is satisfactory during the daylight hours, while the 5 MHz band is usually better at night. During times in the sunspot cycle when radio propagation conditions are favorable, WWV transmits on 20 MHz; this frequency is particularly useful at long distances from the station. Double-sideband AM modulation is used on all frequencies.

Each second is marked by an audible "tick" (a 5-millisecond pulse, audio frequency of 1000 Hz at WWV and 1200 Hz at WWVH); however, the 29th and 59th seconds are not marked by a tick. Once each minute, time is announced by voice in the last 15 seconds of the minute. The two stations are distinguished by a female voice from WWVH at 15 seconds before the minute, and a male voice from WWV at $7\frac{1}{2}$ seconds before the minute. The time is stated as Coordinated Universal Time, which for ordinary navigational purposes can be used as

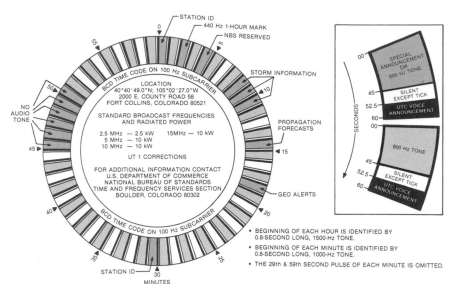

* BEGINNING OF EACH HOUR IS IDENTIFIED BY 0.8-SECOND LONG, 1500-Hz TONE.
* BEGINNING OF EACH MINUTE IS IDENTIFIED BY 0.8-SECOND LONG, 1000-Hz TONE.
* THE 29th & 59th SECOND PULSE OF EACH MINUTE IS OMITTED.

Figure 2227a. Signals from Radio Station WWV.

GMT; see article 2209. The format of the time announcement is the same from both stations; for example, just before 0310 UTC, the announcement, which is recorded, would be "At the tone, three hours, ten minutes, Coordinated Universal Time."

The first pulse of each minute is longer, 800 milliseconds, for emphasis. The first pulse of each *hour* is further emphasized by being of a higher frequency (1500 Hz). The exact time is indicated by the *beginning* of each pulse. Pulses are transmitted in exact synchronization by WWV and WWVH, but propagation delays may result in their being received very slightly out of step if both stations are being heard at the same time.

Audio Tones

In alternate minutes during most of each hour, 500 or 600 Hz audio tones are broadcast. A 440 Hz tone, the musical note *A* above middle *C*, is broadcast once each hour. In addition to being a musical standard, the 440 Hz tone can be used to provide a marker for chart recorders or other automated devices.

There are "silent periods" with no tone modulation. The carrier frequency, however, continues, as do the seconds pulses and the time announcements. On WWV, no audio tones are broadcast at 45 through 51 minutes after each hour, and additionally there are no audio tones for minutes 29 and 59. On WWVH, no audio tones are broadcast for minutes 00 and 30.

High Seas Weather Information

Weather information about major storms in the Atlantic and eastern North Pacific are broadcast in voice from WWV at 8, 9, and 10 minutes after each hour. Similar storm warnings covering the eastern and central North Pacific are given from WWVH at 48, 49, and 50 minutes after each hour. An additional segment (at 11 minutes after the hour on WWV and at 51 minutes on WWVH) may be used when there are unusually widespread storm conditions. These brief messages are designed to tell mariners of storm threats in their areas. If there are no warnings in the designated areas, the broadcasts will so indicate. The ocean areas involved are those for which the U.S. has warning responsibility under international agreement. The regular times of issue by the National Weather Service are 0500, 1100, 1700, and 2300 UTC for WWV and 0000, 0600, 1200, and 1800 UTC for WWVH. These broadcasts are updated effective with the next scheduled announcement following the time of issue. Broadcasts by WWV and WWVH also contain information regarding radio propagation forecasts, geophysical alerts, and official announcements by federal agencies.

Using WWV and WWVH Time Signals

The signals broadcast from WWV and WWVH are in a very useful form for the navigator. The tick transmitted every second is most useful for starting a stopwatch accurately. By beating every second with the incoming signal for about the final 15 seconds of the minute, with a little practice it is possible to start a stopwatch without a readable error—that is, with an error of less than one-fifth of a second.

If UT1 accuracy is required, the DUT1 correction may be noted and applied. This correction, in units of 0.1 second to a maximum of 0.9 second, are encoded into the broadcasts by using double ticks or pulses after the start of each minute. The 1st through the 8th ticks, when doubled, indicate a "plus" correction; doubled 9th through 16th ticks indicate a "minus" correction. For example, if the 1st, 2nd, and 3rd ticks are doubled, the correction is "plus" 0.3 seconds: UT1 = UTC + 0.3; if UTC is 08-45-17, then UT1 is 08-45-17.3. If the 9th, 10th, 11th, and 12th seconds had been doubled, the correction would have been a "minus" 0.4 second and, in the above example, UT1 = 08-45-16.6.

Time Signals from Other Nations

2228 Continuous time signals are also broadcast by the Canadian station CHU near Ottawa, Ontario, on 3,330, 7,335, and 14,670 kHz. Voice announcements of the upcoming minute and hour of Eastern Standard Time (ZD 5) are made in both English and French. The 29th second tick is omitted, as are the 51st to 59th; during this latter period the voice announcement is made. The zero second pulse of each minute is one-half second long; the start of an hour is identified by a pulse of one full second length followed by 12 seconds of silence. The modulation is single-sideband, AM-compatible (A3H) in order that the signals may be heard on either single-sideband or double-sideband receivers. These transmissions can be very useful to vessels off the Atlantic Coast of North America.

Many other foreign nations around the world broadcast time signals on a wide variety of frequencies and schedules; identifying information is given in some cases by Morse code and in other instances in voice. Details will be found in Pubs.

No. 117; changes are published in *Notices to Mariners*. Another source of information on time signal broadcasts is the U.S. Naval Observatory *Time Service Publication, Series 1*.

Time Information from Other Signals

2229 The pulsed signals of Loran-C and Omega electronic navigation systems are precisely timed to atomic standards. Highly accurate time information can be obtained from these transmissions, but this requires access to published technical data; also, coarse time must be known, as no identification of seconds or minutes is transmitted.

A time check can also be obtained from the pulse, or "beep," at the end of each navigational satellite (Transit) transmission every two minutes.

Standard Frequencies

2230 Most time broadcasts, especially those of WWV, WWVH, and CHU, are made on highly accurate frequencies. These signals can assist in the checking and adjustment of radio receiving equipment of all types. Details will be found in the various publications listing time signal transmissions.

Sidereal Time

2231 Although it is not used in practical celestial navigation, a navigator should be familiar with *sidereal time*. Article 1811 explained why the *sidereal day*, which is the time required for the earth to complete one rotation on its axis relative to the vernal equinox, is about 3 minutes and 56.6 seconds shorter than the mean solar day. As sidereal time indicates the position of the stars, their daily shift westward is therefore almost one degree every night. Because of *nutation* (see article 1817), sidereal time is not perfectly constant in rate. Time based on the average rate is called *mean sidereal time*. There is no sidereal date.

Greenwich sidereal time (GST) uses the meridian of Greenwich as its terrestrial reference, while the observer's meridian is the reference for *local sidereal time* (LST).

Some timepieces, often reading in arc rather than in time, are available to keep sidereal time. If set to GST they permit the navigator to read the GHA ♈, which is GST expressed in units of arc, directly from the timepiece at the instant of making a star observation, thus obviating the need to extract GHA ♈ and a correction thereto from the *Almanac*.

Chapter 23

Almanacs; Celestial Phenomena

Introduction

2301 Following a consideration of time—that most important ingredient of navigation—the next logical subject is a review of *almanacs*. These volumes are sources of astronomical data such as Greenwich Hour Angle (GHA) and declination (Dec.) for celestial bodies at any given instant of time. Almanacs also provide much other information necessary and useful in celestial navigation.

Although the *Air Almanac* will be discussed in this chapter, primary attention will be given to the *Nautical Almanac*, which is normally the choice of a marine navigator.

The Development of Almanacs

2302 The early history of celestial observations was briefly covered in chapter 18. Here we will consider how predictions have been developed for direct assistance to the navigator at sea. The Danish astronomer, Tycho Brahe, during the last half of the sixteenth century, spent over twenty years making accurate observations of the heavenly bodies. On the data thus amassed, Kepler based his laws of motion, which were the foundation both of modern astronomy and celestial navigation. The earliest compilations of astronomical calculations for nautical purposes date from the fifteenth century and were published privately by individuals. The first official nautical *ephemeris* or *almanac* was published by the French in 1687; this was followed by the British *Nautical Almanac* in 1765 for the year 1767. In 1852, the United States Nautical Almanac Office published the first *American Ephemeris and Nautical Almanac* for the year 1855; this volume has appeared annually since then. In 1858, the *American Nautical Almanac* was published—the ephemeris section, of primary interest to astronomers, being omitted.

In 1933, the *Air Almanac* was first published in the United States. It was revolutionary, as Greenwich Hour Angle was substituted for Right Ascension; the hour angle, incidentally, was stated to 0.1'. This *Almanac* was discontinued in 1934, but produced again in 1937 by the Royal Greenwich Observatory in somewhat modified form, and published in the United States by the Weems System of Navigation. In 1941, the U.S. Naval Observatory resumed the publication of the *Air Almanac* in the United States.

The British and American editions of the *Nautical Almanac*, which are now identical in content, are produced jointly by Her Majesty's Nautical Almanac Office, Royal Greenwich Observatory, and by the Nautical Almanac Office, U.S. Naval Observatory, but are printed separately in the United States and Britain. The *Nautical Almanac* is prepared to the general requirements of the British Admiralty and the United States Navy, but, of course, meets well the needs of other surface vessel navigators; its purpose is to provide, in convenient form, the astronomical data required for the practice of celestial navigation at sea.

The *Nautical Almanac* is also published, with minor modifications, by a number of foreign nations using their language for page headings, explanatory text, and notes.

Nautical Almanac: Basic Contents

2303 To find an observer's position on earth by observations of celestial bodies, it is necessary to determine the position of the observer relative to the geographical positions of these bodies. The *Nautical Almanac* consists principally of data from which the Greenwich Hour Angle (GHA) and declination (Dec.) of all the celestial bodies used in navigation can be obtained for any instant of Greenwich Mean Time (GMT). In general, these data are presented to the nearest one-tenth minute of arc, and one second of time. The Local Hour Angle (LHA) can then be obtained by means of the equations:

$$LHA = GHA - \text{west longitude}$$
and
$$LHA = GHA + \text{east longitude}$$

bearing in mind that 360° may need to be added or subtracted. LHA, like GHA, is always calculated in a westerly direction. For some methods of sight reduction *meridian angle* (t) is required; this is measured east or west from the observer's meridian to 180°, as discussed in chapter 19. Meridian angle may be readily determined from LHA. Figure 2303 depicts the relationship between longitude (west), GHA, meridian angle (t), and SHA.

There is an "Explanation" section with much useful information following the basic tables of the *Nautical Almanac*.

Figure 2303. Hour angles illustrated on a sphere.

Nautical Almanac: Format

2304 The basic ephemeristic data for all navigational bodies of interest to a mariner covering a three-day period are presented on a pair of facing pages of the *Nautical Almanac*. The left-hand pages are used primarily for the tabulation of data for the stars and navigational planets. These bodies are of navigational interest primarily during morning and evening twilight. The right-hand pages present the ephemeristic data for the sun and moon, to-

gether with the times of twilight, sunrise, sunset, moonrise, and moonset. Sample almanac pages are shown as figures 2304a and 2304b.

The extreme left-hand column of each page contains the dates, days of the week, and the hours of GMT for the three days. It should be noted carefully that *the date is that at Greenwich*; this may be one day earlier or later than the local date at the navigator's position as was explained in article 2218.

Left-hand Pages

The left-hand page for each set of three days gives, for each hour, the GHA of Aries (♈) and the GHA and declination of the navigational planets—Venus, Mars, Jupiter, and Saturn. Also on this page is a tabulation of the SHA of each planet and the time of its meridian passage, and separately, the time of meridian passage of ♈.

A list of 57 selected stars, arranged in alphabetical order together with their SHA and declination is also given. These are the prime navigational stars selected for their magnitude and distribution in the heavens, and are the ones most frequently observed by a navigator.

All tabulations are in degrees, minutes, and tenths of minutes of arc.

Values of v and d

At the bottom of each column of data for a planet there are the v and d values for that body; as these values change slowly, a single entry is given for the three-day period covered by that page.

The d values are the amount in arc by which Dec. changes during each hour; v values are the amount in arc by which GHA departs from the basic rate used in the almanac interpolation tables. The v and d values are for use with the interpolation tables, which are based on a constant rate of change. These latter tables, explained later in this chapter, are included to facilitate the interpolation of GHA and Dec. respectively for intermediate times.

Right-hand Pages

Data for the sun and moon are presented on the right-hand page with GHA and Dec., tabulated to one-tenth minute of arc for each hour. For the moon, additional values for the horizontal parallax (HP) and of v and d are tabulated for each hour. The moon's rate of change of GHA and Dec. varies considerably. For the sun, v is omitted entirely and d is given only once at the bottom of the page for the three-day period.

Also shown on the right-hand pages are data for each day covering the equation of time, meridian passage of the sun and moon, and the age and

JUNE 3, 4, 5 (FRI., SAT., SUN.)

G.M.T.	ARIES G.H.A.	VENUS −4.1 G.H.A.	Dec	MARS +1.3 G.H.A.	Dec	JUPITER −1.5 G.H.A.	Dec	SATURN +0.6 G.H.A.	Dec	STARS Name	S.H.A.	Dec
3 00	251 20.1	225 19.6 N 8	27.0	225 15.5 N 9	38.9	179 21.4 N21	54.8	116 16.2 N18	02.6	Acamar	315 39.3	S40 23.7
01	266 22.6	240 20.0	27.6	240 16.2	39.6	194 23.2	54.9	131 18.4	02.5	Achernar	335 47.4	S57 20.9
02	281 25.1	255 20.4	28.3	255 16.9	40.3	209 25.0	55.0	146 20.7	02.5	Acrux	173 39.3	S62 58.8
03	296 27.5	270 20.8 ··	28.9	270 17.6 ··	41.0	224 26.9 ··	55.1	161 22.9 ··	02.4	Adhara	255 34.2	S28 56.7
04	311 30.0	285 21.2	29.5	285 18.3	41.6	239 28.7	55.1	176 25.2	02.3	Aldebaran	291 20.9	N16 27.7
05	326 32.4	300 21.6	30.1	300 19.0	42.3	254 30.6	55.2	191 27.4	02.3			
06	341 34.9	315 22.0 N 8	30.7	315 19.7 N 9	43.0	269 32.4 N21	55.3	206 29.7 N18	02.2	Alioth	166 44.3	N56 05.1
07	356 37.4	330 22.4	31.3	330 20.4	43.7	284 34.2	55.4	221 31.9 ··	02.2	Alkaid	153 20.0	N49 25.7
08	11 39.8	345 22.8	31.9	345 21.1	44.4	299 36.1	55.4	236 34.2	02.1	Al Na'ir	28 17.7	S47 03.9
F 09	26 42.3	0 23.2 ··	32.5	0 21.8 ··	45.1	314 37.9 ··	55.5	251 36.4 ··	02.0	Alnilam	276 14.2	S 1 13.1
R 10	41 44.8	15 23.6	33.1	15 22.5	45.7	329 39.8	55.6	266 38.7	02.0	Alphard	218 22.9	S 8 33.8
I 11	56 47.2	30 24.0	33.7	30 23.2	46.4	344 41.6	55.7	281 40.9	01.9			
D 12	71 49.7	45 24.3 N 8	34.3	45 23.9 N 9	47.1	359 43.5 N21	55.7	296 43.2 N18	01.9	Alphecca	126 33.7	N26 47.5
A 13	86 52.2	60 24.7	34.9	60 24.6	47.8	14 45.3	55.8	311 45.4	01.8	Alpheratz	358 11.7	N28 57.8
Y 14	101 54.6	75 25.1	35.5	75 25.3	48.5	29 47.1	55.9	326 47.7	01.7	Altair	62 34.4	N 8 48.5
15	116 57.1	90 25.5 ··	36.1	90 26.0 ··	49.1	44 49.0 ··	56.0	341 49.9 ··	01.7	Ankaa	353 42.7	S42 25.5
16	131 59.6	105 25.9	36.7	105 26.7	49.8	59 50.8	56.0	356 52.2	01.6	Antares	112 59.2	S26 22.9
17	147 02.0	120 26.3	37.4	120 27.4	50.5	74 52.7	56.1	11 54.4	01.6			
18	162 04.5	135 26.6 N 8	38.0	135 28.1 N 9	51.2	89 54.5 N21	56.2	26 56.7 N18	01.5	Arcturus	146 20.2	N19 18.1
19	177 06.9	150 27.0	38.6	150 28.8	51.9	104 56.4	56.3	41 58.9	01.4	Atria	108 24.8	S68 59.2
20	192 09.4	165 27.4	39.2	165 29.5	52.5	119 58.2	56.3	57 01.2	01.4	Avior	234 29.5	S59 26.6
21	207 11.9	180 27.8 ··	39.8	180 30.2 ··	53.2	135 00.0 ··	56.4	72 03.4 ··	01.3	Bellatrix	279·01.5	N 6 19.6
22	222 14.3	195 28.1	40.4	195 30.9	53.9	150 01.9	56.5	87 05.7	01.3	Betelgeuse	271 31.0	N 7 24.1
23	237 16.8	210 28.5	41.0	210 31.6	54.6	165 03.7	56.5	102 07.9	01.2			
4 00	252 19.3	225 28.9 N 8	41.6	225 32.3 N 9	55.3	180 05.6 N21	56.6	117 10.2 N18	01.1	Canopus	264 08.7	S52 41.2
01	267 21.7	240 29.3	42.3	240 33.0	55.9	195 07.4	56.7	132 12.4	01.1	Capella	281 15.0	N45 58.4
02	282 24.2	255 29.6	42.9	255 33.7	56.6	210 09.3	56.8	147 14.7	01.0	Deneb	49 49.7	N45 11.9
03	297 26.7	270 30.0 ··	43.5	270 34.4 ··	57.3	225 11.1 ··	56.8	162 16.9 ··	01.0	Denebola	183 01.3	N14 41.9
04	312 29.1	285 30.4	44.1	285 35.1	58.0	240 12.9	56.9	177 19.2	00.9	Diphda	349 23.3	S18 06.6
05	327 31.6	300 30.8	44.7	300 35.8	58.6	255 14.8	57.0	192 21.4	00.8			
06	342 34.0	315 31.1 N 8	45.3	315 36.5 N 9	59.3	270 16.6 N21	57.1	207 23.7 N18	00.8	Dubhe	194 25.0	N61 52.6
07	357 36.5	330 31.5	45.9	330 37.2	10 00.0	285 18.5	57.1	222 25.9	00.7	Elnath	278 47.3	N28 35.2
S 08	12 39.0	345 31.9	46.6	345 37.9	00.7	300 20.3	57.2	237 28.2	00.7	Eltanin	90 58.2	N51 29.5
A 09	27 41.4	0 32.2 ··	47.2	0 38.6 ··	01.4	315 22.1 ··	57.3	252 30.4 ··	00.6	Enif	34 13.6	N 9 46.3
T 10	42 43.9	15 32.6	47.8	15 39.3	02.0	330 24.0	57.4	267 32.7	00.5	Fomalhaut	15 53.9	S29 44.3
U 11	57 46.4	30 32.9	48.4	30 39.9	02.7	345 25.8	57.4	282 34.9	00.5			
R 12	72 48.8	45 33.3 N 8	49.0	45 40.6 N10	03.4	0 27.7 N21	57.5	297 37.2 N18	00.4	Gacrux	172 30.9	S56 59.5
D 13	87 51.3	60 33.7	49.7	60 41.3	04.1	15 29.5	57.6	312 39.4	00.4	Gienah	176 20.1	S17 25.2
A 14	102 53.8	75 34.0	50.3	75 42.0	04.7	30 31.4	57.7	327 41.7	00.3	Hadar	149 25.9	S60 16.1
Y 15	117 56.2	90 34.4 ··	50.9	90 42.7 ··	05.4	45 33.2 ··	57.7	342 43.9 ··	00.2	Hamal	328 31.7	N23 21.2
16	132 58.7	105 34.7	51.5	105 43.4	06.1	60 35.0	57.8	357 46.1	00.2	Kaus Aust.	84 19.4	S34 23.6
17	148 01.2	120 35.1	52.1	120 44.1	06.8	75 36.9	57.9	12 48.4	00.1			
18	163 03.6	135 35.5 N 8	52.8	135 44.8 N10	07.4	90 38.7 N21	58.0	27 50.6 N18	00.0	Kochab	137 18.0	N74 15.1
19	178 06.1	150 35.8	53.4	150 45.5	08.1	105 40.6	58.0	42 52.9 18	00.0	Markab	14 05.4	N15 05.0
20	193 08.5	165 36.2	54.0	165 46.2	08.8	120 42.4	58.1	57 55.1 17	59.9	Menkar	314 43.7	N 4 00.0
21	208 11.0	180 36.5 ··	54.6	180 46.9 ··	09.5	135 44.3 ··	58.2	72 57.4 ··	59.9	Menkent	148 39.3	S36 15.7
22	223 13.5	195 36.9	55.3	195 47.6	10.1	150 46.1	58.2	87 59.6	59.8	Miaplacidus	221 45.7	S69 37.9
23	238 15.9	210 37.2	55.9	210 48.3	10.8	165 47.9	50.3	103 01.9	59.7			
5 00	253 18.4	225 37.6 N 8	56.5	225 49.0 N10	11.5	180 49.8 N21	58.4	118 04.1 N17	59.7	Mirfak	309 19.7	N49 46.7
01	268 20.9	240 37.9	57.1	240 49.7	12.2	195 51.6	58.5	133 06.4	59.6	Nunki	76 31.6	S26 19.4
02	283 23.3	255 38.3	57.0	255 50.4	12.8	210 53.5	58.5	148 08.6	59.6	Peacock	54 01.6	S56 48.2
03	298 25.8	270 38.6 ··	58.4	270 51.1 ··	13.5	225 55.3 ··	58.6	163 10.9 ··	59.5	Pollux	244 01.2	N28 04.8
04	313 28.3	285 39.0	59.0	285 51.8	14.2	240 57.1	58.7	170 13.1	59.4	Procyon	245 28.4	N 5 16.9
05	328 30.7	300 39.3 8	59.6	300 52.5	14.9	255 59.0	58.8	193 15.3	59.4			
06	343 33.2	315 39.6 N 9	00.3	315 53.2 N10	15.5	271 00.8 N21	58.8	208 17.6 N17	59.3	Rasalhague	96 31.3	N12 34.6
07	358 35.7	330 40.0	00.9	330 53.9	16.2	286 02.7	58.9	223 19.8	59.2	Regulus	208 12.5	N12 04.6
08	13 38.1	345 40.3	01.5	345 54.6	16.9	301 04.5	59.0	238 22.1	59.2	Rigel	281 38.5	S 8 13.8
S 09	28 40.6	0 40.7 ··	02.1	0 55.3 ··	17.5	316 06.4 ··	59.1	253 24.3 ··	59.1	Rigil Kent.	140 28.2	S60 44.6
U 10	43 43.0	15 41.0	02.8	15 56.0	18.2	331 08.2	59.1	268 26.6	59.1	Sabik	102 43.3	S15 41.8
N 11	58 45.5	30 41.4	03.4	30 56.7	18.9	346 10.0	59.2	283 28.8	59.0			
D 12	73 48.0	45 41.7 N 9	04.0	45 57.4 N10	19.6	1 11.9 N21	59.3	298 31.1 N17	58.9	Schedar	350 11.7	N56 24.6
A 13	88 50.4	60 42.0	04.7	60 58.1	20.2	16 13.7	59.3	313 33.3	58.9	Shaula	96 58.3	S37 05.2
Y 14	103 52.9	75 42.4	05.3	75 58.8	20.9	31 15.6	59.4	328 35.6	58.8	Sirius	258 58.0	S16 41.3
15	118 55.4	90 42.7 ··	05.9	90 59.5 ··	21.6	46 17.4 ··	59.5	343 37.8 ··	58.8	Spica	158 59.7	S11 02.7
16	133 57.8	105 43.0	06.6	106 00.2	22.2	61 19.2	59.6	358 40.0	58.7	Suhail	223 12.6	S43 20.8
17	149 00.3	120 43.4	07.2	121 00.9	22.9	76 21.1	59.6	13 42.3	58.6			
18	164 02.8	135 43.7 N 9	07.8	136 01.6 N10	23.6	91 22.9 N21	59.7	28 44.5 N17	58.6	Vega	80 56.9	N38 45.8
19	179 05.2	150 44.0	08.5	151 02.3	24.3	106 24.8	59.8	43 46.8	58.5	Zuben'ubi	137 35.2	S15 56.9
20	194 07.7	165 44.4	09.1	166 03.0	24.9	121 26.6	59.9	58 49.0	58.4		S.H.A.	Mer. Pass.
21	209 10.1	180 44.7 ··	09.7	181 03.7 ··	25.6	136 28.5 21	59.9	73 51.3 ··	58.4	Venus	333 09.6	8 58
22	224 12.6	195 45.0	10.4	196 04.4	26.3	151 30.3 22	00.0	88 53.5	58.3	Mars	333 13.0	8 57
23	239 15.1	210 45.3	11.0	211 05.1	26.9	166 32.1	00.1	103 55.7	58.3	Jupiter	287 46.3	11 58
Mer. Pass.	7 09.5	v 0.4 d 0.6		v 0.7 d 0.7		v 1.8 d 0.1		v 2.2 d 0.1		Saturn	224 50.9	16 09

Figure 2304a. *Nautical Almanac*, left-hand daily page (typical).

phase of the moon. Values are given for the semidiameter (SD) of the sun (for the three-day period) and of the moon (for each day).

Additionally, the right-hand pages provide data on sunrise and sunset, moonrise and moonset, and the beginning and ending of twilight. The use of this data is discussed in articles 2317–2322.

Interpolation

2305 To establish the GHA and declination of a body for a specific time of observation other than an exact hour of GMT, it is necessary to interpolate—i.e., calculate intermediate values between those that appear in the hourly tabulation. For the intermediate time, stated in minutes and seconds past the whole hour printed in the tables, the change in GHA and Dec. are assumed to be at a uniform rate. This is not strictly true; however, the error involved is negligible when using the stars. The v and d corrections listed in the previous paragraph are applied for greater accuracy when using bodies within the solar system.

JUNE 3, 4, 5 (FRI., SAT., SUN.)

SUN and MOON

G.M.T.	SUN G.H.A.	SUN Dec	MOON G.H.A.	v	Dec	d	H.P.
3 00	180 30.4	N22 16.2	342 44.5	3.6	S18 46.2	1.2	61.1
01	195 30.3	16.5	357 07.1	3.6	18 45.0	1.2	61.1
02	210 30.2	16.8	11 29.7	3.7	18 43.8	1.4	61.1
03	225 30.1	·· 17.1	25 52.4	3.7	18 42.4	1.5	61.0
04	240 30.0	17.4	40 15.1	3.7	18 40.9	1.7	61.0
05	255 29.9	17.7	54 37.8	3.8	18 39.2	1.8	61.0
06	270 29.8	N22 18.1	69 00.6	3.8	S18 37.4	1.9	61.0
07	285 29.7	18.4	83 23.4	3.9	18 35.5	2.1	61.0
08	300 29.6	18.7	97 46.3	3.9	18 33.4	2.2	60.9
F 09	315 29.5	·· 19.0	112 09.2	3.9	18 31.2	2.3	60.9
R 10	330 29.4	19.3	126 32.1	4.1	18 28.9	2.5	60.9
I 11	345 29.3	19.6	140 55.2	4.0	18 26.4	2.6	60.9
D 12	0 29.2	N22 19.9	155 18.2	4.1	S18 23.8	2.7	60.8
A 13	15 29.1	20.2	169 41.3	4.2	18 21.1	2.9	60.8
Y 14	30 29.0	20.5	184 04.5	4.2	18 18.2	3.0	60.8
15	45 28.9	·· 20.8	198 27.7	4.3	18 15.2	3.1	60.8
16	60 28.8	21.1	212 51.0	4.4	18 12.1	3.3	60.7
17	75 28.7	21.4	227 14.4	4.4	18 08.8	3.4	60.7
18	90 28.6	N22 21.7	241 37.8	4.5	S18 05.4	3.5	60.7
19	105 28.5	22.0	256 01.3	4.5	18 01.9	3.7	60.7
20	120 28.4	22.3	270 24.8	4.6	17 58.2	3.7	60.6
21	135 28.3	·· 22.6	284 48.4	4.7	17 54.5	3.9	60.6
22	150 28.2	22.9	299 12.1	4.7	17 50.6	4.0	60.6
23	165 28.1	23.2	313 35.8	4.8	17 46.6	4.2	60.5
4 00	180 28.0	N22 23.5	327 59.6	4.9	S17 42.4	4.2	60.5
01	195 27.9	23.8	342 23.5	4.9	17 38.2	4.4	60.5
02	210 27.8	24.1	356 47.4	5.1	17 33.8	4.5	60.5
03	225 27.7	·· 24.4	11 11.5	5.1	17 29.3	4.5	60.4
04	240 27.6	24.7	25 35.6	5.1	17 24.7	4.8	60.4
05	255 27.5	25.0	39 59.7	5.3	17 19.9	4.8	60.4
06	270 27.4	N22 25.3	54 24.0	5.3	S17 15.1	5.0	60.3
07	285 27.3	25.6	68 48.3	5.4	17 10.1	5.0	60.3
S 08	300 27.1	25.9	83 12.7	5.4	17 05.1	5.2	60.3
A 09	315 27.0	·· 26.1	97 37.1	5.6	16 59.9	5.3	60.2
T 10	330 26.9	26.4	112 01.7	5.6	16 54.6	5.4	60.2
U 11	345 26.8	26.7	126 26.3	5.7	16 49.2	5.6	60.2
R 12	0 26.7	N22 27.0	140 51.0	5.8	S16 43.6	5.6	60.1
D 13	15 26.6	27.3	155 15.8	5.9	16 38.0	5.7	60.1
A 14	30 26.5	27.6	169 40.7	6.0	16 32.3	5.8	60.1
Y 15	45 26.4	·· 27.9	184 05.7	6.0	16 26.5	6.0	60.1
16	60 26.3	28.2	198 30.7	6.1	16 20.5	6.0	60.0
17	75 26.2	28.4	212 55.8	6.2	16 14.5	6.2	60.0
18	90 26.1	N22 28.7	227 21.0	6.3	S16 08.3	6.2	59.9
19	105 26.0	29.0	241 46.3	6.4	16 02.1	6.3	59.9
20	120 25.9	29.3	256 11.7	6.5	15 55.8	6.5	59.9
21	135 25.8	·· 29.6	270 37.2	6.5	15 49.3	6.5	59.8
22	150 25.7	29.9	285 02.7	6.7	15 42.8	6.6	59.8
23	165 25.5	30.1	299 28.4	6.7	15 36.2	6.8	59.7
5 00	180 25.4	N22 30.4	313 54.1	6.8	S15 29.4	6.8	59.7
01	195 25.3	30.7	328 19.9	6.9	15 22.6	6.9	59.7
02	210 25.2	31.0	342 45.8	7.0	15 15.7	7.0	59.6
03	225 25.1	·· 31.3	357 11.8	7.1	15 08.7	7.0	59.6
04	240 25.0	31.5	11 37.9	7.2	15 01.7	7.2	59.6
05	255 24.9	31.8	26 04.1	7.2	14 54.5	7.3	59.5
06	270 24.8	N22 32.1	40 30.3	7.4	S14 47.2	7.3	59.5
07	285 24.7	32.4	54 56.7	7.4	14 39.9	7.4	59.5
08	300 24.6	32.6	69 23.1	7.5	14 32.5	7.5	59.4
S 09	315 24.5	·· 32.9	83 49.6	7.6	14 25.0	7.6	59.4
U 10	330 24.4	33.2	98 16.2	7.7	14 17.4	7.6	59.3
N 11	345 24.2	33.5	112 42.9	7.8	14 09.8	7.8	59.3
D 12	0 24.1	N22 33.7	127 09.7	7.9	S14 02.0	7.8	59.3
A 13	15 24.0	34.0	141 36.6	8.0	13 54.2	7.9	59.2
Y 14	30 23.9	34.3	156 03.6	8.0	13 46.3	7.9	59.2
15	45 23.8	·· 34.5	170 30.6	8.2	13 38.4	8.0	59.1
16	60 23.7	34.8	184 57.8	8.2	13 30.4	8.2	59.1
17	75 23.6	35.1	199 25.0	8.3	13 22.2	8.1	59.1
18	90 23.5	N22 35.4	213 52.3	8.4	S13 14.1	8.3	59.0
19	105 23.4	35.6	228 19.7	8.5	13 05.8	8.3	59.0
20	120 23.3	35.9	242 47.2	8.6	12 57.5	8.3	58.9
21	135 23.1	·· 36.2	257 14.8	8.7	12 49.2	8.5	58.9
22	150 23.0	36.4	271 42.5	8.8	12 40.7	8.5	58.9
23	165 22.9	36.7	286 10.3	8.8	12 32.2	8.5	58.8
	S.D. 15.8	d 0.3	S.D. 16.6		16.4		16.1

Twilight, Sunrise, Moonrise

Lat.	Naut.	Civil	Sunrise	Moonrise 3	4	5	6
N 72	□	□	□	■	01 33	01 02	00 50
N 70	□	□	□	24 18	00 18	00 26	00 28
68	□	□	□	23 40	24 00	00 00	00 11
66	□	□	01 00	23 13	23 40	23 57	24 09
64	□	□	01 51	22 52	23 24	23 46	24 02
62	□	□	02 22	22 35	23 11	23 36	23 55
60	□	01 18	02 45	22 21	22 59	23 28	23 50
N 58	□	01 55	03 04	22 09	22 49	23 20	23 45
56	□	02 20	03 19	21 59	22 41	23 14	23 40
54	01 11	02 40	03 32	21 49	22 33	23 08	23 36
52	01 45	02 57	03 44	21 41	22 26	23 03	23 33
50	02 09	03 11	03 54	21 34	22 20	22 58	23 30
45	02 50	03 39	04 15	21 18	22 06	22 47	23 22
N 40	03 19	04 00	04 32	21 05	21 55	22 39	23 16
35	03 41	04 17	04 46	20 54	21 46	22 31	23 11
30	03 59	04 32	04 59	20 44	21 37	22 24	23 07
20	04 26	04 55	05 20	20 27	21 23	22 13	22 59
N 10	04 48	05 15	05 38	20 13	21 10	22 03	22 52
0	05 06	05 32	05 55	19 59	20 58	21 54	22 45
S 10	05 22	05 49	06 11	19 45	20 46	21 44	22 39
20	05 38	06 05	06 29	19 31	20 33	21 34	22 32
30	05 53	06 23	06 49	19 14	20 19	21 22	22 24
35	06 01	06 33	07 01	19 04	20 10	21 16	22 19
40	06 10	06 44	07 14	18 53	20 01	21 08	22 14
45	06 20	06 57	07 30	18 40	19 49	20 59	22 08
S 50	06 31	07 12	07 50	18 24	19 36	20 48	22 00
52	06 36	07 19	07 59	18 17	19 29	20 43	21 57
54	06 41	07 26	08 09	18 08	19 22	20 38	21 53
56	06 47	07 35	08 21	17 59	19 14	20 32	21 49
58	06 53	07 44	08 35	17 48	19 05	20 25	21 44
S 60	07 00	07 55	08 51	17 36	18 55	20 17	21 39

Sunset, Twilight, Moonset

Lat.	Sunset	Civil	Naut.	Moonset 3	4	5	6
N 72	□	□	□	■	03 02	05 35	07 40
N 70	□	□	□	02 35	04 17	06 10	08 00
68	□	□	□	03 26	04 54	06 35	08 16
66	23 01	□		03 58	05 21	06 54	08 29
64	22 07	□		04 22	05 41	07 09	08 39
62	21 36	□		04 41	05 58	07 22	08 48
60	21 12	22 41		04 56	06 11	07 33	08 56
N 58	20 54	22 03		05 09	06 23	07 42	09 03
56	20 38	21 37		05 21	06 33	07 50	09 08
54	20 25	21 17	22 48	05 31	06 42	07 58	09 14
52	20 13	21 00	22 13	05 40	06 50	08 04	09 18
50	20 03	20 46	21 48	05 47	06 57	08 10	09 23
45	19 42	20 18	21 07	06 04	07 12	08 22	09 32
N 40	19 25	19 57	20 38	06 18	07 25	08 33	09 40
35	19 10	19 40	20 16	06 30	07 36	08 42	09 46
30	18 58	19 25	19 58	06 40	07 45	08 49	09 52
20	18 37	19 01	19 30	06 57	08 01	09 03	10 02
N 10	18 19	18 42	19 08	07 13	08 15	09 14	10 11
0	18 02	18 24	18 50	07 27	08 28	09 25	10 19
S 10	17 45	18 08	18 34	07 41	08 40	09 36	10 27
20	17 27	17 51	18 19	07 56	08 54	09 47	10 35
30	17 07	17 33	18 03	08 13	09 10	10 00	10 45
35	16 55	17 23	17 55	08 23	09 19	10 07	10 50
40	16 42	17 12	17 46	08 35	09 29	10 16	10 57
45	16 26	16 59	17 36	08 48	09 41	10 26	11 04
S 50	16 06	16 44	17 25	09 04	09 56	10 38	11 12
52	15 57	16 37	17 20	09 12	10 02	10 43	11 16
54	15 47	16 30	17 15	09 21	10 10	10 49	11 21
56	15 35	16 21	17 10	09 30	10 18	10 56	11 26
58	15 22	16 12	17 03	09 41	10 28	11 03	11 31
S 60	15 05	16 01	16 56	09 53	10 38	11 12	11 37

Day	SUN Eqn. of Time 00h	12h	Mer. Pass.	MOON Mer. Pass. Upper	Lower	Age	Phase
3	02 02	01 57	11 58	01 12	13 43	16	◯
4	01 52	01 47	11 58	02 13	14 43	17	
5	01 42	01 37	11 58	03 12	15 39	18	

Figure 2304b. *Nautical Almanac*, right-hand daily page (typical).

These increments and corrections are printed on yellow-tinted pages to facilitate locating them. A sample page is shown in figure 2305. The computations are based on standard apparent motions of the heavenly bodies around the earth, at the rate of 15° per hour for the sun and planets, 15°02.46′ for Aries, and 14°19.0′ for the moon. The values of the correction for v and d are then the excesses of the actual hourly motions over the above adopted values. They are generally positive, except for the v value for Venus which is sometimes negative. Increments and corrections are determined and applied as discussed in article 2309.

Star Positions

2306   The SHA and declination of 173 brighter stars, including the 57 navigational stars listed on the daily pages, are tabulated for each month near the end of the white section of the *Nautical Almanac*. No interpolation is needed, and the data can

36ᵐ   INCREMENTS AND CORRECTIONS   37ᵐ

36	SUN PLANETS	ARIES	MOON	v or Corrⁿ d	v or Corrⁿ d	v or Corrⁿ d
s	° ′	° ′	° ′	′ ′	′ ′	′ ′
00	9 00·0	9 01·5	8 35·4	0·0 0·0	6·0 3·7	12·0 7·3
01	9 00·3	9 01·7	8 35·6	0·1 0·1	6·1 3·7	12·1 7·4
02	9 00·5	9 02·0	8 35·9	0·2 0·1	6·2 3·8	12·2 7·4
03	9 00·8	9 02·2	8 36·1	0·3 0·2	6·3 3·8	12·3 7·5
04	9 01·0	9 02·5	8 36·4	0·4 0·2	6·4 3·9	12·4 7·5
05	9 01·3	9 02·7	8 36·6	0·5 0·3	6·5 4·0	12·5 7·6
06	9 01·5	9 03·0	8 36·8	0·6 0·4	6·6 4·0	12·6 7·7
07	9 01·8	9 03·2	8 37·1	0·7 0·4	6·7 4·1	12·7 7·7
08	9 02·0	9 03·5	8 37·3	0·8 0·5	6·8 4·1	12·8 7·8
09	9 02·3	9 03·7	8 37·5	0·9 0·5	6·9 4·2	12·9 7·8
10	9 02·5	9 04·0	8 37·8	1·0 0·6	7·0 4·3	13·0 7·9
11	9 02·8	9 04·2	8 38·0	1·1 0·7	7·1 4·3	13·1 8·0
12	9 03·0	9 04·5	8 38·3	1·2 0·7	7·2 4·4	13·2 8·0
13	9 03·3	9 04·7	8 38·5	1·3 0·8	7·3 4·4	13·3 8·1
14	9 03·5	9 05·0	8 38·7	1·4 0·9	7·4 4·5	13·4 8·2
15	9 03·8	9 05·2	8 39·0	1·5 0·9	7·5 4·6	13·5 8·2
16	9 04·0	9 05·5	8 39·2	1·6 1·0	7·6 4·6	13·6 8·3
17	9 04·3	9 05·7	8 39·5	1·7 1·0	7·7 4·7	13·7 8·3
18	9 04·5	9 06·0	8 39·7	1·8 1·1	7·8 4·7	13·8 8·4
19	9 04·0	9 06·2	8 39·9	1·9 1·2	7·9 4·8	13·9 8·5
20	9 05·0	9 06·5	8 40·2	2·0 1·2	8·0 4·9	14·0 8·5
21	9 05·3	9 06·7	8 40·4	2·1 1·3	8·1 4·9	14·1 8·6
22	9 05·5	9 07·0	8 40·6	2·2 1·3	8·2 5·0	14·2 8·6
23	9 05·8	9 07·2	8 40·9	2·3 1·4	8·3 5·0	14·3 8·7
24	9 06·0	9 07·5	8 41·1	2·4 1·5	8·4 5·1	14·4 8·8
25	9 06·3	9 07·7	8 41·4	2·5 1·5	8·5 5·2	14·5 8·8
26	9 06·5	9 08·0	8 41·6	2·6 1·6	8·6 5·2	14·6 8·9
27	9 06·8	9 08·2	8 41·8	2·7 1·6	8·7 5·3	14·7 8·9
28	9 07·0	9 08·5	8 42·1	2·8 1·7	8·8 5·4	14·8 9·0
29	9 07·3	9 08·7	8 42·3	2·9 1·8	8·9 5·4	14·9 9·1
30	9 07·5	9 09·0	8 42·6	3·0 1·8	9·0 5·5	15·0 9·1
31	9 07·8	9 09·2	8 42·8	3·1 1·9	9·1 5·5	15·1 9·2
32	9 08·0	9 09·5	8 43·0	3·2 1·9	9·2 5·6	15·2 9·2
33	9 08·3	9 09·8	8 43·3	3·3 2·0	9·3 5·7	15·3 9·3
34	9 08·5	9 10·0	8 43·5	3·4 2·1	9·4 5·7	15·4 9·4
35	9 08·8	9 10·3	8 43·8	3·5 2·1	9·5 5·8	15·5 9·4
36	9 09·0	9 10·5	8 44·0	3·6 2·2	9·6 5·8	15·6 9·5
37	9 09·3	9 10·8	8 44·2	3·7 2·3	9·7 5·9	15·7 9·6
38	9 09·5	9 11·0	8 44·5	3·8 2·3	9·8 6·0	15·8 9·6
39	9 09·8	9 11·3	8 44·7	3·9 2·4	9·9 6·0	15·9 9·7
40	9 10·0	9 11·5	8 44·9	4·0 2·4	10·0 6·1	16·0 9·7
41	9 10·3	9 11·8	8 45·2	4·1 2·5	10·1 6·1	16·1 9·8
42	9 10·5	9 12·0	8 45·4	4·2 2·6	10·2 6·2	16·2 9·9
43	9 10·8	9 12·3	8 45·7	4·3 2·6	10·3 6·3	16·3 9·9
44	9 11·0	9 12·5	8 45·9	4·4 2·7	10·4 6·3	16·4 10·0
45	9 11·3	9 12·8	8 46·1	4·5 2·7	10·5 6·4	16·5 10·0
46	9 11·5	9 13·0	8 46·4	4·6 2·8	10·6 6·4	16·6 10·1
47	9 11·8	9 13·3	8 46·6	4·7 2·9	10·7 6·5	16·7 10·2
48	9 12·0	9 13·5	8 46·9	4·8 2·9	10·8 6·6	16·8 10·2
49	9 12·3	9 13·8	8 47·1	4·9 3·0	10·9 6·6	16·9 10·3
50	9 12·5	9 14·0	8 47·3	5·0 3·0	11·0 6·7	17·0 10·3
51	9 12·8	9 14·3	8 47·6	5·1 3·1	11·1 6·8	17·1 10·4
52	9 13·0	9 14·5	8 47·8	5·2 3·2	11·2 6·8	17·2 10·5
53	9 13·3	9 14·8	8 48·0	5·3 3·2	11·3 6·9	17·3 10·5
54	9 13·5	9 15·0	8 48·3	5·4 3·3	11·4 6·9	17·4 10·6
55	9 13·8	9 15·3	8 48·5	5·5 3·3	11·5 7·0	17·5 10·6
56	9 14·0	9 15·5	8 48·8	5·6 3·4	11·6 7·1	17·6 10·7
57	9 14·3	9 15·8	8 49·0	5·7 3·4	11·7 7·1	17·7 10·8
58	9 14·5	9 16·0	8 49·2	5·8 3·5	11·8 7·2	17·8 10·8
59	9 14·8	9 16·3	8 49·5	5·9 3·6	11·9 7·2	17·9 10·9
60	9 15·0	9 16·5	8 49·7	6·0 3·7	12·0 7·3	18·0 11·0

37	SUN PLANETS	ARIES	MOON	v or Corrⁿ d	v or Corrⁿ d	v or Corrⁿ d
s	° ′	° ′	° ′	′ ′	′ ′	′ ′
00	9 15·0	9 16·5	8 49·7	0·0 0·0	6·0 3·8	12·0 7·5
01	9 15·3	9 16·8	8 50·0	0·1 0·1	6·1 3·8	12·1 7·6
02	9 15·5	9 17·0	8 50·2	0·2 0·1	6·2 3·9	12·2 7·6
03	9 15·8	9 17·3	8 50·4	0·3 0·2	6·3 3·9	12·3 7·7
04	9 16·0	9 17·5	8 50·7	0·4 0·3	6·4 4·0	12·4 7·8
05	9 16·3	9 17·8	8 50·9	0·5 0·3	6·5 4·1	12·5 7·8
06	9 16·5	9 18·0	8 51·1	0·6 0·4	6·6 4·1	12·6 7·9
07	9 16·8	9 18·3	8 51·4	0·7 0·4	6·7 4·2	12·7 7·9
08	9 17·0	9 18·5	8 51·6	0·8 0·5	6·8 4·3	12·8 8·0
09	9 17·3	9 18·8	8 51·9	0·9 0·6	6·9 4·3	12·9 8·1
10	9 17·5	9 19·0	8 52·1	1·0 0·6	7·0 4·4	13·0 8·1
11	9 17·8	9 19·3	8 52·3	1·1 0·7	7·1 4·4	13·1 8·2
12	9 18·0	9 19·5	8 52·6	1·2 0·8	7·2 4·5	13·2 8·3
13	9 18·3	9 19·8	8 52·8	1·3 0·8	7·3 4·6	13·3 8·3
14	9 18·5	9 20·0	8 53·1	1·4 0·9	7·4 4·6	13·4 8·4
15	9 18·8	9 20·3	8 53·3	1·5 0·9	7·5 4·7	13·5 8·4
16	9 19·0	9 20·5	8 53·5	1·6 1·0	7·6 4·8	13·6 8·5
17	9 19·3	9 20·8	8 53·8	1·7 1·1	7·7 4·8	13·7 8·6
18	9 19·5	9 21·0	8 54·0	1·8 1·1	7·8 4·9	13·8 8·6
19	9 19·8	9 21·3	8 54·3	1·9 1·2	7·9 4·9	13·9 8·7
20	9 20·0	9 21·5	8 54·5	2·0 1·3	8·0 5·0	14·0 8·8
21	9 20·3	9 21·8	8 54·7	2·1 1·3	8·1 5·1	14·1 8·8
22	9 20·5	9 22·0	8 55·0	2·2 1·4	8·2 5·1	14·2 8·9
23	9 20·8	9 22·3	8 55·2	2·3 1·4	8·3 5·2	14·3 8·9
24	9 21·0	9 22·5	8 55·4	2·4 1·5	8·4 5·3	14·4 9·0
25	9 21·3	9 22·8	8 55·7	2·5 1·6	8·5 5·3	14·5 9·1
26	9 21·5	9 23·0	8 55·9	2·6 1·6	8·6 5·4	14·6 9·1
27	9 21·8	9 23·3	8 56·2	2·7 1·7	8·7 5·4	14·7 9·2
28	9 22·0	9 23·5	8 56·4	2·8 1·8	8·8 5·5	14·8 9·3
29	9 22·3	9 23·8	8 56·6	2·9 1·8	8·9 5·6	14·9 9·3
30	9 22·5	9 24·0	8 56·9	3·0 1·9	9·0 5·6	15·0 9·4
31	9 22·8	9 24·3	8 57·1	3·1 1·9	9·1 5·7	15·1 9·4
32	9 23·0	9 24·5	8 57·4	3·2 2·0	9·2 5·8	15·2 9·5
33	9 23·3	9 24·8	8 57·6	3·3 2·1	9·3 5·8	15·3 9·6
34	9 23·5	9 25·0	8 57·8	3·4 2·1	9·4 5·9	15·4 9·6
35	9 23·8	9 25·3	8 58·1	3·5 2·2	9·5 5·9	15·5 9·7
36	9 24·0	9 25·5	8 58·3	3·6 2·3	9·6 6·0	15·6 9·8
37	9 24·3	9 25·8	8 58·5	3·7 2·3	9·7 6·1	15·7 9·8
38	9 24·5	9 26·0	8 58·8	3·8 2·4	9·8 6·1	15·8 9·9
39	9 24·8	9 26·3	8 59·0	3·9 2·4	9·9 6·2	15·9 9·9
40	9 25·0	9 26·5	8 59·3	4·0 2·5	10·0 6·3	16·0 10·0
41	9 25·3	9 26·8	8 59·5	4·1 2·6	10·1 6·3	16·1 10·1
42	9 25·5	9 27·0	8 59·7	4·2 2·6	10·2 6·4	16·2 10·1
43	9 25·8	9 27·3	9 00·0	4·3 2·7	10·3 6·4	16·3 10·2
44	9 26·0	9 27·5	9 00·2	4·4 2·8	10·4 6·5	16·4 10·3
45	9 26·3	9 27·8	9 00·5	4·5 2·8	10·5 6·6	16·5 10·3
46	9 26·5	9 28·1	9 00·7	4·6 2·9	10·6 6·6	16·6 10·4
47	9 26·8	9 28·3	9 00·9	4·7 2·9	10·7 6·7	16·7 10·4
48	9 27·0	9 28·6	9 01·2	4·8 3·0	10·8 6·8	16·8 10·5
49	9 27·3	9 28·8	9 01·4	4·9 3·1	10·9 6·8	16·9 10·6
50	9 27·5	9 29·1	9 01·6	5·0 3·1	11·0 6·9	17·0 10·6
51	9 27·8	9 29·3	9 01·9	5·1 3·2	11·1 6·9	17·1 10·7
52	9 28·0	9 29·6	9 02·1	5·2 3·3	11·2 7·0	17·2 10·8
53	9 28·3	9 29·8	9 02·4	5·3 3·3	11·3 7·1	17·3 10·8
54	9 28·5	9 30·1	9 02·6	5·4 3·4	11·4 7·1	17·4 10·9
55	9 28·8	9 30·3	9 02·8	5·5 3·4	11·5 7·2	17·5 10·9
56	9 29·0	9 30·6	9 03·1	5·6 3·5	11·6 7·3	17·6 11·0
57	9 29·3	9 30·8	9 03·3	5·7 3·6	11·7 7·3	17·7 11·1
58	9 29·5	9 31·1	9 03·6	5·8 3·6	11·8 7·4	17·8 11·1
59	9 29·8	9 31·3	9 03·8	5·9 3·7	11·9 7·4	17·9 11·2
60	9 30·0	9 31·6	9 04·0	6·0 3·8	12·0 7·5	18·0 11·3

xx

Figure 2305. *Nautical Almanac,* Increments and Corrections page (typical).

be used in precisely the same way as those selected stars on the daily pages. The stars are arranged in ascending order of SHA.

There are also four star charts that will assist in the identification of celestial bodies and constellations.

Nautical Almanac: Additional Tables

2307 A table is included in the *Nautical Almanac* for correcting sextant observations of the sun, stars, and planets for atmospheric refraction; this is found on the inside front cover and facing page, pages A2 and A3. A corresponding table for moon observations is found on the inside back cover and its facing page, pages xxxiv and xxxv. These tables are based on standard conditions of barometric pressure and temperature; a second table gives additional corrections for nonstandard conditions. Tables for correcting for the dip of the horizon under standard conditions and a special table for moon correction are also included. These tables for correcting the sextant altitude are discussed in more detail in chapter 21. These values do not change as a function of time as do the ephemeristic data in the *Nautical Almanac*.

Nautical Almanac: Accuracy of Data

2308 The tabulated values are in most cases correct to the nearest one-tenth minute, the exception being the sun's GHA, which is deliberately adjusted by up to 0.15' to reduce the error caused by omitting the v correction. The largest imprecision that can occur in GHA or Dec. of any body other than the sun or moon is less than 0.2'; it may reach 0.25' for the GHA of the sun, and 0.3' for the moon. These are extremes; in actual use, it may be expected that less than 10 percent of the values of GHA and Dec. will have errors greater than 0.1'.

Errors in altitude corrections are generally of the same order as those for GHA and Dec., as they result from the addition of several quantities each rounded to 0.1'. The *actual* values, however, of dip and refraction at low altitudes may, in extreme atmospheric conditions, differ considerably from the mean values shown in the tables of the *Nautical Almanac*.

The time values shown are GMT, also referred to as UT1 (see article 2209). This may differ from radio broadcast time signals, which are in UTC, by up to 0.9 seconds of time; step adjustments of exactly one second are made as required to prevent this difference from exceeding 0.9 seconds. Those who require the reduction of observations to a precision of better than one second of time must apply a correction, DUT1, which normally can be determined from the radio broadcast, to each time of observation (see article 2227). Alternatively, the DUT1 correction may be applied to the longitude reduced from the uncorrected time in accordance with the table below:

Correction to time signals	Correction to longitude
-0.9^s to -0.7^s	0.2' to east
-0.6^s to -0.3^s	0.1' to east
-0.2^s to $+0.2^s$	no correction
$+0.3^s$ to $+0.6^s$	0.1' to west
$+0.7^s$ to $+0.9^s$	0.2' to west

Use of the *Nautical Almanac*

2309 The GMT of an observation is expressed as a day and an hour, followed by minutes and seconds. The tabular values of GHA and Dec., and, where necessary, the corresponding values of v and d, are taken directly from the daily pages for the day and hour of GMT; the hour used is always that *before* the time of observation. SHA and Dec. for selected stars are also taken from the daily pages.

The table of Increments and Corrections for the minutes component of the GMT of observation is then selected. The increment for GHA for minutes and seconds of GMT is taken from the line for the number of seconds and the column for the body concerned. The v correction is taken from the right-hand portion of the table for the same GMT minutes opposite the v value given on the daily pages. Both increment and v correction are to be added to the GHA value extracted from the daily page for the whole hour, except for Venus when the v value is prefixed with a minus sign; it is then subtracted.

For the Dec. there is no increment, but a d correction is applied in the same way as for v. Values of d on the daily pages are not marked "+" or "−"; the sign must be determined by observing the trend Dec. value.

Figure 2309 illustrates the determination and recording of data for the sun, moon, Mars, and the star Denebola. The data have been extracted from the daily pages of figures 2304a and 2304b, and the Increments and Corrections page shown in figure 2305.

Solution for the Sun

The use of the *Nautical Almanac* will be illustrated first by the extraction of data for an observation of the sun.

Example: (Figure 2309, sun column)

Body	SUN	MOON	DENEBOLA	MARS
Date (G)	5 JUN	5 JUN	5 JUN	5 JUN
GMT	13-36-35	09-37-08	23-36-56	23-37-22
GHA (h)	15° 24.0'	83° 49.6'	239° 15.1'	211° 05.1'
Incre (m/s)	9° 08.8'	8° 51.6'	9° 15.5'	9° 20.5'
V/V Corr	—	7.6 / +4.8'	—	0.7 / +0.4'
SHA			183° 01.3'	—
Total GHA	24° 32.8'	92° 46.0'	431° 31.9'	220° 26.0'
± 360°			71° 31.9'	
Tab Dec	N 22° 34.0'	S 14° 25.0'	N14° 41.9'	N10° 26.9'
d/d Corr	+0.3 / 0.2	7.6 / -4.8	—	+0.7 / +0.4
True Dec	N 22° 34.2'	S 14° 20.2'	N 14° 41.9'	N 10° 27.3'

Figure 2309. Tabular solutions for GHA and declination using *Nautical Almanac*.

A navigator located at approximately 30° N, 60° W on 5 June ZT 09-36-35 (+4), having observed the sun needs to determine its GHA and Dec. from the *Nautical Almanac*.

Solution: (1) Determine GMT by adding the ZD to the ZT; GMT is thus 13-36-35. (2) On the right-hand page, which includes the data on 5 June (figure 2304b), find the column headed GMT and find the line for the whole hour "13" of the day indicated as "5 Sunday." (3) Follow across this line to the column for the sun; read and record the value for GHA (15°24.0') and Dec. (N22°34.0'); note whether Dec. is increasing, if so the sign of the *d* correction will be +. (4) At the bottom of the Dec. column, read and record the *d* value (0.3'). (5) Turn to the yellow pages for Increments and Corrections and find the page that includes values for 36 minutes of GMT as indicated at the top of the page (figure 2305); find the line for 35 seconds and follow across to the Sun/Planets column; read and record the GHA increment (9°08.8'). [If time was measured more closely than to the nearest second, interpolate as required.] (6) In the column for *v* and *d* corrections, find the line for a *d* value of 0.3'; the *d* correction is read and recorded (0.2'); the sign was previously determined to be (+). (7) Add the GHA increment to the value of GHA for 13 hours GMT on 5 June: 15°24.0' + 9°08.8' = 24°32.8'; this is the GHA of the sun for the time of observation. (8) Add the *d* correction to the value of Dec. for 13 hours GMT on 5 June; N22°34.0' + 0.2 = N22°34.2'; this is the declination of the sun at the time of observation.

Solution for Other Bodies

Referring to figure 2309 and the above procedure for determining GHA and Dec. for the sun, a similar procedure is followed for the other bodies. Following through the problem it will be noted that there is both a *v* and *d* correction for the moon in addition to the correction for minutes and seconds of time after the whole hour of GMT. The south declination of the moon was decreasing with time, resulting in the *d* correction being minus. In the Denebola problem, the GHA ♈ plus SHA star produced a GHA Denebola of 431°31.9' with the result that 360° was subtracted to produce a GHA of 71°31.9'. For the Mars observation, the north declination was increasing with time and the *d* correction was therefore (+). In both the Mars and moon observations, the declination was changing toward the north. In the first case, there was an increase in N Dec., and in the latter there was a decrease of S Dec.

Nautical Almanac: Summary

2310 The coordinates of celestial bodies are tabulated in the *Nautical Almanac* with respect to Greenwich Mean Time. Using the GMT (or in practical terms, UTC) of an observation, the navigator extracts the GHA and Dec. of the body observed. The position of the body establishes one vertex of the navigational triangle; the navigator solves this triangle to obtain a line of position.

The GHAs of the sun, moon, planets, and Aries are tabulated in the *Nautical Almanac* for each hour of GMT, and tables of increments permit interpolation for the minutes and seconds of an observation. A small *v* correction factor applying to the GHA is also shown on the daily pages. The sum of the tabulated GHA, together with the increment for excess minutes and seconds, and the value of the *v* correction for these minutes and seconds, is the GHA of the body at the time of observation. The SHA of the star is taken from the *Nautical Almanac* without interpolation. The SHA of a star is added to the GHA of Aries to obtain the star's GHA.

The declination of the sun, moon, and planets are also tabulated in the daily pages of the *Nautical Almanac* for GMT, as is a *d* factor. The correction to the declination for *d* is obtained from the table of increments for the excess minutes and seconds over the tabulated value. The declination of a star is taken from the *Nautical Almanac* without any correction.

In practice, the navigator always obtains *all* values of GHA and Dec., plus associated data, from the daily pages during one book opening. He then turns to the Increments and Corrections tables for the remaining data. This procedure materially shortens the time required to reduce observations.

Air Almanac: Basic Contents

2311 The *Air Almanac* contains basically the same data as that of the *Nautical Almanac*. The arrangement is designed primarily for the use of aviators, being more convenient for a fast solution; however, small inaccuracies result for some bodies. It is becoming increasingly popular with surface navigators, particularly those on yachts and small craft, but its use is not recommended when maximum precision and accuracy are required.

The *Air Almanac* gives ephemeristic data for each ten minutes of GMT on the daily pages, and due to the great number of tabulations, it cannot conveniently be bound as a single volume covering an entire year. It is issued twice a year, each volume covering a six-month period of time. Two pages, the front and back of a single sheet, cover one calendar day (figures 2311a and 2311b). Thus, at any one opening, the left-hand page contains the tabulation of data for every 10 minutes of time from 12 hours 0 minutes GMT to 23 hours 50 minutes of one day. Data from 0 hours 0 minutes to 11 hours 50 minutes of the following day are presented on the right-hand page. The daily data include GHA and Dec. of the sun, each to 0.1′, the GHA of Aries to 0.1′, and the GHA and Dec. of the moon and of the three planets most suitable for observation at that time, all to the nearest 1′. The volumes are bound with plastic rings to enable the user to tear out the daily pages for more convenient use. In addition, these daily pages give the time of moonrise and moonset, the moon's parallax in altitude, the semidiameters of the sun and moon, and the latter's "age." At the bottom of each column of data (except GHA ♈), an hourly rate of change is given. For the declination of the moon, a "star" symbol following the rate tabulation indicates that a value derived at the end of a six-hour period, which is half of the time interval covered by the page, will be in error by at least

two minutes of arc. These hourly rate tabulations are intended to facilitate computer input processing; they are not used in normal navigation calculations.

On the inside of the front cover there is a table to permit ready interpolation of GHA of the sun, Aries, and planets on the one hand, and of the moon on the other, for time increments between the 10-minute tabulated values of GHA. This table is repeated on a flap that can be folded out from the book. Both of these tables state arc to the nearest whole minute. For greater precision there is also included in the white section in the back of the *Air Almanac* a separate page for the interpolation of GHA sun and one for interpolation of GHA ♈, each giving values of 0.1′ of arc. A star index of the 57 navigational stars in alphabetical order with their magnitudes, SHA, and Dec. to nearest minute of arc is given covering their average position for the six-month period of the *Air Almanac*. For those desiring greater precision, or for stars other than the 57 principal ones, separate tables are included in the white section giving SHA and Dec. of 173 stars to 0.1′ of arc for each month of the period covered. They are listed in ascending order of SHA and are intended for use with an astro-tracker. The value of SHA is combined with GHA ♈ from the daily pages, to obtain GHA of the star.

Air Almanac: Additional Tables

2312 Various other tables, sky diagrams, and other data are included in the back of the book. As far as possible they are arranged in inverse order of use; that is, the more commonly used data, such as refraction and dip corrections, are directly inside the back cover, and thus are more easily located. A table is included in the back pages of the volume to assist in interpolating the time of moonrise and moonset for longitude.

Examples from the *Air Almanac*

2313 Sample daily pages from the *Air Almanac* are shown in figures 2311a and 2311b; for comparison purposes, these are for dates included in the period covered by the sample pages from the *Nautical Almanac*. The table for interpolation of GHA is shown as figure 2313a.

Figure 2313b illustrates the extraction of data from the *Air Almanac* for various bodies. Again, for comparison purposes, the same bodies and times are used as were illustrated in figure 2309 for the *Nautical Almanac*.

Example: Obtain GHA and Dec. of the sun on 5 June ZT 09-36-35 (+4).

(DAY 156) GREENWICH A. M.   JUNE 5 (SUNDAY)

GMT	⊙ SUN GHA	Dec.	ARIES GHA ♈	VENUS −4.1 GHA	Dec.	MARS 1.3 GHA	Dec.	SATURN 0.6 GHA	Dec.	☽ MOON GHA	Dec.
h m	° '	° '	° '	° '	° '	° '	° '	° '	° '	° '	° '
00 00	180 25.5	N22 30.4	253 18.4	225 38	N 8 57	225 49	N10 12	118 04	N18 00	313 54	S15 29
10	182 55.5	30.5	255 48.8	228 08		228 19		120 34		316 18	28
20	185 25.5	30.5	258 19.2	230 38		230 49		123 05		318 42	27
30	187 55.4	. 30.6	260 49.6	233 08 .		233 19 .		125 35 .		321 07 .	25
40	190 25.4	30.6	263 20.0	235 38		235 49		128 06		323 31	24
50	192 55.4	30.6	265 50.4	238 08		238 20		130 36		325 55	23
01 00	195 25.4	N22 30.7	268 20.9	240 38	N 8 57	240 50	N10 13	133 06	N18 00	328 20	S15 22
10	197 55.4	30.7	270 51.3	243 08		243 20		135 37		330 44	21
20	200 25.4	30.8	273 21.7	245 38		245 50		138 07		333 08	20
30	202 55.3	. 30.8	275 52.1	248 08 .		248 20 .		140 38 .		335 33 .	19
40	205 25.3	30.9	278 22.5	250 38		250 50		143 08		337 57	17
50	207 55.3	30.9	280 52.9	253 08		253 20		145 38		340 21	16
02 00	210 25.3	N22 31.0	283 23.3	255 38	N 8 58	255 50	N10 13	148 09	N18 00	342 46	S15 15
10	212 55.3	31.0	285 53.7	258 08		258 21		150 39		345 10	14
20	215 25.2	31.1	288 24.1	260 38		260 51		153 09		347 34	13
30	217 55.2	. 31.1	290 54.6	263 08 .		263 21 .		155 40 .		349 59 .	12
40	220 25.2	31.2	293 25.0	265 39		265 51		158 10		352 23	10
50	222 55.2	31.2	295 55.4	268 09		268 21		160 41		354 47	09
03 00	225 25.2	N22 31.3	298 25.8	270 39	N 8 59	270 51	N10 14	163 11	N17 59	357 12	S15 08
10	227 55.2	31.3	300 56.2	273 09		273 21		165 41		359 36	07
20	230 25.1	31.3	303 26.6	275 39		275 51		168 12		2 00	06
30	232 55.1	. 31.4	305 57.0	278 09 .		278 21 .		170 42 .		4 25 .	05
40	235 25.1	31.4	308 27.4	280 39		280 52		173 12		6 49	03
50	237 55.1	31.5	310 57.8	283 09		283 22		175 43		9 13	02
04 00	240 25.1	N22 31.5	313 28.3	285 39	N 8 59	285 52	N10 15	178 13	N17 59	11 38	S15 01
10	242 55.0	31.6	315 58.7	288 09		288 22		180 43		14 02	15 00
20	245 25.0	31.6	318 29.1	290 39		290 52		183 14		16 26	14 59
30	247 55.0	. 31.7	320 59.5	293 09 .		293 22 .		185 44 .		18 51 .	58
40	250 25.0	31.7	323 29.9	295 39		295 52		188 15		21 15	56
50	252 55.0	31.8	326 00.3	298 09		298 22		190 45		23 40	55
05 00	255 25.0	N22 31.8	328 30.7	300 39	N 9 00	300 53	N10 15	193 15	N17 59	26 04	S14 54
10	257 54.9	31.9	331 01.1	303 09		303 23		195 46		28 28	53
20	260 24.9	31.9	333 31.5	305 39		305 53		198 16		30 53	51
30	262 54.9	. 31.9	336 01.9	308 09 .		308 23 .		200 46 .		33 17 .	50
40	265 24.9	32.0	338 32.4	310 40		310 53		203 17		35 41	49
50	267 54.9	32.0	341 02.8	313 10		313 23		205 47		38 06	48
06 00	270 24.8	N22 32.1	343 33.2	315 40	N 9 01	315 53	N10 16	208 18	N17 59	40 30	S14 47
10	272 54.8	32.1	346 03.6	318 10		318 23		210 48		42 55	45
20	275 24.8	32.2	348 34.0	320 40		320 53		213 18		45 19	44
30	277 54.8	. 32.2	351 04.4	323 10 .		323 24 .		215 49 .		47 43 .	43
40	280 24.8	32.3	353 34.8	325 40		325 54		218 19		50 08	42
50	282 54.8	32.3	356 05.2	328 10		328 24		220 49		52 32	41
07 00	285 24.7	N22 32.4	358 35.6	330 40	N 9 01	330 54	N10 17	223 20	N17 59	54 57	S14 39
10	287 54.7	32.4	1 06.1	333 10		333 24		225 50		57 21	38
20	290 24.7	32.4	3 36.5	335 40		335 54		228 21		59 45	37
30	292 54.7	. 32.5	6 06.9	338 10 .		338 24 .		230 51 .		62 10 .	36
40	295 24.7	32.5	8 37.3	340 40		340 54		233 21		64 34	34
50	297 54.6	32.6	11 07.7	343 10		343 24		235 52		66 59	33
08 00	300 24.6	N22 32.6	13 38.1	345 40	N 9 02	345 55	N10 17	238 22	N17 59	69 23	S14 32
10	302 54.6	32.7	16 08.5	348 10		348 25		240 52		71 47	31
20	305 24.6	32.7	18 38.9	350 40		350 55		243 23		74 12	29
30	307 54.6	. 32.8	21 09.3	353 11 .		353 25 .		245 53 .		76 36 .	28
40	310 24.6	32.8	23 39.8	355 41		355 55		248 24		79 01	27
50	312 54.5	32.9	26 10.2	358 11		358 25		250 54		81 25	26
09 00	315 24.5	N22 32.9	28 40.6	0 41	N 9 02	0 55	N10 18	253 24	N17 59	83 49	S14 24
10	317 54.5	33.0	31 11.0	3 11		3 25		255 55		86 14	23
20	320 24.5	33.0	33 41.4	5 41		5 56		258 25		88 38	22
30	322 54.5	. 33.0	36 11.8	8 11 .		8 26 .		260 55 .		91 03 .	21
40	325 24.4	33.1	38 42.2	10 41		10 56		263 26		93 27	19
50	327 54.4	33.1	41 12.6	13 11		13 26		265 56		95 52	18
10 00	330 24.4	N22 33.2	43 43.0	15 41	N 9 03	15 56	N10 19	268 27	N17 59	98 16	S14 17
10	332 54.4	33.2	46 13.4	18 11		18 26		270 57		100 40	16
20	335 24.4	33.3	48 43.9	20 41		20 56		273 27		103 05	14
30	337 54.4	. 33.3	51 14.3	23 11 .		23 26 .		275 58 .		105 29 .	13
40	340 24.3	33.4	53 44.7	25 41		25 56		278 28		107 54	12
50	342 54.3	33.4	56 15.1	28 11		28 27		280 58		110 18	10
11 00	345 24.3	N22 33.5	58 45.5	30 41	N 9 04	30 57	N10 19	283 29	N17 59	112 43	S14 09
10	347 54.3	33.5	61 15.9	33 11		33 27		285 59		115 07	08
20	350 24.3	33.5	63 46.3	35 42		35 57		288 30		117 32	07
30	352 54.2	. 33.6	66 16.7	38 12 .		38 27 .		291 00 .		119 56 .	05
40	355 24.2	33.6	68 47.1	40 42		40 57		293 30		122 21	04
50	357 54.2	33.7	71 17.6	43 12		43 27		296 01		124 45	03
Rate	14 59.9	N0 00.3		15 00.3	N0 00.6	15 00.7	N0 00.7	15 02.3	S0 00.1	14 26.3	N0 07.3

Moonrise

Lat. N	Moon-rise h · m	Diff m
°		
72	01 02	−11
70	00 26	+03
68	00 00	08
66	23 57	07
64	23 46	10
62	23 36	11
60	23 28	13
58	23 20	14
56	23 14	15
54	23 08	16
52	23 03	17
50	22 58	18
45	22 47	19
40	22 39	20
35	22 31	21
30	22 24	23
20	22 13	24
10	22 03	26
0	21 54	27
10	21 44	28
20	21 34	30
30	21 22	31
35	21 16	32
40	21 08	33
45	20 59	35
50	20 48	36
52	20 43	37
54	20 38	38
56	20 32	39
58	20 25	40
60	20 17	41
S		

Moon's P. in A.

Alt.	+ Corr.	Alt.	+ Corr.
0	59	54	34
10	58	55	33
14	57	56	32
18	56	58	31
21	55	59	30
23	54	60	29
25	53	61	28
28	52	62	27
30	51	63	26
31	50	64	25
33	49	65	24
35	48	66	23
36	47	67	22
38	46	68	21
40	45	69	20
41	44	70	19
42	43	71	18
44	42	72	17
45		73	16
47	41	74	15
48	40	75	14
49	39	76	13
50	38	77	12
52	37	78	11
53	36	79	10
54	35	80	
55	34		

Sun SD 15.8
Moon SD 16'
Age 18d

Figure 2311a. *Air Almanac*, right-hand daily page (typical).

(DAY 156) GREENWICH P. M.   JUNE 5 (SUNDAY)

GMT	☉ SUN GHA	Dec.	ARIES GHA ♈	VENUS −4.1 GHA	Dec.	MARS 1.3 GHA	Dec.	SATURN 0.6 GHA	Dec.	☽ MOON GHA	Dec.
h m											
12 00	0 24.2	N22 33.7	73 48.0	45 42	N 9 04	45 57	N10 20	298 31	N17 59	127 10	S14 01
10	2 54.2	33.8	76 18.4	48 12		48 28		301 01		129 34	14 00
20	5 24.2	33.8	78 48.8	50 42		50 58		303 32		131 59	13 59
30	7 54.1 ·	33.9	81 19.2	53 12 ·		53 28 ·		306 02 ·		134 23 ·	57
40	10 24.1	33.9	83 49.6	55 42		55 58		308 33		136 47	56
50	12 54.1	34.0	86 20.0	58 12		58 28		311 03		139 12	55
13 00	15 24.1	N22 34.0	88 50.4	60 42	N 9 05	60 58	N10 21	313 33	N17 59	141 36	S13 54
10	17 54.1	34.0	91 20.8	63 12		63 28		316 04		144 01	52
20	20 24.0	34.1	93 51.3	65 42		65 58		318 34		146 25	51
30	22 54.0 ·	34.1	96 21.7	68 12 ·		68 28 ·		321 04 ·		148 50 ·	50
40	25 24.0	34.2	98 52.1	70 42		70 59		323 35		151 14	48
50	27 54.0	34.2	101 22.5	73 12		73 29		326 05		153 39	47
14 00	30 24.0	N22 34.3	103 52.9	75 42	N 9 06	75 59	N10 21	328 36	N17 59	156 03	S13 46
10	32 54.0	34.3	106 23.3	78 12		78 29		331 06		158 28	44
20	35 23.9	34.4	108 53.7	80 43		80 59		333 36		160 52	43
30	37 53.9 ·	34.4	111 24.1	83 13 ·		83 29 ·		336 07 ·		163 17 ·	42
40	40 23.9	34.4	113 54.5	85 43		85 59		338 37		165 41	40
50	42 53.9	34.5	116 24.9	88 13		88 29		341 07		168 06	39
15 00	45 23.9	N22 34.5	118 55.4	90 43	N 9 06	91 00	N10 22	343 38	N17 59	170 30	S13 38
10	47 53.8	34.6	121 25.8	93 13		93 30		346 08		172 55	36
20	50 23.8	34.6	123 56.2	95 43		96 00		348 39		175 20	35
30	52 53.8 ·	34.7	126 26.6	98 13 ·		98 30 ·		351 09 ·		177 44 ·	34
40	55 23.8	34.7	128 57.0	100 43		101 00		353 39		180 09	32
50	57 53.8	34.8	131 27.4	103 13		103 30		356 10		182 33	31
16 00	60 23.7	N22 34.8	133 57.8	105 43	N 9 07	106 00	N10 23	358 40	N17 59	184 58	S13 30
10	62 53.7	34.9	136 28.2	108 13		108 30		1 10		187 22	28
20	65 23.7	34.9	138 58.6	110 43		111 00		3 41		189 47	27
30	67 53.7 ·	34.9	141 29.1	113 13 ·		113 31 ·		6 11 ·		192 11 ·	26
40	70 23.7	35.0	143 59.5	115 43		116 01		8 42		194 36	24
50	72 53.7	35.0	146 29.9	118 13		118 31		11 12		197 00	23
17 00	75 23.6	N22 35.1	149 00.3	120 43	N 9 08	121 01	N10 23	13 42	N17 59	199 25	S13 22
10	77 53.6	35.1	151 30.7	123 13		123 31		16 13		201 49	20
20	80 23.6	35.2	154 01.1	125 44		126 01		18 43		204 14	19
30	82 53.6 ·	35.2	156 31.5	128 14 ·		128 31 ·		21 13 ·		206 39 ·	17
40	85 23.6	35.3	159 01.9	130 44		131 01		23 44		209 03	16
50	87 53.5	35.3	161 32.3	133 14		133 31		26 14		211 28	15
18 00	90 23.5	N22 35.3	164 02.8	135 44	N 9 08	136 02	N10 24	28 45	N17 59	213 52	S13 13
10	92 53.5	35.4	166 33.2	138 14		138 32		31 15		216 17	12
20	95 23.5	35.4	169 03.6	140 44		141 02		33 45		218 41	11
30	97 53.5 ·	35.5	171 34.0	143 14 ·		143 32 ·		36 16 ·		221 06 ·	09
40	100 23.5	35.5	174 04.4	145 44		146 02		38 46		223 30	08
50	102 53.4	35.6	176 34.8	148 14		148 32		41 16		225 55	06
19 00	105 23.4	N22 35.6	179 05.2	150 44	N 9 09	151 02	N10 25	43 47	N17 58	228 20	S13 05
10	107 53.4	35.7	181 35.6	153 14		153 32		46 17		230 44	04
20	110 23.4	35.7	184 06.0	155 44		156 03		48 48		233 09	02
30	112 53.4 ·	35.7	186 36.4	158 14 ·		158 33 ·		51 18 ·		235 33 ·	01
40	115 23.3	35.8	189 06.9	160 44		161 03		53 48		237 58	13 00
50	117 53.3	35.8	191 37.3	163 14		163 33		56 19		240 23	12 58
20 00	120 23.3	N22 35.9	194 07.7	165 44	N 9 09	166 03	N10 25	58 49	N17 58	242 47	S12 57
10	122 53.3	35.9	196 38.1	168 14		168 33		61 19		245 12	55
20	125 23.3	36.0	199 08.5	170 45		171 03		63 50		247 36	54
30	127 53.3 ·	36.0	201 38.9	173 15 ·		173 33 ·		66 20 ·		250 01 ·	53
40	130 23.2	36.1	204 09.3	175 45		176 03		68 51		252 26	51
50	132 53.2	36.1	206 39.7	178 15		178 34		71 21		254 50	50
21 00	135 23.2	N22 36.1	209 10.1	180 45	N 9 10	181 04	N10 26	73 51	N17 58	257 15	S12 48
10	137 53.2	36.2	211 40.6	183 15		183 34		76 22		259 39	47
20	140 23.2	36.2	214 11.0	185 45		186 04		78 52		262 04	46
30	142 53.1 ·	36.3	216 41.4	188 15 ·		188 34 ·		81 22 ·		264 29 ·	44
40	145 23.1	36.3	219 11.8	190 45		191 04		83 53		266 53	43
50	147 53.1	36.4	221 42.2	193 15		193 34		86 23		269 18	41
22 00	150 23.1	N22 36.4	224 12.6	195 45	N 9 11	196 04	N10 27	88 54	N17 58	271 42	S12 40
10	152 53.1	36.5	226 43.0	198 15		198 35		91 24		274 07	39
20	155 23.0	36.5	229 13.4	200 45		201 05		93 54		276 32	37
30	157 53.0 ·	36.5	231 43.8	203 15 ·		203 35 ·		96 25 ·		278 56 ·	36
40	160 23.0	36.6	234 14.2	205 45		206 05		98 55		281 21	34
50	162 53.0	36.6	236 44.7	208 15		208 35		101 25		283 46	33
23 00	165 23.0	N22 36.7	239 15.1	210 45	N 9 11	211 05	N10 27	103 56	N17 58	286 10	S12 31
10	167 53.0	36.7	241 45.5	213 15		213 35		106 26		288 35	30
20	170 22.9	36.8	244 15.9	215 45		216 05		108 56		290 59	29
30	172 52.9 ·	36.8	246 46.3	218 16 ·		218 35 ·		111 27 ·		293 24 ·	27
40	175 22.9	36.9	249 16.7	220 46		221 06		113 57		295 49	26
50	177 52.9	36.9	251 47.1	223 16		223 36		116 28		298 13	24
Rate	14 59.9	N0 0.3		15 00.3	N0 0.6	15 00.7	N0 00.7	15 02.2	S0 00.1	14 27.4	N0 08.2

Lat. / Moonset / Diff.

Lat.	Moonset	Diff.
N		
°	h m	m
72	05 35	70
70	06 10	56
68	06 35	51
66	06 54	47
64	07 09	45
62	07 22	43
60	07 33	41
58	07 42	40
56	07 50	39
54	07 58	38
52	08 04	37
50	08 10	37
45	08 22	35
40	08 33	34
35	08 42	33
30	08 49	32
20	09 03	30
10	09 14	29
0	09 25	28
10	09 36	27
20	09 47	25
30	10 00	24
35	10 07	23
40	10 16	22
45	10 26	21
50	10 38	19
52	10 43	19
54	10 49	18
56	10 56	17
58	11 03	16
60	11 12	15
S		

Moon's P. in A.

Alt.	+ Corr.	Alt.	+ Corr.
°	'	°	'
0	59	54	34
7	58	55	33
12	57	56	32
16	56	57	31
19	55	58	30
22	54	60	29
24	53	61	28
27	52	62	27
29	51	63	26
31	50	64	25
32	49	65	24
34	48	66	23
36	47	67	22
38	46	68	21
39	45	69	20
41	44	70	19
42	43	71	18
43	42	72	17
45	41	73	16
46	40	74	15
47	39	75	14
49	38	76	13
50	37	77	12
51	36	78	11
53	35	79	10
54	34	80	
55			

Sun SD 15ʹ8
Moon SD 16ʹ
Age 19d

Figure 2311b. *Air Almanac,* left-hand daily page (typical).

STARS, JAN.—JUNE

No.	Name		Mag.	S.H.A.	Dec.
				° '	° '
7*	Acamar		3·1	315 39	S. 40 24
5*	Achernar		0·6	335 47	S. 57 21
30*	Acrux		1·1	173 39	S. 62 58
19	Adhara	†	1·6	255 34	S. 28 57
10*	Aldebaran	†	1·1	291 21	N. 16 28
32*	Alioth		1·7	166 44	N. 56 05
34*	Alkaid		1·9	153 20	N. 49 26
55	Al Na'ir		2·2	28 18	S. 47 04
15	Alnilam	†	1·8	276 14	S. 1 13
25*	Alphard	†	2·2	218 23	S. 8 34
41*	Alphecca	†	2·3	126 34	N. 26 47
1*	Alpheratz	†	2·2	358 12	N. 28 58
51*	Altair	†	0·9	62 35	N. 8 48
2	Ankaa		2·4	353 43	S. 42 26
42*	Antares	†	1·2	113 00	S. 26 23
37*	Arcturus	†	0·2	146 20	N. 19 18
43	Atria		1·9	108 26	S. 68 59
22	Avior		1·7	234 29	S. 59 20
13	Bellatrix	†	1·7	279 01	N. 6 20
16*	Betelgeuse	†	0·1–1·2	271 31	N. 7 24
17*	Canopus		−0·9	264 08	S. 52 41
12*	Capella		0·2	281 15	N. 45 59
53*	Deneb		1·3	49 50	N. 45 12
28*	Denebola	†	2·2	183 01	N. 14 42
4*	Diphda	†	2·2	349 23	S. 18 07
27*	Dubhe		2·0	194 25	N. 61 52
14	Elnath	†	1·8	278 47	N. 28 35
47	Eltanin		2·4	90 59	N. 51 29
54*	Enif	†	2·5	34 14	N. 9 46
56*	Fomalhaut	†	1·3	15 54	S. 29 45
31	Gacrux		1·6	172 31	S. 56 59
29*	Gienah	†	2·8	176 20	S. 17 25
35	Hadar		0·9	149 26	S. 60 16
6*	Hamal	†	2·2	328 32	N. 23 21
48	Kaus Aust.		2·0	84 20	S. 34 24
40*	Kochab		2·2	137 18	N. 74 15
57	Markab	†	2·6	14 06	N. 15 05
8*	Menkar	†	2·8	314 44	N. 4 00
36	Menkent		2·3	148 39	S. 36 10
24*	Miaplacidus		1·8	221 45	S. 69 38
9*	Mirfak		1·9	309 20	N. 49 47
50*	Nunki	†	2·1	76 32	S. 26 19
52*	Peacock		2·1	54 02	S. 56 48
21*	Pollux	†	1·2	244 01	N. 28 05
20*	Procyon	†	0·5	245 28	N. 5 17
46*	Rasalhague	†	2·1	96 32	N. 12 35
26*	Regulus	†	1·3	208 12	N. 12 05
11*	Rigel	†	0·3	281 38	S. 8 14
38*	Rigil Kent.		0·1	140 29	S. 60 44
44	Sabik	†	2·6	102 44	S. 15 42
3*	Schedar		2·5	350 12	N. 56 25
45*	Shaula		1·7	96 59	S. 37 05
18*	Sirius	†	−1·6	258 58	S. 16 41
33*	Spica	†	1·2	159 00	S. 11 03
23*	Suhail		2·2	223 12	S. 43 21
49*	Vega		0·1	80 57	N. 38 46
39	Zuben'ubi	†	2·9	137 35	S. 15 57

INTERPOLATION OF G.H.A.

Increment to be added for intervals of G.M.T. to G.H.A. of: Sun, Aries (♈) and planets; Moon

SUN, etc.	MOON	SUN, etc.	MOON	SUN, etc.	MOON
m s	° ' m s	m s	° ' m s	m s	° ' m s
00 00	0 00 00 00	03 17	0 50 03 25	06 37	1 40 06 52
01	0 01 00 02	21	0 51 03 29	41	1 41 06 56
05	0 02 00 06	25	0 52 03 33	45	1 42 07 00
09	0 03 00 10	29	0 53 03 37	49	1 43 07 04
13	0 04 00 14	33	0 54 03 41	53	1 44 07 08
17	0 05 00 18	37	0 55 03 45	06 57	1 45 07 13
21	0 06 00 22	41	0 56 03 49	07 01	1 46 07 17
25	0 07 00 26	45	0 57 03 54	05	1 47 07 21
29	0 08 00 31	49	0 58 03 58	09	1 48 07 25
33	0 09 00 35	53	0 59 04 02	13	1 49 07 29
37	0 10 00 39	03 57	1 00 04 06	17	1 50 07 33
41	0 11 00 43	04 01	1 01 04 10	21	1 51 07 37
45	0 12 00 47	05	1 02 04 14	25	1 52 07 42
49	0 13 00 51	09	1 03 04 19	29	1 53 07 46
53	0 14 00 55	13	1 04 04 23	33	1 54 07 50
00 57	0 15 01 00	17	1 05 04 27	37	1 55 07 54
01 01	0 16 01 04	21	1 06 04 31	41	1 56 07 58
05	0 17 01 08	25	1 07 04 35	45	1 57 08 02
09	0 18 01 12	29	1 08 04 39	49	1 58 08 06
13	0 19 01 16	33	1 09 04 43	53	1 59 08 11
17	0 20 01 20	37	1 10 04 48	07 57	2 00 08 15
21	0 21 01 24	41	1 11 04 52	08 01	2 01 08 19
25	0 22 01 29	45	1 12 04 56	05	2 02 08 23
29	0 23 01 33	49	1 13 05 00	09	2 03 08 27
33	0 24 01 37	53	1 14 05 04	13	2 04 08 31
37	0 25 01 41	04 57	1 15 05 08	17	2 05 08 35
41	0 26 01 45	05 01	1 16 05 12	21	2 06 08 40
45	0 27 01 49	05	1 17 05 17	25	2 07 08 44
49	0 28 01 53	09	1 18 05 21	29	2 08 08 48
53	0 29 01 58	13	1 19 05 25	33	2 09 08 52
01 57	0 30 02 02	17	1 20 05 29	37	2 10 08 56
02 01	0 31 02 06	21	1 21 05 33	41	2 11 09 00
05	0 32 02 10	25	1 22 05 37	45	2 12 09 04
09	0 33 02 14	29	1 23 05 41	49	2 13 09 09
13	0 34 02 18	33	1 24 05 46	53	2 14 09 13
17	0 35 02 22	37	1 25 05 50	08 57	2 15 09 17
21	0 36 02 27	41	1 26 05 54	09 01	2 16 09 21
25	0 37 02 31	45	1 27 05 58	05	2 17 09 25
29	0 38 02 35	49	1 28 06 02	09	2 18 09 29
33	0 39 02 39	53	1 29 06 06	13	2 19 09 33
37	0 40 02 43	05 57	1 30 06 10	17	2 20 09 38
41	0 41 02 47	06 01	1 31 06 15	21	2 21 09 42
45	0 42 02 51	05	1 32 06 19	25	2 22 09 46
49	0 43 02 56	09	1 33 06 23	29	2 23 09 50
53	0 44 03 00	13	1 34 06 27	33	2 24 09 54
02 57	0 45 03 04	17	1 35 06 31	37	2 25 09 58
03 01	0 46 03 08	21	1 36 06 35	41	2 26 10 00
05	0 47 03 12	25	1 37 06 39	45	2 27
09	0 48 03 16	29	1 38 06 44	49	2 28
13	0 49 03 20	33	1 39 06 48	53	2 29
17	0 50 03 25	37	1 40 06 52	09 57	2 30
03 21	03 29	06 41	06 56	10 00	

*Stars used in H.O. 249 (A.P. 3270) Vol. 1.

†Stars that may be used with Vols. 2 and 3.

Figure 2313a. *Air Almanac,* tables on inside front cover.

Body	SUN	MOON	DENEBOLA	MARS
Date (G)	5 JUN	5 JUN	5 JUN	5 JUN
GMT	13-36-35	09-37-08	23-36-56	23-37-22
GHA (h + 10m)	22° 54'	91° 03'	246° 46'	218° 35'
Incre (m/s)	1° 39'	1° 43'	1° 44'	1° 51'
SHA	—	—	183° 01'	—
Total GHA	24° 33'	92° 46'	431° 31'	220° 26'
± 360°			71° 31'	
Tab Dec	N 22° 34'	S14° 21'	N14° 42'	N 10° 27'

Figure 2313b. Tabular solutions for GHA and declination, *Air Almanac*.

Solution: (1) Determine GMT by adding ZD to ZT; GMT is 13-36-35. (2) Locate the page that includes the second half of 5 June; locate the line for the hour and next lesser 10-minute interval (13 30). (3) Follow across this line to the column headed "sun"; read and record the GHA (22°54.0') and the Dec. (N22°34.1'). (4) Turn to the table for "Interpolation of GHA" on the inside front cover of the *Almanac* (figure 2313a) and pick out incremental correction in "Sun, etc." column for 6 minutes and 35 seconds (1°39'). *Note:* This is a quickly used table of critical values to the nearest 1'; if a value to 0.1' is needed, there are also interpolation tables for GHA sun and GHA Aries in the white pages at the back of the *Air Almanac*. (5) Add the increment of GHA to the value from the daily page: 22°54.0' + 1°39' = 24°33'; this is the GHA of the sun for the time of observation.

It should be noted here that the *Air Almanac*, with entries for each 10 minutes of time, permits the GHA of the sun to be found more accurately than with the *Nautical Almanac* (unless special procedures are used with the latter). The reason for this is that the *Nautical Almanac*, with tabulated data only for each whole hour, lists GHA adjusted by as much as 0.15' to minimize the error caused by ignoring any *v* correction, as stated in article 2308.

In the *Air Almanac*, tabulated declination is always used without interpolation; the tabular value for the GMT immediately *before* the time of observation is taken. In this example, this is N22°34.1'.

Almanac for Computers

2314 A recent product of the "computer age" is the U.S. Naval Observatory publication, *Almanac for Computers* (prepared by the U.S. Naval Observatory; published by the Government Printing Of-fice and sold by the Superintendent of Documents, Washington, D.C. 20402). This small pamphlet contains mathematical expressions for various items of almanac data and tables of constants to be used in them, together with the necessary instructions. This publication can serve essentially as a complete alternative to the use of a *Nautical* or *Air Almanac*.

The *Almanac for Computers* is designed to facilitate the application of digital computation techniques to problems of astronomy and navigation that require the coordinates of celestial bodies. Although basically intended for use with computers—the tabular data are also available in machine-readable form on punched cards or magnetic tape—the procedures of this publication are within the capabilities of card-programmable personal calculators such as the Texas-Instruments model TI-59, and Hewlett-Packard models HP-41, -67, and -97.

For the navigator, direct calculations to essentially the full level of precision and accuracy of the *Nautical Almanac* are possible for all necessary data of the stars, Aries, planets, sun, and moon, including semidiameter and horizontal parallax where applicable. A given set of constants from the tables is usable for periods of 8 days for the moon, and 32 days for Aries, the sun, and the planets. It is a simple matter to update the constants for subsequent time periods. A set of constants for a star—data are tabulated for 176 stars, including the 57 "selected" stars—is valid for the full year of the publication.

The *Almanac for Computers* also provides for the direct calculation of such celestial phenomena of interest to navigators as sunrise, sunset, and twilight; moonrise and moonset; latitude by Polaris; longitude line of position; motion of body and observer; and others.

POWER SERIES APPROXIMATION OF NAUTICAL ALMANAC DATA

Days 145 thru 150   JD 2445479.5 to 2445485.5   Dates May 25 thru May 30

A = 3.0   B = -49.33333333   W = 145

Term	Moon GHA °	Moon Dec °	Moon H P °	Moon S D °
0	1065.5933	-22.6329	0.9222	0.2513
1	1043.0627	-6.1258	-0.0210	-0.0057
2	-0.7127	5.0806	0.0044	0.0012
3	0.7348	0.3714	-0.0035	-0.0010
4	0.1999	-0.2269	-0.0006	-0.0002
5	-0.0831	-0.0201	0.0033	0.0009
Sums	2108.7949	-23.5537	0.9048	0.2465

Figure 2314. Data page from *Almanac for Computers* (typical).

A separate section in *Almanac for Computers* is provided for the calculation of ephemeristic data of interest to astronomers, in units and to levels of precision and accuracy suited to their needs.

The use of *Almanac for Computers* is not advantageous to a navigator for the reduction of only a few observations. When, however, a considerable number of sights are to be reduced, it is quite convenient to obtain such necessary data as GHA Aries; sun GHA, declination, and semidiameter; or moon GHA, declination, semidiameter, and horizontal parallax by merely punching in the GMT on the keyboard of a personal calculator or general purpose computer. See figure 2314.

A generally similar British publication is Royal Greenwich Observatory Bulletin No. 185, *Compact Data for Navigation and Astronomy* for 1981 to 1985; it is expected that further editions will be published for subsequent years.

Other Ephemeristic Tabulations

2315 In addition to the *Nautical Almanac* and the *Air Almanac*, many special tabulations of ephemeristic data have been made for specific purposes. A number of attempts have also been made to produce a long-term or perpetual almanac. DMAHTC Pub. No. 9, *Bowditch*, Appendix H of Volume II (1975 or 1981) contains one version of a long-term almanac. In the explanation section of each *Nautical Almanac* a brief description is given of corrections that can be applied to use portions of that volume in the succeeding year. These are generally considered to be emergency methods for use when a current edition of the *Almanac* is not available to the navigator.

Volume I of Pub. No. 249 contains information in Table 4 which will permit the computation of GHA ♈ for any time over a nine-year period; this table is updated for each edition of Volume I at five-year intervals. The value of GHA ♈ is determined by adding three tabulated quantities—for (a) month of year, (b) hour of day, and (c) minutes and seconds.

An excellent perpetual almanac is the one prepared in England by Her Majesty's Nautical Almanac Office. It is printed in the sight reduction tables, AP 3270, the British equivalent of Pub. No. 249. It is restricted to the sun, and the entire ephemeris is presented in two pages. The presentation of data is both interesting and original.

TIMES OF CELESTIAL PHENOMENA

Definition of Terms

2317 Sunrise is the first appearance of the sun's *upper limb* above the visible horizon; similarly, sunset is the disappearance of the upper limb below the horizon. Chiefly because of the effect of refraction, as the upper limb appears to touch the horizon at sunset, it is actually more than 30' below the celestial horizon. The times of moonrise and moonset are similarly determined, by contact of the upper limb with the horizon.

Twilight is the period before sunrise when darkness is giving way to daylight, and after sunset when the opposite is true. Three kinds of twilight are shown below;

Twilight	*Lighter Limit*	*Darker Limit*	*At Darker Limit*
Civil	☉ 0°	-6°	Horizon clear; bright stars visible
Nautical	☉ 0°	-12°	Horizon vague
Astronomical	☉ 0°	-18°	Full night

the darker limit of each twilight occurs when the *center* of the sun is that stated number of degrees below the celestial horizon. A navigator is concerned only with civil and nautical twilight.

The conditions at the darker limits are relative and vary considerably under different atmospheric conditions. The duration of twilight is chiefly a function of the observer's latitude; it increases with an increase in latitude.

Information from Published Tables

2318 In the *Nautical Almanac,* the GMT of sunrise and sunset, and the beginnings of morning and endings of evening civil and nautical twilight are tabulated for every three-day period, at various latitudes along the meridian of Greenwich (0°λ), the second of the three being the reference day. The GMT of moonrise and moonset for 0°λ are similarly tabulated in a separate column for each day.

The Local Mean Time (LMT) of sunrise, sunset, and twilight for a given date and latitude are essentially the same in any longitude. This is due to the fact that for a period of one day the change in declination, and more important, the rate of change in hour angle, of the sun is comparatively small. For moonrise and moonset an additional interpolation for longitude is needed.

In the back of each volume of the *Air Almanac,* tables will be found giving the times of sunrise and sunset and the darker limits of civil twilight; times of moonrise and moonset are given on the daily pages. Additionally, the *Tide Tables* (published by the National Ocean Service) include tables for the LMT of sunrise and sunset, with a convenient table for the conversion of LMT to ZT. Moonrise and moonset are tabulated daily for specific cities rather than by latitude.

Time of Sunrise and Sunset

2319 The GMT of sunrise and sunset for the middle day of the three days covered by each page opening in the *Nautical Almanac* is tabulated to the nearest minute of time for selected intervals of latitude from 72° N to 60° S. An extract from this table is shown in figure 2319a. The tabulated times are generally used to obtain the ZT of the phenomena by one of two possible methods. The GMT of sunrise or sunset may be considered to be its LMT, and therefore its ZT on the standard meridian of any zone. To obtain the ZT of the phenomena at a vessel, it is only necessary to convert the difference of longitude between the standard meridian and the vessel into time, adding this difference if the vessel is west of the standard meridian and subtracting if

Lat.	Sunset	Twilight		Moonset			
		Civil	Naut.	3	4	5	6
°	h m	h m	h m	h m	h m	h m	h m
N 72	☐	☐	☐	■	03 02	05 35	07 40
N 70	☐	☐	☐	02 35	04 17	06 10	08 00
68	☐	☐	☐	03 26	04 54	06 35	08 16
66	23 01	////	////	03 58	05 21	06 54	08 29
64	22 07	////	////	04 22	05 41	07 09	08 39
62	21 36	////	////	04 41	05 58	07 22	08 48
60	21 12	22 41	////	04 56	06 11	07 33	08 56
N 58	20 54	22 03	////	05 09	06 23	07 42	09 03
56	20 38	21 37	////	05 21	06 33	07 50	09 08
54	20 25	21 17	22 48	05 31	06 42	07 58	09 14
52	20 13	21 00	22 13	05 40	06 50	08 04	09 18
50	20 03	20 46	21 48	05 47	06 57	08 10	09 23
45	19 42	20 18	21 07	06 04	07 12	08 22	09 32
N 40	19 25	19 57	20 38	06 18	07 25	08 33	09 40
35	19 10	19 40	20 16	06 30	07 36	08 42	09 46
30	18 58	19 25	19 58	06 40	07 45	08 49	09 52
20	18 37	19 01	19 30	06 57	08 01	09 03	10 02
N 10	18 19	18 42	19 08	07 13	08 15	09 14	10 11
0	18 02	18 24	18 50	07 27	08 28	09 25	10 19
S 10	17 45	18 08	18 34	07 41	08 40	09 36	10 27
20	17 27	17 51	18 19	07 56	08 54	09 47	10 35
30	17 07	17 33	18 03	08 13	09 10	10 00	10 45
35	16 55	17 23	17 55	08 23	09 19	10 07	10 50
40	16 42	17 12	17 46	08 35	09 29	10 16	10 57
45	16 26	16 59	17 36	08 48	09 41	10 26	11 04
S 50	16 07	16 44	17 25	09 04	09 56	10 38	11 12
52	15 57	16 37	17 20	09 12	10 02	10 43	11 16
54	15 47	16 30	17 15	09 21	10 10	10 49	11 21
56	15 35	16 21	17 10	09 30	10 18	10 56	11 26
58	15 21	16 12	17 03	09 41	10 28	11 03	11 31
S 60	15 05	16 01	16 56	09 53	10 38	11 12	11 37

Day	SUN			MOON			
	Eqn. of Time 00ʰ	12ʰ	Mer. Pass.	Mer. Pass. Upper	Lower	Age	Phase
	m s	m s	h m	h m	h m	d	
3	02 02	01 57	11 58	01 12	13 43	16	
4	01 52	01 47	11 58	02 13	14 43	17	◐
5	01 42	01 37	11 58	03 12	15 39	18	

Figure 2319a. *Nautical Almanac* portion of a daily page showing evening phenomena; morning phenomena are shown in a similar manner on facing page.

it is east. Each degree of longitude will be 4 minutes of time, and each 15' of longitude 1 minute of time. The same result can be obtained by taking from the table the GMT at the required latitude, and applying to this the longitude converted to time, to give GMT of the phenomena at the local meridian, and finally applying the zone description with the sign reversed. Interpolation for latitude is made by means of a table near the back of the *Nautical Almanac;* a portion of this is reproduced in figure 2319b. When more precise times of sunrise and sunset are desired, they may be obtained by interpolating for the correct day, in addition to the regular interpolation for latitude.

At times, in high latitudes, the sun remains continuously either below or above the horizon. In the former case, the symbol ■ appears in place of a time; in the latter, the symbol ☐ is substituted for the time. These symbols are seen in figure 2319a

TABLES FOR INTERPOLATING SUNRISE, MOONRISE, ETC.

TABLE I—FOR LATITUDE

| Tabular Interval | | | Difference between the times for consecutive latitudes | | | | | | | | | | | | | | |
10°	5°	2°	5m	10m	15m	20m	25m	30m	35m	40m	45m	50m	55m	60m	1h 05m	1h 10m	1h 15m	1h 20m
0 30	0 15	0 06	0	0	1	1	1	1	1	2	2	2	2	2	0 02	0 02	0 02	0 02
1 00	0 30	0 12	0	1	1	2	2	3	3	3	4	4	4	5	05	05	05	05
1 30	0 45	0 18	1	1	2	3	3	4	4	5	5	6	7	7	07	07	07	07
2 00	1 00	0 24	1	2	3	4	5	5	6	7	7	8	9	10	10	10	10	10
2 30	1 15	0 30	1	2	4	5	6	7	8	9	9	10	11	12	12	13	13	13
3 00	1 30	0 36	1	3	4	6	7	8	9	10	11	12	13	14	0 15	0 15	0 16	0 16
3 30	1 45	0 42	2	3	5	7	8	10	11	12	13	14	16	17	18	18	19	19
4 00	2 00	0 48	2	4	6	8	9	11	13	14	15	16	18	19	20	21	22	22
9 00	4 30	1 48	4	9	13	18	22	27	31	35	39	43	47	52	0 55	0 58	1 01	1 04
9 30	4 45	1 54	5	9	14	19	24	28	33	38	42	47	51	56	1 00	1 04	1 08	1 12
10 00	5 00	2 00	5	10	15	20	25	30	35	40	45	50	55	60	1 05	1 10	1 15	1 20

Table I is for interpolating the L.M.T. of sunrise, twilight, moonrise, etc., for latitude. It is to be entered, in the appropriate column on the left, with the difference between true latitude and the nearest tabular latitude which is *less* than the true latitude; and with the argument at the top which is the nearest value of the difference between the times for the tabular latitude and the next higher one; the correction so obtained is applied to the time for the tabular latitude; the sign of the correction can be seen by inspection. It is to be noted that the interpolation is not linear, so that when using this table it is essential to take out the tabular phenomenon for the latitude *less* than the true latitude.

TABLE II—FOR LONGITUDE

| Long. East or West | Difference between the times for given date and preceding date (for east longitude) or for given date and following date (for west longitude) | | | | | | | | | | | | | | | | | | |
	10m	20m	30m	40m	50m	60m	1h + 10m	20m	30m	1h + 40m	50m	60m	2h 10m	2h 20m	2h 30m	2h 40m	2h 50m	3h 00m
0	0	0	0	0	0	0	0	0	0	0	0	0	0 00	0 00	0 00	0 00	0 00	0 00
10	0	1	1	1	1	2	2	2	2	3	3	3	04	04	04	04	05	05
20	1	1	2	2	3	3	4	4	5	6	6	7	07	08	08	09	09	10
30	1	2	2	3	4	5	6	7	7	8	9	10	11	12	12	13	14	15
40	1	2	3	4	6	7	8	9	10	11	12	13	14	16	17	18	19	20
50	1	3	4	6	7	8	10	11	12	14	15	17	0 18	0 19	0 21	0 22	0 24	0 25
60	2	3	5	7	8	10	12	13	15	17	18	20	22	23	25	27	28	30
70	2	4	6	8	10	12	14	16	17	19	21	23	25	27	29	31	33	35
80	2	4	7	9	11	13	16	18	20	22	24	27	29	31	33	36	38	40
90	2	5	7	10	12	15	17	20	22	25	27	30	32	35	37	40	42	45
100	3	6	8	11	14	17	19	22	25	28	31	33	0 36	0 39	0 42	0 44	0 47	0 50
110	3	6	9	12	15	18	21	24	27	31	34	37	40	43	46	49	0 52	0 55
120	3	7	10	13	17	20	23	27	30	33	37	40	43	47	50	53	0 57	1 00
130	4	7	11	14	18	22	25	29	32	36	40	43	47	51	54	0 58	1 01	1 05
140	4	8	12	16	19	23	27	31	35	39	43	47	51	54	0 58	1 02	1 06	1 10
150	4	8	13	17	21	25	29	33	38	42	46	50	0 54	0 58	1 03	1 07	1 11	1 15
160	4	9	13	18	22	27	31	36	40	44	49	53	0 58	1 02	1 07	1 11	1 16	1 20
170	5	9	14	19	24	28	33	38	42	47	52	57	1 01	1 06	1 11	1 16	1 20	1 25
180	5	10	15	20	25	30	35	40	45	50	55	60	1 05	1 10	1 15	1 20	1 25	1 30

Table II is for interpolating the L.M.T. of moonrise, moonset and the Moon's meridian passage for longitude. It is entered with longitude and with the difference between the times for the given date and for the preceding date (in east longitudes) or following date (in west longitudes). The correction is normally *added* for west longitudes and *subtracted* for east longitudes, but if, as occasionally happens, the times become earlier each day instead of later, the signs of the corrections must be reversed.

Figure 2319b. Nautical Almanac, tables for interpolating the times of rising and setting of the sun and moon, and of twilight

where the sun does not set in high latitudes, and the moon, at extreme latitudes, did not come above the horizon on 3 June.

Correction for Latitude Difference

To determine the time at a latitude that is not tabulated, table I is entered, following the instructions listed below the table. It should be noted that the correction table is not linear and that information from the daily pages is always taken for the tabulated latitude smaller than the actual latitude. The entering arguments are:

Latitude difference between the tabulated latitude and the actual one.
Time difference between the times of the occurrence at the tabulated latitudes on either side of the one for which the information is desired.

The latitude interval between tabular entries for sunrise and sunset varies with the latitude concerned, being 10° near the equator, 5° in mid-latitudes, and 2° in higher latitudes. Table I has columns at the left for each of these intervals. The *latitude difference* between the actual latitude and the smaller tabulated latitude is determined and used to select the appropriate line of Table I. For example, if the interval between tabulated latitudes is 2°, and the latitude for which the information is desired is 0°24' greater than the smaller tabulated latitude, the "Tabular Interval" column headed 2° is entered; 0°24' is found on the fourth line down. If the tabular interval were 5°, a latitude difference of 0°24' would be located approximately on the second line down; if it were 10°, this same latitude difference would be located approximately on the first line. The *time difference* is used to determine the column of Table I that is to be used; the time correction is taken directly from the table, with interpolation if necessary to obtain the time of the phenomenon to the nearest minute. The correction thus obtained is applied to the GMT of the phenomenon for the *smaller* tabulated latitude, originally extracted from the daily pages; the sign of the correction is determined by inspection.

To this sum, the longitude converted from arc to time is applied as previously described, to obtain the ZT of the phenomenon for the latitude and longitude.

Sunset Calculation

The procedures described above are illustrated in the typical situation at sea.

Example: Find the ZT of sunset on 5 June at Latitude 41°34.1' N, Longitude 16°46.1' W using the *Nautical Almanac* (figures 2319a and b).

Solution: Enter the appropriate daily page of the *Nautical Almanac* (figure 2319a) and extract and record the LMT of sunset for the next lesser tabulated latitude. In this case, the next lesser latitude is 40° N and the LMT of sunset at that latitude is 1925. Then note the difference of latitude between the tabulated values above and below the latitude for which information is desired, and the difference in the times of the phenomenon between these latitudes including its sign. In this instance, the tabular interval is 5° and the time difference is +17^m (1925 at Lat. 40° N and 1942 at Lat. 45° N). Next, enter Table I of "Tables for Interpolating Sunrise, Moonrise, etc." (figure 2319b) and obtain the correction to the tabulated LMT. In this example, the latitude difference, 41°34.1' minus 40°00.0' or 1°34.1', is applied to the column for Tabular Interval of 5°. The time difference is found between the columns for 15^m and 20^m. Interpolating by eye to the nearest minute, the correction is +5^m. Finally, apply this correction to the LMT for the lesser tabulated latitude (40°) to obtain the LMT of sunset at the given latitude, and convert this time to ZT. For this example, the LMT of sunset at Lat. 41°34.1' N is 1925 + 5 = 1930; the ZT is 1930 + 7^m (for 1°46.1' longitude west of zone central meridian; using the table "Conversion of Arc to Time" to nearest whole minute of time) = 1937.

	Sunset
N 45°	1942
N 40°	1925
Diff for 5°	17 min.
Table I Lat. Corr.	+ 5 min.
1925 + 5 =	1930
DLo Corr.	+ 7
ZT	1937

Answer: The ZT of sunset is 1937.

The above example was done directly from the tabulated data of the *Nautical Almanac* without correction for the fact that 5 June is not the center date of the *Almanac* pages for "June 3, 4, 5" nor for the difference in longitude between the vessel and Greenwich. Such procedure will yield a time of sunrise or sunset sufficiently accurate for the usual uses to which such information is put. If, however, a more precise determination of the time of these phenomena is needed, corrections can be calculated in accordance with procedures explained in the *Nautical Almanac*. In the above example, because of the time of year and latitude, such a correction is negligible; in months near the equinoxes and at high latitudes, corrections can be as much as six to eight minutes.

The procedure for obtaining the time of sunrise from the *Nautical Almanac* is the same as that explained above for sunset.

Procedures for using the *Air Almanac* are illustrated in the following example for the same position and date.

Example: Find the ZT of sunset on 5 June at Lat. 41°34' N, Long. 16°46' W using the *Air Almanac* (figure 2319c).

Solution: The tabular data for sunrise, sunset, and civil twilight are given in the "white pages" of the *Air Almanac* at three-day intervals for the longitude of Greenwich and latitude intervals of 10°, 5°, or 2° similar to the *Nautical Almanac*. These figures may be used for other longitudes without correction. The nearest date is used but interpolation is done for the actual latitude. The *Air Almanac* data for this example are as follows:

	June
Lat.	4
N45	1942
N40	1925

The LMT of sunset at Lat. 41°34' N is found by interpolation to be 1930. Adjusting for longitude, the ZT is 1930 + 7^m (for 1°46' longitude east of zone central meridian) = 1937.

Answer: ZT of sunset is 1937.

Note that in this example the ZT of sunset is the same whether the *Air Almanac* or the *Nautical Almanac* is used. In some instances, slight differences will occur between the results obtained from the use of the two procedures, but these are of negligible practical significance.

Time of Twilight

2320 In celestial navigation, morning and evening twilight are the most important times of the

SUNSET

Lat.	May 17	20	23	26	29	June 1	4	7	10	13	16	19	22	25	28	July 1
	h m	h m	h m	h m	h m	h m	h m	h m	h m	h m	h m	h m	h m	h m	h m	h m
N 72	□	□	□	□	□	□	□	□	□	□	□	□	□	□	□	□
70	□	□	□	□	□	□	□	□	□	□	□	□	□	□	□	□
68	22 18	22 37	23 01	23 43	□	□	□	□	□	□	□	□	□	□	□	□
66	21 39	21 51	22 04	22 17	22 30	22 44	22 58	23 14	23 32	□	□	□	□	□	□	23 46
64	21 12	21 22	21 31	21 40	21 49	21 58	22 06	22 13	22 20	22 25	22 29	22 31	22 32	22 32	22 30	22 26
62	20 51	20 59	21 07	21 15	22	28	21 34	21 40	21 45	21 48	21 51	21 53	21 54	21 54	21 53	21 51
N 60	20 35	20 42	20 48	20 55	21 01	21 06	21 11	21 16	21 20	21 23	21 25	21 27	21 28	21 28	21 27	21 25
58	21	27	33	38	20 43	20 48	20 53	20 57	21 00	21 03	21 05	21 06	21 07	21 07	21 07	21 06
56	20 09	14	20	24	29	33	37	41	20 44	20 46	20 48	20 50	20 50	20 51	20 50	20 49
54	19 58	20 03	20 08	13	17	21	24	27	30	32	34	35	36	36	36	35
52	49	19 54	19 58	20 02	20 06	09	13	15	18	20	22	23	24	24	24	23
N 50	19 41	19 45	19 49	19 53	19 56	20 00	20 02	20 05	20 07	20 09	20 11	20 12	20 13	20 13	20 13	20 13
45	24	27	30	33	36	19 39	19 41	19 43	19 45	19 47	19 49	19 50	19 50	19 51	19 51	19 50
40	19 09	12	15	18	20	22	24	26	28	29	30	31	32	33	33	33
35	18 58	19 00	19 02	19 04	19 06	19 08	19 10	19 12	13	14	16	16	17	18	18	18
30	47	18 49	18 51	18 53	18 54	18 56	18 58	18 59	19 00	19 01	19 03	19 03	19 04	19 05	19 05	19 05
N 20	18 29	18 31	18 32	18 33	18 34	18 35	18 37	18 38	18 39	18 40	18 41	18 41	18 42	18 43	18 43	18 43
N 10	14	15	16	16	17	18	19	20	21	22	22	23	24	24	24	25
0	18 00	18 00	18 00	18 01	18 01	18 01	18 02	18 02	18 03	18 03	18 04	18 05	18 05	18 06	18 07	18 07
S 10	17 46	17 45	17 45	17 45	17 45	17 45	17 45	17 46	17 46	17 46	17 47	17 47	17 48	17 49	17 49	17 50
20	31	30	29	28	28	28	28	28	28	28	28	29	30	30	31	32
S 30	17 14	17 12	17 11	17 10	17 09	17 08	17 07	17 07	17 07	17 07	17 07	17 08	17 08	17 09	17 10	17 11
35	17 04	17 02	17 00	16 59	16 57	16 56	16 56	16 55	16 55	16 55	16 55	16 55	16 56	16 57	16 58	16 59
40	16 53	16 51	16 48	46	45	43	42	41	41	41	41	41	42	42	43	45
45	40	37	34	32	30	28	27	25	25	24	24	24	25	26	27	28
50	24	20	17	14	11	09	16 07	16 05	16 04	16 04	16 03	16 03	16 04	16 05	16 06	16 08
S 52	16 16	16 12	16 09	16 05	16 02	16 00	15 58	15 56	15 55	15 54	15 53	15 53	15 54	15 55	15 56	15 58
54	16 08	16 04	16 00	15 56	15 53	15 50	47	45	44	43	42	42	43	44	45	47
56	15 59	15 54	15 49	45	42	38	36	33	32	30	30	30	30	31	33	35
58	48	43	38	33	29	25	22	19	17	15 16	15 15	15 15	15 15	15 17	18	20
S 60	15 36	15 30	15 24	15 19	15 14	15 10	15 06	15 03	15 00	14 59	14 58	14 57	14 58	14 59	15 01	15 03

Figure 2319c. *Air Almanac, Sunset Tables.*

day, as ordinarily these are the only periods during which a fix may be obtained by nearly simultaneous lines of position from observations of a number of celestial bodies. At the darker limit of nautical twilight, when the sun's center is 12° below the celestial horizon, the horizon is usually only dimly visible, except to an observer with dark-adapted vision, or who is using a telescope of superior light-gathering power. At the darker limit of civil twilight, when the sun's center is 6° below the celestial horizon, during good weather the bright stars are readily discernible to the practiced eye, and the horizon is clearly defined. This is approximately the mid-time of the period during which star observations should ordinarily be made.

The time of the darker limit of civil or nautical twilight is obtained from the *Nautical Almanac* in the same manner that sunrise and sunset data are obtained. The GMT of the phenomenon at the clos-

est tabulated latitude is taken from the daily pages, interpolation for latitude is made in table I, and the ZT of the phenomenon at the desired latitude is then obtained by applying the longitude in time, as discussed in article 2319.

When twilight lasts all night, as happens at times in high latitudes, the symbol //// is shown in lieu of a time; see higher latitudes of figure 2319a.

Example: Find the ZT of the ending of civil twilight on 5 June at latitude 41°36.0' N, longitude 16°54.0' W using the *Nautical Almanac.*

Solution: Enter the appropriate daily page of the *Nautical Almanac* (figure 2319a) and extract and record the LMT for the end of civil twilight for the next lesser tabulated latitude. In this case, the next lesser latitude is 40° and the LMT at that latitude is 1957. Then note the difference between the tabulated values of latitude on either side of the latitude for which the information is desired, and the difference in time of the phenomenon between these tabulated latitudes, and its sign. In this case the tabular interval is 5° and time difference is +21^m (1957 at 40° N and 2018 at 45° N). Next, enter Table I (figure 2319b) and obtain the correction to LMT. This is found on a line for 1°36' in the 5° Tabular Interval Column (between 1°30' and 1°45') and a column for 21^m difference (between 20^m and 25^m); it is +7^m. Finally, apply this correction to the LMT of the lesser latitude (40°) to obtain the LMT at the desired latitude, and convert this time to ZT. In this example, the LMT of the end of civil twilight at latitude 41°36.0' N is 1957 + 7 = 2004; the ZT 2004 + 8^m (for 1°54.0' of longitude west of zone central meridian) = 2012.

Civil Twilight

N 45°	2018
N 40°	1957
Diff for 5°	21 min
Table I Lat. Corr.	+ 7 min
1957 + 7 =	2004
DLo Corr.	+ 8 min
	2012

Answer: ZT of the ending of civil twilight is 2012.

The procedures for finding the ending of nautical twilight, or the beginning of civil or nautical twilight, are similar to the example shown above.

The beginning or ending of civil twilight can be found from the *Air Almanac* following the instructions contained in that publication; the procedures are generally the same as illustrated for sunrise or sunset as described in article 2319.

Time of Moonrise and Moonset

2321 The times of moonrise and moonset are found by first interpolating for the latitude at which they are required, as was done with the sun. However, there must be a second interpolation for longitude, as the times of moonrise and moonset differ considerably from day to day, and at any longitude other than 0° these phenomena will fall somewhere between the times tabulated for consecutive days on the 0° meridian. This results from the fact that the change in hourly rate of increase of GHA for the moon is not precisely 15° per hour, which would be assumed if longitude were merely converted to time as in the case of the sun.

Always remember that the tabulated times of moonrise and moonset are their GMTs at the longitude of Greenwich (0°λ); an observer in east longitude will experience each phenomenon before it occurs at 0° longitude. The GMT of moonrise and moonset in *east* longitude is found by interpolating

between the tabulated time for the given day and the tabulated time for the *preceding* day. For *west* longitude, and the GMT at a given meridian is found by interpolating between the tabulated time for the given day and the tabulated time for the *following* day. (It is for this reason that the *Nautical Almanac* shows moonrise and moonset times for *four* days, the three days of the daily page plus the next day.)

Before interpolating for longitude, however, the times of the required phenomenon on the two days involved must first be interpolated for the required latitude using table I, figure 2319b. The interpolation for longitude is then made using Table II of the "Tables for Interpolating Sunrise, Moonrise, Etc." An extract from this table is shown in the lower part of figure 2319b. GMT is converted to ZT in the usual manner.

Moonset Calculation

A typical calculation of the time of moonset is illustrated below.

Example: Find the ZT of moonset on 5 June at latitude 41°12.4' N, longitude 15°17.1' W using the *Nautical Almanac* (figures 2319a and b).

Solution: Enter the appropriate daily page of the *Nautical Almanac* and extract and record, for the next smaller tabulated latitude, the LMT of the phenomenon at the Greenwich meridian on the given date. In this case the LMT at Greenwich, tabulated for latitude 40° N is 0833 on 5 June. Then extract the equivalent time on the *preceding day if in east longitude,* or on the *following day if in west longitude.* In this example, the LMT at Greenwich, again using 40° N, is 0940 on 6 June, the later day being taken since the position for which information is desired is in west longitude. Then determine the interval between tabulated values of latitude on either side of the one for which information is desired, and the time difference and its sign between the tabulated LMT at each of these latitudes for each of the two days involved. In this case the tabular interval for both days is 5°, and the difference in time is −11^m on 5 June and −8^m on 6 June. Next enter Table I and obtain the correction for latitude to the tabulated LMT at the longitude of Greenwich. The correction is −2^m on 5 June, and −2^m on 6 June. Then apply these corrections to the lesser tabulated latitude (40°), thus completing interpolation to the nearest minute of time for the exact latitude on each day. In this case, the LMT at the longitude of Greenwich at latitude 41°12.4' N is 0831 on 5 June and 0938 on 6 June.

To interpolate for longitude, enter Table II with the longitude (east or west) in the left-hand column, and the difference between the LMT at each date in the line at the top of the table. In this case the longitude is approximately 15° and the time difference is 1^h07^m (0938–0831). Then obtain the correction from the table, using eye interpolation as necessary. In this case the correction to the nearest minute is 3^m. Apply the correction to the LMT of the phenomenon on the date for which the information is desired, in such a way that the time arrived at falls between the LMT at Greenwich on the two dates in question. In most cases this will mean that the correction is added if the longitude is west, and subtracted if it is east. In this case, the correction is added, making the LMT of moonset at the observer's meridian 0834 (since 0831 + 3 = 0834) on 5 June. Finally, convert this LMT to ZT; $0834 + 1^m$ (correction for 0°17.1' of longitude west of zone central meridian) = 0835.

Moonset

N 40°	0833	5 June
N 45°	0822	
Diff for 5°	− 11	
Table I Lat. Corr.	− 2	
LMT (G) 0833 − 2 =	0831	5 June
N 40°	0940	6 June
N 45°	0932	
Diff for 5°	− 8	
Table I Lat. Corr.	− 2	
LMT(G) 0940 − 2 =	0938	6 June
LMT(G)	0831	5 June
Diff between days	1 07	
LMT(G)	0831	5 June
Table II Corr.	+ 3	
LMT(L)	0834	5 June
dLo Corr.	+ 1	
ZT	0835	5 June

Answer: The ZT of moonset is 0835.

The procedure for obtaining the time of moonrise from the *Nautical Almanac* is the same as explained above for moonset.

Calculations for the local times of moonrise and moonset can also be done using the *Air Almanac*. On each daily page (figures 2311a and b) there are data for the 0° longitude occurrence at various latitudes, plus a column headed "Diff.," which gives the half-way difference in order to correct for a longitude other than Greenwich. The correction to be applied to the tabulated GMT of moonrise or moonset is given in the table F4 on the flap headed "Interpolation of Moonrise, Moonset for Longitude" (figure 2321). This table is entered with Diff. and longitude, and the correction, selected without

F4 INTERPOLATION OF MOONRISE, MOONSET FOR LONGITUDE

Add if longitude west
Subtract if longitude east

Longi- tude	DIFF.					
	05	10	15	20	25	30
°	m	m	m	m	m	m
0	00	00	00	00	00	00
20	01	01	02	02	03	03
40	01	02	03	04	06	07
60	02	03	05	07	08	10
80	02	04	07	09	11	13
100	03	06	08	11	14	17
120	03	07	10	13	17	20
140	04	08	12	16	19	23
160	04	09	13	18	22	27
180	05	10	15	20	25	30

Figure 2321. *Air Almanac,* Table F4 for interpolating time of moonrise and moonset (extract).

interpolation, is applied with the sign indicated. This correction cannot be made in extreme conditions, when a symbol (*) is shown in the Diff. column.

Example: Find the ZT of moonset at latitude 41°12' N, longitude 15°17' W using the *Air Almanac* (figures 2311b and 2321).

Solution. Using the exact date and interpolating for latitude, the time is found to be 0830 and the difference 34 minutes. Using the nearest Table F4 arguments, Long. 20°, difference 30^m, a correction of 3^m is found. As the difference is positive and the longitude is west, the correction is additive; the LMT is 0830 + 3 = 0833. The ZT is 0833 + 1 (for longitude 17' west of central meridian) = 0834.

Answer: ZT of moonset is 0834.

Note that this differs from the time found from the *Nautical Almanac* by one minute; the difference is of no practical significance.

The moon appears to make a revolution about the earth in a period averaging 24h 50m; that is to say that moonrise and moonset occur, *on the average,* about fifty minutes later on successive days. However, any given period may vary considerably from the average, and under certain conditions moonrise may occur twice during a single day, or may not occur at all. If moonrise occurs twice on the same day, both times are tabulated in the *Nautical Almanac* and *Air Almanac;* for example, 0002/2355. If moonrise does not occur before midnight of a day, it may be tabulated for that day, but, for example, as 2413. This means that moonrise at the tabulated latitude will not occur at all on the stated day, but at 0013 on the next day. As discussed in article 1816, the phenomenon can occur earlier on successive days. Considerable care must be exercised in interpolation.

Determining Times of Phenomena for a Moving Vessel

2322   In the preceding articles, the methods of obtaining the times of various phenomena have been considered for a specific fixed position. More typical, however, is the need to determine the time of such event for a moving vessel.

To obtain the required time, first examine the vessel's DR track with respect to the tabulated latitudes and GMT in the *Nautical Almanac.* Select the tabulated latitude nearest the DR position for the approximate time of the phenomenon and note the tabulated GMT. This GMT is treated as ZT—for example, a tabulated GMT 1144 is considered as ZT 1144 and the DR position for this time is determined by plot of calculation. Since LMT for any location and ZT seldom differ by more than 30 minutes, this assumption is sufficiently accurate for the initial DR. Using the latitude and longitude of this position, determine the ZT of the phenomenon as described in the preceding articles; this is termed the *first estimate.*

Next, a revised DR position is determined for the time just found. Then the time of the phenomenon is recalculated for the latitude and longitude of the revised DR position; this is the *second estimate.*

Ordinarily, this second estimate will give an acceptably accurate time for the phenomenon. If, however, the two DR positions should prove to differ considerably in longitude, a new determination of the first estimate should be made.

Usually at sea, the maximum obtainable precision is required only for the time of sunrise and sunset; ordinarily, 2 or 3 minutes leeway are permissible in predicting the times of other phenomena. The "Tables for Interpolating Sunrise, Moonrise, Etc." in the back of the *Nautical Almanac* are used, and longitude to the nearest 15′ may be used in converting to time, i.e., to the nearest minute.

Sunset Calculation for a Moving Vessel

The following example illustrates the procedures discussed above.

Example: On 5 June 1977, the 1600 DR position of a ship is Lat. 33°23.3′ N, Long. 65°19.4′ W. The vessel is on course 255°, speed 20 knots.

Required: The ZT of sunset to the nearest whole number, using the *Nautical Almanac* (Figure 2304b).

Solution: (Figure 2322a). By examination of the DR plot and the almanac, the navigator notes that in the band of latitude between 30° N and 35° N, sunset will occur at some time after 1858. At that time, the tabulated latitude nearest to his DR is 35° N. He notes that for this latitude sunset occurs at 1910; he also notes that for latitude 30° N, sunset occurs at 1858, or 12 minutes earlier.

He next plots his expected DR position for 1910; this turns out to be Lat. 33°06.9′ N, Long. 66°32.6′ W.

Using this DR position, he computes the time of sunset by entering the table on the daily page for latitude 30° and extracting the time of 1858. The latitude correction from Table I is $+8^m$ and the correction for difference in longitude between the DR and the central meridian of the time zone is +26 minutes (dLo of 6°32.6′). Adding 1858 + 8 + 26 results in a ZT of 1932 as the *first estimate.*

He plots the 1932 DR position, finding it to be Lat. 33°05.0′ N, Long 66°41.0′ W; now the difference in longitude from the central meridian (computed to the nearest 15′ of arc) is 6°45′, resulting in a recomputed value for dLo correction of +27 minutes. The ZT is adjusted for this additional minute and 1933 is the *second estimate.*

Answer: ZT of sunset is 1933.

	Sunset
N 30°	1858
N 35°	1910
Diff for 5°	+ 12
Table I Lat. Corr.	+ 8
LMT = 1858 + 8 =	1906
dLo Corr.	+ 26
ZT	1932 1st Est.
LMT	1906
dLo Corr.	+ 27
ZT	1933 2nd Est.

Problems involving the times of sunrise, moonrise, moonset, and twilight for a moving ship are solved in a similar manner.

Moonrise Calculation for a Moving Vessel

Moonrise or moonset would be determined on board ship by combining the method set forth in article 2321 with the above. The following example illustrates the solution.

Example: (Figure 2322b). On the evening of 5 June, a ship's 2000 DR position is latitude

Figure 2322a. Plot for determination of ZT of sunset for a moving vessel.

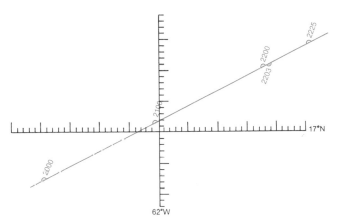

Figure 2322b. Plot for determination of ZT of moonrise for a moving vessel.

16°52.6′ N, longitude 62°19.4′ W. The course is 063°, speed 20 knots.

Required: The ZT of moonrise on the night of 5–6 June, using the *Nautical Almanac* (figures 2304b and 2319b).

Solution: An inspection of the moonrise tables for 5 and 6 June, latitudes 10° N and 20° N, shows that the time of moonrise will be approximately 2230, 5 June. For latitude 10° N and longitude 0°, the time of moonrise will be 2203. The DR position for this time is plotted and found to be latitude 17°11.2′ N, longitude 61°41.2′ W. Next the time of moonrise for this position is calculated as the first estimate; this is 2225. The ship's DR position for the time of the first estimate is plotted and found to be latitude 17°14.5′ N, longitude 61°34.4′ W. The time of moonrise is recalculated for this revised DR position during the same procedures as in obtaining the first estimate; this gives the second estimate of moonrise, 2224.

Moonrise

Calculations of first estimate: Lat. 17°11.2′ N, Long. 61°41.2′ W

20° N	2213 5 June
10° N	2203
Diff for 10°	+ 10
Table I Lat. Corr.	+ 7
2203 + 7 =	2210 LMT, Long. 0°

20° N	2259 6 June
10° N	2252
Diff for 10°	+ 7
Table I Lat. Corr.	+ 5
2252 + 5 =	2257 LMT, Long. 0°
	2210
	+ 47

LMT (Long. 0°)	2210 5 June
Table II Long. Corr.	+ 8
LMT (Ship)	2218
DLo (1°41.2′ W)	+ 7
ZT	2225 1st Estimate

Calculation for second estimate: Lat. 17°14.5′ N, Long. 61°34.4′ W

10° N	2203 5 June
Table I Lat. Corr.	+ 7
	2210 LMT, Long. 0°

10° N	2252 6 June
Table I Lat. Corr.	+ 5
	2257 LMT, Long. 0°
	2210
	+ 47

LMT (Long. 0°)	2210 5 June
Table II Long. Corr.	+ 8
LMT (Ship)	2218
DLo (1°34.4′ W)	+ 6
ZT	2224 2nd Estimate

Times by Calculator or Computer

2323 The calculations shown above in articles 2317–2322 can also be done by using programs for a calculator or microcomputer. In most cases these programs are for the determination of the time of the phenomenon at a fixed location; it is possible, however, to extend the program to include the calculations necessary for determining the time for an observer on a moving vessel.

Chapter 24

Sight Reduction Methods

Introduction

2401 Once an observation of an identified celestial body has been made with a sextant at a precise and accurate time, and the proper corrections made from tabulated data in an almanac, the problem still remains of the conversion of this information to a line of position. This is termed *sight reduction*, and there is a wide variety of methods by which it can be accomplished.

This chapter will continue the step-by-step progression toward a complete celestial navigation solution by considering the more widely used methods of sight reduction, computational and tabular. These include use of the tables of DMAHTC Pub. No. 229, the tables of Pub. No. 249, and the Ageton Method tables now in Pub. No. 9 (*Bowditch*, Volume II), as Table 35 (formerly published separately as H.O. 211). Examples of the use of these publications will be given in this chapter, with complete sight reductions in chapters 26 and 27.

Other, less-used methods of sight reduction are briefly discussed in chapters XX and XXI of *Bowditch*, Volume I (1977 or 1984).

Early Methods

2402 The most widely used sight reduction method in the last century was the *time sight*. A latitude line was obtained by means of an observation of Polaris, or the transit of the sun or of some other body. This latitude line was advanced to the time of an observation of a body located well to the east or west of the observer; the body most frequently used was the sun. With this assumed latitude, a longitude was calculated, originally in time, which gave the time sight its name. The accuracy of the time sight obviously depended on the accuracy of the assumed latitude.

Sine-cosine Equations

The time-sight method remained popular with the merchant service up to World War II. The U.S. Navy was quick to see the advantages of the altitude intercept method of solution conceived by Marcq St.-Hilaire in 1875. For sight reduction by this method, the "cosine-haversine" equations were used for computed altitude and azimuth. These were derived from the classic equations:

$$\sin H = \sin L \sin d \pm \cos L \cos d \cos t \qquad (1)$$

$$\sin Z = \frac{\cos d \sin t}{\cos H} \qquad (2)$$

where H is computed altitude
$\quad L$ is latitude
$\quad d$ is declination
$\quad t$ is meridian angle
$\quad Z$ is azimuth angle

Note: In equation (1), the rules for naming the sign ($\pm$) may be stated as follows:

1. If t is less than 90°:
   a. and L and d have the same name, the sign is +, and the quantities are added;
   b. and L and d have opposite names, the sign is $\sim$, and the lesser quantity is subtracted from the greater.
2. If t is greater than 90°:
   a. and L and d have the same name, the sign is $\sim$, and the lesser quantity is subtracted from the greater;
   b. and L and d have opposite names, the sign is +, and the quantities are added.

These equations are used today when accuracy in reduction is paramount, and many of the "short methods" currently in use are based on them. They, or equations derived from them, are also used for the development of procedures and programs for sight reduction using computers or electronic calculators (Appendix F).

"Short" Methods

The cosine-haversine method remained in general use in the U.S. Navy until about 50 years ago, when Ogura in Japan developed a more convenient solution. This led to the production of other simplified methods, both in this country and abroad. These became known as the "short methods," and included among the American volumes, in the order of their development, the Weems *Line of Position* Book, H.O. 208 by Dreisenstok, and H.O. 211 by Ageton. These methods are still used by some navigators; the H.O. publications are no longer in print, although both the Dreisenstok and Ageton tables are available commercially, and the Ageton tables have been incorporated into the 1975/1981 edition of *Bowditch*, Volume II. A more recent development has been the development of condensed, or "compact," Ageton tables well-suited for small-craft and lifeboat use. The only mathematical skill these demand of the user is the ability to add, subtract, and to interpolate between numbers in a column. They are convenient, in that one small volume permits solution for any latitude, any declination, and any altitude. However, they have now been largely superseded for general use by the "inspection tables," the first of which was H.O. 214, now replaced by more modern tables.

Inspection Tables

2403 Modern sight reduction tables are of the inspection type. They are so called because altitude and azimuth are extracted for a given latitude, meridian angle, and declination by inspection, and no calculation is required (except for some interpolation). These tables are much larger and heavier than the Dreisenstok and Ageton tables, as they consist of vast numbers of precomputed solutions.

Sight Reduction Tables for Marine Navigation, DMAHTC Pub. No. 229, is now the primary inspection method used by surface navigators of the U.S. Navy, Coast Guard, Merchant Marine, and private yachts. *Sight Reduction Tables for Air Navigation*, Pub. No. 249, is the primary method for air navigation and is also popular with some marine navigators. These tables, and the Ageton tables, will be discussed in the articles that follow.

Reduction by Pub. No. 229

2404 The set of tables, entitled *Sight Reduction Tables for Marine Navigation*, are generally referred to as "Pub. 229" (and sometimes by their former number, "H.O. 229"). They are inspection tables of precomputed altitudes and azimuths. This publication is a joint U.S.-British project involving the U.S. Naval Oceanographic Office, the U.S. Naval Observatory, and the Royal Greenwich Observatory; volumes with identical tabular contents are published separately in England.

The Pub. No. 229 tables are published in six volumes, arranged by latitude. Each volume contains data for a 16° band of latitude, north or south, with an overlap of 1° between volumes; for example, latitude 30° appears in both Volumes 2 and 3. In each volume, the latitudes are separated into two non-overlapping "zones" as shown below.

Vol. No.	*First zone of latitude*	*Second zone of latitude*
1	0°–7°	8°–15°
2	15°–22°	23°–30°
3	30°–37°	38°–45°
4	45°–52°	53°–60°
5	60°–67°	68°–75°
6	75°–82°	83°–90°

Use of Assumed Positions

Pub. No. 229 is primarily intended to be used with an *assumed position (AP)*. The latitude of this position is the integral degree *nearest* the vessel's DR or EP latitude; its longitude is artificially selected to give a whole degree of *local hour angle* within 30' of the vessels DR or EP longitude. This procedure is used to fit the format of the tables that present all combinations of latitude, local hour angle (measured westward from the observer's celestial meridian through 360°), and declination at uniform whole degree intervals of each argument. It may, however, also be used for reduction from a DR position, and directions for such procedure are given in each volume.

Pub. No. 229 is designed to provide computed altitudes (Hc) correct to the nearest 0.1' when all corrections are employed, and azimuth angle to 0.1°. Among today's tables it is unique, in that it offers both the maximum degree of precision required by the navigator and also permits the reduction of an observation of *any* navigational body, at *any* altitude, including those of negative value;

there are no limitations of latitude, hour angle, or declination.

Entering Arguments

The primary entering argument (page selection) within each zone of latitude is the *local hour angle;* it is prominently displayed at the top and bottom of each page. The argument heading each column is *latitude,* and the argument for rows is *declination.* For each value of the local hour angle, LHA, in the range 0° to 90° or 270° to 360° (corresponding to t less than 90°), there are two facing pages, which contain the tabulations for declination of 0° to 90° and for 8° of latitude.

Note that the entering arguments (Lat., LHA, and Dec.) are *not* designated as north or south, east or west. The reason for this is illustrated in figure 2404a, where four navigational triangles are shown on the surface of the earth. In each of the four triangles, the AP is at the same latitude north or south of the equator. If the numerical value of the latitude of the AP is assumed to be 33°, then the side between the AP and the pole in *each* triangle, the colatitude, is equal to an arc of 57°. Similarly, the GP in each triangle is at the same latitude, 14° (on the same side of the equator as the AP), making the polar distance in each triangle equal to 76°. Further, the four triangles illustrated are constructed so that the angular distance from the meridian of the AP to the meridian of the GP is equal in each case, making the numerical value of meridian angle, t, the same in all triangles. With the two sides and the included angle of all triangles being numerically equal, the values of computed altitude and azimuth angle obtained by solving each triangle will be numerically equal. Using Lat. = 33°,

LHA = 34°, and Dec. = 14°, the numerical value of Hc (53°44.7') and Z (113.4°) can be obtained from the tabular extract of figure 2404b.

The fact that four triangles can be solved by using one set of entering arguments makes it possible to save considerable space in an inspection table. In figure 2404a note that in each of the four triangles the AP and the GP are on the same side of the equator—both north or both south. In these cases, the latitude and declination are said to have the *same name.* A *second set* of four triangles might be drawn so that in each triangle the AP is on one side of the equator, and the GP is on the other side. If the values of L, Dec., and t are numerically equal for each triangle, the resulting values of Hc and Z will also be numerically the same for all four triangles, and the solution of all four triangles can be achieved using one set of triangles, as before. For this second set of triangles, the latitude and declination are said to have *contrary names,* since they lie on opposite sides of the equator. Since each of the solutions obtained from the tables can apply to any of four triangles, the names north and south (for latitude and declination) or east and west (for meridian angle) are omitted in the tabulation, and must be applied by the navigator as appropriate for the particular triangle being solved. Solutions are provided for both sets of triangles by means of the tables being divided into two parts, *"Latitude Same Name as Declination"* and *"Latitude Contrary Name to Declination."*

Determining Intercept and True Azimuth

To determine the intercept, (a), for plotting the resulting lines of position, Hc is used in each case as obtained from the tables, but azimuth angle, Z, is converted to true azimuth, Zn, which differs for each triangle, since the true direction of the GP from the AP is different in each case. Referring to figure 2404a, the Z in the first triangle is N and E, Zn therefore equals Z. In the second, the Z is S and E; Zn therefore equals 180° − Z. In the third, Z is S and W and Zn equals 180° + Z. In the fourth triangle Z is N and W; Zn therefore equals 360° − Z. When Zn and (a) are determined, the lines of position can be plotted using the methods described in chapter 25.

For each opening of the tables of Pub. No. 229 the left-hand page is always limited to tabulations for declination and latitude of the same name. On the upper portion of the right-hand page are stated the tabulations for declination and latitude of contrary name; in the lower portions of these right-hand pages are given tabulations for the supplementary

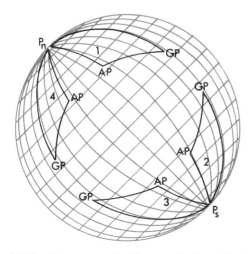

Figure 2404a. Four numerically equal celestial triangles.

34°, 326° L.H.A.   LATITUDE SAME NAME AS DECLINATION

N. Lat. { L.H.A. greater than 180°......Zn=Z / L.H.A. less than 180°......Zn=360°−Z }

Dec.	30° Hc	d	Z	31° Hc	d	Z	32° Hc	d	Z	33° Hc	d	Z	34° Hc	d	Z	35° Hc	d	Z	36° Hc	d	Z	37° Hc	d	Z	Dec.
0	45 53.2	+42.8	126.5	45 17.1	+43.7	127.4	44 40.4	+44.5	128.2	44 03.0	+45.3	128.9	43 25.0	+46.0	129.7	42 46.4	+46.7	130.4	42 07.3	+47.4	131.1	41 27.6	+48.0	131.7	0
1	46 36.0	42.3	125.5	46 00.8	43.2	126.4	45 24.9	44.0	127.2	44 48.3	44.8	128.0	44 11.0	45.6	128.8	43 33.1	46.3	129.5	42 54.7	47.0	130.2	42 15.6	47.7	130.9	1
2	47 18.3	41.7	124.5	46 44.0	42.6	125.4	46 08.9	43.4	126.2	45 33.1	44.3	127.1	44 56.6	45.1	127.9	44 19.4	45.9	128.6	43 41.7	46.6	129.4	43 03.3	47.3	130.1	2
3	48 00.0	41.1	123.4	47 26.6	42.0	124.3	46 52.3	43.0	125.2	46 17.4	43.8	126.1	45 41.7	44.6	126.9	45 05.3	45.4	127.7	44 28.3	46.2	128.5	43 50.6	46.9	129.3	3
4	48 41.1	40.5	122.3	48 08.6	41.5	123.3	47 35.3	42.4	124.2	47 01.2	43.3	125.1	46 26.3	44.2	126.0	45 50.7	45.0	126.8	45 14.5	45.7	127.6	44 37.5	46.5	128.4	4
5	49 21.6	+39.8	121.2	48 50.1	+40.8	122.2	48 17.7	+41.7	123.1	47 44.5	+42.7	124.1	47 10.5	+43.6	125.0	46 35.7	+44.5	125.8	46 00.2	+45.3	126.7	45 24.0	+46.1	127.5	5
6	50 01.4	39.2	120.0	49 30.9	40.1	121.1	48 59.4	41.2	122.1	48 27.2	42.1	123.0	47 54.1	43.0	123.9	47 20.2	43.9	124.9	46 45.5	44.8	125.7	46 10.1	45.6	126.6	6
7	50 40.4	38.4	118.9	50 11.0	39.4	119.9	49 40.6	40.5	120.9	49 09.3	41.5	121.9	48 37.1	42.5	122.9	48 04.1	43.4	123.8	47 30.3	44.3	124.8	46 55.7	45.2	125.6	7
8	51 18.8	37.5	117.6	50 50.4	38.7	118.7	50 21.1	39.8	119.8	49 50.8	40.8	120.9	49 19.6	41.9	121.8	48 47.5	42.9	122.8	48 14.6	43.8	123.7	47 40.9	44.6	124.7	8
9	51 56.3	36.7	116.4	51 29.1	37.9	117.5	51 00.9	39.0	118.6	50 31.6	40.2	119.7	50 01.5	41.2	120.7	49 30.4	42.2	121.7	48 58.4	43.2	122.7	48 25.5	44.1	123.7	9
10	52 33.0	+35.8	115.1	52 07.0	+37.1	116.3	51 39.9	+38.3	117.4	51 11.8	+39.4	118.5	50 42.7	+40.5	119.6	50 12.6	+41.6	120.6	49 41.6	+42.5	121.6	49 09.6	+43.6	122.6	10
11	53 08.8	35.0	113.8	52 44.1	36.2	115.0	52 18.2	37.5	116.1	51 51.2	38.7	117.3	51 23.2	39.8	118.4	50 54.2	40.8	119.5	50 24.1	42.0	120.5	49 53.2	42.9	121.6	11
12	53 43.8	34.0	112.4	53 20.3	35.3	113.6	52 55.7	36.6	114.9	52 29.9	37.8	116.0	52 03.0	39.0	117.2	51 35.0	40.2	118.3	51 06.1	41.2	119.4	50 36.1	42.3	120.5	12
13	54 17.8	33.0	110.8	53 55.6	34.4	112.3	53 32.3	35.7	113.5	53 07.7	37.0	114.8	52 42.0	38.3	116.0	52 15.2	39.4	117.1	51 47.3	40.6	118.3	51 18.4	41.7	119.3	13
14	54 50.7	31.9	109.6	54 30.0	33.4	110.9	54 08.0	34.7	112.2	53 44.7	36.1	113.4	53 20.3	37.3	114.7	52 54.6	38.7	115.9	52 27.9	39.9	117.1	52 00.1	40.9	118.2	14
15	55 22.6	+30.9	108.1	55 03.4	+32.3	109.4	54 42.7	+33.8	110.8	54 20.8	+35.2	112.1	53 57.6	+36.5	113.4	53 33.3	+37.7	114.6	53 07.7	+39.0	115.8	52 41.0	+40.2	117.0	15
16	55 53.5	29.6	106.6	55 35.7	31.2	108.0	55 16.5	32.7	109.3	54 56.0	34.1	110.7	54 34.1	35.6	112.0	54 11.0	36.9	113.3	53 46.7	38.2	114.5	53 21.2	39.4	115.8	16
17	56 23.1	28.5	105.0	56 06.9	30.0	106.4	55 49.2	31.6	107.8	55 30.1	33.1	109.2	55 09.7	34.5	110.6	54 47.9	36.0	111.9	54 24.9	37.3	113.2	54 00.6	38.6	114.5	17
18	56 51.6	27.2	103.4	56 36.9	28.9	104.9	56 20.8	30.5	106.3	56 03.2	32.0	107.8	55 44.2	33.5	109.2	55 23.9	34.9	110.5	55 02.2	36.3	111.9	54 39.2	37.7	113.2	18
19	57 18.8	25.9	101.8	57 05.8	27.6	103.3	56 51.3	29.2	104.8	56 35.2	30.9	106.2	56 17.7	32.5	107.7	55 58.8	34.0	109.1	55 38.5	35.4	110.5	55 16.9	36.7	111.8	19
85	34 06.1	−48.7	3.4	35 06.0	−48.7	3.4	36 05.9	−48.7	3.5	37 05.8	−48.7	3.5	38 05.7	−48.6	3.6	39 05.6	−48.6	3.6	40 05.5	−48.6	3.7	41 05.3	−48.4	3.7	85
86	33 17.4	49.1	2.7	34 17.3	49.0	2.7	35 17.2	48.9	2.7	36 17.1	48.9	2.8	37 17.1	48.9	2.8	38 17.0	48.8	2.9	39 16.9	48.8	2.9	40 16.9	48.8	2.9	86
87	32 28.3	49.2	2.0	33 28.3	49.2	2.0	34 28.3	49.2	2.0	35 28.2	49.2	2.1	36 28.2	49.2	2.1	37 28.1	49.1	2.1	38 28.1	49.1	2.1	39 28.1	49.1	2.2	87
88	31 39.1	49.5	1.3	32 39.1	49.5	1.3	33 39.1	49.5	1.3	34 39.0	49.4	1.4	35 39.0	49.4	1.4	36 39.0	49.4	1.4	37 39.0	49.4	1.4	38 39.0	49.4	1.4	88
89	30 49.6	49.6	0.7	31 49.6	49.6	0.7	32 49.6	49.6	0.7	33 49.6	49.6	0.7	34 49.6	49.6	0.7	35 49.6	49.6	0.7	36 49.6	49.6	0.7	37 49.6	49.6	0.7	89
90	30 00.0	−49.8	0.0	31 00.0	−49.8	0.0	32 00.0	−49.8	0.0	33 00.0	−49.8	0.0	34 00.0	−49.9	0.0	35 00.0	−49.9	0.0	36 00.0	−49.9	0.0	37 00.0	−49.9	0.0	90

34°, 326° L.H.A.   LATITUDE SAME NAME AS DECLINATION

Figure 2404b. Pub. No. 229, typical "same name" page (extract).

LATITUDE CONTRARY NAME TO DECLINATION   L.H.A. 34°, 326°

Dec.	30° Hc	d	Z	31° Hc	d	Z	32° Hc	d	Z	33° Hc	d	Z	34° Hc	d	Z	35° Hc	d	Z	36° Hc	d	Z	37° Hc	d	Z	Dec.
0	45 53.2	−43.3	126.5	45 17.1	44.1	127.4	44 40.4	−44.9	128.2	44 03.0	−45.7	129.0	43 25.0	46.4	129.7	42 46.4	−47.0	130.4	42 07.3	−47.7	131.1	41 27.6	−48.3	131.7	0
1	45 09.9	43.7	127.5	44 33.0	44.7	128.3	43 55.5	45.4	129.1	43 17.3	46.1	129.8	42 38.6	46.7	130.5	41 59.4	47.5	131.2	41 19.6	48.1	131.9	40 39.3	48.7	132.5	1
2	44 26.0	44.3	128.5	43 48.3	45.0	129.3	43 10.1	45.8	130.0	42 31.2	46.4	130.7	41 51.9	47.2	131.4	41 11.9	47.7	132.0	40 31.5	48.4	132.7	39 50.6	48.9	133.3	2
3	43 41.7	44.8	129.4	43 03.3	45.5	130.2	42 24.3	46.2	130.9	41 44.8	46.9	131.6	41 04.7	47.5	132.2	40 24.2	48.1	132.9	39 43.1	48.6	133.4	39 02.1	49.3	134.0	3
4	42 56.9	45.2	130.4	42 17.9	46.0	131.0	41 38.1	46.5	131.7	40 57.9	47.2	132.4	40 17.2	47.8	133.0	39 36.1	48.4	133.6	38 54.5	49.0	134.2	38 12.4	49.5	134.8	4
5	42 11.7	−45.6	131.2	41 31.9	−46.3	131.9	40 51.6	47.0	132.6	40 10.7	−47.5	133.2	39 29.4	−48.1	133.8	38 47.7	−48.7	134.4	38 05.5	−49.2	134.9	37 22.9	−49.7	135.5	5
6	41 26.1	46.0	132.1	40 45.6	46.8	132.8	40 04.6	47.3	133.4	39 23.2	47.9	134.0	38 41.3	48.4	134.6	37 59.0	49.0	135.1	37 16.3	49.5	135.7	36 33.2	50.0	136.2	6
7	40 40.1	46.4	133.0	39 59.0	47.0	133.6	39 17.4	47.6	134.2	38 35.4	48.2	134.8	37 52.9	48.7	135.3	37 10.0	49.2	135.9	36 26.8	49.7	136.4	35 43.2	50.2	136.9	7
8	39 53.7	46.7	133.8	39 12.0	47.3	134.4	38 29.8	47.9	135.1	37 47.2	48.4	135.5	37 04.2	49.0	136.1	36 20.8	49.5	136.6	35 37.1	50.0	137.1	34 53.0	50.5	137.5	8
9	39 07.0	47.0	134.6	38 24.7	47.6	135.2	37 41.9	48.1	135.7	36 58.8	48.7	136.3	36 15.2	49.2	136.8	35 31.3	49.7	137.3	34 47.1	50.2	137.7	34 02.5	50.6	138.2	9
10	38 20.0	−47.4	135.4	37 37.1	−47.9	136.0	36 53.8	−48.5	136.5	36 10.1	−49.0	137.0	35 26.0	−49.4	137.5	34 41.6	−49.9	137.9	33 56.9	−50.4	138.4	33 11.9	−50.8	138.8	10
11	37 32.6	47.6	136.2	36 49.2	48.2	136.7	36 05.3	48.7	137.2	35 21.1	49.2	137.7	34 36.6	49.7	138.2	33 51.7	50.2	138.6	33 06.5	50.6	139.1	32 21.1	51.1	139.5	11
12	36 45.0	48.0	136.9	36 01.0	48.5	137.4	35 16.6	49.0	137.9	34 31.9	49.5	138.4	33 46.9	49.9	138.8	33 01.5	50.3	139.3	32 15.9	50.8	139.7	31 30.0	51.2	140.1	12
13	35 57.0	48.2	137.7	35 12.5	48.7	138.2	34 27.6	49.2	138.6	33 42.4	49.6	139.1	32 57.0	50.2	139.5	32 11.2	50.6	139.9	31 25.1	50.9	140.3	30 38.8	51.3	140.7	13
14	35 08.8	48.4	138.4	34 23.8	49.0	138.9	33 38.4	49.4	139.3	32 52.8	49.9	139.8	32 06.8	50.3	140.2	31 20.6	50.7	140.6	30 34.2	51.2	140.9	29 47.5	51.6	141.3	14
15	34 20.4	−48.8	139.1	33 34.8	−49.2	139.6	32 49.0	−49.6	140.0	32 02.9	−50.1	140.4	31 16.5	−50.5	140.8	30 29.9	−50.9	141.2	29 43.0	−51.3	141.5	28 55.9	−51.6	141.9	15
16	33 31.6	48.9	139.8	32 45.6	49.4	140.3	31 59.4	49.7	140.7	31 12.8	50.2	141.1	30 26.0	50.6	141.4	29 39.0	51.1	141.8	28 51.7	51.4	142.1	28 04.3	51.8	142.5	16
17	32 42.7	49.2	140.5	31 56.2	49.6	140.9	31 09.5	50.0	141.3	30 22.6	50.5	141.7	29 35.4	50.9	142.1	28 47.9	51.2	142.4	28 00.3	51.6	142.7	27 12.5	52.0	143.0	17
18	31 53.5	49.4	141.2	31 06.6	49.8	141.6	30 19.5	50.2	142.0	29 32.1	50.6	142.3	28 44.5	51.0	142.7	27 56.7	51.4	143.0	27 08.7	51.7	143.3	26 20.5	52.1	143.6	18
19	31 04.1	49.6	141.9	30 16.8	50.0	142.2	29 29.3	50.4	142.6	28 41.5	50.8	142.9	27 53.5	51.2	143.3	27 05.3	51.5	143.6	26 17.0	51.9	143.9	25 28.4	52.2	144.2	19
85	25 49.1	+50.5	3.1	26 49.0	+50.6	3.1	27 48.9	+50.6	3.2	28 48.8	+50.6	3.2	29 48.7	+50.7	3.2	30 48.7	+50.6	3.3	31 48.6	+50.7	3.3	32 48.5	+50.7	3.3	85
86	26 39.6	50.4	2.5	27 39.6	50.3	2.5	28 39.5	50.4	2.5	29 39.4	50.5	2.6	30 39.4	50.4	2.6	31 39.3	50.5	2.6	32 39.3	50.5	2.7	33 39.2	50.5	2.7	86
87	27 30.0	50.1	1.9	28 29.9	50.2	1.9	29 29.9	50.2	1.9	30 29.9	50.2	1.9	31 29.8	50.2	2.0	32 29.8	50.3	2.0	33 29.8	50.3	2.0	34 29.7	50.3	2.0	87
88	28 20.1	50.1	1.3	29 20.1	50.1	1.3	30 20.1	50.1	1.3	31 20.1	50.1	1.3	32 20.1	50.0	1.3	33 20.1	50.0	1.3	34 20.1	50.0	1.4	35 20.0	50.1	1.4	88
89	29 10.2	49.8	0.6	30 10.2	49.8	0.6	31 10.2	49.8	0.7	32 10.2	49.8	0.7	33 10.1	49.9	0.7	34 10.1	49.9	0.7	35 10.1	49.9	0.7	36 10.1	49.9	0.7	89
90	30 00.0	+49.6	0.0	31 00.0	+49.6	0.0	32 00.0	+49.6	0.0	33 00.0	+49.6	0.0	34 00.0	+49.6	0.0	35 00.0	+49.6	0.0	36 00.0	+49.6	0.0	37 00.0	+49.6	0.0	90

S. Lat. { L.H.A. greater than 180°......Zn=180°−Z / L.H.A. less than 180°......Zn=180°+Z }   LATITUDE SAME NAME AS DECLINATION   L.H.A. 146°, 214°

Figure 2404c. Pub. No. 229, typical "contrary name" page (extract).

values of LHA, those larger than 90° but less than 270° (t greater than 90°), for declinations of the same name as latitude. The upper and lower sections of each right-hand page are separated by horizontal lines in each column of data; these are known as the *Contrary-Same Lines*, or C-S Lines, and indicate the degree of declination in which the celestial horizon occurs (where the altitude reaches zero). Portions of a left- and right-hand page are shown as figures 2404b and 2404c, respectively.

Assumed Latitude and Longitude

As noted before, the user selects for the assumed latitude (aL), the whole degree *nearest* his DR or estimated position. The user then selects an assumed longitude (aλ) which, when applied to the GHA of the body being observed, will yield a *whole degree* of LHA; *this assumed longitude (aλ) must lie within 30 minutes of arc of the best estimate of the ship's actual longitude at the time of the observation.*

It is obvious that when a number of celestial bodies are observed at about the same time, as in a round of star sights, a different longitude will have to be assumed for each body. In most cases, all the assumed positions will lie along the same assumed parallel of latitude. (The exception occurs when a ship approaches nearer to an adjoining whole degree while observations are being made.) The longitudes assumed should all fall within about 60 minutes of one another, except in higher latitudes when the vessel's course and speed result in a rapid change of longitude, and the period required to obtain the observations is rather protracted.

Columnar Arrangement of Pub. No. 229

To use the tables, the volume that includes the assumed latitude is selected, and the two pages listing the required LHA are found within the appropriate latitude zone of this volume. The appropriate page is then selected for a declination having the same or the contrary name as the latitude. On this page, the vertical column headed by the integral degree of assumed latitude is next found. Declination is listed in vertical columns at the outer edge of each page; the integral whole degree of declination numerically *less* in value to the actual declination is located in this column. Horizontally across from this, in the latitude column, three sets of numerical values are tabulated. The first, under the sub-heading "Hc," is the calculated altitude stated to the nearest 0.1'; in the next column, sub-headed "d" in smaller type, is the actual difference, with sign, to the tabulated altitude for the next higher degree of declination. The third column, subheaded "Z," tabulates the azimuth angle to the nearest 0.1°. Rules are given on each pair of pages for the conversion of Z to Zn.

Interpolation

Interpolation tables, found on four pages inside the front and back covers of each volume, are provided to permit correcting the tabulated altitude for the first difference, d, between the actual declination, and the integral degree of declination used

as an entering argument. The interpolation tables are also designed to permit, where required, correction for the effect of a second difference; this allows full precision to be obtained in the calculated altitude. The linear interpolation tables are sufficiently accurate for altitudes below 60°, and a second difference correction is not required. Above 60°, however, the accuracy of linear interpolation decreases, and a second difference correction will be necessary for some, but not all, reductions. The technique used is termed *double-second difference* and the corrections are listed in the form of tables of critical values at the right side of each block of figures on the pages of the Interpolation Table. In those cases in which second differences are significant, where omission of the correction for second difference might cause an error in excess of 0.25' in the calculated altitude, the value of d is printed in italics, and is followed by a dot (see figure 2404e).

Interpolation Tables

Portions of the interpolation tables are shown in figure 2404d. The main argument in entering these tables is the excess of the actual declination over the integral degree of declination used to enter the main body of the tables. This difference is tabulated in the vertical column at the left-hand edge of each table, under the heading "Dec. Inc." The other argument is the tabulated altitude difference d, which for convenience is divided into two parts, the first being a multiple of 10' (10', 20', 30', 40', or 50'), and the second the remainder in the range 0.0' to 9.9' by tenths of minutes. This interpolation table is a great convenience to the navigator. Its use may occasionally lead to a small error in the Hc not exceeding 0.1'; such error is acceptable in the course of ordinary navigation.

First Difference Correction

The major portion of the correction to convert the tabulated altitude to the calculated altitude is called the *first difference correction*. It is obtained as the sum of two quantities:

The tabulated value corresponding to the Dec. Inc., and the tens of minutes of the altitude difference d, and

The tabulated value corresponding to the Dec. Inc., and the remainder of d in units and tenths. The units are to the right of the tens; note that the decimals here are a vertical argument.

The sum of these two quantities is applied to the tabulated altitude with the sign as shown in the d column of the main tables.

INTERPOLATION TABLE

Left half

Dec. Inc.	10'	20'	Tens 30'	40'	50'		0'	1'	2'	3'	Units 4'	5'	6'	7'	8'	9'	Double Second Diff. and Corr.
28.0	4.6	9.3	14.0	18.6	23.3	.0	0.0	0.5	0.9	1.4	1.9	2.4	2.8	3.3	3.8	4.3	0.8
28.1	4.7	9.3	14.0	18.7	23.4	.1	0.0	0.5	1.0	1.5	1.9	2.4	2.9	3.4	3.8	4.3	2.4 / 0.1
28.2	4.7	9.4	14.1	18.8	23.5	.2	0.1	0.6	1.0	1.5	2.0	2.5	2.9	3.4	3.9	4.4	4.0 / 0.2
28.3	4.7	9.4	14.1	18.9	23.6	.3	0.1	0.6	1.1	1.6	2.0	2.5	3.0	3.5	3.9	4.4	5.6 / 0.3
28.4	4.7	9.5	14.2	18.9	23.7	.4	0.2	0.7	1.1	1.6	2.1	2.6	3.0	3.5	4.0	4.5	7.2 / 0.4 ; 8.8 / 0.5
28.5	4.8	9.5	14.3	19.0	23.8	.5	0.2	0.7	1.2	1.7	2.1	2.6	3.1	3.6	4.0	4.5	10.4 / 0.6
28.6	4.8	9.5	14.3	19.1	23.8	.6	0.3	0.8	1.2	1.7	2.2	2.7	3.1	3.6	4.1	4.6	12.0 / 0.7
28.7	4.8	9.6	14.4	19.2	23.9	.7	0.3	0.8	1.3	1.8	2.2	2.7	3.2	3.7	4.1	4.6	13.6 / 0.8
28.8	4.8	9.6	14.4	19.2	24.0	.8	0.4	0.9	1.3	1.8	2.3	2.8	3.2	3.7	4.2	4.7	15.2 / 0.9
28.9	4.9	9.7	14.5	19.3	24.1	.9	0.4	0.9	1.4	1.9	2.3	2.8	3.3	3.8	4.2	4.7	16.8 / 1.0
34.0	5.6	11.3	17.0	22.6	28.3	.0	0.0	0.6	1.1	1.7	2.3	2.9	3.4	4.0	4.6	5.2	0.8
34.1	5.7	11.3	17.0	22.7	28.4	.1	0.1	0.6	1.2	1.8	2.4	2.9	3.5	4.1	4.7	5.3	2.5 / 0.1
34.2	5.7	11.4	17.1	22.8	28.5	.2	0.1	0.7	1.3	1.8	2.4	3.0	3.6	4.1	4.7	5.3	4.1 / 0.2
34.3	5.7	11.4	17.1	22.9	28.6	.3	0.2	0.7	1.3	1.9	2.5	3.0	3.6	4.2	4.8	5.4	5.8 / 0.3
34.4	5.7	11.5	17.2	22.9	28.7	.4	0.2	0.8	1.4	2.0	2.5	3.1	3.7	4.3	4.8	5.4	7.4 / 0.4 ; 9.1 / 0.5
34.5	5.8	11.5	17.3	23.0	28.8	.5	0.3	0.9	1.4	2.0	2.6	3.2	3.7	4.3	4.9	5.5	10.7 / 0.6
34.6	5.8	11.5	17.3	23.1	28.8	.6	0.3	0.9	1.5	2.1	2.6	3.2	3.8	4.4	4.9	5.5	12.3 / 0.7
34.7	5.8	11.6	17.4	23.2	28.9	.7	0.4	1.0	1.6	2.1	2.7	3.3	3.9	4.5	5.0	5.6	14.0 / 0.8
34.8	5.8	11.6	17.4	23.2	29.0	.8	0.5	1.0	1.6	2.2	2.8	3.3	3.9	4.5	5.1	5.6	15.6 / 0.9
34.9	5.9	11.7	17.5	23.3	29.1	.9	0.5	1.1	1.7	2.2	2.8	3.4	4.0	4.5	5.1	5.7	17.3 / 1.0
35.0	5.8	11.6	17.5	23.3	29.1	.0	0.0	0.6	1.1	1.7	2.3	2.9	3.4	4.1	4.7	5.3	18.9 / 1.1
35.1	5.8	11.7	17.5	23.4	29.2	.1	0.1	0.7	1.2	1.8	2.4	3.0	3.6	4.2	4.8	5.4	20.6 / 1.2
35.2	5.8	11.7	17.6	23.4	29.3	.2	0.1	0.7	1.3	1.9	2.5	3.1	3.7	4.3	4.9	5.5	22.2 / 1.3
35.3	5.9	11.8	17.6	23.5	29.4	.3	0.2	0.8	1.4	2.0	2.6	3.2	3.8	4.4	5.0	5.6	23.9 / 1.4
35.4	5.9	11.8	17.7	23.6	29.5	.4	0.2	0.8	1.4	2.0	2.6	3.2	3.8	4.4	5.0	5.6	25.5 / 1.5
35.5	5.9	11.8	17.8	23.7	29.6	.5	0.3	0.9	1.5	2.1	2.7	3.3	3.8	4.4	5.0	5.6	27.2 / 1.6
35.6	5.9	11.9	17.8	23.7	29.7	.6	0.4	0.9	1.5	2.1	2.7	3.3	3.9	4.5	5.1	5.7	28.8 / 1.7
35.7	6.0	11.9	17.9	23.8	29.8	.7	0.4	1.0	1.6	2.2	2.8	3.4	4.0	4.6	5.2	5.8	30.4 / 1.8
35.8	6.0	12.0	17.9	23.9	29.9	.8	0.5	1.1	1.7	2.2	2.8	3.4	4.0	4.6	5.2	5.8	32.1 / 1.9 ; 33.7 / 2.0
35.9	6.0	12.0	18.0	24.0	30.0	.9	0.5	1.1	1.7	2.3	2.9	3.5	4.1	4.7	5.3	5.9	35.4

Right half

Dec. Inc.	10'	20'	Tens 30'	40'	50'		0'	1'	2'	3'	Units 4'	5'	6'	7'	8'	9'	Double Second Diff. and Corr.
36.0	6.0	12.0	18.0	24.0	30.0	.0	0.0	0.6	1.2	1.8	2.4	3.0	3.6	4.3	4.9	5.5	0.8
36.1	6.0	12.0	18.0	24.0	30.1	.1	0.1	0.7	1.3	1.9	2.5	3.1	3.7	4.3	4.9	5.5	2.5 / 0.1
36.2	6.0	12.0	18.1	24.1	30.1	.2	0.1	0.7	1.3	1.9	2.6	3.2	3.8	4.4	5.0	5.6	4.2 / 0.2
36.3	6.0	12.1	18.1	24.2	30.2	.3	0.2	0.8	1.4	2.0	2.6	3.2	3.8	4.4	5.0	5.7	5.9 / 0.3
36.4	6.1	12.1	18.2	24.3	30.3	.4	0.2	0.9	1.5	2.1	2.7	3.3	3.9	4.5	5.1	5.7	7.6 / 0.4 ; 9.3 / 0.5
36.5	6.1	12.2	18.3	24.3	30.4	.5	0.3	0.9	1.5	2.1	2.8	3.4	4.0	4.6	5.2	5.8	11.0 / 0.6
36.6	6.1	12.2	18.3	24.4	30.5	.6	0.4	1.0	1.6	2.2	2.8	3.4	4.0	4.6	5.2	5.8	12.7 / 0.7
36.7	6.1	12.3	18.4	24.5	30.6	.7	0.4	1.0	1.7	2.3	2.9	3.5	4.1	4.7	5.3	5.9	14.4 / 0.8
36.8	6.2	12.3	18.4	24.6	30.7	.8	0.5	1.1	1.7	2.3	2.9	3.5	4.1	4.7	5.4	6.0	16.1 / 0.9
36.9	6.2	12.3	18.5	24.6	30.8	.9	0.5	1.2	1.8	2.4	3.0	3.6	4.2	4.8	5.4	6.0	17.8 / 1.0
42.0	7.0	14.0	21.0	28.0	35.0	.0	0.0	0.7	1.4	2.1	2.8	3.5	4.2	5.0	5.7	6.4	1.0
42.1	7.0	14.0	21.0	28.0	35.1	.1	0.1	0.7	1.5	2.2	2.9	3.6	4.3	5.0	5.7	6.4	3.0 / 0.1
42.2	7.0	14.0	21.1	28.1	35.1	.2	0.1	0.8	1.6	2.3	3.0	3.7	4.4	5.1	5.8	6.5	4.9 / 0.2
42.3	7.0	14.1	21.1	28.2	35.2	.3	0.2	0.9	1.6	2.3	3.0	3.8	4.5	5.2	5.9	6.6	6.9 / 0.3
42.4	7.1	14.1	21.2	28.3	35.3	.4	0.3	1.0	1.7	2.4	3.1	3.8	4.5	5.2	5.9	6.7	8.9 / 0.4
42.5	7.1	14.2	21.3	28.3	35.4	.5	0.4	1.1	1.8	2.5	3.2	3.9	4.6	5.3	6.0	6.7	10.8 / 0.5
42.6	7.1	14.2	21.3	28.4	35.5	.6	0.4	1.1	1.8	2.5	3.3	4.0	4.7	5.4	6.1	6.8	12.8 / 0.6
42.7	7.1	14.3	21.4	28.5	35.6	.7	0.5	1.2	1.9	2.6	3.3	4.0	4.7	5.5	6.2	6.9	14.8 / 0.7
42.8	7.2	14.3	21.4	28.6	35.7	.8	0.6	1.3	2.0	2.7	3.4	4.1	4.8	5.5	6.2	6.9	16.7 / 0.8
42.9	7.2	14.3	21.5	28.6	35.8	.9	0.6	1.3	2.1	2.8	3.5	4.2	4.9	5.6	6.3	7.0	18.7 / 0.9
43.0	7.2	14.3	21.5	28.6	35.8	.0	0.0	0.7	1.4	2.2	2.9	3.6	4.3	5.1	5.8	6.5	20.7 / 1.0
43.1	7.2	14.4	21.6	28.7	35.9	.1	0.1	0.8	1.5	2.2	3.0	3.7	4.4	5.1	5.9	6.6	22.7 / 1.1
43.2	7.2	14.4	21.6	28.8	36.0	.2	0.1	0.9	1.6	2.3	3.0	3.8	4.5	5.2	5.9	6.7	24.6 / 1.2
43.3	7.2	14.4	21.7	28.9	36.1	.3	0.2	0.9	1.7	2.4	3.1	3.8	4.6	5.3	6.0	6.7	26.6 / 1.3
43.4	7.2	14.5	21.7	28.9	36.1	.4	0.3	1.0	1.7	2.5	3.2	3.9	4.6	5.4	6.1	6.8	28.6 / 1.4
43.5	7.3	14.5	21.8	29.0	36.3	.5	0.4	1.1	1.8	2.5	3.3	4.0	4.7	5.4	6.2	6.9	30.5 / 1.5
43.6	7.3	14.5	21.8	29.1	36.3	.6	0.4	1.2	1.9	2.6	3.3	4.1	4.8	5.5	6.3	7.0	32.5 / 1.6
43.7	7.3	14.6	21.9	29.2	36.4	.7	0.5	1.2	2.0	2.7	3.4	4.1	4.9	5.6	6.3	7.0	34.5 / 1.7
43.8	7.3	14.6	21.9	29.2	36.5	.8	0.6	1.3	2.0	2.8	3.5	4.2	4.9	5.7	6.4	7.1	36.4 / 1.8
43.9	7.4	14.7	22.0	29.3	36.6	.9	0.7	1.4	2.1	2.8	3.6	4.3	5.0	5.7	6.5	7.2	

The Double-Second-Difference correction (Corr.) is always to be added to the tabulated altitude.

Figure 2404d. Pub. No. 229, Interpolation Table (extract).

29°, 331° L.H.A.   LATITUDE SAME NAME AS DECLINATION

N. Lat. { L.H.A. greater than 180°...Zn = Z ; L.H.A. less than 180°........Zn = 360° − Z }

Dec.	Hc	75° d	Z	Hc	76° d	Z	Hc	77° d	Z	Hc	78° d	Z	Hc	79° d	Z	Hc	80° d	Z	Hc	81° d	Z	Hc	82° d	Z	Dec.
0	13 05.0	+59.5	150.2	12 12.9	+59.6	150.3	11 20.8	+59.6	150.4	10 28.6	+59.7	150.5	9 36.4	+59.7	150.5	8 44.1	+59.8	150.6	7 51.8	+59.9	150.7	6 59.5	+59.9	150.8	0
1	14 04.5	59.5	150.0	13 12.5	59.6	150.1	12 20.4	59.7	150.2	11 28.3	59.7	150.4	10 36.1	59.8	150.5	9 43.9	59.8	150.5	8 51.7	59.8	150.6	7 59.4	59.8	150.7	1
65	76 11.4	+50.4	120.9	75 39.1	+52.4	124.2	75 04.0	+54.0	127.3	74 26.4	+55.4	130.2	73 46.7	+56.4	132.0	73 04.9	+57.3	135.2	72 21.5	+58.0	137.5	71 36.6	+58.5	139.5	65
66	77 01.8	49.0	118.5	76 31.5	51.2	122.2	75 58.0	53.1	125.6	75 21.8	54.5	128.8	74 43.1	55.9	131.6	74 02.2	57.0	134.2	73 19.5	57.7	136.6	72 35.1	58.4	138.8	66
67	77 50.8	47.8	116.0	77 22.7	49.9	119.9	76 51.1	52.1	123.6	76 16.4	53.9	127.0	75 39.0	55.4	130.2	74 59.2	56.5	133.0	74 17.2	57.5	135.6	73 33.5	58.2	138.0	67
68	78 38.1	45.1	112.8	78 12.6	48.3	117.3	77 43.2	50.9	121.4	77 10.3	53.0	125.1	76 34.4	54.6	128.5	75 55.7	56.0	131.7	75 14.7	57.1	134.5	74 31.7	57.9	137.1	68
69	79 23.2	42.5	109.4	79 00.9	46.2	118.3	78 34.1	49.2	118.8	78 03.3	51.8	122.9	77 29.0	53.8	126.7	76 51.7	55.4	130.1	76 11.8	56.8	133.3	75 29.6	57.6	136.1	69
70	80 05.7	+39.4	105.4	79 47.1	+43.6	110.8	79 23.3	+47.3	115.8	78 55.1	+50.3	120.4	78 22.8	+52.7	124.6	77 47.1	+54.6	128.4	77 08.4	+56.2	131.8	76 27.2	+57.3	134.9	70
71	80 45.1	35.4	100.9	80 30.7	40.5	106.8	80 10.6	44.8	112.3	79 45.4	48.4	117.4	79 15.5	51.4	122.1	78 41.7	53.7	126.4	78 04.6	55.4	130.2	77 24.5	56.8	133.6	71
72	81 20.5	30.6	95.7	81 11.2	36.4	102.1	80 55.4	41.7	108.3	80 33.8	46.0	114.0	80 06.9	49.6	119.2	79 35.4	52.4	124.0	79 00.0	54.6	128.3	78 21.3	56.2	132.1	72
73	81 51.1	24.8	89.8	81 47.6	31.6	96.7	81 37.1	37.6	103.5	81 19.8	42.9	109.9	80 56.5	47.3	115.8	80 27.8	50.8	121.2	79 54.6	53.5	126.0	79 17.5	55.5	130.3	73
74	82 15.9	18.2	83.2	82 19.2	25.6	90.6	82 14.7	32.6	98.0	82 02.7	39.0	105.1	81 43.8	44.3	111.7	81 18.6	48.7	117.8	80 48.1	52.0	123.3	80 13.0	54.6	128.1	74
89	75 52.0	52.0	2.0	76 52.0	52.0	2.1	77 51.9	51.9	2.3	78 51.9	51.9	2.5	79 51.8	51.8	2.8	80 51.7	51.7	3.1	81 51.6	51.6	3.4	82 51.5	51.5	3.9	89
90	75 00.0	−52.9	0.0	76 00.0	−52.9	0.0	77 00.0	−53.0	0.0	78 00.0	−53.0	0.0	79 00.0	−53.1	0.0	80 00.0	−53.1	0.0	81 00.0	−53.2	0.0	82 00.0	−53.3	0.0	90
		75°			76°			77°			78°			79°			80°			81°			82°		

29°, 331° L.H.A.   LATITUDE SAME NAME AS DECLINATION

Figure 2404e. Portion of a page from Pub. No. 229 with entries requiring a double-second difference correction.

Double-second Difference

The minor portion of the correction is for the *double-second difference*, if required. This is the difference between the tabulated altitude differences (d) on the line directly above and the one directly below the value of d extracted from the table for the first difference. To illustrate: using figure 2404e, enter the main tables with L76° N, LHA29°, and Dec.69° N, Latitude Same as Declination. Note that the value of d is 46.2′, and that it is printed in italics, and followed by a dot; the double-second difference correction is therefore important. The value of d, for Dec. 68° (one line above the selected entry) is 48.3′, and for Dec. 70° (one line below) it is 43.6′; the difference of these values is 4.7′.

The interpolation tables also provide a way to find the value of the double-second difference correction; it is obtained from the vertical column at the extreme right, headed "Double Second Diff.

and Corr." This is a critical-value type of table. Enter it with the 4.7' difference found above and obtain the actual value of the correction, 0.3', by noting that 4.7 falls between 4.0 and 5.6. *This correction is always additive.*

The value of the azimuth angle at times changes significantly with each degree of declination. It must, therefore, be corrected by interpolation for the actual value of the declination.

The following example illustrates azimuth interpolation in the use of Pub. No. 229; it is based on the extracts of figures 2404d and 2404e.

The calculated altitude and azimuth are required for an observation of a body having a declination of 69°34.8' N, and a local hour angle of 29°; the assumed latitude is 76° N.

From the tables Latitude Same as Declination for Dec. = 69°, Hc = 79°00.9', with d = 46.2' (in italics and followed by a dot); Z = 114.3°. These must be corrected for the fractional part of declination using figure 2404d.

Tabular Hc	79°00.9'	
First Diff. Corr. (Tens)	+23.2'	(for 40')
First Diff. Corr (Units and Decimals)	+ 3.6'	(for 6.2')
Second Diff. Corr.	+ 0.3'	(previously
Exact. Hc	79°28.0'	calculated)

Z for 69° = 114.3°; Z for 70° = 110.8: difference for 60' = −3.5°.
Tabulated Z = N114.3W

$$-2.0 \quad (-3.5° \times \frac{34.8}{60})$$

Z = N112.3W
Interpolation Zn =   247.7   (360° − Z)

Possible Errors from Use of an AP

2405   Pub. No. 229, when used with an assumed position, offers sight reductions that are mathematically accurate. However, as with any sight reduction methods designed for use with an assumed position, and which tabulate latitude and meridian or hour angle by integral degrees, resulting lines of position may be somewhat in error under certain conditions. These errors tend to arise when the intercepts are long; they are caused by plotting the intercept and the line of position as rhumb lines on the chart, rather than as arcs of a great and small circle, respectively. These errors are not sufficiently large to require consideration in the ordinary practice of navigation at sea.

It has been found that for any given distance between the true and assumed position, the maximum perpendicular distance from the true position to the plotted line of position is roughly proportional to the tangent of the altitude. The error tends to increase with the altitude of the body, and it is roughly proportional to the square of the difference between the true and assumed positions. Other factors being equal, the error decreases as the latitude increases. In the vicinity of the equator, for an altitude of 75° and a true position differing in both latitude and longitude by 30' from the assumed position, the error will not exceed 1.0 miles; at latitude 60°, it will not exceed 0.7 miles, and the probable error would not be more than 0.3 miles. For an altitude of 60° near the equator, the error will not exceed 0.5 miles. If the difference in both latitude and longitude between the true and assumed positions is reduced to 20', the errors quoted above would be reduced by more than half.

The introductory pages of each volume include a "Table of Offsets," linear distances that can be drawn at right angles to a straight line of position (LOP). This results in a series of points that can be connected to form a better approximation of the arc of a circle of equal altitude, the true LOP. These corrections are offsets of points on the straight LOP plotted at right angles to it; these offset points are joined to obtain a better approximation of the arc of the *small* circle of equal altitude. Usually, the desired approximation of the arc can be obtained by drawing a straight line through pairs of offset points. The magnitudes of these offsets are dependent upon altitude and the distance of the offset point from the intercept line.

Solution by Pub. No. 229 from a DR Position

2406   Pub. No. 229 can also be used for the reduction of an observation using the dead reckoning (DR) position rather than an assumed position (AP); this procedure, however, is more complex and difficult, and it is rarely used. In principle, the method is the measurement of the difference in radii of two circles of equal altitude corresponding to the altitudes of the celestial body from two positions at the same time. One circle passes through the AP (selected, as usual, for whole degrees of latitude and LHA), and the second circle passes through the DR position (or other position from which the computed altitude is desired).

A graphic procedure is followed in which the Hc and intercept are first calculated in the usual way, followed by an offset correction to the plot. Full instructions on this procedure are given in the introductory pages of each volume. This method will give very satisfactory results except when plotting on a Mercator chart in high latitudes.

Other Uses of Pub. No. 229

2407 The tables of Pub. No. 229 can also be used in a number of secondary procedures. These include great-circle sailing problems (article 3015), the solution of general spherical triangles, star identifications (article 2007), and the determination of compass error (article 2803). Instructions for all these procedures are given in the introductory pages, together with several illustrative examples.

Reduction by Pub. No. 249

2408 Another set of precomputed tables bears the name *Sight Reduction Tables for Air Navigation*, now designated as DMAHTC Pub. No. 249. As their name implies, they are designed for use by air navigators. They have, however, also found favor with some surface navigators in cases where their greater speed of use and convenience offsets the less precise positional data so derived. On the high seas, this lessened precision is of little importance, especially on yachts and other small vessels where sextant observations are of somewhat reduced accuracy.

Volume I, Selected Stars

The Pub. No. 249 tables are published in three volumes. Similar to Pub. No. 229, they are inspection tables designed for use with an assumed position, but they differ from that publication in that altitude is stated only to the nearest whole minute of arc, and azimuth values are stated only to the nearest whole degree. The first volume is designed for use with certain selected stars on a world-wide basis; all integral degrees of latitude, from 89° north to 89° south are included. The arguments for entering the tables in Volume I are the nearest whole degree of latitude, specified as North or South; LHA Aries; and the name of the star observed. With this entry, a calculated altitude, Hc, and a true azimuth, Zn (rather than azimuth angle, Z), are obtained. The LHA ♈ is obtained by applying to the GHA ♈ such an assumed longitude (within 30′ of DR or EP longitude) as will give a whole degree of LHA ♈.

For each degree of latitude and of LHA ♈, seven stars are tabulated; see figure 2408a. The names of first-magnitude stars are printed in capital letters; those of second and third magnitude are in upper and lowercase letters. These stars are selected primarily for good distribution in azimuth, for their magnitude and altitude, and for continuity in latitude and hour angle; of these seven, those that are considered best suited for a three-star fix are identified by a diamond symbol ♦. The tabulated altitude and azimuth of the selected stars permits the use of this publication as a starfinder by presetting the sextant and observing in the tabulated direction.

The stars for which data are given in Volume I of Pub. No. 249 have continual slight changes in sidereal hour angle and declination due to the precession and nutation of the earth's axis of rotation. Editions of this publication contain tabulated data

LAT 42°N

LHA ♈	Hc Zn	Hc Zn	Hc Zn	Hc Zn	Hc Zn	Hc Zn	Hc Zn
	♦Alpheratz	ALTAIR	Nunki	♦ANTARES	ARCTURUS	♦Alkaid	Kochab
270	17 41 067	48 59 136	20 33 167	18 23 202	46 28 302	51 20 341	
271	18 22 067	49 29 137	20 43 168	18 06 203	36 50 263	45 51 303	51 05 341
272	19 03 068	49 59 139	20 52 169	17 49 203	36 06 264	45 13 303	50 51 341
273	19 45 068	50 28 140	21 00 170	17 31 204	35 21 265	44 36 303	50 36 341
274	20 26 069	50 56 141	21 07 171	17 12 205	34 37 265	43 59 303	50 22 341
275	21 08 069	51 23 143	21 14 172	16 53 206	33 52 266	43 21 304	50 07 340
276	21 50 070	51 50 144	21 20 173	16 33 207	33 08 267	42 44 304	49 52 340
277	22 32 071	52 15 146	21 25 174	16 12 208	32 23 267	42 08 304	49 37 340
278	23 14 071	52 40 147	21 29 175	15 51 209	31 39 268	41 31 305	49 21 340
279	23 56 072	53 04 149	21 33 176	15 30 210	30 54 269	40 54 305	49 06 340
280	24 39 072	53 26 150	21 36 177	15 07 210	30 10 270	40 18 305	48 51 340
281	25 21 073	53 48 152	21 38 178	14 44 211	29 25 270	39 41 306	48 35 340
282	26 04 073	54 08 153	21 39 179	14 21 212	28 40 271	39 05 306	48 20 339
283	26 47 074	54 28 155	21 40 180	13 57 213	27 56 272	38 29 306	48 04 339
284	27 30 075	54 46 157	21 40 181	13 33 214	27 11 272	37 53 306	47 48 339
	♦Mirfak	Alpheratz	♦ALTAIR	Rasalhague	♦ARCTURUS	Alkaid	Kochab
285	13 22 033	28 13 075	55 03 158	55 07 219	26 27 273	37 17 307	47 32 339
286	13 47 033	28 56 076	55 19 160	54 38 220	25 42 273	36 42 307	47 16 339
287	14 11 034	29 39 076	55 34 162	54 09 222	24 58 274	36 06 307	47 00 339
288	14 36 034	30 22 077	55 47 163	53 39 223	24 13 275	35 31 308	46 44 339
289	15 01 035	31 06 077	55 59 165	53 08 225	23 29 275	34 56 308	46 28 339
290	15 27 035	31 49 078	56 10 167	52 36 226	22 44 276	34 21 309	46 12 339
291	15 53 036	32 33 079	56 20 169	52 04 227	22 00 277	33 46 309	45 56 339
292	16 19 036	33 17 079	56 28 170	51 31 229	21 16 277	33 11 309	45 40 339

Figure 2408a. Pub. No. 249, Volume I, (extract)

for a specific year and an auxiliary table (Table 5) for corrections to be applied to an LOP or fix for years other than the base year. Editions are currently published every five years, but to provide for some overlap, the table of corrections covers a span of eight or more years. Each edition is designated with an *epoch year,* a multiple of five, and may be used for that year (and possibly another) without correction. For example, the basic tables of the Epoch 1985.0 edition may be used without correction for the years 1984 and 1985. The tables of corrections cover the years 1981 through 1989, but the basic data can be used without correction over the span 1982–1987 with errors no greater than 2 miles.

Volume I has other auxiliary tables including altitude corrections for change in position of the observer (primarily for airborne observers), and change in position of the body between time of observation and fix. Polaris latitude and azimuth tables are provided, as well as a table of GHA ♈ to eliminate the need for an *Air Almanac.* Another auxiliary table facilitates conversion between arc and time units.

Volumes II and III

Volumes II and III of Pub. No. 249 are generally similar in format to Pub. No. 229, except that Hc is tabulated only to the nearest whole minute and Z to the nearest whole degree. Both volumes list declination by integral degrees, but only for 0° to 29°; this covers all bodies of our solar system. These volumes are not epoch-limited as is Volume I.

Volume I will normally be used for reducing star sights, although stars with Dec. of 29° or less can be used with Volume II and Volume III; 29 of the 57 selected stars fall into this category. Volume II covers latitudes 0° to 39°, or Volume III covers lati-

tudes 40° to 89°. A portion of a page from Volume II. is reproduced in figure 2408b. The entering arguments are a whole degree of latitude, without name in these volumes, a whole degree of declination of same or contrary name to the latitude, and a whole degree of LHA. In the design of the tables it is intended that the *next smaller value* of declination be used. The tabulated values of LHA provide for negative altitudes because of the large value of the dip at the high operating altitudes of modern planes, which permit the observation of bodies below the celestial horizon.

For each single set of entering arguments, the tables state an altitude expressed to the nearest whole minute of arc, under the heading "Hc." Adjoining this, under the heading *d,* is a value with sign, which is the difference in minutes between the tabulated altitude and the altitude for a declination one degree higher, but at the same latitude and for the same LHA. The third item, under the heading "Z," is the azimuth angle (not Zn as in Volume I). The rules for converting Z to Zn are given on each page.

To correct the tabulated altitude for the difference between the true declination and that used as an entering argument, a multiplication table is in the back of the book; a sample is shown in figure 2408c. With this table, the d value is multiplied by the difference between the true and tabulated declinations, and applied to the tabulated altitude according to the sign shown in the main table.

The "249" tables provide an excellent reduction method for the airborne navigator. Cloud cover rarely presents a problem at the altitudes presently used for long-distance flights, and the seven stars selected for any given time are usually all visible during the hours of darkness. The procedures result in a degree of precision of fix that is in keeping with

DECLINATION (19°–29°) CONTRARY NAME TO LATITUDE

LHA	19° Hc	d	Z	20° Hc	d	Z	21° Hc	d	Z	22° Hc	d	Z	23° Hc	d	Z	24° Hc	d	Z	25° Hc	d	Z	26° Hc	d	Z	27° Hc	d	Z	28° Hc	d	Z	29° Hc	d	Z	LHA
14	36 18	58	164	35 20	58	164	34 22	58	164	33 24	58	164	32 26	58	165	31 28	59	165	30 29	58	165	29 31	58	166	28 33	59	166	27 34	58	166	26 36	59	166	346
13	36 32	58	165	35 34	58	165	34 36	58	165	33 37	58	166	32 39	59	166	31 40	58	166	30 42	59	166	29 43	59	167	28 44	58	167	27 46	59	167	26 47	58	167	347
12	36 45	58	166	35 47	59	166	34 48	58	166	33 49	58	167	32 51	59	167	31 52	59	167	30 53	59	167	29 54	58	168	28 56	59	168	27 57	59	168	26 58	59	168	348
11	36 57	59	167	35 58	59	167	34 59	59	167	34 00	58	168	33 02	59	168	32 03	59	168	31 04	59	168	30 05	59	169	29 06	59	169	28 07	59	169	27 08	59	169	349
10	37 08	-59	168	36 09	-59	168	35 10	-59	169	34 11	-59	169	33 12	-59	169	32 13	-60	169	31 13	-59	169	30 14	-59	170	29 15	-59	170	28 16	-59	170	27 17	-59	170	350
9	37 18	60	169	36 18	59	170	35 19	59	170	34 20	59	170	33 21	59	170	32 22	60	170	31 22	59	170	30 23	59	171	29 24	60	171	28 24	59	171	27 25	59	171	351
8	37 27	60	171	36 27	60	171	35 28	59	171	34 28	59	171	33 29	59	171	32 30	59	172	31 30	59	172	30 31	60	172	29 31	59	172	28 32	59	172	27 32	59	172	352
7	37 34	59	172	36 35	60	172	35 35	59	172	34 36	60	172	33 36	59	172	32 37	60	172	31 37	59	173	30 38	60	173	29 38	60	173	28 38	59	173	27 39	60	173	353
6	37 41	59	173	36 42	60	173	35 42	59	173	34 42	59	173	33 43	60	173	32 43	60	174	31 43	59	174	30 44	60	174	29 44	60	174	28 44	60	174	27 44	59	174	354
5	37 47	-60	174	36 47	-60	174	35 47	-59	174	34 48	-60	174	33 48	-60	175	32 48	-60	175	31 48	-59	175	30 49	-60	175	29 49	-60	175	28 49	-60	175	27 49	-60	175	355
4	37 52	60	175	36 52	60	175	35 52	60	175	34 52	60	176	33 52	60	176	32 52	59	176	31 53	60	176	30 53	60	176	29 53	60	176	28 53	60	176	27 53	60	176	356
3	37 55	60	176	36 55	60	177	35 55	59	177	34 56	60	177	33 56	60	177	32 56	60	177	31 56	60	177	30 56	60	177	29 56	60	177	28 56	60	177	27 56	60	177	357
2	37 58	60	178	36 58	60	178	35 58	60	178	34 58	60	178	33 58	60	178	32 58	60	178	31 58	60	178	30 58	60	178	29 58	60	178	28 58	60	178	27 58	60	178	358
1	38 00	60	179	37 00	60	179	36 00	60	179	35 00	60	179	34 00	60	179	33 00	60	179	32 00	60	179	31 00	60	179	30 00	60	179	29 00	60	179	28 00	60	179	359
0	38 00	-60	180	37 00	-60	180	36 00	-60	180	35 00	-60	180	34 00	-60	180	33 00	-60	180	32 00	-60	180	31 00	-60	180	30 00	-60	180	29 00	-60	180	28 00	-60	180	360

DECLINATION (19°–29°) CONTRARY NAME TO LATITUDE   LAT 33°

Figure 2408b. Pub. No. 249, Volume II, (extract).

TABLE III.—Correction to Tabulated Altitude for Minutes of Declination

d/'	1 2 3	4 5 6	7 8 9	10 11 12	13 14 15	16 17 18	19 20 21	37 38 39	40 41 42	43 44 45	46 47 48	49 50 51	52 53 54	55 56 57	58 59 60	d/'
0	0 0 0	0 0 0	0 0 0	0 0 0	0 0 0	0 0 0	0 0 0	0 0 0	0 0 0	0 0 0	0 0 0	0 0 0	0 0 0	0 0 0	0 0 0	0
1	0 0 0	0 0 0	0 0 0	0 0 0	0 0 0	0 0 0	0 0 0	1 1 1	1 1 1	1 1 1	1 1 1	1 1 1	1 1 1	1 1 1	1 1 1	1
2	0 0 0	0 0 0	0 0 0	0 0 0	0 0 0	1 1 1	1 1 1	1 1 1	1 1 1	1 1 2	2 2 2	2 2 2	2 2 2	2 2 2	2 2 2	2
3	0 0 0	0 0 0	0 0 0	0 1 1	1 1 1	1 1 1	1 1 1	2 2 2	2 2 2	2 2 2	2 2 2	2 2 3	3 3 3	3 3 3	3 3 3	3
4	0 0 0	0 0 0	0 1 1	1 1 1	1 1 1	1 1 1	1 1 1	2 3 3	3 3 3	3 3 3	3 3 3	3 3 3	3 4 4	4 4 4	4 4 4	4
35	1 1 2	2 3 4	4 5 5	6 6 7	8 8 9	9 10 10	11 12 12	22 22 23	23 24 24	25 26 26	27 27 28	29 29 30	30 31 32	32 33 33	34 34 35	35
36	1 1 2	2 3 4	4 5 5	6 7 7	8 8 9	10 10 11	11 12 13	22 23 23	24 25 25	26 26 27	28 28 29	29 30 31	31 32 32	33 34 34	35 35 36	36
37	1 1 2	2 3 4	4 5 6	6 7 7	8 9 9	10 10 11	12 12 13	23 23 24	25 25 26	27 27 28	28 29 30	30 31 31	32 33 33	34 35 35	36 36 37	37
38	1 1 2	3 3 4	4 5 6	6 7 8	8 9 10	10 11 11	12 13 13	23 24 25	25 26 27	27 28 28	29 30 30	31 32 32	33 34 34	35 35 36	37 37 38	38
39	1 1 2	3 3 4	5 5 6	6 7 8	8 9 10	10 11 12	12 13 14	24 25 25	26 27 27	28 29 29	30 31 31	32 32 33	34 34 35	36 36 37	38 38 39	39

Figure 2408c. Pub. No. 249, Volume II or III, Table III (extract).

that of observed altitudes obtained with a sextant using a pendulous mirror, or some other artificial horizon, such as a bubble.

It is also a satisfactory method for small vessels making long ocean voyages. Stowage space in such craft is limited, and the three volumes give world-wide coverage. Of the 173 navigational stars tabulated in the *Nautical Almanac*, 75 are suitable for use with Volumes II or III; 29 of these 75 are among the selected stars. In its degree of precision, Pub. No. 249 is comparable with the accuracy of the sextant observations that can be obtained aboard a small craft in rough water. (On sailing craft, there may be a problem as to the direction in which sights can be taken as a result of the blocking of vision by the sails. The availability of seven selected stars well distributed in azimuth should, however, permit one to obtain enough celestial LOPs to get a fix.) The navigator of a large surface vessel, on the other hand, can, and should, obtain a higher order of precision in his celestial navigation than is possible with the use of these tables; Pub. No. 229 should be the reduction method of his choice if a computer or calculator is not used.

The Ageton Method

2409   A volume entitled *Dead Reckoning Altitude and Azimuth Table* was formerly published as H.O. 211 and is now included in DMAHTC Pub. No. 9 (*Bowditch*), Volume II, as Table No. 35; these are referred to as the *Ageton* tables after their original designer. They are also available as separate tables from commercial publishers in a small volume of roughly 50 pages. There is a single table of log secants and log cosecants (× 100,000), stated for each 0.5' of arc. It is suitable for world-wide use with any declination, and for any altitude. As its name implies, it is intended for use from a DR position. A partial page is shown in figure 2409a.

In this method, two right triangles are formed by dropping a perpendicular from the celestial body to the celestial meridian of the observer. The right angle falls on the celestial meridian at a point that may lie either inside or outside of the navigational triangle. The right triangles are then solved for altitude and azimuth angle from equations derived from Napier's rules.

In figure 2409b the navigational triangle is shown with the parts of the triangle lettered.

In right triangle *PMX*, t and d are known. *R* may be found from equation (1). Knowing *R* and d, *K* may be found by equation (2). *K* is then combined algebraically with *L* to obtain $(K \sim L)$.

In triangle *ZMX*, sides *R* and $(K \sim L)$ are now known. Hc may be found by equation (3). The azimuth, Z, is computed by equation (4).

All equations are in terms of secants and cosecants. The table is arranged in parallel *A* and *B* columns; the *A* columns containing log cosecants multiplied by 100,000, and the *B* columns log secants multiplied by 100,000. This design greatly simplifies the arithmetic of solution.

The tabulation of functions for every half-minute of arc throughout the table is employed so that, in ordinary use, interpolation will not be necessary. If the entry value is midway between two tabular values, use the smaller of the two; the difference in results is not significant, but this procedure will ensure consistency in reductions.

The procedure necessary to obtain the calculated altitude and azimuth by the Ageton method is described in detail in *Bowditch*, Volume II, and in the separate publications of the table. The example shown in figure 2409c illustrates the reduction of an observation by this method; the work form shown will be found convenient, as it indicates where the *A* or *B* values taken from the tables are to be entered and how they are combined.

Example: A navigator whose DR position is L33°21.2' N, λ65°26.4' W observes the sun at a time when its t is 14°12.3' W, and its Dec. is 22°37.7' S. After appropriate corrections are applied to the hs,

′	22° 30′ A	22° 30′ B	23° 00′ A	23° 00′ B	23° 30′ A	23° 30′ B	24° 00′ A	24° 00′ B	24° 30′ A	24° 30′ B	′
10	41412	3491	40516	3651	39641	3815	38786	3983	37951	4155	20
	41397	3494	40501	3654	39626	3818	38772	3986	37937	4158	
11	41382	3496	40486	3657	39612	3821	38758	3989	37924	4161	19
	41367	3499	40471	3659	39597	3824	38744	3992	37910	4164	
12	41352	3502	40457	3662	39583	3826	38730	3995	37896	4167	18
	41337	3504	40442	3665	39569	3829	38716	3998	37882	4170	
13	41322	3507	40427	3667	39554	3832	38702	4000	37869	4173	17
	41307	3509	40413	3670	39540	3835	38688	4003	37855	4176	
14	41291	3512	40398	3673	39525	3838	38674	4006	37841	4179	16
	41276	3515	40383	3676	39511	3840	38660	4009	37828	4182	
15	41261	3517	40368	3678	39497	3843	38645	4012	37814	4185	15
	41246	3520	40354	3681	39482	3846	38631	4015	37800	4187	
16	41231	3523	40339	3684	39468	3849	38617	4017	37786	4190	14
	41216	3525	40324	3686	39454	3851	38603	4020	37773	4193	
17	41201	3528	40310	3689	39439	3854	38589	4023	37759	4196	13
	41186	3531	40295	3692	39425	3857	38575	4026	37745	4199	
18	41171	3533	40280	3695	39411	3860	38561	4029	37732	4202	12
	41156	3536	40266	3697	39396	3863	38547	4032	37718	4205	
19	41141	3539	40251	3700	39382	3865	38533	4035	37704	4208	11
	41126	3541	40236	3703	39368	3868	38520	4037	37691	4211	
20	41111	3544	40222	3705	39353	3871	38506	4040	37677	4214	10
	41096	3547	40207	3708	39339	3874	38492	4043	37663	4217	
21	41081	3549	40192	3711	39325	3876	38478	4046	37650	4220	9
	41066	3552	40178	3714	39311	3879	38464	4049	37636	4222	
22	41051	3555	40163	3716	39296	3882	38450	4052	37623	4225	8
	41036	3557	40149	3719	39282	3885	38436	4055	37609	4228	
23	41021	3560	40134	3722	39268	3888	38422	4057	37595	4231	7
	41006	3563	40119	3725	39254	3890	38408	4060	37582	4234	
24	40991	3565	40105	3727	39239	3893	38394	4063	37568	4237	6
	40976	3568	40090	3730	39225	3896	38380	4066	37554	4240	
25	40961	3571	40076	3733	39211	3899	38366	4069	37541	4243	5
	40946	3573	40061	3735	39197	3902	38352	4072	37527	4246	
26	40931	3576	40046	3738	39182	3904	38338	4075	37514	4249	4
	40916	3579	40032	3741	39168	3907	38324	4078	37500	4252	
27	40902	3581	40017	3744	39154	3910	38311	4080	37486	4255	3
	40887	3584	40003	3746	39140	3913	38297	4083	37473	4258	

Figure 2409a. Pub. No. 9 *(Bowditch)*, Volume II (1975 or 1981), Table 35 (extract).

Figure 2409b. The celestial triangle as solved by the Ageton method.

P. Pole.
Z. Zenith of observer. The azimuth (angle PZM) is also called Z.
M. Heavenly body observed.
L. Latitude of observer.
d. Declination of body M.
t. (or LHA). Local hour angle of body M.
H. Altitude of body M.
R. Perpendicular let fall from M on PZ. This is an auxiliary part.
X. Intersection of R with PZ.
K. Arc from X to the equinoctial. This is an auxiliary part introduced to facilitate solution.
The following equations have been derived:

From triangle PMX—

1. $\csc R = \csc t \sec d.$
2. $\csc K = \dfrac{\csc d}{\sec R}$

From triangle ZMX—

3. $\csc Hc = \sec R \sec (K \sim L).$
4. $\csc Z = \dfrac{\csc R}{\sec Hc}$

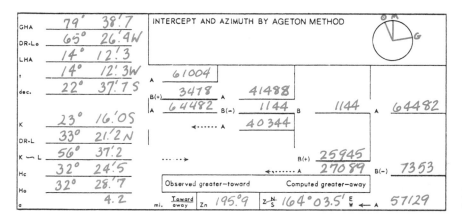

Figure 2409c. Form with sight reduction by the Ageton method.

t AND K ARE BOTH GREATER OR BOTH LESS THAN 90°.
Z IS LESS THAN 90° ONLY WHEN K HAS THE SAME NAME AND IS GREATER THAN L.

'	A 20° B / B 110° A		A 21° B / B 111° A		A 22° B / B 112° A		A 23° B / B 113° A		A 24° B / B 114° A		'
00	46595	2701	44567	2985	42642	3283	40812	3597	39069	3927	60
01	560	706	534	990	611	289	782	603	040	933	59
02	525	711	501	995	580	294	763	608	012	938	58
03	491	715	468	999	549	299	723	613	38984	944	57
04	456	720	436	3004	518	304	693	619	955	950	56
05	46422	2724	44403	3009	42486	3309	40664	3624	38927	3955	55
06	387	729	370	014	455	314	634	630	899	961	54
07	353	734	337	019	424	319	604	635	871	966	53
08	318	738	305	024	393	324	575	640	842	972	52
09	284	743	272	029	362	330	545	646	814	978	51
10	46249	2748	44239	3034	42331	3335	40516	3651	38786	3983	50
11	215	752	207	038	300	340	486	657	758	989	49
12	181	757	174	043	269	345	457	662	730	995	48
13	146	762	142	048	238	350	427	667	702	4000	47
14	112	766	109	053	207	355	398	673	674	006	46
15	46078	2771	44077	3058	42176	3360	40368	3678	38646	4012	45
16	043	776	044	063	145	366	339	684	618	018	44
17	009	780	012	068	115	371	310	689	589	023	43
18	45975	785	43979	073	084	376	280	695	562	029	42
19	941	790	947	078	053	381	251	700	534	035	41
20	45907	2794	43915	3083	42022	3386	40222	3706	38506	4040	40
21	873	799	882	088	41992	392	192	711	478	046	39
22	839	804	850	093	961	397	163	716	450	052	38
23	805	808	818	097	930	402	134	722	422	058	37
24	771	813	785	102	899	407	105	727	394	063	36
25	45737	2818	43753	3107	41869	3412	40076	3733	38366	4069	35
26	703	822	721	112	838	418	046	738	338	075	34
27	669	827	689	117	808	423	017	744	311	080	33
28	635	832	657	122	777	428	39988	749	283	086	32
29	601	837	625	127	747	433	959	755	255	092	31

Figure 2409d. Condensed Ageton tables (extract).

the Ho is 32°28.7'. (See figure 2409c.) The A and B values on the line for "Dec." are taken from the extract of figure 2409a; other values of A and B are from pages not shown. In obtaining Hc, he does not interpolate, as the value for K was not near 90°. If, however, the value for K had been within a few degrees of 90°, the accuracy of the solution would have been inadequate without interpolation; it is good practice to either discard such sights or interpolate the B value in the second column of the form from the A value in the first column.

"Compact" Ageton Tables

As noted in article 2408, the tables of Pub. No. 249 represent a reduction of volume and weight over those of Pub. No. 229. And the Ageton tables provide a further reduction to a booklet of some 50 pages. Now, a yet further reduction has been made to a pamphlet of only 30 small pages for a condensed version of the Ageton tables. These "compact" tables (which actually cover only 9 pages, the remainder are instructions and other explanatory material) are made possible by the use of whole degrees only for columns and whole minutes only for rows, resulting in a reduction to one-fourth of the tabulated entries; see figure 2409d. The overall size of the booklet containing these compact tables was deliberately chosen to make the publication fit into the lid of a typical sextant case.

Use of the compact tables results in some lessening of the accuracy of the position determined, but not to a degree of practical significance in the high-

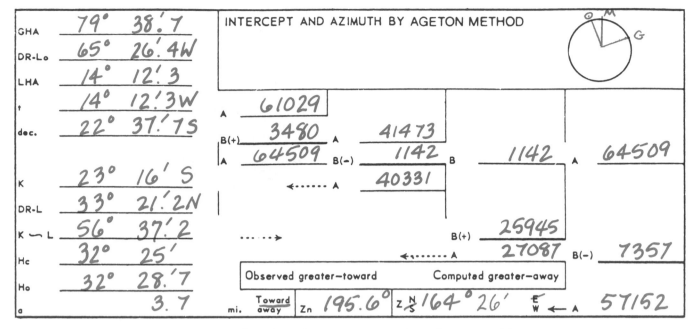

GHA	79° 38.'7			
DR-Lo	65° 26.'4W			
LHA	14° 12.'3			

INTERCEPT AND AZIMUTH BY AGETON METHOD

t	14° 12.'3W
dec.	22° 37.'7S

A   61029

B(+) 3480   A   41473

A   64509   B(−) 1142   B   1142   A   64509

← . . . . . A   40331

K	23° 16' S
DR-L	33° 21.'2N
K ∼ L	56° 37.'2
Hc	32° 25'
Ho	32° 28.'7
a	3.7

. . . . →

B(+) 25945

← . . . . . A   27087   B(−) 7357

Observed greater—toward	Computed greater—away

mi. Toward/away   Zn 195.6°   Z N/S 164° 26'   E/W ← A   57152

Figure 2409e. Form with sight reduction using condensed Ageton tables.

seas navigation of small vessels or for emergency use in survival craft (see chapter 39). An example of the use of the compact tables is shown in figure 2409e. The input data are the same as for the preceding example by the Ageton Method; the differences are slight—less than one mile in intercept and less than one degree in azimuth.

Use with Calculators

The Ageton method, using either *Bowditch,* Table 35 or the compact tables, is gaining popularity as a back-up method for sight reductions by computer or calculator in the case of equipment failure or loss of electric power.

"Concise" Sight Reduction Tables

2410 A new method of sight reduction has recently been added to the list of those available to a navigator; this is through use of the "Concise Tables for Sight Reduction" developed by Rear Admiral Thomas D. Davies, USN (Retired) in conjunction with the Nautical Almanac Office of the U.S. Naval Observatory (Cornell Maritime Press). This method is somewhat reminiscent of the Ageton tables in that the navigational triangle is divided into two right spherical triangles. The difference here, however, is that the construction line is dropped from a different vertex perpendicular to a different opposite side; see figure 2410a. Reduction of a sight involves the extraction of values from a table, but

these are angles in degrees and minutes, not logarithms of secants and cosecants. Various angular values are added or subtracted, but most operations are with two-digit numbers rather than the five-digit extracts from the Ageton tables, a procedure that should lessen the opportunity for error. The

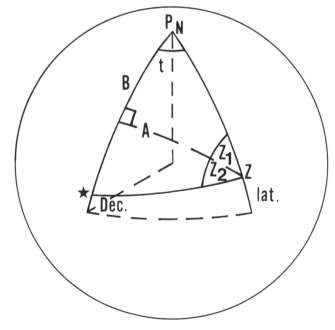

Figure 2410a. The navigational triangle as subdivided for the Davies *Concise Tables for Sight Reduction.*

t		42			43			44			45			46			47			t	
		a	b	c	a	b	c	a	b	c	a	b	c	a	b	c	a	b	c		
45	135	31 42	38 09	56.2	31 08	37 10	55.7	30 34	36 13	55.2	30 00	35 16	54.7	29 25	34 20	54.3	28 50	33 24	53.8	225	315
46	134	32 19	37 39	55.3	31 45	36 41	54.8	31 10	35 44	54.3	30 34	34 47	53.8	29 59	33 51	53.3	29 23	32 56	52.9	226	314
47	133	32 55	37 08	54.3	32 20	36 11	53.8	31 45	35 14	53.3	31 08	34 18	52.8	30 32	33 22	52.4	29 55	32 27	51.9	227	313
48	132	33 31	36 37	53.4	32 55	35 40	52.9	32 19	34 43	52.3	31 42	33 47	51.9	31 05	32 52	51.4	30 27	31 58	50.9	228	312
49	131	34 07	36 05	52.4	33 30	35 08	51.9	32 53	34 11	51.4	32 15	33 16	50.9	31 37	32 21	50.4	30 59	31 27	49.9	229	311
50	130	34 42	35 31	51.4	34 04	34 35	50.9	33 26	33 39	50.4	32 48	32 44	49.9	32 09	31 50	49.4	31 30	30 56	48.9	230	310
51	129	35 17	34 57	50.4	34 38	34 01	49.9	33 59	33 05	49.4	33 20	32 11	48.9	32 40	31 17	48.4	32 00	30 24	47.9	231	309
52	128	35 51	34 22	49.4	35 12	33 26	48.9	34 32	32 31	48.4	33 52	31 37	47.9	33 11	30 44	47.4	32 30	29 52	46.9	232	308
53	127	36 24	33 45	48.4	35 44	32 50	47.9	35 04	31 56	47.3	34 23	31 02	46.8	33 42	30 10	46.3	33 00	29 18	45.9	233	307
54	126	36 57	33 08	47.4	36 17	32 13	46.8	35 35	31 20	46.3	34 54	30 27	45.8	34 12	29 35	45.3	33 29	28 44	44.8	234	306
55	125	37 30	32 30	46.3	36 48	31 36	45.8	36 06	30 43	45.2	35 24	29 50	44.7	34 41	28 59	44.2	33 58	28 08	43.8	235	305
56	124	38 02	31 51	45.2	37 19	30 57	44.7	36 37	30 04	44.2	35 53	29 13	43.6	35 10	28 22	43.2	34 26	27 32	42.7	236	304
57	123	38 33	31 10	44.1	37 50	30 17	43.6	37 06	29 25	43.1	36 22	28 34	42.6	35 38	27 45	42.1	34 53	26 56	41.6	237	303
58	122	39 04	30 29	43.0	38 20	29 36	42.5	37 36	28 45	42.0	36 51	27 55	41.5	36 06	27 06	41.0	35 20	26 18	40.5	238	302
59	121	39 34	29 46	41.9	38 49	28 55	41.4	38 04	28 04	40.9	37 19	27 15	40.4	36 33	26 27	39.9	35 46	25 39	39.4	239	301
60	120	40 04	29 03	40.8	39 18	28 12	40.2	38 32	27 22	39.7	37 46	26 34	39.2	36 59	25 46	38.8	36 12	25 00	38.3	240	300
61	119	40 32	28 18	39.6	39 46	27 28	39.1	38 59	26 39	38.6	38 12	25 52	38.1	37 25	25 05	37.6	36 37	24 20	37.2	241	299
62	118	41 00	27 32	38.5	40 13	26 43	37.9	39 26	25 56	37.4	38 38	25 09	36.9	37 50	24 23	36.5	37 02	23 39	36.0	242	298
63	117	41 28	26 45	37.3	40 39	25 58	36.8	39 52	25 11	36.3	39 03	24 25	35.8	38 14	23 40	35.3	37 25	22 57	34.9	243	297
64	116	41 54	25 58	36.1	41 06	25 11	35.6	40 17	24 25	35.1	39 28	23 40	34.6	38 38	22 57	34.1	37 48	22 14	33.7	244	296
65	115	42 20	25 09	34.9	41 31	24 23	34.4	40 41	23 38	33.9	39 51	22 55	33.4	39 01	22 12	33.0	38 11	21 31	32.5	245	295
66	114	42 45	24 19	33.6	41 55	23 34	33.1	41 05	22 50	32.7	40 14	22 08	32.2	39 23	21 27	31.8	38 32	20 46	31.3	246	294
67	113	43 10	23 28	32.4	42 19	22 44	31.9	41 28	22 02	31.4	40 37	21 21	31.0	39 45	20 40	30.5	38 53	20 01	30.1	247	293
68	112	43 33	22 35	31.1	42 42	21 53	30.6	41 50	21 12	30.2	40 58	20 32	29.7	40 06	19 53	29.3	39 13	19 15	28.9	248	292
69	111	43 56	21 42	29.8	43 04	21 01	29.4	42 11	20 22	28.9	41 19	19 43	28.5	40 26	19 05	28.1	39 33	18 29	27.7	249	291
70	110	44 18	20 48	28.5	43 25	20 08	28.1	42 32	19 30	27.7	41 38	18 53	27.2	40 45	18 17	26.8	39 51	17 41	26.5	250	290
71	109	44 38	19 53	27.2	43 45	19 15	26.8	42 51	18 38	26.4	41 57	18 02	26.0	41 03	17 27	25.6	40 09	16 53	25.2	251	289
72	108	44 58	18 57	25.9	44 04	18 20	25.5	43 10	17 45	25.1	42 16	17 10	24.7	41 21	16 37	24.3	40 26	16 05	24.0	252	288
73	107	45 17	17 59	24.6	44 23	17 24	24.1	43 28	16 51	23.8	42 33	16 10	23.4	41 38	15 46	23.0	40 42	15 15	22.7	253	287
74	106	45 35	17 01	23.2	44 40	16 28	22.8	43 45	15 56	22.4	42 49	15 25	22.1	41 54	14 54	21.7	40 58	14 25	21.4	254	286
75	105	45 53	16 02	21.8	44 57	15 31	21.4	44 01	15 00	21.1	43 05	14 31	20.8	42 09	14 02	20.4	41 12	13 34	20.1	255	285
76	104	46 09	15 02	20.4	45 12	14 33	20.1	44 16	14 04	19.7	43 19	13 36	19.4	42 23	13 09	19.1	41 26	12 43	18.8	256	284
77	103	46 24	14 02	19.0	45 27	13 34	18.7	44 30	13 07	18.4	43 33	12 41	18.1	42 36	12 15	17.8	41 39	11 51	17.5	257	283
78	102	46 38	13 00	17.6	45 40	12 34	17.3	44 43	12 09	17.0	43 46	11 45	16.7	42 48	11 21	16.5	41 51	10 58	16.2	258	282
79	101	46 51	11 58	16.2	45 53	11 34	15.9	44 55	11 11	15.6	43 57	10 48	15.4	43 00	10 26	15.1	42 02	10 05	14.9	259	281
80	100	47 03	10 55	14.8	46 04	10 33	14.5	45 06	10 12	14.2	44 08	9 51	14.0	43 10	9 31	13.8	42 12	9 12	13.6	260	280
81	99	47 13	9 51	13.3	46 15	9 31	13.1	45 16	9 12	12.8	44 18	8 53	12.6	43 19	8 35	12.4	42 21	8 18	12.2	261	279
82	98	47 23	8 47	11.9	46 24	8 29	11.6	45 26	8 12	11.4	44 27	7 55	11.2	43 28	7 39	11.1	42 29	7 24	10.9	262	278
83	97	47 32	7 42	10.4	46 33	7 27	10.2	45 34	7 12	10.0	44 34	6 57	09.9	43 35	6 43	09.7	42 36	6 29	09.5	263	277
84	96	47 40	6 37	08.9	46 40	6 24	08.8	45 41	6 11	08.6	44 41	5 58	08.5	43 42	5 46	08.3	42 42	5 34	08.2	264	276
85	95	47 46	5 32	07.4	46 46	5 20	07.3	45 46	5 09	07.2	44 47	4 59	07.1	43 47	4 49	06.9	42 48	4 39	06.8	265	275
86	94	47 51	4 26	06.0	46 51	4 17	05.9	45 51	4 08	05.7	44 52	3 59	05.6	43 52	3 51	05.6	42 52	3 43	05.5	266	274
87	93	47 55	3 20	04.5	46 55	3 13	04.4	45 55	3 06	04.3	44 55	3 00	04.2	43 55	2 54	04.2	42 56	2 48	04.1	267	273
88	92	47 58	2 13	03.0	46 58	2 09	02.9	45 58	2 04	02.9	44 58	2 00	02.8	43 58	1 56	02.8	42 58	1 52	02.7	268	272
89	91	47 59	1 07	01.5	46 59	1 04	01.5	45 59	1 02	01.4	44 59	1 00	01.4	43 59	0 58	01.4	43 00	0 56	01.4	269	271
90	90	48 00	0 00	00.0	47 00	0 00	00.0	46 00	0 00	00.0	45 00	0 00	00.0	44 00	0 00	00.0	43 00	0 00	00.0	270	270

Figure 2410b. *Concise Tables for Sight Reduction;* Table 1 (extract).

format of the tables is shown in figure 2410b. Some adjustments have been made in Table II to compensate for non-linear differences between values; the effect is to reduce many slight errors while introducing others. The Davies tables should have no error of solution greater than 1' for altitudes of 77 degrees or less, and errors not greater than 2' for nearly all altitudes greater than 77 degrees; these are considered acceptable for practical navigation. Azimuth errors may be as great as 5° for extreme high-altitude observations, higher than 85°.

Beginning with the edition for 1989, the *Nautical Almanac* has been expanded to include these Concise Sight Reduction Tables, with slightly modified and simplified instructions for their use. Also added at the same time were equations and instructions for use of a calculator or computer to determine position from altitudes observed with a sextant. With these two enhancements, the single volume of the *Nautical Almanac* is all that is now needed to reduce sights to the same accuracy as use of Pub. No. 249.

Chapter 25

Celestial Lines of Position

Introduction

2501 After the actions described in chapter 24 and several preceding chapters have been completed, and a navigator has values of altitude intercept and azimuth, the task remains to use these data to determine his position. Actually, a sight reduction will yield a circular line of position, but this cannot be used directly except in the case of quite high altitude observations. In practice, he will plot a minute fraction of that circle, a line so short that it can be considered a straight line in the vicinity of his DR position.

The purpose of this chapter is to explain the techniques whereby celestial altitudes are converted into celestial lines of position (LOP), and how fixes and running fixes are obtained from such lines. Celestial lines of position are usually plotted on special charts called *plotting sheets*. In the interest of simplification, however, the term *chart* will be used throughout this chapter.

Lines of Position

An American, Captain Thomas H. Sumner, discovered the line of position in 1837. Due to thick weather when approaching the English coast, he had been unable to obtain any observations. About 10 A.M. the sun broke through, and he measured an altitude that he reduced to obtain the longitude. However, the latitude he used for the reduction was in doubt, so he solved for longitude twice more, each time using a different latitude. After plotting the three positions on a chart, he was surprised to find that a straight line could be drawn through them. He correctly deduced that his position must lie somewhere along this line, which happened to pass through a light off the English coast. He turned the ship and sailed along that line until the light appeared, thus establishing his position exactly.

Sumner's discovery of the line of position was a great step forward in celestial navigation. Its greatest weakness lay in the fact that to obtain such a line of position, a sight had to be worked twice, using different latitudes. In 1875, Commander Marcq de St.-Hilaire of the French Navy introduced the altitude difference, or intercept method, which has become the basis of virtually all present-day celestial navigation. In this method, the altitude and azimuth, or direction of a body, are calculated for a given instant of time and for a location where the vessel is presumed to be. The difference between the altitude as observed by sextant and the calculated altitude is then determined; this difference, which is called the *intercept (a)*, will be in minutes of arc.

A line is then drawn through the position, corresponding in direction to the calculated azimuth. The intercept is next laid off along the azimuth line, one nautical mile being equal to one minute of arc. It is measured toward the body if the observed altitude is greater than the calculated, and away if it is less. All that remains is to draw the line of position at right angles to the azimuth line.

Terrestial and Celestial LOP Compared

2502 In piloting, a navigator may obtain a line of position in any of several ways; usually such lines represent bearings of a landmark or aid to navigation. In celestial navigation a line of position is a small segment of a circle, which represents distance in nautical miles from the GP of the observed body; it is somewhat similar to the circular LOP obtained from a radar range in piloting. This distance is obtained by converting the altitude of the observed body into miles on the surface of the earth; this distance must then be transformed into a line of position that can be plotted on the appropriate chart. Both celestial and terrestrial lines of position are used in essentially the same manner, and may be advanced or retired as required; usually they are advanced to the time of the last observation so as to result in a common time for two or more LOPs taken in sequence rather than simultaneously.

Labeling Celestial LOPs and Fixes

2503 A neat, carefully labeled plot of navigational information is a prime characteristic of a good navigator. All lines of position and fixes should be drawn and labeled in such a way that no doubt ever exists as to their meaning. The illustrations in this chapter are all drawn and labeled in conformance with the standards that have been generally agreed upon by the various U.S. instructional activities. These standards are:

Assumed position or geographical position. The AP or GP used with an LOP is always marked by an encircled dot and may be labeled "AP" or "GP," as appropriate and numbered consecutively, if more than one appears on a plot.

Advanced AP or GP. The direction and distance an AP or GP is advanced is always shown by a solid line or lines, the end point of which is encircled but not labeled. This is the advanced AP or GP from which an advanced LOP is plotted.

Azimuth line. The direction of the LOP from the AP used to plot the line is always shown by a broken line extending from the AP to the LOP, as indicated by the magnitude and direction of the intercept; no labels.

Line of position. A line of position, whether a straight line or an arc, is always shown by a solid line and labeled with the name of the body "below" the line. The ship's time of the observation may be labeled "above" the LOP, or may be omitted to reduce chart clutter if time is close to that shown at the fix (see below). If the LOP has been advanced or retired for a running fix, the time of observation and the time to which it has been adjusted are both shown if time labels are being used; for example, "1210–1420" for a 1210 line of position advanced to 1420.

Fix. The position found by a fix is encircled and labeled with the time, such as "0726" placed hor-

izontally; the word "fix" is understood and should not be labeled. If a small polygon is formed by an inexact intersection of more than two lines, an encircled dot may be added to indicate the position considered to be the fix.

Running fix. The position found by a running fix is marked in the same manner as a fix, but is labeled as to its special nature; for example, "1628 R Fix" placed horizontally.

Lines of Position from High-altitude Observations

2504 As shown in chapter 19, the radius of a circle of equal altitude is equal to the coaltitude, or 90° minus the altitude. If a body is observed at a very high altitude, the radius will be small, and the resulting circle of equal altitude can be plotted directly on a chart. The center of this circle will be the GP of the body, and the radius will equal the coaltitude. In practice, only that portion of the circle that lies in the vicinity of the ship's DR position need be drawn.

There are two reasons why this direct method of plotting celestial lines of position is not suitable for most celestial observations. The first is that the radii of most circles of equal altitude are very long. For example, for an altitude of 50°, the coaltitude, and therefore the radius, is 40°, which equals 2,400 nautical miles, and for an altitude of 20°, the radius is 4,200 nautical miles. A chart that would permit plotting radii of such magnitudes would be of such small scale that it would not yield the precision in position required in practical navigation.

Secondly, distortion is apparent on the commonly used Mercator projection, and increases with the latitude of the GP. The distortion of such a circle is illustrated in figure 2504a; it would be exceedingly difficult to draw such a line.

If, however, the body is very high in altitude, the coaltitude will be small enough to plot on a navigational chart, and the distortion will be negligible. There is no precise answer as to how great the altitude should be to permit direct plotting as a "high-altitude observation." Typically, all sights with an observed altitude of 87° or more are classed as high-altitude observations and the resulting LOP is plotted directly; the radius in this case would not exceed 180 miles.

Example: The 1137 DR position of an observer is L5°30.5′ N, λ139°57.7′ E, at which time he determines the Ho of the sun to be 88°14.5′. The GP of the sun for this time is determined from an almanac to be L7°14.9′ N, λ140°26.2′ E.

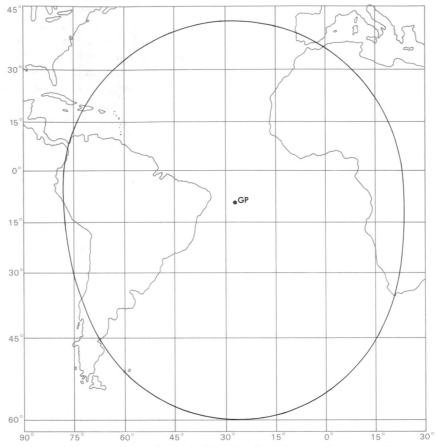

Figure 2504a. Circle of equal altitude plotted on a Mercator chart.

Required: The plot of the 1137 LOP.

Solution: (Figure 2504b) Plot and label the 1137 DR position and the GP, using the latitudes and longitudes given. Since the radius of the circle of equal altitude equals the coaltitude, subtract the observed altitude from 90°, and convert the difference into minutes of arc, which equal nautical miles.

$$
\begin{array}{ll}
 & 90°00.0' \\
\text{Ho} & 88°14.5' \\
\text{Radius} & \overline{1°45.5'} = 105.5 \text{ miles}
\end{array}
$$

Using a radius of 105.5 miles (shown by the broken line), construct an arc with the GP as the center, drawing only that segment that lies in the vicinity of the DR position. Label the resulting line of position as shown, except for the radius shown in this figure, which is normally not drawn.

In actual practice, it is difficult to obtain accurate observations at very high altitudes, since when the sextant is rocked, the observed body travels almost horizontally along the horizon, making it

Figure 2504b. Plot of the LOP from a high-altitude observation.

difficult to establish the vertical. However, at mid-day in the tropics, the navigator must make his LAN observation of the sun, regardless of its altitude, in order to obtain a latitude line of position.

LOP from Other than High-altitude Observations

2505 The great majority of celestial observations are made at altitudes that do not permit direct plotting, as described above; for these, a different method must be employed. This method is usually based on the use of an assumed position (AP), and the solution of the navigational triangle associated with it.

It has been stated that the navigational triangle may be defined by the AP, the elevated pole, and the GP of the body. By solving the triangle, the altitude and azimuth of the body at the AP at the time of observation may be computed. In figure 2505a the circle represents the circle of equal altitude for an observer at M and the point AP is the assumed position selected for the particular observation. By solving the triangle containing AP, the navigator determines the length of the side AP–GP, or coaltitude, which is the radius of the circle of equal altitude through the AP (not shown in figure 2505a).

If the altitude (Ho) obtained by the observer at M is greater than the altitude computed (Hc) by solving the triangle, the observer must be closer to the GP than is the AP; if it is less, he must be farther away. Also, the difference in the radii of the two circles of equal altitude, as illustrated in figure 2505b, is equal to the difference between the coaltitudes obtained from Ho and Hc, respectively. *The difference is the intercept (a)* and is expressed in nautical miles, which equals the difference expressed in minutes of arc.

Azimuth for the LOP

In solving the triangle, the value of the *azimuth angle* (Z) is also obtained; this is used to determine the true direction or *azimuth* (Zn) of the body from the AP (unless Zn is found directly as with Pub. No. 249, Volume I). If the Ho is greater than the Hc, a line representing Zn is plotted from the AP toward the GP; if Hc is the greater, the line will be plotted as the reciprocal of Zn, or away from the GP. This line is a part of the radius of a circle of equal altitude; by laying off a distance equal to (a) along this line, a point on the observed circle of equal altitude is determined. If Ho is greater than Hc, (a) is always labeled T (toward); if it is less, the label is A (away). A useful memory aid in labeling (a) is *Coast Guard Academy* for *Computed Greater Away;* also HoMoTo, for Ho More Toward.

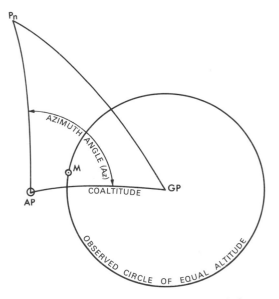

Figure 2505a. A circle of equal altitude and the navigational triangle associated with one AP.

Figure 2505b. The relationship of the altitude difference, (a), to the AP and to the observed circle of equal altitude.

To sum up, to plot a celestial LOP the following must be known:

The position of the AP;
Azimuth of the body, Zn;
The intercept, (a).

The intercept, (a), lies along a partial radius of a circle of equal altitude; it is plotted from the AP in the direction Zn, or towards the body, and labeled T (Ho greater than Hc). If labeled A (Hc greater than Ho), it is plotted in the direction of the reciprocal of Zn. The length of (a) in miles is equal to the difference between Ho and Hc in minutes of arc.

The line of position on which the observer is located is perpendicular to the radius line and passes through its end away from the DR or assumed position. Actually, this LOP is an arc of a circle of equal altitude; for most observations, however, the radius of this circle is so large that the curvature of the LOP is not significant. The LOP resulting from all but very high altitude observations may, therefore, be drawn as a straight line, the resulting error being insignificant in the ordinary practice of navigation. Figure 2505c illustrates the approximation made by using a straight line rather than an arc for plotting a celestial LOP. If a more precise solution is required, the circle can be closely approximated by plotting "offsets" from the straight LOP as covered by article 2405 and the introductory pages to any volume of DMAHTC Pub. No. 229.

Figure 2505c. Plot of the same LOP from the AP and from the GP.

The following example will illustrate that portion of a navigator's work that has just been discussed. The actual plot, as laid down on the chart, is shown in figure 2505d. Note that only two lines are drawn—the dashed line, from the AP, which is the intercept, and the heavy line, which is the LOP. The latter is labeled in accordance with standard practice, the ship's time of the observation being shown above, and the name of the body observed below. In normal practice, the intercept is not labeled; the time may be omitted from the LOP if it is used for a fix that is labeled with time.

Ho	12°37.4'
Hc	12°17.4'
a	20.0' T
Zn	329.2°
aL	35°00.0' S
aλ	76°27.1' W

Figure 2505d. Plot of the LOP from a celestial observation.

Example: At 0623 a navigator determined the Ho of the star Procyon to be 12°37.4'. Selecting a point at L35°00.0' S and λ76°27.1' W as his assumed position, he computes Hc to be 12°17.4' and Zn to be 329.2°.

Required: The plot of the 0623 celestial LOP.

Solution: (Figure 2505d) First, determine the intercept (a) by comparison of Hc with Ho, and designate it "To" or "Away" in accordance with whether Ho or Hc, respectively, is the greater. Plot the AP, using the aL and aλ given. From the AP draw a broken line either toward or away from the direction of the GP, as indicated by Zn and the label of (a). Measure the distance (a) along this line, and at the point so determined, construct a perpendicular. This perpendicular is the 0623 LOP; it is labeled with the time of the observation above the LOP and with the name of the body below the LOP, as shown in figure 2505d.

The Celestial Fix

2506 In piloting, a navigator can fix his position by taking bearings of two or more landmarks or other aids to navigation in rapid succession. For practical purposes, it is generally assumed that these bearings are taken simultaneously, and no adjustment of the lines of position is required. In celestial navigation, observations cannot be taken as rapidly as in piloting, with the result that the lines of position obtained usually must be adjusted for the relatively few minutes of travel of the ship between sights. This means that what is termed a *fix* in celestial navigation is actually constructed using the principles of the running fix used in piloting, since lines of position are advanced or retired to a common time. It is customary to consider the position resulting from observations obtained during a single round of sights as a "fix," with the term *running fix* being reserved for a position obtained from observations separated by a more lengthy period of time, typically more than 30 minutes.

Except when the high-altitude technique is used, each celestial line of position requires an AP (which in some procedures may be the DR position), a segment of the radius (in the direction determined by Zn) equal in length to intercept (a), and the actual LOP constructed perpendicular to the Zn line at the point found by using (a). If three successive celestial observations were taken with small time intervals between them, the resulting APs with their associated lines of position can readily be plotted. To obtain a celestial fix, however, each would have to be advanced or retired to the time desired for the fix, making proper allowance for the travel of the ship during the intervening time. This could be done, as in piloting, by moving each LOP for the correct distance and direction. Because of the larger number of lines required to plot a celestial fix in this manner in a comparatively small area of the chart or plotting sheet, many navigators prefer to *advance the AP rather than the line of position*, thereby plotting the LOP only once. This is the method that will be used throughout this book; it is illustrated in the following examples.

Example 1: The 0515 DR position of a ship on course 176°, speed 14.5 knots, is L35°09.2′ S, λ119°13.7′ E. About this time the navigator observes the stars Antares, Acrux, and Regulus, with the following results:

Body	ANTARES	ACRUX	REGULUS
Time	0515	0519	0525
a	20.3 T	18.1 T	7.0 A
Zn	093.6°	189.5°	311.0°
aL	35°00.0′ S	35°00.0′ S	35°00.0′ S
aλ	118°56.0′ E	119°17.9′ E	119°27.9′ E

Required: The plot of the 0525 celestial fix.

Solution: (Figure 2506a) Plot the 0515 DR position and the DR track from 0515 to 0525. Plot the DR position for the time of each observation. Plot the AP of the earlier sight (Antares) and advance it in the direction and for the distance corresponding to the travel of the ship between the 0515 DR position and the 0525 DR position (2.4 miles in direction 176°). From the advanced AP so obtained, plot the 0515–0525 LOP, labeling it as shown. Note that the line joining the original AP and the advanced AP is plotted as a solid line, and that the advanced AP is *not* labeled. Next, plot the AP of Acrux and advance it for the direction and distance the ship has traveled between 0519 and 0525 (1.4 miles in direction 176°). Plot and label the 0519–0525 Acrux LOP from the advanced AP. Finally, plot the AP for the Regulus sight, and from it plot the 0525 Regulus LOP. The intersection of the three lines of position (or the center of the small triangle so formed) is the 0525 fix. (Note that to reduce the clutter of the plot, times are omitted on the individual LOPs and are shown only for the DR positions and the final fix.)

When a change of course or speed occurs between the times of the observations used in plotting a fix, the procedure used for advancing or retiring a line of position is the same as that used in piloting (article 1112). This is illustrated in the following example.

Example 2: The 0500 DR position of a ship on course 250°, speed 20 knots, is L35°11.0′ N,

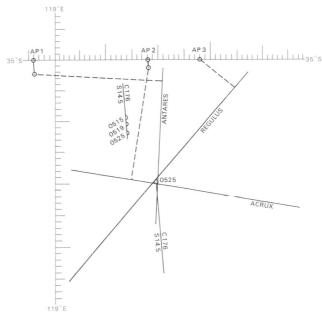

Figure 2506a. A fix determined from three celestial LOPs.

λ78°17.0′ W. At 0535 course is changed to 190°. During morning twilight the navigator observes two bodies with results as follows:

Body	DENEB	VENUS
Time	0525	0550
a	8.1 A	5.3 T
Zn	058.5°	123.9°
aL	35°00.0′ N	35°00.0′ N
aλ	78°09.0′ W	78°27.5′ W

Required: The plot of the 0550 celestial fix.

Solution: (Figure 2506b) Plot the 0500 DR position and the DR track until 0550, indicating the DR position for the time of each observation. Plot the AP of the earlier sight (Deneb) and advance it in the direction and for the distance corresponding to the travel of the ship between the 0525 DR position and the 0550 DR position (7.3 miles in direction 213.4°, as shown by the broken line marked "CMG" for "course made good"). From the advanced AP so obtained, plot the 0525–0550 LOP, labeling it as shown. Plot an AP of the Venus sight, and from it plot the 0550 LOP. The intersection of the two lines of position is the 0550 fix.

A fix obtained using the results of high-altitude observations is plotted in a manner similar to that described above, except that the GP of the body is adjusted if necessary. The method of advancing a high-altitude celestial line of position by advancing its GP is explained in the following example.

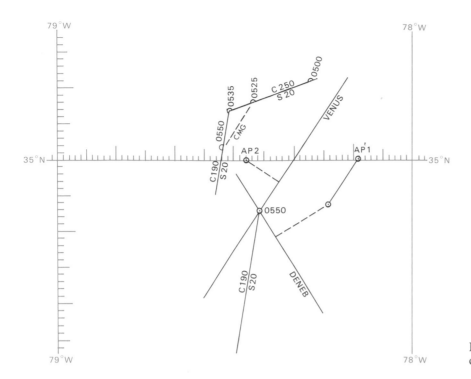

Figure 2506b. A celestial fix with a change of course between observations.

Example 3: The 1200 DR position of a ship on course 270°, speed 20.0 knots, is L23°20.0′ N, λ75°08.4′ W. About this time, the navigator observes the sun twice, with the following results:

Body	SUN	SUN
Time	1154	1206
Ho	88°33.6′	88°00.8′
L GP	22°07.7′ N	22°07.7′ N
λ GP	74°04.2′ W	77°04.2′ W

Required: The plot of the 1206 fix.

Solution: (Figure 2506c) Plot the DR track from 1154 to 1206, indicating the 1154 and 1206 DR positions. Plot the 1154 position of the sun's GP, and advance it for the direction and distance from the 1154 DR position to the 1206 DR position (4.0 miles in direction 270°). Determine the radius of the observed circle of equal altitude about the GP by subtracting the Ho from 90°00.0′. The radius is 86.4 miles (since 90°00.0′ − 88°33.6′ = 1°26.4′ = 86.4 miles). With this radius, and using the advanced GP as the center, swing an arc through the area containing the DR position. This is the 1154–1206 line of position, and is labeled as shown. Plot the 1206 GP of the sun, and determine the radius of the circle of equal altitude about it by subtracting the Ho from 90°00.0′. The radius is 119.2 miles (since 90°00.0′ − 88°00.8′ = 1°59.2′ = 119.2 miles). With this radius, and using the 1206 GP as a center,

swing an arc through the area containing the DR position. The intersection of the two lines of position is the 1206 fix.

Note that there are two possible intersections of two circles of equal altitude, only one of which is shown. In all ordinary circumstances, the intersection nearer the DR position is the fix. In the case shown in figure 2506c, there is no doubt as to the correct intersection, as the body passed to the south of the observer, and the intersection to the north of the GPs used must be the fix. Where doubt exists and the navigator is unable to determine which intersection to use, commence a DR track from both positions, and assume that the ship is on the DR track that is more dangerous until confirmation is obtained.

Running Celestial Fix

2507 When the times of the observations used are separated by a considerable interval (more than 30 minutes in a normal situation), the result is a *celestial running fix* (R Fix). The observations may be of different bodies or successive sights of the same body. Since the time elapsed between observations used to obtain a running fix is usually at least an hour, and frequently considerably longer, the LOP obtained from the earlier observation is plotted for the information it provides. This LOP is then advanced (rather than its AP) to the time of the later observation to establish the R fix, using

Figure 2506c. A celestial fix using high-altitude observations.

the same methods employed in establishing an R fix in piloting.

There is no absolute limit on the maximum time interval between observations used for a celestial running fix. This must be left to the discretion of the navigator who must give consideration to how accurately he knows his course and speed made good during that time interval. In most instances, however, three hours might be considered a practical limit.

It should be noted that in summer, when the sun transits at high altitudes, it changes azimuth very rapidly before and after transit; excellent running fixes may thus be obtained within reasonable periods of time.

Example 1: The 0930 DR position of a ship on course 064°, speed 18.0 knots, is L33°06.4' N, λ146°24.5' W. The navigator observes the sun twice during the morning, with results as follows:

Body	SUN	SUN
Time	0942	1200
a	6.2 A	27.9 A
Zn	134.2°	182.5°
aL	33°00.0' N	33°00.0' N
aλ	146°24.9' W	145°38.0' W

Required: The plot of the 1200 running fix.
Solution: (Figure 2507a) Plot the 0930 DR position, and the DR track to 1200, indicating the 0942 and the 1200 DR positions. Plot the AP with its as-

sociated LOP for 0942. Advance the LOP for the distance and direction from the 0942 DR position to the 1200 DR position (41.4 miles in direction 064°), and label it as shown. Plot the AP and from it the LOP for the 1200 sun observation, labeling it as shown. The intersection of the 0942–1200 LOP and the 1200 LOP is the 1200 running fix. (In this plot, the time is labeled on the 0942 LOP and on the 0942–1200 advanced LOP to ensure proper identification.)

When a change of course or speed occurs between the times of the observations used for obtaining a running celestial fix, the procedures used are the same as those employed in advancing the first LOP to obtain a running fix in piloting.

Using the same observations as in example 1 of this article, the following example illustrates how a running fix is obtained when both course and speed are changed between observations.

Example 2: The 0930 DR position of a ship on course 064°, speed 18.0 knots, is L33°06.4' N, λ146°24.5' W. At 1100 course is changed to 030°, and speed is reduced to 13.5 knots. During the morning, the navigator observes the sun twice, with results as tabulated in example 1.

Required: The plot of the 1200 running fix.
Solution: (Figure 2507b) Plot the 0930 DR position and the DR track to 1200, indicating the 0942 and the 1200 DR positions. Plot the 0942 LOP and advance it for the distance and direction from the

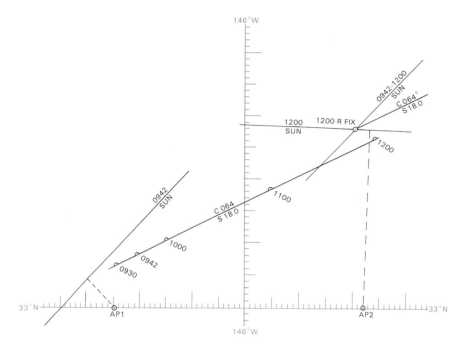

Figure 2507a. A celestial running fix.

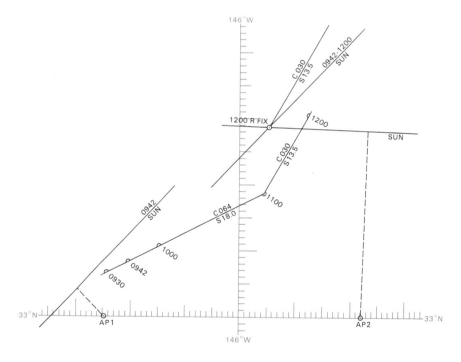

Figure 2507b. A celestial running fix with change of course and speed between observations.

0942 DR position to the 1200 DR position (35.4 miles in the direction 052°). Label it as shown. Plot and label the 1200 LOP. The intersection of the 0942–1200 LOP and the 1200 LOP is the 1200 running fix.

Where a current of known set and drift exists, the position of the running fix may be adjusted to allow for the effect of the current during the time elapsed between the first and second observation.

Errors in Running Celestial Fixes

The errors inherent in the running celestial fix are the same as those for the terrestrial running fix. However, the magnitude of the errors tends to be greater in the celestial fix. The three reasons are:

The celestial LOP is rarely as accurate as the terrestrial LOP;

Information on set and drift is not available at sea to the same degree of accuracy as is usual along a coast or in pilot waters; and

In celestial navigation, the time required to obtain the running fix is usually longer than that required in piloting, thus errors in courses and distances made good affect the accuracy to a greater extent. However, a running celestial fix is frequently the best obtainable indication of position at sea, and is helpful to the navigator.

Fixes Combining Celestial and Other LOPs

2508   A line of position, however obtained, is merely an indication of the position of a vessel, and must be crossed with one or more other LOPs to fix the position. A major objective of all forms of navigation is the determination of position—so that the ship or craft can safely and efficiently be directed from where it is to the desired destination. A navigator should, therefore, use any and all lines of position that he can obtain.

Thus, the navigator might cross a Loran or Omega line with an LOP obtained from a celestial body; an LOP from Consol bearings might be similarly employed. In a like manner, a navigator making a landfall might cross a celestial or some other LOP with a depth curve shown on his chart, determining by echo sounder the time that the curve was crossed. When only one LOP is obtainable at sea, a sounding or series of soundings may be helpful in determining the general area of the vessel's position. Article 1119 describes how soundings can be used in this connection.

All LOPs will not be of the same order of accuracy, but with experience a navigator will learn to evaluate the resulting fix. *It is vital that no opportunity be lost to acquire information that may be helpful in determining the vessel's position.*

Chapter 26

The Complete Celestial Solution

Introduction

2601 The complete solution for a typical celestial navigation sight involves the identification of the body to be observed, the use of a sextant to measure altitude, the accurate determination of the time of the sight, the use of an almanac to extract data, and some method of sight reduction to obtain a line of position, which is then plotted and combined with other LOPs to determine a fix. All these topics have been considered in the six preceding chapters. Here they will be brought together in solutions for typical bodies using the *Nautical Almanac* and the tables of DMAHTC Pub. No. 229, with the necessary actions reviewed briefly in the order in which they are taken. For comparison purposes, this will be followed by reduction of some of the same sights using other publications and methods. (Prior to any celestial observations, it may be necessary to determine the time of certain natural phenomena such as morning and evening twilight, sunrise and sunset, and moonrise and moonset; these were covered in articles 2317–2322.)

Almanac data for these solutions (except for tables of increments and corrections) can be found in chapter 23. Data from Pubs. No. 229 and 249, as well as Table 35 of Pub. No. 9, Volume II, should be taken from the publication concerned.

Note that the observations are reduced in a columnar format. On U. S. naval vessels, the navigator will use forms from the Navigation Workbook as directed by an *OpNav Instruction*. A non-naval navigator may, of course, use any form or format with which he is "comfortable"; it is the result, not the process, that is important. The columnar format, however, is highly recommended since it permits a logically progressive flow of data and calculations in the reduction. Further, it facilitates multiple reductions on a single page, each of which may use some of the same data, such as IC and Dip.

The Combined Coordinate Systems

2602 In chapter 19 the theory of the navigational triangle was considered with reference to positions on the earth's surface; in this case, the vertices of the triangle were the elevated pole, the position of the observer, and the GP of the body. In some respects, however, it is more convenient to consider the triangle with reference to positions on the celestial sphere. In this sense, it is formed by a combination of the celestial equator system of coordinates and the horizon system of coordinates. The vertices of the triangle are now the celestial pole, the observer's zenith, and the body itself, which is located by its coordinates. Note that the navigational triangle as envisioned on the celestial sphere is simply a projection outward of the navigational triangle as envisioned on the earth. Angles and angular distances are identical in each case.

On the celestial sphere shown in figure 2602, the blue lines and labels refer to the triangle portrayed on the sphere, and the black lines and labels refer to the triangle depicted on the earth. In solving the navigational triangle, the navigator first obtains the position of the celestial body at a given time with reference to the celestial equator system of coordinates, by obtaining GHA and Dec. from the *Nautical Almanac*. This establishes the position of the body (and the GP), and defines the relationship of that position to both of the celestial poles. The navigator then selects the proper assumed position (AP), which is in the near vicinity of his DR position

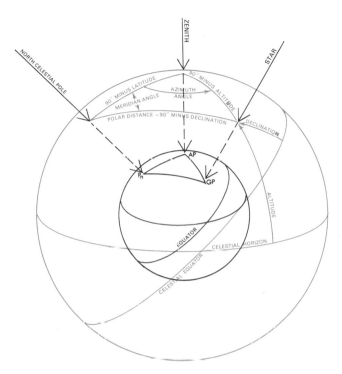

Figure 2602. The combined coordinate systems.

(if the DR position itself is not used). This selection establishes two points on the celestial sphere, both of which may be located in either the celestial equator or the horizon system of coordinates. One point is that occupied by the AP (and its zenith), and the other is the celestial pole nearer the AP. The celestial pole selected is identical with one of the poles used in conjunction with declination in the celestial equator system, and is used in determining both the colatitude and the polar distance sides of the navigational triangle. The pole used is usually called the *elevated pole*, as it is the one above the horizon of the observer. The meridian angle, defined when the AP is selected, determines the angle at the pole between the great circle joining the pole and the zenith, and the great circle joining the pole and the celestial body. Knowing the colatitude, the polar distance, and the meridian angle, the triangle can be solved in terms of the horizon system of coordinates to determine the angle at the zenith, which is azimuth angle, and the arc from the zenith to the body, which is the computed coaltitude. By converting the computed coaltitude to computed altitude (Hc) and comparing it with the observed altitude (Ho) to obtain the altitude difference (a), and by converting the azimuth angle (Z) to true azimuth (Zn), the navigator is able to plot the resulting celestial line of position.

Complete Solutions for Celestial Observations

2603 A navigator will save time, and perhaps reduce the possibility of error, if he extracts the pertinent data for all bodies from the daily pages of the *Nautical Almanac* at one page opening, when working multiple sights for a fix. Similarly, the *v* and *d* corrections, as well as the increments of GHA for minutes and seconds for each body, should be obtained at a single use of the Increments and Corrections Table.

While no additional corrections for nonstandard atmospheric conditions are used in the following examples, a navigator must always bear in mind that these should be included when weather conditions so warrant.

Selections from a Typical Day's Work

2604 The examples of this chapter will represent typical portions of a single day's work in celestial navigation for a navigator; for consideration of what comprises a full day's work, see article 2904. The computations are shown on a typical work form; see figures 2605a and 2606a. Modifications may be made, and an individual navigator should develop a format that is best suited to his procedures. The lines of position and resultant fix from the observations will be shown as a plot in figures 2605b and 2606b.

The situation is that of a salvage tug accompanying a partially disabled tanker; the course is 288°, speed 6.8 knots. At 0400 (time zone +1) on 5 June, the ship's DR position is Lat. 41°02.8′ N, Long. 14°38.0′ W.

The description of the reduction for each type of body, articles 2605–2608, is complete for the illustration of each step involved, even though this results in the repetition of some basic actions. The "simplest" sights, those involving the fewest corrections, are considered first.

Reduction of Star Observations

2605 Two star observations are reduced in the following examples. Note that the Alkaid reduction (Example 2) requires a double-second difference correction.

When observing a star, the navigator measures the sextant altitude of the body and records the time and date of the observation. He also checks the index error of the instrument.

The navigator enters the IC on the form and then the Dip correction as determined from the *Nautical Almanac* for his height of eye. He applies these (and any corrections for instrument or personal errors) to hs to obtain ha. The altitude correction is found in the "Stars and Planets" column of table A2 or the bookmark; this is added to ha to give Ho.

He then converts the time to GMT and Greenwich date, and enters the appropriate daily pages of the *Nautical Almanac* to obtain the GHA of Aries at the whole hours of GMT, and the SHA and declination of the star for that period. Turning to the appropriate Increments and Corrections table, he obtains the increments of GHA of Aries for minutes and seconds. Adding this value to the GHA of Aries and SHA of the star obtained from the daily pages, he obtains the star's GHA at the time of the observation. The Dec. is the value tabulated on the daily page.

The navigator then selects the AP, based on the best estimate of his position, and uses the aλ to determine LHA in whole degrees.

Entering Pub. No. 229 with integral degrees of LHA, aL, and Dec., he obtains the tabulated altitude for the value of the entering argument, d and its sign, and Z. The correction to tabulated altitude for d and Dec. is then taken from the multiplication table in Pub. No. 229, and applied to ht, as is the double-second difference correction if d is printed in *italic* type, to obtain the exact Hc. The navigator corrects Z by mental or written interpolation for the actual value of the declination.

Hc is then compared with Ho to determine (a). By converting Z to Zn, the navigator can then use Zn and (a) to plot the LOP from the AP.

Example 1: On 5 June the 2004 DR position of a ship is Lat. 41°34.8′ N, Long. 17°00.5′ W. At 20-04-08 (watch error 10 seconds fast), the star Capella is observed from a height of eye of 21 feet with a sextant having an IC of +0.2′. The sextant altitude is 15°27.0′.

Required: The AP, (a), and Zn using the *Nautical Almanac* and Pub. No. 229.

Answer: (Solution is shown in Column 2, figure 2605a.)

> aL   42°00.0′ N
> aλ   17°24.8′ W
> a   24.2 Away
> Zn   318.8°

Example 2: Shortly before the above observation, a sight had been taken on another star, Alkaid. The height of eye, IC, and watch error are the same as in the first example; the time was 20-03-06, and the sextant reading was 77°39.3′.

Required: The AP, (a), and Zn, using the *Nautical Almanac* and Pub. No. 229.

Answer: (Solution is shown in column 1, figure 2605a.)

Sight Reduction using Pub. 229

Body		ALKAID		CAPELLA	
IC		+ 0.2	-	+ 0.2	-
Dip (Ht 21 ')			4.4		4.4
Sum			- 4.2		-4.2
hs		77	39.3	15	27.0
ha		77	35.1	15	22.8
Alt. Corr			0.2		3.5
Add'l.					
H.P. ( )					
Corr. to ha			-0.2		-3.5
Ho (Obs Alt)		77	34.9	15	19.3
Date		5 JUN		5 JUN	
DR Lat		41	34.8 N	41	34.8 N
DR Long		17	00.5 W	17	00.5 W
Obs. Time		20-03-06		20-04-08	
WE (S+, F-)			-10 F		-10 F
ZT		20-02-56		20-03-58	
ZD (W+, E-)		+1		+1	
GMT		21-02-56		21-03-58	
Date (GMT)		5 JUN		5 JUN	
Tab GHA	v	209	10.1	209	10.1
GHA incr'mt.		0	44.1	0	59.7
SHA or v Corr.		153	20.0	281	15.0
GHA		363	14.2	491	24.8
±360 if needed				131	24.8
aλ (-W, +E)		17	14.2 W	17	24.8 W
LHA		346		114	
Tab Dec	d	N 49	25.7	N45	58.4
d Corr (+ or -)					
True Dec		N49	25.7	N45	58.4
a Lat (N or S)		42 N Same ~~Cont.~~		42 N Same ~~Cont.~~	
Dec Inc	(±)d	25.7	-32.0	58.4	+42.6
Hc (Tab. Alt.)		77	58.6	15	02.1
tens	DS Diff.	-12.6	6.9	+38.9	
units	DS Corr.	- 0.8	+ 0.4	+ 2.5	+
Tot. Corr. (+ or -)		-13.3		+41.4	
Hc (Comp. Alt.)		77	45.3	15	43.5
Ho (Obs. Alt.)		77	34.9	15	19.3
a (Intercept)		10.4	A/T	24.2	A/T
Z		N 47.9 E		N 41.2 W	
Zn (°T)		047.9°		318.8°	

Figure 2605a. Sight reductions using Pub. No. 229; stars.

> aL   42°00.0′ N
> aλ   17°14.2′ W
> a   10.4 Away
> Zn   047.9°

The lines of position from the above observations and the 2004 fix are shown in figure 2605b.

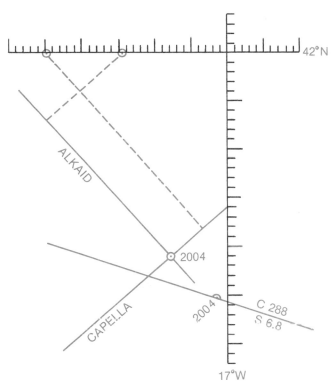

Figure 2605b. Plot of LOPs from sight reductions of figure 2605a.

Complete Solution for a Planet Observation

2606   When observing a planet, a navigator first measures the sextant altitude of the center of the body and records the time and date of the observation. He also checks the index error of the instrument.

The navigator then enters the Index Correction (IC), as determined from the sextant, on the form; any corrections for instrument or personal errors would be entered at this time. Using the *Nautical Almanac* (Table A2 or the bookmark) and his height of eye, he determines the Dip correction and enters it on the form. He next applies these corrections to the sextant altitude (hs) to obtain apparent altitude (ha), which will be used in determining all further corrections. He now determines and records the altitude correction(s) for refraction from the "Stars and Planets" column of Table A2 or the bookmark, including the "add'l" value for Venus or Mars; these are added to ha to yield observed altitude (Ho).

He then converts the time to GMT and Greenwich date, and enters the appropriate daily pages of the *Nautical Almanac* to obtain the GHA and declination at the whole hours of GMT, and the *v* and *d* values for the period, noting the sign of the *d* value by inspection. The *v* is always plus except for Venus, when it can be either plus or minus. (The values of *v* and *d* are normally taken from the bottom of each column; they can also be determined specifically by subtraction between adjacent values of GHA or declination, respectively. Occasionally a difference of 0.1' will be found between these two procedures; this will not make a significant difference in the results.) Turning to the appropriate "Increments and Corrections Table," he obtains the increments of GHA for minutes and seconds, and the corrections to GHA and declination for the *v* and *d* values, respectively. Applying these values to those obtained from the daily pages, he obtains the GHA and Dec. of the planet at the time of observation.

The navigator then selects the AP, based on his DR or best estimate of position, and uses the aλ to determine LHA in whole degrees.

Entering Pub. No. 229 with the integral degrees of LHA, aL, and Dec., the navigator obtains the tabular value for computed altitude (Hc), *d* (noting the sign of the *d* value by inspection), and azimuth angle (Z) for the entering arguments. Z is corrected by interpolation for the actual value of declination. The correction to the tabulated Hc for Dec. Inc. and *d* is then taken from inside the front or back cover of Pub. No. 229 and applied to the tabulated value; a double-second difference correction is applied if the *d* value is printed in italics and followed by a dot. These corrections give the computed altitude, Hc, for the exact declination of the body.

This corrected Hc is then compared with Ho to determine (a). The azimuth angle, Z, is converted to azimuth, Zn. The navigator now completes the reduction by using Zn and (a) to plot the LOP from the AP.

Example 3: On 5 June, the 0417 position of the vessel is Lat. 41°03.4' N, Long. 14°40.4' W. At 04-17-21 by a watch that is 8 seconds fast, the planet Venus is observed from a height of eye of 21 feet, with a sextant having an IC of +0.2'. The observed sextant altitude is 21°13.4'.

Required: The AP, (a), and Zn using the *Nautical Almanac* and Pub. No. 229.

Answer: (Solution is shown in Column 1 of figure 2606a).

aL	41°00.0' N
aλ	14°57.7' W
a	10.1' Toward
Zn	096.4°

Note: This example includes, for the sake of completeness of illustration, a watch error in the calculations. Often in everyday navigation the use of

Sight Reduction using Pub. 229

Body		VENUS		MOON LL		SUN LL	
IC		+ 0.2	−	+ 0.2	−	+ 0.2	−
Dip (Ht 21 ')			4.4		4.4		4.4
Sum			−4.2		−4.2		−4.2
hs		21	13.4	18	56.0	19	17.5
ha		21	09.2	18	51.8	19	13.3
Alt. Corr			2.5	62.4			
Add'l.		03					
H.P. ( )				7.2			
Corr. to ha			−2.2	+	09.6	+	13.3
Ho (Obs Alt)		21	07.0	20	01.4	19	26.6
Date		5 JUN		5 JUN		5 JUN	
DR Lat		41	03.4 N	41	07.9 N	41	07.9 N
DR Long		14	40.4 W	14	58.7 W	14	58.7 W
Obs. Time		04 – 17 – 21		06 – 24 – 43		06 – 25 – 23	
WE (S+, F−)		−8F		− 8F		−8F	
ZT		04 – 17 – 13		06 – 24 – 35		06 – 25 – 15	
ZD (W+, E−)		+1		+1		+1	
GMT		05 – 17 – 13		07 – 24 – 35		07 – 25 – 15	
Date (GMT)		5 JUN		5 JUN		5 JUN	
Tab GHA	v	300 39.3	+0.4	54 56.7	+7.4	285 24.7	
GHA incr'mt.		4	18.3	5	52.0	6	18.8
SHA or v Corr.			0.1		3.0		
GHA		304	57.7	60	51.7	291	43.5
±360 if needed							
aλ (−W, +E)		14	51.7 W	14	51.7 W	14	43.5 W
LHA		290		46		277	
Tab Dec	d	N8 59.6	+0.6	S14 39.9	−7.4	N22 32.4	+0.3
d Corr (+ or −)			+ 0.2		− 3.0		+0.1
True Dec		N8	59.8	S14	36.9	N22	32.5
a Lat (N or S)		41 N	Same Cont.	41 N	Same Cont.	41 N	Same Cont.
Dec Inc	(±)d	59.8	+39.2	36.9	−49.0	32.5	+36.4
Hc (Tab. Alt.)		20	17.9	20	29.2	19	19.9
tens	DS Diff.	29.9		− 24.6		16.3	
units	DS Corr.	9.1	+	− 5.5	+	3.5	+
Tot. Corr. (+ or −)			+ 39.0		− 30.1		+19.8
Hc (Comp. Alt.)		20	56.9	19	59.1	19	39.7
Ho (Obs. Alt.)		21	07.0	20	01.4	19	26.6
a (Intercept)		10.1	A/T	2.3	A/T	13.1	A/T
Z		N 96.4 E		N 133.2 W		N 76.8 E	
Zn (°T)		096.4°		227.8°		076.8°	

Figure 2606a. Sight reductions using Pub. No. 229; planet, moon, and sun.

radio time signals and a comparing watch (or stop-watch) makes this step unnecessary.

The 0417 Venus LOP is shown in figure 2606b.

Complete Solution for a Moon Observation

2607 When observing the moon, the navigator measures the sextant altitude of either the upper or lower limb of the body and records the time and date of the observation. He also checks the index error of the instrument.

He then converts the time to GMT and Greenwich date, and enters the appropriate daily pages of the *Nautical Almanac* to obtain the GHA, v value, which for the moon is always (+), declination, d

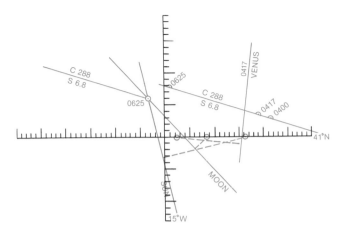

Figure 2606b. Plot of LOPs from sight reductions of figure 2602a.

value (noting the sign of the *d* value by inspection), and HP for the nearest whole hour of GMT. Turning to the appropriate "Increments and Corrections Table," he obtains the increments of GHA for minutes and seconds, and the corrections to GHA and declination for the *v* and *d* values, respectively. Applying these values to those obtained from the daily pages, he obtains the GHA and Dec. of the moon at the time of the observation.

The navigator records the IC on his form. Using the *Nautical Almanac*, he determines the Dip correction for his height of eye; he records this value and the corrections for altitude and HP from the "Altitude Correction Tables—Moon." The latter two corrections are always additive, but if the upper limb is observed, an additional correction of −30′ is made. These corrections are combined with hs to obtain ha and then Ho.

The navigator then selects the AP, based on the best estimate of his position, and selects the aλ to establish LHA in whole degrees.

Entering Pub. No. 229 with integral degrees of LHA, aL, and Dec., he obtains the tabulated altitude for the value of entering arguments, *d* and its sign, and Z. Z is corrected by interpolation for the actual value of the declination. The correction to the tabulated altitude for Dec. Inc. and *d* is then taken from a multiplication table inside the cover of Pub. No. 229 and applied to ht (the tabulated value of h), as is the double-second difference correction if *d* is printed in *italic* type, to obtain Hc.

Hc is then compared with Ho to find (a). By converting Z to Zn, the navigator can then use Zn and (a) to plot the LOP from the AP.

Example 4: On 5 June, the 0625 DR position of the vessel is Lat. 41°07.9′ N, Long. 14°58.7′ W. At 06-24-43 (the watch remains 8 seconds fast), the lower

limb of the moon is observed to be 18°56.0′. (The height of eye and IC are as before, 21 feet and +0.2′ respectively.)

Required: The AP, (a), and Zn using the *Nautical Almanac* and Pub. No. 229.

Answer: (Solution is shown in column 2 of figure 2606a.)

aL	41°00.0′ N
aλ	14°51.7′ W
a	2.3′ Toward
Zn	227.8°

Complete Solution for a Sun Observation

2608 When observing the sun, the navigator measures the sextant altitude of either the upper or lower limb of the body and records the time and date of the observation. He also records the index error of the sextant.

The values of I and IC, with their appropriate signs, would be entered in the form, as would the correction for Dip, obtained from the *Nautical Almanac*. These would be combined with hs to obtain ha.

He then converts the time to GMT and Greenwich date and enters the appropriate daily pages of the *Nautical Almanac* to obtain the GHA and declination at the whole hours of GMT, and the *d* value for the period (noting the sign of the *d* value by inspection). If maximum accuracy were desired, he would also note the SD of the sun from the daily pages.

Ordinarily, the ha is corrected by means of the sun altitude correction tables on the inside front cover of the *Nautical Almanac*, which include corrections for a nominal value of semidiameter, refraction, and parallax. Alternatively, the value of the semidiameter found at the bottom of the sun column in the daily pages of the *Nautical Almanac* may be used together with the value of the refraction correction found under the heading "Stars and Planets," and an additional correction of +0.1′ for parallax to be used for altitude of 65° and less. These corrections are applied to ha to obtain Ho.

Having entered the GHA and declination for the whole hours of GMT, the navigator now turns to the appropriate page of the Increments and Corrections Table, and obtains the increments of GHA for minutes and seconds and the correction to the declination for the *d* value. Applying these values to those obtained from the daily pages, he obtains the GHA and Dec. of the sun at the time of the observation.

With the *Nautical Almanac* still open, the navigator notes the value of IC (as determined from the sextant) and extracts the appropriate value of D. These are combined with hs to obtain ha. The appropriate correction for ☉ or ☽, taken from the Sun Table, is then applied to ha to obtain Ho.

The navigator then selects the AP, based on the best estimate of his position, and chooses an aλ to determine LHA in whole degrees.

Entering Pub. No. 229 with integral degrees of LHA, aL, and Dec., he obtains the tabulated altitude for the value of the entering arguments, d and its sign, and Z. Z is corrected by interpolation for the actual value of the declination. The correction to the tabulated altitude for Dec. Inc. and d is then taken from a multiplication table inside the covers of Pub. No. 229 and is applied to the tabulated computed altitude, as is the double-second difference correction if d is printed in italic type; this is now computed altitude, Hc, for the exact value of declination.

Hc is then compared with Ho to determine (a). Z is converted to Zn. The navigator can now plot the LOP from the AP by using Zn and (a).

Example 5: From the same DR position as in the preceding example, the lower limb of the sun is observed at 06-25-23; sextant reads 19°17.5'.

Required: The AP, (a), and Zn using the *Nautical Almanac* and Pub. No. 229.

Answer: (The solution is shown in column 3 of figure 2606a.)

aL	41°00.0' N
aλ	14°43.5' W
a	13.1' Away
Zn	076.8°

The above reduction was made for refraction under standard conditions. This is not always so; for example, if the temperature were 90°F (32.2°C) and the barometric pressure were 29.23" (990 mb), the refraction correction would have to be calculated in more detail. Using Table A4, a correction of +0.3' is found; this is combined with a value of +15.8' for semidiameter, −2.8' from the "Stars and Planets" column of Table A2, and a parallax correction of +0.1' for the sun's altitude being less than 65°. The correction by this procedure is +13.4'. In this case, the difference is of minor significance, but it would be greater in more extreme conditions of temperature or barometric pressure or both, and at lower apparent altitudes.

The 0625 fix from the moon and sun observations is shown in figure 2606b. The AP for the moon LOP was not advanced because of the short interval between observations and the slow speed of the vessel.

Reduction by Pub. No. 249

2609 As has been noted before, some navigators prefer the greater ease and speed gained through the use of the *Air Almanac* and Pub. No. 249, accepting the lesser degree of precision of the results. (Actually, either almanac could be used with either set of sight reduction tables, but in typical practice, the *Nautical Almanac* is normally paired with Pub. No. 229 and the *Air Almanac* with Pub. No. 249.)

To illustrate the use of the *Air Almanac* and Pub. No. 249 tables, several of the same observations as in the preceding article will be reduced by that method.

The *Air Almanac* has been described in chapter 23, and the Pub. No. 249 tables in chapter 24. Here attention will be focused on their use, with particular reference to the differences between the procedures of the preceding article and those of the A.A./249 method. Comparisons will be made of the results obtained by use of the two different methods.

Reduction of a Star Observation by A.A./249

In the reduction of a star observation, the navigator uses the *Air Almanac* as before to find the dip and refraction corrections and combines them with IC and the sextant reading to obtain Ho to the nearest minute.

If the star observed is not one of the 57 "selected stars," the procedure is the same as previously discussed for Volumes II and III of Pub. No. 249.

If, however, the star is one of the 57 selected stars, the unique procedure of Volume I of Pub. No. 249 can be employed. These tables are entered with whole degrees of latitude and LHA of Aries, and the name of the star, if it is one of the seven tabulated for the latitude and LHA ♈ concerned. Values of Hc and Z can be read directly and the intercept and Zn obtained with great ease and speed.

Note that when Volume I can be used, no incremental corrections of any kind are required. After the LHA and assumed latitude have been determined, a simple table "look-up" is all that is necessary to find Hc and Z. The LHA ♈ can be found from either the *Air Almanac* or the *Nautical Almanac;* note that here in the *Air Almanac* the tabular value is carried to the tenth of a minute, and this degree of precision is correspondingly used in the value of assumed longitude. The assumed latitude is simply the whole degree of latitude nearest the DR position of the vessel at the time of the sight. The GHA ♈ can also be found from Pub. No. 249 without the use of either almanac. Values are taken from table 4 for the month and year, the hour of the day, and the minutes of the hour; these three values are added together to get the GHA ♈ to the nearest whole minute of arc.

Example 1: On 5 June, the 2004 DR position of the vessel is 41°34.8′ N, Long. 17°00.5′ W. At 20-03-06 watch time, a sight was taken on the star Capella. The height of eye was 21 feet, the IC was +0.2′, and the watch error was 10 seconds fast. The sextant reading was 15°26′.

Required: The AP, (a), and Zn using the *Air Almanac* and Pub. No. 249, Volume I.

Answer: (Solution is shown in figure 2609a.)

        aL   42°
        aλ   17°10′ W
        a   16′ Away
        Zn   319°

The line of position just calculated is subject to a correction for the effects upon the tabulated altitude of progressive changes in the declination and SHA of the star due to the precession of the equinoxes, including nutation. Such a correction should be included if the year of the observation is other than the base year of the tables used. Corrections are given in Table 5 of Pub. No. 249, Volume I, for two years before the base year and for five years afterwards. In this case the year of the sight above was not the base year but three years later, necessitating a "P&N" correction for the slight progressive changes in the declination and SHA of the body as a result of the precession of the equinoxes, including nutation. For the appropriate year, Table 5 is entered for the nearest values of LHA and latitude (180° and N40° in this case); interpolation is not used. In the example above, the line of position should be adjusted 2 miles, 120° when plotted. (If several LOPs were determined, a single P&N correction could be applied to the fix, rather than to each LOP individually.) The P&N correction is applicable *only* to sight reductions made with *Volume I* of Pub. No. 249.

Note that although the Zn can be compared directly with the solution by Pub. No. 229 (example 1, article 2605), the intercept value cannot be directly compared, as it is drawn from a quite different assumed position. Figure 2609b shows the LOP as produced by the two methods; the difference is apparent, but slight, and of no particular significance in navigation.

Reduction of a Planet Observation by A.A./249

In using the *Air Almanac* for the reduction of a planet observation, the navigator first enters on his form the IC, the Dip correction (found on the inside

Body	CAPELLA	
IC	+0.2	
Dip		4
Sum		−4
Hs	15	27
Ha	15	23
Alt Corr.		−4
Ho (obs alt.)	15	19
Date	5 JUN 77	
DR Lat	41	34.8 N
DR Long	17	00.5 W
Obs Time	20 -04-08	
WE (S+, F−)		−10 F
ZT	20 -03-58	
ZD (W+, E−)	+1	
GMT	21 -03-58	
Date (GMT)	5 JUN 77	
Tab GHA ♈	209	10
GHA incr'mt.	1	00
GHA ♈	210	10
Aλ (−W, +E)	17	10
LHA ♈	193	
A Lat	42 N	
Hc	15	35
Ho	15	19
a T A	16 ⊤ A	
Zn	319°	
P&N Corr.	2 mi 120°	

Figure 2609a. Sight reductions using Pub. No. 249, Volume III.

back cover), and the refraction correction (from the page facing inside back cover); for marine navigation, use the left-hand column "0" for 0 feet elevation above the earth's surface. (Note that sextant

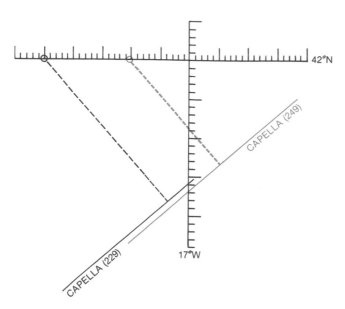

Figure 2609b. Plot of LOPs from reductions of the same sight by Pub. No. 229 and by Pub. No. 249, Volume I.

altitude and corrections are summed to the nearest minute rather than tenth of a minute.) He next locates the applicable daily page and then the line for the GMT just before the time of observation, remembering that tabular entries in the *A.A.* are for each 10 minutes of GMT. The values for GHA and declination are taken from this line and entered on the form. An increment of GHA for the balance of the time is taken from the inside front cover; the same column is used for the sun, Aries, and planets, with a different column for the moon. The GHA of the body is the sum of the angle from the daily page and the increment.

The navigator now selects an assumed position (AP) which has a whole degree of latitude and will yield a whole degree of LHA when its longitude is combined with the GHA of the body.

Volume II or III of Pub. No. 249 is selected as determined by the ship's latitude. The appropriate volume is entered with integral degrees of latitude, declination, and LHA; values are obtained for Hc and *d* to the nearest minute and Z to the nearest degree; the declination correction is obtained from table 5 at the back of the volume and is applied to Hc with the proper sign.

The comparison of corrected Hc and Ho to obtain the intercept (a) and the conversion of Z to Zn is the same as in article 2606.

Example 2: On 5 June, the 0417 position of the vessel is Lat. 41°03.4′ N, Long. 14°40.4′ W. At 04-17-21 by a watch that is 8 seconds fast, the planet

Venus is observed from a height of eye of 21 feet with a sextant having an IC of +0.2′. The observed sextant altitude is 21°13′.

Required: The (a) and Zn using the *Air Almanac* and Pub. No. 249.

Answer: (Solution is shown in column 1 of figure 2609c.)

a   10′ Toward
Zn   096°

Note that this is a solution of the same observation that was reduced by use of the *Nautical Almanac* and Pub. No. 229 in article 2606. The results can be roughly compared without plotting, as the assumed positions are the same except for a fraction of a minute of longitude. The differences in intercept and azimuth, 0.1′ and 0.4°, are negligible.

Reduction of a Moon Observation by A.A./249

In using the *Air Almanac* for reduction of a moon observation, the navigator proceeds as above for the IC, dip, and refraction corrections. From the daily pages, he obtains GHA and declination, plus two other values. Semidiameter is read from the box at the lower right corner and entered on the form; this is combined with the first three corrections to get a value that is used to enter the critical-value table "Moon's P in A" to get the correction for parallax. This final correction is added to obtain Ho.

The tabular value of GHA for the moon is incremental for the balance of time beyond the tabular entry (using a value from the column headed "Moon"); no correction is required to the tabulated declination. An AP is determined as before, so as to give an integral value of LHA when the longitude is subtracted (W) or added (E). Volume II or III of Pub. No. 249 is now used to determine tabular Hc which is corrected for *d* and z. Intercept and Zn are found in the usual manner.

Example 2: On 5 June, the 0625 DR position of the ship is Lat. 41°07.9′ N, Long. 14°58.7′ W. At 06-24-43 (the watch remains 8 seconds fast), the lower limb of the moon is observed to be 18°56′ above the horizon. The height of eye and IC are as before, 21 feet and +0.2, respectively. (These data are the same as used in article 2607.)

Required: The (a) and Zn using the *Air Almanac* and Pub. No. 249.

Answer: (The solution is shown in column 2 of figure 2609c.)

a   2′ Toward
Zn   228°

Body	VENUS		MOON LL	
IC	+0.2		+0.2	
Dip (Ht 21 ')		-4		-4
Ro		-2		-3
S.D.				+16
Sum		-6		+9
hs	21	13	18	56
P in A (Moon)				+56
Ho	21	07	20	01
Date	5 JUN		5 JUN	
DR Lat	41	03.4 N	41	07.9 N
DR Long	14	40.4 W	14	58.7 W
Obs Time	04-17-21		06-24-43	
WE		-8F		-8F
ZT	04-17-13		06-24-35	
ZD	+1		+1	
GMT	05-17-13		07-24-35	
Date (GMT)	5 JUN		5 JUN	
Tab GHA	303	09	59	45
GHA incrmt	1	48	1	06
SHA				
GHA	304	57	60	51
± 360				
a λ (W, + E)	14	57	14	51
LHA	290		46	
Tab Dec	N 9	00	S 14	37
a Lat	41 N	S R	41 N	R C
Dec Inc	00		37	-49
Tab Hc	20	57	20	29
Dec corr		00		-30
Hc	20	57	19	59
Ho	21	07	20	01
a		10 A/T		2 A/T
Z	N 96 E		N 132 W	
Zn	096°		228°	

Figure 2609c. Sight reductions using Pub. No. 249, Volume III.

Here again, compare the results of this reduction with those obtained from the *N.A./229* solution in the preceding article. The differences are slight and without significance in high-seas navigation.

Reduction of a Sun Observation by A.A./249

The procedures for determining the Ho of the sun are basically the same as those just described for the moon, except that there is no parallax correction to the sextant altitude. The procedures for GHA, declination, and LHA are the same for the sun as for the moon.

No example will be shown for the reduction of a sun observation by *A.A./249*; the reader may wish to solve this for himself and compare the slight differences with the *N.A./229* method.

Reduction by Ageton Method

2610 Because of the greater time and effort required, the Ageton method is now seldom used as a primary procedure for sight reduction. The fully qualified navigator should, however, be competent in its use. This method uses the DR position rather than an assumed position, and the intercept distance is thus a relatively direct measure of the accuracy of the DR position. The Ageton method has a considerable advantage for small craft or lifeboat use, as multiple large volumes such as those of Pub. No. 229 are not required. (The Ageton tables can be copied from *Bowditch*, Volume II; they are also published commercially as a slim booklet.) Use of the "compact" Ageton method tables will result in an even further saving of weight and space with little loss of accuracy.

Sextant corrections and almanac data are determined as before, and time calculations are made in the same manner. *Bowditch* Table 35, or other Ageton table, is entered for the various angular values, recording the entry for A or B, or both, as appropriate; note carefully the instruction "When LHA (E or W) is *greater* than 90°, take K from *bottom* of table."

The GHA of the body is entered on the form, and from this is subtracted the DR longitude to obtain the LHA and t angle. The A value for t is found in the tables and entered on the form. The value of declination is entered followed by both the B and A values. Addition, as shown on the form, yields an A value (which is copied again in the fourth column); the corresponding B value is located in the tables and entered in columns 2 and 3. Further additions and subtractions are carried out as shown in figure 2606a, ending in a value for Hc and Z from which (a) and Zn can be derived.

A single reduction will be shown here to illustrate the complete solution by the Ageton method; the observation of the star Capella, previously used, is selected as a typical example.

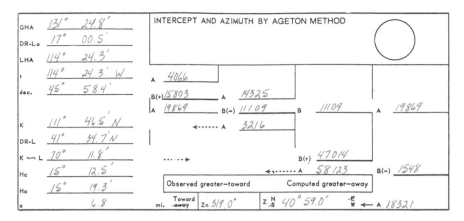

GHA	131°	24.8'
DR-Lo	17°	00.5'
LHA	114°	24.3'
t	114°	24.3' W
dec.	45°	58.4'
K	111°	46.5' N
DR-L	41°	34.7'N
K ↙ L	70°	11.8'
Hc	15°	12.5'
Ho	15°	19.3'
a		6.8

INTERCEPT AND AZIMUTH BY AGETON METHOD

A 4066
B(+) 15803   A 14325
A 19869   B(-) 11109   B 11109   A 19869
←······ A 3216
·····→   B(+) 47014
                        ←······ A 58123   B(-) 1548
Observed greater—toward   Computed greater—away
Toward -away mi. Zn 319.0°   Z ⁿ/ₛ 40° 59.0' ᵉ/w ← A 18321

Figure 2610a. Sight reduction by Ageton method.

Example: On 5 June, the 2004 DR position of the ship is Lat. 41°34.7′ N, Long. 17°01.0′ W. At 20-40-08 (watch is 10 seconds fast), the star Capella is observed from a height of eye of 21 feet with a sextant having an IC of +0.2. The sextant reading is 15°27.0′.

Required: The (a) and Zn using the *Nautical Almanac* and the Ageton method of reduction (table 35 of *Bowditch*, Volume II).

Solution: The following data are extracted from the *Nautical Almanac* and are the same as those in example 5 of article 2604; Ho 15°19.3′; GHA 131°24.8′; Dec. N 45°58.4′. The solution by the Ageton method is shown in figure 2610a.

Answer: a   6.8′ Toward
       Zn   319.0°

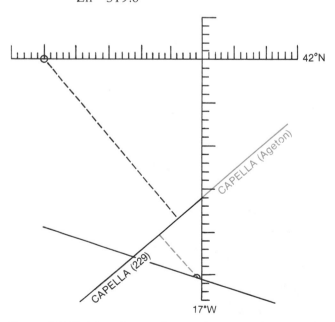

Figure 2610b. Plot of LOPs from reductions of same sight by Pub. No. 229 and by the Ageton method.

Note that the intercept value obtained from the Ageton method is quite different from that resulting from reduction by Pub. No. 229 or 249. This results, of course, from the use of the DR position rather than an assumed position. Sight reduction by the Ageton method can be compared to the results of the other methods only by means of a plot of the corresponding LOPs; see figure 2610b.

Reduction Using "Concise" Tables

2611 Despite their resemblance to the Ageton tables, sight reductions using the Davies "Concise" Tables are made from an assumed position chosen to give whole-degree values of LHA and latitude (as with Pub. No. 229). Step-by-step instructions are included with these tables and will not be repeated here.

Figure 2611 is a reduction using the "Concise" tables of the same observation shown in figure 2605a; except for a lower order of precision, the results are the same.

Solutions by Electronic Calculator

2612 As mentioned in chapter 24, celestial observations can be reduced by computation using a small hand-held electronic calculator. This is more easily done for multiple sights if the calculator can be programmed to repeat the same mathematical processes successively for different input data; it is most easily accomplished if the calculator is "card-programmable," with the process steps recorded for quick insertion into the machine (or if a specialized calculator that has built-in programs is used).

If the vessel is equipped with a microcomputer, or larger model, software programs for sight reduction can be purchased or written on board. Using either a calculator or computer, solutions are

Date _____ DR lat. _____ DR long. _____

Body identity		CAPELLA							
Sextant altitude									
1st correction									
Sum									
2nd correction									
Observed altitude		15-19							
GMT of Sight		21-03-58							
Approximate GHA									
Correction									
GHA of Sun, planet or ♈		210-09.8							
SHA of body		281-15.0							
GHA of body		131-24.8							
Assumed longitude		17-24.8							
Local hour angle		114							
Assumed latitude	N	42							
Table I, lat. & LHA	A	42-45							
1. Table I, lat. & LHA	B	⊖ 24-19	±		±		±		
2. Declination of body	D	⊕ 45-58	⊥		±		±		
Combine B and D	F	⊕ 21-39	±		±		±		
Table I, A and F	H_t	15-54							
3. Table II, A' and Z_2 corr.		⊕ 4	±		±		+		
Combine with H_t		15-58							
4. Table II, F' and P_0 corr.		⊖ 15	±		±		±		
Computed altitude		15-43							
Observed altitude		15-19							
Intercept (A or T)	A	24							
Table I, A and F	P_c	44-50							
5. Table I, lat. & LHA	Z_1	⊕ 33.6	±		±		⊥		
6. Table I, A and F	Z_2	⊖ 74.6	±		±		±		
7. Data from Schedule of Signs		+ 360.0							
8. Combine Z_1 and Z_2	Z	⊖ 41.0	⊥		±		±		
Azimuth	Z_n	319.0							

Figure 2611. Sight reduction using *Concise Tables for Sight Reduction*. (See figure 2605a.)

worked from the DR or best estimate position rather than an assumed position.

No examples are given here of sight reduction by calculator or computer, as the programs and manipulative steps will be dependent upon the specific unit used. No set of sight reduction tables will be needed; a *Nautical* or *Air Almanac* may be required, or the *Almanac for Computers* may be used. With the more widely used card-programmable calculators, the procedures consist of a sequence of program cards, with data being keyed in manually for each program; the calculator internally stores

the results of one program that will be used as partial input for the next program. The final output is a value of intercept and azimuth for a single reduction, or the coordinates of the fix if two or three reductions have been made with internal storage of the separate intercepts and azimuths. As the calculations are made from the DR position, values of azimuth and intercept can be compared directly with Ageton method results, but not to values obtained through use of Pubs. 229 or 249.

With a microcomputer, all that is required is to load the program using a magnetic disk and then enter the data as requested by the "menu" on the screen.

It is again emphasized that a navigator must *not* depend solely on an electronic calculator or computer to the exclusion of a capability to reduce sights by other means (and he must have available the necessary tables for such other means of reduction).

Choice of Reduction Method

2613   In this chapter, complete solutions have been shown for various celestial observations that are *part* of a navigator's daily work at sea (the day's work is covered more fully in chapter 29). Some of these observations were reduced by two or more methods to permit comparison of the results. The basic method of sight reduction shown here, and used by most navigators on large vessels, uses the *Nautical Almanac* and Pub. No. 229. Parallel reductions of some sights were made using the *Air Almanac* and Pub. No. 249. The combinations are not inflexible; many yacht navigators will use the *Nautical Almanac* (because one volume covers a full year) and Pub. No. 249 (because of the lesser space and weight required for the books, and less cost). With each passing year, greater use is being made of personal electronic calculators and computers; the Ageton method is generally favored as a back-up procedure in the event of equipment or electrical power failure.

Special cases of observations and reductions are covered in chapters 27 and 28.

Chapter 27

Latitude and Longitude Observations

Introduction

2701 Not only can "ordinary" celestial sights be taken and reduced to fix a vessel's position relative to her DR track, but there are also "special" observations that can be made for the specific determination of latitude or longitude. These are taken for particular positions of the body observed and are reduced to an LOP by shorter, simpler procedures than are used for the complete solution as discussed in chapter 26. A sight taken when the celestial body is either due north or south of the observer yields an LOP extending in an east-west direction; this is termed a *latitude line*. A longitude observation is obtained when the observed body is either east or west of the observer. The resulting LOP is a *longitude line,* as it extends in a north-south direction.

Latitude lines will be considered first in this chapter, as they have much in their favor—a celestial body changes altitude very slowly at transit, except at very high altitudes. Ordinarily, an experienced observer can obtain a considerable number of observations of a transiting body that will be almost identical in altitude. When one of these observations is reduced, great reliance can be placed on its accuracy.

Any celestial body will yield a latitude line when observed at transit. The two bodies most commonly used, however, are the sun and Polaris. The sun transits the observer's meridian at *local apparent noon* (LAN); the LAN observation is extremely important in navigation, chiefly because it can usually be relied upon to yield the most dependable celestial LOP of the day. The sun should be observed at LAN as a matter of routine aboard every vessel.

A latitude line can also be determined from an observation not exactly at LAN but within 28 minutes of that time through the use of certain compensation tables in *Bowditch* Volume II (see article 2704).

Determining the Time of LAN

2702 To determine the time of LAN accurately, a navigator, while the sun is still well to his east, enters the *Nautical Almanac* for the appropriate day, and finds the tabulated GHA of the sun that is nearest to, but east of, the DR longitude, and he notes the GMT hour of this entry. He then turns to his chart and for this GMT determines difference of longitude in minutes between the sun's GHA and the vessel's longitude at the hour of GMT found in the *Nautical Almanac*. This difference is meridian angle east (tE). The next step is to determine the instant when the sun's hour circle will coincide with the vessel's longitude; this establishes the time of LAN, and is accomplished by combining the rate of the sun's change of longitude with that of the vessel. The sun changes longitude at an almost uniform rate of 15°, or 900' per hour. The rate of the vessel's change of longitude per hour is usually determined by measurement on the chart.

If the vessel is steaming towards the east, its hourly rate of change of longitude is added to that of the sun; if it is steaming west, the rate of change is subtracted from that of the sun.

All that remains is to divide the meridian angle east expressed in minutes, found above, by the combined rate of change of longitude. The answer, which will be in decimals of an hour, should be determined to three significant places. Multiplied by 60, minutes and decimals of minutes are obtained; the latter may be converted to seconds by again multiplying by 60. The answer will be mathematically correct to about four seconds; when added to the hour of GMT obtained from the *Nautical Almanac*, it will give the GMT of the sun's transit (LAN) at the vessel. Any error in DRλ will, of course, affect the accuracy. The zone description may be employed to convert the GMT of LAN to ship's time. The above procedure can conveniently be written as the following equation:

Interval to LAN

$$= \frac{\text{tE in minutes of arc}}{900' \text{ arc} \pm \text{ship's movement in longitude '/hour}}$$

This procedure is illustrated in the following example.

Example: On 5 June, the navigator of a ship proceeding on course 281°, speed 11.5 knots, plans to observe the sun at LAN. At 1145 (+1), he notes that the 1200 DR position will be Lat. 41°17.7′ N, Long. 20°51.6′ W.

Required: The ZT of transit of the sun.

Solution: (Figure 2702) The ship's 1200 DR longitude will be 20°51.6′ W. Entering the *Nautical Almanac* with this value and for this date, 5 June, the nearest, but lesser, GHA of the sun is found; this is 15°24.0′ for 1300 GMT, which is 1200 ship's time. (If the longitude had been east, it would have been subtracted from 360° to get the angular distance west of Greenwich for entry into the *Nautical Almanac*.)

The difference in longitude between the ship and the sun at 1200 (+1) equals 20°51.6′ minus 15°24.0′ or 5°27.6′ or 327.6′. This value is used for tE.

By inspection of the plot of the ship's DR longitude for 1200 and 1300 (figure 2702) the hourly change of longitude, in minutes of arc, is found to be 15.0′. This change is in a *westerly* direction; it will therefore be subtracted from the sun's change,

Figure 2702. Plot for calculating the time of LAN.

which is 900′ per hour. The net hourly rate of change is 900′ minus 15.0′, or 885.0′ per hour. The value of tE is next divided by this net rate, 327.6 ÷ 885.0′, to find the time, in decimal fractions of an hour, after 1200 ship's time at which transit will occur. The answer, rounded off, is 0.37; in minutes 0.37 × 60 = 22.2 minutes or 22 minutes 12 seconds. This is added to 1200 (+1) to get the time of transit, or LAN.

Answer: 12-22-12 ZT.

Alternate Method of Determining LAN

The time of local apparent noon can also be determined from calculations using the time of meridian passage of the sun as tabulated for each day on the right-hand pages of the *Nautical Almanac*; see figure 2304b. This time is given for the meridian of Greenwich, but the rate of change is so slight that it can be used at any longitude without significant error.

The navigator obtains the tabulated value of meridian passage from the *Nautical Almanac*; this is local meridian time (LMT). He then plots the DR position for the vessel for that time in zone time (ZT). He next determines the longitude difference between the DR position and the central meridian of the time zone being used, and converts this to time units. This time difference is applied to the LMT of meridian passage, adding if the DR position is west of the central meridian, subtracting if it is east. The time thus obtained is the first estimate of ZT of transit of the sun.

If the vessel is moving, further computation is required. The navigator plots a new DR position for the first estimate of the ZT of LAN as determined above. Using this new DR longitude, he computes a new ZT correction to the tabulated LMT of meridian passage; this is the second estimate of the ZT of LAN and is used for observations.

This procedure is illustrated using the same situation as in the prior method.

Example: On 5 June, the navigator of a ship proceeding on course 281°, speed 11.5 knots, plans to observe the sun at local apparent noon.

Required: The ZT of transit of the sun.

Solution: The navigator determines from the *Nautical Almanac* that meridian passage is at 1158. He also determines that the ship's longitude at that zone time will be 20°51.1′ W. This is 5°51.1′ west of the central meridian of the (+1) time zone; converted to time units, this is 23ᵐ24ˢ; rounded to 23 minutes and adding to 1158, the first estimate is 1221.

The DR longitude for 1221 ZT is 20°56.9′ W. The time difference for 5°56.9′ is 23ᵐ48ˢ. This is rounded to 24 minutes and added to 1158, giving 1222.

Answer: 1222 ZT.

Note that this procedure computes values to the nearest minute only, consistent with the *Nautical Almanac* tabulations of the time of meridian passage. This is sufficiently precise, as the time of LAN will be used only as the approximate center time for a series of observations.

A determination of the time of LAN is especially necessary when a vessel is running on a generally northerly or southerly course at speed. For a vessel proceeding towards the south, the sun will continue to increase its altitude for a considerable period *after* it actually has crossed the ship's meridian, and an observation made at the moment when it reaches its maximum altitude will yield a latitude that may be considerably in error.

Under most conditions, however, the sun will appear to "hang" for an appreciable period of time at LAN; that is, it will not change perceptibly in altitude. To obtain a latitude line at LAN, the navigator usually starts observing about two minutes before the time of transit, and continues to obtain sights until the altitude begins to decrease. The average of the three or four highest altitudes can be used for the reduction (or a graph can be plotted of altitude vs. time). On a northerly or southerly course several altitudes may be taken before and after that calculated time of transit to ensure that an unpredictable random error did not occur in the sight taken at the time of transit.

Solution of Meridian Altitudes

2703 While meridian altitudes may be solved routinely by means of the inspection tables such as Pub. No. 229, using an assumed latitude, LHA 0°, and a tabulated declination as entering arguments, such tables are not necessary to obtain a solution.

The method of solution is the same for all celestial bodies observed on the upper branch of the meridian; at this instant each azimuth is precisely 000.0°, or 180.0°. In terms of the navigational triangle, it is a special case, in that the elevated pole, the observer's zenith, and the celestial body are all on the same great circle. The LOP obtained from a meridian observation is an exact latitude line.

The semicircle in figure 2703a represents that half of the observer's meridian extending from the north point to the south point of his celestial horizon; it is also occupied by a celestial body (in this

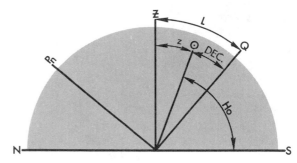

Figure 2703a. Lat. = z + Dec.

case the sun) at the instant of transit. This article will discuss the transit of the sun, as it is the most frequently observed body. However, any celestial body observed when precisely on the navigator's meridian may be used, and the method of reduction would be the same as outlined here for the sun.

In this diagram, Z represents the observer's zenith, Q is the equator, P_n is the north pole, here the elevated pole, N and S represent the north and south points of the observer's horizon, respectively, and $\odot$ the sun on the meridian. The angle z is the zenith distance of the sun, that is, 90° minus the observed altitude; L, $Dec.$, and Ho are the observer's latitude, the declination, and the observed altitude, respectively. The same labeling is used in all diagrams on the plane of the observer's meridian.

Zenith Distance (z)

In reductions to the meridian, *z is named for the direction of the observer from the body;* that is, if the observer is south of the body, z is named *south*. The latitude may then be obtained by applying the angular value of z to the declination, *adding if they are of the same name, and subtracting the smaller from the larger if the names are contrary.* The latitude will have the same name as the remainder; for example, if z is 42° N and the declination is 18° S, the latitude equals 42° N minus 18° S, or 24° N.

Figure 2703a is drawn for an observer in north latitude, who is north of the sun; the observer's altitude of the sun at transit is 71°. The z, therefore, is 90° minus 71°, or 19° N. The sun's declination at the time of transit is 21° N. As the declination is north, and as the observer is north of the sun, z and Dec. are added (19° N + 21° N) to give the observer's latitude, 40° N. Figure 2703b illustrates a case where the observer's latitude and the declination are of opposite name. The Ho is 40°, and the sun is north of the observer, giving a z of 50° S, and the declination is 20° N. In this case Dec. is subtracted from the z (50° S − 20° N) to yield a latitude of 30° S.

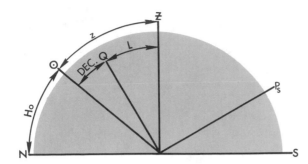

Figure 2703b. Lat. = z − Dec.

Figure 2703c shows an L and Dec. of the same name, but Dec. greater than L. The Dec. is 21° N; Ho is 78°, giving a z of 12° S. Therefore, z is subtracted from Dec. (21° N − 12° S) to yield a latitude of 9° N.

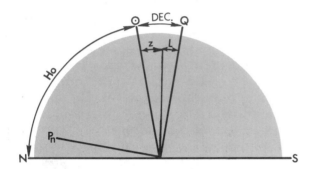

Figure 2703c. Lat. = Dec. − z.

The procedure for the determination of latitude from an observation of the sun at LAN can be summarized in the following two rules:

If the zenith distance and declination are of *same* name, they are added; the *sum* is the latitude of the observer.

If the zenith distance and declination are of *contrary* name, the smaller value is *subtracted* from the larger; the *difference* is the latitude, with the sign of the larger value.

Calculator and computer programs are available for meridian transit solutions, but are hardly necessary in view of the quite simple mathematics involved.

Solutions for Lower-branch Meridian Altitudes

When a body is observed at *lower transit*, on the lower branch of the meridian, the solution differs from that for the upper branch, in that polar distance (p) is used, rather than z; p is the angular distance of the body from the pole or 90° minus Dec. At lower transit, the observer's latitude is

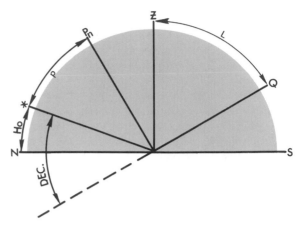

Figure 2703d. Lat. = Ho + p.

equal to the observed altitude plus the polar distance, or L = Ho + p. In figure 2703d a star with a declination of 50° N is observed at lower transit at an Ho of 20°. L therefore equals 20° + 40°, or 60° N.

Reduction to the Meridian Using *Bowditch* Tables 29 and 30

2704 A latitude line of position can be obtained from any observation made within 28 minutes of the time of either upper or lower transit, provided the altitude of the body is between 6° and 86°, the latitude is not more than 60°, and the declination is not greater than 63°. This is termed a *reduction to the meridian,* or *ex-meridian* reduction. The calculations use Tables 29 and 30 in *Bowditch*, Volume II.

An initial *altitude factor* (a) is taken from table 29, using the ship's latitude and the body's declination. For an upper transit, a left-hand page is used if the latitude and declination are of the same name; a right-hand page is used if they are of contrary names. For a lower transit, the factor is taken from below the heavy lines on the last three right-hand pages of Table 29.

The factor (a) derived from Table 29 is used to enter Table 30, together with the time difference from LAN (or meridian angle t in units of arc). Table 30 is entered twice, for the whole units of (a) and for the tenths of that factor; these values are summed. The total is a correction to be applied to the observed altitude, adding for an upper transit or subtracting for a lower transit, to obtain meridian altitude at the time of transit.

Latitude from a Polaris Observation

2705 The latitude of a place is equal to the altitude of the elevated pole, as is illustrated in figure 2705. Both the latitude of the observer, *QOZ*, and

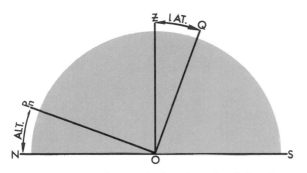

Figure 2705. Latitude equals the altitude of the elevated pole.

the altitude of the pole, *NOPn*, equals 90° minus *PnOZ*. Thus, if a star were located exactly at each celestial pole, the corrected altitude of the star would equal the observer's latitude.

No star is located exactly at either pole, but Polaris is less than a degree from the north celestial pole. Like all stars, it alternately transits the upper and lower branches of each celestial meridian in completing its diurnal circle. Twice during every 24 hours, as it moves in its diurnal circle, Polaris is at the same altitude as the pole, and at that moment no correction would be required to its observed altitude to obtain latitude. At all other times a correction, constantly changing in value, must be applied. The value for any instant may be obtained from the Polaris Tables in the *Nautical Almanac*, the entering argument being LHA♈. The correction is tabulated in three parts; the first is the basic correction applicable under all conditions. This correction, designated a_0 in the *Nautical Almanac*, compensates for the component of the distance between the position of Polaris in its diurnal circle and the north celestial pole, measured along the observer's celestial meridian. The second correction, a_1, is for the DR latitude of the observer, and corrects for the angle at which he views the star's diurnal circle. The third correction, a_2, is for the date and corrects for the small variations in the position of the star in its diurnal circle in the course of a year.

Solution of a Polaris Observation by *Nautical Almanac*

2706 A latitude LOP can be obtained from an observation of Polaris using only the *Nautical Almanac* (or *Air Almanac*) to reduce the observation. An azimuth can also be obtained; see article 2806.

The three Polaris correction tables comprise the last three white pages at the back of the *Nautical*

Almanac. A portion of these tables, showing the arrangement of the three corrections a_0, a_1, and a_2, is reproduced in figure 2706a (the year of the table, normally shown on the top line, has been deleted from this extract). It must be borne in mind that *these three corrections are in addition to the usual corrections applied to all sextant observations to obtain Ho.*

As with any body, the sextant altitude is obtained, and the time and date are recorded. The index error is checked and recorded.

Using the GMT and Greenwich date, the appropriate page of the almanac is entered, and the GHA ♈ for the minutes and seconds are obtained. These are added to the tabulated value for the hours from the daily page to obtain the GHA ♈ at the time of the observation. The DR longitude at the time of observation is applied (subtract west, add east) to get LHA ♈. Note that an assumed position is not used.

To solve a Polaris observation for latitude, find the value of LHA ♈ in the column headings across the top of the Polaris correction tables; these are divided into groups of 10°. Then follow down this column until opposite the single degree of value of LHA ♈ as tabulated in the left-hand column; the exact value for a_0 is then found for the minutes of LHA ♈ by interpolation. Staying in the same vertical column, the value of a_1 is then found in the middle part of the table for the nearest tabulated latitude, without interpolation. Next, the a_2 correction is found in the same column for the current month, again no interpolation.

The arrangement of the tables is such that these three corrections are always *positive* (additive), *but an additional constant of 1° negative is finally applied* to determine the total correction at the time and latitude of the observation. The total correction, therefore, can be negative in some instances.

Customarily, the navigator uses the latitude thus obtained to draw a latitude LOP. If his DR longitude is reasonably accurate, this latitude line will yield acceptable accuracy. If there is considerable uncertainty as to the vessel's longitude, the azimuth of Polaris should be determined. This will be found at the bottom of the Polaris tables, the entering arguments being the nearest 10° of LHA ♈, and the nearest tabulated latitude; no interpolation is required. The LOP is then drawn through the computed latitude and the DR longitude, perpendicular to this azimuth.

Example: The latitude at the time of observation, using the *Nautical Almanac*.

POLARIS (POLE STAR) TABLES
FOR DETERMINING LATITUDE FROM SEXTANT ALTITUDE AND FOR AZIMUTH

L.H.A. ARIES	240°–249°	250°–259°	260°–269°	270°–279°	280°–289°	290°–299°	300°–309°	310°–319°	320°–329°	330°–339°	340°–349°	350°–359°
	a_0	a_0	a_0	a_0	a_0	a_0	a_0	a_0	a_0	a_0	a_0	a_0
°	° ′	° ′	° ′	° ′	° ′	° ′	° ′	° ′	° ′	° ′	° ′	° ′
0	1 43.5	1 38.9	1 33.1	1 26.2	1 18.5	1 10.2	1 01.5	0 52.7	0 44.1	0 36.0	0 28.5	0 22.0
1	43.1	38.4	32.4	25.5	17.7	09.3	1 00.6	51.9	43.3	35.2	27.8	21.4
2	42.7	37.8	31.8	24.7	16.9	08.4	0 59.7	51.0	42.5	34.4	27.1	20.8
9	39.4	33.7	26.9	19.3	11.0	02.4	53.6	45.0	36.8	29.2	22.6	17.0
10	1 38.9	1 33.1	1 26.2	1 18.5	1 10.2	1 01.5	0 52.7	0 44.1	0 36.0	0 28.5	0 22.0	0 16.5
Lat.	a_1	a_1	a_1	a_1	a_1	a_1	a_1	a_1	a_1	a_1	a_1	a_1
°	′	′	′	′	′	′	′	′	′	′	′	′
0	0.5	0.4	0.3	0.3	0.2	0.2	0.2	0.2	0.2	0.3	0.4	0.4
10	.5	.4	.4	.3	.3	.2	.2	.2	.3	.3	.4	.5
20	.5	.5	.4	.4	.3	.3	.3	.3	.3	.4	.4	.5
30	.5	.5	.5	.4	.4	.4	.4	.4	.4	.4	.5	.5
66	.7	.8	.8	0.9	1.0	1.0	1.0	1.0	0.9	.9	.8	.7
68	0.7	0.8	0.9	1.0	1.0	1.1	1.1	1.1	1.0	0.9	0.9	0.8
Month	a_2	a_2	a_2	a_2	a_2	a_2	a_2	a_2	a_2	a_2	a_2	a_2
	′	′	′	′	′	′	′	′	′	′	′	′
Jan.	0.4	0.5	0.5	0.5	0.5	0.5	0.6	0.6	0.6	0.7	0.7	0.7
Feb.	.4	.4	.4	.4	.4	.4	.4	.5	.5	.5	.6	.6
Mar.	.4	.3	.3	.3	.3	.3	.3	.3	.3	.4	.4	.5
Apr.	0.5	0.4	0.4	0.3	0.3	0.3	0.2	0.2	0.2	0.3	0.3	0.3
May	.6	.5	.5	.4	.4	.3	.3	.2	.2	.2	.2	.2
June	.8	.7	.6	.6	.5	.4	.4	.3	.3	.3	.2	.2
July	0.9	0.8	0.8	0.7	0.7	0.6	0.5	0.5	0.4	0.4	0.3	0.3
Aug.	.9	.9	.9	.8	.8	.8	.7	.7	.6	.5	.5	.4
Sept.	.9	.9	.9	.9	.9	.9	.9	.8	.8	.7	.7	.6
Oct.	0.8	0.8	0.9	0.9	0.9	0.9	0.9	0.9	0.9	0.9	0.8	0.8
Nov.	.6	.7	.8	.8	.9	.9	1.0	1.0	1.0	1.0	1.0	1.0
Dec.	0.5	0.6	0.6	0.7	0.8	0.8	0.9	1.0	1.0	1.0	1.0	1.0

Latitude = Apparent altitude (corrected for refraction) $-1° + a_0 + a_1 + a_2$

The table is entered with L.H.A. Aries to determine the column to be used; each column refers to a range of 10°. a_0 is taken, with mental interpolation, from the upper table with the units of L.H.A. Aries in degrees as argument; a_1, a_2 are taken, without interpolation, from the second and third tables with arguments latitude and month respectively. a_0, a_1, a_2 are always positive. The final table gives the azimuth of *Polaris*.

Figure 2706a. *Nautical Almanac*, Polaris Tables (extract).

Answer: (Solution is shown in figure 2706b.)
Lat. 41°00.8′

Solution of a Polaris Observation by *Air Almanac*

2707 An observation of Polaris can also be reduced for a latitude line of position by use of the *Air Almanac.*

Various Q corrections are tabulated for critical values of LHA ♈ (which is found from GHA ♈ and DR longitude in the normal manner). The Q values are applied to the corrected sextant altitude to directly yield latitude.

Example: During morning twilight on 5 June, at approximately 0352 (+1), a navigator observes Polaris. The ship's DR position is Lat. 41°02.5′ N, Long. 14°36.9′ W. The sextant has an IC of +0.2′; the watch is 8 seconds fast; the height of eye is 21 feet. The sextant altitude at 03-52-16 watch time is 41°14′.

Required: The latitude at the time of observation, using the *Air Almanac.*

Answer: (Solution is shown in figure 2707).
Lat. 41°01′ N.

Note that this value, to the nearest whole minute of latitude, is essentially the same as that obtained, to the nearest tenth of a minute, by use of the *Nautical Almanac;* several fewer steps were required by use of the *Air Almanac.*

Observations for Longitude

2708 Longitude observations were in general use until the altitude difference or intercept method, devised in 1875 by Marcq de St.-Hilaire,

IC	+ 0.2	−
Dip (Ht. 28)		4.4
Sum		−4.2
hs	41	14.2
ha	41	−10.0
Alt. Corr		−1.1
TB (hs < 10°)		
Ho	41	08.9
Date	5 JUN 77	
DR Lat.	41°	02.5' N
DR Long	14°	36.9' W
Obs time	03-52-16	
WE (S+, F−)		8F
ZT	03-52-08	
ZD (W+, E−)	+1	
GMT	04-52-08	
Date (GMT)	5 JUN 77	
Tab GHA ♈	313	28.3
GHA Incrmt	13	04.1
GHA ♈	326	32.4
DR Long	14	36.9 W
LHA ♈	311	55.5
a₀	51.1	
a₁	0.5	
a₂	0.3	
Add'n'l		60.0
Sub total	51.9	60.0
Corr to Ho		−8.1
Ho	41	08.9
Lat	41°	00.8 N
True Az		
Gyro Brg		
Gyro Error		

Figure 2706b. Calculation of latitude from a Polaris observation using the *Nautical Alamanc*.

IC	+ 0.2	−
Dip (Ht. 21)		4
Sum		−3.8
hs	41-14	
ha	41-10	
Alt Corr	−1	
TB (hs < 10°)		
Ho	41° 09'	
Date	5 JUN 77	
DR Lat	41° 025' N	
DR Long	14° 36.9' W	
Obs time	03-52-16	
WE	8F	
ZT	03-52-08	
ZD	+1	
GMT	04-52-08	
Date GMT	5 JUN 77	
Tab GHA ♈	326 00	
Incrmt	0 32	
GHA ♈	326 32	
DR Long	14 37	
LHA ♈	311 55	
Q	−8	
Ho	41 09	
Lat.	41° 01' N	

Figure 2707. Calculation of latitude from a Polaris observation using the *Air Almanac*.

was accepted. The longitude obtained was predicated on a latitude; the latter was usually obtained from a LAN sun observation, and carried forward or back by DR. The calculated longitude was therefore accurate only if the DR latitude was accurate. Subsequently, as the accuracy of chronometers was improved, celestial bodies were observed on the *prime vertical*, that is, when their azimuth was exactly 090.0° or 270.0°; this method yielded considerably increased accuracy.

Presently, observations intended solely to yield longitude are seldom required or made. If one is to be made, the most convenient method involves the use of an inspection table, usually Pub. No. 229, to determine the time at which the observation should be made. In the case of Pub. No. 229, it is entered with values of latitude and declination, and the LHA is determined for the time at which

the azimuth equals 90.0° (or 270.0°). The GMT at which this LHA, converted to GHA by applying DR longitude, occurs can then be obtained from the *Nautical Almanac*. For the best results, interpolation should be made for t, Dec., and L. The process is feasible but laborious, and consequently is not often done; calculator and computer programs are available.

Observations on the Beam, Bow, and Stern

2709 Observations made directly on the beam are helpful in determining whether the ship is on the desired track line, while observations obtained dead ahead or astern show how far she has advanced. The sun is the body most commonly used in making such observations. Here, again, Pub. No. 229 may be used to advantage. It is entered with the appropriate latitude and declination, as outlined in article 2708, and the desired azimuth angle, relative to the ship's head, stern, or beam is found. The time for the observation is then determined as for a longitude observation.

Chapter 28

Compass Checks at Sea

Introduction

2801 In the previous chapters, the measurement of compass error (chapter 3) was determined in respect to visible landmarks and aids to navigation. It is not necessary, however, to have such relatively close objects at hand. Compass error on the high seas can be determined from azimuth observations of celestial bodies; the sun is the body most frequently observed. Such observations should be made when the sun is low in altitude, preferably under 20°. All navigators and their assistants should be trained to obtain accurate azimuth observations, and make the necessary calculations.

A prudent navigator, when underway and weather conditions permit, checks the error of his compass once each day; for U.S. naval vessels, regulations require that this be done. Good practice, however, calls for a compass check at least twice a day whenever possible. A check should be made immediately if there is any reason to suppose that a compass has been damaged, or is malfunctioning. Thus far, the celestial navigation portion of this book has been concerned with the solution of navigational triangles to obtain LOPs and fix the position of the vessel. It is often necessary, however, for a navigator to solve navigational triangles for other purposes. This chapter will consider the solution of a navigational triangle to determine true azimuth, and from this, the compass error at sea.

Azimuth Observation

2802 Azimuth observations of celestial bodies are made using an *azimuth circle*, bearing circle, or similar device. An azimuth circle (figure 704) is an instrument whose principal components are a small, hinged, concave mirror and a shielded prism that is located on the ring opposite the mirror. When such an instrument is used to observe the sun's azimuth, it is fitted over a gyrocompass repeater, or the bowl of a magnetic compass, and aligned so that the prism is directly between the mirror and the sun. When the hinged mirror is properly adjusted in the plane of the vertical circle of the sun, a thin, vertical beam of sunlight is cast upon a slit in the prism shield and refracted downward onto the compass card. The line of sunlight on the card indicates the compass azimuth of the sun at that time. Two leveling bubbles are provided with the azimuth circle, as the instrument must be horizontal to indicate an accurate compass azimuth.

An azimuth observation of a star or planet is made using the sight vanes of an azimuth circle or bearing circle, in a manner similar to that used for observing terrestrial bearings (article 704). The moon may be observed for azimuth using either the mirror-prism method or the sight-vane method. Because of the difficulty in seeing the leveling bubbles during darkness, azimuth observations are usually restricted to the sun. A pelorus can also be used to determine the azimuth measurements, although generally with less accuracy.

In practice, the navigator observes the azimuth of a celestial body and notes the time of the observation. He then solves the navigational triangle for his position and determines the true azimuth of the body at the time of the observation. The difference between the true and observed azimuths, properly labeled E or W, is the compass error.

In general, the lower the celestial body, the more accurate the azimuth observations. For most practical purposes, a level of precision of one-half degree is sufficient.

Exact Azimuth by Inspection Tables

2803 The inspection tables for sight reduction, Pub. No. 229, make excellent azimuth tables. (Pub. No. 249 tables can be used for obtaining exact azimuths, but not as precisely, as tabulations are only to the nearest whole degree.)

When Pub. No. 229 is used to determine true azimuth for the purpose of checking the compass, triple linear interpolation usually must be made in order to obtain the required accuracy. The d values in Pub. No. 229 apply only to *altitude* and should not be used when interpolating for azimuth.

Example: The azimuth of the sun is observed at 06-25-42 on 5 June. The 0625 position has been fixed at Lat. 41°06.1′ N, Long. 15°03.1′ W. The azimuth obtained by using a gyro repeater is 076.0°.

Required: Gyro error, using Pub. No. 229 to obtain exact true azimuth.

Solution: (Figure 2803) It is first necessary to determine the exact values of LHA, Dec., and L for the instant of observation of the azimuth. These values are determined as for working a sight, except that the *actual* position of the ship is used rather than an assumed position. Thus the DR longitude, 15°03.1′ W, is used to determine the exact value of LHA at the time of observation. The exact value of Dec. is found to be N22°32.5′ by use of the *Nautical*

Almanac in the usual manner. The DR latitude is taken as the exact value of L at the time of observation. (If a fix obtained from observations and complete reductions at about this time shows the DR position to be significantly in error, the more accurate values of Lat. and Long. of the fix should be used.)

With the exact values of LHA, Dec., and L determined, the appropriate page of Pub. No. 229 is entered for the "tab" values, those tabulated entering arguments *nearest* to the exact values. In this case, they are LHA 277, Dec. N23°, and L41° N. With these "tab" values as entering arguments, the proper page (the "same name" section in this case) is entered and the tabulated azimuth angle, Z, 76.4° is recorded. This value of Z is the *tabulated* ("tab") value, to which the corrections resulting from the necessary interpolation are applied to obtain the azimuth angle for the exact values of LHA, Dec., and L at the moment of observation. Interpolation is made separately for the difference between each of the exact values and the corresponding "tab" values of LHA, Dec., and L; and the algebraic sum of the resulting corrections is applied to the value of tab Z to obtain the exact azimuth angle at the moment of observation. It is sufficiently accurate to reduce these corrections to the nearest tenth of a degree.

An interpolation is made between LHA 277° (Z 76.4°) and LHA 276° (Z 75.8°). The change in Z is

---

EXACT AZIMUTH USING Pub. 229

Body	☉				EXACT		Z DIFF. (+ or -)	CORR. (+ or -)
					Deg	Min		
DR L	41°	06.1′ N		LAT	41	06.1	+ 0.3	0.0
DR λ	15°	03.1′ W		LHA	276	47.1	- 0.6	- 0.1
Date (L)	5 JUN			DEC	22	32.5	+ 0.8	+ 0.4
ZT	06 - 25 - 42					Total (±)		+ 0.3
ZD (+ or -)	+1					Tab Z		76.4
GMT	07 - 25 - 42					Exact Z		76.7
Date (G)	5 JUN					Exact Zn		076.7
Tab GHA	285°	24.7′				Gyro/Compass Brg		076.0
Inc'mt	6°	25.5′				Gyro/Compass Error		0.7 E
GHA	291°	50.2′						
DR λ	- 15°	03.1′ W						
LHA	276°	47.1						

		d(+/-)
Tab Dec	N22° 32.4′	+ 0.2′
d corr	+ 0.1′	
Dec	N22° 32.5′	

NORTH LAT

LHA greater than 180° .... Zn = Z
LHA less than 180° .... Zn = 360° - Z

SOUTH LAT

LHA greater than 180° .... Zn = 180° - Z
LHA less than 180° .... Zn = 180° + Z

Figure 2803. Determination of exact azimuth and gyro error using Pub. No. 229.

−0.6° for a change in LHA of 1° (60′); this is known as the "Z diff." Since the exact value of LHA is 276°47.1′, or 12.9′ less than the "tab" value of LHA, the difference in the value of Z corresponding to this difference in LHA is $\frac{12.9′}{60′}$ of the difference for a 1° change in LHA. Thus the "corr," which is the correction to apply to the value of tab Z because of the difference between the exact value of LHA and the tab value, is equal to $-0.6° \times \frac{12.9′}{60}$ or −0.1°.

An interpolation for declination is made between 23° (Z76.4°) and 22° (Z77.2°) in the same manner as above: 77.2° − 76.4° = +0.8° (Z diff); the exact declination is 60′ − 32.5′ = 27.5′ less than the tab declination of 23°; the correction is $+0.8° \times \frac{27.5}{60} =$ +0.4°.

A similar interpolation is made for latitude between 41° (Z 76.4°) and 42° (Z 76.7°); 76.4° = +0.3°; the exact latitude is 6.0′ greater than the tab latitude of 41°; the correction is $+0.3° \times \frac{6.0}{60} = 0.0°$.

By applying the algebraic sum of the LHA, Dec., and L corrections, as determined above, to the tab Z, the exact azimuth angle at the moment of observation is found to be N76.7° E, which converts to a Zn of 076.7°. The gyro error is found by comparing this exact azimuth with that obtained by observation, 076.0°. Thus 076.7 minus 076.0 equals 0.7°; as the compass is "least" (lesser in value than the true value), the error is "east."

Answer: Gyro error is 0.7° E.

Note that although exact azimuth is calculated to the nearest tenth of a degree, the gyro repeater used for taking the bearing is calculated only to whole degrees, and readings are not possible to a greater precision than a half degree. Thus, gyro error in the above example should more properly be stated as 0.5° E.

In solving problems for exact azimuth using Pub. No. 229, the multiplication of the fractional amount by the amount of the "diff" to obtain the appropriate correction can be accomplished readily by establishing a proportion with dividers on a log scale of speed or distance, such as is found on some charts and on Maneuvering Board forms, and is discussed briefly in article 1404. In establishing the fractions involved, it is well to remember that the denominator of the fractional part of LHA, Dec., and L is always 60′, as the tabulated entering arguments of LHA, Dec., and L are always 1° apart.

As noted above, the other set of commonly used inspection tables, Pub. No. 249, will yield azimuths only to whole degrees. This level of precision is adequate for checking the gross accuracy of magnetic compasses in yachts and other small vessels.

Azimuth by Other Tabular Methods

2804   Exact azimuths can also be calculated from other publications, some now obsolete for general use. These include H.O. 208, H.O. 211 (and other Ageton-method tables), and H.O. 214. As with the inspection tables, these procedures permit simultaneous solution for both azimuth and altitude.

Two other DMAHTC publications, now unfortunately discontinued, were Pub. No. 260, *Azimuths of the Sun and Other Celestial Bodies of Declination 0° to 23°,* and Pub. No. 261, *Azimuth of Celestial Bodies, Declination 24° to 70°.* Pub. No. 260, popularly known as the "Red Azimuth Tables" because of the color of the binding used for most printings, and Pub. No. 261, called the "Blue Azimuth Tables" for the same reason, contain tabulations of azimuth to the nearest *minute* of arc for every ten minutes of time. Present shipboard equipment does not provide azimuth readings of such a high degree of precision, nor is such precision needed for practical navigation. Instructions for the use of the azimuth tables are contained in each of these publications, which are still in use by some navigators.

Azimuth by Amplitude

2805   When using an azimuth to check a compass, a body at low altitude is most desirable, as it is both easy to observe and gives the most accurate results. An *amplitude* observation is one made when the center of the observed body is on either the *celestial* or *visible horizon,* i.e., it is in the act of rising or setting. In the latter case a correction is applied to the observation in order to obtain the corresponding amplitude when the center of the body is on the celestial horizon. The sun is the body most frequently observed in obtaining an amplitude. However, the moon, a planet, or a bright star having a declination not exceeding 24° may also be used. The measurement of amplitudes should be avoided in high latitudes.

Amplitude may be defined as the horizontal angular distance measured N or S from the prime vertical to the body on the celestial horizon. It is given the *prefix* E (east) if the body is rising, and W (west) if it is setting; the *suffix* is N if the body rises or sets north of the prime vertical, as it does with a northerly declination, and S if it rises or sets south of the prime vertical, having a southerly declination.

If a body is observed when its center is on the celestial horizon, the amplitude may be taken directly from table 27 in *Bowditch*, Volume II (figure 2805a).

When observing amplitudes of the sun or moon with a height of eye typical of larger ships' bridges, two assumptions can be made that will yield results sufficiently accurate for practical purposes. The first is that when the *sun's lower limb* is about two-thirds of a diameter above the *visible* horizon, its center is on the *celestial* horizon. The second is that when the *moon's upper limb* is on the *visible* horizon, its center is on the *celestial* horizon. This apparent anomaly is due to the sun's parallax being very small (0.1′) as compared to the refraction, which at this altitude amounts to about 34.5′, whereas the moon's parallax is large (between 54.0′ and 61.5′, depending on the date), while the refraction is about 34.5′.

Planets or stars are on the celestial horizon when they are about one *sun* diameter, or some 32.0′ above the visible horizon.

If a body is observed on the *visible* horizon, the *observed* value is corrected by a value taken from *Bowditch*, Volume II, Table 28 (figure 2805b), according to the rule: For the *sun*, a *planet*, or a *star* apply the correction to the observed amplitude in the direction away from the elevated pole thus increasing the azimuth angle; for the *moon*, apply *half* the correction *toward* the elevated pole. The entering arguments for both tables are latitude and declination Table 28 was computed for a height of eye of 41 feet (12.5 m), but may be used for other values without significant error.

If desired, the correction can be applied with reversed sign to the value taken from Table 27, for comparison with the uncorrected observed value. This is the procedure used if amplitude or azimuth is desired when the celestial body is on the visible horizon.

Example: The DR latitude of a ship is 41°03.8′ N when the declination of the sun is N22°31.9′. The sun, when centered on the visible horizon, bears 059.5° by gyro, giving a compass amplitude of E30.5° N (090°–59.5°).

Required: The gyro error.

Solution: By interpolation in Tables 27 and 28 (figures 2805a and 2805b).

True amplitude	E30.5° N	(Table 27)
Correction	−0.7°	(Table 28,
	E29.8° N	sign reversed
Zn	60.2°	
Compass	59.5°	
Error	0.7° E	

Answer: Gyro error is 0.7° E; or in more realistic terms 0.5° E since, as noted above, observations will be possible only to nearest half-degree.

A computer or electronic calculator can be used instead of the *Bowditch* tables. If the observation is made when the center of the body is on the celestial horizon using the procedures given above for the sun and moon (no Table 28 correction required), true amplitude (A) can be found from the equation.

$$A = \sin^{-1}\left(\frac{\sin d}{\cos L}\right)$$

If the body is observed when its center is on the visible horizon, the equation is

$$A = \sin^{-1}\left(\frac{\sin d - \sin L \sin 0.7°}{\cos L \cos 0.7°}\right)$$

where −0.7° is the value for the altitude of the body used in the preparation of Table 28.

TABLE 27
Amplitudes

Latitude	Declination													Latitude
	18°0	18°5	19°0	19°5	20°0	20°5	21°0	21°5	22°0	22°5	23°0	23°5	24°0	
°	°	°	°	°	°	°	°	°	°	°	°	°	°	°
0	18.0	18.5	19.0	19.5	20.0	20.5	21.0	21.5	22.0	22.5	23.0	23.5	24.0	0
10	18.3	18.8	19.3	19.8	20.3	20.8	21.3	21.8	22.4	22.9	23.4	23.9	24.4	10
15	18.7	19.2	19.7	20.2	20.7	21.3	21.8	22.3	22.8	23.3	23.9	24.4	24.9	15
20	19.2	19.7	20.3	20.8	21.3	21.9	22.4	23.0	23.5	24.0	24.6	25.1	25.6	20
25	19.9	20.5	21.1	21.6	22.2	22.7	23.3	23.9	24.4	25.0	25.5	26.1	26.7	25
30	20.9	21.5	22.1	22.7	23.3	23.9	24.4	25.0	25.6	26.2	26.8	27.4	28.0	30
32	21.4	22.0	22.6	23.2	23.8	24.4	25.0	25.6	26.2	26.8	27.4	28.0	28.7	32
34	21.9	22.5	23.1	23.7	24.4	25.0	25.6	26.2	26.9	27.5	28.1	28.7	29.4	34
36	22.5	23.1	23.7	24.4	25.0	25.7	26.3	26.9	27.6	28.2	28.9	29.5	30.2	36
38	23.1	23.7	24.4	25.1	25.7	26.4	27.1	27.7	28.4	29.1	29.7	30.4	31.1	38
40	23.8	24.5	25.2	25.8	26.5	27.2	27.9	28.6	29.3	30.0	30.7	31.4	32.1	40
41	24.2	24.9	25.6	26.3	26.9	27.6	28.3	29.1	29.8	30.5	31.2	31.9	32.6	41
42	24.6	25.3	26.0	26.7	27.4	28.1	28.8	29.5	30.3	31.0	31.7	32.5	33.2	42
43	25.0	25.7	26.1	27.2	27.9	28.6	29.3	30.1	30.8	31.6	32.3	33.0	33.8	43
44	25.4	26.2	26.9	27.6	28.4	29.1	29.9	30.4	31.4	32.1	32.9	33.7	34.4	44

Figure 2805a. Table 27, Amplitudes, from Pub. No. 9, *Bowditch*, Volume II (extract).

TABLE 28
Correction of Amplitude as Observed on the Visible Horizon

Latitude	Declination													Latitude
	0°	2°	4°	6°	8°	10°	12°	14°	16°	18°	20°	22°	24°	
°	°	°	°	°	°	°	°	°	°	°	°	°	°	°
0	0.0	0.0	0.0	0.0	0.0	0.0	0.0	0.0	0.0	0.0	0.0	0.0	0.0	0
10	0.1	0.1	0.1	0.1	0.1	0.1	0.1	0.1	0.1	0.1	0.1	0.1	0.1	10
15	0.2	0.2	0.2	0.2	0.2	0.2	0.2	0.2	0.2	0.2	0.2	0.2	0.2	15
20	0.3	0.3	0.3	0.3	0.3	0.3	0.3	0.3	0.3	0.3	0.3	0.3	0.3	20
25	0.3	0.3	0.3	0.3	0.3	0.4	0.3	0.3	0.3	0.3	0.3	0.3	0.3	25
30	0.4	0.4	0.4	0.4	0.5	0.4	0.4	0.4	0.4	0.4	0.4	0.5	0.5	30
32	0.4	0.4	0.4	0.4	0.5	0.4	0.4	0.4	0.4	0.4	0.5	0.5	0.5	32
34	0.5	0.5	0.5	0.5	0.5	0.5	0.5	0.5	0.5	0.5	0.5	0.5	0.5	34
36	0.5	0.5	0.5	0.5	0.5	0.5	0.5	0.5	0.6	0.5	0.6	0.6	0.6	36
38	0.6	0.6	0.6	0.6	0.6	0.6	0.6	0.6	0.6	0.6	0.6	0.6	0.6	38
40	0.6	0.6	0.6	0.6	0.6	0.6	0.6	0.6	0.6	0.6	0.7	0.7	0.7	40
42	0.6	0.6	0.6	0.6	0.7	0.7	0.7	0.7	0.7	0.7	0.7	0.7	0.7	42
44	0.7	0.7	0.7	0.6	0.6	0.7	0.7	0.7	0.8	0.8	0.8	0.8	0.9	44
46	0.7	0.7	0.7	0.7	0.7	0.8	0.8	0.8	0.8	0.8	0.8	0.9	0.9	46
48	0.8	0.8	0.8	0.8	0.8	0.8	0.8	0.8	0.9	0.9	1.0	1.0	1.0	48

Figure 2805b. Table 28, Correction of Amplitudes as Observed on the Visible Horizon from Pub. No. 9, *Bowditch*, Volume II (extract).

Azimuth from Polaris Observation

2806 The true azimuth of Polaris is tabulated in the *Nautical Almanac* for northern latitudes up to 65°. Polaris, the "north star," is always within about 2° of true north in these latitudes, and observations of it provide a convenient means of checking the compass, with little interpolation needed. An extract from the *Nautical Almanac* Polaris azimuth table, which appears in the almanac at the bottom of the Polaris latitude tables, is shown in figure 2806.

The entering arguments in the *Nautical Almanac* azimuth table for Polaris are: (1) LHA ♈ and (2) latitude (at intervals of 5°, 10°, or 20°). Interpolation by eye is made if necessary.

Example: The navigator of a ship at Lat. 41°39.2′ N, Long. 17°07.6′ W observes Polaris when the GHA ♈ is 210°25.3′. The observed azimuth by gyro repeater (GB) is 359.0°.

Required: Gyro error by Polaris, using *Nautical Almanac* Polaris Table.

Solution: Using the exact DR longitude (note that an assumed position is *not* used), determine the LHA ♈ for the time of observation. Turn to the three pages of Polaris tables located just forward of the yellow pages, near the back of the *Nautical Almanac*, and locate the column heading encompassing the computed value of LHA ♈. In this case it occurs on the second page of Polaris tables, an extract of which is given in figure 2806. (In this figure the azimuth tables appear directly below the columnar headings, whereas the azimuth portion of the tables is actually at the extreme bottom of the table.) Using the column with a heading of LHA ♈ 190°–199° follow down the column to the appropri-

ate latitude. Using interpolation by eye for latitude, the value of 359.7° is found; this is the true azimuth of Polaris. The gyro error is determined by comparing this with the azimuth observed using the gyro repeater.

DR Lat.	41°39.2′ N	
DR Long.	17°07.6′ W	
GHA ♈	210°25.3′	
DR Long.	17°07.6′ W	
LHA ♈	193°17.7′ W	
Zn	359.7°	(from table)
GB	359.0°	
GE	0.7° E	

Answer: Gyro error 0.7° E. Due to the limitations in the precision with which the compass or a repeater can be read, this would be rounded off to the nearest half-degree, or 0.5° E.

In practice, it is difficult to observe Polaris accurately for azimuth unless the vessel is in a lower latitude, due to the difficulty of observing accurate azimuths at higher altitudes; this difficulty is increased if the vessel is rolling. However, Polaris serves as a useful check on the compass at any time it can be observed, as an azimuth observation of approximately 000° indicates that the compass is reasonably free of error.

Curve of Magnetic Azimuths

2807 The deviation of a magnetic compass on various headings is determined by *swinging ship*. During the process of swinging ship at sea, it is desirable to be able to obtain the magnetic azimuth of the sun at any moment, without the delay that would result if it were necessary to determine each azimuth by triple interpolation from the tables. For

POLARIS (POLE STAR) TABLES
FOR DETERMINING LATITUDE FROM SEXTANT ALTITUDE AND FOR AZIMUTH

L.H.A. ARIES	120°–129°	130°–139°	140°–149°	150°–159°	160°–169°	170°–179°	180°–189°	190°–199°	200°–209°	210°–219°	220°–229°	230°–239°
Lat.					AZIMUTH							
0	359·2	359·2	359·2	359·3	359·4	359·5	359·6	359·7	359·9	0·0	0·2	0·3
20	359·1	359·1	359·2	359·2	359·3	359·5	359·6	359·7	359·9	0·0	0·2	0·3
40	358·9	358·9	359·0	359·1	359·2	359·3	359·5	359·7	359·9	0·0	0·2	0·4
50	358·7	358·7	358·8	358·9	359·0	359·2	359·4	359·6	359·8	0·1	0·3	0·5
55	358·5	358·6	358·7	358·8	358·9	359·1	359·3	359·6	359·8	0·1	0·3	0·5
60	358·3	358·4	358·5	358·6	358·8	359·0	359·2	359·5	359·8	0·1	0·4	0·6
65	358·0	358·1	358·2	358·4	358·6	358·8	359·1	359·4	359·7	0·1	0·4	0·7

Figure 2806. Polaris azimuth table from *Nautical Almanac* (extract).

this reason, it is common practice to determine *in advance* the magnetic azimuths at intervals during the period of swing, and to plot these against time on cross-section paper, fairing a curve through the points. The curve can be constructed by means of azimuths from Pub. No. 229 or from other appropriate tables or procedures.

To construct the curve, the navigator first determines the true azimuth for the approximate mid-time of the period during which the vessel is to be swung, using the method of article 2803. During the time devoted to swinging the ship, the latitude and declination remain essentially constant, and the only one of the three entering arguments to change appreciably is meridian angle. Since meridian angle changes at the nearly constant rate of 1° for each four minutes of time, the azimuth at a time four minutes before or after the mid-time of the swing can be obtained by entering Pub. No. 229 with the same values of Dec. and L used before but with an LHA value 1° greater or less, and applying the same correction to the tabulated value as that used for the mid-time. In practice, the change in azimuth in four minutes (1° of LHA) is usually quite small, and good results are obtained by determining the azimuth in steps of eight minutes (2° of LHA). Thus, having determined the correction to the tabulated azimuth for the mid-time of the swing, the navigator has only to enter Pub. No. 229 with the same values of declination and latitude, and a meridian angle two degrees greater or less, and apply the previously found correction to the tabulated Z to determine the true Z eight minutes earlier or later. A series of such computations provides values of true azimuth at intervals throughout the swing. By converting these values to magnetic azimuth, the navigator can plot this information on cross-section paper and fair a curve through the points, from which the magnetic azimuth can be taken at any time during the period. The above method will provide acceptable accuracy if the total time period is not overly long or close to the time of LAN. For more accurate results, the determination of a separate correction for each solution is recommended.

Example: A ship is to be swung between 1630 and 1730 ZT to determine magnetic compass deviation. The 1700 DR is Lat. 41°28.3′ N, Long. 16°34.2′ W. At that time the declination of the sun will be N22°35.4′ and its meridian angle will be 73°49.3′ W. The variation in the area is 14°32′ W.

Required: A curve of magnetic azimuths for use during the swing.

Solution: Determine the correction to tabulated azimuth angle and the true azimuth for the mid-time of the swing. The correction to tabulated azimuth angle is +0.7° and the true azimuth is 277.6°. Record this information on the middle line of a form such as figure 2807a, and then record ZT at eight-minute intervals before and after the mid-time to provide for the full period of the swing. In this case the time range is 1628 to 1731. Next to each ZT, record LHA at that time. Since the sun is setting for the period of the swing, LHA increases with time in this situation, from 65.8° to 81.8°. Take the nearest whole degree of value, which is the tab LHA value in each case. Then obtain the tabulated Z from Pub. No. 229 for each tab LHA and the constant values of Lat. and Dec. (which are 41° N and N23°, respectively, in this case), and apply the correction for the mid-time (+0.7° in this example) to each tabulated Z to obtain the exact Z for each ZT. Next, convert each Z to Zn and apply the variation for the locality to determine the magnetic azimuth of the sun at each ZT. Finally, plot the magnetic azimuths against zone time on cross-section paper, as shown in figure 2807b.

Answer: See figure 2807b.

It might be noted here that the above procedure is probably more "academic" than practical, as it will seldom be that a ship at sea will have the time to devote to the maneuvers of swinging ship.

ZT	LHA	Tab	Tab Z	Corr	Z	Zn	Var	Mag Zn
	°	°	°		°	°		°
1628	65.8	66	86.6	↑	N87.3W	272.7	↑	287.2
1636	67.8	68	85.4		86.1	273.9		288.4
1644	69.8	70	84.2		84.9	275.1		289.6
1652	71.8	72	82.9		83.6	276.4		290.9
1700	73.8	74	81.7	+ 0.7°	82.4	277.6	14.5°W	292.1
1708	75.8	76	80.5		81.2	278.8		293.3
1716	77.8	78	79.3		80.0	280.0		294.5
1724	79.8	80	78.2		78.9	281.1		295.6
1732	81.8	82	77.0	↓	77.7	282.3	↓	296.8

Figure 2807a. Table of magnetic azimuths.

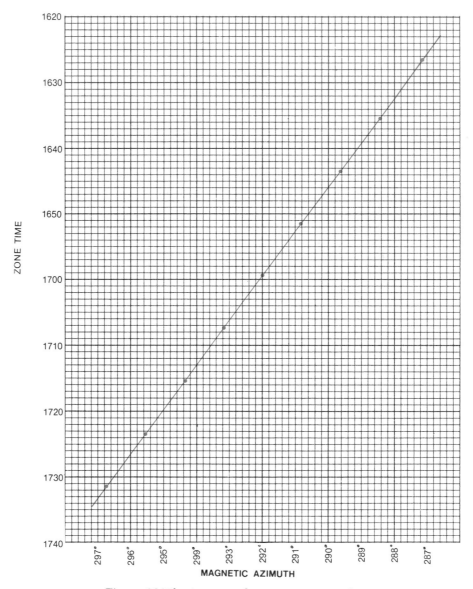

Figure 2807b. A curve of magnetic azimuths.

For an explanation of the use of magnetic azimuths in obtaining deviations of the magnetic compasses aboard ship, see article 321.

Azimuths by Diagram

2808 Various azimuth diagrams have been produced over the years, to permit a graphic determination of azimuth; the Weir diagram was long used by the Navy. Currently the most commonly used azimuth diagram is that designed by Armistead Rust, a portion of which is reproduced in figure 2808.

Importance of Checking Compass Error

2809 Compasses used for navigation, both magnetic and gyro, are highly reliable instruments. Their importance is so great, however, that any error must be quickly and accurately determined. Thus, regular procedures must be followed whenever a vessel is underway.

Compasses can be checked at sea, and any error found, by observing the azimuth of a celestial body and comparing the observed value with the exact value as obtained by computation. The azimuth obtained for plotting an LOP is not sufficiently accurate for this purpose, and interpolation must be made for t, Dec., and Lat. to obtain the exact azimuth when using inspection tables such as Pub. No. 229. This is done by triple linear interpolation, with entering arguments to the nearest 0.1°. The exact azimuth of Polaris, which is always close to 000°, can be obtained from tables in the *Nautical Almanac* (for latitudes up to 65° N). In solutions for exact azimuth by Pub. No. 229 or by Polaris, the best estimate of the ship's position is always used rather than an assumed position.

A reasonably accurate curve of magnetic azimuths, for use in swinging ship, is conveniently obtained by determining the exact azimuth for the mid-time of the period, and applying a constant

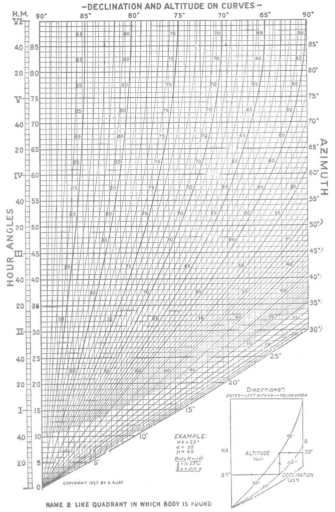

Figure 2808. Armistead Rust azimuth diagram, left half; declination and altitude on the curves.

correction to the tabulated values for the Dec. and L of the mid-time, and for t values that differ from that of the mid-time by whole numbers of degrees.

Chapter 29

The Practice of Celestial Navigation

Introduction

2901 The proper practice of celestial navigation on the high seas is of great importance even in this era of advanced radionavigation systems. Electronic equipment, on the vessel or at shore-based stations, may become unreliable or fail entirely; some will require an external input of information to initialize a subsequent flow of positional data. Even with a radionavigation system functioning apparently normally, it is well to check it periodically from an independent source; celestial navigation is ideal for this purpose. A prudent navigator uses *every* available means to fix his position at sea.

Chapter 17 covered the navigation of a vessel from her berth or anchorage to the point where she took departure on a coastal passage, and then on to her next port. In this chapter, navigation will be summarized for a passage on the high seas, out of sight of landmarks and aids to navigation. A typical day's work of celestial navigation is detailed in article 2904.

Navigation at Sea

2902 On the high seas, it is usually impossible to fix a vessel's position with the same accuracy as can be obtained in piloting; however, a navigator must make every effort to obtain the most accurate fixes possible, and to maintain an accurate DR and EP between fixes. Every opportunity to obtain celestial observations should be seized.

All available means of obtaining positioning data should be employed. Loran, Omega, satellite navigation systems, radio direction finders, Consol, Decca, the echo sounder, and other electronic equipment should be used whenever conditions permit.

The Navigation Team

2903 In the following article a typical minimum day's work in celestial navigation at sea is outlined. The ship's "navigation team" will be discussed here in terms of the personnel available on a U.S. naval vessel; the same general functions will be performed on merchant ships and yachts, but with many fewer people being involved.

Aboard most naval vessels, a considerable share of this work will be performed by the quartermasters. For example, a senior quartermaster usually winds and compares the chronometers, and azimuth observations are usually made and reduced by quartermasters, who also prepare the lists of stars to be observed for the morning and evening celestial fixes. The organization of the navigation team, and the duties of individual quartermasters who are a part of it, will depend upon their training and natural abilities.

The senior quartermasters are frequently good sextant observers, and their sights can be most helpful in augmenting those of the navigator. A navigator should encourage and train his quartermasters to become proficient in all aspects of navigation, and particularly as celestial observers. The greatest limiting factor on the accuracy of celestial navigation is the quality of the sextant observation, and consistently reliable observations can only be obtained after much practice. A quartermaster who can obtain good celestial observations is of great value to his ship and to the navy.

A navigator on a merchant ship may not be so fortunate as his naval counterpart with respect to assistance in taking sights. Normally, nonlicensed deck personnel will not have had any training, and little interest or aptitude, in celestial navigation;

but should a suitable individual be found in the crew, every encouragement and training opportunity should be given. Junior officers will usually desire to sharpen their observational skills by joining the ship's assigned navigator in taking sights, and cadets from maritime academies, if on board, will be active participants as a part of their course of study. On board yachts, the skipper is often also the navigator, but other crewmembers and/or guests can, and should, make observations that can be compared with his sights.

A Training Program

Training in the taking of celestial observations should start with LAN sights when the sun is changing slowly in altitude. Next, observations should be made on that body when its altitude is changing more rapidly; with practice, sights should be possible every 10 to 15 seconds. These should be plotted on graph paper, using 1/2 inch or 1 inch to a minute of arc and to 10 seconds of time; a "line of best fit" is then drawn in, serving to indicate the random errors of the individual observations. Such graphing will soon enable a navigator to identify those individuals with the greater skill. The training program should then progress on to the taking of sights at morning and evening twilight.

A navigator should also see to it that all assisting personnel are properly trained as recorders. An observation is worthless if the latitude or time is omitted or incorrectly recorded.

The training of other persons is one of the most important duties of any navigator.

The Day's Work in Celestial Navigation

2904 Details of a navigating team's work during a day at sea will vary with the navigator and the ship, as well as with other factors, but a typical *minimum* "day's work" during good weather might include the following over a period of 24 hours:

Plot of dead reckoning throughout the period.

Computation of the time of the beginning of morning civil twilight; preparation of a list of stars and planets in favorable positions for observation at that time, with the approximate azimuth and altitude of each body.

Observation of selected celestial bodies and the solution of these observations for a fix during morning twilight.

Preparation of a position report based upon the morning twilight fix.

Azimuth of the sun to determine compass error.

Observation of the sun for a morning sun line (and of the moon and Venus, if available).

Winding of chronometers as necessary, and determination of chronometer error using radio time checks.

Observation of the sun at LAN (and of the moon if it is available) to obtain a ZT 1200 position (running fix or fix), or observations as near LAN as possible in the event of overcast.

Computation of the day's run, from the preceding noon to the present noon.

Preparation of a position report based upon the ZT 1200 position.

Observation of the sun for an afternoon sun line (and of Venus and the moon, if available).

Azimuth of the sun to determine compass error.

Computation of the time of ending of evening civil twilight, and preparation of a list of stars and planets in favorable positions for observation at that time, with the approximate altitude and azimuth of each body.

Observations of the celestial bodies selected and solution of the observations for a fix during evening twilight. If only one or two bodies can be obtained, the afternoon sun line can be advanced and combined with the evening stars for a running fix.

Preparation of a 2000 position report based upon the evening twilight fix and any other positioning data.

Preparation of the check-off list for the Captain's Night Order Book.

Notes on the Day's Work

Venus can frequently be observed in the morning, when it is well west and higher than the sun. Similarly, it can be observed in the afternoon, if it is well east, and therefore considerably higher than the sun.

When the sun is high at transit, it is changing rapidly in azimuth. This permits excellent running fixes to be obtained by combining late morning and early afternoon sun lines with LAN.

During prolonged periods of overcast, the sun does at times break through for a short time. Under such conditions, an observer should be ready to obtain an observation without delay. The sun should be observed even if it is veiled by thin cirrus; rarely does such blurring of the sun's limb cause an error of as much as one minute of arc.

Morning Twilight Observations

2905 The LMTs of the beginning of morning nautical and civil twilights, and of sunrise, are tabulated in the *Nautical Almanac,* and they are used by the navigator principally to assist him in planning for morning twilight observations. He does this by determining the time at which civil twilight begins (article 2320), and obtaining LHA ♈ for that time. By setting his Star Finder (article 2002) for that LHA ♈, he can determine the approximate altitudes and azimuths of celestial bodies that will be visible at that time. If available, Pub. No. 229, Volume I, can be used as an indicator of available and best-located stars.

A table like that shown in figure 2905a is useful in preparing to observe celestial bodies during twilight, as it is of great assistance in locating them in both azimuth and altitude. In addition, it permits the selection of bodies with azimuths, which will be particularly helpful. A body ahead or astern will yield an LOP that makes a *speed line,* thus giving a check on the ship's advance. Similarly, a body observed on the beam will produce an approximate *course line.*

Programs are available for some models of personal electronic calculators that, for an input of latitude, longitude, and date, will compute the time of morning (or evening) civil twilight and the stars that will then be visible, listing altitude to the nearest 1′ and azimuth to the nearest 0.1°. Figure 2905a was prepared by such a procedure. Alternatively, a given time can be entered into the calculator and the positional information of same star cal-

culated. Generally similar programs can be developed for the small computers that are increasingly used aboard ships.

In general, the bodies selected should be well distributed in azimuth. Good practice calls for observing a minimum of five bodies; six or seven are more desirable so that the minimum will still be available if on later reduction one or more do not yield good results due to misidentification or poor altitude data. Of these, four should be reduced, and the resulting LOPs should be advanced for the run between observations. If the resulting quadrangle is of reasonable size, its center is taken as the position of the fix; if not, the other observations are reduced to obtain data for a better position. However, when all the bodies observed lie within 180° of azimuth, the *bisector method,* described in article 2910, should be used in establishing the fix, which may be *external* rather than *internal.*

The table should include many more bodies than the navigator expects to observe, as some may be obscured by cloud cover. Bodies in the altitude range between 15° and 65° are in general the most satisfactory to observe. Azimuth should also be taken into consideration, so that the bodies observed differ by roughly equal amounts in azimuth. The most desirable bodies for observation should be marked by asterisks on the star table, to signify that they are the first choice for observation, as is shown in figure 2905a. The marked stars are se-

Star	Magnitude	H		Zn
		°	′	°
Capella	0.2	10	45	036.4
*Mirfak	1.9	27	25	046.2
Schedar	2.5	52	22	047.9
Hamal	2.2	25	50	081.1
*Alpheratz	2.2	50	55	093.0
Diphda	2.2	12	00	127.2
Formalhaut	1.3	14	22	155.2
*Enif	2.5	57	43	161.3
Nunki	2.1	16	18	210.6
*Altair	0.9	53	49	212.9
*Ralsahague	2.1	36	11	254.5
Vega	0.1	61	49	278.1
*Alphecca	2.3	22	21	287.0
Deneb	1.3	84	07	314.2
Alkaid	1.9	19	33	318.8
Alioth	1.7	18	21	330.4
*Kochab	2.2	38	21	339.5
Dubhe	2.0	15	51	345.9

Figure 2905a. Morning stars, 5 June. DR Lat. 41°02.6′N, Long. 14°37.1′W. Civil twilight 0354.

lected to get good distribution in azimuth, and as being at good altitudes for observation. Polaris, which should be observed, both for an LOP and a check on the compass, is not on the list, as its azimuth will be within about a degree of north, and its altitude will be about the same as the DR latitude.

Rate of Change of Altitude

When there is broken cloud cover, considerable time is often consumed in obtaining observations of a round of stars. As daylight increases, the stars become increasingly difficult to locate, particularly with the naked eye, and allowance must be made for the change in their altitudes. Bodies to the east or west will change altitude much more rapidly than those to the north or south; for example, in the list, Alpheratz, with an azimuth near 090° at twilight, will be increasing in altitude at a rate of about 11.3' per minute of time, while Dubhe will be decreasing in altitude at a rate of only about 3.1'. Alpheratz, therefore, could well have moved out of the field of view of the sextant telescope, if no allowance is made for its motion. The rate of change of altitude in a minute of time may be obtained by the equation:

ΔH per minute = $15 \times \cos \text{Lat} \times \sin Z$, where Z is the angle between the meridian and the body.

This equation was used in preparing the nomogram shown in figure 2905b, which has been found to be helpful.

During morning twilight, the eastern horizon is the first to become sharply defined, and as a general rule, bodies in that direction are observed first. This procedure may be modified by the brightness of a particular body, which may make it visible in the east for some time after all other bodies are hidden from view by the approaching daylight. Conversely, it may be desirable to observe a relatively dim star to the westward as soon as the horizon is clear under it, as it may otherwise be lost to view. In general, the later a star or planet is observed during morning twilight, the more accurate will be its LOP, as the observation will then be made with a more sharply defined horizon. The inexperienced navigator must, however, guard against waiting too long, as the body may then be too faint to see. For this reason, it is often desirable to make an observation of a body as soon as conditions permit, and then a second one of the same body as late as possible.

No difficulty should be experienced in identifying the bodies observed during morning twilight, as the navigator usually has ample opportunity to study them before horizon visibility makes the taking of sights possible. If any doubt does exist, its

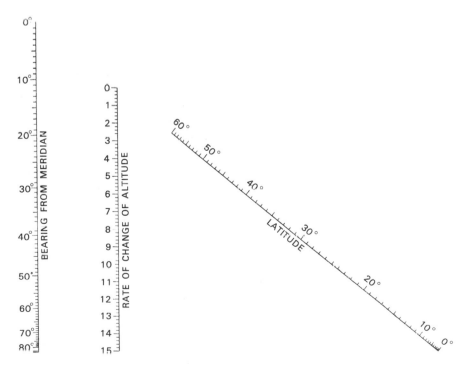

Figure 2905b. Nomogram for determining the change in altitude of a body per minute of time.

azimuth should be noted and recorded for possible use in identifying the body later.

In checking the index error of the sextant, one should use a moderately bright star before making the observations, or the clearest part of the horizon after making the observations.

Daylight Observations

2906 The usual observations made at sea each day include two azimuths made for compass checks. The sun is the body most frequently used for this purpose; the most accurate observations can be made when it is rising or setting, as it is then moving comparatively slowly in azimuth, and minimal error is introduced by any tilt in the azimuth circle. Under conditions where it is very difficult to obtain accurate azimuths with an azimuth circle, it is wise to make an amplitude observation.

Continuing Altitude Sights

When quartermasters who are capable observers are available, it is good practice to observe the sun at frequent and regular intervals; some ships make hourly observations. Even if all these sights are not reduced immediately, it does make valuable data available in the event of sudden overcast.

As stated in article 2904, Venus and the moon should be observed whenever possible in conjunction with the sun to obtain a forenoon fix.

Noon Fix

If only one morning sun sight is to be made, it should be taken with two thoughts in mind. One is that the resulting LOP is to be advanced to noon to obtain a running fix, and the other is that the LAN observation will yield a latitude line, or an approximate latitude line in the event that the sun cannot be observed exactly at LAN. It is desirable that the two LOPs intersect at an angle of 45° or more; on the other hand, the morning sun observation should not be obtained so early that there can be much error due to uncertainty as to the ship's speed and course in advancing it to noon. The two factors depend on the latitude of the observer and the sun's declination. Pub. No. 229 can be used to determine the rate of change of the sun's azimuth, and therefore how long before noon the observation should be made.

LAN should be observed as a matter of routine aboard all vessels. It offers the most accurate celestial line of position, as the sun is not changing altitude perceptibly at LAN, and the horizon is usually sharply defined. In addition to the LAN sight, it may be desirable to obtain a sun line exactly at ZT 1200, so that it will not have to be adjusted to de-

termine the ZT 1200 position, or it may be obtained at another convenient time. Many navigators prefer to make an observation at about ZT 1145, so that it and the morning sun line can be advanced to 1200, and the running fix at that time determined and submitted by 1200. A meridian altitude observation can, of course, be obtained only at the time of transit unless the appropriate correction is applied from *Bowditch* Table 28.

The conditions governing the afternoon sun-line observations are similar to those that apply to the morning sun line. A longitude line in the afternoon is useful for determining the time at which to make evening twilight observations, and since in mid-latitudes it generally will be taken rather late in the afternoon, it affords a good speed check for a vessel on an easterly or westerly course.

The above discussion is based upon the assumption that good weather prevails, and that the navigator can observe the sun at any time. If the sky is overcast, he should not ignore the possibility of obtaining an LOP at any time when the sun might be visible. With skillful use of the sextant shade glasses, the sun often can be observed when behind thin clouds.

If the moon can be observed during daylight, its LOP should be crossed with a sun line obtained at the same time, unless the two bodies are at nearly the same or reciprocal azimuths. Care must sometimes be taken when observing the moon that the correct limb is observed. Venus can often be seen during daylight, when it is higher in altitude than the sun, if the navigator knows its approximate altitude and azimuth, and less frequently Mars and Jupiter can be seen. For observations of Venus and Mars obtained between sunset and sunrise, the "additional correction," found inside the front cover of the *Nautical Almanac*, should be used to compensate for parallax.

Sun Correction Tables

The *Sun Correction Tables*, on the inside front cover of the *Nautical Almanac*, can be used for correcting sextant altitudes except when maximum accuracy is desired. The semidiameter of the sun is averaged in the tables for two six-month periods. Greater accuracy can be obtained by using the refraction correction, listed under "Stars and Planets," and the sun's semidiameter obtained from the bottom of the appropriate page in the *Nautical Almanac*. To these, a parallax correction of +0.1' should be added for altitudes up to 65°.

A lower degree of precision will be achieved if the *Air Almanac* refraction tables are used, but this is still adequate for practical marine navigation.

Low-altitude Sun Sights

Observations of the sun in the altitude range of from 0° to 5° have acquired a reputation for unreliability that they do not wholly deserve. Refraction is somewhat uncertain at low altitudes; however, except under very unusual atmospheric conditions, such sights usually yield acceptable results. To illustrate: In one test 266 observations of the sun were made at altitudes between 0° and 5°; 183 of these yielded LOPs that were within 0.5 mile of the true position, 53 lay between 0.5 and 1.0 mile, 30 were in error by more than 1.0 mile, and only two were in error by more than 2.0 miles, the greatest error being 2.2 miles. These observations were, of course, fully and carefully corrected.

Low-altitude sun sights must be corrected in detail. The fixed sextant error, the IC, and the dip are applied to the sextant altitude (hs) before the refraction correction is taken from the Stars and Planets column of Table A3 of the *Nautical Almanac;* the semidiameter is taken from the daily pages of an almanac, and +0.1' is used as the parallax correction. The "Additional Corrections" to the Altitude Correction Tables should also be used for all low-altitude observations.

It should be noted here that, for some observers, the upper limb of the sun is both easier to observe and yields somewhat more accurate results at low altitudes than does the lower limb.

High-altitude Sun Sights

Observations of the sun at altitudes greater than 80°+ are generally difficult to obtain accurately due to the problem of establishing the vertical. A compensatory advantage, however, is the near absence of observational error from refraction.

When the sun's declination is near the vessel's latitude, morning sun observations make possible the determination of longitude with considerable accuracy. This, in turn, makes possible a highly accurate prediction of the time of local apparent noon, and a high altitude LAN observation can frequently be made with great accuracy.

An azimuth circle is placed on a gyro repeater on the side of the bridge on which the sun will transit and is aligned with the north-south points of the gyro repeater card. The sextant index arm is set to the expected altitude at LAN, and the observer then steps back from the pelorus and places himself so that the azimuth circle vanes are in line when seen through the horizon glass of the sextant. The sun's altitude is obtained for LAN when its image is in contact with the horizon at a point directly above the vanes.

Such a high-altitude LAN observation can be of considerable value, as under such conditions all other sun lines obtained during the day will lie generally in a north-south direction.

Care should be taken in plotting very high altitude observations, those with sextant altitudes of roughly 87° or more. The curvature of the circular line of position becomes so great that a straight line is not a satisfactory approximation. In such cases, it is preferable to plot the entire circle using the geographical position (GP) of the body as the center and the zenith distance (90° − Ho) as the radius. This graphic solution eliminates any need for the use of sight reduction tables. Two circular LOPs can be drawn for observations separated by a short period of time; the DR position will guide the navigator as to which of the two intersections should be used for the fix.

Sea-air Temperature Differences

A difference between the sea surface temperature and that of the air in contact with it tends to affect the value of the dip correction (article 2122). This correction is calculated for "standard conditions," and these are distorted when the air in contact with the sea is warmed or cooled by the water. The resulting error is not serious when a number of bodies well distributed in azimuth are observed, as it may generally be assumed that the anomaly is constant, and will apply equally to each of the bodies observed.

However, when only the sun is available for observation, as is usually the case in the daytime, this anomaly can affect the accuracy of the LOP. This is equally true for several bodies located in a limited sector of azimuth; however, in such a case, the use of bisectors (article 2910) is helpful.

For best results, sea water should be picked up in a dip bucket at some point well forward in the vessel; this is normally done on yachts and smaller ships, but larger vessels often use the intake water temperature as measured in the engine room. However obtained, the water temperature is compared with the dry-bulb air temperature measured at the level where the observations are made. The correction is subtractive when the air is colder than the water (i.e., the sextant altitude will be too great), and additive when the water is colder than the air. This correction should be used only when experienced judgment indicates that it will result in improved observations.

Evening Twilight Observations

2907 Evening twilight observations are similar to morning twilight procedures, with the important difference for an inexperienced navigator that there is little opportunity to identify the bodies in advance of taking sights. Under these conditions, prior computation of the approximate altitude and azimuth is particularly helpful in locating the proper bodies; the azimuth of a body that has been observed, but not positively identified, should always be noted.

In the evening, the stars and planets in the east are usually observed first, subject to their brightness, as that area of the sky darkens first.

Night Observations

2908 Star observations can be made successfully on clear nights, provided the observer's vision is *dark-adapted* and the sextant telescope and mirrors have reasonably good optical qualities. During World War II it was found that if the human eye was exposed to no light other than dull red for a considerable period of time, its night perception was considerably increased. This proved to be of great value to many navigators in the fleet submarines, which, when in enemy waters, could surface only during the hours of complete darkness. (Subsequent research has cast doubt on the necessity for using red light; low intensity appears to be a more decisive factor than the color of the light.) With dark-adapted vision, and using a sextant fitted with a prismatic telescope having a 30-mm objective lens and a magnification of 6x, they obtained satisfactory star fixes. The 6x30 telescope is acceptable for night use, but the 7x50 is superior, as it has about twice the light-gathering power of the 6x30.

In making night observations, it is vital that the readout light on the sextant and the recorder's flashlight be fitted with red bulbs. Red lamp dye is available commercially, and flashlight bulbs dipped in it have proven satisfactory for night use.

Light-amplification Telescopes

Light amplification or night-vision telescopes developed as sniper scopes for the army will, when mounted on a sextant, provide a view of the horizon on a dark night.

Use of an Astigmatizing Shade

When observing bright stars or planets with a dim horizon, it is often desirable to use a pale sun shade to reduce the body's brilliance. An *astigmatizing shade* is also frequently helpful under such conditions. This is a prism that elongates the image of a star into a thin horizontal line. Astigmatizers are fitted on many sextants.

Moonlit Horizons

There is considerable risk of obtaining a false altitude when observing a brilliant moon, or a star or planet near the moon in azimuth, as the moonlight may give a false horizon. This risk is reduced if such observations are made from a point as low as possible in the ship, and it is also wise to have the recorder check the horizon under the moon through a 7x50 binocular to see if the illuminated water is actually at the horizon.

Accuracy of Celestial LOPs and Fixes

2909 The accuracy of an LOP obtained by celestial navigation is only rarely equal to that of the average LOP obtained in piloting. The reasons for this are numerous, and the major ones have been commented upon at appropriate places in this text. Ordinarily, therefore, a navigator should consider a single celestial LOP to be accurate only within one to two miles in either direction. This is considering error in altitude measurement only, and might be increased by a mistake in timing, computation, or plotting. With experience and the cultivation of sound judgment in such matters, a navigator will be able to evaluate some sights as being more accurate than this, and some as probably being less accurate. Also, the accuracy of celestial observations increases with practice; a research program disclosed some years ago that the accuracy of observers in making celestial observations continued to improve even after more than 2,000 observations had been made. Expert observers, under good conditions, can expect a multiple star fix to yield a position that will be accurate within a quarter of a mile.

Analysis of Uncertainties

The following discussion of the theory of errors may be helpful in evaluating positioning data.

A fix or running fix in celestial navigation is determined by two or more lines of position, each of which may be in error. If two lines are crossed at an angle of 90° and each has a possible error of two miles, the situation illustrated in figure 2909a results.

The navigator selects the point where LOP *A-B* intersects LOP *X-Y* as his fix, but if each line is in error by two miles, he will be at one of the corners shown by the broken lines, 2.8 miles from his fix. If one of the lines is in error by two miles and the other is without error, his actual position will be at the intersection of one of the solid lines and one of the broken lines, 2.0 miles from his fix.

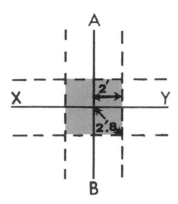

Figure 2909a. Possible error in a fix from two lines of position differing in azimuth by 90° if each LOP has a possible error of two miles.

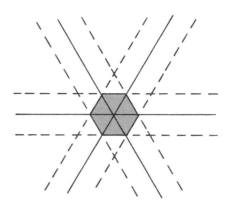

Figure 2909c. Possible error in a fix from three lines of position differing in azimuth by 120° if each LOP has a possible error of two miles.

If two lines are crossed at an angle of 30° and each has a possible error of two miles, the situation illustrated in figure 2909b results. The navigator selects the point where LOP *A-B* intersects LOP *C-D* as his fix, but if each line is in error by two miles, he will be at one of the corners of the parallelogram shown by the broken lines, either 2.1 or 7.7 miles from his fix. If one of the lines is in error by two miles and the other is without error, his actual position will be at the intersection of one of the solid lines and one of the broken lines, or 4.0 miles from his fix.

From the above discussion it can be seen that, when two lines of position are obtained, the navigator may place the most confidence in the resulting fix when the lines intersect at angles of 90°, or nearly 90°, all other factors being equal. A 90° intersection in a *running fix*, however, may not give as reliable a position as can be obtained from two lines of a *fix* that cut at a smaller angle, because of the possible inexactness in advancing the earlier LOP for a running fix.

Use of Multiple LOPs

Whenever possible, a navigator should use at least three lines of position to obtain a fix. If these

lines intersect at angles of 60° and each has a possible error of two miles, the situation illustrated in figure 2909c results. The navigator selects the point where the three lines intersect as his fix, but if each line is subject to error of up to two miles, his actual position may be anywhere within the shaded hexagon of the figure, at a maximum distance of 2.3 miles from the plotted fix.

The accuracy of a fix is not materially increased by plotting more than four lines of position if the lines can be relied on to be equally accurate and are approximately evenly distributed in azimuth. In practice, the usable stars are never perfectly located in azimuth, and five or more lines will usually yield a better idea of the most probable position than will three. When the bodies observed all lie within 180° of azimuth of one another, *bisectors*, which are discussed in the next article, should be drawn and used.

In figure 2909c the three solid lines are shown intersecting at a point. In practice, this rarely happens, and the navigator takes the center of the small figure usually formed as being his fix. The point selected is equidistant from all sides of the figure. It can be determined geometrically or by computation, but in normal practice the navigator estimates it by eye. The size of the figure obtained is not necessarily an indication of the accuracy of the fix.

Constant Error

When a navigator can select three or more bodies to be observed for a fix (as when observing stars), he can guard against a *constant error* in altitude by observing bodies at equal intervals of *azimuth*. A constant error in altitude causes all lines of position to be in error by the same amount and in the same direction, relative to the bodies being ob-

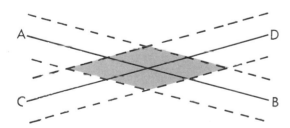

Figure 2909b. Possible error in a fix from two lines of position differing in azimuth by 30° if each LOP has a possible error of two miles.

served. When bodies are observed at equal intervals of azimuth, a constant error will either increase or decrease the size of the figure formed when the lines are plotted, but will have no effect on the center of the figure. Thus, three stars differing in azimuth by 120° (*not* 60°), or four stars differing by 90° should be observed, or five stars differing by 72°, etc. Theoretically, a four-star fix from bodies differing in azimuth by 90° (as N, S, E, and W) should produce only two lines of position, but in all probability a small rectangle will be the result; the center of the rectangle, determined by eye, can be taken as the fix.

Random Error

The factor that has the greatest effect on a single observation is usually *random error*. The reliability of an individual line of position can be considerably improved by making several observations of the same body and averaging the times and altitudes before solving for an LOP; this tends to average out the random errors. Alternatively, if five or more observations of the same body are taken in quick succession, and its azimuth is noted by gyro, the accuracy of the individual observations may be determined by comparing the change of altitude between observation; the rate of change in altitude per second of time being equal to $0.25 \times$ cos Latitude $\times$ sine of the angle between the body and the meridian. If the rate of change is steady for several sights, one of these should be selected for reduction. This equation may be solved extremely rapidly with an electronic calculator or computer.

An alternate method is to make three observations in quick succession and to solve and plot each one. If two LOPs are then in close agreement and a third differs considerably, it is usually safe to assume that the correct LOP lies midway between the two lines that are in agreement. The method is not as tedious as it may at first seem, particularly if solutions are made on a form with multiple columns, as usually the only difference in the solutions are in minutes and seconds of time and the resulting differences in GHA and aλ. Ordinarily, multiple observations are limited to sun lines, as the several bodies observed for a twilight fix serve as a check on each other.

In fixing or estimating the position of a ship, the navigator should not ignore the DR or EP, as these positions are based on other navigational information that may be more or less accurate than a given LOP. A DR or EP should be considered a *circle* with radius equal to the navigator's estimate of its accuracy, if knowledge of course and speed are consid-

ered to be equally good. If the navigator believes that one of these is known more accurately than the other, the DR or EP should be considered a small *ellipse*, with its minor axis extending in the direction indicated by the more accurately known quantity and its major axis extending in the direction indicated by the less accurately known quantity.

From the above, it can be seen that the interpretation of celestial lines of position can be a complex subject—one that calls for sound judgment on the part of an experienced navigator.

Mistakes

The above discussion of "errors" does *not* include "mistakes." *Errors* of navigation are usually either constant or random inaccuracies of the input data used. (See appendix C, article C-02 for a discussion of the difference between accuracy and precision.) In contrast, a *mistake* is a blunder, a completely invalid figure resulting from an incorrect procedure, misreading of an instrument, taking a wrong value from a table, etc. Mistakes vary widely and have no systemic basis, thus no mathematical or graphic analysis can be made of them. The only "cure" is constant attention to detail and thorough checking of procedures. A large mistake is usually readily apparent; a small mistake may go unnoticed, and uncorrected, unless a result is checked by a second instrument or an independent set of calculations. Exact agreement should not be expected, but a wide difference between two solutions should alert a navigator to the possibility of a mistake in one or the other of them.

LOP Bisectors

2910   When a number of bodies with azimuths *all lying within a horizontal 180° sector of arc* are obtained, a constant error (both magnitude and sign) may yield misleading results if the fix is assumed to lie *within* the polygon formed by the LOPs; this is often called an "internal" fix. Such constant errors could result from an uncorrected personal error or from unusual terrestrial refraction, which causes the value of the dip, as obtained from the *Nautical Almanac*, to be considerably in error. This may lead to the fix lying *outside* the polygon, resulting in an "external" fix rather than the usual internal one. Where multiple LOPs well distributed in azimuth are obtained, this problem does not arise, as in this case the error may be assumed to affect all LOPs about equally.

Where three or more observations are made of bodies with azimuths within 180° of each other, it is wise to use *LOP bisectors* to determine the fix.

Each angle formed by a pair of position lines is bisected, being drawn in the direction of the *mean of the azimuths* of the two bodies.

For example, assume that due to cloud cover, it was possible to observe only three stars, the respective azimuths being as follows: star No. 1, 224°; No. 2, 000°, and No. 3, 256°. The resulting LOPs are plotted in figure 2910. Note that arrows have been added to each LOP showing the direction of the celestial body; this is desirable for any plot. LOPs 1 and 2 will be bisected in the direction 292°−112°:

$$\frac{(224° + 000°)}{2} = 112°$$

LOPs 1 and 3 will be bisected in the direction 240°–060°:

$$\frac{(224° + 256°)}{2} = 240°$$

and LOPs 2 and 3 will be bisected in the direction 308°–128°. In figure 2910 these bisectors are drawn in as blue lines.

The most probable position for the fix lies at the center of any small triangle formed by the three bisectors, rather than in the triangle formed by the three LOPs. Note that this external fix shows an apparent greater "error" than is shown by assuming the center of the original triangle, but this is not actually so.

It can be seen in figure 2910 that the external fix is a point equidistant from each LOP in the same direction, "away" in this example. Such a point can also be estimated by eye, taking care to always

be on the same side of each LOP as indicated by the arrows. This technique is more practical at sea than calculating the bisector directions and cluttering up the plot with several additional lines; it should be sufficiently accurate for practical navigation.

The "external" fix should be found and used *only* when there is good reason to believe that there is an error in each observation of constant magnitude and direction. Barring this, the navigator is safer to use the internal fix.

A much more rigorous and detailed mathematical consideration of navigational errors can be found in appendix Q of *Bowditch*, Volume I (1977 or 1984).

Errors Resulting from Selection of the AP

2911 A careful investigation made some years ago in Great Britain showed that for an observer located at the equator when the difference between the true and assumed positions is 30′ in both latitude and longitude, and the altitude of the body observed was 75°, the maximum error will not exceed 1.0 mile; this maximum error will not be more than 0.7 miles at latitude 60°, and the probable error there would be about half this amount. For an altitude of 60° at the equator the error will not exceed 0.5 miles. Being roughly proportional to the square of the difference between the true and assumed positions, if the true position is within 20′ of latitude and longitude of the AP, the errors would be less than half those cited.

It is obvious that these errors are of no great concern in the ordinary course of navigation. They are cited only to show that under special conditions, when the utmost accuracy is required, a reduction should be made from the EP. The use of an electronic hand calculator or a computer, which provides trigonometric functions and other calculations to many decimal places, can yield an accuracy of better than 0.1′; this is better than the limit of precision of sextant observations.

Position Reports

2912 A ship's navigator customarily submits position reports to the captain or master at least three times each day. In the U.S. Navy this is done at ZT 0800, 1200, and 2000. The information required is the zone time and date of the report; the latitude and longitude, and the time the position was last determined; the method used (where a combination of methods are used, it is customary to indicate the method having the predominant effect upon the accuracy of the position); the set and

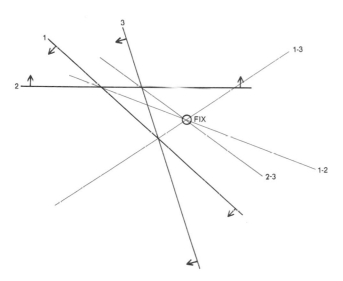

Figure 2910. The use of bisectors showing the external fix (LOPs in black, bisectors in blue).

drift since the last well-determined position; distance made good since the last report (indicate time of last report, and distance in miles); the destination, its distance in miles, and the ETA; the true heading; the error of the master gyro; the variation; the magnetic compass heading, with an indication of which compass is in use; the deviation as most recently determined; the deviation according to the current NavShips 3120/4 table; whether or not degaussing is energized; and any appropriate remarks, such as the clocks having been advanced or retarded since the last report.

The latitude and longitude given are always for the time of the report, while the time at which the last well-determined position was obtained is given in the "determined at" block. Some commanding officers prefer that the time given in connection with the distance made good be the preceding 1200 rather than the time of the last report, since this gives a ready indication of the miles steamed during the elapsed portion of the "navigational day."

The distance made good and distance to go are ordinarily obtained with dividers on the chart if the distance is not too great, or they can be computed, as explained in chapter 30. Gyro and magnetic compass errors are based upon the most recent accurate azimuth observation. Variation is obtained from the pilot chart or sailing chart.

Summary

2913 In this chapter the routine celestial navigation work of the navigator at sea has been listed. While typical, it is not all inclusive, and all of the work done by the navigator and his assistants has not been described. On a non-naval ship the procedures would likely be less formal—and on a yacht even less so—but the basic components of a "day's work at sea" remain valid and should be adhered to as closely as circumstances permit. While this chapter has focused on the daily routine of celestial navigation, on many vessels there will also be the added use of various forms of radionavigation as determined by the equipment on board and the waters used; these are discussed in subsequent chapters.

Only the mechanics of the practice of navigation can be given in a book, and the would-be "navigator" who has mastered this book has mastered *only* the mechanics. The efficiency and judgment of a good professional navigator comes only with experience and really never ceases to increase with more and more experience. The mark of a good navigator is not as much his ability to obtain accurate information as it is his ability to evaluate, interpret, and correctly use the information that is available to him.

Chapter 30

The Sailings

Introduction

3001 Direction and distances for shorter passages are almost always determined graphically, using rhumb lines as a matter of convenience. For longer passages, however, a great circle path (see article 509) can often provide a practical shorter distance with resulting economies of time and fuel; these can be determined graphically as explained in article 3008. There are times, however, when a mathematical solution of course and distance is preferred over a chart plot, or a suitable chart is not available. These calculations are collectively referred to as *sailings*. They were much used in the days before the ready availability of adequate charts and continue today in the internal computations of microprocessors in the receivers of several advanced radionavigation systems; see chapters 32–34 and 38.

When circumstances dictate the determination of course and distance by calculation or by the use of tables, knowledge of the sailings is essential for a navigator, whether he works with paper and pencil or uses a calculator or computer. Great-circle, mid-latitude, and Mercator methods are the only sailings discussed in this chapter as they will provide a suitable solution in almost all situations. Other methods and a more exhaustive treatment of the sailings will be found in *Bowditch*, DMAHTC Pub. No. 9; Volume II (1975 or 1981) of that publication contains tables relating to the sailings with explanations and examples of their use.

Preliminary Considerations

3002 It must be kept constantly in mind that all solutions of sailing problems are made with true directions. Throughout this book, *all directions given are true unless specifically stated otherwise.*

Before proceeding with a discussion of the sailings, it is advisable to be thoroughly familiar with the terms used. In chapter 2, the following terms were introduced: latitude (L), difference of latitude (*l*), longitude (Lo or λ), difference of longitude (DLo), departure (p), distance (D or Dist), course (Cn from mathematical solutions; C as used for plotting), great circles, and rhumb lines. The latitude and longitude of the point of departure will be designated L_1 and λ_1, respectively, and the coordinates of the destination, L_2 and λ_2. The latitude and longitude of the vertex of a great circle (point on circle farthest from the equator) is L_v and λ_v.

Departure (symbol p) is the linear measure, in nautical miles, of an arc of a parallel included between two meridians. The term distinguishes it from difference of longitude (DLo), which is the *angular* measure of the same arc. Regardless of the latitude, the difference of longitude between two meridians remains the same, but the departure between those meridians varies with the parallel along which it is measured. Thus, in figure 3002 the difference of longitude between the meridians is constant, whereas the departure becomes less and less as the poles are approached. Departure must be marked east (E) or west (W) according to the direction in which it is measured.

Figure 3002 illustrates the relationship of DLo and departure at various latitudes. At the equator DLo and departure are identical and equal to the difference in longitude in minutes. The distance between the meridians becomes less with increased latitude and varies as the *cosine* of the latitude—at 60°, the departure is one half of that at the equator

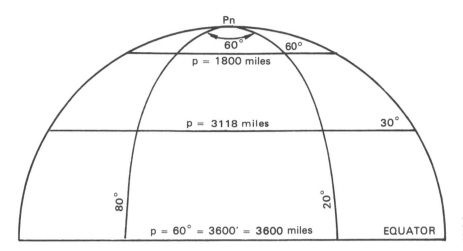

Figure 3002. Departure and difference in latitude.

(cos 60° = 0.5), and the distance around the earth at the 60th parallel is one half the distance around the earth at the equator. The relationship of DLo and p is expressed by the equation, p = DLo cos L, or DLo = p sec L.

Course angle (symbol C) is the inclination of the course line to the meridian, measured from 0° at the reference direction (*north* or *south*) *clockwise* or *counterclockwise* through 90° or 180°. It is labeled with the reference direction (N or S) as a prefix, and the direction of measurement from the reference direction (E or W) as a suffix. The rules for determining the labels and the numerical limits vary with the method of solution. Course angle (C) is converted to *course* (Cn) by following the instructions of the labels. For example:

$$N40° E = 000° + 40° = 040°$$
$$S50° E = 180° - 50° = 130°$$
$$S30° W = 180° + 30° = 210°$$
$$N15° W = 360° - 15° = 345°$$

Middle or *mid-latitude* (Lm) is the latitude of a point that is normally found by taking the *mean* value of L_1 and L_2, both being on the same side of the equator. (A more exact definition exists for "mid-latitude," but it is difficult mathematically and the difference is of no practical significance.)

Meridional parts (M). The length of a meridian on a Mercator chart, as expanded between the equator and any given latitude, expressed in units of 1' of arc of the equator, constitutes the number of meridional parts of that latitude. The meridional parts used in the construction of Mercator charts and in Mercator sailing are tabulated in Table 5 of *Bowditch*, Volume II. In Mercator sailing, M_1 represents the meridional parts of the latitude of the point of departure, and M_2 the parts of the latitude of the destination.

Meridional difference (m). This represents absolute difference $M_1 \sim M_2$ ($M_1 - M_2$ or $M_2 - M_1$ as determined by which is the larger).

The Various Sailings

3003 Several of the more often used "sailings" will be considered in this chapter. The method that gives the most accurate results, and is unlimited in its applications, is *great-circle sailing;* the "cost" of these advantages is a longer mathematical solution of greater complexity. Several other methods involve shorter solutions and give less precise results, although still within acceptable limits for practical navigation; these procedures, which yield rhumb lines, include *mid-latitude sailing* and *Mercator sailing*.

Other sailings of less general usefulness are covered in Volumes I and II of *Bowditch*. Among these are *plane* and *traverse sailing*, in which a small area of the earth's waters is considered to be a flat, or plane, surface with the obvious simplifications in the mathematics of the solution; plane sailing is for a single "leg," and traverse sailing is for two or more legs of a complex set of rhumb lines; these are used by small-craft skippers in navigation contests and predicted log races. *Parallel sailing* is a method involving the interconversion of departure and difference of longitude for a vessel proceeding due east or west; it is now generally obsolete. *Composite sailing* is a modification of great-circle sailing to limit the maximum latitude that otherwise would be reached.

Mid-latitude Sailing

3004 The procedures for *mid-latitude* sailing are based on approximations that simplify the mathematics of the problem and yield somewhat less accurate answers than are obtainable by more rigorous and time-consuming reductions. For ordinary purposes, however, they yield more accurate results than are obtainable in the ordinary navigation of vessels.

Typical mid-latitude sailing problems are: (1) knowing latitude and longitude of points of departure and destination, solving for course and distance; or (2) knowing latitude and longitude of point of departure, and course and distance made good, solving for the latitude and longitude of the point thus reached.

Note carefully that when the course line crosses the equator, the problem *must* be broken down into two separate triangles of north and south latitude and solved separately.

The basic equations for mid-latitude sailing are:

$$p = DLo \text{ (in minutes of arc)} \times \cos Lm \quad (1)$$
$$C = \tan^{-1}(p \div l) \text{ where } l = \text{difference} \quad (2)$$
$$\text{of latitude in minutes of arc}$$
$$Dist = l \times \sec C \quad (3)$$

The use of these equations for the solution of a problem of the first type referred to above is shown in the following example:

Example: A vessel at lat. 8°48.9′ S, long. 89°53.3′ W is to proceed to lat. 17°06.9′ S, long. 104°51.6′ W.

Required: (1) course, (2) distance.

Solution:

L_1	8°48.9′ S		λ_1	89°53.3′ W
L_2	17°06.9′ S		λ_2	104°51.6′ W
l	8°18.0′ S		DLo	14°58.3′ W
l	498.0′ S		DLo	898.3′ W
$\frac{1}{2}l$	4°09.0′ S			
Lm	12°57.9′ S			

DLo	898.3′ W	log	2.95342
Lm	12°57.9′ S	log cos	9.98878 − 10
p	875.4 mi W		2.94220
l	498.0′ S	−log	2.69723
C	S60°21.9′ W	log tan	0.24497
(2) Dist	1007.1	log	2.69723
(1) Cn	240.4°	log sec	0.30586
			3.00309

The solution above is shown through use of logarithms. It can be easily and quickly solved with a small electronic calculator or computer having trigonometric functions. The basic mid-latitude equations (1) and (2) above would be used as shown, but equation (3) might be changed to

$$Dist = l \div \cos C \quad (3a)$$

to better match normal keyboard functions; angles

may have to be converted to degrees and decimal fractions.

If the calculator does not have keys for trigonometric functions, values for them can be found in Table 31 of *Bowditch*, Volume II.

When the latitude and longitude of the point of departure and the course and distance steamed are given, the latitude and longitude of the point of arrival may be found by using the following equations:

$$l = Dist \times \cos C \quad (4)$$
$$p = Dist \times \sin C \quad (5)$$
$$DLo = p \times \sec Lm \quad (6)$$
$$\text{or } DLo = p \div \cos Lm \quad (6a)$$

With l having been found, $\frac{1}{2}l$ is applied to the latitude of the point of departure to find Lm. The latitude and longitude of the point of arrival are found by applying l and DLo, in accordance with their names, to the latitude and longitude respectively of the point of departure.

Example: A vessel at Lat. 37°01.2′ N, Long. 75°53.7′ W proceeds on a rhumb-line course 072.5° for a distance of 850 miles.

Required: (1) Latitude and (2) longitude of point reached at end of run.

Solution (by calculator):

$$l = Dist \times \cos C$$
$$= 850 \times \cos 72.5° = 255.6′ \text{ N}$$
$$= 4°15.6′ \text{ N}$$
$$p = Dist \times \sin C$$
$$= 850 \times \sin 72.5° = 810.7′ \text{ E}$$

l	4°15.6′ N	$\frac{1}{2}l$	2°07.8′ N	
L_1	37°01.2′ N		37°01.2′ N	
(1) L_2	41°16.8′ N			
L_m			39°09.0′ N	

$$DLo = p \div \cos L_m$$
$$= 810.7′ \div \cos 39°09.0′ = 1045.4′$$
$$= 17°25.4′ \text{ E}$$
$$75°53.7 \text{ W}$$
$$(2) \quad 58°28.3′ \text{ W}$$

Answer: Lat. 41°16.8′ N; Long. 58°28.3′ W.

Mercator Sailing

3005 The determination of course and distance on a Mercator chart constitutes a graphic solution of a *Mercator sailing* problem. This sailing may also be solved by computation.

The equations for Mercator sailing are:

$$C = \tan^{-1}(DLo \div m) \quad (1)$$
$$Dist = l \times \sec C \quad (2)$$
$$\text{or } Dist = l \div \cos C \quad (2a)$$

where m is the absolute difference between M_1 and M_2 as taken from table 5 of *Bowditch*, Volume II.

These equations can be conveniently arranged for solution as shown in the following example:

Example: Find the course and distance by Mercator sailing from Cape Flattery Light, Washington, to Diamond Head, Oahu, Hawaiian Islands.

Cape Flattery Light	L_1	48°23.5′ N
	λ_1	124°44.1′ W
Diamond Head	L_2	21°15.1′ N
	λ_2	157°48.7′ N

Solution:

L_1	48°23.5′ N		M_1	3309.2
L_2	21°15.1′ N		M_2	1296.9
l	27°08.4′ S		m	2012.3
l	1628.4′ S			

λ_2	157°48.7′ W
λ_1	124°44.1′ W
DLo	33°04.6′ W
DLo	1984.6′ W

By calculator:

$$C = \tan^{-1}(DLo \div m)$$
$$= \tan^{-1}(1984.6 \div 2012.3) = \tan^{-1} 0.98623$$
$$= 44.6029° = S\ 44°36.2′\ W$$
$$C_n = 180° + 44°36.2′$$
$$= 224.6°$$
$$Dist = l \div \cos C = 1628.4 \div \cos 44.6029°$$
$$= 2287.0\ mi$$

In Mercator sailing, the limits of C are 0° to 90°, labeled N or S to agree with l and E or W to agree with DLo. To convert C to Cn, follow the instructions of the labels. In the above example, start at S (180°). The course is 44°36.2′ to the west, or 180° + 44°36.2′ = 224°36.2′; this is recorded as 224.6°. It is customary to solve for Distance and C to a precision of 0.1′ but to record Cn only to a precision of 0.1°.

These equations can also be used for determining the latitude and longitude of the destination if the course and distance are known, but if the course is near 090° or 270°, an appreciable error in DLo may result.

Mercator sailing problems can also be solved by means of Volume II of *Bowditch* by using values from Table 3 in accordance with instructions in article 1007 of that publication.

Characteristics of Great Circles

3006 Every great circle of a sphere bisects every other great circle. Therefore every great circle, if extended around the earth, will lie half in the Northern Hemisphere and half in the Southern Hemisphere, and the midpoint of either half will be farthest from the equator. This point, where a great circle reaches its highest latitude, is called its *vertex*.

A great circle between two places on the same side of the equator is everywhere nearer the pole than the rhumb line. If the two places are on different sides of the equator, the great circle between them changes its direction of curvature, relative to the rhumb line, at the equator. If the two places are equal distances on opposite sides of the equator, the great circle will bisect the rhumb line between them at the equator.

Since the direction of a great circle is constantly changing, it cannot be drawn on a Mercator chart as a straight line; the course of a vessel attempting to follow such a curved path would have to be continually changed. As this is obviously impractical, the course is changed at intervals, so that the vessel follows a series of rhumb lines. Since for a short distance a rhumb line and a great circle are nearly coincident, the result is a close approximation of the great circle. This is generally accomplished by determining points at regular intervals along the great circle by any one of several methods, plotting them on a Mercator chart or plotting sheet, and steaming the rhumb lines between such points (see article 3008).

It should be apparent that the equator and meridians are special cases, and that many of the statements regarding great circles do not apply to them. If the course lies along one of these great circles, the solution may be made mentally, since the course is constant (these special great circles being also rhumb lines), and the distance is the number of minutes of DLo in the case of the equator and l in the case of a meridian.

Comparison of Rhumb Lines and Great Circles

3007 The difference between the great-circle distance and the rhumb-line distance between two places may amount to several hundred miles. For example, the great-circle distance from Sydney, Australia, to Valparaiso, Chile, is 748 miles shorter than the rhumb-line distance. It is obvious, though, that while the rhumb line is most convenient, it should not be used for all long passages.

Under certain circumstances the great-circle track is *not* materially shorter than the rhumb line between two places. These may be summarized as follows:

1. For a short distance, the rhumb line and great circle are nearly coincident. The difference is about one mile for two places 350 miles apart on the 40th parallel of latitude.
2. The rhumb line between places that are near the same meridian is very nearly a great circle.
3. The equator is both a rhumb line and great circle. Parallels near the equator are very nearly great circles. Therefore, at *low latitudes,* a rhumb line is very nearly as short as a great circle.

The decision to use or not to use great-circle sailing depends on whether the distance to be saved is sufficient to justify the trouble involved, as well as on other considerations, such as the latitude of the vertex, and anticipated weather, currents, shoal water, etc., along the different routes.

Great-circle Sailing by Chart: Gnomonic Projection

3008 The Defense Mapping Agency Hydrographic/Topographic Center publishes a number of charts at various scales using the gnomonic projection and covering the usually navigated portions of the earth; these are listed in the *DMA Catalog of Maps, Charts, and Related Products, Part 2, Volume X.* The point of tangency is chosen for each chart to give the least distortion for the area to be covered. Any great circle appears on this type of chart as a straight line. Because of this property, the chart is useful in great-circle sailing.

However, since the meridians are not shown as parallel lines, no ordinary compass rose can be provided for use in measuring direction over the entire chart, and since angles are distorted, they cannot be measured by protractor or plotter. Latitude and longitude at a particular point on the chart must be determined by reference to the meridians and parallels in the immediate vicinity of the point. Hence, a gnomonic chart is not convenient for ordinary navigational purposes. Its practical use in navigation is limited to solution of great-circle sailing problems.

In use, a straight line connecting the point of departure and the destination is drawn on the chart (upper half of figure 3008). The great circle is then inspected to see that it passes clear of all dangers to navigation. If this requirement is met, the courses are then transferred to a Mercator chart by selecting a number of points along the great circle, determining their latitude and longitude, and plotting these points on the Mercator chart. These points are then connected by straight lines to represent the rhumb-line courses to be steered. The two arrows of figure 3008 indicate a corresponding position on the two charts. It can be seen in figure 3008 that points have been chosen at intervals of 5° of longitude to facilitate the picking off of points and plotting them on the Mercator chart. At this interval the error in using rhumb lines to approximate the great circle is small.

Figure 3008. Transferring a great-circle track from a gnomonic chart to a Mercator chart.

It will be noted that the rhumb-line segments determined in the manner just described are chords of the great circle, as plotted on the Mercator chart. The course and distance for steaming each segment can be determined by measurement on the Mercator chart. Courses and distances of tangents to the great circle can be determined directly from the great-circle charts, but the method is somewhat involved and can best be understood by studying the explanation given on some gnomonic charts. The chord method is easier and is commonly used in practice.

The great-circle distance of a voyage is sometimes determined from a gnomonic chart for comparison with the rhumb-line distance in determining which method will be used.

The great-circle track should be checked on a pilot chart for any potential hazards. If it extends into high latitudes, consideration should be given to modifying it to *composite sailing* in which a great circle track is followed from the point of departure to a *limiting latitude*, thence along that parallel to a point from which another great circle track will take the vessel to her destination.

Great-circle Sailing by Chart: Lambert Conformal Projection

3009   Although most marine navigators use the combination of gnomonic and Mercator charts for great-circle sailing, the use of the Lambert conformal projection is possible. The advantage of a Lambert conformal chart for this purpose is that both great-circle distance and courses for segments of the great circle may be obtained by direct measurement, saving a transfer of points from the gnomonic to the Mercator projection. As stated in chapter 5, any straight line on a Lambert conformal chart is a close approximation to a great circle, and angles are truly represented on this pro-

jection. Although direction can therefore be measured directly on the chart, protractors or plotters must be used, as the meridians are not shown as parallel lines. The course, a rhumb line, of each segment of a great circle is measured at its midpoint.

Since the distance scale of a Lambert conformal chart is so nearly constant that a fixed scale can be used without significant error, distance may be measured either by means of the latitude scale (as on a Mercator chart), by distance scales if printed on the chart, or by use of a special protractor plotter made to the scale of the chart. This latter method permits rapid measurement of both course and distance.

Great-circle Sailing by Conversion Angle

3010   If the difference in the direction of the great circle and rhumb line is known, this difference, called the *conversion angle*, can be applied to either one to obtain the other. In any great-circle sailing, the angle the great circle makes with the meridian at the starting point is referred to as the initial great-circle direction. In many texts this is referred to as the initial great-circle course, even though the course by definition must be a rhumb line.

Conversion angles are tabulated in Table 1 of *Bowditch*, Volume II. If the distance does not exceed approximately 2,000 miles *and* both points (departure and destination) lie on the same side of the equator, the conversion angle can be found to practical accuracy by the equation:

Conversion angle = $\tan^{-1} (\sin Lm \times \tan \frac{1}{2}DLo)$

This equation can be solved graphically by a simple construction as shown in figure 3010. Draw any line *AB*. Draw a second line, *AC*, making an angle with *AB* equal to the mid-latitude between the

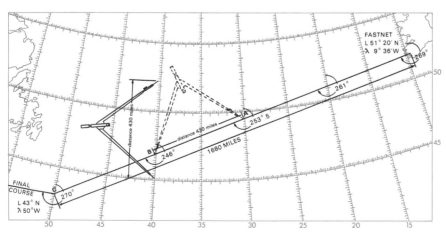

Figure 3009. Great-circle sailing on a Lambert projection chart.

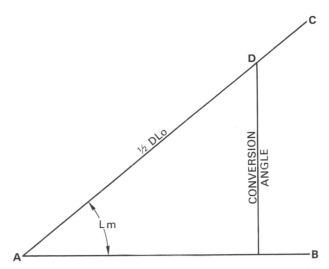

Figure 3010. Conversion angle determined graphically.

point of departure and the destination. From the intersection, measure, to any convenient scale, a number of linear units equal to one-half the number of degrees of DLo, thus locating D. From D drop a perpendicular to the line AB. The number of linear units in this perpendicular, to the same scale used for $\frac{1}{2}$DLo, is the number of degrees of the conversion angle.

The sign of the conversion angle in any given case will be apparent if it is remembered that the great circle is nearer the pole than the rhumb line. For instance, in north latitude if the destination is east of the point of departure, the conversion angle is minus (−); if to the west, it is plus (+).

In practice the conversion angle is usually modified to provide chord courses. This is done by dividing the conversion angle by the number of legs to be used and *subtracting* this from the conversion angle before it is applied to the Mercator (rhumb line) course. At the end of the first leg a new solution must be made for the next leg. This is somewhat more trouble than using a great-circle chart, but eliminates the necessity of a lengthy computation if no great-circle chart is available.

Distance is determined by measuring the length of each rhumb-line leg and adding the figures so obtained.

Great-circle Sailing by Computation: Mathematical Principles

3011 In figure 3011, *1* is the point of departure (L_1, λ_1), *2* the destination (L_2, λ_2); P is the pole nearest *1*, and EQ the equator. The great circles through *P1* and *P2* are meridians. Since latitude is the angular distance of a place north or south of the equator measured along a meridian, *P1*, the angular dis-

tance from the pole to *1*, the point of departure, is $90° - L_1$, or the colatitude. Similarly, *P2* is the colatitude of the destination. However, the term *colatitude*, as used with respect to the destination, is $90° \pm L_2$, since P is chosen as the pole nearest the point of departure. That is, if *2* and *1* are on the same side of the equator, or of the same *name*, the latitude of *2* may be considered (+) and the colatitude = $90° - L_2$. However, if *2* is of opposite name, or on the opposite side of the equator from *1*, it may be considered (−) in which case the colatitude is $90° - (-L_2)$, or $90° + L_2$.

If *1* and *2* are connected by a great circle, a spherical triangle is formed. The length of the arc of the great circle between *1* and *2* is the great-circle distance between these two points. The initial direction from *1* to *2* is the angle *P12*. The angle *1P2* is the DLo, designated t when used in the special case as part of the navigational triangle illustrated in figure 3011. This is the same triangle used in the solution of celestial observations, *1* then being the assumed position of the observer and *2* the point on the earth directly under the celestial body observed. Hence, any method of solution devised for one of these problems can be used for the other. However, some methods devised for solution of celestial observations are better adapted to the solution of great-circle sailing problems than others.

The solution of a great-circle sailing problem involves computation for the distance and initial direction, the position of the vertex, and the coordinates of points along the track. Computation is

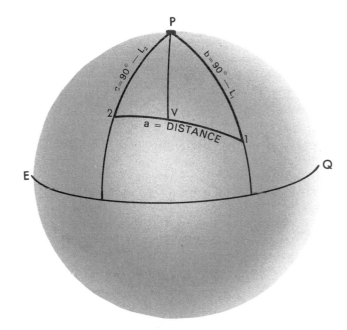

Figure 3011. The navigational triangle as used in great-circle sailing.

somewhat tedious if not done by calculator or computer, but the results are accurate and this method is sometimes the only means available.

Great-circle Sailing by Computation: Distance and Initial Direction

3012 Refer to figure 3012. A perpendicular dropped from the destination, *2*, to the meridian *P1* will divide the oblique navigational triangle *P12* into two right spherical triangles. The length of the perpendicular is designated *R*, and the foot of the perpendicular *y*. The latitude of point *y* is designated *K*, which is always on the same side of the equator as *2*. The arc *1y* represents the *difference* of latitude of points *1* and *y*, regardless of which is greater or whether or not both are on the same side of the equator.

This is designated as $K \sim L_1$. (Here the symbol $\sim$ is used to mean *algebraic* difference.) Thus, if both *K* and L_1 have the same name, the smaller is subtracted from the larger, but if they are of opposite name, their numerical values are added. The value $K \sim L_1$ has no sign or name, being merely a difference. The side *Py* is co-*K*.

If the point of departure and the destination are known, L_1, L_2, and t ($\lambda_2 - \lambda_1$) are the values available for use in the solution. The problem is to find the distance (the side *D* in figure 3012) and the angle C at *1*.

These can be found by the following equations:

$$csc\ R = csc\ t\ sec\ L_2 \tag{1}$$

$$csc\ K = \frac{csc\ L_2}{sec\ R} \tag{2}$$

$$sec\ d = sec\ R\ sec\ (K \sim L_1) \tag{3}$$

$$csc\ C = \frac{csc\ R}{csc\ d} \tag{4}$$

The derivation of these equations is explained in *Bowditch*. Any table of log secants and log cosecants can be used for the solution of these equations, but they are most conveniently arranged in Table 35 of *Bowditch*, Volume II. (These tables of the "Ageton method" were published for many years as a separate volume, H.O. 211. The more compact condensed Ageton tables, see article 2409, may also be used.) In Table 35, column "A" contains log cosecants multiplied by 10^5, and column "B" contains log secants similarly multiplied by 10^5. These values are intended for use without interpolation in most instances, the accuracy being sufficient for practical navigation. In situations, however, where t is near 90°, the results may not be

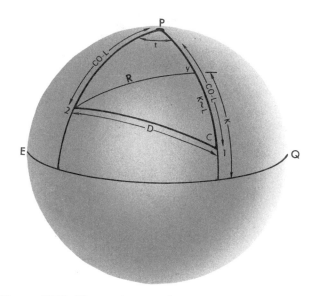

Figure 3012. The navigational triangle divided into two right spherical triangles by a perpendicular from the point of destination to the meridian of the point of departure.

accurate enough; it is advisable to interpolate if it is between 85° and 95°.

Numerous rules for naming the triangle parts north or south, and for entering the tables at the top or bottom of the page, must be carefully followed. These rules, and the equations and method of solution for determining the great-circle distance, the initial direction, the vertex, and additional points along the track are given in article 1016 of *Bowditch*, Volume II (1981) and will not be repeated here. A single complete solution is presented for illustrative purposes in the following article.

Great-circle Sailing by Computation: a Complete Solution

3013 A complete solution for all aspects of the mathematical solution of a great-circle sailing problem using *Bowditch* Table 35 is given in the example below. The equations and the terminology used are as given in the instructions of article 1012, *Bowditch*, Volume II.

Example: (1) Find the initial great-circle direction and distance from Land's End, England (50°04.0′ N, 5°45.0′ W) to St. John's, Newfoundland (47°34.0′ N, 52°40.0′ W) by computation using table 35 of *Bowditch*. (2) Find the latitude and longitude of the vertex. (3) Find the latitude and longitude of points along the great circle at distance intervals of 5° (300 miles) along the great circle, measured in both directions from the vertex.

Solution:

(1)

			Add		Subtract		Add		Subtract
λ_2	52°40.0′ W								
λ_1	5°45.0′ W		Add		Subtract		Add		Subtract
t	46°55.0′ W		A	13646					
L_2	47°34.0′ N		B	17087	A	13191			
			A	30733	B	6041	B	6041	A 30733
K	58°01.0′ N				A	7150			
L_1	50°04.0′ N								
$K \sim L_1$	7°57.0′						B	419	
D	30°29.0′						B	6460	A 29475
Cn	283.7°				C	N76°16.5′ W			A 1258
Dist	1829.0 mi								

(2)

			Add		Subtract	
			Add		Subtract	
L_1	50°04.0′ W		B	19253		
C	N 76°16.5′ W		A	1258	B	62477
L_v	51°25.5′ N		B	20511	A	10691
t_v	17°40.0′ W				A	51786
λ_1	5°45.0′ W					
λ_v	23°25.0′ W					

(3)

d_{v-x}		5°	10°	15°	20°
L_v	A	10691	10691	10691	10691
d_{v-x}	(+)B	165.6	665	1506	2701
L_x	A	10856.6	11356	12197	13392
L_x		51°09.0′ N	50°21.0′ N	49°02.5′ N	47°16.5′ N
d_{v-x}	A	105970	76033	58700	46595
I_x	(−)B	20254	19511	18342	16846
t_{v-x}	A	85716	56522	40358	29749
t_{v-x}		7°59.0′	15°47.5′	23°15.5′	30°16.5′
λ_v		23°25.0′	23°25.0′	23°25.0′	23°25.0′
λ_x		15°26.0′ W	7°37.5′ W	—	— $(\lambda_v - t_{v-x})$
λ_x		31°24.0′ W	39°12.5′ W	46°40.5′ W	53°41.5′ W $(\lambda_v + t_{v-x})$

Note: For some L_x there are two λ_x, one east and one west of the vertex.

In calculations such as the above, it is well to write down the entire form for all parts before doing any of the computation. The mind is thus freed of thinking of what to do next and can focus on the mechanics of the computation. Also, it will be noted that the same quantity sometimes appears in several places. In part (1), for instance, C is found from its A function, (1258). In part (2) both A and B functions are needed. If the B function (62477) is picked out at the same time C is being found, it will save going again to the same place in the table in the solution of part (2). The same A value found in part (1) is used in part (2) regardless of whether it is an exact tabulated number.

It will be noted that but one point is found at distances of 15° and 20° from the vertex, since the points to the east are beyond the point of depar-ture. The number of points needed can be deter-mined by dividing the distance interval (in this example 5° or 300 miles) into the total distance. In determining the number of computations, the position of the vertex must be considered. In some problems the vertex will be located beyond the destination, but its position must be determined in order to calculate the points along the great circle.

Great-circle Sailing by Computation: Verification Procedures

3014 Mathematical errors may occur when a great-circle problem is computed in the foregoing manner. It is advisable to check the answers for gross errors with a small calculator using the following equations. Distances over 1,800 miles and course angles between 0° and 70°, and between 110° and 180°, can be solved with considerable accuracy.

$$D = 60 \cos^{-1} [(\sin L_1 \times \sin L_2) \tag{1}$$
$$+ (\cos L_1 \times \cos L_2 \times \cos t)]$$

$$C = \sin^{-1} [(\cos L_2 \times \sin t) \div \sin D] \tag{2}$$

$$L_v = \cos^{-1} (\cos L_1 \times \sin C) \tag{3}$$

$$t_v = \sin^{-1} (\cos C \div \sin L_v) \tag{4}$$

$$D_v = \sin^{-1} (\cos L_1 \times \sin t_v) \tag{5}$$

$$L_x = \sin^{-1} (\sin L_v \times \cos D_{v-x}) \tag{6}$$

$$t_{v-x} = \sin^{-1} (\sin D_{v-x} \div \cos L_x) \tag{7}$$

Note: Equation (1) above assumed that L_1 and L_2 are both of the same name (both north or both south). If they are contrary (the course crossing the equator), insert L_2 as a negative quantity. In equation (2), d is in angular units, $D \div 60$. These are not the only formats used for such equations; other forms may be found in other sources.

A partial solution by calculator of the previous example yields results as follows:

$$D = 60 \cos^{-1} [(\sin 50°04.0' \times \sin 47°34.0')$$
$$+ (\cos 50°04.0' \times \cos 47°34.0' \times \cos 46°55.0')]$$
$$= 1828.98 \text{ miles}$$
$$C = \sin^{-1} (\cos 47°34.0' \times \sin 46°55.0')$$
$$\div \sin (1828.98 \div 60)$$
$$= \text{N}76.275° \text{ W} = \text{N}76°16.5' \text{ W}$$
$$L_v = \cos^{-1} (\cos 50°04.0' \times \sin 76°16.5')$$
$$= 51.423° = 51°25.4' \text{ N}$$
$$t_v = \sin^{-1} (\cos 76°16.5' \div 51°25.4')$$
$$= 17.667° = 17°40.0' \text{ W}$$
$$\lambda_1 = \underline{5°45.0' \text{ W}}$$
$$\lambda_v = \overline{23°25.0' \text{ W}}$$

Equations (5) through (7) could be similarly solved by calculator for the latitude of intermediate points specified by longitude or longitude intervals to either side of the vertex. (Calculator and computer programs are also available for the computation of the latitude of any point on the great-circle track specified in terms of its longitude—without reference to the vertex.)

Great-circle Sailing by Computation:
Using Pub. No. 229

3015 The tables of DMAHTC Pub. No. 229 are readily adaptable to solutions of great-circle sailing problems, because the point of departure and the destination can always be found on the same page.

Pub. No. 229, and the use of its interpolation tables, is described at some length in article 2404; it will be dealt with only briefly here, to describe its use for finding the great-circle distance and initial direction. By entering the tables with latitude of departure as "latitude," latitude of destination as "declination," and difference of longitude as "LHA," the tabular altitude and azimuth angle may be extracted and converted to distance and course.

The tabular azimuth angle (or its supplement) becomes the initial great-circle course angle, prefixed N or S for the latitude of departure, and suffixed E or W depending upon the destination being east or west of point of departure.

If all entering arguments are integral degrees, the altitude and azimuth angle are obtained directly from the tables without interpolation. If the latitude of destination is not a whole degree, interpolation for the additional minutes of latitude is done as in correcting altitude for any declination increment; if either the latitude of departure or difference of longitude, or both, are nonintegral, the additional interpolation is done graphically.

Since the latitude of destination becomes the declination entry, and all declinations appear on every page, the great-circle solution can always be extracted from the volume that covers the latitude of the point of departure.

Great-circle solutions fall into one of the four following cases:

Case I—Latitudes of departure and destination of same name and great-circle distance less than 90°.

Case II—Latitudes of departure and destination of contrary name and great-circle distance less than 90°.

Case III—Latitudes of departure and destination of same name and great-circle distance greater than 90°.

Case IV—Latitudes of departure and destination of contrary name and great-circle distance greater than 90°.

The introductory pages of Pub. No. 229 provide instructions for the solution of each of these cases. The solution of a Case I problem will be shown below; for comparison purposes, this is the same problem as was worked previously by Table 35 of *Bowditch* and by calculator.

Example: Find the initial great-circle course and distance from Land's End, England (50°04.0' N, 5°45.0' W), to St. John's, Newfoundland (47°34.0' N, 52°40.0' W), by computation using Pub. No. 229.

Solution: (1) Since the latitude of the point of departure, the latitude of the destination, and the difference of longitude (DLo) between the point of departure and destination are not integral degrees, the solution is done from an adjusted point of departure or assumed position of departure chosen as follows: the latitude of the assumed position (AP) is the integral degree of latitude nearest to the point of departure; the longitude of the AP is chosen to provide integral degrees of DLo. This AP, which should be within 30′ of the longitude of the point of departure, is at latitude 50° N, longitude 5°40.0′ W; the DLo is thus 47°.

(2) Enter the tables with 50° as the latitude argument (Same Name), 47° as the LHA argument, and 47° as the declination argument.

(3) From page 96 of Pub. No. 229, Volume 4 (figure 3015a), extract the tabular altitude, altitude difference, and azimuth angle; interpolate altitude and azimuth angle for the declination increment using figure 3015b. The Dec. Inc. is the number of minutes that the actual latitude of the destination exceeds the integral degrees used as the declination argument.

LHA 47°, Lat. 50° (Same), Dec. 47°
  Dec. Inc. 34.0′, d + 22.9′
         ht (Tab. Hc) 59°13.8′
             Tens   11.3′
           Units   1.7′
Interpolated for Dec. Inc. 59°26.8′
          Z 77.1°
          C N77.1°W

Initial great-circle course from AP Cn 282.9°
Great-circle distance from AP
(90° − 59°26.8′ = 30°33.2′) 1833.2 n.mi.

(4) Using the Pub. 229 graphical method for interpolating altitude for latitude and LHA increments, the course line is drawn from the AP in the direction of the initial great-circle course from the AP (282.9°). As shown in figure 3015c, a line is drawn from the point of departure perpendicular to the initial great-circle course line or its extension.

(5) The required correction, in units of minutes of latitude, for the latitude and DLo increments is the length along the course line between the foot of the perpendicular and the AP. The correction applied to the distance from the AP is −4.3′; the great-circle distance is 1828.9 nautical miles.

(6) The azimuth angle interpolated for declination, LHA, and latitude increments is N76.3° W; the initial great-circle course from the point of departure is 283.7°.

The accuracy of Pub. No. 229 in calculating great-circle distance and initial direction is indicated by the fact that the actual distance, rigorously computed, is 1,828.98 miles and the initial direction is 283°43.5′, giving an error of less than 0.1 miles and less than 0.1 degrees.

Points Along a Great-circle Path by Pub. No. 229

If the latitude of the point of departure and the initial great-circle course angle are integral degrees, points along the great-circle path are found by entering the tables with the latitude of departure as the latitude argument (Same Name), the initial great-circle course angle as the LHA argument, and 90° minus distance to a point on the great circle as the declination argument. The latitude of the point on the great circle and the difference of longitude between that point and the point of departure are the tabular altitude and azimuth angle respondents, respectively.

Required: A number of points at 300-mile intervals along the great circle from latitude 50° N, lon-

Figure 3015a. Pub. No. 229, "same name" page (extract).

Dec. Inc.	Tens 10'	20'	30'	40'	50'	Decimals	Units 0'	1'	2'	3'	4'	5'	6'	7'	8'	9'	Double Second Diff. and Corr.	
34.0	5.6	11.3	17.0	22.6	28.3	.0	0.0	0.6	1.1	1.7	2.3	2.9	3.4	4.0	4.6	5.2	0.8	
34.1	5.7	11.3	17.0	22.7	28.4	.1	0.1	0.6	1.2	1.8	2.4	2.9	3.5	4.1	4.7	5.2	2.5	0.1
34.2	5.7	11.4	17.1	22.8	28.5	.2	0.1	0.7	1.3	1.8	2.4	3.0	3.6	4.1	4.7	5.3	4.1	0.2
34.3	5.7	11.4	17.1	22.9	28.6	.3	0.2	0.7	1.3	1.9	2.5	3.0	3.6	4.2	4.8	5.3	5.8	0.3
34.4	5.7	11.5	17.2	22.9	28.7	.4	0.2	0.8	1.4	2.0	2.5	3.1	3.7	4.3	4.8	5.4	7.4	0.4
34.5	5.8	11.5	17.3	23.0	28.8	.5	0.3	0.9	1.4	2.0	2.6	3.2	3.7	4.3	4.9	5.5	9.1	0.5
34.6	5.8	11.5	17.3	23.1	28.8	.6	0.3	0.9	1.5	2.1	2.6	3.2	3.8	4.4	4.9	5.5	10.7	0.6
34.7	5.8	11.6	17.4	23.2	28.9	.7	0.4	1.0	1.6	2.1	2.7	3.3	3.9	4.4	5.0	5.6	12.3	0.7
34.8	5.8	11.6	17.4	23.2	29.0	.8	0.5	1.0	1.6	2.2	2.8	3.3	3.9	4.5	5.1	5.6	14.0	0.8
34.9	5.9	11.7	17.5	23.3	29.1	.9	0.5	1.1	1.7	2.2	2.8	3.4	4.0	4.5	5.1	5.7	15.6	0.9
																	17.3	1.0
35.0	5.8	11.6	17.5	23.3	29.1	.0	0.0	0.6	1.2	1.8	2.4	3.0	3.5	4.1	4.7	5.3	18.9	1.1
35.1	5.8	11.7	17.5	23.4	29.2	.1	0.1	0.7	1.2	1.8	2.4	3.0	3.6	4.2	4.8	5.4	20.6	1.2
35.2	5.8	11.7	17.6	23.4	29.3	.2	0.1	0.7	1.3	1.9	2.5	3.1	3.7	4.3	4.9	5.4	22.2	1.3
35.3	5.9	11.8	17.6	23.5	29.4	.3	0.2	0.8	1.4	2.0	2.5	3.1	3.7	4.3	4.9	5.5	23.9	1.4
35.4	5.9	11.8	17.7	23.6	29.5	.4	0.2	0.8	1.4	2.0	2.6	3.2	3.8	4.4	5.0	5.6	25.5	1.5
35.5	5.9	11.8	17.8	23.7	29.6	.5	0.3	0.9	1.5	2.1	2.7	3.3	3.8	4.4	5.0	5.6	27.2	1.6
35.6	5.9	11.9	17.8	23.7	29.7	.6	0.4	0.9	1.5	2.1	2.7	3.3	3.9	4.5	5.1	5.7	28.8	1.7
35.7	6.0	11.9	17.9	23.8	29.8	.7	0.4	1.0	1.6	2.2	2.8	3.4	4.0	4.6	5.1	5.7	30.4	1.8
35.8	6.0	12.0	17.9	23.9	29.9	.8	0.5	1.1	1.7	2.2	2.8	3.4	4.0	4.6	5.2	5.8	32.1	1.9
35.9	6.0	12.0	18.0	24.0	30.0	.9	0.5	1.1	1.7	2.3	2.9	3.5	4.1	4.7	5.3	5.9	33.7	2.0
	10'	20'	30'	40'	50'		0'	1'	2'	3'	4'	5'	6'	7'	8'	9'	35.4	2.1

Figure 3015b. Pub. No. 229, interpolation table (extract).

Figure 3015c. Correction of great-circle distance when using Pub. No. 229.

gitude 5° W when the initial great-circle course angle is N76° W.

Entering the tables (figure 3015d) with latitude 50° (Same Name), LHA 76°, and with successive declinations of 85°, 80°, 75°, . . . the latitudes and differences in longitude from 5° W are found as tabular altitudes and azimuth angles respectively.

Distance n. mi. (arc)	300 (5°)	600 (10°)	900 (15°)	1200 (20°)
Latitude	51.0° N	51.4° N	51.3° N	50.6° N
DLo	7.7°	15.7°	23.7°	31.5°
Longitude	12.7° W	20.7° W	28.7° W	36.5° W

76°, 284° L.H.A.   LATITUDE SAME NAME AS DECLINATION   N. Lat { L.H.A. greater than 180°......Zn=Z ; L.H.A. less than 180°............Zn=360°−Z

Dec.	45° Hc	d	Z	46° Hc	d	Z	47° Hc	d	Z	48° Hc	d	Z	49° Hc	d	Z	50° Hc	d	Z	51° Hc	d	Z	52° Hc	d	Z	Dec.
0	9 51.0	+43.0	100.0	9 40.5	+43.7	100.2	9 29.8	+44.5	100.3	9 19.0	+45.1	100.5	9 07.9	+45.9	100.7	8 56.8	+46.5	100.8	8 45.4	+47.2	101.0	8 33.9	+47.8	101.1	0
1	10 34.0	42.9	99.3	10 24.2	43.7	99.5	10 14.3	44.3	99.7	10 04.1	45.1	99.8	9 53.8	45.7	100.0	9 43.3	46.4	100.2	9 32.6	47.1	100.3	9 21.7	47.7	100.5	1
2	11 16.9	42.8	98.6	11 07.9	43.5	98.8	10 58.6	44.3	99.0	10 49.2	44.9	99.2	10 39.5	45.7	99.3	10 29.7	46.3	99.5	10 19.7	47.0	99.7	10 09.4	47.7	99.9	2
3	11 59.7	42.7	97.9	11 51.4	43.5	98.1	11 42.9	44.2	98.3	11 34.1	44.9	98.5	11 25.2	45.6	98.7	11 16.0	46.3	98.9	11 06.7	46.9	99.1	10 57.1	47.6	99.3	3
4	12 42.4	42.6	97.1	12 34.9	43.3	97.4	12 27.1	44.0	97.6	12 19.0	44.8	97.8	12 10.8	45.5	98.0	12 02.3	46.2	98.2	11 53.6	46.8	98.4	11 44.7	47.5	98.6	4
70	46 18.0	+6.5	28.7	47 10.5	+7.2	29.2	48 02.7	+8.0	29.8	48 54.7	+8.7	30.3	49 46.3	+9.5	30.9	50 37.6	+10.4	31.5	51 28.6	+11.2	32.2	52 19.2	+12.0	32.9	70
71	46 24.5	5.4	27.3	47 17.7	6.1	27.8	48 10.7	6.8	28.3	49 03.4	7.6	28.8	49 55.8	8.3	29.4	50 48.0	9.0	30.0	51 39.8	9.9	30.6	52 31.2	10.8	31.3	71
72	46 29.9	4.3	25.8	47 23.8	5.0	26.3	48 17.5	5.7	26.8	49 11.0	6.3	27.3	50 04.1	7.1	27.8	50 57.0	7.9	28.4	51 49.7	8.6	29.0	52 42.0	9.4	29.7	72
73	46 34.2	3.3	24.4	47 28.8	3.8	24.8	48 23.2	4.4	25.3	49 17.3	5.1	25.8	50 11.2	5.8	26.3	51 04.9	6.5	26.8	51 58.3	7.3	27.4	52 51.4	8.0	28.0	73
74	46 37.5	2.1	22.9	47 32.6	2.7	23.3	48 27.6	3.3	23.8	49 22.4	4.0	24.3	50 17.0	4.6	24.7	51 11.4	5.3	25.3	52 05.6	5.9	25.8	52 59.4	6.7	26.4	74
75	46 39.6	+1.0	21.5	47 35.3	+1.6	21.9	48 30.9	+2.2	22.3	49 26.4	+2.7	22.7	50 21.6	+3.3	23.2	51 16.7	+3.9	23.7	52 11.5	+4.6	24.2	53 06.1	+5.4	24.7	75
76	46 40.6	−0.1	20.0	47 36.9	+0.4	20.4	48 33.1	+0.9	20.8	49 29.1	1.5	21.2	50 24.9	2.1	21.6	51 20.6	2.7	22.1	52 16.1	3.3	22.6	53 11.5	3.9	23.1	76
77	46 40.5	1.3	18.5	47 37.3	−0.8	18.9	48 34.0	−0.3	19.3	49 30.6	+0.2	19.6	50 27.0	+0.8	20.0	51 23.3	1.3	20.5	52 19.4	1.9	20.9	53 15.4	2.5	21.4	77
78	46 39.2	2.3	17.1	47 36.5	1.9	17.4	48 33.7	1.4	17.7	49 30.8	−0.9	18.1	50 27.8	−0.5	18.5	51 24.6	−0.1	18.9	52 21.3	+0.6	19.3	53 17.9	+1.1	19.7	78
79	46 36.9	3.4	15.6	47 34.6	3.0	15.9	48 32.3	2.6	16.2	49 29.9	2.2	16.6	50 27.3	1.7	16.9	51 24.7	−1.3	17.3	52 21.9	−0.8	17.6	53 19.0	−0.3	18.1	79
80	46 33.5	−4.6	14.2	47 31.6	−4.2	14.4	48 29.7	−3.8	14.7	49 27.7	−3.4	15.0	50 25.6	−3.0	15.3	51 23.4	−2.6	15.7	52 21.1	−2.1	16.0	53 18.7	−1.7	16.4	80
81	46 28.9	5.6	12.7	47 27.4	5.3	13.0	48 25.9	5.0	13.2	49 24.3	4.7	13.5	50 22.6	4.3	13.8	51 20.8	3.9	14.1	52 19.0	3.5	14.4	53 17.0	3.1	14.7	81
82	46 23.3	6.7	11.3	47 22.1	6.4	11.5	48 20.9	6.1	11.7	49 19.6	5.8	12.0	50 18.3	5.5	12.2	51 16.9	5.2	12.5	52 15.5	4.9	12.7	53 13.9	4.4	13.0	82
83	46 16.6	7.8	9.9	47 15.7	7.6	10.0	48 14.8	7.3	10.2	49 13.8	7.1	10.4	50 12.8	6.8	10.6	51 11.7	6.5	10.9	52 10.6	6.2	11.1	53 09.5	5.9	11.4	83
84	46 08.8	8.9	8.4	47 08.1	8.6	8.6	48 07.5	8.5	8.7	49 06.7	8.2	8.9	50 06.0	8.0	9.1	51 05.2	7.7	9.3	52 04.4	7.5	9.5	53 03.6	7.3	9.7	84
85	45 59.9	−9.9	7.0	46 59.5	−9.8	7.1	47 59.0	−9.6	7.3	48 58.5	−9.4	7.4	49 58.0	−9.2	7.6	50 57.5	−9.1	7.7	51 56.9	−8.8	7.9	52 56.3	−8.6	8.1	85
86	45 50.0	11.0	5.6	46 49.7	10.8	5.7	47 49.4	10.7	5.8	48 49.1	10.6	5.9	49 48.8	10.4	6.0	50 48.4	10.2	6.1	51 48.1	10.1	6.3	52 47.7	9.9	6.4	86
87	45 39.0	12.0	4.2	46 38.9	11.9	4.2	47 38.7	11.8	4.3	48 38.5	11.7	4.4	49 38.4	11.7	4.5	50 38.2	11.5	4.6	51 38.0	11.4	4.8	52 37.8	11.3	4.8	87
88	45 27.0	13.0	2.8	46 27.0	13.0	2.8	47 26.9	12.9	2.9	48 26.8	12.8	2.9	49 26.7	12.8	3.0	50 26.7	12.8	3.0	51 26.6	12.7	3.1	52 26.5	12.6	3.2	88
89	45 14.0	14.0	1.4	46 14.0	14.0	1.4	47 14.0	14.0	1.4	48 14.0	14.0	1.5	49 13.9	13.9	1.5	50 13.9	13.9	1.5	51 13.9	13.9	1.5	52 13.9	13.9	1.6	89
90	45 00.0	−15.0	0.0	46 00.0	−15.0	0.0	47 00.0	−15.0	0.0	48 00.0	−15.1	0.0	49 00.0	−15.1	0.0	50 00.0	−15.1	0.0	51 00.0	−15.1	0.0	52 00.0	−15.1	0.0	90
	45°			46°			47°			48°			49°			50°			51°			52°			

76°, 284° L.H.A.   LATITUDE SAME NAME AS DECLINATION

Figure 3015d. Pub. No. 229, "same name" page (extract).

Note: If the values are taken from across the C-S line, the DLo is the supplement of the tabular azimuth angle; the tabular altitudes correspond to latitudes on the side of the equator opposite from the latitude of departure.

Comparison of Various Methods

3016 The "sailings" are mathematical procedures involving computations between latitude and longitude of the departure point, course and speed, and latitude and longitude of the destination. In general, two of these three pairs will be known, and the solution will be for the third pair.

The sailings are not often calculated in modern marine navigation, but when needed they provide a useful solution of course and distance. (Many radionavigation receivers contain internal microprocessors that will continuously compute great-circle course and distance to a destination that has been previously entered; the course may be fed through an interface to an autopilot that will then steer the vessel on a true great-circle path of continuously changing course.) Mid-latitude and Mercator sailing provide less accurate solutions than great-circle sailing, but at a considerable savings of effort and time except when a computer or calculator is used with great-circle sailing; the inaccuracies of these easier methods increase proportionately the longer the distance between the point of departure and the destination.

Chapter 31

Fundamentals of Radionavigation

Introduction

3101 For many decades now navigators have had to consider the great and ever-increasing role in their work played by *electronics*—the science and technology relating to the emission, flow, and effects of electrons in a vacuum, through semiconductors, and in devices and circuitry. The topic of this chapter is *radionavigation*, the application of electronics to a navigator's activities by means of on-board equipment and radio-wave transmissions from a source external to the vessel concerned.

The *radio time signal* was the first such aid to come into use. It made precise time available to the navigator for use in connection with celestial navigation. Subsequently, he was able, on request, to obtain radio bearings from a limited number of shore stations. On some coasts, the direction-finding stations were linked by landline telegraph so that a fix could be determined on shore from several radio bearings and transmitted by radio to the ship; often, though, only one radio line of position was available. This system of shore direction-finding stations is now nearly extinct, having been replaced by ship-borne *radio direction finders* (RDF), which permit a navigator to obtain a bearing on any radio station that is transmitting suitable signals. In many coastal areas, he is able to obtain several such bearings, which enable him to determine his position with considerable accuracy. The wide employment of radio direction finders led to the introduction of the term *radionavigation*. Although the term *electronic navigation* is sometimes used in lieu of radionavigation, it is less precise, as it technically would include the use of any electronic device—depth sounder, log, gyrocompass, etc.—for navigation.

Extensive research has been carried out in this field over the past several decades. The development of long-range airplanes established a need for suitable radionavigation systems. Subsequently, the need arose for systems suitable for Fleet Ballistic Missile submarines, and recently systems for the navigation and guidance of space vehicles.

Dead Reckoning and Positioning Systems

The needs of various types of vessels and aircraft were, in each instance, twofold: systems for position fixing (radionavigation systems), and systems for carrying forward a dead-reckoning position from the last fix (inertial systems, chapter 35). For the latter systems, extremely sensitive and accurate, but expensive, gyros and accelerometers were designed. For position fixing, highly accurate instruments for determining the time of travel of radio signals have been produced, as well as for the measurement of altitude angles of celestial bodies by automatic electro-optical and radiometric tracking. In addition, equipment for measuring the *Doppler shift* of very precisely timed radio signals transmitted by artificial satellites has yielded excellent results. The Doppler shift (named for the Austrian scientist who reported the effect in 1842) is the apparent change in frequency of radiated energy when the distance between the source and the receiver is changing. The classic example used to illustrate Doppler shift is the sound of a fast-moving locomotive's whistle. As the locomotive approaches, the pitch of the sound rises; as it moves away, the pitch lowers. For a long time, Doppler shift was of real interest only to astronomers and science teachers. Later, however, it was realized that the Doppler effect could be used with electromagnetic radiation to measure velocity (and when velocity is known, it can be integrated to obtain distance from a starting point).

In piloting, excellent position fixing is being achieved by both radar and sonar, as currently instrumented. Bathymetric navigation, or navigation by means of continuous soundings of the ocean bottom analyzed by a computer, holds great promise. However, it requires input data in the form of very precise bathymetric charting of the operating area; this is often available to naval vessels, but not to merchant ships and yachts.

The ideal navigation system has yet to be developed. Such a system should be worldwide, self-contained, passive, completely reliable, and highly accurate. Currently, the most promising systems, although they do not meet all the above requirements, are Omega, discussed in chapter 33, and Satellite Navigation, discussed in chapter 34. Omega uses radio signals from land-based transmitting systems, while the Satellite Navigation system depends on signals from one or more satellites traveling in a precisely determined orbit.

Basic Phenomena

3102 The following brief discussion of electronic fundamentals assumes that the reader has some knowledge of basic physics, or has access to appropriate reference books; it is not possible to cover the subject of electronics in detail in a volume such as this.

Frequency

For many decades, alternating current *frequency* was expressed in "cycles per second." This seemed the natural term to indicate the complete reversal of the polarity of the voltage and the direction of flow of the current in alternating current circuits. In recent years, however, this term has been replaced with *hertz*, which is synonymous with "cycles per second"; the older term is still used by some persons, but fewer each year. The new term honors the German scientist, Heinrich Hertz. Larger units are formed in the same manner as for others of the metric system; see appendix D.

$$1 \text{ kilohertz (kHz)} = 1,000 \text{ hertz (Hz)}$$
$$1 \text{ Megahertz (MHz)} = 1,000,000 \text{ Hz}$$
$$\text{or } 1,000 \text{ kHz}$$
$$1 \text{ Gigahertz (GHz)} = 1,000,000,000 \text{ Hz}$$
$$\text{or } 1,000,000 \text{ kHz}$$
$$\text{or } 1,000 \text{ MHz}$$

Electromagnetic Induction

Basic alternating-current theory states that a varying magnetic field, resulting from the flow of alternating current in a circuit, induces a voltage in a conductor placed within the field. In fact, voltage is induced even when there is no conductor in the field. Such a voltage, induced into space, is in effect an electric field. Thus, a varying electric field is created in space by a varying magnetic field. The varying electric field in turn sets up a displacement current, which gives rise to a magnetic field. The varying magnetic field creates an electric field and so on. The process whereby they mutually induce one another is called *electromagnetic induction*. The combination is called the *electromagnetic field;* this effect occurs at all alternating frequencies.

Once the initial field is created, it becomes independent of further electrical input. When the current stops, the field can continue to survive and to propagate itself on out into space, because of the self-sustaining exchange process.

In an electromagnetic radiation field, the electric field lines close on themselves. They are not attached to charges, and the magnetic field lines are not related to current in conductors. The fields are truly independent, as if cut adrift in space.

There is also a connotation of motion in the process. The complete theory was developed about a hundred years ago by James Clerk Maxwell. He correlated a set of four simultaneous partial differential equations, which describe the interrelation of the electric and magnetic components of electromagnetic fields and their relation to electric currents and voltages. These equations stand today as the theoretical basis of electromagnetism, and by their use all problems of electromagnetic fields and radiation can be solved. They are: Ampere's circuital law; Gauss's theorem for the electric field; Gauss's theorem for the magnetic field; and Faraday's law on electromotive force.

These laws, formulated by others, but combined by Maxwell within the concept of the displacement current, facilitate the computation of electromagnetic propagation. To compute the velocity of waves of electromagnetic energy traveling outward into space from the point at which they are created, the characteristics of the medium through which they travel must be considered. Maxwell noted that the computed velocity of radio waves in empty space was 3×10^8 meters per second, a very close value to the measured velocity of light, suggesting that light is a form of electromagnetic radiation. To illustrate the relationship of velocity, wave length, and frequency, consider the measurement of time in the transit of one complete cycle of an electromagnetic field at a specific point on the earth's surface. In the period of time of this measurement, a minute fraction of a second, a complete wavelength of the electromagnetic field would have moved across the point at which the measurement was made. The measured time is the elapsed time required for the electromagnetic field to be moved a distance equal to the wavelength of the field.

Wavelength vs. Frequency

The time of completion of one full cycle is therefore equal to the velocity divided by the wavelength. The frequency, the number of times *per second* the signal completes one full cycle, is given in hertz units. The relationship can be visualized as the greater the wavelength the lower the frequency. The transmission characteristic of a given electronic system is stated either as wavelength or frequency. The relationship is discussed briefly above and can be stated as a simple equation:

$$\lambda = \frac{300}{F}$$

in which λ is the wavelength in meters, F is the frequency in megahertz, and the constant 300 is the velocity of light in meters per microsecond (a more precise figure is 299.793).

Absorption

Absorption accounts for the loss of some of the energy of electromagnetic waves propagated through space that contains material that is not a perfect insulator. In both radio and light waves, the losses caused by absorption are the result of the conversion of some of the field energy into heat, through the collisions of electrons, excited by the electric field, with other particles in the material. The computation of this loss is similar to the computation of power loss in an electrical circuit due to resistance. If the electromagnetic field were radiated into a pure vacuum, no work would be performed by the energy of the field, and its intensity would be maintained. The alternating electric and magnetic fields would continue to be propagated by each other with the same magnitude of energy as that of the initial radiation.

For example, if an electromagnetic field is radiated from an antenna near the surface of the earth, the electrons in the gas atoms of the atmosphere begin to move under the force of the electric field. The greater the length of time that the force continues in one direction, i.e., the lower the frequency of the radiated field, the greater will be the velocity attained by the electrons during each half cycle of the radiated energy. If the movement of the freed electrons were unobstructed, the power expended in their acceleration would be returned to the elec-

tromagnetic wave by the magnetic field that their own motion would produce. However, the electrons, moving at high velocity, collide with atoms of gas and other particles in the atmosphere, thus dissipating significant power in the heat generated by the collisions. Thus, electromagnetic radiation velocity is slightly reduced by increased atmospheric density, or by other material in the propagation medium.

Ground Waves and Sky Waves

3103 The preceding article has discussed briefly the radiation of an electromagnetic field from an antenna into the atmosphere. It next becomes necessary to consider how this field travels outward.

Electromagnetic energy, as transmitted from the antenna, radiates outward in all directions. A portion of this energy proceeds out parallel to the earth's surface, while the remainder travels upward as well as outward, until it strikes one or more layers of ionized gases in the *ionosphere* (see article 3107) and is reflected back to earth; this normally occurs only once but may be repeated as shown by "sky wave 2" in figure 3103a. (These are referred to as "one-hop" and "two-hop" sky waves.) That portion of the radiated energy that follows along the surface of the earth is called the *ground wave;* the energy transmitted at higher angles is termed *sky waves.* The ionosphere and its effect on radio waves is considered in more detail later in this chapter.

In the employment of low frequencies, ground waves become very important, and the conductivity of the earth's crust becomes a major factor in signal attenuation (the decrease in amplitude of a wave or current with increasing distance from the

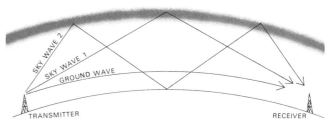

Figure 3103a. Radio ground-wave and sky-wave propagation paths. (Vertical distances in this sketch have been exaggerated for clarity; the distance between the transmitter and receiver is normally hundreds of miles, while the ionosphere is only 30 to 215 miles above the earth.)

source of transmission) by absorption, and its effects on propagation velocity. Because of this conductivity, the electromagnetic field to some extent penetrates the earth's surface. The lower edge of the wave is slightly impeded by its penetration into this medium of increased conductivity, while the upper portion of the wave is not so affected. This results in the lines of force leaning away from the signal source, causing the movement of the electromagnetic wave to curve with the curvature of the earth's surface. It must be remembered that the lines of force of the electric field are perpendicular to the lines of force of the magnetic field, and the direction of motion of the electromagnetic wave is perpendicular to both (figure 3103b).

It is this tendency to follow the earth's curvature that makes possible the transmission of low-frequency ground waves over great distances. Combined with this curvature of the motion of the electromagnetic wave is the energy loss through absorption in the penetration of the earth's surface. This latter effect necessitates the use of high power to achieve long-distance transmission of the ground wave.

The conductivity of the ocean surface is quite constant, and propagation velocity over ocean areas can be predicted quite accurately. The variability of the characteristics of land areas complicates the prediction of its effects on ground-wave transmission.

Only low-frequency radio transmissions curve sufficiently to follow the earth's surface over great distances. Electromagnetic fields at higher frequencies do not penetrate as deeply into the surface, and so encounter less impedance of velocity from the ground. They are slightly curved, but not enough to provide ground-wave signals at great distances from the transmitting antenna.

The *polarization* of the radio wave is described in terms of the orientation of the electric field with respect to the earth, either *horizontal* or *vertical*; for special applications, polarization can also be *circular* or *elliptical* with the plane of polarization rotating about the axis of propagation. In any radio system, the transmitting and receiving antennas should have the same polarization if they are to be the most effective.

Reflection and Refraction

3104 Long-distance transmission of high-frequency radio waves can be achieved by *reflection* and *refraction* of the electromagnetic waves from ionized layers in the upper atmosphere.

Radio waves and light waves are both forms of electromagnetic waves, differing only in frequency. Some of the laws learned in the science of optics are also applicable to radio waves.

Any surface can *reflect* light waves. If the surface is smooth and polished, the light is reflected in a *specular* fashion, as by mirror. Reflection from a rough surface is *diffuse.* Dull, dark-colored surfaces reflect light poorly. When a surface reflects only a portion of the light, the rest is absorbed, and the energy of the absorbed light wave is converted into heat in the material.

Radio waves are also reflected, specularly from smooth surfaces and diffusely from rough surfaces. Surfaces of good conductors reflect, and those with poor conductors absorb. The waves pass through some materials that are electrical insulators, such as glass. Most materials do not completely reflect or completely absorb radio waves, but are imperfect reflectors.

In both light and radio waves, the reflection capability depends upon the magnitude of the surface irregularities as compared to the wavelength of the electromagnetic wave. A sea of ten-foot waves would reflect specularly a radio wave of several hundred meters in length, but a radio signal of a few centimeters wavelength would be reflected diffusely.

When a radio wave is reflected specularly, the character of the wave front is unchanged. As in the behavior of light rays reflected from a sextant mirror, the angle of reflection is equal to the angle of incidence. When reflected from a rough surface, the incident wave front breaks up and is randomly reflected in many different directions.

In free space, an electromagnetic wave travels in a straight line; however, when traveling through an area containing matter or material particles, the wave may be bent or *refracted.* The light from a celestial body, entering the atmosphere at an oblique angle, bends increasingly downward as it contin-

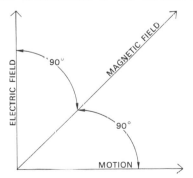

Figure 3103b. Vector relationship of the electric and magnetic fields, and of the motion of the electromagnetic wave.

ues into an atmosphere of increasing density. Similarly, bending in the direction of travel of a radio wave occurs when the wave passes from one medium to another of different permittivity of permeability. Thus, when a wave front enters a medium of different characteristic at an oblique angle, the change in velocity affects the first portion of the wave front entering the new medium before the remainder of the wave is affected, and the alignment of the wave front is changed. The direction of travel, as previously stated, is perpendicular to the wave front; therefore, the direction of travel changes toward the direction of reduced velocity.

Diffraction

3105 When an electromagnetic wave, either radio or light, is partially obstructed by an object of opaque material, the area behind the object is shadowed as the unobstructed portion of the wave front continues in its original direction. In the case of light waves, a shadow is cast by the object; waves that would otherwise reach this area are blocked.

According to Maxwell's equations, the wave-front portion at the edge of the obstructing object does not completely hold to its original direction. A small portion of the energy is propagated into the shadow area. This phenomenon is called *diffraction* (figure 3105). Maxwell's equations predict the intensity of the field to be found in the shadow area.

Interference

3106 If two or more radio waves arrive simultaneously at the same point in space, *interference* results. The combination of such waves is in accordance with the principle of superposition of fields. Each field may be represented by a vector, indicating spatial direction and intensity.

The resultant field direction and intensity of either the electric fields or of the magnetic fields may then be determined by following the rules for vector addition.

Ionization

3107 The daylight portion of the earth's atmosphere is subjected to bombardment by intense ultraviolet rays from the sun. At extremely high altitudes in the atmosphere, the gas atoms are comparatively sparse. Electrons are excited by the powerful ultraviolet electromagnetic forces that reverse polarity approximately 10^{17} times per second. This violent oscillation causes electrons to separate from the positive ions with which they were combined. These freed electrons would eventually find their way to, and combine with, other electron-deficient atoms, but this is prevented by the continuing forces of the ultraviolet rays while in direct sunlight. The region of the upper atmosphere, generally above 30 miles (55 km), where the free ions and electrons exist in sufficient density to

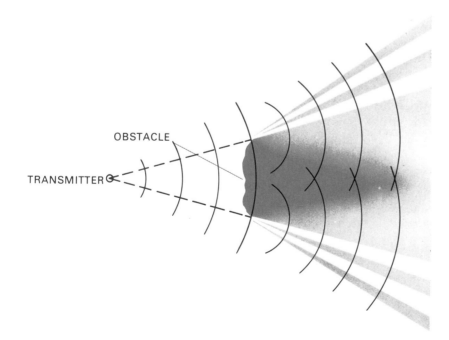

Figure 3105. Diffraction of a wave front.

have an appreciable effect on radio-wave travel, is called the *ionosphere;* the ionization effect reaches its maximum when the sun is at its highest.

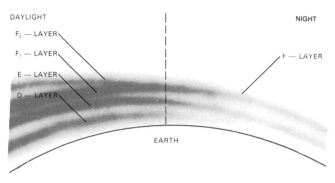

Figure 3108. Layers of ionization; during daytime (left) and at night (right).

Layers of Ionization

3108 The electrons and ions are not uniformly distributed in the ionosphere, but rather tend to form layers. These layers change, disappear, combine, and separate as they are affected by the local time of day, season of the year, and the level of sun-spot activity; the layers are also at times affected by apparent random changes from moment to moment. Four such ionized layers (figure 3108) are involved in the phenomenon of radio-wave propagation. Each layer has thickness with the most intense ionization at the center, tapering off above and below. The greater the intensity of ionization in any layer, the greater is the bending back towards earth of the radio waves; lower frequencies are more easily reflected than are higher frequencies, which have a greater tendency to penetrate the ionosphere and "escape" into space.

D Layer

The ionized layer nearest the earth's surface is termed the *D layer;* its density is considerably less than any of the other three, and it has more of an absorbing than reflecting effect. This layer, which occurs at heights of 30 to 50 miles (55 to 90 km) above the earth apparently exists only during daylight hours and disappears completely at night.

E Layers

Located at a height of about 65 miles (120 km), the *E layer* remains during the night, but with somewhat decreased intensity. Its density is greatest in the region beneath the sun. Irregular areas of very high ionization occur during a large percentage of the time. These areas are referred to as *Sporadic E;* they occur at night as well as in daylight.

F Layers

The ionization designated as F occurs in two separate zones. The F_1 *layer* occurs only in daylight, the freed electrons and ions apparently rejoining to form the normal atoms and molecules of the rarefied air as the stress of the sun's ultraviolet rays diminishes. This layer is usually between 95 and 135 miles (175 to 250 km) above the earth's surface.

The F_2 *layer* varies in both height and density; the variation is diurnal, seasonal, and related to the level of sun-spot activity. It is found at altitudes of 160 to 215 miles (300 to 400 km), where the atmospheric density is extremely low and results in a more complicated diurnal pattern. Due to the molecular collision rates in the very low density of the air at these altitudes, solar energy may be stored for many hours. The gas atoms are relatively few and far between. The release of electrons during the periods of high ultraviolet intensity leaves them moving freely for hours after the sun has disappeared below the horizon. In this condition collisions between free electrons and gas atoms cause other electrons to be dislodged, even during the hours of darkness. Solar energy may be stored in this manner for many hours at these levels.

Some diurnal pattern is discernible at the high levels of the atmosphere. There is a tendency for the F_1 and the F_2 layers to merge during darkness, at a height of about 160 miles (300 km). After sunrise, the upper portion of the layer is again intensified by the sun's rays, and the F_1 layer increases in density as it lowers.

Radio-wave propagation is affected by the various ionized layers in accordance with the wave length or frequency of the radio transmission, and the height and density of the layers of ionization. The ionized layers may either be conducive to the sky-wave transmission of the electromagnetic energy to the area of desired reception, or may hinder or even prevent such transmission, as will be discussed in the following paragraphs.

Electromagnetic Frequency Spectrum

3109 Radiating electromagnetic waves—*radio waves*—occur at all alternating frequencies. The electromagnetic frequency spectrum extends from a single reversal of polarity per second, through the radio frequency spectrum, infrared frequencies, visible light frequencies, ultraviolet ray, X-ray, and Gamma-ray spectrums to approximately 10^{15}

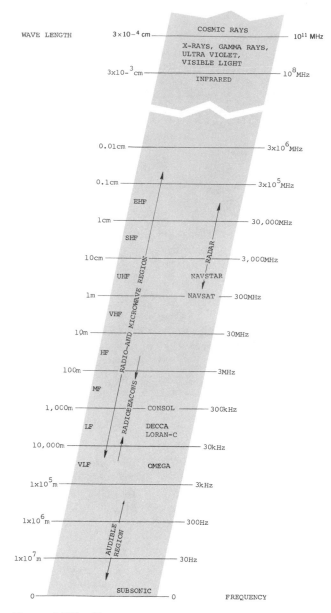

Figure 3109a. Frequency spectrum.

MHz. A diagram of the *electromagnetic* frequency spectrum is shown in figure 3109a.

Radio Frequency Spectrum

3110 The *radio* frequency spectrum relating to navigation extends between narrower limits, from 3 kilohertz (kHz) to 300 gigahertz (GHz). This spectrum is divided into eight frequency *bands* to be described here. (There are two other, lower frequency bands that are not of present interest to this book: VF, or voice frequencies, 300 to 3000 hertz (Hz), and ELF, extremely low frequencies, 3 to 10 kHz.)

Very Low Frequency (VLF)

The *VLF band* includes those frequencies below 30 kHz down to approximately 10 kHz. The primary advantage in employing frequencies in this band is the reliability of propagation over great distances by the use of higher power. VLF ground waves may be propagated for distances as great as 8,000 miles (15,000 km) allowing determination of distance by measuring the time of travel of the wave.

VLF sky waves are reflected from the ionosphere with comparatively little loss of energy because of the short distance they travel within the ionized layer. However, the ensuing reflection from the earth's surface undergoes significant loss by absorption, especially over land areas. Diffraction is also greater in the VLF band than in the higher frequencies. VLF waves will, however, penetrate the surface of the earth (land or water) and hence are used for transmissions to submerged submarines. In the lower part of the VLF band, signals may be received with good readability at depths of 40 to 50 feet (12 to 15 m).

It is much more difficult and expensive to obtain antenna efficiency at these frequencies than at higher ones. Radiation of high power, which is required if good reliability over long distances is to be realized, becomes very costly.

The primary navigational use of the VLF band is for the Omega system discussed in chapter 33.

Low Frequency (LF)

The *LF band* (30 to 300 kHz) is not reflected as efficiently by the ionosphere. Ground losses increase as the frequency is increased and diffraction decreases. However, antennas for use in the LF band are usually more efficient than those in the VLF band. Good ground-wave propagation is still possible over moderate distances. LF signals are usable, to a limited degree, for transmissions to submerged submarines; at 100 kHz, usable signals are available for a short distance beneath the surface.

Navigational time-measurement systems employing the LF band are able to use first-hop sky waves, by applying a correction to compensate for the additional distance of travel of the sky wave. The accuracy obtainable by use of first-hop sky waves is not as good as that obtained with ground waves, although satisfactory for most navigational purposes. For positioning accuracy of less than a mile, ground-wave reception is necessary.

The primary navigational uses of the LF band are: radiobeacons, Loran C, Consol, and Decca (all described in chapter 32).

Medium Frequency (MF)

The *MF band* extends from 300 kHz to 3 megahertz (MHz). Frequencies in this band provide reliable ground-wave propagation over distances of up to approximately 700 miles (1,300 km). Daytime ionosphere absorption is high and limits sky-wave propagation. Long distance sky-wave transmission is possible at night. Antenna requirements are not as stringent as they are in the VLF and LF bands.

The primary navigational systems operating in the MF band are Consol and Raydist; the older Loran-A system also operated in this band. Some radiobeacons operate on frequencies in the band near its lower limit.

High Frequency (HF)

The *HF band* (3 MHz to 30 MHz) is employed for long distance communication; this is made possible by the ionized layers in the ionosphere. At these frequencies, antenna efficiency is much more easily obtained than at the lower frequencies. Communications over long distances are possible with moderate transmitter power. Frequencies must be selected, however, with respect to the conditions prevailing at the moment. Under some conditions, the higher frequencies travel great distances in the ionosphere before being refracted sufficiently to reflect the wave back to earth. Signals entering the ionosphere at an angle of incidence that prevents their being refracted back towards the earth penetrate the ionized layers and are lost in space. In daylight, energy propagated at the lower frequencies of this band has high absorption losses and fades out a short distance from the source. Higher frequencies, during hours of darkness, if reflected at all, return to earth at great distances from the transmitting antenna, so that they skip over dis-

tances of several hundred or more miles. Little or no signals will be received in this "skip zone"; see figure 3110.

An example of the need to select proper frequencies will be found when receiving a National Bureau of Standards time signal from station WWV (see article 2228). This signal can be readily received by day on a standard radio set at 15 MHz at a location 1,300 miles (2,400 km) from Colorado, but the 5 MHz signal must be tuned in at night.

Frequencies in the HF band do not propagate with suitable characteristics for obtaining bearings or distance measurements, thus they are not used for radionavigation systems.

Very High Frequency (VHF) and Ultra High Frequency (UHF)

Frequencies in the *VHF band* (30 to 300 MHz) and the *UHF band* (300 to 3,000 MHz) are widely used for communications. They are basically *line-of-sight* frequencies, as their range is ordinarily limited by the curvature of the earth to distances approximately equal to those at which the top of one antenna could be seen from the top of the other under ideal weather conditions. VHF and UHF frequencies are also used to some extent for communications over several hundred miles in what is termed a *scatter mode* of operation. A small portion of very high power electromagnetic waves in the 30 to 60 MHz frequency range are scattered by particles in the ionosphere and returned to earth, permitting signal reception at ranges of 600 to 1,200 miles (1,100–2,200 km).

A similar scatter effect can be obtained in the *troposphere* by emissions in the 400 to 4,000 MHz range. The troposphere, situated below the stratosphere, is much nearer the earth than the ionosphere. By means of tropospheric scatter, ranges of about 600 miles (1,100 km) have been obtained.

For navigational purposes, VHF and UHF frequencies provide good line-of-sight propagation at

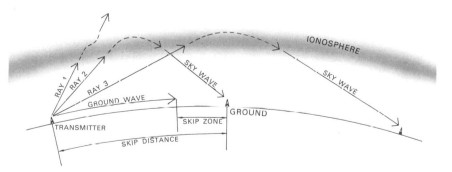

Figure 3110. The effect of the ionosphere on radio-wave propagation.

moderate transmitter power. Systems using VHF include the air navigation techniques of Omni/DME and Shoran. In the lower part of the VHF band will be found the TACAN military air navigation system; some radars use frequencies in the upper regions of the UHF band.

Super High Frequency (SHF) and Extremely High Frequency (EHF)

The *SHF band* (3,000 to 30,000 MHz) and the *EHF band* (30,000 to 300,000 MHz) are used for radar, and for precise distance measurements, within line-of-sight range. The employment of SHF frequencies for radar has resulted in significantly improved definition over the UHF systems. Power requirements are moderate, and very efficient antennas can be employed.

Ducting and Irregularities

3111   Many irregularities occur in the propagation of electromagnetic waves, especially at the higher frequencies. A phenomenon called *radio refractive ducting* occurs over much of the radio frequency spectrum, but particularly on frequencies of the VHF and UHF bands. This phenomenon seems to occur more over oceans than over land, and is generally associated with a temperature inversion at a very low altitude, perhaps 200 or 300 feet (60–90 m), and a sharp decrease in moisture content of the warm air. Very long ranges have been reported when low-power UHF transmitters were employed in experiments with these phenomena. Ducting can be responsible for limiting as well as extending the range of radio transmissions.

Hyperbolic Navigation Systems

3112   *Hyperbolic navigation systems* are based on the theory that the known velocity of travel of electromagnetic waves through space is constant, within acceptable limits. Although it is technically possible to measure the time of travel of a radio wave from the transmitting antenna to a ship, it is the capability of measuring the *time difference* in the arrival of signals from two separate stations that makes practicable the determination of position.

A major advantage of the hyperbolic navigation systems is that position line data may be computed in advance of its use, and printed on charts at convenient units of time-difference value, eliminating the necessity for the navigator to make such computations. A disadvantage lies in the deterioration of accuracy inherent in spherical hyperbolic system geometry.

A hyperbola is the locus of the points at which synchronized signals from the two transmitters comprising a system will arrive at a constant time difference. This time difference is expressed in *microseconds,* or millionths of a second. The receivers employed in these systems therefore provide a readout in microseconds of time difference.

In figure 3112 signals from stations *S* and *M* transmitted simultaneously would have no time difference, but would arrive simultaneously at any point along the center line, as all points along this line are equidistant from points *S* and *M*. All other lines, represented by hyperbolas, would represent points of equal time difference. (In actual hyperbolic navigation systems the transmission for the slave (or subordinate) station *S* is delayed rather than being simultaneous with the master *M*.) The figure represents hyperbolic lines on a plane surface. The appearance of the lines on a navigation chart, which represents a portion of the spherical surface of the earth, will vary somewhat with the chart projection used.

Charts on which the hyperbolic lines are printed are commonly employed for navigation, but if one is not available, published tables can be used. These give the coordinates at which each hyperbola intersects a whole degree meridian or parallel of latitude as appropriate. Many receivers now contain a microprocessor *coordinate converter* that yields a direct readout of latitude and longitude, making radionavigation quite simple.

Two types of time-difference measurement are employed in hyperbolic systems. In one, the matching of electromagnetic wave envelopes of pulses transmitted from the two stations is measured for time difference, resulting in a coarse measurement that locates the receiver on a hyperbolic line with known geographical coordinates. In the other system, matching the *phase* of the electromagnetic waves provides a fine measurement within an area or lane defined by two time-difference hyperbolas, in addition to the coarse measurement obtained by time difference. In phase-matching systems, extreme accuracy is possible under favorable conditions. A precision of about 0.05 microseconds can be obtained, which is equivalent to about 50 feet (15 m). This precision is, of course, degraded by system geometry as distance from the *base line* between the stations increases.

To establish position, a ship or aircraft employs two or more pairs of stations to acquire two or more intersecting lines of position. As with other methods of determining position by means of intersecting position lines, precision in fixing varies

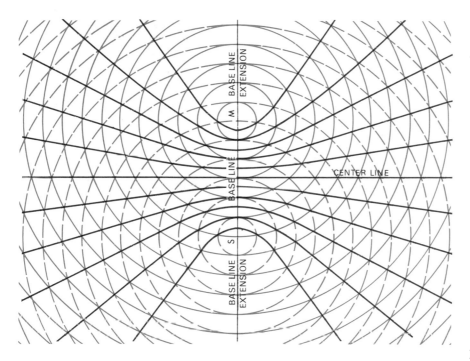

Figure 3112. A family of hyperbolic lines of position.

with the angle of intersection of the lines. Where lines cross at right angles, the area of most probable position is circular, with its center at the intersection of the lines. Where the lines intersect at an acute angle, the area of most probable position is elliptical; the minor axis of this ellipse will be equal to the diameter of the circle formed when the intersection is at 90°. The major axis will be greater; the ratio of its length to the diameter of the circle varies with the cosine of the angle of the intersection.

The development of the first electronic, hyperbolic navigational systems began about 1940. Due to the urgent requirements brought about by World War II, Loran-A came into general military use only a few years later. Following that war, Loran-A was also widely used by merchant shipping, fishing vessels, and some recreational craft. In U.S. waters, a phase-out of Loran-A in favor of Loran-C and Omega was completed at the end of 1980. Loran-D and Decca are other hyperbolic systems.

Short-range hyperbolic systems designed for survey and oceanographic use include Decca Survey, Raydist, and others.

Rho-Theta Navigation

3113 Rho-theta navigation, or, more specifically, range-direction navigation, utilizes a combination of circular or ranging systems for distance measurements, together with azimuthal or direc-

tional measuring systems (figure 3113). The *Omnirange* (VOR) system in general use for aviation throughout the U.S. provides bearing information. A large number of the stations are equipped with distance-measuring equipment (DME) to provide a complete rho-theta system. The military version is known as TACAN. These systems are sufficiently accurate for general navigation purposes, but are limited to a line-of-sight range. As these systems are used by aircraft, often at tens of thousands of feet altitude, line-of-sight ranges may be 100 to 200 miles (185 to 370 km). Marine surface navigators can make only limited use of Omnirange, using sta-

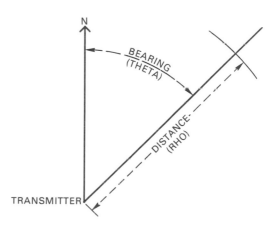

Figure 3113. Rho-theta system of position determination.

tions located near the water out to distances of 5 to 10 or so miles.

The principle of Omnirange navigation is based on the phase comparison between two radiated radio-frequency signals, with the phase varying with a change in azimuth. One of these two signals is nondirectional, with a constant phase throughout 360° of azimuth. This signal is used as the reference phase. The other signal rotates and varies in phase with change in azimuth; it is the variable phase signal.

Special receiver and display equipment on the aircraft translate the received signal into usable information for the pilot, including an indication as to whether the measured direction is "TO" or "FROM" the ground station.

Rho-rho Navigation

3114 In some specialized applications, radionavigation signals are used in what is termed the *rho-rho* mode. Here the travel times of pulses from two or more transmitters are measured, rather than time differences; circular lines of position are thus obtained and plotted. Each receiver must have a highly stable and very accurate "clock" to use this technique.

Accuracy

3115 One of the first questions asked about any navigation system, but particularly in respect to radionavigation, is, "How accurate are its fixes?" This can only be approached by a consideration of what type of "accuracy" is meant, and the standard by which it is measured. The answers can be quite varied.

The type of accuracy of primary interest is *absolute accuracy*, the correctness of the position with respect to the earth and its coordinate system. Other types include *repeatable accuracy* (see article 3116) and *relational accuracy*, the correctness of a position with respect to another position determined by the same system.

Unless otherwise noted, the "accuracy" of the radionavigation systems to be considered in the following chapters is absolute accuracy. This can be measured in a number of ways, and because of the use of different standards, misunderstandings often arise when comparing the various systems. *Root Mean Square (RMS)* error is a statistical measure of the variability of a single LOP; this one-dimensional value is of little use with fixes resulting from multiple LOPs. More suitable is *Circular Error Probable (CEP)*, the radius of a circle within which it is probable that 50% of the fixes will be located. The term CEP is occasionally used for other percentages, such as 67 or 90, with that value included in the statement of accuracy.

Distance Root Mean Square (dRMS) (sometimes termed *Radial Error*) is used when the crossing angles of two LOPs result in an ellipse rather than a circle as an area of probability. This is stated as "2dRMS" if two standard deviations are used. Although there are slight variations depending upon the ellipticity, the usual values are 67% for dRMS and 95% for 2dRMS.

Predictability and Repeatability

3116 In the design and use of all radionavigation systems, two major factors must be carefully taken into consideration for precision work. The first problem, *predictability*, is one of knowing, given the atmospheric conditions, the propagation characteristics of the signal. Predictability is influenced primarily by refraction in the atmospheric medium, and by the conductivity of the surface. One of the basic limitations on predictability is the integrity of the geodetic positioning of the transmitter stations. A minor displacement of an antenna position can cause a major error in prediction of a service area point. Of interest is the geodetic datum, the method of measuring geodetics, the spheroid used, etc. Also a problem in predictability is the translation of coordinates, i.e., hyperbolic to orthogonal and the rigor of the mathematics used.

The second, and closely related, problem is repeatability, the ability of a system to repeat a position. In other words, if the position of a point on the surface of the earth is given in coordinates of the system at one time, "How closely may we return to that exact position at some later time?"

Chapter 32

Basic Radionavigation Systems

Introduction

3201 The preceding chapter discussed the fundamentals of radio waves and their propagation and the general principles of hyperbolic radionavigation. In this chapter, the application of these principles will be considered with respect to certain basic systems—radio direction finding, Loran, Decca, and Consol. More complex systems employing advanced technology—Omega and satellite navigation—will be covered in subsequent chapters, followed by electronic navigation systems not involving radio waves.

The primary advantages of radionavigation systems are their long-range and all-weather availability. Such systems provide information on a vessel's position at sea far beyond such physical aids to navigation as coastal landmarks and offshore buoys. Many radionavigation systems will provide position fixing to a higher degree of accuracy than celestial observations, but their essential advantage is their lack of any need for clear skies and a visible horizon.

The negative side of radionavigation systems includes their complex equipment, need for electrical power, and the fact that signals must be radiated (primarily a disadvantage in time of war). The degrees of complexity will vary considerably in the "basic" systems classification—from simple radio direction finders to automatic signal-acquiring-and-tracking Loran receivers, for example. Well-maintained equipment will have a high degree of reliability, but failures can, and do, occur, often at just the "wrong" time. Also to be considered is the fact that even more complex equipment is based on shore as part of the system and thus is outside the mariner's control as regards operation and maintenance. Alternate sources of power will often be available for shipboard navigational equipment, but the possibility of a total loss of power must not be overlooked when making emergency plans.

Even the most enthusiastic supporters of radionavigation recognize that it has its limitations and that it will probably never completely replace other methods any more than the gyrocompass, valuable as it is, has replaced the magnetic compass. Keep constantly in mind that the methods discussed in this chapter are navigational *aids* and that it is still important to know how to use other methods.

Radio Communications

3202 Although message traffic is the primary function of radio communications, a navigator can also be served in other ways. Probably the most important application is that of time signals (article 2228). Weather information is disseminated both as a part of time-signal broadcasts and in special transmissions for that purpose alone. Information on the establishment or disestablishment of, or defects in, or changes to, aids to navigation are transmitted regularly, including announcements of scheduled interruptions in service for various stations or radionavigation systems. Ships at sea or in remote ports can request and receive written information from *Notices to Mariners* via teletypewriter (teleprinter) communications.

Much information of interest and value to a navigator will be found in DMAHTC Publications No. 117, *Radio Navigational Aids*. Information on weather broadcasts will be found in the publication *Worldwide Weather Broadcasts* of the National Oceanic and Atmospheric Administration. Systems in U.S. waters will be covered by the various volumes of the *Light Lists;* see article 604.

Radio Direction Finding

3203 The simplest and most widespread of radionavigation systems is that of *radio direction finding* (RDF). Equipment for RDF will be found on most medium-sized or larger recreational craft, on fishing vessels of all sizes, and on all ocean-going merchant ships. The extent that RDF is used may vary with the availability of more sophisticated equipment, but it remains a basic radionavigation system.

In the early days of RDF, the actual direction finder was located on shore, taking bearings on transmissions from a ship and then radioing such information to the navigator. Often coastal networks were established, and several simultaneous measurements could yield a fix. Such a network existed along the U.S. coasts during the 1920s and 1930s; shore-based direction finder service is still available in a few foreign locations.

Modern RDF systems for marine navigation use shore-based nondirectional transmitters and ship-based receivers with direction-sensitive antennas. Thus the *radio bearing* is taken aboard the vessel and plotted directly. Bearings are best taken from *marine radiobeacons*, which are designed and constructed solely for this purpose, but they can also be taken on commercial broadcasting stations (standard AM band), aeronautical radiobeacons, and some other stations. (The ability to direction find on other ship stations using medium and high frequencies was essentially lost with the conversion to single-sideband modulation; direction finding on VHF-FM channels is limited to expensive specialized equipment.) A bearing obtained from any of these sources can be used in the same manner as any other line of position. The exact location of the transmitting antenna must be known; nautical charts will show all marine radiobeacons and will often show the position of aeronautical radiobeacons and some commercial broadcasting stations (whose antennas are frequently *not* in the town or city whose name is used in station identification).

Typically, a radio direction finder makes use of the directional properties of a *loop antenna.* If the plane of such an antenna is parallel to the direction of travel of the radio waves, the signal received is of maximum strength. If the plane of the loop is perpendicular to the direction of travel, the signal is of minimum strength or entirely missing. When a dial

is attached to such a loop antenna that can be rotated, the orientation of the antenna and hence the direction of the transmitter can be determined. The pointer indicates the direction of the transmitter from the receiver when the loop is perpendicular to this direction, when the minimum signal is heard. The minimum, generally called the "null," rather than the maximum, is used because a sharper reading is then obtained. Some RDFs use two *fixed* loops at right angles to each other; "rotation" is accomplished by electronic circuitry.

Bearings as read from a radio direction finder aboard a vessel are subject to errors termed *radio deviation.* Each installation must be calibrated and a table of corrections used. See article 3208.

Since radio waves travel a great-circle path, a correction must be applied for plotting long bearings on a Mercator chart; some other chart projections may permit direct plotting of all radio bearings. See article 3207.

Marine Radiobeacons

3204 Many nations operate radiobeacons along their coasts to aid maritime navigation. These transmitting stations are employed both to extend navigational assistance beyond visual range and to replace visual observations at closer distances when fog or other "thick weather" exists. They operate in the upper part of the medium frequency (MF) band and the lower part of the high frequency (HF) band. For purposes of identification, simple characteristics of dots and dashes are used—these are usually, but not always, intended to be read as letters or numbers, or both, in standard Morse code.

Types of Radiobeacons

Radiobeacons have been divided into three specific classifications.

> *Directional radiobeacons* that transmit radio waves in beams along fixed bearings.
> *Rotating radiobeacons* by which a beam of radio waves is revolved in azimuth in a manner generally similar to the beam of light sent out by certain lighthouses.
> *Circular* (or *nondirectional*) *radiobeacons* that send out signals of approximately uniform strength in all directions so that ships may take radio bearings of them by means of the ship's radio direction finders. This is the most common type of radiobeacon.

Full information on the location of marine radiobeacons, frequencies, characteristic identifying signals, hours of operation, type of service, and range is given in DMAHTC Pub. No. 117, *Radio Navigational Aids*; information on radiobeacons in U.S. waters is contained in USCG *Light Lists*. (The existence of radiobeacons is indicated in *Coast Pilots* and DMAHTC *Lists of Lights*, but no operational details are given.) The location of marine radiobeacons is shown on nautical charts by the letters "R Bn" near a chart symbol, the circle of which is *not* indicative of the expected range of radio reception. As permitted by the space available on the chart, some other information may be given, such as the frequency and characteristic signal. Reference should be made to the appropriate publication(s) for full information before any radiobeacon is used. Although any transmitting station can be used, the signal must first be properly identified and the station antenna accurately located on a chart.

The U.S. Coast Guard operates more than 200 nondirectional marine radiobeacons in the frequency band 285–325 kHz. Most of these are located at, or very close to, a primary seacoast light, an offshore light tower, or large navigational buoy; some are located at secondary lights, and some are on the outer ends of jetties at harbor entrances. Where the antenna is separated from the visual aid, the *Light List* gives the direction and distance.

Marine radiobeacons are assigned to specific radio frequencies; stations on the same frequency are spaced geographically far enough from each other to avoid interference, or they are operated on a time-sharing basis. Most major beacons of the U.S. Coast Guard operate continuously, a few as part of a sequenced group. Those in any group transmit on the same frequency and are assigned a specific minute of a six-minute cycle; for example, a radiobeacon assigned sequence II, would transmit during the 2nd, 8th, 14th, 20th, etc., minute of each hour. There may be less than six beacons in a group; one station may transmit in two segments,

or there may be no signals on some segments. Sequenced groups are being eliminated in favor of continuous operation on different frequencies.

The operation of a typical group of sequenced radiobeacons is shown in figure 3204. These are off the New England coast, all operating on 286 kHz. (Another beacon operates on this frequency, but is far away at the Dry Tortugas in the Gulf of Mexico.)

RDF Equipment

3205 Radio direction finder equipment can be either manual (RDF) or automatic (ADF). In the former case, the antenna is rotated by hand until a direction is obtained. The point of minimum signal (null), rather than the maximum, is used as it is sharper and can be judged more precisely. The loop, or other style, antenna can be mounted on top of the receiver or separately. There will be two positions of the antenna, 180° apart, which will give a null; a separate "sense" antenna is used to resolve the ambiguity (unless the correct direction is readily apparent from other information such as the DR position).

Automatic direction finders rotate a loop either mechanically or electronically. A direct-reading visual display continuously indicates the bearing of the transmitter being received, corrected for 180° ambiguity; the operator of an ADF set needs only to tune it to the correct frequency and confirm the identification of the station.

RDFs and ADFs for low and medium frequencies are normally tunable across one or more bands; some models may contain one or more crystals to ensure rapid and accurate tuning. Direction finders for VHF use will be automatic in operation and may be crystal controlled on specific channels.

Radio Direction Finder Stations

3206 In some foreign countries radio direction finder equipment is installed at points ashore, and

Freq. kHz	Group Sequence	Station	Characteristic	Range (mile)	Lat. (N) ° ′ ″	Long. (W) ° ′ ″
286	I	HIGHLAND	HI (•••• ••)	100	42 02 24	70 03 40
	II	NANTUCKET L. S.	NS (■• •••)	100	40 30 00	69 28 00
	III	FIRE ISLAND	RT (•■• ■)	100	40 37 48	73 13 09
	IV	AMBROSE	T (■)	100	40 27 32	73 49 52
	V	GREAT DUCK ISLAND	GD (■■• ■••)	50	44 08 32	68 14 47
	VI	MANANA ISLAND	MI (■■ ••)	100	43 45 48	69 19 38

Figure 3204. Sequenced operation of radiobeacons.

these *radio direction finder stations* will take radio bearings on ships when requested, passing that information by radio. Such stations are also called *radio compass stations*, and can be located by reference to Pub. No. 117, or by the letters "RDF" placed near a radio station symbol on a chart.

Bearings taken by radio direction finder stations, and reported to the ships, are corrected for all determinable errors except the difference between a great circle and a rhumb line, and are normally accurate within 2° for distances under 50 nautical miles.

In some instances, several shore-based radio direction finding stations operate together in a *net*, and a vessel may be advised of its *position* rather than being given bearings; there may be a charge for this service.

Plotting Radio Bearings

3207 Radio bearings are plotted and labeled in the same manner as visual bearings. RDF bearings are, however, usually much less precise and accurate; a position found with one or more radio bearings must be identified as an "RDF fix," or as an estimated position (EP). A new DR track is not customarily plotted from an EP, but a course line should be drawn to determine whether or not there is any possibility of the ship standing into danger. A series of estimated positions obtained from RDF bearings and supplemented by a line of soundings can often provide a vessel's position with acceptable accuracy.

Plotting errors. In addition to the usual possible errors of plotting, there are two additional sources of error that must be avoided. First, be careful to plot from the correct position. If the bearing is observed aboard ship, it must be plotted from the position of the transmitting antenna; if observed at a radio compass station, it must be plotted from the position of the *receiving* antenna. *These locations are not always the same,* nor do they always coincide with an aid to navigation having the same name. Second, radio waves travel great circles and if they are to be plotted on a Mercator chart, a correction may have to be applied to convert the great circle to the corresponding rhumb line between the broadcasting and receiving antennas. A correction is usually not necessary provided the range is under 50 miles. If necessary, the correction will be found in Table 1 of *Bowditch* Volume II, or in DMAHTC Pub. No. 117. (See figure 3207a.) Charts using other projections may permit the direct plotting of all radio bearings.

Arbitrary rules are sometimes used to determine whether or not a radio bearing should be corrected before plotting; these are based on the relative positions of the transmitter and receiver. The amount of the correction depends on the latitude and the difference of longitude. A bearing from a transmitter 200 miles away near the equator or in a nearly north-south direction from the receiver may require a smaller correction than if the distance is 100 miles in an east-west direction in high latitudes. The only way to be sure is to enter a correction table and determine the magnitude of the correction.

Having found the correction, it is necessary to determine its sign before applying it to the observed bearing. This is easy to determine if it is remembered that the *great-circle direction is always nearer the pole than the Mercator direction.* Do not try to remember any other rule; draw a small diagram, mentally or otherwise, for each problem and determine the sign from it. Figure 3207b illustrates

RADIO NAVIGATIONAL AIDS   RADIO DIRECTION—FINDER
                                           AND RADAR STATIONS

200F.   Radio Bearing Conversion Table

Correction to be applied to radio bearing to convert to Mercator bearing

Difference of longitude

Mid. lat.	0.5°	1°	1.5°	2°	2.5°	3°	3.5°	4°	4.5°	5°	5.5°	6°	6.5°	7°	7.5°	Mid. lat.
°	°	°	°	°	°	°	°	°	°	°	°	°	°	°	°	°
4	- - -	- - -	- - -	- - -	0.1	0.1	0.1	0.1	0.2	0.2	0.2	0.2	0.2	0.2	0.3	4
5	- - -	0.1	0.1	.1	.1	.1	.2	.2	.2	.2	.2	.3	.3	.3	.3	5
6	- - -	.1	.1	.1	.1	.2	.2	.2	.2	.3	.3	.3	.3	.4	.4	6
7	- - -	.1	.1	.1	.2	.2	.2	.3	.3	.3	.3	.4	.4	.4	.5	7
8	- - -	.1	.1	.1	.2	.2	.2	.3	.3	.4	.4	.4	.5	.5	.5	8
9	- - -	.1	.1	.1	.2	.2	.2	.3	.3	.4	.4	.5	.5	.6	.6	9
10	- - -	.1	.1	.1	.2	.2	.3	.4	.4	.4	.5	.5	.6	.6	.6	10
11	- - -	.1	.1	.2	.2	.3	.3	.4	.4	.5	.5	.6	.6	.7	.7	11
12	.1	.1	.1	.2	.3	.3	.4	.4	.5	.5	.6	.6	.7	.7	.8	12

Figure 3207a. Radio Bearing Conversion Table (extract from Pub. No. 117).

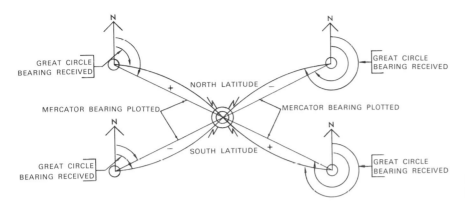

Figure 3207b. Diagram for determination of the sign of a conversion angle.

the four possible situations. The important thing to remember is that the sign depends on the relative position of the *receiver* and the *transmitter*, regardless of which is on your ship.

Accuracy of Radio Bearings

3208 The accuracy of RDF bearings depends on the following factors.

Strength of signals. The best bearings can be taken on transmitters whose signals are steady, clear, and strong. Weak signals and those receiving interference may give inaccurate bearings at best.

Radio deviation. Direction finders are subject to *radio* (or *RDF*) *deviation*, which affects the accuracy of their readings in much the same manner as magnetic compass deviation, although for different reasons. Incoming waves are picked up by metallic objects, particularly items of rigging, and re-radiated in such a way as to cause incorrect nulls on the vessel's RDF. Calibration for these errors can be accomplished by observing simultaneous radio and visual bearings on various headings and preparing an RDF deviation table in terms of *relative bearings*. Any source of signals can be used, but special RDF calibration stations are operated by the Coast Guard at points along all U.S. coasts. Deviation errors should be checked at intervals, particularly after the ship's structure has been altered or major changes have been made in electrical wiring. Bearings should be taken only when other antennas and movable equipment such as davits, cranes, etc., are in the same condition as during calibration.

Reciprocal bearings. With some equipment it is not apparent from which of two directions differing by 180° the bearing is coming. It is usually possible to tell which bearing to use by the dead-reckoning position of the ship, but if there is any doubt, take several bearings and note the direction of change. The station should draw aft. *If a reciprocal bearing is obtained, do not attempt to obtain the correct bear-*

ing by adding or subtracting 180°. The radio deviation correction will probably not be the same.

Night effect. Within half an hour of sunrise and sunset, and to a lesser extent throughout the night, radio bearings may be less accurate than at other times, due largely to polarization effect. This is manifested by a broadening and shifting of the minimum signal.

Land effect. When a radio signal crosses a shore line at an oblique angle, or if it passes over an island or peninsula of high land, the direction of travel may be bent a slight amount in a manner similar to the refraction of light. When a bearing is taken under these conditions, it should be considered of doubtful accuracy.

Personal error. The skill of the operator is perhaps the most important factor in obtaining accurate readings. Frequent practice is essential if this source of error is to be reduced to a minimum.

VHF Direction Finding

3209 Direction finding on VHF-FM signals is not as common as on the lower bands; it can, however, be very useful in certain situations. There are no radiobeacons as such, but the continuous weather broadcasts in U.S. waters by NOAA on frequencies between 162 and 163 MHz can be used if the antenna locations are plotted on the charts being used. Transmissions from Coast Guard stations and Marine Operators should be avoided or used with great caution, as these activities often have more than one transmitting antenna and it cannot be known which one is in use at any given time. VHF direction finding is often useful in a "homing" mode for search-and-rescue operations or when two vessels desire to rendezvous at sea.

Bearings are typically read to a precision of only 5°, but this is usually adequate. A special antenna is required on the vessel and each installation must be carefully checked for radio deviation.

LORAN

Loran Systems

3210 Several related, but distinctly separate radionavigation systems are categorized under the overall heading of Loran, an acronym for *LO*ng *RA*nge *N*avigation. Attention in this chapter will be primarily focused on Loran-C; Loran-A, or standard Loran, has been phased out in U.S. waters, and Loran-D is used only for military operations.

Theory of Loran Operation

3211 The technical principle that distinguishes the various versions of Loran from many other hyperbolic navigation systems is the use of pulse emissions. This permits the nonambiguous measurement of time differences of signals from different stations and further provides the means for discrimination at the receiving location between ground waves and sky waves. The ability to select and use a particular transmission provides maximum accuracy consistent with the system's inherent geometric configuration.

Loran employs shore-based transmitting stations at fixed points sending out carefully synchronized signals. These travel at the speed of light (161,875 nautical miles per second, 299,793 km/s) and cover one nautical mile in 6.18 microseconds (μs).

The time interval between transmissions of signals from a pair of Loran stations is very closely controlled; all Loran-C stations, for example, operate with multiple atomic time standards of extremely high accuracy and stability. As explained in article 3110, lines connecting points of equal *time difference* between the arrival at a receiver of signals from each station take the shape of hyperbolas; any number of hyperbolas can be drawn for various time differences. (See figure 3211.) Since time differences thus define specific fixed curves, these can be either plotted on a chart or their coordinates tabulated; charts with Loran lines are commonly used rather than tables, but these are not required to obtain a line of position with this radionavigation system.

At any given point, then, one line of position can be obtained from one pair of stations. To obtain a fix, at least one additional LOP is needed from another pair of stations or from other means, such as celestial observations.

In actual practice, the signals of both stations are *not* transmitted simultaneously. There is a known, precise time delay between the transmission from the "master" station and the one from the "subordinate" station, but this does not affect the basic principles of a hyperbolic system.

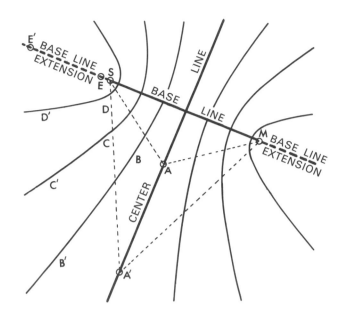

Figure 3211. The basic principle of hyperbolic radionavigation.

Loran-A

3212 The initial system was termed simply *Loran* until the development of later versions; it then became "Loran-A," or "standard Loran." This system operates on medium frequency (MF) channels between 1850 and 1950 kHz. Both ground-wave and sky-wave reception are used, giving different ranges, day and night, and different accuracies of fixes. Daytime use of ground waves extends out to about 500 miles with fixes accurate to 1.5 miles (2.8 km) over 80 percent of the coverage area (accuracy is greatest along the *base line* between the two transmitting stations). The use of sky waves extends the daytime range out to as much as 1,200 miles and as much as 1,400 miles at night; the accuracy of sky-wave fixes is roughly 5 to 7 miles (9–13 km).

Loran-A stations are located at separations of 250 to 600 miles. At one time, there were 83 Loran-A stations in operation giving coverage of both the North Atlantic and North Pacific Oceans, the Gulf of Mexico, and the North Sea, with some extensions into adjacent waters and land areas; now all have been eliminated, except for a few areas in and near Japan.

Loran-C

3213 The need for a more accurate long-range navigation system was recognized during World War II, soon after the development of Loran-A. Between 1952 and 1956 extensive tests were conducted on an improved system, *Loran-C*, and the first operational stations were established along the East Coast of the United States in 1957. Since then coverage has been greatly expanded, with the area of adequate signals in early 1985 as shown in figure 3213. (Greater detail is shown on Chart 5133.) Some 44 stations are now in operation, giving complete coverage of U.S. coastal waters (and also of about two-thirds of the land area of the 48 coterminous states), plus a large portion of the waters of the Northern Hemisphere. Studies have been made of the possible expansion of Loran-C coverage to other areas—such as the Caribbean—but implementation is unlikely because of unfavorable benefit-cost ratios. (A number of separate, but compatible, Loran-C stations are operated by the U.S.S.R., and there are minor systems in several other foreign nations.)

The existing Loran-C system is expected to remain in operation until at least the year 2000. It may ultimately be replaced by the NAVSTAR (GPS) satellite navigation system (see chapter 34) *if* receivers for that system can be developed that are cost-competitive with Loran-C sets.

The Basic Loran-C System

3214 Loran-C is a pulsed, hyperbolic, long-range navigation system available to ships and aircraft by day or night, in all weather conditions, on or over land and sea. It operates on a single frequency centered on 100 kHz. Stations are organized into *chains* of three or more stations, each transmitting pulses that are radiated in all directions. There may also be system area monitoring (SAM) stations.

One station in each chain is designated as the *master station* and transmits the master pulses; the others are *secondary stations*. The secondary stations always transmit in a set sequence after the master station with different predetermined fixed delays. Thus the master pulses are always received first, and time differences increase from a minimum at the secondary station location to a maximum at the master station and beyond. The locations of a constant time difference between the reception of the master pulses and those of a secondary station establish a *Loran LOP*. The same master station and another secondary station can be paired to provide a second LOP and thus a fix. Often the master and a third, or third and fourth, secondary station can be used to provide additional LOPs to confirm and refine the fix. See article 3220 for the plotting of Loran data.

In each repetition interval, individual stations radiate a group of eight pulses spaced 1,000 microseconds apart. Additionally, the master station

transmits a ninth pulse, primarily for identification. Multiple pulses are used so that more signal energy is available at the receiver, improving significantly the signal-to-noise ratio without having to increase the peak power capability of the transmitters. Loran-C can supply position information to a higher degree of accuracy and at greater distances than could be obtained with Loran-A.

In both Loran-A and Loran-C, a time-difference reading is accomplished by electronically comparing the time of arrival of pulses from two transmitters. In addition, Loran-C employs a *cycle-matching* technique for greater precision. A rough measurement is made of the difference in arrival time of the pulsed signals, and this is refined by a comparison of the phase of the signal within each pulse. This phase comparison is made automatically in the receiver and does not involve a separate operation by the navigator.

Because of the use of a lower frequency—100 kHz rather than 1850 or 1950 kHz—and an increased base-line distance between stations—1,000 miles or more—Loran-C is able to provide position information out to approximately 1,200 miles by means of ground waves, and out to more than 3,000 miles with sky waves. The power of a Loran-C transmitter varies with the specific station and is normally between 165 kW and 1.8 MW.

The use of pulse groups and extremely precise timing at each Loran-C station makes possible the sharing of the same frequency by all stations in the system. Identification of the particular groups of stations (chains) must be made by some other means than frequency selection. Accordingly, provision has been made in the Loran-C system for as many as 78 different pulse *group repetition intervals*, abbreviated as GRI. (In theory there could be some 10,000 GRI, but practical considerations lead to the use of not more than 78; actually, even fewer, now only 14, are in current use.) Each station transmits one pulse group—nine pulses for the master station and eight for each secondary station—in each group repetition interval.

Pulse Characteristics

3215 When a pulse is transmitted, the amplitude of the signal starts at zero, rises to a maximum, and then recedes back to zero; all this, of course, occurs in an extremely brief time. This pulse shape can be varied. In Loran-C there is a fast buildup of amplitude to the peak, and the leading edge of the pulse is used for timing signals. Figure 3215 illustrates an idealized pulse shape and the sampling point as determined by the circuitry of the receiver. The shape of the pulse also allows the

Figure 3213. Loran-C coverage diagram, mid-1980s.

LORAN-A COVERAGE IN THE NORTH
ATLANTIC HAS BEEN DISCONTINUED

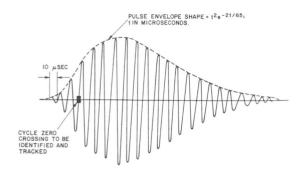

Figure 3215. Loran-C pulse shape, showing sampling point.

receiver to identify one particular cycle of the pulse. This is essential to prevent whole-cycle ambiguities in time-difference measurement and allows the high accuracy of the phase measurement technique to be achieved.

The sampling point is on the leading edge of the pulse in order to differentiate between ground and sky waves. The ground-wave signals of the same pulse will always be received first when signals are being picked up from both paths. The sky-wave lag can be as short as 35 microseconds (μs), making it necessary to use the leading edge of the pulse to ensure that the ground wave is measured before being contaminated by the effects of the sky wave signal. The ability to use ground waves without contamination from the sky wave permits use of precise techniques in time-difference measurements, and permits the use of long base lines with high accuracy synchronization between master and secondary stations.

The sky-wave lag can also be as great as 1,000 μs, and in such cases it would contaminate the ground-wave signal of the next succeeding pulse if the technical characteristics of the Loran-C system did not provide protection.

Within each of the multipulse groups from the master and secondary stations, the phase of the RF carrier is changed with respect to the pulse envelope in a systematic manner from pulse to pulse. The phase of each pulse in an eight- or nine-pulse group is changed in accordance with a prescribed code so that it is either in phase (+) or 180° out of phase (−) with a stable 100 kHz reference signal. The phase code used at a master station is different from the phase code used at a secondary, but all secondaries use the same code. Contamination by preceding sky waves without phase coding would nullify the effect of sampling only the ground wave, thereby degrading the inherent accuracy of the system. The use of phase coding also furnishes the receiver with the necessary information to distin-

guish between time signals from the master and the secondary stations. Phase coding can, to a limited degree, provide protection from interference by non-Loran signals.

Although Loran-C is fundamentally a hyperbolic system, receivers for a few special applications have been modified and equipped with a clock (atomic time standard) comparable to those used at transmitting stations so that the absolute time of arrival of signals can be measured. Thus a computation can be made of the time of travel of each signal, and the distance determined. This yields circular LOPs centered on each transmitter and is termed Rho-Rho, or Range-Range, navigation. Greater useful ranges can be achieved in this mode of operation.

Loran-C Stations

3216 The master and secondary stations of a Loran-C chain are located so that signals from the master and at least two secondary stations may be received through the desired coverage area. (In some instances, a common site is used for a secondary station of two different chains, or for the master of one chain and a secondary of another chain.) For convenience, the master station is designated by the letter *M*, and the secondary stations are designated *W, X, Y,* or *Z*.

For any Loran-C chain, a GRI is selected that will not cause mutual (crossrate) interference with adjacent chains. The designation of a Loran-C rate is by the first four digits of the specific GRI; for example, a GRI of 99300 microseconds is rate 9930. A specific pair, which produce a set of lines of position, are identified by the rate and the letter of the secondary station used with the master—for example, 9930-X.

Figure 3216a. Loran-C "star" configuration of one master and three secondary stations.

Figure 3216b. Loran-C configuration where one station (center) serves as the master station of one chain and a secondary station of another chain.

Chain Operation

3217 The master station transmitter's ninth pulse in each group is used for identification of the master and for "blink." Blinking is used to warn users that there is an error in the transmission of a particular station or stations; it is accomplished by

LORAN-C BLINK CODE

MASTER STATION NINTH PULSE: ■ = APPROXIMATELY 0.25 SECOND
■■ = APPROXIMATELY 0.75 SECOND

UNUSABLE TD (S)	ON-OFF PATTERN
	←———————— 12 SECONDS ————————→
NONE	▬▬▬▬▬▬▬▬▬▬▬▬▬▬▬▬▬
X	■ ■■ ■■ ■
Y	■ ■■ ■■ ■■
Z	■ ■■ ■■ ■■ ■
W	■■ ■■ ■ ■■ ■■ ■
XY	■ ■■ ■■ ■ ■■ ■
XZ	■ ■■ ■■ ■ ■■ ■■
XW	■ ■■ ■■ ■ ■■ ■■ ■
YZ	■ ■■ ■■ ■■ ■ ■■ ■■
YW	■ ■■ ■■ ■■ ■ ■■ ■■ ■
ZW	■ ■■ ■■ ■■ ■ ■■ ■■ ■
XYZ	■ ■■ ■■ ■ ■■ ■ ■■ ■■
XYW	■ ■■ ■■ ■ ■■ ■ ■■ ■■ ■
XZW	■ ■■ ■■ ■ ■■ ■■ ■■ ■■ ■
YZW	■ ■■ ■■ ■■ ■ ■■ ■■ ■■ ■■ ■
XYZW	■ ■■ ■■ ■ ■■ ■ ■■ ■■ ■■ ■■ ■

SECONDARY STATION FIRST TWO PULSES:

TURNED ON (BLINKED) FOR APPROXIMATELY 0.25 SECONDS EVERY 4.0 SECONDS. ALL SECONDARIES USE SAME CODE, AUTOMATICALLY RECOGNIZED BY MOST MODERN LORAN–C RECEIVERS.

Figure 3217. Loran-C blink code.

turning the ninth pulse off and on in a specified code as shown in figure 3217. The secondary station of the unusable pair also blinks by turning off and on the first two pulses of its pulse group. Most modern receivers automatically detect secondary station blink only, as this is enough to trigger alarm indicators.

Synchronization Control

3218 All transmitting stations are equipped with cesium time and frequency standards. The extremely high accuracy and stability of these standards permit each station to establish its own time of transmission without reference to another station. (In the older Loran-A system, subordinate stations were "slaved" to the master station, transmitting only after receipt of the master pulse; this is not so in Loran-C.)

The objective for control of a Loran-C chain is to keep the observed time difference (TD) of each master-secondary pair constant at any location throughout the coverage area. Frequency offsets in the cesium standards and changes in propagation conditions can cause the observed TD to vary. Therefore, one or more SAM stations are established with precise receiving equipment to monitor continuously the TDs of the master-secondary pairs. In some instances, a transmitting station is suitably located and can perform the monitoring function. A control TD is established during system calibration. When the observed TD varies from the control TD by more than one-half the prescribed tolerance, the SAM directs a change in the timing of the secondary station to remove the error. If the observed TD becomes different from the control TD by more than the established tolerance, then a "blink" is ordered to alert all users that the time difference is not usable.

Loran-C Reception

3219 Loran-C receivers normally provide both automatic signal acquisition and cycle matching once the set is turned on.

As a master station is common to two or more pairs, the receiver will automatically give two time differences for two lines of position and automatically track these signals once they have been acquired; some receivers will track more than two station pairs, displaying time differences for those of adequate signal quality. The receiver will give a direct readout of the time differences; if two pairs are being tracked, a single digital display will alternately show each time difference, or there may be a dual display to give both readings simultaneously. Some Loran-C receivers provide a direct readout in latitude and longitude; some models may be coupled to an X-Y coordinate converter that will plot the ship's track.

A Loran-C receiver must be properly installed if it is to operate satisfactorily; this is a task for a qualified technician. The antenna should be mounted as high as possible, but it is even more necessary that it be well away from other antennas, stays, and metallic objects. Do not connect any other equipment to the Loran-C antenna. Equally important is the proper grounding of the antenna coupler and the receiver.

Like all radionavigation systems, Loran-C can be bothered by interference. This can make it difficult to acquire the Loran-C signals and/or make the readings fluctuate more than usual. Most manufacturers provide tunable "notch" filters that can be used to minimize such interference. If a user is always going to remain in the same general area (a radius of several hundred miles from a center point), it will probably never be necessary to readjust these filters once they are properly set by the manufacturer or his local representative.

If the user is going to travel great distances, it will be necessary for the operator to learn how to readjust the filters. This is not a difficult task once he has received some initial training.

To start the acquisition process of the receiver, the GRI of the Loran-C chain to be used is entered into the set. With the long base lines of this system, a single GRI is used over a wide area, such as the U.S. Atlantic and Gulf coasts, or the U.S. Pacific coast. The speed at which the receiver will find the Loran-C signals depends upon the signal strength and how much noise is present. In some receivers, the operator can speed up the process by preselecting the approximate Loran-C readings he expects to read. Most modern receivers will be automatically tracking within five minutes of initial turn-on, and will continue to track until the receiver is turned off. If the vessel is at a known location (at a pier and ready for departure, for example) it will be obvious when the receiver is providing the correct information. In any event, most receivers display some type of an alarm that remains lighted until the receiver is tracking properly.

Initially acquiring Loran-C signals when arriving from far out at sea (several hundred miles or more) is a more difficult problem than that for a vessel made fast to a pier where the Loran-C readings are known. Thus, the receiver may take somewhat longer to acquire the signals. When first entering a Loran-C coverage area, the receiver should be checked frequently to ensure that all alarm lights are out. Sometimes, due to weak signals and high noise, the receiver alarms will go out even though the receiver is not tracking precisely. As the vessel continues to enter the stronger signal area, however, the receiver will automatically recognize that it has made an error and will give the operator an alarm light. This should occur well before entering coastal waters.

Other alarms that may be on a Loran-C receiver include one to indicate that a station is transmitting a "blink" warning (see article 3217), or one indicating that an incorrect cycle is being tracked on one or more signals so that the reading is off by a multiple of 10 microseconds. (This alarm may come on when the receiver is, in fact, tracking properly, but has not yet completed all internal tests to verify correct operation.)

Whenever an alarm light is on, use extreme caution. Do not use a time difference reading unless all alarm lights are out.

Loran-C Positioning

3220 Loran-C is a complex system of radionavigation developed by skilled engineers and maintained by highly trained electronics technicians. However, the *use* of Loran-C for navigation does *not* require technical expertise; determining a vessel's position can be quite simple. A fix can be obtained by using either a chart or a set of tables. Use of a chart is simpler and quicker and yields results of satisfactory precision for ordinary navigation. Use of a tabular solution is more complex, but gives a more precise position; the use of tables also allows a position to be determined if a Loran-C chart does not exist for the area or is not on board.

Charts of U.S. coastal waters published by the National Ocean Service at a scale of 1:80,000 or smaller will have Loran-C lines of position printed on them (using different colors for the various usable pairs of stations). Read one Loran-C time difference from the receiver and find the pair of lines for time-difference values that bracket the observed reading; interpolate by eye or measurement for an exact LOP. Follow the same procedure for a second Loran reading from the receiver; the fix is at the intersection of these lines to an accuracy determined by the range from the Loran transmitters and other factors. If a third time difference and LOP can be obtained, this will improve the accuracy of the fix, and the navigator's confidence in it.

Loran-C lines are primarily shown for offshore waters; they are carried into larger inshore bodies, but not into harbors, rivers, etc., because of the effects of close-by land masses and the consequent lack of the precision and accuracy required for piloting. For example: Loran-C lines are shown on charts of the coastal waters of Virginia and up Chesapeake Bay, but not into Hampton Roads and Norfolk Harbor.

Some Loran-C transmitters are located inland from the coasts—in a few instances, several hundred miles or more. The overland path of signals from these stations results in phase shifts that are difficult to predict accurately. When Loran-C lines were first applied to charts, they were drawn using theoretical values for propagation shifts of the signals. Actual conditions often turn out to be different, resulting from the fact that the pulses travel partly over land and partly over water. The sets of lines bear a correct relationship to each other, but the grid as a whole may be offset from true locations by 1/4 to 2 miles. Field surveys—taking Loran readings at known geographic positions—have resulted in more accurate hyperbolic lattices on later editions of charts (see article 3221).

Each Loran-C chart will carry one of the following notes:

"The Loran-C lines of position overprinted on this chart have been prepared for use with ground-wave signals and are presently compensated only for theoretical propagation delays, which have not yet been verified by observed data. Mariners are cautioned not to rely entirely on the lattices in inshore waters. Sky wave corrections are not provided."

"The Loran-C lines of position overprinted on this chart have been prepared for use with ground-wave signals and are compensated with propagation delays computed from observed data. Mariners are cautioned not to rely entirely on the lattices in inshore waters. Sky-wave corrections are not provided."

There may be continual slight changes in the last digit of the readout of a Loran-C receiver—this is termed "jitter" or jumping. This may occur even though the vessel is not moving; it is caused by noise interfering with the Loran signal. For the most precise navigation, readings should be averaged over a brief period; note the smallest and largest values and average them mentally.

Many receivers have a "Memory" or "Hold" switch. This locks the display on the present reading while the receiver continues to track internally. The memory capability can be most helpful in situations such as a crewman overboard, or marking the location of a float. It must be recognized that the reading shown may be 0.1 or 0.2 microseconds different from the average reading if there is noise jitter present.

In some instances, one or both of the following conditions may cause difficulties for a navigator:

a. The lines of position are almost parallel, thus making it difficult to determine accurately the vessel's position.

b. A small change in the Loran-C reading will cause a large change in the position of the corresponding LOP (i.e., the lines are spaced farther apart than are other sets on the same chart). *Never use a master-secondary pair near their baseline extension;* here the gradients become very large (see figure 3220). There is also the possibility of introducing very large errors in position for lack of knowledge as to which side of the base line the vessel is situated; base-line extensions are labeled on charts.

If either or both of these conditions exist, the proper procedure is to relock one channel of the receiver on the signal of a different secondary station, using the set's instruction manual. To determine which signal to use, examine the chart and find a set of LOPs that result in a good crossing angle (greater than 30°) with the other Loran LOP and/or which shows a small change in position for small changes in time-difference readings.

Loran-C lines are not normally printed on charts at a scale of larger than 1:80,000. Thus, they are not available on harbor charts, but a navigator operating frequently in any given area can make his own "Loran chart" by recording time differences at a series of known positions. He can also record Loran readings at specific critical points, such as turns in channels or designated anchorage berths. The

Figure 3220. Chart with Loran-C lines of position (extract).

Coast Guard has published Loran-C time differences at selected "waypoints" along heavily traveled inland routes such as New York Harbor and Delaware Bay.

DMAHTC Loran-C Charts

Loran-C charts published by the Defense Mapping Agency Hydrographic/Topographic Center have lines of constant time difference based on an all-seawater path. They do *not* include the corrections for propagation over a path that is partially over land. For the most accurate readings (and compatibility of positions where both DMAHTC and NOS charts are available) corrections must also be included from Loran-C Correction Tables (see article 3221).

A further correction is required if sky-wave signals must be used. On many DMAHTC charts with Loran lines, small blocks of figures will be found at regular intervals of the intersections of meridians and parallels. The values given are microseconds to be added to or subtracted from the Loran-C receiver reading. Separate values may be shown for day and night reception, and some areas may have a symbol for one or more station pairs indicating, "Do not use sky waves in this area." The appropriate figure from the nearest block should be applied to the receiver reading before the LOP is drawn. The use of these figures will be explained by use of an example; see figure 3220. The "7980 W" signifies that the sky-wave corrections are for the 7980 W lines of position. The "+13" means that 13 microseconds must be added to the receiver reading; "D" means that this correction is to be applied during daylight navigation only, and "N" has the corresponding meaning for nighttime use. For the 7980 X readings, the "GS-39D" means that 39 microseconds must be subtracted before plotting the LOP if the receiver is tracking a ground-wave master signal and a sky-wave secondary signal during daylight hours. If the letters G and S are reversed, the correction factor applies when receiving a sky-wave master signal and a ground-wave secondary signal. The asterisk on the line for 7980 Z refers to a note elsewhere on the chart that states that sky-wave signals from this secondary station should not be used.

You must, however, be able to know when your receiver is tracking a sky-wave signal. By using the receiver's digital readout and special functions, you can look for one or more of the following indicators of sky-wave tracking.

A signal strength or signal-to-noise ratio much larger than would be expected in the area for a ground-wave signal;

Signal strengths that vary more than normal;
Time differences that vary more than normal;
Large position errors.

When looking for these indications, be sure to determine which specific stations have abnormal signals, since these are the ones for which corrections must be used. Consult the operator manual for the receiver being used for additional information, and remember to use sky-waves with extreme caution, as they are less accurate and much more difficult to use than ground-wave signals.

Correction tables are also published for station pairs using the rho-rho technique. Receivers for this mode of operation must have internal cesium "clocks" for timing.

Positioning by Use of Tables

In almost all Loran-C navigation, charts are used to fix a vessel's position because of the greater ease of so doing. If, however, a chart with overprinted Loran lines is not available, a position can be worked out from *Loran-C Rate Tables*, one for each master-secondary station pair—publications in the 221-(xxxx) series—but this is a much more laborious procedure.

These tables consist of a listing of latitude and longitude for many points along a line representing a given time-difference reading. Enter the table in the T column for the value nearest the reading on the display of the receiver and find the longitudes (or latitudes) closest to and on either side of the DR position. Extract the corresponding latitudes (or longitudes) for these two points. Interpolate as necessary. Plot the two points thus obtained and connect them with a straight line to obtain a segment of a Loran LOP. (Except when the vessel is within about 20 miles of a Loran-C transmitting station, a straight line between the two points can be used without appreciable error.) Repeat this procedure for another station pair with its rate table. Label each line with the time and pair used. The intersection of the lines is the Loran-C fix. If possible, use a third station pair and table.

The *Loran-C Position Tables* contain corrections for the reduction of sky-wave readings to corresponding ground-wave values. When necessary, corrections for the reverse procedure, matching ground waves to sky waves, are also included. Examples in the use of these corrections are provided in the Tables.

Positioning Using Direct-reading Receivers

Increasingly, Loran-C receivers have a "coordinate conversion" capability; an internal microprocessor automatically changes the measured time differences to a display of position directly in latitude and longitude. Many sets can also provide a flow of digital data to a position plotter that will automatically and continuously plot the vessel's position in N-S and E-W coordinates to any selected chart scale within wide limits; this will permit precise return over a previous track for buoy placement, offshore drilling or research tasks, or other applications.

Most Loran-C receivers will compute a great-circle track to a destination described in terms of time differences or latitude and longitude. A number of "waypoints" may be entered and tracks for successive legs computed. These sets can display information such as course and speed being made good (computed from changes in the Loran-derived positions), directions and distance to a previously entered destination or waypoint, cross-track error (distance off course to right or left of direct track), a direct-reading steering indicator, and distance and time to go to the next waypoint or destination plus a warning signal just before that point is reached. One set will even talk to you—using synthesized speech from a microelectronic "chip" to give you selected items from the above list at intervals of six seconds to one hour, as you desire.

Position information in terms of time-difference readings can be transferred between receivers with excellent results. If, however, latitude/longitude data are used, lesser accuracy may occur as different receivers may have different coordinate conversion programs.

Many models of Loran-C receivers can be connected, through an interface unit, to a vessel's automatic steering mechanism (commonly called an "autopilot"). Thus the vessel may be steered, without human action, so as to continuously be on the great circle track previously computed in the receiver.

Once started with accurate time, several receivers can function as a chronometer with an error no greater than about two seconds per month. A Loran-C set often contains highly sophisticated self-testing and signal-status circuitry to give a navigator confidence in its output data.

Remote readout units are available for some Loran-C receivers. These may show position in time differences or latitude/longitude, or may be a steering indicator only. There are also portable receivers powered by an attached battery pack.

Loran-C Position Accuracy

3221 Position accuracy degrades with increasing distance from the transmitting stations as a result of variation in propagation conditions, losses over the signal path, and internal receiver conditions. Accuracies cannot be stated absolutely, but using range as the distance to the master station of the pair, groundwave accuracies may be generally stated as:

> at   200 miles, 50–300 feet (15–90m)
> 500 miles, 200–700 feet (60–210m)
> 750 miles, 300–1,100 feet (90–340m)
> 1,000 miles, 500–1,700 feet (150–520m)

Accuracies are stated as a range of values rather than as fixed amounts, as the error will vary with the position of the receiver with respect to the master and secondary stations, variations from standard propagation conditions, and other factors.

In order to ensure that the Loran-C lines on charts are as accurately located as possible, the Coast Guard and the National Ocean Service have cooperated to conduct *Loran-C verification surveys*. These collect time differences at precisely known locations over a lengthy period, and the data are used to verify or correct the lines shown on previous editions of the applicable charts. Reports are also received by DMAHTC from mariners; these reports list Loran-C readings at known locations or positions that have been fixed by other high-accuracy systems.

Loran C Correction Tables

DMAHTC has prepared a series of *Loran-C Correction Tables*, Pub. No. 221 (xxxx-C). These contain *Secondary Correction Factors*, also called *Additional Secondary Factors (ASF)*, which are used to reduce a Loran-C ground-wave reading to a more accurate value. ASF corrections are needed due to the fact that the signal path is partly over land and partly over water. The table is entered directly with a DR position, or the latitude and longitude of the uncorrected Loran fix, to the nearest 5' of arc to find the correction. This value, in microseconds, is added algebraically to the time-difference reading; correction values can be either positive or negative.

The ASF Correction Tables are published primarily for precision navigators who use electronic computers to convert Loran-C time differences to geographic coordinates. Direct-reading Loran-C receivers with internal coordinate conversion will generally need the application of ASF corrections to obtain their maximum accuracy; most models will require keyboard entry of the values from the tables, but a few sets have internally stored data and make the correction automatically.

ASF corrections can also be used with manual plotting on DMAHTC charts. Although these values

7980-X   23X

LATITUDE	90° 0'	55	50	45	40	35	30	25	20	15	10	5	89° 0'
LONGITUDE WEST													
30° 0'											1.0	1.0	0.9
55											1.0	1.0	1.0
50											1.1	1.0	0.9
45										1.0	1.1	1.0	0.8
40									1.0	1.0	1.0	1.0	0.8
35								1.0	1.0	1.0	1.0	1.0	0.8
30							1.0	1.0	1.0	1.0	1.0	1.0	0.8
25								1.0	1.0		1.0	0.9	0.7
20										0.9	0.9	0.9	0.7
15												0.9	0.6
10		1.1	1.1	1.0	1.1								
5	1.0	1.0	1.1	1.0	1.1	1.1	1.0						
L 29° 0'	1.1	1.0	1.0	1.0	1.0	1.0	1.0	1.0		1.0	0.9	0.9	0.7
A 55	1.0	1.0	1.0	1.0	1.0	1.0	1.0	1.0	0.9	0.9	0.9	0.9	0.7
T 50	1.0	1.0	1.0	1.0	1.0	0.9	0.9	0.9	0.9	0.9	0.9	0.9	0.7
I 45	1.0	1.0	1.0	0.9	0.9	0.9	0.9	0.9	0.9	0.9	0.9	0.9	0.7
T 40	0.9	0.9	0.9	0.9	0.9	0.9	0.9	0.9	0.9	0.9	0.9	0.9	0.7
U 35	0.9	0.9	0.9	0.9	0.9	0.9	0.9	0.9	0.9	0.9	0.9	0.9	0.7
D 30	0.9	0.9	0.9	0.9	0.9	0.9	0.9	0.9	0.9	0.9	0.9	0.9	0.7
E 25	0.9	0.9	0.9	0.9	0.9	0.9	0.9	0.9	0.9	0.9	0.9	0.9	0.7
N 20	0.9	0.9	0.9	0.9	0.9	0.9	0.9	0.9	0.9	0.9	0.9	0.9	0.7
O 15	0.9	0.9	0.9	0.9	0.9	0.9	0.9	0.9	0.9	0.9	0.9	0.9	0.7
R 10	0.9	0.9	0.9	0.9	0.9	0.9	0.9	0.9	0.9	0.9	0.9		0.7
T 5	0.9	0.9	0.9	0.9	0.9	0.9	0.9	0.9	0.9	0.9			
H 28° 0'	0.9	0.9	0.9	0.9	0.9	0.9	0.9						
55	0.9	0.9	0.9	0.9									
50	0.9	0.9	0.9										
45	0.9	0.9											
40	0.9												
35													
30													
25													
20													
15													
10													
5													
27° 0'													

Figure 3221. Loran-C Correction Table (extract).

are usually too small to seriously affect a Loran-C fix plotted on a small-scale chart, they can become as large as ±4 microseconds. The offset for a correction of this magnitude will be minimal on the base line, but in other areas of coverage it can be appreciable because of the expansion of lane width between lines as distance from the base line increases. ASF corrections should be used with caution within 10 miles of land; this area represents an unreliable zone where large variations occur in the magnitude of the correction. Interpolation between correction values will not necessarily improve fix accuracy, as the data are not linear. ASF corrections must *not* be used with charts that have corrected lattices, such as NOS charts.

Each of the tables contains corrections for an entire chain, with separate sections for each master-secondary station pair. Detailed instructions for the use of the tables are included in the front pages of each volume, together with one or more examples.

Use of Sky Waves

Sky-wave reception of Loran-C signals gives greater range, but lesser accuracy. At 1,500 miles, position accuracy may be as poor as 10 miles (18 km); at 2,000 miles, it may degrade to as much as 17 miles (31 km)—these are "worst case" values, and sky-wave accuracies are often better. Corrections can be applied as described in article 3220.

Coverage and Reliability Diagrams

A worldwide *Loran-C Coverage Diagram* is published as DMAHTC Chart No. 5130; see figure 3213. Geographic limits are shown for 95 percent fix accuracy (two standard deviations) of 1,500 feet (457 m) from ground-wave signals with signal-to-noise ratios of 1:3 and 1:10. Boundaries are also shown for sky-wave coverage that will yield a fix of specified lesser accuracy.

In addition, there are *Loran-C Reliability Diagrams* for each chain—Charts No. 5592–5606—

which will show limits of 1:3 and 1:10 signal-to-noise ratios for each station, and boundaries for fix accuracies of 500 feet (152 m), 750 feet (229 m), and 1,500 feet (457 m).

Repeatability

3222 The Loran-C system provides excellent *repeatability;* a Loran-C fix taken many times at a known location will give positions normally varying less than 300 feet (91 m), and often less than 50 feet (15 m). Thus, the knowledge of previously obtained readings at a specific location can be extremely useful if a navigator wants to return to that same spot at a later date; the readings can be used for his return rather than values of latitude and longitude.

The repeatability of Loran-C time-difference readings has led to the use of such coordinates for search-and-rescue operations offshore; these are often *more* useful than geographic coordinates derived from Loran or other sources.

The repeatability capability of Loran-C makes it useful in inshore and harbor navigation where data have previously been taken and recorded. Used in this manner, Loran-C may be employed where its accuracy when used with overprinted charts is not adequate for safe navigation. This local knowledge can be very helpful to a navigator, but he should also make full use of other navigational aids available to him. As every prudent navigator realizes, complete faith should *never* be placed solely on *one* system.

The high order of relative position accuracy of Loran-C permits its use in the early stages of collision avoidance. System errors such as those due to propagation conditions will equally affect all vessels in the same area, and a comparison of Loran-C readings will yield separation distances to a reasonably useful degree of precision.

Other Uses of Loran-C

3223 The inherent stability of the transmitted signals makes the Loran-C system extremely useful for various additional purposes besides precise electronic navigation.

It can serve as a long-range distribution system for time information (UTC) with an accuracy in the order of one microsecond.

It makes possible relative time standardization and synchronization between widely separated receiving locations to accuracies of a few microseconds.

It is useful for electromagnetic wave propagation studies.

These services can be used in conjunction with, and without adversely affecting, navigational accuracy. This time standard, with knowledge of the exact location of the transmitting stations, allows updating of SINS navigational equipment (chapter 35).

Loran-C can be used to track vehicles, whether they be on land, sea, or in the air. The most common use to date has been to track weather balloons, with results that have exceeded the performance of balloon-tracking radar systems and have done so at significantly reduced cost.

The basis for vehicle location systems is retransmission of the Loran-C signals from the vehicle to a base station. With the sophisticated and expensive equipment located at the base station, only inexpensive retransmission modules need be installed in the vehicles. By processing the retransmitted Loran-C signals, the time-difference readings that exist at the vehicle can be determined, thus providing vehicle position on an absolute basis or with respect to the base station. As the existing Loran-C chains cover 92 percent of the population of the 48 "mainland" states, this technique of "land navigation" is believed to have considerable potential for use with emergency and public transportation vehicles, railroad trains, and other units.

This retransmission technique is also being studied as a possible means of locating vessels in distress, and directing search-and-rescue ships and aircraft to their assistance. It is being considered as a method of locating ships in the outer areas of a Vessel Traffic System when they are beyond the range of shore-based radars.

Loran-C for Harbors and Entrances

3224 The current Coast Guard Loran-C program will meet some of the requirements for navigation in "Harbors and Harbor Entrance Areas (HHE)"—another geographic subdivision in the Federal Radionavigation Plan. However, the wide-area Loran-C system for the CCZ (Coastal Confluence Zone) was not designed primarily to have the more precise capability required for the HHE. Studies and experiments are being conducted on possible refinements, including differential Loran-C, signal enhancement by low-powered local transmitters, and complete low-powered local "mini-chains."

Differential Loran-C consists of monitoring the minute variations in signals that occur at a specific location, and then transmitting corrections to local users. Experiments have shown this technique to be effective for increasing the accuracy and effectiveness of Loran-C. Differential techniques show great promise of improving even further the usefulness of the already highly stable Loran-C signals.

A local low-power transmitting station can be used in areas where the CCZ stations do not provide sufficient signal strength to permit rapid and accurate signal processing. This method may also be used for improvement in the intersection angles of Loran lines of position. The navigator of a vessel might use signals from a high-powered CCZ station some distance away in combination with signals from a local low-powered transmitter to obtain the desired quantity and quality of LOPs.

Complete low-power, limited-coverage Loran-C chains have been established in a number of areas by both foreign governmental agencies and commercial enterprises. For example, there is a mini-chain of a master and two secondary stations that covers the Suez Canal, operating in the differential mode to provide real-time vessel location data for the Suez Canal Vessel Traffic Management Service. Other mini-chains operate similarly to the U.S. Coast Guard chains except for having their own coding delays. Since 1972, these systems have been internationally recognized as bonafide Loran-C systems, except that they must operate on a noninterference basis. Some commercially operated chains use a nonstandard phase code sequence of the pulse groups to restrict access to the positional information and/or limit legal liabilities.

Loran-D

3225 Some years ago, the need developed for a low-frequency, hyperbolic navigation system that would be semimobile for military applications. Loran-D, a pulsed-type system, was developed to fill this need. It is designed to be readily transportable, so that lines of position can be furnished in a new area as the need develops, and to minimize downtime required to correct equipment failure.

Like Loran-C, Loran-D operates in the low-frequency band, in the range 90–110 kHz, and its signal characteristics are very similar to those of Loran-C. Three or four transmitting stations operate together on a time-shared basis to provide ground-wave signals of high accuracy out to a maximum range of about 500 miles. Under good conditions it will establish position to within 0.1 mile at a range of 250 miles from the transmitters. Its signals are equally dependable whether over land or water.

Primarily, Loran-D differs from Loran-C in its signal format; it uses repeated groups of 16 pulses spaced 500 microseconds apart.

The system is highly resistant to electronic jamming. This characteristic, and its extreme mobility—stations can be set up anywhere within 24 hours—make it exceptionally useful when areas of operations are changing rapidly. The system is equally satisfactory for use aboard naval vessels or high-speed aircraft.

OTHER SYSTEMS

Decca

3226 The *Decca Navigator System* is unique in that in many geographic areas it is privately owned and operated, supported by funds derived from the sale or lease of receiving equipment used on board ships and aircraft. Decca is a hyperbolic system that uses phase comparison of continuous radio signals, rather than pulses, in the LF band. Each chain normally consists of a master station and three slaves; ideally, the slaves would be equally spaced around the circumference of a circle having a radius of 70 to 80 miles and centered on the master station (see figure 3226a).

For purposes of identification, the slaves are designated with the colors *purple, red,* and *green.* Each station transmits a continuous wave on a different frequency within the limits of 70 and 130 kHz; each is a multiple of a fundamental frequency, f, that lies between 14.00 and 14.33 kHz; different values of f are used to identify chains. The multiple $6f$ is used for the master station and multiples of $6f$, $8f$, and $9f$ for the respective slaves.

With the continuously harmonically related carrier frequencies, the phase relationship of each signal pair determines a line of position, and two or three pairs provide a fix. Decca signals provide information within *lanes,* and *lane identification signals* are transmitted each 20 seconds. Additionally, there are *zones* consisting of 18 green lanes, 24 red lanes, and 30 purple lanes. For identification, each Decca zone is assigned a letter from *A* through *J,* either clockwise or counterclockwise from the base-line extension, depending upon the slave station color; the lettering is repeated every ten zones. Each lane within a zone is given a number with 0–23 being used for red lanes, 30–47 for green lanes, and 50–79 for purple lanes.

In addition to the lane-identification signal mentioned above, each station periodically transmits a *zone identification signal* on a frequency of 8.2 f. This is called the *orange* signal; it is also used for system monitoring and control functions within each chain.

A typical Decca receiver contains four essentially identical sub-receivers, one for each frequency. In-

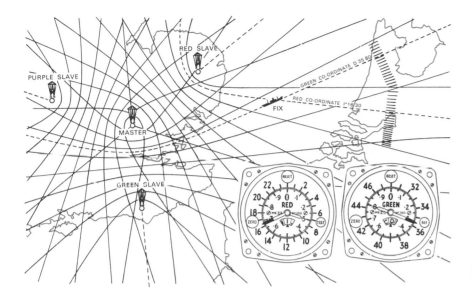

Figure 3226a. Decca lattice for the English Channel.

ternal circuitry provides for a comparison of the phase of the signal from each slave with that of the master.

Charts are published with Decca lines overprinted in colors to match the designation of the slave stations. Two slaves, with the master, provide a fix; the third provides a check on the others and permits better positioning in areas unfavorable to one of the other slave stations. To determine a position, it is only necessary to read three dials called *Decometers*, and then locate the intersection of the two or three lines indicated. No matching of signals or manipulation of dials is required. As with any phase relationship system, the phases of the signals transmitted by master and slave are compared, rather than the travel times. The phase comparison gives a precise measure of the fractional part of a wave-length, or lane, but no indication of the total number of whole lanes existing. An auxiliary means of keeping track of the number of whole lanes is essential. The Mk 21 shipboard receiver, figure 3226b, has a digital Lane Identification Display for this purpose. Lane identification can also be accomplished from an accurate DR plot on the chart.

The average reliable operational day and night range of Decca is about 250 miles. At this distance the average error in a line of position is approximately 150 yards (137 m) in daytime, and about 800 yards (730 m) at night.

Decca coverage extends over much of Western Europe, the Persian Gulf, the Indian subcontinent, the Far East, Australian waters, and the Canadian maritime provinces.

For air navigation, a Decca Flight Log Display, figure 3226c, is available when an automatic system is installed in the aircraft. This roller map display is an X-Y plotter using true coordinates and a strip map showing the exact location of the aircraft at all times.

Figure 3226b. Decca Mk 21 marine receiver (top) and Model 350 T Track Plotter (bottom).

Figure 3226c. Decca Type 966 Flight Log Display Head.

Consol

3227 Consol is a long-range radionavigation system that requires no special receiving equipment. There are stations in several European countries, but none in North America.

Signals are between 190 and 370 kHz and may be received on any LF/MF radio receiver, including most direction finders. If a loop antenna is used, the best results will be obtained by adjusting the antenna to the approximate position of maximum signal; if a communications receiver is used, the automatic gain control must be turned off. A receiver with narrowband selectivity characteristics will give the most satisfactory results under the normally prevailing conditions of atmospheric noise and other interference; the use of a beat frequency oscillator (BFO) is desirable.

Basic Principles

Hyperbolic lines, when extended, approach more and more a straight line, the asymptote. In general, at distances more than 12 times the length of the base line, the lines can be considered as straight. Consol has a very short base line, roughly 2½ miles,

and is sometimes referred to as a "collapsed hyperbolic" system. The system must *not* be used at distances *less than* 25 miles from the transmitting station; beyond this, the lines are, for all practical purposes, straight and are used to obtain a bearing with respect to the mid-point of the base line.

Using Consol

Consol bearings are derived from a count of dots and dashes received; this determines an LOP within a sector roughly 15° wide. Charts are available with Consol lines overprinted for various stations and dot-dash counts, or bearings can be taken from tables in DMAHTC Pub. No. 117A, see figure 3227a. Consol bearings have a maximum accuracy along the perpendicular bisector of the base line through the three transmitting antennas; accuracy decreases as the base-line extension is approached. Useful coverage is thus limited to two areas, each of about 140° extent; see figure 3227b.

During periods of low interference levels, ranges over the sea of 1,000 miles by day and 1,200 miles by night may normally be expected about 90 percent of the time. (If Consol bearings are to be plotted on a Mercator chart, they must first be cor-

Count of dashes	True bearings from station											
0	035.6	057.0	077.0	098.4	127.4	186.6	215.6	237.0	257.0	278.4	307.4	006.6
1	035.4	056.8	076.8	098.2	127.1	186.9	215.8	237.2	257.2	278.6	307.7	006.3
2	035.2	056.7	076.7	098.0	126.7	187.3	216.0	237.3	257.3	278.8	308.1	005.9
3	035.0	056.5	076.5	097.9	126.4	187.6	216.1	237.6	257.5	279.0	308.4	005.6
4	034.8	056.3	076.3	097.7	126.1	187.9	216.3	237.7	257.7	279.2	308.8	005.2
5	034.6	056.2	076.2	097.5	125.8	188.2	216.5	237.8	257.8	279.4	309.1	004.9
6	034.4	056.0	076.0	097.3	125.4	188.6	216.7	238.0	258.0	279.6	309.5	004.5
7	034.2	055.8	075.8	097.1	125.1	188.9	216.9	238.2	258.2	279.8	309.8	004.2
8	034.0	055.6	075.7	096.9	124.8	189.2	217.1	238.3	385.4	280.0	310.2	003.8
54	024.3	047.7	068.0	088.4	112.5	201.5	225.6	256.0	266.3	289.7		
55	024.1	047.5	067.8	088.2	112.3	201.7	225.8	246.2	266.5	289.9		
56	023.9	047.4	067.7	088.1	112.0	202.0	225.9	246.3	266.6	290.1		
57	023.7	047.2	067.5	087.9	111.8	202.2	226.1	246.5	266.8	290.3		
58	023.4	047.0	067.3	087.7	111.5	202.5	226.3	246.7	267.0	290.6		
59	023.2	046.8	067.2	087.5	111.3	202.7	226.5	246.8	267.2	290.8		
60	023.0	046.7	067.0	087.3	111.0	203.0	226.7	247.0	267.3	291.0		

Figure 3227a. Consol dash count to bearing conversion table (extract).

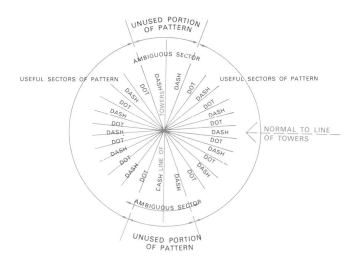

Figure 3227b. Polar diagram of Consol pattern.

rected for the great-circle path that the signals have followed; a correction table for each station is included in Pub. No. 117, see figure 3227c). In general, when ground waves are received, the error over water does not exceed about one-third degree along the perpendicular to the base line, nor about two-thirds of a degree at an angle to the perpendicular. Stated in linear units, this is an error of about 1 mile for each 180 miles from the station along the perpendicular, and for each 90 miles along the bearing line 60° from the perpendicular. This error can usually be reduced considerably by taking a number of readings and getting an average bearing. (A wide variation in successive counts is an indication of sky wave-ground wave interference. These bearings should be used with great caution, or disregarded altogether.)

While Consol cannot be considered a precision system, it is suitable for ocean navigation off the European continent and can be quite useful in some special situations, such as for ships approaching the Straits of Gibraltar from the west, and for ships operating in the western Mediterranean. Bearings should be used with increasing caution as the proximity of possible danger becomes greater. Errors may be expected to be greater at night.

Omnirange Navigation

3228 An aircraft navigation system, VHF Omni-directional Range, or "Omni" for short, has some application to marine navigation. As the name indicates, it operates in the very high frequency band between 108 and 118 MHz. Omni signals are, as the name also indicates, radiated in an all-around pattern and enable the user to get a highly precise bearing on the transmitting station.

A special Omni receiver (quite small and light-weight, but not inexpensive) is required; its operation is quite simple. A direct reading is shown on the face of the indicator, together with an indication of whether it is "To" or "From" the station. The course may be set into the receiver and it will then show any deviation to the right or left.

Ranges are quite limited for surface vessels due to the use of VHF frequencies (line of sight plus a small percentage for bending over the horizon). Although Omni stations are located for their use-fulness to aircraft, many of them will be found close enough to the coastline that they can be received at sea. Omni is thus most useful for "landfall navigation" or obtaining a line of position during coastal passages. (There are, however, many

7510.   Stavanger (LEC).   58°37′32″N., 5°37′49″E.
    FREQ.: 319 kHz. A1.   POWER: 650 W
    CHARACTERISTIC SIGNAL: Call sign 4.5 sec., long dash 19.2 sec., silent 2.5 sec., keying cycle 30 sec., silent 3.0 sec. Total time 40 sec.
    HOURS OF TRANSMISSION: Continuous.
    REMARKS: Coverage areas – 350° to 140° and 170° to 320°. Bearing of line of aerials: 336°59′20″. Distance between aerials: 8,885 f.

7510.1   Stavanger Consol Station—Conversion Table

Difference of longitude	Latitude of Observer																		
	0°	5°	10°	15°	20°	25°	30°	35°	40°	45°	50°	55°	60°	65°	70°	75°	80°	85°	90°
0	0.0	0.0	0.0	0.0	0.0	0.0	0.0	0.0	0.0	0.0	0.0	0.0	0.0	0.0	0.0	0.0	0.0	0.0	0.0
5	1.9	1.9	2.0	2.0	2.0	2.1	2.1	2.1	2.1	2.1	2.1	2.1	2.1	2.1	2.1	2.0	1.9	1.7	0.0
10	3.8	3.9	4.0	4.0	4.1	4.1	4.2	4.2	4.2	4.2	4.2	4.2	4.3	4.3	4.2	4.0	3.8	3.4	0.0
15	5.7	5.8	5.9	6.0	6.1	6.2	6.3	6.3	6.3	6.4	6.4	6.4	6.4	6.4	6.2	6.0	5.7	5.1	0.0
75	31.1	31.7	32.2	32.6	32.9	33.2	33.5	33.6	33.7	33.7	33.6	33.5	33.1	32.6	31.8	30.7	29.0	26.6	0.0
80	33.6	34.2	34.7	35.1	35.5	35.8	36.0	36.2	36.2	36.2	36.1	35.9	35.5	34.9	34.1	32.8	30.8	27.3	0.0
85	36.2	36.8	37.3	37.7	38.1	38.4	38.6	38.8	38.8	38.8	38.6	38.3	37.9	37.2	36.3	34.9	32.8	28.9	0.0
90	38.8	39.5	40.0	40.5	40.8	41.1	41.3	41.4	41.4	41.4	41.2	40.8	40.3	39.6	38.6	37.0	34.7	30.6	0.0

Corrections to be *added* to the Great Circle bearing to obtain the Mercator bearing when the observer is to the East of the station and *subtracted* when the observer is to the West of the station.

Figure 3227c. Radio bearing conversion table for a specific Consol station (typical).

stretches of coastal waters without Omni coverage.)

The Use of Radionavigation Systems

3229   A navigator must be knowledgeable as to which radionavigation systems are available in the waters traveled by his vessel—their capabilities and limitations. He must be able to efficiently use all equipment fitted on his ship for the reception of the signals of such systems, but he must not develop a dependence on the availability and accuracy of any system. Radionavigation systems may become unavailable or ineffective due to loss of ship's power, propagation irregularities, equipment malfunction, or other causes. It is essential that a navigator be skilled in dead reckoning, piloting, and celestial navigation. He must not place his reliance solely on radionavigation systems; he must be able to navigate successfully with the basic tools of the trade—compass and sextant. In the words of the Bible, he must know "the way of a ship in the midst of the sea."

Chapter 33

Omega Navigation System

Introduction

3301 The *Omega Navigation System* is similar to Loran only in that it employs hyperbolic techniques. It uses much lower frequencies that permit wider coverage with fewer transmitters, and a different method for matching the signals from various stations—the cost, lesser precision and accuracy in the positions obtained than with Loran-C. The fundamental principles that underlie Omega date back to the late 1940s, but many years of development and refinement were required before practical implementation could begin. Experimental transmissions began in 1955, but the full system became operational only in 1982.

Omega was developed by the U.S. Navy to provide a worldwide, all-weather positioning system for ships, aircraft, and submarines, both surfaced and submerged, with a nominal accuracy of four miles (7.4 km) for 95 percent of all fixes. Expansion of the Loran-C system was not feasible due to the very large number of stations that would have to be built and operated. Now under the control of the Omega Navigation System Operations Detail (ONSOD) at U.S. Coast Guard Headquarters, in typical situations the system has a fix accuracy of one mile by day and two miles by night.

The Omega electronic navigation system is also currently used by many non-naval vessels, from small yachts to the largest of tankers.

The Omega System

3302 Omega is a long-range (10,000 mi.), shore-based, very low frequency (VLF) navigation system that operates between 10 and 14 kHz. It involves the use of shore-based transmitters, special Omega receivers, propagation correction tables, and special charts or plotting sheets (or lattice tables that permit plotting on conventional charts).

Omega is a global system of eight transmitting stations; two of them are located on U.S. soil, while the other six are operated in cooperation with partner countries. Each station has two transmitters and either an antenna tower approximately 1,400 feet (425 m) high or a valley-span antenna typically 10,000 feet (3,050 m) in length; each station radiates 10 kW on all transmitted frequencies. The stations are carefully sited so that a user will be able to receive signals from at least three stations; normally from four to as many as six stations will be received. This multiple reception will result in an even greater number of signal pairs, each of which provides a line of position. LOPs can thus be selected for optimum crossing angles. (Any two signals may be used as a pair; there are no "master" and "secondary" stations as with Loran-C.) The availability of signals from a number of transmitters also does much to ensure that at least a minimum number of pairs are available even at times of unfavorable propagation conditions. Theoretically, the system provides full global coverage, but economic and political considerations have resulted in transmitter locations that are somewhat less than ideal, and consequently a few limited areas of poor or no signal reception.

Omega receivers are characterized by simplicity of operation, ease of use of the information obtained, simple and compact installation, and acceptable cost. They are so designed that almost any marine navigator with a minimum of training can obtain a fix in a few minutes. An Omega receiver, once set, will continually display a series of lane values, or numbers, on its panel indicator. These numbers roughly correspond to the lines of position on an Omega plotting chart.

A marine navigator records the lane values displayed by his receiver and applies the proper correction data as obtained from the appropriate Propagation Correction Tables (if the corrections have not already been entered into the receiver); see article 3307. He then plots the information on an Omega chart or plotting sheet to establish his ship's position. Most Omega receivers now include internal coordinate conversion with direct display of position in latitude and longitude.

Omega signals can be received out to maximum usable ranges of 4,000 to 10,000 miles from each transmitter, depending upon the bearing of the receiver from the transmitter and favorable propagation conditions. Shorter ranges can be expected at reception points west of stations located near the magnetic equator. Signals are also severely attenuated when a propagation path crosses land that is overlaid with a thick sheet of ice, such as Greenland or Antarctica.

System Description

3303 Omega is a hyperbolic radionavigation system using phase-difference measurements of continuous wave (CW) radio signals. These VLF signals can be transmitted over great distances; only six transmitting stations make the system available in nearly all parts of the globe, with two other stations for redundancy and coverage during repair of an inoperative station. (Each Omega station is assigned a specific month of the year in which to perform nonemergency maintenance that requires off-air time to accomplish. Stations will not be out of operation the entire month, as maintenance is planned to keep "down" time at an absolute minimum; notification of off-air periods are promulgated four to six weeks before the event.)

Omega differs from most other hyperbolic systems, such as Loran, in that it uses a phase-difference technique, rather than a time-difference principle. (Loran-C uses cycle matching, but this is merely for a more precise measurement of time differences. Decca uses phase-comparison techniques, but it is on higher frequencies and is a relatively short-range system.)

The basic Omega measurement is the phase difference of 10.2 kHz signals transmitted from two stations. (As will be seen later, the various Omega stations transmit in sequence rather than continuously. As it is received, each signal is compared with an internal reference oscillator, with these measurements being stored internally for subsequent comparison with other signals, grouped in various pairs.) The phase difference of a station pair yields one hyperbolic line of position (article 3110). A fix can be obtained by using additional LOPs obtained from further phase-difference measurements made on the signals of other pairs of transmitters. At VLF frequencies, signal transmission is reliable, and the velocity of propagation is predictable with errors of only a few microseconds.

The wavelength of the 10.2 kHz signal is approximately 16 miles; phase readings repeat twice for each wavelength or once for every eight miles (figure 3303a). The intervals between zero phase-difference readings are called *lanes*. Along a base line between two stations the lane is eight miles wide; this gradually increases away from the base line to approximately 12 miles. A specific phase difference establishes an LOP *within one* (any one) of these lanes; the proper lane must be known. The counters on the phase indicators on the ship's receiver are set at the beginning of a voyage, and subsequently count the numbers of lanes traversed.

As the hyperbolic lines represent the locus of points at which the differences in the distances from the transmitting stations are equal, and as these distances are measured in units of time representing distances traveled by the radio waves, the relative times of the transmission of signals from all Omega stations must be determined with the utmost precision and accuracy. Each Omega station transmits in a fixed sequence with the length of the transmission in each ten-second period varying between 0.9, 1.0, 1.1, and 1.2 seconds from station to station; these differences aid in the identification of the specific Omega transmitting station. In addition to broadcasting a continuous-wave (no modulation) signal on the basic 10.2 kHz frequency, each Omega station also transmits on three other navigational frequencies, 11.05, 11.33, and 13.6 kHz. The radio frequencies and the timing of the transmissions are governed by extremely accurate cesium frequency standards (four at each station) that are checked and synchronized by reference to the U.S. Naval Observatory Master Clock. (The UTC leap-second adjustments, discussed in article 2209, are *not* made to the Omega time epoch, and "Omega time" may be as much as 15 or more seconds different from UTC.)

The older navigation systems use pulses emitted in the required time relationship, as in Loran, or as in Decca, continuous harmonically related carrier frequencies in which the phase relationship conveys the time information. With a pulse system, all

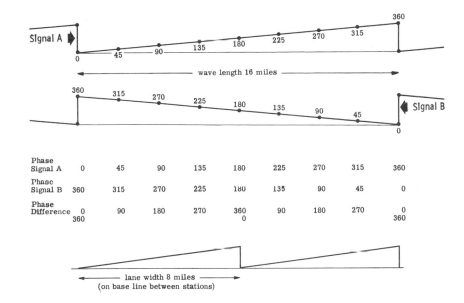

Figure 3303a. Omega 10.2 kHz phase difference measurement.

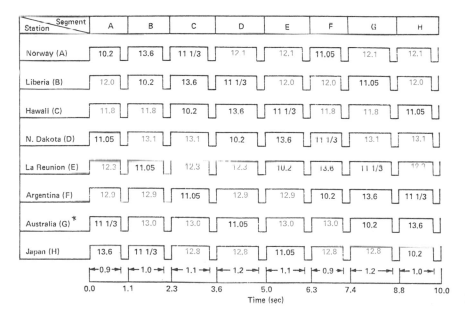

Station	Segment	A	B	C	D	E	F	G	H
Norway (A)		10.2	13.6	11 1/3	12.1	12.1	11.05	12.1	12.1
Liberia (B)		12.0	10.2	13.6	11 1/3	12.0	12.0	11.05	12.0
Hawaii (C)		11.8	11.8	10.2	13.6	11 1/3	11.8	11.8	11.05
N. Dakota (D)		11.05	13.1	13.1	10.2	13.6	11 1/3	13.1	13.1
La Reunion (E)		12.3	11.05	12.3	12.3	10.2	13.6	11 1/3	12.3
Argentina (F)		12.9	12.9	11.05	12.9	12.9	10.2	13.6	11 1/3
Australia (G) *		11 1/3	13.0	13.0	11.05	13.0	13.0	10.2	13.6
Japan (H)		13.6	11 1/3	12.8	12.8	11.05	12.8	12.8	10.2

0.9	1.0	1.1	1.2	1.1	0.9	1.2	1.0
0.0 1.1	2.3	3.6	5.0	6.3	7.4	8.8	10.0

Time (sec)

Figure 3303b. Omega signal format.

Loran stations in a network can transmit on the same radio frequency at different times. However, when continuous carriers are employed, the frequencies used by the various stations must differ, so that they can be identified while retaining a common basis in time. This is why a harmonic relationship is necessary.

Omega to some extent combines both methods. Measurements are made of the relative phase of bursts of a steady carrier transmitted on the same radio frequency at different times. The use of a single frequency is advantageous, since phase shifts within the receiver are of no concern, being the same for all signals. Aside from the very low frequency employed, the chief distinction between

Omega and the older systems is the time-sharing of continuous carrier bursts of relative phase. Each Omega station transmits in a fixed sequence pattern, so that only one station is transmitting on each navigational frequency at any time. Eight stations share a ten-second period, and the receiver can identify each station by its place in the sequence as well as by the exact time duration of its signal; see the portion of figure 3303b relating to 10.2 kHz transmissions. Note that when one station is transmitting on 10.2 kHz in its assigned time slot, a second station is transmitting on 13.6 kHz, a third on 11.33 kHz, and a fourth on 11.05 kHz.

When not transmitting on one of the four frequencies listed above, each Omega station sends out a signal on a specific additional frequency for purposes not related to conventional navigation. These "unique" frequencies are shown as blue numbers in figure 3303b; they can be ignored by navigators at sea.

In addition, Omega differs from other hyperbolic navigation systems in that any two stations from which signals can be received may be paired to furnish a line of position. A navigator may therefore select stations whose signals will yield lines of position crossing nearly at right angles. This geometric excellence, coupled with the range of choices, results in an accuracy in positioning that varies little with geographical location.

In the Omega system, the transmitting stations are located approximately 6,000 miles from one another. With a network of eight stations, at least four stations are available to a navigator at most points on earth, thus yielding a minimum of six possible lines of position. If six stations could be received, he would have a theoretical choice of 15 LOPs.

The U.S.S.R. operates a radionavigation system much like Omega; this consists of three stations using two sets of three frequencies each in the VLF band between 11.9 and 15.6 kHz.

Lane Identification

3304   As discussed above, the measurement of the difference in phase of two received signals, which were synchronized in time at the transmitting station, produces a line of position that can be positively identified with a lane one-half the wavelength in width (figure 3304a). It is therefore mandatory to know in which lane the vessel is located. The Omega receiver provides a counter, or printout, to furnish the navigator with data on the number of lanes that have been crossed since the start of the counter. Lane identification therefore presents no serious problems for vessels, *provided* there is no interruption in the continuous receipt of Omega signals.

An ambiguity in lane identification can be resolved by using the transmission from two stations on a second Omega frequency, 13.6 kHz. This frequency has a wavelength that is exactly one-third shorter than that of the basic frequency, 10.2 kHz. The phase synchronization is adjusted so that one contour of the higher frequency coincides with one contour of the lower frequency. Every *fourth* 13.6 kHz contour will now coincide with every third 10.2 kHz contour, thus establishing a pattern of broad lanes, each extending over three lanes of the basic 10.2 kHz pattern, or over a width of 24 to 32 miles, as determined by lane width. This is illustrated in figure 3304b.

It can thus be determined from the difference of the two phase indications in which of the three 10.2 kHz lanes forming the broad lane the observer is located. If the difference is less than one-third hertz, he is in the first lane; if between one-third and two-thirds, he is in the middle lane; and if between two-thirds and one hertz, he is in the third lane.

A third frequency of 11.33 kHz is also transmitted by all Omega stations; see figure 3303b. The difference between the frequency of this signal and that of the basic 10.2 kHz signal—1.13 kHz—provides for lane ambiguity resolution to 72–96

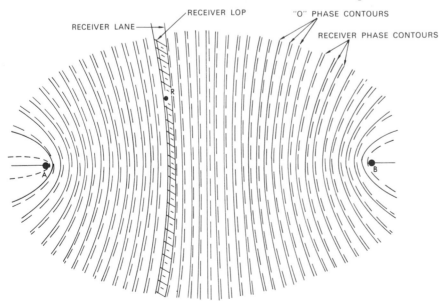

Figure 3304a. Omega lane pattern.

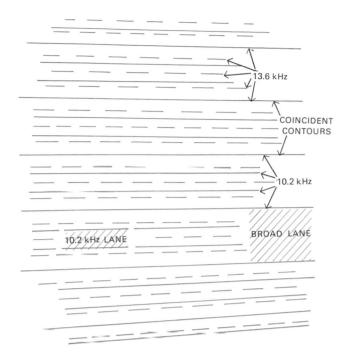

Figure 3304b. Principles of lane resolution.

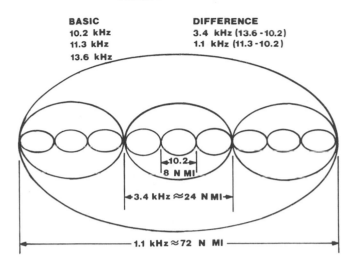

Figure 3304c. Lane resolution relationship using three frequencies.

miles; see figure 3304c. The fourth navigational frequency of 11.05 kHz extends lane resolution out to 288–432 miles and is used primarily in air navigation.

Many Omega navigation receivers can receive only the 10.2 kHz basic signals. With these, an accurate DR track must be maintained, and it may be necessary to employ celestial or other electronic navigation systems to restart an Omega lane count if an interruption to continuous tracking occurs. (Positional accuracy is the same whether one, three, or four frequencies are being received, provided proper lane identification is known; the additional frequencies serve only to resolve questions of lane identification.) In more sophisticated receivers, provisions are made for resolving lane ambiguities and deriving a fix without prior knowledge of position.

Omega Charts

3305 The Defense Mapping Agency Hydrographic/Topographic Center publishes many Omega Plotting Charts at a scale of 1:2,187,400. These are in the 7600/7700 series of chart numbers and are listed in the DMA Chart Catalog, Part 2, Volume X; this publication contains an outline chart of the world indicating graphically the coverage of each chart and areas of two-mile, four-mile, and greater-than-four-mile fix accuracy. (Chart 5132 also shows Omega coverage.) Additionally,

many standard nautical charts for various parts of the world that are overprinted with Omega lines of position are printed by DMAHTC at scales of 1:300,000 and smaller; these are identified in the DMA Chart Catalog, Part 2 regional volumes by the suffix "(Omega)."

The National Ocean Service publishes some nautical charts of U.S. coasts with Omega lines at scales of roughly 1:300,000 to 1:1,200,000 (These generally also have Loran-C lines on a duplicate chart on the reverse side.)

Each Omega chart has two or more sets of lines representing constant phase differences of station pairs (see figure 3305). This permits a navigator to select those that will give him suitable intersection angles—90° for two lines, 120° for three lines, etc. Lines are printed in different colors for greater ease of identification; they are designated by the letters of the station pair and the lane numbers (three or four digits). Lines of position are normally printed for every third lane of any pair. In the margin of the chart, there will be a listing of the Omega pairs for which lines of position are shown on the chart; these are color coded similarly to the printed lines. The station pairs are listed in order of probable best reception.

Since the base line between Omega stations is on the order of 6,000 miles, charted LOPs show relatively little curvature. In some areas, as near a base line bisector, these LOPs may become essentially straight. This characteristic simplifies the navigator's job, particularly in interpolating for percentage of lane between two Omega lines.

Figure 3305. Omega chart showing linear interpolator (extract).

Omega is primarily a long-range radionavigation system and has limitations at relatively close-in ranges. These result from propagation complications as well as the excess curvature of lines. On Omega charts, lines of position are shown dashed within 450 miles of a transmitter. Difficulties can be avoided by using distant pairs of transmitters; for example, a ship near Honolulu should use signals from the Norway and North Dakota stations, but not those from the transmitter in Hawaii.

Only the basic 10.2 kHz frequency is used for the lines printed on Omega plotting charts and overprinted marine charts. LOPs for other frequencies can be derived from this basic frequency but are seldom needed.

Omega Position Tables

3306 Omega charting coordinate tables (called "lattice" tables) are simply Omega lines of position in tabular form. If a navigator so desires, or if he lacks an Omega chart, he may simply plot his Omega information directly onto a conventional chart or plotting sheet. A separate table is used for each station pair for each specific geographic area. These tables are published by DMAHTC as part of the Pub. No. 224 series; a lattice table for a specific pair might be numbered Pub. No. 224(109)A-G

where the "1" specifies the frequency for which the table was prepared (10.2 kHz), "09" indicates the coverage area, and "A-G" identifies the paired stations A and G. (The 26 "Omega areas" are unique to this navigational system and should not be confused with other "areas" or "regions" used with marine navigational charts and publications.) There are more than 260 lattice tables listed in DMA Chart Catalog, Part 2, Volume X; an average of six tables are available for each Omega area.

Each page of an Omega charting table has a number of columns of geographic coordinates for the specific Omega lane value shown at the heading of that column, see figure 3306. In most instances, the readings are tabulated at intervals of one degree of latitude (or longitude). Each column lists all the points, in latitude and longitude, required to plot an Omega line of position; latitude always appears to the left of longitude. Omega hyperbolic lines of position are so nearly straight lines, except when near to a transmitter, that the tabulated points can be joined by straight lines. The Omega lattice tables also include a table of bearings to each of the stations concerned from various points, defined in terms of latitude and longitude.

Since Omega lines of position from each pair of stations fan out in all directions, it is sometimes

T Lat	A-C 985	Δ	A-C 986	Δ	A-C 987	Δ	A-C 988	Δ	A-C 989	Δ	T Long
20 N	96 44.2W	124	96 56.6W	124	97 09.0W	124	97 21.5W	124	97 34.0W	124	
21 N	97 17.2W	125	97 29.7W	124	97 42.1W	125	97 54.7W	125	98 07.2W	125	
22 N	97 50.9W	125	98 03.5W	125	98 16.1W	126	98 28.7W	125	98 41.2W	125	
23 N	98 25.6W	125	98 38.2W	126	98 50.9W	126	99 03.5W	126	99 16.2W	126	
24 N	99 01.1W	127	99 13.8W	127	99 26.6W	127	99 39.3W	127	99 52.0W	127	
25 N	99 37.6W	127	99 50.4W	128	100 03.3W	128	100 16.0W	127	100 28.8W	128	
26 N	100 15.1W	128	100 28.1W	129	100 41.0W	128	100 53.8W	128	101 06.7W	129	
27 N	100 53.8W	130	101 06.9W	129	101 19.8W	129	101 32.7W	129	101 45.8W	130	
28 N	101 33.7W	131	101 46.8W	130	101 59.8W	130	102 12.9W	131	102 26.0W	131	
29 N	102 14.8W	132	102 28.0W	132	102 41.2W	131	102 54.3W	132	103 07.6W	132	
30 N	102 57.3W	133	103 10.5W	132	103 23.8W	133	103 37.2W	133	103 50.6W	133	
31 N	103 41.2W	134	103 54.6W	134	104 08.0W	134	104 21.5W	135	104 35.1W	134	
32 N	104 26.6W	135	104 40.2W	136	104 53.9W	136	105 07.5W	136	105 21.1W	135	
33 N	105 13.8W	137	105 27.6W	137	105 41.4W	138	105 55.2W	137	106 09.0W	137	
34 N	106 02.9W	138	106 16.8W	139	106 30.8W	139	106 44.8W	139	106 58.7W	139	
35 N	106 53.8W	141	107 08.0W	141	107 22.2W	141	107 36.3W	141	107 50.5W	141	
36 N	107 47.0W	143	108 01.4W	144	108 15.8W	143	108 30.2W	143	108 44.6W	143	
37 N	108 42.6W	145	108 57.2W	145	109 11.8W	145	109 26.4W	146	109 41.0W	146	
38 N	109 40.7W	148	109 55.6W	148	110 10.4W	148	110 25.3W	148	110 40.2W	149	
39 N	110 41.6W	151	110 56.8W	151	111 11.9W	151	111 27.0W	151	111 42.3W	152	
40 N	111 45.7W	154	112 01.1W	154	112 16.5W	154	112 32.1W	155	112 47.6W	155	
41 N	112 53.1W	157	113 08.9W	158	113 24.7W	158	113 40.6W	158	113 56.5W	159	
42 N	114 04.3W	161	114 20.5W	162	114 36.8W	162	114 53.1W	162	115 09.4W	163	
43 N	115 19.8W	166	115 36.5W	166	115 53.2W	167	116 09.9W	167	116 26.7W	168	
	43 30.5N	-126	43 17.8N	-126	43.05.2N	-127	42 52.4N	-127	42 39.7N	-127	116 W
	44 14.3N	-123	44 01.9N	-123	43 49.6N	-123	43 37.2N	-124	43 24.7N	-124	117 W
	44 56.1N	-120	44 44.0N	-120	44 31.9N	-121	44 19.8N	-121	44 07.6N	-121	118 W
	45 36.0N	-117	45 24.2N	-118	45 12.3N	-118	45 00.5N	-118	44 48.6N	-119	119 W

Figure 3306. Omega lattice table (extract).

necessary to tabulate the latitude at which the lines intersect meridians; at other times it is necessary to tabulate the longitudes at which the lines intersect parallels of latitude.

For the entire area of coverage, points are listed at intervals of one degree of latitude or longitude from the equator to 60° of latitude, north and south. From 60° latitude to 80° latitude the interval is one degree of latitude or two degrees of longitude; from 80° to 90° latitude the interval of listing is one degree of latitude or five degrees of longitude.

Close to the transmitting stations, where the lines curve sharply, additional points are inserted at intervals of 15 minutes of arc. The spacing of the points has been chosen so that the navigator may safely use a straight line between any two adjacent tabulated points. Within approximately 20 miles of a transmitting station, the curvature of the lines is excessive, and the navigator is cautioned that straight-line segments will introduce appreciable errors. A plot of three consecutive points will always show the amount of curvature present and indicate the true line.

Additional information on the construction of the tables, and their use in navigation without a special Omega chart, will be found in the front pages of each publication.

Propagation Correction Tables

3307 Basic to the operation of the Omega navigation system is the stability of the propagation characteristics of VLF radio waves over great distances, plus the fact that the slight changes that do occur can generally be predicted quite accurately. The VLF Omega frequencies radiate from the transmitting stations to the receiver along the normal "channel" between the earth's surface and the ionosphere. As the ionosphere changes its height from day to night, the path of wave travel varies, and the apparent signal speed also varies from day to night; periods of about two hours at morning and evening twilight show rapid and considerable changes in propagation characteristics. The Omega charts are constructed using standard daytime phase velocity of propagation. Propagation corrections (PPCs) must be applied to each Omega receiver reading to compensate for such deviations from standard conditions. PPCs are calculated in advance and are published in tables for transmitting stations; these tables are part of the DMAHTC Pub. No. 224 series. A specific correction table might be designated Pub. No. 224 (109-C)G, where the "1" indicates its applicability to the 10.2 kHz signals and "09" identifies the area as for lattice tables, the "C" indicates that it is a propagation correction table, and "G" specifies the Omega station concerned. (A figure 3 for frequency would indicate corrections for 13.6 kHz signals.) A brief introduction, which also describes the arrangement and application of the corrections together with illustrative examples, precedes the tabular data within each PPC table. An extract is shown in figure

LOCATION 16.0 N   64.0 W
STATION A   NORWAY

DATE	00	01	02	03	04	05	06	07	08	09	10	GMT 11	12	13	14	15	16	17	18	19	20	21	22	23	24
1-15 JAN	-76	-78	-78	-78	-78	-78	-79	-80	-79	-76	-42	13	-7	-13	-8	-8	-10	-15	-23	-32	-44	-59	-72	-76	-76
16-31 JAN	-74	-76	-76	-76	-76	-76	-76	-78	-76	-70	-37	10	-9	-10	-4	-5	-6	-12	-18	-26	-37	-52	-65	-73	-74
1-14 FEB	-76	-78	-78	-78	-78	-78	-78	-75	-69	-63	-23	4	-8	0	1	0	-1	-7	-14	-23	-32	-50	-66	-74	-76
15-29 FEB	-73	-76	-76	-75	-75	-75	-74	-66	-58	-50	-12	4	-3	5	6	5	5	0	-7	-16	-28	-43	-62	-71	-73
1-15 MAR	-92	-93	-92	-92	-93	-91	-85	-76	-70	-66	-18	-14	-11	-4	1	1	-2	-9	-19	-29	-40	-59	-78	-89	-92
16-31 MAR	-87	-91	-89	-89	-88	-83	-74	-68	-59	-49	-8	-12	-5	1	6	5	5	-1	-10	-21	-33	-49	-71	-83	-87
1-15 APR	-85	-87	-86	-86	-81	-74	-67	-63	-51	-39	-6	-10	-3	0	6	5	2	3	-2	-10	-21	-38	-63	-78	-85
16-30 APR	-78	-78	-80	-78	-69	-66	-58	-50	-37	-28	-4	-7	2	3	7	13	13	13	6	0	-11	-21	-51	-70	-78
1-15 MAY	-78	-83	-83	-83	-74	-70	-55	-53	-39	-27	-11	-9	0	3	5	8	8	8	5	-2	-12	-26	-48	-70	-78
16-31 MAY	-75	-82	-82	-82	-79	-68	-57	-48	-36	-21	-9	-4	3	6	7	8	8	8	6	3	-5	-20	-44	-66	-75
1-15 JUN	-71	-75	-77	-79	-74	-62	-53	-40	-28	-13	-1	0	7	9	11	11	10	11	12	10	5	-10	-36	-61	-71
16-30 JUN	-67	-74	-77	-76	-73	-62	-52	-42	-29	-13	-3	1	6	8	9	9	8	7	5	-3			-31	-58	-67
1-15 JUL	-54	-61	-59	-59	-59	-53	-37	-32	-21	2	11	11	12	16	18	18	17	15	16	14	12	12	-4	-42	-54
16-31 JUL	-57	-64	-64	-63	-62	-57	-45	-38	-26	-5	8	8	10	12	14	15	15	14	13	11	8	9	-6	-43	-57
1-15 AUG	-72	-77	-78	-77	-69	-65	-60	-52	-42	-17	0	-3	-1	4	5	5	5	4	1	-3	-7	-8	-19	-58	-72
16-31 AUG	-71	-78	-78	-74	-65	-64	-60	-51	-41	-17	1	0	1	4	7	5	5	5	1	-4	-9	-14	-25	-59	-71
1-15 SEP	-70	-74	-74	-72	-68	-64	-60	-52	-39	-15	7	4	6	8	9	10	10	7	2	-6	-11	-19	-30	-60	-70
16-30 SEP	-73	-76	-76	-73	-73	-69	-63	-57	-43	-17	10	5	7	9	11	12	9	6	0	-7	-14	-23	-36	-65	-73
1-15 OCT	-81	-81	-77	-79	-79	-75	-70	-59	-48	-24	11	4	6	9	10	9	6	2	-3	-10	-18	-26	-50	-75	-81
16-31 OCT	-82	-82	-81	-80	-81	-81	-75	-65	-56	-31	10	4	3	7	9	8	4	-1	-6	-12	-21	-30	-67	-78	-82
1-15 NOV	-78	-78	-79	-79	-79	-79	-76	-70	-64	-38	16	8	1	6	7	7	3	-1	-5	-12	-23	-42	-71	-79	-78
16-30 NOV	-73	-74	-75	-76	-77	-75	-74	-74	-69	-47	11	18	0	5	6	6	4	1	-5	-12	-26	-47	-67	-73	-73
1-15 DEC	-72	-74	-74	-74	-77	-76	-75	-74	-72	-57	-5	25	4	2	6	6	6	0	-5	-19	-35	-53	-69	-69	-72
16-31 DEC	-72	-73	-73	-72	-71	-71	-71	-71	-75	-65	-24	29	7	2	2	4	4	-2	-9	-18	-34	-53	-66	-72	-72

Figure 3307. Omega propagation correction table (extract).

3307; a graph from this table is also shown. Such graphing is of convenience to a navigator when remaining in the same general vicinity for some time.

These are the only corrections that need to be applied to the receiver display in order to obtain valid readings. Some models of "automatic" Omega receivers have the capability of internally generating and applying propagation corrections from data entered on magnetic tape cassettes.

Continuing efforts are being made to refine the predicted propagation corrections through research and constant monitoring so as to develop more accurate figures. Correction tables are published in new editions when significantly improved data are determined; only the latest edition of correction and lattice tables should be used. Interim changes or corrections to the tables may be disseminated by messages on radio broadcasts of navigational warnings if they are of a magnitude to affect the safety of vessels.

Propagation Disturbances

3308 Since Omega is a phase-difference system, signal phase change characteristics must be predictable. Repeatable propagation characteristics are inherent in the VLF band used; this makes possible the correction tables described above. VLF radio propagation does, however, suffer from occasional unpredictable variations. Solar flares are responsible for the two most important anomalies: Sudden Ionospheric Disturbance (SID) and Polar Cap Absorption (PCA). SIDs are caused by flare-produced X-rays reducing the D-layer ionospheric height in the sunlit hemisphere; occurring during daylight hours only, SIDs typically last 30–60 minutes and cause LOP shifts approximately equivalent to a 4-mile error on the base line. Due to their unpredictability and short duration, real-time user notification of a SID is not practicable. PCAs result from flare-emitted protons that collect at the earth's magnetic poles and cause a reduction in the height of the D-layer. PCA events occur six to eight times a year and *only* affect signals crossing *polar* regions. They usually last several days and can cause LOP shifts equivalent to as much as 8 miles on the base line. The ONSOD provides Omega users with PCA event information in advance by means described in article 3307.

Omega Receivers

3309 To use Omega, a receiver on board a vessel must be capable of determining the phase of the Omega signals in the presence of the usual ambient noise and interference. The format of the signal permits many different modes of receiver operation, ranging from an oscilloscope display of the signal timing with manual alignment of the multiplexing function, to microprocessor-equipped receivers capable of performing all functions and presenting position in the form of geographical coordinates without external aid.

To determine position the receiver and/or operator must be able to:

Recognize the total transmitted pattern to identify the transmission of a given set of stations;

Isolate the signal components;

Determine the relative phases of the isolated signal components with accuracy;

Use the phase reading to determine a line of position.

To use a receiver without internal coordinate conversion to obtain a line of position when the approximate DR position is known, it is only necessary to read the receiver display, note the Greenwich Mean Time, and note these data on the work sheet. The appropriate correction table for the area is then entered, and the diurnal correction for the GMT and date are extracted and noted on the work sheet. This correction is added to the reading taken from the receiver display; the sum provides the required information for plotting one line of position on the Omega chart. A fix can be obtained in two or three minutes from two or more LOPs.

Figure 3309a shows a typical Navy receiver for Omega signals. Graphic recorders provide a continuous record of lane readings, and there is a built-in oscilloscope to aid in synchronization and trouble-shooting. Another Navy receiver, the AN/BRN-7 for submarines, has additional internal circuitry and can directly display position in latitude and longitude; it can receive three Omega frequencies.

Figure 3309b shows a commercial receiver that displays LOP information by a digital readout to .01 lane (1 centilane); PPCs can be pre-inserted by means of the keyboard in order that the lane readings can be used directly without further arithmetic. At the option of the navigator, a single LOP may be displayed, or up to five LOPs cycled at the rate of one every five seconds; the receiver can also feed into a paper-tape recorder for a permanent record. The receiver continuously monitors all transmitting stations, identifies each, and indicates those whose signal-to-noise ratio is adequate for use. (This receiver uses only the 10:2 kHz signals; lane ambiguity must be resolved within 4 miles.) Trackable stations are indicated by lamps on the front panel display. Warning and alarm signals operate whenever there is a malfunction or other problem.

As with Loran-C, sophisticated models of Omega receivers are available. One such set has an internal microprocessor that is loaded with data from an ordinary audio tape cassette; this includes propagation corrections, making unnecessary the use of lengthy tables for such data. An initial position

Figure 3309a. Omega Navigation System receiver as used aboard U.S. naval vessels.

Figure 3309b. Commercial model of Omega receiver.

must be entered by means of the keyboard, but the receiver will then continuously display position in latitude and longitude, and will also print out on paper tape the date, time, and geographic coordinates of the vessel at selected time intervals from one to nine times each hour. If a destination is entered using the keyboard, the unit will compute course and distance for either a rhumb-line or great-circle path; if speed is entered manually, transit time can also be calculated. After starting with the correct time, the receiver will function as a chronometer with an accuracy to within one or two seconds per year. As Omega navigation is dependent upon continuous reception of signals to avoid a loss of lane count, automatic switchover to an internal rechargeable battery occurs on any interruption of primary power, and an alarm signal is sounded.

Omega receivers pose a problem on some small craft, especially sailboats, as they must be left on continuously to maintain the lane count. The primary power drain is not great, but on a continuous basis it can have a significant effect on a boat's batteries. On some models the display can be switched off leaving the remainder of the set running; this reduces the battery drain somewhat.

Antennas for Omega receivers can be very simple in design. Vertical whip antennas, 8 to 10 feet in height, are generally used for shipboard installations. Several special types of antennas are used with aircraft receivers.

Obtaining a Fix from Omega Data

3310 The procedures for obtaining an Omega position will vary somewhat with the specific equipment being used. General procedures can be given here, but reference must be made to the receiver's instruction manual and the material in the propagation correction tables.

In all instances wherever possible, the Omega receiver should be turned on and synchronized while the vessel is at a known position, such as at a pier or in an anchorage. The pairs of transmitters that give acceptable signal strengths are then determined. The propagation corrections for each *station* are determined individually from the appropriate tables for the applicable GMT date and time. Next, the corrections for each *pair* of stations are computed from the individual values by subtracting the PPC for the second station from that for the first station; because this is *algebraic* subtraction, due regard must be given to a minus sign on either or both of the correction values. These pair values are either entered into the receiver or retained for manual application. The correct lane count is entered into the receiver for the known position; the receiver will then automatically track future lane crossings and show percent of lane for each station pair as the voyage progresses.

For each fix, the receiver is read for each pair to be used, and the corrected values are plotted on an Omega chart (or used with Omega position tables to derive geographic coordinates for plotting on a conventional chart). This process is somewhat simpler than positioning by Loran and is much faster than obtaining a fix from celestial observations.

If track is lost during the voyage for any reason, the navigator must then redetermine his position as he did in port and enter the new corrected whole lane counts for his selected station pairs. If the Omega receiver is a single frequency unit, as are most marine units, this redetermined position must be correct to within four miles. In other words, with a lane width of nominally eight miles, a navigator must know his position within half of this lane width in order to determine the proper whole lane count. If his Omega receiver is a dual-frequency unit, that is, it receives signals on both 10.2 and 13.6 kHz, an additional lane width of 24 nautical miles is provided. In this case, the navigator need only know his correct position within ±12 miles, or half of the 24-mile lane width ambiguity. If the Omega set has a capability to receive 11.33

kHz signals also, then the "known" position need only be within ±36 miles of the correct location; or within ±144 miles if all four frequencies, including 11.05 kHz, can be received and used.

Omega need not be used separately from other navigational procedures; it works well in combination with selected daily celestial observations. As Omega involves complex electronic equipment, a prudent navigator maintains his skills with the sextant and sight reduction tables.

Omega Notices and Warnings

3311 A number of methods are used to advise users of items of interest regarding the Omega system, such as off-air periods and propagation disturbances. A recorded status message, updated as changes occur, may be reached by telephone at (202) 245-0298. Similar information can also be obtained via a Western Union "Redilist" service within the United States, or via Telex (892408). If additional information is needed, an ONSOD duty officer can be reached by telephone at (202) 254-0837. All costs for telephone or teletype service must be borne by the user.

Omega status information is also disseminated by HYDROLANT and HYDROPAC messages and/or NAVAREA IV/XII warnings. Status reports are broadcast on WWV (see article 2227) at 16 minutes past each hour and on WWVH at 47 minutes past each hour. Frequencies for these broadcasts are 2.5, 5, 10, 15, and 20 MHz.

An Omega Users Guide has been prepared by ONSOD and can be purchased from the Government Printing Office; it may be available from some local sales agents for charts and navigational publications.

Omega Positional Accuracy

3312 The accuracy of an Omega position is directly related to the accuracy of the propagation correction constants. The published tables are dependent upon the accuracy of predictions, accuracies that increase with continued operation of the system. Monitoring stations build up millions of hours of data, which are analyzed by complex computational procedures to establish refinements to the predictions that were initially made on theoretical and empirical principles. Only after years of data collection and analysis—the process is termed "validation"—will it be possible to realize the true worldwide Omega system daytime accuracy of one to two miles based on one standard deviation, or 68 percent of positions within the stated limits; this may also be stated as within four miles for 95 percent of all fixes. The validation effort is scheduled for completion with a final report issued by mid-1987.

In a manner generally similar to Loran-C, the Omega system offers good "repeatability"; it is often possible to return to a previous position within ¼ mile or better.

Differential Omega

3313 The one to two miles nominal accuracy of the Omega system is adequate for the high seas, but it is not precise enough for coastal areas. Omega accuracy can be improved to approximately one-half nautical mile, or better, by the technique known as *differential Omega*. This technique is based on the principle that propagation corrections will be the same for all receivers within a local area of perhaps 100–200 miles radius. A monitor station whose location is precisely known develops highly refined values of propagation corrections on a continuous basis; these are then transmitted to ships with Omega receivers via any available radio communications link. Several different methods have been used, including modulation of a subcarrier on LF radiobeacon signals and the use of single sideband modulation on a frequency near 1.8 MHz. When these more accurate PPCs are applied to the shipboard Omega receiver, positions can be fixed to within 0.25 miles at distances of 50 miles from the monitoring station, degrading to about 0.5 miles at 200 miles distance, and 1 mile at 500 miles.

Although differential Omega is valuable for its 2:1 or better improvement in accuracy under normal operating conditions, its true worth is achieved at times of sudden ionospheric disturbances (SIDs) and polar cap disturbances (PCDs), when its accuracy is retained while that of the basic system is seriously degraded; at such times the improvement by the differential technique may be as great as 10:1.

Differential Omega also provides a further improved quality of repeatability; the PPC may change from day to day, but fresh data from the monitoring station will ensure the same degree of accuracy on successive applications.

Differential Omega is in relatively wide use in Europe—France has more than 15 such stations in operation. The United States has moved more slowly; one station is providing coverage in the Caribbean (where Loran-C coverage is inadequate and expansion of that system was found not economically justifiable) from the Punta Tuna radiobeacon in Puerto Rico.

The Future of Omega

3314 In general, the advantages and disadvantages of Omega are those of any radionavigation system. The navigator has a relatively simple, fast, and accurate method of determining his position regardless of time of day or weather conditions. On the other hand, he is entirely dependent upon complex electronic equipment, much of which is far distant and not under his control.

Omega has a specific advantage in that it is essentially a worldwide system without gaps in its coverage; thus one relatively small, lightweight, and acceptably priced piece of equipment can be used wherever a vessel travels. Another Omega advantage is that there are only eight stations in the system, and these provide considerable redundancy; a fix can normally be obtained even if one or two, or even more, of the transmitters are off the air.

Since the present Omega system provides worldwide coverage, no expansion in the number of transmitting stations is required or expected. With the advent of the Global Positioning System (see article 3414), the Omega system will continue to be used by the U.S. Navy as a back-up, and so will continue to be available to civilian users. It is likely that Omega will stay in operation until at least the year 2000.

Chapter 34   Satellite Navigation

Introduction

3401 All types of vessels can be navigated by means of radio signals received from orbiting satellites high above the earth. *Satellite Navigation* is a result of the U.S. Navy's NAVSAT program, also known as Project TRANSIT. It is a highly accurate, passive, all-weather, worldwide navigational system, suitable for subsurface and surface navigation. NAVSAT became operational for Polaris submarines in 1964 and was released for civilian use in 1967. It is widely used on major combatant vessels of the U.S. Navy and on commercial ships of the United States and many foreign nations. It is suitable for use on vessels of any size, including yachts, when it is economically justifiable; shipboard receivers and related equipment are somewhat more expensive than other systems such as Omega and Loran. Equipment for receiving NAVSAT signals is now manufactured in at least six countries and marketed in many more.

Doppler Shift

3402 The measurement of radio signals transmitted by NAVSAT is based on the Doppler shift phenomenon—the apparent change in frequency of the radio waves received when the distance between a source of radiation and a receiving station is increasing or decreasing because of the motion of either or both (see article 3101). The rate of change of frequency in either case is proportional to the velocity of approach or recession. In the NAVSAT system the source of signals is in the satellite with the receiver on board the vessel. Motions are complex as the satellite is moving in orbit, the receiver is normally moving with respect to the earth, and the earth itself is rotating in space. The frequency is

shifted upward as the satellite approaches the receiving station and shifted downward as the satellite passes and recedes. The amount of this shift depends on the exact location of the receiver with respect to the path of the satellite. Accordingly, if the satellite positions (orbits) are known, it is possible by a very exact measure of the Doppler shift in frequency to calculate the location of the receiver on earth.

The accuracy obtained by using this Doppler shift technique is possible because the quantities measured, frequency and time, can readily be determined to an accuracy of one part in a billion.

Components of the System

3403 The NAVSAT system (figure 3403a) consists of one or more satellites, (typically five in use and one spare), ground tracking stations, a computing center, an injection station, Naval Observatory time signals, and the shipboard receiver/computer.

Satellite Data

Each satellite is placed in a nominally circular polar orbit at an altitude of about 450 to 700 miles, orbiting the earth in approximately 108 minutes. Only one satellite is used at any given time to determine position. Each satellite stores data that is updated from a ground injection station approximately every twelve hours; it broadcasts the following data every two minutes:

> Fixed and variable parameters describing its own orbit, several thousand bits of data;
> A time reference.

Two frequencies, 150 and 400 MHz, are employed because the ionosphere, which is a dispersion me-

Figure 3403a. Components of the NAVSAT (Transit) navigation system.

dium, bends and also stretches radio waves, causing the satellite to seem closer than it actually is. Each frequency is somewhat differently affected, and by comparing the Doppler signals received on the two frequencies, precise allowance can be made for the ionosphere's effect on the waves. (Receivers for civilian vessels normally use only the 400 MHz signals; this results in a less expensive unit and less precision in position fixing, but still more than required for high-seas navigation.)

The data broadcast by the satellite describe its orbit as a function of time; the variable parameters are correct for the two-minute time interval for which they are transmitted and for those intervals immediately preceding and following that time period. Signals will normally be received for 10 to 15 minutes during each "pass" of a satellite within range of a vessel; this results in five to seven repetitions of the transmitted message for increased accuracy. Data is also included in each broadcast period that will allow an approximation of the orbit if there has been an interruption in the receipt of parameters. The time reference is synchronized with corrected universal time (UT1) from the Naval Observatory. A simplified block diagram of satellite functions is shown in figure 3403b.

The satellites (figure 3403c), sometimes referred to as "birds," use completely solid-state electronics; they are octagonal in shape, and have four

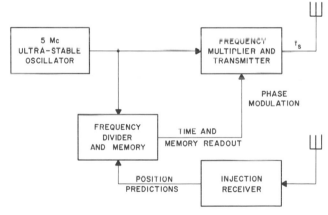

Figure 3403b. Block diagram of a Transit satellite.

windmill-like vanes that carry solar cells for recharging the batteries that power the on-board equipment. The satellites are gravity-gradient stabilized so that the directional antennas are always pointed downward, toward the earth.

Figure 3403d shows an idealized view of four satellites in orbit around the earth. (Actually there are several more in orbit, including spares and older ones that have been switched off.) This constellation of orbits forms a "birdcage" fixed in space within which the earth rotates; a NAVSAT receiver thus passes in turn under each orbit. It is obvious that an increase in the number of satellites would

Figure 3403c. Transit satellite.

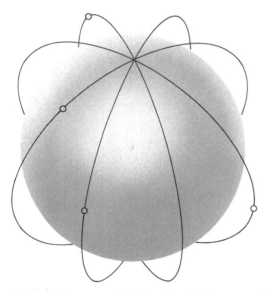

Figure 3403d. Coverage (idealized) with four satellites.

increase the frequency with which a fix could be obtained. In actuality, however, the distribution of orbits is not as ideal as shown in figure 3403d, and the interval between passes becomes irregular. Satellites have a working life of a number of years—12 to 15 in some instances—but precession is not equal among them. Orbits may get closer together or farther apart, upsetting the ideal uniform distribution; more than four satellites may be required to ensure adequate coverage. When orbits get too close, and interference arises, satellite transmitters may be switched off and new birds launched. The original Transit satellites were termed the OSCAR type. More recent ones are designated NOVA satellites; these have doubled transmitter power and other technical improvements.

Position Fixing

3404 A satellite fix can be obtained when there is a direct line from the receiver's antenna to the satellite and the "bird" is more than 15° but less than 75° above the horizon. As a general rule, each satellite will yield four fixes a day—two on successive orbits, and two more on successive orbits some 12 hours later. Ideally, a NAVSAT fix could be obtained about every 90 minutes. As a result of orbital precession, however, intervals become irregular—less than 90 minutes or more than several hours. Fixes are more frequent at higher latitudes as all orbits are closer there. On some passes a satellite may be above the horizon, but either too low or too high for an acceptable position solution.

NAVSAT users are kept informed as to the operational status of the satellites, of the insertion of new satellites into service, and the withdrawal of satellites by SPATRAK messages from the U.S. Naval Astronautics Group, Pt. Mugu, California. The status of operational and non-operational NAVSAT satellites appears quarterly in *Notices to Mariners*.

The Need for Daily Updating

3405 A planet in deep space follows a fixed path around its parent body in accordance with Newton's Laws of Motion. Its orbit is Keplerian, or perfectly elliptical, and its position can be predicted exactly for any given future instant of time. A NAVSAT satellite moves under the earth's gravitational attraction in accordance with the same laws, but as it operates at an altitude averaging about 600 miles, it is subjected to external forces that produce orbital irregularities, or *perturbations*. To make the system acceptable, these perturbations must be accurately predicted, so that the satellite's position can be determined for any instant of time.

The most important of these forces is caused by the earth's shape; satellite navigation is one of the few exceptions when the earth's true oblate spheroid shape must be taken into consideration, and it cannot be used as a "perfect sphere for all practical purposes." Additionally, the earth's gravitational field is irregular; the surface of the ocean is actually as much as 200 meters *higher* in some places than in others. These bulges and dips occur because of gravitational differences resulting from the unequal distribution of mass in the earth's interior. Smaller bulges are due to hills and valleys on the ocean floor. As small as these distances are, they are enough that they have an effect on satellite navigation computations. Figure 3405 shows the earth's gravity model, as sensed by a NAVSAT satellite. The satellite is also subject to slight atmospheric drag, as it is not operating in a complete vacuum. Other external forces that affect it are the gravitational attraction of the sun and the moon, solar photon pressure and solar wind, and electrostatic and electromagnetic forces caused by the satellite's interaction with charged particles in space and in the earth's magnetic field.

Fortunately, all the forces causing perturbations are either sufficiently constant or so localized that they can be reduced to equations that can be programmed into orbital computations.

Satellite Tracking Stations

To determine the precise orbit of each satellite in the system, ground tracking stations are established at exactly determined positions in Hawaii, Minnesota, and Maine. These stations regularly monitor the Doppler signal as a function of time. Concurrently, the U.S. Naval Observatory monitors the satellite's time signal for comparison with corrected Universal Time (UT1). The resulting information is transmitted to the computing center in California for processing.

As the satellite is essentially moving as a planet, and as the perturbations in its orbit are determined by the computer, of all the possible paths permitted by Newton's Laws only one can result in a particular curve of Doppler shift. Thus, at any instant of time, the position of the satellite relative to the

Figure 3405. Contoured plot of mean deviation of sea level.

known location of the tracking station can be determined very precisely.

The computing center, having received these data, computes an orbit for the satellite that best fits the Doppler curve obtained from the tracking stations. This orbital information is extrapolated to give satellite positions for each two minutes of UT1 for the following sixteen hours, and these data are supplied to the injection station for transmission to the satellite about every twelve hours, for storage there and retransmission to receivers on earth. The satellite is in effect a relay station that stores and transmits the data computed at ground stations.

Effect of Vessel Motion

3406 In systems such as Loran or Omega, a fix is derived from at least two station "pairs," each with its own base line. In the case of the Navy Navigation Satellite System, a receiver obtains signals from only one satellite at a time. Instead of measuring range differences from several stations simultaneously, NAVSAT measurements are between sequential positions of the satellite as it passes. This process continues for ten to fifteen minutes, during which the satellite travels some 2,400 to 3,600 miles, providing an excellent base line.

Because NAVSAT measurements are not instantaneous, motion of the vessel during the satellite pass must be considered in the fix calculation. Also, because the satellites are in constant motion relative to the earth, simple charts with lines of position are impossible to generate. Instead, each satellite transmits a set of orbital parameters, permitting its position to be calculated quite accurately as a function of time. By combining the calculated satellite positions, the range difference measurements between these positions, and information regarding motion of the vessel, an accurate position fix can be obtained. Because the calculations are both complex and extensive, a small digital computer is always a part of the receiving equipment. As satellite navigation does not yield continuous positional information (such as Omega), the computer can also be used to keep a dead-reckoning track between each satellite appearance. Speed and heading can be entered manually if not available from other sources. It is preferable, however, to use automatic speed and heading signals to describe the vessel's motion.

Vessel Motion Inputs

3407 To obtain a fix, the vessel's *estimated position* and *velocity of movement* must be entered in the computer. The geographic accuracy of the estimated position is not of great importance; however, the precision and accuracy with which the velocity can be established is important, as will be seen in the following discussion.

On ships equipped with the Ships Inertial Navigation System (SINS) described in chapter 35, the two-minute synchronization signal received from the satellite can be entered into the SINS. In some installations this signal causes the SINS to print out ship's position data coinciding with the two-minute Doppler count. In other installations the SINS general-purpose computer is used to solve the NAVSAT problem rather than employing a separate computer.

If inertial equipment is not available to supply automatic information on the ship's movement to the computer, the course and speed from the gyrocompass and EM log are inserted in the computer. This, of course, is a potential source of error, as the system, for high accuracy, requires an input of the ship's true velocity—that is, her speed and direction of travel relative to the surface of the earth. Data determined from less accurate instruments on small craft, and entered manually, will be even less precise.

Unfortunately, accurate information on the existence of a current and its set and drift are rarely available to the navigator. In round numbers, the error in a NAVSAT fix will be about 0.25 miles for every knot of unknown velocity. A velocity north (or south) error causes a considerably larger error in the fix than a velocity east (or west) error.

The computer insertions can be made in various forms. They may be in the form of an estimated position at a given time plus course and speed, estimated positions at two minute intervals, distance moved in X-Y coordinates, etc. Thus, when two estimated positions are used, the location of the second position must be accurately described relative to the first. The computer must also be fed such initial data as antenna height above or below the *geoid* as corrected for local variations, time and date, and the proper computer program; the first items are entered by use of the keyboard, the program by magnetic tape (if not internally stored).

Shipboard NAVSAT Equipment

3408 Typical NAVSAT shipboard equipment used by a navigator consists of a receiver, a computer, and an input/output unit, normally a keyboard with printer and/or video screen. Equipment used aboard a U.S. Navy ship is shown in figure 3408a. The AN/BRN-3 equipment (figure 3408b) used in fleet ballistic-missile submarines is larger

Figure 3408a. AN/SRN-9 shipboard receiver for satellite navigation.

and somewhat more complex, as both the operation and self-test capability are more fully automated. The BRN-3 is not an integrating Doppler system, as it obtains approximately one-second samples of the signal rather than integrating over a longer period. However, from the navigator's viewpoint they perform similar functions.

A typical commercial receiver is shown in figure 3408c. It is vastly smaller, lighter, and simpler to operate. Necessary data input is entered by means of a telephone-type key pad with additional keys for various functions. (Course and speed can be entered automatically from sensors or manually; variation can be inserted if a magnetic compass is used. It is desirable, but not mandatory, that course and speed remain constant during any satellite pass.) Operation is nearly fully automatic with a direct display of latitude and longitude; computations are done on an internal microprocessor. Power requirement is only 12 watts at 10–30 volts DC. (Other models draw even less, as little as 3 watts average.) There are internal self-testing capabilities to assure the navigator that his set is working properly. Many NAVSAT receivers can be programmed to compute great-circle or rhumb-line courses to a destination, with a number of intermediate waypoints if desired, plus readings of distance to go at any time and an alarm as destination or waypoint is approached. Some receivers will automatically reject a fix of low or questionable accuracy, and so indicate this in the output display. If there should be two satellites "in view" at the same time, the receiver will discriminate between them and select the one providing the best data.

As the input of the information from the satellite is not continuous, a NAVSAT receiver will calculate a steady flow of DR positions using the course and speed input data required for fix computation (plus

Figure 3408b. AN/BRN-3 equipment for submarine use of satellite navigation.

Figure 3408c. Commercial model of satellite navigation receiver.

current set and drift if internally computed or manually entered), or course and speed made good as determined from successive satellite fixes. As a general rule, considering all operational satellites, some 15–25 NAVSAT fixes will be possible each 24-hour day at most locations worldwide.

Obtaining a NAVSAT Fix

3409   The fix determined by the microprocessor in the ship's receiver is based on the Doppler frequency shift that occurs whenever the relative distance between a transmitter and a receiver is changing. Such a change occurs whenever a transmitting satellite passes within range of a radio receiver on earth, and consists of a combination of the motion of the satellite in its orbit, the motion of the vessel over the surface of the earth, and the rotation of the earth about its axis. Each of these motions contributes to the overall Doppler frequency shift in a characteristic way. An increase in frequency occurs as the satellite approaches the ship, in effect compressing the radio waves en route. The received frequency exactly equals the transmitted frequency at the point of closest satellite approach, where for an instant of time there is no relative motion directly along the vector from the satellite to the receiver. The received frequency then decreases as the satellite recedes from the ship's position, thereby expanding the radio waves between them. The shape of the curve of frequency differences and its time of reception depends both on the receiver's position on earth and the satellite's location in space. The reception of these Doppler signals and the resulting computer computations form the basis of the satellite navigation system.

Figure 3409a shows in a simplified form the relationship of time, range, and position. In the diagram, t_1 through t_5 represent the position of the satellite in orbit at the successive transmissions that occur at two-minute intervals. S_1 through S_5 represent the slant range between the satellite and the ship. p_1 through p_5 represent the position of the

ship referenced to the time at which the receiver recognizes the satellite synchronization signal $t_1 + \Delta t_1$ through $t_5 + \Delta t_5$, where Δt represents the time interval for the signal to travel from the satellite to the receiver aboard the ship.

The integral Doppler measurements (figure 3409b) are simply the count N 1–2 of the number of cycles received between $t_1 + \Delta t_1$ and $t_2 + \Delta t_2$, the count N 2–3 of the number of Doppler cycles between $t_2 + \Delta t_2$ and $t_3 + \Delta t_3$ and so on for all two-minute intervals during the satellite pass.

Four or five two-minute Doppler counts are obtained during a typical satellite pass. Each Doppler count consists of a constant plus a measured slant range difference between the receiver and the satellite at positions defined by the navigation message. The measured range differences are truly known only if the constant, but unknown, frequency difference, ΔF, between the satellite's oscillator and the receiver's reference oscillator can be determined.

To calculate a position fix, the Doppler counts and the satellite message are fed to a digital computer. The computer is also provided with an initial estimate of the ship's latitude and longitude and an estimate of the frequency difference ΔF. The computer then compares calculated range differences from the known satellite positions to the estimated ship's position with those measured by the Doppler counts, and the navigation fix is obtained by searching for and finding those values of latitude, longitude, and ΔF that make the calculated range differences agree best with the measured range differences. Because the geometry is complicated, only simple, linearized equations are used, and the computations are performed repeatedly until the solution converges. Many repetitions are normally required, and a fix is obtained within a few minutes on a typical small digital computer or internal microprocessor.

Output Data

3410   An AN/SRN-9 NAVSAT receiver output is on printed tape. Figure 3410a depicts an output of satellite orbit data, and figure 3410b illustrates a typical printout of positional information. (The explanations shown at the right in each of these illustrations are, of course, not printed on the tape.) Note that for naval use minutes of latitude and longitude are shown to four decimal places.

As seen in figure 3408c, the output from a commercial satellite navigation receiver is in alphanumeric format on a video screen or digital display with lat/long data to the nearest tenth of a minute

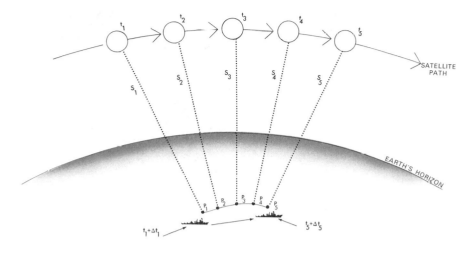

Figure 3409a. Integrated Doppler measurements of satellite signals.

Figure 3409b. Frequency variation with time as measurement of slant range changes.

	Units	Title and Symbol
+ + 1 2 8 1 . 0 8 1 5	Minutes	Time of Perigee (t_p)
+ . 4 2 7 5 8 1 7	Deg/Min	Mean Satellite Motion − 3 ($\dot{M}$ − 3)
+ 3 2 0 . 2 0 3 4	Degrees	Argument of Perigee (ϕ_p)
+ . 0 0 2 1 4 3 1	Deg/Min	Argument of Perigee Change Rate ($1\dot{\phi}1$)
+ 0 . 0 1 1 1 1 5	None	Eccentricity
+ 0 7 3 7 4 . 0 1	Kilom.	Orbit Semi Major Axis (A_0)
+ 2 1 1 8 . 4 8 2	Degrees	Right Ascension of the Ascending Node (ω_N)
− . 0 0 0 0 6 3 6	Deg/Min	Right Ascension Change Rate ($\dot{\omega}_N$)
+ 0 . 0 1 5 7 0 7	None	Cosine of the Inclination Angle
+ 1 3 4 . 2 8 0 2	Degrees	Right Ascension of Greenwich at Time of Perigee (ω_G)
+ 0 . 9 9 9 8 7 7	None	Sine of the Inclination Angle
3 9 7 7 4 9 2 .	Cycles	(Doppler Count)

Figure 3410a. Tape printout from a receiver showing satellite orbit.

+ 0 3 9 0 9 7 7		Latitude : 39°09.7782' North
8 2		
− 0 7 6 5 3 8 3	Fix Result	Longitude : 76°53.8350' West
5 0		
+ 3 1 9 6 2 1 9		Offset Frequency : 31,962.19 Cycles

Figure 3410b. Tape printout of a vessel's position.

(although internal calculations employ more decimal places). Some commercial receivers provide output data in a format suitable for direct connection to a printer.

Other possible output data include present heading and speed; course and speed made good since a given time; and time to go to destination (or next waypoint) at present speed. An internal back-up battery is often included to prevent any interruption in the accumulation of data from a temporary loss of primary power.

Time Signals

3411 The time signal transmitted by the satellite, which occurs at the two-minute mark, is accurate to better than 0.02 seconds. It may be used conveniently as an accurate chronometer check. With the NAVSAT receiver locked to the satellite signal, the two-minute signal will be heard as a "beep." Many receivers will provide a digital display of current GMT date and time plus local date and time with accuracy to nearest second.

Many receivers will indicate time since the last NAVSAT fix, and after a full set of satellite passes, the time of a number of future passes. Several models reduce total power consumption by going into a very low drain mode until shortly before the next satellite pass is expected; this is particularly advantageous on small craft with limited battery capacity.

NAVSAT Accuracy

3412 NAVSAT fixes have a high order of accuracy and repeatability. For a fixed location, a dual-frequency receiver can be expected to give a fix within 50 yards (46 m) and a single-frequency receiver to within 100 yards (91 m). As previously noted, accuracy of fix for a vessel underway is dependent upon precise and accurate knowledge of own ship's motion. Typically, a Transit fix of a moving vessel can be as accurate as 0.1 mile (185 m).

Combined Equipment

3413 A more recent development than either Loran-C, Omega, or NAVSAT is a receiver that will

Figure 3413. A receiver that combines position data from the Omega and satellite navigation systems.

operate on *two* of these systems simultaneously, *or even all three!* Typically, this is NAVSAT combined with either Omega or Loran-C. The latter systems give continuous positions better than the DR data normally carried forward from the last satellite fix; the high-accuracy NAVSAT fixes are used, when available, to make any slight adjustments needed to update the flow of information from Loran-C or Omega.

The "ultimate" equipment uses all three radio-navigation systems. NAVSAT positional information is paired with the flow of data from the other two systems where Loran-C is available in addition to Omega. As the accuracy of Loran-C is so much greater than Omega, there is little, if anything, to be gained by pairing them, except perhaps when entering or leaving a Loran-C coverage area.

GLOBAL POSITIONING SYSTEM

The GPS System

3414 A second-generation satellite navigation system is under development to replace NAVSAT—this is the *Global Positioning System,* generally referred to as *GPS* or *NAVSTAR.* When fully operational, the NAVSTAR system will ensure the continuous accessibility of navigation satellite signals worldwide. GPS satellites are in higher orbits than those of NAVSAT, 10,898 miles above the earth, transmitting position and time messages. This highly sophisticated tri-service military project is designed to meet a defense requirement for extremely accurate instantaneous position (in three dimensions), velocity (in three directions), and time information, all with user equipment of reduced size and weight and with considerably improved reliability. It is planned that a less-sophisticated version of NAVSTAR will be available to civilian users; see article 3417.

On full system deployment, the Global Positioning System will be composed of:

Satellites—eighteen in use, with three spares, each of which will complete two revolutions of the earth per day, transmitting continuously on 1575.42 and 1227.6 MHz.

Control Stations—consisting of a master station and a few monitor units located in the United States that fine tune the satellites when they pass over each day.

User Equipment—lightweight, small, and relatively inexpensive receivers that may be installed on ships, aircraft, and ground vehicles, or carried as a man-pack; there are also very small hand-held receivers powered by AA dry cells, not much larger than a paperback book and weighing only 24 ounces. Initially, receivers are expected to be quite expensive, but costs will come down, as they did with NAVSAT equipment, as production volume increases and technology advances.

GPS System Operation

3415 Signals are received from several satellites at the same time (the higher orbits make this possible) in a one-way ranging mode using extremely precise timing of transmissions. Information from three satellites is necessary for two-dimension (lat/long) positioning and horizontal velocity; a fourth signal is required to add the third dimension (altitude and vertical rate of change). Normally, output data will be available continuously, but over large geographic areas there will be times each day when the 18-satellite configuration will yield poor four-satellite geometry; additionally, the failure of a satellite might result in only three-satellite availability in some areas. The limitations of such a situation can be overcome, and acceptable three-dimension results achieved, if the receiver contains a highly precise and highly accurate time standard. This "clock" can be kept updated during the times that a normal full four-satellite navigation is available; long-term stability is not required.

The satellite signals are demodulated, time-correlated, and processed to derive precise time, position, and velocity information. These data can be presented in a variety of ways to meet the different requirements of various users. GPS, when fully

operational, is to provide position within 8 meters (8.7 yd) horizontally and 10 meters (10.9 yd) vertically; velocity to 0.1 knot; and time to a fraction of a microsecond. These highly precise data are obtained only from signals that have been "coded" for military security; "clear" or uncoded signals can provide less precise positioning information, within about 200 meters (219 yds). (During periods of war or international crisis, the uncoded signals could be turned off to prevent their use by hostile forces, while the secure, high-precision coded signals would remain usable by friendly units.)

System Development

3416 The NAVSTAR program is divided into three phases with a different number of satellites in each phase. In Phase I six "birds" provide periodic coverage for the United States. During Phase II additional satellites will be launched providing a worldwide, two-dimensional navigation capability with position within 300 meters (328 yds) and velocity within 2 knots. The Phase III configuration, consisting of the full 18 satellites, plus several spares, in three orbital planes, will supply continuous real-time, three-dimensional navigation information to users around the world. The launching of satellites was delayed due to the Challenger shuttle disaster, but full operational availability of the system is expected in the early 1990s.

Pending the availability of the full operational system, GPS is being used in hybrid equipment with other radionavigation systems such as NAVSAT, or alongside other receivers such as Omega.

Nonmilitary Use of GPS

3417 NAVSTAR signals will, of course, be able to be received by civilian users—ships, boats, aircraft, and others; it can be used in land vehicles to show a moving cursor on a digitally stored map displayed on a small TV-like screen. Under normal circumstances, however, only the "C-A" (for Course-Acquisition) code will be readable by nonmilitary users, and this will result in the lesser positional accuracy as described in article 3416. There is also the program of "Selective Availability" that would further degrade the accuracy of GPS positional data for nonmilitary users because of national security reasons; variable artificial errors would be introduced, intentionally contaminating the signals. Even these signals will, however, be adequate for normal offshore navigation.

Where greater accuracy is required, several possibilities exist. The full-accuracy NAVSTAR system employing "P" (for Precise) coded signals could be allowed to certain nonmilitary users under tightly controlled circumstances. Such users would probably be offshore petroleum and mining operations, but could include other scientific and technical activities.

Another possibility is use of a "differential GPS" mode of operation, much like differential Omega as described in article 3313. This could provide highly accurate positional information within a limited local area for such applications as harbor approach and inland navigation; it could always be quickly shut down if it was necessary for security reasons. In this technique, a fixed station at a highly accurately determined location would continuously receive NAVSTAR signals, compare the indicated position with the known position, and broadcast offset corrections to the GPS coordinates. With

such a system, accuracies to the order of 10 meters might be achieved as far out as a distance of several hundred miles from the fixed station by using only the C-A coded signals.

The high developmental costs of GPS, and its considerable continuing operational expenses, have led to consideration of recouping a portion of these costs through a system of licensing civilian users. Technically, this might be done by the mandatory inclusion in each receiver of a plug-in module that would have to be replaced, for a fee, on an annual basis. This is probably feasible for the very limited number of full-precision users, but logistical problems make such a program of questionable practicability for the expected large numbers of low-accuracy users of NAVSTAR in civilian ships, boats, and aircraft. No firm decision has yet been reached in this matter.

Chapter 35   Inertial Navigation

Introduction

3501 Inertial navigation is the process of measuring accelerations in known spacial directions and employing the Newtonian laws of motion to direct the motions of a vessel—aircraft, ship, or submarine. A single integration of acceleration with respect to time yields velocity; a second integration provides distance data that can be used to give position fixes based on departure from a known starting location. The basic components used in an inertial navigation system are gyros, accelerometers, and digital computers.

Ship's Inertial Navigation System (SINS)

3502 The *Ship's Inertial Navigation System* (SINS) has been developed by the U.S. Navy as an accurate, all-weather, dead-reckoning system. It employs gyroscopes, accelerometers, and associated electronics to sense turning rates and accelerations associated with the rotation of the earth, and with a vessel's movement relative to the surface of the earth.

Since Newton's Laws of Motion remain valid throughout the entire range of speeds of any vessel, inertial navigation, which is based on these laws, can be of tremendous assistance to a navigator. Inertial systems can furnish a wide range of information in addition to position coordinates. They provide a continuous readout of latitude, longitude, and ship's heading, as well as information on roll, pitch, and velocity, which is useful for the stabilization of other instruments. They are capable of extreme accuracy; their accuracy depends directly on how faithfully the component gyroscopes and accelerometers mechanize the laws of motion. Constant advances are being made both in the design and manufacturing processes of this precision instrumentation. In addition, every effort is made to locate and eliminate each possible source of error, no matter how minute. The SINS system is of necessity extremely complex compared to other navigational methods—consequently, it has a high initial cost and requires expert maintenance and operating personnel.

Generally similar, but often somewhat less elaborate, inertial systems are available for civilian applications requiring very high accuracies, such as offshore geophysical surveys. These are used with externally referenced systems, primarily the Transit navigational satellite system described in chapter 34.

Development of SINS

3503 Inertial navigation systems were originally developed for military aircraft and missiles; subsequently they came into use in spacecraft. The Ship's Inertial Navigation System was developed for the Polaris submarines; its use has now been extended to include surface ships and attack-class submarines. Inertial navigation is used in long-distance commercial airline flights, but is little-used on merchant vessels because of the considerable cost of the equipment and the availability of other systems.

Principles of Operation

3504 Inertial systems derive their basic name from the fact that gyroscopes and accelerometers (described in article 3506) have a sense of *inertia* in that they have a tendency to maintain their orientation in accordance with Newton's Laws. Any deviation from their original orientation can be sensed and measured with proper instrumentation.

Accelerometers measure the individual components of horizontal and vertical accelerations, while the gyroscopes stabilize the accelerometers in a desired orientation. A computer, which is also included in the system, determines position and velocity by integrating the acceleration components sensed in the vehicle and also calculates orientation corrections caused by motion over the earth, rotation of the earth, and other factors.

Chapter 3 discussed the basic concept of the gyroscope in introducing the principles of the north-seeking gyrocompass. In inertial systems three gyro axes (article 3505) are used to establish a stable platform for the accelerometers. The platform must remain horizontal with reference to the surface of the earth, while the gyroscopes, in their gimbaled mounts, are generally torqued so as to have two horizontal axes and one vertical axis. They are generally not fixed in space, although they could be in certain configurations. Certain errors in SINS increase with time, so that after an extended period the readout data become unacceptable; the system must then be corrected or updated. This is achieved by the *systems approach,* in which the inertial system with its own internal monitoring is supplemented by external sources of data on position, attitude, and velocity. These data sources have limited errors that are not a function of elapsed time; they include celestial trackers, Loran and other radionavigation systems, navigation satellites, speed logs, etc.

Gyroscopes

3505 A *gyroscope* is, in effect, a miniaturized version of the earth, used here to hold an inertial platform in alignment. When affected by disturbing torques, it cannot maintain direction in space as well as the earth does, because of its much smaller mass, which is only partially offset by its much higher speed of rotation. (See articles 327–330). For this reason it is necessary to use several motors and gear drives or direct-drive torquers to drive the gimbals in response to the gyroscope's signals to maintain platform stabilization. A "package" consisting of three gyroscopes, two for the horizontal axes and one for azimuth, can control the alignment of a platform from which accelerometer measurements are made. The velocity meters (accelerometers) can be mounted on the gyro-stabilized platform. Velocity signals from these accelerometers are used to precess or torque the gyroscopes in their respective axes. This feedback from one instrument to the other produces an oscillation, which can best be visualized by considering a simple pendulum that has motion across

the vertical when any force is applied to it, rather than simply moving to a new position and stopping.

Rate Gyroscopes

A simplified schematic of a *rate gyroscope,* having a single degree of freedom, is shown in figure 3505a. The precessional rotation around the output axis is restrained by a spring. The amount of precession around this axis is a function of the *rate* of rotational motion around the input axis rather than the *amount* of rotation, as in the case of an integrating gyroscope. The rate of rotation around the input axis results in an output torque that is opposed by a restraining force illustrated by the spring device. The gyro will precess through angle θ until precessional torque is balanced by the force exerted by the spring. It follows, then, that as long as the *rate* of input remains constant the gyro will maintain its position. When the rate of input decreases, the gyro will feel the force of the spring applied as an input torque, and this torque will cause the rotor to return toward its normal position. The angle θ is always proportional to the angular input rate.

Rate Integrating Gyroscopes

Three rate gyros are normally used on the platform, the z axis of the platform being vertical. Axes x and y may be aligned north and east or in other azimuthal directions, depending upon the coordinates used in designing the system.

The basic sensing element of a modern SINS system, such as the Mark 3 Mod. 4 or 6, is the *rate integrating gyroscope* (figure 3505b). The accuracy of the SINS data output depends largely upon the ability of such a gyro to maintain its orientation; this ability, while based to a great extent on the

Figure 3505a. Schematic of a rate gyro.

Figure 3505b. Rate integrating gyro.

internal construction of the gyro, also depends upon the accuracy of calibration and alignment of the system, which are the responsibility of the shipboard operator. Basic information on gyroscopic precession was given in chapter 3. It is summarized here, and is illustrated in figure 3506b when applied to a gyroscope having a single degree of freedom. For a given torque around the input axis (*IA*), a given angular rate of precession about the output axis (*OA*) is generated, assuming the angular momentum of the wheel stays constant. The rule for precession can be stated as follows: a spin axis (*SA*) precesses about the output axis (*OA*) toward the input axis (*IA*) about which the torque is applied. In other words, with the force exerted by a torque acting directly on the wheel, the precession of the wheel is in the direction of the force rotated around 90° in the direction of wheel rotation, as shown in figure 3505c.

Accelerometers

3506   Inertial navigation is based on the sensing of movement of the vehicle and integrating this movement or acceleration with respect to time to determine velocity and distance (position). The stable platform established by means of gyroscopes is used to establish the horizontal for the *accelerometers*. In actual practice, the accelerometers need not be physically mounted on the gyro platform; they can be installed on an accelerometer platform controlled by the gyros.

Acceleration-sensing instruments may be of three basic types:

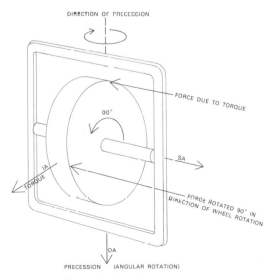

Figure 3505c. The rule for precession.

Figure 3506a. Gravity and acceleration effects on a bubble.

Figure 3506b. Illustrations of accelerometer action and integration for velocity and distance.

An *accelerometer* in which the output is a measure of acceleration;

A *velocity-meter*—a single-integrating device with an output signal proportional to velocity; and

A *distance meter*—a double-integrating device with an output signal proportional to distance traveled.

The term "accelerometer" is often used to denote any one of these instruments.

The Complete System

3507 Two basic physical principles can be stated that summarize the use of gyroscopes and accelerometers in an inertial navigation system.

Linear momentum of a rotating mass remains constant unless an external force is applied.

Angular momentum of a rotating mass remains constant unless an angular torque is applied.

By practical application of the first principle, if acceleration is accurately measured, and is integrated twice with respect to time, then the distance traveled is determined. Applying the second principle, a gyroscope can be used to find the direction. Having determined both distance and direction, a dead-reckoning navigation system is created.

Figure 3507a shows the schematic of a gimbaled inertial design using separate gyroscopes and accelerometers for the three axes, *x*, *y*, and *z*.

Figure 3507b shows a complete inertial system, the Autonetics Mark 2, Mod. 1 *Inertial Autonaviga-*

Figure 3507a. Components of an inertial guidance platform.

Figure 3507b. Mark 2, Mod. 1 Inertial Autonavigator.

tor. The arrangement of the internal component parts is visible, with the cover removed from the binnacle. In the cabinet at the left of the photograph, the top section contains windows for the readout of latitude, longitude, roll, pitch, and velocity. The central section contains the system control panel, and the lower section holds a digital computer designated VERDAN (Versatile Digital Differential Analyzer).

Figure 3507c shows the SINS Mark 3 Mod. 5 installed aboard ship; other Mods. are essentially similar to this model. The binnacle is at the left,

and the various consoles with their functions marked are at the right. Another piece of equipment, which is not illustrated here, is the AN/WSN-1(V)2 Dual MINISINS.

Inaccuracies in Inertial Navigation

3508   Inertial systems are not subject to the various errors of dead-reckoning navigation outlined in article 1201, grouped together under the heading "current." In theory the inertial system is limited in ultimate accuracy only by the degree of perfection of the instrumentation used. Imperfections

Figure 3507c. Mark 3, Mod. 5 Ship's Inertial Navigation System (SINS).

TYPEWRITER TAPEREADER CABINET

ELECTRONIC CONTROL CABINET

SINDAC COMPUTER

DATA OUTPUT CONSOLE

BINNACLE

can, of course, arise in many of the various parts of the assembled system.

When the inertial system is used aboard ship over a considerable period of time, the dominant error sources are the gyro-loop uncompensated drift rates. These drift rates are composed of many variables, depending on the mechanization and configuration of the system. They may be due to imperfections in manufacturing, to instabilities arising subsequent to the installation of the system, or they can be caused by vehicle movement or position. The ultimate result, however, is that they appear as gyro platform drift, causing erroneous presentation of the output data. The principal known causes of this apparent gyro drift are outlined below.

Article 3505 stated that an accelerometer is sensitive only to acceleration along one axis. If two accelerometers are mounted with their sensitive axes at right angles to one another, they can be used to measure any arbitrary acceleration in the plane in which they are mounted. Assuming for the sake of simplicity that the system is so designed that one accelerometer is mounted with a north-south axis while the other is in the east-west axis, then in measuring accelerations along any course each will measure one component of the acceleration. These components can be integrated separately and interpreted as distances traveled north-south or east-west from the assumed starting point.

Errors in Alignment

Obviously, an exact *initial alignment* of the platform is necessary. If there is a misalignment in azi-

muth of the system, and the vessel is traveling on a precise course of 000°, the east-west accelerometer will detect a very slight signal that will produce an erroneous indication that the vessel has moved slightly to the east or west, and the north distance readout will be slightly too low.

Earth Rate

As the earth completes one rotation about its axis in 24 hours, the accelerometer platform must be continuously adjusted to remain level with respect to the earth during this entire period. If the platform is permitted to tilt, the accelerometer will sense a component of gravity. This adjustment for the computed *earth rate* is automatically applied to the platform by the computer system. While the computed earth rate may be equal in *magnitude* to the true earth rate, if its *direction* is incorrect due to a misalignment of the platform in heading, there will be an error in the rate supplied to the platform. The resultant error in the accelerometer platform position is generally known as the "24-hour error," as it is based upon erroneous sensing of the daily rotation of the earth.

Aligning the Platform Using the Earth Rate

The fact that the computed earth rate must match the true rate is used in aligning the inertial platform. With the system at rest, the platform is leveled and aligned as closely as possible in azimuth. The accelerometer outputs are then monitored, and any indicated acceleration is considered to be the result of platform tilt caused by residual error in the azimuth alignment. Azimuth alignment is then corrected until no measurable platform tilt is detected. When this procedure is followed, the platform is aligned by using the earth's rate of rotation as a reference.

The orientation of the inertial package when carried over the surface of the earth must be adjusted for the curvature of the earth in order that it will remain level. When the computer arrives at an incorrect value of the angular distance traveled by the vehicle, because of incorrect alignment or other errors in the system effectively causing an error in the direction of earth rate, it will supply an incorrect signal to the drive motor used for leveling the accelerometer platform. This causes the accelerometer, which cannot distinguish between gravity and vehicle acceleration, to sense a gravity component, and an erroneous acceleration signal is fed back through the closed loop. The attempt of the system to correct itself produces an undamped oscillation, which in a properly designed system would have a period of 24 hours (figure 3508).

Gyro Drift

Since a gyroscope cannot be constructed to be mechanically perfect, some *drift rate* will always be present. This drift of the platform tends to produce an acceleration error that increases linearly with time. Due to the closed feedback loop, however, the accelerometer platform oscillates about a zero mean error rather than building up a linear error. Constant components of gyro drift tend to cause offsets in the position and heading sinusoids, as well as a ramp in longitude. Thus, as indicated in figure 3508, there will be a consistent pattern of error propagation with respect to time resulting from unpredictable gyro drift, producing an error in the indicated position of the vehicle.

Miscellaneous Sources of Error

The precise requirements of an inertial system make it necessary to take secondary effects into account; these are caused by the Coriolis effect, and the earth's shape, which is not perfectly spherical. These error sources are automatically compensated for by the computer. For long periods of inertial navigation, dynamic coupling between various parts of the system produces a small rate error that must also be considered.

It must be realized that error sources can better be described statistically than as constants. Using this concept, the long-term build-up of errors can be determined and reduced more readily than by attempting to evaluate and use only constant error sources.

Reset Procedures

3509   The early methods of resetting the system were based on the assumption that the drift rate remained constant during the sampling period. This did not prove entirely satisfactory because accurate drift rate measurements can be made only at intervals, and it was not always true that the drift rate was essentially constant, or that any random errors were accurately known. Accurate position information, external to the inertial system, is needed and is used to recalibrate or reset the SINS, regardless of the reset technique. These data are fed through the computer, which calculates and applies proper torquing to the stabilized platforms. All of the data that is fed to the computers needs to be smoothed out, as frequent resetting or use of data that may itself be inaccurate can cause errors in determining and correcting the drift rate of the system.

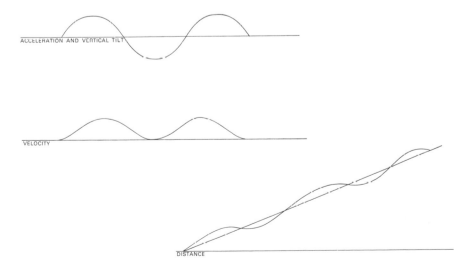

Figure 3508. System errors plotted against time.

Use of a Monitoring Gyroscope

3510 New methods of monitoring the SINS gyros are constantly being developed. One method of determining the drift rate is by employing a *monitoring gyro*.

Including a monitor (a rate gyro) in the system improves performance because it senses and supplies data to the computer on any uncompensated fixed or slowly varying components of drift in the *x* and *y* gyros; a significant reduction in the random error component is also obtained. The monitoring technique utilizes a redundant gyro mounted on a rotating platform. An integrating rate gyro, with high-gain feedback from pickoff to torquer, is used to effectively yield an accurate rate gyro. This platform, an integral part of the *heading* gimbal, rotates about an axis parallel to the heading gimbal axis, and does not compensate the *z* axis, or *heading* gyro. Reversal of the direction of the input axis of the monitor inertial component, with respect to the navigational component, represents the basic technique used. Case reversal is instrumented by successively positioning the monitor table to each of the four quadrant positions, under control of a computer program. The monitoring gyro provides an output at each quadrant that is equivalent to the relative drift between the controlling gyro and the monitoring gyro. The torque applied from the computer to the monitor gyro for earth rate and vessel's velocity over the earth is the same as the torque computed for the gyro being monitored. Since the SINS system computes the vessel's position from accelerations resulting from the vessel's movement, it is important that gyro drift be known as accurately as practicable. The monitoring gyro improves overall performance of the system by detecting gyro drift that has not been compensated; it particularly helps to maintain heading accuracy.

System Updating

3511 Because of the errors just discussed, inertial navigation systems must have the capability of being updated or reset through the computer. Continuous compensation can be made for a known gyro drift. Discrete position information obtained, for example, from a NAVSAT, Omega, Loran-C, bathymetric, or celestial fix, can also be used to damp the system by manual or automatic insertion of the position into the computer.

The process of navigation involves various coordinate systems. Regardless of the system of coordinates chosen for the internal operation of the system, the computer must deal with three reference systems, as well as with the vector angles defining the angular relationship of the reference systems. These vector angles can be described in an overly simplified manner as follows:

1. The vector angle relating the platform coordinate system, defined by the sensitive axes of the inertial instruments on the platform, to a true coordinate system such as latitude and longitude.
2. The vector angle relating the computer coordinate system, defined by information available to the computer, to a true coordinate system.
3. The vector angle relating the platform coordinate system to the computer coordinate system.

This latter vector angle can in part be attributed to the misalignment of the platform, resulting in a slightly different set of coordinates from those programmed in the computer. The interrelationship of vector angles in the coordinate systems outlined above can always be stated as:

$$\text{vector no. } 1 = \text{no. } 2 + \text{no. } 3$$

Stellar Inertial Navigation

A *star tracker* mounted on an inertial system can be used for determining a celestial fix, but even more importantly, it can be used to determine the platform drift rate representing a major portion of the vector angle described in no. 3. The star tracker could be physically mounted on the stable element of the inertial system; in actual use it is often remotely located. A computer in the system can automatically compute elevation angle or altitude, and azimuth angle, from the ephemeristic data stored in its memory section, and from its knowledge of ship's position. Disregarding errors in driving the telescope, it would be possible to point the telescope directly at the star, provided the coordinate system in the computer and the platform coordinates were coincident. The platform-mounted telescope will, however, have a pointing error equivalent to vector angle no. 3.

The telescope on the star tracker generally scans around or across the line of sight to the star. In this process it does have the ability to track the star, thereby permitting a determination of the deviation in altitude and azimuth angles from those computed. These error data, extrapolated over a period of time, can be used in determining drift rate of the gyro platform. In this monitoring system it is necessary to use either two trackers tracking different stars, or one tracker alternately tracking two stars. This is because a star tracker, when used as a monitor, must be capable of measuring the angular deviation between the actual line of sight to the star and the computed line. The tracker can measure only components normal to the line of sight; it cannot detect angular errors about the line of sight. However, the error components obtained from two stars can be resolved in the computer to determine the total error.

Since the stellar-monitored system has the capability of determining a gyro drift rate, it can be used for *alignment* of the platform attitude, as well as to correct the *computed* azimuth orientation without physically rotating the platform. It must be remembered that the stellar monitor system will introduce its own slight error caused by refraction compensation errors, ephemeristic errors, timing errors, and mechanical pointing errors. They may be considered as essentially constant while tracking a star for a short period of time. While alternately tracking two stars, the stellar-monitoring error will generally be random in nature.

Coordinate Systems

3512 Previous articles have mentioned various coordinate systems relating to inertial navigation. The gyros in the inertial system are the inertial instruments that define the frame of reference in which acceleration is measured. This frame of reference is mathematically described by the particular coordinate system chosen, and mechanically defined by causing the gyro to precess at angular rates as dictated by the coordinate system. The design and arrangement of components and the coordinate system employed within the instrumentation is not strictly a navigational function and will not be discussed in detail. The readout on a SINS system is normally given in the familiar terms of latitude and longitude, even though the computer may go through various conversions and computations to arrive at this readout. The operating manual for the SINS Mark 3 Mod. 5 explains the operation of that particular instrumentation on the basis of the following three coordinate systems, which are familiar to the navigator and will be reviewed briefly.

The *ship's coordinate system* is defined by the longitudinal axis, the athwartship axis, and the vertical or deck-to-keel axis, which, in the case of a submarine, can be defined as the optical axis of the main periscope. The angular quantities measured in the ship's coordinate system are relative bearing or relative azimuth, and elevation—the angle measured in a vertical plane from the deck plane to the line of sight. The ship's coordinate system is

related to the horizontal plane in the local geographic coordinate system by the angles of roll, pitch, and heading.

The *local geographic coordinate system* is located at the ship's position and is based on the direction of the vertical and the direction of north (figure 3512a). The quantities measured in the local geographic system are velocity north and velocity east (and *depth* when used in a submarine). Heading is measured about the vertical from north clockwise to the projection in the horizontal plane of the ship's fore-and-aft axis. It can be considered as a local coordinate system, and the angle relating this system to the equatorial coordinate system is latitude.

The *equatorial coordinate system* consists of the earth's polar axis, the intersection of the plane of the ship's local meridian with the plane of the equator, and an axis directed east perpendicular to both these axes (figure 3512b). The intersection of the equatorial coordinate system axes is therefore

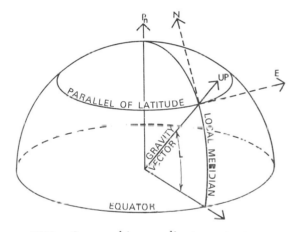

Figure 3512a. Geographic coordinate system.

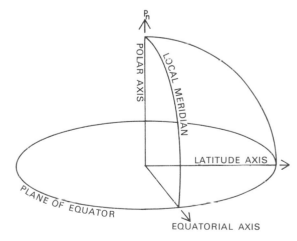

Figure 3512b. Equatorial coordinate system.

at the center of the earth. The latitude axis and the east axis of the local geographic system are parallel. Ship's motion in longitude is measured about the polar axis of this system, while motion in latitude is measured about the latitude axis.

Computers in Inertial Navigation

3513 Due to the technical and mathematical complexity of inertial navigation systems, a *computer* must be included as an integral part of the overall system. Within this chapter, various references have been made to the functions of the computer. The computers used in modern SINS systems are usually general-purpose digital computers, but they are used in a very special purpose application. The words "general purpose" merely imply that the computer could be programmed without a hardware change to solve any general problem instead of the specific computations related to inertial navigation.

The computer for a SINS system could be analog rather than digital, although the digital type is now almost exclusively used, and its functions would vary somewhat depending upon the acceleration instruments employed, the system accuracy required, and the choice of coordinate system. In general, the computer will send torquing signals to the gyros and accelerometers, in addition to computing present position and velocity.

Electrostatically Supported Gyro Navigators

3514 Since unpredictable gyro drifts are major contributors to errors in inertial systems, techno-logical advances have been used to attempt to reduce their effects.

A major source of drift is frictional torque within the gyro. This can be minimized by suspending the gyro electrostatically in a vacuum. Further, torquing of a gyro tends to cause drift rates to be unstable; therefore, once up to speed, these electrostatically supported gyros are not torqued. The gyro-stabilized accelerometer platform should then be space-referenced. Any required transformation of coordinate systems is done in the computer, which also models and predicts the residual gyro drifts on the basis of calibrations. The accuracy of this drift prediction allows significantly longer intervals between system updatings from external fix sources than would be required for conventional SINS.

Such inertial navigators using electrostatically supported gyros can be used independently or as a monitoring device for SINS.

Caution

3515 It is vitally important to always remember that for all the precision and accuracy of inertial systems, the output is merely an estimated position and not a fix. Only external means (visual bearings, radionavigation systems, NAVSAT, celestial observations, etc.) will provide the exact location of a vessel at a given time. The best inertial equipment must be updated at intervals, as frequently as circumstances permit. The navigator who puts blind faith in the output of his inertial systems invites disaster.

Chapter 36

Bathymetric Navigation

Introduction

3601 The navigation of a surface vessel or submarine can also be accomplished by use of the topography of the ocean floor to obtain positioning data. This is *bathymetric navigation* and can be used even in considerable depths of water. Positions are determined relative to the known locations of specific geological features of the ocean bottom.

Modern electronic technology permits the taking of soundings in waters of considerable depth, including making a profile of the bottom if desired. (The principles of electronic depth sounding were covered in article 716.)

Side Echoes and Multiple Returns

3602 In theory, echoes are returned from the bottom from all points within the sound cone; in actual practice, the first echoes tend to mask the later ones, and there may be a significant delay between the return of the first and the later echoes. It must be borne in mind that the first return will come from that portion of the bottom that is *nearest* the ship, and that *this portion is not necessarily directly below the ship*. This phenomenon is known as a *side echo*. Subsequent returns will be from other portions of the bottom. In comparatively shallow water, *multiple returns* may occur when the bottom is a good sound reflector. The echo returns from the bottom and is recorded as the depth, but it is also reflected for a second trip downward by the vessel's hull and the water's surface, and then back up for a second reading. Two or more returns can occur in shallower water, particularly when the bottom is of hard material such as sand or rock. Reducing the

echo-sounder gain will usually remove indications of multiple return (some models feature automatic gain control).

Another phenomenon that may be puzzling is the appearance at times of a false bottom, suspended in the water. This is caused by echoes returned from the *deep scattering layer*, also called the *phantom bottom*. In daytime it is encountered at depths of about 200 fathoms (366 m); it usually moves nearer the surface at night. It is caused by echoes reflected from light-shunning plankton and other minute marine life. At times, this layer is sufficiently dense to mask echoes from the actual bottom. Schools of fish, or a single large fish, also return an echo, making the echo sounder particularly useful to fishermen. Any sharp discontinuity within the water causes sound to be reflected, and an echo sounder often can detect the boundary of a layer of fresh water overlying heavier salt water.

A rocky bottom reflects almost all the sound striking its surface, while soft mud tends to absorb it, thus returning a weaker signal. A layer of mud or silt overlying rock frequently yields two echoes.

A navigator must always bear in mind that depths shown on charts may be inaccurate due to changing bottom conditions, such as silting or the formation of sandbars since the survey was made. It is also possible that protruding underwater obstacles may have been missed during the survey. It is important to use the depth sounder continuously in a deep-draft vessel approaching shallow water or operating on soundings. Modern surveys are, however, much more accurate and reliable than those conducted before the introduction of electronic positioning systems. Electronic systems permit not only an accurate establishment of the sur-

Figure 3602. A typical bottom profile.

vey vessel's position, but extend the range of operations farther from shore. More important, they are able to maintain an automatic plot of positions related to time. By use of a depth sounder in place of the old hand lead a continuous recording of depths is made and is correlated with the position of the survey vessel. Data are often forwarded from the survey vessel to the charting agency by means of magnetic tape.

Echo-sounding Equipment

3603 The AN/UQN-4 precision echo sounder is a standard model in use by the U.S. Navy; it has features typical of commercial sounders used on merchant ships.

The UQN-4 is essentially an improved version of an earlier model, the AN/UQN-1. It transmits and receives on 12 kHz using solid-state components and has a digital display of depth in feet or fathoms.

The transducer beam width is 30°. The signal frequency is crystal controlled, and emission consists of a pulse with a maximum peak output of 1,000 watts. The pulse duration and repetition rate are given in the following table. Two pulse lengths are available for each of the deeper range settings.

Range	Short Pulse	Long Pulse	Pulse Repetition Rate
600 feet	0.33 ms		120 per minute
600 fathoms	2.46 ms	26.67 ms	20 per minute
6,000 fathoms	20.00 ms	160.00 ms	2 per minute

In lieu of automatic transmission (auto pinging), the operator can key a single pulse manually. In addition to the numerical depth readout, the UQN-4 has a strip chart recorder, which is greatly improved over previous models.

The UQN-4 has two additional features that were not available on its predecessors. It is fitted with a draft adjustment, which permits the depth readout to be adjusted so that it states depth below the lowest portion of the ship, such as a sonar dome, and provision is made for automatic tracking. A selected depth is set manually into the numerical depth readout circuit. A *Lost Tracking Indicator* is illuminated whenever a depth of 200 feet (61 m) greater or less than the preset depth is encountered.

Various commercial models of echo sounders for merchant ships and small craft are described in chapter 7.

Use of an Echo Sounder in Navigation

3604 Soundings shown on NOS and DMAHTC charts are obtained by echo sounders using an assumed standard velocity of sound in sea water and are uncorrected for any variation in salinity, density, or temperature. This lack of correction is actually desirable because conditions in any given area remain reasonably constant, and thus the subsequent echo-sounder readings of a ship (also uncorrected) may be directly compared with the charted values.

In bathymetric navigation, the wide-beam characteristics of a typical depth sounder may be advantageous. Often a sea-bottom feature would go undetected by a ship not directly over it were it not for the wide cone of sounding pulses. Because of the cone configuration, the deeper such a feature lies, the greater the horizontal distance at which the ship can locate it. From the bathymetric navigation standpoint, the fact that such an off-track feature is recorded at a depth greater than its true depth is a meaningful clue to its position. The minimum depth recorded by a ship over a seamount will be identical to that shown on the chart only if the ship

Figure 3603. AN/UQN-4 Depth Finder.

passes directly over the top, assuming that the charted depth is in fact correct. If the top of the seamount still lies within range of the sound cone, it will be recorded even though the ship is to one side. However, the minimum depth will be recorded as deeper than shown on the navigation chart because of the greater oblique distance from the transducer. Within a reasonable range of values, the difference in minimum depths (between charted and recorded values) will yield distance horizontally from the vessel to the projected point of the seamount top at the surface.

Line of Soundings

When using the echo sounder in ordinary navigation, the *line-of-soundings* method may be used to advantage as an aid in determining position; this technique is described in article 1119. A closely related procedure is covered in article 3607.

The National Ocean Service is producing a series of *bathymetric maps* of the waters adjacent to portions of the coast of the United States. These maps extend seaward somewhat beyond the 100-fathom curve, and show the contour of the bottom in considerable detail. Such maps can be of great assistance in fixing position by means of the depth finder.

Even where a line of soundings cannot be matched to a chart or bathymetric map, echo-sounder data can still be of value to a navigator. While an isolated measurement of depth cannot, of itself, yield a position due to the repetition of the same depth at many spots, it can provide "negative" information that questions the validity of a fix obtained by other means and starts the navigator on a search for better data.

Use of Bottom "Landmarks" for Navigation

3605 Charted "landmarks" on the ocean floor can often assist the navigator in determining position. Such marks include *submarine canyons, trenches, troughs, escarpments, ridges, seamounts,* and *guyots*. These terms in general describe submarine topographical features that are similar to their counterparts found on dry land. An *escarpment* is a long steep face of rock, or long submarine cliff. A *seamount* is an elevation of relatively small horizontal extent rising steeply towards, but not reaching, the surface. A *guyot* is a flat-topped seamount, rather similar to the mesas found in the southwestern United States. *Canyons* are found off most continental slopes; they are relatively steep-sided, and their axes descend steadily. A canyon, when crossed approximately at right angles, is easily recognized on a depth sounder or recorder. It will serve to establish a line of position, and the maximum depth noted, when crossing the axis, may further aid in determining position. Trenches, troughs, ridges, and escarpments are often found on the ocean bottom, which may otherwise be featureless; they also can be useful in yielding a line of position. Many guyots occur in the Pacific, and are useful in positioning. A line of position may also be obtained when crossing the line of demarcation between an ocean basin, which is usually very flat, and the surrounding bottom mass.

Precise Positioning Using Seamounts

3606 If the apex of an identified isolated seamount is located by means of an echo sounder, a precise position can be determined. If several seamounts are located in the same area, identification must be made by individual shape as well as minimum depth.

Echo sounders on many vessels typically generate a 60° cone of sounding pulses. The geometry of such a cone will now be considered in terms of isolated features on the sea bed such as a seamount; this is known as the *side-echo technique* (the name is something of a misnomer in this case, as the technique actually concerns position to one side of a feature rather than the phenomenon previously discussed under this name.) Basically, the technique involves two passes near a seamount at right angles with each other. The point of minimum depth on each track is noted and lines at right angles to the track are drawn at these points; the intersection of these lines locates the seamount with respect to the ship.

Although the procedures are not difficult, several important concepts must be kept in mind. Seamounts (or seaknolls) are large features. The notion that they are steep-sided, as seen on echograms with large vertical exaggeration, must be dispelled. The tops are never so sharp or well defined as they appear on the echogram. Charted values indicating a unique minimum depth can be incorrect; the depth can be wrong; or (more probably) it may have been charted in the wrong position. Knowledge of whether the feature was compiled from a survey or from random tracks is essential for confidence in use of the reference chart. One records the minimum sounding of a seamount identical to the depth on the chart only when the ship passes directly over the top or very close to it. A recorded value shallower than seen on the chart indicates the chart is in error (or the sounding gear is in error, or it is the wrong seamount). It is desirable to know the nature of the equipment used by the ship(s) that produced the data upon which the chart is based, and of course one must know the limitations of his own equipment. All of these must be kept in mind. There is also the possibility of using incompatible features, and an isolated seamount is best chosen despite the greater difficulty in initial detection.

The 60° Signal Cone

The first echo return comes from the portion of the sea bed that is nearest the vessel, and this portion is not necessarily directly below the vessel; in such a case, the depth finder is indicating a side echo. This can be very helpful, because if the seamount apex lies within the sound cone, the depth recorded by the depth finder cannot exceed the depth of the apex multiplied by 1.154. In addition, the horizontal distance from the apex to the ship cannot exceed half the depth indicated by the depth finder (figure 3606a). (These factors must be modified if the depth sounder being used has a cone of sound pulses other than 60°.)

Ordinarily, to obtain a fix by means of locating the summit of a seamount, a position some distance away is determined as accurately as possible, and then a course is set for the apex. The distance of

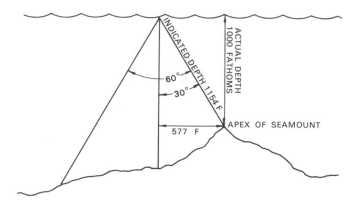

Figure 3606a. The geometry of a 60° sound cone.

the departure position from the apex will depend in part on the existing current, sea, and wind conditions.

Figure 3606b shows the contour lines surrounding the apex of a seamount. Assume that a ship obtained a good running fix due south of the apex, and is approaching on a course of 000°. It is possible that this course will take the ship directly over the summit, in which case the depth finder will give a minimum reading of 1,126 fathoms (the depth at the summit), and provide a fix. Unfortunately, this seldom occurs.

Figure 3606c shows the DR plot as the ship approaches the location of the summit. Soundings are recorded every minute on the plot and also the minimum sounding obtained (times are omitted in this figure for clarity). The shallowest sounding obtained is 1,169 fathoms, and a line is drawn at right angles to the heading line for this sounding. As the soundings begin to increase, it is obvious the ship has passed the area of the summit; a right turn is made to come to a course of 270°, crossing the

Figure 3606b. Bottom contour chart.

Figure 3606c. Determining position by means of a seamount.

original track at an angle of 90°. The turn to starboard is adjusted so that the new course will pass as close as possible to the summit's assumed position. Soundings are again noted every minute, as is the minimum sounding, which is 1,149 fathoms. A perpendicular to the ship's course line is again drawn for this minimum sounding.

The intersection of the two perpendicular lines passing through the minimum recorded depths locates the summit of the seamount relative to the ship; the direction and distance separating the intersection of these two lines from the charted position of the seamount is the offset of the ship's track from the seamount. Adjustment of the track may be accomplished by shifting all recorded times and soundings by the direction and distance of the offset.

It is possible that the selected track will pass so far to the side of the seamount that the top lies *outside* the cone of sounding pulses. This is apparent if the navigator observes a minimum depth greater than 1,300 fathoms; this means that the ship was more than 1,300 yards to the side of the top. For a 60° sound cone, the geometry of the situation leads to this rule of thumb; the deepest value recorded with the seamount top still retained within the cone is twice the distance from ship to seamount top horizontally. Obviously, it is to the advantage of the navigator to choose, if a choice is possible, a seamount with deep minimum depth, other considerations being equal. In the event that the top does not lie within the sound cone, the ship's position

can be determined only approximately. It would be desirable to make another pass on a reciprocal course, displaced to one side as indicated by the approximate position, in order to attempt a more precise location of the seamount top.

It should also be noted that this method, while entirely feasible, requires that the vessel be diverted from her track towards her destination in order to make the second pass by the seamount at right angles to the first passing. Such a diversion is not normally welcomed by vessel owners, and for ships on normal ocean passages this method is rather more theoretical than practical.

Contour Advancement

3607 Somewhat similar to the line-of-soundings method (described in article 1119) is the *contour advancement technique*. If the area has been precisely surveyed and compiled, this technique can yield highly accurate and repeatable results. No bathymetric anomalies such as seamounts, canyons, or ridges are required; but some variation in depths is necessary. In this case, it is the slopes that are of interest. Ideally, a slope of more than one degree, but no more than four or five degrees, is required. The slope should not be constant, because this method will not work well if the linear distance between contours is equal.

In noting that some slope is required, the presence or absence of contour lines and the scale of chart used must be kept in mind. Areas that appear devoid of contours and flat on one chart may, upon use of a larger-scale chart, show some relief or slope. After finding that a given area is not absolutely level, the contour advancement method is facilitated by use of the largest-scale chart available.

Refer to figure 3607a as the base chart. The DR track is shown as a dashed line, with observed depths marked off at increments equal to the charted contour interval. These data were obtained while the ship was steaming across the area, using the 700-fathom curve as referencing contour. This is a time-distance plot and is based on ship speed and recorded depths. For example, if the ship had been steaming in the same direction for several miles (over this slope), it would be recording incremental depths differing in time from the recording of the charted depths. The recorded contour crossings are merely extended to the area on this chart and plotted in relative position on the DR track.

By starting with the 700-fathom curve as the first one crossed, the curve is traced onto an overlay and becomes the *reference contour*. The assumed track

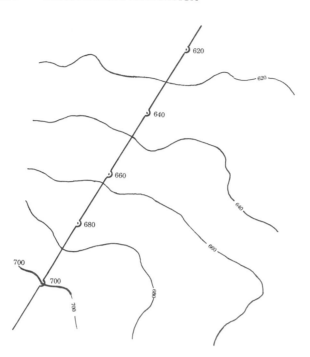

Figure 3607a. Chart extract showing DR track and successive depth contours.

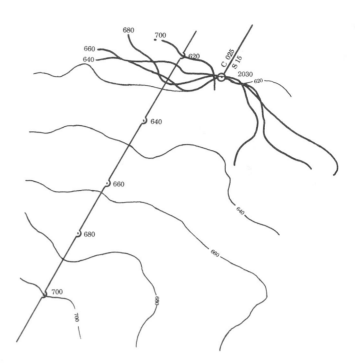

Figure 3607b. Transparent overlay showing contours successively advanced and position of vessel at common intersection.

is also indicated on the overlay. The next step is to shift the overlay in the direction of travel until the reference contour (700 fathoms) matches the plotted (not contoured) position of the next depth for which a contour exists (680 fathoms). Now the 680-fathom curve is traced. It should intersect the reference contour at one or more positions. The overlay is again advanced along the direction of travel to the point where the reference contour intersects the plotted 660-fathom curve. This contour (660 fathoms) is now traced. The three contours that are now traced should intersect at a point off the assumed track, or some triangle or error will be indicated that can be further defined by continuation of the "advancement." The intersection of lines becomes the position that is used to adjust the ship's track. This adjustment is a linear shift of the DR track and is a fix modified by the time (and therefore positional) lag after determination.

This description may appear complex in the absence of an overlay. Actually, the technique is a simple one and easy to master. Figure 3607b depicts the overlay after the contours have been traced by advancement of the 700-fathom curve.

Use of Sonar in Navigation

3608 *Sonar* (SOund NAvigation Ranging) operates in the same manner as the echo sounder, except that it radiates its signal in a generally hori-

zontal, rather than a vertical, direction. Excellent ranges on underwater objects may be obtained with sonar, and as the sonar transducer can be rotated horizontally, acceptably precise and accurate bearings may also be obtained.

Sonar can be of great assistance in piloting in thick weather, particularly in rocky areas.

For example, when the harbor of Newport, Rhode Island, is closed due to very heavy fog, a vessel returning to port can come to anchor out of the channel south of Brenton Reef and west of Seal Ledge in a very precisely determined position. Subsequent changes in sonar ranges and bearings would give immediate notice, should she drag her anchor (figure 3608).

In arctic regions, sonar is sometimes helpful in locating ice when steaming at slow speed, as approximately nine-tenths of the ice mass is located below the water surface. Large bergs may sometimes be detected at a range of 6,000 yards or more, but the actual service range is usually less. Growlers may be picked up at ranges of between 1,000 and 2,000 yards; even smaller pieces may be detected in time to avoid them.

Summary

3609 Bathymetric navigation is an advanced technique of the general art and science of positioning ships at sea, but one whose potential should not

Figure 3608. Use of sonar in piloting.

be overlooked by any navigator, especially for specialized situations. An interesting device developed by the Navy for its Deep Submersible Rescue Vehicle program is the altitude/depth sonar, which shows the vehicle's "altitude" above the ocean bottom and the depth below the surface for cruising and search purposes. Nuclear submarines cruising beneath polar ice packs are able to use the sounding equipment both upward and downward, as well as ahead.

Bathymetric navigation is a developing technique, and continued refinements and improvements can be expected in the future, both in equipment and procedures.

Chapter 37   Doppler Navigation

Introduction

3701 Many navigation systems and techniques measure a vessel's position at a given moment in time; others determine its course and speed with respect to the water in which it is traveling. If it were possible to continuously and accurately measure the direction and distance a vessel traveled *with respect to the earth*, then position could be fixed at all times following departure from a known location. Advancing technology has produced several such methods, including inertial navigation systems covered in chapter 35. Another technique is *Doppler navigation* using acoustic waves. The general principles of the Doppler effect have been discussed previously (article 3101) and its use with radio waves was described for satellite navigation (articles 3402 and 3408).

Acoustic Doppler Systems

3702 Acoustic Doppler navigation systems are capable of giving a constant readout of speed and distance traveled to a high degree of accuracy. Some models can additionally show speed on the athwartship axis for a measurement of offsetting influences such as current. In shallower waters —depths less than 250 feet (76 m)—some Raytheon units can be switched to a "mooring mode" in which speeds on both the fore-and-aft and athwartship axes can be resolved down to 0.01 knot to facilitate docking, anchoring, or mooring to a buoy.

A limitation of Doppler navigation systems is the depth of water under the vessel. Typically, units can operate from bottom echoes in waters no deeper than 1,500 feet (460 m). In greater depths "water-mass tracking" must be employed, using reflections from particulate matter in the water with somewhat reduced accuracy of speed and distance measurements.

Doppler systems can simultaneously be used for depth measurement, often with a preset alarm capability. All information derived from the system— speed, distance traveled, and depth—can be transmitted in digital form to a navigational computer. Here, distance can be combined with heading information from a gyrocompass for an accurate continuing computation of latitude and longitude.

Acoustic Doppler Principles

3703 The basic principles of acoustic Doppler navigation will be illustrated by an example that considers the sonic energy as being transmitted horizontally through the water, rather than diagonally downwards, as is actually the case in marine Doppler navigation. Energy is transmitted as a continuous wave, rather than in pulses as for echo sounding. If the sonic projector shown in figure 3703a is considered as being stationary in the water while transmitting sound on a frequency f, the transmitted energy in the form of sound waves moves away from the transmitter at the speed of sound, C. This speed is affected primarily by the temperature, salinity, and density of the sea water. The energy travels outward in the form of waves, alternating between pressure crests and troughs. The distance between consecutive crests or troughs is the *wavelength*, λ, of the acoustic wave.

The wavelength is equal to the speed of sound divided by the frequency, or $\lambda = C \div f$. Therefore, in a period of time each pressure crest travels a distance d equal to C multiplied by t. In the illustra-

Figure 3703a. Pattern of acoustic waves transmitted from a stationary underwater projector.

Figure 3703b. Pattern of acoustic waves transmitted from a moving underwater projector.

tion it can be seen that the wavelength in feet (λ) and the distance (d) that a given pressure crest has traveled are one and the same.

Figure 3703b depicts a ship carrying the projector (transducer) moving through the water at a velocity V, and the resulting wave being monitored at a fixed point some distance away from the projector. When transmitted at the same fixed frequency (f, as above), the waves, with their pressure crests, are generated at the same time intervals or frequency. The pressure crests are closer together in the water due to the forward velocity of the vessel. The new compressed wavelengths, λ', are equal to the prior undisturbed wavelengths minus the distance traveled at velocity v between pressure crests. Since wavelength and frequency vary inversely in any medium having a fixed speed of sound, the shortened wavelength caused by the ship's velocity results in an increase in frequency

received at the monitoring point. Stated somewhat differently, the motion of the source of sound waves toward the stationary observer results in a greater number of pressure crests reaching the observer in a given unit of time; this means a higher frequency of the acoustic waves. The change in frequency is known as the *Doppler shift*.

If the stationary observer in figure 3703b is replaced by a reflector, as shown in figure 3703c, the transmitted energy will be reflected back to the ship. By adding a hydrophone (another transducer) and receiver, the distance to the object can be determined by measuring the elapsed time between transmission of an outgoing signal and the return of the echo, a sonar distance. In addition, by measuring the Doppler shift of the echo, the ship's speed relative to the reflector can be determined.

In Doppler navigation the ocean floor is normally used as a reflector, as no reflective surfaces are

PROJECTOR

HYDROPHONE

OBSERVER
(REFLECTOR)

RECEIVED FREQUENCY
EQUALS $\frac{C-V}{\chi}$

Figure 3703c. Pattern of acoustic waves reflected back to a moving transmitter/ receiver.

available in the horizontal plane. A highly directional sound projector and hydrophone are therefore depressed to a predetermined angle below the horizontal. If a second projector and hydrophone, facing in the opposite direction to the first pair and depressed to the same angle, are added, the Doppler shift, as received by the two hydrophones, can be compared. If the Doppler shift, as obtained from the after hydrophone, is subtracted from the shift as obtained from the forward hydrophone, the value of the shift due to horizontal motion will be doubled; in addition, any shift due to vertical motion will be canceled. It follows that if four projectors and hydrophones equally distributed in bearing are employed, relative direction and distance measurements can be very precisely determined. In some systems, only three projector/receiver units are used, with one being common to the two pairs.

Sonic Signals Transmitted through Sea Water

3704 So far, only the Doppler shift has been considered, with no thought to the medium—sea water—through which it is transmitted. The existing characteristics of the water can have a significant effect on Doppler navigation, the major considerations being their effect on the *speed of sound*, on *signal attenuation*, and on *volume reverberation*.

Speed of Sound

As was stated in article 3703, the wavelength, λ, of a transmitted sound wave is equal to the speed of sound, C, divided by the frequency, f, or $\lambda = C \div f$. The *speed of sound* in water is affected by such factors as salinity, temperature, and pressure (which increases with depth). It can vary by approximately 3 percent on either side of the standard

value, which is generally taken as 4,935 feet per second (1,504 m/s) in sea water near the surface with a temperature of 60°F (15.6°C) and salinity of 34 parts per thousand. Note that this speed differs from the more-rounded figure of 4,800 feet per second (1,463 m/s) commonly used in echo-sounding and bathymetric navigation.

An uncompensated variation in the speed of sound as great as 3 percent could cause an unacceptable error in a Doppler navigation system. Errors resulting from such a cause can be largely eliminated by transmitting a signal on a constant wavelength rather than on a constant frequency, or by constantly adjusting the depression angle of the transmitter and hydrophone array to compensate for a change in the velocity of sound. Both methods offer certain advantages, but neither is generally considered to be the ultimate answer to the problem. The two methods have been combined with considerable success in some Doppler instrumentation.

Signal Attenuation

The acoustic energy of the sonic signal is dissipated as it passes through the water; this phenomenon is called *signal attenuation*. As path losses increase with increased frequency due to signal attenuation, tradeoffs between power and frequency must always be taken into consideration in the design of Doppler navigational equipment.

Volume Reverberation

In addition to the reflected echo from the bottom, acoustic energy is returned from debris, bubbles, minute marine life, and from thermal boundaries in the water; this is collectively termed *volume re-*

verberation. The noise caused by volume reverberation can at times drown out the echo reflected from the bottom. This effect is used to advantage with some types of Doppler equipment, as discussed in article 3706.

Application of Doppler Principles

3705 The Doppler navigational system as originally developed by the Raytheon Company employed four beams of sonic energy, spaced 90° apart. These beams were directed outward and downward at equal angles of inclination from the horizontal. The sonic energy was transmitted from *transducers*, which were activated by an electrical signal from the transmitter. In addition to radiating the outgoing sonic signal, the transducers served as hydrophones, in that they also picked up the echo of the signal, reflected from the ocean floor, and converted the acoustic echo back into electrical energy. This energy passed into the receiver, where it was amplified, and the input from the four transducers was compared to produce the Doppler frequency. It also determined the relative strength of the frequencies, thus providing a sense of motion and its direction.

If the transducer array remained fixed in bearing relative to the ship's center line, motion would be stated relative to the vessel's coordinate system; that is, the readout would show motion relative to the vessel's heading and would indicate speed over the bottom and cross-track errors (lateral displacement relative to the track). To make it a true navigational system, a transducer array can be constantly oriented to true north by the vessel's gyrocompass, which also serves to stabilize the array and maintain it in a horizontal plane, regardless of any roll or pitch. Motion is thus indicated in the north-south and east-west directions, and readout is both the true direction and distance traveled from a point of departure expressed as distance north or south and east or west. Therefore the system can present a constant indication of position, expressed as latitude and longitude, and can also continuously plot position on a chart, using an X-Y coordinate plotter. In lieu of continually orienting the transducer array to true north, N-S and E-W components of the vessel's motion can be derived by a microprocessor program.

Accuracy

Geometric arrangement and sonic factors, both of which affect the performance of the system, have been considered briefly. Another limitation on the accuracy of the system is the heading accuracy supplied by the gyrocompass employed. A high-quality gyrocompass under good operational conditions will have a bearing uncertainty of 0.1°, or about six minutes of arc. The Doppler navigational system using a heading reference in which this error remained constant would indicate a position to within about 0.17 percent of the distance traveled from the departure point, and the ship might be to the right or left of the intended track by this amount. As the errors introduced by the gyro usually tend to be random rather than constant, they average out to a considerable extent. Many runs have been made with this equipment to a considerably higher degree of accuracy than the 0.17 percent error would seem to indicate.

The chief limitation in Doppler navigation using the ocean floor as a reflector is not system accuracy, but rather that it is effective only in depths not exceeding approximately 1,500 feet (460 m) because of signal attenuation; accuracy degrades somewhat with increasing depth.

Doppler Navigation in Deep Waters

3706 Volume reverberation was mentioned in article 3704 as sometimes having an adverse effect on the Doppler navigational system, as an echo returning from the ocean floor was masked by an echo from thermal gradients, stratified layers of minute marine life, etc. Because of this volume reverberation in sonar transmissions, with a continuous-wave transmitter, part of the acoustic energy is reflected back and produces a signal level. Consequently, Doppler navigation is possible *relative to the water mass*, regardless of water depth.

Volume reverberation is thus not an unmixed liability, as it makes possible the use of the Doppler navigational system as an accurate DR system at any sea depths. Motion is sensed relative to the water mass and is accurately read out as a change in position. This equipment can be extremely helpful at sea in indicating deviations from the intended heading, such as steering errors.

Doppler Navigation Equipment

3707 A new generation of Doppler navigational instrumentation has been developed with two very different types of vessels primarily in mind; these are the "super-jumbo" tankers, displacing 300,000 tons or more, and research submarines, often termed deep-submergence vehicles.

These two highly diverse types have one characteristic in common—they are little affected by wave action. At its operating depths, the deep submergence vehicle will be quite unaffected by sur-

Figure 3707. Doppler system readout showing speed, distance traveled, and depth, with depth alarm available.

face conditions, while the giant tanker, due to its enormous mass, is much less affected than are most other surface ships.

Because of this greatly improved stability, the Doppler systems developed for these vessels do not need to employ a gyro-stabilized pendulous array of transducers. Instead, the four transducers are rigidly affixed to the ship's bottom plating, in such a position that under normal conditions of loading, their axes are directed downwards at a specific angle; usually they are located well forward of the midships point. Stabilization is achieved internally by electronic means.

This system of mechanically fixed transducers will perform the same functions and permit the same degree of accuracy as discussed above, and the system should greatly benefit both types of vessels. The deep submergence vehicle, operating in a medium that prohibits almost all conventional navigation, is no longer at the mercy of unknown and variable currents. It can complete an accurate and detailed survey of the ocean floor, and return to the point from which the survey was started.

For the giant tanker, this equipment furnishes a continuous and accurate DR plot at sea; it is of even greater benefit when entering or operating in port. As these ships have large drafts, often well in excess of 80 feet (24 m), they cannot totally rely on the usual aids to navigation to keep in safe waters. Instead, they must often restrict their movements to a limited portion of the normally used channel. The Doppler system will be of great assistance in such operations, and can often warn of potential trouble before such could be detected by plotting visual bearings.

Use of Doppler Equipment in Docking

3708 Pilots and conning officers have frequently experienced difficulty in sensing slight lateral motion in large vessels, such as tankers, during the final stages of coming alongside a berth. Since the momentum involved is tremendous, serious damage can result from even a comparatively slight contact with a pier or camel.

To detect such slight motion, a more sensitive "mooring mode" can be used, or a pair of auxiliary transducers may be installed. These are placed on the athwartship axis, and are intended solely to detect lateral or turning motion when coming alongside a pier and when the engines are stopped. Propeller noise would seriously affect their efficiency when underway.

Chapter 38

Navigational Computers

Introduction

3801 The past two decades have brought great advances in computer capabilities, with almost unbelievable reductions in size, power requirements, and cost. And with these advances have come the increasing application of computers to navigation. While many basic methods for obtaining fixes have not changed, the "machinery" used continues to improve in speed, precision, and accuracy. Acronyms and terms such as NAVDAC, VERDAN, MARDAN, SINS, MINISING, INS, microelectronics, and digital, have become a part of a navigator's vocabulary. These terms relate to computers; how computers affect a navigator, and some of the computers used in navigation, are covered in this chapter.

Computers for Navigation

3802 A *computer* is an electronic device especially designed for the solution of complex mathematical calculations. When separate subsystems are combined to make a single complex navigational system, such as SINS (chapter 35), the solution becomes much too involved and lengthy for a navigator to undertake using the old conventional methods. Therefore computers, with their essential mathematical programming and information storage capability, are employed to do the navigator's work. Computers are now installed in aircraft, submarines, and in limited numbers, in surface vessels. They may be programmed for one specific task: for instance, Loran-C or Omega supplying a continuous latitude-longitude readout on an *x-y* plotter or on dials; or a series of tasks, as when used in the *Integrated Navigation System* or INS (article 3807). In order to provide answers to the various navigational problems, either an *analog* or *digital* computer, or a combination of both, may be required.

A *calculator* is a smaller (usually hand-held) and less-capable device that is much like a computer. It is able to compute quite complex mathematical problems, but at a much slower rate, has much less data storage capabilities, and is usually less convenient to use in terms of the input and output of data. Nevertheless, calculators, too, can play an important role in navigation, on large vessels as well as small craft; see appendix F.

Analog Computers

3803 An *analog computer* solves a particular physical problem instantaneously through the use of an equivalent electrical circuit that is mathematically identical to the physical problem; that is, the electrical circuit is designed to be *analogous* to the problem.

It should be noted that the solution of the physical problem by an analog computer is instantaneous; in other words, the electrical analog produces a continuous solution at every instant of time. Generalizing, analog computers may be said to yield instantaneous solutions to time-varying physical problems. The analog computer is not versatile; if the physical problem itself, rather than merely its parameters, is changed, a new analog must be designed. Analog computers are therefore usually designed to furnish repeated solutions to a very specific type of problem. It is obvious that the accuracy of the solution of a physical problem by an electrical analog is limited by the tolerances of the circuit component. The limited versatility and precision of analog computers has led to the concentration of developmental work on digital computers.

Digital Computers

3804   A *digital computer* is a complex electronic device that calculates the solution of a mathematical statement to a specified degree of numerical precision through a prearranged sequence or algorithm of simple arithmetic operations such as addition, subtraction, multiplication, and division. Digital computers employ the *binary* code of numbers that uses only two digits, 0 and 1; electronically this can be off and on, pulse and no pulse, or high and low levels of voltage. Bits are combined into "words" or *bytes* of varying length, typically 8, 16, or 32 bits.

Several important advantages and disadvantages inherent in digital computers should be noted. The digital computer forms the solution through a sequence of arithmetic operations known as *instructions*. A *program* is defined as an ordered sequence of instructions. The digital computer performs only one of these operations or instructions at a time, although at an almost unimaginable rate of speed.

Clearly, the digital computer solution is *not* instantaneous, as it obviously requires a finite, although extremely brief, time to form and sum the first terms of a series expansion. However, it is important to note that the solution can be made more accurate by merely summing more terms. Finally, the input variable need not be continuous; that is, the independent variable is treated as a discrete value, and the solution is the numerical result of the summation for that value.

The finite time required for the digital computer solution must be less than the time between significant changes of the input variable; otherwise, the solution would be seriously in error. Fortunately, the computation frequency of an electronic digital computer can be made much greater than the frequency of changes for most variables in the real world. The functions can be accomplished at the rate of 10 million or more operations per second.

A major advantage of the digital computer over the analog computer is its versatility. Analog computers usually require a hardware change to solve a new problem of a different form, but the digital computer may be reprogrammed to solve a new problem merely by rearranging the existing instructions already fed into the computer, or by preparing new instructions. In other words, a new problem of a different form merely requires a "software" change to the program of a digital computer. A large number of different programs for a single computer can be prepared in advance and stored, to be called up and used as later required.

NAVDAC

3805   The *NAVigation Data Assimilation Computer* (NAVDAC) is a real-time (precise time or clock time), general-purpose, digital computer originally designed for the Polaris submarine program. This computer has four primary functions:

Coordination—the control of all equipment in the entire system.
Data gathering for fixes from external fix sources.
Processing of fix data for reduction to SINS reset parameters.
Resetting SINS and *monitoring* results.

From these four functions it can be seen that NAVDAC is an integrator for the various navigational instruments, including the inertial system, velocity measuring devices, gyrocompasses, electronic navigation systems such as NAVSAT, Loran-C, Omega, and celestial altitude measurements, etc. It is, in fact, the central system for combining the individual components into a single operating system. Data from the individual input sources are processed by NAVDAC, drawing, when necessary, on its data storage or "memory" component, and the resultant information is used to determine the corrections to be applied to SINS, to indicate ship's position, etc. The data storage component has a tremendous capacity; for example, it stores the sidereal hour angle and declination for each of about 200 stars. All data are regularly updated, as required.

Since NAVDAC uses more than one fix-determining input, it must be able to filter the data received, correlate and weigh it, make logical and statistical decisions, perform coordinate conversions, and generate control functions. Consequently, a standard of accuracy and reliability previously unattainable is possible by means of the redundancy from multiple data sources. In addition to all this, the computer is able to carry out self-checking procedures for verifying the large number of computations that it has undertaken. NAVDAC has provided accuracies of data fully commensurate with the requirements of marine navigation.

Figure 3805a shows the role of NAVDAC in the operational system, together with its inputs and outputs, as well as its employment of both analog and digital computer information. Figure 3805b shows the NAVDAC data flow with input from an external electronic navigation system. Operation with any other system would differ only in the source and type of input. The function of the NAV-DAC computer has been described, since it is representative of the computer solution required for navigation of modern nuclear submarines. Other computers provide similar solutions. A later version, the MARDAN computer, used with the Auto-

netics N7F SINS, has a self-contained buffer allowing intercommunication with the other computers. It has a capacity of 4,096 words and a speed of up to 400 iterations per second. The Sperry SINDAC computer was shown in figure 3507c, in a shipboard installation.

MINDAC

3806 The *Mi*niature *I*nertial *N*avigation *D*igital *A*utomatic *C*omputer (MINDAC), is a general-purpose digital computer in a SINS system designed primarily to calculate present ship's position from heading and velocity input data, and to provide

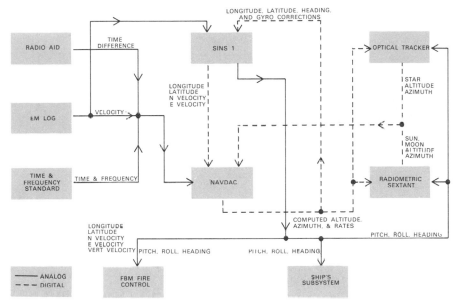

Figure 3805a. Block diagram of navigation system with NAVDAC.

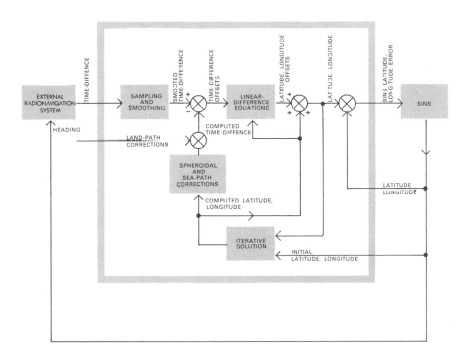

Figure 3805b. NAVDAC operation with input from an external radionavigation system.

appropriate bias and torquing signals to the gyros in order to keep the SINS inertial platform aligned to the vertical. In addition, it provides periodic readout of the ship's velocity and position to the central data processor, and resets the platform to the correct position when necessary at the operator's command.

While there are other computers that perform these same functions, MINDAC is the primary inertial platform alignment computer designed for use in the Integrated Navigation System described hereafter. It is also used aboard submarines and aircraft carriers with the Sperry Mk 3 Mod. 6 SINS.

Integrated Navigation System (INS)

3807 The *Integrated Navigation System* (INS) consists of a Ship's Inertial Navigation System (SINS), to which are added an automatic star tracker, a multispeed repeater, and instrumentation to provide accurate data on attitude (roll, pitch, and heading) for radar stabilization. The system also supplies velocity (north, east, or vertical), and latitude and longitude coordinates for ship control and navigation.

As may be seen in figure 3807, the INS receives inputs from a number of sources, processes the data, positions the star tracker (for day and night observations), and gives an output of navigation data and heading. This enables the proper positioning of the tracking equipment (radar) for immediate acquisition of the tracked object. INS is a subsystem of the complete *Ship's Position and Attitude Measurement System*, the components of which are also shown in figure 3807.

Future Computer Use

3808 Every year sees advances in computer design capabilities that were not even "dreams" a few years ago. The principal improvements have been made in the quantity of data that can be stored internally ("memory"), and the speed of operation. This has been achieved by the ever-increasing density of components on integrated circuits—ICs or "chips"; this has reached the almost unbelievable figure (in 1984) of some 450,000 transistors on a square chip a quarter of an inch on each side, and the density continues to expand with newer manufacturing processes. The advances in the general field of computers are, of course, reflected in those used for navigation.

Closely related to the use of computers for position fixing is their application to collision avoidance. One such application uses the U.S. Navy standard minicomputer AN/UYK-20 with the appropriate program loaded by means of a AN/USH-26 cartridge magnetic tape unit. Input is from the vessel's radar, and a dual output is available—alpha-numeric data added to the radar display plus a tabular listing of course, speed, closest point of approach, etc., for each "target" within range. Displays can be installed in CIC, at the navigator's station, and on the bridge. Use of the computer permits a conning officer to enter a *proposed* evasive action and immediately and fully see its potential effect on the situation before that action is ordered. The system is also very useful in taking station on a formation guide. For navigation, the essential features of a chart can be entered into the display, again through the use of digital data on magnetic tape, or a paper chart can be scanned by a high-resolution TV camera and so entered into the display.

In addition to computers used solely for navigation and collision avoidance—as described above—there are those intended for general shipboard use on a time-shared basis. The latter type is of very considerable interest to operators of large commercial vessels, as it fits in well with the present trend towards automation in such ships.

It seems probable that all naval vessels of the destroyer type as well as many of the larger military planes will soon be equipped with digital computers designed for navigation. Such a computer might give a continuous DR readout in latitude and longitude, based on data received from the gyrocompass and ship's log, as does the *Dead Reckoning Analyzer Indicator* (DRAI) currently in use. However, with the computer, the DR position could be updated on command from the navigator, based on any navigational data obtained, even a single line of position. In such a case, the computer would select the most probable position, and give, in effect, an EP. The computer would have its own time source, in the form of a quartz crystal clock or even a cesium atomic time standard, and a memory section capable of storing the SHA and Declination of a limited number of stars—those currently in use for morning and evening observations. GHA and Dec. of the sun, moon, and planets would be entered in the computer by means of a typewriter keyboard as required.

The computer would have a remote electronic readout of the altitude shown on the sextant; the latter would be fitted with a button to signal when the body was on the horizon, and the computer would note both time and altitude and almost instantaneously reduce the sight for computed altitude and azimuth, and determine the intercept. Several observations would yield a satisfactory fix

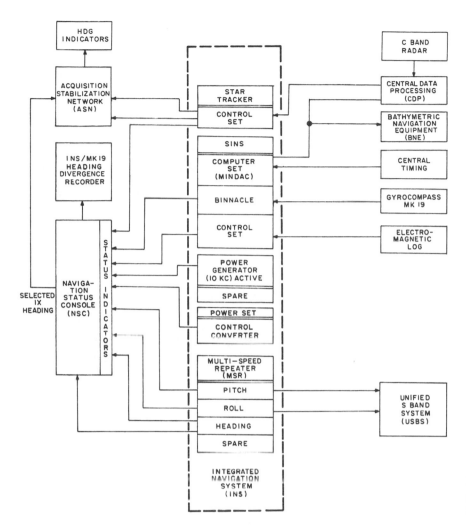

Figure 3807. INS data and signal inputs and outputs from and to external equipment.

automatically, the computer being able to differentiate between an internal and external fix (article 3009).

The navigator could thus take several observations of each body, without ever losing it from view, and these observations would be averaged by the computer in order to determine an excellent fix.

When used with such radionavigation systems as Loran-C, Omega, and NAVSAT, a computer is able to update a position continuously in terms of latitude and longitude based on the signals received.

Shipboard computers in many instances have the capability of solving both plane and spherical triangles. Great-circle distances and bearings (or initial headings) from the ship's position can be obtained almost instantaneously.

Computers in Non-naval Vessels

3809 The use of computers on merchant ships is steadily increasing and has even extended to smaller vessels and yachts. *Data loggers* have been

used with success to monitor the performance of both the main and auxiliary power plants aboard merchant ships for many years. Their function is to scan perhaps 300 or more test points at a rate of 2 to 25 or so readings per second, depending on the required control. The scanning sensors are transducers with rapid response, converting physical measurements into electrical signals. These signals are processed by the data logger for display, and an alarm may be actuated if any measurement exceeds a safe value.

The data logger has greatly increased power-plant efficiency; however, unlike the computer, it cannot exert any control function. The growing trend towards automation in the merchant service and the decreasing cost of computers, combined with increased reliability, versatility, and flexibility, all lead towards the increased use of computers in merchant ships. These computers are generally of the multipurpose type, and are programmed to serve several or all the ship's departments. For the engine room, such a computer can carry out all the functions of a data logger, and in addition, it can be programmed to take immediate corrective action when required. The fresh water supply can be monitored, and the evaporators started as needed. All in all, it can make possible a reduction in the number of men needed in the engineering spaces of a ship.

Such a computer can also be extremely valuable for navigation. In merchantmen, the mate on watch traditionally has performed all the navigator's duties during his tour on the bridge. Sight reduction and plotting can be time consuming, and sometimes may have to be slighted when other immediate problems demand attention. The computer can be programmed to do all this; in fact, if desired, it could be designed to perform all the navigational functions described in article 3808.

Of particular interest to commercial operators is the use of the computer for ship weather routing (chapter 41). The computer's memory section can store data on the ship's resistance moment, performance under various conditions of load, draft, sea state, and the resulting motion. Based on these data, and an input of weather and sea state reports, the computer can supply an immediate recommendation on the optimum course and speed to be employed.

It is expected that this ability of the computer to recommend optimum course and speed under conditions of adverse weather, as well as the improved accuracy in navigation it permits, will lead to greatly increased economy of operation.

A basic element of computers—the *microprocessor*—has found its way into many electronic navigation devices such as receivers for Loran-C, Omega, and NAVSAT, and even some depth sounders. This has now been expanded for small craft with an "Integrated Marine System" from Texas Instruments that takes inputs from navigation sensors (digital compass, knotmeter, Loran-C, NAVSAT, Omega, etc.), engine systems (temperatures, pressures, fuel and water levels, and flow rates, etc.), and general vessel systems (bilge levels, fume and fire detectors, rudder angle, trim tab position, etc.). Output is on a TV-like video monitor in terms of graphic plots, bar graphs, or alpha-numeric statements; data can also be printed out and/or recorded on magnetic tape cassettes for reference.

Chapter 39

Lifeboat Navigation

Introduction

3901 Despite the best of intentions and efforts, there is always the possibility that a navigator will one day find himself in a lifeboat with severely limited facilities and capabilities. As a survivor of a disaster at sea, he may need to practice his navigation skills in order to reach a place of safety. In addition, lifeboat navigation differs in that it is impossible to travel any considerable distance to windward even in a powered survival craft, and in that any destination must be carefully selected. It is also impossible to bring a lifeboat in to a beach through heavy surf without risking the loss of all hands; this has a direct bearing on the selection of a landfall and navigation toward it.

As long as ships ply the seas, ships will go down; and a prudent navigator must *plan ahead* for the possibility that his ship may be one of them. He cannot expect that there will be sufficient time to organize his equipment *after* the word is passed to abandon ship. In addition to being thoroughly familiar with the use of available equipment, he must be able to improvise and must know what actions are possible if either sextant, watch, reduction tables, or almanac is lost.

Advance Preparations

3902 The best way to lessen the severity of an emergency is to always be prepared for it. When the emergency occurs, it may be too late to "plan"; only "execution" is possible. There are several ways to prepare for the emergency of abandoning ship. The surest way is to make up an emergency navigational kit for *each* lifeboat and life raft, place it in a waterproof container, and lash it securely in place. The following items are desirable even if they cannot all be included in a kit for each lifeboat.

Charts, Publications, and Tools

Charts. The best charts for survival craft use are pilot charts for the area to be traveled. Both winter and summer charts should be included. The aircraft position charts, published by the National Ocean Service, are also excellent. They are prepared on the Lambert conformal conic projection; in addition to variation, they give data permitting the plotting of lines of position from Consol stations, if within an area of coverage, and if a radio receiver is available. Other plotting materials that may prove useful include a pad of Maneuvering Board sheets (the 10-inch DMAHTC Chart 5091 will be more convenient in a lifeboat than the 20-inch Chart 5092) and sheets of graph paper, preferably graduated in five or ten lines per inch.

Sextant. If possible, the ship's sextant should be taken into a lifeboat. If this is not possible, there are inexpensive plastic ones that should be in each survival craft; these are sufficiently precise and accurate for lifeboat navigation.

Almanac and star chart. If at all possible a *Nautical Almanac* and a *Star Finder* should be available. Failing the latter, charts in the *Nautical Almanac* may be used, although many navigators prefer the star chart included in the *Air Almanac*; the star chart from a superseded almanac may be saved for emergency use. A *Long-term Almanac* is included in *Bowditch*, Volume II (1975 or 1981), Appendix H. With the instructions for its use and auxiliary tables, it comprises six pages and supplies data on the sun and 30 of the selected stars. It does not become outdated and is surprisingly accurate; the maximum error in altitude computed by it should not exceed 2.0′ for the sun, and 1.3′ for the stars. It is wise to have these pages photocopied and included with each set of sight reduction tables to be used in boats. It is necessary to include copies of the refraction and dip tables from the *Nautical Almanac*, as these tables are not a part of the *Bowditch Long-term Almanac*. Copies of almanacs for recent years can be put in lifeboat navigation kits with instructions on the simple corrections to be applied for use in the current year. These are usable for the sun, Aries, and stars, with data being sufficiently accurate for emergency situations.

Tables. Although the two volumes of *Bowditch* constitute a considerable bulk to take into a lifeboat, consideration should be given to such action because of the vast amount of information contained therein. As an alternative, only Volume II with its tables, plus chapter XXVI of Volume I, could be taken into the boats.

Volume II of *Bowditch* now includes the Ageton tables for sight reduction, formerly published separately as H.O. 211. These are the most compact set of tables for sight reduction; they are used from a DR position, which is sometimes advantageous in lifeboat navigation. Condensed versions of the Ageton tables are now available in a compact size that easily fits within a sextant case.

For vessels operating only in a relatively limited ocean area, or repeatedly along certain routes, photocopy extracts could be made of just those pages of Pub. No. 229 or 249 that might be needed.

A 10-inch slide rule with sine/cosine scales permits a rapid reduction of observations for altitudes and azimuths. Equations for use with slide rules are given in article 3912. Altitudes to 30° may be solved to an accuracy of about 2′ if care is used; an accuracy of roughly 5′ may be obtained up to 50°. Electronic hand calculators, which have almost completely replaced slide rules in recent years, are of no value in lifeboats because of their dependence upon batteries that will quickly become discharged with no power source for recharging (except for a few newer models that are solar-powered).

Battery-powered radio. A small transistorized radio receiver can be of great value in obtaining time signals, especially if it has a short-wave band. It should be used sparingly to conserve battery power; spare batteries should be brought into the lifeboat if they are readily available and time permits.

EPIRB. Although not directly related to the navigation effort being made in the lifeboat, each craft should be equipped with an *Electronic Position In-dicating Radiobeacon* (EPIRB) type A or B. This small unit transmits a distinctive signal on the emergency frequencies (121.5 and 243.0 MHz) guarded by long-range civil and military aircraft; it can be received by high-flying planes out as far as 200 miles. An EPIRB can serve not only to alert authorities of a ship sinking, but also subsequently as a navigation aid for aircraft and ships searching for survivors.

Radar reflector. Folding radar reflectors are available, made of metal mesh or aluminum plates. Such a reflector returns a strong echo, and will make it much easier for search craft to locate a lifeboat by radar, particularly if the reflector is elevated. Aluminum kitchen foil may serve as a substitute, but with much less effectiveness.

Plastic bags. Fairly heavy plastic bags, such as are used for packaging ice cubes, are of great value for storing books, instruments, radio, etc., and keeping them dry in a lifeboat. The types that securely seal with a plastic "zipper" that changes color are especially valuable.

Notebook. Various items of general information from this chapter and any other desired information should be copied in advance. *Do not depend on memory.* Enough blank pages should be left to permit computations and for a log to be kept.

Plotting equipment. Be sure to include pencils, erasers, a protractor (very important), and some kind of straightedge; one measuring in metric units is preferable for its decimal subdivisions. Dividers and compasses may prove useful, but are not essential. A knife or some means of sharpening pencils should be provided.

American flag merchant ships are required by law to keep certain equipment in their lifeboats; however, this is all survival gear, and includes no navigational equipment beyond a simple magnetic compass.

Information

In addition to physical items of equipment, knowledge of certain facts is most useful and may be of great value under some conditions. Typical of such items are:

Positions. The approximate latitude and longitude of several ports, islands, etc., in the area in which the ship operates. This will prove useful if no chart is available. In addition, the approximate position of the ship should be known at all times. A general knowledge of the charts of the region in which the ship operates is often useful.

Currents. A general knowledge of the principal ocean currents in the operating area is valuable if no chart showing currents is available.

Weather. A general knowledge of weather is useful. The particular information of value in emergencies is a knowledge of prevailing winds at different seasons in the operating area, and the ability to detect early signs of approaching storms and to predict their paths relative to the course of the lifeboat.

Stars. The ability to identify stars may prove valuable, particularly if no star chart is available.

Whatever plan is adopted for preparation in case of an emergency, *be sure there is a definite plan.* Do not wait until the order to "abandon ship" to decide what to do. It may then be too late.

Abandoning Ship

3903   When the abandon ship order is given, the amount of preparation that can be made for navigation will depend on the time available. There is usually some warning. There are some things that must of necessity be left to the last moment, but it is not wise to let this list grow large. All actions in support of lifeboat navigation that will be required in an actual emergency should be a part of every abandon-ship drill.

A check list should be available without a search. The number of items on it will depend on the degree of preparation that has been made. The following minimum list assumes that a full navigational kit is available in the survival craft. Anything short of this should be taken into consideration in making the check list. Before leaving the ship, check the following:

Watch error. Determine the error and write it down. Be sure you know what kind of time your watch is keeping. Do not attempt to set it, but see that it is wound. It may be possible to take along a chronometer. Wristwatches of the "quartz" type, especially if their rate is known, will probably provide time of fully sufficient accuracy for lifeboat navigation; they do not require winding and generally are quite water-resistant, making them suitable for the wet environment of a boat. Having such a watch will lessen the need for radio time signals for celestial navigation.

Date. Check the date and write it down in the notebook, note the zone time being maintained.

Position. Write down the position of the ship. If possible, record also the set and drift of the current and the latitude and longitude of the nearest land in several directions. It may be easier to take along the chart or plotting sheet giving this information.

Navigational equipment. Check the navigational equipment in the craft. Look particularly to see that there is a compass, chart, and watch. If anything is missing, is it possible to get it from the ship? Do not abandon the ship's sextant. If a portable radio is available, take it along.

See that all equipment is properly secured before lowering the boat.

Getting Organized in the Lifeboat

3904   The first consideration after abandoning ship is to decide whether to remain as close as possible to the scene, or try to reach land or a heavily traveled shipping lane. This will generally depend on whether or not a distress signal was sent, and acknowledged, before the vessel was abandoned, and when help might be expected to arrive. Even if it is decided to remain at the scene, navigation will still be required to keep the survival craft as close as possible to the reported position despite winds and currents that would carry it away.

If no assistance can be expected, a navigator must always bear in mind that long voyages in poorly equipped lifeboats *can* be made, as proved by Captain Bligh, of HMS *Bounty*, who sailed 3,000 miles when cast adrift in an open boat. He must also remember that morale is a factor of the highest importance if a long journey is to be attempted.

The first few hours in a lifeboat may prove the most important. If medicine for seasickness is available, take it at once, even before leaving the ship if possible.

There must be a definite understanding of who is to be in charge, not to exercise autocratic rule, but to regulate the cramped life in the lifeboat and avoid confusion. Extreme fairness and equality are important if good teamwork and high morale are to be maintained. *If there are several boats in the water, considerable advantage is to be gained by their staying together, if possible.*

Before setting out on any course, it is important to make an *estimate of the situation.* Do not start out until you know where you are going; determine this carefully and deliberately. This may be the most important decision of the entire journey; make it carefully.

First, determine the number of watches available, and determine as accurately as possible the error of each watch. Learn from each owner all that is available regarding the rate and reliability of his timepiece. Record this information and establish a regular routine for winding those watches having a spring-driven movement, and checking them.

Record the best-known latitude and longitude of the point of departure and the time of day. Let this be the beginning of a carefully kept log.

In choosing the first course, carefully study all factors. *Do not set the course until you are sure the best possible one has been determined.*

A number of factors will influence the decision. If a pilot chart is available, study it minutely and be sure you are thoroughly familiar with the average current and prevailing winds to be expected. Consider the motive power available and the probable speed. It may be better to head for land some distance away, if wind and current will help, than for nearby land that will be difficult to reach.

Note the location of the usually traveled shipping routes. These are shown on the pilot chart. If more than one suitable course is available, choose the one that will take you nearest to a well-traveled shipping route. Remember, in selecting a course, that the upwind range of even a powered lifeboat is very limited. Captain Bligh knew that there were islands within about 200 miles upwind, but he knew he could not reach them; his decision to take the long 3,000-mile downwind journey made survival possible.

Consider the size and height of any nearby land, and the navigation equipment available. Remember that the horizon is quite close when the observer is standing in a lifeboat; the distance to the horizon in miles is about 1.17 times the square root of the height of eye in feet. (Square roots can be determined by trial-and-error calculations if no table or slide rule is available.) Consider the probable accuracy with which positions can be determined. A small low island some distance away may be extremely hard to find with crude navigational methods; it may be advantageous to head for a more distant, but higher and more easily seen, landfall.

If the destination is on a continental land mass at a known latitude, it is often wise to direct one's course toward a point somewhat north or south of that place, and then when land is reached, run south or north along the coastline to the objective. This will eliminate the uncertainty as to which way to turn that will exist if land is reached at what is believed to be the correct latitude, but the destination is not sighted.

Will accurate time be available? Remember that the latitude can be determined accurately without time, but the longitude will be no more accurate than the time. If there is any question of the ability to maintain reasonably accurate time (each four seconds error in time results in 1' error in the longitude), do not head straight for the destination, but for a point that is certain to take the boat to the east or west of the destination, and then when the latitude of the destination has been reached, head due west or east and maintain the latitude. This method was successfully used for centuries before the invention of the chronometer.

Having decided upon the course to follow and the probable average speed, including help from current and wind, estimate the time of reaching the destination and set the ration of water and food accordingly.

Assess the knowledge, ability, and aptitude of all on board and assign each of them certain responsibilities. *Establish a definite routine.*

If adequate distress signals were sent before abandoning ship, you can expect that rescue ships or planes will conduct a search, and it will probably be best to remain as near as possible to the last reported position of the ship.

Morale

3905 An important part of the trip back to safety is the maintaining of a high morale. With great determination and cool judgment almost any difficulty can be overcome. This is proved by many great tales of the sea. The story of Captain Bligh, previously mentioned, is perhaps one of the greatest illustrations of the value of patience and determination.

Morale and navigation are closely interrelated. Good health and morale will materially aid in the practice of good navigation. The capability to navigate adequately will definitely contribute toward hope of survival, an essential ingredient of good morale.

A regular routine and a definite assignment of duties is valuable from the standpoint of morale. Include in the routine regular periods for reading aloud from the Bible if one is available. This will not only provide a means of occupying time, but will constitute a source of encouragement and add to the faith and determination of the crew. Remember, also, the high value placed on prayer by those who have been through the experience of abandoning a ship at sea.

Dead Reckoning

3906 *Dead reckoning* is always important, but never more so than when in a lifeboat. Determine as accurately as possible the point of departure and keep a record of courses, speeds, estimated ocean currents, and leeway. Do not be too quick to abandon a carefully determined estimated position for an uncertain fix by crude methods. Unless really accurate methods of navigation are available, consider all positions as EPs and carefully evaluate all information available. The real test of a navigator is how accurately he can evaluate the information at hand and from it determine his true position. Upon this ability may depend the question of whether the lifeboat arrives at its destination.

Take full advantage of all conditions. When the wind is favorable, make all the distance possible in the desired direction. It may sometimes be advantageous to change course slightly to make greater speed in a direction differing somewhat from the desired course. If the wind is definitely unfavorable, put out a sea anchor and reduce the leeway.

Attempt to keep a plot of the track of the boat. Plotting in an open boat may be difficult; it may be easier to keep account of movements mathematically by means of the traverse table in article 3909.

Direction

3907 At the very start of the voyage it is well to check the accuracy of the compass on the course to be steered. The variation can be determined from the pilot chart, but to find the deviation, if this is not accurately known, locate a bit of wreckage in the water or throw overboard an object that will not drift too much with the wind and take the reciprocal magnetic course to the one desired. After this has been followed for some distance (a half mile to a mile), turn and steer for the object. If there is no deviation, the compass course will be the reciprocal of that first steered. If it is not, the desired compass course is half way between the reciprocal of the first course and the compass course back to the object.

Underway the compass error should be checked at regular intervals. In the Northern Hemisphere Polaris can be considered to be due north except in very high latitudes (above L 60° N the error can be greater than 2°). When Polaris is directly above or below the pole the azimuth is 000° in any latitude. When the sun, or any body, reaches its highest altitude, it can be considered to be on the celestial meridian, bearing 180° or 000°. These are true directions, and yield compass error directly, not deviation. If an almanac and a method of computation are available, the true direction of any body can be determined at any time by the usual methods of computing azimuth.

If a compass is not available, an approximation of a straight course can be steered by towing a line secured at the gunwale amidships. If the boat deviates from a straight track, the line will move away from its neutral position approximately parallel to the side of the craft. With a cross sea this method is less accurate, but may be better than nothing at all. Do *not* steer by a cloud on or near the horizon; these move with the wind and a curved, rather than straight, track will result. At night the boat can be kept on a reasonably straight course north or south, east or west by steering by Polaris or a body near the prime vertical.

Speed

3908 Throughout the trip, speed should be determined as accurately as possible. Ability to estimate speed will be developed by practice. One crude method of measuring speed is to throw a floating object overboard at the bow and note the time required for the boat to pass it. For this purpose a definite distance should be marked off along the gunwale. Make this as long as practicable, but a length that will facilitate calculations—a length that is divisible into 100 a whole number of times, such as 25, 20, 16.7, or 10. In round figures, a boat traveling 100 feet in 1 minute is moving at a speed of 1 knot. If, for example, the length marked off is 25 feet (one-fourth of 100 feet) and an object is thrown overboard at the forward mark, it should be opposite the after mark in 15 seconds (one-fourth of one minute) if the boat is making 1 knot, 7.5 seconds if the speed is 2 knots, 5 seconds if 3 knots, etc. If the distance were 16.7 feet (one-sixth of 100 feet), the times would be 10 seconds for 1 knot, 5 seconds for 2 knots, etc. A table or curve of speed vs. time can easily be made. Speed determined in this manner is relative to the *water* and not speed made good over the bottom.

Since objects available for throwing overboard may be scarce, a light line, such as used for fishing, may be attached to the object and the other end secured to the boat so that the object can be recovered and used again; this line must be able to run out freely. Alternatively, a small drogue can be improvised from a piece of cloth and a light line; this makes a good log line. Knot the line at intervals similar to those listed above or multiples of these. As the drogue is streamed aft, the time between the passage of two knots through the hand is noted. The drogue should be some distance astern before starting to take time; the knot at which time is started should therefore be 25 feet (7.6 m) or so forward of the drogue. *Be sure the line can run out freely.*

Even without a watch, the method can still be used. A member of the crew who has practiced with a chronometer, such as a quartermaster who has been responsible for checking a comparing watch with a chronometer, may have become quite proficient at counting seconds and half seconds. A half-second counter can be improvised by making a simple pendulum. Attach any small heavy weight to a light line. If the pendulum is 9.8 inches long (24.9 cm) to the center of the weight, the period (over and back) is 1 second. If the length is 39.1 inches (99.3 cm) long, the period is 2 seconds. The boat should be reasonably steady when this technique is used, as any pitching or rolling will affect the regular swinging of the pendulum.

Traverse Table

3909 A simple traverse table can have many uses; it is especially valuable if a graphic plot cannot be made of the boat's travel. In the first table below, the course is given in the first four columns, the difference of latitude in minutes per mile distance along the course in the fifth, and the departure or miles east or west per mile distance in the sixth. To find *l* and p multiply the tabulated value by the distance; the course determines whether the values are north or south, east or west.

Course				*l*	*p*
°	°	°	°		
000	180	180	360	1.00	0.00
005	175	185	355	1.00	0.09
010	170	190	350	0.98	0.17
015	165	195	345	0.97	0.26
020	160	200	340	0.94	0.34
025	155	205	335	0.91	0.42
030	150	210	330	0.87	0.50
035	145	215	325	0.82	0.57
040	140	220	320	0.77	0.64
045	135	225	315	0.71	0.71
050	130	230	310	0.64	0.77
055	125	235	305	0.57	0.82
060	120	240	300	0.50	0.87
065	115	245	295	0.42	0.91
070	110	250	290	0.34	0.94
075	105	255	285	0.26	0.97
080	100	260	280	0.17	0.98
085	095	265	275	0.09	1.00
090	090	270	270	0.00	1.00

Lm	p to DLo	Lm	p to DLo	Lm	p to DLo
°		°		°	
0	1.00	30	1.15	60	2.00
5	1.00	35	1.22	65	2.37
10	1.02	40	1.30	70	2.92
15	1.04	45	1.41	75	3.86
20	1.06	50	1.56	80	5.76
25	1.10	55	1.74	85	11.47

These tables can be used for the solution of any right triangle. For the distance covered by a lifeboat during one day, the earth can be considered a plane without appreciable error. Apply the difference in latitude to the latitude at the beginning of the run. To convert p to DLo, multiply p by a factor

taken from the table below. The mid-latitude is the entering argument. Both differences of latitude and difference of longitude are in minutes. The course indicates the direction in which to apply them.

A photocopy of the above two tables should be made and fastened into the notebook that is a part of each lifeboat navigation kit.

Example: A lifeboat leaves Lat. 28°37′S, Long. 160°12′E and follows course 240° for 80 miles.

Required: The latitude and longitude at the end of this run.

Solution: Enter the first table with C240° and find *l* = 0.50, p = 0.87. Since the distance is 80 miles, the difference in latitude is 80 × 0.50 = 40′. Since the course is 240°, this is a southerly change; hence the latitude after the run is 28°37′S + 40′S = 29°17′S.

Enter the second table with the mid-latitude 29° S and take out "p to DLo" as 1.14 by interpolation. The DLo is then 80 × 0.87 × 1.14 = 79′; this is westerly. Thus the longitude after the run is 160°12′E − 79′W = 158°53′E.

Answer: Lat. 29°17′S, Long. 158°53′E.

If desired, the values of *l* and p can be found graphically by constructing the triangle of figure 3909a. A Maneuvering Board sheet (chapter 14) is useful for this purpose, but not essential. The conversion from p to DLo can also be made graphically, as shown in figure 3909b. However, it is usually as easy to plot directly on a chart or plotting sheet as to make graphic solutions in the way just described.

Measuring Altitudes

3910 If a sextant is available, the altitude of a celestial body can be measured as described in chapter 21. Be sure to determine the index correction. To assure optimum observations when using a sextant in a lifeboat or in any other small craft, the observer should obtain his altitude at the instant the crest of a wave is directly under his position in the boat. The height of eye used in calculations should be the height in calm water plus one-half of the height of the waves. If no sextant is available, altitudes can be measured in several ways, including the following:

Protractor. A protractor, a Maneuvering Board sheet fastened securely to a board, or any graduated circle or semicircle can be used in any of several ways.

In figure 3910a a weight is attached to the center of curvature by a string that crosses the outer scale. If a plotter such as the one shown in figure 721a is used, a hole for attaching the string is already pro-

Figure 3909a. Traverse sailing.

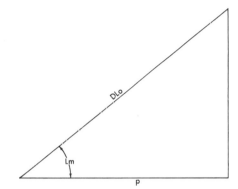

Figure 3909b. Converting p to dLo graphically.

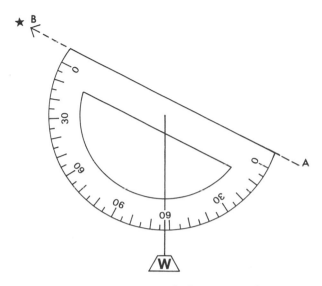

Figure 3910a. Measuring zenith distance with a protractor.

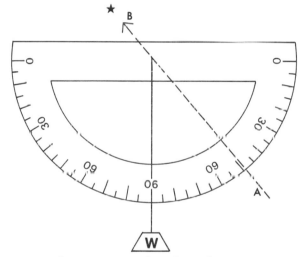

Figure 3910b. Measuring altitude with a protractor.

vided. The observer sights along the straightedge of the protractor, *AB*, towards the body. Another person reads the point on the scale where it is crossed by the string. This is the zenith distance if the protractor is graduated as shown in figure 3910a; the altitude is 90° minus this reading. In figure 3910a, the reading is 62½° and hence the observed altitude is 27½°. Several readings should be taken, some with the protractor reversed; all of these are averaged for a more accurate value. This method should not be used for the sun unless the eyes are adequately protected.

In figure 3910b the weight is attached to a pin at the center of curvature and the protractor held horizontally, as indicated by the string crossing at 90°. The assistant holds the protractor and keeps the string on 90°. The observer moves a pin, pencil point, or other thin object along the scale until this pin and the center one are in line with the body. The body is then in direction *AB*. When the protractor is used in this way, the altitude is indicated directly. In figure 3910b an altitude of about 49° is being measured. This method should not be used for the sun unless the eyes are protected.

For the sun, either of the above methods can be used if a pin is mounted perpendicularly at the cen-

ter of the protractor. In the first method the reading is made when the shadow of the pin falls on 0°. In the second method the reading is made at the shadow.

There are several other variations of the use of the protractor. In the second method the weight can be omitted and the assistant can sight along the straightedge at the horizon. An observation can be made without an assistant if the weight is attached at the scale at 90° and a loop of string placed over the pin at the center of curvature for holding the device. If preferred, a handle can be attached at 90° on the scale and the weight hung from the center of curvature, the protractor being inverted. The first method can be used without an assistant if the

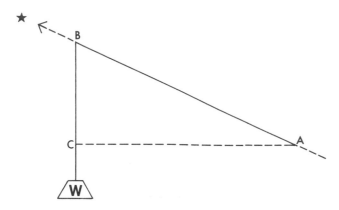

Figure 3910c. Measuring altitude without a protractor.

string is secured in place by the thumb and forefinger when the observation is made.

If no protractor is available, but there is handy a Maneuvering Board pad, one of these sheets may be fastened to any flat surface that can be raised to eye level. The same procedures are used as with a more conventional protractor; pins stuck into the board make sighting easier and more accurate.

If no scale graduated in degrees is available, place two pins or nails in a board (figure 3910c) and attach a weight to *B* by means of a string. Sight along *AB* and line up the two pins with the body. If the sun is being observed, hold the board so that the shadow of *B* falls on *A*. When *A* and *B* are lined up with the body, secure the string in place with the thumb and forefinger. From *A* draw *AC* perpendicular to the string. The traverse table can then be used to find the angle, entering the difference of latitude column with length *BC* or the departure column with *AC*. In either case the length is given in units of *AB*. That is, if *AB* is 10 inches, the length *BC* or *AC* in inches is divided by 10 before entering the table. A simple way is to divide *AC* by *BC* and use the table below, entering the L/H column with *AC* ÷ *BC*.

Length of shadow. If a bucket or other container is available, altitudes of the sun can be determined by measuring the length of a shadow. Drive a nail or other pointer in a board and float the board on water (the boat must be steady). The top of the pointer should be pointed for accurate results. If a nail is used, drive it through the board and turn the board over. Measure carefully the length of the shadow. Turn the board approximately 180° in azimuth and measure again. Divide the average of the two readings by the height of the pin and enter the following table (or any table of natural cotangents) to find the altitude.

In this table *L* is the length of the shadow and *H* is the pin height.

Alt.	L/H	Alt.	L/H	Alt.	L/H
°		°		°	
5	11.430	35	1.428	65	0.466
10	5.671	40	1.192	70	0.364
15	3.732	45	1.000	75	0.268
20	2.747	50	0.839	80	0.176
25	2.145	55	0.700	85	0.087
30	1.732	60	0.577	90	0.000

Example: The length of the shadow of a pin 4.0 inches long is 6.3 inches, or similar dimensions in metric units.

Required: The altitude of the sun.

Solution: L ÷ H = 6.3 ÷ 4 = 1.575. Interpolating in the table, the altitude is found to be 32.6°.

Answer: h = 33°.

Note: In all calculations of lifeboat navigation, care must be taken *not* to carry the calculations to a finer degree of precision than is warranted by the input data. In the above example, the length of the pin was stated to be 4.0 inches—this is two significant figures. It would be unwarranted, with such a statement of one element of the equation, to state altitude to the tenth of a degree, three significant figures in this example; even the exactness of "33°" is less than justified by this method and with this data. In lifeboat navigation it is self-delusion (perhaps dangerously so) to carry calculations to the same degree of refinement as done on a larger vessel. Even if a marine sextant and exact time by radio is available, the movement of a small boat, the uncertainty of the height of the observer's eye, and similar factors, do not justify position measurements more precise than a whole minute and azimuths to a whole degree—and even this level of precision is subject to question.

When using any of the methods described, several observations should be made, and the average used with the average time. If possible, reverse the device for half the readings.

Whatever method is used, *measure* the altitude, however crude the method. Do not attempt to estimate it, for estimates are seldom as accurate as the crudest measurement. If a damaged sextant is available, try to repair it. If the mirrors are broken, plain glass held in place by chewing gum or anything else available will usually be satisfactory.

Correction of Measured Altitudes

3911   If altitudes are measured from the visible horizon, they are corrected in the usual way, as explained in chapter 21. Altitudes of the sun should be corrected for refraction, mean semidiameter, and dip. Altitudes of stars should be corrected for refraction and dip. If a weight is used to establish the vertical, or if the length of a shadow is measured, there is no correction for dip. If the sun's altitude is measured by means of a shadow, whether the length of the shadow is measured or the shadow falls across a scale or another pin, the center of the sun is measured, and hence no correction for semidiameter is needed.

Refraction. Approximate altitude corrections for refraction can be found as follows:

Alt. °	5	6	7	8	10	12	15	21	33	63	90
Corr. '	9	8	7	6	5	4	3	2	1	0	

The critical type table shown above provides corrections from 5° to 90°. If crude methods of observing the altitudes are employed, it may be sufficiently accurate to apply the correction only to the nearest 0.1°. For this procedure, altitudes above 20° can be considered to have no correction and those between 5° and 20° to have a correction of 0.1°. Observations below 5° should not be made if they can be avoided. The correction for refraction is always subtractive and must be applied to observations of all bodies, regardless of the method used.

If a slide rule is available, the refraction correction for altitudes above 10° may be found accurately by multiplying the cotangent of the altitude by 0.96°.

Mean semidiameter. The mean semidiameter of the sun is 16′ and the actual value does not differ from this by more than 0.3′. If the lower limb is observed, the correction is (+) and if the upper limb is observed, the correction is (−).

Dip. The correction for dip, in minutes of arc, is equal to the square root of the height of eye in feet, to sufficient accuracy for lifeboat use. (The *Nautical Almanac* tables do not give a dip correction for height of eye less than 8 feet or 2.4 m). This correction is used for all bodies whenever the visible horizon is used as a reference; it is always (−). Dip may be determined more exactly with a slide rule; multiply the square root of the height of eye in feet by 0.97, or the square root of the height of eye in meters by 1.76.

Parallax. No correction is made for parallax, unless the moon is used, for it is too small to be a consideration in lifeboat navigation when other bodies are observed.

Horizon Sights

3912 A line of position may be obtained without a sextant or other altitude-measuring instruments by noting the time a celestial body makes contact with the visible horizon. The body most suitable for such observations is the sun, and either the upper or lower limb may be used; the best practice would be to time both when they contact the horizon, and use the mean of the two resulting intercepts. Binoculars, if available, will assist in determining the instant of contact; there must be no clouds on the horizon in that direction.

Such observations will usually yield surprisingly accurate results; they will certainly be more satisfactory than LOPs obtained from measurements made by improvised altitude-measuring devices.

The uncorrected altitude is noted as 0°0′, and carefully corrected for dip, refraction, and semidiameter. The correction for dip is made by adding its value numerically to the value of the refraction correction. Thus, if the semidiameter is 16.0′ and the height of eye is 6 feet 6 inches, the corrections to an upper limb sun horizon sight would be as follows:

Height of eye 6′6″	Dip −	2.5′
0° H, Refraction	−	34.5′
☉	SD −	16.0′
Correction		53.0′

The corrected altitude would be 0° minus 53.0′ or −53.0′. Under nonstandard atmospheric conditions, the additional corrections for temperature and barometric pressure should be applied, if a thermometer and barometer are available; in actual lifeboat circumstances, however, this is unlikely.

The sight may be reduced by the tables of Pub. No. 229 or the Ageton (H.O. 211) tables in *Bowditch*, Volume II. It must be remembered that when *both* Ho and Hc are negative, the intercept will be *"towards" if Ho is numerically less than Hc*, and vice versa; this is the *reverse* of the normal procedure.

Very low altitude sights may also be reduced quite rapidly by means of a slide rule having sine/cosine scales, using the equation

$$\sin Hc = \sin L \sin D \pm \cos L \cos d \cos t.$$

Hc is negative, if its sine is negative. Accurate solutions may be obtained at very low latitudes; as at altitudes below 2°, a sine may be read to about 0.2′ on a 10-inch slide rule. Azimuth angle may be obtained by means of the equation:

$$\sin Z = \frac{\cos d \sin t}{\cos Hc}$$

At very low altitudes, the division by cosine Hc may be ignored, as in such cases the cosine approaches unity. (See article 2402 for naming the sign.)

Any low-altitude observations may yield results that are in error by a few miles under conditions of abnormal terrestrial refraction. However, Captain P.V.H. Weems, USN (Retired) made ten horizon sights at sea on six different occasions, which gave an average error of 1.95 miles and a maximum error of 4.0 miles.

An azimuth of the sun should be obtained at the same time the horizon sight is made, as a check on the accuracy of the compass.

The Green Flash

The *green flash* is a common phenomenon in the tropics, and occurs at the moment the sun's upper limb touches the horizon. It is caused by refraction of the light waves from the sun as they pass through the earth's atmosphere; there must be no low clouds on the horizon in the direction of the sunset. These light waves are not refracted, or bent, equally, the longer waves of red light being least refracted, the shorter blue and violet waves being more refracted. The red, orange, and yellow light is cut off by the horizon when the blue and violet light is still momentarily visible. These blue and violet rays cause the green flash.

It is estimated that at sea in the tropics, the green flash may be seen as often as 50 percent of the time; it is, of course, easier to observe at sunset. The green flash usually lasts for a period of between one-half and one second.

Using the time of the green flash to obtain a line of position is merely a variation of the horizon sight described in the previous article. It is somewhat easier to use the time of the flash than to determine the instant the sun's upper limb disappears below the horizon when there is no green flash.

A green flash sight is corrected and reduced similarly to the horizon sight, described above.

Lines of Position

3913 If tables are available for computation of Hc, lines of position are used in the usual way, as explained in chapter 25. However, if no such tables are available, latitude and longitude should be determined separately, as was done before the discovery of the line of position by Captain Sumner in 1837.

If accurate time is not available, it will not be possible to determine longitude. In this case, no attempt should be made to steer directly for the destination unless a whole continent is involved. Instead, the course should be set for a point well to the eastward or westward of the destination and when the latitude has been reached, a course of 090° or 270°, as appropriate, should be followed, as mentioned earlier in the chapter. If a single wrist watch is used for time and the journey is likely to be a long one, the time may be of questionable accuracy before the end of the voyage. If the watch is in error by 1 minute, longitude will be inaccurate by 15'. If the destination is a small island, the course should be set for a point 50 to 100 miles, or more, according to the maximum reasonable error in time, to the eastward or westward. In making this estimate allow for large watch rates, since the rate in a lifeboat will probably not be the same as aboard ship. Watches controlled by quartz crystals will give consistently better results than others.

Finding Latitude

3914 The latitude of a position can be determined in the Northern Hemisphere by means of an altitude observation of Polaris, and in any latitude by means of meridian altitudes, as explained in chapter 27.

Latitude by Polaris. If a Polaris correction table is not available, the correction can be estimated in the following way: A line through Polaris and the north celestial pole, if extended, passes between ε Cassiopeiae and Ruchbah (the two left-hand stars of *Cassiopeia* when it appears as a W) on one side and Alkaid and Mizar (the last two stars in the handle of the big dipper) on the other. In both constellations these are the trailing stars in the counterclockwise motion about the pole. Polaris is on the side of the pole toward *Cassiopeia.* The correction depends only on the angle this line makes with the vertical. The accompanying critical-value type of table gives the correction. If *Cassiopeia* is above Polaris, the correction is (−); if the *Big Dipper* is above, the correction is (+). If no correction table is available, it may be possible to estimate the correction from the relative positions of the two constellations. In figure 3914a the angle is 40°, and from the table the correction is found to be 0.8°. Since *Cassiopeia* is above the pole, the correction is −0.8°.

Meridian altitude. At survival craft speed, the most accurate results by the meridian altitude method are usually obtained by observing the highest altitude. For this purpose, a number of observations should be made before and after meridian transit. If graph paper is available, plot the altitude vs. time and fair a curve through the points. A typical curve is shown in figure 3914b. Although the highest altitude measured is 40.0°, the meridian altitude is found to be 39°58'. For this plot altitudes were observed to the nearest 0.1° at five-minute intervals. If preferred, altitudes can be observed at less frequent intervals, perhaps each half hour, during the entire day. At a stationary point the

Angle °	0	14	30	40	48	56	62	69	75	81	87	90
Corr. °		1.0	0.9	0.8	0.7	0.6	0.5	0.4	0.3	0.2	0.1	0.0

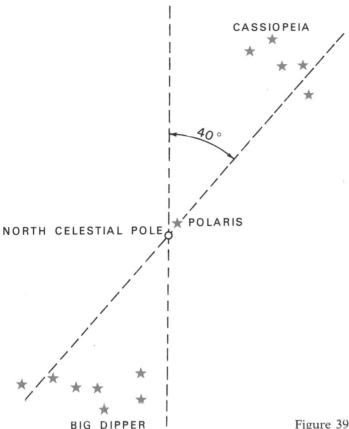

Figure 3914a. Estimating the Polaris correction.

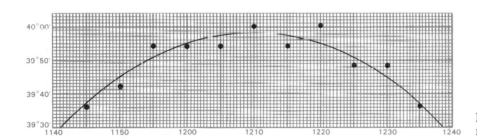

Figure 3914b. Curve of altitudes near meridian transit (typical).

curve should be symmetrical before and after meridian transit; at lifeboat speeds it should approach symmetry. The highest altitude is independent of time, which is used only to space the observations at any desired interval. Approximately equal intervals can be estimated by using a pendulum, as explained in article 3908, or by counting at an even speed to any desired amount.

When the meridian altitude has been determined, combine it with the body's declination to find the latitude, as explained in chapter 27.

The latitude can also be found by the duration of daylight, as described in article 3916.

Obtaining the Declination of the Sun

3915 If tables of the declination of the sun are not available, an approximate value can be found as follows:

Draw a circle, the larger the better, and draw horizontal and vertical diameters. Label the left intersection of the diameter and the circle March 21 and the right intersection September 23. Label the top of the circle June 22 and the bottom December 22. Divide each quadrant into a number of spaces equal to the number of days between the limiting dates. Divide the vertical *radius* into 23.45 linear units with 0 at the center, positive above the center and negative below the center. To find the declination, draw a horizontal line from the date to the vertical diameter and read off the declination in degrees. See figure 3915. A compass rose or a Maneuvering Board sheet is convenient for this purpose. If the latter is used, consider the radius 1 and multiply the reading by 23.45 to find the declination. The maximum error of this method is about half a degree; not good, but better than nothing at all.

The declination can also be found by means of the traverse table, as follows: Refer to figure 3915. Find the angle *A* between the radius to the nearest solstice (June 22 or December 22) and the given date. Enter the traverse table with this as a course and take out *l*, the difference of latitude. Multiply this value by 23.45 and the answer is declination in degrees. To find the angle *A*, find the number of days between the given date and the nearest solstice. Divide the latter by the former and multiply by 90°. For example, in figure 3915 there are 93 days between March 21 and June 22 and 36 days between May 17 and June 22.

$$A = \frac{36}{93} \times 90° = 34.8°$$

From the traverse table the value of *l* is 0.82. The declination is

$$\text{Dec.} = 0.82 \times 23.45° = 19.2°$$

Finding Longitude

3916   In figure 3914b the highest point on the curve represents meridian transit, or LAN; it can be seen that the time of transit is 1210. At this moment, the sun is the same distance west of Greenwich as the observer, and if a table of GHA of the sun is available, or if the equation of time is known, the approximate longitude can be determined. (Without a fairly accurate timepiece there is, of course, no method for determining longitude.)

The time of meridian transit can be found by picking off two points on this curve at which the altitude is the same, and noting the respective times meridian transit occurs midway between them.

Greater accuracy may be obtained if the observations for equal altitude are made when the sun's rate of change of altitude is greater than that

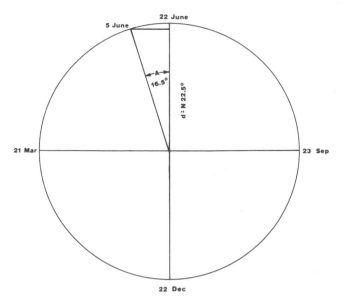

Figure 3915. Determination of the approximate declination of the sun graphically.

shown in figure 3914b—say an hour before and after transit in this case. A better practice would be to obtain a series of altitudes before transit, plotting them against time, then drawing in a line of best fit, which over a period of a few minutes would be represented by a straight line. Then, after transit, the sextant would be reset to the last and highest altitude obtained before LAN, and when the sun reached this altitude, a new series of sights would be begun. These also should be plotted. Note that actual observations do not have to be used; equal altitudes, with their times, may be taken from the lines of best fit. The time of meridian transit is the midpoint of the times of pairs of equal altitudes.

This method can be used with any body. If no means of measuring an altitude is available, the instant at which the body bears 180° or 000° true should be noted.

If a star is used, it is necessary to have its GHA. If its SHA is known, its GHA can be found approximately, by knowing that GHA ♈ in time units equals GMT on 23 September. GHA ♈ in time units is 90° more than GMT on 22 December, 180° more on 21 March, and 270° more on 22 June. GHA ♈ in time units gains approximately 4 minutes per day on GMT. The GHA of a star is equal to GHA ♈ + SHA.

The equation of time can be found approximately from the table below.

Linear interpolation in this table does not produce very accurate results because of the uneven variation of the equation of time. The value varies from year to year also, as does declination, but almost repeats every four years. If an almanac is available, it should be used.

Date	Eq. T	Date	Eq. T	Date	Eq. T
	m s		m s		m s
Jan. 10	−7 29	May 10	+3 41	Sept. 10	+2 53
20	11 02	20	3 39	20	6 25
30	13 21	30	2 42	30	9 51
Feb. 10	14 21	June 10	+0 50	Oct. 10	12 51
20	13 53	20	−1 16	20	15 05
28	12 43	30	3 23	30	16 15
Mar. 10	10 30	July 10	5 08	Nov. 10	16 04
20	7 41	20	6 10	20	14 25
30	4 39	30	6 19	30	11 25
Apr. 10	−1 27	Aug. 10	5 19	Dec. 10	7 20
20	+1 01	20	3 24	20	+2 33
30	2 47	30	−0 43	30	−2 25

Example: The altitude of the sun is 30° at $11^h21^m14^s$ and again at $12^h06^m32^s$ on 15 July. The watch is keeping +9 ZT.

Required: Find the longitude, using the equation of time table above.

Solution: The time of transit is midway between the two times given, or at $11^h43^m53^s$. The GMT is 9 hours later, or $20^h43^m53^s$. The equation of time on 15 July is -5^m39^s. Hence, the Greenwich apparent time (GAT) is $20^h43^m53^s - 5^m39^s = 20^h38^m14^s$. The GHA is equal to GAT ± 12^h, or $8^h38^m14^s = 129°33.5'$. This is the longitude.

Answer: Long. 129°34′W. (Although times are shown to have been measured to the precision of the nearest second, note that the altitude of the sun is only stated to the nearest *degree*, implying a relatively crude and inexact technique. In this instance, longitude should be given only to the nearest minute, and that degree of precision is of doubtful validity.)

If the only watch should run down, it can be started again *approximately* by working this problem in reverse. That is, start with the best estimated longitude and find the GAT, then the GMT, and finally the ZT. Set the watch according to this time. Do this at the first opportunity after the watch runs down, while the EP is still reasonably good.

Longitude can also be determined by the time of sunrise or sunset, if a sunrise-sunset table is available. The process is somewhat similar to that just described for meridian transit. Find the LMT of sunrise or sunset from the table. Note the exact watch time of the phenomenon and from this find the GMT. The difference between GMT and LMT is

the longitude. This depends on a knowledge of the boat's latitude. It has the advantage that the only equipment needed is a watch and sunrise-sunset table. It is, however, not very accurate, and longitude so obtained will not be as reliable as that taken from a horizon sight line of position, using the same latitude.

Latitude can be determined in this way, too, but even less accurately. Near the equinox, it is practically worthless and of little value at any time near the equator. To use the method, the times of sunrise *and* sunset are noted, and the total period of daylight determined. This is a function of the latitude on any given date. The latitude having this length of daylight is determined from the almanac. This is perhaps the least accurate way of finding latitude and should be used only when there is no means of measuring altitude. The time of day need not be accurate, for only the *duration* of daylight is needed.

Estimating Distance Off

3917 If land or a ship is seen, it may be of value to know its approximate distance. To determine this, it is necessary to know approximately its height or some other dimension. If an object of known height (such as a mountain peak) appears over the horizon, the distance in nautical miles from the top of the object to the horizon is equal to $1.17\sqrt{H}$, where H is the height of the object above sea level in feet. This is approximately equal to 7/6 of the square root of the height in feet of the object; as noted before, the square root of a number can be found by trial-and-error method of multiplying successive approximations. (The expression is $2.12\sqrt{H}$ when H is in meters.) To this must be added the distance from the observer to his horizon found in the same manner for his height of eye.

Example: A mountain peak 2,000 feet high appears over the horizon of an observer whose eye is 8 feet above sea level.

Required: The distance of the mountain peak from the observer.

Solution: The distance from the top of the mountain to the horizon is $1.17\sqrt{2000} = 52.3$ miles. The distance from the observer to the horizon is $1.17\sqrt{8} = 3.3$ miles. Hence, the distance of the mountain is 52.3 + 3.3 = 55.6 miles.

Answer: D = 56 miles, approximately. (The degree of precision with which the height of the mountain and the height of eye in a moving small boat are known does not permit a more precise statement of distance, regardless of the refinement of the calculations.)

If an object is fully visible and its height is known, or if the length between two visible points is known, the distance can be found by simple proportion. Hold a scale at arm's length and measure the length subtended by the known height or length. Distance is then found by the proportion

$$\frac{D}{d} = \frac{H}{h} \quad \text{or} \quad D = \frac{dH}{h}$$

where D is the distance in feet, d is the distance in inches of the rule from the eye, H is the height (or length) of the object in feet and h is the length of the rule subtended by the object in inches. See figure 3917. If H is in miles, the distance D is also in miles. If H is in feet and D is desired in nautical miles, the formula becomes

$$D = \frac{dH}{6000h}$$

Example: An island 1.2 miles long subtends a length of 3.5 inches for an observer holding a rule 21 inches from his eye.

Required: The distance of the island from the observer.

Solution: Solving the formula.

$$D = \frac{dH}{h} = \frac{21 \times 1.2}{3.5} = 7.2 \text{ miles.}$$

Answer: D = 7 miles, approximately.

In using this method with a length, be careful to use the length *at the visible height* (the shore line and a low beach may be below the horizon), and be sure that the length is perpendicular to the line of sight (which may not be the same as the greatest length). If a height is employed, be sure the *visible* height is used.

A variation is to measure the angle subtended and determine the length graphically. That is, in figure 3917 if the angle at E is known, the distance

D at height H can be determined by drawing a figure to scale.

Miscellaneous Guidance

3918 The position of the celestial equator is indicated in the sky by any body of 0° declination. The sun's declination is 0° about 21 March and 23 September. The star δ Orionis (the northernmost star of *Orion's* belt) is nearly on the celestial equator. Such a body indicates the approximate east point of the horizon at rising and the west point at setting, at any latitude.

A great circle through Polaris, Caph (the leading star in *Cassiopeia*), and the eastern side of the square of *Pegasus* (Alpheratz and Algenib) represents approximately the hour circle of the vernal equinox. The local hour angle of this circle is the LHA ♈. The LHA ♈ in time units can also be determined approximately by knowing that the autumnal equinox (about 23 September) LHA ♈ and LMT are identical. Every half a month thereafter the LHA ♈ in time units *gains* one hour on LMT. Hence, on 15 January it is approximately 7^h30^m fast on LMT.

Protect the watch and wind it regularly if necessary. If a watertight container is available, that is a good place for the watch, especially while launching the lifeboat, but make sure that this container is inside a compartment or is secured to the lifeboat by a lanyard.

In the interest of being picked up at the earliest possible time, remember that metal is a better radar reflector than wood, and the higher the reflector the greater the range at which it might be picked up. If there is a possibility that radar-equipped planes or ships are searching for your lifeboat, try to rig up some kind of metal corner reflector that will produce a stronger pip on the rescuer's radar screen. Also, do not forget to weigh the possibility of rescue in determining whether to

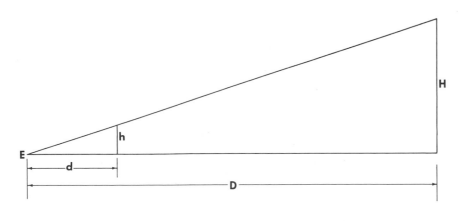

Figure 3917. Finding distance by simple proportion.

leave the vicinity of the stricken ship and in setting the course.

Keep out of the direct rays of the sun as much as possible to avoid sunburn, dehydration of the body, eye infection, and eye strain. Good physical condition is a prerequisite to good navigation under difficult conditions.

Rig a sail, even if one must be improvised.

Navigation without Instruments

3919   The ancient Polynesians were able to navigate successfully without mechanical instruments or timepieces by using their knowledge of the heavens and the lore of the sea. Few persons today have acquired this knowledge, hence this chapter has been principally devoted to using, or improvising, instruments and methods familiar to most naval and merchant marine officers and quartermasters and yacht navigators.

The declination of any star is equal to the latitude of the point on earth directly beneath the star; the GP, and for lifeboat accuracy the declination of the stars, can be assumed to remain fixed. This is the key to no-instrument celestial navigation. In the South Atlantic, for example, Alphard will pass overhead at Ascension Island. Farther north Alkaid passes directly over Land's End, England; Newfoundland; Vancouver Island, south of the Aleutians; and over the Kuril Islands, north of Japan.

A rough determination of latitude can therefore be made by observing the passing of a star of known declination directly overhead. (The determination of "directly overhead" is not easily done; use the opinions of several persons for an average result.) By comparing the star's declination with the known latitude of land areas, a position east or west of the land areas can be determined. Ancient navigators were able to sail to the proper latitude, then sail directly east or west to a known island by this process.

Directions to land can be determined by observing the flight of birds or by typical cloud formations over islands. A steady course can be steered by maintaining a constant angle with the direction of swells or wave motion. Nearby land can sometimes be detected by sounds or even by a particular smell. A complete dissertation on using the lore of the sea and sky for navigation is beyond the space limitation of this text, but it is mentioned here to illustrate the necessity of using any and all available data or knowledge when routine navigation methods are not available.

The Importance of Lifeboat Navigation

3920   Anyone spending a part of his life at sea or over the water should consider it good insurance to be adequately prepared for an emergency. A man does not refuse to buy fire insurance for his house just because he hopes it will never burn down, or even because relatively few houses do burn. The cost of insurance is too inexpensive and the consequences of a fire too great to ignore this important item. As long as there is a possibility, however remote, of having to abandon ship, a suitable preparation for this emergency is good insurance. A navigator's very life and those of others may depend on his preparation. It may be too late when the order to abandon ship is given.

One of the essential items of preparation is a thorough knowledge of *fundamentals*. Practically all of the information given in this chapter consists of the application of fundamentals.

A major decision is whether to remain in the area of the abandoned vessel, or make way for the nearest land or shipping lanes. If a distress message has been sent and acknowledged, efforts should be made to stay in the vicinity reported; even this requires continual navigation because of winds and currents that would carry you away. If the distress is unknown to the authorities, plans should be made to proceed toward land or areas of greater concentration of shipping where there would be a greater probability of being sighted and rescued.

Once you have boarded a lifeboat or life raft, make a careful estimate of the situation. The methods to be used and the procedure to be followed depend on the particular situation, what tools and information are available. Use the most accurate methods available. Do not, however, be misled by the level of detail to which your calculations can be taken; remember the relative crudity of your instruments and the difficult conditions under which they are used. Carry calculations only to a justifiable degree of precision, and label them "approximate" when appropriate; plan further actions with a full awareness of the inexactness of your information. Use imagination and ingenuity in making use of the materials at hand. If more than one method of doing anything is available, use all of them and check one against another.

Establish a regular routine and keep busy. *Navigate* with whatever means are available; do not guess if there is any way of making a measurement or estimate.

Chapter 40   Polar Navigation

Introduction

4001 Navigation in the higher latitudes can be very different, and much more difficult, than in nonpolar regions. Probably the best advice that can be given to a polar navigator is to use every available method and evaluate the results by considering the relative value of each item of positional data obtained. No method used here is truly new or unique; it is rather the application of standard procedures to different circumstances.

After first reviewing the geography of polar and subpolar regions, the following broad areas of interest will then be considered: chart projections, environmental factors (as they relate to navigation), determination of direction and distance, fixing position, and determination of the times of celestial phenomena.

The Polar Regions

4002 No single definition is completely satisfactory in defining the limits of the *polar regions*. Astronomically, the parallels of latitude at which the sun becomes circumpolar, at about latitudes 67.5° north and south, are considered the lower limits. Meteorologically, the limits are irregular lines that, in the Arctic, coincide approximately with the tree line. For purposes of this book, the polar regions will be considered to extend from the geographical poles to latitude 70°. The *subpolar regions* are a transitional area extending for an additional 10° to latitude 60°.

Arctic Geography

4003 The *Arctic Ocean* is a body of water, a little smaller in area than the continental United States—an ocean that is almost completely surrounded by land. Some of this land is high and rugged and covered with permanent ice caps; part of it is low and marshy when thawed. Permanently frozen ground underneath, called *permafrost*, prevents adequate drainage, resulting in large numbers of lakes and ponds and extensive areas of *muskeg*, soft spongy ground with characteristic growths of certain mosses and tufts of grass or sedge. There are also large areas of *tundra*, low treeless plains with vegetation consisting of mosses, lichens, shrubs, willows, etc., and usually having an underlying layer of permafrost.

The central part of the Arctic Ocean is a basin with an average depth of about 12,000 feet (3,660 m); the bottom is not level, and there are a number of seamounts and deeps. The greatest depth is probably something over 16,000 feet (4,880 m); at the pole the depth is 14,150 feet (4,310 m). Surrounding the polar basin is an extensive continental shelf, broken only in the area between Greenland and Spitsbergen. The many islands of the Canadian archipelago lie on this shelf. The Greenland Sea, east of Greenland, Baffin Bay, west of Greenland, and the Bering Sea, north of the Aleutians, all have their independent basins. Due to ice conditions, surface ships cannot penetrate to the pole, but some have successfully reached quite high latitudes.

Antarctic Geography

4004 The *Antarctic*, or south polar region, is in marked contrast to the Arctic in physiographical features. It is a high mountainous land mass, about twice the area of the United States, surrounded by the Atlantic, Pacific, and Indian Oceans. An extensive polar plateau, covered with snow and ice, is about 10,000 feet (3,050 m) high. The average height of Antarctica is about 6,000 feet (1,830 m), which is higher than that of any other continent, and there are several mountain ranges with peaks rising to more than 13,000 feet (3,960 m). The height at the South Pole is about 9,500 feet (2,900 m).

The barrier presented by land and the tremendous *ice shelves* in the Ross Sea prevent ships from reaching very high latitudes. Much of the coast of Antarctica is high and rugged, with few good harbors or anchorages.

Navigation Concepts in Polar Regions

4005 Many of the concepts of measurements used in normal navigation take on new meanings, or lose their meaning entirely, in the polar regions. In temperate latitudes, one speaks of north, south, east, and west when he refers to directions; of latitude and longitude; of time; of sunrise and sunset; and of day and night. Each of these terms is normally associated with specific concepts and relationships. In the polar regions, however, each of these terms has a somewhat different significance, requiring a reappraisal of the concepts and relationships involved.

In lower latitudes, the lengths of a degree of latitude and a degree of longitude are roughly comparable, and meridians are thought of as parallel lines, as they appear on a Mercator chart, or as nearly parallel lines. Not so in polar regions, where meridians radiate outward from the pole like spokes of a great wheel, and longitude becomes a coordinate of direction. An aircraft circling the pole might cover 360° of longitude in a couple of minutes. Each of two observers might be north (or south) of the other if the north (or south) pole were between them. At the north pole all directions are south, and at the south pole all directions are north. A visual bearing of a mountain peak can no longer be considered a rhumb line. It is a great circle, and because of the rapid convergence of meridians, must be plotted as such.

Clock time as used in temperate zones has little meaning in polar regions. As the meridians converge, so do the time zones. A mile from the pole the time zones are but a quarter of a mile apart. At the pole the sun rises and sets once each year, the moon once a month. The visible stars circle the sky endlessly, essentially at the same altitudes; only half the celestial sphere is visible from either pole. The planets rise and set once each sidereal period (from 225 days for Venus to 29½ years for Saturn). A day of 24 hours at the pole is not marked by the

usual periods of daylight and darkness, and "morning" and "afternoon" have no significance. In fact, the day is not marked by any observable phenomenon except that the sun may make one complete circle around the sky, maintaining essentially the same altitude and always bearing south (or north).

The system of coordinates, direction, and many of the concepts so common to our daily lives are manmade. They have been used because they have proved useful. If they are discarded near the poles, it is because their usefulness does not extend to these regions. A new concept must be devised for use in the polar regions. It should differ as little as possible from familiar methods, while taking full cognizance of changed conditions.

Charts

4006 The familiar Mercator chart projection will normally not be used in higher latitudes, since distortion becomes so great as the poles are approached. Variations of the Mercator projection can be used, thus retaining some advantages without the unacceptable distortion imposed by having the tangency of the cylinder occur at the equator. This is done *by rotating the tangent cylinder through 90°*. If this is done, the cylinder is tangent to a meridian, which becomes the "fictitious equator." Parallels of latitude become oval curves, with the sinusoidal meridians extending outward from the pole. The meridians change their direction of curvature at the pole; see figure 4006. Within the polar regions the parallels are very nearly circles, and the meridians diverge but slightly from straight lines. The distortion at L 70° is comparable to that at L 20° on an ordinary Mercator chart. Within this region a straight line can be considered a great circle with but small error. If the cylinder is tangent to a meridian, the projection is called *transverse Mercator*. If it is placed tangent to an oblique great circle, the projection is termed *oblique Mercator*.

Other projections used in polar regions are the stereographic, gnomonic or great circle, azimuthal equidistant, and a modified Lambert conformal. Near the pole, all of these and the transverse Mercator projection are so nearly alike as to be difficult to distinguish by eye. All are suitable, and all can be used with a grid. On the gnomonic chart a great circle is a straight line, and on the others it is very nearly so. Distance and grid direction (see article 4007) are measured in the accustomed manner.

In practice these polar charts are used in a manner similar to the Lambert for measuring course and distance and for plotting position (chapter 5).

The real problem of polar charts does not involve the projection to be used. The latitude and longi-

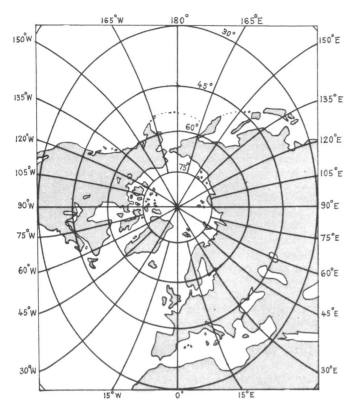

Figure 4006. A polar transverse Mercator chart with the cylinder tangent at the 90°E–90°W meridian.

tude lines can be drawn to the same accuracy as on any other chart, but the other information shown on polar charts is sometimes far from accurate. Arctic regions are being traveled more and more, and publications and charts are improving, but many areas have not been accurately surveyed. The result is that in less-traveled areas such as Greenland and Alaska coastlines are inaccurate or missing, topography is unreliable, and soundings are sparse. Lines of magnetic variation are located principally by extrapolation. Even the positions of the magnetic poles are only generally stated, and vary irregularly. The navigator must, therefore, be acutely aware of the lack of accuracy and completeness of his charts, and take greater than usual precaution to ensure that a safe course is steered. Any advance-warning device is most useful, and should be fully used. Coastal topography or irregular soundings may indicate pinnacles some distance offshore, and if ice conditions permit use of sonar on a forward-looking echo sounder, this should be employed.

A straight line across a polar chart can be considered a great circle within the limits of practical navigation. On the transverse Mercator chart this is a fictitious rhumb line making the same angle with fictitious meridians.

The most easily used projection for polar ship operations is often considered to be the Lambert conformal. Plotting is a bit of a problem, but land masses are most accurately portrayed, and courses steamed in ice being somewhat erratic, the advantage of a rhumb line course being a straight line is not missed. For this or any other of the usual high-latitude chart projections, an AN or aircraft plotter is most convenient (article 721).

Grid Direction

4007 Some navigators consider that in polar regions it is convenient to discard the conventional directions of true north, east, etc., except for celestial navigation, and substitute grid north, grid east, etc. That is, directions can be given in relation to the common direction of all fictitious grid meridians across the chart. The relationship between grid direction and true direction depends on the orientation of the grid. The system generally accepted places grid north in the direction of the north pole from Greenwich, or 000° on the Greenwich meridian is 000° grid (at both poles). With this orientation the interconversion of true and grid directions is very simple. If G is grid direction and T is true direction, in the Northern Hemisphere,

$$G = T + \lambda W$$
$$G = T - \lambda E$$
$$T = G - \lambda W$$
$$T = G + \lambda E$$

In the Southern Hemisphere the signs are reversed. It is not necessary to remember all of these equations, for the last three follow naturally from the first. Grid direction of a straight line remains constant for its entire length, while true direction changes continually, with change in longitude.

In figure 4007 the grid direction from *A* to *B* is 057° and from *B* to *A* is 237°, the reciprocal. However, at *A*, longitude 20° W, the true direction is 037° (T = G − λW = 57° − 20° = 37°). At *B*, longitude 100°E, the direction is not 237°, but 237° + 100° = 337°.

It is most convenient to give all directions in relation to grid north. Even azimuths of celestial bodies can be converted to grid directions if desired, both for plotting lines of position and for checking the directional gyro. If wind directions are given in terms of the grid, confusion is minimized, for a wind blowing in a constant grid direction is following widely different true directions over a relatively short distance near the pole. Since drift correction angle relative to a grid course is desired, wind direction should be given on the same basis. A grid direction is indicated by the let-

Figure 4007. Grid navigation.

ter *G* following the direction, as Zn 068°G, or by placing the letter *G* before the nature of the direction, as GH 144°, for grid heading 144°.

The lines of equal magnetic variation all pass through the magnetic pole and the geographic pole, the former because it is the origin of such lines, and the latter because of the convergence of the meridians at that point. Convergency, however, can be combined with variation to obtain the difference between grid direction and magnetic direction at any point. This difference is called *grid variation* or *grivation*. Lines of equal grid variation can be shown on a polar chart in lieu of lines of ordinary variation. These lines pass through the magnetic pole, but not the geographic pole. Hence, even when a magnetic compass is used, grid navigation is easier than attempting to maintain true directions.

Grid sailing as described may be useful for air navigation, but is not likely to be needed for surface ship operations because 82° N is the probable limit of navigation, and speeds are usually so low that other more normal plotting methods can be effectively used.

Environmental Factors

4008 The effects of polar operations in navigation are many and varied. A thorough study of *Sailing Directions* or *Coast Pilots* is necessary, including those available from foreign nations. For example,

the Danish *Pilot* for Greenland contains some excellent land profiles. *Aircraft charts* can also be very useful, since the topography shown is an essential factor in marine navigation. The *Ice Atlas*, NavOceanO Pub. No. 700S3, gives good average seasonal data for the North Atlantic Ocean although up-to-date information from satellite, long-range aircraft, or helicopter ice reconnaissance is more useful. There is also the Oceanographic Atlas of the Polar Seas, NavOceanO Pub. No. 705, Part I for the Antarctic and Part II for the Arctic. In some areas, it may be necessary to work from aerial photographs or preliminary charts, and soundings will be lacking. Whatever the circumstance, the navigator must plan ahead and obtain all information from whatever source.

Occasionally, a review of old *Cruise Reports*, or even accounts by early explorers, will yield useful data. A volume of *Sailing Directions for Antarctica*, DMAHTC Pub. No. 27, has been published, and updated with changes. It contains a large amount of information, which recent expeditions into the area have proved to be quite accurate, if incomplete.

Rather than paraphrase the many authoritative references available on the higher latitudes, a brief summary of the more prevalent features is presented as a background relating to the general environment in which navigation must be accomplished.

Seasonal conditions. Normally cruises will be scheduled during the daylight periods, that is, during the summer months for the area involved. During these periods the sun may not set at all, and consequently there may be no navigational twilight. Ice conditions will be more favorable, as will the weather generally, except at the turn of the seasons. Fog at the ice edge is frequently encountered, and good radar navigation is imperative. Warm-water currents also cause fog, not just at the ice edge but near cooler land masses as well. There may be days with below-freezing temperatures, or raw and damp days, but for the most part the weather will be cool and pleasant. Gales are few. Cold-weather precautions should be taken. Aside from the *Sailing Directions* and other sources already suggested, there are several Army Engineer manuals on cold-weather operations, and also the *Naval Arctic Manual.* There is a special series of *Ice Plotting Charts* and *Sheets* for the arctic area. There is also additional information in the ATP and NWP series of naval publications for those to whom such documents are available.

Cruising in the off season, though unlikely, is possible and is apt to increase as ship capabilities and the needs of commerce expand. Severe low temperatures, ice conditions, and gales may be expected, especially at the turn of the season. During the dark period, there may be enough light to take good celestial sights, although there may be no actual navigational twilight. The mid-winter period will probably be clear and very cold. Bare flesh will stick to metal instruments. Elaborate cold-weather precautions are essential for engineering equipment as well as for personnel.

Magnetic anomalies and *storms* are prevalent, the *Aurora* (*Borealis* and *Australis*) will be visually attractive but troublesome to communications and magnetic compasses.

Mirage effect. This phenomenon, due to abnormal refractions, occurs whenever there is a severe difference between surface and air temperatures. In summer in the north, for example, when the water and ice are much colder than the air above, multiple images may be seen. Landfalls may appear many miles before they are expected.

Piloting and DR. Unknown tidal and ocean currents, or ice conditions, will make a good DR very hard to keep. Close observations for any clues of set and drift are most useful; for example, grounded icebergs may show tidal erosion as well as a wake. If observed for long periods, they serve as a rough tide gauge. Depth can also be estimated from grounded bergs, using 1 foot (or meter) above the waterline as equal to 6 feet (or meters) below. Pit logs may not be practical, but timing objects passing alongside can give a rough indication of speed through the water or ice.

Upon entering a harbor or unfamiliar waters it is good practice to send a small boat ahead with a portable echo sounder plus a radio for communications.

One of the principal hazards to marine navigation in polar regions is ice. In some regions icebergs are very numerous. In the upper part of Baffin Bay, for instance, south of Cape York, literally hundreds of icebergs may be visible at one time. During periods of darkness or low visibility, radar is essential in avoiding collision. This method is usually quite adequate, icebergs often being picked up before they are capable of being seen. Smaller icebergs, about the size of a small house, are called *growlers;* these break off from larger icebergs and constitute the chief hazard to marine navigation. When the sea is smooth, it is usually possible to detect growlers in time to avoid them without difficulty, but if the sea is rough, they may not be picked up because of excessive sea return near the ship. It must be remembered that about 90 percent of an iceberg is *below* the surface of the water, so that in a rough sea, a growler is practically awash. Sonar has proved useful in detecting the presence of such ice. Broken ice presents no particular difficulty, but when heavy pack ice is encountered, further progress is usually impossible. Sometimes a *lead* or strip of open water where the ice has cracked and drifted apart permits a ship to continue for some distance into pack ice, but this can be carried too far, into a dangerous situation.

Fog is rather frequent in some polar regions during the summer, but is seldom of long duration. Most of the precipitation in the summer is in the form of rain, which can be quite plentiful in some areas, but is usually light, although steady. Overcast conditions can persist for days.

Direction

4009 The determination of direction is perhaps the single most difficult problem. Magnetic compasses become largely useless due to the weakness of the horizontal component of the earth's field and the large and somewhat unpredictable variations, plus the typical magnetic storms encountered. Gyrocompasses with proper speed and latitude corrections entered are reasonably accurate, but the directive force weakens as the poles are approached. Flux-gate gyros have been recommended, but are usually available only in aircraft.

Any gyroscopic device will degrade in accuracy in higher latitudes, and will lose all directive effect at the geographic poles. It is therefore necessary to take almost continuous error observations on a celestial body, normally the sun. One practical method is to mount an *astrocompass* on or parallel to the ship's centerline. An astrocompass is illustrated in figure 4009. A sun compass can be useful, but needs a shadow from the sun to give useful data. The astrocompass can be used with the sun or *any other body*.

The *sky compass*, operating on polarized sunlight, has been used successfully. It is valuable in that the sun need not be seen, therefore an overcast does not mean a total loss of direction; a clear zenith, however, is needed for full accuracy. The usual azimuths of celestial bodies can also be used, of course, and precomputed tables or curves make the process practical and timely. Since acceleration errors in gyrocompasses (from turns or abrupt speed changes) are greater in higher latitudes, timely error determination is essential.

Bearings

Bearings may be difficult to plot over long distances, due to the problems encountered with chart projections, but considering the bearings as great circles and plotting them as such according to the chart projection employed will solve the problem (use radio-bearing correction procedure). Bearings generally may be a problem due to poor charting. In this case, redundancy of observations is important, and an attempt to fix the position of objects while the ship is stopped, to give good visual or radar navigational references for a stretch of steaming, is recommended.

Distance

4010 Determining distance may also require some ingenuity. *Distance off* may be measured by radar, or by stadimeter or sextant if heights are known. *Distance to go* will depend on good fixes and good charts. *Distance run* will require the use of some of the older piloting techniques (such as doubling the angle on the bow if running on a steady course and speed), or a chip log, or timing the passage of objects alongside the ship for a known distance. Fixed or almost stationary objects such as bergs can also be used and plotted on a Maneuvering Board sheet as known fixed targets to solve for own course and speed; radar can be useful for this purpose. In open water, pit logs or engine turns can be used as usual with only normal problems as to accuracy. To prevent damage, pit logs

Figure 4009. An astrocompass.

and retractable sonar gear must be retracted when entering ice.

Dead Reckoning

4011 A DR plot must be carefully and attentively kept, particularly in ice. Every movement of the vessel must be recorded with the best possible accuracy. Some ships operating in ice detail one or two men full time to this task alone. At times a ship's movements may be too erratic to permit plotting, and the average course and speed must be carefully estimated. An *automatic course recorder* is very useful if the gyro is kept corrected. Speed must be estimated or obtained as described above. With practice, a useful estimate of speed can be made by an experienced man. Since many polar cruises require close navigation, it is better to keep up all plots rather than to prepare historical records after the fact. The latter records are also desirable, but timely fixes and good DR projections are operationally necessary for safe navigation at the present moment. It is frequently good practice to proceed very deliberately, or even stop, in order not to lose track. If a DRT has a dummy log input, speed estimates can be entered and a track without set can be developed easily.

Position Fixing

4012 *Fixing position* can be quite a project, and occasionally there will be considerable doubt.

Skillful piloting is essential, in addition to a good DR plot. A navigator must never miss an opportunity for an LOP; he cannot know when there will be another opportunity. He must obtain all information possible, even though some of it may be incomplete or of questionable accuracy. An alert conning officer may notice uncharted dangers or those on the track if the ship is off course. Occasionally land, water, or ice reflections can be useful in navigating as well as conning, and the watch officer may be the one to observe them first.

Visual methods of position fixing are always good, particularly as charts of polar areas improve, but there will be an almost total absence of such aids to navigation as buoys, lights, and sound signals.

Radar can serve as a warning device as well as for navigation. A good rule is to use only radar ranges. One helpful technique, particularly in first establishing a position in an unfamiliar area, is to prepare a tracing of the PPI picture, which can then be matched with the chart. Many targets should be plotted on the tracing; target separation should, when possible, be about 5°. This will simplify matching the tracing to the chart, as any error in bearings will not affect the accuracy of determining the ship's position; position is determined by matching the contours on the tracing to those on the chart, rather than by the use of bearings.

One useful wrinkle when using radar in ice is to reduce radiated power, if possible. This reduces range but increases ice definition (resolution), so that leads are more easily perceived. Some radars have an automatic setting for this, others would require reducing magnetron current. Shorter wavelength radars give better resolutions.

Celestial Navigation

4013 Celestial navigation is of prime importance in polar regions, although its practice may be very different from that to which a navigator is accustomed. He must acquire new techniques, familiarize himself with new tools, accustom himself to functioning in a very different environment, and never miss the opportunity to obtain a line of position.

Navigation during the summer months involves the problem of positioning the vessel by altitude measurements of the sun only (except for occasional use of the moon), as continuous daylight prevents any observations of stars or planets. A navigator, therefore, must depend almost solely on single lines of position of the sun. In very high latitudes, a particular difficulty may arise twice a year. After the sun has set below the horizon, (or shortly before it rises for the summer) there may be a period of days or even several weeks when the sun is not available, yet the sky is too bright for observation of other bodies; at this time, it will not be possible to make any use of celestial navigation.

Tools and techniques that have been found useful will be discussed in the following paragraphs. But we must first consider *time*, on which all celestial navigation is based, as the nature of time itself is somewhat affected in the polar regions.

Time

In previous chapters, the importance of time was stressed, since each four seconds of error of the navigational watch may introduce an error of as much as one minute of longitude. At the equator this is 1 mile (1.85 km); at latitude 60°, it is 0.5 mile (0.93 km); at latitude 88°, it is only 0.035 miles (65 m). Thus, at this latitude a watch error of 2 minutes would introduce a maximum error of about 1 mile (1.85 km). That is, the maximum change of altitude of a body, at a fixed point of observation, is one minute of arc in two minutes of time, and the average error is not more than half this amount. Thus, for celestial navigational purposes precise time is of little consequence in polar regions. At the pole all bodies circle the sky at a constant altitude, except for a very slow change due to the changing declination. Because time zones lose their significance near the poles, it is customary to keep all timepieces set to GMT while in polar regions.

Lower Altitude Sights

Navigators in temperate climates usually avoid observations of bodies below 15°, and most of them never observe bodies lower than 10°. In polar regions the only available body may not exceed an altitude of 10° for several weeks. At the pole the maximum altitude of the sun is 23°27'; the moon and planets may exceed this value by a few degrees. Hence, in polar regions sights must be taken without regard for any lower limit for observations.

The reason for avoiding low altitudes in temperate latitudes is the variable amount of refraction to be expected. In polar regions refraction varies over much wider limits than in lower latitudes. Because of the low temperatures in polar regions, the refraction correction for the sextant altitudes should be adjusted for temperature, or a special refraction table for this area should be used. Refraction is known to vary with temperature and barometric pressure, but there are other factors that are imperfectly known. Refractions of several *degrees* have occasionally been observed, resulting in the sun appearing several days before it was expected in the spring, or continuing to appear for days after it should have disappeared below the horizon. Since abnormal refraction affects both the refraction and dip corrections, bubble sextant altitudes, if the average of a number of observations is used, are sometimes more reliable in polar regions than marine sextant altitudes on the natural horizon.

Tools and Techniques

A marine sextant is the basic tool for polar navigation, although it is difficult at times to obtain a good horizon. Sun and moon observations will usually be made at lower altitudes than the navigator is accustomed to using; they must be carefully corrected for refraction. As for all observations made in the polar regions, the "Additional Corrections" for nonstandard temperature and barometric pressure, contained in the *Nautical Almanac*, should be applied. An artificial horizon can be improvised when required. The conventional mercury horizon can rarely be used even aboard a stationary ship; it can, however, be used to advantage on the ice. For ship use, a pan of lubricating oil makes an acceptable horizon. It may be placed on a leveled gyro repeater and should be shielded from the wind.

When the horizon is poorly defined and a star at high altitude is visible, it may be desirable to take both direct and *back* (or *over-the-shoulder*) sights. In this latter technique, the observer faces *away* from the body and measures the *supplement* of the altitude (180° − sextant reading = observed altitude). The arc that appears when "rocking" the sextant is inverted, with the highest point on the arc the position of perpendicularity; practice is required for accuracy in taking back sights. The results of the direct and back sights are compared, and usually averaged.

Bubble Sextants

An aircraft bubble sextant, or a marine sextant with bubble attachment (Article 2104), can be used advantageously in the polar regions. It takes some practice to become accustomed to its use, and a considerable number of sights of each body should always be taken and averaged. Results obtained with the bubble sextant will be improved if there is no ship's motion; it may be desirable to take all way off the ship while sights are being made. Some navigators suspend the bubble sextant from a spring, to help damp out undesired motion.

The best celestial fixes are obtained by erecting a theodolite on shore, or on firm ice. If it is equipped with a 30-power telescope, high-magnitude fixed stars, situated at reasonably high altitudes, should be visible on clear days, even with the sun above the horizon. This is particularly true if they lie approximately 90° from the sun in azimuth. For nighttime star observations, the theodolite serves best if it is fitted with a prismatic astrolabe.

Celestial Observations

During the long polar day—which at Thule, Greenland, in latitude 76°32'N, lasts for four months—the only body regularly available is the sun, which circles the sky, changing azimuth about 15° each hour. The moon will at times give a second line of position; but when it is near the new or full phase, such a line will be nearly parallel to the sun line and hence of little value in fixing a position. An average of several observations of the sun, obtained every two hours, can provide a series of running fixes. An even better practice is to make observations every hour and establish the most probable position for each hour.

The best celestial fixes are usually obtained from star observations made during twilight. With increased latitude, the period of twilight lengthens, permitting additional time for observation. With this increase, the period when the sun is just below the horizon also lengthens, and it may be difficult to pick up stars or planets unless a sextant with a high-magnification telescope and large mirrors is available.

In the Arctic, with such an instrument, Capella, Deneb, and Vega should be among the first stars visible, particularly when situated approximately at right angles in azimuth to the position of the sun below the horizon. In the Antarctic, the first stars to look for are Rigel Kentaurus, Acrux, Canopus, Hadar, and Achernar. The brighter planets will be the next bodies to become visible if they are high in declination. A bright aurora may delay the observation of stars and planets after sunset; at times, however, it may assist in defining the horizon. With dark-adapted vision and good sextants, a navigator can frequently obtain excellent observations throughout the polar night. The moon should, of course, be observed whenever it is available. Polaris, because of its high altitude and difficult azimuth determination, has very limited use.

Other conditions besides long periods of darkness complicate the problem of locating the horizon in high latitude. Low fog, frost smoke, or blowing snow may obscure the horizon when the sun is clearly visible. Nearby land, hummocked sea ice, or an extensive ice foot may be troublesome, particularly at low heights of eye. As previously stated, an artificial horizon sextant can be most helpful under such conditions, and can supply good lines of position if the observer is practiced in its use and averages a number of observations.

When using the marine sextant aboard ship, the value of the dip correction should be determined by the height of eye *above the ice at the horizon*. This can usually be established with reasonable accuracy by observing nearby ice. Due to the frequently considerable anomalies in refraction, the tabulated refraction should always be corrected for non-standard temperature and barometric pressure. When stars are available, several, well distributed in azimuth, should be observed to minimize errors due to abnormal refraction. The center of the geometric figures formed by the LOPs should be taken as the fix. Any error in dip or refraction will alter the size of the polygon, but will not appreciably change the location of its center. Other difficulties experienced aboard ship include the fact that false horizons sometimes appear, and during summer, when ships are most likely to be in polar regions, the sky in some areas is usually overcast. Further, a geographic position is not as important to a ship as a position relative to adjacent land, which may not be accurately charted. When stars are available, it is good practice to observe those of relatively high altitudes, since these are least affected by abnormal refraction.

The plotting of lines of position in polar regions is no more difficult than elsewhere. However, it must be remembered that an azimuth line is in reality a great circle. In moderate latitudes it is approximated on a Mercator chart by a rhumb line. Over the short distance involved no appreciable error is introduced by this practice. Similarly, the line of position, actually part of a small circle on the earth, is also drawn as a straight line without loss of accuracy unless the altitude is very high, when it is actually drawn as a circle. These are discussed in more detail in chapter 25.

In polar regions, rhumb lines are not suitable because they no longer approximate great circles. This is shown in figure 4013a in which a fix is plotted on a Mercator plotting sheet in the usual way. The solid lines show the actual lines that should be used. In figure 4013b this same fix is shown plotted on a transverse Mercator chart. Note that both the azimuth line and the line of position are plotted as straight lines, as on a Mercator chart near the equator. The assumed position is selected as in any latitude and located by means of the graticule of actual latitude and longitude. The fix is also given

Figure 4013a. High-altitude celestial fix plotted on a Mercator plotting sheet.

in terms of geographic coordinates. In plotting the azimuth line, the direction can be converted to grid azimuth, or plotted directly by means of true azimuth. If the latter method is used, care must be taken to measure the direction from the meridian of the AP. An aircraft plotter or protractor is usually used for this purpose.

Sextant altitudes are corrected in the same manner in polar regions as elsewhere, except that refraction should be corrected for temperature, or a special refraction table used, as indicated above. Coriolis corrections, needed for bubble sextant observations made from a moving craft, reach extreme values near the poles and should not be neglected.

Computed altitude can be calculated in polar regions by any of several methods, including the Ageton tables now in Volume II of *Bowditch* as table 35. It can be determined more easily, however, by Pub. No. 229. If its level of precision is acceptable, Pub. No. 249 offers a rapid reduction, but Volume I is restricted to a limited number of stars.

If a body near the zenith is observed, the line of position is plotted as a circle, with the GP as the center, as in any latitude.

The Geographic Pole as Assumed Position

One special method of plotting lines of position is available above 80° latitude. By this method the pole is used as the AP. The Hc can then be determined by means of the almanac. The altitude of a

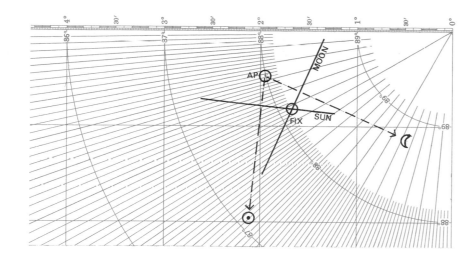

Figure 4013b. The celestial fix of figure 4013a plotted on a transverse Mercator chart.

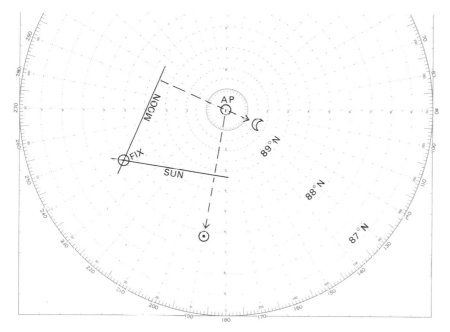

Figure 4013c. The celestial fix of figure 4013a plotted on a Maneuvering Board sheet used as azimuthal equidistant chart. The pole is used as the assumed position.

body is its angular distance from the horizon; the declination is its angular distance from the celestial equator. At the pole the horizon and celestial equator coincide, making the altitude equal to the declination. This is why a body with fixed declination circles the sky without change in altitude. At the pole all directions are south (or north), and hence azimuth has no significance. The lines radiating outward from the pole, similar to azimuth lines in moderate latitudes, are meridians. Hence, in place of azimuth, GHA is used, for it indicates which "direction" the body is from the pole.

To plot a sight by this method, enter the almanac with GMT and determine the body's declination and GHA. Using the declination as Hc, compare it with Ho. If Ho is greater, it is a "Toward" case, as usual. Measure the altitude difference (a) from the

pole along the meridian indicated by the GHA, and at the point so found erect a perpendicular to the meridian. If Hc is greater, an "Away" case, measure (a) along the meridian 180° from that indicated by the GHA, or *away* from the body (figure 4013c).

In the early days of air exploration in polar regions, this method was quite popular, but with the development of modern tabular methods, it has fallen into disuse, except within 2° of the pole, or above latitude 88°, where it is sometimes used. This, of course, is a very small area. If a ship is near the meridian of the GP of the body (or its reciprocal), the method is entirely accurate at any latitude, even though the altitude difference might be quite large, for this is simply a different way to plot meridian altitudes. However, the straight line used as the line of position is actually the arc of a small circle on the earth. The radius of the circle depends on the altitude of the body. For bodies near the horizon, the straight line of position, a close approximation of a great circle, can be used for some distance from the meridian of the GP without appreciable error. However, as the altitude increases, the discrepancy becomes larger. Tables have been prepared to show the distance from the straight line to the circle of equal altitude at different altitudes and for several hundred miles from the meridian of the GP, on a polar stereographic projection. With modern methods available, the pole is not generally used as the AP in an area where such a correction is needed.

Lines of position are advanced in the same manner as in lower latitudes. If a grid course is being followed, the AP or line of position is advanced along the grid course. The use of the pole as the AP does not complicate this practice.

Other methods of using celestial navigation in polar regions have been suggested. Among these are the use of sets of altitude curves for different bodies printed on transparent paper or plastic, to be used as a template over the chart; these methods also include the use of various types of computers.

From overall considerations, tables such as Pub. No. 229 or Pub. No. 249 are the best for celestial navigation in polar regions.

Radionavigation

4014 Other means of fixing position include various radionavigation techniques and systems.

Radiobeacons, when available, can be used. Beware of plotting errors due to chart projection and attenuation over ice or snow. Radio direction finders may be used to effect a rendezvous between ships or aircraft. On the surface, this is particularly useful in fog when there are many radar returns such as from icebergs. Radio reception in high latitudes suffers from ionospheric disturbances, but the short distances involved here should make RDF use possible. It is important to keep radio deviation tables up-to-date.

Consol, available in a small portion of the north polar region, is useful but not precise, as is true of any bearing technique at extreme range.

Loran-C is available in some portions of the polar regions and is quite precise when properly used. See Chart No. 5130 for coverage.

Omega is available in polar regions but is subject to propagation distortions resulting from solar flares.

Navigational satellites give excellent fixes, but not continuously, with good precision and reliability. They are essential for polar vessels, and receiver-computers are available to civilian navigators.

Inertial navigation systems will prove very useful in polar cruising, but must be updated periodically from external sources of information. Inertial systems have been used as the primary means of navigation by submarines transiting the pole under the ice.

Sunrise, Sunset; Moonrise, Moonset

4015 Sunrise, sunset, moonrise, and moonset, as stated in article 4004, do not have the same significance in polar regions as in lower latitudes. At the poles, any change in altitude of a body is occasioned only by a change in declination. Since the maximum rate of change of declination of the sun is about 1' per hour, and the sun is about 32' in diameter, the entire sun would not be visible for about 32 hours after "sunrise," or the moment of first appearance of the upper limb, if refraction remained constant. In an aircraft high above the pole the sun might be visible more than a week before it appears to an observer at the surface. Because of large variations in refractions, even the *day* of sunrise is difficult to predict in polar regions.

Ordinary sunrise, sunset, moonrise, and moonset tables are not available above 72° N or 60° S latitudes, nor would they be of much value if they were published. The method usually used is that provided by graphs in the *Air Almanac* as shown in figures 4015a, b, and c; comparable diagrams are not found in the *Nautical Almanac*.

The semiduration of sunlight is found by means of the graph in figure 4015a. The manner of its use is illustrated by the dashed lines.

Example: Find the LMT of sunrise and sunset at L 78° on March 8. Find the GMT if the observer is in λ 93° W.

Solution: From 8 March on the scale at the bottom of the graph draw a line vertically upward to the top of the diagram. To the nearest minute the time indicated by the dots is 1211. This is the LMT of meridian transit, or the center of the period of sunlight. Next, draw a horizontal line from L 78° N at the left (or right) margin to intersect the vertical line. At the point of intersection interpolate by eye between the curves. The semiduration of sunlight so found is 4^h40^m. Hence, the sun will rise 4^h40^m before meridian transit, or at 0731, and set 4^h40^m after meridian transit, or at 1651. The GMT is

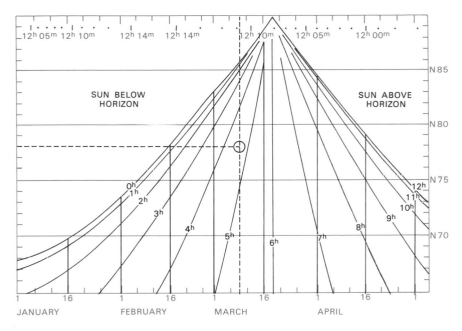

Figure 4015a. Semi-duration of sunlight graph from the *Air Almanac.*

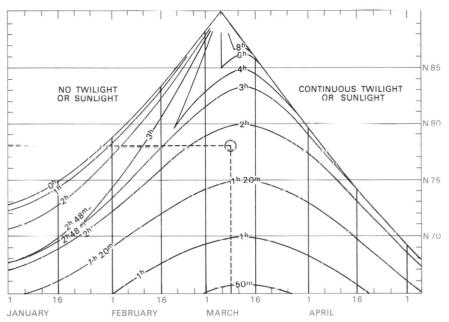

Figure 4015b. Duration of twilight graph from the *Air Almanac.*

6^h12^m *later*, so that sunrise occurs at 1343 and sunset 2303. These values are approximations.

Answers: Sunrise, LMT 0731, GMT 1343; sunset, LMT 1651, GMT 2303.

The duration of civil twilight is found in a similar manner by the use of figure 4015b.

Example: Find the LMT and GMT of beginning of morning twilight and ending of evening twilight for the example above.

Solution: Draw a vertical line through 8 March and a horizontal line through L 78° N. At the intersection interpolate between the two curves. The value found is about 1^h45^m. Hence, morning twilight ends 1^h45^m after sunset.

Answers: Morning twilight, LMT 0546, GMT 1158; evening twilight, LMT 1836, GMT 2448 or 0048 the following day.

The time of moonrise and moonset is found from figure 4015c in a manner similar to finding sunrise and sunset. The time of transit of the moon, of course, is not always near 1200 but may be any time during the day. The phase of the moon is shown by its symbol, the open symbol being full moon and the filled symbol new moon.

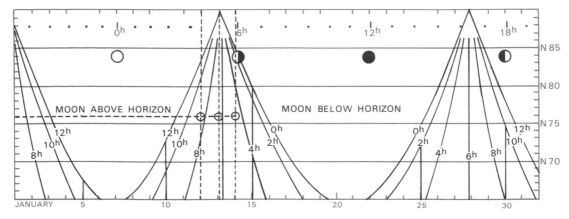

Figure 4015c. Semi-duration of moonlight graph from the *Air Almanac*.

Example: Find the LMT, ZT, and GMT of both moonrise and moonset at L 76° N, 70° W on 12 January, and the phase this day.

Solution: The vertical line through 12 January indicates that the moon will be on the celestial meridian at LMT 0425. The semiduration of moonlight is 8^{h}00^m. Hence, moonrise occurs 8 hours before, and moonset at 1225. Similarly, for the following day moonrise occurs at 2230 the day before and moonset occurs at 1130. The next moonrise will occur at 0100 on 14 January.

	Moonrise	
Tab	2230	12 Jan.
Tab	0100	14 Jan.
Diff	150	
150 × 70.0/360	(+) 29	
LMT	2259	
dλ	(−) 20	
ZT	2239	12 Jan.
ZD	(+) 5	
GMT	0339	13 Jan.

	Moonset	
Tab	1225	12 Jan.
Tab	1130	13 Jan.
Diff	55	
55 × 70.0/360	(−) 11	
LMT	1214	
dλ	(−) 20	
ZT	1154	12 Jan.
ZD	(+) 5	
GMT	1654	12 Jan.

The phase is gibbous, about two days before last quarter.

Answers: Moonrise, LMT 2259, ZT 2239, GMT 0339 (13 Jan.); moonset, LMT 1214, ZT 1154, GMT 1645; phase, gibbous, about two days before last quarter.

There are comparable graphs for sunlight, twilight, and moonlight for the south polar region. These are not printed in the almanacs, but are available free from the U. S. Naval Observatory in Washington, D.C., in Circular No. 147.

Land Navigation

4106 Marine navigation of a ship may develop into land navigation as shore parties are sent out on various missions, or the vessel becomes icebound and may even have to be abandoned. Land navigation across stretches of ice surface is not essentially different from that of surface vessels or aircraft, with one important exception. The navigator of a land vehicle or party can stop and obtain a stable platform for measuring altitudes, directions, etc., without being bothered by bubble acceleration or vibrations.

Navigation in such circumstances usually consists of proceeding by dead reckoning for a convenient period (often several days) and checking the position by accurate celestial observation at favorable times. At such times the accuracy of the compass is also checked. An aircraft-type flux-gate compass is generally most suitable for maintaining direction, except in the immediate vicinity of the magnetic poles, where it is usually necessary to steer for prominent landmarks and check the direction at frequent intervals. Dead reckoning on land is complicated by the necessity of frequently changing course to avoid obstructions.

Summary

4017 Throughout this chapter emphasis has been placed on the problems and difficulties that will be encountered in polar regions to underscore the need for an understanding of the conditions to be met and for adequate planning and preparation *before* entering the regions. This having been done, the polar regions can be navigated with confidence.

Planning is important in any operation; it is vital to the success of polar navigation. The first step to adequate planning is the acquisition of maximum data on the operational area. *Sailing Directions* should be procured. The Defense Mapping Agency Hydrographic/Topographic Center and the Naval Polar Oceanography Center should be consulted to obtain any pertinent data. Planning should not be confined solely to navigational matters; the navigator should seek information on ice, climate, and weather, as well as information gained from previous operations in the area. Forecasts on anticipated ice and weather conditions should be obtained before departure and updated by radio whenever possible.

Piloting in polar regions is burdened with many difficulties, and at best yields only a general indication of position. It is, however, a most important means of navigation in these regions. For celestial observations, a bubble sextant should be obtained, and the navigator should familiarize himself with its operation.

The entire cruise may well be unusual and interesting, as well as professionally challenging. The navigator's role is vital to the safety of the vessel, and his skillful and ingenious use of a variety of navigation methods will contribute significantly to the success of the operation.

Chapter 41

Ship Weather Routing

Introduction

4101 At the very beginning of this book the basic definition of navigation was qualified by including "safely" and "efficiently." *Ship weather routing* can materially aid in the achievement of these different, yet related, goals. It can be specifically defined as the process of selecting an optimum track for an ocean passage by making long-range predictions of wind, waves, and currents, and their effect on the vessel, which may be large or small. In more general terms, it is taking advantage of all meteorological and hydrographic information to achieve the safest and most economical passage for a ship or yacht. This is essentially routine in aircraft operation, but not as widely used in marine navigation as it might be.

Optimum Track Ship Routing

In the U.S. Navy, weather routing is called *Optimum Track Ship Routing* (OTSR) and is done by the Naval Eastern Oceanography Center for the Atlantic and by the Fleet Numerical Oceanography Center for the Pacific. Several commercial meteorological activities provide similar services for merchant ships and yachts.

Purpose of Weather Routing

4102 As shown in earlier chapters, the shortest distance between any two points on the surface of the earth is the arc of the great circle connecting them. Although this represents the shortest linear distance, it may not represent the most desirable track for a vessel; another route may produce a least-time track. In the case of passenger vessels, the optimum route is quite often the one that will maximize conditions of passenger safety and comfort. In other operations, minimum fuel consumption may be the determining factor; or, in the case of some cargo vessels, particularly those carrying deck loads, the optimum track may be one that will present the least hazard to the cargo. In general, routes are prepared that combine these considerations. It has always been recognized by seamen that waves, whether breaking seas or swells, have the greatest adverse effect on the movement of a ship through the water. Optimum track routing is therefore normally used to route ships along a track to avoid areas where the waves are expected to be the highest.

The desirability of optimum track routing cannot be overemphasized. For a one-month period, a group of insurance underwriters reported that due to bad weather, 105 merchant ships sustained hull or cargo damage of sufficient seriousness to result in insurance claims. During the same month, bad weather was a contributing factor in the total loss of 7 ships and damage to 253 others.

Fundamentals of Weather Routing

4103 The basic inputs to any ship routing process are present weather conditions and forecasts; forecasts may be short-range (roughly a week), extended-range (a week to a month), and long-term (more than a month). From such forecasts, predictions are made of probable sea states. Other inputs are vessel type, speed, extent of loading, and nature of cargo.

The output from a weather routing advisory service is normally in the form of an *initial route recommendation* prepared and made available to the vessel two or three days in advance of the planned sailing date. Subsequently, the advisory service may recommend advancing or delaying the day or hour of the departure. Also available from advisory services are generalized *planning routes* that are developed more from seasonal data than from present and forecast weather patterns. These use information from Pilot Charts (and other sources), but are more detailed and specific.

After a vessel sails, its progress along the recommended route is monitored with respect to developing weather patterns. *Diversions* are recommended in terms of change of course or speed to avoid or minimize the effects of adverse weather and sea conditions—conditions that might require a speed reduction by one-third or an increase in transit time of six hours or more. A recommendation of storm *evasion* may be made if conditions become dangerous enough that the planned route should be disregarded and the vessel should take independent action to avoid hazardous conditions.

An essential element of any ship weather-routing system is an efficient two-way communications system. By having the vessel report present conditions, the advisory agency can confirm or modify its forecasts; by receiving changes in routing, the vessel can take advantage of knowledge more recent than that which went into the initial route recommendation.

Predictions of Sea Conditions

4104 Standard wave-forecasting techniques are used to derive predictions of wave heights from the isobaric pattern of winds on the weather chart. Empirical tests have been made to determine ship speed versus wave conditions for various types of vessels; this information is further divided into the effect of head seas, following seas, and beam seas. Figure 4104a shows a typical graph presenting this information.

Synoptic wave charts are prepared showing the size and type of waves over large areas of the ocean. Data for the preparation of these charts is gathered from commercial and military vessels, and from the meteorological services of various governments. *Prognostic* wave charts are more widely used than the synoptic charts for route selection, because wind and wave conditions often change rapidly at a given point—as in the vicinity of a rapidly moving cold front. They are prepared from sea-level atmosphere charts, as well as from data in the synoptic charts. Figure 4104b is a section of a typical prognostic wave chart of the North Atlantic.

Figure 4104c shows a surface pressure system lying along a ship's proposed track, *A-B*, and the distribution and direction of waves connected with this pressure system. The barometric pressures are in millibars; the wave heights are in feet (1 foot = 0.3 m). The *isopleth* lines give the mean wave heights for waves within each area. The pressure system and wave pattern are assumed to remain static for each 24-hour period.

The various techniques of forecasting sea conditions are constantly being improved. The use of upper air charts and jet stream analysis has proven valuable for longer term predictions covering the duration of a voyage. Significant upper air meteorological features often appear on the upper level

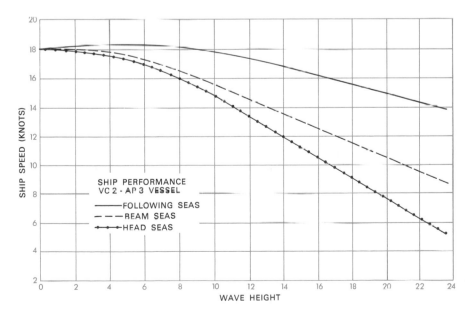

Figure 4104a. Relationship between wave heights and ship's speed made good for a typical merchant vessel.

Figure 4104b. Prognostic wave chart.

SURFACE WEATHER CHART   WAVE CHART

Figure 4104c. Surface pressure system and associated wave heights.

charts before they are reflected in surface conditions, thus permitting the analysis and the forecasting of marine weather. Ocean areas that will become hazardous may thus be determined before the condition actually develops.

Current, Wind, and Waves

4105   The effects of ocean currents on the movement of a ship in relation to the earth would be easy to determine if the exact current set and drift were known; as the vessel moves through the water, the entire water mass is also being moved by the current effect. By adding the vectors representing the vessel's course and speed and the set and drift of the current, the vessel's movement relative

to the earth could be precisely determined. (Receivers for several radionavigation systems can provide direct, continuous data on course and speed made good, ascertained from successive determinations of position.) This is quite similar to the wind drift problem of an aircraft in which the track of the aircraft over the earth is the result of the two vectors representing heading and air speed, and wind direction and velocity. However, there is one important difference affecting a vessel in the ocean current problem. The vessel is not completely immersed in the moving medium; approximately one-third of the hull is immersed and affected by the current, while the remainder of the hull is being affected by air resistance. This latter effect is negligible at low speeds and in no-wind conditions, but it becomes more serious as the relative wind speed increases. Vessel movement can be aided by a favorable current, but the prediction of the location and velocity of such a current at a given time is not in most cases accurate enough to be the determining factor in optimum track ship routing. Currents help in the final determination of a route where the wind and wave conditions also suggest the same choice.

Wind Effect

Wind effect on the movement of a vessel is difficult to compute. It varies with the ship's type, load, and on the direction and strength of the wind relative to the exposed hull and superstructure; container ships with their massive deckloads are particularly affected by surface winds. It is known that for a given wind velocity, a head wind will slow the movement of a vessel more than a following wind will increase her speed; in fact, if a following wind produces moderate to large waves, forward movement can be slower rather than faster; see the solid line in figure 4104a.

Wave Effects

Wave effects on a vessel are also difficult to determine, and the computations of mathematical models seldom agree with actual experiences. This is due in part to the fact that uniform wave heights are used in computation while a great range of heights is actually present in a storm. The prediction of wave effects on different types of vessels represents the result of large numbers of empirical tests analyzed to produce average values. A combination of reported wave heights and wind values from prognostic charts is used to draw *isopleths*, or lines of equal wave heights, on the chart. Details of theory and the construction of wave charts to apply these values to actual operations is beyond the scope of this book. Additional information will be found in Naval Oceanographic Office Pubs. No. 148, 601, 602, and 604; also Special Publication No. 1 and Technical Report No. 148.

Guidance for ship weather routing in various ocean areas can be found in *Bowditch* (1977 or 1984), Volume 1, articles 2405 and 2406. These generalized statements are based on the overall probability of storm generation at various seasons of the year; they provide a base of information to which can be applied specific extended and long-range forecasts for more exact ship routing. The goal of careful route planning is to minimize the later need for diversion.

Construction of a Least-time Track

4106 Either as an adjunct of weather routing advice, or in lieu thereof, a vessel that has the capability of receiving and printing facsimile radio weather charts can benefit from the construction of "least-time" tracks like those prepared ashore by a routing service prior to departure.

The basic concept involves the determination of a day's run that would be obtained on various courses. A great circle is normally drawn on the chart between point of departure, or present position if already at sea, and the destination. Diverging lines radiating from the point of origin represent the possible tracks, as shown in figure 4106a. Using a chart of average wave height and the ship's performance curve to determine speed on the various tracks, a 24-hour passage can be computed for each possible track. The points on each line representing a 24-hour passage are then connected with a smooth curve that represents the loci of possible positions of the vessel after one day's travel. Additional diverging tracks are then drawn, the origin of each being perpendicular to curve S, at its starting point. Using the wave chart for the second day, the second day's run is constructed and a curve S_2 is drawn through these points. A point of tangency of an arc, centered at the destination B, to curve S_2 would indicate the point nearest the destination that can be reached after two days' travel.

Least-time tracks can be carried forward for as many days as reliable meteorological forecasts are available. Such advanced plans, however, should be rechecked each day as additional weather and wave forecasts are received. Figure 4106b shows a plot carried forward for five days. The least-time track is plotted in reverse from the farthest point of advance (found in the preceding paragraph as the point of tangency) back to the point of origin. Each section of the intended track will be perpendicular to its respective curve.

Computers now being introduced aboard merchant vessels can digest weather and sea data inputs, and present an almost instantaneous recommendation as to the optimum course and speed to permit maximum safety and economy. The use of computers on board vessels is discussed in more detail in chapter 38.

Routing to Avoid Storms

4107 For an extended trip it may be impossible to avoid all storms; sometimes the vessel will be able to avoid the actual storm center, but not all the storm seas and swells associated with the sys-

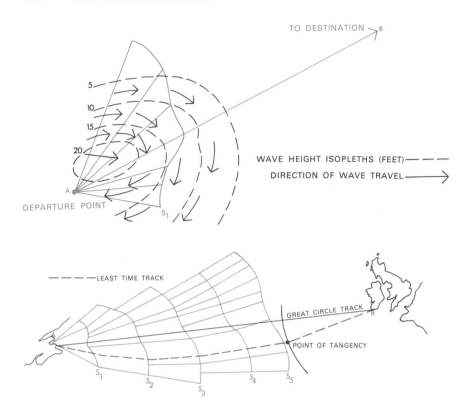

Figure 4106a. Possible routes for the first day's travel (black lines outward from *A*).

Figure 4106b. Least time track for five days' travel.

tem. The use of long-range forecasts and all available weather data to avoid storms is an art that is mastered by a thorough understanding of both navigation and meteorology. The following examples illustrate the use of weather routing on a long voyage using the forecasts of the movements of storm centers expected to be encountered.

Figure 4107 shows a developed semistationary storm and a series of deepening lows in the Northern Hemisphere. A ship is bound to the westward from *A* to *B*.

Prolonged heavy head seas are to be expected to the south and southwest of the storm center, and moderate head seas to the south and southwest of the center of the second low-pressure area.

To avoid these head seas, a marked diversion to the north of the storm center is indicated; this new path, shown as a dotted line, should also take the ship to the north of the second low.

Another situation is the existence of a very intense Northern Hemisphere storm pattern with a series of lows that will be moving northeastward along a cold front. In this case, it is not possible to pass safely to the north of the storm. The ship therefore should divert well to the south. This will cause continuous head winds, but will avoid possible damage due to heavy seas.

A reduced speed *after* adverse weather and sea conditions are encountered will probably mean a

longer time of exposure for the ship and her crew and cargo. The objective of weather routing and storm avoidance planning is to make any necessary diversion early enough and of great enough magnitude to entirely avoid the threatening conditions; a greater distance may have to be traveled, but if speed can be maintained (or nearly so), then little delay may result; information can also be found in DMAHTC Pubs. No. 117A and 117B.

Transmissions of Weather Data

4108 Various U.S. Navy radio stations, and foreign stations also, transmit facsimile weather charts and other data on regular schedules. Weather broadcasts by radiotelephone and radiotelegraph are made by many stations throughout the world. NOAA publication *Worldwide Marine Weather Broadcasts* furnishes a complete listing of such transmissions.

Results of Weather Routing

4109 Experience indicates that considerable savings in time and fuel are usually obtained by using ship weather routing, and that damage can frequently be avoided. The many variables involved, and the uncertainty of the time that would have been used in following a great circle make exact comparisons impossible. From the experience gained in thousands of passages, it is apparent

Figure 4107. Storm avoidance.

that the savings in time, fuel, and passenger and cargo safety, as well as reduced cargo and vessel damage, have made this system very worthwhile, and the navigator should familiarize himself with the techniques required for optimum ship routing. In order to gain this familiarization, the Naval Oceanographic Office Special Publication, *Applica-tion of Wave Forecasts to Marine Navigation*, Pub. No. SP-1, should be consulted for further detailed information.

The use of a weather routing service is purely advisory to the navigator and captain of any vessel. The captain fully retains his responsibility for the safe and efficient movement of his vessel.

Appendix A

Abbreviations

Included in this appendix are the abbreviations and symbols that are commonly used in the practice of navigation. The abbreviations and symbols used on charts are described in Chart No. 1, which is included at the back of this book.

A   ampere; amplitude; augmentation; away (altitude difference)

a   altitude intercept (altitude difference, Hc ~ Ho); assumed

$a_0, a_1, a_2,$ First, second, and third Polaris sight-reduction correction (from *Nautical Almanac*)

AA   *Air Almanac*

AC   alternating current

ADF   automatic direction finder

AF   audio frequency

aL   assumed latitude

aLo   assumed longitude

AM   amplitude modulation

Amp   amplitude

AP   assumed position

App   apparent

atm   atmosphere

AU   astronomical unit

Aug   augmentation

Az   azimuth angle. (Z also used)

aλ   assumed longitude

B   bearing; bearing angle; barometric correction (altitude); body (celestial body)

BFO   beat frequency oscillator

Bn   beacon

C   Celsius (centigrade); chronometer time; compass (direction); correction; course (vessel); course angle

Note: Some variations in capitalization may occur.

CB   compass bearing

CC   chronometer correction; compass course

CCZ   Coastal Confluence Zone

CE   chronometer error; compass error

CH   compass heading

CIC   Combat Information Center

cm   centimeter

CMG   course made good

Cn   course (as distinguished from course angle)

CNO   Chief of Naval Operations

co-   the compliment of (90° minus)

COA   course of advance

COG   course over ground

co-L   colatitude

comp   compass

corr   correction

cos   cosine

cot   cotangent

CPA   closest point of approach

Cpgc   course per gyro compass

cps   cycles per second

Cpsc   course per standard compass

Cp stg c   course per steering compass

CRT   cathode ray tube

csc   cosecant

CW   continuous wave

C − W   chronometer time minus watch time

D   deviation; dip (of horizon); distance; drift (current)

d   declination; difference; distance

DB   danger bearing

DC   direct current

Dec.   declination

Dec. inc.   declination increment

deg   degree

Dep   departure

Dest destination
Dev deviation
DG degaussing
diff difference
dist distance
D. Lat. Difference of latitude
DLo Difference of longitude (arc units)
DMAHTC Defense Mapping Agency Hydro-graphic/Topographic Center
DME distance measuring equipment
DR dead reckoning, dead reckoning position
Dr drift
DRA dead reckoning analyzer
DRAI dead reckoning analyzer indicator
DRM direction of relative movement
DRT dead reckoning tracer
DSD Double-second difference
DST daylight saving time
dur duration
DUT₁ time signal correction
dλ difference of longitude
E East; error
e Earth (wind triangle and relative movement problems); base of Naperian logarithms
EHF extremely high frequency
EM log electromagnetic log
EP estimated position
Eq. T equation of time
est estimated
ETA estimated time of arrival
ETD estimated time of departure
F Fahrenheit; fast; phase correction (altitude)
f frequency; latitude factor
fath fathom, fathoms
FM frequency modulation
fm fathom, fathoms
ft foot, feet
FTC fast time constant (radar)
G Greenwich, Greenwich meridian (upper branch); grid
g Greenwich meridian (lower branch); acceleration due to gravity
GB grid bearing
GC grid course
GE gyro error
GH grid heading
GHA Greenwich hour angle
GHz gigahertz
GMT Greenwich mean time
Govt government
GP geographical position
GPS Global Positioning System
Gr Greenwich
GRI group repetition interval
GST Greenwich sidereal time

GV grid variation
GZn grid azimuth
h altitude (astronomical); height above sea level
ha apparent altitude
HA hour angle
Hc computed altitude
Hd head
Hdg heading
HE height of eye
HF high frequency
HHW higher high water
HLW higher low water
Ho observed altitude
Hor horizontal
HP horizontal parallax
H_{pgc} heading per gyro compass
H_{psc} heading per standard compass
H_{pstgc} heading per steering compass
hr hour
hrs hours
hs sextant altitude
HT height
ht tabulated altitude
Ht. eye height of eye
HW high water
Hz hertz (cycle per second)
I instrument correction
IC index correction
IFF identification friend or foe
IMU inertial measurement unit
in inch, inches
INS integrated navigation system
J irradiation correction
K knot; knots; Kelvin (temperature)
kc kilocycles (kilohertz)
kHz kilohertz
km kilometer, kilometers
kn knot; knots
kt knot; knots
kW kilowatt
L latitude; lower limb correction for moon (from *Nautical Almanac*)
L₁ latitude of departure
L₂ latitude of destination
l difference of latitude
LAN local apparent noon
LAT local apparent time
lat latitude
LF low frequency
LHA local hour angle
LHW lower high water
LL lower limb
LLW lower low water
Lm mid-latitude; mean latitude

LMT   local mean time
log   logarithm; logarithmic
log$_e$ natural logarithm (to base e)
log$_{10}$ common logarithm (to base 10)
Lo(λ)   longitude
long   longitude
LOP   line of position
Lv   latitude of vertex
LW   low water
λ_1   longitude of departure
λ_2   longitude of destination
λv   longitude of vertex
M   magnetic; maneuvering ship (in relative plot of relative movement problems; meridian (upper branch); meridional parts
m   maneuvering ship (in speed triangle of relative movement problems); meridian (lower branch); meridional difference; meters
mag   magnetic; magnitude
max   maximum
MB   magnetic bearing
mb   millibars
MC   magnetic course
Mer. Pass.   meridian passage
MF   medium frequency
MH   magnetic heading
MHHW   mean higher high water
MHW   mean high water
MHWN   mean high water neaps
MHWS   mean high water springs
MHz   megahertz
mi   mile, miles
mid   middle
min   minute, minutes
MINDAC   Miniature Inertial Navigational Digital Automatic Computer
MLLW   mean lower low water
MLW   mean low water
MLWN   mean low water neaps
MLWS   mean low water springs
mm   millimeter
mph   miles (statute) per hour
MPP   most probable position
ms   millisecond
MZn   magnetic azimuth
N   North
NA   *Nautical Almanac*
Na   nadir
NASA   National Aeronautics and Space Administration
naut   nautical
NAVDAC   Navigational Data Assimilation Computer
NAVSAT   Navy navigation satellite system
NAVSTAR   Global Positioning System

nm   nautical mile, nautical miles
n mi   nautical mile, nautical miles
NOAA   National Oceanic and Atmospheric Administration
NOS   National Ocean Service (formerly National Ocean Survey)
Nt M   nautical mile
P   atmospheric pressure; parallax; planet; pole
p   departure; polar distance
PC   personal correction
PD   polar distance; position doubtful
pgc   per gyro compass
P in A   parallax in altitude
Pit log   Pitot-static log
PM   pulse modulation
Pn   North pole; North celestial pole
Pos   position
posit   position
PPC   propagation correction
PPI   plan position indicator
PRF   pulse repetition frequency
PRR   pulse repetition rate
Ps   South pole; South celestial pole
psc   per standard compass
p stg c   per steering compass
Pt   point
pub   publication
PV   prime vertical
Q   Polaris correction
QQ'   celestial equator; equator
R   reference craft (relative movement problems); refraction
r   reference ship (in speed triangle of relative movement problems)
RA   right ascension
RB   relative bearing
R Bn   radiobeacon
RDF   radio direction finder
rel   relative
rev   reversed
RF   radio frequency
R Fix   running fix
RMS   root mean square
RPM   revolution per minute
S   sea-air temperature difference correction; slow; South; speed
s   second, seconds
SD   semidiameter
sec   secant; second, seconds
SH   ship's head (heading)
SHA   sidereal hour angle
SHF   super high frequency
SI   international system of units (metric)
sin   sine
SINS   Ship's Inertial Navigation System

SMG   speed made good
SOA   speed of advance
SOG   speed over the ground
SRM   speed of relative movement
SSCNS   Ship's Self-Contained Navigation System
STC   sensitivity time control
st.m   statute mile
T   air temperature correction; temperature; time; toward (altitude difference); true (direction)
t   meridian angle; elapsed time
Tab   tabulated value
tan   tangent
TB   true bearing; combined temperature-barometric correction
TC   true course
TD   time difference (Loran)
T$_G$ ground-wave reading (Loran)
T$_{GS}$ ground-wave-sky-wave reading (Loran)
TH   true heading
TR   track
Tr   transit
TZn   true azimuth
U   upper limb correction for moon (from *Nautical Almanac*)
UHF   ultra high frequency
UL   upper limb
UT   Universal Time (UT$_1$, UT$_2$)
UTC   Coordinated Universal Time

V   variation; vertex
v   excess of GHA change from tabulated value for one hour
Var   variation
vel   velocity
VHF   very high frequency
vis   visibility
VLF   very low frequency
VOR   very high frequency omnirange
W   watch time; West
w   wind (wind triangle problems)
WAC   World Aeronautical Chart
WE   watch error
X   parallactic angle
yd   yard
yr   year
Z   azimuth angle; zenith
z   zenith distance; zone meridian (lower branch)
ZD   zone description
Zn   azimuth (as distinguished from azimuth angle)
ZT   zone time
Δ   A small increment, or the change in one quantity corresponding to a unit change in another variable
λ   longitude; wave length (radiant energy)
μs   microsecond
π   ratio of circumference of circle to diameter $=3.14159 +$

Appendix B   Symbols

Positions

⌒   dead reckoning position
⊙   fix
⊡   estimated position
△   symbol used for one set of fixes when simultaneously fixing by two means, e.g., visual and radar; sometimes used for radionavigation fixes

Mathematical Symbols

$+$ plus (addition)
$-$ minus (subtraction)
$\pm$ plus or minus
$\sim$ absolute difference (smaller subtracted from larger)
$\times$ times (multiplication)

$\div$ divided by (division)
x^2 square of number x
x^3 cube of number x
x^n nth power of number x
$\sqrt{}$ square root
$\sqrt[n]{}$ nth root
$=$ equals
$\neq$ not equal to
$\approx$ nearly equal to
$>$ is greater than
$<$ is less than
$\geq$ is equal to or greater than
$\leq$ is equal to or less than
∞ infinity
.....   repeating decimal

Appendix C

Standards of Precision and Accuracy; Mathematical Rules

Standards of Precision and Accuracy

C-01 The adoption of a set of standards for the precision and accuracy of navigational measurements must be tempered somewhat by their application to a specific vessel in a specific set of circumstances. A large ship will be navigated more precisely than a small boat; a vessel of any size more accurately in good weather than in a storm.

Precision

C-02 In navigation, "precision" is used to mean the fineness of the degree of measurement; thus a value of 12.0 is a more *precise* value than one of 12; the former has three significant digits, the latter has two.

In some scientific fields, "precision" is related to the degree to which a given set of measurements of the same sample agree with their mean; this definition is not applicable in navigation.

Accuracy

C-03 *Accuracy* relates to the closeness of a measured value to the true (correct, exact) value.

Precision and accuracy are not the same, and only the proper term should be used in each instance. A measured value should not be stated to a degree of precision that is greater than the accuracy of its measurement.

Any quantity derived by interpolation from a table should be expressed to the same degree of precision as are the tabulated values.

Any quantity derived from a mathematical calculation should not be expressed to any higher degree of precision than that of the *least* precise term used in the calculation.

Levels of Precision

C-04 The levels of precision of measurement and calculation used in this book are:

Altitude	0.1'
Azimuth	0.1°
Bearing	0.1°
Compass Error	0.5°
Current: Set	1°
Drift	0.1 knot
Course	0.1°
Deviation	0.5°
Distance	0.1 mile
Height of tide	0.1 foot
Latitude	0.1'
Longitude	0.1'
Speed	0.1 knot
Time DR	1 minute
Celestial	1 second
Variation	0.5°

In expressing any quantity to *tenths*—when there are no tenths—the ".0" should be shown to indicate the degree of precision; for example,

15 miles—means to the nearest mile;
15.0 miles—means to the nearest 0.1 mile.

Rounding Off

C-05 The following rules have been used to round off the results of mathematical computations which contain digits without significance.
1. If the digit to be rounded off is a "4" or less, it is dropped or changed to a zero. (633 is rounded to 630; 1.24 is rounded to 1.2.)
2. If the digit to be rounded off is a "6" or larger, the preceding digit is raised to the next higher

value and the rounded digit is dropped or changed to zero.

> 1.27 is rounded to 1.3
> 787 is rounded to 790

3. If the final digit is a "5", the preceding digit is *increased* or *decreased* so that it will be an *even* number and the rounded digit is dropped or changed to zero.

> 1.25 is rounded to 1.2
> 1.35 is rounded to 1.4

> 425 is rounded to 420
> 775 is rounded to 780

4. If more than one digit is to be rounded off, these digits are *not* rounded off separately in sequence. For example, 1.348 is rounded to 1.3 in one operation, and *not* in steps, first to 1.35 and then to 1.4.

Note: Calculations involving the use of a calculator or computer may be internally rounded off in a slightly different manner.

Appendix D   The Metric System

Introduction

D-01 The "Metric Conversion Act of 1975" declared the policy of the United States to be an increased use of the metric system of measurement on a voluntary basis, with the goal of "a nation predominantly, although not exclusively, metric." This edition, therefore, introduces metric units as parenthetical equivalents to the customary (English) units. Some charts are now using metric units for depths and heights, although it is expected that nautical miles and knots will continue in marine use for distance and speed.

The Modern Metric System

D-02 The correct name for the "metric" system is the *International System of Units*, abbreviated as *SI* (from the name in French). This is a thoroughly modernized metric system based on very precise standards and relationships between units. SI provides a logical and consistently interrelated system of measurement for science, industry, commerce, and other areas of human effort, including, of course, navigation.

The modern metric system is built upon a foundation of seven *base* units, plus two *supplementary* units.

The Base Units

D-03 The *base units* and their symbols are:

Quantity	SI unit name	Symbol
Length	meter[†]	m
Mass (weight)	kilogram	kg
Temperature	kelvin	K[‡]
Time	seconds	s
Electric current	ampere	A
Amount of substance	mole	mol
Luminous intensity	candela	cd

[†]The spelling in SI is "metre" but "meter" has been adopted for U.S. use.

[‡]The commonly used unit of temperature is the "degree Celsius," °C (formerly called "centigrade"); the size of the unit is the same, the zero point is different. If kelvins are used, note that the unit is "kelvin (K)" and not "degree kelvin (°K)."

The Supplementary Units

D-04 The *supplementary units* and their symbols are:

Quantity	SI unit name	Symbol
Plane angle	radian	rad
Solid angle	steradian	sr

Unit symbols should be used rather than abbreviations; e.g., "A" rather than "amp" for ampere. Unit symbols are not changed for the plural form. Most symbols are written in lower-case letters; exceptions are those named after persons in which cases the symbol is capitalized. Periods are not used after symbols (except at the end of a sentence). In the expression of a quantity, a space is left between the numerical value and the symbol; e.g., 35 mm rather than 35mm, but a hyphen is normally inserted in the adjectival form; e.g., 35-mm film. No space is left, however, between a numerical value and the symbols for degrees, minutes, or seconds.

In the field of navigation, the SI units most often encountered will be those of length, time, and angular measurement; note that the unit of time is the same in both metric and customary (English) systems.

Derived Units

D-05 SI units for all other quantities are *derived* from the above nine base and supplementary units. All are defined as products or ratios without numerical factors. Some are expressed in terms of the base units concerned; others have been given special names of their own.

Typical of the derived units that are combinations of the base units are:

Quantity	SI unit name	Symbol
Area	square meter	m^2
Volume	cubic meter	m^3
Density	kilogram per cubic meter	kg/m^3
Speed, velocity	meter per second	m/s
Acceleration	meter per second squared	m/s^2

Typical of derived units with special names are:

Quantity	SI unit name	Symbol	Expression in terms of other units
Frequency	hertz	Hz	s^{-1}
Force	newton	N	$kg \cdot m/s$
Pressure, stress	pascal	Pa	N/m^2
Energy, work	joule	J	$N \cdot m$
Power	watt	W	J/s
Electrical potential	volt	V	W/A
Electrical resistance	ohm	Ω	V/A

Some derived units combine base and special names; typical of these are:

Quantity	SI unit name	Symbol
Electrical field strength	volt per meter	V/m
Specific energy	joule per kilogram	J/kg

Derived units resulting from multiplication are normally written out with a space between units; e.g., newton meter (acceptable, but less desirable is the hyphenated form, "newton-meter"). With symbols, a raised dot ($\cdot$) is used to indicate the product of the two units; e.g., $N \cdot m$; an exception is watt hour which is written "Wh" without the raised dot.

Powers may be expressed as words, such as "squared" or "cubed," which follow the names of units. An exception is that powers expressed as words may precede the names of units of area and volume.

In division, the word "per" is used rather than a solidus (/) when units are spelled out; e.g., meter per second, not meter/second. When symbols are used, any of the following forms may be used; m/s or $\frac{m}{s}$ or $m \cdot s^{-1}$.

Multiples and Submultiples

D-06 Units larger and smaller than the base and derived units are formed by adding prefixes decimally to make multiples and submultiples. The symbol for the prefix is added to the symbols for the base or derived unit.

1,000,000,000	10^9	giga	G
1,000,000	10^6	mega	M
1,000	10^3	kilo	k
100	10^2	hecto	h
10	10^1	deka	da
0.1	10^{-1}	deci	d
0.01	10^{-2}	centi	c
0.001	10^{-3}	milli	m
0.000,001	10^{-6}	micro	μ

There are others—larger multiples and smaller submultiples—than those shown above (for a total of 16 prefixes), but these are of little or no interest in navigation.

It is important to note that the kilogram is the only SI unit that integrally includes a prefix. Because double prefixes are not to be used, the standard prefixes, in the case of mass, are to be used with gram (g) and not with kilogram (kg).

Retained Customary Units

D-07 Certain "customary" (English) units that are not a part of the SI (metric) system are in such wide use that it is not practical to abandon them. Among those accepted for continued use with SI units in the United States are:

degree, angle (°) $= (\pi/180)$ rad
minute, angle (') $= (1/60)° = (\pi/10,800)$ rad
second, angle (") $= (1/60)' = (\pi/848,000)$ rad
liter (L)* $= 10^{-3}\ m^3$
metric ton (t) $= 10^3\ kg$

*The international symbol for liter is the lowercase letter "l" which can easily be confused with the numeral "1"; accordingly, the symbol "L" is recommended for U.S. use.

In those cases where their usage is well established, certain other customary units will continue to be acceptable "for a limited time, subject to future review." Of interest to navigators in this category are:

nautical mile

knot

bar, millibar (atmospheric pressure)

Unacceptable Units

D-08   The Metric Conversion Act of 1975 authorizes the Secretary of Commerce to make "interpretations and modifications" of the International System of Units for U.S. usage. Several such official decisions have been made; these form the basis for the preceding articles. Metric units, symbols, and terms not in accordance with the published decisions are no longer acceptable for continued use in the United States. The officially acceptable list includes many units not discussed above, but these are generally not used in navigation.

Conversion

D-09   As long as both "customary" and "metric" units are in wide use, a navigator will be faced with the task of converting from one to the other. The conversion factors shown here have been rounded off for practical use and do not, in most instances, yield exact values. (The metric equivalents shown in this book have been rounded to roughly the same degree of precision of value as the customary unit.)

Customary units to metric

Known value	Multiplied by	To find
inches (in)	25.4	millimeters (mm)
feet (ft)	0.3048	meters (m)
yards (yd)	0.9144	meters (m)
statute miles (s mi)	1.609	kilometers (km)
nautical miles (n mi)	1.852	kilometers (km)
ounces, weight (oz)	28.35	grams (g)
pounds (lb)	0.4536	kilograms (kg)
ounces, liquid (oz)	30.28	milliliters (mi)
quarts (qt)	0.9464	liters (L)
gallons (gal)	3.785	liters (L)
Fahrenheit temperature (°F)	5/9 after subtracting 32	Celsius temperature (°C)

Metric units to Customary

centimeters (cm)	0.3937	inches (in)
meters (m)	3.281	feet (ft)
meters (m)	1.094	yards (yd)
kilometers (km)	0.6214	statute miles (s mi)
kilometers (km)	0.5400	nautical mi (n mi)
grams (g)	0.03527	ounce (weight) (oz)
kilograms (kg)	2.205	pounds (lb)
milliliters (ml)	0.03302	ounces (liq.) (oz)
liters (L)	1.057	quarts (qt)
liters (L)	0.2642	gallon (gal)
Celsius temperature (°C)	9/5 then add 32	Fahrenheit temperature (°F)

Procedures for Conversion

When converting from customary units to metric, or from metric to customary, care must be taken not to have a converted value implying a higher degree of precision than the original value. The number of digits retained in the converted value should be such that precision is not exaggerated. For example, a length of 250 feet converts exactly to 76.2 m. If, however, the 250-foot length has been obtained by rounding to the nearest 10 feet, the converted value should be stated as 76 m; if it has been obtained by rounding to the nearest 50 feet, the metric length should be given as 80 m.

The proper conversion procedure is to multiply the given quantity, customary or metric, by the conversion factor in full exactly as given above, and then to round the product to the appropriate number of significant digits (for rounding, see article C-04). For example, to convert 15.2 feet to meters, multiply 15.2 by 0.3048 and obtain 4.63296; this is rounded to 4.63 m. Do not round either the conversion factor or the quantity before multiplying them.

Conversion by Calculator

Conversion in either direction between customary and metric units is easily accomplished using a personal electronic calculator such as those described in appendix F. Ordinary multiplication can be performed using the conversion factors listed above, or other appropriate values. Many more advanced models, however, are internally programmed for direct keyboard conversions without reference to the factor involved.

Appendix E

Conversion Table for Feet, Fathoms, and Meters

Meters	Feet	Fathoms	Meters	Feet	Fathoms	Feet	Meters	Feet	Meters	Fathoms	Meters	Fathoms	Meters
1	3.28	0.55	61	200.13	33.36	1	0.30	61	18.59	1	1.83	61	111.56
2	6.56	1.09	62	203.41	33.90	2	0.61	62	18.90	2	3.66	62	113.39
3	9.84	1.64	63	206.69	34.45	3	0.91	63	19.20	3	5.49	63	115.21
4	13.12	2.19	64	209.97	35.00	4	1.22	64	19.51	4	7.32	64	117.04
5	16.40	2.73	65	213.25	35.54	5	1.52	65	19.81	5	9.14	65	118.87
6	19.69	3.28	66	216.54	36.09	6	1.83	66	20.12	6	10.97	66	120.70
7	22.97	3.83	67	219.82	36.64	7	2.13	67	20.42	7	12.80	67	122.53
8	26.25	4.37	68	223.10	37.18	8	2.44	68	20.73	8	14.63	68	124.36
9	29.53	4.92	69	226.38	37.73	9	2.74	69	21.03	9	16.46	69	126.19
10	32.81	5.47	70	229.66	38.28	10	3.05	70	21.34	10	18.29	70	128.02
11	36.09	6.01	71	232.94	38.82	11	3.35	71	21.64	11	20.12	71	129.84
12	39.37	6.56	72	236.22	39.37	12	3.66	72	21.95	12	21.95	72	131.67
13	42.65	7.11	73	239.50	39.92	13	3.96	73	22.25	13	23.77	73	133.50
14	45.93	7.66	74	242.78	40.46	14	4.27	74	22.56	14	25.60	74	135.33
15	49.21	8.20	75	246.06	41.01	15	4.57	75	22.86	15	27.43	75	137.16
16	52.49	8.75	76	249.34	41.56	16	4.88	76	23.16	16	29.26	76	138.99
17	55.77	9.30	77	252.62	42.10	17	5.18	77	23.47	17	31.09	77	140.82
18	59.06	9.84	78	255.91	42.65	18	5.49	78	23.77	18	32.92	78	142.65
19	62.34	10.39	79	259.19	43.20	19	5.79	79	24.08	19	34.75	79	144.48
20	65.62	10.94	80	262.47	43.74	20	6.10	80	24.38	20	36.58	80	146.30
21	68.90	11.48	81	265.75	44.29	21	6.40	81	24.69	21	38.40	81	148.13
22	72.18	12.03	82	269.03	44.84	22	6.71	82	24.99	22	40.23	82	149.96
23	75.46	12.58	83	272.31	45.38	23	7.01	83	25.30	23	42.06	83	151.79
24	78.74	13.12	84	275.59	45.93	24	7.32	84	25.60	24	43.89	84	153.62
25	82.02	13.67	85	278.87	46.48	25	7.62	85	25.91	25	45.72	85	155.45
26	85.30	14.22	86	282.15	47.03	26	7.92	86	26.21	26	47.55	86	157.28
27	88.58	14.76	87	285.43	47.57	27	8.23	87	26.52	27	49.38	87	159.11
28	91.86	15.31	88	288.71	48.12	28	8.53	88	26.82	28	51.21	88	160.93
29	95.14	15.86	89	291.99	48.67	29	8.84	89	27.13	29	53.04	89	162.76
30	98.43	16.40	90	295.28	49.21	30	9.14	90	27.43	30	54.86	90	164.59
31	101.71	16.95	91	298.56	49.76	31	9.45	91	27.74	31	56.69	91	166.42
32	104.99	17.50	92	301.84	50.31	32	9.75	92	28.04	32	58.52	92	168.25
33	108.27	18.04	93	305.12	50.85	33	10.06	93	28.35	33	60.35	93	170.08
34	111.55	18.59	94	308.40	51.40	34	10.36	94	28.65	34	62.18	94	171.91
35	114.83	19.14	95	311.68	51.95	35	10.67	95	28.96	35	64.01	95	173.74
36	118.11	19.69	96	314.96	52.49	36	10.97	96	29.26	36	65.84	96	175.56
37	121.39	20.23	97	318.24	53.04	37	11.28	97	29.57	37	67.67	97	177.39
38	124.67	20.78	98	321.52	53.59	38	11.58	98	29.87	38	69.49	98	179.22
39	127.95	21.33	99	324.80	54.13	39	11.89	99	30.18	39	71.32	99	181.05
40	131.23	21.87	100	328.08	54.68	40	12.19	100	30.48	40	73.15	100	182.88
41	134.51	22.42	101	331.36	55.23	41	12.50	101	30.78	41	74.98	101	184.71
42	137.80	22.97	102	334.65	55.77	42	12.80	102	31.09	42	76.81	102	186.54
43	141.08	23.51	103	337.93	56.32	43	13.11	103	31.39	43	78.64	103	188.37
44	144.36	24.06	104	341.21	56.87	44	13.41	104	31.70	44	80.47	104	190.20
45	147.64	24.61	105	344.49	57.41	45	13.72	105	32.00	45	82.30	105	192.02
46	150.92	25.15	106	347.77	57.96	46	14.02	106	32.31	46	84.12	106	193.85
47	154.20	25.70	107	351.05	58.51	47	14.33	107	32.61	47	85.95	107	195.68
48	157.48	26.25	108	354.33	59.06	48	14.63	108	32.92	48	87.78	108	197.51
49	160.76	26.79	109	357.61	59.60	49	14.94	109	33.22	49	89.61	109	199.34
50	164.04	27.34	110	360.89	60.15	50	15.24	110	33.53	50	91.44	110	201.17
51	167.32	27.89	111	364.17	60.70	51	15.54	111	33.83	51	93.27	111	203.00
52	170.60	28.43	112	367.45	61.24	52	15.85	112	34.14	52	95.10	112	204.83
53	173.88	28.98	113	370.73	61.79	53	16.15	113	34.44	53	96.93	113	206.65
54	177.17	29.53	114	374.02	62.34	54	16.46	114	34.75	54	98.76	114	208.48
55	180.45	30.07	115	377.30	62.88	55	16.76	115	35.05	55	100.58	115	210.31
56	183.73	30.62	116	380.58	63.43	56	17.07	116	35.36	56	102.41	116	212.14
57	187.01	31.17	117	383.86	63.98	57	17.37	117	35.66	57	104.24	117	213.97
58	190.29	31.71	118	387.14	64.52	58	17.68	118	35.97	58	106.07	118	215.80
59	193.57	32.26	119	390.42	65.07	59	17.98	119	36.27	59	107.90	119	217.63
60	196.85	32.81	120	393.70	65.62	60	18.29	120	36.58	60	109.73	120	219.46

From DMAHTC Pub. No. 9, Volume II, Table 21.

Appendix F

The Use of Electronic Calculators and Computers in Navigation

Introduction

F-01 The use of small, hand-held *electronic calculators* is now so ubiquitous in everyday life that it is hardly necessary to begin a consideration of their use in navigation with any review of their origin and development. The cost of the smaller models has been so reduced—to a very few dollars—that they are available to essentially everyone.

Electronic computers have come later to navigation than calculators, but they have followed generally the same developmental pattern—increasing capability, with decreasing size and decreasing price, and ever-increasing usage. The computing power of small electronic calculators will meet most, if not all, of the requirements of a navigator, but a computer can be used, and in some instances will be found more desirable.

We must not overlook another electronic marvel, the *microprocessor*—more and more becoming a part of sophisticated navigational equipment. This is a small *integrated circuit* (IC) package, essentially a tiny dedicated computer that is part of the circuitry of a larger electronic device. These "chips" enhance the capabilities and make easier the use of many types of electronic equipment from depth sounders to radar, from Loran to Omega to satellite navigation receivers. They process incoming signals, average values over periods of time and "remember" them, convert microsecond intervals of time differences to latitude and longitude, and carry out many other functions to facilitate the work of a navigator.

Electronic Calculators

F-02 The basic hand-held electronic calculator (now available even as part of a wristwatch!) has four "functions"—add and subtract, multiply and divide. The next move upward in sophistication is the provision of one or more *memories* for the temporary storage of data. To be really useful for navigation, however, a few more functions are needed; fortunately, these are available for only a slight increase in price. Such added capabilities include the ability to calculate squares and square roots of numbers, plus simple trigonometric functions. Many models also have internally stored constants such as "pi" (π) and the ability to calculate immediately the reciprocal of the value displayed. These models are generally referred to as *scientific calculators*—they were once called "slide-rule" calculators, but we now have a generation of navigators to whom a slide rule is only a tool from the past!

The calculators just described are fully capable of meeting the needs of a navigator for his routine computations, but not with the greatest possible ease. Now there is an improvement—*programmable* models in which the program, the sequence of instructions, need be entered only once for any number of repeated calculations of the same type using different input data and providing different answers. Initially, such calculators lost all the stored program instructions, and any data in memory, when the unit was switched off. More recent models have the capability of retaining the contents of their memories for extended periods of time, eliminating the bothersome chore of reentry, a step that can occasionally involve human error.

The next step upward for increasing capability and ease of use is the *card programmable* calculator, with a considerable number of individually addressable memories. (Unfortunately, this is also the next step up in cost!) With such models, the program steps need be entered only once; they can then be recorded onto a small magnetic card. At any later date, this card can be passed through the calculator, quickly and flawlessly reentering the program. A "library" of cards for the solution of different programs can be purchased or gradually built up by a user. The use of such cards can be extended to the input of data, and also the extraction of results for storage and later use. (A variation of the magnetic card is a small module containing an IC chip that is inserted or plugged into the calculator.)

Related to programmable calculators, and probably the ultimate step in sophistication, are the *stored program* models that have a number of navigational programs permanently built into their memories; these are frequently referred to as "hard-wired" units. Such calculators are very easy to use since the display will often "prompt" the user as to the entry of the next item of data required. Such models do, however, have a disadvantage in that they are limited to the specific navigational calculations for which they have a stored program, plus a limited number of simple, nonprogrammed arithmetic and trigonometric functions; they are not programmable for other functions.

Caution

An individual's ability to use an electronic calculator for the solution of navigational problems must *not* be substituted for the ability to solve such problems by other means *without* the assistance of a calculator.

A calculator is a marvelous device, but it is quite complex and relatively fragile; with few exceptions, it has not been designed and manufactured for use and storage in a marine environment. A navigator may be able to use a calculator, and will surely gain from such use, *but he should not be entirely dependent upon it.*

Characteristics of Calculators

F-03 Electronic calculators normally compute to a level of precision of from six to twelve or more digits. Many models, however, provide for rounding down to a preselected number of decimal places in the display or printout, if desired, without decreasing the level of precision used for internal calculations. In all applications, especially in navigation, caution must be continually exercised that this very high degree of precision in computation does not lead the user to place a higher degree of confidence in his results than is warranted by the level of precision and accuracy of the input data. Furthermore, the number of significant figures shown in the answer must be taken into considera-tion—a calculated result should contain no more significant figures than the least number in any item of input data. For example, a calculator might well be capable of producing a dead-reckoning position to degrees, minutes, and hundredths of minutes—yet this level of precision would not be justified if speed were only known to the nearest knot, and course only to the nearest degree. Calculator-derived solutions to a celestial observation might yield a fix to a hundredth of a minute, yet if the sextant observation had been made under difficult conditions, the position might be valid only to the nearest minute, if even to that level of precision. Loran-C receivers often display position information to two decimal places in minutes of latitude and longitude, a level of precision not always warranted by the validity of time-difference measurements. While calculator results can be accepted as fully *accurate* (provided that the data and functions have been correctly keyed in), judgment must be used in deciding upon the level of *precision* to be given to the output data.

Initially, electronic calculators used light-emitting diode (LED) displays, and some models still do. More recently, however, a shift has been made to readouts using liquid crystal displays (LCD). Each of these has its advantages and disadvantages—where one is better, the other is less desirable. Power consumption (battery drain) can be a major consideration, especially in small craft where recharging may not be practicable; here the LCD type is clearly superior. Readability in bright light, such as on deck or in an open cockpit, is another area in which the LCD exhibits superiority. At night, or in dim light, however, an LED display will be clearly readable, whereas LCD numbers will be difficult or impossible to read (many LCD calculators have an internal light for the display, but these are often inadequate). A final difference is that the digits of an LCD display are almost always larger, and hence easier to read, than those of a LED readout.

Special Features

Some calculators that are capable of computing trigonometric functions also have internal programming and special keys for polar-to-rectangular coordinate conversion, and the inverse; this can increase the speed and ease of solution of a number of navigational problems.

A capability to convert measurements between commonly used metric and customary (English) units will be found in some calculators. Several basic statistical functions are internally programmed in many models.

In more advanced calculators, numbers may be entered and displayed either in conventional format or in *scientific notation*—expressed as a number (mantissa) that has a single digit to the left of its decimal point followed by a variable number of digits to the right of the decimal point as selected by the user, plus a power-of-ten (exponent). This makes possible calculations involving very large or very small quantities. A variation of this is *engineering notation* in which there may be one, two, or three digits to the left of the decimal point, chosen so as to make the exponent a multiple of three—to fit standard metric prefixes such as micro, kilo, mega, etc.

The number of functions on the more capable units has reached the point where it is no longer possible to have a separate key for each one and remain a "hand-held" or "pocket" calculator. Two functions are then assigned to each key, selected by a *second function* or *shift* key much the same as is done on a typewriter for uppercase letters and special characters. The most advanced models may even use a single key for three functions, with two "shifts."

Several models of programmable calculators can provide an optional paper-tape printout of the stored program, a trace of the calculations, or merely a printout of the results. In various designs, this capability is either built into the unit or achieved by coupling the hand-held calculator to a separate printer.

Most calculators now have at least one memory, and such is almost essential for any navigational work. Probably the majority will have multiple memories, each individually addressable. As noted above, the trend is toward memories that will retain their information for a period of days, weeks, or longer after the unit is switched off to conserve battery power. But even so, only one program or set of data can be so stored. Where a number of different programs will be used over a period of time—or repetitive entry of considerable amounts of data is necessary, as with values from the *Almanac for Computers*—a capability to record to magnetic cards will be much appreciated by the user.

A major advancement in personal calculator design arrived with the capability to use solid-state, semiconductor memory units in the form of small plug-in modules or cartridges. A single such unit, which can be less than 0.8 inch (2 cm) square, can hold as many as 5,000 program steps and replace an entire "library" of as many as 25 programs stored on magnetic cards. At about the same time as this advancement, the number of internal memory registers was considerably increased, and provision was made for varying the proportion of registers between use for program steps and use for data storage. Some calculators can use both modules and magnetic cards; a combination of plug-in modules programmed by the manufacturer, plus cards that store programs prepared by the user, makes a very powerful hand-held personal calculator.

Specific Models

In this appendix, reference to specific models is avoided as much as possible because of the rapid advancement in calculator design and the frequent introduction of new models, which often leads to the discontinuance of older units.

Data Entry Techniques

F-04   In the development of electronic calculators, two quite different techniques have come into use for the entry of data into the devices. One is generally termed *algebraic entry*, and the other is named *Reverse Polish Notation* (for reasons that need not be considered here). The various calculator manufacturers have adopted one or the other of these procedures; strong proponents speak for each technique, and usually against the other, but either is quite suitable for use in all navigational calculations.

It is beyond the scope of this appendix to discuss either algebraic entry (AE) or Reverse Polish Notation (RPN) in detail; such information can best be obtained from the instruction manual for the calculator being used. In very broad terms, it can be said that RPN provides a somewhat more "powerful" programming technique, but at a cost of greater complexity in use. RPN, with its more difficult procedures, is more easily used by individuals with mathematical experience. On the other hand, algebraic entry, with its "plain English" approach, is more easily understood by the average person.

Calculator Programs

F-05   Any mathematical problem of reasonable scope can be solved using an electronic calculator by merely pressing the correct keys in proper sequence to enter the data and perform the mathematical operations—this is true whether the problem is long or short, simple or complex. The sequence of steps taken, the keys pressed, is a *program*, although this term is not normally used unless the sequence is thought out and reduced to writing in advance of execution. If the problem is lengthy or complex, or the same problem is to be solved repeatedly with different input data, *programming* in advance is desirable both from the point of time saved and the reduction of possibility of error. A program simply consists of a statement of the sequence of operations that will be repeated in each solution of the problem, with appropriate entry points for the insertion of data. Programming is merely logical thinking, the organization of the flow of the various steps of the solution. For most complex solutions, there may be no one single "best program"; the efforts of different persons will yield somewhat different programs, all of which should yield the same solution to the program.

The effort required to prepare an efficient program for the solution of a problem is quickly repaid by the ease with which that problem is solved a second or third or more times. With card-programmable models, this advantage reaches its maximum; the program need be prepared manually and entered into the calculator only once, no matter how many times, or how much later, it is needed.

The many navigational problems that can be solved more easily, quickly, and accurately with an electronic calculator—and the many different models that can be used—make it impractical to cover programming in detail in this appendix. That topic could fill a book, and indeed several have been written about it. (See *The Calculator Afloat* by H. H. Shufeldt and Kenneth Newcomer, published by the Naval Institute Press.)

Sources of Programs

Many navigational problems can be solved using programs furnished by the calculator manufacturer or taken from relevant books. Programs for various models have been prepared by the manufacturers to cover a wide variety of applications; some are furnished with the unit when it is purchased, and others can be bought separately as the need arises. Such programs may have been developed by the manufacturer's staff or have been contributed by users. Other programs are often available from formal or informal groups of users of similar model calculators. Users can frequently improve on or extend purchased programs.

At times, however, a navigator may not have a program available for the specific problem at hand, or he may want to try writing a more efficient program. No prior education or experience in computer programming is necessary for the level involved with the small calculators being considered here. It is, however, valuable to follow certain basic procedures. In general terms, he should first search available texts and reference works—this book,

Bowditch, etc.—for the appropriate equation(s) to solve the problem. These can be as simple as D = ST, or it can be as complex as $\sin h = \sin L \sin d \pm \cos L \cos d \cos t$ or

$$\sin Z = \frac{\cos d \sin t}{\cos h},$$

or even more complex; see equations such as those in articles 908 and 1012. The equations so found may not be in the best format for calculator solution and may have to be rearranged algebraically. In other cases, a new equation may have to be developed by extension, or by a combination of basic relationships.

Flow Charts

When a suitable equation has been found or developed, it is then broken down into a series of mathematical functions and machine operations depending upon the basic nature of the calculator being used (the use of AE or RPN, the number of memories available, etc.). This is sometimes termed the *algorithm*. Although not strictly necessary, it is often helpful in complex problems to prepare a *flow chart* (or *flow diagram*), especially if branching or subroutines are involved, or if multiple related programs are to be used. A flow chart outlines what is happening, and in what sequence, when a program is running; it is a graphic representation of the reasoning behind the structure of the program. A complete flow chart will include not only the instructions placed in the calculator's memory, but what also must be done manually on the keyboard, such as starting the program and inserting the data. More on flow charts and diagrams will be found in the instruction manuals of advanced calculator models.

Program Entry and Debugging

When the program has been written down on paper, it should be keyed into the calculator and immediately saved on a magnetic card if this is possible. The program should then be run with simple data, or with data that will yield a known solution. If the program runs correctly the first time, fine; but if there are "bugs," these must be located and corrected, and the program re-recorded. (The reason for recording the program immediately after entry is that at times in debugging operations human error can cause the total loss of the program from the calculator's memory; with it recorded, it is much easier to start over. When the program checks out, a new recording is made and the initial faulty program is erased.)

From here on, the program can be run as many times as necessary, inserting the appropriate data in each run. With card-programmable models, the program can be entered into a calculator's memory at any later date in only a few seconds' time.

A calculator navigation "library" may consist of a set of magnetic cards or a plug-in module containing a number of programs, or a combination of these two storage methods. Often the solution of a complex problem may require the use of several prepared programs from different cards or from a single module.

Electronic Computers

F-06 General-purpose *digital computers* are divided into three main classifications based on decreasing physical size and operational capabilities—*mainframe computers, minicomputers,* and *microcomputers.* A mainframe computer often occupies much of a medium-to-large size room; a minicomputer is typically the size of a desk and one or two standing cabinets. Although a minicomputer might make it to sea on a very large vessel, it is the microcomputer that a navigator will most likely encounter—the capabilities are less than the other classifications, but far more than he needs in his day's work.

Microcomputers

Microcomputers themselves are divided into general categories based on size. The largest group is normally termed "desk-top"; a computing unit about the size of a portable typewriter, a viewing monitor similar to a medium-size television receiver, a keyboard that may be a part of the computing unit or a separate unit at the end of a cable or infrared beam, a printer (also about the size of a portable typewriter), and perhaps other peripheral units such as disk drives.

There are also "portable" microcomputers that have a smaller monitor screen and are physically packaged so that a single unit may be closed up and carried by a handle. In view of the size and weight of these models, and the fact that they require connection to a 117-volt AC power source, they more properly should be referred to as "transportables." A more recent development is the truly portable models commonly called "lap portables" (also termed "briefcase" or "notebook" computers because their size roughly matches such objects). These are much smaller and lighter, use an LCD type of display rather than a cathode-ray tube, and operate from an internal rechargeable battery. Although the screen will be smaller, and the keyboard may be more limited, these units possess a significant computing capability, quite sufficient for navigation. Their size and internal power source makes practicable their use in even the smallest of craft. (Another system of categorization of microcomputers is "professional," "personal," or "home," in descending scale of capability and cost.)

Program entry is normally accomplished by use of *magnetic disks* in disk drive units; the day of cassette tape programs is essentially gone. Disks of 5¼-inch diameter are generally used—the so-called "floppy disks"—but smaller sizes are coming into wider use. Keyboards are another means of program entry, but the length and complexity of programs generally results in the use of disks. Data, of course, is entered using the keyboard. Computer memories are generally "volatile"—their contents are lost when the unit is turned off—but the use of magnetic disks makes the saving of programs and data quite simple.

The typical navigator at sea on a large vessel or yacht may not have the programming knowledge and experience to write his own, but there are programs available for purchase on disks, or programs can be obtained from someone who has developed the capability of writing them. Program disks will generally be unique to one specific brand of computers or family of related computers, and will need at least minor rewriting to be applied to other models.

Calculators in Navigation

F-07 "Once upon a time" a slide rule was of considerable assistance to a navigator trained in its use—time and effort were saved, and accuracy was enhanced to some degree. Now, however, the slide rule is all but totally replaced by electronic calculators—and, in some cases, by computers—which can supply the answers to navigational problems from simple distance-time-speed calculations to the determination of the latitude and longitude of a fix from multiple celestial observations.

The simplest four-function calculators are generally limited to the solution of the most elementary problems. A slight increase in speed may be gained over paper-and-pencil methods, but the main advantage is in the accuracy of computations *if* care is taken in keying-in the data and functions to be executed. The time it takes to look up trigonometric values in tables, and the necessity for having such tables at hand, makes the use of these simple calculators impractical for more complex problem solving.

More advanced models that include a capability for trig functions can be of considerable use in the solving of current sailing problems or positioning using two bearings on the same object; as with all calculator applications, there is greater ease and speed of solution, plus increased precision and accuracy. If such a calculator has multiple memories, polar-rectangular coordinate conversion, and conversion between degrees-minutes-seconds and degrees plus decimal minutes, even wider applications are possible. These calculators have the capability of reducing celestial observations, but the length of the process, and the necessity to perform each step individually for each reduction, normally makes such application rather tedious.

Use in Celestial Navigation

Calculator use for celestial navigation really comes into its own with programmable models, especially those with the capability of reading stored programs from magnetic cards or solid-state modules. Such units are also useful for any navigation application involving complex equations or extensive data, such as dead reckoning, current and tide predictions, and great circle or composite sailing. Calculations can also be made for the most probable position based on one or two or more lines of position. Relative motion problems, too, are very suitable for calculator solution.

The calculators with internally stored "hardwired" programs represent the ultimate in ease and speed of solution and have increased protection from operator error. These require only the entry of input data, and not much of that since some can internally compute almanac data. Convenience and accuracy are increased by the action of the calculator in "prompting" the user, actually asking for the next item of data to be entered.

The need to use the *Nautical Almanac* (or *Air Almanac*) in celestial sight reductions may not be eliminated in all models of calculators, but where almanac data is required it can be obtained by direct computation from the tables of the U.S. Naval Observatory publication, *Almanac for Computers*, most easily by using prerecorded magnetic cards for the entry of both program and mathematical constants.

It should be noted that there are two different approaches in the calculator reduction of celestial observations, procedures that are nearly the opposite of each other. With a calculator that has internally stored programs, or one that can "load" such programs from magnetic cards or modules, the answer can be obtained by merely pressing a few keys to enter the raw input data. No knowledge of celestial triangles, nor of the use of precomputed tables (Pubs. No. 229 and 249), is necessary; the

process has truly become "push-button navigation." On the other hand, a navigator knowing the geometry involved and the basic equations that are applicable can use a simpler, less-capable calculator to solve the equations and obtain the answers needed. The "push-button navigator" runs the risk of being completely incapable of making a sight reduction if his calculator fails. His more knowledgeable counterpart, however, can continue to function in such circumstances, albeit more slowly and with more mental effort, using the precomputed tables or even simple tables of sine and cosine values.

It is for this reason that preprogrammed calculators (internally or externally) are not allowed in most scholastic or licensing examinations. The "push-button-only" navigator is not a safe navigator; the "fully qualified" navigator, who is knowledgeable in both techniques, can use the "easy-quick" method when available, but he is fully competent to meet situations in which the only "calculator" available is his own brain.

Computers in Navigation

F-08 Only rarely will computers found on vessels be used solely for navigation. The more likely situation is the availability of a general-purpose microcomputer that has programs for ship's business (cargo and stores inventory, personnel records, payroll, etc.). This does not mean, however, that it cannot be used for navigation, as the other applications will not require its operation full-time. Use of a computer in navigation will closely parallel the use of a calculator that loads its programs from a magnetic card or solid-state module. Normally, once the program is loaded from a disk, it will call for the entry of data by on-screen prompts. Actually, the use of a computer will offer few advantages over the use of an advanced model of calculator; its use will probably result from its availability in the absence of a suitable calculator. If programs are available, some computers can offer the desirable additional feature of graphic presentations not available with calculators.

Summary

F-09 This appendix has dealt with electronic calculators and microcomputers more in generalities than specifics because of the fast-changing nature of these devices in a rapidly advancing field of technology. The capabilities of today's calculators, and especially computers, make models of just a few years ago appear quite crude and obsolete, while the capabilities of models just a few years in the future cannot now even be guessed.

Caution

It cannot be emphasized too strongly that the only safe way to use an electronic calculator or computer for the solution of navigational problems is with a full knowledge and understanding of the basic equations. Blind reliance on purchased prerecorded magnetic cards or plug-in modules, or programs prepared by other persons, can only lead to disaster. There must be available a back-up "manual" capability—for celestial sight reduction this is often the Ageton method, using either the full or condensed tables. (Use of the Ageton method is logical, for it, like calculator and computer solutions, computes from the DR position rather than from an assumed position as used in Pubs. No. 229 and 249.) Calculators and computers can be a great help, but the only true "brain" available to solve any problem is that gray matter in the navigator's head.

Index

Chart No. 1

United States of America

Nautical Chart Symbols
and Abbreviations

Eighth Edition
NOVEMBER 1984

Prepared jointly by

DEPARTMENT OF COMMERCE
National Oceanic and Atmospheric Administration
National Ocean Service

DEPARTMENT OF DEFENSE
Defense Mapping Agency
Hydrographic/Topographic Center

Published at Washington, D.C.
DEPARTMENT OF COMMERCE
National Oceanic and Atmospheric Administration
National Ocean Service
Washington, D.C. 20230

INTRODUCTION

General Remarks—This publication (Chart No. 1) contains symbols and abbreviations that have been approved for use on nautical charts published by the United States of America. A Glossary of Terms used on the charts of various nations is also included. The user should refer to DMAHTC Pub. No. 9, **American Practical Navigator** (Bowditch), Volume I, for the use of the chart in the practice of navigation and more detailed information pertaining to the chart sounding datum, tides and currents, visual and audible aids to navigation, etc.

Numbering—Terms, symbols, and abbreviations are numbered in accordance with a standard format approved by a 1952 resolution of the International Hydrographic Organization (IHO). Although the use of IHO-approved symbols and abbreviations is not mandatory, the United States has adopted many IHO-approved symbols for standard use. Style differences of the alphanumeric identifiers in the first column of the following pages show the status of symbols and abbreviations.

VERTICAL FIGURES indicate those items for which the symbols and abbreviations are in accordance with resolutions of IHO.

SLANTING FIGURES indicate those symbols for which no IHO resolution has been adopted.

SLANTING FIGURES ASTERISKED indicate IHO and U.S. symbols do not agree.

SLANTING LETTERS IN PARENTHESIS indicate that the items are in addition to those appearing in the IHO STANDARD LIST OF SYMBOLS AND ABBREVIATIONS.

Metric Charts and Feet/Fathom Charts—In January 1972 the United States began producing certain new nautical charts in meters. Since then many charts have been issued with soundings and contours in meters; however, for some time to come there will still be many charts on issue depicting sounding units in feet or fathoms. Modified reproductions of foreign charts are being produced retaining the native sounding unit value. The sounding unit is stated in bold type outside the border of every chart and in the chart title.

Chart Modernization—Chart symbols and labeling are brought into reasonable agreement with uniform international charting standards and procedures as quickly as opportunity affords. An example of this is the trend toward using vertical type for labeling items referred to the shoreline plane of reference, and slant type for all items referred to the sounding datum. This is not completely illustrated in this publication but is reflected in new charts produced by this country in accordance with international practices.

Soundings—The sounding datum reference is stated in the chart title. In all cases the unit of depth used is shown in the chart title and in the border of the chart in bold type.

Drying Heights—On rocks and banks that cover and uncover the elevations are above the sounding datum as stated in the chart title.

Shoreline—Shoreline shown on charts represents the line of contact between the land and a selected water elevation. In areas affected by tidal fluctuation, this line of contact is usually the mean high-water line. In confined coastal waters of diminished tidal influence, a mean water level line may be used. The shoreline of interior waters (rivers, lakes) is usually a line representing a specified elevation above a selected datum. Shoreline is symbolized by a heavy line (A9).

Apparent Shoreline is used on charts to show the outer edge of marine vegetation where that limit would reasonably appear as the shoreline to the mariner or where it prevents the shoreline from being clearly defined. Apparent shoreline is symbolized by a light line (A7, C17).

Landmarks—A conspicuous feature on a building may be shown by a landmark symbol with a descriptive label. (See I 8b, 36, 44, 72.) Prominent buildings that are of assistance to the mariner may be shown by actual shape as viewed from above (See I 3a, 19, 47, 66). Legends associated with landmarks when shown in capital letters, indicate conspicuous or the landmarks may be labeled "CONSPIC" or "CONSPICUOUS."

Buoys—The buoyage systems used by other countries often vary from that used by the United States. U.S. Charts show the colors, lights and other characteristics in use for the area of the individual chart. Certain U.S. distributed modified reproduction charts of foreign waters may show shapes and other distinctive features that vary from those illustrated in this chart.

In the U.S. system, on entering a channel from seaward, buoys on the starboard side are red with even numbers, on the port side, black or green with odd numbers. Lights on buoys on the starboard side of the channel are red or white, on the port side, white or green. Mid-channel buoys have red and white or black and white vertical stripes and may be passed on either side. Junction or obstruction buoys have red and green or red and black horizontal bands, the top band color indicating the preferred side of passage. This system does not apply to foreign waters.

IALA Buoyage System—The International Association of Lighthouse Authorities (IALA) Maritime Buoyage System (combined Cardinal-Lateral System) is being implemented by nearly every maritime buoyage jurisdiction worldwide as either REGION A buoyage (red to port) or REGION B buoyage (red to starboard). The terms "REGION A" and "REGION B" will be used to determine which type of buoyage is in effect or undergoing conversion in a particular area. The major difference in the two buoyage regions will be in the lateral marks. In REGION A they will be red to port; in REGION B they will be red to starboard. Shapes of lateral marks will be the same in both REGIONS, can to port; cone (nun) to starboard. Cardinal and other marks will continue to follow current guidelines and may be found in both REGIONS. A modified lateral mark, indicating the preferred channel where a channel divides, will be introduced for use in both REGIONS. Section L and the color plates at the back of this publication illustrate the IALA buoyage system for both REGIONS A and B.

Aids to Navigation Positioning—The aids to navigation depicted on charts comprise a system consisting of fixed and floating aids with varying degrees of reliability. Therefore, prudent mariners will not rely solely on any single aid to navigation, particularly a floating aid.

The buoy symbol is used to indicate the approximate position of the buoy body and the sinker which secures the buoy to the seabed. The approximate position is used because of practical limitations in positioning and maintaining buoys and their sinkers in precise geographical locations. These limitations include, but are not limited to, inherent imprecisions in position fixing methods, prevailing atmospheric and sea conditions, the slope of and the material making up the seabed, the fact that buoys are moored to sinkers by varying lengths of chain, and the fact that buoy body and/or sinker positions are not under continuous surveillance but are normally checked only during periodic maintenance visits which often occur more than a year apart. The position of the buoy body can be expected to shift inside and outside the charting symbol due to the forces of nature. The mariner is also cautioned that buoys are liable to be carried away, shifted, capsized, sunk, etc. Lighted buoys may be extinguished or sound signals may not function as the result of ice, running ice, other natural causes, collisions, or other accidents.

For the foregoing reasons a prudent mariner must not rely completely upon the position or operation of floating aids to navigation, but will also utilize bearings from fixed objects and aids to navigation on shore. Further, a vessel attempting to pass close aboard always risks collision with a yawing buoy or with the obstruction the buoy marks.

Colors—Colors are optional for characterizing various features and areas on the charts. For instance the land tint in this publication is gold as used on charts of the National Ocean Service; however, charts of the DMA show land tint as gray.

Heights—Heights of lights, landmarks, structures, etc. are referred to the shoreline plane of reference. Heights of small islets or offshore rocks, which due to space limitations must be placed in the water area, are bracketed. The unit of height used is shown in the chart title.

Conversion Scales—Depth conversion scales are provided on all charts to enable the user to work in meters, fathoms, or feet.

Improved Channels—Improved channels are shown by dashed limit lines with the depth and date of the latest examination placed adjacent to the channel or in a channel tabulation.

Longitudes—Longitudes are referred to the meridian of Greenwich.

Traffic Separation Schemes—Traffic separation schemes show established routes to increase safety of navigation, particularly in areas of high density shipping. These schemes were established by the International Maritime Organization (IMO) and are described in the IMO publication "Ships Routing".

Traffic separation schemes are generally shown on nautical charts at scales of 1:600,000, and larger. When possible, traffic separation schemes are plotted to scale and shown as depicted in Section P.

Names—Names on nautical charts compiled and published by the United States of America are in accordance with the principles of the Board of Geographic Names.

Correction Dates—The dates of New Editions are shown below the lower left border of the chart. These include the date of the latest Notice to Mariners applied to the charts.

U.S. Coast Pilots, Sailing Directions, Light Lists, Lists of Lights—These related publications furnish information required by the navigator that cannot be shown conveniently on the nautical charts.

U.S. Nautical Chart Catalogs and Indexes—These list nautical charts, auxiliary maps, and related publications and include general information relative to the use and ordering of charts.

Special and Foreign Symbols—Some differences may be observed between the symbols shown in Chart No. 1 and symbols shown on certain special charts and reproductions of foreign charts. A glossary of foreign terms and abbreviations is generally shown on charts on which they are used, as well as in the Sailing Directions. In addition, an extensive glossary is found at the back of this publication.

TABLE OF CONTENTS

A   The Coastline

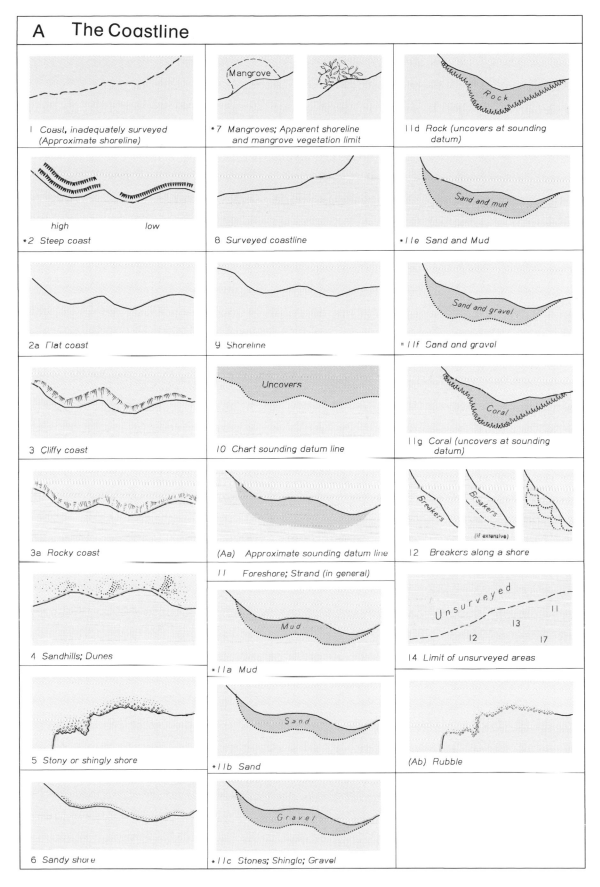

1   Coast, inadequately surveyed
    (Approximate shoreline)

*2 Steep coast
    high   low

2a Flat coast

3   Cliffy coast

3a Rocky coast

4   Sandhills; Dunes

5   Stony or shingly shore

6   Sandy shore

*7 Mangroves; Apparent shoreline
    and mangrove vegetation limit

8   Surveyed coastline

9   Shoreline

10 Chart sounding datum line

(Aa) Approximate sounding datum line

11 Foreshore; Strand (in general)

*11a Mud

*11b Sand

*11c Stones; Shingle; Gravel

11d Rock (uncovers at sounding
    datum)

*11e Sand and Mud

"11f Sand and gravel

11g Coral (uncovers at sounding
    datum)

12 Breakers along a shore
    (if extensive)

14 Limit of unsurveyed areas

(Ab) Rubble

B		Coast Features		C		The Land	

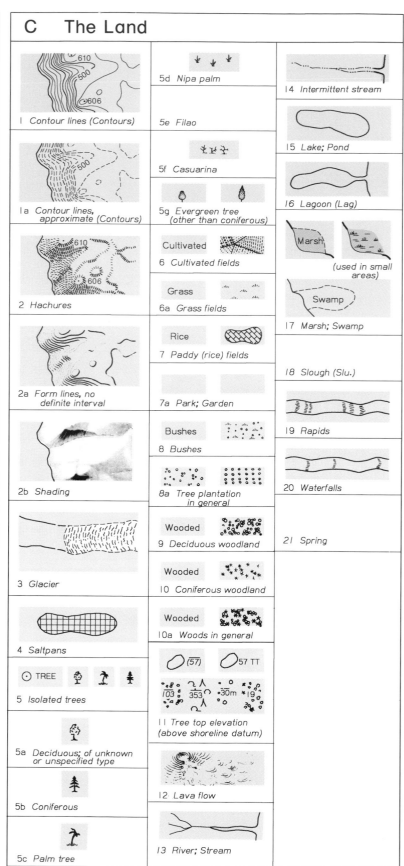

B Coast Features

1	G	Gulf
2	B	Bay
(Ba)	B	Bayou
3	Fd	Fjord
4	L	Loch; Lough; Lake
5	Cr	Creek
5a	C	Cove
6	In	Inlet
7	Str	Strait
8	Sd	Sound
9	Pass	Passage; Pass
	Thoro	Thoroughfare
10	Chan	Channel
10a		Narrows
11	Entr	Entrance
12	Est	Estuary
12a		Delta
13	Mth	Mouth
14	Rd	Road; Roadstead
15	Anch	Anchorage
16	Hbr	Harbor
16a	Hn	Haven
17	P	Port
(Bb)	P	Pond
18	I	Island
19	It	Islet
20	Arch	Archipelago
21	Pen	Peninsula
22	C	Cape
23	Prom	Promontory
24	Hd	Head; Headland
25	Pt	Point
26	Mt	Mountain; Mount
27	Rge	Range
27a		Valley
28		Summit
29	Pk	Peak
30	Vol	Volcano
31		Hill
32	Bld	Boulder
33	Ldg	Landing
	Lndg	Landing
34		Tableland
		Plateau
35	R, Rk, Rks	Rock, Rocks
36		Isolated rock
(Bc)	Str	Stream
(Bd)	R	River
(Be)	Slu	Slough
(Bf)	Lag	Lagoon
(Bg)	Apprs	Approaches
(Bh)	Rky	Rocky
(Bi)	Is	Islands
(BJ)	Ma	Marsh
(Bk)	Mg	Mangrove
(Bl)	Sw	Swamp

C The Land

1 Contour lines (Contours)

1a Contour lines, approximate (Contours)

2 Hachures

2a Form lines, no definite interval

2b Shading

3 Glacier

4 Saltpans

5 Isolated trees

5a Deciduous; of unknown or unspecified type

5b Coniferous

5c Palm tree

5d Nipa palm

5e Filao

5f Casuarina

5g Evergreen tree (other than coniferous)

6 Cultivated fields

6a Grass fields

7 Paddy (rice) fields

7a Park; Garden

8 Bushes

8a Tree plantation in general

9 Deciduous woodland

10 Coniferous woodland

10a Woods in general

11 Tree top elevation (above shoreline datum)

12 Lava flow

13 River; Stream

14 Intermittent stream

15 Lake; Pond

16 Lagoon (Lag)

17 Marsh; Swamp
(used in small areas)

18 Slough (Slu.)

19 Rapids

20 Waterfalls

21 Spring

D   Control Points

1	△	Triangulation point (station)	4	⊕ Obs Spot	Observation spot
1a		Astronomic station	5	⊼ o BM	Bench mark
2	⊙	Fixed point (landmark, position accurate)	6	View X	View point
			7		Datum point for grid of a plan
(Da)	o	Fixed point (landmark, position approximate)	8		Graphical triangulation point
3	· 256	Summit of height (Peak) (when not a landmark)	9	Astro	Astronomical
			10	Tri	Triangulation
(Db)	◎ 256	Peak, accentuated by contours	(Df)	C of E	Corps of Engineers
(Dc)	✹ 256	Peak, accentuated by hachures	12		Great trigonometrical survey station
			13		Traverse station
(Dd)	✺	Peak, elevation not determined	14	Bdy Mon	Boundary monument
(De)	⊙ 256	Peak, when a landmark	(Dg)	◇	International boundary monument

E   Units

1	hr, h	Hour	11	M, Mi / NMi, NM	Nautical mile(s)	21	′	Minute (of arc)
2	m, min	Minute (of time)				22	″	Second (of arc)
3	sec, s	Second (of time)	12	kn	Knot(s)	23	No	Number
4	m	Meter	12a	t	Tonne (metric ton equals 2,204.6 lbs)	(Ea)	St M, / St Mi	Statute mile
4a	dm	Decimeter						
4b	cm	Centimeter	12b	cd	Candela (new candle)	(Eb)	μsec, μs	Microsecond
4c	mm	Millimeter	13	lat	Latitude	(Ec)	Hz	Hertz (cps)
4d	m²	Square meter	14	long	Longitude	(Ed)	kHz	Kilohertz (kc)
4e	m³	Cubic meter	14a		Greenwich	(Ee)	MHz	Megahertz (Mc)
5	km	Kilometer(s)	15	pub	Publication	(Ef)	cps, c/s	Cycles/second (Hz)
6	in, ins	Inch(es)	16	Ed	Edition	(Eg)	kc	Kilocycle (kHz)
7	ft	Foot, feet	17	corr	Correction	(Eh)	Mc	Megacycle (MHz)
8	yd, yds	Yard(s)	18	alt	Altitude	(Ei)	T	Ton (U.S. short ton equals 2,000 lbs)
9	fm, fms	Fathom(s)	*19	ht; elev	Height; Elevation			
10	cbl	Cable length	20	°	Degree			

F   Adjectives, Adverbs, Nouns, and Other Words

1	gt	Great	25	discontd	Discontinued	(Fe)	cor	Corner
2	lit	Little	26	prohib	Prohibited	(Ff)	concr	Concrete
3	Lrg	Large	27	explos	Explosive	(Fg)	fl	Flood
4	sml	Small	28	estab	Established	(Fh)	mod	Moderate
5		Outer	29	elec	Electric	(Fi)	bet	Between
6		Inner	30	priv	Private, Privately	(Fj)	1st	First
7	mid	Middle	31	prom	Prominent	(Fk)	2nd, 2d	Second
8		Old	32	std	Standard	(Fl)	3rd, 3d	Third
9	anc	Ancient	33	subm	Submerged	(Fm)	4th	Fourth
10		New	34	approx	Approximate	(Fn)	DW	Deep Water
11	St	Saint	35		Maritime	(Fo)	min	Minimum
12	CONSPIC	Conspicuous	36	maintd	Maintained	(Fp)	max	Maximum
13		Remarkable	37	aband	Abandoned	(Fq)	N'ly	Northerly
14	D, Destr	Destroyed	38	temp	Temporary	(Fr)	S'ly	Southerly
15		Projected	39	occas	Occasional	(Fs)	E'ly	Easterly
16	dist	Distant	40	extr	Extreme	(Ft)	W'ly	Westerly
17	abt	About	41		Navigable	(Fu)	Sk	Stroke
18		See chart	42	N M	Notice to Mariners	(Fv)	Restr	Restricted
18a		See plan	(Fa)	L N M	Local Notice to Mariners	(Fw)	Bl	Blast
19		Lighted, Luminous				(Fx)	CFR	Code of Federal Regulations
20	sub	Submarine	43		Sailing Directions			
21		Eventual	44		List of Lights	(Fy)	COLREGS	Int'l Regulations for Preventing Collisions at Sea, 1972
22	AERO	Aeronautical	(Fb)	unverd	Unverified			
23		Higher	(Fc)	AUTH	Authorized	(Fz)	IWW	Intracoastal Waterway
23a		Lower	(Fd)	CL	Clearance			
24	exper	Experimental						

G Ports and Harbors

1		Anch	Anchorage (large vessels)
2		Anch	Anchorage (small vessels)
3		Hbr	Harbor
4		Hn	Haven
5		P	Port
6		Bkw	Breakwater
6a			Dike
7			Mole
8			Jetty (partly below MHW)
8a			Submerged Jetty
(Ga)			Jetty (small scale)
9		Pier	Pier
10			Spit
11			Groin (partly below MHW)
*12	ANCH PROHIBITED	ANCH PROHIB	
			Anchorage prohibited
			(Screen optional)
12a			Anchorage reserved
12b	QUARANTINE ANCHORAGE	QUAR ANCH	Quarantine anchorage
*12c			Quarantine Anchorage
*12d			Quarantine Anchorage
*12e		FISH PROHIB	Fishing prohibited
13	Spoil Area		Spoil ground (Dump Site)
(Gb)	Dumping Ground		Dumping ground (depths may be less than indicated) (Dump Site)
(Gc)	Disposal Area 92 depths from survey of JUNE 1972 85 90 87		Disposal area (Dump Site)
(Gd)	Ⓟ		Pump-out facilities

14		Fsh stks	Fisheries; Fishing stakes
14a			Fish trap; Fish weirs (actual shape charted)
14b			Duck blind
15			Tunny nets
15a	Oys	Oys	Oyster bed
16		Ldg,Lndg	Landing place
17			Watering place
18		Whf	Wharf
19			Quay
20	Ⓐ ⑭		Berth
*20a	⑭ ⑭ Ⓑ		Anchoring berth
20b	3		Berth number
21	Dol		Dolphin
22			Bollard
22a		S P M	Fixed single point mooring structure (lighted)
23			Mooring ring
24	⊖		Crane
25			Landing stage
25a			Landing stairs
26	⊕	Quar	Quarantine
27			Lazaret
28	Harbor Master ⚓	Hbr Mr	Harbormaster's office
29	⊖	Cus Ho	Customhouse
30			Fishing harbor
31			Winter harbor
32			Refuge harbor
33		B Hbr	Boat harbor
34			Stranding harbor (uncovers at LW)
35			Dock
36			Drydock (actual shape on large scale charts)
37			Floating dock (actual shape on large scale charts)
38			Gridiron; Careening grid

G   Ports and Harbors

39		Patent slip;Slipway; Marine railway
39a	Ramp	Ramp
40		Lock (point upstream)
41		Wetdock
42		Shipyard
43		Lumber yard
44	Health Office	Health officer's office
45	Hk	Hulk (actual shape on large
45a		scale charts)
* 46	PROHIBITED AREA PROHIB AREA	Prohibited area (screen optional)
46a	10	Calling-in point for vessel traffic control
47		Anchorage for seaplanes
48		Seaplane landing area
* 49	Under construction	Work in progress
* 50		Under construction
51		Work projected
(Ge)	Subm ruins	Submerged ruins
(Gf)	Dump site	Dump site

H   Topography

1		Road (Rd) or Highway (Hy)
(Ha)	20 50 95	Highway markers
2		Track, Footpath or Trail
3	CONRAIL Same grade Ry. above Ry. below	Railway (Ry) (single or double track) Railroad (RR)
(Hb)		Abandoned railroad
3a		Tramway
3b		Railway station
3c		Tunnel (railroad or road)
3d		Embankment, Levee
3e		Cutting
3f	Cswy	Causeway
4	OVERHEAD POWER CABLE AUTHORIZED CL 140 FT TOWER TOWER	Overhead power cable (OVHD PWR CAB)
5		Power transmission line
5a		Power transmission mast
6	Tel	Prominent telegraph or telephone line
7		Aqueduct; Water pipe
8	Viaduct	Viaduct
8a		Pipeline
9	Pile Piling Post Piling	Pile; Piling; Post
9a	Pile Piling Post	Pile, Piling, Post
10		Highway (See H 1)

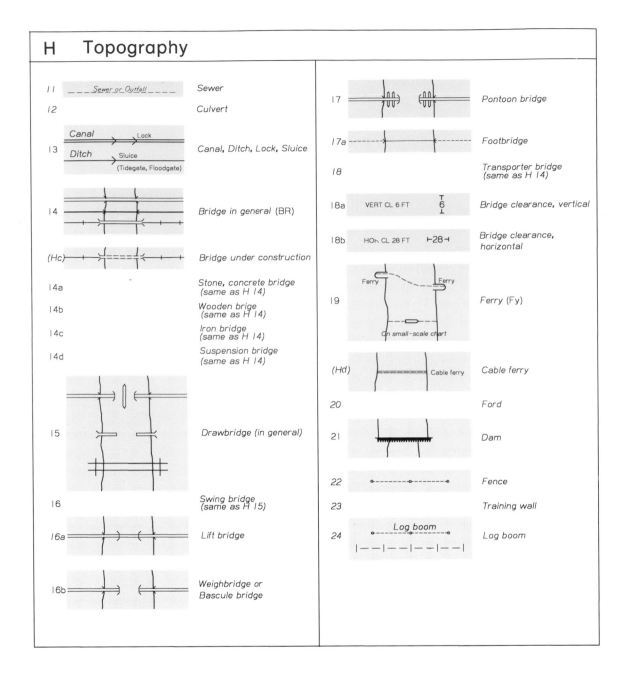

11	_Sewer or Outfall_	Sewer
12		Culvert
13	Canal · Lock / Ditch · Sluice (Tidegate, Floodgate)	Canal, Ditch, Lock, Sluice
14		Bridge in general (BR)
(Hc)		Bridge under construction
14a		Stone, concrete bridge (same as H 14)
14b		Wooden brige (same as H 14)
14c		Iron bridge (same as H 14)
14d		Suspension bridge (same as H 14)
15		Drawbridge (in general)
16		Swing bridge (same as H 15)
16a		Lift bridge
16b		Weighbridge or Bascule bridge
17		Pontoon bridge
17a		Footbridge
18		Transporter bridge (same as H 14)
18a	VERT CL 6 FT	Bridge clearance, vertical
18b	HOh CL 28 FT ⊢28⊣	Bridge clearance, horizontal
19	Ferry ... Ferry · On small-scale chart	Ferry (Fy)
(Hd)	Cable ferry	Cable ferry
20		Ford
21		Dam
22		Fence
23		Training wall
24	Log boom	Log boom

I Buildings and Structures

I		City or Town (large scale)
(Ia)		City or Town (small scale)
Ia	(30)	Height of a structure
2		Suburb
3	Vil	Village
3a		Buildings in general
4	Cas	Castle
5		House
6		Villa
7		Farm
8	Ch	Church
8a	Cath	Cathedral
8b	SPIRE Spire	Spire; Steeple
9		Roman Catholic Church
10		Temple
11		Chapel
12		Mosque
12a		Minaret
(Ih)		Moslem Shrine
13		Marabout
14	Pag	Pagoda
15		Buddhist Temple; Joss-House
15a		Shinto Shrine
16		Monastery; Convent
17		Calvary; Cross
17a	Cem	Cemetery, Non-Christian
18		Cemetery, Christian
18a		Tomb
19		Fort (actual shape charted)
20		Battery
21		Barracks
22		Powder magazine
* 23		Airplane landing field
* 24		Airport, large scale

(Ic)		Airport, military (small scale)
(Id)		Airport, civil (small scale)
25		Mooring mast
26	St	Street
26a	Ave	Avenue
26b	Blvd	Boulevard
27	Tel	Telegraph
28	Tel Off	Telegraph office
29	PO	Post office
30	Govt Ho	Government house
31		Town hall
32	Hosp	Hospital
33		Slaughter house
34	Magz	Magazine
34a		Warehouse; Storehouse
35	MON o Mon	Monument
36	CUP o Cup	Cupola
37	ELEV o Elev	Elevator
(Ie)	Elev	Elevation; Elevated'
38		Shed
39		Zinc roof
40	Ruins o Ru	Ruins
41	TR o Tr	Tower
(If)	ABAND LT HO	Abandoned lighthouse
42	WINDMILL	Windmill
43		Watermill
43a	WINDMOTOR	Windmotor
44	CHY o Chy	Chimney; Stack
* 45	S'PIPE oS'pipe	Water tower; Standpipe
46		Oil tank; Gas tank; Gasholder; Gasometer
47	Facty	Factory
48		Saw mill
49		Brick kiln
50		Mine; Quarry
51	o Well	Well
52		Cistern
53	TANK o Tk	Tank
54		Noria
55		Fountain
61	Inst	Institute
62		Establishment
63		Bathing establishment
64	Ct Ho	Courthouse

I Buildings and Structures

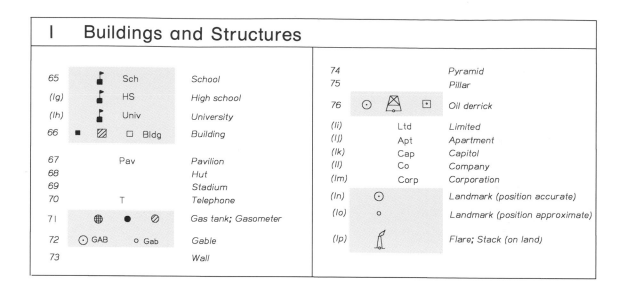

65	Sch	School	
(Ig)	HS	High school	
(Ih)	Univ	University	
66	■ ▨ □ Bldg	Building	
67	Pav	Pavilion	
68		Hut	
69		Stadium	
70	T	Telephone	
71	⊕ ● ⊘	Gas tank; Gasometer	
72	⊙ GAB o Gab	Gable	
73		Wall	

74	Pyramid	
75	Pillar	
76	Oil derrick	
(Ii)	Ltd	Limited
(Ij)	Apt	Apartment
(Ik)	Cap	Capitol
(Il)	Co	Company
(Im)	Corp	Corporation
(In)	⊙	Landmark (position accurate)
(Io)	o	Landmark (position approximate)
(Ip)	Flare; Stack (on land)	

J Miscellaneous Stations

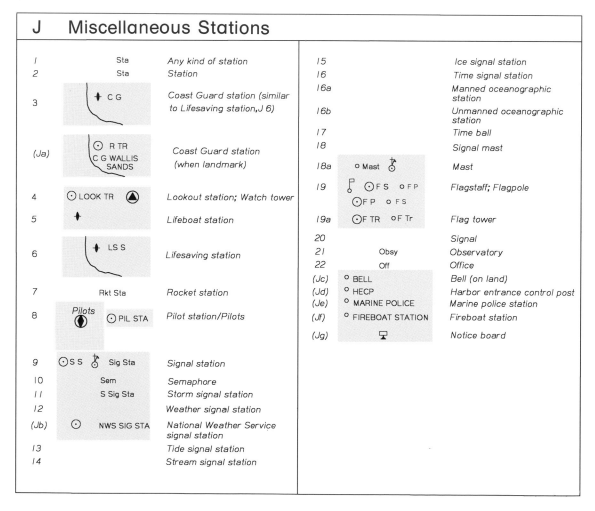

1	Sta	Any kind of station
2	Sta	Station
3	◆ C G	Coast Guard station (similar to Lifesaving station, J 6)
(Ja)	⊙ R TR C G WALLIS SANDS	Coast Guard station (when landmark)
4	⊙ LOOK TR ▲	Lookout station; Watch tower
5	◆	Lifeboat station
6	◆ LS S	Lifesaving station
7	Rkt Sta	Rocket station
8	Pilots ◕ ⊙ PIL STA	Pilot station/Pilots
9	⊙S S Sig Sta	Signal station
10	Sem	Semaphore
11	S Sig Sta	Storm signal station
12		Weather signal station
(Jb)	⊙ NWS SIG STA	National Weather Service signal station
13		Tide signal station
14		Stream signal station

15		Ice signal station
16		Time signal station
16a		Manned oceanographic station
16b		Unmanned oceanographic station
17		Time ball
18		Signal mast
18a	o Mast ☥	Mast
19	⌐ ⊙F S oF P ⊙F P o F S	Flagstaff; Flagpole
19a	⊙F TR oF Tr	Flag tower
20		Signal
21	Obsy	Observatory
22	Off	Office
(Jc)	o BELL	Bell (on land)
(Jd)	o HECP	Harbor entrance control post
(Je)	o MARINE POLICE	Marine police station
(Jf)	o FIREBOAT STATION	Fireboat station
(Jg)	⌐	Notice board

K   Lights

I	⚡ ✦ ● ★ •	Position of light	
*2	Lt	Light	
(Ka)	❀	Riprap surrounding light	
3	Lt Ho	Lighthouse	
4	•AERO ★ AERO	Aeronautical light	
4a		Marine and air navigation light	
*5	•Bn ⚓ ⚡	Light beacon	
6	⚓ ⚓	Light vessel; Lightship	
8		Lantern	
9		Street lamp	
10	REF	Reflector	
11	⚡------	Leading light	
11a	⚡ Lts in line 270°	Lighted range	
12		Sector light	
13	GREEN RED	Directional light	
14		Harbor light	
15		Fishing light	
16		Tidal light	
17	• ★ ● Priv maintd	Private light (maintained by private interests; to be used with caution)	
21	F	Fixed (steady light)	
22	Oc; Occ	Occulting (total duration of light more than dark)	
23	Fl	Single-Flashing (total duration of light less than dark)	
(Kb)	L Fl	Long-Flashing (2 sec or longer)	
	Fl (2+1)	Composite group-flashing	
23a	Iso; E Int	Isophase (light and dark equal)	
24	Q; Qk Fl	Continuous Quick Flashing (50 to 79 per minute; 60 in US)	
	Q(3)	Group Quick	
25	IQ; Int Qk Fl; I Qk Fl	Interrupted Quick Flashing	

25a	S Fl	Short Flashing	
(Kc)	VQ; V Qk Fl	Continuous Very Quick Flashing (80 to 159 - usually either 100 or 120 per minute)	
	VQ (3)	Group Very Quick	
	IVQ	Interrupted Very Quick	
	UQ	Continuous Ultra Quick (160 or more - usually 240 to 300 flashes per minute)	
	IUQ	Interrupted Ultra Quick	
26	Al; Alt	Alternating	
27	Oc (2); Gp Occ	Group-Occulting	
	Oc(2+3)	Composite group occulting	
28	Fl (2); Gp Fl	Group Flashing	
28a	S-L Fl	Short-Long Flashing	
28b		Group-Short Flashing	
29	Γ Fl	Fixed and Flashing	
30	F Gp Fl	Fixed and Group Flashing	
30a	Mo (A)	Morse Code light (with flashes grouped as in letter A)	
31	Rot	Revolving or Rotating light	
41		Period	
42		Every	
43		With	
44		Visible (range)	
(Kd)	M; Ml; N Mi	Nautical mile	
(Ke)	m; min	Minutes	
(Kf)	s; sec	Seconds	
45	Fl	Flash	
46	Oc; Occ	Occultation	
46a		Eclipse	
47	Gp	Group	
48	Oc; Occ	Intermittent light	
49	SEC	Sector	
50		Color of sector	
51	Aux	Auxiliary light	
52		Varied	
61	Vi	Violet	
62		Purple	
63	Bu; Bl	Blue	
64	G	Green	

K Lights

No.	Abbr	Description	No.	Abbr	Description	No.	Abbr	Description
65	Or; Y	Orange	72	Prov	Provisional light	80	Vert	Vertical lights
66	R	Red	73	Temp	Temporary light	81	Hor	Horizontal lights
67	W	White	(Kg)	D; Destr	Destroyed	(Kh)	VB	Vertical beam
67a	Y ; Am	Amber	74	Exting	Extinguished light	(Ki)	RGE	Range
(Ko)	Y	Yellow	75		Faint light	(Kj)	Exper	Experimental light
68	OBSC	Obscured light	76		Upper light			
68a	Fog Det Lt	Fog detector light	77		Lower light	(Kp)		Lighted offshore platform
70	Occas	Occasional light	78		Rear light			
71	Irreg	Irregular light	79		Front light	(Kq)		Flare (Flame)

L Buoys and Beacons

No.	Symbol	Description	No.	Symbol	Description
*1	o	Approximate position of buoy	*21	Tel	Telegraph-cable buoy
*2		Light buoy	*22		Mooring buoy (colors of mooring buoys never carried)
*3	BELL BELL	Bell buoy	22a		Mooring
*3a	GONG GONG	Gong buoy	*22b	Tel Tel	Mooring buoy with telegraphic communications
*4	WHIS WHIS	Whistle buoy	*22c	T T	Mooring buoy with telephonic communications
*5	C	Can or Cylindrical buoy	*23		Warping buoy
*6	N	Nun or Conical buoy	*24	Y	Quarantine buoy
*7	SP	Spherical buoy	24a		Practice area buoy
*8	S	Spar buoy	*25	Explos Anch	Explosive anchorage buoy
*8a	P	Pillar or Spindle buoy	*25a	AERO	Aeronautical anchorage buoy
*9		Buoy with topmark (ball)	*26	Deviation	Compass adjustment buoy
*10		Barrel or Ton buoy	*27	BW	Fish trap (area) buoy (BWHB)
(La)		Color unknown	*27a		Spoil ground buoy
(Lb)	FLOAT	Float	*28	W	Anchorage buoy (marks limits)
*12	FLOAT FLOAT	Lightfloat	*29	Priv maintd	Private aid to navigation (buoy) (maintained by private interests, use with caution)
13		Outer or Landfall buoy	30		Temporary buoy
*14	RW BW	Fairway buoy (RWVS; BWVS)	30a		Winter buoy
*14a	RW BW	Midchannel buoy (RWVS; BWVS)	*31	HB	Horizontal bands
*15	R "2"	Starboard-hand buoy (entering from seaward - US waters)	*32	VS	Vertical stripes
*16	"1" "1"	Port-hand buoy (entering from seaward - US waters)	*33	Chec	Checkered
*17	RB BR RG GR RB	Bifurcation buoy	*33a	Diag	Diagonal bands
*18	RB BR RG GR BR	Junction buoy	41	W	White
*19	RB BR RG GR RG	Isolated danger buoy	42	B	Black
*20	RB BR RG GR G	Wreck buoy	43	R	Red
*20a	RB BR RG GR G	Obstruction buoy	44	Y	Yellow
			45	G	Green
			46	Br	Brown
			47	Gy	Gray

L   Buoys and Beacons

48	Bu	Blue
48a	Am	Amber
48b	Or	Orange
* 51		Floating beacon (and variations)

* 52   Fixed beacons (unlighted or daybeacons)

▲R Bn △RG Bn		Triangular beacon
▲Bn		Black beacon
▪G Bn □GR Bn □W Bn		Square and other shaped beacons
□Bn ✦		Color unknown
		Variations

53	⊥Bn □ ▲	Beacon, in general
54	⚲ ✦	Tower beacon
55		Cardinal marking system
56	△Deviation Bn	Compass adjustment beacon
57		Topmarks
58		Telegraph-cable (landing) beacon

* 59	Piles Piles	Piles	
	Stumps	Stumps	
		Stakes, perches	
(Lc)	⊙MARKER ∘Marker		Private aid to navigation
61	⊙CAIRN ∘Cairn △ ⌂		Cairn
62			Painted patches
63	⊙		Landmark (position accurate)
(Ld)	∘		Landmark (position approximate)
64	REF		Reflector
65	⊙MARKER		Range targets, markers
(Le)	W Or Y Y		Special-purpose buoys
	W Or Y Y		
66			Oil installation buoy
67	▫		Drilling platform
70	NOTE: Refer to IALA Buoyage System description on page 48 for aids used in certain foreign waters.		
71			LANBY (Large Auto. Nav. Buoy); Superbuoy
72			TANKER terminal buoy (mooring)
73	ODAS		ODAS (Oceanographic Data Aquisition System)
(Lg)	∘Art		Articulated light (floating light)

M   Radio and Radar Stations

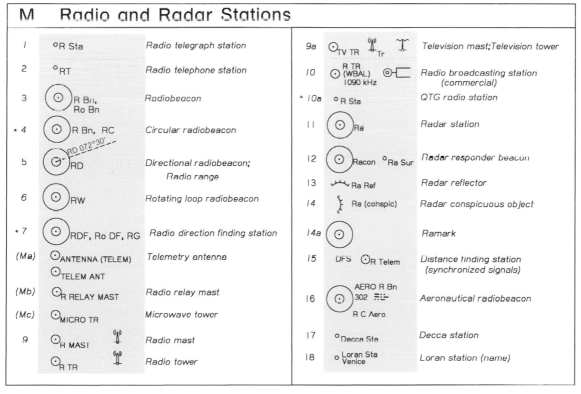

1	∘R Sta	Radio telegraph station
2	∘RT	Radio telephone station
3	⊙R Bn, Ro Bn	Radiobeacon
* 4	⊙R Bn, RC	Circular radiobeacon
5	⊙RD 072°30' RD	Directional radiobeacon; Radio range
6	⊙RW	Rotating loop radiobeacon
* 7	⊙RDF, Ro DF, RG	Radio direction finding station
(Ma)	⊙ANTENNA (TELEM) ⊙TELEM ANT	Telemetry antenna
(Mb)	⊙R RELAY MAST	Radio relay mast
(Mc)	⊙MICRO TR	Microwave tower
9	⊙R MAST	Radio mast
	⊙R TR	Radio tower

9a	⊙TV TR Tr	Television mast; Television tower
10	R TR (WBAL) 1090 kHz	Radio broadcasting station (commercial)
* 10a	∘R Sta	QTG radio station
11	⊙Ra	Radar station
12	⊙Racon ∘Ra Sur	Radar responder beacon
13	Ra Ref	Radar reflector
14	Ra (conspic)	Radar conspicuous object
14a	⊙	Ramark
15	DFS ⊙R Telem	Distance finding station (synchronized signals)
16	AERO R Bn ⊙302 R C Aero	Aeronautical radiobeacon
17	∘Decca Sta	Decca station
18	∘Loran Sta Venice	Loran station (name)

M Radio and Radar Stations

19	CONSOL Bn 190 kHz MMF ⚬	Consol (Consolan) station
(Md)	AERO R Rge 342 ⚬	Aeronautical radio range
(Me)	Ra Ref Calibration Bn	Radar calibration beacon

(Mf)	LORAN TR SPRING ISLAND	Loran tower (name)
(Mg)	R TR F R Lt	Obstruction light
(Mh)	RA DOME DOME (RADAR) Ra Dome Dome (Radar)	Radar dome
(Mi)	uhf	Ultrahigh frequency
(MJ)	vhf	Very high frequency

N Fog Signals

1	Fog Sig	Fog-signal station
2		Radio fog-signal station
3	GUN	Explosive fog signal
4		Submarine fog signal
5	SUB-BELL	Submarine fog bell (action of waves)
6	SUB-BELL	Submarine fog bell (mechanical)
7	SUB-OSC	Submarine oscillator
8	NAUTO	Nautophone
9	DIA	Diaphone
10	GUN	Fog gun
11	SIREN	Fog siren
12	HORN	Fog trumpet

13	HORN	Air (foghorn)
13a	HORN	Electric (foghorn)
14	BELL	Fog bell
15	WHIS	Fog whistle
16	HORN	Reed horn
17	GONG	Fog gong
18	⊚	Submarine sound signal not connected to the shore
18a	⊚∿	Submarine sound signal connected to the shore
(Na)	HORN	Typhon
(Nb)	Fog Det Lt	Fog detector light
(Nc)	Mo	Morse Code fog signal

O Dangers

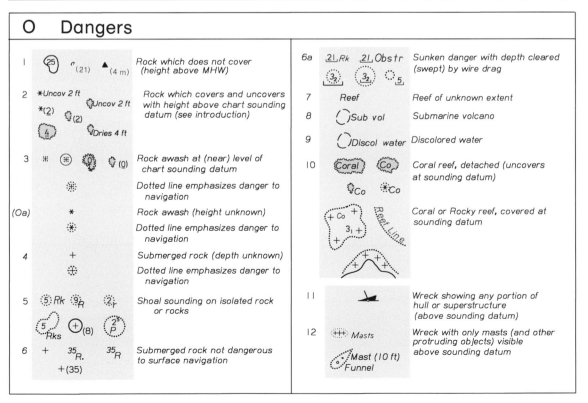

1	25 (21) ▲ (4 m)	Rock which does not cover (height above MHW)
2	*Uncov 2 ft Uncov 2 ft *(2) (2) (4) Dries 4 ft	Rock which covers and uncovers with height above chart sounding datum (see introduction)
3		Rock awash at (near) level of chart sounding datum
		Dotted line emphasizes danger to navigation
(Oa)	*	Rock awash (height unknown)
		Dotted line emphasizes danger to navigation
4	+	Submerged rock (depth unknown)
		Dotted line emphasizes danger to navigation
5	5 Rk 9 R 2 r 5 Rks (8) 2.5 P	Shoal sounding on isolated rock or rocks
6	+ 35 R. 35 R +(35)	Submerged rock not dangerous to surface navigation

6a	21 Rk 21 Obstr 3.2 3.2 5	Sunken danger with depth cleared (swept) by wire drag
7	Reef	Reef of unknown extent
8	Sub vol	Submarine volcano
9	Discol water	Discolored water
10	Coral Co Co Co	Coral reef, detached (uncovers at sounding datum)
	+Co + 3₁ + Reef Line	Coral or Rocky reef, covered at sounding datum
11		Wreck showing any portion of hull or superstructure (above sounding datum)
12	Masts Mast (10 ft) Funnel	Wreck with only masts (and other protruding objects) visible above sounding datum

O   Dangers

13		Old symbols for wrecks
13a		Wreck always partially submerged
14		Sunken wreck dangerous to surface navigation (less than 11 fathoms over wreck)
14a		Sunken wreck covered 20 to 30 meters
15		Wreck over which depth is known
15a		Wreck with depth cleared by wire drag
15b		Unsurveyed wreck over which the exact depth is unknown, but is considered to have a safe clearance to the depth shown
16		Sunken wreck, not dangerous to surface navigation
17		Foul ground, Foul bottom
17a		Mobil bottom (sand waves)
18	Tide rips	Overfalls or Tide rips
	Symbol used only in small areas	
19	Eddies	Eddies
	Symbol used only in small areas	
20	Kelp	Kelp, Seaweed
21	Bk	Bank
22	Shl	Shoal
23	Rf	Reef
23a		Ridge
24	Le	Ledge
25	Br or	Breakers
26		Submerged rock
27	Obstr	Obstruction
(Ob)	Obstr °Well	Submerged well
	Obstr Well	Submerged well (buoyed)
(Oc)	Obstruction (fish haven)	Fish haven (artificial fishing reef)
		(actual shape)

28		Wreck
29	Wreckage Wks	Wreckage
29a		Wreck remains (dangerous only for anchoring)
* 30	Subm piles Subm piling / Subm piles Stakes, Perches	Submerged piling
* 30a	°° Snags °° Stumps	Snags; Submerged stumps
31		Lesser depth possible
32	Uncov	Dries
33	Cov	Covers
34	Uncov	Uncovers
35	③ Rep (1983)	Reported (with date)
	☀ Eagle Rk (rep 1983)	Reported (with name and date)
36	Discol	Discolored
37		Isolated danger
38		Limiting danger line
39	+ rky +	Limit of rocky area
41	PA	Position approximate
42	PD	Position doubtful
43	ED	Existance doubtful
44	P Pos	Position
45	D	Doubtful
46	Unexam	Unexamined
(Od)	LD	Least Depth
(Oe)	⊡ Subm Crib / □ Crib (above water)	Crib
(Of)	⊡ ■ Platform (lighted) HORN	Offshore platform (unnamed)
(Og)	⊡ ■ Hazel (lighted) HORN	Offshore platform (named)

P Various Limits, etc.

I		Leading line; Range line
2		Transit
3		In line with
4		Limit of sector
5		Channel, Course, Track recommended (marked by buoys or beacons)
5a	←→ DW ←→	Recommended track for deep draft vessels (defined by fixed marks)
5b	←→ DW83 ft ←→	Depth is shown where it has been obtained by the cognizant authority
(Pa)		Alternate course
6	— Ra — Ra —	Radar-guided track
6a		Established traffic separation scheme. One-way traffic lanes (separated by line or zone)
6b		Established traffic separation scheme: Roundabout
	○	If no separation zone exists, the center of the roundabout is shown by a circle
6c	DW	Recommended direction of traffic flow
7		Submarine cable (power telegraph, telephone, etc.)
7a	Cable Area	Submarine cable area
7b		Abandoned submarine cable (includes disused cable)
8		Submarine pipeline
8a	Pipeline Area	Submarine pipeline area
8b		Abandoned submarine pipeline
9		Maritime limit in general
(Pb)	RESTRICTED AREA	Limit of restricted area
*10		Limits of national fishing zones
(Pc)		U.S. Harbor Line

II		Limit of dumping ground, spoil ground
12		Anchorage limit
*13		Limit of airport
*14		Limit of sovereignty (Territorial waters)
*15		Customs boundary
*16		International boundary (also State boundary)
17		Stream limit
18		Ice limit
19		Limit of tide
20		Limit of Navigation
21	— — < — — > — —	Recommended track (not marked by buoys or beacons)
21a	DW DW	Recommended track for deep draft vessels (track not defined by fixed marks)
21b	>DW83 ft.> DW76 ft> DW83 ft DW76 ft	Depth is shown where it has been obtained by the cognizant authority
22		District or province limit
23		Reservation line (Options)
24	COURSE 053° 00' TRUE ⊙ MARKERS ⊙ MARKERS	Measured distance
25	PROHIBITED AREA	Prohibited area (Screen optional)
(Pd)	SAFETY FAIRWAY	Shipping safety fairway (two-way traffic)
(Pe)		Limits of former mine danger area
(Pf)	17386	Reference larger scale chart
(Pg)		Limit of fishing areas (fish trap areas)
(Ph)		3-mile Territorial Sea Boundary 12-mile Contiguous Zone Boundary; headland to headland line
(Pi)		COLREGS demarcation line

Q   Soundings

1	SD	Doubtful sounding
2	$\overline{65}$	No bottom found
3	(23) • —1036	Out of position
4	(5)	Least depth in narrow channels
5	30 FEET APR 1984	Dredged channel (with controlling depth indicated)
6	21 FEET OCT 1983	Dredged area
7	6	Swept channel
8	2	Drying (or uncovering) heights above chart sounding datum
9	89 17 119 15	Swept area, not adequately sounded (shown by purple or green tint)
9a	29 23 3 22 8 30 19 21 18 7	Swept area adequately sounded (swept by wire drag to depth indicated)

10		Hairline depth figures
10a	19 8_2 $7\frac{3}{4}$	Figures for ordinary soundings
11		Soundings taken from foreign charts
12	8_2 19	Soundings taken from older surveys (or smaller scale charts)
13	8_2 10	Echo soundings
14	8_2 19	Sloping figures
15	8_2 19	Upright figures
16	(25) (2)	Bracketed figures
17	6	Underlined sounding figures (drying)
18	3_2 6_1	Soundings expressed in fathoms and feet
22		Unsounded area
(Qa)	6 5 2 ft	Stream

R   Depth Contours and Tints

Feet	Fm/Meters			
0	0			
6	1			
12	2			
18	3			
24	4			
30	5			
36	6			
60	10			
120	20			
180	30			
240	40			

Feet	Fm/Meters	
300	50	
600	100	
1,200	200	
1,800	300	
2,400	400	
3,000	500	
6,000	1,000	
Approximate depth contour		
Continuous lines, with values		

——— 5 ——— (blue or black)——— —100———

S   Quality of the Bottom

1	Grd	Ground	11	Rk, rky	Rock; Rocky	(Sb)	Vol Ash	Volcanic ash
2	S	Sand	11a	Blds	Boulders	17	La	Lava
3	M	Mud; Muddy	12	Ck	Chalk	18	Pm	Pumice
4	Oz	Ooze	12a	Ca	Calcareous	19	T	Tufa
5	Ml	Marl	13	Qz	Quartz	20	Sc	Scoriae
6	Cy; Cl	Clay	13a	Sch	Schist	21	Cn	Cinders
7	G	Gravel	14	Co	Coral	21a		Ash
8	Sn	Shingle	(Sa)	Co Hd	Coral head	22	Mn	Manganese
9	P	Pebbles	15	Mds	Madrepores	23	Sh	Shells
10	St	Stones	16	Vol	Volcanic	24	Oys	Oysters

S   Quality of the Bottom

25	Ms	Mussels	42	h; hrd	Hard	60	gn	Green
26	Spg	Sponge	43	stf	Stiff	61	yl	Yellow
27	K	Kelp	44	sml	Small	62	or	Orange
28	Wd	Seaweed	45	lrg	Large	63	rd	Red
	Grs	Grass	46	sy; stk	Sticky	64	br	Brown
29	Stg	Sea-tangle	47	bk; brk	Broken	65	ch	Chocolate
31	Spi	Spicules	47a	grd	Ground (Shells)	66	gy	Gray
32	Fr	Foraminifera	48	rt	Rotten	67	lt	Light
33	Gl	Globigerina	49	str	Streaky	68	dk	Dark
34	Di	Diatoms	50	spk	Speckled	70	vard	Varied
35	Rd	Radiolaria	51	gty	Gritty	71	unev	Uneven
36	Pt	Pteropods	52	dec	Decayed	(Sc)	S/M	Surface layer and Under layer
37	Po	Polyzoa	53	fly	Flinty	76		Freshwater springs in seabed
38	Cir	Cirripedia	54	glac	Glacial			
38a	Fu	Fucus	55	ten	Tenacious	(Sd)		Mobile bottom (sand waves)
38b	Ma	Mattes	56	wh	White	(Se)	Si	Silt
39	f; fne	Fine	57	bl; bk	Black	(Sf)	Cb	Cobbles
40	c; crs	Coarse	58	vi	Violet	(Sg)	m	Medium (used only before S (sand))
41	so; sft	Soft	59	bu	Blue			

Foreign Bottoms   See glossary

T   Tides and Currents

1	HW	High water	10	ISLW	Indian spring low water
1a	HHW	Higher high water	11	HWF&C	High-water full and change (vulgar establishment of the port)
2	LW	Low water			
(Ta)	LWD	Low-water datum	12	LWF&C	Low-water full and change
2a	LLW	Lower low water	13		Mean establishment of the port
3	MTL	Mean tide level	13a		Establishment of the port
4	MSL	Mean sea level	14		Unit of height
4a		Elevation of mean sea level above chart (sounding) datum	15		Equinoctial
5		Chart datum (datum for sounding reduction)	16		Quarter; Quadrature
			17	Str	Stream
6	Sp	Spring tide	18	2 kn	Current, general, with rate
7	Np	Neap tide	19	2 kn	Flood stream (current) with rate
7a	MHW	Mean high water	20	2 kn	Ebb stream (current) with rate
8	MHWS	Mean high-water springs			
8a	MHWN	Mean high-water neaps	21	° Tide gauge	Tide gauge; Tidepole; Automatic tide gauge
8b	MHHW	Mean higher high water			
8c	MLW	Mean low water	23	vel	Velocity; Rate
9	MLWS	Mean low-water springs	24	kn	Knots
9a	MLWN	Mean low-water neaps	25	ht	Height
9b	MLLW	Mean lower low water	26		Tide

16

T   Tides and Currents

27		New moon	34		Place for which tabulated tidal stream data are given
28	●	Full moon	35		Range (of tide)
29		Ordinary	36		Phase lag
30		Syzygy	(Tb)		Current diagram, with *explanatory note*
31	fl	Flood	(Tc)	CRD	Columbia River Datum
32		Ebb	(Td)	GCLWD	Gulf Coast Low Water Datum
33		Tidal stream diagram			

U   Compass

1	N	North
2	E	East
3	S	South
4	W	West
5	NE	Northeast
6	SE	Southeast
7	SW	Southwest
8	NW	Northwest
9	N	Northern
10	E	Eastern
11	S	Southern
12	W	Western
21	brg; My	Bearing
22	T	True
23	mag	Magnetic
24	var	Variation
25		Annual change
25a		Annual change nil

26	+15°	Abnormal variation; Magnetic attraction
27	deg	Degrees
28	dev	Deviation
29		Compass roses

The outer circle is in degrees with zero at true north. The inner circles are in points and degrees with the arrow indicating magnetic north.

ALBANIAN CHARTING TERMS

K, koder, kodra . . . . hill

ARABIC CHARTING TERMS

Dj, djebel . . . . mountain, hill
G, geb, gebel . . . . mountain, hill
J, jab, jabal, jabel . . . . mountain, hill
Jazirat, jazt . . . . island, peninsula
Jeb, jebel . . . . mountain, hill
Jez, jezirat . . . . island, peninsula
Jl . . . . mountain, hill
K, khawr . . . . inlet, channel
Si, sidi . . . . tomb
W, wad, wadi, wed . . . . valley, river, river bed

CHINESE CHARTING TERMS

Chg, chiang . . . . river, shoal, harbor, inlet, channel, sound

DANISH CHARTING TERMS

B . . . . bay, bight
Banke, bk . . . . bank
Bugt . . . . bay, bight
Fj, fjord . . . . inlet
Grd, grund . . . . shoal
Havn, havnen . . . . harbor
Hd . . . . headland
Hm . . . . islet
Hn . . . . harbor
Hne . . . . islets
Holm, holmene . . . . islet, islets
Hoved . . . . headland
K, kap . . . . cape
N, nord, nordre . . . . north, northern
One, oyane, oyene . . . . islands
Pt, pynt . . . . point
Skaer, skjaer, skr . . . . rock above water
Sd, sund, sundet . . . . sound

DUTCH (NETHERLANDS) CHARTING TERMS

As . . . . ash

B, baai . . . . bay
Bas . . . . woods in general
BaZ . . . . notice to mariners
Berg, bg . . . . mountain
Bk . . . . bank, broken
Br . . . . brown, latitude
Bu . . . . blue

CG . . . . coast guard station
Cy . . . . clay

D . . . . dark
Dia . . . . diaphone
Dm . . . . decimeter

Eb . . . . ebb

F . . . . fine
Fla . . . . chimney with flare

G . . . . gravel, shingle, green, gulf
Gb . . . . checkered, ground
GEB . . . . range
Gr . . . . great, large
Gs . . . . gray

H . . . . cape, hook, head, headland, hour
Hk . . . . reformed church
Horizontale lichten . . . . horizontal lights
HW . . . . high water

K . . . . creek, cape
Kenb, kenbaar . . . . conspicuous, remarkable
Kl, klein . . . . little, small
Kn . . . . knot
Krt . . . . see chart
Kt . . . . chalk

L . . . . light, longitude
LAT . . . . lowest astronomical tide
LW . . . . low water
LWS . . . . low water springs

M . . . . meter, mud, muddy, nautical mile
Min . . . . minute
Ml . . . . marl
Mond, monding . . . . mouth
Mosselen, Ms . . . . mussels

N . . . . north
No . . . . number
Nw, nwe . . . . new

O . . . . oysters
OMS . . . . submarine fog signal

Pas . . . . passage, pass
Pt . . . . point

R . . . . red, river, stream
Rf, rif . . . . reef
Ru . . . . ruins

S . . . . sand, south
Sh . . . . shells
Sk . . . . ooze
Sp . . . . speckled
SS . . . . signal station
St . . . . saint
Stn . . . . station

Tr . . . . tower

V . . . . volcanic
Vm . . . . fathom
Vs . . . . flagstaff, flagpole
Vss . . . . established traffic separation scheme
Vt . . . . foot, feet

W . . . . white

Y . . . . yellow, amber

ZW, zwart . . . . black

FINNISH CHARTING TERMS

K . . . . rock, reef
Kallio . . . . rock
Kari . . . . rock, reef
Kivi . . . . rock
Luodet, luoto, lu . . . . rock(s)
Ma, matala . . . . shoal
Sa, saaret, saari . . . . island(s)
Torni, tr . . . . tower

FRENCH CHARTING TERMS

A, Ae . . . . inlet, aeronautical
Ant . . . . front light
App, appr . . . . approach
Arch, archipel . . . . archipelago
Arg . . . . clay
+Astro . . . . astronomic station
Aux . . . . auxiliary light

V Abbreviations of principal foreign terms, (Glossary)

B	boulders, bay, shoal, white, blue	F el	isophase light
Baie	bay	Feu	light
Bal tel	telegraph-cable (landing beacon)	F f	fixed (steady light)
Bc	bank	Fin	fine
B de sauv	lifeboat station	Fjd	fjord
Bk, bks	bank, banks	Fl	large river, single-flashing (total duration of light less than dark)
Bl	blue		
Blanc	white	Fla	oil derrick
Blds	boulders	Fo	occulting light
Ble	battery	Fque	factory
Blk	black	Fr	suburb
B M	low water	FS	flag tower
BM	bench mark	Ft	fort
Bn	basin	FV	revolving, rotating light
Bo, boue	ooze, boulder		
Br	broken, stream	G	coarse, gulf, large, great
Brk	broken	Ga, gal	shingle, gravel
		Gaz	gas tank
C	cape, cove, inlet	Gd	ground
Ca	calcareous	Gde	large, great
Cal	calcareous, channel, narrows	Gg	fog gong
Cap	cape	Gl	glacier
Carre, carriere	mine	Glu	sticky
Cath	cathedral	Gp	group
C de G	coast guard station	Gr	gravel, gray
Ch, Chal, chan	channel, narrows, chimney, stack	Grd	ground
Chap	chapel		
Chat, chau	castle	H	hard
Chau d'eau	water tower, standpipe	Hul hop	hospital
Chee	chimney stack	Ild	head, headland
Chen	channel	H de V	town hall
Chk, chl	channel, narrows	Hn	haven
Chle	chapel	Hr	height, harbor
Chno	range	Hrd	hard
Cl	bell buoy, fog bell	Ht fd	shoal
Cler	steeple	Huit	oysters
Co, cor	coral		
Coll, colline	hill	I, is, Ile, ilot, it, its	island, islands, islet
Coq	shells	Ineg	uneven
Cq	shells	Inf	lower, lower light
Cr	creek	Int	inlet, intensified, inner
Crl	coral	Intd, interdit	prohibited
D	dark, hard	J	yellow
Dec	uncovers	Jct	junction
Det, detr	strait, destroyed		
Detroit	strait	L, lac	lake, loch, lough
Detruit	destroyed	Lag	lagoon
Dist	district	Lav	lava
Dk	dark	Ldg	landing
Dn	dolphin	Le, les	ledge, ledges
Dne	customhouse	Lndg	landing
Duc d'Albe	dolphin	Lum	luminous
Dur	hard		
		M	marl, mud, soft
E, eclat	flash	Mad	madrepores
Egl	church	Mat	varied
El	electric	ME	neap tide
Emb, embre	mouth	Mge	anchorage
Ent	entrance, inlet	Mane	mountain
Entp	magazine	Mid	middle
Entree	entrance, inlet	Mlg	anchorage
Env	about	Mn	minute, mill
Ep	wreck	Mnt	monument
Est	east, estuary	Mou	soft
Ev	every, eventual	Mouil, mouillage	anchorage
Ext	outer	Moul	mussels
		Moy	middle
F	ooze, light, unwatched light, fine	Mt, mts	mount, mountain
F Aero	aeronautical light	Mus	mussels
F b ae	fixed and group flashing light	MWL	low water datum
F b e	fixed and flashing light		
F det br	fog detector light	N	knots, black, north
Fd	fjord, ground	NL	new moon
F e	single flashing light		

V   Abbreviations of principal foreign terms, (Glossary)

Nrs	narrows
Nv	new
O	annual change nil, occulation
Obs	obstruction
Obsc, obscd	obscured light
Occas	unwatched light, occasional light
Org	orange
P	port
Pas	passage
Pav	pavilion
Peb	pebbles
Pen	peninsula
Pi	stones
Pic	peak
Pierres	stones
Pit, pite	small, little
Pk	peak
Pl	full moon
Pla	tableland, sunken flat
Pm	high water
Pn	peak
Post	rear light
Pr I	peninsula
Prom	promontory
Pt, pte	landing, point
PTT	post office
Pyr	pyramid
Q	quay
R	river, rock, submerged rock, radio telegraph station, road, roadstead, red
Ra	radar responder beacon
RaRa	radar station
Rau	stream
Rav	ravine
RC	circular radiobeacon
RC Aero	aeronautical radiobeacon
Rd	road, roadstead, directional radiobeacon, radio range
Re	rock, submerged rock
Regl	standard
Relt	bearing
Rem	remarkable
Rer	rock, usually above water
Resr	oil tank
Rf, rfs	reef, reefs
RG	radio direction finding station
Rge	range of mountains
Rgl	standard
Riv	river
Rk, rks	rock, rocks
R Lta	riprap surrounding light
Ro Bn	radiobeacon
Ro Tel	radio telephone station
Ro Tr	radio tower
Rsv	oil tank
RT	radio telephone station
RW	rotating loop radiobeacon
S	sand, sector, south
Sal br	fog-signal station
Sante, ste	health officer's office
Sbrv	color of sector, white, red, green
Sect	sector
Sf	stiff
SG	sand and gravel
Sft	soft
Sh	shoal
Shin	shingle
Shl	shoal
Sif	fog whistle
Sif Gg	whistle buoy

Sir	siren
Sm	submarine, statute mile
Sm, sml	small
So, sft	soft
Som	summit
Sous-marin	submarine
Sp, spr	spring tide
St, ste	Saint
Stf	stiff
Stn	station
Str	strait
Stk	sticky
Sup	higher
Sy	sticky
Syz	syzygy
T	tufa
Tel	telegraph
Temp, tempre	temporary
The, tour, tr	tower
Tr	tufa
U	minutes
Us	factory
V	green, vertical lights
Var	varied
VC	see chart
VE	spring tide
Vig	lookout station, watchtower
Vio	violet
Vis	visible (range), conspicuous
Vol sm	submarine volcano
VPl	see plan
Vue	view point
Vx	old
W, wh	white
WT	watertower, standpipe
Y	nautical mile

GAELIC CHARTING TERMS

Bo, bogha	sunken rock
E, eilean, eileanen, en	island(s), islet(s)
Ru, rubha	point
Sg, sgeir, sgr	rock

GERMAN CHARTING TERMS

A, amt, anslalt	office, establishment
Ankpl	anchorage
Anl	jetty
Anst	approach
Auff	conspicuous
Aust	oysters
B	bay
Bntt	battery
Beabs	projected
Ber	correction
Bk	beacon in general, fixed beacon
Bl, blau	blue
Blink, blitz	long flash, short flash
Blk, blz	long flash, short flash
Blk (1&2)	composite group long flashing light
Blk (2)	group long flashing light
Blz	short flashing light
Blz-Blk	short-long flashing light
Blz (1&2)	composite group short flashing light
Blz (3)	group short flashing light
Bn	well
Bnt	varicolored
Br	brown, chocolate, latitude
Bucht	bay

Dev-Dlb	deviation dolphin		Kst-W	coast guard station
Dev-Tn	compass adjustment buoy		Ku	cupola
Di	diatoms			
Dkl	dark		Laz	lazaret
Drchf	passage, pass		Lcht-TM	light
			Ldg-Pl	landing, landing place
Ehem	ancient		Lg	longitude
Einf	inlet		Lv	lava
Eis-s	ice signal station			
Enge	narrows		M	oysterbed
E-werk	electric works		Mdg	mouth
Expl, explosiv	explosive		Meeresarm	loch, lough
			Mgl	marl
F	fine, fixed light		Mk	marker
Fbr	factory		Ml-Bk	mile beacon
Fd	fjord		MNpHW	mean high water neaps
Fhrwss	channel		MNpNW	mean low water neaps
Fi, fi-hfn	fishing light, fishing harbor		Mo(K)	morse code light, according to character
Fj	fjord		MSpHW	mean high water springs
Fkl	quick flashing light		MSpNW	mean low water springs
Fkl unt	interrupted quick flashing light		Mt	middle
Fl	river		Mt-F	middle light
Flgtm	flag tower		Mun-Vers Gbt	explosives dumping ground
Fls, fls,	rock, rocky		MW	mean tide level
FluB	river			
Fr	foraminifera		N	north
			NF	radio list
G	yellow, gulf		NfS	notices to mariners
Gas-T	gas tank, gasometer		N-L	fog light
Gb	coarse		N-lich, nörlich	northern
GB	large, great		NO	northeast
Gbg	range		Not-S	distress signal station
GbK	shingle		Nr	number
Gd	ground		N-S	fog signal station
Gef-S	danger signal station		N-Such-F	fog detector light
Gel	extinguished		NW	low water
Gelb	yellow			
Gem	reported		O	east
Ger	lesser		Ober feuer, ob-f	rear light, upper light
Gez-F, gezeitenfeuer	tidal light		Obs	observatory
Ggf	eventual		Od, oder	or
Gl	globigerina		Öl-T, öltank	oiltank
Glt	isophase light		Or	orange
Gl-Tn	bell buoy			
Gn	green		P-A	post office
Gr	gray		Pf, pfähle	pile
Grs	see-weed, grass, mattes		Priv	private
			Pt	pteropods
			Pyr	pyramid
H	light			
Hfn	haven, harbor, port		Qm-F	cross light
Hg	hill		Qrt-Tn	quarantine buoy
H-I	peninsula		QTG kustenfunkstelle r	QTG-radio station
Hk	point		Qu	quartz
Hl-Tn	whistle buoy			
Hs	house		R	QTG-radio station, reef, red
Ht	hard, hut		Ra	radar, radar scanner, radar station
HW	high water		Ra-Ku	radar cupola, radar dome
			Ra-Mst	radar mast
I	Institute		Ra-Trn	radar tower
			RC	circular radiobeacon
K	gravel		RC (Aero)	aeronautical radiobeacon
Ka	calcareous		Rcht-Bk	leading beacon
Kai	quay		Rcht-F	leading light
Kas	barracks		RD	directional radiobeacon, radio range
Kb-Bk	telegraph cable beacon		Rf	reef
Kb-Tn	telegraph cable buoy		RG	radio direction finding station
Kblg	cable length		Rgd	sand reef
Kl	little		R-S	lifeboat station, lifesaving station
Klippe, klp	rock, sunken rock		Ru	ruins
Kl St	pebbles		RW	consol station, rotating loop radiobeacon
Kn	knot			
Kor, koralle	coral			
Kr	chalk		S	black, station, south
Krhs	hospital		Sc	scoriae

V Abbreviations of principal foreign terms, (Glossary)

Sch	shells
Sch-H	obstruction, depth unknown
Sch-H	sunken danger with depth, cleared by wire drag (in German waters by diver)
Schl	ooze, castle
Schp	shed
Schutt-S	spoil ground
Schw	sponge, faint
Sd	sand, sound
Sdkor	sabellaria
SFKl	very quick flashing light
Sgn	signal
Sgn-S	international signal station
Shb	sailing directions
Siel	sewer
Sk	mud, muddy
Skr	vertical
S-lich	southern
Sm	nautical mile
SMt	seamount
SO	southeast
Sp	summit, peak
St	flinty, stones
Stg	fucus, kelp
Str	strait
Strm-S	storm signal station
T	clay, and
Tafel	board
Tg-F	daytime light
Tlws	partly
Tm-Bk	tower beacon
Tst	tufa
Ton	clay
T-S	telegraph office
U	and
Ua	etc, other
Ubr	occulting light
Ubr(2)	group occulting light
Ubr(2&3)	composite group occulting light
U-F	front light, lower light
Und	and
Ungf	approximate
Unr gd	foul ground
Unr (mun)	foul (explosives)
Unr unrein	foul, wreck, remains dangerous only for anchoring
Unrein (munition)	foul (explosives)
Unterfeuer	front light, lower light
Untf	shoal
Usw	and so on
U-Wss-Gl	submarine fog bell (action of waves)
U-Wss-Gl	submarine fog bell (mechanical)
V	volcanic
Va	cinders
Vdklt	obscured
Verb	prohibited
Viol	violet
Vrd	concealed
Vrsdt	shoaled
Vrst	intensified
Vsw	experimented
W	lookout station, watch tower, white
Wache, wachtturm	lookout station, watch tower
Warn-F, warnfeuer	obstruction light
Wch	soft
Wchs Blk wr	long flashing light alternating, white-red
Wchs Blz wr	short flashing light alternating, white-red
Wchs Ubrwr	occulting light alternating white-red
Wchs(2)wgn	group alternating light, white-green

Wchs wr	alternating light, white-red
Weiß-rot	group alternating light, white-red
Wgr	horizontal
Wk	wreck
W-S	weather signal station
WSS-S	tide signal station
WSS-T	water tank
W-Tm	lookout station
Z, zäh	tenacious, sticky
Zbr	broken
Zgl	brick kiln
Zolla-A, zoll-w	custom-house
Zrst	destroyed
Z-S	refuge for shipwrecked mariners
Zt-S	time signal station
Ztwl	temporary, temporary buoy
Ztws	occasional

GREEK CHARTING TERMS

Ak, akra, akrotirion	cape
Ali, angali	bight, open bay
Ang, angirovolion	anchorage
If, ifaloi, ifalos	reef(s)
Kolpos, ks	gulf
Limin, In	harbor
N	island
Nes	islet
Nis, nisidhes, nisis	islet(s)
Nisoi, nisos	island(s)
Noi	island
O, ormos	bay
Pot, potamos	river
Sk, skopeloi, skopelos	reef(s)
Ves	rocky islets
Vis	rocky islet
Voi, vos	rock(s)
Vrakhoi	rock(s)
Vrakhonisides	rocky islets
Vrakhonisis	rocky islet
Vrakhos	rock(s)

ICELANDIC CHARTING TERMS

Fjordhur, fjr	fjord
Gr, grunn	shoal

INDONESIAN CHARTING TERMS

Abu	cinders
Abu-abu	gray
Adjaib	remarkable
Arus	stream
Atap seng	zinc roof
Aum kabut	fog whistle
Badai	storm
Bagus	fire
Bahan peledak	explosive
Bajangan	shading
Bakobako	mangroves
Balai kota	town hall
Bandar	harbor, port
Bangunan	building
Barak	barracks
Baru	new
Barat	west
Barat daja	southwest
Barat laut	northwest
Baringan	bearing
Batre	battery
Batu	stones
Batu besar	boulder
Batu bulat-bulat	boulders
Batu karang	rock, rocky
Belukar	bushes
Berbatu-api	flinty

V Abbreviations of principal foreign terms, (Glossary)

Berduri	spicules	Kudus	saint
Berpasir	gritty	Kuning	yellow
Besar	great	Kwarsa	quartz
Besar (luas)	large		
Biara	monastery, convent	Laguna	lagoon
Biasa	ordinary	Lahar	lava, lava flow
Biru	blue	Lembah	valley
Budjur	longitude	Liat	tenacious, sticky
Bukit	hill	Limban	footbridge
Bukit pasir	sandhills, dunes	Lintang	latitude
Busuk	rotten	Listrik	electric
		Luar	outer
Dalam	inner	Luas	large
Dalam air	submarine	Lumpur	mud, muddy
Danau	lake	Lumut	mussels
Daratan	land		
Dengan	with	Mudrepora	madrepores
Depa	fathom	Mata air	spring
Deradjat	degrees	Membusuk	decayed
Derwerga	wharf, quay	Menit	minute
Desimeter	decimeter	Merah	red
Detik	second	Mesdjid	mosque
Deviasi	deviation	Millimeter	millimeter
Diatoms	diatoma	Mil laut	nautical mile
Dibawah air	submerged	Millautdjam	knots
Dihentikan	discontinued	Muara	mouth
Dikenal	conspicuous	Muda	light
Dirusak	destroyed		
Diterangi	see plan	Nomor	number
Djalan masuk	entrance		
Djam	hour	P	white
Djarak	distant	Pagar	fence
Djingga	orange	Palem	tide gauge, tide pole
Duk	dock	Pasang	flood
		Pasir	sand
Galangan	shipyard	Patah	broken
Gamping	chalk	Paviljun	pavilion
Gelangkepil	mooring ring	Peg, pegunungan	range, mountain range
Gelap	eclipse	Pelabuhan	road, roadstead
Geredja	church, chapel	Pembetulan	correction
Gerundjal	uneven	Penataran	establishment
Glester	glacier	Pendaratan	landing place, leading stage, stairs
Gubug	shed, hut	Penerbitan	publication
Gudang	magazine	Pengeluaran	edition
Gunung	mountain	Penggaraman	saltpans
		Penggergadjian	saw mill
H	black	Penting	prominent
Halus	soft	Periode	period
Hidjau	green	Perseroan	company
Hitam	black	Pertambangan	mine, quarry
		Peritjobaan	experimental
Institut	institute	Peternakan	farm
Intji	inch	Pteropods	pteropoda
		Pulau	island
Kaki	foot	Puntjak	summit, peak
Kaku	stiff	Puri	castle
Kampung	village	Putih	white
Kasar	coarse		
Katedral	cathedral	Rabuk	marl
Kelompok	group	Rawa	marsh, swamp, slough
Kepulauan	archipelago	Rintangan	obstruction
Kapur	chalk	Ruangan	pillar
Keran	crane	Rumah	house
Kerang	shells, oysters	Rumput	grass
Kerangka	a number of sunken ships		
Keras	hard	Sawah	paddy fields
Kerikil	gravel, shingle, pebbles	Scoria	scoriae
Ketjepatan	velocity, rate	Sedjati	true
Ketjil	little	Sekolah	school
Ketjil (sempit)	large	Sektor	sector
Kira-kira	approximate, about	Selat	strait
Koral	coral	Selatan	south
Kota	city or town	Semenandjung	peninsula
Kpn	archipelago	Sentimeter	centimeter
Kr, krueng	river	Seperempat	quarter, quadrature

23

Stadion	stadium
Suar atas	upper light
Suar bawah	lower light
Suar belakang	rear light
Suar darurat	auxiliary light
Suar depan	front light
Sumur	well
Sungai	river, stream
Surut	ebb
Taman	park, garden
Tandjung	cape
Tanggul	embankment, levee
Tangki	tank
Telegrap	telegraph
Telepon	telephone
Teluk	bay, gulf, creek, cove
Tembok	wall
Tempat	ground
Tengah	middle
Tenggara	southeast
Terbatas	pyramid
Tertutupes	glacial
Terusan	tunnel (railroad or road), cutting
Tiang	wreck masts visible
Tiangkepil	dolphin
Tiap-tiap	every
Timur	east
Tinggi	height, altitude
Tjandi	temple
Tjerlang	flash
Tjiatan	narrows
Tjoklat	brown, chocolate
Topan	typhoon
TPSB	great trigonometrical survey station
Triangulasi	triangulation
Tua	old
Tua, gelap	dark
Udjung	cape
Ug	cape
Unga	violet
Utara	north
Variasi	variation
W, wai	river

ITALIAN CHARTING TERMS

A	kelp
A band	flagstaff, flagpole
Aco	ancient
Aff	dries
Alb	hotel
All to, allineamento e rotta	leading line, range line
AM	high water
AN	notice to mariners
Anc, anco	anchorage
Ant	front
Appr	approximate
AR	antenna radio
Ar	orange
Arcgo	archipelago
A seg	signal mast
Astr	astronomical
Aum ann	increasing annually
Aus	auxiliary
A var nulla	annual change nil
Azz, azzurro	blue
B	bay
Ba, baia	bay
Banco	bank
Battigia	foreshore: strand (in general)
Bco	bank

Bianco	white
BM	low water
Bna	quay
Boc,	mouth
Bq	quarantine buoy
Br	dolphin
Briccole	dolphin
Bt	mooring buoy with telephonic communications
Btg	mooring buoy with telegraphic communications
BVB	compass adjustment buoy
C	cape
Cal	wharf
Cala	cove
Cam Neb	fog bell
Cam Stm	submarine fog bell
Can	channel
Cann Neb	fog gun
Capo	cape
Cas	castle
Cl	cove
Cle	hill
Cma	summit
Cna	range
Co	cape
Coclo, cocuzzolo	boulder
Colle	hill
Comlo	gable
Convto abb	monastery, convent
Cop	covers
Corne da nebbia	fog horn
Cosp, cospicuo	conspicuous
Cn	shells
Cr	coral
Czo	mountain, mount
Decl	variation
Depo	warehouse, storehouse
Dim ann	decreasing annually
Dir	directional
Dr	dredged
Eccl	occulation
EF	list of lights
Elettr	electric
Eso	estuary
Est	east
Eta	entrance
F	mud, muddy, river
Fca	factory
Fce	brick kiln
Fdo	fjord
F(Ff)	fixed light
Fi Neb	fog whistle
F Lam	fixed and flashing light
F Lam	fixed and group flashing light
Flo	chimney, stack
Fna	fountain
G	yellow
Gde	great
Grp	group
Gta	jetty
H	altitude
I	island, islands, islet, islets
IMAM	mean establishment of the port
Inf	lower, lower light
Int	intermittent light, occulting light
Irreg	irregular

V Abbreviations of principal foreign terms, (Glossary)

ISAM	high water full and change (vulgar establishment of the port)
Iso	isophase
Ist, istitut	institute
Ito	islet
Lam	flash
Lam	group flashing light
Lam L	long flashing light
LM	mean sea level
LRS	chart datum (datum for sounding reduction)
Lum	lighted, luminous
M	madrepores, magnetic, mountain, mount
Mag	magazine
Mar	maritime
MAMQ	mean high water neaps
MAMS	mean high water springs
MBMQ	mean low water neaps
MBMS	mean low water springs
Mgna	mountain, mount
Mlo, molo	mole, pier
Mun	town-hall
Nauto	nautophone
NE	new edition
Nord	north
Nord Est	northeast
Nord Ouest	northwest
NC	new chart
Nvo	new
Occas	occasional light
Off	factory
Orriz	horizontal light
Osc	obscured light
Osp	hospital
Oss	observatory
Ost	obstruction
Ouest	west
P	square
Pali	piles, stakes, stumps, perches
Pass	pass, passage
Pco	peak
Per	period
PG	coast guard station
Pgio	mound, small hill
Pietre	stones
Pil	pillar
Pl	piles, stakes, stumps, perches
Pla	peninsula
Ple	groin
Plo	little, small
Po	hill
Port, portolano	sailing directions
Post	rear
PPTT	telegraph office
Pref	government house
Prio	promontory
Prog	projected
Provv	provisional light
P sb	landing
Pta	point, summit
Pte	bridge
Pto	haven
Pubbl	publication
Pzo	peak
R	radio telegraph station, rock, rocky, red
Ra	road, roadstead, radar station
Ra (cosp)	radar conspicuous
Ra Rifl	radar reflector

RC	circular radiobeacon
RC AERO	aeronautical radiobeacon
RD	directional radiobeacon, radio range
Rdf	radio broadcasting station
Rel	wreck showing any portion of hull or superstructure
RG	radio direction finding station
Rifl	reflector
Ril	bearing
Rist	reprint
RT	radio telephone station
R Telem	distance finding station (synchronized signals)
RW	rotating loop radiobeacon
S	sand, saint, south
Sc	quick flashing light, ridge of rocks
Sca	shoal
Scaf	wreck
Sci, sco	rock(s), reef(s)
Scogliera	ridge, ridge of rocks
Scogli, scoglio	rock(s), reef(s)
Scop Em	uncovers
Scra	ridge
Se, secca	shoal(s)
Seg	signal
Seg Neb	fog signal station
Segnale	signal
Sem, semaforo	semaphore
Serb, serbatolo bafta	oil tank
Serra	range of mountains
Set, settore	sector
SMt	seamount
Somm	submerged
Sopp, soppresso	discontinued
Sra	range of mountains
Stab	establishment
Ste	station
Ste Pt	pilot station
Ste Salo	lifeboat station
Ste Seg	signal station
Stm	submarine
Sto, stretto	strait
Sud	south
Sud Est	southeast
Sud Ouest	southwest
Sup	higher, upper
T	intermittent stream, torrent
Tam	temporary light
Tav	table-land
Tel	telegraph
Telno	telephone
Torre	tower
Tre	tower
Tre Ved	lookout station, watchtower
Tro Neb	fog trumpet
TV	television mast or tower
Uff	office
V	green, true, street
Va	villa
Vedi piano	see plan
Verde	green
Vert	vertical
Vietato	prohibited
Viol	violet
Vle	valley
Vno	volcano
Vo	old
VP	see plan
Vto	prohibited
Vto Anco	anchorage prohibited

Zo .... elevation of mean sea level
above chart datum

JAPANESE CHARTING TERMS

B .... bay
Byoti .... anchorage
Cab .... cable length
Dake, de .... mountain, hill
Destd .... destroyed
Ga, gawa .... river
GTS .... great trigonometrical survey station
H .... height
Ha, hana .... cape, point
Hakuchi .... roadstead
Hi .... roadstead
Hn .... haven
Hr .... harbor
Irie .... loch, lough
Irikuti .... entrance
Ja, jima .... island
Ka .... river
Kaikyo, ko .... strait
Kaiwan .... gulf
Kako .... estuary
Kawa .... river
Ko .... loch, lough, strait
Koro .... passage
Kuti .... mouth
Kyoko .... fjord
LL .... list of lights
Ma .... village
Machi, mi .... town
Mi, misaki, mki .... cape
Mura .... village
Sa .... island
Saki .... cape, point
San .... mountain
Sankakusu .... delta
Sdo .... sound, pass, channel
Seto .... narrows, strait
Shima .... island
Si .... cape, point
Sn .... mountain
So .... narrows, strait
Suido .... sound, pass, channel
Take, te .... hill, mountain
Wan .... bay
Ya, yama .... mountain
Zaki .... cape, point
Zan .... mountain
Zi .... cape, point
Zn .... mountain

MALAY CHARTING TERMS

A, ayer .... stream
Bandar .... seaport
Batang .... river
Batu .... rock
Bdr, bendar .... seaport
Bt .... hill
Btg .... river
Bu .... rock
Bukit .... hill
Gg .... shoal, reef, islet
Gg .... mountain
Gosong, gosung .... shoal, reef, islet
Gunong .... mountain
Gusong .... shoal, reef, islet
Kali .... river
Kampong, kampung .... village
Karang .... coral reef, reef
Kg .... village
Kg .... coral reef, reef
Ki .... river
Kla, kuala .... river mouth

Lab, labn, labuan, labuhan .... anchorage, harbor
Ma, muara .... river mouth
Parit .... stream, canal, ditch
Pelabohan, pln .... roadstead, anchorage
PP .... group of islands
Prt .... stream, canal, ditch
Pu, pulau .... island
Pulau-pulau .... group of islands
Pulo, pulu .... island
Selat .... strait
SH .... strait
Si .... river
Sungai, sungei .... river
Tandjong, tandjung, tanjong .... cape
Telok, teluk .... bay
Tg .... cape
Tk .... bay

NORWEGIAN CHARTING TERMS

Aero .... aeronautical
Ankerplass .... anchoring berth, anchorage
Aust .... east
Austre .... eastern

Bae .... rock (submerged rock)
Bake .... tower beacon
Bakre fyr .... rear light
Banke .... bank
Bekk .... river, stream
Berg .... mountain, mount, hill
Bg .... mountain, hill
Bifyr .... auxiliary light
Bla .... blue
Bl, blink .... flash
Blokk .... boulder
Blot .... soft
Br .... brown
Br, bredde .... latitude
Bukt .... bay, bight
By .... city, town

Dia, diafon .... diaphone
Dm .... decimeter
Dnl .... sailing directions
Duc d'albe .... dolphin

Efs .... notice to mariners
Elv .... river, stream

F .... fine, rock, rocky, fixed
Famm .... fathom
Farbar .... navigable
Fast .... stiff, fixed
Favn .... fathom
Fd, fdn .... fjord
Fin .... fine
Flak .... rock (submerged rock), bank
Flo .... flood
Flu .... sunken rock
Fm .... occulting
Fm bl .... fixed and flashing
Fm n fm gpoc .... group occulting light
Fm oc .... occultation
Fremre .... front light
Fv .... fathom
Fyr .... light
Fyrskip .... light vessel, light ship

G .... green, coarse
Gl .... yellow
Gml .... old
Gn .... green
Godt synlig .... conspicuous
Gong .... fog gong
Gp .... group

V Abbreviations of principal foreign terms, (Glossary)

Gp hbl, gp hurtigbl	interrupted quick flashing light
Gp lynbl	group short flashing light
Gr	gravel
Gr, gra	gray
Grad	degree, degrees
Gron	green
Grov	coarse
Grunne	ground, rock (submerged rock), shoal
Grus	gravel
Gs	sea-weed, grass
Gul	yellow
H	white
Hamn	harbor
Havn, havneby	harbor, port
Hbl	quick flashing light
Hd	altitude, height
Hefte	ostruction
Hn	harbor
Holme	islet
Hv, hvert	every
Hvit	white
HW	high water
In	inner
K	cape
Kai	quay, wharf
Kbl	cable
Kil	cove
Klakk	rock (submerged rock)
Kn	knots
Kr	coral
L	little, small, clay
Lavere	lower, front light
Lav kyst	flat coast
Lbl	short flashing light
Ldg	longitude
Lei	channel
Lengde	longitude
Lille	little, small
Lop	channel
Loa	pilot station always attended (on older charts)
Ls	pilot office
LW	low water
Lykt	light, light beacon
Lynbl, lynblink	short flashing light
Lys	light
Lysboye	light buoy
Lysende	lighted, luminous
Lysflate	light-float
M	middle, with, nautical
Magn	magnetic
Med	with
Mil	nautical mile
Myr	marsh, swamp
N	north, nautical mile, northern
Ned	lower
Nes	head, headland
No	northeast, number
Nord	north
Np	neap tide
Nr	number
Nut	peak
Ny	new
Os	estuary mouth
Ost	east
Ov	higher, upper, rear (light)
Ovre	upper
Oy	island

P	post office
Pilar	pile, pillar
Pir	pier
Pos	position
Pr	private
Puller	bollard
Pynt	point, head, headland
R	mooring ring
Rad mast	radio mast, radio tower
Rad st	radio broadcasting station
RC	circular radio beacon
RD	direction radiobeacon, radio range
Red	road, roadstead
Rev	reef, ridge
RG	radio directing finding station
Rod	red
RS	lifesaving station
R st	radio telegraph station
RT st	radio telephone station
RW	rotating loop radio beacon
S	second (of time), southern, south, black
Sec, sek	second (of time)
Sekt, sektor	sector
Sem, semafor	semaphore
Sg	shingle, pebbles
Sk	chimney, stack
Skall	rock (submerged rock)
Skalle	shoal
Skjaer, skjart	shoal
Skjer	rock (submerged rock)
Skjerane	rocks above water
Skolt	rock (submerged rock)
Sl	mud, muddy, ooze
So	southeast
Sor	south
Sp	spring tide
St	saint, large, stones
Stake	spar buoy
Stein	stones
Sto	ramp
Stor	large
St St	boulders
Svart	black
Syd	south
Sydlige	southern
Sydvest	southwest
Synl, synlig (rekkevidde)	visible (range)
T	ton
Taren	sunken rock
Tarn	tower
Tn	sunken rock
TS	telegraph station
Tydelig	conspicuous
Uren bunn	foul ground
Ute av bruk	abandoned
Ute av posisjon	out of position
Uv	submarine
Uv kl	submarine fog bell
V	cairn, tower beacon, western
Vest	west
Vg	bay, cove
Vks	alternating light
Vrak	wreck
Vorr	submerged jetty
Vs	weather signal station
Yt, ytre	outer
Zo	elevation of mean sea level above chart datum

V Abbreviations of principal foreign terms, (Glossary)

PERSIAN CHARTING TERMS

B, bandar . . . . harbor
Jab, jabal . . . . hill, mountain
Jazh, jazireh . . . . island, peninsula
K, khowr . . . . inlet, channel
R, rud . . . . river

POLISH CHARTING TERMS

Jez, jezioro . . . . lake
Kan, kanal . . . . channel
Miel, mielizna . . . . shoal
R, rzeka . . . . river
Wa, wyspa . . . . island
Zat, zatoka . . . . gulf, bay

PORTUGUESE CHARTING TERMS

A . . . . sand, yellow, range of tide
Aband . . . . abandoned
Aero . . . . aeronautical
Aerom. . . . . marine or air navigational light
Aeroporto . . . . airport
Aero RC . . . . aeronautical radiobeacon
AF, Af . . . . Shoal, fine sand
Afl . . . . muddy fine sand
Ag . . . . coarse sand, spire, steeple, compass
                                                            adjustment buoy
Aguada . . . . watering place
Agua descorada . . . . discolored water
Al . . . . muddy sand
Alf . . . . custom-house
Alg . . . . kelp, sea-weed
Alt . . . . alternating light
Am . . . . neap tide, marine and air navigation
                                                            light, yellow
Amarra . . . . cable length
Amarracao . . . . mooring
Amb, ambar . . . . amber
AN . . . . notices to mariners
Anc . . . . roadstead
Ang . . . . cove
Ant, anterior . . . . front, front light
Antigo . . . . ancient
Apito . . . . fog whistle
Apodrecido . . . . rotten
Aprox . . . . approximate
Ar . . . . clay
Arborizado . . . . woodland
Arco vis . . . . sector of visibility
Arg . . . . clay
Arm . . . . warehouse, storehouse
Arq . . . . archipelago
Arr . . . . brook
Ars . . . . Arsenal
At, AT . . . . lookout tower, power transmission line
Aux . . . . auxiliary light
Av . . . . spring tide, avenue
Az . . . . blue

B . . . . gravel, bay, white
Bal . . . . beacon, range targets (markers)
Barragem . . . . dam
Bat, bateria . . . . battery
Bb . . . . fathom
Bc, Bco . . . . bank
BM . . . . low water
BM AM . . . . mean low water neaps
BM AV . . . . mean low water springs
BM de AV da India . . . . Indian spring low water
Br . . . . white, fathom
Bt . . . . tenacious
Buz . . . . fog horn
Buz elt, buzina de neveoiro electrica . . . . electric fog gun
Bxa, Bxas, Bxio, Bxo . . . . shoal

C . . . . strand, shingle, cape, gravel

Cabeco de poco . . . . wellhead
Cabo . . . . head, headland
Cabo submarino . . . . submarine cable
Cach . . . . waterfalls
Cada . . . . every
Cal . . . . inlet, calcareous
Calhau . . . . strand
Calvario . . . . calvary, cross
Camp . . . . spire, steeple
Can, canal . . . . channel
Canalizacoes subm . . . . submarine pipeline area
Canhao de nevoeiro (cerracao) . . . . fog gun
Cap . . . . chapel
Carta . . . . chart
Casa de campo . . . . villa
Cast . . . . castle, brown
Casuarina filao . . . . filao
Cat, catedral . . . . cathedral
Cem . . . . cemetery (non-christian)
Cerca de . . . . about
Ch, Chm, CH . . . . chimney, stack, elevation of top of
                                                            building
Ci . . . . cirripeda
Cin, Cin F . . . . ash, cinders
Cin, cinzento . . . . gray
Cir . . . . cirripeda
Cist, cisterna . . . . cistern
Cl . . . . light (quality of bottom)
CM . . . . town-hall
Cme . . . . summit
Co . . . . shells, cape
Cob, cobre . . . . covers
Col . . . . hill
Com . . . . reported
Comp ag . . . . compass adjustment beacon
Compia . . . . company
Con . . . . shells, cape
Con, conv . . . . convent
Consp . . . . conspicuous
Cor . . . . coral, shoal
Cord . . . . range of mountains
Cor do sector . . . . color of sector
Corr . . . . correction
Corr, corrente . . . . stream
Cre . . . . chalk
Crista sub . . . . ridge
Cruz . . . . cross
CS . . . . wreck, telegraph cable buoy
Ct . . . . quick flashing light
Ctl(int) . . . . interrupted quick flashing light
CtR . . . . continuous very quick light
CtRI . . . . interrupted very quick light
CtR (n) . . . . group very quick light
CTT . . . . post and telegraph office
CtU . . . . continuous ultra quick light
CtUI . . . . interrupted ultra quick light
Cume . . . . summit
Cup . . . . cupola
Cz . . . . gray

D . . . . diatoms, distance, delta, doubtful, hard
DA . . . . water tower, stand-pipe
DC . . . . oil tank
Decl . . . . variation
Des . . . . landing
Des, descb, descobre
    (periodicamente) . . . . uncovers, dries
Descor, descolorido . . . . discolored
Desigual . . . . uneven
Dest . . . . destroyed
Det . . . . decayed
Dia . . . . diaphone
Dist . . . . distant
Distr . . . . district
D Mg . . . . variation

V Abbreviations of principal foreign terms, (Glossary)

Dol	dolphin		GTS	great trigonometrical survey station
Duque de alba	dolphin		Gw	Greenwich
Duro	hard			
DW	deep water route		H	amplitude of a tidal component (half of the range), height, elevation, hour
E	dark, red		Hor, Horiz	horizontal lights
Ecl	eclipse		Hora	time signal station, hour
Ed	edition			
Electr, elt	electric		I	intermittent light, island
Elev, elevador	elevator		Ig	church
Empena	gable		Igp	creek
En ch, enchente	flood		Igreja	church
Enf	in line (range)		IH	sale place of charts and nautical publications of the instituto hidrografico
Ens	cove			
Ent	entrance, magazine		Il	islet (islets)
Equin, equinocial	equinoctial		Ilheu	islet
Erv mar	sea-weed, grass		In	discontinued
ES	signal station		Inf	lower, lower light
Esc	school, dark, scoriae		Inst	institute
ES(corr)	stream signal station		Int	inner, intermittent light
ES(gelo)	ice signal station		Inter	intermediate, intermediate light
ES(mare)	tide signal station		Irreg	irregular light
ES(meteor)	weather signal station		Is, Iso	isophase light
Esp	sponge		Ita	islet
Espic, espiculas	spicules			
Esponja	sponge		J, jarda	yard
ES(temp)	storm signal station			
Est	stadium		L	mud, muddy, lake, light
Estab	established		La, lama	sandy mud, lagoon, orange
Estal, estaleiro	shipyard		LAN	list of navigational aids
Estb	established		LAR	list of radio navigational aids
Est salv	lifesaving station		L. aux	auxiliary light
Esto	creek		Laz, lazareto	lazaret
Estr	strait		LC	full moon
Exp	experimental		Ld	ooze
Explos	explosive, explosive fog signal		L det nev	fog detector light
Ext	outer		L dir	directional light
Extr, extremo	extreme		LF	list of lights
			L int	intermittent light
F	fixed light, branch, fine		l irreg	irregular light
Fab	factory		List listrado	streaky
Fal	cliff, bluff		LN	new moon
Faz	farm		L/ocas	occasional light
Fc	fucus		Lp	flash, flashing light
Fd	fjord		L part	private light
F Gr Lp	fixed and group flashing light		LpC	short flashing light
F Lp	fixed and flashing light		LpCl	short-long flashing light
For	foraminifera		Lp R	quick flashing light
Foz	mouth		L prov	provisional light
Fr	faint light		LpRIn	interrupted quick flashing light
FRl	fixed and flashing light		LpUR	ultra quick flashing light
FRl Agr(n), FRl(n)	fixed and group flashing light		LpURIn	interrupted ultra quick flashing light
Ft, Fte	fort, small lighthouse		L rot	rotating light
Fu	fucus		L temp	temporary light
			Lv	lava
G	corse, gulf, phase lag		Lz	light
Gas	gasometer, gas tank			
Gasoduto	gas pipeline		M	meter, nautical mile, bearing
GC	Coast Guard station		Mad	madrepore
Gde	great		Mag	magnetic
Gelos	ice signal station		Mal, malhado	speckled
Cgo	fog gong, gong buoy		Mang	manganese
Gl	globigerina		Mangal	mangrove
Glac, glaciares	glacial, glaciers		Manganesio	manganese
Gol	narrows		Mangrulho	dolphin
Gongo	fog gong		Mangue	mangrove
Gov	government house		Mant, mantido	maintained
Gp	group		Marabuto	marabout
Gr	great, large		Mare	tide
Gr Lp	group flashing light		Mareg, maregrafo	tide gauge
Gr Lp C	group short flashing light		Mares	tide signal station
Gr Lp MR	group very quick flashing light		Mar, maritimo	maritime
Gr Lp R	group quick flashing light		Mas, MAST, Mast	mast, signal mast
Gr Oc	group occulting light			

MAST AT	power transmission mast
MAST (Mas)TV	television mast
MASTROS	wreck of which only the masts are visible
Mat	boulder
Md	ground (shells), middle
Med	middle
Merc	magazine
Meteo	weather signal station
Mex, mexilhao	mussels
Mg	magnetic, marl
Min	minute of time
Ml	soft
MN	bench mark
Mo	hill
Mo	morse code light
MON, Mon	monument
Most	monastery, convent
Mt	mountain, mount
Mt sub	seamount
Mun	municipality
Na sa	our lady
Nauto	nautophone
Navegavel, Navg	navigable
NC	new chart
NE	new edition
NM, nm	mean sea level, mean tide level
No	number
No	knot
Nora	noria
Nos	knots
Not, notavel	remarkable
Novo	new
NR	chart datum (for sounding reduction)
NS	our lord, our lady
NV	unwatched light
Obs	observatory
Obsc	obscured light
Obst, Obstr	obstruction
Oc	occulting light
Ocas	occasional, occasional light
Ocid, occidental	western
Oc Agr (n), Oc (n)	group occulting light
Oc (n t m)	composite group-occulting light
Ocultacao	occultation
Ol	brick kiln
Oleoduto	oil pipe
Ord ordinario	ordinary
Os, Ost	oysters
O sub	submarine oscillator
P	broken, black, harbor, port, haven, preliminary, stones
Pa	branch
Pad, padrao	standard
Pag, pagode	pagoda
Par	gray
Part	private, privately, private aid to navigation
Pas, Pass	passage, pass
Pc	peak
Pcel	bank, shelf
Pe	foot
Ped, pedregoso	flinty
Pen	peninsula
Peq	small, little
Per	period
Pesq	fish haven
PICO SUB	seamount
Pil, pilar	dolphin, pile, pillar
PILOTOS	pilot station
Pinhal	coniferous woodland
Pir, piramide	pyramid

Plan	tableland
PM	high water
PM AM	mean high water neaps
PM AV	mean high water springs
Po	peak, polyzoa
Poco	well
Pod	rotten
Pol	polyparia, polyzoa, inch
Pontao	hulk
Pos, posicao	position
Post	rear, rear light
Poste	post
Pp	pumice
Pr	black, beach
Prados	grass fields
Prel	preliminary
Princ	principal light
Proem, proeminente	prominent
Prof menor, Profundidade minima em canais (ou rios) estreitos	least depth in narrow channels
Proib	prohibited
Proj	projected
Prom	promontory
Prov	provisional, provisional light
Pt	pteropods
Pta	point
Ptal	head, headland
Pub, Publ	publication
Purp, purpura	purple
Q	quarantine, quarantine buoy, quarter, quadrature, broken, farm
QC	2nd quarter
QM	1st quarter
Qta	farm
Qtel	barracks
Qtz	quartz
R	true course, street, rock, rocky, river, stream, radiotelegraph station, measured distance, recommended track
Ra	river, stream, radar guided track, radar station
Rad	radiolaria
Rada	road, roadstead
Rap	ramp
Rc	rock
Rch	creek
Rd, RD	radiolaria, directional radiobeacon
Red	small
Res	tank
Res met, Residuos metalicos	mattes
Rest	spit of land
RF	radiobeacon
Rfe	reef
RG	radio direction finding station
Rl	flashing light
Rl Agr(n)	group flashing light
Rl L	long-flashing light
Rl(n)	group flashing light
Rl(n+m)	composite group flashing light
Riba	river, stream
Ric	bar
Rio	river
RN	bench mark
Rocha	rock, rocky
Rot	revolving light, rotating light
RT	radio telephone station
Ru, ruinas	ruins
RV	true course
RW	rotating loop radiobeacon
S	pebbles, saint, second of time, syzygy
Sa	range of mountains, gritty

Sarg, sargaco	kelp, sea-tangle
Sc	small bay
Sem	semaphore
Ser	fog siren, saw mill
Set, setentrional	northern
Simb	symbol
Sin ac sub	submarine sound signal with platform
Sinais	signal station
Sinal	signal
Sino	fog bell
Sino sub	submarine fog bell
Sir	fog siren
Sizigia	syzygy
So	height of mean sea level above the zero of tidal staff
St, Sta, sto	saint, farm
Sub	submarine
Subm	submerged
Sup	higher, upper light
T	ton, temporary light, ground
Temp	temporary light
Temp bud, Templo budista	buddhist temple, joss-house
Tempo	storm signal station
Tf, TF	tufa, federal territory
T oleo	oil tank
Tr	tower, reed horn, power transmission mast
Trib	courthouse
Tufo	tufa
U	unit of height
Ur	bank, shelf
V	see, ooze, true, green
Va, vale	valley
Var	stranding harbor (dries at low-water)
Var, variado	varied
Vau	ford
Vaz, vazante	ebb
Vd	green
Velho	old
Vel, velocidade	velocity, rate
Ver	see
Vert	vertical, vertical lights
Vi	violet
Vig	lookout station, watch tower
Viol	violet
Vis, visivel (alcance)	visible (range)
Vm	red
Vsc	sticky
Vul	volcano
Vul sub	submarine volcano
X	schist
Z	azimuth (bearing)
Zero hidrografico (plano de reducao de sondas), ZH	chart datum (datum for sounding reduction)
Zo	elevation of MSL above chart datum
Zv	true bearing

ROMANIAN CHARTING TERMS

Br, brat, bratu, bratul	branch, arm
C, cap, capu, capul	cape
I, insula	island
L, luc, locu, lucul	luke
O, ostrov, ostrovu, ostrovul	river island

RUSSIAN CHARTING TERMS

Banka, banki, bka, bki	bank(s)
B, bukhta	bay, inlet
G, gavan	harbor, basin
G, gora	mountain, hill
Ga, guba	bay, inlet, creek
Kam, kamen	rock
M, mys	cape
O, ostrov, ostrova	islands
Oz, ozero	lake
Pol, poluostrov	peninsula
Proliv, prv	channel, strait
R, reka	river
Z, zaliv	gulf, bay

SPANISH CHARTING TERMS

A	gritty, yellow, sand, orange, amber
A de Bda	flagstaff, flagpole
A de la M	range (of tide)
Abr, abra	haven
ACo	sand and gravel
Ad, aduana	customhouse
Aero	aeronautical
Aeromar	marine and air navigation light
AF	sand and mud
Agua	water tower, standpipe
Al	alternating
Alg	kelp, seaweed, seaweed grass
Alm	magazine
Alm	mussels
Alm Dep	warehouse, storehouse
Alr	about
Alt	alternating, alternating light
Am	yellow
An	narrows, orange
Anch	anchorage, bridge clearance (horizontal)
Ang, angostura	narrows
Ant	front light
Antg	ancient
Apag, apagdo, apagada	extinguished light
Aproxte	approximate
Ar	clay
Arc	clay
Arch, Archo, archipielago	archipelago
Arrf, arrecife	reef, rock (uncovers)
Arro	stream, creek
AS	signal mast
Aserr, aserrado	saw mill
Astrm, Astro	astronomical
At	faint light
Aux	auxiliary light
Av, avd	avenue
Az	blue
B	bay, white, reed horn
Ba, bahia	bay
Bajo	shoal
Bal	beacon (in general), bathing establishment
Banco	bank
Bat, bateria	battery
Bca	mouth
Bco	bank
Bd, bdo	soft
Bjmar	low water
BM	low water
Bo, boca	shoal
Br, braza	fathom
Bulevar	boulevard
Bzo	arm (of the sea), loch, lough, lake
C	cape, small, fog bell, shells, every, shingle, post office, quarter, quadrature
Ca	mountain range, shells, calcareous, house
Cable	cable length
Cabo	cape

V Abbreviations of principal foreign terms, (Glossary)

Cada	every
Cal, caleta	inlet, tufa
Calle	street
Cam Send Hlla	track, footpath, trail
Can, canal	channel, sound, canal, fog gun
Canal	dredged channel
Carbon	cinders
Carta	chart
Cas, castillo	castle
Casa	house
Cat	cathedral
Cbl	cable length
Cc	shells
Cd	new candle
Ce	summit
Cerro	hill
Cha	chimney
Cima	summit
Cisterna	cistern
Cj	gravel
Cjo	farm
Cl	light (quality of bottom), coral
Claro	light (quality of bottom)
CN	post office
Co	gravel, hill
Col, colina	hill
Comp, agj	compass adjustment beacon
Con	with
Consp, conspicuo	conspicuous
Cord	range
Corr	correction
Corto	small
Cr	coral
Cra	mountain, range
Cre	summit
Crec	flood
Cruz	calvary, cross
Ct	quick flashing light
Cte	stream (current)
Ctl	int. quick flashing light
Cto	convent, quarter, quadrature
CtR	continuous very quick flashing light
Cu	quartz
Cubo, cubierto	covers
D	doubtful, delta, flash, flashing light, hard, diaphone
Darna	dock
De	drydock, floating dock
Demora, demarcacion	bearing
Des	flashing, landing place
Descol	discolored, discolored water
Descubo, descubierto	uncovers
Desemb	landing place
Dest, Desto	decayed, destroyed
Diaf	diaphone
DL	riprap surrounding light
Dm	city or town (small scale)
Do	reported
Dta	delta
E	east, sponge, explosive fog signal, station, eclipse
Ea	farm
E B Salv	lifeboat station
Ec	scoriae
E de l P	mean establishment of the port
Elec, Elect	electric
Enf	in line with
Ens, Ensa	bay, creek, cove
Ent, entr	entrance
Entrante	flood
Ep	sponge
Equin, equinicial	equinoctial
ES	signal station

E Salv	lifesaving station
Esc	scoriae, school
E S Horaria	time signal station
Esp	sponge
Esq	schist
Est	estuary
Estabdo, establecide	established
Este	east
Esto	stadium
Estr	strait
Event	eventual
Exp, Exper	experimental
Expl, Explos, Explosivo, Expvo	explosive
Ext, exterior	outer
F	fixed light, mud, muddy, fine
F D, Fd	fixed and flashing light, fjord
F Des	fixed and flashing
F Gp D	fixed and group flashing
F Gr D	fixed and group flashing
Fabca	factory
FC	railway
Fca	factory
Fdo	ground, fjord
Fdo So	foul ground, foul bottom
Fm	fathom
Fo	lighthouse, light
Fond	anchorage
Fondo Aero	anchorage for seaplanes
Fondo Prohdo	anchorage prohibited
Fondo sucio	foul ground, foul bottom
Freu	sound
Frontispicio, Fronton	gable
Fte	fort
G	phase lag, gray, coarse, revolving or rotating light, pebbles
Gde	great
Gj	flinty
Gja	farm
Gl	glacial, globigerina
Go	gulf, shingle
Gob, gobo	government house
Gong, Gongo, gong de niebla	fog gong
Gp	group
Gp Ct	group quick flashing light
Gp D	group-flashing light
Gp Oc	group occulting light
Gp Rp	group very quick flashing light
Gr	group, gray, large, gravel, shingle, chalk, Greenwich
Grd	great, large
Gr D	group flashing light
Gr Dc	composite group flashing light
Gr Des	group flashing light
Gris	gray
Gr Oc	group occulting light
Gru	coarse
Gs	coarse
H	hour, height, altitude, elevation, bridge clearance (vertical)
Hlla	track, footpath, trail
Hor, hort	horizontal light
I	island, islet
Ig, Igla	church
Inf, inferior	lower, lower light
Ins, instituto	institute
Int, Interior	inner
Ip	stiff
IQ	interrupted quick flashing
Irreg	irregular light
Is	island
Iso, Isof	isophase light

Ite (Ites)	islet (islets)
IUQ	int. ultra quick flashing light
IVQ	int. very quick flashing light
Kn	knot, knots
L	light, large, ooze, lake, pond, loch, lough
La	lagoon
Laz, lazareto	lazaret
Lum	lighted, luminous
Lv	lava
M	meter, minute (of time), nautical mile, speckled
Mn	mountain
Mad, madrepora	madrepore
Mag	magnetic
Mal	jetty (partly below MHW)
Mco	magnetic
Md	middle, madrepores
M de S	mean low-water springs
M de Sic	spring tide
Mdo	speckled
Me, medio	middle, mole
Mejillon	mussels
Mj	mussels
Ml	ground (shells)
Mlle	mole
Mma	swamp
Mna	mountain, mount
Mo	morse code light, head, headland
Mol	windmill
Mon	monument
Mons, monasterio	monastery
Mr	marl
Ms de C	neap tide
Ms de S	spring tide
Mta	tableland (plateau)
Mte, Mtna	mountain, mount
Mte sub	seamount
Mto	monument
Municipio	town hall
Murulla, muro	wall
Mv	bearing
N	north, knot, nautophone, black, nautical mile
Naut, Nautof, nautofono	nautophone
Nav	navigable
N de R	bench mark
Nj, nja	orange
N M	mean tide level
NMM	mean sea level
No	number
Noray	dolphin
Not	notable
NRS	chart datum (datum for sounding reduction)
Ns	knots
Nv, nvo	new
O	dark, submarine oscillator
Obs, obsn	obstruction
Obco	observatory
Obston, obstr	obstruction
Obsv	observatory
Oc	occultation, occulting light
Ocas, Ocasl	occasional, occasional light
Occ	occulation, occulting light
Occidental	western
Of	office
Of de pto	harbormaster's office
Oficina	office
Of Tel	telegraph office

Ord, ordinario	ordinary
Os	oysters
Osc	submarine oscillator, dark, obscured light
Ost	oysters
O sub	submarine oscillator
P	peak, brown, stones, position, shoal sounding on isolated rock
Pal	wreck with only masts visible (above sounding datum)
Part	private, privately
Paso	passage, pass
Pblo	village
Pc	peak
Pd	pebbles
P de O	observation spot
P de R	point of reference
Penl, penla	peninsula
Peq	little
Pet	oil tank
Pg	sticky
Pie	foot, feet
Pil, pilares	pilar
Pl de R	chart datum (datum for sounding reduction)
Plmar	high water
Ply	beach
P M	high water
Pm M de S	mean high-water springs
PnFo	light vessel, lightship
Pn	passage, pass
Pob	village
Pod, podrido	rotten
Pol, Polv, polvorin	powder magazine
Posn, posicion	position
Pq	small
Pr	brown
Prof men	lesser depth possible
Prof min	least depth in narrow channels
Proh, prohdo	prohibited
Prom, promo	promontory, prominent
Prov, Provo	provisional light
Proy, proyecto, proyo	projected
Pta	point
Pte	bridge
Plo	harbor, port
Publ, publicacion	publication
Pz	pumice
Q	stream, quick flashing light
Qb	broken
Queb, quebrada	stream
Quebrado	broken
R	red, radio fog-signal station, radio telegraph station, rock, river, qtg radio station
Ra	isolated rock, radar station, radar guided track
Rada	road, roadstead
Ram	ramark
RC	circular radiobeacon
Rcso	rocky
RD, Rd	directional radiobeacon, radiolaria
Rda	road, roadstead
Rdf	radio broadcasting station
Ref	hut
Regla	standard
RF, RFo	Radiobeacon
RG	radio direction finding station
Rga	ridge
Ria	creek
Rs	rocks, ruins
Rso	rocky

RT . . . . radio telephone station
Ru . . . . dumping ground
R Telem . . . . distance finding station
Rui, ruinas . . . . ruins
RW . . . . rotating loop radiobeacon

S . . . . station, south, fog signal, second (of time), signal, syzygy, saint, sector
S A S . . . . submarine fog bell (mechanical)
S A So . . . . submarine fog bell (action of waves)
S C Bal . . . . cardinal marking system
S G . . . . unwatched light
S Mt . . . . seamount
S S . . . . signal station
Sa . . . . mountain range
SD . . . . doubtful sounding, lesser depth possible
Seg . . . . second (of time)
Sem . . . . semaphore
Senal . . . . signal
Sic . . . . syzygy
Sil, silb, silbato . . . . fog whistle
Sir, sirena . . . . fog siren
Sn . . . . saint
So . . . . low-water datum, sound
Son . . . . morse code fog signal
SSN . . . . submarine fog signal
Sta, sto . . . . saint
Subm . . . . submarine
sumdo, sumg, sumgd . . . . submerged
Sup . . . . higher, upper light
Supdo, Suprim . . . . discontinued

T . . . . temporary, temporary light, ton, tufa
Tba . . . . tomb
Te . . . . tower
Te bal . . . . tower beacon
Tejar . . . . brick kiln
Tel, telegrafo . . . . telegraph
Tem . . . . temporary, temporary light
Tfno . . . . telephone, mooring buoy with telegraphic communications
Tn . . . . ton
Tri, Triang, triangulacion . . . . triangulation
Trompa, Trompeta de niebla . . . . fog trumpet
T V . . . . television mast, television tower

U . . . . unit of height, ultra quick flashing light
UQ . . . . ultra quick flashing light

V . . . . true, green, valley, volcano, ebb, lookout tower
Valle . . . . valley
Var . . . . variation
Var an, Variacion anua . . . . annual change
VC . . . . see chart
Vc . . . . volcanic
V de T . . . . triangulation point (station)
Ve . . . . valley
Verd . . . . true
Vert . . . . vertical lights
Verto, Vertedero de draga . . . . spoil area
Vi . . . . violet
Vigia . . . . lookout station, watch tower
Vis . . . . visible (range)
Vj . . . . old
Vo . . . . true
Vol, volcan . . . . volcano
VP . . . . see plan
VQ . . . . very quick flashing light
Vt . . . . streaky

Zo . . . . elevation of mean sea level above chart sounding datum, chart datum (datum for sounding reduction)

Zona C Subm . . . . submarine cable area
Zona Can Subm . . . . submarine pipeline area

SWEDISH CHARTING TERMS
B . . . . bay, bight
Berg, berget, bg, bgt . . . . mountain
Bk . . . . bank
Bukt . . . . bay, bight
Fj, fjard . . . . fjord
Gra, grund . . . . shoal
Hamm, hamnen . . . . harbor
Hd . . . . headland
Hm . . . . islet
Hn . . . . harbor
Holm, holmen . . . . islet
Huvud . . . . headland
K, kap . . . . cape
N, nord, norr, norra . . . . north, northern
Sk, skar, skaret . . . . rock above water

THAI CHARTING TERMS
Kh, khao . . . . hill, mountain
Laem, lm . . . . cape, point
Mae nam, MN . . . . river

TURKISH CHARTING TERMS
Ad, ada, adacik, adasi . . . . island, islet
Br, burnu, burun . . . . point, cape
Ca, cay, cayi . . . . stream, river
Da, dag, dagi . . . . mountain
De, dere, deresi . . . . valley, stream
Li, liman, limani . . . . harbor
Te, tepe, tepesi . . . . hill, peak

YUGOSLAV CHARTING TERMS
Br, brda, brdo . . . . mountain(s)
Gr, greben, grebeni . . . . rock, reef, cliff, ridge
Hr, hrid, hridi . . . . rock
L, luka . . . . harbor, port
O . . . . islet(s)
O, otoci . . . . island(s)
Otocic, otocici . . . . islet(s)
Otok . . . . island(s)
Pl, plicina . . . . shoal
Pr, prolaz . . . . passage
Sk, skolj, skoljic . . . . island, reef
U, uvala, uvalica . . . . inlet
Z, zaliv . . . . gulf, bay

Index of Abbreviations

Index of Abbreviations

Index of Abbreviations

Lt	Light	K 2		NW	Northwest	U 8
lt	Light	S 67		NWS	National Weather Service	
Ltd	Limited	li			Signal Station	Jb
Lt Ho	Lighthouse	K 3				
LW	Low water	T 2		**O**		
LWD	Low water datum	Ta		OBSC	Obscured (light)	K 68
				Obs Spot	Observation spot	D 4
M				Obstr	Obstruction	O 27
M, Mi	Nautical mile	E 11; Kd		Obsy	Observatory	J 21
M	Mud, Muddy	S 3		Oc, Occ	Occulting (light),	
m	Medium	Sg			Occultation	K 22, 46
m	Meter	E 4, d, e		Oc, Occ	Intermittent (light)	K 48
m²	Square meter	E 4d		Occas	Occasional (light)	F 39; K 70
m³	Cubic meter	E 4e		ODAS	Oceanographic Data	
m, min	Minute (of time)	E 2; Ke			Aquisition System	L 73
Ma	Marsh	Bj		Off	Office	J 22
Ma	Mattes	S 38b		Or, or	Orange	K 65; L 48b; S 62
mag	Magnetic	U 23		OVHD		
Magz	Magazine	I 34		PWR CAB	Overhead power cable	H 4
maintd	Maintained	F 36		Oys	Oysters, Oyster bed	S 24; G 15a
max	Maximum	Fp		Oz	Ooze	S 4
Mc	Megacycle	Eh				
Mds	Madrepores	S 15		**P**		
Mg	Mangrove	Bk		P	Pebbles	S 9
MHHW	Mean higher high water	T 8b		P	Pillar (buoy)	L 8a
MHW	Mean high water	T 7a		P	Pond	Bb
MHWN	Mean high water neaps	T 8a		P	Port	B 17; G 5
MHWS	Mean high water springs	T 8		PA	Position approximate	O 41
MHz	Megahertz	Ee		Pag	Pagoda	I 14
MICRO TR	Microwave tower	Mc		Pass	Passage, Pass	B 9
mid	Middle	F 7		Pav	Pavilion	I 67
min	minimum	Fo		PD	Position doubtful	O 42
Mkr	Marker	Lc		Pen	Peninsula	B 21
Ml	Marl	S 5		PIL STA	Pilot station	J 8
MLLW	Mean lower low water	T 9b		Pk	Peak	B 29
MLW	Mean low water	T 8c		Pm	Pumice	S 18
MLWN	Mean low-water neaps	T 9a		Po	Polyzoa	S 37
MLWS	Mean low-water springs	T 9		P O	Post Office	I 29
mm	Millimeter	E 4c		P, Pos	Position	O 44
Mn	Manganese	S 22		priv	Private, Privately	F 30
Mo	Morse code light,			Priv maintd	Privately maintained	K 17; L 29
	Fog signal	K 30a; Nc		Prohib	Prohibited	F 26
mod	Moderate	Fh		prom	Prominent	F 31
MON	Monument	I 35		Prom	Promontory	B 23
Ms	Mussels	S 25		Prov	Provisional (light)	K 72
μsec, μs	Microsecond (one millionth)	Eb		Pt	Point	B 25
MSL	Mean sea level	T 4		Pt	Pteropods	S 36
Mt	Mountain, Mount	B 26		pub	Publication	E 15
Mth	Mouth	B 13		P F	Pump-out facilities	Gd
MTL	Mean tide level	T 3		PWI	Potable water intake	
My	Bearing	U 21				
				Q		
N				Quar	Quarantine	G 26
N	North, Northern	U 1, 9		Q, Qk Fl	Quick flashing (light)	K 24
N	Nun, Conical (buoy)	L 6		Qz	Quartz	S 13
N M, N Mi	Nautical mile	E 11				
NAUTO	Nautophone	N 8		**R**		
NE	Northeast	U 5		R	Red	K 66; L 15, 43
N'ly	Northerly	Fq		R	River	Bd
NM	Notice to Mariners	F 42		R	Rocks	B 35
No	Number	E 23		Ra	Radar station	M 11
Np	Neap tide	T 7		Racon	Radar responder beacon	M 12

Index of Abbreviations

Ra (conspic)	Radar conspicuous object	M 14
RA DOME	Radar dome	Mh
Ra Ref	Radar reflector	Lf; M 13
Ra Sur	Radio responder beacon	M 12
RBHB	Red and black horizontal bands	L 17, 18, 19, 20, 20a
R Bn	Red beacon	L 52
R Bn	Radiobeacon	M 3, 4, 16
RC	Circular radiobeacon	M 4
Rd	Radiolaria	S 35
rd	Red	S 63
Rd	Road, Roadstead	B 14; H 1
RD	Directional Radiobeacon, Radio range	M 5
RDF, Ro DF	Radio direction finding station	M 7
REF	Reflector	K 10; L 64
Rep	Reported	O 35
Restr	Restricted	Fv
Rf	Reef	O 23
RG	Radio direction finding station	M 7
Rge	Range	B 27
RGE	Range	Ki
Rk	Rock	B 35
Rk, rky	Rock, Rocky	S 11
Rky	Rocky	Bh
R MAST	Radio mast	M 9
Ro Bn	Radiobeacon	M 3
Rot	Rotating (light), Revolving	K 31
RR	Railroad	H 3
R RELAY MAST	Radio relay mast	Mb
R Sta	Radio telegraph station, QTG Radio station	M 1, 10a
RT	Radio telephone station	M 2
rt	Rotten	S 48
R TR	Radio tower	M 9
Ru	Ruins	I 40
RW	Rotating loop radiobeacon	M 6
RW Bn	Red and white beacon	L 52
RWVS	Red and white vertical stripe	L 14, 14a
Ry	Railway	H 3

S

S	Sand	S 2
S	South, Southern	U 3, 11
S	Spar (buoy)	L 8
Sc	Scoriae	S 20
Sch	Schist	S 13a
Sch	School	I 65
Sd	Sound	B 8
SD	Sounding doubtful	Q 1
SE	Southeast	U 6
sec, s	Second (time; geo, pos.)	E 3; Kf
SEC	Sector	K 49
Sem	Semaphore	J 10
S Fl	Short flashing (light)	K 25a
sft	Soft	S 41
Sh	Shells	S 23

Shl	Shoal	O 22
Si	Silt	Se
Sig Sta	Signal station	J 9
SIREN	Fog siren	N 11
Sk	Stroke, strike	Fu
S-L Fl	Short-long flashing (light)	K 28a
Slu	Slough	Be; C 18
S'ly	Southerly	Fr
sml	Small	F 4; S 44
Sn	Shingle	S 8
Sp	Spring tide	T 6
SP	Spherical (buoy)	L 7
Spg	Sponge	S 26
Spi	Spicules	S 31
S'PIPE	Standpipe	I 45
spk	Speckled	S 50
S Sig Sta	Storm signal station	J 11
St	Saint	F 11
St	Street	I 26
St	Stones	S 10
Sta	Station	J 1, 2
std	Standard	F 32
stf	Stiff	S 43
Stg	Sea-tangle	S 29
stk	Sticky	S 46
St M, St Mi	Statute mile	Ea
Str	Strait	B 7
Str	Stream	Bc; T 17
str	Streaky	S 49
sub	Submarine	F 20
SUB-BELL	Submarine fog bell	N 5, 6
Subm, subm	Submerged	F 33; O 30
Subm Ruins	Submerged ruins	Gd
SUB-OSC	Submarine oscillator	N 7
Sub Vol	Submarine volcano	O 8
Subm W	Submerged Well	Ob
SW	Southwest	U 7
sw	Swamp	Bl

T

t	Tonne	E 12a
T	Ton	Ei
T	Telephone	I 70; L 22c
T	True	U 22
T	Tufa	S 19
TB	Temporary buoy	L 30
Tel	Telegraph	I 27; L 22b
Telem Ant	Telemetry antenna	Ma
Tel Off	Telegraph office	I 28
Temp	Temporary (light)	F 38; K 73
ten	Tenacious	S 55
Thoro	Thoroughfare	B 9
Tk	Tank	I 53
TR, Tr	Tower	I 41; L 63; Ld; M 9a
Tri	Triangulation	D 10
T.T.	Treetop	C 11
TV TR	Television tower (mast)	M 9a

U

uhf	Ultra high frequency	Mi
Uncov	Uncovers; Dries	O 2, 32, 34
Univ	University	Ih

Index of Abbreviations

unverd	Unverified	Fb
unev	Uneven	S 71
μsec. μs	Microsecond (one millinoth)	Eb
UQ	Continuous Ultra Quick	Kc

V

var	Variation	U 24
vard	Varied	S 70
VB	Vertical beam	Kh
vel	Velocity	T 23
Vert	Vertical (lights)	K 80
VERT CL	Vertical clearance	H 18a
vhf	Very high frequency	Mi
Vi, vi	Violet	K 61; S 58
View X	View point	D 6
Vil	Village	I 3
Vol	Volcanic	S 16
Vol Ash	Volcanic ash	Sb
VQ, V Qk Fl	Very quick flashing (light)	Kc
VS	Vertical stripes	L 32

W

W	West, Western	U 4, 12
W, wh	White	K 67; L 41; S 56
W Bn	White beacon	L 52
Wd	Seaweed	S 28
Whf	Wharf	G 18
WHIS	Fog whistle	N 15
Wk	Wreck	O 15, 15a, 28
Wks	Wrecks, Wreckage	O 29
W Or	White and orange	Le
W'ly	Westerly	Ft

Y

Y, yl	Yellow	L 24, 44; S 61
yd, yds	Yard(s)	E 8
1st	First	Fj
2nd, 2d	Second	Fk
3rd, 3d	Third	Fl
4th	Fourth	Fm
°	Degree	E 20
'	Minute (of arc)	E 21
"	Second (of arc)	E 22

AIDS TO NAVIGATION

IN

UNITED STATES WATERS

MODIFIED U.S. AID SYSTEM
LATERAL AIDS AS SEEN ENTERING FROM SEAWARD

NOTE: WHEN USED ON THE INTRACOASTAL WATERWAY, THESE AIDS ARE ALSO EQUIPPED WITH SPECIAL YELLOW STRIPS, TRIANGLES, OR SQUARES. WHEN USED ON THE WESTERN RIVERS (MISSISSIPPI RIVER SYSTEM), THESE AIDS ARE NOT NUMBERED. (MISSISSIPPI RIVER SYSTEM ABOVE BATON ROUGE AND ALABAMA RIVERS)

AIDS TO NAVIGATION ON NAVIGABLE WATERS
except Western Rivers and Intracoastal Waterway

LATERAL SYSTEM AS SEEN ENTERING FROM SEAWARD

PORT SIDE
ODD NUMBERED AIDS
GREEN OR WHITE LIGHTS

FIXED
FLASHING
OCCULTING
QUICK FLASHING
EQ INT

"9"
Fl G 4sec

LIGHTED BUOY

"7"

C"7"

CAN

SG

DAYMARKS

G "1"

MID CHANNEL
NO NUMBERS—MAY BE LETTERED
WHITE LIGHT ONLY

MORSE CODE
Mo(A)

BW "N"
Mo(A)

BW C"T"

CAN   LIGHTED   NUN

BW N"B"

A
MB

BW "A"
DAYMARK

JUNCTION
MARK JUNCTIONS AND OBSTRUCTIONS
NO NUMBERS—MAY BE LETTERED
INTERRUPTED QUICK FLASHING

WHITE OR GREEN   WHITE OR RED

BR "M"
I Qk Fl G

RB "D"
I Qk Fl R

LIGHTED

PREFERRED CHANNEL TO STARBOARD
TOPMOST BAND BLACK

PREFERRED CHANNEL TO PORT
TOPMOST BAND RED

BR "N"

RB "L"

CAN   NUN

JG   JR

GR "A"   RG "B"

STARBOARD SIDE
EVEN NUMBERED AIDS
RED OR WHITE LIGHTS

FIXED
FLASHING
OCCULTING
QUICK FLASHING
EQ INT
GROUP FLASHING (2)

8
R"8"
Fl R 4sec

LIGHTED BUOY

6
R N"6"

NUN

2
I R

DAYMARK   R "2"

BUOYS HAVING NO LATERAL SIGNIFICANCE—ALL WATERS

SHAPE HAS NO SIGNIFICANCE
NO NUMBERS—MAY BE LETTERED
MAY BE LIGHTED
ANY COLOR LIGHT EXCEPT
RED OR GREEN

W Or C

SPECIAL PURPOSE

FIXED
FLASHING
OCCULTING

N W C"N"

ANCHORAGE

BW C

FISH NET AREA

GW C

DREDGING

UNLIGHTED

DANGER

EXCLUSION AREA

DAYMARKS HAVING NO LATERAL SIGNIFICANCE
MAY BE LETTERED

NW   NR   NG   NB

SUBMERGED DANGER JETTY   A   A   M

W Bn   RW Bn   GW Bn   BW Bn

AIDS TO NAVIGATION ON THE INTRACOASTAL WATERWAY

AS SEEN ENTERING FROM NORTH AND EAST—PROCEEDING TO SOUTH AND WEST

PORT SIDE
ODD NUMBERED AIDS
☐ GREEN OR ☐ WHITE LIGHTS

FIXED ═══════ OCCULTING ▬▬ ▬
FLASHING ▬ ▬ ▬ QUICK FLASHING ▪▪▪▪▪▪
EQ INT ▬▬ ▬▬

"3"
Fl G 4sec

LIGHTED BUOY

"9"
C"9"

CAN

SG-I

1

G
"1"

DAYMARKS

SG-SY

5

G
"5"

DUAL PURPOSE DAYMARKS

5
C"5"

DUAL PURPOSE BUOYS

TR-SY

6

R
"6"

6
R
N"6"

JG-SY

A

GR
"A"

JR-SY

D

RG
"D"

SW 7530-01-GF2-5560

JUNCTION
MARK JUNCTIONS AND OBSTRUCTIONS
NO NUMBERS—MAY BE LETTERED
INTERRUPTED QUICK FLASHING

☐ WHITE OR ☐ GREEN LIGHTS   ☐ WHITE OR ☐ RED LIGHTS

J
BR "J"
I Qk Fl G

N
RB "N"
I Qk Fl R

PREFERRED CHANNEL

A
TO STARBOARD
TOPMOST BAND
BLACK

BR
C"A"

CAN

S
TO PORT
TOPMOST BAND
RED

RB
N"S"

NUN

A

GR
"A"

JG-I

B

RG
"B"

JR-I

MID CHANNEL MORSE CODE ▬▪ ▬▬▪ NO NUMBERS—MAY BE LETTERED
☐ WHITE LIGHT ONLY

B

MB-I   **DAYMARK "B"**

BW
"B"

T
BW
C"T"

N
BW
Mo(A)
"N"

B
BW
N"B"

CAN   LIGHTED   NUN

**DUAL PURPOSE MARKING USED WHERE THE
ICW AND OTHER WATERWAYS COINCIDE**

INTRACOASTAL WATERWAY
JOINT WATERWAY

6
R
N"6"

N

7
N"26"

R
N"4"

C"25"

6
N"6"

JOINT WATERWAY

R
N"8"

C"3"
C"5"

C"7"
R
N"28"

INTRACOASTAL WATERWAY

C"29"

5

When following the ICW from New Jersey through Texas, a △ should
be kept to your starboard hand and a ☐ should be kept to your port hand,
regardless of the color of the aid on which they appear.

STARBOARD SIDE
EVEN NUMBERED AIDS
■ RED OR ☐ WHITE LIGHTS

FIXED ═══════ OCCULTING ▬▬ ▬
FLASHING ▬ ▬ ▬ QUICK FLASHING ▪▪▪▪▪▪
EQ INT ▬▬ ▬▬
GROUP FLASHING (2) ▬▬ ▬ ▬▬ ▬

8
R"8"
Fl R 4sec

LIGHTED BUOY

6
R
N"6"

NUN

TR-I

2

R
"2"

DAYMARK

TR-TY

6

R
"6"

6
R
N"6"

DUAL PURPOSE DAYMARKS

DUAL PURPOSE BUOYS

SG-TY

5

G
"5"

5
C"5"

JG-TY

C

GR
"C"

JR-TY

B

RG
"B"

44

AIDS TO NAVIGATION ON WESTERN RIVERS
(MISSISSIPPI RIVER SYSTEM)

AS SEEN ENTERING FROM SEAWARD

PORT SIDE

☐ GREEN OR ☐ WHITE LIGHTS
FLASHING

LIGHTED BUOY

CAN

PASSING DAYMARK — SG

CROSSING DAYMARK — CG

176.9
MILE BOARD

JUNCTION

MARK JUNCTIONS AND OBSTRUCTIONS
INTERRUPTED QUICK FLASHING

PREFERRED CHANNEL TO STARBOARD
TOPMOST BAND BLACK

PREFERRED CHANNEL TO PORT
TOPMOST BAND RED

☐ WHITE OR ☐ GREEN LIGHTS

☐ WHITE OR ☐ RED LIGHTS

LIGHTED

CAN

NUN

JG

JR

STARBOARD SIDE

☐ RED OR ☐ WHITE LIGHTS
GROUP FLASHING (2)

LIGHTED BUOY

NUN

PASSING DAYMARK — TR

CROSSING DAYMARK — CR

123.5
MILE BOARD

RANGE DAYMARKS AS FOUND ON

NAVIGABLE WATERS – EXCEPT – ICW – MAY BE LETTERED

| KGW | KWG | KWB | KBW | KWR | KRW | KRB | KBR | KGB | KBG | KGR | KRG |

INTRACOASTAL WATERWAY – MAY BE LETTERED

| KGW-I | KWG-I | KWB-I | KBW-I | KWR-I | KRW-I | KRB-I | KBR-I | KGB-I | KBG-I | KGR-I | KRG-I |

SN 7530-0-4GF2-5530

45

UNIFORM STATE WATERWAY MARKING SYSTEM

STATE WATERS AND DESIGNATED STATE WATERS FOR PRIVATE AIDS TO NAVIGATION

REGULATORY MARKERS

BOAT EXCLUSION AREA

EXPLANATION MAY BE PLACED OUTSIDE THE CROSSED DIAMOND SHAPE, SUCH AS DAM, RAPIDS, SWIM AREA, ETC.

DANGER

THE NATURE OF DANGER MAY BE INDICATED INSIDE THE DIAMOND SHAPE, SUCH AS ROCK, WRECK, SHOAL, DAM, ETC.

CONTROLLED AREA

TYPE OF CONTROL IS INDICATED IN THE CIRCLE, SUCH AS SLOW, NO WAKE, ANCHORING, ETC.

INFORMATION

FOR DISPLAYING INFORMATION SUCH AS DIRECTIONS, DISTANCES, LOCATIONS, ETC.

BUOY USED TO DISPLAY REGULATORY MARKERS

MAY SHOW WHITE LIGHT
MAY BE LETTERED

AIDS TO NAVIGATION

MAY SHOW WHITE REFLECTOR OR LIGHT

MOORING BUOY

WHITE WITH BLUE BAND

MAY SHOW WHITE REFLECTOR OR LIGHT

RED-STRIPED WHITE BUOY

MAY BE LETTERED
DO NOT PASS BETWEEN BUOY AND NEAREST SHORE

BLACK-TOPPED WHITE BUOY

MAY BE NUMBERED
PASS TO NORTH OR EAST OF BUOY

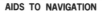

RED-TOPPED WHITE BUOY

PASS TO SOUTH OR WEST OF BUOY

CARDINAL SYSTEM

MAY SHOW GREEN REFLECTOR OR LIGHT

MAY SHOW RED REFLECTOR OR LIGHT

SOLID RED AND SOLID BLACK BUOYS

USUALLY FOUND IN PAIRS
PASS BETWEEN THESE BUOYS

PORT SIDE ———— LOOKING UPSTREAM ———— STARBOARD SIDE

LATERAL SYSTEM

SN 7530-01-GF2-5540

INTERNATIONAL ASSOCIATION OF LIGHTHOUSE AUTHORITIES (I.A.L.A.) MARITIME BUOYAGE SYSTEM

L 70   Buoys and Beacons IALA* Buoyage System

Where in force, the IALA System applies to all fixed and floating marks and occasionally lighthouses, sector lights, range marks, lightships and LANBY's (large automatic navigational buoys).

The standard **buoy shapes** are cylindrical (can) ⌷, conical △, spherical ○, pillar (including high focal plane) ⌸, and spar ∤, but variations may occur, for example: lightfloats ⌷. In the illustrations below, only the standard buoy shapes are used. In the case of fixed **beacons** (lighted or unlighted), only the shape of the topmark is of navigational significance.

Lateral Marks (used in conjunction with a conventional direction of buoyage) are generally for well-defined channels.
There are two international Buoyage Regions—A and B—where Lateral marks differ

Port-hand Marks are red with can topmarks (if any). Lights are red and have any rhythm except Fl(2+1)R

REGION A

Preferred channel to Starboard
Fl(2+1)R, if lighted
RGR

Symbol showing direction of buoyage where not obvious

Preferred channel to Port
Fl(2+1)G, if lighted
GRG

Starboard-hand Marks are green with conical topmarks (if any). Lights are green and have any rhythm except Fl(2+1)G

Port-hand Marks are green with can topmarks (if any). Lights are green and have any rhythm except Fl(2+1)G

REGION B

Preferred channel to Starboard
Fl(2+1)G, if lighted
GRG

Preferred channel to Port
Fl(2+1)R, if lighted
RGR

Starboard-hand Marks are red with conical topmarks (if any). Lights are red and have any rhythm except Fl(2+1)R

A preferred channel buoy may also be a pillar or a spar. All preferred channel marks have three horizontal bands of color

---

All marks other than Lateral Marks are the same in REGIONS A and B

UNLIGHTED MARKS	LIGHTED MARKS

Cardinal Marks indicating navigable water to the named side of the marks

Topmark: 2 black cones

Time (seconds)
White light   0   5   10   15

North Mark
Black above yellow

NW   NE

West Mark   Point of interest   East Mark

Yellow with black band   Black with yellow band

SW   SE

South Mark
Yellow above black

North Mark   VQ or Q   BY

East Mark   VQ(3)5s or Q(3)10s   BYB   Period

South Mark   VQ(6)+L Fl.10s or Q(6)+L Fl.15s   YB   Period

West Mark   VQ(9)10s or Q(9)15s   YBY   Period

The same abbreviations are used for lights on spar buoys and beacons. The periods, 5s, 10s and 15s, may not always be charted.

Isolated Danger Marks, stationed over dangers with navigable water around them.

Body: black with red band(s)
Topmark: 2 black balls

BRB   BRB   BRB   BRB   Fl(2)   White light

Safe Water Marks, such as mid-channel and landfall marks.

Body: red and white stripes
Topmark (if any): red ball

RW   RW   RW   RW   RW   RW   Iso. or Oc. or L Fl.10s, or Mo(A)   White light

---

Special Marks, not primarily to assist navigation but to indicate special features.

Body (shape optional): yellow
Topmark (if any): yellow X

Y   Y   Y etc   Y   Y   Y   Fl.Y etc   Yellow light

BEACONS with IALA System topmarks are charted by upright symbols, eg.   BYB   R   BRB   R (minor beacon) or, on smaller-scale charts: Bn R   Bn G

Beacon towers are charted: R   G   BRB   BYB   etc. (occasionally lighted)

RADAR REFLECTORS on buoys and beacons are not generally charted.

COLOR ABBREVIATIONS under symbols, especially those of spar buoys, may be omitted, or may be at variance with symbols shown above.

LIGHTFLOATS: The IALA System is not usually applied to large lightfloats (replacing manned lightships) but may be applied to smaller lightfloats.

∗IALA is an abbreviation of International Association of Lighthouse Authorities.

IALA MARITIME BUOYAGE SYSTEM
LATERAL MARKS REGION A

PORT HAND

STARBOARD HAND

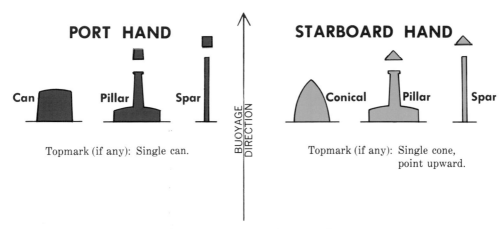

Topmark (if any): Single can.

Topmark (if any): Single cone,
point upward.

BUOYAGE DIRECTION

Lights, when fitted, may have any phase
characteristic other than that used
for preferred channels.

Examples

 Quick Flashing
Flashing
Long Flashing
Group Flashing

PREFERRED CHANNEL
TO STARBOARD

PREFERRED CHANNEL
TO PORT

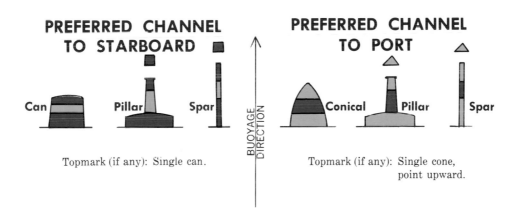

Topmark (if any): Single can.

Topmark (if any): Single cone,
point upward.

BUOYAGE DIRECTION

Lights, when fitted, are composite
group flashing Fl (2 + 1).

IALA MARITIME BUOYAGE SYSTEM
LATERAL MARKS REGION B

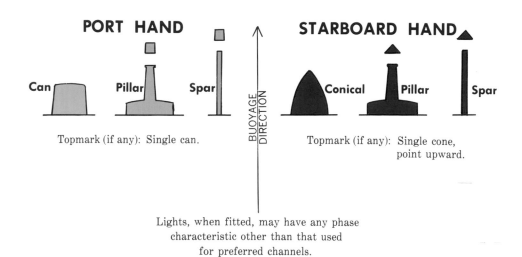

PORT HAND

Can Pillar Spar

Topmark (if any): Single can.

STARBOARD HAND

Conical Pillar Spar

Topmark (if any): Single cone,
point upward.

BUOYAGE DIRECTION

Lights, when fitted, may have any phase
characteristic other than that used
for preferred channels.

Examples
Quick Flashing
Flashing
Long Flashing
Group Flashing

PREFERRED CHANNEL TO STARBOARD

Can Pillar Spar

Topmark (if any): Single can.

PREFERRED CHANNEL TO PORT

Conical Pillar Spar

Topmark (if any): Single cone,
point upward.

BUOYAGE DIRECTION

Lights, when fitted, are composite
group flashing Fl (2+1).

IALA MARITIME BUOYAGE SYSTEM
CARDINAL MARKS REGIONS A AND B

Topmarks are always fitted (when practicable).
Buoy shapes are pillar or spar.

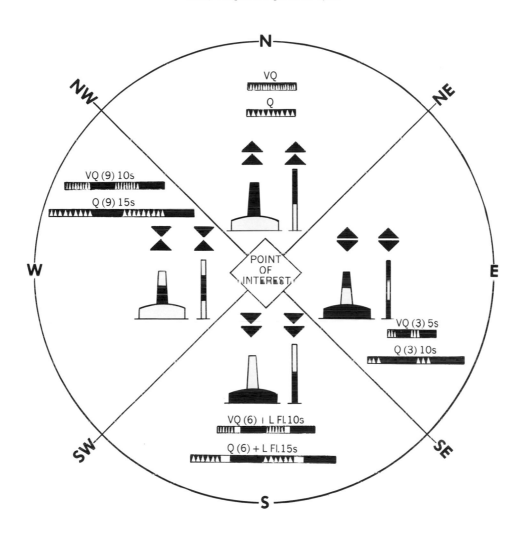

Lights, when fitted, are **white** . Very Quick Flashing
or Quick Flashing; a South mark also has a
Long Flash immediately following the quick flashes.

IALA MARITIME BUOYAGE SYSTEM
REGIONS A AND B

ISOLATED DANGER MARKS

Topmarks are
always fitted
(when practicable).

Light, when fitted, is
white
Group Flashing (2)

 Fl (2)

Shape: Optional, but not
conflicting with lateral
marks; pillar or spar
preferred.

SAFE WATER MARKS

Topmark (if any):
Single sphere.

Light, when fitted,
is **white**
Isophase or Occulting,
or one Long Flash
every 10 seconds or
Morse "A".

Iso

Occ

L Fl.10s

Morse "A"

Shape: Spherical
or
pillar or spar.

SPECIAL MARKS

Topmark (if any):
Single X shape.

Light (when fitted) is
yellow and may have
any phase characteristic
not used for white lights.

Examples

Fl Y

Fl(4) Y

Shape: Optional, but not
conflicting with
navigational marks.

The Naval Institute Press is the book-publishing arm of the U.S. Naval Institute, a private, nonprofit professional society for members of the sea services and civilians who share an interest in naval and maritime affairs. Established in 1873 at the U.S. Naval Academy in Annapolis, Maryland, where its offices remain today, the Naval Institute has more than 100,000 members worldwide.

Members of the Naval Institute receive the influential monthly naval magazine *Proceedings* and substantial discounts on fine nautical prints, ship and aircraft photos, and subscriptions to the Institute's recently inaugurated quarterly, *Naval History*. They also have access to the transcripts of the Institute's Oral History Program and may attend any of the Institute-sponsored seminars regularly offered around the country.

The book-publishing program, begun in 1898 with basic guides to naval practices, has broadened its scope in recent years to include books of more general interest. Now the Naval Institute Press publishes more than forty new titles each year, ranging from how to books on boating and navigation to battle histories, biographies, ship guides, and novels. Institute members receive discounts on the Press's more than 300 books.

For a free catalog describing books currently available and for further information about U.S. Naval Institute membership, please write to:

Membership Department
U.S. Naval Institute
Annapolis, Maryland 21402

or call, toll-free, 800-233-USNI.